Management
A Focus on **Leaders**

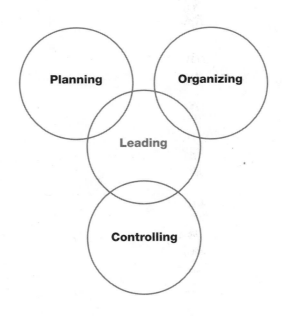

Management
A Focus on **Leaders**

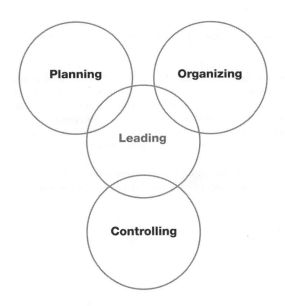

Planning

Organizing

Leading

Controlling

Annie McKee
Teleos Leadership Institute

Prentice Hall

Boston   Columbus   Indianapolis   New York   San Francisco   Upper Saddle River
Amsterdam   Cape Town   Dubai   London   Madrid   Milan   Munich   Paris   Montreal   Toronto
Delhi   Mexico City   São Paulo   Sydney   Hong Kong   Seoul   Singapore   Taipei   Tokyo

Chapter Opener Credits: Page 56: Image CDH Design/iStockphoto; Page 338: Image iQoncept/ShutterStock; Page 378: Image mosrafa fawzy/ShutterStock; Page 456: Image Devation/Edwin Verbruggen/ShutterStock

Editorial Director: Sally Yagan
Editor in Chief: Eric Svendsen
Acquisitions Editor: Kim Norbuta
Director of Editorial Services: Ashley Santora
Editorial Project Manager: Claudia Fernandes
Editorial Assistant: Carter Anderson
Director of Marketing: Patrice Lumumba Jones
Director of Development: Steve Deitmer
Development Editor: Laura Town
Marketing Manager: Nikki Ayana Jones
Marketing Assistant: Ian Gold
Senior Managing Editor: Judy Leale

Operations Specialist: Arnold Vila
Creative Director: John Christiana
Interior and Cover Designer: Blair Brown
Senior Art Director: Blair Brown
MyLab Product Manager: Joan Waxman
Editorial Media Project Manager: Denise Vaughn
Production Media Project Manager: Lisa Rinaldi
Full-Service Project Management/Composition:
    S4Carlisle Publishing Services
Printer/Binder: Courier/Kendallville
Cover Printer: Lehigh-Phoenix Color/Hagerstown
Text Font: 10/12 Minion

Credits and acknowledgments borrowed from other sources and reproduced, with permission, in this textbook appear on appropriate page within text.

Library of Congress Cataloging-in-Publication Data
McKee, Annie, 1955-
Management: a focus on leaders/Annie McKee.
    p. cm.
Includes bibliographical references and index.
ISBN-13: 978-0-13-257590-4 (alk. paper)
ISBN-10: 0-13-257590-6 (alk. paper)
1. Leadership. 2. Management. I. Title.
HD57.7.M3959 2011
658.4—dc22

                    2010017698

10 9 8 7 6 5 4 3 2 1

Prentice Hall
is an imprint of

www.pearsonhighered.com

ISBN 10: 0-13-257590-6
ISBN 13: 978-0-13-257590-4

With admiration for his scholarship and his passion
for the natural world,
With respect for his strength, his humor, and the gifts
of insight he gave to us, and
With profound gratitude for the time we had together,
the fun we had and the love we all shared,
I dedicate this book to my brother, Robert Wigsten, 1961–2009.

Brief Table of Contents

Chapter 1: Managing and Leading Today: The New Rules **pg. 2**

Chapter 2: The Leadership Imperative: It's Up to You **pg. 16**

Chapter 3: Motivation and Meaning: What Makes People Want to Work? **pg. 56**

Chapter 4: Communication: The Key to Resonant Relationships **pg. 94**

Chapter 5: Planning and Strategy: Bringing the Vision to Life **pg. 136**

Chapter 6: The Human Side of Planning: Decision Making and Critical Thinking **pg. 176**

Chapter 7: Change: A Focus on Adaptability and Resiliency **pg. 210**

Chapter 8: Workplace Essentials: Creativity, Innovation, and a Spirit of Entrepreneurship **pg. 252**

Chapter 9: Organizing for a Complex World: Structure and Design **pg. 292**

Chapter 10: Teams and Team Building: How to Work Effectively with Others **pg. 338**

Chapter 11: Working in a Virtual World: Technology as a Way of Life **pg. 378**

Chapter 12: Organizational Controls: People, Processes, Quality, and Results **pg. 418**

Chapter 13: Culture: It's Powerful **pg. 458**

Chapter 14: Globalization: Managing Effectively in a Global Economic Environment **pg. 496**

Chapter 15: Sustainability and Corporate Social Responsibility: Ensuring the Future **pg. 544**

Chapter 16: Managing and Leading for Tomorrow: A Focus on Your Future **pg. 590**

Contents

The World Has Changed (pg. xxi)
Acknowledgments (pg. xxxi)
About the Author (pg. 1)

Chapter 1: Managing and Leading Today: The New Rules (pg. 2)

Why Do Managers Have to Be Leaders? (pg. 4)
  Today, Everyone Needs to Be a Leader (pg. 4)
  What Being a Leader Means for You (pg. 4)
  PERSPECTIVES: Dolores Bernardo (pg. 5)

What Is the Difference between a Manager and a Leader? (pg. 7)
  PERSPECTIVES: John Fry (pg. 7)
  Traditional Views of Managers and Leaders (pg. 8)
  What Managers *Actually* Do (pg. 9)
  PERSPECTIVES: Jill Guindon-Nasir (pg. 11)

What Is the Other Side of the Leadership Coin? (pg. 11)

A Final Word: Changing World, Changing Expectations of Managers and Leaders (pg. 13)

KEY **TERMS** (pg. 14)

VISUAL **SUMMARY** (pg. 15)

Chapter 2: The Leadership Imperative: It's Up to You (pg. 16)

Leadership: Whose Responsibility Is It? (pg. 18)
  We All Need to Become Great Leaders (pg. 18)
  PERSPECTIVES: Lawton Fitt (pg. 19)
  Leadership Is Learned (pg. 19)

What Is the Secret to *Effective* Leadership? (pg. 20)
  Competencies Explained (pg. 20)
    Five Components of Competencies (pg. 21)
    Threshold and Differentiating Competencies (pg. 21)
    Technical, Cognitive, and Relational Competencies (pg. 22)
    Competency Models (pg. 22)
  Social and Emotional Competencies and Resonant Leadership (pg. 22)
    Self-Awareness: The Foundation of Social and Emotional Intelligence (pg. 24)

What Is the Secret to *Influential* Leadership? (pg. 25)
  Sources of Power Exist in Different Forms (pg. 26)
  Empowerment (pg. 27)
    Empowered Employees and Empowering Organizations (pg. 27)
  STUDENT'S CHOICE: Big City Leader in a Small-Town Plant (pg. 28)
    Empowerment and Theories X, Y, and Z (pg. 29)
    The Empowerment Movement Today (pg. 29)

What Is the Secret to *Responsible* Leadership? (pg. 30)
  Developing Values and Ethics (pg. 30)
  Levels of Ethics (pg. 31)
    Individual Ethics (pg. 31)
    Professional Ethics (pg. 32)
    Organizational Ethics (pg. 32)
    Societal Ethics (pg. 32)
  Business Ethics: It's Complicated (pg. 33)
    Ethics in Business and the Role of Law (pg. 33)
      Laws Often Follow Ethical Violations (pg. 33)
      When Laws Force People to Change: The International Anticorruption and Good Governance Act of 2000 (pg. 34)
    Dealing with Ethical Dilemmas at Work (pg. 34)
  BUSINESS CASE: The Washington Post: A Lesson of Lasting Impact (pg. 35)
    Defining Ethics through Leadership (pg. 35)
  How to Handle Everyday Decisions Ethically (pg. 36)
    What Happens When It Goes Wrong: The Slippery Slope (pg. 36)
    Rationalizing Unethical Behavior (pg. 37)
    When All Is Said and Done, Ethical Behavior Is Up to You (pg. 38)

How Do Theories and Models Explain Management and Leadership? (pg. 39)
  Trait Theories of Leadership (pg. 39)
  Behavior Models and Approaches to Leadership (pg. 40)
    Ohio State Studies: Consideration and Initiating Structure (pg. 40)
    University of Michigan Studies: Production- and Employee-Oriented Behavior (pg. 40)
    Leadership Grid (pg. 41)
  Contingency Approaches to Leadership (pg. 42)
    Fiedler's Contingency Theory (pg. 42)
    Situational Leadership Theory (pg. 42)
    Path-Goal Theory (pg. 43)
    Leader Substitutes Model (pg. 43)
  The Study of Leadership Continues (pg. 43)

Is It Time to Take a Stand for Transformational Leadership? (pg. 44)

What Is HR's Role in Supporting Excellent and Ethical Leadership? (pg. 45)
  The HR Cycle (pg. 45)
  Ethical Leadership Development (pg. 46)
  HR's Leadership Roles (pg. 47)
    Whistle-Blower Protection (pg. 48)

What Can We All Do to Become Great Leaders? (pg. 48)

    Self-Aware Leaders Are Authentic (pg. 49)

    Self-Aware Leaders Inspire Trust (pg. 50)

    Inspirational Leaders: Integrity, Courage, and Ethical Leadership (pg. 50)

A Final Word on Leadership (pg. 51)

KEY **TERMS** (pg. 52)

VISUAL **SUMMARY** (pg. 54)

Chapter 3: Motivation and Meaning: What Makes People Want to Work? (pg. 56)

What Is Motivation? (pg. 58)

What Makes Work Meaningful? (pg. 58)

    The Flow Experience (pg. 59)

    Motivation: It's Up to You (pg. 60)

    PERSPECTIVES: Bonaventure Agata (pg. 60)

    Great Leaders Inspire and Motivate Us (pg. 60)

What Is the Link between Motivation and Psychology? (pg. 61)

    Intrinsic Motivation (pg. 62)

    Extrinsic Motivation (pg. 62)

    BUSINESS CASE: Google: Motivation for Innovation (pg. 63)

    Locus of Control (pg. 63)

    Motivation and the Big Five Dimensions of Personality (pg. 64)

Which Theories of Motivation Are Important to Know? (pg. 65)

What Are Basic and Higher-Order Needs Theories of Motivation? (pg. 66)

    Hierarchy of Needs (pg. 67)

    ERG Theory (pg. 67)

    Two-Factor Theory (pg. 68)

Why Are the Three-Needs, Equity, Expectancy, and Goal-Setting Theories Popular? (pg. 69)

    Three-Needs Theory (pg. 69)

        Need for Achievement (pg. 69)

        Need for Affiliation (pg. 70)

        Need for Power (pg. 70)

            Personalized versus Socialized Power (pg. 71)

            Socialized Power, Prosocial Behavior, and Ubuntu (pg. 71)

        Measuring Needs for Achievement, Affiliation, and Power (pg. 71)

    Equity Theory (pg. 72)

        Equity Theory and Cognitive Dissonance (pg. 73)

        Is Equity Theory Relevant Today? (pg. 73)

        Restoring Equity: What Managers Can Do (pg. 74)

    Expectancy Theory (pg. 75)

    Goal-Setting Theory (pg. 76)

        Smart Goals (pg. 77)

        "Doing" and "Being" Goals (pg. 77)

What Are Learning Theories? (pg. 78)

    Operant Conditioning Theory (pg. 78)

        Positive Reinforcement (pg. 78)

        Punishment (pg. 79)

            "What Did I Do Wrong?" (pg. 79)

            "Why Me?" (pg. 79)

            "I Must Be an Awful Person." (pg. 80)

            "I Can't Believe My Manager Did That in Front of Everyone." (pg. 80)

        Operant Conditioning: Does It Really Work? (pg. 80)

    Social Learning Theory (pg. 81)

        Vicarious Learning: The Bobo Doll Experiment (pg. 81)

        Self-Reinforcement: Don't Wait for Others to Reward You (pg. 81)

        Self-Efficacy (pg. 82)

How Can We Integrate Theories of Motivation? (pg. 83)

    STUDENT'S CHOICE: Lance Armstrong and LIVESTRONG (pg. 83)

What Role Does HR Play in Motivation? (pg. 84)

    Compensation and Reward Programs (pg. 84)

    The Job Characteristics Model (pg. 85)

What Can We All Do about Motivation? (pg. 86)

    Self-Awareness and Motivation (pg. 86)

    Empathy and Motivation (pg. 87)

A Final Word on Motivation and Meaning at Work (pg. 88)

KEY **TERMS** (pg. 88)

VISUAL **SUMMARY** (pg. 91)

Chapter 4: Communication: The Key to Resonant Relationships (pg. 94)

Why Is Communication Central to Effective Relationships at Work? (pg. 96)

    PERSPECTIVES: Karen Lombardo (pg. 96)

How Do Humans Communicate? (pg. 97)

    Language: Our Human Specialty (pg. 97)

        Verbal and Sign Language (pg. 98)

        Written Language (pg. 99)

        Denotation and Connotation (pg. 100)

    Nonverbal Communication: Our Bodies, Our Voices, and Pacing (pg. 100)

        Body Language (pg. 101)

        Vocal Intonation, Volume, and Pacing in Communication (pg. 101)

How Do We Communicate and Interpret Sophisticated Information? (pg. 102)

    Expressing Emotions: How Nonverbal Behavior Gives Us Away When It Comes to Feelings (pg. 102)

    A Sophisticated Skill: Interpreting Emotions, Opinions, and Facts at Work (pg. 103)

How We Manage Our Image through Communication (pg. 103)

    Saving Face (pg. 103)

    A Strategy for Saving Face and Keeping Relationships Healthy (pg. 104)

How Do We Manage Our Image through Communication
Making Sense of Information (pg. 104)

What Is the Interpersonal Communication Process? (pg. 106)

    Models of Communication (pg. 107)

        The Shannon-Weaver Model of Communication (pg. 107)

        The Schramm Model of Communication (pg. 107)

        The Berlo Model of Communication (pg. 107)

    Effective and Efficient Communication (pg. 108)

    Choosing "Rich" or "Lean" Communication Channels (pg. 108)

How Do We Use Information Technology to Communicate at Work? (pg. 110)

    E-Mail and Text Messaging (pg. 110)

    Web Conferencing and Videoconferencing (pg. 110)

    BUSINESS CASE: IBM: IBM and Second Life (pg. 111)

What Are Common Barriers to Effective Communication? (pg. 112)

    When Language Gets in the Way of Communication (pg. 112)

        Dialects (pg. 112)

        Jargon: A Shortcut to Communication That Can Backfire (pg. 113)

    Poor Communication: It Happens Too Often! (pg. 114)

    Selective Perception and Stereotyping: The Enemies of Communication (pg. 114)

    The Interaction of Communication and Power (pg. 115)

Why Is It Challenging to Communicate in a Socially Diverse World? (pg. 116)

    Communication and Culture (pg. 116)

        Nonverbal Behavior in Cross-Cultural Communication (pg. 116)

        Communication in High-Context and Low-Context Cultures (pg. 117)

    Yes, Men and Women Communicate Differently (pg. 117)

    Communication and the Age Factor (pg. 118)

What Is Organizational Communication? (pg. 119)

    Direction of Communication Flow (pg. 119)

    STUDENT'S CHOICE: Anthony Idle and Liberty Building Systems (pg. 120)

    Organizational Communication Networks (pg. 121)

    Formal vs. Informal Communication (pg. 122)

    PERSPECTIVES: Peter Oliver (pg. 123)

    What Every Manager Deals with Sooner or Later: Crisis Communication (pg. 124)

    The Power of Storytelling (pg. 125)

What Can HR Do to Ensure Effective Communication and Resonant Relationships in Organizations? (pg. 126)

    Communicating Labor Laws (pg. 127)

    Gathering and Communicating Employee Engagement Information (pg. 127)

What Can We All Do to Improve Communication and Build Resonant Relationships at Work? (pg. 128)

    A Few Basic Rules for Sending Clear and Powerful Messages (pg. 129)

    When to Break the Rules (pg. 129)

A Final Word on Communication and Leadership (pg. 131)

KEY **TERMS** (pg. 132)

VISUAL **SUMMARY** (pg. 134)

Chapter 5: Planning and Strategy: Bringing the Vision to Life (pg. 136)

How Do People Plan for the Future? (pg. 138)

    Planning Defined (pg. 138)

    Exploring How People Think about and Plan for the Future (pg. 139)

        Goal-Oriented Planning (pg. 139)

        Directional Planning (pg. 139)

        Action-Oriented Planning (pg. 140)

What Does Planning Look Like in Organizations? (pg. 141)

    Plans: More Than Goals and Metrics (pg. 141)

    Types of Plans Used in Organizations (pg. 142)

How Do You Plan in Uncertain Times? (pg. 143)

    Creating Plans That Can Change: A Modular Approach (pg. 144)

        Goals, Subgoals, Milestones, and Action Steps: Mapping the Journey to Your Destination (pg. 144)

        Modular Planning: What We Can Learn from Blackjack (pg. 145)

    Scenario Planning (pg. 146)

What Is a Mission? Why Does Vision Matter? (pg. 147)

    PERSPECTIVES: Luis Ottley (pg. 147)

    Mission Clarity Leads to Better Choices (pg. 147)

    Vision: Our Highest Aspiration (pg. 149)

What Is Strategy? (pg. 150)

    Strategy Links Mission, Vision, Goals, and Actions (pg. 150)

    BUSINESS CASE: 3M: Investing in the Future (pg. 150)

    Types of Strategies (pg. 151)

        Corporate Strategies (pg. 152)

        Business Strategies (pg. 155)

        Functional Strategies (pg. 156)

What Needs to Be Considered in a Strategic Planning Process? (pg. 156)

Environmental Scanning (pg. 157)

Economic Environment (pg. 157)

Sociocultural Environment (pg. 157)

Legal and Tax Environment (pg. 157)

Political Environment (pg. 158)

Technological Environment (pg. 158)

Natural Environment (pg. 158)

Last but Not Least: The Industry Environment (pg. 159)

Stakeholder Analysis (pg. 159)

STUDENT'S CHOICE: FreshDirect: Great Service Is Only a Click Away (pg. 160)

What Are the Steps in the Strategic Planning Process? (pg. 161)

Step 1: Review or Evaluate Mission, Vision, Goals, and Strategies (pg. 162)

Steps 2 and 3: Conduct Internal and External Analyses (pg. 162)

SWOT Analysis: A Popular Approach to Internal and External Analysis (pg. 162)

Drawbacks of SWOT Analysis (pg. 163)

Step 4: Craft Strategies (pg. 163)

The BCG Matrix: One Way to "See" a Business (pg. 164)

Drawbacks of the BCG Matrix (pg. 164)

Steps 5 and 6: Implement and Evaluate Strategies (pg. 165)

Implementing a Plan Is Sometimes Called "Execution" (pg. 165)

Evaluation and "Must-Wins" (pg. 165)

What Is HR's Role in Planning and Strategy? (pg. 166)

Recruiting Employees (pg. 166)

Selecting the "Right" Employees (pg. 167)

Succession Planning (pg. 167)

Workforce Growth and Reductions (pg. 167)

What Can We All Do to Support Effective Strategic Planning? (pg. 169)

Pattern Recognition: A Key Element of Strategic Planning (pg. 169)

Developing a Personal Vision (pg. 170)

A Final Word on Planning and Strategy (pg. 171)

KEY **TERMS** (pg. 172)

VISUAL **SUMMARY** (pg. 174)

Chapter 6: The Human Side of Planning: Decision Making and Critical Thinking (pg. 176)

What Is Decision Making? (pg. 178)

Decision Making Defined (pg. 178)

Types of Decisions (pg. 178)

STUDENT'S CHOICE: Tackling the Big Issues at Antares (pg. 180)

How Do Cognitive and Emotional Processes Affect Decision Making? (pg. 181)

Reason and Logic in Decision Making (pg. 182)

Cognitive Processing: Perceptions Impact How We Understand Information (pg. 182)

Schemas: The Brain's Filing System for Information (pg. 182)

Stereotypes (pg. 183)

The Halo Effect (pg. 184)

Emotions: A Legitimate and Important Part of Decision Making (pg. 185)

Intuition in Decision Making (pg. 186)

How Can You Apply a Systematic Approach to Making Decisions? (pg. 187)

Step 1: Identify the Problem (pg. 188)

Step 2: Establish the Decision Criteria (pg. 189)

Step 3: Allocate Weights to Decision Criteria (pg. 190)

Step 4: List Alternatives (pg. 190)

Step 5: Analyze Alternatives (pg. 191)

Step 6: Choose an Alternative (pg. 192)

Step 7: Implement the Decision (pg. 192)

Step 8: Evaluate the Decision (pg. 193)

How Can People Make Good Decisions with Incomplete Information? (pg. 194)

Bounded Rationality (pg. 194)

PERSPECTIVES: Gavin Patterson (pg. 195)

80/20 Rule (pg. 196)

How Can You Improve Your Critical Thinking Skills and Make Better Decisions? (pg. 197)

Critical Thinking Defined (pg. 197)

BUSINESS CASE: Wikipedia: Critical Thinking Required (pg. 198)

Critical Thinking Errors and How to Avoid Thinking Traps (pg. 199)

What Can HR Do to Support Good Decision Making and Critical Thinking? (pg. 201)

Brainstorming (pg. 202)

The Delphi Technique (pg. 202)

What Can We All Do to Improve Critical Thinking and Decision Making? (pg. 203)

Mindfulness: The Secret to Conscious Decision Making (pg. 203)

Double-Loop Learning (pg. 204)

A Final Word on Decision Making and Critical Thinking (pg. 205)

KEY **TERMS** (pg. 206)

VISUAL **SUMMARY** (pg. 208)

Chapter 7: Change: A Focus on Adaptability and Resiliency (pg. 210)

What Is Change and How Do You React to It? (pg. 212)

Change: What It Means to You (pg. 212)

Change Is Constant (pg. 213)

Why Do Organizations Change? (pg. 214)

STUDENT'S CHOICE: Patagonia (pg. 215)

When Social Changes Come to Work: Diversity, Inclusion, and Change (pg. 216)

Gender, Ethnicity, and Pay (pg. 217)

Age Demographics and Change (pg. 217)

Shifts in the World's Economies (pg. 218)

What Is the Difference between Incremental and Transformational Change? (pg. 220)

Revolutionary and Evolutionary Change: "Slow" Is Not Always Better (pg. 221)

Incremental Changes That Led to a Worldwide Financial Crisis (pg. 221)

The Long Story Leading to a Global Recession (pg. 222)

Maybe No One Noticed There Was a Problem (pg. 222)

Which Models Can Help Us Understand Change? (pg. 224)

Lewin's Force Field Analysis Model of Change (pg. 224)

Consider the Context: The "Whole Picture" (pg. 225)

Consider the Power of Culture (pg. 227)

Studying a System *Changes* the System (pg. 227)

Change Is Constant: The Permanent White-Water Metaphor (pg. 227)

What Practical Models Can Help Us Manage Change in Organizations? (pg. 228)

Kotter's Eight-Stage Change Model (pg. 228)

Kotter Stages 1 through 5: Preparing for Change (pg. 228)

Kotter Stage 1 (pg. 228)

Kotter Stage 2 (pg. 230)

Kotter Stage 3 (pg. 230)

Kotter Stage 4 (pg. 231)

Kotter Stage 5 (pg. 231)

Kotter Stages 6 through 8: Change (pg. 231)

Kotter Stage 6 (pg. 231)

Kotter Stage 7 (pg. 231)

Kotter Stage 8 (pg. 231)

Gregory Shea's Work Systems Model (pg. 231)

Shea's Levers of Change in the Work System Model (pg. 232)

Shea on How to Choose *What* to Change (pg. 233)

How Do *People* Change? (pg. 235)

Change: It Is Not Always Easy for People (pg. 235)

The Psychology and Neuropsychology of Individual Change (pg. 235)

Intentional Change (pg. 236)

PERSPECTIVES: Mark McCord-Amasis (pg. 237)

Leading Change in Groups, Organizations, and Communities (pg. 238)

Gestalt Cycle of Experience Applied to Change (pg. 238)

The Gestalt Cycle of Experience and Change in Groups, Organizations, and Communities (pg. 239)

The Gestalt Cycle of Experience: It Works for Groups Even When Controversial Changes Need to Be Explored (pg. 240)

BUSINESS CASE: Cambodia: Combatting the Spread of HIV (pg. 241)

What Can HR Do to Foster Effective Change? (pg. 242)

Organization Development Defined (pg. 242)

Action Research (pg. 243)

Leadership Competency Development and Change (pg. 243)

What Can We All Do to Support Change? (pg. 244)

Become a Change Agent (pg. 245)

Caring for Others during Change: Empathy, Inspiration, and Managing Resistance (pg. 245)

Facing Change with Courage (pg. 246)

STUDENT'S CHOICE: Horses as Healers (pg. 247)

A Final Word on Change (pg. 248)

KEY TERMS (pg. 249)

VISUAL SUMMARY (pg. 250)

Chapter 8: Workplace Essentials: Creativity, Innovation, and a Spirit of Entrepreneurship (pg. 252)

Why Are Creativity, Innovation, and Entrepreneurship at the Heart of Business? (pg. 254)

Hypercompetition (pg. 254)

Adopt a Long-Term Outlook and Embrace Innovation (pg. 254)

PERSPECTIVES: Joe Steier (pg. 255)

What Is Creativity? (pg. 256)

Creativity Defined (pg. 256)

Convergent and Divergent Thinking (pg. 257)

The Left vs. Right Brain Myth (pg. 257)

The Neuroscience of Creativity: Thinking *and* Feeling (pg. 258)

How Can We Encourage Creativity at Work? (pg. 259)

Developing a Culture Where Creativity Is Valued (pg. 259)

"The Weird Rules of Creativity" (pg. 260)

What Is Innovation and Why Is It Important? (pg. 262)

STUDENT'S CHOICE: Innovation: It's Everywhere (pg. 262)

Innovation: What It Looks Like in the World of Business (pg. 263)

BUSINESS CASE: Seventh Generation: Innovation and a Long-Term View (pg. 264)

Most Innovative Companies and Products (pg. 265)

How Can We Foster Innovation in People and Companies? (pg. 267)

  PERSPECTIVES: Dato' Nooraishah Ahmad Tajuddin (pg. 267)

  Structures That Promote Innovation (pg. 268)

    Skunk Works® (pg. 268)

    Idea Incubators (pg. 269)

  Innovative Divisions Outside an Organization's Bureaucratic Hierarchy (pg. 269)

What Is Entrepreneurship? (pg. 270)

  The Importance of Small Businesses in Our Economies (pg. 271)

  STUDENT'S CHOICE: Cooperatives in Zambia (pg. 271)

  Profile of an Entrepreneur (pg. 273)

  Social Entrepreneurship (pg. 274)

How Does a New Business Get Started? (pg. 274)

  Questions to Ask When Starting a Business (pg. 275)

  Writing a Business Plan (pg. 276)

  Where Does the Money Come From? (pg. 277)

  The Life Cycle of a Start-Up Business (pg. 277)

    Stage 1: Start-Up (pg. 277)

    Stage 2: Growth (pg. 278)

    Stage 3: Maturity (pg. 278)

    Stage 4: Decline or Renewal (pg. 278)

  How to Avoid Common Pitfalls and Succeed as an Entrepreneur (pg. 279)

    Good Leadership and Management Will Result in Success (pg. 279)

    Develop Your Employees (pg. 279)

    Remember Your Business Plan and Understand Your Finances (pg. 280)

    Stay Flexible (pg. 280)

    Manage Growth and Measure Success (pg. 280)

    Marketing Matters (pg. 280)

    Focus on Customer Service (pg. 280)

    Be a Good Community Member (pg. 281)

  BUSINESS CASE: R&R Health and Fitness Center: Kathleen and Rhett Reddell (pg. 281)

What Is Intrepreneurship? (pg. 282)

  Intrepreneurship: How It Works in a Health Care Company (pg. 282)

  PERSPECTIVES: Joe Steier (pg. 282)

  Building Support for Ideas (pg. 283)

What Is HR's Role in Supporting Creativity, Innovation, and Entrepreneurship? (pg. 284)

  Laws and Regulations That Entrepreneurs Must Understand (pg. 284)

  Minimize Bureaucracy to Support Creativity and Innovations (pg. 285)

What Can We All Do to Be More Creative, Innovative, and Entrepreneurial? (pg. 285)

  Becoming More Creative (pg. 285)

  Thinking Outside the Box (pg. 286)

A Final Word on Creativity, Innovation, and Entrepreneurship (pg. 287)

KEY **TERMS** (pg. 288)

VISUAL **SUMMARY** (pg. 290)

Chapter 9: Organizing for a Complex World: Structure and Design (pg. 292)

  Why Study Organizational Structure? (pg. 294)

  How Do Traditional Concepts Affect Our Views about Organizational Structure Today? (pg. 294)

    Hierarchy in Organizational Structures (pg. 295)

      Authority (pg. 296)

      Responsibility (pg. 297)

      Accountability (pg. 297)

    Span of Control in Organizational Structures (pg. 297)

    Centralization of Decision Making in Organizational Structures (pg. 298)

  What Is an Organizational Chart? (pg. 299)

  How Can We "See" Organizations and Their Structures in Nontraditional Ways? (pg. 301)

    Open Systems Theory: No Organization Is an Island (pg. 301)

      Organizations Are Naturally Open to Their Environments (pg. 301)

      Understanding Open Systems and Complex Issues (pg. 303)

    STUDENT'S CHOICE: Organizing to Fight Malaria (pg. 303)

    Mechanistic and Organic Organizations (pg. 304)

    Gareth Morgan's Metaphors for Organizations (pg. 305)

    Organizations as Spiders and Starfish (pg. 305)

  How Are Organizations Classified and Legally Structured? (pg. 308)

    Common Forms of Ownership (pg. 310)

      Sole Proprietorship (pg. 310)

      Partnership (pg. 311)

      Corporation (pg. 311)

      How Corporations and Partnerships Can Be Structured Legally: S Corporations and LLCs (pg. 312)

    Structural and Legal Relationships with Outside Entities (pg. 312)

      Cooperative Contracts (pg. 312)

      Licensing Agreements (pg. 313)

      Franchising (pg. 313)

      Wholly Owned Affiliates (pg. 314)

      Strategic Alliances (pg. 314)

What Are Common Contemporary Organizational Structures? (pg. 315)

"Tall" and "Flat" Organizational Structures (pg. 316)

BUSINESS CASE: IDEO: Empowering Employees (pg. 317)

Departmentalization and Organizational Structure (pg. 318)

Divisional Structures (pg. 318)

Functional Departmentalization (pg. 319)

Product Departmentalization (pg. 319)

Process Departmentalization (pg. 319)

Customer Departmentalization (pg. 320)

Geographic Departmentalization (pg. 320)

Matrix Structure (pg. 320)

Hybrid Structure (pg. 321)

Networked Organizational Structures and Power Dynamics (pg. 322)

How Is Work Structured? (pg. 323)

Tasks (pg. 324)

Jobs (pg. 324)

What Factors Affect the Design of Organizational Structures? (pg. 325)

The Relationship between Structure and Strategy (pg. 325)

Structure Follows Strategy (pg. 325)

Strategy Can Be Determined by Structure (pg. 325)

Structure and Strategy: An Iterative Process (pg. 326)

The External Environment (pg. 326)

Technology (pg. 327)

Company Size and Geography (pg. 327)

Company Size (pg. 327)

Geography (pg. 327)

Organizational Design: It's Not Always Deliberate! (pg. 328)

What Is HR's Role in Organizational Design and Structure? (pg. 329)

Job Analysis (pg. 329)

What Can We All Do to Work Effectively within Our Organizations' Structures? (pg. 330)

Managing and Leading the Informal Organization (pg. 330)

PERSPECTIVES: Carol de Wet (pg. 331)

Managing "Up" (pg. 332)

A Final Word on Organizational Structure (pg. 333)

KEY TERMS (pg. 333)

VISUAL SUMMARY (pg. 336)

Chapter 10: Teams and Team Building: How to Work Effectively with Others (pg. 338)

Why Do Leaders Need Teams? (pg. 340)

BUSINESS CASE: Charles H. Ramsey: Philadelphia Police Commissioiner Charles H. Ramsey on Leadership (pg. 340)

Groups and Teams: Where We Learn, Live, and Work (pg. 341)

Groups Are Mysterious (pg. 341)

How Does Leadership Behavior Affect Group Dynamics? (pg. 342)

How Do Groups Change over Time? (pg. 344)

Bruce Tuckman's Model of Group Development (pg. 344)

Stage 1: Forming (pg. 344)

Stage 2: Storming (pg. 344)

Stage 3: Norming (pg. 344)

Stage 4: Performing (pg. 344)

Stage 5: Adjourning (pg. 345)

Susan Wheelan's Integrated Model of Group Development (pg. 345)

Stage 1: Dependency and Inclusion (pg. 345)

Stage 2: Conflict and Counterdependence (pg. 345)

Stage 3: Trust and Structure (pg. 347)

Stage 4: Productivity and Work (pg. 347)

Stage 5: Termination (pg. 347)

Group Development: A Useful but Limited Way to Explain What Happens in Groups (pg. 347)

How Do Group Dynamics Impact Team Effectiveness? (pg. 349)

Group Roles (pg. 349)

How Roles Develop in Groups (pg. 350)

Stanford Prison Experiment (pg. 350)

Group Norms (pg. 351)

Group Norms Need to Be Explicit (pg. 351)

Emotional Intelligence and Group Norms (pg. 352)

PERSPECTIVES: Police Commissioner Charles H. Ramsey (pg. 352)

Status and Power in Groups (pg. 353)

Social Status (pg. 354)

How We "Get" Social Status (pg. 354)

Status and Influence in Groups (pg. 354)

Personal Power in Groups (pg. 355)

Power and Influence in a Leaderless Group (pg. 355)

Diversity Is a Group Dynamic (pg. 356)

We Differ in How We Take In and Process Information (pg. 356)

Personality Tests Can Help Us Understand Diversity (pg. 356)

David Kolb's Learning Styles (pg. 357)

Paradoxes of Group Life (pg. 358)

How Do Teams Function at Work? (pg. 359)

Describing Work Teams (pg. 359)

Self-Directed Work Teams (pg. 359)

High-Performance Teams (pg. 360)

STUDENT'S CHOICE: Mark Arnoldy— GlobeMed (pg. 361)

How Can We Deal with the Challenges of Working in Groups? (pg. 362)

The Big Six Challenges We Face in Groups (pg. 362)

Membership (pg. 362)

Participation (pg. 362)

Communication (pg. 363)

Influence (pg. 363)

Social Loafing (pg. 364)

Emotions (pg. 364)

Conformity and Groupthink (pg. 364)

Avoiding Dysfunctional Conformity in Groups (pg. 365)

What Role Does Conflict Play in Groups? (pg. 366)

Functional and Dysfunctional Conflict (pg. 366)

Sources of Conflict (pg. 366)

Trust: The Basis for All Conflict Resolution Strategies (pg. 368)

Conflict Management: Negotiating to Find the Win-Win (pg. 368)

How Can HR Support Effective Team Performance? (pg. 369)

Focus on Teams: HR's Contributions (pg. 369)

Resonant Team Building (pg. 369)

Resonant Team Building: Getting Started (pg. 369)

Resonant Team Building: Visioning (pg. 370)

What Can We All Do to Create and Sustain Resonant Teams? (pg. 370)

Listening to What People Actually Say (pg. 371)

Active Listening (pg. 371)

Leading a Resonant Team (pg. 372)

A Final Word on Teams and Team Building (pg. 373)

KEY TERMS (pg. 374)

VISUAL SUMMARY (pg. 376)

Chapter 11: Working in a Virtual World: Technology as a Way of Life (pg. 378)

How Do Advances in Information and Communication Technologies Change Life and Work? (pg. 380)

The Winning Formula: ICTs + People = Successful Communication and Information Sharing (pg. 380)

Sociotechnical Systems Theory (pg. 381)

ICTs and Working in a Virtual World (pg. 381)

How Did Technology Affect Life and Work during the Industrial Revolutions? (pg. 382)

Technology and the First Industrial Revolution (pg. 382)

Technology and the Second Industrial Revolution (pg. 383)

Africa, India, South America, and China during the Era of Western Industrialization (pg. 384)

Africa during the Era of Industrialization (pg. 384)

India during the Era of Industrialization (pg. 385)

South America during the Era of Industrialization (pg. 385)

China during the Era of Industrialization (pg. 386)

The World Economic Stage as Western Industrialization Waned (pg. 386)

The Post-Industrial Society and the Third Industrial Revolution (pg. 387)

Information + Communications Technology = Profound Social Change (pg. 387)

Social Change = Changes at Work (pg. 388)

Job Migration (pg. 388)

Global Logistics (pg. 388)

How Have Computing and Telecommunication Technologies Evolved? (pg. 389)

Computing Technology: From a U.S. Defense Strategy to Web 2.0 (pg. 389)

The Internet, Intranets, Extranets, and the "Cloud" (pg. 390)

The Evolution of Telecommunications (pg. 391)

How Do People Use ICTs at Work? (pg. 392)

E-Mail (pg. 392)

PERSPECTIVES: Rachel Kamau (pg. 393)

Text Messages (pg. 394)

Using Emoticons (pg. 394)

Teleconferences, Videoconferences, and Web Conferencing (pg. 394)

Groupware (pg. 395)

Social Networks (pg. 396)

Putting It All Together: When Business Goes Multimedia (pg. 396)

PERSPECTIVES: Sheila Robinson (pg. 396)

Where and How Is Virtual Work Conducted? (pg. 397)

Telecommuting (pg. 398)

The Hybrid Worker (pg. 399)

Virtual Teams (pg. 399)

Making Virtual Teams More Effective (pg. 399)

Trust and Accountability in Virtual Teams (pg. 400)

What Is a Virtual Organization? (pg. 401)

BUSINESS CASE: Avon: Ahead of Its Time (pg. 402)

Components of Virtual Organizations (pg. 402)

Models of Virtual Organizations (pg. 403)

Traditional Organizations Are Evolving to Better Use and Offer Virtual Services (pg. 404)

The Evolution of Virtual Banking (pg. 404)

STUDENT'S CHOICE: Using the Internet to Change Lives: One Entrepreneur at a Time (pg. 405)

The Evolution of Virtual Consumer Sales (pg. 406)

The Evolution of Virtual Education and Training (pg. 406)

What Are the Challenges of Working in a Virtual World? (pg. 408)

  The Challenges of the 24/7 Virtual Work World (pg. 408)

  Technology and Information Overload (pg. 408)

  The Challenge of Knowledge Management (pg. 409)

What Can HR Do to Support Virtual Work? (pg. 411)

  The Privacy Question: HR's Role in Monitoring Employee Electronic Communications (pg. 411)

  Establishing Guidelines for On-the-Job Social Networking (pg. 411)

What Can We All Do to Work Most Effectively in a Virtual World? (pg. 412)

  Virtual Relationships Are *Real* Relationships (pg. 412)

  Using E-Mail Effectively at Work (pg. 413)

  Taking Charge of Virtual Teams (pg. 413)

A Final Word on Working in a Virtual World (pg. 414)

KEY **TERMS** (pg. 415)

VISUAL **SUMMARY** (pg. 416)

Chapter 12: Organizational Controls: People, Processes, Quality, and Results (pg. 418)

What Is the Organizational Control Process? (pg. 420)

What Historical Perspectives Help Us Understand Control in Organizations? (pg. 421)

  Frederick Taylor and Scientific Management (pg. 421)

  Elton Mayo and the Hawthorne Studies (pg. 422)

  Mary Parker Follett: Control Is More Than Telling People What to Do (pg. 423)

  The Human Touch (pg. 423)

  STUDENT'S CHOICE: Spartan Surfaces (pg. 424)

What Are Common Control Systems? (pg. 425)

  Bureaucratic Control Systems (pg. 425)

  Adhering to Rules versus Objective Assessment of Behavior and Outputs (pg. 426)

  Normative Control (pg. 427)

  Levers of Control (pg. 427)

What Conventions and Forces Guide Organizational Control Processes? (pg. 429)

  Corporate Governance (pg. 429)

  Audits (pg. 430)

  Legislation and Sarbanes-Oxley (pg. 430)

    Legislation and Controls (pg. 430)

    Sarbanes-Oxley and Controls (pg. 431)

  When Customers Control (pg. 432)

  BUSINESS CASE: Threadless: Customer Control (pg. 432)

What Are the Typical Steps in the Control Process? (pg. 433)

  Creating Standards and Metrics (pg. 433)

  Measuring Performance (pg. 434)

  Comparing Performance to Standards (pg. 434)

  Taking Corrective Action (pg. 435)

  Feedback Processes (pg. 435)

    Feedback Control (pg. 436)

    Feed-Forward Control (pg. 436)

    Concurrent Control (pg. 436)

  Integrating Feedback (pg. 436)

What Should Companies Control? (pg. 437)

  Controlling Financial Performance (pg. 437)

    Financial Controls (pg. 438)

    Accounting Controls (pg. 438)

    Beyond Budgeting (pg. 440)

  Controlling Service: Customer Relationship Management (pg. 441)

  Quality Control (pg. 442)

    Business Process Reengineering (pg. 442)

    Total Quality Management (pg. 443)

  PERSPECTIVES: Rafidah Mohammad Noor (pg. 444)

    Six Sigma (pg. 444)

    Lean Management (pg. 445)

    ISO 9000 and 14000 (pg. 445)

    Baldrige Award (pg. 446)

What Can HR Do to Help Control for Effectiveness and Efficiency at Work? (pg. 447)

  The Performance Management Process (pg. 447)

  Management by Objectives: Use with Caution (pg. 448)

  Gathering Information about Employee Performance (pg. 448)

  Performance Review (pg. 449)

What Can We All Do to Enhance Effectiveness and Efficiency at Work? (pg. 450)

A Final Word on Organizational Control (pg. 451)

KEY **TERMS** (pg. 452)

VISUAL **SUMMARY** (pg. 454)

Chapter 13: Culture: It's Powerful (pg. 456)

What Is Culture? (pg. 458)

  Values (pg. 458)

  Attitudes (pg. 459)

  Norms (pg. 459)

Why Is Culture Important at Work? (pg. 461)

  PERSPECTIVES: Michael Gaines (pg. 461)

What Are the Dimensions of National and Organizational Culture? (pg. 462)

  Hofstede's Dimensions of Culture (pg. 462)

  The GLOBE Project Value Dimensions (pg. 464)

  Culture: It's Complicated! (pg. 466)

    Subcultures (pg. 467)

    Culture Change (pg. 467)

How Can We Describe Organizational Cultures? (pg. 468)

The Competing Values Model of Organizational Culture (pg. 468)

"Strong" and "Weak" Cultures (pg. 469)

BUSINESS CASE: McKinsey: They Get You for Life (pg. 470)

STUDENT'S CHOICE: Tying One On at Vineyard Vines: Poised for Progress, Maintaining Family Culture (pg. 470)

How Can We Study Organizational Culture? (pg. 472)

Edgar Schein's Levels of Culture (pg. 472)

Observable Artifacts: The Top Level of Schein's Organizational Culture Model (pg. 472)

Values: The Middle Level of Schein's Organizational Culture Model (pg. 473)

Basic Assumptions: The Deepest Level of Schein's Organizational Culture Model (pg. 473)

Myths and Heroes, Taboos, Sacred Symbols, and Language (pg. 473)

Myths and Heroes (pg. 474)

Taboos (pg. 474)

Sacred Symbols (pg. 475)

Language (pg. 476)

Leaders and Managers as Ethnographers (pg. 477)

Organizational Culture: What's Important Today? (pg. 479)

Innovative Cultures (pg. 479)

Customer Service Cultures (pg. 479)

Diversity Cultures (pg. 480)

Ethical Cultures (pg. 480)

Cultures That Support Sustainability and Service (pg. 482)

Cultures That Support the Whole Person: Mind, Body, Heart, and Spirit (pg. 483)

How Can HR Support the Development of Positive Organizational Cultures? (pg. 484)

HR's Role in Creating an Inclusive Culture: A "Push" Strategy (pg. 484)

Promoting Diversity and Inclusion in the Workplace and the EEOC (pg. 484)

Preventing Sexual Harassment in the Workplace (pg. 487)

How HR Can Help Diagnose and Develop Culture: A "Pull" Strategy (pg. 488)

What Can We All Do to Create Positive and Powerful Organizational Cultures? (pg. 489)

Develop Your Cultural Intelligence (pg. 489)

Leading Culture Change (pg. 490)

A Final Note on the Power of Culture (pg. 491)

KEY **TERMS** (pg. 492)

VISUAL **SUMMARY** (pg. 494)

Chapter 14: Globalization: Managing Effectively in a Global Economic Environment (pg. 496)

What Is Globalization and Why Does It Matter? (pg. 498)

Technology's Role in Fostering Rapid Globalization (pg. 498)

Globalization Matters Because It Is Changing Our Lives (pg. 499)

How Have International Political and Economic Changes Fostered Globalization? (pg. 500)

The End of the Cold War (pg. 500)

Events That Shook the World during the Cold War (pg. 501)

The Lasting Impact of the Cold War (pg. 502)

Fluid Boundaries and the Softening of the Nation-State (pg. 502)

Social and Economic Changes Sweep across the World (pg. 503)

What Key Economic Factors Are Affecting Global Business? (pg. 504)

Global Trade (pg. 504)

Global Investment (pg. 504)

Global Finance and Debt (pg. 504)

What Must Be Considered When Developing a Global Strategy? (pg. 505)

Reviewing Legal and Organizational Design Issues (pg. 505)

Global Strategy and Culture (pg. 506)

Exporting Disney (pg. 506)

Crafting an *International* Strategy (pg. 507)

PERSPECTIVES: Vittorio Colao (pg. 507)

What Are the Opportunities and Risks in a Global Business Environment? (pg. 508)

Opportunity: Expand Markets and Sales (pg. 508)

Opportunity: Access to Expertise While Saving Money (pg. 509)

Opportunity: Improve Operations (pg. 509)

Risk: Uncertainty Due to Government Involvement and Political Instability (pg. 509)

Risk: Growing Too Fast and False Economies of Scale (pg. 510)

Risk: Partnerships Can Increase Exposure (pg. 510)

Risk: Political and Popular Disapproval (pg. 510)

What Opportunities Exist in Emerging Markets? (pg. 511)

Brazil (pg. 512)

Brazil: The Past (1889–1985) (pg. 512)

Brazil: The Present (1985–2009) (pg. 513)

Brazil: The Future (2010 and Beyond) (pg. 514)

Advantages and Disadvantages of Doing Business with Brazil (pg. 515)

Russia (pg. 516)

    Russia: The Past (1917–1989) (pg. 516)

    Russia: The Present (1989–2009) (pg. 516)

    Russia: The Future (2010 and Beyond) (pg. 518)

    Advantages and Disadvantages of Doing Business with Russia (pg. 518)

India (pg. 519)

    India: The Past (2500 B.C.E. to 1990) (pg. 521)

    India: The Present (1991–2009) (pg. 521)

    India: The Future (2010 and Beyond) (pg. 522)

    Advantages and Disadvantages of Doing Business with India (pg. 523)

China (pg. 524)

    China: The Past (1912–1989) (pg. 524)

    China: The Present (1989–2009) (pg. 525)

    China: The Future (2010 and Beyond) (pg. 526)

    Advantages and Disadvantages of Doing Business with China (pg. 526)

A Final Word on Emerging Markets (pg. 528)

STUDENT'S CHOICE: Zambia: On the Threshold of Globalism (pg. 528)

How Has the Growth of Worldwide Trade Alliances Affected Globalization? (pg. 529)

    World Trade Organization (pg. 529)

    The European Union (pg. 529)

    The North American Free Trade Agreement (pg. 530)

    Central America Free Trade Agreement (pg. 531)

    South American Trade Alliances (pg. 531)

    Asian Trade Alliances (pg. 532)

        Association of Southeast Asian Nations (pg. 532)

        Asia-Pacific Economic Cooperation (pg. 532)

How Do Global Regulators Affect Economies and Social Issues? (pg. 533)

    Group of Twenty (pg. 533)

    The World Economic Forum (pg. 533)

    United Nations Economic and Social Council (pg. 534)

What Is HR's Role in Supporting Global Business? (pg. 535)

    The Expat Experience: Team-Based Learning (pg. 535)

    BUSINESS CASE: IBM: Building a Culture of Collaboration (pg. 536)

    Coaching for Success: Helping Employees and Managers Adjust to Globalization (pg. 536)

What Can We All Do to Succeed in a Global Environment? (pg. 537)

    The Intersection between Personal Ethics, Societal Ethics, and Company Ethics (pg. 537)

    Competencies That Support Working Abroad (pg. 538)

A Final Word on Globalization (pg. 539)

KEY **TERMS** (pg. 539)

VISUAL **SUMMARY** (pg. 542)

Chapter 15: Sustainability and Corporate Social Responsibility: Ensuring the Future (pg. 544)

Why Are Sustainability and Corporate Social Responsibility Important in Today's World? (pg. 546)

What Is Sustainability? (pg. 546)

    Sustainability: People Have Been Practicing It for Generations (pg. 547)

    Why Sustainability Is Important Today: The "Big Three" Reasons (pg. 547)

        1. Climate Change and Global Warming (pg. 548)

        Potential Effects of Climate Change and Global Warming (pg. 549)

        Facing the Threat of Climate Change: It's Up to All of Us (pg. 551)

        2. The Call for Business Ethics and Social Responsibility (pg. 551)

        3. An Economic Crisis That Swept the World (pg. 552)

What Are the Three Pillars of Sustainability? (pg. 553)

    The Bhopal Disaster (pg. 553)

    Tracking Companies That Focus on Sustainability (pg. 555)

What Is Environmental Sustainability? (pg. 556)

    The History of the Conservation and Ecology Movements in the United States (pg. 556)

    Reducing Greenhouse Gas Emissions: World Leaders Try to Agree on a Course of Action (pg. 558)

        The Kyoto Protocol (pg. 559)

        The United Nations Climate Change Conference of 2009 (pg. 561)

    Reliance on Fossil Fuels: It Can't Last Forever (pg. 561)

    The Green Economy and Green Jobs (pg. 562)

    Pollution, Waste, and Environmental Sustainability (pg. 563)

    Plants, Animals, and Environmental Sustainability (pg. 564)

    What Else Are We Doing to Foster Environmental Sustainability? (pg. 565)

What Is Social Sustainability? (pg. 566)

    BUSINESS CASE: Ashoka: A Proactive Approach to Social Sustainability (pg. 567)

    Child Labor (pg. 567)

    Slavery in the World Today (pg. 568)

    Safety and Risk at Work (pg. 571)

What Is Economic Sustainability? (pg. 572)

    BUSINESS CASE: Generation Investment Management: Al Gore and David Blood (pg. 573)

STUDENT'S CHOICE: Passion and Partnership: One Road to Economic Sustainability (pg. 574)

What Is Corporate Social Responsibility? (pg. 575)

PERSPECTIVES: Mary McNevin (pg. 577)

How Can Companies Approach Corporate Social Responsibility? (pg. 578)

The Obstructionist Approach (pg. 580)

The Defensive Approach (pg. 580)

The Accommodative Approach (pg. 580)

The Proactive Approach (pg. 580)

What Is HR's Role in Sustainability and Corporate Social Responsibility? (pg. 581)

Telecommuting (pg. 582)

Supporting CSR through Employee Service Programs (pg. 581)

What Can We All Do to Support Sustainability and Corporate Social Responsibility? (pg. 584)

A Final Word on Sustainability and Corporate Social Responsibility (pg. 585)

KEY **TERMS** (pg. 585)

VISUAL **SUMMARY** (pg. 587)

Chapter 16: Managing and Leading for Tomorrow: A Focus on Your Future (pg. 590)

Why Do "Great Leaders Move Us"? (pg. 592)

PERSPECTIVES: Chade-Meng Tan (pg. 592)

What Are "Moon Shots for Management"? (pg. 593)

How Can You Continue Your Journey to Becoming a Resonant Leader? (pg. 595)

What Can You Do to Develop Your Leadership? (pg. 596)

Making Leadership Development Fun—and Effective (pg. 596)

Exploring Your Vision and What You Want to Change (pg. 597)

A Final Word on Managing Yourself (pg. 606)

VISUAL **SUMMARY** (pg. 607)

Endnotes (pg. E-1)

Index (pg. I-1)

Glossary/Index (pg. G-1)

The World Has Changed

The pace and scope of change in the world and in organizations during the past 10 years have been unprecedented. In this environment, staying ahead of the curve and being adequately prepared for work, management, and leadership has been challenging—even daunting. At the same time, a massive shift in the balance of economic power is under way, with many of the world's largest economies slowing down as other economies continue to grow and gain power, bringing prosperity to many and a new world order. This new world order has the potential to bring education, opportunities, better working conditions, and better lives to millions of people around the world. The path to this future, however, also has the potential to be divisive and to cause fear and anger—emotions that generally lead to trouble.

These challenges have been magnified a hundredfold as the very fabric of our economic system has come under great strain, resulting in years of uncertainty, economic woes, and global instability in many countries, industries, and institutions. Many believe that this trying situation is a direct result of a failure of leadership, at all levels and in many sectors.

As we face the opportunities and challenges of the social and economic changes that are rocking our world, we need to rethink how we do business and how organizations around the globe relate to one another. We need to learn how to lead in this challenging and exciting new era.

As the world changes, people are struggling with how to behave, manage their organizations, and lead others in an unfamiliar landscape. In too many cases in recent years, this has led prominent people and businesses to engage in unethical and illegal behavior, harming millions and destroying formerly great institutions. People won't stand for this anymore. Partly because we now have so much access to information, and partly because more and more people realize that we truly are interconnected and the actions of one affect all of us, people everywhere are demanding that businesses serve society rather than the other way around. Along with this demand for greater transparency and more ethical business practices, there is growing recognition that economic, social, and environmental sustainability are imperatives for which we are all responsible. Taken together, the rebalancing of world economic power, the call for ethical leadership, and the focus on sustainability add up to profound changes for our societies and our businesses.

We believe that these changes may be a once-in-a-lifetime wake-up call and an opportunity for students everywhere to take charge and take responsibility for becoming the leaders of the future. In the years to come, you will be cleaning up the messes of the past while sailing in the uncharted waters of new possibilities as you work, manage, and lead in the next generation of organizations that will emerge from today's crises and social transformations. The tremendous opportunities that our new world order offers to people, organizations, and societies are unprecedented, and they will require bold new ways of relating to one another, managing ourselves and our institutions, and most of all, leading powerfully at all levels of business and society. Today, *everyone* needs to be a leader.

In recent years, we have done extensive research and talked with countless business leaders, faculty, deans, and others about what is happening in our world. We have asked instructors to consider what is currently taught in management courses—as well as what should be taught—and we've asked people what needs to change in how the leaders of the future are taught. Across the board, we hear the same message: "Although some of the theories and perspectives of the past are relevant today, much of what we teach and test for is not preparing students to lead. And if everyone, at every level, is now expected to lead, we need to shift what we teach about work, organizations, management, and especially leadership."

So, to better serve you, the student, we have embarked on a bold and exciting project. During 2009 and 2010, we worked with principles of management professors from colleges and universities of all sizes and with management professionals from all over the world to develop a powerful new textbook that will help define what is taught about management and leadership in college and university courses everywhere.

Our Vision

Our vision is to bring the study of management solidly into the twenty-first century. We will provide you with foundational and groundbreaking material to support you in new ways of learning. We'll present relevant and exciting ideas, models, theories, examples, and stories—all written in a straightforward, engaging, and interesting manner. This book and its supplements will also directly address the challenges and opportunities in our changing world in order to better prepare you to be a leader now and in the future.

Major Themes

When undertaking this project, we realized that our task was daunting in many ways. First, we needed to put leadership at the forefront of our approach, while at the same time emphasizing the idea that being a leader is not something that happens later. You need to lead *now*. We knew that we would need to include the best of our field's basic research and foundational models, as well as new research that has emerged in fields as varied as management, neuropsychology, sociology, and information technology. We also undertook what we believe to be the key to truly understanding management and leadership today: integration of the traditional views of management. After all, in our complex, global, ever-changing world, activities related to planning, organizing, controlling, and leading are never isolated. Finally, we realized that many of you, if not all, have grown up with the Internet and are accustomed to short bursts of communication—communication that is less formal and more lively than what is found in most textbooks. We therefore knew we needed to write a book that people today would find interesting, engaging, and *fun* to read.

To accomplish these goals, we kept the following themes in our hearts and minds:

- **Leadership**—Leadership is a central theme of this book and is deeply embedded within each chapter. The importance of leadership at all levels in organizations is stressed throughout the text, in ways that will both engage you intellectually and stimulate your desire for additional learning and development. Our approach to leadership is steeped in the best and most current research and it is *practical*: We want you to learn how to lead in today's challenging and exciting global environment.

- **Tradition meets NOW**—Our goal is to teach theories and research in a way that is relevant to you by providing material you can apply to your life both today and later in your career. We studied, reviewed, reread, and discovered both new and old research and held it up to the light of day, asking ourselves: Is this relevant? Is the research sound? Is this way of understanding leadership and organizations something students can use now and also later in their careers? And, for the older models and research, do the concepts still hold up in today's very different world? In truth, although many theories of the past are still relevant, not all of them teach you what you need to know to be successful in today's complex organizations. In these cases, we have shown you how to use your own judgment when deciding which models to adopt and use and which to simply be aware of.

In this book we are marrying the best of the old with the best of the new and providing a solid foundation of current knowledge, seminal works, and practical application that will support you both in life and at work.

- **Integration of the foundations of management**—As management changes, how we view management must also change. Scholars and faculty (as well as businesspeople) have known for years that management cannot be viewed as individual silos of planning, organizing, leading, and controlling. That's even more true today, when nothing is static, communication and change are constant, and far more people throughout organizations are leading and making decisions about the future, about how to organize resources, and about how to manage complexities related to quality and efficiency. Although we have kept the basic framework that so many people are familiar with (it is useful, after all), we have put leadership at the center of the model, and we've encouraged you to think about management as a complex whole, rather than a series of isolated topics.

- **Integration of today's most important topics**—We believe that in today's organizations, there are several areas of study (and life) that must be integrated into the study of management. Key among these are the following:

  - Ethics and the responsible use of power

  - Social, technological, and organizational change

  - The need for innovation

  - Globalization as a fact of life for everyone today

  - The power of human diversity

  - Resonant leadership, driven by social and emotional intelligence

  - A focus on creating sustainable organizations and communities that support our larger, global community and our natural environment.

These topics are addressed specifically in certain chapters and are *woven throughout the text* as well.

- **Engaging, outcome-driven writing style**—We have sought to write this book in a way that engages your heart and your mind, with a solid focus on scholarship and a friendly and inviting tone. You will be able to understand management and leadership concepts and apply them to your current situation, as well as to your work in the future. We have taken an outcome-driven approach, focusing on how you can apply the knowledge, theories, and concepts in this course *now*.

  As any faculty member will tell you, the transformation of scholarly work into language that students can relate to is not easy. We have undertaken this task in hopes that our style will encourage you to read more, so you will have language to discuss even the most complex topics and will bring more to the discussions and activities in your classroom.

- **Aesthetics that support engagement and learning**—We have noticed that far too many textbooks are "packed" with stuff: boxes, pictures, diagrams, and chunks of text all over the page. We've been told by faculty and students alike that this is distracting—not to mention that much of this material makes books more expensive. For these reasons, we have decided on a minimalist approach and an elegant layout. We've included only the best exhibits, pictures, and icons—the ones that really add something to the learning experience. In addition to those exhibits that support research and models, we have created four "special" visual models that support our most important concepts in the text. The first is our integrated model of management and leadership, found at the beginning of each chapter, which shows how the traditional functions of management are actually linked with leadership at the center. We've also created icons to remind you of the importance of social and emotional intelligence, and two icons that depict human resources' ever-more-important leadership role in supporting businesses and organizations today.

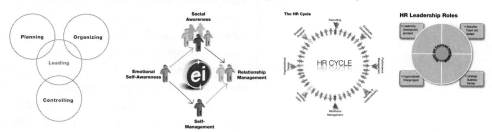

We've also created a visually appealing and helpful summary at the end of each chapter for you—the student—to study along with lists of key terms so you won't have to hunt through the book to find them.

Hallmark Chapter Features

We have written this book to bring concepts alive so you can see yourself in the ideas as you read. In addition to a straightforward and personal writing style, we have created several features that are intended to help you learn while focusing your attention on the real world. These features are as follows:

- **"What Can We All Do to . . .?"** At the end of every chapter we have included a section called "What Can We All Do to . . .?" This section brings home key *practical* lessons related to the chapter content. Here, you can integrate some of what you have learned to see how you can use this information both now and in the future. We've taken some of the best traditional action-oriented theories and models, added some of the newest thinking and research from scholar-practitioners, and combined them in these sections to help you focus on developing self-awareness and skills in the areas of leadership, ethics, social and emotional intelligence, critical thinking, creativity, communication, and team building.

- **Real life, real leaders: We went to the best leaders we know for their perspectives.** In each chapter we have included at least one "Perspectives" feature, in which outstanding leaders share thoughts and wisdom about current topics and about leadership in general. These individuals are well known to the author and were carefully selected for their outstanding leadership, their ethics, and their twenty-first-century worldview. These leaders are special. What they have to say matters—and they've said it in a way that is relevant to you. They're not talking about life in the rarified air of the executive suite—they are sharing ideas, advice, and compelling stories that are relevant to you now.

- **"Student's Choice": You've told us what you care about in leaders and organizations.** Just as we went to great leaders for their best ideas, we also went to your fellow students for theirs. In each chapter, there is at least one "Student's Choice" feature—a case adapted by the author from a case written by current students about leaders and organizations they believe are exemplary. These students were given simple instructions: Choose a leader and/or an institution that you think is making a difference, and tell us what we can learn from this person or this organization. The resulting stories are fascinating in their variety, but they all have one thing in common: They reflect what other students believe to be great leadership and important topics in today's world.

- **"What Can HR Do to . . .?"** We believe that HR has a special role in supporting people and organizations, because HR professionals are at the center of change initiatives and many other challenges inherent in managing and leading today. In addition to the traditional "HR cycle" and the technical support this function provides, HR leadership roles are vitally important today. HR professionals need to *lead*—to provide advice and coaching, to serve as change agents, and to create a learning architecture that will enable people to learn how to lead. To that end, we have included a special section in each chapter that addresses how human resources supports people and the organization as a whole through processes, programs, and activities related to leadership, organization, planning, change, and guiding/managing activities around efficiency and effectiveness.

- **We've made learning *personal* with sets of "Most Popular Discussion Questions."** Throughout the text we draw your attention to how concepts, models, and theories currently affect you, as well as how important this material will be later in life. To support this, at the end of every major section throughout the book, we have included provocative questions that draw your attention to your own experience and cause you to think deeply about and analyze issues. These questions support both your learning and your instructor's teaching. Your instructor may assign these questions, use them in large group discussions, or give them to small groups to discuss and debate.

What's Special about Each Chapter?

Within this book, we've included all of the important and traditional topics found in principles of management and other foundational courses, supported by both seminal and cutting-edge new research. We have also added many topics that are of particular importance today, such as ethics, social and emotional intelligence, critical thinking, creativity, sustainability, and working in a virtual world. Each chapter includes unique material that supports your development now and prepares you to work effectively and lead others in organizations.

Chapter 1—Managing and Leading Today: The New Rules Chapter 1 starts with one of the foundational beliefs of this textbook: *Today, everyone needs to be a leader.* We address the question, "What's the difference between *management* and *leadership*?" We explain that although there are differences, the two roles—manager and leader—are not necessarily distinct. Most employees will need to do *both*, and do both well.

Chapter 2—The Leadership Imperative: It's Up to You Chapter 2 is all about leadership—what it is, how you can develop leadership competencies, and what major theories have contributed to our understanding of leadership. We begin the chapter by sharing what we believe to be the secrets of effective, influential, and responsible leadership: engaging and developing your social and emotional intelligence; sensible and conscientious use of power; and constant attention to ethics and values.

Chapter 3—Motivation and Meaning: What Makes People Want to Work? Chapter 3 covers all major theories of motivation, paying special attention to whether research actually supports the models and the extent to which these models are used explicitly or implicitly in organizations. We also focus on motivation more holistically, pointing out how essential it is for people to find meaning in their work and to engage in it with passion, focus, and creativity.

Chapter 4—Communication: The Key to Resonant Relationships Chapter 4 looks at the many ways humans communicate (e.g., verbal, nonverbal, sign) and how we can use our communication skills to create vibrant, positive environments that foster effective results—or the opposite. We share information about sophisticated skills involved in interpreting emotions, facts, and opinions, as well as how we manage our image through our words and gestures. We also address issues of communication that are important in our technology-driven, increasingly diverse workplaces and communities.

Chapter 5—Planning and Strategy: Bringing the Vision to Life This chapter focuses on the skills and tools necessary to plan in the midst of uncertainty and constant change. We explore how people envision the future, how to create plans that are designed to be changed, and how even the best plans will fall short if they are not grounded in a powerful vision that is personally meaningful to people in organizations. Strategy is also defined and discussed as a dynamic process in which scanning multiple aspects of the environment is the key to ultimate success.

Chapter 6—The Human Side of Planning: Decision Making and Critical Thinking Chapter 6 is unique in that it goes far beyond traditional approaches to rational decision making. In addition to the usual practical steps in the decision-making process, we explore the cognitive, perceptual, and emotional factors that affect people's ability to take in, interpret, and use information when making decisions. We also look at the role of intuition, and how to hone the art and science of making decisions without full information (which is the norm at work and in life today). The latter half of the chapter is dedicated to another important area of study: critical thinking. Along with social and emotional intelligence, many organizations are putting critical thinking at the top of the list of skills that employees, managers, and leaders need today.

Chapter 7—Change: A Focus on Adaptability and Resiliency Chapter 7 is *practical*. In this chapter we direct your attention to how *you* deal with change and how important it is for all of us—employees, managers, and leaders alike—to learn how to change ourselves and to deal well with changes in our societies and our organizations. For example, we address social changes such as diversity in our workplaces and the shifting balance of economic power. We look at revolutionary and evolutionary change, challenging the notion that gradual changes are always less risky. Finally, we present several old and several new change models as practical ways to support people and organizations in positively and powerfully facing change.

Chapter 8—Workplace Essentials: Creativity, Innovation, and a Spirit of Entrepreneurship Chapter 8 focuses on what organizations of all kinds need from us today: new perspectives, new ways of doing things, innovation, and an entrepreneurial spirit. Delving into neuroscience, we demystify creativity by explaining cognitive and emotional processes that are natural to all of us. Creativity is something we *all* can do—not something reserved for geniuses or certain types of people. We also explore creativity's cousin, innovation. We look at the driving forces behind innovation, showing what innovation *really* looks like in organizations. Finally, we explore entrepreneurship, by sharing models and processes that support people in starting their own businesses. Then, we explore the entrepreneurial attributes that all organizations want to see in their employees: passion; good judgment and risk taking; and the ability to get one's ideas taken up by others. We also cover an increasingly important factor in our world's economies: social entrepreneurship.

Chapter 9—Organizing for a Complex World: Structure and Design

In Chapter 9, we show how many organizational structures seem straightforward and easy to understand if we consider elements such as hierarchy, roles, and responsibilities. Then we take the discussion much further—we look at new and creative ways to understand how people, jobs, functions, and processes are *really* coordinated, as well as how both formal and informal organizational structures are powerful drivers of people's behavior and organizational results. We take a systems perspective and explain this in a way that is easy to understand. We also bring the conversation to a practical level, including discussions of how businesses and organizations are legally structured and descriptions of contemporary organizational structures.

Chapter 10—Teams and Team Building: How to Work Effectively with Others

In this chapter we present the seminal research on group development, as well as several newer and highly researched models. We focus attention on several aspects of group dynamics that are critical in organizations today: the importance of creating group norms based on social and emotional intelligence; the power of social roles; how we deal with status and power in groups; and diversity of perspective as a powerful force in groups at work. We also consider how to make our teams as effective as possible and take a fresh look at how to deal with common problems we encounter in teams at school, at work, and in our communities. We examine conflict, and we explore trust as the foundation for conflict resolution and negation. To conclude the chapter, we give straightforward advice on how to build resonant teams that are fun, effective, and productive.

Chapter 11—Working in a Virtual World: Technology as a Way of Life

Chapter 11 is dedicated to the opportunities and challenges inherent in working in our increasingly virtual world. In this chapter we share historical perspectives regarding the advances of technology through the First, Second, and now Third Industrial Revolutions, looking at what occurred both in the West and in other parts of the world (e.g., India, China, Africa) that are industrializing *now*. We also cover recent (and very rapid) advances in information and telecommunications technologies that have revolutionized how and where we work, and we discuss how to build trust and relationships in virtual teams. In addition, we explore how virtual organizations are structured, governed, and led, as well as how they do business. As is true throughout the book, this chapter is full of straightforward discussions about how people can address some of the challenges inherent in this new way of working—by learning new skills while not forgetting that even in a virtual environment, people are at the heart of an organization's success.

Chapter 12—Organizational Controls: People, Processes, Quality, and Results

In our discussions with faculty as we wrote this book, many instructors mentioned that "control" was one of the least engaging and most difficult subjects for students. Yet, as we've discovered in our work in the business world, control is at the top of many companies' lists in terms of priorities. To try to rectify this divide, we start this chapter by locating "control" in historical perspectives about management, in order to show how the processes we see now have evolved over time. Then, using real-world examples and straightforward language, we explain how controls are *used* in organizations, including some of the benefits and the disadvantages. We next cover some contemporary quality control systems and processes, again giving a balanced perspective about their pluses and minuses. We also look at one of the most important control processes in any organization: self-management.

Chapter 13—Culture: It's Powerful Throughout this textbook we focus your attention inward: on your life, your work, and your dreams for the future. In this chapter, we start the discussion of culture by exploring attitudes and norms. If we understand how these factors drive our own and others' behavior, we can begin to make more conscious decisions about how to manage ourselves and our relationships at work. We go on to study foundational and more contemporary research about culture, as well as to explore how cultures change over time, using present-day examples. We also share creative ways to look at culture and powerful models to help "diagnose" culture so that you will be equipped to understand what's working and what's not working in your organizations. Then, we look at certain types of cultures (e.g., ethical) that organizations are trying to build today and how inclusive cultures result in more effective organizations (and are, in fact, mandated by law).

Chapter 14—Globalization: Managing Effectively in a Global Economic Environment Chapter 14 is a comprehensive overview of the historical and current conditions of our interconnected, global world. We look at economic factors and social issues, and at how important it is that we understand the complexity, opportunities, and challenges inherent in a global economy. We present all of this in a way that is intended to both inform and intrigue you. In this chapter we pay special attention to historical and current events and forces in emerging economies—especially those of Brazil, Russia, India, and China. These four countries (and a few others) are growing at unprecedented rates, changing the face of global economics and politics. You need to know what's happened to get us to this point, and you must also understand the possibilities and challenges of the future. To that end, we focus attention on what you can do personally to develop competencies that will support you in working in a global environment.

Chapter 15—Sustainability and Corporate Social Responsibility: Ensuring the Future We have included a chapter on environmental, social, and economic sustainability because these topics are at the forefront of current political, economic, and organizational debates. You and your peers are no doubt engaged in these debates, and we want to share perspectives, facts, controversies, and the many possibilities that are ours to seize. So, in this chapter, we explore climate change, economic development, and various social issues that are affecting individuals, organizations, and nations today. We take on some tough topics: global warming, social/economic issues such as child labor and slavery, and the tension between short-term profit and the long-term health of organizations and communities. We also look at philanthropy, what corporate social responsibility looks like, and what it means for organizations and employees. Throughout the chapter, we draw your attention to your role with respect to these issues and what you can do *now* to be part of the debate.

Chapter 16—Managing and Leading for Tomorrow: A Focus on Your Future This is the last chapter in the textbook, but it is designed to be the next step on your path to becoming a great leader. In this chapter we share our own and others' advice about what managers and leaders will need to do, be, and become to help our organizations and our world. Then, we bring it back to you—a leader of the future. To support your development, we share a few simple but ultimately profound exercises that will help you chart your course, realize your dreams, and contribute your very best to your organizations, your communities, and the world.

Student Supplements

CourseSmart eTextbook   CourseSmart is an exciting new choice for students who are looking to save money. As an alternative to purchasing the print textbook, you can purchase an electronic version of the same content. With a CourseSmart eTextbook, you can search the text, make notes online, print out reading assignments that incorporate lecture notes, and bookmark important passages for later review. For more information or to purchase access to the CourseSmart eTextbook, visit www.coursesmart.com.

MyManagementLab   mymanagementlab (www.mymanagementlab.com) is an easy-to-use online tool that personalizes course content and provides robust assessment and reporting to measure individual and class performance. All of the resources you need for course success are in one place—flexible and easily adapted for your course experience. Some of the resources include an eText version of all chapters, quizzes, video clips, simulations, assessments, and PowerPoint presentations that engage you while helping you study independently.

Acknowledgments

I would like to express my deepest gratitude to the many wonderful people who have helped create this book. Your contributions helped shape our vision at every step of the way, and your ideas, insights, expertise, enthusiasm, and support have been tremendously valuable—thank you. Most of all, thank you for your passion for learning and education, for your dedication to creating and sharing knowledge that will truly support the leaders of the future, and for your commitment to making a difference in the world.

To my **editorial team**, Laura Town and Chris Allen Thomas: Your creativity and tireless commitment to excellence are inspiring. I am deeply grateful to both of you for your incredible writing, editing, research, ideas, passion, and good humor, and for helping shape our vision and this book at every step of the way. Thank you so very much.

 Laura Town, Founder, Williams Town Communications, and Development Editor
Williams Town Cummunications

 Chris Allen Thomas, Manager, Research and Knowledge, *Teleos Leadership Institute*

I would also like to thank the team at **Williams Town Communications** for your professionalism and outstanding work on this book. To Sarah Wagner Felde and Rachael Mann, thank you!

To our **editorial review board**: You have each contributed to the vision of this book in so many ways, and your writing, research, editing, guidance, feedback, and advice have been outstanding. I appreciate all that you have done, and I feel honored to know you and to have worked with you on this book. Thank you. A special thank you to Jim LoPresti and Steven Stovall, whose contributions were extraordinary! In addition to our core editorial review board, special thanks also to my editorial support team. Your talents, knowledge, and enthusiasm are much appreciated.

 Stephen Adams, *Salisbury University*

 Suzanne Rotondo, *Teleos Leadership Institute*

 Frances Johnston, *Teleos Leadership Institute*

 Mike Shaner, *Saint Louis University*

 Bella L. Galperin, *University of Tampa*

 Steven Austin Stovall, *Wilmington College*

 Martha A. Hunt, *New Hampshire Technical Institute*

 Charlotte D. Sutton, *Auburn University*

 Mary Jo Jackson, *University of South Florida, St. Petersburg*

 Gabriela Albescu, *Academy of Economic Studies in Foreign Languages, Bucharest, Romania; Alumni of AIESEC International*

 William T. Jackson, *University of South Florida, St. Petersburg*

 Ondrej Gandel, *University of Economics, Prague, Czech Republic; Alumni of AIESEC International*

 Mary Beth Kerly, *Hillsborough Community College*

 Carloyn Merritt, *Arcadia University*

 Delores Mason, *2YourWell-Being*

 Bobbie Nash, *Teleos Leadership Institute*

 Eddy Mwelwa, *Teleos Leadership Institute*

 Juliane Wigsten, *student, Boston University*

 Jim LoPresti, *University of Colorado at Boulder*

 Christina Yerkes, *Teleos Leadership Institute*

 Clint Relyea, *Arkansas State University, Jonesboro*

Thank you as well to our **editorial reviewer team**. Your feedback on each and every one of the chapters was extremely helpful. As a writer, I truly recognize the value of outside review. The time, attention, and professionalism you gave to this process was outstanding. I am deeply grateful for your review and feedback—and I acted on it! Thank you very much to Stephen Braccio, Vaughn College; Syed Kazmi, Brown Mackie—Fort Wayne; Martha Spears, Winthrop University; Kathleen Davis, Temple University; Janice Ferguson, Bryant and Stratton College; Chuck Foley, Columbus State Community College; Pat Galitz, Southeast Community College; Dan Hallock, University of Northern Alabama; David Hearst, Florida Atlantic University; and Deborah Windes, University of Illinois.

The team at **Pearson Education** has worked tirelessly to bring this vision to life. Thank you all so very much. I have great respect for all that you have contributed—your great ideas, knowledge, and expertise. Special thanks to Sally Yagan, for your vision; to Kim Norbuta for bringing the vision to life; and to Blair Brown for your artistic genius.

Thank you, Pearson team: Blair Brown, senior art director and interior cover designer; John Christiana, creative director; Steve Deitmer, director of development; Claudia Fernandes, editorial project manager; Ian Gold, marketing assistant; Nikki Ayana Jones, marketing manager; Patrice Lumumba Jones, director of marketing; Judy Leale, senior managing editor; Kim Norbuta, acquisitions editor; Carter Anderson, editorial assistant; Ashley Santora, director of editorial services; Eric Svendsen, editor in chief; Arnold Vila, operations specialist; and Sally Yagan, editorial director.

Thanks also to John Makheta, director, Business Development & Strategic Alliances; and Judy Chartrand, Director, Talent Assessessment along with their team at Pearson's Talent Lens Assessment Group.

Thank you, too, to the entire team at **S4Carlisle Publishing Services**, especially Heather Willison, senior project editor; Laura Davis, pager; Beverlee Day, indexer; Susan Konzen, editorial assistant; Kim Weinschenk, illustrator; Lorretta Palagi, copyeditor; and Julie Lewis and Mark Kwicinski, editorial proofreaders.

This book is meant to bring "real life" into the classroom. To all of the **resonant leaders** who contributed time, wisdom, guidance, and real-life experience through your stories, heartfelt thanks: Bonaventure Agata, CSL Behring; Dolores Bernardo, Google; Vittorio Colao, Vodafone Group Plc.; Carol de Wet, Franklin and Marshall College; Lawton Fitt, Thomson Reuters Board of Directors; Niall FitzGerald, Thomson Reuters Board of Directors; John Fry, president, Drexel University; Michael Gaines, CSL Behring; Gail Goodman, Constant Contact; Jill Guindon-Nasir, Ritz-Carlton Hotel Company; Rachel Kamau, Signature HealthCARE; Karen Lombardo, Gucci Group; Mark McCord-Amasis, GlaxoSmithKline; Mary McNevin, McCain Foods; Rafidah Mohamad Noor, AKEPT Malaysia; Peter Oliver, British Telecom Group; Luis Ottley, Fieldstone Middle School; Gavin Patterson, British Telecom Group; Spencer Phillips, MINI Cooper Dealership; Charles H. Ramsey, Philadelphia Police Department; Sheila Robinson, Diversity Woman; Joe Steier, Signature HealthCARE; Kathleen and Rhett Reddell, R&R Fitness; Dato' Nooraishah Ahmad Tajuddin, AKEPT Malaysia; Chade-Meng Tan, Google; and Dan Teree, Ticketfly.

I am also deeply grateful to the **student leaders** who contributed their ideas and their beliefs about what it takes to be a great leader and a successful organization today. You are the future! Thanks to each of you for sharing your wonderful cases: Leah Despain, University of Arkansas; Shaun Hatch, University of Arkansas; Bob Kern, University of Colorado at Boulder; Ryan Killgore, University of Arkansas; Emily King, University of Colorado at Boulder; Julie Lessiter, University of Arkansas; Leonard Mesa, Arkansas State University; Chikasha Muyembe, University of Zambia; Mwitwa Muyembe, University of Zambia; Mulenga Mwenda, University of Zambia; Ben Parker, University of Iowa; Sean Planchard, University of Colorado at Boulder; Chris Allen Thomas, University of Pennsylvania; Mindy Walker, University of Arkansas; Juliane Wigsten, Boston University; and Spenser Wigsten, University of Binghamton.

To my **Teleos Leadership Institute colleagues**: Thank all of you for all that you do to help others be the very best they can be. Your commitment to great leadership and resonant teams, organizations, and communities is inspirational! Thank you to the core team and our wonderful associates: Frances Johnston, Marco Bertola, Eddy Mwelwa, Bobbie Nash, Suzanne Rotondo, Alberto Castigliano, Lee Chalmers, Fiona Coffey, Kaye A. Craft, Delores Mason, Cordula Gibson, Shirley Gregoire McAlpine, Ellie Hale, Ian Hale, Judy Issokson, Janet Jones, Jeff Kaplan, Hilary Lines, Jochen Lochmeier, Gianluca Lotti, Delores Mason, Robert McDowell, Michael McElhenie, Nosisa Mdutshane, Bill Palmer, Laura Peck, Linda Pittari, Gretchen Schmelzer, David Smith, Felice Tilin, Kristin von Donop, Lothar Wüst, Chantelle Wyley, Christina Yerkes, Greg Yerkes, and Amy Yoggev.

To the many **friends and colleagues** who have helped shape the ideas and research in this book, I trust I have honored your contributions. Special thanks to my friends Richard Boyatzis, Peter Cappelli, Daniel Goleman, Peter Kuriloff, Greg Shea, and Kenwyn Smith. Thank you, too, to all the colleagues near and far who have influenced my thinking about leadership: Darlyne Bailey, Ann Baker, Laura Mari Barrajón, Diana Bilimoria, Susan Case, Cary Cherniss, Judy Cocquio, Luigi Cocquio, Harlow Cohen, David Cooperrider, Charlie Davidson, Arne Dietrich, Christine Dreyfus, Charles E. Dwyer, Ella L. J. Edmondson, Rob Emmerling, Jim Fairfield-Sonn, Ingrid FitzGerald, Mary Francone, Ronald Fry, Jonno Hanafin, Hank Jonas, Lennox Joseph, Jeff Kehoe, Toni Denton King, David Kolb, Lezlie Lovett, Carolyn Lukensmeyer, Doug Lynch, Tom Malnight, Jacqueline McLemore, Cecilia McMillen, Mary Grace Neville, Ed Nevis, Roberto Nicastro, Eric Nielson, John Nkum, Dennis O'Connor, Joyce Osland, Asbjorn Osland, Arjan Overwater, William Pasmore, Mary Ann Rainey, Peter Reason, Leslie Reed, Ken Rhee, Craig Seal, Joe Selzer, Dorothy Siminovitch, David Smith, Melvin Smith, Gretchen Spreitzer, Sue Taft, Scott Taylor, Ram Tenkasi, Tojo Joseph Thachankary, Felice Tilin, Lechesa Tsenoli, Bill van Buskirk, Kees van der Graaf, Susan Wheelan, Jane Wheeler, and Judith White

Finally, to **my family**, you inspire me! Heartfelt thanks to Eddy Mwelwa, Rebecca Renio, Sean Renio, Sarah Renio, Andrew Murphy, Toby Nash, Murray R. Wigsten Sr., Carol Wigsten, Murray R. Wigsten Jr., Matthew Wigsten, Mark Wigsten, Lori Wigsten, Jeff Wigsten, Samantha Hagstrom, Bobbie Nash, Mildred Muyembe, Ginny Lindseth, Jon Lindseth, Rita MacDonald, Warren Wigsten, Betty Wigsten, Ellie Browning, and Buzz Browning.

About the Author

Annie McKee has coauthored three groundbreaking books on leadership: *Primal Leadership* (with Daniel Goleman and Richard Boyatzis), *Resonant Leadership* (also with Boyatzis), and *Becoming a Resonant Leader* (with Boyatzis and Frances Johnston). She serves as adjunct professor at the Graduate School of Education at the University of Pennsylvania and guest lecturer at the Wharton School's Aresty Institute of Executive Education. McKee is the founder of the Teleos Leadership Institute, a consultancy serving managers and leaders of businesses and not-for-profits all over the world. She received her doctorate in organizational behavior from Case Western Reserve University and her baccalaureate degree, summa cum laude, from Chaminade University in Honolulu. Her life's work has been to support individuals in reaching their full potential as employees, leaders, and people as they contribute to their families, organizations, and communities. As she puts it, "My mission is to, one by one, with leader after leader, help others embrace the hope that carries me through my life. If I can help people experience hope and find their dreams, and give them the power to realize them, I will consider my life worthwhile."

Managing and Leading Today:
The New **Rules**

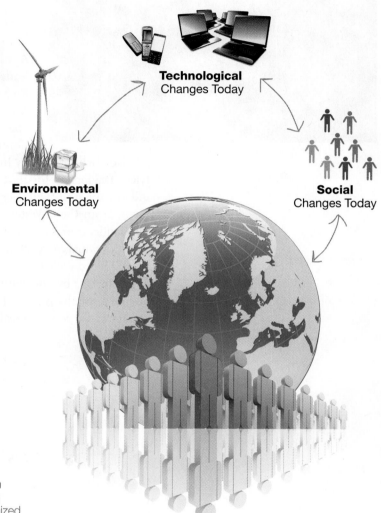

Technological
Changes Today

Environmental
Changes Today

Social
Changes Today

Chapter Outline

Find out what you already know about the concepts in this chapter by going to www.mymanagementlab.com and taking the **Pre-Test.** Your results will generate a customized study plan for Chapter 1.

1. Why Do Managers Have to Be Leaders? (pp. 4–7)

2. What Is the Difference between a Manager and a Leader? (pp. 7–11)

3. What Is the Other Side of the Leadership Coin? (pp. 11–13)

4. A Final Word: Changing World, Changing Expectations of Managers and Leaders (pp. 13–14)

Go back to www.mymanagementlab.com and take the **Post-Test** to verify your understanding of the concepts. **To experience and apply** the concepts, explore the additional material associated with Chapter 1.

PEARSON
mymanagementlab

>Part 1: Leading and Managing for Today and the Future (Chapters **1**, 2, 3, 4)
Part 2: Planning and Change (Chapters 5, 6, 7, 8, 9)
Part 3: Organizing Human Systems (Chapters 10, 11)
Part 4: Controlling Quality, Culture, and Yourself (Chapters 12, 13)
Part 5: Leading and Managing for the Future (Chapters 14, 15, 16)

Planning and Change

8. Workplace Essentials: Creativity, Innovation, and a Spirit of Entrepreneurship

7. Change: A Focus on Adaptability and Resiliency

9. Organizing for a Complex World: Structure and Design

6. The Human Side of Planning: Decision Making and Critical Thinking

5. Planning and Strategy: Bringing the Vision to Life

Organizing Human Systems

10. Teams and Teambuilding: How to Work Effectively with Others

11. Working in a Virtual World: Technology as a Way of Life

Leading and Managing for Today and the Future

16. Managing and Leading for Tomorrow: A Focus on Your Future

1. Managing and Leading Today: The New Rules

14. Globalization: Managing Effectively in a Global Economic Environment

2. The Leadership Imperative: It's Up to You

4. Communication: The Key to Resonant Relationships

3. Motivation and Meaning: What Makes People Want to Work?

1. Managing and Leading Today: The New Rules

15. Sustainability and Corporate Social Responsibility: Ensuring the Future

Controlling Quality, Culture, and Yourself

12. Organizational Controls: People, Processes, Quality, and Results

13. Culture: It's Powerful

3

1. Why Do Managers Have to Be Leaders?

In recent decades we have seen environmental, technological, and social changes that have had profound effects on individuals, families, communities, and governments around the world. These changes have affected the ways in which businesses and organizations are designed, organized, managed, and led, as well as the ways in which people do their jobs and relate with one another at work. Along with these changes come new responsibilities for leaders, managers, and employees alike.

Today, Everyone Needs to Be a Leader

In organizations today, *everyone needs to be a leader*. The challenges and opportunities we face are huge. Each and every one of us must contribute the best of who we are—our talents, skills, and creativity—to address issues that require us to make ethical and responsible business decisions. More and more people around the world have access to information, technology, and a better way of life. We also need to deal with today's challenging global economic and social changes. For example:

- The balance of world economic and political power is shifting, resulting in turmoil and uncertainty, as well as great hope.
- Partly because of better access to food, clean water, and health care, the human population is growing at an unprecedented rate, as is the demand for resources such as land, water, education, and jobs. (See ■Exhibit 1.1.)
- Although rapidly expanding access to computers and telecommunications means that people around the world are far more interconnected now than in the past, increased industrialization and globalization mean that environmental resources are at risk. Meanwhile, ongoing shifts in the world's climate are also cause for concern.
- Despite great progress, there is still the potential for some groups and individuals to continue to be left out of the advances and benefits that positive economic changes, better telecommunications, and advanced information technology can provide.

As these points illustrate, today's world is complex. So are our organizations and businesses. Gone are the days when some people led, some managed, and others just blindly followed orders. In the jobs you have had and in your career going forward, you will be called on to do all three: lead, manage, and follow.

■Exhibit **1.1**

The human population is growing, which is putting a strain on the world's natural and economic resources.

Robert Eaton/Alamy Images

What Being a Leader Means for You

What do these changes mean for you in the workplace? In short, they mean that you will be called on to respond ethically, positively, and powerfully to the many transformations that are occurring in our world. You will have to know your own values as well as your organization's ethical code. You will need to be able to make good decisions—often very quickly and without complete information. To do so, you will need to know how to think analytically, while also relying on your intuition. You will need to be able to build strong, trusting relationships with others and to communicate well with people at all levels of the organization. To do so, you will need to develop your self-awareness and your capacity for empathy and managing yourself well in stressful situations. You will also need to understand and manage your own and others' emotions. (This is called emotional intelligence.)[1] Self-awareness, self-management, and empathy, among other skills, will enable you to inspire people, build powerful and effective teams, deal with conflict, and guide, coach, and mentor others.[2]

Each and every day, you have choices about what you do, how you live your values, and how you influence others. You have opportunities all the time to *lead* other people, no matter what role you hold in an organization. Think about your own experience: Have you worked in a job where you had a manager who directed what you did every day? Were you also influenced by colleagues and your boss's boss? Did you manage *yourself* some of the time? It is highly unlikely that all your instruction and guidance came from your manager, and it's even less likely that you were influenced only by people above you, or that you yourself had no influence. Rather, you were guided by all of the people around you, as they were by you.

Dolores Bernardo, Global Diversity and Inclusion Manager at Google, is a brilliant young leader whose mission is to support Google's unique, diverse, and innovative culture. Her charge is to support *all* of Google's employees in being their best selves at work—and in being the best leaders they can be. Let's look at what she says about what it means to lead today.

Perspectives

I think of leadership as a verb—it's about taking action. It's about inspiring others to come along with you. It's about taking the time to reflect. And it's about taking the time to build connections and relationships with people so they believe in what you are trying to do—and so they believe in you.

Anyone can be a leader at Google. That's the only way any of our companies will succeed today. If every single Googler feels empowered to innovate, to create new products and improve on existing ones, we'll not only keep up with the changes that are happening around us, we'll be the change. Each one of us needs to think this way: we can't just respond to change, we have to lead change. Our success hinges on our ability to understand the needs of all Google's hundreds of millions of users. The unique perspective that each person brings to leadership is what makes Google's products serve our diverse user community.

Dolores Bernardo, Global Diversity and Inclusion Manager at Google

Source: Personal interview with Dolores Bernardo conducted by Annie McKee, 2009.

But what if we all recognized this situation and every one of us thought of ourselves as a leader? What if you decided to truly see yourself as a leader now, rather than waiting until you've been given a senior level job? What if we all took seriously our responsibility to inspire others, reflect on our actions, and build positive, powerful relationships? It's common sense: If we all acted this way, we'd have a much better chance of harnessing the brain power we need to face the challenges and opportunities in our organizations, our communities, and the world.

Still, many people don't see themselves as leaders. Why is this? Part of the reason is that from the time we were small, we have been taught that leadership and authority go hand in hand with certain roles: parent, school principal, business owner. And it's true: All of these roles require leadership. What's different today is that we can't hide behind our roles and rely on others to lead—instead, leadership is up to all of us. Therefore, it's essential that we adjust our understanding of what it means to be a manager, versus what it means to be a leader.

Most Popular » Discussion Questions

1. Think about the groups you are part of, including groups associated with your family, friends, school, and work. Who looks to you for leadership in these groups? What do they want from you? How do you inspire them to follow you?
2. Think about Dolores Bernardo's statement that "leadership is a verb." What does this statement mean to you?
3. Complete the "Whom Do You Lead" exercise to help see that, in fact, you are a leader (■Exhibit 1.2).

■Exhibit **1.2**
Whom Do You Lead?

Whom Do You Lead?

1. On the chart on the following pages, brainstorm and write a list of several of the groups you belong to. Break these groups down as much as you can (e.g., instead of writing "family," note the various branches and groups within your family; instead of writing "work," describe your immediate team, the organization around it, and groups that you touch or have some responsibility for). Be sure to also list groups in which your authority is informal, and your "title" isn't the only source of your power. Finally, consider other arenas where you guide, advise, and help people.

2. Next to each group, label or name your role (e.g., "sister" or "brother"; "oldest cousin"; "team leader"; etc).

3. For each position, formal and informal, describe your role (e.g., "I am the person everyone comes to when there is a conflict in the family"; "I am the one who knows the professor"; "I am the designated team leader").

4. For each of your roles, write who looks to you for guidance, help, and vision and describe what they look for from you. Be as specific as you can (e.g., "My family looks to me to resolve problems. . ."; "My team looks to me to understand their needs, provide help, remove obstacles, and share information"; "My boss looks to me to deliver on my promises").

My groups	My role	Description of my role	People and groups who turn to me for help, guidance, or direction	What people look for from me

Continued on next page>>

■Exhibit **1.2**
Continued

My groups	My role	Description of my role	People and groups who turn to me for help, guidance, or direction	What people look for from me

Source: Adapted from Annie McKee, Richard Boyatzis, and Frances Johnston. 2008. *Becoming a resonant leader.* Boston: Harvard Business School Press.

2. What Is the Difference between a Manager and a Leader?

Manager
An individual who makes plans; organizes and controls people, production, and services; and who regulates or deploys resources.

Leader
A person who is out in front, influencing and inspiring people to follow.

What's the difference between a manager and a leader? To answer this question, we must first consider what each of the words means. *Manager* is a derivation of the verb *manage*, and it comes from the Italian *maneggiare* (to handle). Back in the 1500s, the word referred to the handling of horses. The root of *maneggiare* comes from the Latin word *manus* (hand). Notice that *handle*—meaning *to control*—has a similar origin, in this sense: A person's hand is his or her primary tool for physically controlling the environment. The meanings of these words were eventually extended to business and the control of resources.

The word *leader* can be traced back to Old English *lædan* (to guide; to cause to go with one). It is also a form of *liðan* (to travel). So, a word leader can be interpreted as someone who guides others on a journey. As you can see, this way of looking at leadership is about *influencing* rather than forcing people to go in a particular direction.

Using these definitions, a **manager** can be described as an individual who makes plans; organizes and controls people, production, and services; and who regulates or deploys resources. A **leader**, in contrast, is a person who is out in front, influencing and inspiring people to follow.[3] There is no reason whatsoever that a manager can't be a leader, or that a leader can't manage. In fact, the political, social, and technological changes of recent years require us all to do both. (See ■Exhibit 1.3.)

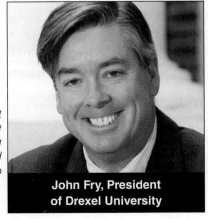

Perspectives

Here's what John Fry, president of Drexel University in Philadelphia, says about leading and managing:

We have to focus on actually <u>getting things done</u> and <u>inspiring people</u> to be their very best. In order to bring about big changes, you have to really understand the workings of the institution. You have to

John Fry, President of Drexel University

understand the numbers: How does this place work financially? You have to understand the structure: How do the various groups, like faculty, staff, and students, interact with one another? And you have to understand some of the nuts and bolts issues that need to be addressed.

But it's more than simply management: The job of a leader is to clear the path. You

Continued on next page>>

Perspectives   **Continued**

need to focus people on their essential greatness, which allows them to tackle some of the difficult issues. You're not trying to create the aura of a powerful leader; you're trying to create the aura of a powerful community. If this works, long after you are gone the community will carry on successfully and with confidence.

The worst kind of leader is the kind where the place crashes and burns after he or she leaves. To avoid this, you need to manage and lead in a way that people are inspired to learn to work together to get things done.

Source: Personal interview with John Fry conducted by Annie McKee, 2009.

■Exhibit **1.3**

The Dali Lama, spiritual leader of Tibet, meets with Nancy Pelosi, the first female speaker of the U.S. House of Representatives.

krtphotoslive/Newscom

As John Fry points out in the *Perspectives* feature, we all need to manage *and* lead. But much of the research on managerial and leadership behaviors reinforces the assumption that only a few individuals (usually those at the top of an organization) are responsible for activities such as strategic planning, crafting and communicating a vision, or inspiring people to pursue organizational goals. Today, this type of differentiation between management and leadership is no longer useful.

However, we should still look at the early research and perspectives on which this differentiation between management and leadership was based. Once we understand these assumptions, we can begin to adjust them to fit today's world.

Traditional Views of Managers and Leaders

Traditionally, managers are viewed as people who perceive an organization as something that needs to be organized, controlled, and maintained. In contrast, leaders are traditionally viewed as people who look at the "big picture" and view the environment as a blank canvas on which they can test their creative ideas for driving an organization toward success.

Managers have been encouraged to focus their energies on problem solving and controlling resources, while leaders have been encouraged to focus on vision and the environment. Managers have been taught to see the *independence* of their tasks and responsibilities in relation to their division or functional unit, whereas leaders have been encouraged to view and oversee the *interdependence* of all tasks, people, and functions in the organization, rather than picturing them as isolated, self-contained "silos."

Managers are expected to be tactical, carrying out the strategic vision of their leaders like good soldiers. Managers are tasked with establishing and administering order and control in order to reduce complexity. In contrast, a leader is expected to thrive on chaos and possess a unique vision for the organization. Research has sought to articulate these perceived differences, as shown in ■Exhibit 1.4.

In summary, one could say that managers have traditionally been expected to occupy themselves with the status quo and how they can work within these parameters. Leaders, on the other hand, have been called on to ask important questions about the organization's future: "Where are we going?" "How are we going to get there?" and "What if?" Also, whereas a manager has historically been seen as someone who does things "right," a leader is more often pictured as someone who can be called on to "do the right thing."

■Exhibit **1.4**

A Traditional View of What Managers and Leaders Do	
Managers Tend to . . .	**Leaders Tend to . . .**
• *Control resources.* • *Be problem solvers.* • *Seek efficiency.* • *Be comfortable with order.* • *Be concerned with how things get done.* • *Play for time and delay major decisions.* • *Seek compromises.* • *Identify goals that arise out of necessity.* • *Adopt impersonal attitudes toward goals.* • *Coordinate and balance opposing views.* • *Avoid solitary activities.* • *Work from low-risk positions.* • *Avoid displaying empathy.*	• *Create and provide resources through motivation.* • *Be comfortable with uncertainty.* • *Function well in chaotic environments.* • *Be concerned with what events and decisions mean to people.* • *Seek solutions that do not require compromise.* • *Take highly personal attitudes toward goals.* • *Identify goals that arise out of desire.* • *Inspire strong emotions.* • *Be comfortable with solitude.* • *Work from or seek out high-risk activities.* • *Have meaningful, highly personal mentorship relationships.* • *Be empathic and actively read others' emotional signals.*

Source: Adapted from Zaleznik, Abraham, 1992. Managers and leaders: Are they different? *Harvard Business Review*
(March–April): 126–35.

What Managers *Actually* Do

So what exactly does a manager do? During the 1970s and 1980s, noted scholar Henry Mintzberg decided to answer that question by following managers on the job and recording their daily activities. Mintzberg's findings are important and continue to be relevant today. Whereas the prevailing opinion of managers' behavior prior to this research was one of thoughtful planning and careful execution of everyday activities, Mintzberg discovered that a manager's work was fraught with meetings, pressure to deliver performance results, and a great deal of "fire fighting," or constantly addressing unexpected issues. Managers, according to Mintzberg, put in long work hours and work at an intense pace.[4]

Based on this research, Mintzberg came up with a solid outline for a manager's "job description" as described in ■Exhibit 1.5. Each of the three broad categories—informational, interpersonal, and decisional—is a category into which multiple associated roles fall. In particular, the informational category includes the roles of monitor, disseminator, and spokesperson; the interpersonal category includes the roles of figurehead, leader, and liaison; and the decisional category includes the roles of entrepreneur, disturbance handler, resource allocator, and negotiator.[5]

Mintzberg's work is important in that it took a serious look at the actual behavior of managers and offered valuable insight into managerial roles and their attending activities. What's also important to note about this research is that many of these roles and activities are now expected of more people—people who may not formally be called "managers." That's because during the past two decades, many businesses and organizations have streamlined operations and decision making. Whereas it used to be that only managers—and many times, senior managers—did things like disseminate information, foster innovation, or negotiate contracts, nowadays nonmanagerial staff is often empowered to do these things.

As you will see in Chapter 2, *The Leadership Imperative: It's Up to You*, a vast amount of research has been done on leadership behavior. The early studies about leadership looked at personal characteristics and physical, intellectual, and psychological traits. Later research focused on leadership behaviors and styles and the importance of being

■Exhibit **1.5**

Henry Mintzberg's Managerial Roles

Category	Role	Organizational Function	Example Activities
Informational	Monitor	Responsible for information relevant to understanding the organization's internal and external environment	Handle correspondence and information such as industry, societal, and economic news and competitive information
	Disseminator	Responsible for the synthesis, integration, and forwarding of information to other members of the organization	Forward informational e-mail; share information in meetings, conference calls, webcasts, etc.
	Spokesperson	Transmit information to outsiders about organizational policy, plans, outcomes, etc.	Attend management meetings; maintain networks between the organization and stakeholders
Interpersonal	Figurehead	Symbolic leadership duties involving social and legal matters	Attend ceremonies; greet visitors; organize and attend events with clients, customers, bankers, etc.
	Leader	Motivate, inspire, and guide employees' actions; provide opportunities for training; support appropriate staffing	Build trusting relationships with employees; build effective teams; manage conflict
	Liaison	Build and maintain relationships between the organization and outside entities	Work on external boards; create and maintain social networks (real and virtual) with key stakeholders
Decisional	Entrepreneur	Scan the organizational environment for opportunities; foster creativity and innovation	Participate in strategy and review meetings for new projects or continuous improvement
	Disturbance handler	Manage organizational problems and crises	Participate in strategy and review meetings that involve problems and crises; get involved directly with key issues and people
	Resource allocator	Take responsibility for allocation of all types of organizational resources	Create work schedules; make authorization requests; participate in budgeting activities
	Negotiator	Represent the organization during any significant negotiations	Negotiate with vendors and clients; settle disputes about resource allocation

Source: Mintzberg, Henry. 1975. *The Nature of Managerial Work.* New York: Harper & Row.

able to adapt one's approach to a particular situation. More recently, research has focused on bringing various fields of study together to help us understand what it means to lead effectively. For example, research in the areas of management, psychology, and neuroscience is helping us understand that leadership competencies, social and emotional intelligence, ethics, and the responsible use of power are key to great leadership. Emerging from this research is the growing understanding that one of the foundations of good leadership is self-awareness: the capacity to reflect on, articulate, and understand one's emotions, thought processes, and physical responses to certain situations (like stress). Throughout this book, we will encourage you to develop self-awareness. To see what one effective and successful leader has to say about this topic, see the *Perspectives* feature.

Perspectives

Jill Guindon-Nasir is responsible for the Leadership Center for Ritz-Carlton. Ritz-Carlton is one of the best known and finest hotel brands in the world. But they're also known for something else: their outstanding customer service which is provided by each and every employee, no matter their role in the organization. The Ritz-Carlton Leadership Center is one of the places that provides training to employees, as well as for other companies—it's that good. Jill says this about why self-awareness is so important to leadership:

Resonant leadership and emotional intelligence are <u>huge</u>. Employees want a real person—genuine, authentic, caring, and able to connect. In order to do this, you have to be it. People see through you: You have to know yourself, know your values, and be clear with people about what

**Jill Guindon-Nasir
of the Leadership Center
for Ritz-Carlton**

you stand for. You have to have passion, and people need to see your passion. They don't want a "flavor of the month" leader. They want consistency. You need to be clear and honest about what you believe in, and be very open about it. You need a calling and a cause—people want to know who you are and what you stand for. And you have to be a risk-taker. Sometimes you're going to be standing alone. People will follow you when they see that you are doing what you said you would do, courageously.

In the end, you have to be true to yourself before you can lead others. First, you need to lead yourself.

Source: Personal interview with Jill Guindon-Nasir conducted by Annie McKee, 2009.

In this section, we have looked at the traditional views of what managers and leaders do, and we've made a case that at work, everyone needs to be both a manager and a leader. We all need to learn skills that will enable us to plan, organize people and resources, and control processes. We also need to learn to show people who we are and what we stand for and to demonstrate skills and competencies that will enable us to inspire others to follow our lead. Finally, we need to learn how to follow others. Leadership is not a one-way street. We all lead, and we all follow.

Most Popular » Discussion Questions

1. Think about the last time you worked on a project with a group at work or in school. What did you and others do that could be described as "managerial" behavior? What did you and others do that could be described as "leadership" behavior?
2. Consider Mintzberg's managerial roles in Exhibit 1.5. Which of these roles are easy for you to play or come naturally? Which roles do you think you need to learn more about or learn how to do better?
3. Consider Jill Guindon-Nasir's words: "In the end, you have to be true to yourself before you can lead others. You need to lead yourself." What does this mean to you?

3. What Is the Other Side of the Leadership Coin?

Without followers, there are no leaders. So although we must strive to develop self-awareness and to develop our values, ethics, and competencies in such a way that we can lead others responsibly, we also need to learn how to follow.[6] Although bookstores and workshops are full of information on how to be a good leader, there is less about what it takes to be an effective follower. That is in part because in American culture and many others, the term *followership* has a very negative connotation.[7] How many times have you heard the term "mindless sheep" in relationship to followers? This attitude is a significant problem in today's flatter, more networked organizations where the line between who is leading and who is following can be quite blurred.[8]

Barbara Kellerman of the Harvard Business School proposes that it is not just leaders who can be judged as effective or ineffective.[9] The same process, she believes, also holds true for followers. Think about your own experience: More than likely you have been in the position of trying to lead a group in which one or more of the members simply doesn't want to follow. They want to do their own thing, they resist being influenced, or they cause disruption in the group. Many times, this kind of behavior doesn't arise because people fundamentally disagree with what is being asked of them—they just don't want anyone else directing their activities. In today's highly interconnected complex organizations, this attitude just doesn't work. Good followers, according to Kellerman, take the time and effort to invest in who and what their leaders are all about.[10]

Barbara Kellerman also proposes a way to look at how engaged we are when following others. In her model, good followers actively support good leaders and respond appropriately to bad leaders. As you can see in ■Exhibit 1.6, there are five types of followers: isolates, bystanders, participants, activists, and diehards.

Other leadership scholars are beginning to take notice of the importance of understanding different types of followership. For example, one of the most respected leadership scholars in the world, Warren Bennis, notes that the characteristics of both leadership and followership are likely to be different from culture to culture.[11] As organizations become more globally integrated, these cultural differences are likely to become increasingly important.

Large organizations are complex systems, and their fate in a globally competitive environment may very well depend on how well the organizational leaders understand and respond to the needs of the rank-and-file members, as well as how we all learn to follow when things change and the "rules" are different.[12]

Research on followership or the study of it in practice has been largely overlooked until recently. Indeed, followers have a power all their own that is important to the effective functioning of an organization. The Wharton School's Michael Useem helps us understand this power in his book *Leading Up: How to Lead Your Boss So You Both Win.*[13] Other scholars have suggested other effective followership tools, such as effective resistance and managing up as being useful for all of us to learn.[14] **Managing up** is a term used to describe how followers can influence leaders.

Managing up
A followership tool that enables followers to influence leaders.

Isolates
Followers who are nonresponsive or indifferent to leaders.

Bystanders
Followers who are not engaged.

Participants
Followers who are actively engaged and make an effort to be supportive and have impact.

Activists
Followers who feel strongly about their organization and leaders and act accordingly.

Diehards
Followers who are passionate about an idea, a person, or both and will give all for them.

■Exhibit **1.6**

Types of Followers

- **Isolates:** Isolates are nonresponsive or indifferent to their leaders. They are typically found in large organizations. They do their jobs and make no effort to stand out.

- **Bystanders:** Bystanders are exactly what the name implies. They are not engaged in the life of the organization. They are observers and spectators rather than active participants, passively doing their jobs and offering little active support.

- **Participants:** Participants are actively engaged and make an effort to support and impact the organization. If they agree with a leader, they will support him or her. If they disagree, they will oppose the leader.

- **Activists:** Activists feel even more strongly about their organizations and leaders than participants and act accordingly. When supportive, they are eager, energetic, and engaged. When they disagree strongly with what a leader does, they are vocal and will take action.

- **Diehards:** Diehards are passionate about an idea, a person, or both and will give all for them. When diehards consider something worthy, they become dedicated.

Source: Kellerman, Barbara. 2007. What every leader needs to know about followers. *Harvard Business Review* 85(12): 84–91.

So, although we started this chapter with the statement "Today, everyone needs to be a leader," we now add ". . . and everyone needs to be an effective follower."

Most Popular » Discussion Questions

1. When have you been a good follower? What inspired you or encouraged you to take up this role in a positive way?
2. When has following others been difficult for you? What were the reasons you found it difficult? What did you do?
3. What do you do when you are expected to follow someone, yet you know what he or she is doing is wrong or could be done better? How effective are you at influencing that person from the follower position? What could you do better?
4. Can you think of ways to be a better leader? A better manager? A better follower?

---

4. A Final Word: Changing World, Changing Expectations of Managers and Leaders

Niall FitzGerald, Deputy Chairman of Thomson Reuters.

In this chapter we have made a case for learning to be a good leader, manager, and follower. Our world today requires this from all of us. People everywhere are facing great challenges and great opportunities, and business has a huge role to play in helping all of us create a better future.

We end this chapter with a few words from Niall FitzGerald, a distinguished and world-renowned leader. Following the meltdown of the world's financial services that began in 2007, Niall reflected on our responsibility as businesspeople and leaders to create a better world. Here's part of what he said about the crises and changes that we face today, and what we need to do about it:

> . . .This is a crisis that affects many: Young people cannot find jobs; those in or near retirement see the value of their pension funds decline. Charities watch their investments fall in value, property owners owe more money than their homes are worth. [Yet there is still] a culture of "reward for failure" for business leaders who remain unwilling to acknowledge any responsibility for their part in the crisis. No acceptance by so-called leaders of their accountability. An economic, but also a moral, failure. . . .
>
> It is important that we examine more basic concepts that have to do with the way that business works and the way in which it relates to the world around it. . . .
>
> So I shall talk about the lessons of freedom and responsibility. About how business must earn freedom and sustain it by acting responsibly. I shall explain why responsible behavior is central to business strategy. . . .
>
> And I shall suggest that we judge business leaders by wider criteria than profit and that they accept accountability for the impact their actions have on society.
>
> In short, business leaders must behave properly. . . Yet businesses were not created to be moral beings. They might operate in ways that we might regard as moral or immoral, but their primary purpose was the creation of wealth. . . .The question is how do we get business operating in a more consistently beneficial fashion?
>
> Business leaders need to acknowledge what's gone wrong and move to rebuild trust in business. Trust is not a property that can be bought. It is a quality that must be earned. There are times in life we may take people on trust, but we rarely trust them again when they let us down. Someone once said, "Trust departs on a fast horse and returns if ever slowly on foot. . . ." This is how businesses rebuild trust—brick by brick. That may be a slow process, but it is also a rewarding one.

What are the principles that encourage trust? Perhaps the main one is embodied in all the great religions of the world, the idea that we do unto others as we would have them do unto us. . . .

It makes sense for business [leaders] to behave better. . .They should behave in a socially responsible way not because they think they ought to—attractive as that moral probity might be—but because it is absolutely in their longer-term commercial interests to do so. For a business to be sustainable in the long term it needs a properly functioning society around it. Intelligent business leaders realize that they share responsibility for building and maintaining that society.

Don't think this is easy. Commercial decisions do not necessarily have obvious and indisputable social benefit. There are tensions between commercial opportunity and social impact. Tough trade-offs have to be made. . . .

So let us have companies set out their values and standards of behavior, apply them in a way that is consistent with their culture, and then be prepared to explain why they take the actions they have. . . .

From now, businesses and customers are looking for partners they can trust. Society is entitled to demand better leadership.[15]

Key Terms

1. Why Do Managers Have to Be Leaders? (pp. 4–7)

Key Terms None

---

2. What Is the Difference between a Manager and a Leader? (pp. 7–11)

Key Terms

Manager An individual who makes plans, organizes and controls people, production and services, and who regulates or deploys resources. p. 7

Leader A person who is out in front, influencing and inspiring people to follow. p. 7

3. What Is the Other Side of the Leadership Coin? (pp. 11–13)

Key Terms

Managing up A followership tool that enables followers to influence leaders. p. 12

Isolates Followers who are nonresponsive or indifferent to leaders. p. 12

Bystanders Followers who are not engaged. p. 12

Participants Followers who are actively engaged and make an effort to be supportive and have impact. p. 12

Activists Followers who feel strongly about their organization and leaders and act accordingly. p. 12

Diehards Followers who are passionate about an idea, a person, or both and will give all for them. p. 12

4. A Final Word: Changing World, Changing Expectations of Managers and Leaders (pp. 13–14)

Key Terms None

Chapter 1 Visual Summary

1. Why Do Managers Have to Be Leaders? (pp. 4–7)

Summary: It is important for you to know what leadership means to you. In organizations today, everyone must be a leader because globally, many social, political, and economic changes must be faced. You will be called upon to make good decisions, act ethically, and inspire others throughout your career.

2. What Is the Difference between a Manager and a Leader? (pp. 7–11)

Summary: Managers and leaders have traditionally been seen as different. The managerial role has been traditionally viewed as one that reduces complexity, whereas leaders are expected to "thrive on chaos." The truth, however, is that everyone needs to develop both managerial and leadership skills. We all need to be able to see the "big picture," as well as be able to plan, organize, and control people and resources.

3. What Is the Other Side of the Leadership Coin? (pp. 11–13)

Summary: All leaders need to be able to follow, and all followers need to be able to lead. Indeed, it is hard to imagine any role in work or society that does not include both leading and following in some fashion. Approaching leadership and followership as skills to be developed is a critical challenge for today's managers. Furthermore, the concept of "managing up" reminds us that responsible followership includes the ability to help your boss become a better leader.

4. A Final Word: Changing World, Changing Expectations of Managers and Leaders (pp. 13–14)

Summary: Today's world is calling on all of us—employees, managers, and leaders alike—to take responsibility for our organization's actions. Society is calling on business, and on us, to lead in a socially responsible way.

16. Managing and Leading for Tomorrow: A Focus on Your Future

14. Globalization: Managing Effectively in a Global Economic Environment

1. Managing and Leading Today: The New Rules

Leading and Managing for Today and the Future

2. The Leadership Imperative: It's Up to You

4. Communication: The Key to Resonant Relationships

3. Motivation and Meaning: What Makes People Want to Work?

15. Sustainability and Corporate Social Responsibility: Ensuring the Future

Resonant Leadership

Ideal Self

Real Self

Mindfulness

Experimenting

Learning Plan

The Leadership Imperative:

It's Up to **You**

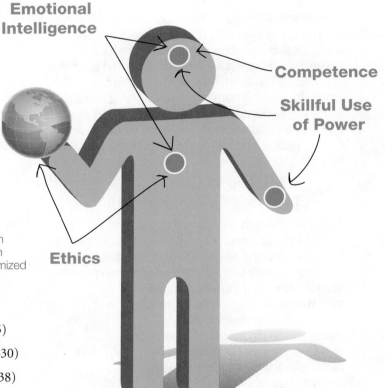

Emotional
Intelligence

Competence

Skillful Use
of Power

Ethics

Chapter Outline

Find out what you already know about the concepts in
this chapter by going to www.mymanagementlab.com
and taking the **Pre-Test.** Your results will generate a customized
study plan for Chapter 2.

1. Leadership: Whose Responsibility Is It? (pp. 18–20)

2. What Is the Secret to *Effective* Leadership? (pp. 20–25)

3. What Is the Secret to *Influential* Leadership? (pp. 25–30)

4. What Is the Secret to *Responsible* Leadership? (pp. 30–38)

5. How Do Theories and Models Explain Management and
   Leadership? (pp. 39–44)

6. Is It Time to Take a Stand for Transformational Leadership?
   (pp. 44–45)

7. What Is HR's Role in Supporting Excellent and Ethical
   Leadership? (pp. 45–48)

8. What Can We All Do to Become Great Leaders?
   (pp. 48–51)

9. A Final Word on Leadership (p. 51)

Go back to www.mymanagementlab.com and take the **Post-Test**
to verify your understanding of the concepts. **To experience and apply**
the concepts, explore the additional material associated with Chapter 2.

> **Part 1:** Leading and Managing for Today and the Future (Chapters 1, **2**, 3, 4)
Part 2: Planning and Change (Chapters 5, 6, 7, 8, 9)
Part 3: Organizing Human Systems (Chapters 10, 11)
Part 4: Controlling Quality, Culture, and Yourself (Chapters 12, 13)
Part 5: Leading and Managing for the Future (Chapters 14, 15, 16)

8. Workplace Essentials: Creativity, Innovation, and a Spirit of Entrepreneurship

7. Change: A Focus on Adaptability and Resiliency

9. Organizing for a Complex World: Structure and Design

Planning and Change

6. The Human Side of Planning: Decision Making and Critical Thinking

5. Planning and Strategy: Bringing the Vision to Life

16. Managing and Leading for Tomorrow: A Focus on Your Future

1. Managing and Leading Today: The New Rules

Leading and Managing for Today and the Future

14. Globalization: Managing Effectively in a Global Economic Environment

Organizing Human Systems

10. Teams and Teambuilding: How to Work Effectively with Others

11. Working in a Virtual World: Technology as a Way of Life

2. The Leadership Imperative: It's Up to You

4. Communication: The Key to Resonant Relationships

3. Motivation and Meaning: What Makes People Want to Work?

2. The Leadership Imperative: It's Up to You

15. Sustainability and Corporate Social Responsibility: Ensuring the Future

12. Organizational Controls: People, Processes, Quality, and Results

Controlling Quality, Culture, and Yourself

13. Culture: It's Powerful

17

1. Leadership: Whose Responsibility Is It?

Senior executives in our businesses and organizations should know how to lead. But in recent years, we have seen far too many examples of businesspeople failing miserably as leaders. For example, if we look at the corruption and scandals at Enron and World-Com, Bernie Madoff's Ponzi scheme, and the subprime mortgage debacle, we can see abuse of power, incompetency magnified by greed, major flaws in character, and a breakdown in values and ethics. These scandals—and the people behind them—ruined lives and tipped entire economies into recession and disarray.

Here's the catch, though: It takes more than a few bad apples to do this kind of damage. In most cases, there were only a few architects of the fraud scheme and only a few people directly involved in unethical practices. However, many people were either indirectly involved or probably saw the signs that something was gravely wrong. So, whose responsibility is it to make sure that people wield power responsibly, that they enact good leadership, and that they uphold ethical standards?

To answer that question, let's move a little closer to home, to the kinds of experiences many of us have had with leaders. Think about the jobs you have held, the teams you have been part of, and the schools you have attended. Chances are, in all of those situations, you had opportunities to see leadership up close. How many bosses, team leaders, teachers, or counselors have you had who were excellent leaders? How many were average or even bad leaders? Most of the time, when we ask people in organizations this question, they remember far more average or bad leaders than good. That simply isn't acceptable today. Our businesses, institutions, and communities require all of us to lead—and to lead well. The world is faced with great opportunities and even greater challenges. Therefore, all of us need to learn how to use power responsibly, how to apply our skills, and how to live by our values and ethics.

Now, think about your own behavior at work, on teams, and in your community. You have had opportunities to lead people, either formally or informally. How much attention did you pay to learning how to use your power effectively so you could influence others positively? Did you ensure that you lived your values consistently? Did you consciously develop leadership skills? If you are like most people, you had every intention of doing all of the above, and you probably worked hard at being a good leader. But maybe because of the pressures of the job or because of the difficulty in "studying" your own behavior, you paid less attention to improving your leadership than you might have wanted. Maybe you even noticed situations—or were part of situations—that made you feel uncomfortable and were not in line with your values, yet you didn't speak up. This happens to all of us at one time or another. The key to great leadership is recognizing that each of us has the obligation to use power responsibly, study our own leadership behavior, seek to improve, and constantly stand up for the values and ethics that guide us and our organizations.

Lawton Fitt is a prominent member of the Thomson Reuters board of directors, and she is well known for her financial brilliance and excellent leadership. She can teach us some valuable lessons about what it means to lead today, as you can see in the Perspectives feature.

We All Need to Become Great Leaders

As Lawton Fitt knows, in today's challenging business world we do not have the luxury to assign certain behaviors and values to leaders alone. In successful organizations, everyone understands the link between their jobs and the company's strategy. In addition, because the best organizations are more complicated and must be more adaptable, far more people need to motivate others, to paint a compelling picture of the future, to engage people's passion, to build enthusiasm, and to direct people's energy.

At all levels in organizations, we are regularly faced with new challenges and we need to know how to respond. Take change, for example—change is everywhere, and it's constant in

Perspectives

Lawton Fitt's career has been—and continues to be—stunning. At a young age, she became a valued member of the Goldman Sachs investment banking team, and she soon went on to become one of the most successful leaders in the company. She describes great leadership this way:

To me, business is about more than getting people to perform tasks effectively. People bring their lives to work. As a leader, you need to create an organization that has a vision and mission that people can feel proud of—and emotionally engaged with. You just can't shy away from this. An emotional connection to the organization and to work is very important and deeply satisfying to people. It's what makes people want to do their best, to make decisions that they, and everyone, can be proud of.

Lawton Fitt, Board Member of Thomson Reuters

And the best leaders are human. They have deep self-knowledge, they learn from experience, and they are willing to share what they know. They care about the long-term outcomes of their actions—especially when it comes to people.

If you are just trying to take the hill without considering the consequences for people, you won't wear well as a leader. People may take the first hill with you, maybe even the second. But after that, if they see that you don't care about them and don't respect them, they just won't follow you.

Source: Personal interview with Lawton Fitt conducted by Annie McKee, 2009.

organizations. Those of us who expect continuity and stability simply will not be effective at work, and we certainly won't be good leaders. If, however, you see change as an opportunity and embrace it with enthusiasm and hope, you will be seen as an outstanding leader.

People who rely on managers and others to "do the right thing" while they themselves adopt any means at hand to achieve their goals risk making unethical decisions. They also risk treating people badly and creating an unhealthy, dissonant environment that does not support organizational effectiveness. You, however, can choose to explore your values and ethics and rely on them to guide your choices. You can also learn to use your power and to influence people and groups so that *everyone* is better off. Maybe most importantly, if you seek to *learn how to lead,* develop leadership competencies, and increase your capacity for self-awareness, you are on the road to becoming a great leader.

Leadership Is Learned

The good news is that you can learn how to be a great leader. Despite what you might have heard, *leaders are not born—they are made.* We learn how to lead as a result of our experiences and by deliberately improving our leadership skills, learning to wield power responsibly, and attending to our values so we can make ethical decisions. Managers and employees can—and must—become leaders by seeking out learning experiences and developing the abilities that support vision, inspiration, and influence. This takes courage. It's always easier to point at "them"—those faraway leaders who can be credited or blamed for everything. In reality, though, there's no such thing as "them." It's just "us."

Today more than ever before, everyone needs to learn how to lead. That's what this chapter is about: How you—as a person, employee, or manager—can become a great leader. To start, you will discover three secrets to becoming an outstanding leader:

- *Emotional and social competence:* The secret to e*ffective* leadership
- *Power:* The secret to *influential* leadership
- *Ethics:* The secret to *responsible* leadership

You will also study several theories that seek to explain leadership, with a special focus on transformational leadership. You will then learn how HR can support excellent leadership. Finally, you will discover what we can all do to ensure that we are great leaders in work and in life.

2. What Is the Secret to *Effective* Leadership?

Competencies
Capabilities or abilities that include both intent and action, and that can be directly linked to how well a person performs on a task or in a job.

■Exhibit **2.1**
The iceberg as a metaphor.

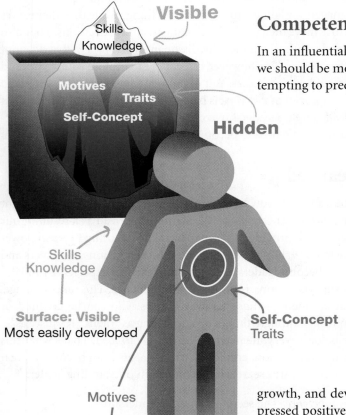

The secret to effective management and leadership is that we must master competencies related to social and emotional intelligence. **Competencies** are capabilities or abilities that include both intent and action, and that can be directly linked to how well a person performs on a task or in a job.[1] When it comes to management and leadership, the competencies that make the difference are related to social and emotional intelligence. Social and emotional intelligence are abilities linked to self-awareness, self-management, social awareness, and relationship management. Before exploring social and emotional competencies in depth, let's define competencies and look at why they are important for everyone at work.

Competencies Explained

In an influential article published in 1973, scholar David McClelland argued that we should be more concerned with competencies than with intelligence when attempting to predict the potential success of students and employees.[2] One reason McClelland and his colleagues were searching for factors other than intelligence was because they were aware that intelligence tests tend to have cultural biases built into them that result in inaccurate scores for people outside the majority culture. Furthermore, they had evidence that these tests were poor predictors of occupational success. In fact, as far back as 1959, research pointed out that there is little correlation between intelligence test scores and success at work.[3]

McClelland and well-known scholar Richard Boyatzis then sought to determine exactly what *was* related to success on the job. They found that when a person demonstrates a competency, he or she is acting intentionally and behaving in a way that leads to successfully accomplishing a task. For example, if a manager engages an employee in a conversation about performance, the manager is demonstrating a competency called "developing others" if he or she (1) intended to guide and direct the employee's behavior toward more effective performance, growth, and development, and (2) gave specific, constructive feedback and expressed positive expectations for the employee's improvement.[4]

Competencies also involve other levels of personal characteristics that impact intention and action: motives, enduring personal traits, self-concept, knowledge, and skills. As you can see in ■Exhibit 2.1, knowledge and skills are more easily observed. For this reason, knowledge and skills are often the focus of development in training programs. Motives, traits, and self-concept are "below the water line" and are not as easy to develop as knowledge and skills. However, in order for people to develop competencies, *all* levels must be attended to. In fact, if the deeper aspects of a competency are not attended to, the likelihood that the competency will be improved is much lower. Let's look at each aspect of competencies in more detail.

Five Components of Competencies

Motives are needs or drives that fuel action. Motives are closely linked to McClelland's three-needs theory of motivation, which is discussed in Chapter 3. According to McClelland, people are often driven by three needs: to achieve personal goals, have influence, and build positive relationships with others. *Traits* are psychological or physical characteristics and/or consistent ways of responding to situations. For example, race car drivers have good hand-eye coordination and a tendency to remain calm in stressful situations. *Self-concept* includes attitudes, values, and self-image—all powerful drivers of actions. For example, a self-confident person who values honesty will be more likely to take action when he or she sees unethical behavior.

Knowledge is information that a person has at his or her disposal or the ability to find information when needed. For example, when you complete this course, you will have gained information about management and leadership. You should also have gained knowledge about how to evaluate theories of management and leadership, and you should understand how to use research to inform your use of theories in the future.

Finally, *skills* are learned abilities that are needed to perform tasks, such as the ability to type, use the Internet for research, or analyze financial data. Most professions require distinctive knowledge and skills. A surgeon, for example, needs to be skilled in the use of surgical equipment, and he or she must have a knowledge of human anatomy. Similarly, an accountant needs to be skilled in the use of spreadsheet programs and have a knowledge of tax laws.

Threshold and Differentiating Competencies

Some competencies are necessary just to do a job (threshold competencies), whereas others support outstanding performance (differentiating competencies). Threshold competencies include basic expertise, experience, and many cognitive abilities.[5] For example, threshold competencies for a restaurant manager include the ability to calculate the amount of food and beverages to buy each month, plan a schedule for the wait staff, and use spreadsheet programs.

Competencies related to social and emotional intelligence, pattern recognition, and systems thinking differentiate superior leaders from average leaders. (This will be examined later in the chapter.) To return to the example of the restaurant manager, differentiating competencies would include the ability to manage personal emotions when things go wrong and to inspire people with a powerful vision.

In recent years, the threshold and differentiating competencies that used to be expected only of senior managers have become expected of almost everyone at work. For example, almost all professionals need to be able to type. As hard as it is to believe, that competency used to be reserved for secretaries and assistants. Everyone also needs to be proficient in common software programs and able to use the Internet, among other technical competencies. Today, most jobs also require some degree of systems thinking and other cognitive competencies that support critical thinking and good decision making. Furthermore, because people often work with less direct supervision than in the past, relational competencies such as self-management and the ability to understand and influence others are essential in order to set goals and engage colleagues in attaining them.

Technical, Cognitive, and Relational Competencies

Early research indicated that competencies fall into one of three categories: technical, cognitive, or relational. People who are adept at technical competencies are proficient in the use of tools and processes related to a specialized field. Technical skills are especially critical in areas such as engineering, finance, and information technology.

Cognitive competencies include things like the ability to see the "big picture" in systems such as groups and organizations. Seeing the big picture means that you can recognize that various bits of information are not isolated; they actually form a pattern (this is called pattern recognition). Another example of a cognitive competency is the ability to analyze complex situations and to understand how all things and people relate to one another (this is called systems thinking). These two cognitive competencies—pattern recognition and systems thinking—are crucial in many jobs today.[6]

Finally, relational competencies support the development of strong working relationships with colleagues, direct reports, senior management, and customers. These competencies are often called "people skills," and they include self-awareness, self-management, empathy, and inspirational leadership, among others. Relational competencies support us in building teams, coaching, monitoring performance, and providing feedback.

Competency Models

People need to develop numerous competencies in order to be effective in their jobs and as leaders. This is where competency models come in. A **competency model** is a set of competencies that are directly related to success in a job and are grouped into job-relevant categories. Thousands of competency models are in use in organizations today. The best ones are well researched and based on the study of people, jobs, and organizational contexts. This is the case with one early comprehensive model, presented in ■Exhibit 2.2, which was created by Richard Boyatzis.[7] This model is grounded in extensive research, including 2,000 interviews with managers in both the private and public sectors. This research demonstrated that certain competencies distinguished superior managers from average performers. Within Boyatzis' model, these competencies are organized into five clusters: action skills, leadership skills, directing skills, managing skills, and focus on others.[8]

Over the years since their original research was conducted, Boyatzis and his colleagues have extended their studies to include thousands of people performing in a wide array of jobs around the world. Their conclusion was that when it comes to leadership, one subset of competencies makes all the difference: competencies related to social and emotional intelligence.[9]

Competency model
A set of competencies that are directly related to success in a job and are grouped into job-relevant categories.

Social and emotional intelligence
Competencies linked to self-awareness, self-management, social awareness, and relationship management that enable people to understand and manage emotions in social interactions.

■Exhibit **2.2**

The comprehensive management competency model organizes competencies in five clusters.

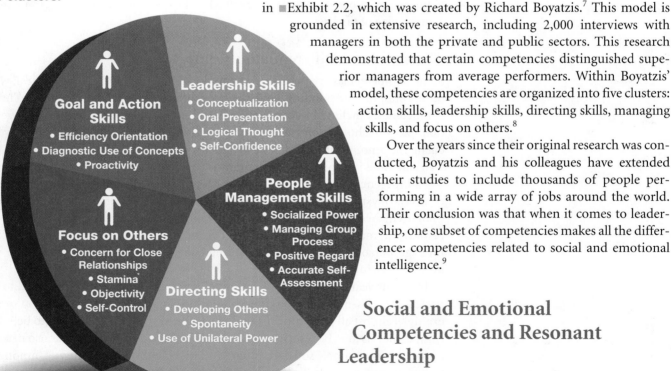

Goal and Action Skills
• Efficiency Orientation
• Diagnostic Use of Concepts
• Proactivity

Leadership Skills
• Conceptualization
• Oral Presentation
• Logical Thought
• Self-Confidence

People Management Skills
• Socialized Power
• Managing Group Process
• Positive Regard
• Accurate Self-Assessment

Focus on Others
• Concern for Close Relationships
• Stamina
• Objectivity
• Self-Control

Directing Skills
• Developing Others
• Spontaneity
• Use of Unilateral Power

Source: Based on Boyatzis, Richard E. 1982. *The competent manager: A model for effective performance.* Hoboken, NJ: Wiley-Interscience.

Social and Emotional Competencies and Resonant Leadership

Popularized by Daniel Goleman in 1995, the term *emotional intelligence* and, more recently, the phrase **social and emotional intelligence** refers to competencies linked to self-awareness, self-management, social awareness, and relationship management (■Exhibit 2.3). These competencies enable people to understand and manage their own and others' emotions in social interactions.[10]

Social and emotional intelligence competencies enable people to understand and manage their own and others' emotions in social interactions.

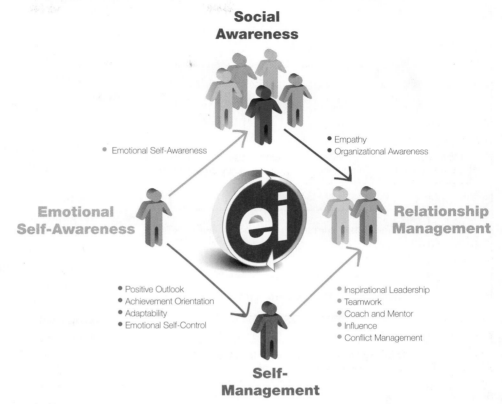

Source: Based on Boyatzis, Richard E. 2008. Competencies in the 21st century (Guest Editorial). *Journal of Management Development* 27(1): 5–12. McKee, Annie, Boyatzis, Richard, Johnston, Frances (2008). *Becoming A Resonant Leader: Develop Your Emotional Intelligence, Renew Your Relationships, Sustain Your Effectiveness.* Boston: Harvard Business Press.

Resonant organizations
Organizations characterized by a powerful and positive culture in which people have a shared sense of excitement and commitment to mutual goals.

Resonant leaders
Socially and emotionally intelligent, visionary people who lead and manage in ways that enable everyone to contribute their very best.

Self-awareness
The ability to notice and understand one's emotions and their effects.

Social and emotional competencies also enable people to create resonance in relationships, groups, and organizations. **Resonant organizations** are characterized by a powerful and positive organizational culture in which people have a shared sense of excitement and commitment to mutual goals. **Resonant leaders** are socially and emotionally intelligent, visionary people who lead and manage in ways that enable everyone to contribute their very best.[11]

The study of social and emotional intelligence emerged from research about competencies, multiple intelligences (the different ways intelligence can be demonstrated), the study of personality, the psychology of emotion, and neuroscience.[12] This concept has gained tremendous popularity in organizations in recent years, because research emphasizes the link between emotional and social competence and a person's effectiveness as a leader, manager, and employee.[13] These competencies help us create resonant environments that support people in being their very best.[14]

For example, the competency called **self-awareness** is the ability to notice and understand one's emotions and their effects. We have all seen people who *don't* have this competency: the friend yelling at us who says, "I'm not angry!" or the boss with a face like a thundercloud who says, "It's a great day, isn't it?" These kinds of interactions are confusing and can be destructive. The same boss using this competency effectively would recognize that he is angry, maybe as a result of a flat tire on the way to work. He'd know that his mood impacts his employees, so he would take a few minutes to calm down before coming to the office. Or he might say something like, "Sorry, I know I look upset—I had a bad morning."

Part of the reason that attending to one's own and others' emotions is so critical to leadership is that emotions are linked to our ability to think clearly, make good decisions, and

■Exhibit **2.4**

Neurophysiology, personality, motives, traits, and values are all related to competencies.

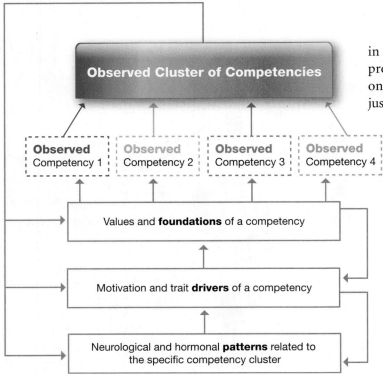

Source: Adapted from Boyatzis, Richard E. 2008. Competencies in the 21st century (Guest Editorial). *Journal of Management Development* 27(1): 9.

Limbic resonance
Refers to the fact that emotions are contagious and a powerful driver of our feelings, thoughts, and behaviors.

focus on tasks. Our brains are complex structures, and there is an important relationship between neurophysiology (how the brain works), psychology (personality, motives, and traits), and values (deeply held beliefs about how to act on our ideals).[15] This relationship is shown in ■Exhibit 2.4.

Let's look at social and emotional intelligence in action in a hypothetical—but common—experience. You have probably walked into a crowded room and, although no one said anything, you knew something was wrong. You could just feel it. Because you were aware of the uneasiness in the room, you may have decided to behave differently than if things had seemed calm or upbeat.

Some people call this intuition, but it is really a complex combination of competencies and the fact that emotions are contagious. By closely attending to subtle clues such as people's facial expressions, body language, who was sitting with whom and the like, you were using *empathy,* a social awareness competency. And by deciding to behave differently than you normally would, you were employing emotional self-control. You may also have been relying on emotional self-awareness, if you recognized that the minute you walked into the room you began to feel anxious, even though you had no personal reason to feel this way.

Catching emotions from other people happens all the time. **Limbic resonance** is a term used to describe how emotions are both contagious and a powerful driver of our feelings, thoughts, and behaviors.[16] Scholars Annie McKee, Richard Boyatzis, and Frances Johnston put it this way: "Just as [emotions] travel like electricity in our brains and bodies, feelings travel rapidly *between* people. . . . We are constantly tuning in to the emotional state of someone standing next to us, and it affects how we feel, what we think, and what we do."[17]

Back to the example of walking into a charged atmosphere: By employing emotional self-awareness, self-management, and empathy, you increase the likelihood that you (1) can avoid catching people's negative emotions, (2) are prepared to deal with conflict or trouble in the group, and (3) are one step ahead in trying to understand what is happening in the group and what you might do to help solve the group's problems.

Self-Awareness: The Foundation of Social and Emotional Intelligence

Self-awareness is at the heart of social and emotional intelligence, and social and emotional intelligence are at the heart of great leadership. So, to become a great leader, you must focus on developing self-awareness. But how can you do this? To start, just ask yourself questions such as these:

• What am I feeling, and how are these feelings affecting my thoughts and actions?
• What values are important to me, and how do I use them when making decisions?
• Do I see myself as powerful? Why or why not?

As you continue to read this chapter, you have the opportunity to develop self-awareness by consciously applying the concepts described in the text to *yourself.* For instance, in the next section you have a chance to reflect on power: How do *you* influence people? How do *you* respond to others attempts to influence you? Later, we will discuss ethics. You can then reflect on *your* ethics and values. This kind of reflection will improve your self-awareness and your social and emotional intelligence. As a result, you will become a more effective leader.

Most Popular » Discussion Questions

1. Review the competency model in Exhibit 2.2. Which of these competencies do you regularly use when you work with a team? Choose two competencies and describe how you developed them and how you can improve.
2. Think about a situation in which you believe you were at your best as a leader. What happened? What did you do? What were the results? Review the social and emotional competencies in Exhibit 2.3. Which of these did you demonstrate in this situation?
3. Reflect on a situation where you "caught" someone else's emotions. What was the impact on you? Do you have ways to manage yourself so you can choose when to take on other's moods or not?

---

3. What Is the Secret to *Influential* Leadership?

Power
Influence over or through others.

Organizational politics
Involve many things, including internal competition and the pursuit of personal goals at the expense of others or the organization.

Using power effectively is the secret to influential leadership. **Power** is influence over or through others. Power is the ability to get people to do what one desires by changing how those people think, feel, or act. Because we all need to be leaders at work, we all need to understand how to use our power. That seems obvious. However, it is surprising how often people minimize or misuse their own power and deal poorly with others' power. This is partly because many people are uncomfortable with the idea of wielding power and with the idea that others might use power to influence them. Another reason many people are nervous about power is because the common view of "power" is that with it come victims. In other words, people are constantly on the alert for abuse. People also have difficulty with power at times because it is linked closely to culture, as you will see in Chapter 13. Different cultures view, use, and distribute power differently. In today's multicultural organizations, it is especially important to develop the ability to understand, manage, and use power in ways that are cross-culturally acceptable.[18]

Researchers who study power conclude that it is essential for all of us to understand the sources of power in ourselves and others to be able to work most effectively and to achieve our own and the organization's goals.[19] If you have a clear idea about how power is used in your organization, you will be more likely to make ethical decisions, influence others, and deal well with destructive organizational politics. **Organizational politics** involve many things, including internal competition and the pursuit of personal goals at the expense of others or the organization. As distasteful as they are to most people, organizational politics are a reality in most organizations. And if you don't understand them, you can't help change the situation for the better. Worse, you can become a victim of destructive political dynamics.

Power is a fact of social life in organizations, and managers and leaders need to understand how to use it for the benefit of their employees, the organization, and the people and communities that the organization serves. A useful framework for understanding power is presented in ■Exhibit 2.5. This framework describes five sources of power that a person can draw on when trying to influence others: legitimate power, reward power, coercive power, expert power, and referent power.

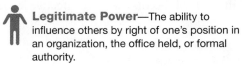

■Exhibit **2.5**

There are five sources of power that people can use to influence others.

Legitimate Power—The ability to influence others by right of one's position in an organization, the office held, or formal authority.

Reward Power—The ability to influence others by giving or withholding rewards such as pay, promotions, time off, attractive projects, learning experiences, and the like.

Coercive Power—The attempt to influence others through punishment.

Expert Power—The ability to influence others through a combination of special knowledge and/or skills.

Referent Power—Power that comes from personal characteristics that people value and want to emulate and that cause people to feel respect or admiration.

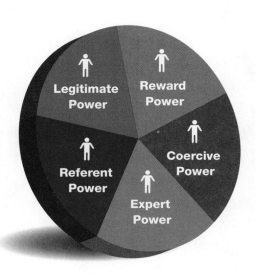

Sources of Power Exist in Different Forms

Legitimate power
The ability to influence others by right of one's position in an organization, the office held, or formal authority.

Reward power
The ability to influence others by giving or withholding rewards such as pay, promotions, time off, attractive projects, learning experiences, and the like.

Coercive power
The attempt to influence others through punishment.

Expert power
The ability to influence others through a combination of special knowledge and/or skills.

Legitimate power is the ability to influence others by right of one's position in an organization, the office held, or formal authority. For example, in your school, numerous people have legitimate power, including the president, deans, and instructors. These individuals have the authority to influence people and processes. As an illustration, instructors may include an attendance policy in the syllabus that requires you to attend all classes.

Reward power is the ability to influence others by giving or withholding rewards such as pay, promotions, time off, attractive projects, learning experiences, and the like. Rewards can also take the form of acknowledgment, praise, attention, and respect. *How* a manager uses reward power affects motivation and group morale. When we feel that rewards are granted in a fair and equitable manner, we tend to be highly motivated. On the other hand, when we believe that managers use rewards unfairly or to control us, we tend to react badly. We can quickly become demoralized, resist our manager's influence, and feel less inclined to do our best on the job.

Coercive power is the attempt to influence others through punishment. A better term for coercive power may be *corrosive power*, because this source of power can be, and often is, highly destructive. Punishment is not motivating, and it can have serious negative side effects for the individuals punished, the entire group, and the relationship between employees and managers. At times, the use of coercive power and punishment is necessary, for example, when an employee behaves unethically, sexually harasses another employee, or can't or won't correct serious performance problems. In these and other serious situations, punishment such as firing or demotion might be a necessary last resort.

In far too many instances, however, managers and leaders rely too heavily on coercive power. Explanations for this phenomenon range from incompetence to insecurity. Whatever the reasons, the result is almost always the same: fearful, angry, or resentful employees who comply only when necessary, and a dissonant environment that saps people's creativity and resilience.[20]

Expert power is the ability to influence followers through a combination of special knowledge and/or skills. For example, Colin Browne is a graduate of the University of Delaware. He is also a master carpenter. For big projects, such as building an addition on a house or remodeling a kitchen, he employs architects, electricians, painters, and other carpenters—all of whom are well-respected professionals. Because Colin is known to be an expert when it comes to carpentry, and because he is also known to be

Referent power
Power that comes from personal characteristics that people value and want to emulate and that cause people to feel respect or admiration.

■Exhibit **2.6**
Colleen Barrett has legitimate and referent power.

Getty Images, Inc./Bloomberg/Contributor/Mike Fuentes

Empowerment
Trusting employees to make decisions and to take responsibility for their decisions and actions.

artistic and to pay attention to aesthetics, members of the construction teams regularly consult him and gladly accept his advice. Colin is particularly effective at influencing people because of the way he uses his expert power—he is always respectful of others, never acts as if he is better than his colleagues, and shares his passion for his work in a way that inspires people.

Many people develop expertise over the course of their careers, as Colin has. But it is important to note that expert power is especially important to entry-level employees and new managers as well. Because it's less likely at this point in one's career to be able to use legitimate, reward, or coercive power, tapping into one's expertise and sharing it in a way that supports others can help you be more effective.

Referent power comes from personal characteristics that people value and want to emulate and that cause people to feel respect and admiration. When employees feel that a manager or leader cares for them, is admirable, and will do the right thing even if it means taking personal risks, they often feel a strong sense of loyalty and choose to follow willingly.

Like expert power, referent power is very useful early in one's career. Without the benefit of reward, coercive, or legitimate power, new employees and new managers need to rely on their personal characteristics and expertise to get others' attention and respect. Referent power is also important throughout the later parts of one's career. Take the example of Colleen Barrett, now president emeritus at Southwest Airlines. Her rise through the company was nothing short of amazing—from legal secretary and assistant, to corporate secretary, to vice president, and finally, to president from 2001 through 2008. Barrett was one of the architects of Southwest's successful business model and legendary employee- and customer-focused culture.

Barrett gained legitimate power at Southwest, and she used reward power as well. But anyone who ever met her knows that it is her referent power—her respect for people, her humility and humor, and her focus on doing the right thing—that sets her apart as a leader. In other words, people follow Colleen Barrett because they want to.[21] Moreover, Colleen *shares* her power with others—this is called empowerment (■Exhibit 2.6).

Empowerment

Possibly one of the most important ways to wield power is to share it. This is because no single individual has all the answers or can make all the decisions. Effectively running an organization takes everyone's knowledge and good judgment. Good managers find ways to involve everyone, so that everyone's input can be used. This is what is known as empowerment.

Empowerment is trusting employees to make decisions and to take responsibility for their decisions and actions.[22] Noted scholar Gretchen Spreitzer points out that empowerment can be seen as a form of organizational democracy.[23] In democratic societies, people contribute time, talent, energy, and ideas. They engage in the process of governing by voting, expressing concerns, and contributing to their communities. It is much the same in organizations. Democratic participation fueled by empowerment is demonstrated by members' ability to self-govern, to voice concerns, and to contribute ideas. And as you will see in Chapter 3, participation and empowerment are also important parts of motivation.[24]

Empowered Employees and Empowering Organizations

Empowered employees have a say in how things get done—they have a voice at work, and they use it.[25] Because they are encouraged to point out problems without fear, empowered employees can improve work processes. Also, if they have some control over the products or services they create or deliver, these employees will be motivated to contribute to decisions to improve work design, production processes, and quality. They can also take responsibility for organizing their work and setting goals individually or in self-managing teams. Empowered employees tend to be more engaged and committed, which drives them to surpass average performance.

An empowering organization will have systems and processes that encourage employee involvement, such as suggestion programs, ethics hotlines, or quality circles (structured groups that examine and improve work processes). These organizations may also have support programs that enable employees to deal directly with conflicts, such as mediation processes or access to ombudspersons. Additionally, empowering organizations often feature compensation programs that support collaboration and quality, such as profit-sharing plans.

Micromanagement
The practice of overcontrolling others and their work, as well as paying far too much attention to details and how employees do their work.

Finally, empowering organizations discourage micromanagement. **Micromanagement** is the practice of over controlling others and their work, as well as paying far too much attention to details and how employees do their work. Micromanagement is common and destructive. It is a waste of everyone's time, employees and managers alike. And it causes employees to feel resentful, discouraged, and disrespected—a recipe for ineffectiveness and dissonance in the culture.

Empowering organizations support managers and leaders in learning new management skills that focus on excellent communication, accurate assessment of employees' abilities, group and team facilitation, and creating an environment that is marked by trust, commitment, and openness to learning.[26] These skills help managers avoid the pitfalls of micromanagement. You can see how empowerment really works in Leonard Mesa's *Student's Choice*.

Student's Choice

Leonard Mesa

Big City Leader in a Small-Town Plant

Sam began working as a supervisor for Riviana, one of the biggest rice retailers in the United States, in the fall of 2000. He worked in the Houston, Texas, production facility, where he supervised a crew that operated production lines and maintained sanitation and safety requirements. The Houston production plant was located only 10 miles away from the company's corporate headquarters, which meant that vice presidents and even the CEO often stopped by to visit the plant and talk with supervisors. Rather than being scared of the visits, Sam looked at them as his opportunity to shine.

He and the other managers promoted an environment where the employees were empowered to act quickly and decisively when choices had to be made. As a result, the people Sam supervised were happy, motivated, and worked hard. Four years later, Sam was offered a promotion to manager in a different department located in the small, rural town of Carlisle, Arkansas. After discussions with his wife and the other managers at the Carlisle facility, Sam decided that taking the promotion was the best decision for both the family and his career.

Sam was excited to get to work, but before arriving at the new plant, he determined that what he *wasn't* going to do was make big changes until he had a thorough understanding of the people and the operations. On the first day, he took the opportunity to meet the entire staff, and he invited all employees to provide a few details about themselves, explain their responsibilities, and ask him questions. He also spent the first two months at his new position learning what he could about the culture, the processes, and their relation to the rest of the organization. More importantly,

he learned about each one of the people who worked at the facility. In those two months, Sam built solid relationships with the machine operators, as well as with the other managers. This gave Sam an opportunity to understand the culture. He also learned about the unique challenges the plant faced.

Leading a new group of employees in a new environment was difficult. Back in Houston, the people he supervised spoke freely and were not afraid to make decisions. This new group of employees were motivated and hard working, but they rarely offered suggestions for improvement or acted independently. They had not been empowered to do so in the past—and they were not expecting to be empowered now. Desiring to change this situation, Sam started forging alliances with other managers who would be most influential in facilitating change and who had similar values with regard to employee empowerment. They put a lot of work into building trust with the employees and implementing localized policies that encouraged communication and employee decision making. In less than a year, the small changes began to have a big impact in terms of decreased absenteeism and lower employee turnover, fewer work injuries, and higher quality of work output. Some of the other managers became interested in what Sam was doing differently. He found that they, too, wanted to do their best but had never been encouraged to experiment with alternative leadership styles.

By creating a more empowered workforce, Sam and the managers were able to make significant changes in the facility's approach to sanitation, documentation, and production, while also improving the quality of the products manufactured at the plant. Together, they were able to start implementing much-needed changes—changes that improved organizational effectiveness *and* organizational culture.

Source: Adapted from a case by Leonard Mesa.

Empowerment and Theories X, Y, and Z

Researchers have been concerned with employee involvement and empowerment for several decades. Beginning in the 1960s, first Douglas McGregor and then William Ouichi proposed Theories X, Y, and Z to describe three starkly different attitudes about the degree to which people take responsibility for their work.[27] Each of these theories is presented here.

Theory X states that the average employee is inclined to be lazy, without ambition, and irresponsible. This attitude toward workers can result in micromanagement (the opposite of empowerment). Besides being insulting, Theory X results in poor relationships with employees, a dissonant and unpleasant environment, and eventual burnout for the manager. It's simply impossible to guide employees' every move, and stand ready to reward or punish behavior all the time. Today's workplace doesn't allow for that.

Theory Y states that workers are inherently ambitious, responsible, and industrious, and that they will work hard to help an organization reach its goals. This stance fosters an environment that is conducive to employee involvement, participation, and decision making—in a word, empowerment. Most people thrive in such an environment.

Theory Z states that in organizations that have strong, relational cultures, employees have discretionary freedom in local decision making and are trusted to work autonomously. In other words, they are empowered.

Although on the surface Z organizations look ideal, it is nearly impossible to imagine a present-day organization that will offer lifetime employment, another characteristic Ouchi points to. And, Z organizations are often described as benevolent but paternalistic.[28] In organizations like this, kind but nevertheless directive leaders control the most important processes and decisions. This can backfire over time, because it can result in a workforce that is overly dependent on management. Despite these drawbacks, however, the Z approach can generate positive morale and loyalty. Leaders who follow a course of benevolent paternalism are genuinely concerned about their employees, and employees show loyalty in return. Furthermore, research indicates that benevolent paternalism works in many cultures, which is important to know in today's global environment.[29]

The Empowerment Movement Today

The movement to empower people in organizations has become popular in recent years. This is happening for several reasons. First, there aren't as many levels of hierarchy as there used to be in most organizations—organizations are "flatter" today. **Flat organizations** have few levels of hierarchy, which drives a need for more people to make decisions. Second, organizations have become much leaner, meaning that fewer people are doing the work than in the past, and people are often exceedingly busy. It simply is not practical for managers and leaders to make all of the decisions all of the time. When work is well organized, and when employees manage day-to-day activities and are empowered to make certain kinds of decisions, the more senior managers can spend their time on bigger issues such as spotting industry trends and creating a resonant environment that sparks passion and leads to excellent performance.

The empowerment movement is also taking hold because it has become clear that the person closest to the work process can often make better decisions than managers or leaders who are farther removed from the process. Finally, empowerment is more important today than ever before because the nature of the employment contract is changing. In the past, the employment equation went something like this: "I will come to work and do my best to fulfill the organization's expectations in exchange for respect, reasonable pay, decent working conditions, and a promise of lifetime employment." Today, the equation is more like this: "I will share my talents and expertise with this organization only as long as I am fairly compensated, have opportunities to learn and grow, can do and be my best, and feel that my contributions are valued."[30] If these conditions are not met, people can and will leave.

Theory X
A belief system that holds that the average employee is inclined to be lazy, without ambition, and irresponsible.

Theory Y
A belief system that holds that workers are inherently ambitious, responsible, and industrious, and that they will work hard to help an organization reach its goals.

Theory Z
A belief system that holds that in organizations with strong, relational cultures, employees have discretionary freedom in local decision making and are trusted to work autonomously.

Flat organizations
Organizations that have few levels of hierarchy, which drives a need for more people to make decisions.

Empowering people at work is good for organizations. When scholars at the Brookings Institution, a well-known think tank, consolidated all major studies on empowerment, they found that "[i]f you sum it all up, employee participation has a positive impact on business success. It is almost never negative or neutral."[31]

Most Popular » Discussion Questions

1. Discuss a situation from your experience in which power was abused. How was it abused, and what were the consequences for you personally and for others?
2. Think of a leader who has influenced you directly. What sources of power did this leader draw on? What was the effect of his or her use of these sources of power on you?
3. Discuss the pros and cons of an empowered workforce. Draw on your own experience at work and in school to support both sides of the argument.
4. How can empowerment support democratic processes? How might participation, empowerment, and democratic processes at work have an effect on people's behavior outside work?

---

4. What Is the Secret to *Responsible* Leadership?

The secret to responsible management and leadership is ethics. The relationship between leadership and ethics is simple: How we lead is determined by what we value. The behavior of any individual—in business, politics, medicine, law, or any other field—is determined by the underlying values, principles, and beliefs that contribute to the person's code of ethics.

Organizations also have both explicit and implicit codes of ethics. In this section, we first look at how people develop values and ethics. Then, you will see what happens when individuals lose sight of values and ethics. To further explain how ethics affect us at work, we then examine levels of ethics and important aspects of business ethics. Finally, we look at how people rationalize unethical behavior and how you can handle everyday decisions ethically.

Developing Values and Ethics

Ethics
A set of values and principles that guide the behavior of an individual or a group.

Ethics is a set of values and principles that guide the behavior of an individual or a group. The word *ethics* comes from the Greek word *ethos*, meaning "moral character" or "custom." Aristotle refers to ethics as being greatly aided by inner self-control and virtue.[32] Saint Augustine considered it our "inner dwelling place," our heart.[33] That inner dwelling place houses our fundamental orientation toward our lives, including our values.

Values
Ideas that a person or a group believes to be right or wrong, good or bad, attractive or undesirable.

Values are ideas that a person or a group believes to be right or wrong, good or bad, attractive or undesirable. Values are beliefs about how things should or should not be; they impact how we behave, and they form the basis of our ethical code. An **ethical code** is "a system of principles governing morality and acceptable conduct."[34] A leader's ethical code is of paramount importance to an organization. We look up to our leaders in life and at work, and many scholars believe that the example a leader sets can be considered "the most important weapon in the ethics arsenal" of an organization.[35]

Ethical code
A system of principles governing morality and acceptable conduct.

Terminal values
Personal commitments we make to ourselves in relation to our life's goals.

The two kinds of values we deal with as leaders are *terminal* and *instrumental*. **Terminal values** are personal commitments we make to ourselves in relation to our life's goals. These values are what we desire for ourselves and others in life, such as freedom, wisdom, love, equality, and a world at peace. Other examples of terminal values include happiness, pleasure, self-respect, inner harmony, and family security.[36]

Instrumental values
Preferred behaviors or ways of achieving our terminal values.

Instrumental values are preferred behaviors or ways of achieving our terminal values. Examples of instrumental values include ambition, competence, creativity, honesty, integrity, and intellectual ability.

How do we develop and adopt values and ethics? Values are learned, like a language. As children, we quickly learn we are rewarded for good behavior and punished for bad behavior. This is the beginning of our moral development. We learn about values and ethics from our parents, friends, teachers, and spiritual figures, and even from the books we read and the movies we watch. We also learn on the job, often adopting the values and ethics of the organizations we work for, and we emulate the behavior and values of our leaders.

In this era of global instability, what you believe and how you choose to act on your values is more relevant than ever before. The study of personal values and ethics at work is extremely important—maybe the most important topic in this book. The last 10 years have seen an inordinate number of blatant ethical transgressions and breaches of trust in every sector of our society. Each of us is responsible for changing this—and to do so, you need to start with yourself. You must identify those values that you will never compromise, no matter what.

Levels of Ethics

According to scholar Edwin Epstein, there are four distinct levels of business-related ethics: individual, professional, organizational, and societal.[37] Each of these levels of ethics can have a powerful effect on our behavior. As we sort out what "the right thing to do" is, we need to understand each of these levels and how they might affect us.

Individual Ethics

Individual ethics
A personal code of conduct when dealing with others.

Individual ethics refers to a personal code of conduct when dealing with others. An individual's ethical code is formed and influenced by his or her social environment, including family, friends, school, religious organizations, and so on. Although individual ethics derive from personal values, it is also true that people have multiple identities linking them ideologically to professions, employers, and society. These other levels of ethics, described in ■Exhibit 2.7, have a profound effect on people's behavior at work.

■Exhibit **2.7**

Levels of ethics affect people's behaviors.

 Individual Ethics—A personal code of conduct when dealing with others.

 Professional Ethics—Standards that outline appropriate conduct in a given profession.

 Organizational Ethics—The values and principles that an organization has chosen that guide the behavior of people in the organization and/or what stakeholders expect of the organization.

 Societal Ethics—Principles and standards that guide members of society in day-to-day behavior with one another.

Professional ethics
Standards that outline appropriate conduct in a given profession.

Professional Ethics

The profession you choose will likely have its own set of ethical standards. **Professional ethics** are standards that outline appropriate conduct in a given profession. Professional ethics are often written and explicit. For example, the American Society for Training and Development, the Conference Board, the Financial Accounting Standards Board, the American Medical Association, and unions are all guided by explicit professional codes of ethics. Some organizations, like the American Institute of Certified Public Accountants (AICPA), have lengthy codes of ethics. Just a small part of AICPA's code reads as follows:

> These Principles of the Code of Professional Conduct of the American Institute of Certified Public Accountants express the profession's recognition of its responsibilities to the public, to clients, and to colleagues. They guide members in the performance of their professional responsibilities and express the basic tenets of ethical and professional conduct. The Principles call for an unswerving commitment to honorable behavior, even at the sacrifice of personal advantage.[38]

Of course, conflicts and differences of opinion often arise when it comes to professional ethics. For example, most of us are familiar with the complexity of ethics within the medical field. Not everyone agrees on everything, and some ethical issues, such as assisted suicide, are extremely controversial and present no easy answers.

When you choose to join a profession, you also choose its ethical code. This is an important decision, requiring that you know your own values well so that you can choose a profession that fits with what you believe. The same is true when you join an organization.

Organizational ethics
The values and principles that an organization has chosen that guide the behavior of people within the organization and/or what stakeholders expect of the organization.

Organizational Ethics

Organizational ethics are the values and principles that an organization has chosen that guide the behavior of people within the organization and/or what stakeholders expect of the organization. Organizational ethics often permeate a company's culture and are codified it's mission. They also frequently reflect a company's beliefs, values, and practices about how employees, customers, and the environment are to be treated.

For example, it may be less expensive to dump chemical waste illegally than to dispose of it properly, but a company's ethical stance will hopefully drive managers to make the decision to incur the cost rather than damage the environment. Similarly, a firm in the United States may discover that labor is much cheaper abroad, which could potentially save the company millions of dollars. However, the company's ethics may direct managers to consider matters such as working conditions before making the decision to relocate operations. Ethical situations such as these define an organization and its reputation.

Societal ethics
Principles and standards that guide members of society in day-to-day behavior with one another.

Societal Ethics

Finally, **societal ethics** are principles and standards that guide members of society in day-to-day behavior with one another (■Exhibit 2.8). Societal ethics are related to culture, and they are sometimes supported by laws, social conventions, and even language. Societal ethics often include beliefs, values, and practices related to issues such as justice, individual freedom, equality, equal employment opportunity rights, and how companies should impact the environment.

Societal ethics are at the "macro" end of the ethics spectrum. At this level, values unite the individuals in a society under a particular set of political and cultural ideologies that guide behavior. In some cases, certain societal ethics are strongly held by everyone. For example, in the United States, Britain, and Germany (among other countries), it is considered unethical to employ children as laborers, and an increasing number of companies will not buy products from suppliers who use child labor. Some organizations in certain countries around the world do employ children, but that does not mean everyone in those countries agrees with this practice or finds it ethical. That is because there are often differences even within societies with respect to ethics and ethical practices.

■Exhibit **2.8**

In the United States, it is considered unethical to drink and drive.

Michael C. Gray/Shutterstock

Senator Ted Kennedy worked toward equal access to health care for several decades before his death in 2009.

Stakeholders
Any constituent potentially impacted by an organization's actions, either inside or outside the organization.

What happens when certain ethics are not held by everyone within a society? One example of a debate about societal ethics is the long-standing argument over access to health care in the United States. As far back as 1964, the late Senator Edward Kennedy (■Exhibit 2.9) called for the United States to move toward a system in which everyone had access to health care, not just those people who could afford it. A number of ethical dilemmas surround this issue. The discussion is especially heated because of at least two separate ideologies—government-influenced social equity versus free-market capitalism. These two sides of the argument around health care in the United States illustrate very different points of view about the government's responsibility with respect to the welfare of citizens.

When debates about ethics become pronounced or heated in society, it is often a sign that changes have occurred. As you will see in Chapter 13, values are closely tied to culture—and cultures change. Probably the best way to deal with ethical debates at the societal level is to engage in them openly and transparently, involving as many people and points of view as possible.

Business Ethics: It's Complicated

Now that we have looked at the individual, professional, organizational, and societal levels of ethics, let's consider how ethics impact business. Business ethics can be complex. For one, different stakeholders often have different beliefs about how a business should enact values and ethics. **Stakeholders** consist of any organization, group, or person either internal or external to a company who has a stake in the company's success or failure. For example, think about an energy company. One group of stakeholders might believe that the company should provide the cheapest energy to the most people, which could mean using existing energy sources (such as coal) and spending little, if any, money on researching alternative sources of energy. Another group of stakeholders expects the company to not only invest in research about alternative energy sources, but to seek them out and use them now. Both groups believe their stance is ethical.

Another reason business ethics are complicated is because increasingly, business is global. Many companies do business in two, four, or even dozens of countries. It is common to find that the values and ethics of these countries are in conflict. Another result of globalism is that values, cultures, and loyalties are rapidly shifting and unpredictable.

There are also so-called "irreducible" differences in values, norms, and practices between various cultures.[39] Sometimes people just disagree about right and wrong, and it is very difficult to find common ground. When confronted with these factors, it is possible that people will adopt a relativist approach—tolerance of a wide range of ethical views, with the end result being that a unified set of ethical standards is impossible. Alternatively, people may make moral choices in uncertainty and against a variety of potentially conflicting ethical standards.[40] For an individual, this can mean that you constantly have to examine and choose *which* code of ethics to follow.[41]

Ethics in Business and the Role of Law

Conflicting views regarding ethical and unethical behavior make it difficult for people and companies to decide on an appropriate course of action in some situations. That's where the law comes in. Many laws concerning business ethics exist today. For instance, there are laws against fraud and bribery. How a company can treat its employees or customers is dictated by laws, and there are also laws to protect the environment. All of these laws are in one way or another related to societal values and ethics.

Laws Often Follow Ethical Violations

When situations occur that overstep the bounds of what most people in a society consider fair and just business practices, new legislation typically follows in some form. For example, in 2002, in the wake of the Tyco, Enron, Arthur Andersen, Adelphia, and WorldCom scandals, Congress passed the Sarbanes-Oxley Act (formally known as the Public Company Accounting Reform and Investor Protection Act of 2002).[42] This legislation established new standards and improved on existing ones for all U.S. public company boards, management, and accounting firms. Although no legislation can or will prevent scandals such as Enron or WorldCom from happening again, new laws can establish strict guidelines and oversight to ensure that unethical behavior is less likely to occur.

When Laws Force People to Change: The International Anticorruption and Good Governance Act of 2000

But what happens when you need to require that people act in accordance with a company's ethics and your government's laws, even if this requires them to violate their personal ethical codes? This issue is on the top of many multinational companies' agendas as U.S. laws relating to corruption become more pervasive—even outside the borders of the United States. According to the U.S. Department of State Web site:

> Congress passed the *International Anticorruption and Good Governance Act of 2000* (IAGGA) (Public Law 106-309) on October 5, 2000. The purpose of this legislation is "to ensure that United States assistance programs promote good governance by assisting other countries to combat corruption throughout society and to improve transparency and accountability at all levels of government and throughout the private sector."[43]

This sounds good, right? And it is. But consider how difficult it has been, and will continue to be, for the companies that must adhere to this—even when doing business in lands where practices such as hiring family members first, regardless of their qualifications, is considered the right thing to do. (That's called nepotism, by the way.) Or what about when bribery is a natural part of business? These challenges are real, and they are not going to go away soon.

It's also important to know that the laws governing business ethics apply to both organizations *and* their leaders. Until the 1970s, the study and analysis of business ethics focused only on individuals. Since that time, the focus has shifted toward the organization. Organizations have values, mind-sets, cultures, goals, and objectives, much the same as individuals. Therefore, in terms of ethics, organizations are treated as individuals, both conceptually and legally.

Business ethics are complicated because the world's societies are complicated. What that means is that we have to learn to recognize how to handle ethical dilemmas in life and at work.

Dealing with Ethical Dilemmas at Work

Ethical dilemmas
Situations in which it appears that acting ethically would prevent the achievement of an objective.

As you can see, acting on values and ethics at work is not always easy, and it's not always clear what to do. In fact, everyone encounters **ethical dilemmas**—situations in which it appears that acting ethically would prevent the achievement of an objective. For example, imagine witnessing an auto accident. The car is flipped over. The driver is conscious, but he can't get out of the car on his own. Gasoline is dripping steadily from the car. You ask the driver how he feels. He tells you that his back is numb and his head is throbbing. You want to pull him free from the car in case it explodes or catches fire. However, you are also concerned that if you pull the driver from the car, you may hurt him—and if this happens, you may be sued. You know that some states have "Good Samaritan" laws that protect people from being sued in situations like this, but you don't know if your state has such a law. What should you do?

It is not unheard of, for example, for people to request time off to attend religious services and be denied. Supervisors making these decisions are most likely not malicious, and may not even be intending to discriminate—but they are. Even good intentions in situations like this (e.g., perceived fairness to other employees) can still result in unethical and even illegal behavior.

In many cases, "right" and "wrong" are hard to determine, especially when situations are clouded by opinions and conflicting points of view. The best solutions to ethical dilemmas can only be determined by people who are in dialogue with one another and thinking deeply about what is best for all. Scholars suggest, in fact, that ethics are "practiced" when ethical issues are made visible and discussed as complex problems.[44] In the previous example, it is not hard to see that conversations would have led to the right decision: Allow the employees time off for religious observance. Let's now look at a case involving extremely controversial issues, and one woman's approach to dealing with risky ethical dilemmas.

The Washington Post   **Business** Case

A Lesson of Lasting Impact

Katharine Meyer Graham (1917–2001), known to many simply as "Kay," was at the helm of the *Washington Post* during the publication of articles on the infamous Watergate scandal that earned the paper the Pulitzer Prize for Public Service. Graham later won her own Pulitzer in 1998 for her memoir *Personal History*. Throughout her many challenges and triumphs, Graham—considered to be one of the most influential people of the twentieth century—remained a true example of strong, authentic, and ethical leadership.[45]

Although she eventually earned worldwide acclaim for her leadership ability, Katharine Graham's journey was not easy. After the death of her father, control of the family-run paper passed to her husband, Philip. Then, following Philip's suicide in 1963, Graham assumed the mantle of leadership—something she had never planned to do.[46] As she put it,

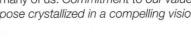
Katharine Graham

> . . . I set out to learn. What I essentially did was to put one foot in front of the other, shut my eyes, and step off the edge. The surprise was that I landed on my feet.[47]

Like many successful people, Kay treated problems as challenges to be addressed.[48] After her unexpected rise to leadership at the paper, she faced some difficult choices. Key among these was whether to run a series of articles based on the secret Pentagon Papers, which were first published by the *New York Times*. She ultimately took the courageous and ethical stance: to run the articles. These articles examined U.S. political and military involvement in Vietnam from 1945 through 1967. Later, under her leadership, the paper published Bob Woodward and Carl Bernstein's Watergate articles, which eventually brought down the Nixon presidency.

Needless to say, publishing these articles was risky. Kay and her board were under tremendous pressure, and one might wonder why Kay would want to be at the center of such controversy.[49] According to Kay, it started with passion, purpose, and true commitment to values: "To love what you do and feel that it matters— how could anything be more fun?"[50]

Graham lived for the meaning her work provided. Such a sense of meaning and purpose allows a leader to feel part of something bigger, generating a long-lasting sense of contribution and significance. This, in return, creates a positive cycle of reinforcement that continues to build an even stronger sense of meaning.[51] It also leads to a deep commitment to getting it right and loyalty to organizational ethics and goals. This kind of commitment is contagious; people feel it, want to join, and give their all.

Meaning was at the center of Kay's leadership, and vision is what gave her the strength and determination to transform the old-fashioned *Post* into a modern newspaper with national appeal. Kay's vision was simple and compelling: a commitment to speak the truth for the service of people, the organization, and community.[52] Kay communicated her vision consistently: "She spoke with her newspaper; she spoke with her money; she spoke with her presence; most essentially, she spoke with her decency."[53]

Katharine Graham's leadership legacy offers a lesson for many of us: *Commitment to our values and a deep sense of purpose crystallized in a compelling vision can change the world.*

Photo Source: Richard Ellis/Alamy Images

Defining Ethics through Leadership

Katharine Graham influenced her company's ethics, as do the best leaders today. Many companies formalize leaders' beliefs about ethical conduct. For example, Google's Code of Conduct starts out somewhat provocatively with a one-liner: "Don't be evil." Co-founders Sergey Brin and Larry Page go on to define what exactly is expected of all employees when they are asked not to be evil:

"'Don't be evil.' Googlers generally apply those words to how we serve our users. But 'Don't be evil' is much more than that. Yes, it's about providing our users unbiased access to information, focusing on their needs and giving them the best products and services that we can. But it's also about doing the right thing more generally—following the law, acting honorably and treating each other with respect.

The Google Code of Conduct is one of the ways we put 'Don't be evil' into practice. It's built around the recognition that everything we do in connection with our work at Google will be, and should be, measured against the highest possible standards of ethical business conduct."[54]

Needless to say, "Don't be evil" is harder to do than to talk about, and Google, like any other company, faces its share of ethical dilemmas. In some cases, people disagree violently about whether some actions the company has taken are good or bad. Still, we can see that leaders at Google have set an extremely high standard that they are not afraid to talk about. *Everyone* at Google knows the code, and virtually all decisions are weighed with this code in mind. When leaders have the courage to set a standard this high and then try their very best to adhere to it, the world knows, and employees can feel proud of where they work.

How to Handle Everyday Decisions Ethically

Rules, regulations, and even inspirational codes of conduct can't guide our every move. In the end, it comes down to individual people and the decisions they make. In other words, it comes down to you: your values, your code of ethics, your decisions, and your behavior.

Before sharing some tips on how you can handle everyday decisions ethically, we need to look at what can happen when we *violate* our ethics, as well as one of the biggest problems when it comes to ethics: rationalizing unethical behavior.

What Happens When It Goes Wrong: The Slippery Slope

If you don't know what your personal "line in the sand" is, you may inadvertently make some very bad decisions or be part of situations that will not make you feel proud of yourself. Let's look at someone who many people believed was a great man, but who stepped way over the ethical line by defrauding people and breaking the law.

Until 2009, Bernie Madoff was a well-known and well-respected financier. But over many years, he deliberately defrauded people by running an elaborate Ponzi scheme.[55] A Ponzi scheme involves taking money from people who believe they are investing it legitimately, then paying dividends and the like from investors' money instead of from profits. Here is what happened: Madoff solicited funds from friends, charities, and everyday people—even people he knew well.[56] He told these friends and clients that he was investing their money in stocks, but he didn't do this. Fabricated monthly statements were issued, and although some people suspected something was wrong, these red flags were ignored.[57] Madoff's closely guarded financial records also caused concern for researchers at *Barron's,* but nothing came of that either.[58] Madoff schemed successfully for several years, even escaping six botched investigations by the U.S. Securities and Exchange Commission (SEC). He was only caught after admitting his guilt to his two sons.[59] On March 12, 2009, Madoff pleaded guilty to 11 felony counts. Prosecutors estimated the dollar amount of the fraud at $64.8 billion, including fabricated gains and estimated actual losses of $18 billion, lost by nearly 4,800 investors.

Could one man pull off a fraud of this magnitude without help? It's unlikely, and at the time of this writing, the evidence is still being reviewed. What we can be certain about, however, is that one man's ethics somehow became compromised to the point that he defrauded people for years, repeatedly and with dire consequences.

Most people will never compromise their values and ethics the way Madoff did. However, it is likely that at some point in your life, you will be faced with choices that challenge your sense of right and wrong. Most of us don't want to violate our own ethical code, but consider these common situations:

- You have written an outstanding paper for a particular class, and it fits a new assignment for another class perfectly. Despite your new instructor's clear request for original work, you are considering using the old paper.
- You overhear a friend or colleague lying about why he missed class or work. When the instructor or boss jokingly asks you to tell her what really happened, you decide not to "rat out your friend."
- You find yourself joining in with a group of friends to make fun of someone. It gets out of control, and you stop saying things about the person, but you don't try to stop what's going on.
- You have found a job that is perfect for you. It requires that you have completed your degree. Knowing you will finish in a few months, you are considering indicating that you *are* done, rather than you *will be* done.

This list shows that living our values and sticking to our ethical code can be difficult because ethics are not always crystal clear, and some of our values can actually be in conflict with other values. Unfortunately, we are quite clever at finding reasons for violating our own beliefs, values, and ethics.

Rationalizing Unethical Behavior

On the day Andrew Fastow, former CFO of Enron, was indicted by a federal court, some employees at Enron's accounting firm, Arthur Andersen, were busy shredding incriminating documents that amounted to approximately one ton of paper.[60] This fraudulent activity and attempted cover-up not only resulted in convictions, but also in the demise of Arthur Andersen. In the end, thousands of people lost their jobs, and thousands more lost money. But how could employees at one of the nation's oldest and most respected accounting firms have justified these actions?

People typically use any one of many reasons to justify unethical behavior. One common justification is the stance that once in a while, everyone violates ethics, so it's really no big deal. And many people believe that they will not get caught, or that it's just a one-time thing and no one will really be hurt. These justifications are often true. But does this make them right? Probably not. First, how can someone say they have certain values and ethics and deliberately not hold to them? What went through the minds of those leaders at Enron? Did they find yet another justification? "My boss told me to." "I will get fired if I don't." "I'm not *really* sure what I am shredding." "There's no law against shredding documents."

At the societal level, every genocide in history has involved people violating their ethics and values. For example, at some point in time, soldiers must have questioned themselves when they followed those hideous orders in the concentration camps of Nazi Germany, or when officials of a brutal dictatorship killed millions in Cambodia, or when mobs swarmed the countryside of Rwanda during yet another attempt at genocide. Surely these people asked themselves questions, but then they denied their values and ethical codes anyway. Excuses were no doubt used: "We have to do it to achieve our goals." "They're somehow a threat, or ungodly, evil, or inhuman." Either way, the people who carried out these atrocities had to find ways to shut themselves off from the truth—and from their feelings.

In organizations, people often use similar excuses: "We won't win unless we do it this way." "The ends justify the means." "If I don't do it, I'll be fired." Another common justification is that if behavior is not illegal, it is not unethical either. This is not the case, of course, as rules and law generally follow social standards rather than precede them.

Another way some people justify unethical behavior is the age-old "*They're* doing it, and if I don't, I will lose out." This is called *pluralistic ignorance,* and some scholars believe it is currently a root cause of many corporate ethical scandals.[61] This seems to be a reformulation of Garrett Hardin's influential essay, "The Tragedy of the Commons," which describes what happens when one party attempts to maximize its access to resources to maximize personal, organizational, or national benefits, assuming everyone else is doing the same.[62] In these situations, a limited communal resource can be quickly depleted. Tragedy of the commons examples abound, such as the behavior and debate around water use in the western United States, or the question about who should "use" the Brazilian rain forest: farmers, loggers, or no one.

Or, closer to home, consider the following excuses for unethical behaviors: "I only had a couple of beers. It's ok for me to drive." "I called in sick—sure, I'm not really sick, but everyone does it once in a while." "It's just one paper off the Internet. I don't usually do this, but I have to pass this course." Are any of these excuses valid?

Maybe the saddest reason for violating ethics is that some people simply don't think about them. These people don't know who they are or what they stand for.

When All Is Said and Done, Ethical Behavior Is Up to You

As you read about some of the ways people justify unethical behavior, you may have recognized yourself. You aren't alone. Most adults have experienced situations in which they have compromised their values and acted outside of their ethical codes. If you want to prevent this in the future, the first step is to become clear about what you believe in. This has been mentioned several times in this chapter, and it cannot be overemphasized: Examine your values, create your own personal code of ethics, and challenge yourself to attend to these guidelines at work and in life.

As you clarify your values and ethics, it helps to also examine the kinds of situations that tempt you to cross the line. Does this happen when there is social pressure? Do you tend to conform, even when you sense it is wrong? What about when you are afraid of failing? Or do you compromise just a little bit when the "prize" is something you really want? If you understand what conditions put you at risk, you can try to avoid them. Better yet, you can try to understand why you feel as you do in these situations and change your reaction.

When it comes to making the ethical decisions that are part of everyday life and work, you can ask yourself a few basic questions. Certainly, the "golden rule" is a good guideline. How would I feel if I were treated this way? Would I feel confident in telling my boss, my family and friends, or society as a whole about the decision I have made? Can I look at myself in the mirror and know for certain that my conscience is clear of any doubt that my decision is ethical and in line with my values? If the answer to any of these questions troubles you, think again. Talk with someone. Reach out to people you trust for advice. Get support. It takes self-awareness, clear thinking, and courage to consistently behave ethically. But, as you know, great leaders make the tough decisions.

Most Popular » Discussion Questions

1. Consider your favorite restaurant. Are the values and ethics of this company apparent? What are they, and how do employees demonstrate them?
2. Does your college have a formal code of conduct for students? If so, read it. What parts of it fit with your personal values and code of ethics? Are there any aspects of it that are in conflict with your values? What are these conflicts, and how can you reconcile them?
3. Have you ever rationalized unethical behavior (yours or someone else's)? Why and how did you do this?
4. Think of an ethical dilemma you have faced. What are some of the factors that made the situation difficult to resolve?

5. How Do Theories and Models Explain Management and Leadership?

So far, we have discussed the essentials of outstanding leadership: social and emotional intelligence competencies, effective use of power, and ethics. We now turn our attention to major theories that have informed scholars' and practitioners' beliefs about management and leadership during the past 75 years. As a student of management and as a responsible leader in life and work, you must understand and be able to discuss these theories. It is also important that you know their limitations, recognize which models are not well supported by research, and understand which models are most relevant today.

Trait Theories of Leadership

Traits are enduring and distinguishing personal characteristics that may be inherited, learned, or developed. Traits include psychological characteristics such as optimism, pessimism, self-confidence, and sociability, as well as physical characteristics such as energy and stamina. A person's traits also include things like intelligence, maturity, and integrity.

In the early 1900s, leadership **trait theories** were prominent. Trait theories are models that attempt to explain leadership effectiveness by articulation of physical, psychological, and social characteristics, as well as abilities, knowledge, and expertise. In many cases, early theorists focused on studying people thought to be excellent leaders, so this method came to be called the "Great Man Approach." Many of these studies in fact focused only on men, and in many cases the studies paid an inordinate amount of attention to characteristics such as height, "bearing" (e.g., military posture), and neatness.[63] These studies were seriously flawed, and subsequent research did not support a relationship between these traits and leadership success.[64] Another inaccurate assumption in many of these theories was that all traits—physical and psychological alike—were immutable. In fact, some of what these researchers considered traits can and do change over time.

Trait theories operate implicitly and powerfully when it comes to what people believe about leadership. Unfortunately, much of what people believe about leadership traits is based on unfounded research, folklore, or even cultural stereotypes. For example, ask three people what they believe to be a good leader's most important characteristics. You are likely to get a wide range of responses, only some of which may be relevant to leadership. Also, it is highly unlikely that all three people will agree about which traits are most important—what one person feels are the five most important qualities of a leader may be another person's bottom five, and researchers might say none of them are important! For these reasons, it is important to understand what implicit trait models you may have developed and to compare these with what research suggests.

Despite the fact that a good deal of the research on traits has been flawed, several categories of traits or characteristics do seem to be somewhat related to leadership. Numerous studies have been conducted over the years, and the results of these studies are presented in ■Exhibit 2.10. These traits and characteristics can be shown in six categories: personality, physical characteristics, intelligence and ability, social background, work-related characteristics, and social characteristics.[65]

Some of the characteristics in Exhibit 2.10 are actually traits, whereas others are more correctly described as knowledge, competencies, or expertise. Although each of these characteristics affects leadership, rarely do good leaders possess all of the traits listed in the exhibit. Moreover, some people who possess many of these characteristics are not effective leaders at all. This is because traits or characteristics alone are not sufficient to explain a person's effectiveness as a leader. Because of this, in the mid-1960s, researchers began to turn their focus toward how leaders *behaved* rather than what qualities they seemed to possess.

Traits
Enduring and distinguishing personal characteristics that may be inherited, learned, or developed.

Trait theories
Models that attempt to explain leadership effectiveness by articulation of physical, psychological, and social characteristics, as well as abilities, knowledge, and expertise.

■Exhibit **2.10**

Leadership Traits Identified in Research[66]					
Personality	Physical Characteristics	Intelligence and Ability	Social Background	Work-Related Characteristics	Social Characteristics
Emotional intelligence Emotional control/ stability Empathy Integrity/honesty Conscientiousness Self-monitoring Flexibility/ adaptability Open to experience Comfortable with uncertainty/chaos Divergent thinking Assertive/ aggressive Extroverted Enthusiastic Confident	Age Energetic Appearance/ grooming	Cognitive ability Intelligence Knowledge Creativity Comprehension skills Oral and written communication skills	Education Social status Mobility	Achievement drive Responsibility/ power drive Motivation to lead Vision Stewardship Task/performance orientation Entrepreneurial Explicit/tacit knowledge of the business Competence expertise Administrative expertise	Ability to influence and persuade Ability to inspire Charisma Empowerment of others Ability to delegate Administrative expertise Trust/credibility Diplomatic Shows appreciation Desires to serve others Team oriented

Behavior Models and Approaches to Leadership

The behavioral approach to studying and understanding leadership effectiveness goes beyond personal characteristics and traits. It looks at the actual behaviors leaders engaged in when guiding and influencing others. These models drew on disciplines such as sociology, psychology, and anthropology, and they examined human interaction in an organizational environment.

Ohio State Studies: Consideration and Initiating Structure

Toward the middle of the twentieth century, researchers at Ohio State University surveyed leaders and found two major dimensions of behaviors associated with leadership: consideration and initiating structure.[67] **Consideration** refers to people-oriented behaviors such as respect, openness to employees' ideas, and concern for employees' well-being. Leaders who emphasize consideration would likely create trusting, supportive, and amiable environments marked by open communication and teamwork.

Initiating structure includes behaviors related to task and goal orientation, such as giving clear directions, monitoring employees' performance, and planning and setting work schedules and deadlines. Leaders who emphasize structure are likely to emphasize efficiency and effectiveness and to support employees by identifying what needs to be done in order for them to succeed at the job or task. The Ohio State studies started a trend that focused on which style was the "best."[68]

University of Michigan Studies: Production- and Employee-Oriented Behavior

Around the same time the Ohio State studies were under way, researchers at the University of Michigan began studying the behavior of effective supervisors.[69] They identified two dimensions of behavior. The first dimension, *production-oriented behavior*, focuses on efficiency, costs, adhering to schedules, and meeting deadlines. These super-

Consideration
People-oriented behaviors such as respect, openness to employees' ideas and concern for employees' well-being.

Initiating structure
Behaviors related to task and goal orientation, such as giving clear directions, monitoring employees' performance, and planning and setting work schedules and deadlines.

visors focused their energies on job tasks and work procedures and regarded employees as a means to the end of achieving work goals.

Supervisors who favored production-oriented behavior tended to be less effective than those favoring *employee-oriented behavior*. Supervisors who favored the employee-oriented behavior approach were supportive of employees, emphasized relationships, and focused on engaging employees through setting and assisting in the attainment of high-performance goals. The study concluded that employees preferred employee-oriented behavior and would perform better when supervisors embraced it.

Leadership Grid

Researchers Robert Blake and Jane Mouton of the University of Texas built on the University of Michigan and Ohio studies.[70] In 1964, they proposed that managerial behaviors could be plotted along horizontal and vertical axes measuring concern for people and concern for production, and then could be grouped into management or leadership styles. Now called the *Leadership Grid*, this model is still in use today, and it has been periodically updated.[71] Five of the leadership styles are well known and are presented in ■Exhibit 2.11. As you can see, behavioral emphasis on people is measured on

■Exhibit **2.11**

The leadership grid presents five leadership styles.

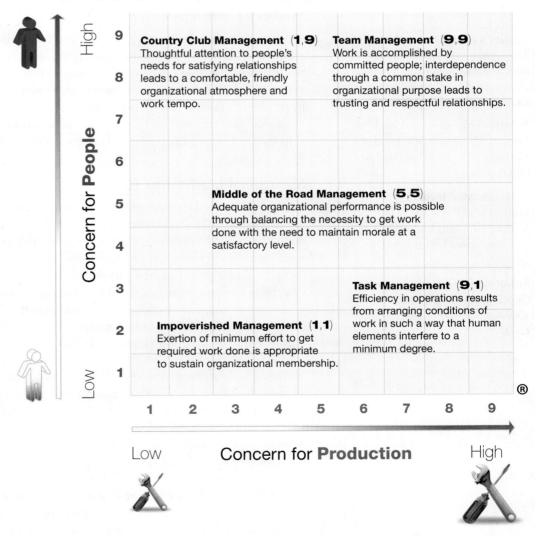

the vertical axis, and the focus on production is shown on the horizontal axis. Although the model indicates the positive attributes of each style, the research team contended that the team management style worked best.[72]

Contingency Approaches to Leadership

Contingency approaches to leadership are based on the perspective that when it comes to leadership and management, one size does not fit all. These models and theories of leadership take into account leader behavior *and* various aspects of the organizational situation and/or characteristics of followers. In other words, different situations call for different approaches. For example, leading a small team of people in an entrepreneurial start-up will call for a different approach than leading a large division of a multinational company. In the start-up, you will rely heavily on interpersonal communication, strong personal relationships, and inspiring people by painting a picture of the future. In a large division, you can't possibly have personal relationships with everyone, so you will need to rely on reaching people in other ways—via webinars, speeches, e-mail, and the like. You will also need to rely on organizational processes and culture to guide people's behavior. Contingency models state that many different variables come into play, and that each situation is unique and requires its own approach. In the next four sections, we will look at several contingency approaches to leadership.

Fiedler's Contingency Theory

Fiedler's contingency theory, developed by Fred Fiedler in 1967, states that leadership effectiveness is dependent on the characteristics of the leader and the characteristics of the situation.[73] Fiedler proposed that *leader style* is either task oriented or relationship oriented. **Relationship-oriented leaders** emphasize good relationships and being liked by employees. **Task-oriented leaders** focus on accomplishments and seek to ensure that employees perform well on the job. The theory also states that changing one's leadership style is difficult. Effectiveness, therefore, is dependent on matching a leader's style to the situation.[74]

Situational Leadership Theory

Situational leadership theory links leader style with followers' readiness for tasks. This model, developed by Paul Hersey and Ken Blanchard, focuses on followers' readiness to do their jobs and leaders' responsibility to notice this and adapt accordingly.[75] The term *readiness* refers to the extent to which employees are capable, confident, and willing to complete an assigned task or perform well on the job. These factors enable a leader to determine how much guidance and direction employees need.

The model suggests that when leaders attend to these factors, they can then vary their level of attention to task and relationship behaviors and choose one of four styles to employ. The four leadership styles identified by Hersey and Blanchard are listed here:

- *Telling style:* Appropriate when followers are unable, unwilling, or insecure—they need clear direction, close supervision, and guidance
- *Selling style:* Appropriate when employees are unable to complete tasks, but they are willing and/or confident
- *Participating style:* Can be used when employees are able, but unwilling or insecure
- *Delegating style:* Can be used when employees are able, willing, or confident

The situational theory is somewhat appealing in that it focuses on *followers* and their competencies and capabilities, or their progress from immaturity to maturity. Leaders who can accurately diagnose followers' readiness are more likely to match their leadership behavior to employee needs. That said, the model assumes that leaders can accurately read followers' readiness. Unfortunately, that is not always the case. You may have

---

Contingency approaches to leadership
Models and theories of leadership that take into account leader behavior and various aspects of the organizational situation and/or characteristics of followers.

Fiedler's contingency theory
Theory stating that leadership effectiveness is dependent on the characteristics of the leader and the characteristics of the situation.

Relationship-oriented leaders
Leaders who emphasize good relationships and being liked by employees.

Task-oriented leaders
Leaders who focus on accomplishments and seek to ensure that employees perform well on the job.

Situational leadership theory
Contingency model that links leader style with followers' readiness for tasks.

had an experience in which a leader didn't match his or her style to your level of readiness. Maybe you worked on a team, for example, where the leader gave far too many instructions and treated you as if you didn't know what you were doing. This, by the way, is a common mistake for new managers. They think they have to direct everything, and they ignore the fact that they need to adjust their behavior to people and situations.

Path-Goal Theory

Path-goal theory

A contingency approach to leadership stating that the leader is responsible for motivating employees to attain goals.

Path-goal theory states that a leader is responsible for motivating employees to attain goals.[76] The path-goal theory is based on the expectancy theory of motivation, covered in Chapter 3. In this model, effective leaders boost employee motivation (and presumably effectiveness) by illuminating the path toward organizational and personal goals and linking rewards to goal attainment. Leaders must ensure that the path to the goal is free of obstacles, that goals are meaningful, and that rewards are valued. Path-goal theory supports the notion that leaders can change their behaviors and styles.[77] According to this theory, leaders can choose to behave in four different ways, depending on employees' goal-related needs and expectations, as shown in ■Exhibit 2.12.

■Exhibit **2.12**

Path-goal theory: Choose a style that helps people reach their goals.

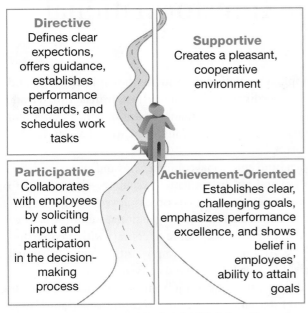

Directive
Defines clear expectations, offers guidance, establishes performance standards, and schedules work tasks

Supportive
Creates a pleasant, cooperative environment

Participative
Collaborates with employees by soliciting input and participation in the decision-making process

Achievement-Oriented
Establishes clear, challenging goals, emphasizes performance excellence, and shows belief in employees' ability to attain goals

Source: House, Robert J., and T. R. Mitchell. 1986. Path-goal theory of leadership. In *Decision making: An organizational behavior approach*, ed. J. M. Pennings. Princeton, NJ: Markus Wiener Publishers.

Leader Substitutes Model

Leader substitutes model

A contingency model of leadership that states that certain characteristics of people or of the situation can make direct leadership unnecessary.

The **leader substitutes model** states that certain characteristics of people or of the situation can make direct leadership unnecessary.[78] For example, when employees are knowledgeable, well trained, and highly motivated, people often don't need close supervision. They will self-regulate to get the job done.

This theory is quite useful, because it challenges the traditional idea that people *have* to be managed and led, and that if they are not, they will avoid work entirely or not work to their full potential. The notion that people need to be cajoled, told, and controlled, colors many of the early theories of management and leadership. Today, most people assume that others are willing and capable. This, then, leads to the possibility of "substituting" personalized leadership with clear goals and a compelling vision, along with an empowering, resonant culture.

Contingency approaches to leadership are quite popular today, and many variations and models are used in organizations. For a student of management, probably the most useful lesson is that it is important to attend to one's own leadership behavior as well as the situation, employees' abilities, confidence, self-efficacy, and motivation. Understanding these dimensions can be quite helpful in determining how to influence, engage, and support people.

The Study of Leadership Continues

As you can see from this discussion of common theories and models that seek to explain leadership, there is tremendous interest in this topic. This interest makes sense: If we can better understand how to guide, direct, and influence people, organizations will be more effective and probably more enjoyable places to work. Each of the theories you have studied in this section has a kernel of wisdom. To utilize the theories, however, you need to discern what aspects of the research apply to work and organizations today. This means you need to be an educated consumer of knowledge—carefully evaluating the models that you hold implicitly and explicitly. You also need to be able to discern which models are operating in the minds of others and in organizations. Very often, these models are not overt or explicit—they are embedded in organizational culture and systems. It can be difficult to identify which model or models are operating. If you do, however, you will be in a much better position to understand what drives behavior in an organization.

Most Popular » Discussion Questions

1. Study the common leadership traits in Exhibit 2.10. Which of these traits do you believe are important to leadership? Why? Are there any traits that you believe are irrelevant to leadership? What are they? Which traits do you have?
2. Which theories of leadership stand out as more relevant for today's business environment than others? Explain.
3. Consider a situation you have experienced personally where you were expected to lead. Using contingency theories, describe your preferred approach to leadership, the context (e.g., people, what else is going on in the group or organization, etc.), and other people's abilities and willingness to work on the task.

6. Is It Time to Take a Stand for Transformational Leadership?

Transformational leaders
People who have social and emotional intelligence and who can inspire others to seek an extraordinary vision.

Transactional leaders
People who follow a traditional approach to management in which leader and follower behavior is an instrumental exchange.

Transformational leaders are people who have social and emotional intelligence and who can inspire others to seek an extraordinary vision. In contrast, **transactional leaders** are people who follow a traditional approach to management in which leader and follower behavior is an instrumental exchange (e.g., "You do the work I assign to you, and I will reward you for your effort").[79]

As you saw in the sections on social and emotional competencies and empowerment, the most effective leaders go far beyond an instrumental exchange—they attend to *people*. Transformational leaders value people and focus on employees' needs for personal growth and inspiration. Transformational leaders are passionate about what they do, and they share their passion with everyone they come in contact with. People find transformational leaders compelling. And maybe most importantly, transformational leaders do the right thing in the right way, as Ed Breen did at Tyco.

In July 2002, Ed Breen accepted one of the toughest jobs in the corporate arena: He became chairman and CEO of Tyco International. Tyco had recently joined the league of organizations infamous for their greed and fraud. Former CEO L. Dennis Kozlowski had been sentenced to up to 25 years in prison for plundering the company. Not only was there still a top layer of managers who could have been involved in the many questionable and unethical practices during Kozlowski's tenure, but the company was also hamstrung with enormous debt and struggling to assimilate nearly 400 acquisitions. Breen had a big challenge, summed up by an incident during a meeting with employees when a woman stood up and said she was embarrassed to wear her Tyco T-shirt to her child's soccer games. He told her, "I don't blame you."[80]

In his first week at Tyco, Breen made a transformational leadership decision. He fired 290 of the company's top 300 executives. He then turned his sights on the board and asked them to resign or not seek reelection—something that had never happened in a company that size before. Breen then closed Tyco's expensive Manhattan offices and moved to West Windsor, New Jersey. Ordering company-wide consolidations, Breen paid down $11 billion of Tyco's $28 billion debt.

According to Breen, when making and implementing tough, transformational decisions, CEOs and managers at all levels must feel *passion* and *compassion*: "These are the two words I always keep in my mind even though they might seem like soft words coming from a hard-hitting CEO." Compassion is important, Breen says, because "[a]s you move up, you need to be a team player. You need to care about other people. If you don't, you won't move up. . . . Believe me, people see. They know who the team players are and who the individual players are."[81]

Under the guidance of a transformational leader such as Breen, employees will enthusiastically accept the organization's vision and goals as a part of their own personal vision.[82] That's because followers of transformational leaders see something bigger than themselves in the leadership vision. They see a vision that is meaningful to them—a vision that inspires them to actively move toward the future.[83]

One of the words often associated with transformational leaders is *charisma*. Charismatic leaders are self-confident without being arrogant, honest in their dealings with their employees, and they communicate clearly. They have *presence*. Researchers describe five behavioral attributes of charismatic leaders that define transformational leadership[84]:

- Vision and articulation
- Sensitivity to the environment
- Sensitivity to people's needs
- Personal risk taking
- Unconventional behavior

Transformational leaders also have a high degree of social and emotional intelligence. They are self-aware in that they know how their emotions affect themselves and others, and they use their emotions to create resonance, excitement, and optimism. Transformational leaders are visionary, and they know how to convey their visions in ways that make people feel inspired and committed. Transformational leaders are change agents.

In this section, we have introduced a way of thinking about leadership that goes to the heart of what is needed today, from everyone at every level. Transformational leadership requires that you develop social and emotional intelligence competencies, understand and live your values and ethics, and manage your power wisely. It may seem that leading this way is something that you will learn to do over time—this is true. It is also true that you can learn *now*.

Most Popular » Discussion Questions

1. Describe the difference between transactional and transformational leadership.
2. How important is it for a leader to be transformational? Why? Use your experience to support your position.
3. Think about your leadership abilities, especially your social and emotional intelligence, and how you inspire people. What would it take for you to be able to use these skills more often and effectively?

---

7. What Is HR's Role in Supporting Excellent and Ethical Leadership?

The role of human resources (HR) in leadership can be summed up in one word: *support*. This support takes a variety of forms, some technical, and some more strategic. In this section we look at a traditional model outlining HR's responsibilities, followed by a more recent conceptualization of how HR can support leaders practically—and strategically—by adopting certain key roles.

The HR Cycle

As you can see in ■Exhibit 2.13, HR is responsible for a number of key activities. These are often considered the areas of technical expertise that HR manages to support of an

■Exhibit **2.13**
The HR cycle.

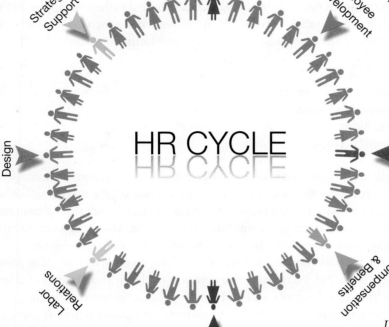

organization. Each of these areas is discussed below, followed by an example of how HR can address ethical leadership through training:

Recruiting: Handling employee selection, hiring, succession planning, and staffing from both outside and inside the organization.

Employee development: Providing leadership development and job or career-related training for employees through a variety of means, such as training programs, tuition reimbursement, seminars, cross-training, online learning, and different forms of self-directed learning.

Performance management: Providing processes and programs to identify, measure, and plan for the development of employees' skills.

Compensation and benefits: Providing schemas and technical processes to support employee compensation and benefits such as health care, flexible vacation time, flexible work schedules, travel, the company car, the executive washroom, the corner window, status, sense of purpose, etc.

Workforce management: Managing the size and shape of the workforce through activities such as organizational development and programs to support strategic issues.

Labor relations: Managing relations between internal and external groups (e.g., trade unions) that set standards for how employees are to be treated.

Organizational design: Studying organizational design issues and creating or recreating job descriptions, work design, organizational structures, and interorganizational relationships.

Strategic support: Conducting research and providing support on people-related issues.

HR's role in supporting great leadership cannot be underestimated. In this section, we focus on one of the most important roles HR can hold in this arena: training for and supporting ethical leadership.

Ethical Leadership Development

As the organizational function in charge of employee training and development, HR has an obligation to deliver programs that address issues related to ethical leadership. These programs must be designed to clarify the organization's code of ethics and reinforce the importance of professional ethics, as well as to embed ethical leadership in all levels of the organization. Companies can develop organizational ethics in many different ways. For example, within a development program, employees can be provided the opportunity to learn the company's ethical code and explore their own values as well as professional, organizational, and societal ethics. These are not easy topics, and lecture-style programs simply won't work. In order to be successful, these programs need to be:

- Relevant to employees' experiences
- Focused on developing good judgment
- Focused on reflection and dialogue
- Fully and visibly supported by management

In the next section, we will look at another way that HR can support ethical leadership, and how HR professionals themselves can take up leadership roles.

HR's Leadership Roles

During most of the last century, HR professionals were largely relegated to the "back office." In many cases, even the most senior HR employees were not consulted on strategic issues. The HR function (often called "personnel") was expected to provide the technical services necessary to hire, pay, and train professionals, as well as deal with labor unions and the like. HR was not expected to be "at the table" when big decisions were made or to provide more than technical advice. That view has changed, and so have the roles that HR professionals need to hold. These roles require nothing less than that HR professionals revolutionize what their function does and how it is perceived.

As you progress in your career, you will no doubt deal with HR on many levels, and you may even join the profession yourself. As you can see in ■Exhibit 2.14, there are several exciting ways to rely on the support of HR professionals and to develop yourself.[85] Today, HR professionals are called upon to lead in their roles as executive coach and advisor, strategic business partner, organizational change agent, and leadership development architect. This represents a new way of looking at HR, which we will address throughout this book. For now, let's look at just one way HR can be a strategic business partner when it comes to developing an ethical culture: by creating and managing whistle-blower programs.

■Exhibit **2.14**

The four HR leadership roles include social and emotional intelligence at the center.[86]

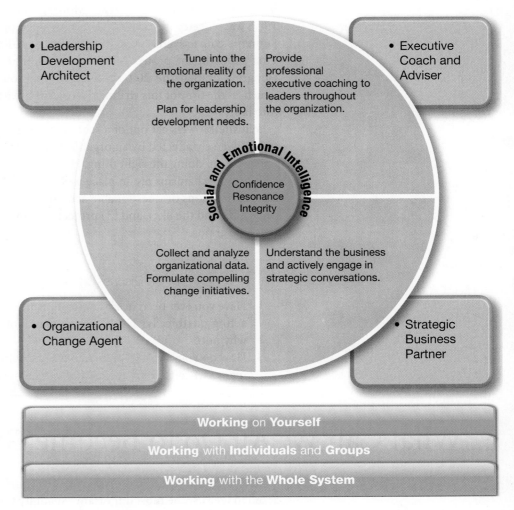

Leadership Development Architect
Tune into the emotional reality of the organization.
Plan for leadership development needs.

Executive Coach and Adviser
Provide professional executive coaching to leaders throughout the organization.

Social and Emotional Intelligence
Confidence
Resonance
Integrity

Organizational Change Agent
Collect and analyze organizational data. Formulate compelling change initiatives.

Strategic Business Partner
Understand the business and actively engage in strategic conversations.

Working on Yourself

Working with Individuals and Groups

Working with the Whole System

Source: Annie McKee and Frances Johnston.

Whistle-Blower Protection

Codes of conduct and ethics training are useful, but they certainly do not guarantee that ethical issues will not arise. To ensure that an organization can address ethical behavior strategically, HR must often provide mechanisms that both support the culture and encourage individual people in changing their behavior. For example, if a company wants to foster ethical behavior but people are afraid to speak up, the company might institute a whistle-blower program.

Cynthia Cooper, former vice president of internal audit at WorldCom, is a classic example of a whistle-blower. Cooper and her team worked secretly at night to uncover the multibillion-dollar fraud at their organization in 2002. When her investigation was complete, Cooper exposed the scandal by informing WorldCom's board of directors that the company had hidden $3.8 billion in losses through the use of phony bookkeeping.[87] Whistle-blowers are employees who expose illegal and/or unethical practices within their companies to either their employers or to outside organizations and authorities.

Of course, "telling" on others is something that many cultures discourage. Think of your childhood, for example: Weren't the kids who "told" on people called names and shunned? It's much the same in organizations, where there are often strong, implicit rules against exposing questionable processes. However, if employees don't expose these problems, who will?

It is to a company's advantage to protect whistle-blowers and not treat them like disloyal employees. However, many people argue that employees should keep certain information to themselves; also, people are sometimes punished for blowing the whistle. Fortunately, the United States has laws to protect whistle-blowers. The first federal law in this area was passed in 1912.[88] More recently, the Whistleblower Protection Act of 1989 was enacted to protect government employees.[89] However, in 2006, the U.S. Supreme court severely weakened the act by ruling that whistle-blowers did not have First Amendment protection from employer retaliation.[90] In response, members of Congress drafted the 2007 Whistleblower Protection Enhancement Act (HR 985), which, at the time of this writing (2010), has bipartisan support but has yet to be passed into law.[91]

Whistle-blowers act out of a sense of loyalty—loyalty to *all* stakeholders who stand to be adversely affected by an organization's ethical or legal transgressions. To support employees in doing the right thing, HR has a responsibility to (1) know the law; (2) ensure that mechanisms are in place to support employees in identifying and reporting ethical violations or questionable activities (e.g., anonymous hotlines, ombudsperson programs, and the like), and (3) protect employees from harm should they need to use these programs.

Most Popular » Discussion Questions

1. Have you ever been in a situation in which people were—or were considering—acting unethically? Did you consider "blowing the whistle" on them? Why or why not?
2. How do you think HR can help build a culture in which people feel safe speaking up when they see things that seem to be unethical?

---

8. What Can We All Do to Become Great Leaders?

When members of the Stanford Graduate School of Business's Advisory Council were asked to identify the most important capability for leaders to develop, their answer was nearly unanimous: self-awareness.[92] If we are to understand how our *view* of the world affects our *place* in that world, we need to be vigilant in understanding all that contributed to who we are. This is one aspect of self-awareness.

So much of what we learn and who we are as people is "second nature"—and often unexamined. That's because from a very young age, we develop the beliefs and moral principles that will shape our lives. Our parents, our religious affiliations, our teachers, our friends, and our broader social networks all influence our personal code of ethics and set the standards by which we make decisions—both for ourselves and, later, when we are in positions of responsibility, for others. Developing self-awareness helps us have a clear vision of what we stand for and what we will do in any given situation, as well as the courage to act on our core values without thought of compromise.

As you learned in this chapter, there are a number of competencies related to social and emotional intelligence that are essential to good leadership. (See ∎Exhibit 2.15.) Throughout this text we will draw your attention to these competencies. In this section we will focus on two of them: self-awareness and inspirational leadership.

In this chapter you have been asked to reflect on your competencies, your values, and your behavior. As you progress along the path toward deeper self-awareness, you may find that you are more authentic in your relationships and better able to inspire trust. You may even find that deepening your knowledge of yourself enables you to be more confident and to display courage and integrity in the face of challenges. Let's look at how authenticity, trust, integrity, and courage can support you in becoming a better leader.

Self-Aware Leaders Are Authentic

Authenticity
Genuine presentation of one's thoughts, feelings, and beliefs.

Authenticity is the genuine presentation of one's thoughts, feelings, and beliefs. This characteristic has been identified as an essential leadership trait by numerous researchers.[93] Authenticity requires a high degree of self-awareness because, after all, how can you be genuine if you don't really know yourself? Authentic leaders are committed

∎Exhibit **2.15**

Social and emotional intelligence competencies enable people to understand and manage their own and others' emotions in social interactions.

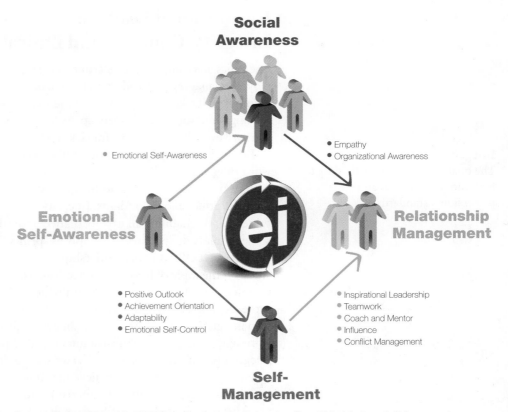

Source: Boyatzis, Richard E. 2008. Competencies in the 21st century (Guest Editorial). *Journal of Management Development* 27(1): 5–12.

to honesty, both with themselves and with those around them. Because of this emphasis on truth, an authentic leader's behavior and words exhibit a refreshing strength coupled with humility.

Authenticity is often linked with self-esteem: People with low self-esteem are more likely to misinterpret their own feelings, particularly negative ones, due, in part, to fear of rejection or their insecurity.[94] However, high self-esteem allows people to publicly present their thoughts, feelings, and beliefs nondefensively, which others experience as authenticity. So, one powerful step you can take as you develop self-awareness and the capacity for authenticity is to focus on your self-esteem. It is imporant to recognize that you have special gifts and talents that no one else has, and to know that you can use these gifts for good as a person and as a leader.

Self-Aware Leaders Inspire Trust

When it comes to leadership, trust is the expectation by employees that a leader will act in an ethically justifiable manner, will have their best interests at heart, and will strive to achieve the organization's goals.[95] Research on trust provides some advice about how you can build trust with others at work.

Scholars also propose that a leader's trust in followers and followers' trust in leaders are based on perceptions of ability, benevolence, and integrity in previous encounters. In addition, studies suggest that subordinates' trust in leaders is positively related to such things as job performance and satisfaction, organizational and goal commitment, and belief in the truth of information. One study found that team members' trust was primarily facilitated by three practices: consulting team members on decisions, communicating a group vision, and homogeneity of values.[96] Without trust, people are secretive and serve their own needs first, and they become uncooperative, defensive, and suspicious. If a leader has not earned the trust of the people he or she leads or manages, then this leader is unlikely to be successful in the long run.

Inspirational Leaders: Integrity, Courage, and Ethical Leadership

The ethics of a company are determined in large part by the choices and decisions that employees, managers, and leaders make on a daily basis. It takes integrity to make ethical decisions, and it takes courage to act on these choices. Therefore, integrity is often seen as the starting point for ethical leadership. As Molière wrote, "If everyone were clothed with integrity, if every heart were just, frank, kindly, the other virtues would be well-nigh useless."[97]

Integrity
The quality of steadfastly holding to high moral principles and professional standards.

But what is integrity when it comes to ethics? **Integrity** is derived from the Latin word *integrare*, which means "to be whole." A typical dictionary definition of integrity with respect to ethics refers to the quality of steadfastly holding to high moral principles and professional standards. Integrity is related to concepts such as honesty, truthfulness, and reliability, all of which affect ethical decision making and action. In fact, some scholars define *integrity* simply as "principled behavior."[98]

Project GLOBE (Global Leadership and Organizational Effectiveness) is a worldwide study on the topic of leadership effectiveness. (You will read more about this project in Chapter 13.) This study shows that the perception of a leader's integrity is important for leadership effectiveness across all cultures.[99] Some scholars also believe that leadership integrity is more important than ever before because today's knowledge economy is fraught with ecological unsustainability and political uncertainty, meaning that our integrity is constantly challenged as we seek to do the right thing.[100]

Finally, some researchers believe that integrity involves consistency between words and actions (the opposite of hypocrisy), and that the outcomes of leadership integrity are trust and reciprocal integrity, as well as satisfaction with leaders and leadership performance.[101]

Leaders with integrity take responsibility for their actions, are principled, are transparent, do what they say they will do, and never compromise their ethics. These leaders are perceived as credible. People believe in them, in what they say, in their vision, and in their commitment to doing the right thing. It's not always easy to act on one's integrity, though, because strong forces can push us toward compromise. What it takes to avoid this situation is courage.

What is courage? Courage isn't the lack of fear; it is the ability to overcome fear.[102] Certainly, fear plays a huge part in whether a person acts or refuses to act on his or her code of ethics. Courage means facing our fears and doing the right thing anyway. But fear isn't the biggest obstacle to courage. Conformity is the real enemy. As commentator Jim Hightower once wrote, "Even a dead fish can go with the flow."[103] Maybe you've had an experience in which the pressure to conform was strong, yet you knew that conforming would be a violation of your personal code of ethics. As with courage in other situations, courage in leadership involves taking risks, including the risk of going against the crowd. **Courage**, then, can be defined as the willingness and ability to face fear, danger, uncertainty, or pain without giving up whatever course of action you believe is necessary and right.

At one time or another, every great person has to find the courage to step away from the crowd and do the right thing. This can be hard, even painful.[104] But it's worth it. When you come upon injustice, injury, or wrongdoing and make the brave decision to act—to take on the risk of confronting the situation and boldly trying to change it—then you will know you are truly a courageous leader.[105]

Courage
The willingness and ability to face fear, danger, uncertainty, or pain without giving up whatever course of action one believes is necessary and right.

Most Popular » Discussion Questions

1. Sometimes we think about self-awareness as understanding our mind (intellect), body (physical self), heart (emotions), and spirit (values). For each of these areas, discuss two or three things that you believe define who you are as a person.
2. When leading a team, how do you build trust between yourself and others? Among team members?
3. Discuss the role of integrity in college life, both in the classroom and outside it.
4. Consider people's tendency to want to conform. It is actually natural to want to be part of a group. Think about yourself: When do you tend to conform, and when do you step away from the crowd? Give examples and link them to self-awareness and inspirational leadership.

---

9. A Final Word on Leadership

Throughout this book, we will emphasize that everyone is a leader—or can become a leader, if he or she chooses. We all influence others every day, and you can too. In this chapter you have had opportunities to reflect on some very important aspects of leadership, such as the social and emotional intelligence competencies you need to develop, how to use your power effectively, and how to ensure that your values and ethics are at the center of your leadership. These "keys to success" are vital today—and part of what it takes to be a transformational leader.

You have also learned about some of the more popular theories of leadership developed during the past few decades. Knowing these theories and being able to evaluate them is an important part of being an informed citizen, as well as an informed leader.

As we move into a variety of compelling topics related to leadership and management, you will be well served to turn back to this chapter often, to link what you learn to how you can be an outstanding leader.

Key Terms

1. Leadership: Whose Responsibility Is It? (pp. 18–20)

Key Terms None

2. What Is the Secret to *Effective* Leadership? (pp. 20–25)

Key Terms

Competencies Capabilities or abilities that include both intent and action, and that can be directly linked to how well a person performs on a task or in a job. p. 20

Competency model A set of competencies that are directly related to success in a job and are grouped into job-relevant categories. p. 22

Social and emotional intelligence Competencies linked to self-awareness, self-management, social awareness, and relationship management that enable people to understand and manage emotions in social interactions. p. 22

Resonant organizations Organizations characterized by a powerful and positive culture in which people have a shared sense of excitement and commitment to mutual goals. p. 23

Resonant leaders Socially and emotionally intelligent, visionary people who lead and manage in ways that enable everyone to contribute their very best. p. 23

Self-awareness The ability to notice and understand one's emotions and their effects. p. 23

Limbic resonance Refers to the fact that emotions are contagious and a powerful driver of our feelings, thoughts, and behaviors. p. 24

3. What Is the Secret to *Influential* Leadership? (pp. 25–30)

Key Terms

Power Influence over or through others. p. 25

Organizational politics Involve many things, including internal competition and the pursuit of personal goals at the expense of others or the organization. p. 25

Legitimate power The ability to influence others by right of one's position in an organization, the office held, or formal authority. p. 26

Reward power The ability to influence others by giving or withholding rewards such as pay, promotions, time off, attractive projects, learning experiences, and the like. p. 26

Coercive power The attempt to influence others through punishment. p. 26

Expert power The ability to influence others through a combination of special knowledge and/or skills. p. 26

Referent power Power that comes from personal characteristics that people value and want to emulate and that cause people to feel respect or admiration. p. 27

Empowerment Trusting employees to make decisions and to take responsibility for their decisions and actions. p. 27

Micromanagement The practice of overcontrolling others and their work, as well as paying far too much attention to details and how employees do their work. p. 28

Theory X A belief system that holds that the average employee is inclined to be lazy, without ambition, and irresponsible. p. 29

Theory Y A belief system that holds that workers are inherently ambitious, responsible, and industrious, and that they will work hard to help an organization reach its goals. p. 29

Theory Z A belief system that holds that in organizations with strong, relational cultures, employees have discretionary freedom in local decision making and are trusted to work autonomously. p. 29

Flat organizations Organizations that have few levels of hierarchy, which drives a need for more people to make decisions. p. 29

4. What Is the Secret to *Responsible* Leadership? (pp. 30–38)

Key Terms

Ethics A set of values and principles that guide the behavior of an individual or a group. p. 30

Values Ideas that a person or a group believes to be right or wrong, good or bad, attractive or undesirable. p. 30

Ethical code A system of principles governing morality and acceptable conduct. p. 30

Terminal values Personal commitments we make to ourselves in relation to our life's goals. p. 30

Instrumental values Preferred behaviors or ways of achieving our terminal values. p. 31

Individual ethics A personal code of conduct when dealing with others. p. 31

Professional ethics Standards that outline appropriate conduct in a given profession. p. 32

Organizational ethics The values and principles that an organization has chosen that guide the behavior of people within the organization and/or what stakeholders expect of the organization. p. 32

Societal ethics Principles and standards that guide members of society in day-to-day behavior with one another. p. 32

Stakeholders Any constituent potentially impacted by an organization's actions, either inside or outside the organization. p. 33

Ethical dilemmas Situations in which it appears that acting ethically would prevent the achievement of an objective. p. 34

5. How Do Theories and Models Explain Management and Leadership? (pp. 39–44)

Key Terms

Traits Enduring and distinguishing personal characteristics that may be inherited, learned, or developed. p. 39

Trait theories Models that attempt to explain leadership effectiveness by articulation of physical, psychological, and social characteristics, as well as abilities, knowledge, and expertise. p. 39

Consideration People-oriented behaviors such as respect, openness to employees' ideas and concern for employees' well-being. p. 40

Initiating structure Behaviors related to task and goal orientation, such as giving clear directions, monitoring employees' performance, and planning and setting work schedules and deadlines. p. 40

Contingency approaches to leadership Models and theories of leadership that take into account leader behavior and various aspects of the organizational situation and/or characteristics of followers. p. 42

Fiedler's contingency theory Theory stating that leadership effectiveness is dependent on the characteristics of the leader and the characteristics of the situation. p. 42

Relationship-oriented leaders Leaders who emphasize good relationships and being liked by employees. p. 42

Task-oriented leaders Leaders who focus on accomplishments and seek to ensure that employees perform well on the job. p. 42

Situational leadership theory Contingency model that links leader style with followers' readiness for tasks. p. 42

Path-goal theory A contingency approach to leadership stating that the leader is responsible for motivating employees to attain goals. p. 43

Leader substitutes model A contingency model of leadership that states that certain characteristics of people or of the situation can make direct leadership unnecessary. p. 43

6. Is It Time to Take a Stand for Transformational Leadership? (pp. 44–45)

Key Terms

Transformational leaders People who have social and emotional intelligence and who can inspire others to seek an extraordinary vision. p. 44

Transactional leaders People who follow a traditional approach to management in which leader and follower behavior is an instrumental exchange. p. 44

7. What Is HR's Role in Supporting Excellent and Ethical Leadership? (pp. 45–48)

Key Terms None

8. What Can We All Do to Become Great Leaders? (pp. 48–51)

Key Terms

Authenticity Genuine presentation of one's thoughts, feelings, and beliefs. p. 49

Integrity The quality of steadfastly holding to high moral principles and professional standards. p. 50

Courage The willingness and ability to face fear, danger, uncertainty, or pain without giving up whatever course of action one believes is necessary and right. p. 51

9. A Final Word on Leadership (p. 51)

Key Terms None

Chapter 2 Visual Summary

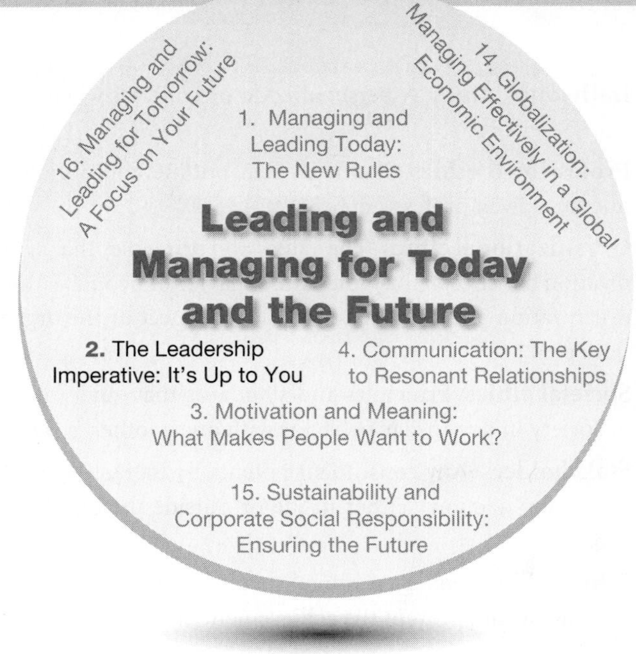

1. Leadership: Whose Responsibility Is It?   (pp. 18–20)

Summary: In today's organizations, it is important for everyone to learn how to lead others and use power responsibly, regardless of position. That's because all of us share the responsibility of ensuring that those in power behave fairly and ethically. The good news is that leadership can be learned. And although it can be challenging to step up to leadership, you can do it now—you don't need to wait until you have a senior position at work. It is essential, however, that we seek emotional connections with our work and our colleagues in order to create healthy organizational environments that prepare us to lead one another through the challenges we face in organizations today.

2. What Is the Secret to *Effective* Leadership?   (pp. 20–25)

Summary: To be an effective leader or manager, mastering social and emotional intelligence competencies—abilities tied to things like self-awareness, self-management, social awareness, and relationship management—is essential. Like other competencies, social and emotional intelligence determine how effectively a leader performs and are based on the motives, traits, self-concept, knowledge, and skills the leader brings to the job. There are two levels of competencies—those that are necessary to do a job and those that support outstanding performance—and three categories that can be used to further subdivide competencies according to technical, cognitive, and relational components. No matter how you classify competencies, however, research suggests that social and emotional intelligence make all the difference in terms of an individual's ability to create resonant relationships, communicate effectively, and be truly aware of the environment. Special attention must also be given to self-awarness, the foundation of social and emotional intelligence.

The circle diagram shows:
- 16. Managing and Leading for Tomorrow: A Focus on Your Future
- 1. Managing and Leading Today: The New Rules
- 14. Globalization: Managing Effectively in a Global Economic Environment

Leading and Managing for Today and the Future

- 2. The Leadership Imperative: It's Up to You
- 4. Communication: The Key to Resonant Relationships
- 3. Motivation and Meaning: What Makes People Want to Work?
- 15. Sustainability and Corporate Social Responsibility: Ensuring the Future

3. What Is the Secret to *Influential* Leadership? (pp. 25–30)

Summary: Effective use of power is the key to influential leadership, and power can take several forms—legitimate, reward, coercive, expert, or referent. Each form of power has its place and its uses, and some forms yield more consistently positive long-term results than others. Sharing power by empowering others is one of the most important ways to ensure that you are using your power constructively. Empowerment not only gives employees a sense of ownership of their jobs, but it is essential for the success of organizations today as they become both flatter and leaner and call on their employees to take on more responsibilities.

4. What Is the Secret to *Responsible* Leadership? (pp. 30–38)

Summary: Responsible leadership calls for living our values and acting ethically. Individual, professional, and organizational ethics often determine what we consider moral and how we behave within organizations—and across society as a whole. Business ethics, in particular, can be complicated by a number of factors, including conflict with personal values, ethical differences across cultures, varying levels of ethical commitment among organization members, and integration of governmental regulations. It can be difficult to do what's right; when all is said and done, however, as a leader, you must know your values and live by an ethical code of conduct that you can be proud of.

9. A Final Word on Leadership   (p. 51)

Summary: We all have the potential to be leaders if we so choose because we all influence the people around us, whether we realize it or not. It is a good idea, therefore, for all of us to develop social and emotional intelligence competencies. Understanding the various theories of leadership is one step toward this goal; knowing your values and your ethics is another. As you learn about other important management topics, it is important to keep their relationship to leadership in mind and learn how to continually integrate it into all that you do.

8. What Can We All Do to Become Great Leaders?   (pp. 48–51)

Summary: Self-awareness is one of the key components of becoming a great leader, because it allows us to understand our place in the world and grants us the courage to act on our core values without compromise. Leaders who possess self-awareness are authentic and inspire trust in their followers. They also show integrity and courage when faced with challenging ethical situations. It can be difficult to develop self-awareness because it requires you to put your ethics and your sense of what is right above what is popular, but the final payoff in terms of living up to your ethics and inspiring others to do the same is worth the effort.

7. What Is HR's Role in Supporting Excellent and Ethical Leadership?   (pp. 45–48)

Summary: HR is responsible for supporting leaders in a variety of technical and strategic areas, such as recruiting excellent employees and managing all aspects of the staffing process, maintaining positive relationships with trade groups, providing leadership development and training, and offering strategic support in people-related issues. HR professionals also lead their organizations by taking on the roles of executive coach, strategic business partner, change agent, and leadership development architect. HR can support ethical behavior and leadership through ethics training and whistle-blowing protection programs.

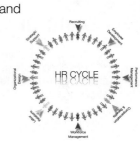

6. Is It Time to Take a Stand for Transformational Leadership?   (pp. 44–45)

Summary: Transformational leaders are emotionally and socially intelligent and seek to inspire people with vision. This type of leadership tends to foster passion and accountability in employees and create a resonant work environment. It ultimately ties together values, ethics, and responsible use of power in a leadership approach that can be very effective in terms of motivating employees.

5. How Do Theories and Models Explain Management and Leadership?   (pp. 39–44)

Summary: Theories describing the characteristics of great leaders have been around for many years and are based on a variety of qualities, ranging from immutable physical characteristics, to conscientiousness, to confidence, just to name a few. Despite the reality that many of these theories are not based in fact, many people unfortunately subscribe to them. Behavior models also seek to explain what makes a leader effective, and they come a little closer to hitting the mark through their emphasis on behaviors and approaches to work, colleagues, and subordinates. Contingency theories go even further, emphasizing situational factors and personal abilities above characteristics and behaviors. Nevertheless, no single theory or model can explain great leadership in its entirety, and a wise leader draws inspiration from a variety of sources.

Motivation and Meaning:

What Makes People Want to **Work**?

Chapter Outline

Find out what you already know about the concepts in this chapter by going to www.mymanagementlab.com and taking the **Pre-Test.** Your results will generate a customized study plan for Chapter 3.

1. What Is Motivation? (p. 58)

2. What Makes Work Meaningful? (pp. 58–61)

3. What Is the Link between Motivation and Psychology? (pp. 61–65)

4. Which Theories of Motivation Are Important to Know? (pp. 65–66)

5. What Are Basic and Higher-Order Needs Theories of Motivation? (pp. 66–69)

6. Why Are the Three-Needs, Equity, Expectancy, and Goal-Setting Theories Popular? (pp. 69–78)

7. What Are Learning Theories? (pp. 78–82)

8. How Can We Integrate Theories of Motivation? (p. 83)

9. What Role Does HR Play in Motivation? (pp. 84–86)

10. What Can We All Do about Motivation? (pp. 86–87)

11. A Final Word on Motivation and Meaning at Work (p. 88)

Go back to www.mymanagementlab.com and take the **Post-Test** to verify your understanding of the concepts. **To experience and apply** the concepts, explore the additional material associated with Chapter 3.

Part 1: Leading and Managing for Today and the Future (Chapters 1, 2, **3**, 4)
Part 2: Planning and Change (Chapters 5, 6, 7, 8, 9)
Part 3: Organizing Human Systems (Chapters 10, 11)
Part 4: Controlling Quality, Culture, and Yourself (Chapters 12, 13)
Part 5: Leading and Managing for the Future (Chapters 14, 15, 16)

8. Workplace Essentials: Creativity, Innovation, and a Spirit of Entrepreneurship

7. Change: A Focus on Adaptability and Resiliency

9. Organizing for a Complex World: Structure and Design

Planning and Change

6. The Human Side of Planning: Decision Making and Critical Thinking

5. Planning and Strategy: Bringing the Vision to Life

16. Managing and Leading for Tomorrow: A Focus on Your Future

1. Managing and Leading Today: The New Rules

Leading and Managing for Today and the Future

2. The Leadership Imperative: It's Up to You

4. Communication: The Key to Resonant Relationships

3. Motivation and Meaning: What Makes People Want to Work?

10. Teams and Teambuilding: How to Work Effectively with Others

Organizing Human Systems

11. Working in a Virtual World: Technology as a Way of Life

14. Globalization: Managing Effectively in a Global Economic Environment

15. Sustainability and Corporate Social Responsibility: Ensuring the Future

12. Organizational Controls: People, Processes, Quality, and Results

Controlling Quality, Culture, and Yourself

13. Culture: It's Powerful

3. Motivation and Meaning: What Makes People Want to Work?

1. What Is Motivation?

We spend almost a third of our *lives* working. We work as students, employees, carpenters, dancers, musicians, electricians, small business owners, artists, professional sports players, farmers, consultants, accountants, caregivers—you name it. We all work, and we work a lot. Including school, most of us will spend an astounding 60 years or more working in one capacity or another. That's a good reason to understand what motivates us to do our best, and how we can find meaning and satisfaction in work. And if you happen to be a teacher, a parent, a manager, or a leader, it is essential to understand what motivates other people to contribute their very best to their families, teams, or organizations.

Motivation

The result of a complex set of psychological influences and external forces or conditions that cause a person to behave in a certain way while maintaining a certain level of effort and degree of persistence.

What, exactly, is motivation? **Motivation** is the result of a complex set of psychological influences and external forces or conditions that cause a person to behave a certain way while maintaining a certain level of effort and degree of persistence.[1] For example, consider yourself right now—you are reading this chapter and preparing for class. You may be studying because you have been told you must. Perhaps you are cramming for a test, and you need to do well. Or, maybe you are self-motivated because you enjoy the class and are curious about management and leadership. That's also psychological—your curiosity is causing you to put effort into studying and sticking with it.

In this chapter, we look at how you—as a student, employee, manager, or formal or informal leader—can keep yourself and others passionately engaged in meaningful work and *motivated to produce results.* You will learn why meaning in life and work is so important to human beings and why work is more than simply a means to an end. You will also learn a fundamental truth about motivation: It takes personal effort, great leadership, and a positive environment to sustain passionate engagement with work.

Numerous theories attempt to explain human motivation. We discuss many of these theories in this chapter. We also cover what HR can do to support a motivated workforce and what we all can do to support motivation and create meaningful work.

> **Most Popular »** Discussion Questions
>
> 1. Make a list of all the jobs you have had, paid and unpaid, including your "job" as a student. What kind of work did you find most enjoyable in these jobs, and why?
> 2. Describe a situation in which you had to motivate other people. How did you do it?

---

2. What Makes Work Meaningful?

In 1963, Victor Frankl wrote about his life as a prisoner in the Nazi concentration camps.[2] Without ignoring the horrors of the camps, Frankl described how the search for meaning in day-to-day activities and finding a sense of control, if only over his attitude and spirit, were the keys to survival. His powerful reflection helps us see how important it is for people to find meaning in existence, no matter how dreadful life is at the moment. In Frankl's case, doing so was a matter of life and death—finding meaning and a sense of control helped him to survive.

Although most of us are not fighting for survival, we still search for meaning in our work. But what *is* meaningful work? A well-known story puts it this way: Three men are found smashing boulders with hammers. When asked what they are doing, the first man says, "Breaking big rocks into little rocks." The second man says, "Feeding my family." The third man says, "Building a cathedral."[3] (See ∎Exhibit 3.1.) No matter what you are doing, if you are convinced that you are doing meaningful work—as these three people were—there's no cost too high: Your curiosity, commitment, and passion will soar. You will be energized and enthusiastic, and you will draw on all of your talents. You'll be motivated to work—and work hard.

■Exhibit **3.1**

What Makes Work Meaningful to You?

In the story, the three men described what they were doing quite differently. Let's assume each man found meaning in the work.

- Why might "Breaking big rocks into little rocks" be meaningful?
- Describe how "Feeding my family" could be meaningful.
- Why might building a cathedral be meaningful?

In these examples, meaning may have come from artistry, craftsmanship, love, responsibility, or spirituality. Maybe you had other answers, too. Are any of these answers more or less meaningful to you? If so, that's a hint about what you find meaningful.

- Think about work you have done at school or in your community that you found meaningful. Why was this work meaningful to you? (For example, was it fun? Were you learning? Were you helping people?)

■Exhibit **3.2**

Victor Frankl searched for meaning even while imprisoned in Nazi concentration camps.

Depmicrostock/Newscom

Flow

A state of intense concentration and complete engagement in a task, along with full use of one's talents to accomplish the task.

The Flow Experience

At about the same time that Victor Frankl was writing about meaning (■Exhibit 3.2), researchers like Mihaly Csikszentmihalyi began studying what it is like to experience deeply satisfying work.[4] When we become truly engrossed in a task that matches our skills and requires full use of our talents, and when the level of challenge is exactly what we want and need, we experience what Csikszentmihalyi calls "**flow**." Sometimes we talk about this as being "in the zone." When in this state, people can work productively for long hours, ignoring hunger, thirst, weariness, and distractions.

Have you ever had a flow experience? You might remember a time when you were writing a paper—you'd done the research, the topic was inherently interesting, and despite the anxiety you felt about producing a long document, you dove in. Soon, you became completely engrossed, moving back and forth between your writing and your sources, and going to the Internet to check facts. You felt alive and completely in control of the process. At some point, you probably "woke up" from your intense focus and realized that many hours had passed. You'd missed a meal or two, or maybe you didn't even hear your phone ring. That's flow! Or maybe you've experienced flow while painting, dancing, or playing sports. Everything seems to work just as it should—your mind, your body, your emotions are all in synch. The outcome of your efforts is fantastic: Your paper is outstanding, your painting is beautiful, your dance is technically perfect and artistically inspiring, or your performance on the field is your very best.

Csikszentmihalyi and colleagues associate the following conditions with flow:

- Intense focus
- A sense that one's actions and the task are in synch
- A sense of control over one's actions
- A lack of awareness that time is passing
- A focus on the activity itself, rather than the hoped-for outcome.[5]

Wouldn't it be great if work could always "flow"? When we are passionately engaged in meaningful work, we tend to be more committed, more resilient, even more creative and adaptable. We can work "*smarter*"—not just more efficiently, but also more effectively.

Motivation: It's Up to You

As you will discover in this chapter, motivation is linked to psychology, and many psychological theories attempt to explain what motivates us at work. Before we explore this research, however, it helps to think about some of the basics. First, human thoughts, emotions, and behavior are at the center of motivation. Ultimately, you motivate yourself, no matter what is happening around you. Second, leaders have a tremendous impact on the degree to which employees are motivated in the workplace. Finally, the overall work environment—the psychological conditions and the emotional reality of the climate—impacts people's desire to do well and affects their capabilities and motivation. Let's look at how one very impressive leader has sought and found passion in his work in the following *Perspectives* feature.

Perspectives

Bonaventure Agata, CSL Behring Senior Director of Global Commercial Development

Bonaventure Agata lives a fascinating life. Born and educated in Kenya, he is passionate about human health. Maybe Bonaventure is passionate about health because he grew up in a part of the world where, he contends, a vast majority of the population has little access to health care. Maybe it is because his father, a physician, told the story of entering medical school only to realize that his own father (Bonaventure's grandfather) could have lived longer had the right health care and drugs been available. Bonaventure has dedicated his life to health care (and to his family, of course). He says the following about leadership, meaning, and passion at work:

You have to love what you do. Your ideals and your values have to align with the organization's or you shouldn't *be there. You need to make sure people understand where you come from—you have to be honest with them. People won't follow you if they don't trust you. And you need to understand where others come from as well—who they are, what motivates them, what drives them. Today, you have to be passionate about what you do. And you have to have high energy—you've got to be ready for action all the time. When you're doing something, you need to be fully engaged, active, and energetic. This links to passion. You have to feel what you do.*

Source: Personal interview with Bonaventure Agata conducted by Annie McKee, 2009.

The comments and perspective of Bonaventure Agata are his own personal views and not necessarily those of CSL Behring.

Bonaventure Agata teaches us some powerful lessons. First, it is up to each one of us to discover what we are passionate about and to find work that inspires us to excel. There is no perfect job, but if we are clear about what motivates us, we will be more likely to (1) choose the right career and jobs and (2) find aspects of almost any job to engage our passion. This calls for self-awareness—the foundation of emotional intelligence. Self-awareness enables us to make good choices and to discover ways to infuse work with meaning, passion, fun, and great outcomes.

Great Leaders Inspire and Motivate Us

Self-awareness is important when you want to motivate others. As a leader, you can impact individuals, groups, and even entire organizations through your behavior. When you lead people, you cast a powerful shadow that either encourages or inhibits people's motivation to engage in their work and join together to accomplish goals. This is true for informal leaders as well as people who hold titles and roles. What you do, say, and feel matters to others. In fact, they may even adopt your attitudes, beliefs, and behavior—for good or bad. Knowing yourself and understanding how people see you enables you to understand what kind of shadow you cast on the people around you. Being mindful of your leadership shadow allows you to create an environment that draws out the best in people: an environment that is ripe with hope, inspiration, and resonance.

■Exhibit **3.3**

A resonant environment is characterized by excitement, energy, optimism, efficacy, and hope.

Sean Prior/Shutterstock

Hope
A state of mind that includes optimism, an image of a future that is challenging but realistic, and a belief that we can do something to move toward this vision.

Resonant environment
A work environment characterized by excitement, energy, optimism, efficacy, and hope.

How can you tell what type of shadow you're casting? Companies spend millions of dollars every year hiring consultants and coaches to help people recognize and understand how they affect the work environment and other people's motivation and commitment. Wouldn't it be better if self-awareness became an essential part of the leader's repertoire?

As a leader, you can develop self-awareness. You can also learn how to inspire others. One way to inspire and motivate people is to help them feel hopeful about the future. Hope is particularly important when it comes to motivation. Hope has been discussed in many ways in spiritual literature, philosophy, and psychology. When it comes to work and motivation, **hope** is described as a state of mind that includes optimism, an image of a future that is challenging but realistic, and a belief that we can do something to move toward this vision.[6] When people feel hopeful, they are psychologically and physically more resilient, more determined, and better able to envision how to achieve goals.[7] A hopeful state of mind supports people in managing motivation, energy, and effort while engaged in tasks at work.

A challenge for managers and leaders is to create a sense of hope among employees. This can be done in a number of ways, such as by tying work to a clear, compelling vision or by ensuring that employees see how their contributions make a difference. In addition, leaders can foster a sense of hope by helping employees focus on success and what's possible, rather than constantly dwelling on problems. But remember—a vision must be realistic. Attempting to spark hope by painting a picture of an unrealistic future will ultimately backfire.

As a leader, you can impact people's motivation to work hard and succeed simply by creating the right kind of environment.[8] We are profoundly affected by the "mood" of people, groups, and organizations. You probably know this from your own experience—when working in situations where relationships are good, the mood is upbeat and hopeful, which helps us do our best. Good leaders know they must create such a work environment. They create what we call *resonance* in their relationships, groups, and organizations.[9] A **resonant environment** at work is characterized by excitement, energy, optimism, efficacy, and hope—positive and powerful emotions when it comes to motivation (■ Exhibit 3.3). Positive emotions matter because emotions impact our ability to motivate ourselves and others.

In the next section, we look at other psychological conditions that can affect motivation.

Most Popular » Discussion Questions

1. What sort of work do you find meaningful? Be specific.
2. When do you experience flow? What does this experience feel like to you?
3. Think about a situation in which you were a leader. What sort of shadow did you cast, and how effective were you in motivating people? What led to your success, and what could you have done better?
4. Think about a time when your emotions affected your motivation. Describe the experience and your reactions, including the outcomes.

---

3. What Is the Link between Motivation and Psychology?

To understand motivation, we need to understand a bit about people: Are we motivated to achieve an internal state that is in some way satisfying? This is called *intrinsic motivation.* Or are we *extrinsically* motivated, seeking tangible outcomes that can be seen and measured outside of ourselves? How does our perception of control over our actions and environment link to motivation? What aspects of personality affect motivation? The following sections address these questions.

Intrinsic Motivation

Intrinsic motivation
An internal sense of satisfaction derived from the work itself and/or the desire to engage in activities even in the absence of external rewards in order to feel a sense of satisfaction, to use or improve one's abilities, or to learn.

Csikszentmihalyi's work on flow concentrates largely on **intrinsic motivation**, which is defined as an internal sense of satisfaction derived from the work itself and/or the desire to engage in activities even in the absence of external rewards in order to feel a sense of satisfaction, to use or improve one's abilities, or to learn.[10] When behavior is intrinsically motivated, a person may be very interested in a task, seek a sense of accomplishment, or want to make a worthwhile contribution to other people or the organization.

Intrinsic motivation is the basis for **self-determination theory (SDT)**, developed by Edward Deci and Richard Ryan.[11] Self-determination theory is concerned with people's need for *empowerment* (to feel competent and have a reasonable degree of autonomy) and their need for *relatedness* (to care for and be related to others). Research has shown that when people work for supervisors who foster self-determination, they are positive about their work.[12] Not surprisingly, then, when supervisors are controlling, employees show more negativity. People are more satisfied and motivated when they are allowed and encouraged to take control of their environment, act with autonomy, and actively seek relatedness with others.

Self-determination theory (SDT)
Theory of motivation that is concerned with people's need for empowerment (to feel competent and have a reasonable degree of autonomy) and their need for relatedness (to care for and be related to others).

The research around self-determination theory supports the idea that intrinsic motivation is a powerful driver of people's behavior and performance at work.[13] On the job, intrinsic motivators include interesting and appropriately challenging work, the opportunity to learn, and a chance to contribute to something that impacts people and society in a positive way. For students, intrinsic motivators may include the chance to share ideas where both relationships and results are positive in class or the opportunity to work on a self-directed project as part of an effective team.

Self-determination theory suggests that satisfaction of the needs for competence, autonomy, and relatedness has a positive effect on intrinsic motivation. When these factors are present, we may even value *extrinsic* motivation more.[14] But what is extrinsic motivation, and what are some common extrinsic motivators?

Extrinsic Motivation

Extrinsic motivation
Motivation that is the result of forces or attractions outside of the self, such as material rewards, social status, or avoidance of unpleasant consequences.

Extrinsic motivation is the result of forces or attractions outside of the self, such as material rewards, social status, or avoidance of unpleasant consequences. Examples of extrinsic motivators at work include pay, benefits, and job security. For a student, extrinsic motivators might be a good grade or the instructor's approval.[15] ■Exhibit 3.4 illustrates other common extrinsic motivators and lists intrinsic motivators for comparison.

■Exhibit **3.4**

Intrinsic and Extrinsic Motivators

Intrinsic Motivators	Extrinsic Motivators
The satisfaction of doing something well	Pay and other material rewards
Interesting and appropriately challenging tasks	Avoiding being fired
Autonomy/empowerment	People's approval
Learning	Social status
Contributing to others in a meaningful way	Fame
Relatedness	Grades

Google

Motivation for Innovation

Google is revered for its focus on innovation. Recently, Google has gained acclaim in another area: motivation in the workplace. What lies beneath Google's success in becoming a company many of us would love to work for?

When it comes to headquarters, Google is second to none. Located in Mountain View, California, it is only a stone's throw from the Shoreline Park wetlands.[16] Bikes are placed all around the campus to help "Googlers" get around. Beach volleyball courts, swimming pools, gyms, numerous cafés, and dozens of micro-kitchens with snacks are just some of the facilities that the company offers its employees.[17] Who wouldn't love to work for a company that provides opportunities for fun, exercise, and great food?

Although comfortable facilities and free meals can help explain why Google is one of the best places to work, there's more.[18] What immediately stands out about Google's approach is that leaders understand that creating a resonant environment is the key to innovation and success. They recognize that morale and innovation are not merely the result of a flashy workplace or progressive bonus structure. What also matters is how the company's leaders ensure that people are intrinsically motivated, engaged, and passionate.

To this end, Google employs a strategy that is also used at Princeton and 3M. The strategy is designed to release people's creativity and provide them with a way to contribute their best.[19] It goes something like this:

- Seventy percent of people's time should be dedicated to core business tasks.
- Twenty percent of time can be dedicated to projects related to the core business.

- Ten percent of time can be dedicated to projects *unrelated* to the core business. This is when Googlers can dive into something *new*, something that could be *big*.[20]

Some of Google's most progressive and innovative projects, such as Google Earth, Google News, and Google Local, were a result of this process.[21] For these kinds of results to occur, we can assume that (1) employees are actually doing work other than their assigned projects, (2) employees are passionate and creative in these new pursuits, and (3) the company dedicates resources and establishes support structures that allow employees to pursue these projects.

Using processes like these, Google enables a thousand flowers to bloom and carefully selects which ones need to be harvested. As CEO Eric Schmidt explains, "Innovation always has been driven by a person or a small team that has the luxury of thinking of a new idea and pursuing it. . . . Innovation is something that comes when you're not under the gun."[22]

Google encourages sharing ideas and creativity

At Google, staff are encouraged to initiate their own out-of-the-box projects, develop and release them, and then have the courage to accept the outcome—success, they hope, but setbacks are also tolerated. That's a big lesson: For people to be truly motivated to take chances on new projects, they have to feel that it is okay to fail.

Google's recipe for success is clear and simple: Create an environment that is supportive of people's physical and emotional health; provide a structure that encourages people to share their best ideas and be creative; and engage people's higher selves in the pursuit of doing good work while providing good services. This is what motivation is all about.

Photo Source: iStockphoto.com

Let's look at how motivators can be put into practice with people who work at Google. You only have to think about what motivates you to realize that intrinsic and extrinsic motivators are both important drivers of your behavior, effort, and persistence. You may study long and hard for an exam because you want a good grade and the instructor's approval (extrinsic motivation). You may also enjoy learning (intrinsic motivation). It's the same at work: Both intrinsic and extrinsic motivators are important drivers of behavior. As a manager, team leader, or colleague, it is important to understand how to motivate people so they can be personally productive while also contributing to the achievement of team and organizational goals. This means you need to understand what contributes to both extrinsic and intrinsic motivation. One psychological concept often linked with both intrinsic and extrinsic motivation is *locus of control*, which we explore next.

Locus of Control

Locus of control
Our perception of the degree to which we have control over what happens in our lives.

Locus of control is a concept developed by psychologist Julian Rotter in 1954. As the phrase implies, locus of control refers to our perception of the degree to which we have control over what happens in our lives.[23] The concept allows us to place ourselves (and others) along a continuum of perceived control over our actions, outcomes, and fate. One end of the continuum is an internal locus of control, and the other end is an external locus of control.

If you have a high *internal locus of control,* it means you believe you can impact your environment and your fate. You take personal responsibility for the outcomes of your actions. Conversely, a high *external locus of control* indicates that you believe others and the environment have a great impact on you and the results of your efforts. If this is the case, you may not take responsibility for your actions, or you may not try hard to achieve results. Why would you try hard if you think that your efforts won't make a difference? Most of us know people who give up too quickly or who are quick to blame others. These people are not positive or inspiring, and they are often difficult to work with.

It is much more pleasurable to work with people who have a high internal locus of control. They believe they can get things done, they take responsibility, and they generally have a positive outlook. Where do you feel your locus of control is on the internal-external continuum?

The amount of control we feel we have over outcomes impacts our energy and motivation. Other aspects of personality that affect our level of motivation are discussed next.

Motivation and the Big Five Dimensions of Personality

To understand how theories of motivation have been developed, it helps to understand certain aspects of psychology and personality. In this section, we focus on what are commonly called the "Big Five" dimensions of personality.[24] These five dimensions were derived from numerous early studies, one of which included 18,000 personality characteristics![25] Since the average English speaker's vocabulary is around 17,000 words, a list that long is clearly not useful.[26] So, researchers worked to consolidate the descriptors, resulting in ever-smaller lists.[27] Eventually, 16 personality traits were identified, and these were collapsed into the Big Five.[28] These traits are summarized in ■Exhibit 3.5.

Studies have examined the effects of these dimensions of personality on leadership and motivation. For example, studies suggest that extraversion correlates with inspirational leadership and motivation.[29] In a study of sales representatives, researchers found that extraverts were more likely to be motivated to gain status and power, which helped them to do well as sales reps. Employees scoring high in conscientiousness were motivated to accomplish tasks, which also led to increased job performance.[30]

■Exhibit **3.5**

The Big Five Dimensions of Personality

- *Openness to experience* (versus conformity, closed-mindedness): Imaginativeness, openness to new ideas, and curiosity
- *Conscientiousness* (versus undirectedness): Self-discipline, planning, and achievement
- *Extraversion* (versus introversion): The desire to seek out others and to have a positive, energetic, social attitude and emotions
- *Agreeableness* (versus antagonism): Compassion, cooperativeness, and willingness to compromise
- *Emotional stability* (versus neuroticism): Psychological consistency of mood and emotions

Source: Copyright © 1963 by the American Psychological Association. Reproduced with permission. The Big Five Dimensions of Personality. Source: Norman, W. T. 1963. Personality measurement, faking, and detection: An assessment method for use in personnel selection. *Journal of Applied Psychology*, 47(4): 225–241. The use of APA information does not imply endorsement by APA.

Now, let's explore several models of motivation that have been developed over the years, starting with an overview. As you read the next few sections, consider carefully which models make the most sense to you.

Most Popular » Discussion Questions

1. What is the difference between intrinsic and extrinsic motivation?
2. How can you increase a person's sense of intrinsic motivation on a project team? What extrinsic motivators might encourage people to participate fully on a team?
3. How does locus of control affect you in college?

---

4. Which Theories of Motivation Are Important to Know?

In the next few sections, you will learn about several major theories of motivation that attempt to explain why people are driven to behave as they do. Remember that these theories and models are backed by research to varying degrees. Strangely, some of the theories of motivation that are least supported by research are the most commonly taught and referenced in organizations. Because of this, we will point out supporting research—or lack thereof—so that you can form your own educated opinion. You do not need to embrace all of the theories described in this chapter—but you should be familiar with them so that you can understand their application at work, in school, and in teams.

Many theories of motivation emerged during the twentieth century. ■Exhibit 3.6 shows a time line of when the theories covered in the next few sections were introduced, and ■Exhibit 3.7 summarizes the main focus of each.

As a student, employee, or manager, you need to understand what each theory of motivation says about human behavior. You also need to know what the research indicates: Do these theories really explain motivation? If so, to what extent? How can you use these theories, both individually and in conjunction with each other? You have already read about Deci and Ryan's self-determination theory as it relates to intrinsic motivation. In the next several sections, we are going to explore other major theories of motivation in detail.

■Exhibit **3.6**

Theories of Motivation: Time Line		
Year	**Theorist**	**Theory**
1953	B. F. Skinner	Operant conditioning theory
1954	Abraham Maslow	Hierarchy of needs theory
1959	Frederick Herzberg	Two-factor theory
1961	David C. McClelland	Three-needs theory
1963	John Stacey Adams	Equity theory
1964	Victor Vroom	Expectancy theory
1968	Edwin Locke	Goal-setting theory
1969	Clayton P. Alderfer	ERG theory
1977	Albert Bandura	Social learning theory
1985	Deci and Ryan	Self-determination theory

■Exhibit **3.7**
Visual summary of theories of motivation

HIERARCHY OF NEEDS THEORY
Basic and higher-order needs motivate behavior in ascending order

ERG THEORY
Needs for existence, relatedness, and growth can all motivate at once

TWO-FACTOR THEORY
Higher-order factors motivate, and inadequate hygiene factors can lead to dissatisfaction

THREE-NEEDS THEORY
Needs for achievement, affiliation, and power drive thoughts, feelings, and behavior

EQUITY THEORY
Inputs, outputs, and perceived fairness can be used as a formula to determine level of motivation

EXPECTANCY THEORY
Effort affects performance, and performance is moderated by perceived value of outcomes

GOAL-SETTING THEORY
Specific, measurable, achievable, results-based, time-specific goals motivate

SELF-DETERMINATION THEORY
The needs for empowerment and relatedness contribute to motivation

OPERANT-CONDITIONING THEORY
People are motivated by reinforcement

SOCIAL LEARNING THEORY
The motivation to learn and change behaviors is linked to self-efficacy and vicarious learning

---

Most Popular » Discussion Questions

1. What motivated you to go to college?
2. You are about to study nine theories of motivation. This will take effort and persistence. Take a few minutes to list a few intrinsic and extrinsic motivators that will help you stay focused as you read.

---

5. What Are Basic and Higher-Order Needs Theories of Motivation?

Needs theories assume that people engage in activities to satisfy certain needs and desires. Thus, Maslow's hierarchy of needs, Alderfer's ERG theory, and Herzberg's two-factor theory all help explain the interaction between motivation and people's physical and psychological needs. Each of these theories looks at basic needs, such as what we require for life, and higher-order needs—the things that make life worth living.

■Exhibit **3.8**
Maslow's hierarchy of needs.

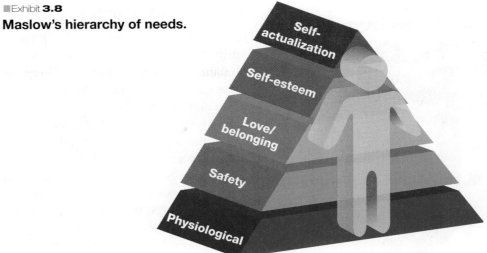

Hierarchy of Needs

Hierarchy of needs
A model stating that people are motivated to satisfy physiological, then safety and security, then love and belonging, then self-esteem, and finally self-actualization needs, in that order.

Abraham Maslow's **hierarchy of needs** is one of the best-known needs theories of motivation.[31] This theory posits that people are motivated to satisfy first physiological, then safety and security, then love and belonging, then self-esteem, and finally self-actualization needs, as depicted in ■Exhibit 3.8. Self-actualization describes a state of being in which a person seeks truth, perfection, and meaningfulness—something most people try to attain throughout their lives.

This theory is still taught in many courses and training programs all around the world, possibly because it is simple and easy to understand. Of course, ease and simplicity are not necessarily sound reasons for adopting a theory. Maslow's theory has not been well supported by research (or common sense). An often-criticized aspect of the theory is the notion that you must first satisfy the lower-order needs before progressing to the higher-level of needs. Another often-questioned element of Maslow's theory is the idea that once a need is met, it ceases to be a motivator. Also, the hierarchy of needs theory states that people will only seek to satisfy self-actualization needs after all other needs have been met. This has too been criticized.

If you've ever been poor or lived through a natural disaster, you can probably recognize flaws in Maslow's theory. Even when you were worried about how you would buy food or pay rent, didn't you still care about your friends and loved ones? Even when you felt unsafe and insecure because your community had been ravaged by a storm, didn't you still seek to find meaning, truth, and beauty in life? Didn't you look for the proverbial "silver lining"? As these situations illustrate, people are complicated, and Maslow's simple hierarchy does not explain everything that motivates us.

Still, the needs that Maslow identified are important to people. As a manager or a team member, you must recognize when these needs are affecting people. Then, you can make decisions about whether satisfying these needs will keep people engaged and committed to their work.

ERG theory
Theory that people are motivated to satisfy needs related to existence, relatedness, and growth, and these needs can all be activated at the same time.

■Exhibit **3.9**
ERG theory focuses on needs related to existence, relatedness, and growth.

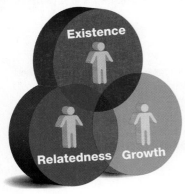

ERG Theory

Basing his theory on the work of Maslow, Clayton Alderfer developed **ERG theory**, which states that people are motivated to satisfy needs related to Existence, Relatedness, and Growth, and that these needs can all be activated at the same time.[32] According to Alderfer, these are needs that people *want* to satisfy, and although people will be immediately compelled to satisfy existence needs, the needs for relatedness and growth can be powerfully motivating at the same time. (See ■Exhibit 3.9.)

Motivators and hygiene factors.

Two-factor theory (motivator-hygiene theory)
Theory that two distinct sets of factors, called motivators and hygiene factors, affect job satisfaction, motivation, or job dissatisfaction.

Motivators
Factors that positively impact motivation, such as the needs for recognition, responsibility, achievement, and opportunities for growth and development.

Hygiene factors
Both physical and psychological aspects of a job that can lead to dissatisfaction, including salary, working conditions, supervision, relationships with coworkers, and level of job security.

Two-Factor Theory

Like Maslow and Alderfer, Frederick Herzberg sought to explain how the desire to satisfy needs can act as a motivator. He also looked at what might cause dissatisfaction and detract from motivation. Herzberg's resulting **two-factor theory**, sometimes called the **motivator-hygiene theory**, states that two distinct sets of factors, called motivators and hygiene factors, affect job satisfaction, motivation, or job dissatisfaction.[33] Until Herzberg proposed his theory, most people felt that job *satisfaction* and job *dissatisfaction* were at two ends of a continuum. Herzberg proposed that satisfaction and dissatisfaction are actually two entirely different scales that need to be considered separately when determining whether people are satisfied and motivated to do their jobs or not. (See ■Exhibit 3.10.)

Herzberg called the factors that lead to job satisfaction **motivators**. Motivators are higher-order needs, such as the needs for recognition, achievement, and opportunities for growth and development. When these factors are present, people are satisfied and motivated. In contrast, when motivators are absent, Herzberg suggested that people are neutral about work, as shown in ■Exhibit 3.11.

Hygiene factors do not motivate, but they affect the level of *dissatisfaction* with a job. Hygiene factors are both physical and psychological aspects of a job that can lead to dissatisfaction, including salary, working conditions, supervision, relationships with coworkers, and level of job security. To illustrate how this works, think about the last time you received a raise. What was the net amount of that raise per week? Was that enough to keep you motivated to get up and go to work, ready to do the best you possibly could, for the next 52 weeks? If you are like most people, a raise would give you a momentary sense of excitement. However, if you found the job boring and didn't feel a sense of accomplishment, even a large raise would not be a powerful motivator for very long.

Like Maslow's hierarchy of needs, Herzberg's two-factor theory is taught in management training programs, despite the fact that research has not, for the most part, supported this theory.[34] Still, this theory is helpful in that Herzberg was one of the first researchers to study white-collar workers and focus on job design and job enrichment.[35] These two topics are discussed later in the chapter.

■Exhibit **3.11**

Hygiene factors and motivator equations as proposed by Frederick Herzberg.

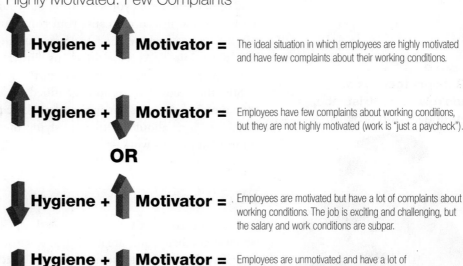

Highly Motivated: Few Complaints

Hygiene + Motivator = The ideal situation in which employees are highly motivated and have few complaints about their working conditions.

Hygiene + Motivator = Employees have few complaints about working conditions, but they are not highly motivated (work is "just a paycheck").

OR

Hygiene + Motivator = Employees are motivated but have a lot of complaints about working conditions. The job is exciting and challenging, but the salary and work conditions are subpar.

Hygiene + Motivator = Employees are unmotivated and have a lot of complaints about working conditions.

Unmotivated: Many Complaints

6. Why Are the Three-Needs, Equity, Expectancy, and Goal-Setting Theories Popular?

As research continued to expand our understanding of motivation, several theories began to stand out: three-needs theory, equity theory, expectancy theory, and goal-setting theory. These theories have been studied extensively and are quite popular.

Although these theories are quite different from one another, they all focus on linking intention, behavior, effort, and outcomes. Many of the assumptions underlying these theories impact how motivation is often viewed in modern organizations. This section explores each of these theories and how they apply to you and to work today.

Three-Needs Theory

Three-needs theory
Theory stating that people are motivated by needs for achievement, affiliation, and power.

David McClelland's **three-needs theory** focuses on people's needs for achievement, affiliation, and power.[36] McClelland and others often refer to these needs as motives. McClelland's research on these needs was extensive and has been followed up with numerous studies around the world.[37] Many of these studies have involved managers, making the results particularly important. Let's look at each of these needs individually, and then we'll consider their relevance in the workplace. (See ■Exhibit 3.12.)

Need for Achievement

Need for achievement (nAch)
The desire to engage in challenging and complex activities, meet and exceed personal goals, and to seek excellence.

The **need for achievement (nAch)** is the desire to engage in challenging activities, to meet and exceed personal goals, and to seek excellence. The need for achievement can include a desire to do better than others, but people who are high in nAch most often

■Exhibit **3.12**
McClelland's three-needs theory.

Need for Achievement:
Desire to engage in challenging activities, meet and exceed personal goals, and seek excellence.

- Defines success as reaching a personal standard of excellence
- Exhibits a relentless desire to succeed
- Enjoys regular feedback

Need for Affiliation:
Desire for warm, fulfilling, and close personal relationships.

- Expends time and energy building relationships
- Concerned with others' feelings, desires, and needs
- Avoids conflict

Need for Power:
Desire to have influence, control, and responsibility, either directly or through social status.

- Seeks control and social status
- Gratified by promotion, titles, and symbols of power
- Less susceptible to stress that accompanies power and responsibility ("power stress")[38]

seek to reach a personal standard of excellence. People who are high in nAch also like regular feedback, and they tend to have a relentless desire to succeed in whatever they do. nAch can be a powerful and positive force because it drives people to be and do their very best.

Research indicates that people with high nAch do well early in their careers, when individual contribution is valued.[39] However, few of today's jobs call for individual contribution alone. Even entry-level jobs usually require people to work in teams on complex projects with others. Tasks and responsibilities need to be negotiated, and goals and standards have to be agreed on. This can be difficult when people on the team are motivated by strong need for achievement.

Later, as a person gains more responsibility and begins to manage others, the need for achievement can really get in the way. Why does this happen? When excellence is the goal and personal standards are the measure of success, managers don't always have much patience with other ways of doing things, especially if others are in the process of learning. These managers would often prefer getting the job done correctly and as fast as possible, rather than training people. At worst, people who are high in nAch can become micromanagers. **Micromanagers** try to do everything themselves and criticize everyone else's efforts. Clearly, this creates a negative environment and results in people not giving their best effort. So, as valuable as high personal standards and desire for success can be, people with a high need for achievement must take care not to let it harm relationships or teamwork.

Micromanagers
People who try to do everything themselves and criticize everyone else's efforts.

Need for Affiliation

The **need for affiliation (nAff)** can be described as the desire for warm, fulfilling, and close personal relationships. People who are high in nAff are concerned with others' feelings, care about people's desires and needs, and will expend tremendous time and energy building trusting relationships. These individuals value friendship and camaraderie and will often try to create a sense of team spirit at work. They may avoid conflict and are keen to resolve it in ways that leave relationships intact.

People high in nAff are often great coworkers, as they tend to create environments that are marked by care, empathy, and compassion. Many people thrive in this sort of environment. Problems can arise, however, when a strong nAff drives employees or managers to consistently avoid disrupting relationships. This can result in outcomes that are destructive in the long term. For example, a manager who is high in nAff might avoid giving direct feedback on performance. This can lead to ongoing performance issues. Alternatively, the manager may suppress conflict that is a healthy expression of differing opinions. Another possibility is that a high-nAff manager might build strong friendships with some employees (those with similar needs) and not with others, leading to perceptions of inequity, unhealthy competition, or internal conflict.

Need for affiliation (nAff)
The desire for warm, fulfilling, and close personal relationships.

Need for Power

The **need for power (nPow)** is the desire to have influence, control, and responsibility, either directly or through social status. Research indicates that the need for power is associated with attaining significant positions of responsibility, such as top management jobs. People who are high in nPow seek control and social status and are gratified by promotions, titles, and the like. It also seems that people high in nPow are less susceptible to "power stress"—chronic stress associated with the constant pressure, heavy responsibilities, long hours, and hard work that leaders and managers face today.[40]

So what is the downside of a high need for power? In today's organizations, single-minded ambition for the sake of controlling others is destructive. These kinds of managers and leaders create dissonance, and they wreak havoc on teams and organizations. However, these people can also be strangely attractive, because they exude confidence and strength. We often find ourselves drawn to these people, and we may even seek to emulate them. So, it is important to recognize when and how to manage the downside of the need for power both in ourselves and with others.

Need for power (nPow)
The desire to have influence, control, and responsibility, either directly or through social status.

Personalized power

A need for power that drives people to seek control through assertive or aggressive behavior, often for personal gain.

Socialized power

An expressed need for power that is based on a desire to support the welfare of others, a group, society, or the common good.

Prosocial behavior

Any behavior that seeks to protect the welfare of society or the common good.

Personalized versus Socialized Power

One way to manage a high need for power is to consciously channel it toward the good of the group, rather than simply toward personal gain. In fact, McClelland and colleagues make a distinction between *personalized power* and *socialized power*.[41] Individuals high in **personalized power** seek control through assertive or aggressive behavior, often for personal gain.[42] However, individuals high in **socialized power** desire to support the welfare of others, a group, society, or the common good. People high in socialized power seek to change their environments through *prosocial behavior*.[43] **Prosocial behavior** is any behavior that protects the welfare of society or the common good.[44] People motivated by socialized power often experience satisfaction from the accomplishments of others and shy away from notoriety themselves. An example would be a supervisor whose joy comes from watching employees succeed on their own, using skills that he or she has taught them.

Socialized Power, Prosocial Behavior, and Ubuntu

Socialized power and *prosocial behavior* are becoming popular as service, sustainability, and corporate social responsibility become more prominent aspects of organizational visions and strategies. Although the terms "socialized power" and "prosocial behavior" may be relatively new, the concepts are not. For example, in some cultures, such as many in sub-Saharan Africa, the good of the group is put ahead of individual needs or desires. This is captured in the word *Ubuntu*. *Ubuntu* is a Nguni word, but it can also be found in the Zulu and Xhosa cultures, as well as in many others throughout the southern half of the African continent. *Ubuntu* is roughly translated as "I am because you are." Zulu and Xhosa proverbs sum up this philosophy of life and relationships in the following phrase: "A person is a person through other people." Zulu—"Umuntu, ngumuntu, ngabantu"; and Xhosa— "Umntu, ngumntu, ngabanye abantu." In 2008, Nelson Mandela (■Exhibit 3.13) described *Ubuntu* this way:

> Ubuntu does not mean that people should not enrich [take care of] themselves. The question therefore is: Are you going to [fulfill your needs] in such a way as to enable the community around you to be able to improve? These are the important things in life. And if one can do that, you have done something very important, which will be appreciated.[45]

Ubuntu is a mindset that motivates people to direct power toward the good of the group. Today, scholars such as Barbara Nussbaum are applying the concept of *Ubuntu* to business.[46] The *Ubuntu* philosophy is an important contribution to people's understanding of how to work well together and how to link what "I" need with what "we" need. Consciously attending to this "I/we" dilemma can help engage socialized power—which can and does impact groups and organizations positively.[47]

Measuring Needs for Achievement, Affiliation, and Power

Yet another of McClelland's contributions to the study of motivation was his work in measuring nAch, nAff, and nPow.[48] To assess which needs were impacting people's thought processes and intentions, McClelland used a tool called the Thematic Apperception Test (TAT).[49] The TAT is a projective test: Test-takers are asked to look at pictures that show people alone or interacting with others, and they are then asked to write a short story describing what they believe is happening in the pictures. The pictures evoke different ideas for different people, and some of these differences can be traced to each person's needs for achievement, affiliation, and power.[50] When a trained researcher reads the TAT stories, he or she can measure thoughts, feelings, and actions that indicate the presence of the three needs.

Try this for yourself. Look at the picture in ■Exhibit 3.14 and write a few paragraphs about what you think is going on, how the person feels, and what he might be thinking. As you reread your story, do you see any evidence of achievement, affiliation, or power needs?

This is an interesting exercise, and it can give you some insights about your motives. It is important to note, however, that many projective tests (the TAT included) have low

■Exhibit **3.13**

Nelson Mandela is a proponent of prosocial behavior and *Ubuntu*.

Geof Daniels/Eye Ubiquitous/Alamy

■Exhibit **3.14**

The Thematic Apperception Test (TAT).

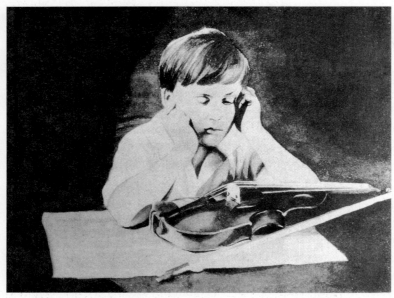

© Spencer Grant/PhotoEdit Inc.

Equity theory
Theory stating that an individual's level of motivation is a result of comparing personal inputs and outcomes, and also of comparing one's efforts and rewards with others' efforts and rewards.

reliability and validity, which means that they don't measure the "truth" about personality or, in this case, needs. Still, these types of tests help us explore how we think about things, which can give us an idea about what is important to us.

McClelland and his colleagues have contributed significantly to our understanding of how our psychological needs influence motivation and how we might think about measuring our needs. Let's now turn to look at equity theory—yet another way to understand motivation.

Equity Theory

John Stacey Adams' **equity theory** suggests that we all keep a mental ledger comparing personal inputs and outcomes, and also comparing one's efforts and rewards with others' efforts and rewards.[51] This theory is about people's perceptions of fairness: Do my contributions (inputs) and what I receive as a result (outcomes) match what others like me are giving and receiving? Do I get what I believe I deserve? The answer to these questions affects our motivation.

To illustrate equity theory, consider this example: Two recent graduates have accepted jobs as analysts in an accounting firm. Both graduated from good schools with good grades, and both have the same work responsibilities, pay, and titles (analyst). During the first six months on the job, one of them comes to work at 8:00 A.M. as expected, and leaves at 5:00 P.M., as she was told she could. The other analyst arrives early, and when he feels it is beneficial to him and to his team, he stays later than 5:00 P.M. Sometimes, he is there as late as 8:00 or 9:00 P.M., and he has even worked a few weekends. He doesn't resent doing the work; in fact, he enjoys it and feels a sense of accomplishment. However, as time goes on, he becomes frustrated by the fact that he still receives the same salary as his counterpart, and that the department manager treats both of them exactly the same way. He believes things are out of balance and unfair. This perception of inequity causes him to feel anxious and tense, and he feels pressure to restore balance.

Equity theory states that the analyst (and indeed, all people) will respond to this type of situation in one of four ways:

- First, he might simply ignore the perceived inequity and cope with the stress related to his perception of unfairness.
- Second, he could decide to stop working so hard (i.e., he could change inputs).
- Third, he could ask for a raise or try to get his supervisor to recognize his efforts and reward him with special assignments (i.e., he could try to change outcomes).
- Fourth, he could attempt to see the situation differently (i.e., he could change his perception of his and his colleague's inputs and outcomes). For example, the analyst may come to see that his colleague is actually doing as much work as he is and the quality is the same. She just doesn't take as many breaks during the day as he does.

In this example, the analyst is comparing himself with another individual, called a *referent*. A referent is another individual, a group, or oneself in a situation that is assessed for comparison purposes. In the previous example, the analyst compared himself with a specific coworker. He might have also compared his salary to that of the analysts in another company, or perhaps even compared his own experience in this position to his experience in another job. For example, have you ever started a new job that is similar to one you had in the past, but with a lower salary? Here, you are the referent, because you are comparing your current input-outcome ratio to a ratio from your own past. A referent can also be a person's beliefs about one's worth and value. This belief can be a result of what a person has learned over the years from family, teachers, and bosses. Hopefully, these beliefs are informed by self-awareness.

You can see why self-awareness is important here: Far too many people have inaccurate pictures of the value of their contributions. If people have inflated pictures of themselves, they may constantly feel as if they aren't getting what they deserve. Such people can be very unpleasant to work with. On the other hand, when people believe that their input is less valuable than it really is, they often lack self-confidence. This can be a problem because self-confidence is a critical part of working successfully in organizations today, because increasingly, people need to be bold enough to make decisions on their own.

Let's look at another example of how consideration of equity can affect someone. Imagine that you found a fellow employee's pay stub on the floor, and you saw that she makes several thousand dollars more than you do when you both have exactly the same jobs. What do you do? It's doubtful that you would just feel happy for her. According to equity theory, you would likely do one of four things to regain your sense of equity: try to ignore it, minimize your own performance so that you feel your effort matches your salary, ask your boss for a raise, or find a reason to change your perception about the fairness of the situation.

Let's reverse the situation. What if the pay stub indicated you were being paid more than your coworker was? Would you go to your boss and ask for a reduction in salary? That's highly unlikely. Still, you might feel uncomfortable and want to restore equity, so you might start helping your colleague more, or even suggest to your boss that she deserves a raise.

Equity Theory and Cognitive Dissonance

In the example, you believed that your inputs and your colleague's were similar, yet you were being rewarded more, which did not seem fair. You experienced an inner conflict, which is called cognitive dissonance. **Cognitive dissonance** is a state of psychological stress arising from the attempt to process conflicting ideas, attitudes, or beliefs.[52] To alleviate cognitive dissonance, you might change your perception of your input. You might, for example, choose to believe that your contributions are actually more valuable than others', or that you are in some ways "better" than others, so you deserve to be paid more.

Cognitive dissonance can lead to problems. When we experience it, we sometimes talk ourselves into believing things that just aren't true. Seeing ourselves, other people, and the world accurately is of vital importance to leadership. Some scholars suggest that leaders who are capable of managing cognitive dissonance are more likely to sustain ethical leadership over time.[53] This is in part linked to the social and emotional intelligence competencies of self-awareness, empathy, and organizational awareness. We need to see ourselves and each other accurately. We also need to see situations clearly and accurately in order to see equity expectations accurately.

Equity theory helps us understand the link between people's perceptions and their behavior and how this equation affects motivation. It also gives managers an important road map for motivating employees: Manage the perceived ratio of inputs to outcomes. When people perceive the balance between inputs and outcomes to be fair, they are motivated to contribute. In contrast, when they perceive the equation to be out of balance, they may experience cognitive dissonance or change their behavior in ways that affect the level or quality of outcomes, harming team efforts and interfering with the accomplishment of goals.

Is Equity Theory Relevant Today?

Attending to equity is especially important today. In many organizations, people are working harder than ever before. Organizations have been requiring more of people for years. "Do more with less" is a common mantra. Many companies have downsized

Cognitive dissonance
A state of psychological stress arising from the attempt to process conflicting ideas, attitudes, or beliefs.

numerous times while maintaining the scope of the work that needs to be accomplished. In 1990, studies showed that Americans were working fully one month more per year than they were 20 years earlier.[54] Unfortunately, things have only gotten worse since then.[55] People are working early mornings, into the evenings, on weekends, and even during their vacations. Even though Americans are working more, in many cases the rewards have not increased proportionately.

For many people, the equity equation is wrong, and they feel the need to restore balance. However, rarely does someone approach a manager and say, "Sorry, I don't think this situation is fair, so I am not going to work as hard anymore." People attempt to restore balance in more subtle ways, and those ways can be extremely destructive for an organization. For example, some people justify spending a lot of time texting or on social networking sites because they believe they are not being paid enough and have a "right" to spend time this way. Then, there are those who show up for work and do only the bare minimum. These employees are physically present. However, mentally and psychologically, they are absent.

To further compound the problem, this kind of work environment can be insidiously destructive. Emotions are literally contagious, and the negativity, passivity, and dissonance that accompany widespread perceptions of inequity affect everyone.[56] Even employees who perceive equity and balance in their own input-outcome equation can become demoralized as a result of working in such an environment.

Restoring Equity: What Managers Can Do

As a manager, you must be alert for perceived inequity—especially in an environment where everyone is working very hard. Look for signs that people are not comfortable with their own or others' contributions and rewards. Talk to people. Find out what they are thinking and feeling. If you discover that your employees perceive inequity, find out exactly why. If they are right, you will need to restore a sense of equity by helping people change inputs and/or outcomes to restore balance.

If equity actually *does exist*, you will need to help people reframe the situation and change perceptions. For example, consider a manager who heard through office gossip that his employees thought he was playing favorites when assigning overtime. In actuality, the manager wasn't playing favorites. He realized, however, that perceptions are as powerful as reality and that he needed to find a way to prove that he was fair. The next week, he placed all eligible employees' names in a bowl. During a break, he asked one of the employees to pull names for the next week's overtime assignments. The result: the selection process was seen to be fair and the grumbling stopped.

This manager had his eyes and ears open and was able to learn of people's dissatisfaction. It is not enough to rely solely on office gossip, however. To ferret out and understand perceived inequity, managers need to be engaged in honest and authentic communication with their employees. Too many managers shy away from these difficult but ultimately rewarding discussions. The best managers and leaders, however, have the courage to find out the truth and act on it—whenever possible.

It is unrealistic to think that most managers can fix everything. Due to economic pressures, most organizations need employees to work hard, and for professionals, the hours are often long. It might also be impossible to pay people more for the work they do. Cost-of-living or routine yearly raises are a thing of the past for many companies. It can be difficult to change the equity equation using concrete rewards like money.

Still, some managers find ways to be creative and try to balance the equation. For example, one leader of a luxury goods company was greatly disturbed that she could not give her valued employees the pay raises they'd asked for and that she believed they deserved. What did she do? First, she told the employees that she valued them tremendously, that they deserved raises, and that she wanted them to stay and be happy. Then, she bought sushi from a fantastic restaurant and invited everyone to the showroom for drinks, food, and fun. She also requested permission to give her best employees more vacation time. She told them, "I can't give you money, and you know how sorry I am about that. But I can give you time. Take the week between Christmas and New Year's Day off, paid. Take your birthday off, paid. And since it's summer, let's close the offices at 4:00 P.M. on Fridays." This manager used every approach she could to restore a sense of equity: praise and recognition, opportunities for fun, and time off with pay.

Expectancy Theory

Expectancy theory

Theory stating that motivation is affected by the relationships among effort and performance, performance and outcomes, and the perceived value of outcomes.

Effort

A person's input, which will be affected by the person's perception about whether the effort will lead to an acceptable level of performance.

Performance

The extent to which a task or work is completed successfully.

Instrumentality

A person's belief about the degree to which performance will result in realizing certain outcomes.

Valence

The value placed on outcomes.

Expectancy theory goes beyond equity theory in that it looks at the degree to which people value the outcomes they receive as a result of their efforts. The theory is attributed to Yale professor Victor Vroom, who, along with others, engaged in extensive research on the relationship between effort (input), performance, rewards (outcomes), and the perceived value of the outcomes (valence).[57] **Expectancy theory**, then, is a theory stating that motivation is affected by the relationship among effort and performance, performance and outcomes, and the perceived value of outcomes. Let's look at each component of the theory:

- **Effort**: A person's input, which will be affected by the person's perception about whether the effort will lead to an acceptable level of performance.
- **Performance**: The extent to which a task or work is completed successfully.
- **Instrumentality**: A person's belief about the degree to which performance will result in realizing certain outcomes.
- **Valence**: The value placed on outcomes. Outcomes can be extrinsic, such as money, or intrinsic, such as a sense of achievement.[58]

The resulting formula is as follows:

$$\text{Motivation} = \text{Valence} \times \text{Expectancy} \times \text{Instrumentality}^{[59]}$$

Let's look at an example to see how expectancy theory works in the real world. Say your instructor has given you a team assignment: Select a leader whom you admire; analyze his or her leadership competencies; then write a paper, create a set of slides, and give a presentation to the class. In your first team meeting, you discover that all four people on the team are individually confident that they can do well on the project. You also find out that two of the team members are good writers and two have excellent computer and graphics skills. All of you enjoy giving class presentations and have delivered successful presentations in the past.

You leave the first group meeting confident that if everyone works hard, your group will write a good paper, create a good slide set, and give a great presentation to the class. In other words, you have high *expectations* that your collective *efforts* will result in excellent *performance*. So far, you are motivated to work on this assignment.

But what if you have had this professor before, and you know that he rarely gives an A to his students? Everyone on your team wants an A—this grade is a highly desired *outcome* that has high *valence* for all of you. In this situation, however, your perception of the link between excellent task performance (a great paper and presentation) and the desired outcome (an A) is not positive. You do not believe that your efforts will be *instrumental* in helping you achieve the outcome you desire. Therefore, according to expectancy theory, you will not be motivated to work on this assignment.

As another example, picture a consumer goods company in which senior management determined that the company should increase revenue in its beauty products business by 12 percent over the next three years. When rolled down through the divisions, this meant that each brand was expected to increase revenue by anywhere from 8 to 20 percent, depending on the expectations of what could be accomplished in particular geographic areas. The senior executives were excited by this goal. More than a few of them were high in need for achievement, so this stretch goal was exciting and motivating—so much so, in fact, that the executives were somewhat blind to the realities in certain geographic areas.

As the strategy was rolled out, managers in these areas raised a number of objections, not the least of which was the fact that a recent recession had impacted sales of beauty products considerably. Despite these objections and the fact that sales were going down in many regions, the managers were told by corporate headquarters to hit their targets anyway. Let's follow one manager's thoughts and actions as this plan was implemented.

Bill believed in his company, his products, and his division's capabilities. He truly wanted to achieve the targets for several reasons. He wanted to see how the company and its divisions could grow. Bill also expected a promotion, and he knew that his team's compensation was tied directly to achieving the new financial targets. The outcomes, then, had high valence for Bill. For a while, he drove himself and his team as hard as possible. They invested in new marketing plans, engaged a new advertising company, and even changed the packaging on a few of their key products. They worked long hours without complaint. Bill worked weekends and skipped his vacation. In the past, Bill and his team's efforts led to excellent results, and they expected a similar outcome.

This time, however, things just weren't turning out the same. No matter how hard the team worked or how many hours people put in, their performance constantly fell short of their own and others' expectations. Then, halfway through implementation of the new marketing plan, the budget was cut. Bill was told that the advertising campaign could only be implemented in two of four regions. Also, the new packaging took much longer than expected, partly because of mandatory layoffs that left the design team understaffed. Bill came to believe that his team's efforts couldn't possibly lead to reaching the goal. Over time, the situation spiraled downward. Bill's team members were not motivated because they no longer believed their efforts would result in achieving their goals either.

Although it may seem far-fetched that a company's executives would embark on a strategy with so little chance of success, this scenario has become common. Recent years have seen an almost obsessive focus on short-term (usually quarterly) growth results in publicly traded companies—to please investors, analysts, and the like.[60] In many cases, this pattern has led managers to try to force their organizations and employees to achieve ever more unrealistic goals. Managing companies in such a way is detrimental to both the long-term sustainability of the business and the health and welfare of employees.

Because of problems like these, responsible leaders must ask themselves an important question: To what end do we motivate our employees to work? In this example, if senior management had tied the company's strategy more closely to its mission, they may not have been so single-minded about growth in a declining market. Instead, they may have chosen to direct managers' and employees' attention toward creating more recession-proof products or finding more effective ways to manufacture their current products. In other words, they would have motivated employees to engage in different activities, with different measures of performance and different outcomes.

Goal-Setting Theory

As illustrated in the previous section, some goals (like unrealistic sales targets) are not sufficient to motivate people to achieve excellence—simply because they are the wrong goals! But, if the right goals *have* been chosen, how can they be used to motivate behavior?

Goal-setting theory

Theory which states that people are motivated by the process of identifying and achieving goals, and that the characteristics of these goals will have an impact on motivation, performance, and results.

Scholars Edwin Locke, Gary Latham, and colleagues have conducted extensive research on the relationship between goals and motivation.[61] A goal is an outcome that a person, group, or organization is attempting to achieve, accomplish, or attain. Locke and others studied the goal-setting process and subsequently developed the **goal-setting theory**, which states that people are motivated by the process of identifying and achieving goals, and that the characteristics of these goals will have an impact on motivation, performance, and results.[62]

■Exhibit **3.15**

SMART goals motivate many people.

SMART goals

Term describing goals that are specific, measurable, achievable, results-based, and time-specific.

Smart Goals

As we saw in the example about Bill and his sales team, not all goals are helpful. The best goals include certain characteristics, such as being specific and challenging. Let's look at this in practice: Say that two friends want to get in shape. One says to himself, "I'm going to eat better and exercise." The other decides to lose five pounds and to be able to run three miles easily within eight weeks. Her subgoals include (1) working out for half an hour every morning, (2) eating a salad every day for lunch, and (3) cooking dinner at home except on weekends. Which goals do you think are more likely to drive behavior? The first person's goals are vague. It's not clear what he will do or how he will measure his success. In contrast, the other person's goals present a specific set of challenges and outcomes. This person has created a **SMART goal**. SMART goals are specific, measurable, achievable, results-based, and time-specific, as shown in ■Exhibit 3.15.[63] Goals that meet the SMART criteria tend to be motivating for many people, and they are more often achieved than goals that violate one or more of the SMART criteria.

Once a SMART goal has been determined, commitment, an appropriate level of complexity, and feedback on our progress are three important factors that influence the goal's power to motivate us. Feedback tells us where we are in relation to our goals and how far we have to go to achieve them—it's like a SMART goal GPS. Now, I see why commitment is so important. Commitment seems like an obvious condition for motivation: Who wants to work hard to achieve a goal that he or she doesn't care about? Amazingly, building commitment to goals is often overlooked by managers. To illustrate this, consider Tanya, who works at a sports retail store. One day, she gets an e-mail from her manager telling her that her goal is to sell 10 percent more running shoes this month than she did last month. No explanation is given for why Tanya needs to achieve the goal or why it should matter to her personally. The consequences of Tanya's success or failure are absent. Also, the situation in the department seems to have been ignored: One sales clerk is out on maternity leave, and another is on vacation. Why should she care about this new goal—one that seems to have come out of nowhere? What level of commitment would she have to this goal?

Now, imagine that Tanya's manager Maria handles the situation differently. Maria sets up a special meeting with Tanya, maybe over coffee. In a relaxed manner, she praises Tanya for her work in the shoe department, sharing specific, positive feedback from customers. She indicates that because of Tanya's performance, management wants her to attend a training session that will prepare her for a promotion. Then, Maria describes some of the initiatives that have been suggested for the store, including improving sales of particular brands of sports apparel and shoes. She asks Tanya's opinion on this, including what she might need in order to increase sales by 10 percent. Wouldn't Tanya be more likely to commit to the goal in this scenario?

"Doing" and "Being" Goals

Goal setting as a way to motivate people is embraced by many businesses. However, some scholars argue that many assumptions related to goal setting are based on early twentieth-century manufacturing models that focused on a machine-like equation for achieving results.[64] According to these researchers, the typical goal-setting model works for so-called "doing" goals that are clear-cut (e.g., "Increase sales by 10 percent over the next year"), but it is less appropriate for so-called "being" goals, for which there is no definitive ending (e.g., "Become a better sales organization").

SMART goals tend to be "doing" goals. As opposed to "being" goals, which focus on an ongoing transformation, SMART goals zero in on a limited end point.[65] Thus, goal-setting processes that worked well in industrial organizations do not necessarily allow for the stepwise change and transformation that today's knowledge-based, innovative organizations need.

The three-needs, equity, expectancy, and goal-setting theories are well researched and continue to have significant impact on organizations. Despite some drawbacks, they are useful. In the next section, we consider a different but equally well-researched approach: learning theories. Learning theories are especially useful because they focus on learning and change, both of which are essential in today's organizations.

Most Popular » Discussion Questions

1. Which needs do you believe affect your motivation most: achievement, affiliation, or power?
2. Think about a time when you used socialized power—a time when you influenced others in a powerful and positive way that benefited them. What did you do? What was the outcome?
3. What outcomes matter most to you when considering equity (e.g., money, respect, opportunities for learning)?
4. Have you ever experienced cognitive dissonance? Why? What did you do about it?
5. Discuss a situation in which you felt either highly motivated or highly demotivated as a result of considering the factors in expectancy theory, such as the relationship between your effort, performance, and the extent to which you valued the outcome.
6. Do goals motivate you? Why or why not?

---

7. What Are Learning Theories?

Learning theories are closely linked to the study of motivation because they help us understand how people change their behavior. These theories also help us understand how people can be motivated to change their behavior (learn) as a result of experience, consequences, and practice. Two theories in particular, operant conditioning theory and social learning theory, provide useful guidelines for motivating people to learn.

Operant Conditioning Theory

Operant conditioning theory
Theory that learning and behavior changes occur when behavior is reinforced, and when behavior is not reinforced or is punished, it will eventually cease.

Reinforcement
Consequences associated with behavior.

Operant conditioning theory is based on the premise that learning and behavior changes occur when behavior is reinforced, and when behavior is not reinforced or is punished, it will eventually cease. In other words, this theory states that learning occurs through reinforcement. **Reinforcement** refers to the consequences associated with behavior. Behavioral psychologist B. F. Skinner is the scholar most closely associated with this theory.[66] His work continues to have a profound effect on the field of psychology, and the operant conditioning model can be seen in numerous organizational processes. The most common applications of operant conditioning at work include positive reinforcement, negative reinforcement, extinction, and punishment. ■Exhibit 3.16 summarizes each of these methods.

Although we can easily find examples of all types of reinforcement processes in organizations, two are of particular importance: positive reinforcement and punishment. They are important because they are both used extensively in many organizations and they have a profound effect on people's self-image and motivation.

Positive Reinforcement

Positive reinforcement is powerful because it tends to motivate people profoundly. Think about your own experience: When you are praised or given a bonus or a day off for work done well, don't you feel good about yourself and excited to do well again? You are likely to feel good about your boss or your organization too. That's the other reason positive re-

■Exhibit **3.16**

Operant Conditioning: How It Works		
Type of Reinforcement	How the Consequence Is Applied	Real-World Example
Positive reinforcement	Addition of a positive consequence following a desired behavior	Bonuses are given to the employee who sells the first car each month
Negative reinforcement	Removal of a negative consequence following a desired behavior	Manager ceases sending harsh reminder e-mails once a report is turned in
Extinction	Withholding of a consequence following a certain behavior	A new employee regularly asks for feedback, and when she gets none, she stops seeking it
Punishment	Addition of a negative consequence following an undesired behavior	A factory worker fails to meet production quotas and her salary is docked

inforcement can be a powerful motivator at work: It contributes to a resonant environment, one in which people feel optimistic, energized, and safe.

Take the example of a project team leader—we will call him Marco. Marco is expected to turn in a progress report to his manager, Celeste, every Friday. Until recently, Marco gave the report to Celeste at 5:30 P.M. One week, he finished the report in the morning and gave it to her at noon. Celeste was thrilled. For the first time, she would not have to stay late to review the report! She thanked Marco profusely, praising his time management, thoughtfulness, and professionalism. She even offered to take him to lunch.

Marco truly enjoyed the praise and recognition, and he had a good time at lunch. He and Celeste talked through some of the more difficult aspects of the project and made a plan. They got to know each other better, which both of them enjoyed. These pleasant experiences motivated him to finish the report early the following week. He did so and passed it on to Celeste by 10:00 A.M., again receiving praise and an offer of lunch.

Punishment

Punishment can be highly destructive to individuals and the organizational environment. Although it might be necessary to stop unlawful, unethical, or harmful behaviors (theft, sexual harassment, and the like), punishment is best used as a "last resort" approach to changing behavior. Here are a few examples of what can happen as a result of misusing punishment, as well as information about what a manager can do to minimize the negative effects.

"What Did I Do Wrong?"

Unfortunately, people often do things that are unacceptable simply because they don't know the rules or have not been socialized to the organization's work processes, culture, or ethics. It is actually surprising how often people are punished without truly understanding why. This leads to mistrust, suspicion, and confusion—not the optimal circumstances for people to perform at their best. As a manager, if you *have to* use punishment, you *must* link it clearly with the undesired behavior. Make sure an employee understands what he or she did, why it was wrong, and how the consequences relate to the undesired behavior.

"Why Me?"

It is surprising how often managers blame and punish the wrong person or the wrong team. One common example is the "blame the messenger" syndrome. The person who brings bad news to the boss "gets it." When people are blamed and punished for things they didn't do and/or couldn't control, they feel a profound sense of injustice.

In such situations, we learn not to trust our environment or the people in it. We become defensive and self-protective. Needless to say, this kind of environment is not conducive to healthy autonomy, creativity, or positive risk taking—all behaviors that are much needed in many organizations today. So, if you must punish, be *sure* you know the real source of the undesired behavior.

"I Must Be an Awful Person."

Punishment can harm self-respect and self-image. As a leader, part of your job is to ensure that your people are confident, believe in themselves, and are proud of their contributions. This state of mind is conducive to productivity and commitment to collective goals. So, if you need to stop someone from doing something, and punishment is the only way to achieve this, it is important to separate the behavior (what the person is doing/has done that is wrong) from the person (the totality of that individual's humanity: mind, body, heart, and spirit).

Let's say, for example, that an employee has been having outbursts of temper in team meetings, causing serious disruption in the team's ability to work together. You have spoken to the person and have tried rewarding good behavior. Nothing has worked. Finally, you decide to remove the person from the team (a much-valued assignment). You do not talk about the behavior as part of the person's character or personality (e.g., "You never handle yourself well" or "You just don't fit on this team"). You are careful to share, as objectively as possible, the link between the outbursts and others' ability to work on the team. You are compassionate with the individual, and you offer help: connection with the HR department, ongoing mentoring, and a coach.

"I Can't Believe My Manager Did That in Front of Everyone."

Punishment is bad enough. But punishment in front of other people is simply an unacceptable way to address a problem. Why? It almost always fails to accomplish the goal. The shame that most people feel when publicly chastised is profound. Shaming someone poses a threat to that person's identity, which in many cases causes people to fight back.[67] Some people go "underground," hiding everything from the manager. Others may strike back in retaliation or even sabotage the manager, the group, or the organization.

Public punishment not only affects the individual negatively, it affects everyone present—and usually many others who hear about it. In fact, punishing one person in a group can be tantamount to punishing everyone. Unfortunately, most of us have had the experience of being punished in public. Maybe we've had our faults and shortcomings pointed out to others. Maybe we've been criticized harshly during a team meeting. What was your reaction when you were punished in front of others? What lessons can you take from your life experience into your work or management roles?

Even when punishment is done "well," it is an extremely risky way to attempt to motivate people. As you can see, an organization is much better off training for good behavior, rather than having to punish bad.

Operant Conditioning: Does It Really Work?

Operant conditioning can be seen everywhere in organizational life and, in fact, may be at the heart of many people's assumptions about what motivates people. Think about it: Paychecks, bonuses, incentive programs, the threat of being fired for poor performance, criticism, feedback, and praise—all are examples of operant conditioning at work. But does operant conditioning really motivate people? Is motivation as simple as perfecting the behavior-consequence formulas used in this theory? Although it seems clear that certain behaviors can be learned and changed through reinforcement, the method is not a panacea and can even have negative consequences. For example, dozens of studies show that people who expected financial incentives performed at lower levels than those who expected no reward.[68] This could be linked to an argument that extrinsic rewards do not affect emotional or cognitive commitment, especially when intrinsic motivators are absent.

The Achilles' heel of many incentive programs is that they rely wholly on extrinsic motivators—and once these motivators are removed, desired behaviors may die out. To ensure that performance continues at a high level, incentives must be kept in place or, very often, increased over time. This is why some organizations seek to transform employees by converting extrinsic motivation to intrinsic motivation, which requires more than a carefully planned operant conditioning program.

These findings should be taken seriously. They indicate that operant conditioning programs at work may not have the desired effect on motivation and behavior change. Next, we look at social learning theory, which to a certain extent addresses some of the concerns associated with operant conditioning.

Social Learning Theory

Social learning theory
Theory stating that people learn new behaviors by observing others and that self-reinforcement and self-efficacy support learning and behavior change.

Albert Bandura is well known for his work on **social learning theory**.[69] Social learning theory states that people learn new behaviors by observing others, and that self-reinforcement and self-efficacy support learning and behavior change. Social learning theory helps us understand how people can learn by watching others, reinforcing their own behavior, and believing that they can be successful. Let's look at what research says about social learning theory as it applies to work motivation today.

Early studies showed that people learn from watching others and that employees who were close to supervisors or leaders imitated their behavior.[70] This greatly influenced later learning theorists, such as Julian Rotter, whose work on locus of control you read about earlier in this chapter. Rotter proposed that an individual's behavior has an impact on the motivation of others to engage in similar behavior.[71] By observing the consequences of others' actions, an observer is able to calculate the likelihood of positive or negative outcomes and act accordingly.

Vicarious Learning: The Bobo Doll Experiment

Bandura built on this early research and conducted fascinating studies. With his now-famous Bobo doll experiment, he showed how people will replicate the behavior they observe.[72] In this experiment, children in one group witnessed adults behaving aggressively with an inflatable doll (Bobo). Other children witnessed adults calmly engaged in activities without being aggressive. The groups of children exposed to aggressive treatment of the doll were more likely to replicate this aggression later. They had "modeled" their behavior on the adults they observed. This is called vicarious learning.

Vicarious learning happens at work all the time. For instance, in many pharmaceutical companies, new hires are paired with experienced sales reps as they make their rounds of doctors' offices and hospitals. The new hires watch, listen, and learn how to build relationships with their customers, how to encourage them to try new drugs, and how to manage their time.

Self-Reinforcement: Don't Wait for Others to Reward You

Bandura's work also indicates that people engage in self-reinforcement to motivate themselves.[73] For example, maybe you've promised yourself an evening out when you finish this chapter. At work, people might self-reinforce by stopping to feel a sense of accomplishment when they do a good job or plan a nice lunch for the team.

Self-reinforcement is not easy at work today, because many people are extremely busy. It takes time and effort to actually reward ourselves. Self-reinforcement is even more important today, however, because managers simply don't have the time to reinforce people constantly. In our increasingly autonomous jobs, we need to find ways to motivate ourselves.

Self-Efficacy

Self-efficacy
The degree to which a person believes that he or she is capable of successfully performing a behavior, accomplishing a task, or achieving a goal.

Although vicarious learning and self-reinforcement are valuable in learning and motivation, self-efficacy might be the most important concept in this theory. **Self-efficacy** is the degree to which a person believes that he or she is capable of successfully performing a behavior, accomplishing a task, or achieving a goal.[74] Self-efficacy plays a key role in motivation because the stronger a person's belief that he or she is capable of performing a task, the more motivated he or she will be to direct attention, increase efforts, and "stick with it" in order to succeed.[75]

Self-efficacy is important for students and employees alike. Research indicates that "self-efficacious students work harder, persist longer, persevere in the face of adversity, have greater optimism and lower anxiety, and achieve more."[76] At work, it is not hard to think of examples in which self-efficacy plays a part in overall success. Imagine, for example, someone who has just been hired to work in the marketing department of a graphic arts business. He loves graphic arts and is quite talented—but that's not his job. His duties include finding, calling, and visiting potential clients to interest them in the firm's activities. He is essentially a salesperson. But say he comes to the job believing that no matter what kind of training he receives, he will never be a good salesman. In college, he tried to raise money for a club and failed. He describes himself as shy with strangers and doesn't think he's very good at small talk. Can you imagine him succeeding as a salesperson?

Is this young professional doomed to fail? Scholars suggest not: Self-efficacy can be improved. What can you do to improve your self-efficacy? First, you can deliberately gain experience with the work you need to do. You can also consciously model your behavior on a successful colleague or friend. It also helps if people around you are supportive and encouraging. Finally, it helps if you are passionately engaged with your work. When you feel strongly about what you are doing, your energy will be directed and more intense.[77] Try not to feel discouraged as you learn. It is far better to focus on the positive, because this sparks creativity and resilience.[78]

In summary, social learning theory contains powerful messages for how we can improve our own and others' motivation. Many companies use the theory explicitly, and many more use it implicitly. In the example of the sales rep earlier in this section, the company is using principles of social learning theory. It is supporting the development of sales skills and self-efficacy by pairing new hires with experienced reps. In addition, the company provides several experiential training sessions for the new reps, led by experienced and encouraging instructors. And, managers in charge stay very close to the new reps and their partners, modeling behavior while encouraging and creating a sense of energy, optimism, and positive outcomes. When applied in these ways, social learning theory greatly improves motivation and performance.

Most Popular » Discussion Questions

1. Consider rewards and punishments or other reinforcements you have experienced at work. What was the effect on your motivation to learn or change your behavior?
2. Think about a time when you learned by modeling your behavior on someone else. Was this learning experience successful? Why or why not? What could have made it more successful?
3. What self-reinforcers work for you? Why? Are they actually helpful, or do they have "side effects" that might be harmful to you?
4. How did you develop self-efficacy? Consider your family, school, friends, sports, and the like.

8. How Can We Integrate Theories of Motivation?

Trying to apply so many motivation theories can be overwhelming. So where do you start? First, if you find a theory that you can easily embrace and implement, use it. Don't make the mistake, however, of thinking any one theory has all of the answers or can be applied in every situation. You need to have more than one theory in your toolbox. To practice integrating theories of motivation, consider the following *Student's Choice* case about Lance Armstrong. How can you use theories of motivation to explain Lance Armstrong's success in cycling and as a leader? Some hints: His success in cycling could be tied to a need for achievement, implementation of an excellent goal-setting program, and a strong sense of self-efficacy. His ongoing motivation to make the Lance Armstrong Foundation successful could be tied to his need for socialized power. Can you think of other ways to apply the theories to this case?

Student's Choice

Mindy Walker

Lance Armstrong and LIVESTRONG

Lance Armstrong is an athlete, a cancer survivor, a philanthropist, and a leader. He is also motivational, inspiring millions. While most people first think of him as a record-breaking cyclist, his story of beating cancer is astonishing. Armstrong didn't stop there: Showing true compassion and concern for people affected by cancer, he established a foundation to support them.

Lance Armstrong began his athletic journey at the age of 13. By age 16, he was a professional triathlete. By the time he was 20, he was cycling competitively and winning races. Just two short years later he won the Tour de France for the first time. His career was booming and everything seemed possible. Clearly this was a man motivated to succeed and win.

Then tragedy struck. At the age of 25, Lance Armstrong was diagnosed with testicular cancer. After surgery, the doctor informed him that he had a 50 percent chance of survival. Armstrong, however, remained upbeat and used visual imagery to help beat the disease. After intense chemotherapy, his cancer went into remission. Armstrong went on to win six more Tour de France races and, after a brief retirement, he even captured third place in the race at age 38.

Although it may have been tempting for Armstrong to rest on his laurels after his legendary fight with cancer and his remarkable cycling career, he wanted to do even more with his life. He became an advocate for cancer research and created the Lance Armstrong Foundation. The foundation offers educational programs and support for people affected by cancer and also supports research. The foundation's philosophy is based on the belief that "unity is strength, knowledge is power and attitude is everything."[79] It's more than just words: This foundation has had an impact. In conjunction with Nike, the foundation launched an awareness campaign around the now-famous yellow wristband with the word *LIVESTRONG* on it. This yellow wristband has swept the world, symbolizing hope, knowledge, and a will to live. The sales have raised millions to support the foundation's mission.

Armstrong encourages people to maintain a positive attitude and to never give up. He has not forgotten his struggle with cancer and he hopes to encourage and motivate others to fight the disease and win. Lance Armstrong is a great example of believing in yourself and looking toward the future. His commitment to curing cancer is powerful, exciting, and inspirational.[80]

Source: Adapted from a case written by Mindy Walker.

Most Popular » Discussion Questions

1. What do you think motivates Lance Armstrong? Use the three-needs, expectancy, and goal-setting theories together to explain your answer.
2. Use social learning theory to explain how an athlete can motivate himself or herself, as well as others.
3. Does Lance Armstrong motivate you? How and why?
4. Pick three motivation theories and apply each to getting students to study.

9. What Role Does HR Play in Motivation?

As the "people" function of an organization, one of HR's core responsibilities is to ensure that the workforce is energized, committed, and motivated. Two important ways in which HR supports motivation include creating and administering compensation plans, which can affect extrinsic motivation, and considering the characteristics of jobs, which can affect intrinsic motivation.

Compensation and Reward Programs

Many people value money highly (expectancy theory would say it has high valence). Money enables people to satisfy basic needs (Maslow's hierarchy of needs and the ERG theories suggest that this is essential for motivation), and pay can be a measure of one's success or status (satisfying the need for achievement or power). Pay can also allow people to compare their input and output with others, thereby giving them an opportunity to determine equity. Pay can be linked closely with goal attainment, or it can be used as positive reinforcement. Money can even be a factor in social learning theory, because people may have a strong desire to model their behavior on others who receive a high salary.

Any way you look at it, money is a powerful motivator. HR is often responsible for supporting managers in determining in what manner, when, and how much people are paid, as well as what other forms of compensation are available. Pay can be determined by considering an individual's performance, the performance of a group, or the entire organization's performance. Types of compensation plans include the following:

Individual compensation
A plan in which compensation is determined by considering an individual's performance.

- **Individual compensation:** When compensation plans are based on individual performance, they will be most effective and most motivating when people can see the link between their performance and their compensation, when compensation is considered fair, and when individuals have opportunities to learn and improve their performance.

Group compensation
A plan that bases an individual's compensation on the performance of a group or groups and/or the organization as a whole.

- **Group compensation:** This type of plan bases an individual's compensation on the performance of a group or groups and/or the organization as a whole. Group compensation plans are often used when it is difficult to measure individual performance or when collaboration is required to accomplish goals. These schemes tend to be most effective when the link between individual contribution, group performance, and compensation is clear. They also tend to be more effective when the groups function well, meaning that the groups have a shared purpose, constructive norms, and healthy relationships. Some researchers have argued that when applying these schemes, cultural attitudes toward individualism versus collectivism need to be considered and reconciled.[81]

Merit-based compensation
A plan in which compensation is determined by the level of performance of an individual or group.

- **Merit-based compensation:** This type of plan is based on the performance level of an individual or group, as opposed to factors such as years with the organization. Very few organizations have "pure" merit-based compensation schemes; most companies balance evaluation of merit and performance with factors such as tenure and role in the organization. Still, many organizations have merit pay schemes that allow managers to offer or increase compensation within a certain range for specific roles. For example, in a large retail clothing chain, a certain type of job may be compensated with a salary of $30,000 to $34,000 per year. This is the range that a manager has to work with when hiring employees and when rewarding performance with increased compensation.

Compensation package
A plan in which wages, bonuses, and "fringe" benefits (such as health insurance, retirement plans, vacation, tuition reimbursement, and stock options) are all monetized.

Money is not the only component of compensation. HR managers must also take into account other benefits that employees may receive. Compensation can include anything that can be monetized. HR is often responsible for creating **compensation packages**,

Compensation schedule
A plan defining how payment structures and terms of payment (including regular pay, commissions, and bonuses) are dispersed to employees.

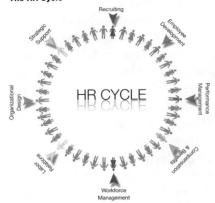

The HR Cycle

plans in which wages, bonuses, and "fringe" benefits (such as health insurance, retirement plans, vacation, tuition reimbursement, and stock options) are all monetized.

How compensation is dispersed is also something HR needs to consider. **Compensation schedules** define how payment structures and terms of payment (including regular pay, commissions, and bonuses) are dispersed to employees. Wages and salaries are almost always paid at regular intervals, and in many companies, raises are also given at predictable times. Bonuses and special compensation such as sales commissions may be given at intervals or intermittently, usually determined by individual or collective performance.

The Job Characteristics Model

Job characteristics model
Framework that states that people need certain qualities in their job to be intrinsically motivated and satisfied with their work.

Job enrichment
Building intrinsic motivators, such as opportunities for learning, more control over how tasks are accomplished, and leadership opportunities, into the structure of a job.

Job enlargement
Combining several simple jobs into one larger job.

Job rotation
Moving employees from one job or one job site to another to increase satisfaction and productivity.

Well-known scholars J. R. Hackman and G. R. Oldham proposed a model that describes the specific conditions that lead to intrinsic motivation in job performance.[82] They identified three types of variables: psychological states contributing to intrinsic motivation, job characteristics that facilitate these psychological states, and personal attributes that determine positive response to job complexity and challenge. The model has come to be known as the **job characteristics model**. The job characteristics model is a framework that states that people need certain qualities in their job to be intrinsically motivated and satisfied with their work. This model describes five job characteristics that can lead to motivation, job satisfaction, and productivity (■Exhibit 3.17).

As job designers, HR managers have a responsibility to create jobs that combine the appropriate level of each of the core dimensions of the job characteristics model. This ensures that employees can experience their work as meaningful, feel responsibile for outcomes, work, and know how their efforts actually impact the final results. Job characteristics can enhance personal and work outcomes such as motivation, job satisfaction, and work performance. To enhance the five core job dimensions, HR can use the following types of activities:

- **Job enrichment**: Building intrinsic motivators, such as opportunities for learning, more control over how tasks are accomplished, and leadership opportunities, into the structure of a job.
- **Job enlargement**: Combining several simple jobs into one larger job.
- **Job rotation**: Moving employees from one job or one job site to another to increase satisfaction and productivity.

■Exhibit **3.17**
Ideal outcomes of the job characteristics model.

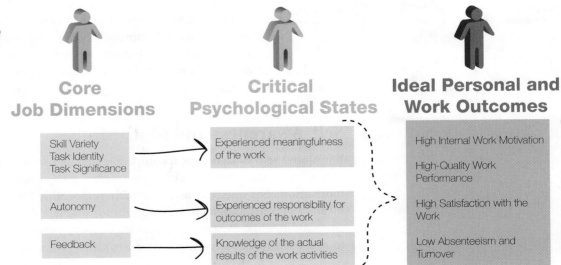

These job characteristics can add to a job's appeal. However, it is important to remember that this model does not suggest that "more is always better"; rather, it suggests that an *appropriate* level of these characteristics can support motivation. For example, too much freedom and autonomy can cause employees to feel unsupported.

Imagine, for example, that you've just started a job as a buyer for a luxury goods company. It's your first day. You find your office, say hello to a few people nearby, and start to set up your desk. The people who hired you—your manager and the HR director—are nowhere to be found. You busy yourself as best you can, expecting direction from someone, but that direction never comes. A few hours later, the HR director sends you an e-mail with forms to complete. Late that afternoon, your manager shows up and says, "Hi! Great to see you here! Are you settling in okay? Good. See you Friday." Then, he leaves. Most people would agree that's too much autonomy! It's also possible to have "too much" of any one of the other job characteristics identified in this model as well!

A final note on the job characteristics model: Although it is widely used in organizations, it has shortcomings. For example, one study purports that factors other than this model's five characteristics can also lead to increased productivity, happiness, and motivation. Examples of such factors include the needs for respect, growth, and trustworthy leadership, as well as the desire to be a member of the in-crowd and to impact decisions about one's job.[83]

Most Popular » Discussion Questions

1. Pay is often considered a primary motivator. Is it for you? Why or why not? Use theories presented in this chapter to support your stance.
2. Can an employee impact the design of his or her own job? How? Give examples.

---

10. What Can We All Do about Motivation?

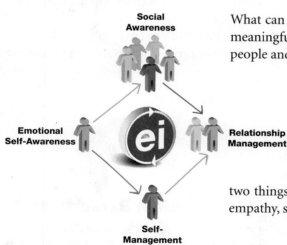

What can you do to motivate yourself and others and ensure that everyone's work is meaningful? Of course, you can apply various theories and concepts of motivation to people and situations. To do this, you must integrate different theories and viewpoints about motivation. That's not all, however: You must also understand what motivates *you* and causes you to perceive work as meaningful. This is self-awareness, a foundational social and emotional intelligence competency. You also need to understand what motivates others, and you must learn how to respond to their needs. This is empathy, another important social and emotional intelligence competency. Both self-awareness and empathy are discussed next. As you read, think about one or two things that you can do to improve your self-awareness and build skills related to empathy, such as accurately reading other people's emotions.

Self-Awareness and Motivation

Emotional self-awareness is a competency related to social and emotional intelligence.[84] Why do you need to develop a high degree of self-awareness with respect to motivation? For one, you are ultimately responsible for motivating yourself. This means you must understand the conditions that enable you to feel engaged and excited about work. When you are aware of these conditions, you will be better able to make sensible choices about your work and your career. Knowing what you find meaningful and what motivates you also allows you to consciously support yourself during times when you are faced with work that isn't as fulfilling as you'd like. Remember Holocaust survivor Victor Frankl from the beginning of the chapter? There wasn't much to motivate him and others in the prison camps. However, Frankl found ways of looking at life that gave a sense of meaning to his daily activities. If you know yourself, you can also do this whenever you are faced with difficult work or life circumstances.

Understanding feelings and moods is an important aspect of effective leadership. Understanding your own feelings about work, effort, and goals, as well as your own needs, desires, and hopes, can help you understand your own motivation (or lack thereof). With self-awareness, you can monitor your response to work and adjust your stance consciously. You can make decisions about what sort of work is meaningful and motivating to you, and you can either seek this kind of work or attempt to design features into your job that will enhance your motivation.

Empathy and Motivation

Empathy
Accurately interpreting the emotions, needs, and desires of others.

When we work with, manage, or lead other people, we need to be cognizant of which needs and desires might be affecting them, as well as how their thoughts and feelings are impacting their behavior. "Reading" others' behavior requires **empathy**. Empathy includes accurately interpreting the emotions, needs, and desires of others.[85] Studies repeatedly show that empathy is a critical component of effective management and leadership.[86] When you empathize, you are better able to connect with people and motivate them to meet their own needs, your needs, and the needs of the organization. Also, when others believe that you understand them and care about their hopes, desires, and needs, they are motivated to join you and, in many cases, follow your lead.

The capacity for empathy takes on special importance in multicultural settings, which are extremely common today, both domestically and internationally. Different cultures experience work and motivation in different ways. Therefore, we must be able to read others and their cultures so that we can understand which theories are applicable and how they should be applied.

Many issues can complicate how we motivate people in a multicultural setting. First, although the theories you learned in this chapter have value, many of these theories of motivation have a decidedly Western bent.[87] Differences in values and social norms affect expectations about appropriate management behavior, job security, compensation structures, performance evaluation, career development, and motivation strategies. Any person who works in a multicultural or cross-cultural setting must understand how his or her own and others' cultures affect behavior. This requires that we develop abilities related to social awareness, including empathy.

Most Popular » Discussion Questions

1. Think about a relationship with a school or work colleague that you are motivated to improve. Practice self-awareness by examining your role in this relationship: What are you doing to make it better? What have you done to create the current problems? What emotions have driven your behavior?

2. For the same relationship, practice empathy. What do you think is driving the other person's behavior? What motivates him or her to act in certain ways? What emotions is he or she expressing?

11. A Final Word on Motivation and Meaning at Work

As you have seen, there are many theories that attempt to explain motivation and many other factors to consider when trying to keep yourself and others engaged and passionate about work. As you study more about management and leadership, you will likely find that exploring motivation and meaning at work will become more and more important. That is because almost everything we do as employees, managers, or leaders involves harnessing talent and energy in the service of doing something well.

Or, at least it should. We began this chapter by talking about how important it is for people to find meaning in work. Sigmund Freud is widely believed to have said, "Love and work are the cornerstones of our humanness."[88] We'll leave love up to you. As for work, we can't emphasize enough how important it is for you to find ways to use your talents, engage your passion, and bring others along with you on the search for meaningful work. You can start by developing self-awareness and empathy to deepen your understanding of what motivates you, as well as what motivates others.

Key Terms

1.   What Is Motivation?   (p. 58)

Key Terms

Motivation The result of a complex set of psychological influences and external forces or conditions that cause a person to behave in a certain way while maintaining a certain level of effort and degree of persistence. p. 58

2.   What Makes Work Meaningful?   (pp. 58–61)

Key Terms

Flow A state of intense concentration and complete engagement in a task, along with full use of one's talents to accomplish the task. p. 59

Hope A state of mind that includes optimism, an image of a future that is challenging but realistic, and a belief that we can do something to move toward this vision. p. 61

Resonant environment A work environment characterized by excitement, energy, optimism, efficacy, and hope. p. 61

3.   What Is the Link between Motivation and Psychology?   (pp. 61–65)

Key Terms

Intrinsic motivation An internal sense of satisfaction derived from the work itself and/or the desire to engage in activities even in the absence of external rewards in order to feel a sense of satisfaction, to use or improve one's abilities, or to learn. p. 62

Self-determination theory (SDT) Theory of motivation that is concerned with people's need for empowerment (to feel competent and have a reasonable degree of autonomy) and their need for relatedness (to care for and be related to others). p. 62

Extrinsic motivation Motivation that is the result of forces or attractions outside of the self, such as material rewards, social status, or avoidance of unpleasant consequences. p. 62

Locus of control Our perception of the degree to which we have control over what happens in our lives. p. 63

4. Which Theories of Motivation Are Important to Know? (pp. 65–66)

Key Terms None

5. What Are Basic and Higher-Order Needs Theories of Motivation? (pp. 66–69)

Key Terms

Hierarchy of needs A model stating that people are motivated to satisfy physiological, then safety and security, then love and belonging, then self-esteem, and finally self-actualization needs, in that order. p. 67

ERG theory Theory that people are motivated to satisfy needs related to existence, relatedness, and growth, and these needs can all be activated at the same time. p. 67

Two-factor theory (motivator-hygiene theory) Theory that two distinct sets of factors, called motivators and hygiene factors, affect job satisfaction, motivation, or job dissatisfaction. p. 68

Motivators Factors that positively impact motivation, such as the needs for recognition, responsibility, achievement, and opportunities for growth and development. p. 68

Hygiene factors Both physical and psychological aspects of a job that can lead to dissatisfaction, including salary, working conditions, supervision, relationships with coworkers, and level of job security. p. 68

6. Why Are the Three-Needs, Equity, Expectancy, and Goal-Setting Theories Popular? (pp. 69–78)

Key Terms

Three-needs theory Theory stating that people are motivated by needs for achievement, affiliation, and power. p. 69

Need for achievement (nAch) The desire to engage in challenging and complex activities, meet and exceed personal goals, and to seek excellence. p. 69

Micromanagers People who try to do everything themselves and criticize everyone else's efforts. p. 70

Need for affiliation (nAff) The desire for warm, fulfilling, and close personal relationships. p. 70

Need for power (nPow) The desire to have influence, control, and responsibility, either directly or through social status. p. 70

Personalized power A need for power that drives people to seek control through assertive or aggressive behavior, often for personal gain. p. 71

Socialized power An expressed need for power that is based on a desire to support the welfare of others, a group, society, or the common good. p. 71

Prosocial behavior Any behavior that seeks to protect the welfare of society or the common good. p. 71

Equity theory Theory stating that an individual's level of motivation is a result of comparing personal inputs and outcomes, and also of comparing one's efforts and rewards with others' efforts and rewards. p. 72

Cognitive dissonance A state of psychological stress arising from the attempt to process conflicting ideas, attitudes, or beliefs. p. 73

Expectancy theory Theory stating that motivation is affected by the relationships among effort and performance, performance and outcomes, and the perceived value of outcomes. p. 75

Effort A person's input, which will be affected by the person's perception about whether the effort will lead to an acceptable level of performance. p. 75

Performance The extent to which a task or work is completed successfully. p. 75

Instrumentality A person's belief about the degree to which performance will result in realizing certain outcomes. p. 75

Valence The value placed on outcomes. p. 75

Goal-setting theory Theory which states that people are motivated by the process of identifying and achieving goals, and that the characteristics of these goals will have an impact on motivation, performance, and results. p. 76

SMART goals Term describing goals that are specific, measurable, achievable, results-based, and time-specific. p. 77

7. What Are Learning Theories? (pp. 78–82)

Key Terms

Operant conditioning theory Theory that learning and behavior changes occur when behavior is reinforced, and when behavior is not reinforced or is punished, it will eventually cease. p. 78

Reinforcement Consequences associated with behavior. p. 78

Social learning theory Theory stating that people learn new behaviors by observing others and that self-reinforcement and self-efficacy support learning and behavior change. p. 81

Self-efficacy The degree to which a person believes that he or she is capable of successfully performing a behavior, accomplishing a task, or achieving a goal. p. 82

8. How Can We Integrate Theories of Motivation? (p. 83)

Key Terms None

---

9. What Role Does HR Play in Motivation? (pp. 84–86)

Key Terms

Individual compensation A plan in which compensation is determined by considering an individual's performance. p. 84

Group compensation A plan that bases an individual's compensation on the performance of a group or groups and/or the organization as a whole. p. 84

Merit-based compensation A plan in which compensation is determined by the level of performance of an individual or group. p. 84

Compensation package A plan in which wages, bonuses, and "fringe" benefits (such as health insurance, retirement plans, vacation, tuition reimbursement, and stock options) are all monetized. p. 84

Compensation schedules A plan defining how payment structures and terms of payment (including regular pay, commissions, and bonuses) are dispersed to employees. p. 85

Job characteristics model Framework that states that people need certain qualities in their job to be intrinsically motivated and satisfied with their work. p. 85

Job enrichment Building intrinsic motivators, such as opportunities for learning, more control over how tasks are accomplished, and leadership opportunities, into the structure of a job. p. 85

Job enlargement Combining several simple jobs into one larger job. p. 85

Job rotation Moving employees from one job or one job site to another to increase satisfaction and productivity. p. 85

---

10. What Can We All Do about Motivation? (pp. 86–87)

Key Terms

Empathy Accurately interpreting the emotions, needs, and desires of others. p. 87

---

11. A Final Word on Motivation and Meaning at Work (p. 88)

Key Terms None

Chapter 3 Visual Summary

1. What Is Motivation?   (p. 58)

Summary: Almost half of our adult waking lives is spent working in our careers. That's why it is important to understand what motivates us, as well as how we can make our work meaningful and satisfying. Motivation results from internal psychological influences and external forces. Numerous theories in this chapter attempt to explain where motivation comes from and how it works. Along with these theories, you will also learn why it is important for people to find meaning in life and work—and why it takes personal effort and leadership to motivate yourself and others.

16. Managing and Leading for Tomorrow: A Focus on Your Future

14. Globalization: Managing Effectively in a Global Economic Environment

1. Managing and Leading Today: The New Rules

Leading and Managing for Today and the Future

2. The Leadership Imperative: It's Up to You   4. Communication: The Key to Resonant Relationships

3. Motivation and Meaning: What Makes People Want to Work?

15. Sustainability and Corporate Social Responsibility: Ensuring the Future

2. What Makes Work Meaningful?   (pp. 58–61)

Summary: Work can be meaningful to people in different ways, depending on their experiences, their needs, and their goals. When work is meaningful to you, you may find yourself so engrossed in what you are doing that you achieve "flow," or a state of being "in the zone." When this happens, you are highly motivated and able to meet challenges fully. Motivation is a psychological state and, ultimately, it is up to you to find what connects you to your work in a meaningful way. This is not to say that leadership is unimportant. On the contrary, organizations choose leaders because of their ability to inspire and motivate. An effective leader does this by instilling hope and creating a resonant work environment.

3. What Is the Link between Motivation and Psychology?   (pp. 61–65)

Summary: There are two forms of motivation that get people working: intrinsic and extrinsic. Intrinsic motivation is that which we provide for ourselves, while extrinsic motivation refers to what is offered to us by others when we do a good job. Self-determination theory examines the relationship between intrinsic motivation and workplace performance, noting that competence, autonomy, and relatedness are at the heart of this form of motivation. Extrinsic motivation, such as pay and benefits, also encourages us to do our best, because these rewards are recognition by others for our hard work. Other factors that contribute to motivation include certain personality characteristics, such as locus of control. Having a high locus of control means that you believe you have power over your environment, so your actions are meaningful. People who have a high locus of control are inspiring and enjoyable to work with because they readily take responsibility for their actions.

4. Which Theories of Motivation Are Important to Know?   (pp. 65–66)

Summary: There are several major theories of motivation, and each one says something unique about human behavior. As a manager, it is important for you to familiarize yourself with these theories so you will be better able to understand what motivates both you and the people who work for you. You also need to understand which of these theories are supported by research, as well as how they are used in organizations.

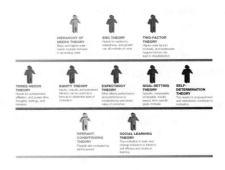

5.   What Are Basic and Higher-Order Needs Theories of Motivation? (pp. 66–69)

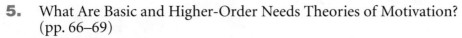

Summary: Needs theories view human motivation as the desire to satisfy various types of needs. We all have these needs, from the most basic ones related to survival (e.g., food, water, safety, health) to higher-order needs related to self-fulfillment and a sense of purpose. One influential theory is Maslow's hierarchy of needs, which states that people fulfill their needs in order, starting with the most basic and working toward higher-level needs. This theory is not supported by research. A second influential theory is ERG theory, which stands for existence, relatedness, and growth. This theory of motivation states that different types of needs can be activated at the same time. Still another theory, two-factor theory, argues that people are influenced by two sets of factors—motivators and hygiene factors—each of which have different effects on job satisfaction, dissatisfaction, or motivation. Motivators, such as the desire for recognition, impact both motivation and job satisfaction, whereas hygiene factors, such as working conditions, do not affect motivation—but do affect job *dis*satisfaction.

6.   Why Are the Three-Needs, Equity, Expectancy, and Goal-Setting Theories Popular?   (pp. 69–78)

Summary: Several theories of motivation—the three-needs, equity, expectancy, and goal-setting theories—are especially popular in organizations. Although these theories are each unique, they all focus on the link between intention, behavior, effort, and outcomes.

David McClelland's three-needs theory tells us that individuals are motivated through needs associated with the desire for achievement, affiliation, or power. People who are driven by achievement seek new challenges and get a sense of satisfaction from achieving personal excellence; people who have affiliation needs are motivated by relationships with others; and people who are driven by power seek control and influence over others. However, not all power is bad. Power can be harnessed to bring about positive change in society and improve the welfare of others; this is called socialized power. For instance, the African concept of *Ubuntu* is a mind-set that motivates people to use power for the good of the group.

Equity theory is based on a mental "accounting" that compares our effort to the rewards we get and/or how our efforts and rewards compare to those of others. According to this theory, people are motivated to the extent that they feel these equations are equitable and fair. When we perceive that our effort is undervalued or overvalued, we may develop cognitive dissonance, in which we experience stress while attempting to process conflicting attitudes, beliefs, or ideas. Cognitive dissonance compels us to resolve our inner conflict by changing our beliefs or our behavior.

Expectancy theory holds that in addition to inputs and outcomes, people also consider the degree to which they value these outcomes (called "valence"). Outcomes that have a high degree of valence can motivate us to work harder, as long as we believe that our efforts will be instrumental in achieving the desired outcome.

Finally, goal-setting theory tells us that "SMART" (specific, measurable, achievable, results-oriented, and time-specific) goals motivate many people. To the extent that we can create meaningful, challenging goals, we can improve motivation in many cases.

11. A Final Word on Motivation and Meaning at Work (p. 88)

Summary: When work is meaningful, people are inspired, motivated, and passionate about what they do. When you study more about management and leadership, you will learn that motivation and the search for meaning are powerful factors that allow us to tap into our energy, skill, and talent and become truly effective at work.

10. What Can We All Do about Motivation? (pp. 86–87)

Summary: It is your responsibility to motivate yourself and the people you work with. To accomplish this, you can start by understanding and integrating the different theories of motivation that have been presented in this chapter. You can also develop your social and emotional intelligence, beginning with self-awareness. Self-awareness will help you make sensible decisions about how to choose meaningful work and/or make work more satisfying. You also need to understand how to motivate others, which starts with empathy.

9. What Role Does HR Play in Motivation? (pp. 84–86)

Summary: HR plays an important role in motivation at work. For one, HR creates and administers compensation packages, which are motivating for most people. These extrinsic motivators need to be combined and managed appropriately and equitably for their effect in recruiting and retaining good employees. Different forms of compensation can yield different types of motivation—for example, group compensation can motivate teamwork and collaboration. Compensation packages include more than money (e.g., health insurance, status, and opportunities for enrichment). This means that HR should pay attention to making sure that people find work meaningful and thereby motivating—such as by encouraging lifelong learning and designing work to be intrinsically satisfying. In fact, the job characteristics model suggests that HR leadership can improve motivation by paying attention to job factors that lead to satisfying work and better work outcomes.

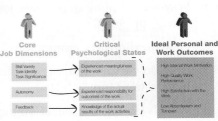

8. How Can We Integrate Theories of Motivation? (p. 83)

Summary: No one theory of motivation is wholly effective by itself, so it is important to find ways of integrating multiple theories into your personal and professional lives.

7. What Are Learning Theories? (pp. 78–82)

Summary: Learning theories answer many questions about motivation. For instance, operant conditioning holds that we learn and are motivated to change our behavior depending on whether that behavior is reinforced, punished, or ignored. Positive reinforcement is a powerful driver of individual performance, and it also helps create a resonant environment. Punishment may be necessary when laws are broken or to address egregious behavior, but it is extremely destructive and should be avoided. Operant conditioning underlies many organizational incentive programs, but it's too simplistic and relies too much on extrinsic motivation.

Social learning theory tells us that we learn by observing. Vicarious learning allows us to model our behavior on that of others and to make choices based on our observations of the consequences of others' behavior. Both self-reinforcement and self-efficacy—or the belief that we can do something—are important parts of social learning theory.

Communication:

The Key to **Resonant Relationships**

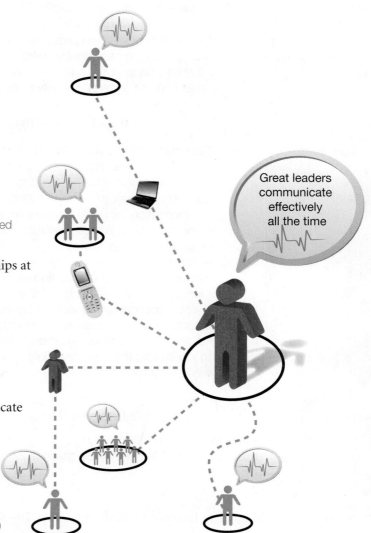

Great leaders communicate effectively all the time

Chapter Outline

Find out what you already know about the concepts in this chapter by going to www.mymanagementlab.com and taking the Pre-Test. Your results will generate a customized study plan for Chapter 4.

1. Why Is Communication Central to Effective Relationships at Work? (pp. 96–97)

2. How Do Humans Communicate? (pp. 97–102)

3. How Do We Communicate and Interpret Sophisticated Information? (pp. 102–106)

4. What Is the Interpersonal Communication Process? (pp. 106–109)

5. How Do We Use Information Technology to Communicate at Work? (pp. 110–111)

6. What Are Common Barriers to Effective Communication? (pp. 112–116)

7. Why Is It Challenging to Communicate in a Socially Diverse World? (pp. 116–119)

8. What Is Organizational Communication? (pp. 119–126)

9. What Can HR Do to Ensure Effective Communication and Resonant Relationships in Organizations? (pp. 126–128)

10. What Can We All Do to Improve Communication and Build Resonant Relationships at Work? (pp. 128–131)

11. A Final Word on Communication and Leadership (p. 131)

Go back to www.mymanagementlab.com and take the Post-Test to verify your understanding of the concepts. To experience and apply the concepts, explore the additional material associated with Chapter 4.

> **Part 1:** Leading and Managing for Today and the Future (Chapters 1, 2, 3, **4**)
Part 2: Planning and Change (Chapters 5, 6, 7, 8, 9)
Part 3: Organizing Human Systems (Chapters 10, 11)
Part 4: Controlling Quality, Culture, and Yourself (Chapters 12, 13)
Part 5: Leading and Managing for the Future (Chapters 14, 15, 16)

8. Workplace Essentials: Creativity, Innovation, and a Spirit of Entrepreneurship

7. Change: A Focus on Adaptability and Resiliency

9. Organizing for a Complex World: Structure and Design

Planning and Change

10. Teams and Teambuilding: How to Work Effectively with Others

Organizing Human Systems

11. Working in a Virtual World: Technology as a Way of Life

6. The Human Side of Planning: Decision Making and Critical Thinking

5. Planning and Strategy: Bringing the Vision to Life

16. Managing and Leading for Tomorrow: A Focus on Your Future

1. Managing and Leading Today: The New Rules

14. Globalization: Managing Effectively in a Global Economic Environment

Leading and Managing for Today and the Future

2. The Leadership Imperative: It's Up to You

4. Communication: The Key to Resonant Relationships

3. Motivation and Meaning: What Makes People Want to Work?

15. Sustainability and Corporate Social Responsibility: Ensuring the Future

4. Communication: The Key to Resonant Relationships

12. Organizational Controls: People, Processes, Quality, and Results

Controlling Quality, Culture, and Yourself

13. Culture: It's Powerful

95

1. Why Is Communication Central to Effective Relationships at Work?

Success at work is based in part on your ability to share information and to influence others—two main purposes of communication in the workplace (■Exhibit 4.1). Effectiveness at work also includes the ability to share one's values, to inspire others, and to create resonance in relationships through positive communication that helps create an environment where everyone can be and do their best.[1]

From your own experiences in school, work, and life, you have developed the capacity to communicate who you are, what you need, and what you think and feel. You've learned to communicate in ways that help you build relationships, manage conflict, influence others, share knowledge, and collaborate with others. Good leaders and successful employees pay a great deal of attention to *what* they communicate. Good communicators also pay attention to *how* they share information, present themselves to others, influence people, and build relationships. Let's examine how one dynamic leader describes the importance of communication at work.

■Exhibit **4.1**

Communication is essential to success at work.

Mira/Alamy Images

Perspectives

Karen Lombardo is a dynamic leader who serves as the Executive Vice President of Global Human Resources for the Gucci Group. In addition to the Gucci brand, the Gucci Group include eight luxury brands, such as Bottega, Veneta, Yves Saint Laurent, Balenciaga, and Stella McCartney. Because brand leaders have competing agendas, it is up to Karen to support them in rallying around a common vision and mission. As Karen puts it:

Karen Lombardo, Executive Vice President of Global Human Resources for the Gucci Group

People often feel as if they are in isolation—but very rarely is anything in isolation in a company—or in the world for that matter. Look at the decisions made in the financial industry before the 2008 recession—decisions about subprime mortgages and bonuses for executives, for example, ended up affecting millions of people who had nothing to do with those mortgages and never saw a penny in bonus money.

Every single decision you make has a ripple effect. Everything you say and do impacts people in ways that you can barely imagine. That's why you have to under-

stand that how you communicate as a leader will make a difference—for better or worse. If you stray from your values, you will get into trouble. And you can't hide it when you are coloring the truth or shading it to make a point or to make yourself feel better about something—people can sense this a mile away. If you think you can fool anyone by shading the truth, then you are the fool.

When you tell the truth, you will be respected. And if you enjoy what you are doing and you do it with pride and integrity, people will be inspired and motivated. If you show people through your words and your actions that you have their best interests at heart—as well as the company's—they will trust you, and they will follow you. And at work, just as in life, you can't be something you're not. You have to find a way to communicate authentically who you are and what you believe in. If you can do this, you can be a real leader.

Source: Personal interview with Karen Lombardo conducted by Annie McKee, 2009.

As Karen Lombardo so eloquently points out, what we communicate through our words and our actions *does* matter. If you tell your employees that you are committed to the growth of each and every one of them and back it up with action, that message will ripple out to others—fast. If you are genuinely passionate about what you do at work, people will know. If your actions contradict what you say, people will know that too.

Commenting on the contemporary business environment, former Levi Strauss CEO Robert Haas noted: "We are at the center of a seamless web of mutual responsibility and collaboration, a seamless partnership, with interrelationships and mutual commitments."[2] At the center of this seamless web of relationships is communication. When we communicate at work, we inform, persuade, inspire, and motivate. We build—or destroy—relationships based on how and what we communicate interpersonally.

In this chapter, we will discuss a number of ways that you can improve your communication skills and your ability to build **resonant relationships**—vibrant and supportive relationships that foster respect, inclusion, and open and honest dialogue. To begin this chapter, we will explore how we use both verbal and nonverbal language to communicate thoughts and emotions. We will introduce interpersonal communication models that demonstrate how we send and receive information. You will also learn how to use communication to manage your image at work and in life. Then, we will discuss technology and communication, followed by tips on overcoming common communication barriers. You will learn about the special challenges of communication in today's socially diverse organizations, how to navigate communication networks effectively, and how to use storytelling as a powerful communication tool. Finally, you will learn what HR can do to improve communication in organizations and what we all can do to communicate effectively and build resonant relationships at work.

Resonant relationships
Vibrant and supportive relationships that foster respect, inclusion, and open and honest dialogue.

Most Popular » Discussion Questions

1. Karen Lombardo says, "[A]t work, just as in life, you can't be something you're not. You have to find a way to communicate authentically who you are and what you believe in." What does this mean to you?
2. Reflect on a time when something you said had unintended and unpleasant effects. What happened? What could you have done to avoid this outcome?
3. When you begin working with a group or team (on a class project, for example), what strategies do you use to help people get to know each other and build resonant relationships?

---

2. How Do Humans Communicate?

Communication comes from the Latin *communicatus/communicare*, meaning "to impart or share."[3]

Communication
The act of conveying a message from one person or group to another person or group.

Communication is the act of conveying a message from one person or group to another person or group. Human communication is incredibly complex. We share *everything*: our ideas, hopes, dreams, joys, anger, and fears by talking, singing, dancing, painting, writing, smiling, frowning, crying, laughing, kissing, hugging—the list goes on and on. We communicate with words, both spoken and written. We also communicate nonverbally through facial expressions, posture, gestures, and the like. Each of these types of communication is discussed next.

Language: Our Human Specialty

Many animals have communication systems that can be considered "language," but none of their languages are as complex as human language, and no animals use language as creatively as we do. Renowned linguist Noam Chomsky points out that the cognitive abilities for creativity, language, and symbolism evolved fairly recently among our human ancestors and that the creative function of human language has not been found to exist in animal communication systems.[4] Psychology professor Michael Corballis says that, unlike animals, "Humans use language, not just to signal emotional states or territorial claims, but to shape each other's minds."[5]

Although no one can place an exact date on when humans first began to use spoken language, it seems to have emerged around 50,000 years ago. Scholars believe that language and the ability to reason evolved together, that language is tied to our ability to *think*, and that even the earliest forms of language probably included gestures and sounds associated with both thoughts and feelings.[6]

Verbal and Sign Language

Language is a systematic form of communication that is composed of a set of sounds and symbols shared by people. Oral language is a combination of sounds that are symbols for our ideas and feelings. For example, the word *table* is a set of sounds that symbolizes what English speakers understand as a four-legged piece of furniture with a flat surface on top. The phrase "I love you" is a set of three sounds that symbolize a complex set of feelings—attraction, respect, commitment, and protectiveness, among others.

You might wonder how words evolve. Do they in some way relate or describe an object, thought, or feeling? In fact they don't. Most words are arbitrary except for the case of onomatopeia (words that mimic sounds). There is no relationship between the combination of sounds and our thoughts, feelings, and ideas. The word *table* could just as easily be the word *horse*. As you can see in ■Exhibit 4.2, there are many ways to combine sounds to create words that have meaning for us.

Hand gestures can indicate thoughts and feelings as well. These gestures are called sign language and are used by people who have impaired hearing or speech, as well as their friends, families, and coworkers.

The World Federation of the Deaf estimates that there are about 70 million deaf people in the world, and 80 percent of these live in developing countries.[7] Although dozens of sign languages and hundreds of dialects are used throughout the world, only a few are used among large numbers of people. The largest sign language by use is Spanish Sign Language, with 28 million users, followed by 2 million users of Chinese Sign and 1.6 million users of French Sign.[8] British Sign Language is used by about 250,000 users, according to the British Deaf Association.[9] According to data posted on Gallaudet University's Web site, there are between 500,000 and 2 million users of American Sign Language in the United States, and Canada uses it too. Estimates vary wildly, and a firm number of ASL users have been elusive.[10]

As you can see in ■Exhibit 4.3, even though both Britons and Americans use English as their spoken language, the two countries' sign languages are completely different. Users who know only one of the two languages would not be able to understand each other.[11]

Language
A systematic form of communication that is composed of a set of sounds and symbols shared by people.

■Exhibit **4.2**

"I love you" in different languages.

English	I love you
German	Ich liebe dich
Spanish	Te amo
Tagalog	Mahal kita
Japanese	愛しています (aishiteimasu)
Zambia Nyanja language Zambia Bemba language	Nikukonda Nalikutemwa
Hindi	Females to males: Maiṅ tumse pyār kartī hūṅ Males to females: Maiṅ tumse pyār kartā hūṅ
Russian	Я тебя люблю (ya tebya l'y bk'u)
American Sign Language	

Exhibit **4.3**

The American and British Sign Languages are different from each other.

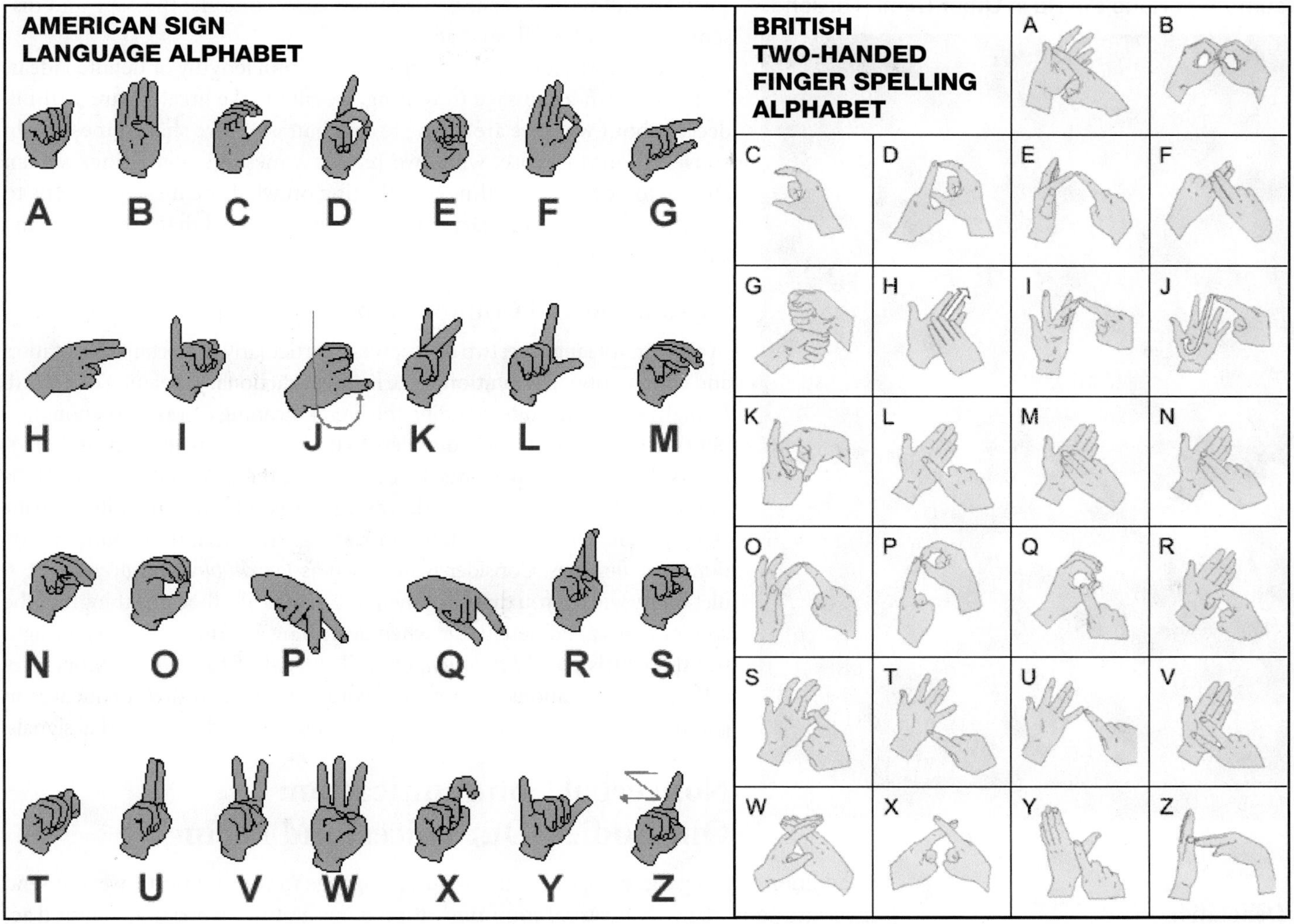

Exhibit 4.3 — American Sign Language Alphabet and British Two-Handed Finger Spelling Alphabet.

Looking at the vast differences between the American and British Sign Languages, it is easy to understand why an international sign language has been developed. International Sign Language (ISL) has been formally developing since the nineteenth century and arose because of interactions between people who spoke different sign languages, the same way pidgin languages came into being.[12] A **pidgin** is a language that uses signs, words, or phrases from more than one language, allowing people to communicate without learning one another's language.

Along with oral and sign language, people have developed another way to symbolize thoughts and feelings: written language.

Pidgin
A language that uses signs, words, or phrases from more than one language, allowing people to communicate without learning one another's language.

Written Language

It is difficult to say when our ancestors first began using written symbols to communicate. More than 25,000 years ago, people were drawing on cave walls; were these the first "written" stories? It's hard to tell. But it is clear that for thousands of years, people have used symbols drawn or scratched on stone, wood, and other materials to express and share thoughts and emotions (Exhibit 4.4). Writing as we know it probably emerged around 7,000 years ago, although no one knows for sure.

Examples of common forms of written communication used at work include e-mails, text messages, memos, posters, books, manuals, contracts, and articles in the company newsletter. Many of these are now online, of course. One significant advantage of written communication is that it produces a permanent record. Why is that important?

■Exhibit **4.4**

Prehistoric color drawings discovered on the summit of Kaho Pla Ra in Uthai Thani, Thailand.

Whitehead Images/Alamy Images

Denotation
The literal or dictionary meaning of a word.

Connotation
The associations, feelings, and judgments that accompany a word.

Nonverbal communication
Any gesture, expression, physical action, or vocal intonation, pitch, or volume that communicates a message either intentionally or unintentionally.

Written records can be useful when someone needs to refer to an original communication for clarification or to sort out any disagreement. They also allow participants to reproduce the original message and disseminate it both easily and accurately.

Written communication is especially helpful lengthy or detailed ideas. When we craft a message in writing, we often take greater care to think deeply about what we are trying to say than when we share a message in conversation. Likewise, when we receive a message in writing, we can choose to devote more time to reflecting on what the message means to us or what the person sharing the message intended than we can during a direct conversation.

Denotation and Connotation

In all forms of language, two concepts are particularly important: denotation and connotation. **Denotation** is the literal or dictionary meaning of a word. It might seem like understanding the literal meaning of words is enough—but there's more. **Connotation** refers to the associations, feelings, and judgments that accompany words. Understanding the connotation of words is important because communication extends beyond simple definitions to include personal, social, and cultural meanings that cannot be found in dictionary definitions. Consider words such as *fat*, *chubby*, and *overweight*. A dictionary will tell you that all of them mean basically the same thing, but the connotations are different. Or, when describing a strong person, you might use the words *powerful*, *tough*, or *resilient*. All of these descriptors have different connotations. As a result, word choice has real consequences in communication—as do gestures, tone of voice, and other nonverbal signals.

Nonverbal Communication: Our Bodies, Our Voices, and Pacing

In addition to using signed, spoken, and written language to communicate, we also send messages nonverbally. **Nonverbal communication** is any gesture, expression, physical action, or vocal intonation, pitch, or volume that communicates a message either intentionally or unintentionally. Nonverbal communication is extremely important.

According to anthropologist Ray Birdwhistell, only about 35 percent of what we convey to others is communicated with words.[13] Other scholars have come up with even more striking figures. For instance, scholars Albert Mehrabian and Susan Ferris argue that words only account for about 7 percent of the important information conveyed in interpersonal communication.[14] Think about the last time you had a conversation with someone. Did you notice how he or she was looking at you? Did you notice facial expressions, hand gestures, tone of voice, how slowly or quickly he or she spoke, and how close he or she stood to you? What do you think the person was communicating nonverbally?

Learning how to decode others' nonverbal behavior and manage your own might be the most important communication skill you can learn. Nonverbal communication signals to people what we are thinking and feeling. Our nonverbal messages can be far more nuanced and more accurate than what we convey with words. That is partly because emotions impact our bodies. For example, there are numerous minute facial muscles that respond to our feelings. Others can see and interpret these minute movements and often interpret our true feelings and messages. Nonverbal communication is linked to a process called limbic resonance. Limbic resonance describes the complex neurological and psychological processes that enable people to decipher and then mirror one another's emotions.[15] By carefully attending to nonverbal communication, we can manage the limbic resonance process more consciously, thereby allowing us to monitor and manage communication and relationships more effectively.

Accurately reading nonverbal signals is linked to your capacity to empathize—a critical social and emotional intelligence competency. Learning to manage your own nonverbal signals involves emotional self-awareness and self-management—two other important competencies for leaders.

The fact than much nonverbal behavior happens naturally is both good and bad—it facilitates fast and accurate communication, for example. But, it can also show others more or different information than you might intend. Aspects of nonverbal communication that you should pay special attention to are body language, vocal intonation, volume, and the rate, or pacing, of your speech.

Body Language

Body language
Hand gestures, facial expressions, eye contact, physical touch, proximity to others, or any other physical gesture that has the capacity to convey meaning.

Body language includes hand gestures, facial expressions, eye contact, physical touch, proximity to others, or any other physical gesture that has the capacity to convey meaning. When you want to direct someone's attention to a man entering a room, for example, you might nod in his direction while maintaining eye contact with your conversation partner. You might point or raise your eyebrows in the man's direction. You might go even further and use facial expressions or gestures to tell your partner what you think and feel about this man. You could also add to your nonverbal message by varying how obvious your signals are. If, for example, you point and laugh loudly, it may convey that you don't care about his feelings, that you consider yourself more powerful than him, or, depending on your facial expression, that you are friends.

We respond to people's body language with nonverbal feedback. In the example of the man entering the room, for instance, he may communicate that he knows you are drawing your friend's attention to him by waving or joining in the laughter if he interprets your gestures as friendly, or he may tense up and scowl if he senses you are making fun of him.

Vocal Intonation, Volume, and Pacing in Communication

Vocal intonation is the variation and pattern of the rise and fall of pitch in speech. Changes in your pitch can signal that you are saying something worthy of increased attention, or that you are adjusting the meaning of your words. For example, the simple sentence "She's really nice" can mean very different things depending on which words you emphasize and the tone of your voice when you say the sentence. Intonation also signals whether you are making a statement or asking a question, and it can communicate surprise, irony, uncertainty, anger, compassion, sympathy, and many other emotions.

Voice volume also signals what you are trying to convey. You may increase the volume of your voice, or lower it, to capture people's attention. In some cultures, softly spoken words indicate deference, shyness, or insecurity. In others, they can indicate power (i.e., you do not have to speak loudly to get attention).

How fast or slowly you talk and how much or little you vary this rate is called pacing. Like intonation and volume, pacing can draw attention to what you are saying and convey your thoughts and feelings. For instance, you might slow down to emphasize the importance of specific instructions or to make sure others have a chance to ask questions.

Variation in how we use our voices is helpful because it holds people's attention. Everyone has struggled to stay focused on a lecture that was delivered in a monotone: The lack of vocal emphasis makes it hard to pay attention. If you learn to speak in a way that captures and keeps people's attention, you will be a more effective communicator.

Body language, vocal intonation, volume, and pacing are all intertwined in communication. Mastering the art of sending and interpreting nonverbal language enables us to be better communicators because we can then share thoughts and emotions more effectively. Good communicators use all aspects of language well, including verbal and/or sign as well as nonverbal. In the next section, we will look at sophisticated communication skills that allow us to interpret complex messages and present ourselves in social situations.

3. How Do We Communicate and Interpret Sophisticated Information?

In this section, we will discuss four sophisticated topics related to communication: expressing emotions through our nonverbal behavior; interpreting emotions, opinions, and facts; communicating "who we are" and how we want others to see us; and interpreting objective and subjective information.

Expressing Emotions: How Nonverbal Behavior Gives Us Away When It Comes to Feelings

When you communicate, you transmit sophisticated information about your thoughts and emotions. Expressing and interpreting emotions is an ability that humans are born with, although people differ in their ability to do so effectively. According to noted scholar Paul Ekman, people of all cultures immediately recognize at least six basic emotional expressions: happiness, sadness, fear, anger, disgust, and surprise.[16] Many other emotions are more subtly expressed or culture specific in terms of how people convey them. With the right knowledge and practice, we can effectively learn to read others' feelings and moods more accurately[17] (■Exhibit 4.5). We can also learn how to express our emotions in ways that make others more likely to understand us.

At best, managing our expression of emotions is done consciously and the feelings we express are in synch with our words. Often, however, our nonverbal language gives "voice" to emotions that we are unaware of or are trying to hide. For a variety of reasons, people can be reluctant to communicate their emotions, so they will try to mask them.[18] In many cultures, the communication of one's inner emotional state is not acceptable in certain situations. Scholars also note that we sometimes want to communicate our emotions but hold back; when that happens, others recognize that we are hiding our feelings.[19]

For instance, you may have been in a situation where a decision was being discussed. You disagreed with the direction the conversation was going and were very unhappy about the decision the group was about to make. You hid your feelings because it seemed that everyone else was happy with the choice. It's entirely possible, however, that your nonverbal behavior gave clues about your real feelings. Your nonverbal messages might be interpreted accurately, or not—causing confusion and miscommunication. For example, not knowing why you looked agitated, may have caused the others to wonder "What's wrong with her?" or "Is she mad at me?"

Nonverbal behavior can also give clues about emotions related to cognitive dissonance or lying.[20] Masking, hiding, or denying emotions takes a lot of energy—it is difficult and draining. In fact, the stress that results from hiding our feelings is associated with an assortment of social and psychological problems.[21]

■Exhibit **4.5**

Observing body language is one way to determine the moods and feelings of others.

mm-images/Alamy Images

A Sophisticated Skill: Interpreting Emotions, Opinions, and Facts at Work

Accurately conveying and reading emotions is essential in life and at work. It is especially important for leaders at all levels in an organization. That's because emotions impact decision making, accomplishment of goals, and the quality of work relationships.[22] Consider this example: A manager is meeting with employees to create a new process to schedule work shifts during the holidays. The business needs to stay open at all times, and employees have made numerous complaints about the demanding hours. Some employees are always asked to work holidays, which they resent. Other employees are rarely asked to work holidays, which means they do not have the opportunity to earn overtime wages.

At the meeting, the manager notices that employees are uncomfortable. She interprets this as people being upset with *her* (she is wrong—they are just frustrated with the situation). She chooses to ignore the nonverbal signals. When someone tries to bring up his or her feelings about the problems, she changes the subject. She is afraid that the employees will verbally attack her and she will be unable to control the meeting. The employees sense her resistance, and several of them become angry: "Doesn't she trust us to have a reasonable conversation?" Others think, "If we can't talk about our problems and feelings, how will we ever find a good solution?" Still others are just confused: "What is this manager's problem?" This meeting is off to a bad start—and it will not end with the best solution. Had the manager been more confident and skilled at reading people's emotions, this likely would have been a more productive meeting.

The preceding example illustrates several points: emotions are conveyed constantly; reading them accurately is important; and we all need skills to deal with conflicting opinions and different emotions. The example also illustrates another sophisticated topic related to communication: how we communicate and protect our self-image. Part of the reason this manager did not want to address the emotions she saw in her group was that she wanted to maintain her self-image as a manager who doesn't lose control. Let's look at how managing image and identity is an important part of the communication process.

How We Manage Our Image through Communication

In Japan, there is a saying that everybody has two faces—one to keep to yourself and one to present to others. We all choose identities that suit us for the different roles we have in society—leader, manager, student, friend, employee. We support each of our identities by carefully choosing our words and behavior to show and maintain the image we want to present.[23]

The identities we create for public view are what is known as *face*. **Face** is the public representation of an aspect of our identity that we want others to accept.[24] We want others to agree with how we portray ourselves or, at the very least, not challenge us.[25] For example, you may see yourself as a loyal friend. When someone is in trouble, you will say things like "I'll be there for you." If your friend is really upset, he might say, "No you won't—you're too busy with your own problems." This is a challenge to your identity—the public face you want to present. If this identity is important to you, you'll be upset and want to prove to your friend that you are indeed loyal.

Saving Face

When someone challenges the identity you present, you may take steps to "save face" or to avoid "losing face."[26] Maintaining face is especially complicated in the work environment, where people often play many roles. At work, people often expect us to do things that may not fit with our image of ourselves or that interfere with the identity we are attempting to display. We may have to change our self-presentation, acting in ways that we

Face

The public representation of an aspect of our identity that we want others to accept.

might not otherwise choose. Some of these challenges to our preferred identity are made as explicit requests (on-record), whereas others are more indirect (off-record).

For example, you may attempt to recruit a volunteer for a project by using an indirect, off-record approach. You say, "This project is *so* important and I really want to make the deadline. I am really worried that I won't be able to do it alone." Expressing your need this way allows a person to see you as a diligent worker trying to get something done on time. That is the "face" you want the person to see and accept. To allow you to save face, the person may agree to help you without having been asked directly (allowing him to present the image of a great team member). Alternatively, he might say, "I wish I could help, but since I can't, let me help you find someone else." Many of our communication strategies are designed to make off-record requests like this because, as you can see, they allow both parties to maintain face.

A Strategy for Saving Face and Keeping Relationships Healthy

When an explicit, on-record request is made, it is harder for both parties to maintain face. Someone might have to give in and change how they are presenting themselves. In this case, a strategy may be needed to allow both parties to maintain face. Researchers Penelope Brown and Stephen Levinson created a model that helps us understand how "politeness" can support a strategy for maintaining relationships when either indirect or direct requests are made:[27]

- *Positive politeness* refers to the messages we send that indicate we accept another's face. In the previous example of an indirect request, your colleague might show his acceptance of your face by saying "I'd be happy to help—we all need that project to come in on time!" Positive politeness is a process of reinforcing shared or common values and seeking common ground—in the example, the idea that "we are in it together on this project."
- *Negative politeness* is a strategy of recognizing the other person's "territory," independence, time, and resources as private and valuable. For instance, when a direct request for help is required, instead of saying "I need you to help me with this project," you might say, "I need your help, but I know how busy you are." Your colleague might then respond, "Thanks so much for recognizing how busy I am. Let me see what I can do."

Every interaction, then, is an attempt to show others our preferred self-image while allowing others to do the same. It is amazing that we actually communicate successfully on a day-to-day basis, given how complex this process is. We are able to do this, in large part, by understanding the rules of communication politeness within a society.

Different cultures have different preferences for how people share who they are, and how they express themselves politely. The risk of offending others and endangering important relationships is higher in cross-cultural interactions, even when making the most sincere attempts to be polite. Effective leaders recognize that they must manage this complex social dance and also maintain an image that will enable them to influence others.

Communication is complicated, especially when it comes to emotion and important information such as one's image and identity or cultural rules of interaction. How do we make sense of it all? Let's look at one way to categorize information so we can understand and use it more effectively.

Making Sense of Information

One way to categorize how we understand and share information has been proposed by scholar Ken Wilbur.[28] Wilbur's model allows us to categorize information we encounter in the world as being:

- Related to a single person (*individual*) versus related to a group, organization, or community (*collective*) **and**
- Inside a person or group (*interior*) versus outside a person or group (*exterior*).

■Exhibit **4.6**

Wilbur's Model for Categorizing How We Understand and Share Information[29]		
	Interior (Subjective)	**Exterior (Objective)**
Individual	My values	My behavior
Collective	Our culture	Our common language

As you can see in ■Exhibit 4.6, this categorization scheme is clever in that it allows us to more clearly see how information "fits together."

Wilbur's model is particularly useful in organizations because it forces people to discipline themselves when sending and interpreting information. To illustrate how using this model can improve communication in organizations, consider this example: Senior managers in the sales and marketing division of a company determine that in order to track costs more efficiently and effectively, a more rigorous process for tracking employee expenditures during business trips needs to be used. Managers purchase a software program that allows employees to input expense data on trips, including the specific type of expense (hotel, food, gas, etc.). Employees are trained and expected to use this new program to better track all expenses.

This new process is a big change for employees and for the company. Until the change, expenses had been managed with an honor system—employees could simply write a list of expenses and attach receipts (if they had them) at the end of the month, and they would be reimbursed. Now, they have to enter every last penny for others to monitor.

Six months into the program, the senior management team is meeting to discuss the effectiveness of the new expense-tracking process. Two of the managers are responsible for almost all of the employees who have to use the new system, and they have heard numerous complaints. They are quite sure that the process is doomed to fail, because "all" of the employees hate it. The two other managers on the team are from the finance department. They are delighted with the fact that they now have what they believe to be good information about expenses. It is easy to see how this team could argue endlessly about whether the new process is working or not.

Imagine if this team had organized their conversation by plotting the information they had in Wilbur's four quadrants. ■Exhibit 4.7 indicates what the information might look like.

Discussing what the management team knew about the employees' subjective experience, as well as the factual data about how well the program was working, would be a very different conversation than the "It's horrible" versus "It's fantastic"

■Exhibit **4.7**

Applying Wilbur's Model to Evaluate the New Expense Tracking System		
	Interior (Subjective)	**Exterior (Objective)**
Individual	**1** "I do not feel trusted by my manager anymore" *or* "This system could help us, but it is not easy to use."	**3** Logs expenses once a month instead of every week as required.
Collective	**2** Mixed feelings about the system: It violates some values (trust and trustworthiness) but supports others (commitment to accurate reporting of data).	**4** 60% compliance with turning expense reports in weekly; no data regarding how accurate the reports are.

debate that might arise without this kind of analysis. For instance, the conversation could be focused on what certain individuals felt about the program (Box 1) and how the program did or did not jive with the culture of the organization (Box 2). The conversation could also include clear and specific information about the *facts* (Boxes 3 and 4): how individuals were actually using the program, and statistics about numbers of people using it, how often, and so forth. This conversation would more likely result in the discovery that there were mixed feelings about the system and that fixing some of the software glitches would help tremendously with the roll-out.

So far, we have discussed what communication is and how people share thoughts, feelings, and information. Let's turn now to several models that researchers have developed to understand the interpersonal communication process.

Most Popular » Discussion Questions

1. Do you think people can "read" your emotions easily? Why or why not? Give examples. Does this serve you well or get in the way of communication and relationships?
2. What "face" do you present at school? At work? At home? If these are different, explain why.
3. Analyze a recent communication you have had with someone. Describe how you each attempted to maintain face and how you used positive and negative politeness in the interaction.
4. Consider a recent controversial situation at your school or workplace. Use Ken Wilbur's model to "plot" information about the problem, including your individual interior and exterior states (feelings and behavior) and interior and exterior information (culture and actual facts).

Sender
A person who encodes and sends a message through a communication channel.

Message
Information.

Receiver
A person who receives and decodes a message.

Channel
The medium through which a message is transmitted from a sender to a receiver.

Encoding
The process of converting information from one format into another before sending it.

Decoding
The process of converting information from one format into another in order to understand it.

Feedback
The process by which a receiver indicates to a sender through words or nonverbal signals that a message has been received or that more communication is desired.

4. What Is the Interpersonal Communication Process?

Most interpersonal communication models focus on how people send messages to receivers. In these models, a **sender** is a person who encodes and sends a **message** (information) through a communication channel to a **receiver**, a person who receives and decodes the message. A communication **channel** is the medium through which a message is transmitted from a sender to a receiver.

When communicating, you first choose a message to share with another person. Then, you translate that message into a shared language, some combination of words and nonverbal behavior that the receiver can comprehend. When you convert your thoughts and emotions into a message, you are encoding. **Encoding** is the process of converting information from one format into another before sending it. To illustrate encoding, imagine that you are watching a beautiful sunset and you want to communicate the experience. You have experienced visual stimuli, which you convert into words to describe the colors, the sun, the scenery—you have now *encoded* the message.

Once you have encoded your message, you send it through a channel to a receiver. You (the sender) may choose to send your message about the sunset in a text message (the channel) to a friend (the receiver). When the message reaches the receiver, he or she attempts to interpret what the sender conveyed. This is called *decoding*. **Decoding** is the process of converting information from one format into another in order to understand it.

Feedback is the next step in the communication process (■Exhibit 4.8). **Feedback** occurs when a receiver indicates to the sender through words or nonverbal signals that the message has been received or that more communication is desired. That message might be a simple confirmation that the original message was received—a nod, "mmhmm," a restatement of the message, or questions for clarification. A

■Exhibit **4.8**

Interpersonal communication involves a sender, a message, and a receiver.

Jose Luis Pelaez Inc./Blend Images/Alamy

Feedback loop
The process of sharing information back and forth between sender and receiver.

Noise
Anything that interferes with the transmission or receipt of a message.

feedback loop is the process of sharing information back and forth between sender and receiver, and it is complete when both sender and receiver feel that the message has been fully conveyed and accurately interpreted.

Now that you understand the basic components of the communication process, we will explore three models of communication that attempt to explain exactly how the process works.

Models of Communication

The communication process has been studied extensively, and at least three different models are commonly used to help explain how it works. One early model is the Shannon-Weaver mathematical model,[30] which is quite straightforward in that it shows communication to be a linear process. The Schramm model builds on the Shannon-Weaver model by showing how communication is interactive.[31] Finally, Berlo's model includes complex factors, such as culture, as critical components of the communication process. Each of these models is discussed next.

The Shannon-Weaver Model of Communication

The Shannon-Weaver model shows how information is encoded by a sender, transmitted through a channel, and decoded by a receiver.[32] The model points out how messages can be misinterpreted due to noise. **Noise** is anything that interferes with the transmission or receipt of a message. Noise can be sound; it can also be things like a mumbled spoken message, poor grammar, or body language that does not fit the words. To lessen the impact of noise, we need to learn how to listen—really listen—to the messages people are trying to share with us.

The original Shannon-Weaver model shows communication flowing in one direction, from a sender to a receiver. This model has been criticized because it is not representative of the way humans actually communicate, which is not strictly linear and is influenced by many other factors in addition to "noise."[33] Moreover, the model does not indicate how people distinguish important ideas from those that lack any value, or are even nonsense.[34] Later models attempted to compensate for these shortcomings by showing communication as bidirectional (■Exhibit 4.9).

The Schramm Model of Communication

In 1954, communication studies pioneer Wilbur Schramm introduced a simple model of communication which emphasized that communication is an interactive process. Rather than a simple unidirectional model from sender to receiver, the Schramm model showed communication as a bidirectional (although still linear) process.[35]

The Berlo Model of Communication

In 1960, David Berlo offered a model of communication that elaborated on the process of encoding and decoding messages.[36] The advantage of the Berlo model over the other two is that it recognizes the importance of communication skills, attitudes, knowledge, society, and culture in both encoding and decoding messages.

All three of these models attempt to explain how we send and receive messages, what can get in the way, and how best to understand one another. Let's now look at effective and efficient communication and at how the complexity, or richness, of the message and channel can affect the communication process.

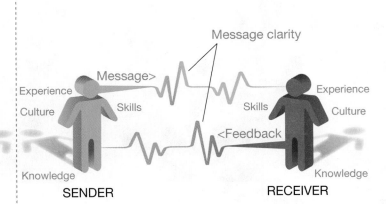

Communication degraded by noise   **Maximized communication**

NOISE SOURCE

Interruption of message

Message>

<Feedback

SENDER   RECEIVER

Message clarity

Experience

Message>

Culture   Skills

Experience

Skills   Culture

<Feedback

Knowledge   Knowledge

SENDER   RECEIVER

■Exhibit **4.9**

MODEL OF COMMUNICATION
Interpersonal communication is enriched when "noise" is minimized and people can fully express themselves to one another.

Effective communication
The result of information conveyed accurately from sender to receiver.

Efficient communication
Sharing information using the fewest possible resources (time, money, and effort).

Effective and Efficient Communication

Effective communication is the result of information conveyed *accurately* from sender to receiver. When communication is not effective, the consequences can be disastrous. For example, consider NASA's ill-fated Mars Climate Orbiter, which was destroyed by friction and stress as it entered the Martian atmosphere in 1998. This $327.6 million project ended in failure due to a simple miscommunication between two teams on the project: One team had used metric units, but the other had used U.S. customary measurements (i.e., inches and pounds). As a result, upon entering Mars' atmosphere, the vehicle crashed. Although ineffective communication does not always yield such horrific misfortune, it can lead to poor performance, unhappy employees, and disappointed customers. Good communicators make sure that their audience understands their messages by soliciting and listening to feedback to ensure full understanding.

Sharing information using the fewest possible resources (time, money, and effort) is considered **efficient communication**. Although we should all endeavor to achieve both, effective communication and efficient communication are often in conflict. For example, when managers take the time to share information in individual conversations with direct reports, the communication is more likely to be effective, but it can be extremely time consuming and inefficient. On the other hand, a brief company-wide e-mail is an efficient means of communicating, but there is no assurance that receivers of the message will understand its intended meaning. In fact, so-called efficient communication can be extremely destructive. Take this example: One manager we know worked for a company that sent an e-mail that read "Due to a decrease in sales, we will lay off 20% of our workforce. Donuts in the break room!" Imagine what this "efficient message" did to morale in this company.

As these examples show, when deciding how to balance effective and efficient communication, we must consider the channel we use to send the message. Some channels are "rich," meaning they allow complicated information to flow back and forth between senders and receivers. Other channels are "lean" and do not have the capacity to carry as much information.

Choosing "Rich" or "Lean" Communication Channels

Different communication channels can carry different types and amounts of information.[37] A rich channel can carry more information than a lean channel and is less likely to result in vague or ambiguous messages.[38] Rich channels allow for messages that are targeted to a specific receiver, offer opportunities for feedback, and incorporate a full range of verbal and nonverbal signals, all of which help a receiver achieve full understanding. Rich channels are often used to send messages that are not routine, are emotionally charged, or may be confusing when a receiver is more likely to have difficulty decoding the message.

The richest channel is face-to-face communication in pairs or small groups. In such settings, nonverbal communication is possible and feedback can be fluid. There are many good reasons why a manager will choose a one-on-one conversation over other options. A discussion about poor work performance, for instance, is a highly personal and sensitive conversation that could result in miscommunication or a damaged work relationship if conducted over the telephone. Similarly, many people prefer to deal with complex issues face-to-face in small group communication, which can be rich and varied.

Other types of communication slide further along the spectrum from rich to lean. Presentations are less personalized than interactive meetings, and the feedback loop may be somewhat more constrained. On the other hand, presentations allow a sender to reach a wider audience while keeping some of the advantages of face-to-face communication (e.g., the presenter can use body language). Videoconferences also lack some of the immediacy of the other channels and potentially distort or hide body language, but they can save a company the money and time that would be necessary to convene geographically dispersed participants. Similarly, a telephone conversation removes body language from the communication process, but because it allows for intonation and pacing, it retains some of the advantages of the richer face-to-face communication channel.

On the leaner end of the spectrum are different forms of written communication. Written personal communication, as the name suggests, has the advantage that messages can be tailored to specific receivers. However, e-mails, letters, and personalized memos, the most common forms of written personal communication, lack many signals that are associated with oral channels (e.g., nonverbal signals) and feedback can be difficult, slow, or even impossible. Still, the targeted nature of the message and the low resource cost make written personal communication an appropriate channel when we need to efficiently convey simple information to specific individuals.

The leanest of all possible channels is impersonal written communication, such as a company newsletter, which lacks nonverbal signals and a feedback loop and is tailored for a large audience. It is probably the best way to communicate messages that are fairly straightforward and do not justify the more intensive use of time or other resources.

Communication channels and models are important to understand because they help explain the interpersonal communication process. These concepts were originally developed to explain direct, spoken communication or written communication that was shared on paper. The onset of technology, however, has led to a vast expansion in the various ways we can communicate through writing, video images, and the spoken word. We will explore the role of technology at work in depth in Chapter 11; in the following sections, we will consider how it is affecting communication at work.

Most Popular » Discussion Questions

1. Choose a recent interpersonal communication experience of which you were a part. Apply the three models of communication discussed in the preceding section to describe what happened.
2. Is communication a linear process—first in one direction and then in reverse? Explain your answer with examples from your experience.
3. How do you give feedback in a conversation? For example, do you use body language? Do you ask questions? Do you restate what you heard? Do you talk about an experience that is similar to what you have heard?

5. How Do We Use Information Technology to Communicate at Work?

In 1855, the U.S. Congress authorized a study on the use of camels to transport mail from Texas to California. This method didn't work well. Stagecoaches were much better at this task, and they could get mail across the country in less than 30 days, weather permitting. Then came the first rapid communication system in the United States: the Pony Express. The Pony Express was a mail delivery system that used horses to travel the nearly 2,000 miles from Missouri to California in only a few days. A rested horse was used at each 10-mile interval, and riders were changed every 100 miles. It was a marvel of ingenuity that lasted for 18 months, to be replaced by the transcontinental telegraph.[39]

As this example suggests, technology has fundamentally changed the way we communicate in our lives and at work. We now communicate with people we may never meet in person, getting to know them professionally and personally. Even language barriers are breaking down with the advent of portable, handheld electronic translation dictionaries and Internet translation services. Technology has also placed pressure on modern societies to develop new rules and conventions for proper communication behavior. For instance, many companies have guidelines for how to use e-mail, and text messaging has developed its own language system.[40]

E-Mail and Text Messaging

E-mail and its sister technology, text messaging, have made it possible to communicate in writing over long distances in a matter of seconds.[41] The benefits are obvious: We can share written messages in real time with people who are far away, who can then provide feedback and build on our ideas. Many people have migrated from communicating with friends and family via e-mail to text messaging. At work, however, e-mail is king. Most people use it constantly, and it is important to learn how to use it professionally: E-mails should include pleasant and somewhat formal greetings and closures; accurate grammar, sentence structure, and the like; and an appropriate amount of information.

The use of e-mail and text messages, however, does present challenges:

- Emotions in e-mail messages often fall short of reaching the receiver, and they can be inaccurately interpreted.
- We have little tolerance for long electronic messages, which means that vital information is often eliminated from communication or not read.
- The interpretation of silence or a nonresponse is difficult, given the possibility of instantaneous reply. Without a response, a sender may jump to conclusions that are inaccurate.[42]
- E-mail invites people to be lazy communicators: "Forward" and "cc" are shortcuts people often use too much.
- E-mail and text messages are not private and can be monitored and retrieved by employers or other authorities.[43]

Web Conferencing and Videoconferencing

Web conferencing combines telecommunications and computing by connecting people by phone or video, while simultaneously enabling all participants to view the same documents online and to work on the documents together. Early versions of web and videoconferencing technology required expensive equipment, specialized technicians, and a special location. Today, any individual with a webcam and Internet service can connect with others who have the same tools. Both web and videoconferencing are richer communication channels than e-mail—they allow for more sharing of contextual information and emotion and more access to nonverbal behavior.

Organizations are using these and other new technologies in ever more creative ways, revolutionizing how people communicate at work. The following *Business Case* shows how IBM used a "virtual world" to share information and build effective working relationships among employees and technology experts.

IBM

IBM and Second Life

In 2008, IBM held a three-day conference for more than 200 participants. This was not a typical conference. The venue was futuristic—almost surreal. There were no drinks or snacks, or even a restroom. The attendees were dressed casually. Most unusual, however, was that there were no "people" at the conference. Instead, attendees were composed of pixels and polygons. IBM employees and others participated in the conference virtually through their avatars in a secure *Second Life* environment.

Second Life, which is a virtual world created by Linden Lab, provided IBM with the virtual space for their conference.[44] The environment allowed people to interact through their avatars, attend keynote speeches and breakout sessions, visit a library, and gather as a community. The format was not entirely new

IBM

to IBM—the company had been experimenting with the *Second Life* environment as a way to conduct employee orientation sessions and other events.[45] The size, scope, and complexity of this conference, however, was impressive.[46]

The conference used virtual social networking technology to bring large numbers of leaders together to "talk," share information, learn from one another, and build relationships—all from the comfort of their own offices. The conference was an opportunity to gain inspiration and practical knowledge about the impact of virtual reality on communication and relationships between and among people in organizations. There was also a financial benefit associated with the new initiative—bringing people together without incurring travel expenses represents a significant cost-saving approach to organization-wide communication and collaboration.[47]

Photo Source: Photosani/Shutterstock

The benefits of this type of virtual world communication are becoming clear, but what are the costs associated with it? Can people communicate fully in such a world? Will individuals who are adept at maneuvering their avatars have richer communication opportunities than those who are not as technically proficient? Is there a hidden time cost in creating "good" avatars that are capable of representing people and employees as they really are? Who controls the environment? HR? Managers? Employees themselves? Are there any rules and, if so, what are they? These questions and many others will need to be addressed in order for this technology to be successfully integrated into the business environment on a large scale.

E-mail, texting, web and videoconferencing, social networking, and many other information technologies have brought dramatic changes in how we can communicate. Yet despite the advances made, we still encounter significant barriers to effective communication at work.

Most Popular » Discussion Questions

1. Consider two situations: one in which information technology helped you build a relationship, and one in which it inhibited the development of a relationship. How did technology help in the first instance and get in the way in the second?
2. Imagine that your manager has sent an e-mail telling you that she is not pleased with the report you turned in and that you need to "fix it." She does not give you specific ideas about what to do. You would much rather she had called you, and now she is traveling so you have to respond via e-mail. Draft an e-mail that would get you the information you need, without causing her to become defensive.

6. What Are Common Barriers to Effective Communication?

Communication is anything but simple. To be effective, we must try to overcome some of the most common barriers to effective communication. The first barrier we will explore in this section is how language itself can inhibit communication. Then we will examine poor communication skills as well as how misunderstandings occur due to people's biases. We will also consider the role that power and authority play in communication at work.

When Language Gets in the Way of Communication

In many companies today, people speak several (and sometimes dozens of) different native languages. Most companies adopt one language as the standard—often English—and expect senior-level managers and executives to learn that language. Although this seems like a reasonable way to solve the problem, it is far easier said than done. Even when people are considered fluent in a second language, large differences exist in how well they understand the more nuanced aspects of the language, such as emotional expression or humor.

Globalization and migration have produced an increasingly diverse workforce, and language barriers are clearly one potential area of difficulty. Without a shared language, communication can be difficult, even harmful. For example, a pair of researchers describe the following encounter between a Japanese manager and an American employee at an automotive factory. The Japanese manager, noticing that the employee was a very hard worker, attempted to translate a common phrase of encouragement ("gambatte, kudasai"), but what actually came out was "You must work harder." The hard-working American employee was, understandably, quite upset.[48]

In this and countless other situations, literal or near literal translations rarely work or at best lose a great deal of meaning from one culture to another, with the result that the intended meaning can be lost or seriously misunderstood. Another source of misunderstanding is when people use humor across cultural boundaries. The use of humor can make the person who doesn't "get" the joke feel awkward.

You might be saying to yourself, "Why don't they just get an electronic translator?" That is a good idea, and it can help. On the other hand, however, literal translation rarely works in complex messages. Languages are representative of cultures, so words translated literally often mean something entirely different in another language. For example, when Kentucky Fried Chicken entered the Chinese market, they discovered that their slogan "finger lickin' good" came out as "eat your fingers off."[49]

Several other common barriers to communication are linked to language. First, it can be challenging for people to get used to one another's accents. Second, native speakers tend to speak their own language quickly and often violate some of the rules of grammar and pronunciation. For example, Americans often drop the "g" in words ending in "ing" and combine the sounds of one word with those of the next (e.g., "going to" becomes "gonna," "should have" becomes "shoulda"). These habits can make it difficult for nonnative speakers to follow a native speaker's conversation. Third, it is tiresome for people to speak a second language all day, because doing so takes intense concentration. Finally, even within a language (such as English), a single word can have several different meanings (■Exhibit 4.10).

Dialects

Problems can also arise when people speak the same native language but use different dialects. A dialect can be a form of language spoken in a particular region, such as Southern

**To the British, *punting* means using a long pole to move a boat down a river.
To Americans, it means drop-kicking a football.**

Left: Chris Ballentine/Paul Thompson Images/Alamy;
Right: Dennis MacDonald/Alamy Images

English in the United States or the variants of English used in the five different boroughs of New York City.[50] A dialect may also be spoken by people who are from the same socioeconomic background. For example, William Labov studied language differences in a New York department store, showing that different dialects were used, depending in part on the socioeconomic status of the speaker(s).[51] Dialects also exist among racial and ethnic groups.

Besides the dialects that can be found within a country, dialects exist across countries that share the same language. For example, the Spanish spoken in Madrid is different from that spoken in Mexico, and there are significant differences between the English dialects in the United States, England, Australia, India, and South Africa.

Jargon: A Shortcut to Communication That Can Backfire

Jargon
Terminology that has been specifically defined in relation to certain activities, professions, or groups.

Another language barrier at work is entirely of our own making: Many professions and organizations develop their own sublanguage, called jargon. **Jargon** is terminology that has been specifically defined in relation to certain activities, professions, or groups. Depending on the technicality of the jargon, it may be nearly impossible for a person outside the group or field to understand.[52] Typical examples are the medical jargon that doctors, nurses, and health care workers use; the legal jargon lawyers use; and the financial jargon stock market analysts use.

This textbook is introducing you to managerial jargon, which can be useful in communicating with others in the fields of management, strategy, and leadership. However, you may be greeted with quizzical looks if you try to use the same terms when speaking to friends at the local pub. Other common jargon in business includes the term *sacred cows*, which refers to people, products, or processes that cannot be changed, and *C-suite*, which refers to the people who hold the top offices in a company, such as the chief executive officer and the chief financial officer.

In addition to jargon, people in companies often adopt acronyms as shortcuts to describe what they do or how they do it. An acronym is an abbreviation of a phrase that uses the first letter of every word in the phrase. For example, *ASAP* is an acronym for "as soon as possible," and *JIT* stands for "just in time," which describes a specific type of inventory control process. *SOPs* is an acronym for "standard operating procedures," which are rules for how things must be done. Teams and divisions in organizations are often referred to by acronyms, such as when the senior executive team is called the *EC*, for "Executive Committee," or when human resources is referred to as *HR*.

Language matters at work. As a manager—or an employee, for that matter—it is important to remember that language can foster inclusion or exclusion from the communication process.[53] Languages that are limited to a small group (such as jargon, some dialects, or a language spoken only by executives) can cause company-wide problems. In contrast, language can be a unifying force—when people share the same language and use it well, they can share information smoothly and effectively.

Poor Communication: It Happens Too Often!

Competent communication refers to the ability to encode and decode messages in culturally appropriate ways. Competence includes knowledge of the rules of conversation, such as when to talk and how much to say.[54] Competent communicators know the rules of grammar, express thoughts clearly and concisely, use adequate and situationally appropriate vocabulary, and express emotion appropriately.

Poor communication skills can often hurt an otherwise well-crafted message. Remember that it is the sender's job to encode a message in a way that has meaning for him or her, as well as for the audience. This means that we need to learn how to express our thoughts, opinions, and feelings in words that others can understand. We also need to organize our communication in a way that others can follow. Too simple or too complex a vocabulary can be a barrier to communication, depending on the audience. How can you decide what to say and how to say it? That's where empathy comes in: Many barriers to communication can be avoided by simply reading one's audience accurately.

The grammar we use and how we express ourselves at work do matter. An e-mail that is filled with misspellings, errors in grammar, and missing punctuation will hurt the credibility of the writer and force readers to spend extra time decoding the message. Speakers who mumble or mispronounce words create similar difficulties for their listeners. People who interrupt others or do not share information also hinder the communication process. Whether written, spoken, or signed, a message that is missing important information or simply does not make sense is highly problematic at work.

But barriers to communication are not the fault of senders alone. It's also up to receivers to ensure that barriers are minimized. In particular, when we are receiving messages, we can avoid all sorts of communication problems if we simply *listen*. People speak at 125 to 175 words per minute (WPM), but they can listen intelligently to 400 to 800 WPM.[55] Because of the difference between how fast we can send information versus how fast we can receive it, it is easy for us to let our minds wander and think about other things when someone is speaking. The cure for this is to *pay attention* to nonverbal behavior, cultural information, and emotional expressions.[56]

Focusing fully on a message means listening to what others are saying and noticing their nonverbal behavior, while also mentally summarizing the main points, exploring what the person is sharing, generating a few explanations about the message, and determining what other information would be useful.[57] These activities take concentration and effort, but are worth it, because poor listening can be a barrier to accurately interpreting a message. So can biases and stereotyping.

Selective Perception and Stereotyping: The Enemies of Communication

Both senders and receivers can harm the communication process by relying on personal biases when encoding or decoding messages. One manifestation of biases is called **selective perception**. Selective perception is consciously or unconsciously focusing on certain parts of a message and ignoring others. When people do this, they may only pay attention to the information that they consider most interesting or that supports their beliefs. Or, they may

Selective perception
Consciously or unconsciously focusing on certain parts of a message and ignoring others.

pay more attention to negative or threatening aspects of a message and miss everything else. For example, suppose your manager says, "I really appreciate what you have done this week. You really hit the ball out of the park. There's one small thing I'd like you to fix, though—that last section of the report still isn't quite accurate. I'll need you to take another crack at it." If you are like many people, you will completely ignore the praise and focus on the criticism. This may be a serious misinterpretation of the manager's message.

Selective perception can reinforce stereotypes. **Stereotypes** are rigid and often negative biases used to describe or judge individuals based on their membership in a social group. Selective perception and stereotyping are often linked to prejudice. For example, a young manager who believes that older workers are resistant to change might notice each and every time an older person argues about a new idea and completely miss the fact that this happens only about one in ten times. As this situation illustrates, when communication involves stereotypes, valuable information is lost, twisted, or otherwise compromised.

Poor listening, selective perception, and stereotyping are somewhat obvious barriers to communication. In organizations, we face another barrier that is less obvious but also a problem: dealing with power dynamics.

The Interaction of Communication and Power

Communication is affected by the amount of power senders and receivers have and the organizational role they occupy.[58] For example, if a peer whom you like and trust says, "I'm not sure the report you showed me was complete or accurate," you are likely to interpret this message as honest and helpful. If your manager says the same thing you will probably interpret the message differently. You might interpret it as criticism, as a threat, or as a veiled message about your overall performance. Your interpretations in these examples would be based in part on the power relationships between you and your peer and you and your manager. Going back to the example of the manager's comment, you may feel fearful and become defensive. Conveying this to your manager verbally or nonverbally could cause him to wonder what's wrong with you—and communication spirals downward from there.

Managing your reaction to power in the communication exchange requires self-awareness and self-management. When you understand your immediate response to powerful people, you are more likely to respond so that the relationship remains healthy. Likewise, when you have power, it is wise to remember that "your whisper is heard as a shout." By understanding this, you can consciously manage how you communicate so you are less likely to spark a negative or fearful response.

Power can be used as a means to control different elements of the communication process, including who is privileged to send and receive information. Power is also important because it often determines which communication networks you participate in ("who you know"). For example, in many organizations senior managers have access to information that others do not. But power isn't only related to formal roles and hierarchy—it can be linked to social groups as well.

In many organizations, people who are similar to one another along certain demographic lines (e.g., culture, race, gender, or ethnicity) are often members of the same communication networks. These social networks may or may not have access to certain kinds of information. This means that accessing particular ideas or information is sometimes dependent on being of a particular class, race, gender, or ethnicity.[59] At their worst, these networks are closed—meaning that unless you are part of the group, you don't have access to the group's information; or, if you are a member of a group with less power, you may be shut off from vital information. This is problematic in organizations, of course, and many companies are doing their utmost to ensure that people who need access to information are involved in dialogues so that information can flow quickly and accurately among everyone.[60] However, networks of people who share the same interests still tend to develop, and business gets done when these people come together to pursue those interests.

Stereotypes
Rigid and often negative biases used to describe or judge individuals based on their membership in a social group.

One well-known symbol of this type of network is the golf course, which has played a legendary role as the place where business relationships are developed and deals are done. Golf and private clubs are linked with the "old boys' club," the name for networks of informal relationships through which power and influence have tended to flow. Often in the past, places like golf and private clubs were exclusive: Women, people of color, and other groups were not welcome, which means they were excluded from important business conversations. This is still true to some extent today. For instance, Catalyst is a well-respected research firm focused on women in the workforce. One of the key findings of a Catalyst survey of women executives in Fortune 1000 companies was that women in the twenty-first century were still hindered by the same barriers that blocked access to informal networks in 1996.[61] In fact, exclusion from relationship-building activities such as golfing was cited by women who took the survey as the second-largest barrier to advancing their careers to the most senior positions.[62]

Power is one aspect of diversity in organizations, but it is by no means the only dimension that affects communication. In the next section, we will explore both the challenges and the opportunities of communication in a socially diverse workplace.

Most Popular » Discussion Questions

1. Reflect on your communication skills (oral and written). If you could magically get better at two of these skills, what would they be? Why would you want to improve those skills?
2. Do you sometimes engage in selective perception? What sorts of topics (e.g., politics, religion) or situations (e.g., conflict) cause you to pay more attention to certain things and less to others?
3. Reflect on powerful people you know personally—either formal leaders or those who have informal power, such as popular people. How would you describe the way that you react to them and to their power and how you communicate with them? How do they communicate with you?

---

7. Why Is It Challenging to Communicate in a Socially Diverse World?

■Exhibit **4.11**

It can be challenging to communicate in a diverse world.

Pictor International/ImageState/Alamy

One of the major challenges to communication arises from one of the greatest *benefits* of a globalized world: diversity in the workforce. Language and cultural differences affect communication, as do gender and age differences (■Exhibit 4.11).

Communication and Culture

Many aspects of culture affect communication in a diverse workforce. We discussed issues related to language, selective perception, and stereotypes earlier in the chapter. We also discussed nonverbal behavior, which deserves special attention in a cross-cultural setting.

Nonverbal Behavior in Cross-Cultural Communication

Another challenge to cross-cultural communication is that acceptable nonverbal behavior differs from one group to another.[63] A failure to recognize that body language requires attention in cross-cultural communication can produce unfortunate misunderstandings. Something as simple as shaking hands, for example, requires different techniques as one goes from country to country, and it is even completely inappropriate in some parts of the world. The "thumbs up" sign and the "OK" sign used in the United States are considered obscene gestures in some places. People in different cultures also have varied expectations about personal space.

Language and nonverbal behavior have obvious links to culture and need to be attended to and managed in cross-cultural settings. Other cross-cultural differences may be less obvious, such as the importance of group identity. Now we will turn our attention to a framework that examines how the strength of group identity affects communication styles.

Communication in High-Context and Low-Context Cultures

According to anthropologist Edward Hall, cultures differ in their communication preferences, with some being "high-context" and others being "low-context."[64] A high-context culture is one in which there is a strong group identity and a relatively closed boundary. High-context cultures rely on shared history and shared views that can be difficult for outsiders to understand. This can make cross-cultural communication difficult. In a low-context culture, it is easier for outsiders to communicate with insiders because there is less emphasis on shared history and identity.

Although Hall's theory can be helpful, one problem with it is that all cultures have sub-groups that are higher or lower context than the norm. For instance, the United States is classified as a low-context culture, but it is easy to find examples where a high degree of context is important, such as in tightly organized communities based on religion or ethnicity, or when a profession uses exclusive acronyms and jargon. In other cases, we switch between high- and low-context communication on a regular basis. Who has not been the "outsider" on an "inside joke" or been told "You had to be there" in order to understand a story being swapped by a couple of friends? Despite the fact that high- and low-context cultures are not pure categories, the model can still help explain communication problems in diverse work groups.

Communication in diverse groups is complex, and it can be difficult. It is essential, however, that we learn how to do it effectively because today's organizations are diverse, as are customers, consumers, and clients. According to Harvard professor David Thomas, diversity will be the core of successful organizational strategies, and it takes dedication and commitment to ensure that people can communicate effectively and succeed in these organizations.[65] We must remember, however, that diversity does not just apply to people of different cultural backgrounds; it also applies to people of different genders and ages.

■Exhibit **4.12**

Men and women communicate differently.

Marcin Balzerzak/Shutterstock

Yes, Men and Women Communicate Differently

We have all heard that it sometimes seems like women and men come from different planets. When it comes to communication, this view is not so far from the truth. Gender has an effect on how we communicate (■Exhibit 4.12). A great deal of research has been done on the differences between men's and women's communication preferences—and even more speculation about it has appeared in popular books, magazines, and Web sites.[66]

Before looking at the research about gender communication, you should note that communication is *learned*. That means that whatever tendencies we see in the research, women and men are not born communicating differently, and everyone can learn new ways to communicate. That said, let's look at what some research says about common gender-related tendencies.

Men and women often approach the communication process with distinct sets of values and intentions.[67] Generally speaking, men tend to assert independence, so they use communication to define their status relative to others. Women tend to seek connections, and they are more oriented to the types of communication that forge relationships.[68]

How do these differences translate into specific communication styles? Men are more likely to assert ownership and avoid asking questions or offering apologies for fear of admitting weakness or fault. Men may also be more likely to offer candid and direct feedback. Conversely, women are less likely to boast, and they are more likely to admit uncertainty, apologize, and temper their communication with positive feedback.[69]

Robin Lakoff, one of the first linguistics scholars to closely examine gender and language, notes that the way women are talked about, as well as the way they are expected to speak, reflect attitudes that marginalize women.[70] Social training in how to use language begins in early childhood, when girls are expected to speak politely—to talk like ladies—rather than use the rough or crude language boys are allowed to use. Girls are also socialized to use language that expresses uncertainty, such as phrasing statements as questions.[71] One of the leading scholars studying gender differences, Deborah Tannen, says that girls learn that sounding too sure of themselves may make them unpopular, whereas boys are allowed to use language to promote their status.[72] Boys and girls also learn that girls should not be as aggressive as their male counterparts.

Although women are increasingly taking on top management roles, management professor Judith Oakley notes that different behavioral norms are expected for women in what she refers to as "behavioral double binds."[73] A double bind is when we expect something of a person, and then when he or she does it, we criticize him or her. For example, in many industries senior leaders are expected to be assertive, competitive, and aggressive. Yet, women who act this way are often seen in a negative light by male and female peers, direct reports, and bosses. Expectations are changing, however, in part because there is a growing realization that the communication strengths associated with women are actually the behaviors most needed in today's organizations. Competencies linked to cooperation, flexibility, empathy, and relationship skills are seen as assets in a global marketplace.[74]

Just as it is important to recognize that there are general differences in how men and women communicate, it is also essential to avoid treating these general differences as absolutes or unchangeable patterns.[75] Doing so only results in stereotyping, which you will recall undermines our ability to communicate effectively.

Communication and the Age Factor

Like other cultural barriers, the differences that exist between members of different generations have the potential to interfere with communication in the workplace. A young worker who assumes that an older worker is unwilling to listen to the ideas of a junior employee is as guilty of stereotyping as the older worker who believes all that young people have a sense of entitlement.

Generation Y, sometimes called the Millennials, is the generation whose members were born between approximately 1980 and 1995. They are entering the workforce in vast numbers—making their mark on work and society in much the way the Baby Boomers did in the 1960s and 1970s.

According to many scholars, the Baby Boomers and the Millennials have some difficulties communicating with one another. The Millennials tend to value more directness than previous generations and to look for clear, candid communication and more frequent feedback from managers. Millennials also want more flexibility to work and communicate in ways that are comfortable to them, are accustomed to using technology to communicate, and are also more likely to favor electronic communication over face-to-face communication when given the choice.

A frequent complaint about Millennials heard from Boomers is that Millennials have a sense of entitlement and don't want to work or put in the hours and years it takes to succeed. But a recent study by Randstad USA found that despite their ambition and the directness of their communication, Millennial workers are aware of the limits to their competence and are realistic about the qualities that are important in today's workplace.[76]

In this section you have learned about the challenges and opportunities that are inherent in communication within and among socially diverse groups. It is an exciting time to learn how to communicate effectively in our complex and diverse world. Organizations must also adjust for a new world and new ways to share and disseminate information.

Most Popular » Discussion Questions

1. Consider a group that you have worked with that is socially or otherwise diverse. Take a close look: Were there barriers to communication? What were they? How did the group overcome them? How did the group's diversity enrich communication?
2. Do you think your culture is high- or low-context? Explain.
3. Do you belong to any groups at school that are "closed" to others? What is the impact of this on your relationships with people outside of these groups?
4. Describe how your gender affects your verbal and nonverbal communication.
5. Have you noticed how your age affects the way you communicate or the way others communicate with you? Describe and explain.

Downward communication
The flow of information from higher in an organizational hierarchy to lower.

Upward communication
The flow of information from lower in an organizational hierarchy to higher.

8. What Is Organizational Communication?

So far in this chapter we have focused largely on interpersonal communication—how thoughts and emotions travel from one person to another or within a small group. In organizations, communication must flow among many people and in many directions using a variety of channels simultaneously. How easy or difficult is it to communicate efficiently and effectively within an organization of 100 people? 1,000 people? 100,000 people? Well, it's as easy or as difficult as we make it. Some processes work, and some don't. In this section we will explore how communication happens within organizations, including direction of communication flow, communication networks, formal versus informal communication, and communication during crises. We will conclude the section with an exploration of a powerful tool for communication within organizations: storytelling.

Direction of Communication Flow

Communication moves in all sorts of directions in an organization: up, down, across, and back again. Consider a manager who directs employees to complete a research project. The employees divide up the work, complete their tasks, combine the data into a report, and submit the results to the manager, who may pass it further up in the organization. Information is flowing in several directions, in each case accomplishing a slightly different purpose.

In this example, the project begins with **downward communication** (■Exhibit 4.13), which is the flow of information from higher in an organizational hierarchy to lower. Downward communication within an organization is often a manager giving direction, providing information, or offering feedback to subordinates.

Upward communication is the flow of information from lower in an organizational hierarchy to higher. An example of upward communication is when a report is given to the manager. Upward communication can be damaged when people filter information as it is shared up the hierarchy.

■Exhibit **4.13**

An example of downward communication is when a manager shares information with her team.

Manager

Employees

Filtering

The deliberate miscommunication of information, including changing the information or modifying, eliminating, or enhancing particular parts of a message.

Filtering is the deliberate miscommunication of information, including changing the

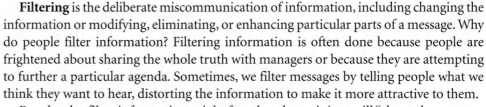

■Exhibit **4.14**

Horizontal communication is the flow of information between people.

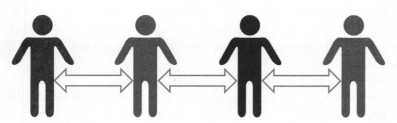

Horizontal communication

The flow of information between individuals at the same or similar levels of an organizational hierarchy.

Filtering is the deliberate miscommunication of information, including changing the information or modifying, eliminating, or enhancing particular parts of a message. Why do people filter information? Filtering information is often done because people are frightened about sharing the whole truth with managers or because they are attempting to further a particular agenda. Sometimes, we filter messages by telling people what we think they want to hear, distorting the information to make it more attractive to them.

People who filter information might fear that the recipient will "shoot the messenger" or that they will have to admit their mistakes. Maybe they simply want to keep the boss happy. Whatever the reason, filtered messages are almost always inaccurate and often just plain wrong. To discourage filtering, managers and leaders need to create a level of trust between themselves and workers, ensure that communication channels are open and easily accessible, and discourage a culture that allows people to further individual agendas at the expense of others or the organization.

Organizations also depend on **horizontal communication**, which is the flow of information between individuals at the same or similar levels of an organizational hierarchy (■Exhibit 4.14). In the course of their work, people often need to coordinate or collaborate with team members or other colleagues. Horizontal communication is not confined to lower-level employees, because managers also depend on horizontal communication to coordinate projects, share work, or consult with fellow managers.

Obviously, communication flows in all directions in organizations. Let's look at how it works in real life, at a company called Liberty Building Systems.

Ryan Kilgore

Anthony Idle and Liberty Building Systems

In 2008, Australia native Anthony Idle was named general manager of Liberty Building Systems and transferred to Memphis, Tennessee.[77] The parent company of Liberty, BlueScope Steel, had recently acquired Varco Pruden Buildings of Memphis, and leadership wanted Idle to oversee integration of the two companies' operations and systems.

After accepting the job, Idle had little time to adjust to his new role. He quickly assessed the company's position and developed a blueprint for restructuring. Then, he assembled his management team to explain his plan and their roles, highlighting several key projects that required immediate attention (*downward communication*).[78] Once the projects had been outlined, Idle and the department managers selected employees to work on each project. The management team was careful to choose employees who were responsible and knowledgeable about the specific areas, and they also made sure that every employee within the facility was involved in at least one project.[79]

As teams were selected and the tasks were outlined, Idle scheduled weekly meetings for the project teams so that team members could discuss progress and determine how to complete their tasks with an emphasis on productivity and profitabil-

ity (*horizontal communication*). Also, as the projects progressed, Idle met with the team leaders on a regular basis to discuss their results, review any recommendations for changes to the plan, and implement any new ideas generated as a result of the systems integration (*upward* and *downward communication*).[80]

Then, in Liberty's monthly business meetings, Idle shared a presentation describing the progress of all of the projects relative to the overall blueprint. He also shared this information with all Liberty employees (*organization-wide downward communication*). Prior to all of these meetings, Idle carefully analyzed the information and input from the team leaders and department managers; then, during the meetings, he addressed each point, applauding the successes of the teams. Of course, he also concentrated on those areas in which expectations had not been met, publicly recommitting support to these projects. Idle's leadership and inclusion of all Liberty personnel in the restructuring allowed everyone to see the efforts that were being made, as well as where improvement still needed to occur.

Anthony Idle remained proactive in each of Liberty's projects throughout the time they were being planned and implemented. Between weekly update meetings and monthly business reviews, he spent much of his time interacting with employees and customers to get their feedback regarding the changes within the company. At one point, an employee suggested that all workers be encouraged to visit a local jobsite in order to get a better

Continued on next page>>

understanding of how Liberty Buildings are assembled in the field. The employee found a local jobsite, worked with the contractor to arrange a visit, and took a group of employees to the site. Idle also attended the field visit, taking notes and pictures to help with training and quality issues. The group members asked the building owner, the contractor, and the field personnel for their feedback on the system, and they used this information to better understand how they could improve quality for the customer and reduce production costs for the company.

On his return to the office, Idle met with the employee who had suggested the field visit to discuss what had been learned, with a focus on how to best address problems, maximize the positives, and provide a better quality product for the customer. The employee was thrilled to be consulted in this way, and he left the meeting committed to finding more innovative ways to improve the business.

Source: Adapted from a case by Ryan Killgore.

Internal communication
Communication that stays within, and is defined in relation to, the structure of an organization.

External communication
Communication that occurs when members of an organization communicate with people on the outside.

Communication network
The pattern of communication among a group of people.

Wheel network (hub-and-spoke network)
A communication network in which one person acts as a central conduit for all information.

Clearly, Anthony Idle of Liberty Building Systems knew how to use both interpersonal and organizational communication to support his vision for the company. Through his carefully laid out plan, he ensured that everyone who needed information received it in a timely manner (including himself). He also ensured that the communication processes—up, down, and across the organization—resulted in people feeling included, respected, and valued. He supported communication with clients and other stakeholders as well.

Most of the information discussed so far in this section has been about **internal communication**, or communication that stays within, and is defined in relation to, the structure of an organization. **External communication**, which occurs when members of an organization communicate with people on the outside, is also a critical component of effective organizational communication. Both internal and external communication can be categorized by the pattern, or communication network, through which information flows.

Organizational Communication Networks

Regardless of the direction of any specific communication flow, the pattern of communication among a group of people can be explained by the kind of **communication network** in which they are operating.

A **wheel network** is sometimes called a **hub-and-spoke network** (■Exhibit 4.15). In this type of network, one person acts as a central conduit for all information. The manager

■Exhibit **4.15**
In a wheel network, also called a hub-and-spoke network, one person acts as a central conduit for all information.

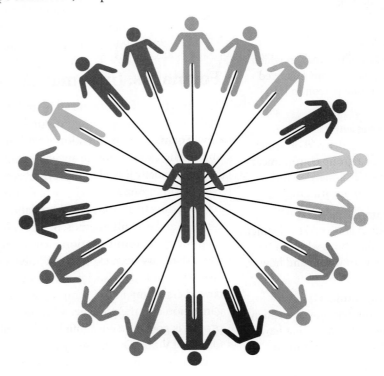

■Exhibit **4.16**

A chain network is one in which information passes in an organized sequence from one person to the next.

■Exhibit **4.17**

The all-channel network is one in which all members of a group communicate with everyone else as needed for maximum flow of information.

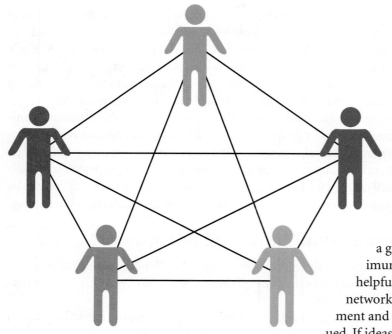

who directs several employees to complete parts of a larger project has created a wheel network to manage communication flow. This arrangement can be very efficient, because one person controls the flow of information, but it can also isolate and limit the contributions of individual group members, who communicate with one person rather than a team.

Another familiar pattern of communication is the **chain network** (■Exhibit 4.16), in which information passes in an organized sequence from one person to the next. Communication in a chain network often moves upward or downward in a specific order according to hierarchical relationships. Because each person has to wait on someone else to do his or her part, it can be an inefficient way to communicate. The clear structure, however, makes the communication process easy to manage because information flows along a clearly defined linear path.

The **all-channel network** is one in which all members of a group communicate with everyone else as needed for maximum flow of information (■Exhibit 4.17). This can be both helpful and challenging. Because many people are involved, this network structure can result in a high level of employee commitment and engagement—people feel that their contributions are valued. If ideas do indeed flow freely, this network can be highly effective and even efficient. However, it is equally likely that this network will be inefficient, because information (including contradictory information) can flow in a chaotic manner.

Formal vs. Informal Communication

The structure of an organization and its communication network often define how formal communication should occur—who talks to whom about what, when, where, and how. **Formal communication** is communication governed by distinct and known rules about who can communicate with whom and how they should do it. Formal communication is usually linked to the formalized power relationships within the hierarchy. Examples of situations in which formal communication often occurs include performance reviews, directives from HR about labor policies, scheduled project updates (meetings or e-mail), and e-mails, memos, or webcasts to all employees about organizational changes.

Informal communication is communication that moves through channels other than those that have been explicitly defined within an organization. Informal communication is usually linked to social networks outside the formal organizational structure. The coworkers sitting in the company cafeteria who casually discuss recent changes in an organization and the manager who runs into a subordinate in the elevator and asks how a project is going are engaging in informal communication. Peter Oliver, Chief Operating Officer, TV and Online Services at British Telecom Group, understands the importance of informal communication in organizations.

Chain network
A communication network in which information passes in an organized sequence from one person to the next.

All-channel network
A communication network in which all members of a group communicate with everyone else as needed for maximum flow of information.

Formal communication
Communication governed by distinct and known rules about who can communicate with whom and how they should do it.

Informal communication
Communication that moves through channels other than those that have been explicitly defined within an organization.

Perspectives

Peter Oliver is a young and dynamic leader at British Telecom Group, a large telecommunications company in the United Kingdom. Peter has considerable responsibilities and is well-respected by employees, peers, and senior management for his talent and his leadership ability. Part of the reason Peter is so successful is that he truly understands the importance of informal communication in the company. He puts it this way:

We are here in the head office—which can seem very far away from the business. In order to understand what is really going on, what people need, and what the business needs, you have to spend time in operations. You have to get out and meet people—talk to them, relate to their points of view, put your-

Peter Oliver, Chief Operating Officer, TV and Online Services at British Telecom Group

self in their shoes. You'll never get this kind of insight if you wait for it to come through formal channels.

You need to get out there, find people who are doing the jobs—grab a cup of tea, and just talk. What's working? What's not? How are things going? People don't want to talk to you in "management speak," they want to have a real conversation without the hierarchy getting in the way. Having these kinds of conversations builds great rapport and relationships. And respect. And, you get insights that you would never get from a manager's report.

Source: Personal interview with Peter Oliver conducted by Annie McKee, 2009.

Grapevine
An informal process of sharing information among and between coworkers about what is happening in an organization.

Peter Oliver's advice shows us why informal communication is so important: It provides an excellent means to gather and share information, and it helps build relationships. Informal communication provides a much-needed social outlet for people. Talking about families, the news, or even the weather are important ways for people to simply connect during the day. Informal communication also provides avenues for people to share information and build relationships outside of the boundaries of the hierarchy. In some cases, as Peter Oliver points out, this is the best way to gather useful feedback and information that can help the business overall. Another reason informal communication is essential is that formal channels can become unavailable, ineffective, or inefficient means of communicating.

There is nothing inherently good or bad about informal communication. When it is benefiting an organization, informal communication increases efficiency of information flow, helps workers feel fully informed, and can enhance creativity. On the other hand, when used inappropriately or maliciously, informal communication can facilitate the rapid spread of inaccurate or incomplete messages. For example, false rumors of an impending downsizing will certainly affect the performance of employees, as will inaccurate rumors of actual plans for downsizing.

A common name for an informal communication channel is "the grapevine." The **grapevine** is an informal process of sharing informal among and between coworkers about what is happening in an organization. Traditionally, the grapevine has been word of mouth. Today, however, the grapevine has been augmented by e-mail, blogging, texting, twittering, and any number of other electronic communication processes. The topics range from professional (e.g., the status of a big account) to personal (e.g., the dating habits of the new manager). Whatever the subject, the grapevine is often where people in an organization get much of their information.

The grapevine is not completely reliable, of course, but it often contains surprisingly accurate information. The level of accuracy usually depends on the organization. Organizations whose leaders are more open and frank with their employees are likely to find that the grapevine contains more dependable information.

There is no doubt that informal communication networks such as the grapevine have an important role in organizational life. One scholar has even gone so far as to suggest that the majority of information is communicated through the grapevine in many organizations.[81] Although it might be hard to quantify exactly how much information is actually shared in this way, it's clearly quite a bit, and it is particularly important for managers to understand the grapevine's role.[82]

How are leaders and managers supposed to respond to the grapevine? For starters, managers need to accept the grapevine rather than fight it. Attempts to punish people for using the grapevine as a communication channel will backfire. Because it is a highly efficient communication channel, the grapevine can be a good tool for disseminating information quickly. Using it in this way means understanding how it works within one's particular organization: Through whom does most information travel? How exactly is information disseminated?

One way for managers to tap into the grapevine is to spend time engaging in spontaneous conversations with employees in person, on the phone, or via webcam. This is sometimes called *management by walking around*. Informal communication such as this removes some of the barriers that result from status differences, which helps information move up the hierarchy, and it provides a way for employees to share feedback in a less threatening situation. Increased contact between managers and employees also creates a greater level of comfort for employees who might otherwise be more guarded about what they communicate.

In addition to using the grapevine to improve organizational communication, a good manager will increase the accuracy of information in the grapevine and control the impact of negative rumors, which can undermine the morale of employees. How does one do that? Responding with accurate, or at least more complete, information is one measure, as is simply communicating more information. People are less likely to jump to conclusions about management decisions when they feel like the organization is being open and honest. Communicating accurate information is generally considered a good management practice. This practice becomes even more important in a crisis.

What Every Manager Deals with Sooner or Later: Crisis Communication

Quoting Greek philosopher Aeschylus, President John Kennedy noted: "In war, truth is the first casualty."[83] Similarly, in times of crisis, communication can be the first casualty in organizations. How do managers keep honest, open communication flowing when serious issues are threatening the organization? If a manager remains calm and focuses his or her attention on gathering as much detailed information as possible, communicates information as openly as possible, and responds swiftly to the crisis, much confusion and misrepresentation of the facts can be avoided.

Sometimes, however, leaders can jump to conclusions in a crisis, or try to calm people down by being overly optimistic. For example, during the aftermath of Hurricane Katrina in New Orleans, President George W. Bush told the head of the Federal Emergency Management Agency (FEMA), Michael Brown, "Brownie, you're doing a heck of a job."[84] In actuality, FEMA's actions were far from effective. In another case, soon after a passenger attempted to ignite a bomb on a Delta flight on December 25, 2009, the head of the U. S. Department of Homeland Security, Janet Napolitano said, "The system worked."[85] Most people would not agree, as an individual apparently attempted to detonate a bomb on the plane. Clearly, no one wants to make these kinds of communication errors in a crisis—yet it happens all the time.

Not all of us will have to manage crises like the aftermath of a hurricane or a national security issue. Most people do, however, have to manage crises at work and communicate effectively before, during, and after. Many situations call for the special attention crisis communication deserves: when a layoff is imminent, under way, or just over; when a business grows (or shrinks) much faster than expected; or when a natural disaster affects people, the company, or business assets. If you need to communicate effectively during a crisis, the trick is to assess the situation and remain calm and coherent so that you can receive and relay the critical information needed to bring the crisis to a satisfactory resolution.

Because not everyone deals well with crises, and because organizations need to be perceived as aligned around responses, communication scholar W. Timothy Coombs argues that it is important for organizations to have designated spokespersons. A spokesperson's primary responsibility is to manage the accuracy and the consistency of the organization's message. When multiple spokespersons are involved, their communications and actions must be coordinated to ensure that messages are consistent and not contradictory. Coombs also strongly recommends that people who speak for the organization have strong listening skills, the ability to think quickly, and media training.[86]

As you have seen in this section, communication in organizations is complicated. Still, when it comes down to exactly what organizational communication is, it is simply just information flowing among people. Scholar Karl Weick notes that even with the wide variety of communication channels and technologies available to us, organizational communication is still dominated by people's natural urge to talk with one another, to communicate as fully as possible, and to engage in conversation. In fact, Weick goes so far as to say that conversation is the fundamental activity in organizations.[87]

Weick's premise makes sense in light of what we know about organizational learning as well as communication theory. People need to connect with one another before communication can be effective.[88] One very powerful way to connect with people and to share information is through storytelling. Stories capture people's imagination—and their attention—and are an effective way to convey complex information.

The Power of Storytelling

Storytelling is the art of creating or delivering a narrative—a description of events that people can relate to, learn from, and remember. Stories are powerful tools because they do more than merely convey information: They are a meaningful and enjoyable way to share ideas, lessons, and values. Good stories are persuasive, appealing, and a good way to shape an organization's culture (■ Exhibit 4.18).[89]

Leaders throughout history have relied on storytelling as an effective means of motivating others, especially during times of uncertainty and rapid change.[90] Stories are far more persuasive and effective than abstract concepts. Rather than presenting sterile, mundane data, a manager or leader can present important organizational information in a way that resonates with people, that engages their imagination and stimulates commitment and enthusiasm. This is because emotional content is inherent in stories, which adds another dimension to the communication process. Stories capture our imaginations. They evoke sights, sounds, smells, and other sensory experiences that the presentation of abstract concepts or data simply cannot.

Storytelling is one of the ways to handle the principal—and most difficult—challenges of leadership: sparking action, getting people to work together, and leading people into the future. The right story at the right time can help an organization get ready for a new idea and course of action. Storytelling doesn't replace analytical thinking; it supplements it by enabling us to imagine new perspectives and new worlds.

But just how does one tell a good story? ■Exhibit 4.19 lists some basic rules that any storyteller can follow to achieve maximum effect with his or her story.

■Exhibit **4.18**

Stories Are Persuasive and Effective Leadership Tools[91]	
Stories Are	**Stories Can Be**
• Simple • Enduring • Appealing to people across the organization • A fun way of delivering meaning	• Integral to an organization's culture • A useful form of training • A great method for empowering people • An excellent means to pass on corporate values and traditions

■Exhibit **4.19**

Seven Rules for Telling Good Stories

1. The story should be about a real person. Using a real person makes the story more credible to your audience.
2. The story should have a strong sense of time and place. This puts the story into a context that people can relate to and will remember: "Two years ago when I was manager of Snuffy's Restaurant in Toledo, Ohio. . . ."
3. The story should be focused, simple, and clear. Too much detail and rambling will cause your audience to lose interest.
4. The story should be told in colorful and animated language. This engages the audience's imagination and captures interest.
5. A good story uses emotions carefully and powerfully. Empathy, surprise, meaningful insight, compassion and even tactful and controlled outrage will engage your audience's attention. It is emotional content that separates raw, boring data from a good illustration of the story's point.
6. Along with emotions, you can also use gestures to add emphasis and a touch of theatre. After all, storytelling is a performance art.
7. Be yourself. Be authentic and sincere. You want people to believe you.

Source: Adapted from Kouzes and Posner 2002, *The Leadership Challenge,* 3d edition. San Francisco: Jossey-Bass.

Storytelling, when done right, is truly one of the most powerful and effective tools for engaging and inspiring people to get behind a vision or mission. Stories help create the culture that becomes the heart and soul of the organization.

> **Most Popular »** Discussion Questions
>
> 1. Describe a downward communication process used recently in your school or at work. What channels were used? How effective was the communication? How could it be improved?
> 2. Using Exhibits 4.15, 4.16, and 4.17, which depict organizational communication networks, plot a network that represents how you and your faculty communicate in this course.
> 3. Does your school or work have a grapevine? What role do you play in this communication channel?
> 4. Using the seven rules of effective storytelling (Exhibit 4.19), create a story about your success on a difficult school or work project. Make sure that someone hearing the story will learn from your experience.

9. What Can HR Do to Ensure Effective Communication and Resonant Relationships in Organizations?

Many people and functions within an organization are responsible for ensuring effective communication. Large organizations often have divisions dedicated specifically to internal and external communication; legal departments also have a role in communication. In almost all organizations, HR plays a key role in communication, either alone or in conjunction with other departments. HR is often responsible for ensuring that everyone in an organization is fully informed about these topics:

- *Labor laws:* Local, state, and federal laws that guide processes such as hiring and firing employees, as well as how workers are to be treated on the job.

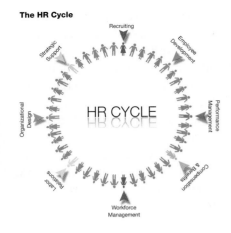

The HR Cycle

- *Workforce data:* Information that can impact the company's ability to succeed, such as information about the labor pool (both inside and outside the organization), morale, and organizational culture.

Communicating Labor Laws

Laws and labor relations regulations that guide how employees must be treated at work have proliferated during the past few decades. As you will see in Chapter 13, the United States has a comprehensive set of laws that protect employees, as do many other countries. Two of HR's responsibilities are to be current on all relevant laws and labor relations regulations and to be sure that all levels of employees and management are trained and understand laws that impact how they must do their jobs. Labor relations is a key aspect of HR's technical support of the organization.

But knowing the laws is only the first step. The real challenge for HR professionals is to communicate information about the laws in a way that people in the organization can understand. You can imagine, for example, how simply sending an e-mail with attachments of all the laws wouldn't help people learn how to apply them. Talented HR professionals use a variety of communication channels and techniques to share and teach relevant labor laws, including written communication, workshops, small group seminars, coaching, and directly advising managers on specific issues.

Gathering and Communicating Employee Engagement Information

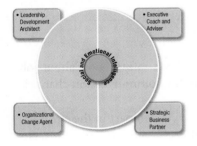

HR Leadership Roles

HR is often responsible for gathering, organizing, and disseminating information about things like the talent pool, compensation, and employees' skills. Data related to the workforce can be difficult to collect and manage, which is why there are many advanced software applications in use in different organizations. These are often managed by HR.

Other information that HR is often responsible for managing is, in some ways, even harder to collect and use: information about employee morale and engagement. To be effective in one of the key HR roles, that of strategic business partner, HR professionals must be able to advise managers and leaders by relying on factual information, not just their opinions about what is going on in the workforce.

Employee morale
The collective mood or spirit in an organization.

Employee morale is the collective mood or spirit in an organization. Employee morale affects people's ability to do their jobs well and the organization's ability to achieve its goals. High morale is often linked to things like enthusiasm, commitment, trust, belief in the organization's mission and vision, esprit de corps, and faith in leadership. High morale is often linked with employee satisfaction and positive organizational results. Low morale often appears as the opposite of high morale, as well as a general malaise, sense of impending doom, or fear of failure. Typical manifestations of low morale are high employee turnover, absenteeism, and illness, as well as a dissonant climate and lower productivity.

Qualitative research
A process of gathering and analyzing subjective data, such as information from conversations, interviews, or answers to open-ended questions on a survey.

Collecting information about morale can be complicated. Sometimes, HR professionals gather information through conversations and observation of employees and managers at work. This anecdotal information can be helpful, of course, but in order for it to be accurate, more rigorous methods of data collection are necessary. In some cases, HR professionals will engage in **qualitative research**, which is a process of gathering and analyzing subjective data, such as information from conversations, interviews, or answers to open-ended questions on a survey.

Quantitative research
A process of gathering information that can be converted to numbers, then analyzed using statistics and other mathematical tools.

Another method that is used widely relies on **quantitative research**, which is a process of gathering information that can be converted to numbers, then analyzed using statistics and other mathematical tools. To study employee morale this way, HR often administers surveys that allow employees to rank, or otherwise rate, various aspects of morale, such as the degree of trust they have in leaders, the effectiveness of managerial communication, the extent to which teams are effective, and the like. Surveys like this are often called *people surveys, employee opinion surveys, employee engagement surveys,* or *job satisfaction surveys*.

The benefits of surveys are that they can be cost effective (as opposed to the time-consuming and therefore expensive interviews and focus groups) and efficient, because they can reach lots of people very quickly. One outcome of a good survey is that HR professionals may have a wealth of information, and another outcome is that people will likely feel positive about the effort because they have been included. A well-designed survey can also provide benchmark information. **Benchmark information** allows HR professionals and managers to compare their scores with the average, high, and low scores of similar organizations. (In Chapter 13, we will discuss two specific qualitative research methods that are widely used in organizations.)

Unfortunately, one major downside of gauging employee morale in this way is that surveys only measure what is asked. In other words, if you ask the wrong questions or if the survey is incomplete, the data will not be useful. In fact, this information can be harmful, because it can direct HR and managers' attention to the wrong problems. A second problem associated with surveys is their low return rate. Rarely will everyone—or even close to everyone—respond to a survey, and because only data from those who choose to respond is measured, the resulting information could be skewed. For example, it is not unheard of for only disgruntled employees to respond to surveys, resulting in an inaccurate picture of overall morale. Still, regardless of the shortcomings of the survey method, it is popular and widely used.

Benchmark information
Information that allows HR professionals and managers to compare their scores with the average, high, and low scores of similar organizations.

Most Popular » Discussion Questions

1. How does your school's HR department disseminate information about job openings, labor laws, and employee policies? Are the communication channels appropriate? Why or why not?
2. Describe a situation in which morale played an important part in the effectiveness of a group or organization to which you belonged. What was the impact of high or low morale? Was anyone responsible for monitoring morale? If so, how did they do it, and how did they communicate their findings to the group?

---

10. What Can We All Do to Improve Communication and Build Resonant Relationships at Work?

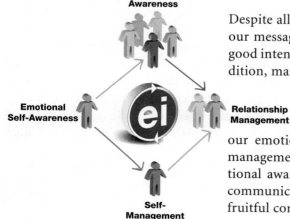

Social Awareness

Emotional Self-Awareness

Relationship Management

Self-Management

Despite all the barriers to effective communication at work, we still manage to get our messages across most of the time. How do we accomplish this? It starts with good intentions. Most of us want to be understood and to understand others. In addition, many of us have learned to communicate skillfully, as well as to anticipate potential breakdowns in the communication process before they occur. We all employ social and emotional intelligence when communicating. For example, we tune in to others—that's empathy. We manage our emotions when communicating—that's emotional self-awareness and self-management. We also track and use communication networks—that's organizational awareness. In this section, we will cover a few tips for ensuring that you communicate well, and we'll also discuss how to improve your ability to engage in fruitful conservations.

■Exhibit **4.20**

Checklist for Effective Communication
☑ Be sure you know what message you want to send.
☑ Determine the most appropriate channel for your message.
☑ Simplify your language to match your audience.
☑ Remember that jargon can hurt communication when it is unfamiliar to the receiver, but it may improve communication when it is familiar.
☑ Create a level of trust that makes people feel comfortable passing bad news up and down the hierarchy.
☑ Be careful about poor or inadvertent use of inappropriate nonverbal signals.
☑ Practice empathy when communicating. Accurately reading others' responses will enable you to help them understand your message.

A Few Basic Rules for Sending Clear and Powerful Messages

Paying attention to communication basics can go a long way in helping you become an effective communicator. This is particularly true when it comes to sending messages. After all, you can control the quality of your own communication. Your job is to ensure that your intended audience understands your message. You therefore need to be clear, avoid ambiguity, and be concise. You must also provide just the right level of necessary information—not too much and not too little.

Soliciting and listening to feedback increases the likelihood that your message will be understood. After communicating with a coworker or an employee, a good manager asks questions tactfully to test whether his or her message was received. In some cases, people produce this sort of feedback without prompting, or they provide nonverbal signals that demonstrate either understanding (e.g., a nod) or confusion (e.g., a furrowed brow). It is up to you—the sender of a message—to pay attention and tend to these responses to complete the feedback loop. To ensure that you send clear, powerful messages that are most likely to be heard accurately, you can start by following the guidelines in ■Exhibit 4.20.

Obviously, we want to communicate effectively, and following these guidelines will help. Paradoxically, however, the best communicators not only follow the rules, but they also know when and how to break them.

When to Break the Rules

Influential language philosopher H. Paul Grice devised a set of four maxims—or general rules—to guide effective conversations. Grice's four maxims are as follows:

- *Quality:* Be truthful.
- *Quantity:* Share the right amount of information.
- *Relevance:* Make your contribution relevant to the matter at hand.
- *Manner:* Be clear, and avoid ambiguity or vagueness.[92]

Grice made the point that these four rules are not always observed. Rather, the guidelines represent what we try to do when we cooperate in the communication process. When one or more of these rules are violated, the type and manner of the violation carries important information about the speaker's values, emotions, and motives. In other words, we make sense of each other by trying to understand how, when, and why the rules are broken.

For example, when we sense that someone is not being completely truthful, we often begin to question why this might be. Is the person pursuing a particular agenda? Is he or she afraid to tell us the truth? Similarly, when someone shares what seems to be too little information, we may question the person's knowledge or capability or again wonder about his or her personal agenda. On the other hand, if someone shares too much information—goes on and on about a topic, for example—we might speculate about why it is so important to him or her or question his or her communication skills. Finally, if a message is ambiguous or vague, we will often wonder whether a person is trying to hide something, or we might think that the person doesn't know what he or she is talking about. ■Exhibit 4.21 shows how Grice's maxims might be violated and what the communication often looks like when violations occur.

Consider a simple example: You are visiting a colleague's office around 1:00 P.M. and you are hungry. If you followed Grice's guidelines, you might simply say, "I want something to eat." You tell the truth, giving just enough information. It's relevant in that many people eat lunch at this time of day. You are specific. In some situations, this would be an appropriate way to communicate what you want.

It's also entirely possible, however, that you would take a very different approach. You might ask your colleague if he or she has had lunch, or you might casually mention that you missed breakfast. Neither of these messages will necessarily be interpreted as a request for food, leaving room for your colleague to choose how to respond. In this situation, the rules are violated. Quality is violated because you did not tell your colleague that you were hungry. Quantity is violated because you actually offered no information about the topic—your hunger. You also violated relevance by bringing up breakfast at 1:00 in the afternoon, and your manner was not clear because you were indirect.

Of course, even though all of the rules were broken, we sense immediately that your indirect request was more polite than the direct one. It made no explicit demands, but you did hint at the real issue in a way that could be understood. This al-

■Exhibit **4.21**

Breaking communication rules through indirect requests.[93]

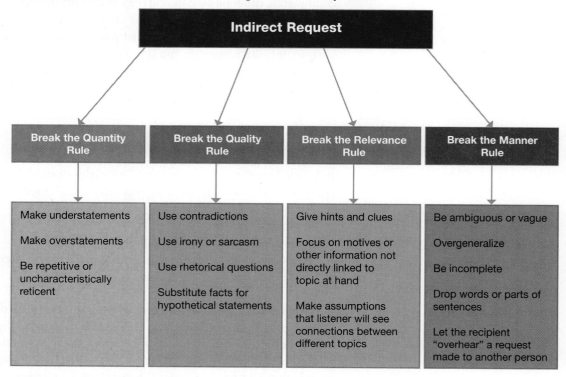

Source: Based on Brown, Penelope, and Stephen C. Levinson. 1987. *Politeness: Some universals in language usage,* p. 214. New York: Cambridge University Press.

lows your colleague to recognize and take actions to please you. If for some reason your colleague does not want lunch, has already eaten, or does not want to have lunch with you, he or she will not be embarrassed, he or she can save face, and the relationship will remain intact.

This example shows that on some occasions, we will deliberately break communication rules in order to keep our relationships positive and resonant. Successful leaders know how to communicate in ways that build relationships and create resonance among and between people. In this kind of environment, direct or threatening requests aren't needed often. The organization fueled by positive relationships seems to run itself.

At work, we are all responsible for effective communication. Leaders and managers have a special role, because they are charged with ensuring that employees have the information they need, understand organizational goals and values, and are inspired to do their jobs.

For leaders at any level, communication comes with responsibility. When we communicate with others, we can influence, persuade, or inform. What and how we communicate can help others, or we can create obstacles that prevent them from doing their jobs or reaching their goals. We can support people, or we can hurt them. As you engage others in communicating about life, work, politics, religion, current affairs, relationships, or just about anything, it is worth thinking about what, exactly, you hope to accomplish as you share your views, attempt to persuade, or engage them in conversation. Far too many conflicts occur as a result of misguided or poor communication or, even worse, skilled communication used to harm others or further personal agendas at the expense of others.

Most Popular » Discussion Questions

1. Consider your "message sending" skills in interpersonal communication. What are your strengths and weaknesses?
2. Reflect on a situation in which you deliberately broke the conversation rules around quality, quantity, relevance, or manner. Why did you do it, and what was the result?
3. During the next day or so, consciously monitor your *intentions* when communicating. Then, reflect on these intentions and how they affect both you and others.

---

11. A Final Word on Communication and Leadership

This textbook presents many different theories of leadership, several of which are radically different from one another. However, all of these theories do have one thing in common: They all state that leaders at all levels have the ability to construct or shape the social reality of their organizations through communication.[94] When you think about leadership as *the ability to control communication,* it becomes apparent to you that some people who are nominally labeled as leaders actually have relatively little leadership power, whereas others who are not traditionally thought of as leaders (e.g., secretaries and administrative assistants) have an abundance of leadership power by virtue of their positions within the communication networks of an organization.[95] People who are at the center of communication networks usually have numerous positive relationships. They create resonance, they get and share information, and they have tremendous influence, no matter what formal role they hold. In today's diverse and global organizations, well-networked people who understand how to communicate cross-culturally will be the most successful leaders.

Key Terms

1. Why Is Communication Central to Effective Relationships at Work? (pp. 96–97)

Key Terms

Resonant relationships Vibrant and supportive relationships that foster respect, inclusion, and open and honest dialogue. p. 97

2. How Do Humans Communicate? (pp. 97–102)

Key Terms

Communication The act of conveying a message from one person or group to another person or group. p. 97

Language A systematic form of communication that is composed of a set of sounds and symbols shared by people. p. 98

Pidgin A language that uses signs, words, or phrases from more than one language, allowing people to communicate without learning one another's language. p. 99

Denotation The literal or dictionary meaning of a word. p. 100

Connotation The associations, feelings, and judgments that accompany a word. p. 100

Nonverbal communication Any gesture, expression, physical action, or vocal intonation, pitch, or volume that communicates a message either intentionally or unintentionally. p. 100

Body language Hand gestures, facial expressions, eye contact, physical touch, proximity to others, or any other physical gesture that has the capacity to convey meaning. p. 101

3. How Do We Communicate and Interpret Sophisticated Information? (pp. 102–106)

Key Terms

Face The public representation of an aspect of our identity that we want others to accept. p. 103

4. What Is the Interpersonal Communication Process? (pp. 106–109)

Key Terms

Sender A person who encodes and sends a message through a communication channel. p. 106

Message Information. p. 106

Receiver A person who receives and decodes a message. p. 106

Channel The medium through which a message is transmitted from a sender to a receiver. p. 106

Encoding The process of converting information from one format into another before sending it. p. 106

Decoding The process of converting information from one format into another in order to understand it. p. 106

Feedback The process by which a receiver indicates to a sender through words or nonverbal signals that a message has been received or that more communication is desired. p. 106

Feedback loop The process of sharing information back and forth between sender and receiver. p. 107

Noise Anything that interferes with the transmission or receipt of a message. p. 107

Effective communication The result of information conveyed accurately from sender to receiver. p. 108

Efficient communication Sharing information using the fewest possible resources (time, money, and effort). p. 108

5. How Do We Use Information Technology to Communicate at Work? (pp. 110–111)

Key Terms None

6. What Are Common Barriers to Effective Communication? (pp. 112–116)

Key Terms

Jargon Terminology that has been specifically defined in relation to certain activities, professions, or groups. p. 113

Selective perception Consciously or unconsciously focusing on certain parts of a message and ignoring others. p. 114

Stereotypes Rigid and often negative biases used to describe or judge individuals based on their membership in a social group. p. 115

7. Why Is It Challenging to Communicate in a Socially Diverse World? (pp. 116–119)

Key Terms None

8. What Is Organizational Communication? (pp. 119–126)

Key Terms

Downward communication The flow of information from higher in an organizational hierarchy to lower. p. 119

Upward communication The flow of information from lower in an organizational hierarchy to higher. p. 119

Filtering The deliberate miscommunication of information, including changing the information or modifying, eliminating, or enhancing particular parts of a message. p. 120

Horizontal communication The flow of information between individuals at the same or similar levels of an organizational hierarchy. p. 120

Internal communication Communication that stays within, and is defined in relation to, the structure of an organization. p. 121

External communication Communication that occurs when members of an organization communicate with people on the outside. p. 121

Communication network The pattern of communication among a group of people. p. 121

Wheel network (hub-and-spoke network) A communication network in which one person acts as a central conduit for all information. p. 121

Chain network A communication network in which information passes in an organized sequence from one person to the next. p. 122

All-channel network A communication network in which all members of a group communicate with everyone else as needed for maximum flow of information. p. 122

Formal communication Communication governed by distinct and known rules about who can communicate with whom and how they should do it. p. 122

Informal communication Communication that moves through channels other than those that have been explicitly defined within an organization. p. 122

Grapevine An informal process of sharing information among and between coworkers about what is happening in an organization. p. 123

9. What Can HR Do to Ensure Effective Communication and Resonant Relationships in Organizations? (pp. 126–128)

Key Terms

Employee morale The collective mood or spirit in an organization. p. 127

Qualitative research A process of gathering and analyzing subjective data, such as information from conversations, interviews, or answers to open-ended questions on a survey. p. 127

Quantitative research A process of gathering information that can be converted to numbers, then analyzed using statistics and other mathematical tools. p. 127

Benchmark information Information that allows HR professionals and managers to compare their scores with the average, high, and low scores of similar organizations. p. 128

10. What Can We All Do to Improve Communication and Build Resonant Relationships at Work? (pp. 128–131)

Key Terms None

11. A Final Word on Communication and Leadership (p. 131)

Key Terms None

Chapter 4 Visual Summary

1. Why Is Communication Central to Effective Relationships at Work? (pp. 96–97)

Summary: Communication forms the basis for relationships in all aspects of your life and is at the heart of working effectively with other people. Successful leaders and employees understand this and pay attention to what and how they share information with others. This enables them to build resonant relationships that foster respect and lead to positive resolutions when conflicts arise.

2. How Do Humans Communicate? (pp. 97–102)

Summary: Communication can take on several different forms, including verbal and nonverbal signals. Verbal communication is made up of words and may be spoken, signed, or written. It is affected by both the actual meaning of the words and their connotations. Nonverbal communication is made up of gestures, facial expressions, and voice qualities that are far harder to consciously control and are more nuanced than verbal communication. Learning to control and align verbal and nonverbal communication will make your message more likely to be received correctly and believed.

3. How Do We Communicate and Interpret Sophisticated Information? (pp. 102–106)

Summary: Good communicators master sophisticated skills such as managing emotion in the communication process. Much of what is shared between and among people is emotional, and these emotions have a tremendous impact on your communication and your ability to maintain healthy relationships.

Good communicators also recognize that we are constantly communicating an image—how we want others to see us—and that saving face is important in relationships. Good communicators also treat information in a sophisticated manner, categorizing it as relevant to the individual or a group, and recognizing whether it is subjective or objective.

16. Managing and Leading for Tomorrow: A Focus on Your Future

14. Globalization: Managing Effectively in a Global Economic Environment

1. Managing and Leading Today: The New Rules

Leading and Managing for Today and the Future

2. The Leadership Imperative: It's Up to You

4. Communication: The Key to Resonant Relationships

3. Motivation and Meaning: What Makes People Want to Work?

15. Sustainability and Corporate Social Responsibility: Ensuring the Future

4. What Is the Interpersonal Communication Process? (pp. 106–109)

Summary: In its most basic form, communication involves a sender conveying an encoded message via a communication channel to a receiver who decodes it and provides feedback to the sender. Several models have been developed to analyze this process and explain why messages are sometimes misinterpreted, including the Shannon-Weaver model, the Schramm model, and the Berlo model. Regardless of the model used to analyze the process, the effectiveness and efficiency of communication are important factors to consider when crafting messages, and should inform whether a message is sent via a rich or a lean communication channel. The richer the channel, the less likely the message is to be misinterpreted.

5. How Do We Use Information Technology to Communicate at Work? (pp. 110–111)

Summary: Technology has expanded the communication channels available to us (e.g. email, text, web or video conferencing). This is good from the perspective that information can be shared more quickly and easily than ever before. However, technology adds complexity, because of the challenges it presents when it comes to communicating emotions, providing complete and understandable messages, and managing the volume of messages that come and go via email and other technologies.

11. A Final Word on Communication and Leadership (p. 131)

Summary: The best leaders, both formal and informal, build strong resonant relationships and powerful social networks. People who can do this in today's diverse organizations will be successful.

10. What Can We All Do to Improve Communication and Build Resonant Relationships at Work? (pp. 128–131)

Summary: Paying attention to communication basics is one of the best things you can do to become a more effective communicator—speaking clearly, concisely, and unambiguously are good starters. Knowing the four rules of quality, quantity, relevance, and manner will help too, as will knowing how and when it is appropriate and necessary to break these rules. At work, how you communicate affects your relationships. One of your most important jobs is to communicate in ways that increase resonance in your relationships.

9. What Can HR Do to Ensure Effective Communication and Resonant Relationships in Organizations? (pp. 126–128)

Summary: In most organizations, HR plays an important role in communicating important information about labor laws, workforce data, and a variety of other issues related to people. Beyond simply informing people about these issues, HR is responsible for ensuring that people understand and apply the information they receive. HR also is responsible for assessing employee morale and engagement and serves as a research hub for these areas.

8. What Is Organizational Communication? (pp. 119–126)

Summary: Organizational communication can be top-down, bottom-up, and/or horizontal. Organizational communication involves several types of communication networks, including wheel networks, chain networks, and all-channel networks. Both formal and informal communication regularly take place within an organization, and the grapevine is a powerful communication tool. Storytelling is an effective tool that many leaders and managers are increasingly relying on to share messages in organizations.

7. Why Is It Challenging to Communicate in a Socially Diverse World? (pp. 116–119)

Summary: It can be difficult to communicate effectively with individuals different from yourself because each person develops communication skills within his or her own culture. Language can get in the way, as can different expectations about nonverbal behavior. The strength of group identity also affects communication in diverse settings. Gender and age can also lead to communication challenges, largely due to the fact that the different genders and generations have been socialized to communicate in different ways. With all these differences, however, its important to recognize that communication is learned.

6. What Are Common Barriers to Effective Communication? (pp. 112–116)

Summary: Even when people have the best intentions and rich communication channels are used, some common barriers still exist that can get in the way of effective communication. One of these barriers is language; even when speakers all use the same language, they may do so with different dialects, accents, and jargon that create problems. Another common barrier is poor communication skills on both the part of the sender and receiver of a message. Barriers such as selective perception, stereotypes, and prejudice can also harm communication, as can unexamined power relationships.

Planning and Strategy:

Bringing the **Vision to Life**

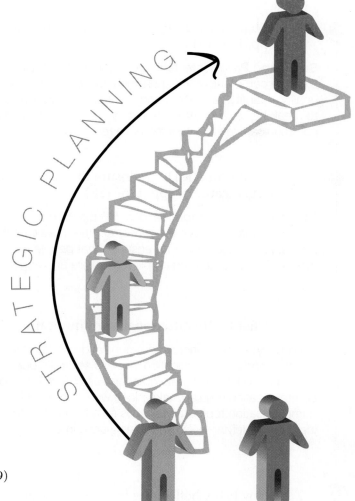

STRATEGIC PLANNING

Chapter Outline

Find out what you already know about the concepts in this chapter by going to www.mymanagementlab.com and taking the **Pre-Test**. Your results will generate a customized study plan for Chapter 5.

1. How Do People Plan for the Future? (pp. 138–140)

2. What Does Planning Look Like in Organizations? (pp. 141–143)

3. How Do You Plan in Uncertain Times? (pp. 143–146)

4. What Is a Mission? Why Does Vision Matter? (pp. 147–149)

5. What Is Strategy? (pp. 150–156)

6. What Needs to Be Considered in a Strategic Planning Process? (pp. 156–161)

7. What Are the Steps in the Strategic Planning Process? (pp. 161–166)

8. What Is HR's Role in Planning and Strategy? (pp. 166–168)

9. What Can We All Do to Support Effective Strategic Planning? (pp. 169–170)

10. A Final Word on Planning and Strategy (p. 171)

Go back to www.mymanagementlab.com and take the **Post-Test** to verify your understanding of the concepts. **To experience and apply** the concepts, explore the additional material associated with Chapter 5.

Part 1: Leading and Managing for Today and the Future (Chapters 1, 2, 3, 4)
Part 2: Planning and Change (Chapters 5, 6, 7, 8, 9)
Part 3: Organizing Human Systems (Chapters 10, 11)
Part 4: Controlling Quality, Culture, and Yourself (Chapters 12, 13)
Part 5: Leading and Managing for the Future (Chapters 14, 15, 16)

8. Workplace Essentials: Creativity, Innovation, and a Spirit of Entrepreneurship

7. Change: A Focus on Adaptability and Resiliency

9. Organizing for a Complex World: Structure and Design

Planning and Change

6. The Human Side of Planning: Decision Making and Critical Thinking

5. Planning and Strategy: Bringing the Vision to Life

16. Managing and Leading for Tomorrow: A Focus on Your Future

1. Managing and Leading Today: The New Rules

14. Globalization: Managing Effectively in a Global Economic Environment

10. Teams and Teambuilding: How to Work Effectively with Others

Organizing Human Systems

11. Working in a Virtual World: Technology as a Way of Life

Leading and Managing for Today and the Future

2. The Leadership Imperative: It's Up to You

4. Communication: The Key to Resonant Relationships

3. Motivation and Meaning: What Makes People Want to Work?

15. Sustainability and Corporate Social Responsibility: Ensuring the Future

12. Organizational Controls: People, Processes, Quality, and Results

Controlling Quality, Culture, and Yourself

13. Culture: It's Powerful

5. Planning and Strategy: Bringing the Vision to Life

1. How Do People Plan for the Future?

How do *you* think about the future? Do you envision exactly where you will be, who you will be with, and what you will be doing in a few years? Do you think about how you will use your values to guide the choices you make, trusting that you will encounter opportunities along the way and end up with work you love, great relationships with family and friends, and a good life? Or do you think more about today than tomorrow, concentrating on meaningful activities in the moment rather than images of the future?

Planning focuses on moving from where you are now to a future that is different. Interestingly, people think about the future in different ways. Some people focus on outcomes: They set goals for themselves (and maybe others) and then work diligently and single-mindedly to achieve them. Other people are highly action oriented: They are content to work hard in the moment, and they spend very little time thinking beyond immediate tasks or projects. Still others focus on direction and a meaningful vision: They think about their own and their organization's future as part of a personally meaningful vision, and they coordinate activities around these less-specific yet compelling images.[1]

The fact that people have different ways of thinking about the future and planning is one of many issues that arise when it comes to organizational planning and strategy. Most organizational plans are almost entirely focused on specific goals and objectives, leaving out or underemphasizing the image of a meaningful future state and the joy and creativity that can emerge when people are in a state of flow—focused completely and fully in creative activities in the moment.[2]

Regardless of how we think about the future or plan, *human beings are purposeful creatures.* The Greek word *teleos* captures our stance: We purposefully move toward a future that is better than today, one that we find meaningful, perfect, and complete.[3] This is what we do in our organizations, too: We seek to identify a noble purpose, a mission, and a vision, as well as a way to get there through strategies, goals, and actions. If you can first master how you approach the future and then find ways to engage others in the planning process, you will be more successful in managing the dynamics that accompany the constant process of creating and adapting plans in your work, in teams, and in organizations.

But how do leaders and managers ensure that people plan so that an organization's vision, strategy, goals, and actions are linked strategically? This chapter will answer that question. First, you will learn about planning and types of plans commonly used in organizations. Then, you will look at how an organization's success begins with clarity of purpose, including clarity about why it exists, who it serves, and what it does. For most organizations, this is articulated in a mission statement and brought to life through a powerful vision. You will also learn how an organization's mission and vision can be realized through strategic planning, which will be explained as a six-step process. Finally, you will assess HR's role in the planning process, as well as what we can all do to ensure a sound mission, a compelling vision, and the capacity to act on strategic plans.

Planning Defined

Planning
The cognitive, creative, and behavioral process of developing a sequence of activities intended to achieve a goal or move toward an imagined future state.

So what exactly is planning, and how do people do it? **Planning** is the cognitive, creative, and behavioral process of developing a sequence of activities intended to achieve a goal or move toward an imagined future state. Scholars have looked at organizational planning in many ways. Most would agree with scholar Henry Mintzberg, who sees planning as a formal process that includes analysis, creativity, and synthesis of ideas. This process helps people identify steps, activities, and decisions that can be integrated to move people—and organizations—toward a desired future state.[4]

Unfortunately, some of the key elements in this view are often ignored in organizational planning, such as creativity and synthesis of ideas.[5] Goal setting is often the primary driver of organizational planning, overshadowing a meaningful vision of the future and in-the-moment creativity. This happens in part because many people believe that short-term, visible, and measurable goals are the way we think about the future, which is not always the case. Let's look at how goal setting supports some people in planning for the future, how action orientation supports creativity, and how directional planning ensures that the overall vision doesn't get lost in the process.

Exploring How People Think about and Plan for the Future

The way that humans conceptualize the future is complicated. How we plan depends in part on certain personality traits, including a temperamental disposition toward optimism or pessimism. More importantly, how we think about the future and plan is dependent on what we have learned from our family, our school, our culture, and even the norms and practices in the organizations in which we work.[6] In other words, we learn the skills associated with planning from other people and from the social environment around us—including organizations. Let's look at three particular ways in which planning can be described.

Goal-Oriented Planning

The goal-setting process is often confused with planning. In reality, goal setting is only one aspect of the planning process—an aspect that focuses on clearly delineated, specific actions and outcomes that will move people toward a clearly defined end point. **Goal-oriented planning** involves determining the activities and steps that will get us from an existing state to a clearly defined end state. This process may involve forward planning (devising a set of steps that arrive at the goal), backward planning (devising a set of steps from the goal to the existing state), or both.

For example, say that the manager of a high-end jewelry store wants to create a new display in the store's front cabinet (■Exhibit 5.1). Forward planning steps might include emptying the cabinet, cleaning the cabinet, identifying pieces to display, installing new shelves, and placing the jewelry on display. Backward planning might start with a sketch of the manager's vision for what the store should look like, including how customers will approach the jewelry cabinet, view it, and access it. From the sketch, the manager might then consider moving the cabinet, changing the lighting, and using a particular color scheme in and around the cabinet.

Directional Planning

Not all planning is goal oriented. Often we choose steps based on the general direction we intend to go, as well as the behaviors and actions we prefer. **Directional planning** identifies a domain (general area of activity) and direction (preferred values and activities) rather than specific goals.[7] This means that some people make decisions—even daily decisions—based on personal and organizational values that are

Goal-oriented planning
The process of determining the activities and steps from an existing state to a clearly defined end state.

Directional planning
The process of identifying a domain (general area of activity) and direction (preferred values and activities) rather than specific goals.

■Exhibit **5.1**

A manager in a jewelry store planned this display.

iStockphoto/Stockphoto.com

clear guidelines for behavior that help chart a path toward realizing a vision. Such planning involves a different kind of goal focus—a *path goal* as opposed to a *destination goal.*

For instance, while in college (the "domain"), you have many opportunities to take interesting electives and get involved with clubs, social activities, sports, and the like. You may not have a clear plan about how your electives or group memberships will affect your career. You don't link your actions directly to specific goals, but you do choose what to do based on which activities fit your values and preferences.

Action-Oriented Planning

Action orientation
Directing one's full attention to the task at hand.

Some people avoid goal setting and also fail to identify a general path toward the future. Instead, their energy is directed toward immediate and short-term actions. Obviously, an overemphasis on immediate tasks could interfere with planning for the future. On the other hand, **action orientation**, or the ability to direct one's full attention to the task at hand, is quite important and can also be fulfilling. For example, you may be the type of person who procrastinates when it comes to things like writing a paper for class, but once you start, you become fully engaged in the task. You're not doing it to get an *A*, and you don't even think much about how it relates to success in school. You just love working on the assignment—and you do it well—which moves you toward the future!

These three approaches to planning have value, and you should understand them so that you can create plans that will capture other people's (and your own) interest and commitment.

Planning is not something people do once in a while or something only top managers or leaders do. Plans are created and implemented every single day in organizations, by virtually every employee. Managers, of course, are asked to plan continuously. They create some plans that will begin and end in a single day and others that will stretch out for years. From planning budgets and meetings to crafting plans for staffing and operations, managers juggle many plans all at once. Planning is an essential part of every manager's job. That's why it is important for everyone to learn the various skills involved in planning: visioning, goal setting, and linking actions to goals and vision.

If individual planning is complex, imagine what planning for dozens, or maybe even thousands, of people involves. In the next section, you will discover how plans can be used—and misused—in organizations, and what types of plans are typically developed.

Most Popular »   Discussion Questions

1. Define *planning* and explain why it is both a rational process and a creative process.
2. What approach do you tend to use when planning for the future? Do you focus more on goals, vision, or current activities?
3. What effect does your approach to planning have on your success in school? At work? In your social life?
4. Which of the following things do you think you should learn more about and practice: setting goals, envisioning a future that is meaningful to you, or finding ways to be "in the flow" when engaging in work or school activities?

2. What Does Planning Look Like in Organizations?

A simple view of planning in organizations is that it is the process of identifying goals and charting a path to attain them. In fact, goal setting is often seen as *the* way to plan in organizations. However, as you have learned, not everyone is goal oriented. In addition, organizations are extremely complex, especially when it comes to large-scale changes related to technology, core business, or culture. Significant change is constant in organizations today, which means we need the stability of a meaningful vision. Overreliance on goal setting can result in too much attention to short-term objectives. It can also result in overemphasis on the skills associated with goal setting, at the expense of competencies that support visioning and the execution of plans.

Plans: More Than Goals and Metrics

Let's look at an example to illustrate what can happen when people rely too heavily on goal setting and metrics to assess progress when trying to create change. Recently, a large manufacturing company embarked on a new and daring plan to enable people in emerging markets to access their products and services at a reasonable cost. This was driven by a new CEO, who powerfully and publicly set out to redefine the company's mission. People inside the company were inspired, and the market and general public responded favorably.

This kind of change required significant alterations in the organization's culture and leadership practices, so the CEO and his team charged HR leaders with developing a "change program." Over many months, dozens of people explored what aspects of the company's leadership practices, cultural norms, and even values needed to change. They created a process that would first engage senior leaders and then many more people in exploring the new vision, while also engaging in action-oriented projects to bring this vision to life.

Six months into the change project, it fell apart. Strong resistance to focusing on purpose and action projects had emerged—in large part because the change program was not following a typical goal-oriented process. Instead, this program was emergent and dependent on people's emotional engagement, and the company (including the CEO and his team) simply couldn't tolerate the ambiguity. In the change program's place, a more typical process was selected that focused on operational efficiency. (The process the company finally adopted is called lean management, which you will learn about in Chapter 12.)

The new program set out to create and measure progress on specific projects, as well as on business and financial goals. Although this was useful, the program focused *only* on goals and metrics—it did not attend to changing people's understanding of the company's new mission, or how they might need to alter their daily activities and mindset. As a result, two years out from the CEO's brave new vision, the company has changed very little.

The plan that was ultimately chosen in this organization looked "good"—there were clear goals, objectives, milestones, and action steps. Project managers toiled endlessly to create spreadsheets outlining actions and due dates. Tasks and roles were clearly assigned. Outcomes were linked to metrics so goal attainment could be measured. But this plan failed in that it did not do what was required: It did not change leadership practices or organizational culture, and it did not result in shifting the organization so that it could fulfill the new mission in emerging markets. This failure was due in part to the fact that the company's leaders took a simplistic view of how to change the organization. In particular, they confused goals and metrics with a robust plan.

The sheer complexity of planning inside multifaceted organizations is daunting. To move and change organizations, plans must be both rational and creative, and they must *link* mission and purpose with goals and activities. A good plan helps people focus constantly on an overarching vision, goals, and activities. Purpose and vision alone are not enough, and neither are goals and metrics. Moreover, actions, events, and strategies should not happen haphazardly.

A new entrée at a restaurant, for example, does not magically show up on the menu. Processes and steps take place that the customer never sees prior to the introduction of the dish. For instance, managers lead market research activities to find out if the entrée is something customers will enjoy and order. They also oversee the wording in the menu so that the entrée will sound appetizing to patrons. They work with kitchen staff to determine when and how to order ingredients and how to cook the entrée in a timely manner. Finally, they evaluate the success of the new entrée by examining sales figures regularly after the item is added to the menu.

Why go through all this trouble? Wouldn't it simply be easier to say, "Let's add a new double bacon cheeseburger to our menu?" The problem with this approach is that adding the wrong menu item could be a costly decision in terms of both time and money. If the new burger is not something patrons of this restaurant will order, the costs associated with stocking the ingredients, training staff to prepare the dish, changing the menu, and so forth will be a heavy burden. Even if the choice of menu item is good—meaning customers like and order it—the restaurant may not profit from the addition of the new entrée if adequate planning hasn't gone into marketing, advertising, buying and stocking ingredients, teaching cooking techniques, and the like.

Missteps can have subtle but serious consequences. Let's continue with this example. Say the restaurant is known to provide healthy, fresh food—in fact, doing so is part of the company's mission. The restaurant's customers and staff alike have, therefore, come to expect healthy food. When a new item that doesn't fit the restaurant's image is added (such as a double bacon cheeseburger), this can cause customers to feel let down or confused. Employees may also wonder if the restaurant's mission is changing, and they may feel discouraged by having to offer an item that customers do not want.

If we were to examine this example in more depth, we would discover that adding a new entrée actually requires the creation of several different types of plans. For example, the new entrée may fit into a larger, long-term plan to broaden the restaurant's appeal and attract new customers. There would also likely be a short-term marketing plan, as well as a plan for the day the entrée is first introduced. In the next section, we will look at the types of plans that are typically used in organizations.

Types of Plans Used in Organizations

At first glance, it might seem that all plans are the same. However, distinct differences exist in the types of plans that managers typically use in organizations, as seen in ∎Exhibit 5.2. To illustrate these different types of plans, let's look at the fictitious example of a clothing store called Classic Style. As you can see in the table, Classic Style's various plans differ in terms of scope, time frame, and how often they are used.

At any given time, a company can have many different types of plans. It is important for the management team to ensure that the goals of the various plans are not in conflict with one another. Better yet, the plans need to be carefully coordinated as they are created—and as they change. Many organizational plans simply fall apart during implementation because various parts of the organization lose sight of how their piece of the plan fits into the whole.

■Exhibit **5.2**

Types of Planning Used by Classic Style Clothing Store		
Type of Plan	**Definition**	**Example Plan**
Short-term plan	Typically created for a period of one year or less; has a definite end point	Plan for hiring two employees over a three-month period
Long-term plan	Often in place for three or more years; end point not always determined; can be complex and require substantial resources	Plan for doubling the number of retail stores in four years
Single-use plan	Used once for a unique situation	Plan for issuing stock on publicly traded markets
Standing plan	Designed for repeated, ongoing activities	Plan for preparing monthly budget reports
Operational plan	Detailed outline of how goals are to be achieved	Plan for managers' and clerks' sales training, customer service training, and sales targets
Strategic plan	Typically a far-reaching plan that articulates and synthesizes mission-driven, strategic goals for a business	Plan for moving from in-store sales to sales only over the Internet
Financial plan	Plan for providing financial resources to support an organization's activities	Plan for financing start-up costs of the new Internet business
Contingency plan	Designed to respond to a crisis or a failed plan; a "backup plan"	Plan for getting stock to stores in the event of a transportation strike
Project plan	Outlines specific actions, time frames, roles, responsibilities, objectives, and outcomes for particular work projects to be done by one or more people	Plan for helping managers better understand employees' attitudes about leadership practices; in this instance, the team would outline the steps necessary to collect information, analyze data, create reports, and share results with managers and employees

---

Most Popular » Discussion Questions

1. Think about a sports team, club, or committee to which you belong. How does this group plan for the future? Review the preceding section to describe what your group does or has done in the past. What could you and other members do to improve the planning process?
2. It is never too early to start thinking about your plans for your life and work after college. What short-term plans do you currently have that are related to your life after college? What long-term plans have you created?
3. Think of a time when a plan did not go as you expected. How did you react? What did you do? Did you have a contingency plan? Did it work?

---

3. How Do You Plan in Uncertain Times?

An early definition of *plan* was "scheme of action" or "design." "Plan" was adapted from a fifteenth-century word "plane," meaning a level or flat surface. First recorded in 1706, the word and its origins bring to mind a linear process—clear, two-dimensional movement from one state to another.[8] But that's not how life works, and it's not what planning is really like either. Most plans in organizations are complex, coordinated with other plans, and often nonlinear. Plans aren't—or shouldn't be—static or unchangeable. The minute a plan becomes rigid, it becomes irrelevant. That's because things change, and if the plan can't change too, it's likely to fail. Sure, it's important to keep overarching goals, purpose, and vision in mind. However, as individuals, groups, and organizations move toward any vision, their plans and goals almost always need adjustment.

Creating Plans That Can Change: A Modular Approach

The best course of action to ensure that plans are dynamic and can be adapted when change occurs is to (1) clearly link plans to mission and vision and (2) include multiple subgoals that are discrete and individually planned.[9] We will discuss mission and vision later in the chapter. First, let's focus on how to create dynamic plans that can be changed easily.

As complex as it sounds, goals need to be created with the knowledge that they may have to be changed, and other related actions or subgoals may also need to be inserted into the plan. Let's look at how the metaphor of a journey can help us create plans that can change.

Goals, Subgoals, Milestones, and Action Steps: Mapping the Journey to Your Destination

To begin, let's consider the definitions of goals, subgoals, milestones, and action steps and explore how to map the journey to your destination:

- *Goals:* According to the *American Heritage Dictionary*, a goal is "[t]he purpose toward which an endeavor is directed; an objective."[10] The word *goal* originally meant "end point of a race," and it was possibly derived from the Old English *gal*, meaning "obstacle."[11] Goals (and especially subgoals) that are "SMART" are specific, measurable, achievable, results based, and time specific.[12]
- *Subgoals:* A subgoal is a goal that is created to help attain another, bigger goal. A larger goal can be decomposed into several smaller subgoals, which are easier to solve and often far more concrete than the overarching goal.[13]
- *Milestones:* The term *milestone* comes from the practice of marking distance on ancient highways through the placement of stones at periodic intervals ("miles"). On modern highways, milestones have been replaced by mile markers, but the concept is essentially the same. Today, the term *milestone* refers to getting somewhere or to marking distance traveled ("arriving *at* a milestone"). For example, you may have set yourself the following goal: "Get an *A* in this class." A milestone marking progress to this goal occurs at the end of each month, when you measure your class attendance record: "I've made it two months now without missing a class!" Milestones help us mark progress toward a goal or subgoal.
- *Action steps:* As the term implies, action steps are individual actions that support goal or subgoal attainment. The word *steps* implies a linear process over time. Action steps, however, are not always organized to follow a time sequence, nor are they always linear. For example, for the goal "Get an *A* in this class," you might have identified action steps related to the subgoal "Get an *A* on the midterm exam" that include the following: eat nutritious food all semester; party with friends only on weekend nights; study the text and notes weekly; and attend all classes. These things happen at various times and in various ways, not in any specific sequence. It's good to practice this type of nonlinear planning because it is a form of logic that is highly prized and extremely useful in leadership.

The four definitions outlined here are one way of looking at goal setting. In fact, the metaphor *goals are destinations* is based on this model: You set destinations (goals and subgoals), take steps to get there (action steps), and mark your progress (milestones). You are metaphorically on a journey, and as Confucius reminds us, "A journey of a thousand miles begins with a single step." A journey is a metaphor for what plans allow us to do: move from here to there.[14]

Good plans include steps, markers, and destinations. Useful plans include macro goals that can be broken down into modular subgoals. These subgoals should be designed in a way that allows for continual evaluation, flexibility, and adaptation of subgoals and action steps. This is a modular approach to planning: After each subgoal is achieved, we recalculate the actions needed to achieve the next subgoal or reach the next milestone.[15]

Modular Planning: What We Can Learn from Blackjack

We can learn a little bit about modular planning from mathematician Andrey Markov, who showed us that analyzing what *might* happen next can help us adapt our plans.[16] For instance, expert blackjack players *plan* how to win—and card counting in blackjack is a Markov process (■Exhibit 5.3). Each card value from 2 through 9 has a 1/13 probability of appearing, a 10 or a face card has a 4/13 probability of appearing, and an ace has a 1/13 probability in a complete deck of cards. Each turn of a card, however, changes the probability of what card can appear next because there is one less card (and not just any card!) in the deck. Expert blackjack players mentally calculate this change and plan accordingly.[17]

■Exhibit **5.3**

Card counting in blackjack is a Markov process.

Tony French/Alamy Images

If card sharks can plan for change, managers can too. Effective managers realize that change is inevitable in the business world—and it's not as predictable as in blackjack. In the last few years, the business landscape has seen recession, double-digit unemployment, very low interest rates, and the collapse of iconic, century-old companies. Change—constant and dramatic change—is the environment for twenty-first-century managers. The ability to adapt to these changes in a timely manner sets the successful employees, managers, and leaders apart from the mediocre. Therefore, although plans, goals, and subgoals are important guides, we must all recognize when these items need to be revised, and act accordingly.

For example, suppose a sales manager plans to support her growth region, which, according to recent sales reports, is North Carolina. The manager's goal is to hire two new sales representatives for territories in that state. Subgoals include articulation of the following:

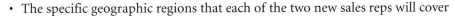

- The specific geographic regions that each of the two new sales reps will cover
- The products the reps will sell
- The clients the reps will serve
- The recruiting and hiring process
- A training plan

Just before hiring the reps, however, the manager is shown reports that clearly reveal a much stronger growth trend in Texas than in North Carolina. The manager has limited resources and can't hire for both regions. She now has at least two choices: She can continue with her staffing plan in North Carolina while going through the long and risky process of requesting a budget increase, or she can revise her plan. The best decision seems straightforward and logical—she'll probably be better off changing her plan. Many people, however, have difficulty changing plans. They might have become emotionally attached to the first course of action, or they might feel frustrated about all the work that has led to nothing. Some people are even blind to the need for change. As employees, managers, and leaders, it serves us well to get used to the idea that plans almost always change. Better yet, we can prepare for change.

■ Exhibit **5.4**

In the 1960s, Shell Oil created a scenario plan for the business should war break out in the Middle East.

Peter Jordan/Alamy Images

Scenario Planning

In the previous example, the manager and her team could have gathered as much information as possible about the regions and developed several scenarios for staffing should one or another region begin to grow unexpectedly. This is called scenario planning. **Scenario planning** is a dynamic, systematic process in which people envision all of the "what if" scenarios for given situations and plan for several likely possibilities.[18] A classic example of scenario planning is the alternative plans that Shell Oil Company created in the 1960s (■ Exhibit 5.4). Company leaders played out different scenarios based on the possibility that the countries where Shell secured its oil could experience political turmoil. Later, when the 1973 Arab–Israeli War broke out, the price of oil more than quadrupled. Shell was better prepared than its competitors because this was a scenario leaders had anticipated, and they had a plan in place for maintaining the company's supply of oil despite the price increase.[19]

Managers, leaders, and employees who are nimble and proactive in how they approach planning are more likely to achieve personal and organizational success than those who long for stability and hold on to the status quo. Still, most people and most organizations need something they can be sure of—a north star or guiding light. This comes in the form of an organization's mission and vision, as discussed in the next section of the chapter.

Scenario planning
A dynamic, systematic process in which people envision all of the "what if" scenarios for given situations and plan for several likely possibilities.

Most Popular » Discussion Questions

1. Why is it important to learn to plan—and to change plans—in today's world and work environment? Give examples from your experience.
2. Research an industry you find interesting, or one in which you are considering working after college. What changes have occurred in the industry or the environment in the past five years that likely caused leaders to change plans?

4. What Is a Mission? Why Does Vision Matter?

Mission statement
A statement that describes what an organization is, what it does, and what it stands for.

An organization's mission articulates the organization's fundamental purpose. A **mission statement** describes what an organization is, what it does, and what it stands for. In other words, this statement explains the purpose of the business—its raison d'être. One scholar who has studied hundreds of mission statements from American businesses says, "A mission statement is an enduring statement of purpose for an organization that identifies its scope of operations in product and market terms, and reflects its values and priorities."[20] Clear mission statements are not just created to make people feel proud of their organization (although they do that too). Mission statements are concrete: They guide what people *do* at work. Let's look at what Dr. Luis Ottley has to say about this.

Perspectives

Luis Ottley, Principal of Fieldstone Middle School

Dr. Luis Ottley is the principal of Fieldstone Middle School in New York City. The school has a long and well-respected tradition of providing students with an outstanding education while enabling them to focus on their unique strengths. When it comes to mission, Dr. Ottley states the following:

*To be a great leader today, you have to have a clear sense of the purpose that will guide how you make decisions. When you have a purpose and that purpose is clear, you can create a win-win situation. A clear sense of purpose also opens the door to collaboration— all of a sudden, we're not talking about what you do, or what I do. We are talking about **what we can do together** to achieve the same goals.*

Now, you don't have to love the people you work with, but you do have to be in relationships with them. That means you have to understand and respect them, and they you. Relatedness allows you to enroll people, to bring them along, to engage them with the mission. It allows you to tap into passion. So, when you invest time and energy in relationships, you will get so much more from people. When they know we are all in it together, and that we all care a lot, you get much more robust decisions, stronger commitment, and people will give their all.

Source: Personal interview with Luis Ottley conducted by Annie McKee, 2009.

As Luis Ottley shows us, a clear sense of purpose plus positive relationships helps Fieldstone Middle School be at its best. The same is true for businesses. In strategic terms, an organization's mission is what sets it apart by articulating its **competitive advantage**, or anything that positively distinguishes one organization from others. For instance, an organization's competitive advantage might be the quality of the products or services offered, or it could be the speed of delivery or the caliber of employees.

A mission also creates a rationale for working that unifies employees. A powerful mission will help managers and leaders make decisions, motivate employees, create unity, and integrate short- and long-term goals. In a similar way, an organization's vision serves to inspire employees and customers alike. A **vision** describes what the organization wants to become—its future identity—which can be realized through the successful accomplishment of its mission. An organization's vision is often articulated in a **vision statement**. ■Exhibit 5.5 illustrates several mission and vision statements that will give you an idea of what these particular organizations aspire to.

Competitive advantage
Anything that positively distinguishes one organization from others.

Vision
A description of what an organization wants to become—its future identity—which can be realized through the successful accomplishment of its mission.

Vision statement
An articulation of a company's vision.

Mission Clarity Leads to Better Choices

Without a well-established mission, an organization may lose focus. For example, suppose an entrepreneur decided to start a small coffee shop in her hometown. She has some money and finds a few friends to invest in the shop. After renting a store, she purchases expensive equipment, buys fancy tables and chairs, contracts with suppliers to

■Exhibit **5.5**

Examples of Mission and Vision Statements

	Mission Statement	Vision Statement
Big Brothers Big Sisters[21]	The Big Brothers Big Sisters mission is to help children reach their potential through professionally supported, one-to-one relationships with mentors that have a measurable impact on youth.	The Big Brothers Big Sisters vision is successful mentoring relationships for all children who need and want them, contributing to brighter futures, better schools, and stronger communities for all.
Toyota Motor Sales[22]	To attract and attain customers with high-valued products and services and the most satisfying ownership experience in America.	To be the most successful and respected car company in America.

Source: Big Brothers Big Sisters Mission and Vision Statements; Toyota Motor Sales Mission and Vision Statements.

provide high-end ingredients for her coffees, and hires three employees. She distributes flyers at the local supermarket and advertises online.

Almost right away, sales are good. So good, in fact, that the entrepreneur decides to offer ice cream. Sales continue to improve and after a year in business, she's flush with cash and decides to add a deli—signing more contracts with suppliers, buying more equipment, and hiring more employees. The little coffee shop has now become a full-fledged restaurant. The owner is delighted—she feels like she's made it. But now, the environment in the restaurant is bustling and noisy, when it used to be quiet and serene. Gone are the comfortable chairs and calming music. The owner thinks this change is the price of growth.

Customers notice the change, too—and they don't like it. Sales begin to plateau. Accounts payable increase faster than revenue. The owner must take action, so she lets a couple of her employees go. Customers now find themselves waiting longer for their orders, and the remaining employees feel overworked. Soon, sales are in a steep decline. The owner tries juggling the coffee, ice cream, and deli, but all three areas of the business are slipping out of her grasp. Now, she's personally doing more of the work, and creditors are requesting immediate payment. The business is on a slippery slope from which it will be difficult to recover.

What went wrong here? Isn't growth the goal of any business? Not necessarily, and certainly not this way. This entrepreneur lost her focus—or maybe she never had one. What if she had been clear that the purpose of her business was simply to make and sell excellent coffee drinks in a relaxing environment? Her mission statement may then have read, "We provide top-of-the-line coffee and coffee drinks to local professionals in a beautiful, relaxing environment." With this mission to guide her when she was flush with cash, she might have chosen to open another coffee shop rather than entering into first one, then two, then three totally different businesses. Or, she could have upgraded her equipment or contracted with suppliers for unique ingredients. Maybe she could have supported her star employees through tuition assistance—preparing them to manage new shops. As this example shows, leaders have many choices. Without a well-defined mission and vision for guidance, a company is a ship without a rudder, floating aimlessly.[23] Clarity about the organization's mission, its fundamental purpose, and how it is different from its competitors can help make choices easier, more logical, and more likely to lead to success.

Vision: Our Highest Aspiration

Once leaders are clear about an organization's mission, they need to tie that mission to a vision that is clear, compelling, and accessible. A vision is both aspirational and inspirational. It describes a future that an organization has not yet attained, but one that can be accomplished with the right planning and strategies. Employees and customers alike can be inspired by an organization's vision, which can result in a committed workforce and loyal customers.

The best leaders are capable of imagining a future for an organization that is stimulating, exciting, and clear. They can see what is possible, and they have the wherewithal to link what is possible with the current reality and to bring about change. Scholars note that the creation of a concrete and meaningful vision is partly the result of systems thinking. Systems thinking involves taking in as much information as possible about people, the organization, and its environment, and then using that information to understand complex cause-and-effect relationships and to predict what could happen in the future.[24]

Who establishes an organization's mission and vision, and how do they do it? In small, entrepreneurial start-ups, it is often the founder (or founders) of the company who define the mission and vision. In larger organizations, it is often the top leaders, including the president or CEO, vice presidents of business divisions, finance and HR leaders, and possibly others. In many companies, HR leaders drive this process by doing research and creating opportunities for the executives to engage in conversations about the vision. They also engage employees in dialogue, debating and fine-tuning the vision to make the vision and mission come alive in the business.

Sometimes employees drive the process more directly, with the support of leadership and HR. This has become quite popular in recent decades because effective leaders understand the importance of getting buy-in from employees, especially on things as central as an organization's mission and vision. Leaders and managers expect more of themselves and their employees these days—all the more reason to have a compelling and inspiring vision to keep people focused, energized, and committed.

Some companies, such as Johnson & Johnson, set their mission many years ago—it is a pillar on which the organization is built, and the company is (rightly) proud of it. Sometimes, though, fundamental changes in mission and vision are necessary. Technology, globalization, and the advent of new industries can drive profound change in an organization's central purpose.[25]

A company's mission and vision therefore need to be carefully tended to, communicated, and *used* to guide choices. Mission and vision direct the organization's choices about plans, goals, and activities, and they facilitate the strategic planning process, as you will see in the next section.

Most Popular » Discussion Questions

1. Take a look at your college's mission statement. What does it tell you about the institution? Do you feel it accurately describes what your college is and does?

2. One tactic some college seniors use to prepare for the job market is to write their own personal mission statement. You can try this, too. Write a personal mission statement that captures who you are. You might start with answering these big questions: Who are you? What do you stand for? What's your purpose in life and in work?

3. Choose a company that you admire. Perhaps it is one you buy from repeatedly or one whose products you have always dreamed of buying. What do you see as that company's competitive advantage? Were you initially attracted to this company because of its competitive advantage?

5. What Is Strategy?

Imagine a football team running onto the field to play the first game of the season. All of a sudden it becomes clear that no one on the team knows who the quarterback is. Eleven players are on the field without any preparation or sense of how they are going to win the game. These players probably would not be successful, even if their mission (play football) and vision (win the division championship) were clear. It's the same with organizations. Mission and vision alone, as critical as they are, are not enough. Just as coaches and players need strategies, so do leaders, managers, and employees.

But what, exactly, is strategy? The history of the word is telling. From Greek to French, and then to English in 1810, *strategy* meant "the art of a general." Indeed, the Greek word *strategia* meant "office or command of a general," and it was composed of *stratos* ("that which is spread out") and *agos* ("leader"). So, historically, the word meant to spread leadership beyond a leader's direct reach. Strategy, then, can become a partial substitute for personal leadership because it directs people's behavior, guides thinking, and drives actions. In other words, with a good strategy, the "general" does not have to do everything.

Tom Malnight is a professor of strategy at IMD, a leading international business school in Switzerland. He believes that strategy begins with answering questions such as: What value does the company add to the market? How are we making money? How will we grow or maintain our position? In addition, it is important to honestly assess the competition with these types of questions: What value do our competitors bring to the marketplace? Why or how is their strategy better than ours? Why might some customers prefer their company to our company?[26]

Creating a strategy means assessing the current reality, challenging assumptions, seeing things from multiple perspectives, and creating alternatives.[27] This in turn means taking some risks, because challenging assumptions invariably means leaving a comfort zone. Malnight advocates stepping up to risk by thinking in terms of "what must we do" as opposed to "what can we do." By defining what we must do to achieve our mission or long-term goals, a path to achievement can be developed by choosing actions that are necessary, as opposed to actions that are easy or convenient.

Strategy Links Mission, Vision, Goals, and Actions

A strategy helps an organization realize its mission and brings its vision to life. Whether it is a collegiate soccer team, a small local start-up, or a huge multinational corporation, every organization needs a strategy to guide decisions, direct behavior, and organize activities. In this section we will explore a number of important concepts related to strategy. First, though, let's look at what one well-known company did to create and sustain innovation through its strategy.

3M

Business Case

Investing in the Future

3M is known for the Post-it® Note.

3M is a successful company, and its products—including Post-it Notes, Buf-Puf facial sponges, and Scotch Tape—are well known. 3M is renowned for its innovation and focus on the future. As George Buckley, chairman, president, and CEO of 3M, notes, "If you don't invest in the future and don't plan for the future, there won't be one."[28]

Many people are familiar with the famous story about the invention of the Post-it Note. Arthur Fry, a 3M employee, was a choir member in his free time and got annoyed that his bookmark wouldn't stay in place. "It was during the sermon," Fry remembers, "that I first thought, what I really need is a little bookmark that will stick to the paper but will not tear the paper when I remove it."[29] After this realization, Fry dedicated time to experimenting with the idea. Ultimately, his efforts generated what became the adhesive behind the hugely popular Post-it Note.[30]

Innovations like this keep companies relevant. And to stay relevant, businesses like 3M must constantly shift goals and

Continued on next page>>

3M **Continued**

strategies.[31] For example, during the 1990s, 3M's management decided that they needed a very new approach to keep up with changes in the market. The company's leaders took a bold step in their new strategy: They banked on innovation. Leaders planned for a 30 percent growth in revenue from *new* products, and they intended to keep revenue coming from new products going forward.[32] But how did 3M plan for, create, and sustain innovation? Let's look at two lessons about planning and change that are worth learning.

Lesson 1: Strategy Is a Navigation of Future and Current Realities

First, 3M decided that strategy should not be a divine act that happens in boardrooms, where only a few are allowed to enter the debate. Rather, they understood that strategy must be a living process happening throughout the organization at all times. The new role of strategy, as understood by 3M, was to support the organization's need to deliver results today and simultaneously adapt for the future.[33]

What did it take to make this change? 3M redefined its decision-making processes to allow for fluidity and timeliness. For example, it streamlined vendor and human resources management processes so typical activities (such as hiring people) could be completed in less than three months. The company later went on to generate a system that allows such processes to be completed within an average of three weeks.[34] Moreover, it understood that none of the efforts to change would work without quality leaders. 3M accordingly developed leaders who not only manage processes but also lead through vision, mission, and inspiration.[35]

Lesson 2: Get into Other People's Shoes: Your Customers, Competitors, and Employees

The challenges 3M's leaders faced along the way were the usual ones associated with change management: tension among groups, fear of change, complacency, and so on. Most challenging, though, was the realization that the company couldn't find the solution to these problems alone. What followed was a bold step to open up dialogue both inside and outside the organization to find the best solutions.[36] 3M started by asking itself about its stakeholders: Who were the ones who could critically influence the company's path to sustained success? No surprise here—the answer was the organization's consumers, customers, competitors, and employees.

3M got into its customers' shoes and realized that "lead users" (or customers who use a product frequently) were ahead of the product development curve and were likely to start thinking up the next solution even before developers could.[37] In response, 3M developed the *lead customers methodology*, which is built on the notion that innovation is driven by customers. As part of this process, 3M managers conduct regular focus group interviews, and they invest in relationship building between developers and lead customers.[38]

The first initiative to test this approach was set up in 1996 in 3M's Medical-Surgical Markets Division. The team was asked to generate a breakthrough innovation concerning the materials that are employed to avoid infections in surgery.[39] Using a small group of lead customers from across the medical system as their sounding board, the division managers came up with three entirely new products. Since then, the lead customer methodology has been adopted across the entire business.[40]

3M also got into its competitor's shoes and increased its focus on competitor information.[41] 3M now uses competitor data at the core of its planning process, ensuring that key data is timely and available to all decision makers within the organization.[42]

Finally, 3M walked in its employees' shoes. Consequently, to help foster innovation, 3M employees now have 15 percent of their time free to invest in special projects.[43] This framework enables them to experiment with outside-the-box ideas: "Most of the inventions that 3M depends on today came out of that kind of individual initiative," says Bill Coyne, retired senior vice president of research and development.[44]

3M has succeeded in learning these lessons and making innovation a central driving force in the company. But change is a constant process, and perhaps 3M's biggest success has been making change a constant factor in its strategic planning processes.

We can learn many things from 3M's long-term strategic focus on innovation. Not the least of these lessons is that strategy and strategic planning are not one-time events. At its best, strategy is a living, breathing process that includes multiple activities, frameworks, and linkages.

Most strategies, even for teams or small businesses such as local coffee shops, are complex. For large, multidivision and/or multinational companies, this complexity is multiplied exponentially. ■Exhibit 5.6 shows a simplified view of the components of most strategies. You can imagine that the full picture for any of these institutions would be extensive and complex.

Types of Strategies

One of the ways leaders and managers attempt to manage the complexity of strategic planning in larger, complex organizations is to categorize types of strategies. One way to categorize strategies is to describe them by the part of the organization they support. Corporate strategies are designed for the entire organization. Business strategies

■Exhibit **5.6**

Components of Strategies

	Mission	Vision	Long-Term Strategic Goals	Short-Term Goals and Subgoals	Tactics and Actions
College Women's Soccer Team	Engage players, students, faculty, staff, and alumni in the noble game of soccer.	Become the top women's college soccer team in the United States.	1. Create and maintain an exemplary training program. 2. Build the bench for the next three years.	1. Win the season. 2. Create and implement this year's recruiting program.	1. Assess each player for training needs. 2. Identify top high schools from which to recruit.
Start-Up Coffee Shop	Provide the best coffee in the city in an atmosphere that both customers and staff enjoy.	Become *the* place in our city where local people enjoy coffee and friends.	1. Open two more coffee shops within three years. 2. Buy the shop we now rent.	1. Identify and select suppliers. 2. Provide technical training for all baristas. 3. Provide customer service training for all employees.	1. Conduct a taste test during a local street fair. 2. Test and buy comfortable furniture.
Large Multidivision Food Corporation	Provide healthy, tasty food for the people of the world.	Become the company of choice when it comes to good food all over the world.	Snacks Division: 1. Streamline and reduce number of brands. 2. Expand research and development to support creation of products that are desirable and that meet caloric and fat restrictions.	1. Evaluate each brand in major markets. 2. Implement testing and measurement to ensure that all snacks meet caloric and fat restrictions.	1. Examine financial reports by brand for the past three years; create a forecast by market. 2. Conduct analysis of research and development operations to determine HR and technical needs.

are designed for particular divisions or lines of business. Functional strategies guide key areas of the business, such as human resources, finance, and marketing. Within each major category of strategies, there can be other types of strategies that support achievement of organizational, business, or functional goals.

Corporate Strategies

Growth strategy
A corporate strategy that involves expansion of operations and/or an increase in market share.

As can be seen in ■Exhibit 5.7, a company has several options for strategies at the corporate level. For instance, companies can decide to follow a **growth strategy** to expand operations and/or increase market share. A growth strategy might include plans for

■Exhibit **5.7**

Corporate Strategies		
Corporate Strategy	**Focus**	**Example**
Growth	Expansion into new market(s) and/or increasing market share. May be accomplished through expanding business, acquiring or merging with other businesses, or joint ventures.	Annick Goutal is a French fragrance company that created a growth strategy in 2009. The strategy called for expansion: creation of new products, doing business in new territories, and increasing the number of stores that sell the company's products from 11 to 40.[45] In comparison, the largest wine company in the world, Constellation Brands, grew through acquisition. In 2004, Constellation acquired Robert Mondavi for just over $1 billion in cash.[46] Later, in 2007, Constellation purchased Fortune Brands, makers of Clos du Bois, Geyser Peak, and Wild Horse wines, for $885 million.[47]
Stability	Maintaining current market position.	In the early 1990s, Powell Flute Company of New England was known for making the best handcrafted flutes in the world. So, when the company learned of a new technology for hole placement on the flute body, there was a great deal of debate as to whether the company could adopt this method and still retain its identity as Powell Flutes, as well as maintain existing sales levels. Balancing the need for change and retaining a stable market image and identity required that company leaders focus carefully on maintaining certain aspects of the artisans' craft and the organizational culture, while simultaneously learning and changing.[48]
Retrenchment	Defensive posture to hold off threats while turning a company around.	In 2000, lingerie retailer Frederick's of Hollywood filed for Chapter 11 bankruptcy protection. Using a turnaround strategy, CEO Linda Lore utilized the opportunities of Internet sales, redesigned the company's retail stores, and surveyed 18,000 participants to find out what customers' perceptions of the firm were.[49] In just a little over one year, the turnaround strategy worked, and Frederick's emerged from bankruptcy.
Divestiture	Selling off or folding a particular division.	In 1998, German automaker Daimler purchased American carmaker Chrysler for $35 billion. Within fewer than 10 years, dramatic financial losses led Daimler to essentially pay Cerberus Capital Management more than $600 million to take Chrysler off its hands.[50]

things like enhanced and innovative marketing, soliciting capital to expand into new territories, or plans to improve productivity.

There are several ways a company can implement a growth strategy. One alternative is to employ an **acquisition strategy**. An acquisition strategy involves joining with other businesses by buying, merging with, or taking over other companies. This might include acquiring companies in the same industry or in industries that support the core business. It may also require purchasing altogether different businesses.

Although acquisitions seem like a great way to grow, the phrase "buyer beware" can apply. Noted scholar Harbir Singh and colleagues studied acquisitions of technology firms and argue that sometimes integration can decrease innovation in an acquired firm, particularly for firms that have not launched products prior to being acquired.[51] Of course, acquisition-related problems are not limited to tech firms. Factors such as the differing languages and cultures of two organizations can slow down the integration process in any strategic merger or acquisition.[52] Such complications exist regardless of whether

Acquisition strategy
A corporate strategy that involves joining with other businesses by buying, merging with, or taking over other companies.

Joint venture
A formal arrangement between two or more entities to engage in activities together and to share risk.

the organizations' employees *actually* speak different languages, because each organization has its own culture and its own way of using words.[53]

Strategic alliances, which are often called **joint ventures**, are another way for organizations to implement a growth strategy. A joint venture is a formal arrangement between two or more entities to engage in activities together and to share risk. For example, the San Francisco Bay Joint Venture was created under the Migratory Bird Treaty Act. Public and private organizations such as conservation and land development groups came together in this joint venture with a common mission to preserve and restore wetlands in and around the San Francisco Bay.[54]

Another example of a joint business venture is Walmart's partnership with Bharti Enterprises, an Indian company. In 2009, Walmart started doing business in India for the first time. However, the Indian Walmart is not the typical Walmart you see in cities across America. Rather, the retail giant formed a joint venture in 2006 with Bharti, one of India's leading business groups, to plan for and ultimately conduct business in India while complying with strict government restrictions on foreign competition with India's domestic businesses. The new Indian Walmart is a wholesale business catering to the specific needs of vegetable vendors, hospitals, restaurants, and hotels, operating under the name BestPrice Modern Wholesale (■Exhibit 5.8).[55]

When contemplating a joint venture, issues regarding whether, how quickly, and to what degree to integrate must be considered. Professor Harbir Singh notes that costs of coordination can be high, and they must be monitored and moderated.[56] Often, organizations attempt to manage coordination by developing bureaucracies and lots of rules, which often slow things down. Interestingly, however, trust tends to decrease the need to rely on rules and bureaucracy. This means that in complex joint ventures where the cost of coordination may be high, it is well worth leaders' time and effort to build trusting relationships and an environment that fosters confidence and collaboration.

Stability strategy
A corporate strategy that is intended to maintain a company's current position.

A choice to remain relatively static would call for a **stability strategy**. This strategy is intended to maintain a company's current position. Perhaps due to a struggling economy or to disruptive societal or technological changes, a company's top managers might decide

■ Exhibit **5.8**

Here, consumers in India are shopping at a wholesale store similar to the one Walmart opened as BestPrice Modern Wholesale.

David Pearson/Alamy Images

that the best approach is to simply maintain the current position. This is not a strategy of doing nothing, however. In fact, during crises or challenging times, a company might have to adopt dramatic measures to ensure stability, such as restructuring, closing plants, or initiating layoffs in order to maintain its current position in the market.

A third type of corporate strategy is a **retrenchment strategy**. This kind of strategy is adopted when a company needs to regroup and defend itself while turning the business around. An example of this would be General Motors in 2009, after the company was purchased, in part, by the U.S. government. At that time, CEO Rick Wagoner was either fired or pressured to resign and a new CEO, Fritz Henderson, took his place. Henderson sought to create a strategy to turn General Motors around and restore it to the successful company it once had been.

Finally, a **divestiture strategy** is one in which a company sells off or folds a particular division, business, brand, product, or service line. Sometimes companies do this so they can focus on their core businesses. Daimler, for example, essentially paid a capital management firm to take control of Chrysler less than a decade after purchasing the American automaker for a sum of $35 billion.

Business Strategies

At the business level, companies craft strategies that support a particular division of the business, brand, product, or service line to remain or become successful in the marketplace. As you can see in ■Exhibit 5.9, one business-level strategy is **differentiation**, which involves providing a product or service that is perceived as unique by customers. Swedish-based retailer IKEA has differentiated itself with the layout of its stores. Apple's iPhone was instantly perceived as unique. *Time* magazine even declared the iPhone the "Invention of the Year."[57] Unique products and services are often related to an organization's core competencies. A **core competency** is an activity that an organization does very well. These sets of skills or knowledge are those which customers readily identify with the company, as well as those that set the company apart from its competitors.[58]

Cost leadership is a strategy of providing the lowest prices in the industry for a particular product, product line, or service. In grocery retailers, the "store brand" is typically the lowest-priced item in each category. The grocer is utilizing a cost leadership strategy by pricing common goods such as canned vegetables, cookies, and pasta lower than their name-brand competitors.

A **niche strategy** caters to a narrow segment of the market. Companies such as Rolex, Bulgari, and Lamborghini Gallardo all cater to a specific niche in the market—

Retrenchment strategy
A corporate strategy that is adopted when a company needs to regroup and defend itself while turning the business around.

Divestiture strategy
A corporate strategy in which a company sells off or folds a particular division, business, brand, product, or service line.

Differentiation
A business strategy of providing a product or service that is perceived as unique by customers.

Core competency
An activity that an organization does very well, that is readily identified by customers, and that sets the company apart from its competitors.

Cost leadership
A business strategy of providing the lowest prices in the industry for a particular product, product line, or service.

Niche strategy
A business strategy that caters to a narrow segment of the market.

■Exhibit **5.9**

Business-Level Strategies		
Business Strategy	**Focus**	**Examples**
Differentiation	Providing unique products, services, or features	Apple iPhone (when released) IKEA store design
Cost leadership	Being most competitive (lowest priced) in terms of the cost of a product or service	Grocery store brand products, which are lower-priced than other items on the store's shelves
Niche	Catering to a particular segment of the market or a particular demand	Rolex watches and Gucci bags (high-price status symbols) Richforth Limited (school uniform manufacturer)
Vertical integration	Seeking cost savings and efficiency through operating businesses along the supply chain	BP: oil discovery, recovery, refinement, and gas stations Heroin cartel: own and operate poppy farms, heroin manufacturing plants, shipping fleet; manage sales force on the ground

namely, upper-income customers. These luxury goods are marketed in entirely different ways than mainstream products. One is not likely to see a commercial for them during the evening news. Another example of a product for a niche market is the "minivan," which is targeted at families with small children.

Finally, **vertical integration** is a strategy of acquiring or developing businesses along the **supply chain**. A supply chain includes all of the resources, products, services, and operations that contribute to producing and selling goods or services. An example of vertical integration would be a pasta manufacturer that elects to buy farms that produce semolina wheat, a key ingredient in pasta. Owning the farms may cut costs and help the company control quality.

Functional Strategies

Examples of functions include human resources, finance, marketing, sales, information technology, facilities, health and safety, risk management, and legal services. Many large businesses have divisions or departments for these functions. In smaller companies, services are often assigned to individuals or provided by consultants or specialized businesses.

Functional strategies are departmental strategies that are developed to help an organization achieve its goals. For example, if a differentiation strategy was selected, the marketing team might develop a strategy to enhance advertising, focusing on the unique features of the business or products. This strategy could include plans for brochures, videos, television ads, or other sales material to show customers the unique features and benefits of new products. Meanwhile, the operations team might retool a manufacturing facility to prepare for an increase in production for a particular product.

As you can see, strategy and strategic planning are multifaceted and complex. How are these strategies developed? Where do managers and strategists start, and what steps do they follow? In the next section, you will learn about strategic planning—how it is typically done, as well as some guidelines for avoiding common problems.

Most Popular » Discussion Questions

1. Consider a product you see advertised on television, on the Internet, or in magazines. What business strategy do you think the company is employing?
2. Using the Internet, review facts about a company you know well. What is the company's corporate strategy? What are its business strategies? Functional strategies?
3. For the same company as in Question 2, compare its strategies with the company's mission and vision. Are these all aligned? In what ways? If not, describe the lack of alignment.

Vertical integration
A business strategy of acquiring or developing businesses along the supply chain.

Supply chain
All of the resources, products, services, and operations that contribute to producing and selling goods or services.

Functional strategies
Departmental strategies that are developed to help an organization achieve its goals.

6. What Needs to Be Considered in a Strategic Planning Process?

Strategic planning
The process of examining an organization's internal and external environments and determining major goals that will help the company realize its mission and move toward its vision.

Strategic planning is the process of examining an organization's internal and external environments and determining major goals that will help the company realize its mission and move toward its vision. The strategic planning process addresses the following questions: What is the state of the business, both internally and in the market? What are the goals that will enable the business to achieve its mission? What activities and tasks will the business need to engage in to achieve these goals?

Strategic planning is a complex and multilayered process that often begins with an examination of the competitive landscape; the social, technological, and natural environment; and stakeholders' needs and expectations. Each of these is discussed in the following sections.

Environmental Scanning

Environmental scanning
The process of assessing social and natural conditions that have the potential to affect an organization.

Environmental forces and conditions can have a profound impact on strategic planning and an organization's success or failure.[59] **Environmental scanning** is the process of assessing social and natural conditions that have the potential to affect an organization. Let's look at this process in practice.

Today, many people are concerned about the cost of oil and gas, as well as the negative impact of burning fossil fuels on the natural environment. In response, people in the United States and elsewhere have become increasingly concerned about the fuel efficiency of their cars. These conditions affect the automobile industry. For example, when the U.S. government began funding the creation of hybrids in the American auto market, Japanese automakers noticed. Moving quickly, they invested heavily in the creation of hybrid vehicles and beat the American automakers in introducing products to the market. The result? The Toyota Prius hybrid was a best-selling car in both 2008 and 2009. As this example illustrates, successful companies pay careful attention to aspects of the economic, sociocultural, legal and tax, political, technological, natural, and industrial environments when formulating strategies.

Economic Environment

The economic environment encompasses the local, regional, national, and global economic conditions that affect an organization's ability to achieve its mission and attain its goals. The state of the economy will determine how easy or difficult it is for a company to access capital to invest in the business, whether the company has access to credit, and, if so, how much it will cost. For example, the recession that began in late 2007 affected businesses in many ways. Layoffs, cost cutting, limits on the availability of capital, and even bankruptcies result from economic conditions like this. Strategists who scan economic environments examine the current climate, but they also try to predict the state of the economy in the coming months and years.

Sociocultural Environment

Societies change and evolve. As social changes occur, managers must attempt to understand how these trends will help or hurt a business. For example, by 2005, low-carb and no-carb diets had taken America by storm. Restaurants that traditionally served high-carbohydrate meals such as pasta or pizza were significantly impacted by this societal shift.[60] Similarly, the rise of social networking tools such as Twitter represents a cultural change in how people communicate.[61] Twitter has affected businesses as varied as music, news, education, and book publishing firms. Sociocultural evolutions—and revolutions—will continue, and managers must stay abreast of these changes and adapt their strategies quickly.

Legal and Tax Environment

Laws are powerful guidelines that inform what an organization can and cannot do. Larger companies often have an entire legal team to keep abreast of new and pending laws, as well as to ensure that the firm complies with existing laws. Smaller organizations are more likely to retain legal assistance only when needed. In either case, knowing and abiding by international, federal, state, and local legislation are important. The price of acting outside the law can be high—in many ways.

For example, Shell Oil paid a $5.8 million fine in 2009 for violations of the Clean Air Act.[62] Imperial Sugar was fined $8.8 million by the Occupational Safety and Health Administration for a 2008 explosion that left 13 employees dead and more than 40 injured.[63] On a smaller scale, countless businesses have felt the pinch when county and local governments have assessed fees for legal violations related to things as varied as zoning, chemical emissions, and fair labor practices, to name just a few.

Consider the effects of tax laws. States, counties, and cities can all adopt taxation policies that either support businesses or not. Take the city of Philadelphia. Like many cities, it levies a tax on businesses. Here's how that tax has progressed in the last 20-plus years: When compared to other large cities in the United States in 1987, Philadelphia had a large business tax burden that was considered unfriendly to business.[64] More than a decade later, the problem had not abated. In 2001, of the 20 largest cities in the country, most did not levy a business tax, while Philadelphia had a 6.5 percent business income tax rate, second only to New York City. Additionally, Philadelphia was one of the few large cities that levied a tax on business gross receipts. This was in addition to the high resident wage tax (over 4.5 percent at that time). Philadelphia was the only one of the 20 largest cities that had all three taxes, giving the city a reputation of being extremely unfriendly to business.

By 2003, Philadelphia's personal income tax for residents was 462 percent higher than the average rate in the 20 largest cities. Business net income tax, at 6.5 percent, was more than 900 percent higher than the average of the 20 largest cities.[65] The *Philadelphia Business Journal* analyzed business taxes in Philadelphia and other major business hubs and concluded that Philly was not the place to be—not by a long shot.[66]

In the wake of the financial crisis that began in 2007, the city's wage tax is to be reduced to 3.7974 percent for residents. The city was set to phase in an elimination of the gross receipts tax and reduction of the net income tax to 6 percent to be completed in 2017; however, this was changed to 2022, and reductions are not set to begin until 2014.[67] This example illustrates how profoundly the tax law environment can impact businesses.

Political Environment

The United States has a stable political environment. However, this is not the case in other parts of the world, so keeping tabs on the political climate is a necessity when doing business globally. For example, Somalia, Afghanistan, and Sudan have experienced grave political instability that has lasted for several years. Companies that want to do business in these countries need to be highly attuned to the special circumstances, conditions, and costs associated with manufacturing goods or providing services in these nations. In addition, politically negotiated international trade agreements can help or hinder a business. (We will explore trade agreements in depth in Chapter 14.)

Technological Environment

The "information revolution" has changed business practices profoundly. Some businesses, such as Facebook and Yahoo!, exist solely because of the advent of the Internet. Others companies have used the Internet to enhance their sales by permitting customers to purchase products online. Additional technological advances exist as well. For example, Coca-Cola added a system to its warehouse operations whereby workers speak into a device to fill orders and verify quantities. This voice-based application has literally freed the warehouse employees' hands: They no longer carry handheld computers, which supports a safer and more efficient process for filling orders.[68] When formulating strategies, leaders need to recognize that technologies will change, resulting in both opportunities and potentially more competition.

Natural Environment

The natural environment is a focal point for many businesses today because of the threat and the impact of global warming, the realization that the supply of fossil fuels is finite, and the widespread attention paid to land use and threats to biodiversity. Companies such as IBM, Dell, and Intel are all taking steps to become more energy efficient. They are likely doing this to save costs, but they are probably also responding to the rising awareness that use of alternative energy sources will set companies apart from their competitors. Estée Lauder, for instance, is setting targets for reductions in greenhouse emissions. Walmart is working with its suppliers to provide more energy-efficient flat-screen TVs to consumers.[69] In situations like these, the implications in terms of costs, resources, and even public image must be considered by strategists.

Of course, there are a number of other ways in which the natural environment might affect strategy and strategic planning:

- Weather patterns can influence choice of business location and business services. For example, knowledge that an area is prone to tornadoes would factor into site selection and construction plans.
- Terrain may affect decisions about the distribution of goods. For example, a company that is selling ice cream in Indonesia would need to have a plan for distribution to hundreds of islands.
- Vegetation and wildlife often need to be taken into account. Consider the Brazilian rain forest: Millions of acres have been burned or developed in recent years, raising questions about land use and development.
- Nature is unpredictable (witness the eruption of Iceland's Eyjafjallajokull volcano in Iceland in 2010). The best strategies include contingency plans and risk management strategies to guide actions when unpredictable events occur.

Last but Not Least: The Industry Environment

Industry
A collective group of companies that provide the same or similar products and services.

An **industry** is a collective group of companies that provide the same or similar products and services. For example, Domino's, Papa John's, and Donato's are all specific companies in the pizza industry. The five forces model was developed by Harvard professor Michael Porter in 1979 as a framework to analyze the industry in which a company resides and competes.[70]

Each of the five forces is presented below, along with questions managers might ask to determine where a company fits within its industry. The five forces model—and the answers to the questions this model provokes—contribute to an evaluation of a company's competitive position in the market.

- *Competitive rivalry within the industry:* Within the industry, how intense is the rivalry? Are competitors "cutthroat" or more laissez-faire?
- *Threat of new entrants:* What is the likelihood that a new competitor will enter the industry? Do barriers currently exist to keep new competitors at bay?
- *Threat of substitutes:* How easy is it for customers to substitute something similar? Can the products or services in the industry be substituted?
- *Bargaining power of suppliers:* Are suppliers and vendors to the industry powerful enough to hold a great deal of bargaining power? Is it difficult to negotiate with suppliers?
- *Bargaining power of customers:* Do customers have strong bargaining power? Can they demand lower prices or more services because of their position?[71]

The five forces model has been adapted over the years. For example, a sixth force called *complementors* is sometimes added to help evaluate strategic alliances.[72] To explain this force by way of a metaphor, remember that complementary colors make each other brighter. Similarly, businesses that serve as complementors to one another enhance each other's potential.

Stakeholder Analysis

When scanning the environment, one of the most important arenas to explore is what people want from a business. The case of FreshDirect illustrates this concept quite clearly.

Shaun Hatch

FreshDirect: Great Service Is Only a Click Away

FreshDirect isn't the only online grocer in the United States, or even in New York, but it is extremely successful. FreshDirect stands out as having found ways to succeed in a challenging industry. This industry is challenging for a number of reasons. First of all, grocery shopping online is less interesting than the in-store experience, which is why companies seek ways to make the pricing of groceries highly competitive. This means that profit margins are lower. In addition, distribution costs are very high.[73] So how does FreshDirect manage to flourish? By keeping its focus on the New York metropolitan market and on its customers.

FreshDirect is an online grocery store that operates in New York City. The company has been in business since 1999, delivering fresh foods to the doorsteps of online shoppers. FreshDirect's chairman and CEO, Rick Braddock, is the former CEO of Priceline.com. Since joining the company, Braddock has used his knowledge of stakeholders and the Internet sales environment to improve customer service at FreshDirect. Further, the company sought to do more than simply provide better products at a lower price; they also wanted to make the customer feel cared for.[74]

FreshDirect has been successful in large part because it listens to its customers and plans accordingly. Based on customer feedback, Braddock and his team developed initiatives to increase customer value and build relationships.[75] For instance, one of FreshDirect's customers' most frequent requests has been for socially responsible packaging. Thus, FreshDirect has been working hard to eliminate the number of boxes used in packaging and shipping. Something else that sets FreshDirect apart from its competition is its extensive customer database. This database tracks your favorite foods and reminds you when you forget to order something that you tend to purchase frequently. In fact, almost 20 percent of FreshDirect customers are prompted by the reminders and increase their orders on average by two items, or about 10 percent.[76]

Finally, much of FreshDirect's success can be traced to the company's understanding of the unique challenges of selling on the Internet. Braddock and his team quickly realized that selling food online can be difficult, especially because the people who are ordering the food can't touch or smell it—the "squeeze" factor is missing. In response to this barrier, FreshDirect came up with a rating system for its products—in particular, its produce—so that shoppers know what grade of food to expect when it arrives at their doorstep. According to Braddock, more than 60 percent of its customers use this rating system to make produce purchases.[77]

Through these and other innovative solutions to common barriers to online grocery shopping, Richard Braddock has been able to turn FreshDirect into a respected and even beloved addition to the Big Apple.

Source: Adapted from a case written by Shaun Hatch.

Stakeholder

Any constituent potentially impacted by an organization's actions, either inside or outside the organization.

The FreshDirect case focuses on one group of stakeholders—customers. A **stakeholder** is any constituent potentially impacted by an organization's actions, either inside or outside the organization. Some stakeholders, such as customers and employees, have a greater deal of influence on an organization, but other stakeholders who wield less influence can still be important. For example, the local community where a firm is based may have little interaction with the company, but maintaining a positive image in the community and in the local press is vital.

One way to look at stakeholders is to see them as individuals, groups, or organizations that have a participatory interest in a particular outcome. This includes all those who have an *effect* on the outcome of a plan, project, or policy, as well as any person or any group *affected by* the outcome.[78]

■Exhibit 5.10 shows a stakeholder map—a visual representation of people and groups that can impact and/or will be impacted by an organization's actions.[79] In a typical analysis, stakeholders can be placed into one of three groups:

- *Key stakeholders:* Those who have significant influence or importance
- *Primary stakeholders:* Those who are directly affected by an organization's actions
- *Secondary stakeholders:* Those who are indirectly affected by an organization's actions.[80]

Stakeholder analysis

An audit of all stakeholders and an analysis of how each stakeholder will be affected by an organization's decisions, and/or how the stakeholder can affect the organization.

Sometimes, a list of stakeholders can be quite extensive, and it is often difficult to determine which stakeholders are key, primary, or secondary. For this reason, stakeholder analysis is an important part of strategic planning. A **stakeholder analysis** includes an audit of all stakeholders and an analysis of how each stakeholder will be affected by an organization's decisions, and/or how the stakeholder can affect the organization. Stakeholder analysis was

Exhibit **5.10**
The stakeholder map shows all the groups and people who are affected by an organization's actions.

publicly debated in 2008 and 2009 when the U.S. government was deciding whether to bail out Ford, Chrysler, and General Motors, the country's three largest domestic automakers. Although it seemed unfair to bail out companies whose strategies over many years had left them unable to compete in the world market, other stakeholders far removed from these companies would have been dramatically affected by their demise. One widely publicized estimate was that nearly 2 million domestic jobs were in some way directly connected with the U.S. auto manufacturing industry. Clearly this stakeholder analysis was an important part of the government's decision-making process.[81]

Most Popular » Discussion Questions

1. How often do you think an organization should develop a strategic plan? What might cause an organization to change strategies?
2. Think of an organization to which you belong (school, work, community group, social, or sports club). Does this group have a strategic plan? Who developed it? Who is aware of it, and who is not? How has the plan's development and dissemination impacted the organization?
3. Think about a big decision in your life. Draw a stakeholder map to include the people or groups who will be affected by your decision. Code them as *key, primary,* or *secondary* stakeholders. Reflect on how this map can help you in stakeholder management.

---

7. What Are the Steps in the Strategic Planning Process?

In 2009, Toyota President Akio Toyoda stated that his company was in a "near rock-bottom crisis." This is a dramatic statement from the company that knocked down General Motors in the United States and was the world's top-selling automaker in 2008. What went wrong? A massive recall of vehicles, quality issues with multiple Toyota brands, and a highly publicized wrongful death suit all plagued the company within a short time frame.[82]

When big, unexpected changes like this occur, strategic plans often need to change.[83] So how do managers develop a new strategic plan? The strategic planning process can be seen as a series of sequential steps (Exhibit 5.11). Each step must be completed so that the information gained can be used for the next step.[84] In the next few sections, we will use this stepwise model to discuss how leaders can develop and implement strategic plans.

The strategic planning process involves six steps.

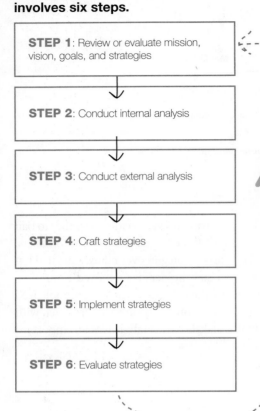

STEP 1: Review or evaluate mission, vision, goals, and strategies

STEP 2: Conduct internal analysis

STEP 3: Conduct external analysis

STEP 4: Craft strategies

STEP 5: Implement strategies

STEP 6: Evaluate strategies

SWOT analysis
A technique that examines strengths, weaknesses, opportunities, and threats that may affect achievement of strategic mission and vision.

Step 1: Review or Evaluate Mission, Vision, Goals, and Strategies

Obviously, mission and vision should guide the choice of strategic goals. Mission and vision are critical in engaging employees in the difficult and exciting challenge of implementing strategies. Once vision and mission are reviewed and agreed on, an effective strategic planning process examines the current strategic goals. Have these goals been achieved? If not, why not? Are these goals still relevant in today's business environment?

Remember, though, that strategic planning is more than just goal setting. It is a creative integration and synthesis of decisions, goals, and actions. To evaluate the current state, the organization's existing strategies need to be identified. Here, managers should ask:

- What strategies have we been using?
- Why did we choose these strategies in the past?
- Which strategies are providing us with measurable success?
- Which ones did not work?
- Are these the strategies that we should be using?

The answers to these questions provide insight into what the current strategic goals are, which strategies have been successful, and which have not.

Steps 2 and 3: Conduct Internal and External Analyses

Clarity about mission, vision, goals, and current strategies provides a big picture of the existing situation. Once this situation has been reviewed, strategists can begin a deeper, systematic analysis of the business. To do this, managers and leaders examine what is going on inside the organization: internal strengths, core competencies, and weaknesses, as well as internal stakeholders' needs, desires, and demands.

Factors outside the organization can also impact the company. For example, rising fuel prices may hurt a trucking company but help oil companies. A decline in home sales, as occurred in 2009, affects realtors, construction companies, and the banks that provide home loans. These examples point to why strategists also examine what's happening *outside* the organization. This analysis focuses on aspects of the external environment, such as opportunities and threats, and external stakeholders' needs, desires, and demands.

SWOT Analysis: A Popular Approach to Internal and External Analysis

One way to look at what is going on inside and outside an organization is to conduct a **SWOT analysis**.[85] SWOT is an acronym for strengths, weaknesses, opportunities, and threats that may affect achievement of strategic mission and vision. It is a technique that involves analyzing the internal and external factors that will affect the achievement of business objectives.[86] SWOT analysis is a popular tool for strategic planning because it can help managers examine what is potentially helpful or harmful to the process of attaining strategic goals, as illustrated in ■Exhibit 5.12.

A **strength** is any positive characteristic or activity that an organization possesses that can have a positive impact on the organization. For instance, home improvement chain Lowe's can count a recognizable name, strong presence on the East Coast, and reliable customer service among its strengths. One type of strength that is often the focus of SWOT analysis is an organization's core competencies. German-based chemical giant

■Exhibit **5.12**

A SWOT analysis examines an organizations strengths, weaknesses, opportunities, and threats.

(Internal)

Strengths: Any positive characteristic or activity that an organization possesses that can have a positive impact on the organization

Weaknesses: Any characteristic or activity that an organization possesses that can have a negative impact on the organization

(External)

Opportunities: Any situation, condition, or event that is favorable to the organization

Threats: Any situation, condition, or event that can negatively impact an organization

(Maximize)   **(Minimize)**

Strength

Any positive characteristic or activity that an organization possesses that can have a positive impact on the organization.

Weakness

Any negative characteristic or activity that an organization possesses that can have a negative impact on the organization.

Opportunity

Any situation, condition, or event that is favorable to an organization.

Threat

Any situation, condition, or event that can negatively impact an organization.

BASF's core competency is innovation.[87] This sets it apart from competitors, and BASF's customers easily recognize the difference.

A **weakness** is any characteristic or activity that an organization possesses that can have a negative impact on the organization. A food manufacturer who has had to recall meat, for instance, might experience a fairly long-lasting negative image among consumers.

The other half of SWOT analysis is the identification of opportunities and threats that could impact the organization. An **opportunity** is any situation, condition, or event that is favorable to the organization. For example, an airline's management may have identified an opportunity if their research indicates that a major city is underserved by the industry and the city's airport has the capacity for more flights every day.

In contrast, a **threat** is any situation, condition, or event that can negatively impact an organization. For example, leaders at Starbucks likely perceived a threat to their high-end coffee drinks when Dunkin' Donuts began to advertise less expensive, tasty coffee and customers began to respond, in part because of a downturn in the economy and Starbucks' reputation for being expensive. Some threats aren't as obvious, such as slowly growing consumer trends or the emergence of a social trend that changes consumer habits. Many organizations therefore have systems in place to monitor potential threats and plan responses. Morgan Stanley, for example, goes through a series of drills to prepare for computer hackers, natural disasters, and terrorism.[88]

Drawbacks of SWOT Analysis

SWOT analysis can be helpful, but it has some drawbacks. First, even SWOT proponents note that simply filling in the four boxes with brainstormed lists isn't enough—long lists of unevaluated information are often little more than a case of "garbage in, garbage out." Scholars have thus attempted to evaluate the SWOT technique by asking users the following questions about the items generated for each category:

- How many points are listed as strengths, weaknesses, opportunities, and threats?
- Are these points described clearly and specifically?
- Were the items weighted or prioritized? If so, how?
- Was the information used in decision making? If so, how?[89]

The researchers found that the items created through SWOT analysis were almost never prioritized, grouped, weighted, or organized beyond the general categories. The study revealed that items were brief, clarification was rarely sought, and independent verification was rarely if ever conducted. Another problem that affects the quality of SWOT analysis is that many people have only vague ideas about their organizations' real strengths.[90] Additionally, the researchers found that in making SWOT lists, the distinction between internal and external factors was frequently violated. Surprisingly, completed SWOT analyses were rarely utilized as input in subsequent strategic planning.[91]

Taken as a whole, scholars' critiques indicate that the SWOT technique can be useful, but only if it is conducted as a true analysis, not simple list making. A good SWOT analysis requires the time and attention of people who are willing to *think* about the current state of the company.

Step 4: Craft Strategies

As you can see, a great deal of work takes place prior to formulating a strategy. Steps 1 through 3 ensure that the right strategy is selected. Then, in step 4, managers take all the information they have collected and analyzed and formulate strategic goals and plans for the organization.

But crafting strategy is more than simply saying "Let's do this." Even though a great quantity of information has been amassed about the company, its competitors, and the various environments, strategists need to grapple with where to expend resources to support different parts of a business, such as divisions, product lines, brands, or individual products or services. The BCG matrix is one common method for looking at this type of problem.

The BCG Matrix: One Way to "See" a Business

A **diversified company** is a company that has two or more distinct divisions that produce different products or services. General Electric (GE), for example, makes everything from appliances and jet engines to light bulbs. For diversified companies such as GE, Procter & Gamble, and Newell Rubbermaid, strategy does not take a one-size-fits-all approach. Different divisions of these companies perform better than others and have varying needs.

For this reason, large corporations often use an analysis tool developed by the Boston Consulting Group (BCG). This tool is called the **BCG matrix**, and it illustrates how a business unit, product, service, brand, or product portfolio is performing in terms of market share and market growth.[92] Managers can use the BCG matrix to categorize businesses or products by how much market share they have and their growth potential. As you can see in ■Exhibit 5.13, the resulting categories are called stars, question marks, cows, and dogs.

Let's look at how the BCG matrix works. As shown in Exhibit 5.13, the horizontal axis illustrates market share. **Market share** describes the percentage of the market that a product, service, or business unit has captured. For example, there is fierce competition for market share of paid search advertising on the Internet, which is tied to market share of search engine browsing. These statistics are monitored closely by Google, Microsoft, Yahoo!, and many other companies.

Plotted on the vertical axis, the **market growth rate** is a measure of growth in the market for given products or services. The top of the vertical axis represents high market growth rate, whereas the bottom of the axis represents low market growth rate. Take, for example, the market for Apple's iPhone, which is categorized as a "smart phone." The market for smart phones is growing—and fast. Estimates suggest that the market will grow by more than 30 percent per year through 2012—which represents a huge opportunity for Apple and other smart phone producers.[93]

By mapping products or business lines in this way, a company can make decisions about how to support certain aspects of a business. For instance, dogs can be liquidated, whereas investing in stars could turn them into cash cows. Question marks are the most difficult. They may have the potential to generate a lot of income if they capture market share, but they can also be a drain on financial resources. For large companies, the challenge is to craft strategies that support a good balance among products and business lines.

Drawbacks of the BCG Matrix

The BCG matrix has its drawbacks.[94] First, the matrix is most useful for large conglomerates with a variety of different units, which was more common in the 1980s than it is

Sidebar definitions

Diversified company
A company that has two or more distinct divisions that produce different products or services.

BCG matrix
An analysis tool used to illustrate how a business unit, product, service, brand, or product portfolio is performing in terms of market share and market growth.

Market share
The percentage of the market that a product, service, or business unit has captured.

Market growth rate
A measure of growth in the market for given products or services.

■Exhibit **5.13**

The BCG matrix analyzes a company's products.

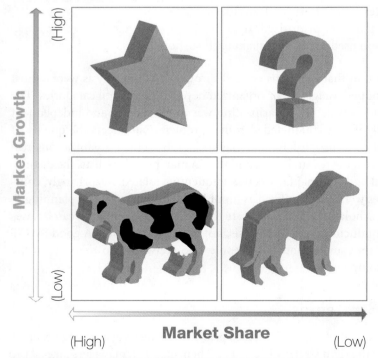

Market Growth (High) / (Low)

Market Share (High) / (Low)

Source: The BCG Portfolio Matrix from *The Product Portfolio*, © 1970. The Boston Consulting Group.

today.[95] Another problem is that the BCG matrix oversimplifies the relationship between market share and income generation. Market share is not a reliable indicator of future profitability in a rapidly shifting technological landscape. In fact, no matter how elegant the model, there is no single reliable indicator that can replace human interpretation and good analysis.[96]

Steps 5 and 6: Implement and Evaluate Strategies

The reasons for strategic planning are somewhat obvious. Without a well-thought-out, carefully crafted plan, a company stumbles along—it might be successful or it might not be. However, even a perfect strategic plan is useless if it is never enacted. Imagine spending time in meetings, working long hours over the weekend, and exchanging countless memos and e-mails in order to develop a strategic plan. Everyone agrees that it is a fine plan, but it gets filed away with no action taken. Unfortunately, this occurs in companies of all sizes. That is why the implementation of a plan is more important than the creation of the plan itself. Without implementation, the strategic plan is nothing more than a good idea.

Implementing a Plan Is Sometimes Called "Execution"

Consultant Ram Charan has dedicated a good deal of his work to examining how leaders implement plans. Charan and his colleagues have found that a crucial element of strategy that is often overlooked is execution—or getting the job done. According to Charan, the discipline of executing plans requires leaders to do the following:[97]

- Make assumptions about the business environment
- Assess organizational capability
- Link strategies to operations and identify the people to carry out the strategies
- Coordinate the efforts of people in charge of carrying out the strategies
- Create a clear and explicit reward system based on outcomes
- Develop the mechanisms for challenging and changing assumptions as the business environment changes

Executing plans is a form of accountability.[98] Charan suggests that most of the time, a CEO fails not because of ideas, but rather because of failure to follow through on commitments.[99] Other scholars take a broader view, suggesting that high-performing companies are successful because of their focus on both planning *and* execution.[100]

Evaluation and "Must-Wins"

But even the best of plans is not flawless in perpetuity, no matter how well it is implemented. All kinds of factors and conditions can lay waste to the most carefully constructed plans. The inability to adapt a plan in the event of a crisis can wreak havoc on the planning process.

Evaluation of strategies is and should be a continual process. Well-known professor and scholar Tom Malnight believes that strategy implementation and evaluation is a process of constantly determining which strategies are the "must-win battles."[101] Malnight's position is that managers and leaders need to continually examine organizational priorities. Everything is not equally important; therefore, strategic decisions about the allocation of resources must be made—and changed when necessary. The initiatives, programs, projects, and so forth that are essential to the realization of important goals are the must-win battles, and care must be taken to ensure that sufficient resources are in place to ensure victory. Malnight argues that the average organization can only wage a few must-win battles at any given time. This may mean refocusing the organization to do fewer things, but do them better. This process needs to be continual, and it needs to be timely. In today's fast-paced environment, constant attention to change—and possibly changing priorities—can give a company the edge it needs.

8. What Is HR's Role in Planning and Strategy?

HR Leadership Roles

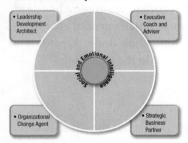

In decades past, the human resources department was relegated to the back corners of the corporate office, being viewed primarily as the "compensation and benefits" staff. In recent years, however, this philosophy has evolved to one of inclusion of—and reliance on—HR for advice and support around business strategies. Progressive companies and forward-thinking CEOs now see partnering with HR as an opportunity to work with business experts and consultants who can impact an organization's strategy in a positive manner.[102] In fact, linking HR activities to strategy is essential, especially when it comes to the "people strategy." HR ensures that the right people are in the right jobs and that they are supported by the organization in ways that allow them to help realize the organization's mission, vision, and strategy.

In this section, we will focus on how HR can support strategy and planning through ensuring that the right numbers and right kinds of people are in the workforce. This can include recruiting, selection, and succession planning, as well as overall plans for workforce growth or reductions.

Recruiting Employees

How do companies find individuals who have the necessary qualifications to fill a job? The process of attracting qualified candidates for jobs is known as **recruiting**. What once involved simply placing an ad in the Sunday paper has turned into a complex process of casting a targeted net into the labor pool to find talented individuals who can support an organization's strategy and fit into its culture. Today, companies compete to find "stars" in the labor pool, and they use a variety of ways to locate these candidates.

The first place many HR professionals look is within their own organization. When an open position exists, internal recruiting includes two primary approaches. The first and by far least expensive and easiest method is to place a job posting on the company's intranet or bulletin boards, in HR newsletters, and so forth. A second method of internal recruiting is through the use of an HR inventory. An **HR inventory** is an internal system that maintains information about people within an organization. It identifies relevant skills, training needs, career plans, and other information about employees.[103] These systems are used to identify talent in the organization, and as positions open up in the company, the HR inventory can provide a list of qualified candidates.

Of course, there are occasions when HR recruiters must look outside the firm for talent. It may be that no one within the organization is qualified, or there may be a need

Recruiting
The process of attracting qualified candidates for jobs.

HR inventory
An internal system that maintains information about people within an organization, including skills, training needs, career plans, and other information about employees.

to bring in fresh ideas and approaches. External recruiting methods are numerous and include such things as visits to colleges, career fairs, use of online recruiting and placement companies (such as Monster.com), postings on the company Web site, social networking, and the like.[104] HR will also often tap employment agencies, professional recruiters (sometimes called "headhunters"), and competitors. Some of these methods are quite expensive; for instance, professional recruiters can earn up to 100 percent of a candidate's first-year salary for their services.

Selecting the "Right" Employees

Selection is the act of choosing whom to hire from among a group of qualified applicants. But what does "qualified" mean? This is where the HR professional must make some important determinations. Obviously, the right kind of experience for the job is necessary, as are the appropriate number of years of experience. In addition, college degrees, certifications, and specific skills are often considered. But, other criteria are also weighed. Will a candidate fit in an organization's culture? Can he or she get along with others? Is he or she the type of candidate who can be promoted into other positions in the company in the future? Questions such as these help the recruiter assess a candidate's "fit" with the company. From a planning perspective, HR professionals must ensure that they are hiring individuals who will achieve the organization's goals while adhering to the mission and vision of the firm.

Succession Planning

On September 11, 2001, two planes slammed into the twin towers of the World Trade Center in New York, and more than 2,700 people lost their lives—a tragedy for families, friends, and the world. It was also a tragedy for many businesses, and the event became an important wake-up call for companies: In a situation in which a large percentage of the staff is suddenly gone, what can you do? For example, the Port Authority of New York and New Jersey had 2,000 employees in the World Trade Center, and it lost 84 of them that day—including its executive director. Financial services firm Cantor Fitzgerald lost 658 people—two-thirds of its total workforce and all of the employees in its headquarters offices at the time.[105] The New York City Fire Department lost 343 of its 11,000 firefighters in a matter of moments.[106]

Beyond the sudden loss of numerous employees—as in the case of the World Trade Center—attrition is constant and creates the need for a well-developed succession plan. A **succession plan** is a plan for filling management positions in the event those positions are vacated. Sucession planning is an important part of HR professionals' overall strategic planning process. This is particularly important today in some countries becasue of demographics. For example, as Baby Boomers retire during the next two decades, other individuals will need to be developed to fill management vacancies.

So far, we have been talking about specific processes to manage recruiting, selecting, and hiring individuals. In order for these processes to truly support the workforce, HR professionals must understand how to craft the size and shape of the workforce in a way that supports the organization's strategy.

Workforce Growth and Reductions

In the event that an organization's strategy calls for expanding the workforce significantly, HR will need to plan carefully and implement an effective growth strategy. Certainly, this is a good problem to have! A rush to fill these positions with just any "warm body," however, can ultimately affect the performance of the entire organization. Constant communication with managers at every level of the organization and

Selection
The act of choosing whom to hire from among a group of qualified applicants.

The HR Cycle

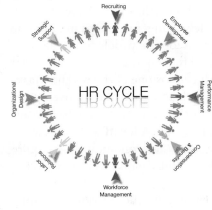

Succession plan
A plan for filling management positions in the event those positions are vacated.

strong recruiting processes will result in hiring enough of the right kind of employees in the right parts of the business. Many HR professionals find recruiting to support a growth strategy to be demanding and rewarding. It's a chance to truly reshape a business.

Unfortunately, not all HR planning is positive or fun. The flipside to a growth period is a downturn, which results in the need to reduce the workforce across the business or in certain areas. Perhaps the toughest part of any manager's job is the task of terminating an employee. Often an individual's job is an integral part of that person's identity. In fact, when we first meet someone new, one of our first questions is "What do you do for a living?" When a job is taken away through a termination, a person's livelihood is affected—and so is the person's self-image. Firing or laying off workers is one of the toughest parts of an HR professional's job.

HR managers are often the architects of downsizing plans, and they also support managers in terminating employees. There are several types of termination situations. A reduction in force is the dismissal of employees due to economic reasons, technological advancements, or redundancy of work. In 2008 and 2009, the United States, Europe, and many other parts of the world saw drastic and devastating reductions in force due to the global recession. Companies were often left with too few people to do the work that was needed, and individuals and families suffered tremendously.

Planning for and implementing a workforce reduction is one of the toughest tasks HR professionals face. Imagine sitting in a meeting with a list of 100 or more employees, most of whom you know well and most of whom are doing a great job. Your responsibility is to decide which 20 people you need to lay off. A **layoff** is a termination with the possibility of rehire once conditions improve. When conditions that require layoffs are in place for a long time (such as during the extended global recession that began in 2007), rehiring is usually a distant dream.

What makes these situations so difficult is that employees who did nothing wrong have to be let go. A reduction in force takes jobs away from people due to company changes—not necessarily the employees' performance. An effective HR manager is one who handles these situations with professionalism and treats the people who are losing their jobs with dignity.

Yet another type of workforce reduction is firing people. This is called **for-cause termination**, and it involves the dismissal of an employee for breaking a company policy, failing to perform, or failing to adjust to company values, norms, or culture.

Terminations—whether for cause or workforce reductions—are important factors in strategic planning. Obviously, fewer workers will impact a company's productivity. In many cases, fewer workers also means that remaining employees have to take on additional responsibilities—sometimes to the point that people burn out. Workforce reductions also affect morale profoundly. The people who remain can feel guilty, angry, or fearful—feelings that don't support effectiveness on the job. HR, then, has to deal the the ramifications of workforce reductions as well.

Layoff

A termination with the possibility of rehire once conditions improve.

For-cause termination

The dismissal of an employee for breaking a company policy, failing to perform, or failing to adjust to company values, norms, or culture.

Most Popular » Discussion Questions

1. Describe a selection process in which you have participated (either at work, at school, or in a social club). Was the selection process strategic? In what ways? Was it tied to the mission, vision, or strategic goals of the organization? If so, in what ways?

2. Think about an organization to which you belong, such as a sports team, musical group, or social club. Is there a succession plan that will help replace members as they move on? What are the characteristics of the plan? Is it effective?

3. Do you know anyone who has been fired or laid off from a job? How was it done? What was the impact on the person? How would you handle firing or laying off an employee?

9. What Can We All Do to Support Effective Strategic Planning?

When it comes right down to it, plans are great, and good plans are even better. But unless people act on these plans, they're worthless. So, what can we all do to ensure that our personal, work, and strategic plans come to life? We can start by developing our ability to analyze current situations and see how the patterns we recognize relate to the future. We can also make sure that crafting our personal vision is something we do regularly.

To become an expert strategic planner, you must develop your pattern recognition skills. This competency enables you to analyze situations—both internal and external to an organization—thereby allowing you to engage in strategic planning more effectively. To be a truly successful strategic leader, your personal vision must be in line with your organization's. When your vision and your goals are in synch with what your organization needs from you, you will be more fulfilled at work and more likely to do your best. How to develop pattern recognition skills and create a personal vision is discussed in the following sections.

Pattern Recognition: A Key Element of Strategic Planning

The following statement is often attributed to A. A. Milne, famous British author and creator of the beloved Winnie-the-Pooh characters: "Organizing is what you do before you do something, so that when you do it, it is not all mixed up." When we organize our thoughts, we are engaging systems thinking and pattern recognition, the two cognitive competencies expected of MBA students, because these competencies are linked to effective leadership.[107]

Pattern recognition is central to cognition: It is a higher order competency that is important to analytical thought.[108] Pattern recognition is the process of taking in raw information and mentally organizing it into a model or blueprint that helps explain a situation. This is a critical skill because leaders must be able to make connections when information is not perfectly clear (which is quite often the case).

Recognition of patterns is a central aspect of situational awareness, which is the ability to quickly identify relevant patterns, integrate them into decision-making processes, and act accordingly.[109] Decision making and planning in real-world situations often rely on the use of "fuzzy logic."[110] This means that patterns encountered in the real world are rarely exactly the same as those held in memory, so we need to be able to recognize vague, or "fuzzy," patterns and make them more clear.

How can you develop pattern recognition? Interestingly, you probably already have. Our educational processes are geared toward developing this skill; from learning to read, to solving math problems, to writing term papers, we have all been taught to look for patterns in information. Beyond what you have already been taught, you can enhance your capacity for pattern recognition by becoming more aware of your automatic thought processes. This is called *mindfulness*. Esteemed scholar Ellen Langer explains it this way: "When we are mindless, we are like programmed automatons, treating information in a single-minded and rigid way, as though it were true regardless of the circumstances. When we are mindful, we are open to surprise, oriented in the present moment, sensitive to context, and above all, liberated from the tyranny of old mindsets."[111] So, the single most important thing you can do to develop your capacity for pattern recognition is to pay attention—really pay attention—to what you encounter in the world. Then, ask questions. Challenge yourself to see things differently than you normally would. Come up with more than one explanation for what you see, think, or experience. Next, try to link various bits of information together in unique and novel ways. This calls for a certain amount of playfulness, as well as good-natured willingness to be wrong. In the end, though, mindfully attending to the information in your environment will give you more access to the right answers, and it will permit you greater success as you plan for the future.

Developing a Personal Vision

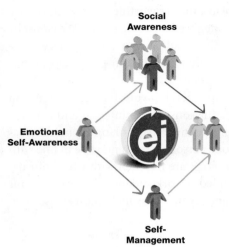

Another way to improve your planning skills is to practice on the most important plan of all: your life plan. Like a good strategic plan, a life plan starts with a personal mission (what you believe to be your purpose in life) and a vision (your aspirations for yourself as a person). We call this your "ideal self." Articulating your ideal self is the first step in intentional change, which is the process of creating a life vision, learning goals, milestones, and action steps.[112] This entire process is covered in depth in Chapter 16. For now, let's focus on the first step: creating a personal vision.

As scholars Annie McKee, Richard Boyatzis, and Frances Johnston wrote in *Becoming a Resonant Leader*, "Our dreams help to determine what we become, because a compelling and meaningful vision provides us with the optimism, strength, energy, and efficacy we need to move confidently toward the future."[113] Our dreams feed our personal vision and our image of our ideal self. Hope—a belief in a more positive, feasible future, and a sense that we can make it happen—also feeds our vision. And our core identity—our values, beliefs, and philosophy—is also a key element. As a way to begin to articulate a personal vision, reflect on the following questions and statements:

1. What is your highest purpose in life? What do you think you are meant to do and be?
   If I could accomplish only one thing in life, it would be to. . . .
   Something I would like to do before I die is. . . .
   If I could change anything in the world, it would be. . . .
2. If I had as much money as I could ever need, I would. . . .
3. In 10 years, my ideal life will include (reflect on loved ones, friends, work, lifestyle—anything that is important to you). . . .

Now, simply take the time to jot down a few themes you see in your responses to these questions. By doing this, you will begin to get a sense of your ideal self. You will also practice pattern recognition, another key tool in planning.

As you look at the themes that emerged from answering these questions, you are likely to see some of what's important in your life now and in the future. Considering your life holistically, write a few paragraphs that describe your ideal life in five years. Include key relationships, roles, work, where you live, your lifestyle and anything else that is important to you.

Most Popular » Discussion Questions

1. Why is it important for you to create a personal vision now, while you are in college? How might this help you choose a career or find an organization where you will fit in well?
2. Who in your life today can help you think about your future? What advice do you think they might give you about your personal vision?
3. To practice pattern recognition, think about your group of friends. What similarities exist among them? What are some differences? How is your "group" different from other groups on campus or at work?

10. A Final Word on Planning and Strategy

We started this chapter by considering the different ways people envision and plan for the future. As you have seen, managers and leaders have different options in terms of planning methods, and many different kinds of plans can be created and adopted by organizations. Planning is a complex and multifaceted process that any manager will tell you doesn't always work. There is much for us to learn about planning and strategy from the models and theories presented in this chapter. On the other hand, it is important to know that many plans and strategies are compromised because of inattention to certain aspects of the planning process or its implementation. Henry Mintzberg, mentioned earlier in the chapter, and other scholars have criticized strategy formulation because it often devolves to a formal planning process that creates a stepwise, primarily quantifiable process. This essentially reduces strategy to an algorithm—an impossible oversimplification in today's businesses.

In the next chapter, we will address these problems directly, by considering what is really needed to create and implement a successful plan: decision making and critical thinking—the human side of planning.

Key Terms

1. How Do People Plan for the Future? (pp. 138–140)

Key Terms

Planning The cognitive, creative, and behavioral process of developing a sequence of activities intended to achieve a goal or move toward an imagined future state. p. 138

Goal-oriented planning The process of determining the activities and steps from an existing state to a clearly defined end state. p. 139

Directional planning The process of identifying a domain (general area of activity) and direction (preferred values and activities) rather than specific goals. p. 139

Action orientation Directing one's full attention to the task at hand. p. 140

2. What Does Planning Look Like in Organizations? (pp. 141–143)

Key Terms None

3. How Do You Plan in Uncertain Times? (pp. 143–146)

Key Terms

Scenario planning A dynamic, systematic process in which people envision all of the "what if" scenarios for given situations and plan for several likely possibilities. p. 146

4. What Is a Mission? Why Does Vision Matter? (pp. 147–149)

Key Terms

Mission statement A statement that describes what an organization is, what it does, and what it stands for. p. 147

Competitive advantage Anything that positively distinguishes one organization from others. p. 147

Vision A description of what an organization wants to become—its future identity—which can be realized through the successful accomplishment of its mission. p. 147

Vision statement An articulation of a company's vision. p. 147

5. What Is Strategy? (pp. 150–156)

Key Terms

Growth strategy A corporate strategy that involves expansion of operations and/or an increase in market share. p. 152

Acquisition strategy A corporate strategy that involves joining with other businesses by buying, merging with, or taking over other companies. p. 153

Joint venture A formal arrangement between two or more entities to engage in activities together and to share risk. p. 154

Stability strategy A corporate strategy that is intended to maintain a company's current position. p. 154

Retrenchment strategy A corporate strategy that is adopted when a company needs to regroup and defend itself while turning the business around. p. 155

Divestiture strategy A corporate strategy in which a company sells off or folds a particular division, business, brand, product, or service line. p. 155

Differentiation A business strategy of providing a product or service that is perceived as unique by customers. p. 155

Core competency An activity that an organization does very well, that is readily identified by customers, and that sets the company apart from its competitors. p. 155

Cost leadership A business strategy of providing the lowest prices in the industry for a particular product, product line, or service. p. 155

Niche strategy A business strategy that caters to a narrow segment of the market. p. 155

Vertical integration A business strategy of acquiring or developing businesses along the supply chain. p. 156

Supply chain All of the resources, products, services, and operations that contribute to producing and selling goods or services. p. 156

Functional strategies Departmental strategies that are developed to help an organization achieve its goals. p. 156

6. What Needs to Be Considered in a Strategic Planning Process? (pp. 156–161)

Key Terms

Strategic planning The process of examining an organization's internal and external environments and determining major goals that will help the company realize its mission and move toward its vision. p. 156

Environmental scanning The process of assessing social and natural conditions that have the potential to affect an organization. p. 157

Industry A collective group of companies that provide the same or similar products and services. p. 159

Stakeholder Any constituent potentially impacted by an organization's actions, either inside or outside the organization. p. 160

Stakeholder analysis An audit of all stakeholders and an analysis of how each stakeholder will be affected by an organization's decisions, and/or how the stakeholder can affect the organization. p. 160

7. What Are the Steps in the Strategic Planning Process? (pp. 161–166)

Key Terms

SWOT analysis A technique that examines strengths, weaknesses, opportunities, and threats that may affect achievement of strategic mission and vision. p. 162

Strength Any positive characteristic or activity that an organization possesses that can have a positive impact on the organization. p. 162

Weakness Any negative characteristic or activity that an organization possesses that can have a negative impact on the organization. p. 163

Opportunity Any situation, condition, or event that is favorable to an organization. p. 163

Threat Any situation, condition, or event that can negatively impact an organization. p. 163

Diversified company A company that has two or more distinct divisions that produce different products or services. p. 164

BCG matrix An analysis tool used to illustrate how a business unit, product, service, brand, or product portfolio is performing in terms of market share and market growth. p. 164

Market share The percentage of the market that a product, service, or business unit has captured. p. 164

Market growth rate A measure of growth in the market for given products or services. p. 164

8. What Is HR's Role in Planning and Strategy? (pp. 166–168)

Key Terms

Recruiting The process of attracting qualified candidates for jobs. p. 166

HR inventory An internal system that maintains information about people within an organization, including skills, training needs, career plans, and other information about employees. p. 166

Selection The act of choosing whom to hire from among a group of qualified applicants. p. 167

Succession plan A plan for filling management positions in the event those positions are vacated. p. 167

Layoff A termination with the possibility of rehire once conditions improve. p. 168

For-cause termination The dismissal of an employee for breaking a company policy, failing to perform, or failing to adjust to company values, norms, or culture. p. 168

9. What Can We All Do to Support Effective Strategic Planning? (pp. 169–170)

Key Terms None

10. A Final Word on Planning and Strategy (p. 171)

Key Terms None

Chapter 5 Visual Summary

1. How Do People Plan for the Future? (pp. 138–140)

Summary: People plan for the future in different ways; some are goal focused, others are driven by direction and vision, and still others are action oriented. A good plan reflects these different preferences by incorporating an organization's vision, strategy, goals, and actions into a cohesive whole.

2. What Does Planning Look Like in Organizations? (pp. 141–143)

Summary: When engaging in organizational planning, leaders must not focus solely on goals and metrics; rather, they must seek to link the organization's mission and purpose with particular goals and activities. Often, this means crafting multiple types of plans—such as short-term, long-term, single-use, standing, operational, strategic, financial, contingency, and project plans—all of which must be coordinated with one another.

8. Workplace Essentials: Creativity, Innovation, and a Spirit of Entrepreneurship

7. Change: A Focus on Adaptability and Resiliency

9. Organizing for a Complex World: Structure and Design

Planning and Change

6. The Human Side of Planning: Decision Making and Critical Thinking

5. Planning and Strategy: Bringing the Vision to Life

STRATEGIC PLANNING

3. How Do You Plan in Uncertain Times? (pp. 143–146)

Summary: A good plan is flexible so that it can be adapted to changing environments and conditions. To ensure adaptability, it's helpful to employ a modular approach to planning—after all, it's easier to change individual goals, subgoals, milestones, and action steps than to adjust an entire plan. It's also a good idea to envision various "what if" scenarios for given situations and prepare for several likely possibilities.

4. What Is a Mission? Why Does Vision Matter? (pp. 147–149)

Summary: When crafting a plan, leaders and managers must carefully consider their organization's mission and vision. A clear mission articulates an organization's purpose and competitive advantage. It also unifies employees. Similarly, a good vision inspires people both within and beyond the organization to strive for a better tomorrow. Together, a strong mission and vision can help a company make better choices—but they cannot do so unless they are clearly communicated to all members of the organization.

5. What Is Strategy? (pp. 150–156)

Summary: A strategy helps an organization realize its mission and bring its vision to life. All strategies are complex, and they exist in a variety of forms. The three primary categories of strategies are corporate strategies, which are designed for an entire organization; business strategies, which are designed for particular divisions or lines of business; and functional strategies, which guide how different support services within an organization can help the entire organization achieve its goals.

10. A Final Word on Planning and Strategy (p. 171)

Summary: Although the models and theories presented in this chapter can greatly assist leaders, managers, and others in crafting effective plans, it's important to remember that strategy formulation is ultimately a human process.

9. What Can We All Do to Support Effective Strategic Planning? (pp. 169–170)

Summary: To support effective strategic planning, you can develop your capacity for pattern recognition. Pattern recognition is a complex and extremely important competency that allows us to make sense of information today and plan for tomorrow. In addition, you can strive to develop a personal vision that will support you in planning for the future you desire.

8. What Is HR's Role in Planning and Strategy? (pp. 166–168)

Summary: Human resource professionals have several responsibilities when it comes to planning and strategy formulation. Beyond participating in the planning process directly, these individuals are also charged with recruiting appropriate job candidates; selecting those candidates that will best support the organization's vision, mission, and goals; creating succession plans so people can advance and positions can be filled; and managing periods of workforce growth and reduction.

7. What Are the Steps in the Strategic Planning Process? (pp. 161–166)

Summary: Strategic planning consists of a series of steps. First, the organization must evaluate its mission, vision, goals, and existing strategies. After that, all internal and external factors that might affect the organization's ability to achieve its objectives should be analyzed. Following analysis, the organization can craft specific strategies and put them into place. Finally, the organization must evaluate the strategies it has chosen to determine whether they have been effective.

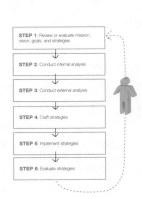

6. What Needs to Be Considered in a Strategic Planning Process? (pp. 156–161)

Summary: Strategic planning is a complex and multilayered process. Before beginning this process, it's important to examine the various forces at work in an organization's economic, sociocultural, legal, political, technological, natural, and industry environments. In addition, the needs and expectations of the organization's stakeholders must be taken into consideration.

The Human Side of Planning:

Decision Making and
Critical Thinking

Chapter Outline

Find out what you already know about the concepts in this chapter by going to www.mymanagementlab.com and taking the **Pre-Test**. Your results will generate a customized study plan for Chapter 6.

1. What Is Decision Making? (pp. 178–181)

2. How Do Cognitive and Emotional Processes Affect Decision Making? (pp. 181–187)

3. How Can You Apply a Systematic Approach to Making Decisions? (pp. 187–193)

4. How Can People Make Good Decisions with Incomplete Information? (pp. 194–196)

5. How Can You Improve Your Critical Thinking Skills and Make Better Decisions? (pp. 197–201)

6. What Can HR Do to Support Good Decision Making and Critical Thinking? (pp. 201–203)

7. What Can We All Do to Improve Critical Thinking and Decision Making? (pp. 203–205)

8. A Final Word on Decision Making and Critical Thinking (p. 205)

Go back to www.mymanagementlab.com and take the **Post-Test** to verify your understanding of the concepts. **To experience and apply** the concepts, explore the additional material associated with Chapter 6.

Part 1: Leading and Managing for Today and the Future (Chapters 1, 2, 3, 4)
Part 2: Planning and Change (Chapters 5, **6**, 7, 8, 9)
Part 3: Organizing Human Systems (Chapters 10, 11)
Part 4: Controlling Quality, Culture, and Yourself (Chapters 12, 13)
Part 5: Leading and Managing for the Future (Chapters 14, 15, 16)

8. Workplace Essentials: Creativity, Innovation, and a Spirit of Entrepreneurship

7. Change: A Focus on Adaptability and Resiliency

9. Organizing for a Complex World: Structure and Design

Planning and Change

6. The Human Side of Planning: Decision Making and Critical Thinking

5. Planning and Strategy: Bringing the Vision to Life

16. Managing and Leading for Tomorrow: A Focus on Your Future

14. Globalization: Managing Effectively in a Global Economic Environment

Organizing Human Systems

10. Teams and Teambuilding: How to Work Effectively with Others

11. Working in a Virtual World: Technology as a Way of Life

1. Managing and Leading Today: The New Rules

Leading and Managing for Today and the Future

2. The Leadership Imperative: It's Up to You

4. Communication: The Key to Resonant Relationships

3. Motivation and Meaning: What Makes People Want to Work?

15. Sustainability and Corporate Social Responsibility: Ensuring the Future

6. The Human Side of Planning: Decison Making and Critical Thinking

12. Organizational Controls: People, Processes, Quality, and Results

Controlling Quality, Culture, and Yourself

13. Culture: It's Powerful

1. What Is Decision Making?

Plans are only as good as the decisions that go into them. Even the most detailed, precise plan will not be helpful if the people who created the plan failed to analyze issues, check and double-check their assumptions, and avoid common errors, such as ignoring information that does not fit with their beliefs. To help you avoid these pitfalls, this chapter addresses the human side of planning: decision making and critical thinking. Both processes are essential to effective management and leadership—and both involve a variety of factors, including emotion, intuition, logic, and perception. Indeed, these factors affect not just your decisions in the workplace, but also your decisions in *all* aspects of life.

It is difficult to engage in effective decision making and critical thinking without understanding what each process entails. Developing such an understanding is the purpose of this chapter. We begin with a brief definition of decision making, along with a look at different categories of decisions. We also discuss the role of logic, emotion, and intuition and explore ways in which perception and bias can either help or hinder the decision-making process. In the next section, we turn to a common model that will help guide you in making important decisions. We also share research about how to make decisions when information is incomplete (which is common). Next, we shift our focus to critical thinking, examining what it involves and how you can improve your skills in order to make better decisions. You'll also learn about several common errors that impede decision making. Finally, the chapter concludes with an examination of what HR can do to support managers and leaders in effective decision making and critical thinking, as well as what we can all do to develop our capabilities in these areas.

Decision Making Defined

Decision making
A cognitive, emotional, and neuropsychological process involving thoughts, feelings, and neurological functioning that results in making a judgment or choosing from alternatives.

Decision making is a cognitive, emotional, and neuropsychological process involving thoughts, feelings, and neurological functioning that results in making a judgment or choosing from alternatives. Making decisions includes the following tasks:

- Collecting information related to a dilemma, problem, or opportunity
- Reacting to and considering this information
- Incorporating emotional responses to possible choices with information about those choices
- Evaluating alternatives using logic, reasoning, emotion, or intuition
- Reacting and responding to risk and uncertainty
- Making a judgment or choosing a course of action

This definition may be broader than those you have encountered in the past, because decision making is often taught as a purely rational process involving *only* cognitive assessment of problems, rational consideration of alternatives, analysis of costs and benefits, and selection of a course of action. Decision making does, of course, involve complex cognitive processing, logic, and reasoning. We now know, however, that decision making is *not* a purely cognitive process. It also involves neurological activity that can cause us to pay attention to certain information and ignore other data while making choices.[1] Decision making involves becoming aware of and using intuition and varied emotional responses to information and choices.[2]

Types of Decisions

Every single day, you make decisions about things you barely even think about, such as whether to brush your teeth, what to have for breakfast, or what to wear. At work, you don't think much about where to sit, how to turn your computer on, or whether to say hello to your manager. These and many other daily decisions are quick and easy, so we may not think about them for more than a moment or two.

At other times, we agonize over which direction to choose, which alternative to select, or which solution to try. Think about some of the major decisions you have made in life. When you were young, you might have been faced with the decision about which sport to pursue, what instrument to play, or which kids to be friends with. Later, you may have had to choose whether to take a part-time job during the school year or in the summer, weighing financial need and a desire for experience against how the job might compromise your grades or interfere with your social life. Other important decisions such as whom to date, what career to pursue, and where to live can also be very difficult to make. These types of decisions require you to think about what you are doing and what you want now, *and* they also require you to consider your future. You'll need to consider the kind of life you want, the kind of people you want to surround yourself with, your financial needs or desires, and the kind of work you want to do for the next several years or perhaps your whole life!

Just as in life, decisions at work can be easy and automatic, or they can be complicated and difficult. For example, a manager can quickly decide whether to bring bagels or donuts to an early morning meeting. This is a fairly straightforward, routine decision. In contrast, a manager who is deciding whether to open a new manufacturing plant has a much more complicated challenge. This decision is unique, has far-reaching consequences, and involves any number of facts and opinions (not to mention people).

Decisions can be classified depending on how often and how easily they are made. Decisions that are routine in nature and occur with some frequency are known as **programmed decisions** (■Exhibit 6.1). For instance, the selection of a classroom for this course was most likely a programmed decision, because within the college environment, this type of choice occurs with regularity and is based on known factors such as instructor preference, number of students enrolled, and the number or types of available classrooms. Within a business setting, programmed decisions could include such things as ordering office supplies, choosing where to hold weekly staff meetings, scheduling employee vacations, or determining whether customer returns will be accepted without a receipt. When things are working well within an organization, programmed decisions such as these are easy, seamless, and cost effective.[3] Thus, many organizations dedicate a great deal of attention to making decisions as routine—or programmed—as possible.

Programmed decisions
Decisions that are routine in nature and occur with some frequency.

■Exhibit **6.1**
Buying a soda is a programmed decision, whereas buying a house is a nonprogrammed decision.

Bill Lyons/Alamy Images

iStockphoto.com

Nonprogrammed decisions
Decisions that are not routine and/or involve unique information or circumstances.

In contrast, decisions that are not routine are called **nonprogrammed decisions** because they are novel and involve unique information or circumstances. Two examples of nonprogrammed decisions that you have likely faced are choosing which college to attend and which major to select.

Like individuals, business organizations also face a potentially vast array of nonprogrammed decisions. In fact, some choices are encountered only once in an organization's history—whether to declare bankruptcy or to sell shares on a publicly traded market, for instance. Additional examples of nonprogrammed and strategic organizational decisions include the following:

- Choosing to expand the business geographically
- Choosing to invest in a new product line
- Choosing to eliminate or dramatically reduce an entire class of jobs, such as administrative support
- Choosing to institute a wage freeze
- Choosing to change the company's logo or Web site
- Choosing to relocate the company's headquarters

These are nonprogrammed strategic decisions that will likely be made by senior managers. Managers, however, are not the only ones who have to make tough decisions. For instance, what do you do if a more senior employee wants to go out on a date with you? He or she is not your manager, and you'd really like to go, but this person leads some of your project teams. Or what do you do if you feel someone in your work group is behaving in an unethical manner, such as by spending three to four hours a day at work surfing the Internet? Or what if someone is selling goods that "fell off of the truck" (i.e., have been taken from the loading dock)? Or at school, what if someone in class obtains a copy of a midterm before the exam? The answers may seem pretty obvious on the surface. In actuality, however, they involve making very difficult decisions. For instance, you might think: "Will I get in trouble if I go out on this date?" "What if my manager doesn't believe me about what people are doing?" "What if the person I report does not get fired and is still working in the next cubicle after I say something to my manager or human resources?" "What if I am not really sure that he or she is actually doing these things?" These kinds of questions can lead to a hard time making decisions and often cause emotional turmoil.

Nonprogrammed decisions like these occur infrequently, take more time to evaluate, often involve numerous people and stakeholders, and have significant implications in terms of personnel, time, and money. When a business is facing significant changes in the market, when technology changes, or when a growth strategy is chosen, leaders will be faced with numerous nonprogrammed decisions, as illustrated by the case of Annabel, a new manager at a design and manufacturing company.

Julie Lessiter

Student's Choice

Tackling the
Big Issues at Antares

Annabel was the vice president of sales at Antares, a British design and manufacturing company owned and run by her father for 25 years until he retired in 2005. Antares designed "gadgets and gidgets" (common-sense, practical, simple design improvements for the household that made life easier). Annabel's father was a su-

perb design engineer, and shortly after he began the company, he hired her to help him grow his firm.

Annabel had recently graduated from college with a business degree, and although she did not have much real-world experience, she was extremely intelligent and personable. On her first day of work at Antares, Annabel decided to make sure that she got to know everyone so they would have a chance to see what kind of manager she hoped to be—focused on business *and* on developing relationships with people. Annabel personally met everyone on that first day, and she organized a

Continued **on next page>>**

reception so all of the company's employees could get together to socialize.

As you might imagine, not everyone was happy when the boss's daughter was hired right out of school to help run the company. When they realized, however, that Annabel simply wanted what was best for the company and its employees and that she was mindful of others' opinions when making decisions, people started coming around.

Annabel also decided that she needed to collect quite a bit of information about how things were done at Antares *before* making big decisions. Therefore, she spent her first six months with the company reviewing operations and asking each employee for suggestions, comments, and ideas about how to increase sales. Annabel learned of several serious issues, including errors in some accounting processes and high employee turnover. She also discovered that several employees had great ideas for solving these and other problems.

Annabel wanted everyone at Antares to feel that they had a say in the operation of the business, regardless of their position. She saw people as a key source of information—their knowledge and ideas were critical to the changes that she would need to implement in order for the business to grow and mature. This stance served Annabel well. One of the ways that Annabel and her team shifted people's attitudes and improved knowledge sharing was to hold an open forum with all Antares employees each month to talk about the company's progress and collectively address issues. When employees had opportunities to get to know each other, information and creativity flowed and great decisions were the result. Annabel also encouraged staff members to create a company-sponsored softball league (in which she played), as well as a group that got together to have meals at various restaurants around town.

This combination of updated business practices and social activities yielded positive results for Antares. Relationships quickly became more cohesive and collaborative. Also, the right information was getting to the right people efficiently, so managers could make informed decisions and implement them faster and more effectively than ever before. Sales of the company's products increased 10 percent during Annabel's first six months. After that, they increased steadily an additional 10 percent each year. Many employees' attitudes improve after Annabel arrived, and both absenteeism and turnover dropped. Annabel had built a sound and trusting relationship with her employees. Furthermore, she had made Antares a place where people wanted to be and where all employees were genuinely concerned about the success of the business.

Source: Adapted from a case written by Julie Lessiter.

Annabel faced a significant number of nonprogrammed decisions during her first year at Antares and, luckily, she recognized them as such. She took the decisions seriously, considering facts and feelings. She took her time evaluating situations, rather than jumping to the wrong conclusions. Part of the reason that Annabel was successful was that she recognized how complicated decision making can be.

Throughout this chapter, we will be discussing some of the reasons that decision making can be complicated and difficult. We will also be sharing research, models, and tips that can help you make better decisions. To begin this process, in the next section we will look at several important inputs to the decision-making process.

Most Popular » Discussion Questions

1. Why, in your opinion, does decision making include thoughts *and* feelings?
2. Consider a decision you have made in life. What were your thoughts and feelings about the situation and your choices?
3. Identify three nonprogrammed decisions that you need to make this year. Describe what is unique about each of these decisions. What information will you need in order to make these choices?

2. How Do Cognitive and Emotional Processes Affect Decision Making?

Many people believe that decision making is a purely rational process, and that if we analyze a situation deeply enough, a perfect decision will emerge. Making decisions includes reason and logic, of course, but it also includes *how* we apply reason and logic. For instance, people process information differently, so it is important to understand certain aspects of cognitive processing. Because emotion is a part of the decision-making process, we also need to understand how our feelings affect our thoughts about the problems we are trying to solve, the information we gather, and the choices we identify. Intuition also has an important impact on many decisions, so we need to understand what it is—and what it is not.

Reason and Logic in Decision Making

Organizational scholar James March and his coauthor Chip Heath note that the most common way of describing the process of decision making as a rational choice and that, in popular usage, the term *rational* is used synonymously with *intelligent* or *successful*.[4] Rational decision making follows the logic of consequences: If I do X, then Y will happen as a result. Rational decision making is the foundation of decisions in realms such as computer programming and mathematics.[5] A computer follows an algorithm of pure logic, which means that given the same set of inputs, the output will be identical each time. In other words, it is *deterministic*, which means that outcomes are determined by inputs.

Most decisions are more complicated than that because we make choices that seem like they will lead to a certain outcome based on weighing preferences, expectations, and alternatives.[6] Reasoning is a "psycho-logic" process in which we seek out evidence, beliefs, and consequences to support different alternatives when faced with a decision.[7] This means that pure, or formal, logic is rarely a part of human decision making.

Cognitive Processing: Perceptions Impact How We Understand Information

People's decision-making abilities often differ based on how well they understand and manage their own thought processes. In this section, we will explore several aspects of cognitive processing that can either help—or greatly harm—our decision-making abilities.

Schemas: The Brain's Filing System for Information

To understand how we process and interpret information, it helps to understand what cognitive psychologists refer to as *schemas*. Schemas are conceptual maps in our minds that allow us to understand and mentally categorize information as we receive it.[8] To simplify this with a metaphor, think about a massive filing system that we have created over our entire lives that is filled with our experiences. The system has billions of files, each carefully labeled with an idea, an experience, or an emotion. Most of the files are very complex and include numerous subfolders. For example, you might have a file for "Management Course." Within that file will be everything you have ever heard about, experienced, thought, or felt about this course.

When new information comes to us, the first thing we try to do cognitively is to file the information. If we have a file into which the new information can easily fit, we store it there. If we don't, we either try to force the information to fit into our filing system or we create a new file. To illustrate this, consider Lucas Johnston-Peck, a very bright 7-year-old boy. When Lucas was younger, his parents read stories to him every evening. One of the stories was about animals, and Lucas began to link the pictures in the book with words. He learned that a small furry animal with pointy ears and whiskers that said "meow" was a cat. He learned that a larger animal that said "woof" was a dog, and that an even larger brown animal with round ears that said "grrr" was a bear. Lucas was developing schemas—new files—that enabled him to quickly file information about certain animals.

During the period of time when Lucas was learning about animals, his aunt visited—with a *dog* named *Bear*. At first, Lucas insisted that this was impossible and refused to call the dog by name. Very quickly, however, Lucas adjusted his filing system to include the concept that dogs could be named Bear. Lucas didn't know it, but he was engaging in a sophisticated cognitive process called accommodation: Lucas was adapting his existing filing system to include new information. This is one sign of an intelligent human being.

The term *accommodation* was initially proposed by famous developmental psychologist Jean Piaget to describe one way of approaching new information. **Accommodation** is the process of adapting one's cognitive categorization system to allow for new information, new schemas, and new ways of understanding information.[9]

According to Piaget, another way to deal with new information is through assimilation. Had Lucas tried to force the new information into his filing system by giving the dog a new name, for example, he would have been engaging in assimilation. **Assimilation** is the process of integrating or forcing new information to fit existing cognitive categorization systems.[10] When we assimilate new information, we force it to fit the schemas we have in place. This is when cognitive schemas get us into trouble: If we are forcing information to fit what we believe to be true, we are not seeing information clearly and we will likely make poor decisions as a result.

To illustrate how assimilation happens at work, consider two brothers in a family business. As a child and during high school and college, the older brother, Greg, saw himself as the serious, scholarly one. His younger brother Marty was involved in lots of activities, had a busy social life, and was considered by many to be the "life of the party." When Greg later hired Marty to make his parents happy, he refused to give Marty any serious responsibilities. Greg continued to shoulder the burden of the business without sharing it with Marty, because he did not believe that his brother *could* actually contribute. Marty—who was actually a very good manager, well liked by employees, and adept at motivating people—became fed up after a few years of this and left the family business to start a competitor, thereby creating a schism in the family.

The problem in this situation wasn't Marty; it was Greg's inability to change the way he *saw* Marty. Greg could not change his habitual way of judging his brother. He literally could not understand that Marty was actually more competent than he gave him credit for. Underlying this example are common problems related to cognitive processing that often get in the way of good decision making at work: stereotypes and the halo effect.

Stereotypes

Stereotypes are oversimplified ideas or beliefs that are particularly rigid and difficult to change. They often apply to people and are often destructive. When applied to people, stereotypes are simplified schemas that attribute a common set of characteristics to all members of a particular group.

Stereotypes reduce people's cognitive processing load because they are automatic and do not require conscious effort.[11] Many stereotypes are harmful and cause us to misjudge people and situations. Other stereotypes are used on a daily basis to facilitate positive social interactions. For example, when we talk to the pharmacist at the local drug store, we have certain stereotypes about the profession and the kind of information he can share with us. Pharmacists, in turn, have certain stereotypes about customers, such as that they may be ill or worried about a family member.

Social stereotypes can facilitate easy decisions about how to behave if they are based on accurate assumptions. However, when stereotypes about a person or group are based on incorrect or derogatory assumptions, they can be extremely destructive. Stereotypes linked to racial, gender, political, religious, sexual preference, and other identities often lead to discrimination and form the basis for denying rights, liberties, or resources to certain groups of people.

We often assume that damaging stereotypes are no longer present in the workplace. Unfortunately, this is not the case. For instance, a female executive recently flew into Cleveland on business, and her company arranged for a driver to pick her up at the airport. Upon

---

Accommodation
The process of adapting one's cognitive categorization system to allow for new information, new schemas, and new ways of understanding information.

Assimilation
The process of integrating or forcing new information to fit existing cognitive categorization systems.

arrival, the executive saw the driver waiting, holding a sign with her name—Dr. Auld—written on it. When she introduced herself, he looked at her blankly and said, "Oh, I was expecting a man. They told me it was *Doctor* Auld." When the executive expressed surprise and jokingly said something about the stereotype, the man said, "It's not a stereotype; it's common sense." This particular situation is a perfect example of a rigid stereotype that resulted in the driver making two very bad decisions: looking for a man (hence, missing his customer) and expressing discriminatory views (only men can be doctors).

One long-lasting consequence of this man's prejudice was that the car company lost a customer, illustrating how applying stereotypes can result in serious problems. When stereotypes are used, relationships are harmed. Often the effects are far more extensive: People are misjudged, overlooked, or treated unfairly; customers are lost; contract negotiations break down; or groups are pitted against one another.

Although the egregious use of stereotypes in the previous example was easy to recognize, sometimes the use of stereotypes is more subtle. For instance, a manager who is originally from New York may believe that people from her home state are more cosmopolitan than employees from other states and are better suited for travel assignments. She may also believe that graduates from her alma mater are better educated than graduates of other colleges and therefore a better fit for certain assignments. This might look like simple favoritism, but it is actually poor decision making based on stereotypes.

Here's the dilemma: Whether obvious or subtle, everyone has stereotypes. Clearly, stereotypes that are harmful to individual members of groups are simply destructive and, as responsible leaders, we cannot tolerate them in ourselves or in others. Nor can we allow them to influence the decisions we make. Other stereotypes are more reasonable and perhaps worth using, such as our assumptions about the pharmacist–customer interaction. However, even these need to be constantly scrutinized: Do the underlying assumptions still apply? Do they apply in *this* situation? Should I let go of preconceived notions and view this situation as new and different? In all cases, we must continually examine our own stereotypes in order to improve the way we make decisions.

The Halo Effect

Halo effect

The phenomenon in which we judge something or someone positively based on a previous positive experience or association with someone or something we admire.

The halo effect is somewhat like a stereotype in that it is a cognitive bias that people use to process information more quickly. The **halo effect** occurs when we judge something or someone positively based on a previous positive experience or association with someone or something we admire.[12] Every astute student has learned this lesson: If you are enthusiastic and engaged in the first few classes, do extremely well on the first test or paper in a course, and seek out the instructor for a chat about the subject matter, that professor just might go easy on you for the rest of the semester. In this example, the halo effect may be interfering with the professor's objectivity and possibly even decisions about grades. This happens at work, too, and can result in favoritism.

According to personality theory, judgments regarding an individual's first-noticed trait or behavior can have a cascading effect on subsequent interpretations of other personality traits.[13] One characteristic in particular seems to draw forth the halo effect: attractiveness. That's one reason why people pay so much attention to how they look, and it's also why the halo effect is the bread and butter of marketing. For instance, in brand marketing, a halo effect can be noticed when positive perceptions of one product extend to positive perceptions of other unrelated products because of a marketing campaign that ties them together. Celebrity spokespersons are used in marketing precisely because the positive feelings people have for the celebrities are projected onto the things these celebrities endorse.

Similarly, a negative halo effect, or "devil effect," can be seen when a negative judgment is made based on first-noticed characteristics or an association with someone or something that we do not like. For example, the student who cracks jokes and seems to be ignoring the professor may, unfortunately, be graded more harshly than his seatmate, who is quiet and looks studious. It is the same at work—the employee who misses

■Exhibit **6.2**

How do you think scandals affect celebrity endorsements of products?

a deadline soon after starting a job may be judged more negatively and harshly by unthinking managers long after the incident is over. Or, returning to marketing campaigns, we often see "guilt by association"—when a celebrity suddenly falls out of the public graces and the products he or she endorses become less popular (■Exhibit 6.2).

Cognitive processing, stereotypes, and the halo effect are powerful because they operate at a subconscious level. Some researchers have demonstrated that even when confronted with evidence that our judgments are biased, we may still be completely unable to identify how our thoughts are affecting our behavior and our decisions.[14] To make the best decision possible, therefore, we need to become more aware of some of our habitual thought processes and learn to examine them. That's true with emotions, too.

Emotions: A Legitimate and Important Part of Decision Making

Emotions have a profound effect on decision making, yet common decision-making processes have largely ignored this fact. How do we know emotions have an effect on decision making? For one thing, patients who have experienced damage to sections of the brain that process emotions but no damage to their cognitive centers (the "thinking brain") have tremendous difficulty making even the simplest decisions in life.[15] Second, neuroscientists now recognize that powerful emotions like fear, love, and anger are processed through centers in the brain that can trigger what is called the sympathetic nervous system. This is a part of our nervous system that activates things like heart rate, blood pressure, and large muscle contraction and also tells us what to focus on and what to screen out.[16] This is likely a survival mechanism that helps us realize when we are in danger (fight-or-flight situations) or when we might be able to connect with others (comfort, nurture, make friends, or mate). Our emotions, then, affect what we take in, what we ignore, and our perceptions of people and situations. Clearly this will affect decision making.[17]

Many times, emotions are extremely helpful because they point us in the right direction when making choices. At other times, however, they can get us into trouble. If, for example, our emotions simply "flood" our brains, we can often be completely unaware of anything else. Here is a common example: You've fallen in love. Your new partner is (in your view) the most perfect human being on the planet. You want to spend every minute of every day with him or her. Nothing else is important—not school, not work, not friends or family. You make some questionable decisions in these areas, while also totally ignoring those little signs that he or she isn't perfect—that short temper, or chronic lateness, or texting constantly while with you. A few months down the path, when the flood of emotions recedes, where might you be?

Another way that emotions affect decision making is related to whether a problem, situation, or choice is framed in a negative or positive way. When a choice is framed in negative terms, people may steer away from it. One famous example involves a decision that was framed in two different ways, but where the choices involved resulted in two identical outcomes. In the simulated situations, the research subjects were leaders faced with a disease outbreak. Two scenarios were proposed: One choice was presented in terms of how many people would live, the other in terms of how many people would die. Even though it was easy to see that either outcome would result in 200 people living and 400 people dying, subjects consistently chose the option that focused on how many would live. The researchers believed this happened because the research subjects experienced more positive emotions when thinking about people surviving.[18]

Finally, emotions are tied to our belief systems, and they have a great deal to do with preferences. Emotions guide us as we sift through the vast amount of information we face on a daily basis.[19] Emotions inform our preferences in making choices. Without emotions, we would just be automatons with no free will.

Intuition in Decision Making

The power of intuitive understanding will protect you from harm until the end of your days.

—Lao Tzu, ancient Chinese philosopher[20]

The only real valuable thing is intuition.

There is no logical way to the discovery of these elemental laws. There is only the way of intuition, which is helped by a feeling for the order lying behind the appearance.

—Albert Einstein, genius known for developing the theory of relativity[21]

Definitions of intuition abound. Some people view intuition as a sort of mystical knowledge. Others talk about intuition as if it were instinct—something encoded in our DNA like a spider's innate ability to spin a web or a baby's natural development of language skills. It is also something often attributed to women rather than men, as suggested by the common phrase "woman's intuition."

It's true that intuitive knowledge is not borne purely of rational thought. But if intuition does not come from logic, is it also "illogical"? Does intuition lack sense and reason, or does it simply lack direct access to sense and conscious reason?

Intuition

Tacit knowledge, or knowledge that we have access to at an unconscious level.

Intuition is not biologically encoded in DNA—it is not instinctive knowledge. **Intuition** is tacit knowledge: knowledge that we have access to at an unconscious level. Intuition is knowing something without any evidence that this understanding comes as a result of rational thought processes. This can be described as a form of memory that links past experiences and emotions with complex processing of a current situation.[22] For example, when we speak or listen to our native language, we have intuitive knowledge of how to form sentences, link verbs and nouns, use pronouns, and manipulate words in countless ways. Intuition also plays a role in the big decisions in life: who to date or marry, which job to take, even which car to buy. How do we know when intuition is at play?

For one thing, many people experience intuition as a "gut feeling." You may have had these kinds of feelings when deciding to go somewhere, do something, or try something new. For some reason, you just knew what the right decision was. If someone asked you to explain it, you couldn't. That is another clue: If you can't explain your thoughts or feelings about a decision you want to make, it could be that you are drawing on unconscious experiences and emotions and applying them to the situation at hand. Another way we can determine whether a decision is intuitively based is to consider whether it is accompanied by memories of past experiences and emotions.[23]

Herbert Simon studied the role of intuition in expert chess players' decision making. Chess is rightly perceived to be an intensely cerebral game of strategy that relies heavily on logic and intellect (■Exhibit 6.3). However, top chess experts intuitively single out the move they will make from hundreds of potential moves within the first few seconds. Even when they take a long time to make a move, most of that time is spent examining the chosen move for potential weaknesses or flaws.

Expert's knowledge, Simon argues, comes from an experientially based skill of seeing information holistically, rather than in bits. Each pattern is linked to similar patterns stored in memory and is accessible at an unconscious level. Simon suggests that the intuitive processing of expert knowledge is the same for all people, whether they are chessmasters, physicians, or managers.[24]

People process information and make decisions both intuitively *and* rationally, often engaging in below-the-surface and deliberate processes at the same time.[25] Intuition is tacit—an unconscious experiential system of processing that is automatic. The tacit system operates at a subconscious level of cognition, and its work is filtering out information that is not relevant and organizing what is left into packaged, holistic patterns. Conscious analysis is a deliberate process that we are aware of and can control. Many researchers agree that the type of activity a person is engaged in has a

Chess players rely on their logic and intuition.

Yadid Levy/Alamy Images

strong influence on whether tacit (intuitive), explicit (analytical), or both cognitive systems are used when making decisions.[26]

Taking intuition into the realm of leadership, scholars Daniel Goleman and Richard Boyatzis note that intuition is a powerful tool that leaders can learn to use to make decisions. Their research indicates that intuition can be found in the brain—in particular, the cells that regulate emotion are wired to other cells that notice patterns and make judgments. They conclude that leaders should not fear acting on intuition, provided they are correctly attuned to other people and the situation.[27]

You now have a deeper understanding of the many processes that affect decision making: logic, cognitive processing, bias, emotion, and intuition. Let's look at a model that can help you organize all of this as you take steps toward making a decision.

Most Popular » Discussion Questions

1. Think about an experience you have had that challenged the way you think (your schema, or cognitive filing system). What was the situation? How did you react emotionally? What logical process did you employ to explain the new information?

2. In this section, we noted that taking in new information can require accommodation—that is, adapting your cognitive filing system to include new ways of understanding people and situations. Have you ever consciously done this? What was the situation? Was this easy or hard for you? How did accommodation help you?

3. How does emotion impact you when making important decisions? Are there certain kinds of decisions that trigger your emotions more than others? Why is this so?

4. Do you pay attention to your intuition? Why or why not?

---

3. How Can You Apply a Systematic Approach to Making Decisions?

Decision-making process
The steps taken when choosing a course of action.

When we talk about a **decision-making process** in this section, we are referring to the steps taken when choosing a course of action. The type of decision-making process selected depends on the nature of the problem, the availability of information, and the alternatives being considered. In addition, an individual's values play a role in the type of decision-making process that is ultimately chosen. How complex the decision is, how many people need to be involved, and the extent of the consequences are also factors that need to be considered when selecting or creating a decision-making process.

Some problems and decisions are simple, and the consequences of a bad choice are not serious. These decisions are straightforward and present themselves along with sufficient information. In comparison, complex decisions tend to necessitate a structured and elaborate decision-making process. This is the case for a number of reasons. For one, identifying a problem (i.e., what needs to be decided) can be challenging and confusing. In the earlier case study, for instance, Annabel noticed that turnover was quite high and recognized that she needed to determine the reason(s) for this situation. Were people leaving because the pay was too low or because working conditions were poor? Were there lots of good jobs in the area, and people simply had better opportunities? Or were employees leaving Antares because they felt disempowered and demoralized? Several different issues might have caused people to leave their jobs, each of which would have led to a different decision about how to resolve the issue.

Another complicating factor in complex decisions is that the decision maker frequently lacks all of the information he or she requires. For instance, several alternative choices may exist, and you may not be able to predict the outcome of these choices perfectly. Take the example of choosing a major in college. You can't know everything—or even very much—about how a particular course of study will affect your career or your life. Emotions play a part in a decision like this, as do intuition and your habitual way of processing information. Plus, you have so many available alternatives! Still, you must make a decision—but how? This is when it helps to have a model or a structured process to follow to better organize your thoughts and feelings about a decision, the information you collect, and the number of possible choices.

A common decision-making model has emerged from research about how customers choose what products to buy.[28] This model is outlined in ■Exhibit 6.4. As you can see, it consists of eight sequential steps for rationally identifying a problem and then choosing and implementing a specific alternative. The following sections take a closer look at each of the distinct steps in this process.

■Exhibit **6.4**

Eight-Step Decision-Making Model

Step 1: Identify the problem.

Step 2: Establish the decision criteria.

Step 3: Allocate weights to decision criteria.

Step 4: List alternatives.

Step 5: Analyze alternatives.

Step 6: Choose an alternative.

Step 7: Implement the decision.

Step 8: Evaluate the decision.

Step 1: Identify the Problem

In the first step of the eight-step decision-making process, the problem must be properly identified.[29] In a decision-making scenario, a problem exists whenever a desired state is not in line with the actual state. For example, say that in a department store, the desired state is for sales to increase by 6 percent this quarter, but so far, sales have declined by 10 percent. What is the problem here? Obviously, the problem is that sales are dropping. But why? One possible contributing factor is that the department store has a high rate of absenteeism. At any given time, at least one out of every ten employees is home sick. When so many people are out, other employees have to work harder and longer to meet the store's objectives. If this is determined to be the primary problem causing low sales, managers might decide to hire new employees, or they might entice people to work longer hours by paying overtime or bonuses.

However, the absenteeism could also be a symptom of a larger problem. The real problem might be that the store's supervisors are ineffective and difficult to get along with. They are not motivating employees. In fact, supervisors are causing employees to experience a great deal of stress—hence, the higher rate of absenteeism and the drop in sales. If the store's managers correctly identify the supervisors' leadership abilities as the root problem, they will realize that simply hiring new employees isn't the right decision. Instead, the managers might decide to provide the supervisors with opportunities to develop their leadership competencies.

As you can see, correctly identifying the problem is critical to effective decision making. Too often in organizations (and in life, for that matter), people derail the decision-making process in its very first step by incorrectly identifying the central problem. For that reason, it is important to take the process slowly and to carefully consider what, exactly, serves as the source of more obvious problems.

Let's look at another issue related to problem identification that you can probably relate to. During the first or second year of college, most students are required to select a major. This can be a difficult decision, often because a student has many interests or because he or she isn't sure which career to pursue. However, the real problem may be even deeper.

Take the example of Jason (■Exhibit 6.5). Jason is under pressure from his parents to pursue a degree in accounting, but he is not sure that he wants to be an accountant. Regardless of how thoroughly he weighs his alternatives and imagines his career, he still can't make a decision. That's because Jason is actually faced with a bigger problem than simply choosing a major—in effect, he is deciding whether to follow his desires or to pursue his parents' plan. This situation is very emotional for Jason, but he knows he must gather the courage to decide for himself. Jason will have to talk honestly with his parents about what he wants, and what they want as well.

Step 2: Establish the Decision Criteria

In the second step of the decision-making process, the decision criteria are established. For instance, if the problem is that a manager must choose between two job candidates who have both interviewed well, then the decision criteria might be level of education, years of experience, grade point average, specific knowledge, job skills, and specific abilities.

To get a better idea of how such criteria are established, let's return to the example of choosing a major. Let's say that Jason has realized that the real problem is that he wants to major in management and eventually own a business, but his parents want him to major in accounting. Jason's father is especially insistent about this, because he is a successful accountant in a large firm, and he believes a similar career path will provide Jason with a satisfying job and a good salary. To help himself better understand the alternatives, Jason brainstorms a set of decision criteria. He then phrases each criterion as a question in order to create the following list:

- Which major will allow me to follow my dream of becoming a business owner?
- Which major will ensure that I am prepared to get a job after college if I can't start my own business right away?
- Which major will help me obtain a broad education in business management?
- Which major will accept the elective credits I already have?
- Which major will allow me to finish college in four years?

■Exhibit **6.5**

Jason knows that choosing a major will have an impact on his career.

iStockphoto.com

- Which major will ensure that my parents aren't worried about me or my career opportunities?
- Which major will permit me to take classes with my girlfriend?

Jason may continue brainstorming decision criteria until he comes up with a fairly long list. Obviously, some of the criteria will be more important to him than others—and that's where the next step in the decision-making process comes into play.

Step 3: Allocate Weights to Decision Criteria

The third step in the decision-making process involves prioritizing the decision criteria and assigning weights to them based on their relative importance. Although this may sound complicated, the reality is that people prioritize decision criteria all the time. For example, whether you realize it or not, you probably assign weights to your criteria when choosing where to go for lunch. In this situation, your decision criteria might be quantity of food, price, flavor, healthiness of food, and convenience, and you may place the greatest weight on price and the lowest on convenience, or perhaps the highest on healthiness and the lowest on price. In any case, the way you prioritize your criteria will affect your ultimate decision.

But what about Jason's decision criteria? After much soul searching, Jason has decided that he must follow his own path. However, he also wants to please his parents and relieve their fears regarding his future job security. Accordingly, Jason prioritizes his decision criteria as follows, beginning with the most important criterion and moving toward the least important:

1. Which major will allow me to follow my dream of becoming a business owner?
2. Which major will allow me to finish college in four years?
3. Which major will help me obtain a broad education in business management?
4. Which major will ensure that I am prepared to get a job after college if I can't start my own business right away?
5. Which major will ensure that my parents aren't worried about me or my career opportunities?
6. Which major will accept the elective credits I already have?
7. Which major will permit me to take classes with my girlfriend?

Jason is passionate about following his dream of being a business owner—that's why he gives this criterion the most weight in his decision-making process. He also knows that he must finish college within four years for financial reasons. Jason is aware that the job market is tight, and it's important to him to be prepared to support himself and to get a job if he needs one before starting his own business. In addition, Jason understands that by preparing himself for a job and finishing college in four years, he can alleviate his parents' anxiety and please them as well as himself. Finally, as he assigns weights to his list of criteria, Jason realizes that he doesn't mind taking more electives and that taking classes with his girlfriend is really not that important in the grand scheme of things.

Assigning weights to decision criteria is obviously subjective and includes thoughts, emotions, and intuition. That's why you must carefully consider the logic behind your prioritization and also be honest with yourself. In Jason's case, it was hard for him to admit that his parents' wishes were quite low on his list, but he had to be honest about this situation in order to arrange his criteria in a way that most accurately represented his own wants and needs.

Step 4: List Alternatives

During the fourth step of the decision-making process, a list of alternatives is generated. This is the part of the process in which the decision maker outlines all of the possible choices that can be made. To better understand this step, consider the example of a company that has five manufacturing plants around the country. The company has experienced a drop in sales and has decided to close one of its plants. Before arriving at this conclusion, the company's senior management had considered dozens of alternative actions, most of which were aimed at keeping all five plants open. For instance, the managers explored alternatives such as reducing the overall workforce, halting production of a new line of goods, and reducing management bonuses. Although the managers were as creative as possible, they ultimately determined that the only alternative that would solve the company's financial problems was closing one entire plant. Now, the company's leaders must decide which plant to close, and they have just five alternatives.

As yet another example, say that a restaurant is facing the problem of declining sales. Here, the restaurant owner's initial list of alternatives might include cutting prices, having a sales contest among servers, changing the menu offerings, offering lunch specials, offering free drinks, increasing advertising, and sending press releases to local newspapers about the restaurant. As this wide and varied list demonstrates, outside-the-box thinking can play a critical role when facing a complex decision.

How might this step progress for Jason? At first glance, Jason's list of possible alternatives seems simple:

1. Choose to major in management.
2. Choose to major in accounting.

As Jason examines his choices more creatively, he realizes that he has at least three other choices as well:

3. Choose a dual major in both management and accounting.
4. Choose to major in management and minor in accounting.
5. Choose to major in accounting and minor in management.

Thanks to some creative thinking, Jason now has five alternatives. Note that at this point, Jason is not making any effort to "qualify" or compare his alternatives—that comes during the next step in the decision-making process. For now, just generating a list of possible courses of action is the goal.

Step 5: Analyze Alternatives

In step 5 of the decision-making process, each alternative is evaluated. Here, the decision maker must ask whether each alternative is truly a viable option, or whether it is cost or time prohibitive. This step is made easier by the decision criteria that were established in step 2, and also by the weights that were assigned in step 3. Ultimately, the decision maker takes an objective look at each alternative and determines which one (or ones) can realistically be implemented. For instance, in the restaurant example, the owner may elect to throw out the alternative of changing menu offerings because this can't be done without the high costs associated with reprinting menus, ordering ingredients from different suppliers, and training the kitchen staff to cook new items.

What should Jason do? As he looks over his list of five potential options, Jason (■Exhibit 6.6) notes that all are realistic, feasible, and seem to fit his decision criteria. However, when he begins to analyze the options more closely, Jason comes to the conclusion that majoring in accounting is out of the question. For one, majoring in accounting will not prepare Jason to own his own business. (Remember, this is Jason's most important decision criteria.) Even if he pairs accounting with a minor in management, Jason still doesn't think that this will be enough. He also knows that he cannot

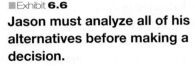
■Exhibit **6.6**

Jason must analyze all of his alternatives before making a decision.

complete a dual major within four years (his second most important criteria), so he takes that option off his list. Hence, Jason is left with only two alternatives:

1. Choose to major in management.
2. Choose to major in management and minor in accounting.

Jason believes that he can make a case for either of these two alternatives that will satisfy his decision criteria and possibly help his parents feel less anxiety about his future.

Step 6: Choose an Alternative

Step 6 in the decision-making process involves choosing one alternative from the list. Based on the evaluation conducted in step 5, one alternative may emerge as the best choice. In Jason's case, for instance, a clear choice has emerged: major in management and minor in accounting. This choice meets all of Jason's criteria—specifically, it allows him to pursue his dream, finish school in four years, obtain a broad education, and prepare himself to get a job. Because of the minor in accounting, Jason feels his parents will be less anxious about his decision to major in management. As an added bonus, he knows his father will be pleased that he has some interest in the accounting field.

Satisficing
Choosing an alternative that is adequate but not perfect.

In many cases, choices are not as clear as Jason's; there may be several good options, for example, or none that are perfect. Similarly, time and other constraints might make it impossible to carry out a full and thorough investigation during each step in the decision-making process. In such instances, **satisficing** may be necessary.[30] Satisficing means choosing an alternative that is adequate but not perfect. For example, when you are deciding where to go for lunch, the best decision based on price and the quality of the food might be the $4.99 pizza buffet on the other side of campus. You are satisficing if you go to the cafeteria because it is "good enough" for a quick lunch.

Satisficing happens in organizations all the time. People need to rely on past experiences, good judgment, and input from others to make the best decision possible, even when a perfect alternative does not exist. This process will be discussed more later in the chapter.

Step 7: Implement the Decision

The seventh step in the decision-making process is actually implementing the decision. Here, you put things into action. For the chosen alternative to be successful, the right amount of time, money, and resources must be dedicated to carrying out the decision. For instance, to return to the restaurant example, if the owner decides that the best option is to offer lunch specials, then several actions have to occur. Promotional signs need to be created. Servers have to be trained to remind customers about the specials. A break-even point will need to be determined so that the restaurant owner knows how many more lunches he must sell at the reduced price to begin to make a profit. The kitchen staff has to be alerted that certain entrées may be ordered in greater numbers than normal. Last but not least, the restaurant's managers will need to ensure that an ample supply of ingredients is available to meet the potential increase in demand.

Let's go back to Jason's decision and see how he implements it. Jason first contacts his adviser and fills out the appropriate forms. He then finds out what the management department expects of him by meeting with the chair of the department, signing up for an orientation session, and so on. As he plans his courses for the next four semesters, Jason also begins thinking about his senior thesis or project. Lastly, Jason makes plans to talk with his parents, which is a difficult yet vitally important step in implementing his decision.

Step 8: Evaluate the Decision

In the eighth and final step of the decision-making process, the decision is evaluated. Although this step is often forgotten and ignored, it is one of the most important parts of the entire process. After all, how can you know whether the decision was correct if you don't evaluate the outcomes? In our restaurant scenario, for example, suppose that the owner decided to offer lower-priced lunch specials to ameliorate declining sales. If no evaluation takes place, the owner will not know whether the restaurant is now profitable, breaking even, or losing money. What if sales continue to decline? What if the cut in prices was so severe that the restaurant is now losing money on certain entrées? Is it making up the difference somewhere else? Evaluation of decisions is essential in organizations and an important part of managing a business.

Of course, it is difficult (if not impossible) to evaluate many decisions immediately. In the restaurant, for instance, initial sales figures might be misleading. There could be an increase in sales the first week when customers first notice the cut in prices, but this might do little to offset the restaurant's overall drop in revenue. Alternatively, there could be a gradual increase in sales that slowly helps the restaurant get back on track.

Decisions that are emotionally charged and that involve several people are often even harder to evaluate. Let's go back to Jason (■Exhibit 6.7). Immediately upon making his decision, Jason may feel a huge sense of relief. He may feel proud of himself and convinced that he made the right decision. Therefore, at this point, his evaluation of his decision would be very positive. One year into his major, however, when faced with a semester full of difficult courses, he may have second thoughts. At times like this, it often helps to revisit the decision criteria, because remembering why you did something in the first place can help you evaluate your decision more fairly over time.

In summary, the eight-step process presented in this section is a useful tool when making decisions. It forces us to consider each aspect of decision making, from identifying the "real" problem (as opposed to symptoms) to carefully considering the available alternatives and making an informed choice. The model is rational and easy to follow. The problem, however, is that most decisions are not made under conditions that are purely rational. This is because "perfect" rational decisions require that we have access to all necessary information and use this information in a perfectly logical manner. In reality, neither condition ever occurs. For this reason, scholars have looked at how we can make decisions when conditions are not perfect, such as when we do not have access to all the information we'd like.

■Exhibit **6.7**

Jason is proud of his decision.

iStockphoto.com

Most Popular » Discussion Questions

1. Do you use a process such as the one outlined in this section to make decisions? Why or why not? If you do not use this method, what do you do? How well does it work for you? Give examples.
2. Consider a problem that you are currently facing that requires a decision. Brainstorm five different ways of articulating the problem, including at least two in which the problem as you currently see it is actually a symptom of a different problem.
3. Apply the eight-step process discussed in this section to a decision you are currently grappling with. Now, ask yourself some tough questions: Are you being realistic and honest with yourself about the decision criteria, the weights you assigned to them, and even your alternatives? Are you "too close" to the problem to decide on an effective course of action? Why? What can you do to change that?
4. Do you evaluate your big decisions regularly? How?

4. How Can People Make Good Decisions with Incomplete Information?

Rarely, if ever, can we make use of *all* the information potentially available to us when making a decision. Doing so simply isn't practical. Try this: Imagine that your professor has asked you learn everything you can about decision making and summarize it in a paper. To begin the assignment, you search "decision making" on the Internet—and you immediately realize you can't possibly attend to all the information available. Indeed, at the time of this writing, there are no fewer than 78,700,000 sites dealing with the topic![31] In organizational life today, employees and managers are faced with this kind of situation all the time. There is an almost unlimited amount of information available to us, and we just can't use it all. When it comes to almost all complex decisions, we simply cannot know everything about our problems, our alternatives, or the future consequences of our decisions. Let's look at two ways we can deal with these problems: working with bounded rationality and remembering the 80/20 rule.

Bounded Rationality

From Aristotle to Kant, philosophers have implored people to rely on reason and logic when approaching life's choices.[32] It may be true that if all the information needed to make a decision were available, accessible, and accurate, and if all humans were perfectly rational all the time, then decisions would be universally logical and perfect as well. In reality, however, even the simplest decisions can involve an amount of information that is literally impossible to process in an efficient and effective manner. Also, for most decisions, no matter how extensively we research the problems and alternatives, it is unlikely that we will discover *everything*. Finally, even if we could access all the information we need, what we do with that data is not always logical. As influential social scientist Herbert Simon points out, humans are far from perfect rational beings.[33]

In the real world, decisions are often rushed and irrational. There will always be either too little, too much, or flawed information to consider; as humans, we usually won't be able to take in or evaluate all of the information available; and there is never enough time to evaluate all information or all possible choices. Rather than fight this, it might serve us to accept that our decision-making process is constrained. Herbert Simon and colleague James March call this bounded rationality.[34] **Bounded rationality** is an approach to decision making that accepts that all decisions are made under conditions or constraints that limit rationality. Such conditions include the following:[35]

Bounded rationality
An approach to decision making that accepts that all decisions are made under conditions or constraints that limit rationality.

- Information will never be complete or completely accurate.
- We cannot always evaluate the quality of the information we get.
- It is basically impossible for humans to rationally evaluate all information or all possible choices.
- People are not purely rational: Emotions, intuition, biases, and the like are always present.
- We simply don't have the time to implement the rational decision-making process in its purest form.

Many recent studies have shown that there are limitations to the amount and quality of information people can and do use when making decisions.[36] Daniel Kahneman, who received the Nobel Prize in 2002 for his work on bounded rationality, notes that although we are not poor reasoners, we frequently act without full *consideration* of information, suggesting that the cognitive costs of getting and processing information are very important factors in how we make decisions.[37] Moreover, when analyzing data, we often make judgments according to personal mental models—biases and stereotypes, for example—that result in choices that are not purely rational.[38]

What this means is that it is hard work to contemplate and analyze information, we will never be purely objective and rational, and we make trade-offs. We mentally balance the "cost" of gathering and processing information, and at some point we are willing to run the risk that something is potentially eliminated from framing a problem, from considering alternatives, or from selecting a solution.[39]

So, to make any decision at all, we need to decide how much and what type of information to seek, how much time we can actually allot to the process, and how to best manage the decision-making process given the limitations and the approaches of the people involved. Under these conditions, we can arrive at satisfactory (but possibly not optimal) solutions—in other words, we can satisfice.[40]

All leaders constantly grapple with the reality that decisions must be made under imperfect conditions. Truly outstanding leaders, though, understand how to make the best decisions possible and how to implement these decisions with everyone's full support. Gavin Patterson, CEO of British Telecom (BT) Retail, is one such leader.

Perspectives

Gavin Patterson is a dynamic, engaging leader at British Telecom (BT), Britain's premier telecommunications company. Gavin is quite young to be a CEO, but his success is no accident. Gavin knows the business inside and out—and he is passionate about it and about the people he serves. He is smart, hardworking, and emotionally intelligent. Also, when it comes to making tough decisions and ensuring that people are with him, Gavin has some good advice:

Gavin Patterson, Director, British Telecom Group, and CEO, British Telecom (BT) Retail

First, you have to truly understand what you are trying to accomplish and where you are going. That's not always as easy as it sounds, because the environment is shifting so quickly—you have to be clear about your general direction and focus on your values and principles. You can't wait until you have every single piece of information, or for all the alternatives to become clear. There's just too much information, things are changing too fast, and many of the decisions we make are too complex for this kind of clarity. So, you need to be ruthless in terms of what input you take and what you discard. You need to be able to make decisions without constant back and forth, constant starts and stops. And you

need to do this in a way that engages people, rather than pushing them away—you need their input, and you need them to be with you.

Once you make a decision, you need to simplify it for people—make it as clear as you possibly can what was decided, why, and what needs to be done. You need to give people confidence that they can achieve the goals. You need to let them know that you believe in them. More than anything, it's important to create the right atmosphere—one that is filled with passion and commitment. You want an environment that is marked by positive and powerful competitiveness around delivery, and that balances supportiveness with challenge and excitement. People need to feel that they can be themselves and bring the best of themselves to the work that has to be done. They need time to laugh, have fun—and work hard. In this kind of atmosphere, people are willing to debate the hard decisions, come to a conclusion, and move forward.

Source: Personal interview with Gavin Patterson conducted by Annie McKee, 2009.

As Gavin Patterson knows, most decisions have to be made without complete or perfect information, by people who are also not perfect or purely rational. To further complicate matters, decisions at work often involve many people—all of whom need to support both the decision process and the ultimate outcome. Recognizing this reality allows us to pay more attention to the kind of information we *do* have access to, as well as to how we convey this information to others. In this area, one rule of thumb that seems to have caught on is called the 80/20 rule.

80/20 Rule

In the early 1900s, economist Vilfredo Pareto noted that 80 percent of the land in Italy was owned by 20 percent of the population. Then, a few decades later, management theorist Joseph Juran came to the conclusion that in manufacturing, 20 percent of the problems in a production process cause 80 percent of the quality issues.[41] Juran called this effect the Pareto principle, in honor of Vilfredo Pareto. Also known as the 80/20 rule, this principle is commonly used as a rule of thumb to quickly see possible causal relationships, such as that 80 percent of sales come from 20 percent of clients or that 80 percent of a company's work is done by 20 percent of its employees. Other examples might be that 80 percent of your disciplinary write-ups are caused by only 20 percent of your employees, or that 80 percent of a restaurant's sales come from just 20 percent of the patrons—the "regulars."

What does the 80/20 rule have to do with decision making? Most of what we do at work is complicated and linked to many other things. We often have to make decisions about *what* to focus on. The 80/20 rule tells us that 20 percent of what we do each day results in 80 percent of our output, suggesting that it can be productive to focus on the 20 percent.

Obviously, the 80/20 rule isn't 100 percent accurate (especially if you don't identify the 20 percent correctly!). Rather, it's a guideline that many people find useful because it helps us determine what to focus on at work. If you approach problems assuming that the 80/20 rule is in effect, then you are likely to consider causes, alternatives, and decisions differently than if no rule of thumb applies. For example, managers who want to leverage the sources of their success might be inclined to focus more attention on a vital few clients, their star employees, or their regular patrons. Alternatively, they might focus on the 20 percent causing problems—underperforming employees, for example. Sometimes, when making decisions about how to solve problems, focusing on the 20 percent is wise. In other cases, however, it is not. The assumptions underlying the 80/20 rule are helpful in guiding our attention when we attempt to understand a challenge or a problem. However, it is critical to always remember that this rule is merely a guideline.

In this section, we've reviewed how the paradox of always having too much information—but never really having it all—is a major factor in most decisions. This problem, coupled with our inherent irrationality, can impact our ability to make good choices. To deal with these problems, we must learn to make decisions under conditions of bounded rationality and to use rules of thumb such as the 80/20 rule to help guide our thought processes. In the next section, we will discuss critical thinking—yet another way of understanding and using the information we have available to us to improve our decision-making ability.

Most Popular » Discussion Questions

1. Consider a decision you have made this year. Did you have all the information you needed to make it? Why or why not? How did you know when you had enough information to proceed? How did you manage to make the decision if you didn't have all of the information you desired?
2. Use the concept of bounded rationality to explain how you make decisions.
3. Do you believe the 80/20 rule is a useful model for attempting to understand organizational strengths and weaknesses? Why or why not? Give one example in which the model would be helpful and one in which it could result in a bad decision.

5. How Can You Improve Your Critical Thinking Skills and Make Better Decisions?

As helpful as the eight-step process described earlier in the chapter can be, decision making is difficult, especially when there are many variables and consequences to consider. When it comes right down to it, *people* identify problems, generate alternatives, and make decisions. The ultimate quality of any decision is dependent on the quality of the thinking that goes into it. In this section, we will consider how you can hone your critical thinking skills so you can make better decisions.

Critical Thinking Defined

Critical thinking
The disciplined intellectual process of evaluating situations or ideas and making appropriate judgments or taking certain actions.

For many people, the word *critical* has negative connotations—it may bring to mind judging others or their ideas. However, critical thinking is *not* about criticizing. Rather, **critical thinking** is the disciplined intellectual process of evaluating situations or ideas and making appropriate judgments or taking certain actions. It is a structured intellectual process that we use to objectively examine ideas, assumptions, knowledge, and reasoning in order to determine their logic and validity and to determine a course of thought or action.[42]

Scholars Goodwin Watson and Edwin Glaser have studied critical thinking in depth, and they have devised categories of skills along with a well-known self-assessment instrument for measuring these skills. Their test, the Watson-Glaser Critical Thinking Appraisal, is composed of five skill sets that these researchers have linked to critical thinking skills: inference, recognition of assumptions, deduction, interpretation, and evaluation of arguments.[43] ■Exhibit 6.8 provides a definition for each of these skill sets.

Critical thinking is *very* important in most jobs today. In virtually every industry, people have to make more decisions than in years past, there is less direct supervision, and there are more opportunities to access and weigh information as a normal part of work. Employees who can take the vast amount of information they will encounter during the day—reports, e-mails, meeting notes, budgets, and so on—and form appropriate assumptions about that data before making key decisions are incredibly valuable to organizations. In some cases, entire service lines and even businesses are built around critical

■Exhibit **6.8**

Critical Thinking Skills and Definitions	
Critical Thinking Skill	**Definition**
Inference	The reasoning involved in drawing conclusions from evidence or known information
Recognition of assumptions	The ability to recognize statements or information that have been assumed to be true or taken for granted
Deduction	A type of inference that reasons from general premises to specific conclusions
Interpretation	The meaning or significance of a collection of facts
Evaluation of arguments	The ability to judge the strength of an argument based on logical criteria

thinking, as is the case in the fields of consulting, software development, and supply chain management.

To better understand the importance of critical thinking, consider how much information is now shared through social networking. From blogs to wikis, information is generated at an ever-faster pace and available to more and more people. But how do we know that what we read is accurate? As consumers of information, we need to understand how to think critically about what we read. For companies like Wikipedia, whose mission is to involve as many people as possible in the creation and generation of knowledge, contributors' critical thinking skills will be a main factor in success or failure. Let's look at Wikipedia in some depth in the following *Business Case* feature. As you read through it, consider how critical thinking impacts Wikipedia's "product" at all steps in the creation and delivery process.

Wikipedia   **Business** Case

Critical Thinking Required

It was the American inventor Ward Cunningham who pioneered the idea of the *wiki*—a collaborative, computer-based environment that enables people in different locations to simultaneously work together on shared files. However, it was businessman Jimmy Wales and philosopher Larry Sanger who took this idea and revolutionized how knowledge is compiled and shared in the twenty-first century through the creation of Wikipedia.[44]

As with many great inventions, the "big idea" behind Wikipedia sounds simpler than it really is: Allow people to compile knowledge, and enable individuals everywhere to have free access to this knowledge.[45] In Wikipedia, *everyone* can write and edit articles. The final product is not the result of research conducted by a small group of highly sophisticated individuals, but rather the result of mass collaboration. Its 3 million English-language entries alone make Wikipedia far larger than the 2005 edition of the *Encyclopaedia Britannica*, which contained only 65,000 articles.

The advent and immense popularity of Wikipedia has inevitably impacted popular culture, and the word *wiki* has become an official part of the English language.[46] People all over the world turn to Wikipedia each day for information about every subject imaginable, and many large organizations and corporations have begun using the site as a fast, simple way to share information about themselves with a global audience.[47] Despite this generally positive reception, several serious objections have arisen regarding Wikipedia and similar sites that allow unlimited, unsupervised access to information. For one, some companies see this movement as a threat to their intellectual property.[48] If everything goes "open source," how will

companies sell "their" ideas, their patents, and their copyrighted material?

Also, the open nature of Wikipedia's system makes it easy for people to deface entries, delete others' opinions, or push one-sided views. Sometimes, extreme measures must be taken to prevent this from happening, such as in 2004, when entries about U.S. presidential candidates John Kerry and George W. Bush had to be locked for most of the year.[49] Still, thanks to Wikipedia's numerous devoted editors, obscenity and other problems are usually quickly recognized and corrected. In fact, according to one MIT study, any obscenity that is randomly inserted on Wikipedia is removed within an average of 1.7 minutes.[50]

Still, at the core of each of these criticisms is the fact that many people believe that Wikipedia is an unreliable source of information. This is why many teachers forbid students from using the site when doing papers and projects.

Despite such concerns, it's obvious that Wikipedia is here to stay, and that it continues to change how people gather, think about, create, and share information. In this new information-sharing environment, critical thinking skills—along with ethics and personal responsibility—are perhaps more important than ever before. Not only do Wikipedia's contributors need to think carefully about what they add to the site, but its editors must make quick judgments and move rapidly when they discover something is amiss. Perhaps most importantly, because Wikipedia's users can never be 100 percent sure that everything they find on the site is accurate, they must continually use their critical thinking capabilities to determine the validity of what they read on the screen.

Photo Source: Helder Almeida/Shutterstock

As this case study demonstrates, many factors play a role in Wikipedia's success—with one primary factor being contributors', editors', and users' capacity for critical thinking. Indeed, people's ability to understand existing knowledge, examine assumptions, deduce specific conclusions, interpret complex data, and evaluate arguments are key when it comes to the generation and management of knowledge in environments of all types, not just in communal platforms like Wikipedia. Whether you're receiving information from Wikipedia or from a newspaper, a network news program, or even a faithful friend or coworker, it's essential that you evaluate that information critically. After all, each and every bit of data we receive represents the work of some person somewhere who has his or her own opinions, agenda, experiences, and worldview—and these things ultimately influence that person's message, whether intentionally or not.

As organizations move to empower employees to make more—and more important—decisions, the need to analyze situations (and people) has become part of everyday work at all levels in an organization. To be a successful manager, you will need to master critical thinking. Much of this comes from experience: The more complex situations you face in your career, the better your critical thinking skills become. You don't have to wait until you are older, however; you can improve your critical thinking now by learning to avoid common thinking errors.

Critical Thinking Errors and How to Avoid Thinking Traps

Critical thinking is a dynamic process with many opportunities for making mistakes. *One common mistake people often make is jumping too quickly to a conclusion.* Perhaps we have encountered a similar situation numerous times, such as the manager who has seen countless employees complain about the hours they are scheduled to work. Because of this experience, when a new employee suddenly asks why he is scheduled to work on a Saturday morning, the manager might jump to the conclusion that the employee doesn't like working weekends and is trying to find a way out of it. However, the employee might actually want to know whether he can work all day Saturday in addition to the morning, or whether he can work both Saturday and Sunday mornings. This particular employee may not have any problem at all with the Saturday morning shift.

Second, *critical thinking errors frequently occur because people don't have the courage to carry out the entire critical thinking process, especially when it means confronting others with new ways of looking at things.* By our nature, we often want to "fit in" and not go against the crowd, which can make critical thinking difficult in a group setting. If our urge to conform is greater than our need to make effective choices to solve a problem, we are in danger of shortchanging the critical thinking process. Taking actions or offering suggestions that are not popular may feel uncomfortable. It's not easy to be the one who is different from the rest of the team. When you do speak up, however, you may discover that others were thinking the same things you were. Good leaders have the courage to see things as they are, speak up, work through problems completely, and act on solid decisions.

Finally, *critical thinking errors occur when we assume from the outset that we are right.* Do you know anyone who is convinced that they are never wrong? We all do, and unfortunately, these people's perceived, self-proclaimed perfection is a sign that they are unable to engage in critical thinking. These individuals assume from the start that they are right, when in reality, they may only be partially correct or even entirely wrong. Being open to suggestions from others and taking time to learn more about a situation facilitates critical thinking, which contributes to good decisions.

Scholars John Hammond, Ralph Keeney, and Howard Raiffa have provided a very useful guideline to add to the critical thinking errors discussed so far. Their model, which you can see in ■Exhibit 6.9, allows us to see specifically where people get "trapped" when trying to make decisions and what we can do about it.[51]

Let's take two of these thinking traps and look at how they played out in real situations:

Supporting the status quo: Supporting the status quo affects decisions both inside and outside an organization. Take this example: Within two months of taking the job, a prominent medical services firm's CEO realized that her CFO and team were not

■Exhibit **6.9**

Thinking Traps in Decision Making		
"Thinking Trap"	Explanation	Avoidance Strategy
Anchoring	Giving too much value to the first piece of information received. The result is that you might stop gathering information prematurely, or the overvalued information may bias your perception of new information.	Seek out diverse perspectives that challenge your views. Generate more than one hypothesis to explain information you encounter. Pursue multiple lines of analysis.
Status quo	Favoring decisions that perpetuate the current situation.	Question the value of the current situation: Is it really good/right/the only way? Ask yourself whether you would choose the status quo if it wasn't "the way things are." Don't be afraid of the effort or cost of change.
Sunk costs	Making choices that justify flawed past decisions.	Consider the perspectives of individuals who weren't involved in the earlier decisions. Avoid encouraging fear of failure. Know when to quit.
Confirming evidence	Selectively seeking out information that supports your point of view.	Question whether you are seeking all relevant information or whether you are favoring only information that supports your point of view. Seek out voices that argue against you. Avoid "yes men."
Estimating and forecasting	Being unduly influenced by memories of powerful examples.	Consider whether examples in memory on which you base estimates are extremes. Obtain actual data rather than relying on impressions.
Framing	Being overly influenced by how a problem is explained or seen.	Consider alternative ways to see and articulate a problem. Consider whether the problem has been articulated with a sufficient amount of detail.

Source: Adapted from Hammond, John S., Keeney, Ralph L., and Raiffa, Howard. 1998. The hidden traps in decision making. *Harvard Business Review* 76(5): 47–58.

up to par. First, the team was far too large. Whereas comparable firms' finance teams were about 50 people, this one was 120. Second, there were numerous errors in financial reports, even those that went to the board. Third, the CFO was known to be an abrasive, unpleasant manager—employees had been complaining about him for years.

It seems obvious what the CEO needed to do, right? It was time for a new CFO and extensive restructuring of the function. The new CEO, however, felt that for at least a year, she needed to keep the team in place. Why? First of all, the chairman of the board wanted her to: He had been involved in hiring the CFO and wanted him to stay. Second, the CEO had just come from a job where in her first six months, she completely changed her top team. This action had resulted in her being despised and mistrusted during her entire term as senior vice president. She did not want that experience again! She decided that the status quo would do for a while.

Unfortunately, during the year that the CEO gave herself before making changes, serious discrepancies were found in the finance area. Money was missing, reports had been doctored, and the like. The CEO was in big trouble.

Sunk costs: This is a common problem in many organizations. For example, in one company we know, managers had decided to invest heavily in one particular type of diet food. They spent millions, and the project was the "one to be on" because of the visibility and hype around how popular it was going to be when it hit the market. Ultimately, the product flopped—badly. Consumers didn't like the taste, didn't like the ingredients (lots of chemicals), and felt it was too expensive. Rather than going back to the drawing board, this company launched a massive ad campaign—spending many more hundreds of thousands of dollars. The result: Product sales went up minimally. Consumer feedback was still exactly the same: Taste, ingredients, and cost were still huge problems. What did the company do? Another marketing campaign! And all because they were trapped by the "We've come this far, we just need to keep going" mentality. They did not know when to quit.

As you have gathered throughout this chapter, decision making is complicated. There are many things to consider, from accurate diagnosis of a problem, to dealing with imperfect information, to understanding how your own emotions and thought processes can help or harm your ability to make good decisions. In the next section, we will look at approaches that can help you think more clearly as you make the many important decisions that accompany you throughout life and at work.

Most Popular » Discussion Questions

1. Review Exhibit 6.8, which describes critical thinking skills. Which of these skills do you believe are strengths for you? Which do you need to work on? (*Note:* You can explore these skills more deeply by logging in to MyManagementLab and taking the Watson-Glaser Critical Thinking Appraisal).

2. Do you ever jump to conclusions or shortcut a critical thinking process when making a decision? Have you ever found that you shut out information because you believed you were right? Most of us have done this. Think about a specific example and reflect on the outcome and what you could have done better.

3. Review Exhibit 6.9 about "thinking traps." Consider a decision you need to make in the near future, and imagine what would happen if you fell into one of the thinking traps. Now, review the avoidance strategies and apply a few to your reflection about the decision.

---

6. What Can HR Do to Support Good Decision Making and Critical Thinking?

Group decision making is the process whereby two or more individuals are involved in making a decision. Many companies use teams and committees to tackle major problems and decisions because different employees bring different viewpoints to the discussion and may represent different constituencies. For example, a team attempting to solve the problem of cutting company expenses might be more effective if it involves a broad group of employees in addition to the company's accountants. Employees representing operations, human resources, and marketing might bring balance and perspective to the discussion and ensure that critical business functions are not arbitrarily eliminated.

Regardless of the exact scenario, most of the time, it's helpful to have more than one person involved in making complex decisions. Two brains (or more) are almost always better than one. Unfortunately, it's often impractical to simply ask all relevant parties for input individually. There are, however, some very good techniques that HR can teach people to help groups gather input at various points in the decision-making

HR Leadership Roles

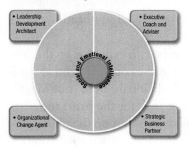

process. As the function that often supports leaders in solving problems, HR is well placed to use and teach techniques that help people make better decisions. In this section, we will concentrate on two such methods: brainstorming and the Delphi technique.

Brainstorming

Brainstorming
The process of generating a list of ideas within a group.

Brainstorming is the process of generating a list of ideas within a group. Brainstorming requires virtually no preparation time and can be facilitated by anyone. The process involves gathering a group of interested individuals and asking them for ideas about an issue, decision, criterion, alternative, etc. Brainstorming can be helpful at any point in a decision-making process. Each person offers ideas without any critique—good or bad—from other participants.[52] The process continues until everyone is out of new ideas. During the brainstorming session, one person records each idea on a white board, flipchart, or computer. Once the ideas have been exhausted, the group begins the process of critiquing and prioritizing the ideas, discussing each idea's merits and ease of implementation.

To illustrate how brainstorming could help an organization, say that an HR professional facilitates a brainstorming session with managers after a crisis, such as when products must be recalled. The group might generate numerous ideas, such as how to find a quick and seamless way to implement the recall, change their marketing approach, engage in more PR activities, sponsor charitable events, or hire a spokesperson. As a facilitator, the HR professional will want this first discussion to go on as long as possible, and he or she will need to challenge people to continue thinking. Many times, once the easiest answers are on the table, people quit thinking. This means that if you are facilitating a brainstorming session, you may need to encourage people to keep going.

Once you have a good list of ideas, you will next need to push people to prioritize. This can and usually will result in conflict, so be ready to facilitate that, too. After priorities are clear, it is important for the group to determine what to do with the ideas, who is responsible, and so forth.

The Delphi Technique

Delphi technique
A technique in which a panel of experts is asked to reach agreement after responding to a series of questions.

Brainstorming often includes non-expert participants; sometimes, however, companies need experts to weigh in on a particular manner. One way to gather this type of advice is through use of the **Delphi technique**, in which a panel of experts is asked to reach agreement after responding to a series of questions. Based on the assumption that group judgments are more valid than individual judgments, the Delphi technique is a kind of focus group of experts, each of whom comes up with ideas regarding a topic and provides justifications for those ideas. The ideas and justifications are then synthesized and summarized before moving to the next round of questions. This method was designed at the RAND Corporation during the Cold War as a method for forecasting military technology developments, but it has useful applications in all types of business.[53]

To manage the Delphi technique, a group of individuals with expertise on the subject is chosen.[54] These individuals may be managers within the company who are intimately familiar with the problem, or they may be individuals from outside the organization who have relevant knowledge. It is not necessary for the panel members to actually meet face to face; the discussions can take place online or on the phone. The process begins with an open-ended question that the experts freely discuss with one another. Once an agreement has been reached among the experts, the next question is discussed. This process continues until a solution to the problem is reached.

The HR Cycle

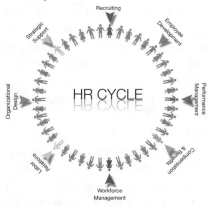

---

1. Consider a problem that you are experiencing at school or work. (It doesn't have to be a serious problem, just something that is bothering you.) Brainstorm all of the possible reasons for this problem. Try to get up to fifty!

2. How does generating a very long list of reasons for a problem change how you see that problem?

---

7. What Can We All Do to Improve Critical Thinking and Decision Making?

We all make hundreds of decisions every single day. Most are small and of little consequence, some are important, and some are life changing. It serves us well to be able to learn how to make good decisions—consciously and conscientiously. It also serves us well to learn from our experiences, so we can apply all that we learn today to the decisions we will make tomorrow. In this section, we will look at how practicing mindfulness will help us attend to the problems and opportunities we need to decipher, as well as reflect consciously on the process of making decisions. Then, we will look at how a method called double-loop learning can help us learn from our experience.

Mindfulness: The Secret to Conscious Decision Making

One of the most important ways to improve your ability to make good decisions is to make the process as conscious as possible. Although this might seem obvious, the fact is that most decisions are extremely complicated and involve dozens—if not hundreds or even thousands—of factors. Because our brains are extremely efficient machines when it comes to processing data, a good deal of this information is processed automatically and unconsciously.

Let's think about what to order for lunch to illustrate this point. Imagine yourself standing in line, waiting to order your meal. You've consciously noticed the two choices that appeal to you—the salad and the burger. You've noticed the nutrition information, and you're remembering eating both of these items before with pleasure. You have weighed how hungry you are, and you've decided that either option would be fine. While all of this is happening more or less consciously, any number of other factors are operating beyond your awareness. For example, the picture of the burger is brighter and more colorful on the menu board, so it captures your attention. You *always* have the burger—it's a habit—and you've told your friend over and over that the burger is the best thing on the menu. You *love* pickles, which come on the burger but not the salad. The door opens and a cold wind blows in, making a hot lunch more attractive. Meanwhile, someone walks by with the salad and you register—albeit unconsciously—how small it is. Also, you didn't sleep much last night and your body is craving the quick energy fats and sugars would provide . . . and on and on.

Obviously, this example does not represent the many more complex decisions all of us face, such as where to live, what career to pursue, or how to motivate our teams or manage resource allocation in our departments at work. Still, this simple scenario does illustrate what often happens when making small and large decisions: Much of the process happens mindlessly. It doesn't have to be this way.

Scholars Ellen Langer and Jon Kabat-Zinn believe that we can greatly improve our capacity to take in information, learn, and make decisions by developing the capacity for mindfulness.[55] **Mindfulness** is a state in which we are awake, aware, and attuned to

Mindfulness
A state in which we are awake, aware, and attuned to ourselves, others, and our environment.

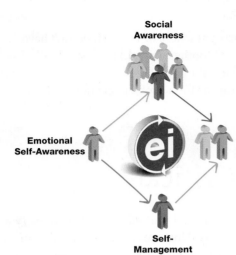

ourselves, others, and our environment. Mindfulness enables us to be more fully aware of all that is happening inside us—physically, psychologically, and cognitively—while also being tuned in to what is going on around us in the immediate and more distant environment.[56] Mindfully attending to your lunch decision, for example, might mean recognizing that your habit of ordering the burger causes you to select it without thinking or that what you really need is sleep, not fats and sugar. Alternatively, mindfully attending to this decision might cause you to notice that the door blew open for an instant, but you quickly warmed up when the door closed. You might also consciously recognize that the brightly colored, appealing picture is an advertising ploy—the real burgers don't look like the picture at all.

What would it be like if you were living more mindfully? Would you examine your choices more carefully and make better decisions? Might you be healthier, choose a better diet, get more exercise, or even engage in different social activities? Would you be less stressed? Would you have an easier time dealing with information and choices? Research suggests that all of this is true.[57]

But how do you develop mindfulness? Some people believe that practicing mindfulness means you have to meditate every day or examine yourself constantly. Neither is the case, although reflective practices like meditation can help. For example, you might decide that for 10 minutes a few times a week, you will focus on a few good things you have done or been part of recently. Or, you might commit to walking to class more often, running again, or enjoying some other individual physical activity. While doing this, you don't think about all of the issues, problems, and stress you have—you simply pay attention to yourself and your environment. Or, you can adopt the simplest practice of them all: Just pay more attention to what you think, feel, and do. For most of us, developing mindfulness can involve some simple—but profound—changes in what we do and think.

Double-Loop Learning

There are two ways to slide easily through life: to believe everything or to doubt everything. Both ways save us from thinking.

—Alfred Korzybski[58]

In this chapter, we have stressed many times that it is important to examine your thought processes, feelings, and approaches to decision making. If you want to take it one step further, you can also focus on improving your capacity for learning from experience. Why might you want to do this? Doing so will help ensure that as you proceed in life and at work, you will get better and better at understanding common problems, generating more solutions, and charting a course for implementing decisions that work well.

Surprisingly, many people don't pay much attention to learning from experience unless something occurs that is a huge wake-up call, like being caught driving while under the influence of alcohol. Even in serious learning situations like this, some people simply never learn how bad decisions can lead to devastating consequences. For example, a person will have the experience (drinking too much, driving, and getting caught). Then he will ultimately suffer the subsequent experiences that come along with that bad decision, including court appearances, fines, driving school, and even jail. The person knows that what he did was risky, so in the future, he does not drink and drive—unless he is "sure" he won't get caught or he thinks he is under the legal limit. He has changed his behavior, but not the underlying beliefs that allowed him to drink and drive in the first place, such as "It's no one else's business" or "The law has no right to control my behavior" or "I am an excellent driver and alcohol doesn't compromise my abilities."

This is an example of **single-loop learning**, a process that results in taking in feedback and changing behavior, but not changing underlying beliefs about one's self, others, or the environment. People use these underlying beliefs to explain what happens and why, as well as what to do in certain situations.

Single-loop learning
A process that results in taking in feedback and changing behavior, but not changing underlying beliefs about one's self, others, or the environment.

Double-loop learning
A process that focuses on changing underlying beliefs as well as behavior.

The process of **double-loop learning** focuses on changing underlying beliefs as well as behavior.[59] In the example about driving drunk, the person could have examined his belief that his needs and desires were more important than people's safety, or he may have come to realize that alcohol does indeed impair his driving skills. With these new mental models in place, he won't *ever* drive while under the influence.

Consider this scenario at work: Suppose a manager has an underlying belief that goes something like this: "Once an employee starts questioning my decisions, we're on a path that will end in me having to fire her. Such behavior is insubordination, and that is not allowed at work, and especially not on my watch." With this belief in place, the manager may start paying more attention to the employee's behavior in general and taking notes on any apparent questioning of authority. If single-loop learning is in operation here, the employee is very likely to be fired, even if the questions she brought to her manager were intended to be helpful.

If, however, this manager challenges his own assumptions and beliefs as this scenario plays out, he has a chance to truly learn from the experience. Say that he notices that the employee's questions are always raised respectfully, politely, and in private. He starts attending more carefully to the content of the questions (safety of the group of employees, a few good ideas about improving quality). As he does this, he begins to see that questioning one's manager isn't always bad, and it can indeed be helpful. He is changing his underlying beliefs and his behavior. That's double-loop learning.

We can reinforce double-loop learning by deliberately challenging or testing our assumptions on a regular basis. This requires a conscious effort to overcome our natural tendency to retain the beliefs that guide our actions.[60]

Most Popular » Discussion Questions

1. Do you have a daily practice that allows you to reflect, calm down, and become more mindful? Brainstorm several other things you can do to foster mindfulness.
2. For one week, take 15 minutes a day to simply sit, walk, or lie down and breathe, trying not to think about anything at all. Just focus on breathing. At the end of the week, reflect on this experience and how it has affected you.
3. Consider a situation where you believe you made a bad decision. Are you applying single-loop or double-loop learning to the situation?

---

8. A Final Word on Decision Making and Critical Thinking

Of the skills essential to effective management and leadership, decision making and critical thinking are among the most important. Although many of the decisions you face on a daily basis are simple and perhaps even routine, others are far more complex. To make the best choices possible when confronted with complex decisions, you need to understand the many inputs to the decision-making process: logic, cognitive processes, emotion, and intuition.

It is also important to use a systematic approach to support decision making, such as by identifying the problem; establishing the decision criteria; allocating weights to these criteria; listing, analyzing, choosing, and implementing alternatives; and evaluating your decision. Furthermore, you must be aware of what strategies you can employ when faced with either too little or too much information about the situation at hand.

Of course, none of the aforementioned actions is possible without the ability to engage in critical thinking. Unlike decision making, critical thinking is not a stepwise endeavor; rather, it is a dynamic process. You can improve your decision-making and critical thinking skills by practicing mindfulness, remembering that pure rationality isn't always possible, and understanding how unexamined biases may be hindering your ability to think clearly.

Key Terms

1.   What Is Decision Making? (pp. 178–181)

Key Terms

Decision making A cognitive, emotional, and neuropsychological process involving thoughts, feelings, and neurological functioning that results in making a judgment or choosing from alternatives. p. 178

Programmed decisions Decisions that are routine in nature and occur with some frequency. p. 179

Nonprogrammed decisions Decisions that are not routine and/or involve unique information or circumstances. p. 180

2.   How Do Cognitive and Emotional Processes Affect Decision Making? (pp. 181–187)

Key Terms

Accommodation The process of adapting one's cognitive categorization system to allow for new information, new schemas, and new ways of understanding information. p. 183

Assimilation The process of integrating or forcing new information to fit existing cognitive categorization systems. p. 183

Halo effect The phenomenon in which we judge something or someone positively based on a previous positive experience or association with someone or something we admire. p. 184

Intuition Tacit knowledge, or knowledge that we have access to at an unconscious level. p. 186

3.   How Can You Apply a Systematic Approach to Making Decisions? (pp. 187–193)

Key Terms

Decision-making process The steps taken when choosing a course of action. p. 187

Satisficing Choosing an alternative that is adequate but not perfect. p. 192

4.   How Can People Make Good Decisions with Incomplete Information? (pp. 194–196)

Key Terms

Bounded rationality An approach to decision making that accepts that all decisions are made under conditions or constraints that limit rationality. p. 194

5.   How Can You Improve Your Critical Thinking Skills and Make Better Decisions? (pp. 197–201)

Key Terms

Critical thinking The disciplined intellectual process of evaluating situations or ideas and making appropriate judgments or taking certain actions. p. 197

6. What Can HR Do to Support Good Decision Making and Critical Thinking? (pp. 201–203)

Key Terms

Brainstorming The process of generating a list of ideas within a group. p. 202

Delphi technique A technique in which a panel of experts is asked to reach agreement after responding to a series of questions. p. 202

7. What Can We All Do to Improve Critical Thinking and Decision Making? (pp. 203–205)

Key Terms

Mindfulness A state in which we are awake, aware, and attuned to ourselves, others, and our environment. p. 203

Single-loop learning A process that results in taking in feedback and changing behavior, but not changing underlying beliefs about one's self, others, or the environment. p. 204

Double-loop learning A process that focuses on changing underlying beliefs as well as behavior. p. 205

8. A Final Word on Decision Making and Critical Thinking (p. 205)

Key Terms None

Chapter 6 Visual Summary

1. What Is Decision Making? (pp. 178–181)

Summary: Decision making is a far more complicated process than many people understand. Decision making is complex; it involves cognitive, neuropsychological, and emotional processes. When making judgments or choices, we need to consider both the information available to us and how we react to it. This is especially true when making nonprogrammed decisions—decisions that are not routine.

2. How Do Cognitive and Emotional Processes Affect Decision Making? (pp. 181–187)

Summary: Decision making is commonly understood to be a rational process, but reasoning and logic are only two of the tools a decision maker should use. We need to also understand how our cognitive processes affect our judgments, watching out for misunderstandings and stereotypes. In addition, we need to examine our emotions and intuition, two legitimate sources of information that can positively affect decision making.

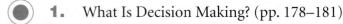

■Exhibit **6.4**

Eight-Step Decision-Making Model

Step 1: Identify the problem.
Step 2: Establish the decision criteria.
Step 3: Allocate weights to decision criteria.
Step 4: List alternatives.
Step 5: Analyze alternatives.
Step 6: Choose an alternative.
Step 7: Implement the decision.
Step 8: Evaluate the decision.

8. Workplace Essentials: Creativity, Innovation, and a Spirit of Entrepreneurship

7. Change: A Focus on Adaptability and Resiliency

9. Organizing for a Complex World: Structure and Design

Planning and Change

6. The Human Side of Planning: Decision Making and Critical Thinking

5. Planning and Strategy: Bringing the Vision to Life

3. How Can You Apply a Systematic Approach to Making Decisions? (pp. 187–193)

Summary: The eight steps of decision making include identifying the problem, which needs to be done very carefully, and establishing and prioritizing decision criteria. Once you know what you're trying to do, and what's most important to you in how you do it, you can move on to list, analyze, choose, and then implement an alternative. The final step, and the one that is most often overlooked, is to evaluate the decision and recognize whether the problem was solved appropriately and completely.

4. How Can People Make Good Decisions with Incomplete Information? (pp. 194–196)

Summary: We are navigating the information age with this paradox: We have both too much and not enough information when making decisions. We must make decisions under conditions of bounded rationality, meaning that we will always be constrained by time, amount and quality of information, and our own inability to be perfectly rational. One tool to help under these conditions is the 80/20 rule, which helps us see causal relationships.

8. A Final Word on Decision Making and Critical Thinking (p. 205)

Summary: Critical thinking skills are essential to long-term success in any endeavor. When approaching complex decisions, we all need to recognize and rely on reason, conscious cognitive processing, emotion, and intuition.

■ Exhibit **6.8**

Critical Thinking Skills and Definitions	
Critical Thinking Skill	**Definition**
Inference	The reasoning involved in drawing conclusions from evidence or known information
Recognition of assumptions	The ability to recognize statements or information that have been assumed to be true or taken for granted
Deduction	A type of inference that reasons from general premises to specific conclusions
Interpretation	The meaning or significance of a collection of facts
Evaluation of arguments	The ability to judge the strength of an argument based on logical criteria

7. What Can We All Do to Improve Critical Thinking and Decision Making? (pp. 203–205)

Summary: As emphasized throughout the chapter, the key to becoming a better decision maker is to clearly understand the emotions, rationality, intuition, and cognitive processes that affect decisions. One way to understand this is to practice mindfulness—that is, being aware of ourselves and our environment—which can lead to an understanding of what is really motivating us to make one decision or the other. Mindfulness can lead to the deeper process of double-loop, rather than single-loop, learning. In double-loop learning, we learn from our experiences and change our underlying beliefs, not just our behavior.

6. What Can HR Do to Support Good Decision Making and Critical Thinking? (pp. 201–203)

Summary: HR can guide employees and managers to make the best decisions by ensuring that groups allow different informed viewpoints to be heard. Two techniques that bring out the best of what a group has to offer are brainstorming and the Delphi technique. Brainstorming allows your group to bypass the fear of criticism that can shut down promising ideas. The Delphi technique allows you to use a group of experts to review a situation and come to a conclusion based on their knowledge and expertise.

5. How Can You Improve Your Critical Thinking Skills and Make Better Decisions? (pp. 197–201)

Summary: Developing and using our critical thinking skills is paramount at work today—and elsewhere in our lives. Do you draw accurate conclusions from evidence? Can you recognize the assumptions you're making about a situation and their validity? Can you understand specific issues by analyzing general information? Are you able to evaluate arguments using logical criteria? Do you work hard to interpret a collection of facts? If so, you're applying critical thinking skills to the decision-making process and increasing the odds that you'll make a good decision.

Change:

A Focus on Adaptability and **Resiliency**

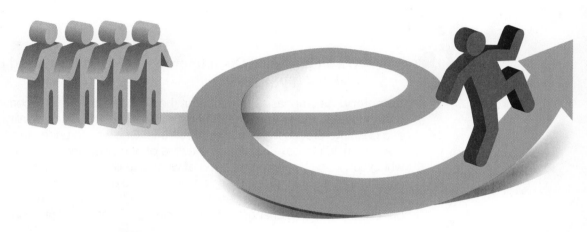

Chapter Outline

Find out what you already know about the concepts in this chapter by going to www.mymanagementlab.com and taking the **Pre-Test.** Your results will generate a customized study plan for Chapter 7.

1. What Is Change and How Do You React to It? (pp. 212–214)

2. Why Do Organizations Change? (pp. 214–219)

3. What Is the Difference between Incremental and Transformational Change? (pp. 220–224)

4. Which Models Can Help Us Understand Change? (pp. 224–228)

5. What Practical Models Can Help Us Manage Change in Organizations? (pp. 228–234)

6. How Do *People* Change? (pp. 235–242)

7. What Can HR Do to Foster Effective Change? (pp. 242–244)

8. What Can We All Do to Support Change? (pp. 244–248)

9. A Final Word on Change (p. 248)

Go back to www.mymanagementlab.com and take the **Post-Test** to verify your understanding of the concepts. To experience and apply the concepts, explore the additional material associated with Chapter 7.

Part 1: Leading and Managing for Today and the Future (Chapters 1, 2, 3, 4)
> **Part 2:** Planning and Change (Chapters 5, 6, **7**, 8, 9)
Part 3: Organizing Human Systems (Chapters 10, 11)
Part 4: Controlling Quality, Culture, and Yourself (Chapters 12, 13)
Part 5: Leading and Managing for the Future (Chapters 14, 15, 16)

8. Workplace Essentials: Creativity, Innovation, and a Spirit of Entrepreneurship

7. Change: A Focus on Adaptability and Resiliency

9. Organizing for a Complex World: Structure and Design

10. Teams and Teambuilding: How to Work Effectively with Others

Planning and Change

Organizing Human Systems

6. The Human Side of Planning: Decision Making and Critical Thinking

16. Managing and Leading for Tomorrow: A Focus on Your Future

14. Globalization: Managing Effectively in a Global Economic Environment

11. Working in a Virtual World: Technology as a Way of Life

5. Planning and Strategy: Bringing the Vision to Life

1. Managing and Leading Today: The New Rules

Leading and Managing for Today and the Future

7. Change: A Focus on Adaptability and Resiliency

2. The Leadership Imperative: It's Up to You

4. Communication: The Key to Resonant Relationships

3. Motivation and Meaning: What Makes People Want to Work?

15. Sustainability and Corporate Social Responsibility: Ensuring the Future

12. Organizational Controls: People, Processes, Quality, and Results

Controlling Quality, Culture, and Yourself

13. Culture: It's Powerful

211

1. What Is Change and How Do You React to It?

Benjamin Franklin said that nothing is certain but death and taxes. Today we add "and so is change."

Pictorial Press/Alamy Images

Change
To alter, adjust, modify, or transform someone or something.

At the age of 83, Benjamin Franklin said about the American Constitution, "Everything appears to promise that it will last; but in this world nothing is certain but death and taxes."[1] Today, we might say "nothing is certain but death, taxes, and *change*" (■Exhibit 7.1).

In the past few decades, change has been constant in many people's lives, as well as at work. This was not the case for the tens of thousands of years that preceded the eighteenth century. During most of human history, the way we lived and worked remained more or less the same from generation to generation. Changes occurred, of course, such as migration, marriage, birth, and death, but these changes were considered "normal." Customs and traditions guided people about how to behave when these predictable changes happened. These customs and traditions, such as how families behaved before, during, and after weddings, helped people deal with the disruption, anxiety, and excitement that accompany change. And although our ancestors experienced unpredictable shifts and changes such as the domestication of animals, the taming and riding of horses, and iron production and tool forging, these changes were very gradual and intermittent. People had decades or even centuries to adjust to them. This is not true anymore. Change is now constant, and we need to understand how to work, manage, and lead when the future is not predictable.

What exactly is change? **Change** means to alter, adjust, modify, or transform someone or something. As you can see in ■Exhibit 7.2, the word *change* can be used as either a noun or a verb, and many words and phrases in English are synonymous with the word *change*. The meanings of these synonyms run the gamut from mild change (adjustment) to massive, transformational change (an about-face).

There usually isn't a direct relationship between the number of words to describe something and its importance to people. Scholars note, however, that the richness of vocabulary related to concepts can be an important indicator of what people care about, value, and pay attention to.[2] For instance, people who share a profession (such as lawyers or doctors), a social group (such as members of the PTA or teenagers), or a type of relationship (such as mothers and young children) develop a specialized way of talking with one another about things they share that are important to them.[3]

Within such groups, a larger vocabulary is used to describe important concepts. Given the rate and pace of change humans have experience during the last two centuries, it's not surprising that our language allow us to describe change in many ways.[4] In businesses and organizations we talk about change a lot, and we have many ways to describe change because it happens almost every day.

Change: What It Means to You

How do you feel about change? When you started college, you probably had to change a lot of things, such as your lifestyle, how you spend time, and maybe where you live. What were your emotional responses to the changes you had to make? How did you cope with these changes? Chances are you felt mixed emotions: exhilaration about starting college and the changes this would bring; excitement about the future; and openness to doing things in new ways. Or, you might have felt uncertain about how to organize your time, handle the workload, or make new friends. Maybe you even felt fear or sadness about what you were leaving behind.

People react to change in many different ways. For some, a move across town or a change in jobs is experienced as tumultuous and difficult, even when it is welcomed. Others aren't bothered at all. When faced with making a big change like starting college, taking a new job, getting married, or having a child, most people experience emotions

■Exhibit **7.2**

The Many Ways We Say "Change"

Change Is a Noun

"about-face, addition, adjustment, advance, break, compression, contraction, conversion, correction, development, difference, distortion, diversification, diversity, innovation, metamorphosis, modification, modulation, mutation, novelty, permutation, reconstruction, refinement, remodeling, replacement, reversal, revision, revolution, shift, substitution, surrogate, switch, tempering, transformation, transition, transmutation, turn, turnover, variance, variation, variety, vicissitude; exchange, flip-flop, interchange, swap, trade, turnaround."[5]

Change Is a Verb

"accommodate, adapt, adjust, alter, alternate, commute, convert, diminish, diverge, diversify, evolve, fluctuate, make innovations, make over, merge, metamorphose, moderate, modify, modulate, mutate, naturalize, recondition, redo, reduce, reform, regenerate, remake, remodel, renovate, reorganize, replace, resolve, restyle, revolutionize, shape, shift, substitute, tamper with, temper, transfigure, transform, translate, transmute, transpose, turn, vacillate, vary, veer, warp; barter, displace, exchange, interchange, invert, remove, reverse, supplant, swap, switch around, trade, transmit."[6]

---

as varied as joy, fear, resentment, excitement, and hope. Most people also experience a combination of willingness to change as well as resistance to it. That's part of the reason change is so complicated: It forces us to cope with conflicting emotions, disruptions to habits, and the need to give up things that are familiar.

The ability to deal with change is one of the most important things you can learn. The ability to adapt and change personally and to inspire others to change is at the center of great leadership and management and also a big part of being an effective employee today. We make radical changes such as moving to a new location or changing jobs more often today than we did in the past. Consider this: The most commonly reported statistic with regard to job change is that people change careers an average of three times over the 40 years most of them will be in the workforce.[7] However, these statistics don't reflect how often we change *jobs*, as opposed to careers. The U.S. Bureau of Labor Statistics (BLS) found that in 2008, the median length of time employees had worked for their current employer was only 4.1 years.[8] Among major occupations, managers in general had the longest tenure, at 5.1 years, with engineering and architecture managers in particular having the longest tenure at 6.4 years.[9] If you act according to these numbers, you are likely to change jobs *ten times* over the course of your working life.

Change Is Constant

The environment within which today's organizations operate is becoming increasingly dynamic and competitive—things change all the time at work. Change is constant at work and in life due to factors such as advancing technology and social, economic, and political shifts around the world. These shifts are happening at an unprecedented pace and are affecting billions of people. Old ways of life are being replaced by radical new ways of approaching basic human activities: communication, health, lifestyles, birth, and death.

Is constant change a bad thing? Imagine living in a world that did not involve change. Tomorrow would be the same as today (which would be boring). Technology would stay the same (meaning there would be no new computers, phones, cars, or energy sources). Social norms, such as how people relate to one another, who's on top, and who's not, would stay the same (which would mean hopelessness for some people, such as the poor or those who experience discrimination). With no new services, products, or markets, competition would be static, and the world's economy would be flat. This sounds awful, doesn't it? Yet, people complain about change all the time and have trouble understanding it, coping with it, and managing it. To be successful in our dynamic organizations today, you need to understand change on a personal level, and also how to support others as they face change in how they work and live.

In this chapter, we will first look at why organizations change, as well as the difference between incremental change and transformational change. Then we will explore models that explain the forces for and against change, and how change is constant in today's organizations. We will also look at practical approaches to organizational change, followed by how people change and how we can foster enthusiasm for change in groups, organizations, and communities. We will conclude by looking at HR's role in organizational change, and what we all can do to embrace change and help others do the same.

Most Popular » Discussion Questions

1. List a few major changes you have experienced in life (such as moving, divorce in the family, illness, starting college, or starting or ending a relationship). Now, using the synonyms for change in Exhibit 7.2, list some words that describe each of these changes. Can you see any patterns in the words you chose? What do those patterns suggest to you?

2. List several major changes that you have experienced. Now, organize them into two categories: "Changes I Initiated and Wanted" and "Changes That Were Forced on Me." Some of your life experiences may fall in the middle of these two extremes, but try to put them in the category that fits best. How do you feel about each of these lists? What were the differences in how you dealt with changes in the two categories?

3. Consider the following sentence: "The environment within which today's organizations operate is becoming increasingly dynamic and competitive—*things change all the time at work*." Do you believe this is true? Why or why not?

---

2. Why Do Organizations Change?

Why do organizations change? Organizations change because they must in order to remain relevant, productive, and profitable. Organizations that do not change quickly enough risk becoming obsolete.

Organizations choose to change—or are forced to change—for at least three reasons. The first reason organizations change is obvious: Technology, especially information technology and telecommunications, affects what organizations and people can do at work and how they do it. We address this in detail in Chapter 11. For now, we'll simply say that changes in technology affect almost every aspect of organizational life and work, including communication; manufacturing processes; how goods are transported, bought, and sold; and the increased capability of organizations of all sizes to produce and distribute goods and services globally.

Another major driver of organizational change during the past 50 years has been globalization, which has been fueled by advances in transportation and information technologies.[10] Different patterns of social interaction, enhanced competition, shifts in world politics, and expanded markets all accompany globalization.

The third reason organizations are changing so rapidly is also linked to a movement that hasn't fully taken root yet—namely, environmentalism and the need to ensure a sustainable world.[11] Sustainability is explored more fully in Chapter 15. For now, it's enough to know that the "Green Revolution" has been under way for a long time and is having profound effects on organizations and businesses because there are now more laws regulating things like carbon emissions—not to mention the fact that sustainability is a worldwide social movement that is just getting started.[12] Many businesspeople's commitment to supporting environmental sustainability—while making a profit—has driven them to search for new and better ways to manage their businesses, as you can see in the following *Student's Choice* feature.

Ben Parker

Patagonia

These days, it seems like many people spend a lot of time talking about the green movement but do very little to protect the planet. Thankfully, there are individuals who actually contribute to the cause—and some of them manage to make a great deal of money doing so. One such person is Yvon Chouinard, owner of Patagonia, Inc.

Chouinard was born in 1938 to rugged French-Canadian parents who raised him with an appreciation for the outdoors. To clarify just what "rugged" means, Chouinard recalls sitting next to the wood-burning stove of his house in rural Maine, watching his father perform amateur dental extractions on his own mouth simply because he thought the dentist charged too much for something he could do himself. Later, when his family moved to California, 14-year-old Yvon took up falconry as a hobby, capturing falcons from their cliffside nests and domesticating them for hunting. It was during these falcon-catching excursions that Chouinard was introduced to rock climbing, because in order to reach the nests, he had to rappel from above. Chouinard quickly became dissatisfied with the climbing equipment available to him, so he decided to begin making it himself. Soon, Chouinard's equipment gained local acclaim for its high quality, and he was able to transform his hobby into a profitable business.[13]

It was at this point that Chouinard's environmental conscience first intersected with his business interests. In particular, Chouinard noticed that some of his company's equipment had been left in the cracks of Yosemite's high granite walls, where it was starting to damage the rock. Shortly thereafter, Chouinard Equipment Company ceased all operations, and Yvon sold the business to some friends, who turned it into rock-climbing equipment juggernaut Black Diamond Equipment.

Chouinard's business knack didn't end with the sale of his climbing gear company, however. A few years before closing up shop, he had started another business with his wife, Malinda Pennoyer, selling Scottish rugby shirts to climbers. Chouinard called the new company Patagonia.[14] Patagonia grew quickly, and as early as 1991, several experts predicted that the company would be worth $1 billion by 2002.

Here again, Chouinard's environmental conscience intervened. Chouinard didn't want Patagonia to be a billion-dollar company that littered landfills with its products. He wanted it to be a responsible company that taught its consumers and the

rest of the corporate world that bigger wasn't better and that quality and longevity were far more important than the bottom line. So, Patagonia became an experiment—a company designed entirely around sustainable business practices.[15]

Over the years, Chouinard has repeatedly shown that if people change their thinking, they can run a business that both makes a good profit and promotes environmental stewardship. Some lessons that can be taken from Patagonia include the following:

- Consider the "waste stream"—that is, understand the waste your company is producing and then stop it. During the last decade, Patagonia has launched an environmental audit on every one of its products to understand the precise effects that manufacturing the products has on the environment, as well as to find ways to streamline the company's production practices.
- Innovate in recycling. For example, Patagonia collects its old polyester clothes and sends them to Japan, where they are melted down to their original polymer and rewoven into new items.
- Create sustainable business buildings. Patagonia focuses on renewable power sources like wind and solar energy, employs compost and edible landscaping, uses recycled paper, and so forth. As of 2009, the Patagonia headquarters provided 62 percent of its own daily power, in addition to reusing rainwater, having a compost system for all on-campus food, and using recycled paper within the warehouse. Chouinard has said that he will be unsatisfied until Patagonia is 100 percent sustainable.[16]

Patagonia is also leading the way in green business practices with what Chouinard calls the "Earth tax." Here, Patagonia takes a percentage from its annual bottom line and "pays a tax" to the planet by supporting numerous environmental charities. Chouinard has even started a nonprofit called "1% for the Planet," in which every company that joins promises to give 1% of its yearly earnings to an association of environmental groups.[17]

Chouinard thinks that in order to change society's approach to the environment, companies need to start demanding more of each other and their customers. In other words, we all need to change—not only for our own sakes, but also for the sake of our planet.[18]

Source: Adapted from a case by Ben Parker.

Amazon.com's business model enables the company to tap niche markets.

Gary Lucken/Alamy

When Social Changes Come to Work: Diversity, Inclusion, and Change

As the previous case illustrates, social changes such as an increased focus on sustainability affect many organizations today. Another social change that is linked directly to changes in organizations is increased diversity among the employee base, customers, and consumer markets.[19] As it turns out, diversity is good for business.[20] Consider the following:

1. Recognition of consumer diversity opens up many new opportunities for businesses to capitalize on selling to multiple niche markets (■Exhibit 7.3). For instance, Amazon.com and eBay are prime examples of companies that have tapped niche markets.
2. Acknowledging cultural diversity in global markets by tailoring products and services to local needs offers companies a competitive advantage. For example, KFC menus around the world feature different dishes designed specifically for local populations.[21]
3. Educational and skills diversity offers companies new and potentially revolutionary opportunities to access a wide base of relevant knowledge. For example, Walt Disney Imagineering taps experts from 150 disciplines.[22]
4. Diversity in the workplace—including skills, background, gender, ethnicity, religion and sexual orientation—can improve decision-making quality and facilitate strategic organizational change because it provides the opportunity for greater breadth of perspective.
5. Valuing diversity in the workplace pays off in terms of employee workplace satisfaction and can lead to significant savings in terms of employee engagement and productivity.[23]
6. Countries and regions throughout the world have a wide range of laws that enforce cultural, racial, gender, and linguistic diversity in the workplace, and these laws are constantly changing.

To illustrate the first point on this list, Amazon.com and eBay showed the world how to capitalize on the "long tail" of the market.[24] The concept of the long tail refers specifically to diversity in consumer interests and geographic distribution. For instance, for a particular type of product, you might have only a small handful of customers in a given region, and no bricks-and-mortar store would ever survive selling just that product. If you had access to all of the customers in all of the different regions in the nation, however, you could have a booming business. This is what Amazon.com does—and does well. Throughout 2009, the worst year for businesses since perhaps the Great Depression, Amazon continued to do extremely well.

Even education is getting into the business of marketing to the long tail. With increasingly sophisticated online courses, it is now possible for smaller schools to diversify their educational offerings, even if the physical location of the school only has one or two students interested in a particular subject. By aggregating students nationally—or even globally—schools can provide significant class sizes and quality interaction.[25]

The case for diverse employees in the workplace is a bit more complicated. Part of the problem, diversity scholar David Thomas notes, is that we have been trained to confuse issues of racial, gender, and ethnic equity with issues of diversity. When **diversity** is understood as "the varied perspectives and approaches to work that members of different groups bring,"[26] you can see how diversity can improve decision making, as well as approaches to complex things like organizational change.

Of course, demographic differences are also important aspects of diversity, and there continues to be a need to foster positive relationships, effective communication, and employment equity across the many ethnic, racial, class, and gender boundaries in our society. Many businesses still grapple with serious problems in their attempts to change their organizational cultures to be more inclusive so that people from all backgrounds and with diverse demographic characteristics can work together effectively. Despite

Diversity
The varied perspectives and approaches to work that members of different groups bring.

many laws, problems in areas such as pay equity still exist among various groups. We will now look at diversity and inclusion issues that are driving changes in our organizations. Each of the topics discussed in the following sections involves important and pressing issues that organizations must address. These issues include changing cultures to be more inclusive and responsive to diversity and changing organizational systems (such as pay and benefits) to foster equity.

Gender, Ethnicity, and Pay

As of 2008, the most recent year for which the Bureau of Labor Statistics (BLS) has data, in the United States, Asians (as a group) working full time earn more on average across occupations than whites (16 percent), African Americans (46 percent), and Latinos (63 percent). Whites earn 26 percent more than African Americans and 40 percent more than Latinos. African Americans earn 11 percent more than Latinos. The lowest paid of these groups is Latinas, who earn almost 6 percent less than their male counterparts.

Women comprise 30 percent of the full-time white workforce. African American women make up about 35 percent of the full-time African American workforce, while among Latinos, women comprise only 27 percent. Among Asians, women make up 31 percent of the full-time workforce. Full-time female workers, as a whole, earned 80 cents for every dollar men earned. The pay gap is much smaller among the most disadvantaged groups—African Americans and Latinos—where women earned just under 90 cents for every dollar their male counterparts earned. Asian women showed the greatest pay equity gap, earning only 78 cents for every dollar Asian men earned. There are less than half as many women as men in management, professional, and related occupations, and they earn about 12 percent less than their male counterparts. In management occupations alone, women earn 19 percent less, and there are about one-third fewer women in these roles. When it comes to executive management positions, the story is not much better: Women chief executives receive just over 84 percent of the pay of their male counterparts.[27]

Fortune magazine, which tracks the progress of women in the top 1,000 corporations in the United States, reported that in the Fortune 500, there were 15 women CEOs, or just 3 percent.[28] The story is even worse for the Fortune 1000, where there were only 28, or 2.8 percent.[29] This contrasts with the BLS data, which uses a very large sample of large, medium, and small organizations in the public, private, and nonprofit sectors. The BLS finding was that just under 20 percent of all chief executives are women.[30] Although this number is better than those for top corporations, it is still quite small considering the fact that in 2008, women made up 42 percent of the workforce.[31]

These statistics reflect some improvements over past years in terms of pay equity and the representation of certain groups in the workplace. However, we have a long way to go in this change process.

Age Demographics and Change

Another demographic aspect of diversity that drives change in businesses and organizations in terms of what they do and how they market to consumers and clients is the changing average age of populations around the world. ■Exhibit 7.4 lists examples of averages for various countries worldwide.

Populations are shrinking and getting older on average in the North and West (the United States, Europe, and the United Kingdom, for example). The number of people under age 25 in the United States in 2010 was about 106 million, or about 34 percent of the population.[32] In Western Europe, the number is 109 million, or a little over a fourth of the population.[33] Populations in the South and East are much younger. For example, in Latin America and the Caribbean, the number of people under age 25 was 271 million, or about 46 percent of the population.[34] In India, there are 568 million people under age 25, or about 48 percent of the population.[35]

■Exhibit **7.4**

Approximate Numbers of People under Age 25 in 2010[36]		
Country	Number of People under Age 25	Percentage of Population under Age 25
United States	106 million	34%
India	568 million	48%
Brazil	87 million	43%
Germany	20 million	25%
United Kingdom	18 million	30%
Russia	41 million	29%
China	466 million	35%
Latin America and the Caribbean	271 million	46%
Western Europe	109 million	25%
Sub-Saharan Africa	534 million	63%

Just as demographics are shifting and causing organizations to consider how to best employ, lead, and manage a diverse workforce, those same organizations are grappling with how to change their products and services in response to massive shifts in the world's economies and the balance of power. This issue has become one of the defining factors driving change in organizations.

Shifts in the World's Economies

The economies of the West and North (particularly Europe, the United Kingdom, and the United States) have held sway in most of the world for several hundred years. Today, however, a distinct shift in the balance of power is underway. Economies in the East and South, such as those of China, Brazil, and India, are quickly overtaking the traditional powers in terms of economic growth. Consider what is happening in India versus what is happening in the United States, as reported by the *Wall Street Journal* in January 2010:

India's economy is expected to grow at a fast clip this fiscal year ending March 31, top ministers said Friday, highlighting that the expansion will be one of the fastest among major economies that shrugged off a global downturn.

While Prime Minister Manmohan Singh expects the economy to grow around 7%, Finance Minister Pranab Mukherjee is hopeful for a more optimistic 7.75% expansion.

"We are equally optimistic that we can return to, and sustain, an annual growth rate of 9 to 10% in a couple of years," Mr. Singh said at a conference for overseas Indians.

"The rapid growth of India's economy in the last few years has helped lift millions of people out of poverty," he added.

India's economic expansion averaged 9% for four years through March 31, 2008, before slowing to 6.7% in the last fiscal year amid the global slowdown.[37]

Compare this to what the U.S. economy has seen in recent years (see ■Exhibit 7.5). This picture is partly the result of the worst recession in many years, and growth rates did begin to improve in 2010. Still, the trend remains that strong economies such as India, China, and others are growing much faster than the U.S., U.K., and other Western economies.

Long-term growth rates in countries such as the United States are considered to be around 2 to 3 percent. However, as mentioned in the previous quote, fast-growing

■Exhibit **7.5**
United States GDP Growth Rate, adjusted for inflation, 2006–2009*.[38]

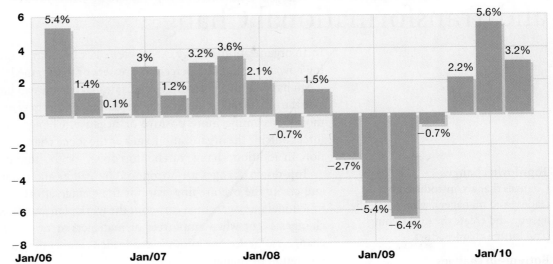

*Figures that go into calculating GDP are constantly changing, and adjustments are made retroactively.

economies such as India have been seeing upwards of 7 percent annual growth, as has China. Although these high rates of growth won't be sustained indefinitely, they are happening now and have been for some time. Comparative growth trends are shifting. Countries in the East and South are growing more quickly, whereas economies in the North and West are slowing down. This means that the world's businesses have to shift strategies quite dramatically.

As you can imagine, large social and global trends can have a profound effect on organizations and businesses. The rate and pace of these macro changes are increasing on a local, national, and global level. What does this mean for businesses and organizations? Business and organization leaders need to understand change and how to respond to it. Accordingly, in the next two sections, we look at how change happens (incrementally or radically) and how we can respond to it (adaptation or transformation). Then, we look at models that can help us understand how to manage change in organizations, groups, and individuals (including ourselves).

Most Popular » Discussion Questions

1. In recent years, businesses have become more global, and populations have become more diverse. In addition, sustainability has become more important than ever to many businesses. What kinds of changes might an organization have to engage in to deal with these societal shifts?

2. Do you believe that the focus of business and economic growth is moving "West to East and North to South"? Present evidence for your argument.

3. How will the growth of economies in the East and South affect American companies such as auto manufacturers, banking institutions, and professional services firms?

4. What do you think today's workers, managers, and leaders need to do *on a personal level* to cope with technological, social, and economic changes?

3. What Is the Difference between Incremental and Transformational Change?

In an organization, change can be viewed as any shift in the work environment, including how it is organized, perceived, created, or maintained. Change can be anticipated or it can happen unexpectedly. Organizational change can happen as a result of forces inside the organization, such as the development of a new product or service or employee morale becoming more positive or negative. Change can also happen as a result of forces outside the organization, such as the social changes discussed in the previous section. In addition, change can be "top down" or "bottom up."

Top-down changes

Changes that are introduced by leaders and managers, who define the agenda and create the overarching plan for the change effort.

Bottom-up changes

Changes that occur when employees or managers at various levels spark a movement for change, influence one another and leaders, and contribute to the planning and implementation of change.

Top-down changes are introduced by leaders and managers, who define the agenda and create the overarching plan for the change effort.[39] The company's business and functional managers then carry out the work plan and implement changes. **Bottom-up changes** occur when employees or managers at various levels spark a movement for change, influence one another and leaders, and contribute to the planning and implementation of change.

Whatever the reasons for change or where it originates, change can be either incremental or sudden. According to scholars David Nadler and Michael Tushman, there are four approaches to organizational change, as you can see in ■Exhibit 7.6.

According to this model, leaders and organization members can either anticipate the need for change or react to change that occurs in the organization or the environment. Change can be incremental, occurring in small steps over a long time, or it can involve dramatic shifts in strategy or ways of working or doing business.[40]

In this model, the four ways of dealing with change are called *tuning*, *adaptation*, *reorientation*, and *re-creation*. Tuning and adaptation are incremental approaches. Tuning is an anticipatory approach (what we might now call *proactive*) that is adopted in response to expected changes in the internal or external environment. For example, an organization might choose not to fill empty positions if leaders anticipate a decrease in sales.

Adaptation is another incremental approach to change made in response to an event or series of events. Adaptation is reactive in the sense that changes are planned after unforeseen changes in the internal or external environment or the organization have occurred. For example, adaptation occurs when you develop new manufacturing processes after the development or modification of products.

Strategic approaches to change include reorientation and re-creation. Both of these approaches involve completely changing ways of working and doing business—shaking things up, if you will. Reorientation is anticipatory, whereas re-creation is reactive. Reorientation is an organization-wide strategic change made in anticipation of a future occurrence. These changes involve a basic redirection of the organization, such as changing a business model or shifting from a store front to a primarily online presence due to anticipated changes in consumer shopping preferences. Re-creation is strategic change brought about by external events.

General Electric, one of the oldest companies in the United States, underwent dramatic strategic change in the 1990s that involved both reactive and anticipatory approaches. Senior leadership decided to shift the company's strategy and began moving more of GE's operations overseas. They did this because being centered primarily in the United States was hurting the company in an era of increasing globalization.[41] This was a reactive approach. At around the same time, GE invested heavily in research on environ-

■Exhibit **7.6**

Different ways of dealing with change can be seen in organizations.

	Incremental	Strategic
Anticipatory	Tuning	Reorientation
Reactive	Adaptation	Re-creation

Source: Adapted from Nadler, David A., and Michael Tushman.1989. Organizational frame bending: Principles for managing reorientation. *Academy of Management Executive* 3: 196.

mentally friendly technology long before such concerns were proven to be profitable. This was anticipatory. Today, GE is a major supplier of efficient energy-producing wind turbines and other innovative green products.[42]

Many people argue that the American auto industry missed opportunities to anticipate changes in recent years (for example, they did not adequately forecast the need for more fuel-efficient cars). Failing to anticipate business and social changes and act accordingly means that the U.S. auto industry has had to react to changes—an expensive and difficult situation. Business results have been poor, and during the economic recession that began in late 2007, both General Motors and Chrysler were forced into bankruptcy, while shares of Ford stock dropped dramatically in price toward the end of 2008 before subsequently recovering.

Revolutionary and Evolutionary Change: "Slow" Is Not Always Better

Nadler and Tushman suggest that, to the extent possible, leaders, managers, and employees should anticipate change and move toward the future more strategically. They also suggest that incremental change is easier to manage. Although this is partially true, there are at least two things to consider. First, we simply cannot anticipate everything that might happen, especially during a time when many aspects of technology, society, and our world's economies are changing at warp speed. Unexpected changes can also result from unpredictable natural forces, such as the earthquake in Haiti in 2010. This catastrophic event caused the world to react with an enormous outpouring of compassion, money, and aid. When an event like this occurs, many aid organizations, governments, and businesses that provide medical supplies, food, water, and transportation can suddenly find themselves under tremendous pressure to provide assistance quickly, without any warning whatsoever.

Incremental change, on the other hand, happens subtly over time and is sometimes hard to detect. In many cases, this allows leaders to plan for change, adapt these plans as they go, and engage in an orderly change process. Shouldn't we always implement change in this way? Not necessarily, and the metaphor of the boiling frog shows us why:

> They say that if you put a frog into a pot of boiling water, it will leap out right away to escape the danger. But, if you put a frog in a kettle that is filled with water that is cool and pleasant, and then gradually heat the kettle until it starts boiling, the frog will not become aware of the threat until it is too late. The frog's survival instincts are geared towards detecting sudden changes.[43]

The frog fable is a warning to pay attention *both* to obvious threats *and* to more slowly developing ones. Like frogs, people are hardwired to notice dramatic changes and *do* something. We often take incremental changes in stride, sometimes not examining them too carefully. But we (and our companies) must pay attention to slowly changing trends in the environment and not just devote our attention to sudden changes. Consider what happened to the world's financial institutions in the years leading up to the recession that began in 2007.

Incremental Changes That Led to a Worldwide Financial Crisis

The financial crisis that exploded on the scene in late 2007 has been called the worst economic crisis since the Great Depression. How did it occur? What went wrong? Well, many things, actually. The wheels were set in motion decades ago. Incremental changes over many years in financial policies, lending policies, the commodities market, and consumerism eventually led to a situation in which what the system was capable of doing was dramatically different from what it needed to do in a suddenly changed economic landscape.

■Exhibit **7.7**

The roots of the economic recession that began in 2007 can be traced back to President Ronald Reagan's deregulation of the banking industry in 1982.

Nik Wheeler/Alamy Images

Investment banks
Institutions that raise capital, trade securities, and assist with mergers and acquisitions.

Net capital rule
Rule that guides how much debt an institution can hold.

Leveraging money
A practice that allows financial institutions to increase the amount of debt they handle in proportion to the amount of money they hold.

The Long Story Leading to a Global Recession

The story of the events that contributed to the devastating recession of recent years began almost three decades ago. A number of incremental changes in both U.S. Federal Reserve policy and financial services institutions were adopted over the course of the 20 to 30 years prior to the recession. Many of these changes did not seem radical and, in fact, some were not even noticed by many people—to our collective detriment. Let's look at how some of these changes happened.

In 1982, President Ronald Reagan's administration took steps toward federal deregulation of the U.S. banking industry (with the help of Congress, of course).[44] This meant that banks had more freedom of choice about the terms and conditions of their financial products, such as loan structures and the like (■Exhibit 7.7). Then, when President Clinton's administration tore down the walls between commercial banks and investment banks in 1999, more potential problems loomed. That's because **investment banks**, which are institutions that raise capital, trade securities, and assist with mergers and acquisitions, tend to take far more risks than commercial banks. With deregulation, commercial banks were allowed to take even more risks than before, which they did. More and more financial institutions subsequently moved toward a culture of risk taking that proved entirely unsafe.[45]

At the same time, many banks were moving from being privately owned to publicly traded, and shareholders were demanding short-term gains. The U.S. Securities and Exchange Commission's relaxing of the **net capital rule**, which guided how much debt an institution could hold, also had a profound effect because banks could drastically increase the practice of **leveraging money**, which allowed them to increase the amount of debt they handled in proportion to the amount of money they held.[46] The result was a dramatic increase in debt. As we neared the year 2000, countries such as China increased exports to the United States dramatically and underwrote U.S. debt, while Presidents Bill Clinton and George W. Bush encouraged home ownership through their support of lower interest rates and similar measures.[47]

Maybe No One Noticed There Was a Problem

Those of us who have looked to the self-interest of lending institutions to protect shareholders' equity, myself included, are in a state of shocked disbelief.

–Former chairman of the U.S. Federal Reserve Alan Greenspan to Congress in its 2008 investigation of the financial crisis (■Exhibit 7.8)[48]

■Exhibit **7.8**

Alan Greenspan was chairman of the U.S. Federal Reserve from 1987 until 2006.

Scott J. Ferrell/Congressional Quarterly/Alamy

When President Reagan removed Paul Volcker and appointed Alan Greenspan as chairman of the U.S. Federal Reserve in 1987, no one imagined that Greenspan would become the most revered chairman of the "Fed" in decades and then fall so far off this pedestal that he probably will have to explain himself for the rest of his life.[49] Following the September 11, 2001, terrorist attacks and a series of high-visibility corporate scandals, Greenspan sought to keep the economy going (and the president and U.S. citizens happy) by cutting federal interest rates to 1 percent by 2003. This meant that money was cheap and easy to borrow.

The low interest rates held for a long time, which helped fuel a housing boom in 2002 and 2003. A *housing boom* is a way to describe a high level of activity in the housing market, resulting in rapidly increasing home values.[50] Because of low interest rates and a variety of other factors, more and more people were able to buy houses. In many cases, they were buying houses that were extremely expensive and more than they could actually afford. Easy credit, predatory lending, and subprime lending led to an unsustainable housing boom, which quickly inflated housing prices. *Predatory lending* is a term used to describe deceptive or unfair practices such as not disclosing the legal or financial terms of a mortgage or charging exorbitant fees when a mortgage is originated. **Subprime lending** is a term describing the practice of lending money to people who normally would not qualify for a mortgage because they have maxed-out credit cards, a poor debt-to-income ratio, or bad credit. From 1997 to the peak of the housing bubble in 2006, median home sale prices increased 124 percent.[51] Subprime lending jumped from about 8 percent of loans to 20 percent in 2005.[52]

During this time, investors were buying up U.S. cash at historically low prices and using the money to invest in high-interest markets overseas.[53] Globally, there was roughly $70 trillion seeking higher yields than U.S. treasury bonds were paying. This led to the development of financial innovations such as mortgage-backed security and collateralized debt obligations that were considered "safe" investments. These were based on the supply chain of mortgages, and they further fueled the bubble.[54]

These factors, when taken together, meant banks were carrying far too much debt. They also meant that much of this debt would never be paid back because people had been encouraged to take on loans they could not afford, and because the terms of their mortgages changed dramatically after a few years in ways that caused them to suffer financially and even declare bankruptcy. It's not as if no one noticed what was happening. As Paul Volcker predicted in 2005:

> *I don't know whether change will come with a bang or a whimper, whether sooner or later. But as things stand, it is more likely than not that it will be financial crises rather than foreign policy foresight that will force the change.*[55]

Despite a few outcries, the situation continued to heat up. New ways of commoditizing debt, such as the expanding derivatives market, also contributed to the growing problem. Derivatives are extremely complicated financial instruments that are very difficult to measure and value, because they represent the anticipated future value of underlying financial products such as bonds or currency. Financial genius Warren Buffett famously called derivatives "financial weapons of mass destruction," and argued that although they generate reportable earnings, those earnings are based on "wildly overstated" estimates "whose inaccuracy may not be exposed for many years."[56] In fact, the incorrect pricing of risk in loans, especially subprime loans, led to the overnight collapse of some of the world's largest financial institutions, including AIG, Lehman Brothers, and Bear Stearns.[57]

Although any one of the many changes that occurred between 1982 and 2007 probably would not have led to global recession on its own, together, these incremental changes were disastrous. Somehow the world's leaders and financial wizards didn't see the problem coming. In the next section, we will discuss some approaches that can help leaders pay more attention to change processes and also help people cope with the change process itself.

Subprime lending
The practice of lending money to people who normally would not qualify for a mortgage because they have maxed-out credit cards, a poor debt-to-income ratio, or bad credit.

Most Popular » Discussion Questions

1. Consider some changes that you have experienced and plot them on the model in Exhibit 7.6. Explain what happened in a change that you experienced as tuning. Then, explain a change that caused you to adapt, reorient, and re-create yourself or some aspect of your life. Which of these was easiest for you? Which had the best outcome?

2. Have you seen any evidence of incremental or evolutionary changes in your school or where you work? If so, what are they? Are the leaders of the institution or organization taking an incremental approach, or is change a haphazard process? Give evidence for your point of view.

3. What revolutionary changes have you seen in a business or institution you are familiar with? What caused this organization to change radically? What was the effect on you?

4. Consider the difficult financial crisis that began in 2007. Do you know people who suffered from this recession or who had to change the way they lived or worked? How and why?

---

4. Which Models Can Help Us Understand Change?

There are many different views of how change occurs and how individuals react to the process of change. In this section, we look at one popular and useful model created by social scientist Kurt Lewin that examines how forces for and against change affect what happens. Then, we look at a metaphor that helps us explain and understand the idea that change is a constant in modern life, work, and organizations.

Lewin's Force Field Analysis Model of Change

In 1951, social scientist Kurt Lewin proposed a powerful way of understanding change in organizations that incorporated group dynamics, field theory, and action research into a combined systems perspective.[58] The model that bears his name is still widely used today because it remains relevant for complex modern organizations. Lewin's change model, which is usually called *force field analysis*, can be applied to any level of human systems: an individual, a group, an organization, a community, and so on.

As you can see in ■Exhibit 7.9, Lewin's model looks at change as having three distinct phases. Prior to the beginning of a change process, a system is seen as frozen, and the status quo is firmly in place. Later, in the first stage of the change process, the system begins to "unfreeze." Then, in the second phase, change occurs. Finally, in the third stage, the system refreezes, settling into a new status quo. The model as originally presented argues that social habits are fixed, or frozen. To initiate change, these social habits have to "unfreeze," which requires "[breaking] open the shell of complacency . . . [by causing] an emotional stir-up" to bring these habits into consciousness, where they can be worked on.[59] After desired changes are activated, a process of refreezing occurs that locks in new ways of feeling, thinking, and behaving.

In each of Lewin's stages, dynamic forces are at work that are both driving change and preventing it. When these forces are balanced, no change occurs and the status quo remains in place. In contrast, when driving forces become more powerful than restraining forces, the system begins to unfreeze—old habits are questioned, old patterns of behavior don't seem to work as well, and people might feel anxious and uncertain. If the driving forces continue to be powerful enough, change can occur.

■Exhibit **7.9**

Lewin's force field analysis model of change helps us look at forces for and against change.

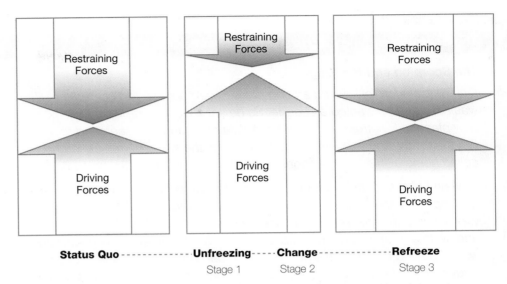

Source: Based on Lewin, Kurt. 1952. Group decision and social change. In *Readings in social psychology*, ed. E. Maccoby, T. Newcomb, and E. Hartley, 459–73. New York: Holt, Rinehart, & Winston.

Then, in the third stage, the forces for and against change are once again balanced, which allows people and the organization to settle into new habits, processes, and activities.

Lewin's approach to change has many of the right elements, and some of them are not obvious in the model.[60] Namely, Lewin emphasized that change can be effectively implemented only if the entire context is considered. Culture and values must be addressed overtly, as well as goals, mission, business practices, and the like.

Consider the Context: The "Whole Picture"

Lewin believed that change at any level of a system has to include a deep understanding of the context in which behaviors, patterns, and habits have developed.[61] This means that it's not enough to simply look at a person, group, or organization—you have to look at the entire picture and how each part of a system is linked to and related to the other parts. The well-known parable in ■Exhibit 7.10 shows us what this means.

The poor frog in the parable misses a few things about the big picture—namely, that the scorpion *was* a scorpion, after all. The frog also failed to explore the situation: Why did the scorpion want to cross the river? How important was it? What was on the other side? More scorpions? Did the scorpion really care about living or dying? Were there other scorpions around, with their own agendas? Was there anything else that would prevent the scorpion from being a scorpion? What, after all, was the reason the scorpion wanted to change, and could he?

Considering the context of organizational change is extremely important. Take, for example, what Apple's leader Steve Jobs had to say about the context—the market environment—that existed at the time the iPod Nano was introduced. The iPod was already dominating the market when Steve Jobs challenged his top executives and engineers to develop a product to replace it. "Playing it safe is the most dangerous thing we can do," Jobs warned.[62] At the time, iPod claimed 74 percent of the market for digital music players, which might convince some people and companies to relax. Jobs, however, didn't want to give the competition any time to catch up, and that meant ensuring that the only company to make the iPod obsolete would be Apple. The result of this was the very successful iPod Nano. Steve Jobs and Apple didn't follow the rules of the industry, and as a result, they kept the competition off balance and inspired the company's team of creative workers.[63]

The Scorpion and the Frog Is a Well-Known Parable

The Scorpion and the Frog

One day, a scorpion looked around at his desert home and decided that life was hard and he wanted a change. So he set out on a journey to look for a new place to live, trekking through the dust and sand and scorched rocks. Days went by, and everywhere he looked was the same barren desert he had called home all his life. His hopes began to sink, until one day he came to a river!

Now on his side of the river, the land was the same that he was used to—cactus and rock and sand and other scorpions. But, lo and behold, on the other side was a lush paradise. There were trees and even grass. But the river was wide and swift, and the scorpion realized that he had a problem. He couldn't see any way of getting to the other side. So he scurried up and down the river bank, looking for a bridge or a fallen tree or some large rocks—anything that would help him reach his goal.

There was nothing. The little scorpion despaired of ever getting across the river and settled down on his haunches, contemplating the unfairness of life. Suddenly, out of the corner of his eye, he spied a frog sitting by itself in the rushes along the bank of the other side of the river. Maybe, just maybe, the frog could be convinced to help him get across.

"Hellooo, Mr. Frog!" the scorpion shouted across the river. "I would very much like to be on your side of this river. Would you be so kind as to help me?"

"Hrrmph, Mr. Scorpion! If I try to help you, you are just going to reward me with death!" said the frog with self-assured certainty.

"But," replied the scorpion, "if I kill you, then I could not get to your side of the river, for you see, I really want to leave this desert and be over there."

This seemed to make sense to the frog, who hadn't really had that much experience with scorpions before. But he was still unsure. "What about when I get you across? You could still kill me once I have helped you!"

"Well . . . ," answered the scorpion, "you see, if you bring me to your side of this river, I will be so grateful for your help, it would be terribly unjust to turn around and kill you for your kindness, now wouldn't it?"

*"But . . . but . . . ," sputtered the frog, "after all, you **are** a scorpion!"*

*"This is true," agreed the scorpion. "But you see, I am a **changed** scorpion. I have been traveling these past days looking for a new life. I have worked **very hard**! And I see that on your side of the river, there is enough for everybody. Why would I waste all my hard work?"*

The frog, being a kind and trusting sort, finally agreed to take the scorpion across the river. He swam across to the scorpion and settled himself right along the edge of the bank to let his passenger climb upon his back. The scorpion crawled on, his sharp claws gently pricking the frog's slippery hide, and the frog slid back into the river. The scorpion was elated! Here he was, having overcome all kinds of obstacles, and now his goal was within reach. The trees on the other side of the river were becoming larger and larger. The splish, splish of the river had a soothing effect, and the scorpion began to relax.

*But then the scorpion looked back. He realized he was losing a **lot**. The food he liked, the feel of warm sand at night . . . and the chance to find a mate. That did it. Life wouldn't be worth living.*

Halfway across the river, the frog suddenly felt a sharp stinger sink deep into his back. His vision became blurry, and his limbs grew weak. Using the last of his strength, he turned his head to see the scorpion pulling his stinger out from the frog's back.

"You fool!" croaked the frog, "Now we are both going to die, and for what?! Why on earth did you do that?"

The scorpion sadly shrugged as they began to sink, and said, "I guess it is just my nature."

Consider the Power of Culture

Lewin also believed that change only occurs when group and cultural norms, values, and dynamics are addressed. In other words, it isn't enough to simply try to change individuals, because the power of culture almost always trumps a person's desire to change—even when it is sincere. That's because culture is a powerful restraining force that helps maintain the status quo. In Chapter 13, you will learn about the various attributes of culture. For now, consider aspects such as shared values and beliefs and accepted behaviors—that is, "the way we do things around here."

Think about this from your own experience. It's likely that when you started college, you learned new things about how to behave with people, build new friendships, and communicate. Maybe you were a bit shy before college or perhaps you were one of the "stars" back home. Upon entering this new "system"—college—you realized that you would have to learn new behaviors, and maybe even a new way of seeing yourself. You might have become more outgoing so you could meet new friends. You might have realized that there were many "stars" in college, and you'd have to behave somewhat differently than you did before. You likely made a number of changes to how you behave, how you perceive others, and even how you see yourself.

Then something very strange happened. On your first visit home, after having changed many of your "old" ways of behaving, you found yourself slipping into your old habits. Almost immediately, you took up the roles you had always held with your parents, siblings, and friends, behaving in much the same way you did before you left. If you didn't return to these old behaviors, you might have found that people were not particularly happy with you and tried to push you back to your old ways. This happens a lot—and for the reasons Lewin pointed out. The norms and expectations of the groups we belong to are powerful drivers of our behavior.

When trying to change a situation, *you need to understand the situation as it is before trying to change it.* Change must start with a significant examination of what currently exists, such as forces for and against change; culture, beliefs, and values; and behaviors, processes, and structures—which brings us to Lewin's third point about change.

Studying a System *Changes* the System

According to Lewin, the very act of studying a system changes it.[64] Social scientist Edgar Schein agrees, noting that you cannot hope to understand how to change a system unless you know what the system is changing from.[65] Also, because all systems are in a constant state of change, it is important to identify and locate those elements that are already at work to produce change. In essence, you need to continually find ways to take a snapshot of where the organization is at the moment and use that information to spark the desire for change.

Lewin proposed a process for studying human systems while simultaneously changing them, called action research, that we will discuss later in the chapter. Action research assumes that the act of studying a group, organization, or community results in change—regardless of whether the researchers intend this or not. That means that while we study human systems, we need to understand and manage the changes that occur *because* of our research. For example, say you're part of a team that is experiencing lots of conflict. You want to understand this, so you "study" the group by asking each team member questions such as, "Why do you think we fight so often?" Simply by asking these questions, you draw people's attention to how they're acting. Increased attention will most likely cause people to monitor their behavior more carefully, which might result in less conflict.

Change Is Constant:
The Permanent White-Water Metaphor

Although Lewin's model is extremely useful when considering change in human systems, it does have some drawbacks. The most notable drawback is this model appears to indicate that a system starts in a fixed or static place and ends that way—static, albeit different.

Peter Vaill is a well-known organizational change theorist who coined the term *permanent white water*. **Permanent white water** is a metaphor that refers to the fact that organizational systems face unrelenting turbulence and constant change.[66] As a result, managers have to accept that they have limited control over their environments.

However, in *real* white-water rapids, expert rafters know how to use paddles, body weight, posture, currents, and the quiet water near the shore to help them deal with the dangers of navigation. As organization scholars Gregory Shea and Robert Gunther point out, managers and leaders everywhere need to learn the equivalent skills for dealing with fast-paced and constant change in organizations and the environment.[67] In fact, whatever role you have today, you will need to be a creative lifelong learner, steering yourself toward new skills and the information you'll need to deal with constant change.[68]

Kurt Lewin's force field analysis model is helpful in understanding change, and the permanent white-water metaphor helps us see that change is constant and must be managed. Now, let's look at some practical ways to actually implement change.

Permanent white water
Metaphor that refers to the fact that organizational systems face unrelenting turbulence and constant change.

Most Popular » Discussion Questions

1. Think about a change you attempted this year in school (such as a change in study habits, your social life, or your extracurricular activities). What are the forces *for* this change (those that help you) and the forces *against* this change (those that interfere)? What might you do to capitalize on the forces that help you while minimizing those that do not?
2. Review the parable of the scorpion and the frog in Exhibit 7.10. Have you ever felt like the frog? Have you missed important information or asked the wrong questions when deciding to do something new? Can you see any patterns in the information you tend to pay attention to or tend to miss when making changes in your life or at work?
3. How does the permanent white-water metaphor apply to your life?

---

5. What Practical Models Can Help Us Manage Change in Organizations?

In this section, we turn our attention to practical models of change that enable us to manage change in organizations. Scholar-practitioners John Kotter and Gregory Shea help us consider what we should pay attention to and do when implementing change. Both Kotter's and Shea's models help us focus our efforts when attempting to bring about organizational change.

Kotter's Eight-Stage Change Model

As you can see in ■Exhibit 7.11, Harvard Business School professor John Kotter's well-known approach to organizational change involves eight clearly defined steps.

Kotter Stages 1 through 5: Preparing for Change

Kotter Stage 1

John Kotter, like Kurt Lewin, believes that in order for a change process to actually begin (with any hope of continuing), the first stage of any change process in an organization must *ensure that people feel an urgent need for change*. Everyone involved, or potentially involved, needs to have both a cognitive understanding of why change is necessary and an emotional investment in what needs to be done and why. Sometimes leaders attempt to expose a "burn-

■Exhibit **7.11**

John Kotter's Approach to Implementing Organizational Change
What to Do to Ensure Effective Implementation of Change
Stage 1: Ensure that people feel an urgent need for change.
Stage 2: Get the right people involved to lead change.
Stage 3: Create a new strategic vision.
Stage 4: Make sure the new vision is effectively communicated.
Stage 5: Empower a broad group of change agents.
Stage 6: Successfully pull off short-term victories.
Stage 7: Consolidate the victories and go after more changes.
Stage 8: Solidify the change in the organizational culture.

Source: Based on Kotter, John P. 1996. *Leading change*. Boston, MA : Harvard Business School Press.

ing platform," a common metaphor used in organizations to describe something that is on the horizon or a trend that is currently under way that absolutely must be attended to.

To see how Kotter's first stage has played out in reality, consider the pharmaceutical industry. In this industry, the business model has revolved around research, development, and marketing of "blockbuster" drugs. Blockbuster drugs have tended to be company "jewels." Developing these drugs requires a huge investment of money and time, but if the drugs are taken up by the market, they provide huge amounts of revenue to the company for the entire time the company holds the patent. Examples of 2005 blockbuster drugs include Lipitor, Plavix, and Nexium (see ■Exhibit 7.12).[69] As you can see, these medications made a *lot* of money.

During 2005, when these drugs were blockbusters, total spending on prescription drugs was approximately $602 billion worldwide, with more than 41 percent of these

■Exhibit **7.12**

Top Three Blockbuster Drugs in 2005

1. Lipitor
    a. Treats: High blood pressure
    b. Annual Sales: $12.9 billion
    c. Annual Growth: 6.4%
    d. Manufacturer: Pfizer
    e. Approved: December 1996
    f. Patent Expiration: June 2011[70]
2. Plavix
    a. Treats: Heart disease
    b. Annual Sales: $5.9 billion
    c. Annual Growth: 16%
    d. Manufacturer: Bristol-Myers Squibb and Sanofi-Aventis
    e. Approved: November 1997
    f. Patent Expiration: November 2011[71]
3. Nexium
    a. Treats: Heartburn
    b. Annual Sales: $5.7 billion
    c. Annual Growth: 16.7%
    d. Manufacturer: AstraZeneca
    e. Approved: March 2000
    f. Patent Expiration: 2019, but on 27 May 2014, AstraZeneca will license this drug to another manufacturer to settle a lawsuit[72]

sales occurring in the United States. According to a 2007 report, "The top 100 block-buster drugs generated sales of $252.5 billion, accounting for 35.5 percent of the total pharmaceutical market."[73]

However powerful this business model has been, many market analysts and pharmaceutical executives believe that this way of doing business is on the way out. It won't end right away, of course, because industry practices and an organizational system geared toward creating and marketing blockbusters are well entrenched. However, the pressures related to the costs and time needed to develop these drugs, the inevitable loss of patents, the public's growing impatience with marketing strategies that deliberately sow the seeds of fear or foster a perceived need for a particular drug, and the call for pharmaceutical companies to behave in a socially responsible manner together add up to one thing: Change is coming. Wise industry leaders in the drug industry are paying attention.

For instance, one of the world's largest pharmaceutical companies recently indicated a major strategic shift. Following a quarterly earnings report that was 33 percent higher than Wall Street expected, Andrew Witty, CEO of GlaxoSmithKline, announced that GSK has taken some bold moves to put the company at the forefront of changes in drug research and marketing. For example, in 2009, GSK took a peer-to-peer (P2P) approach to research and development, turning the traditional model of pharmaceutical research on its ear.[74] The company is developing a "patent pool" to which it will contribute 13,500 of the molecules its researchers have developed, allowing for greater open source research. This means that researchers outside GSK can work toward joint solutions using the company's innovations.

In addition, 60 scientists around the world will have access to GSK's research centers to conduct their work.[75] This is an "open lab" project. By making innovation publicly available, GSK can enlist the creative energies of researchers around the world to develop much needed and less expensive drugs to treat illnesses in developing and undeveloped countries—the so-called "neglected diseases," which "are a low risk area for drug firms to experiment with open data."[76]

One of the interesting aspects of GSK's decision to create open labs to support the development of drugs for emerging markets is that it is an approach to change that moves away from a fear-based response toward an innovative and inspirational approach instead. This indicates a shift in how the company perceives change. Rather than seeing change as a "burning platform" that must be avoided, the company is moving *toward* something: a creative research process that can help the world's poor. Rather than simply frightening employees about the future, this company's leaders are inspiring people to change by working toward new business realities: new ways of doing research and new markets. The company's leaders are clear about the changes they want, and they're bringing employees along with them. In fact, at JP Morgan's 28th Annual Healthcare Conference in January 2010, Witty indicated a move away from the blockbuster approach, noting that in order to successfully diversify GSK, the company had to get out of the business of pushing "white pills in Western markets" and into the business of solving real needs in emerging markets.[77] An inspiring vision indeed, and one that is likely to help employees want to address urgent needs for change in the company.

Kotter Stage 2

According to Kotter, the second stage of any change process involves *getting the right people involved to lead change.* This can include people at all levels, but it must include senior leaders. Without senior leadership involved, most change efforts will fail. Sometimes this takes the form of a "change council" that is composed of senior leaders, people from all levels of the organization, representatives of all major functions, and expert advisers who understand change and/or the issues the organization is facing.

Kotter Stage 3

Kotter's stage three involves the *creation of a new strategic vision* for the organization. A new strategy is often created at the top of the organization by the senior team and/or the board of directors. But when preparing for large-scale change, it is important to gather information and to involve key people from throughout the organization.

Kotter Stage 4

In stage 4, steps must be taken to *make sure the new vision is effectively communicated* throughout the organization. If people know what's going on and why, they are far more likely to be willing to make changes—even difficult ones. Something to note about this kind of communication is as follows: Rarely do impersonal forms of communication (such as company-wide e-mails) work. Leaders have to find ways to inspire and excite people, and they need to help people understand how the new organizational vision supports *individuals'* hopes and dreams.

Kotter Stage 5

After people understand the new vision, it is time to *empower a broad group of change agents*. This means finding, training, and creating a plan for a broad group of people to actively support the change process. Change agents work to continue to communicate, inspire, and mobilize people to engage in new behaviors, attitudes, and even values. They must, of course, have the skills to help people be enthusiastic about the change and to deal with the details of change implementation.

Although empowering change agents is an important part of the model, it is a stage that often fails in organizations. Part of the reason for this failure is that change agent skills, such as managing resistance, engaging in inspirational leadership, and displaying personal resilience, are not necessarily what people learn at work. In fact, in many organizations, skills related to sponsoring and encouraging change are discouraged.

Kotter Stages 6 through 8: Change

Kotter Stage 6

Kotter's sixth stage, *successfully pull off short-term victories*, is somewhat counterintuitive. Kotter says that in stage 6, leaders should set their sights on identifying opportunities for small victories that bring confidence that the change process is going in the right direction, rather than going after one big, splashy, noticeable change.

Kotter Stage 7

Stage 7 of Kotter's model involves *consolidating the smaller victories and going after more and bigger changes*. By this time, people's hearts and minds will have shifted, and they will be inspired and motivated to continue and to take on even bigger, more significant change efforts.

Kotter Stage 8

Finally, in the last stage of Kotter's change process, the *new ways of thinking and doing must be solidified in the organizational culture*. This can take the form of changing some of the "symbols" of the culture (such as the mission statement), emphasizing and capitalizing on the "good stories" that have emerged about the new organization, or embedding the new ways of being and doing into organizational systems and processes.

Kotter argues that organizational change often fails because leaders ignore or overlook one or more steps in this model. For instance, without selecting and empowering a coalition of leaders to implement change, obstacles become barriers. Overconfidence after accomplishing small gains might make leaders believe that they have achieved success. Even when the vision of change is successfully accomplished with significant gains, the failure to embed the change into the organizational culture can lead to long-term failure.

Kotter's model has and continues to be used quite extensively as a framework for implementing change in organizations. Let's now look at another practical model that, when coupled with Lewin's force field analysis and Kotter's approach, will further improve the chances of successfully implementing change in an organization.

Gregory Shea's Work Systems Model

Gregory Shea, Wharton's expert on organizational transformation, sees today's businesses and institutions as complex, dynamic systems that are constantly undergoing change. Shea has developed a model of organizations called the work systems model

■ Exhibit **7.13**

Gregory Shea's work systems model shows how complex organizations are.

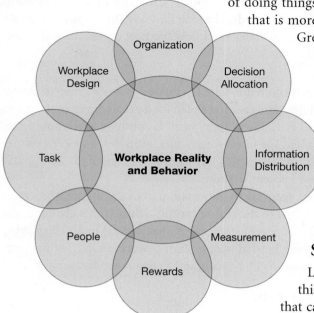

Source: Adapted from Shea, Gregory P. 2001. Leading change. In *Medicine and business: Bridging the gap*, ed. S. Rovin, p. 47. Gaithersburg, MD: Aspen Publishers. Used with permission of Shea & Associates, Inc. © Shea & Associates, Inc.

(shown in ■ Exhibit 7.13) that shows how complex organizations are, as well as how many aspects of an organization must be considered—and leveraged—when trying to bring about change.[78]

In this model, change efforts are directed toward the center: a new and better way of doing things, a more effective and efficient organization, and an overall context that is more likely to result in success, employee satisfaction, and resonance. As Gregory Shea puts it:

> *Change involves creating a different workplace reality. People do things differently. To get that to happen, you must first figure out the workplace reality that you want. 'What will be happening in this office setting, that production area, or within that cross-national, continental, or global virtual team?' 'What scenes will they live out that will embody the change, that will be the change?' If you can't see it, then you can't design for it. If you can't design for it, then you just dramatically cut your chances of getting and sustaining it. So, first things first: what constellation of behaviors or scenes or film clips are you trying to bring to life?*[79]

Shea's Levers of Change in the Work System Model

Let's take a moment to look at Shea's model in more detail. First of all, in this model, a *lever* is an aspect of an organizational system or subsystem that can be studied, attended to, emphasized, or ignored during the change process. The selection of which levers to study and influence is extremely important. Depending on the type of change needed or desired, this decision can make or break the change process. Each of the levers is a potential contributor to or inhibitor of successfully introducing change to the whole system. This is the case because change in any one part of the system has an impact on the *entire* system.

For example, Children's Medical Center of Dallas used the people, rewards, and task levers in a change process it implemented in response to a growing need for more effective doctor–patient communication in a region where native Spanish speakers are the fastest growing population. The hospital was increasingly facing problems because many of its doctors were not fluent in Spanish and many of its patients were not fluent enough in English to accurately describe their symptoms or understand their doctors' or nurses' instructions. The hospital first tried hiring several dozen professional medical translators, but doing so was costly, and this new cadre of translators was hard to manage.

Then, the hospital system turned to its own population. Many of the employees who were working as receptionists and in other areas of the hospital were bilingual, but they did not have fluency in medical language. The hospital's leaders thus decided to offer volunteers free training in both English and Spanish medical language, awarding bonuses and a pay raise to people who successfully passed the training, along with the additional title of "language liaison." Now, when translation service is needed, doctors can tap a staff member in the immediate vicinity with confidence.[80]

In this example, leadership first tried to fix the situation by changing the organization (hiring outside translators). This didn't work, partly because they were only shifting one lever—the overall structure of the organization. Then leadership addressed several more levers in concert. By asking for volunteers and providing training, they influenced the *people* lever, and by evaluating people's success in the training program, they influenced the *measurement* lever. By adding new duties and responsibilities, the *task* lever was influenced. And finally, bonuses and pay raises influenced the *reward* lever.

This situation shows us that it is important to pick the right levers, as well as to choose enough levers on which to focus. Shea cautions that paying attention to just one or two levers is a mistake. He notes, "In my experience working with organizations on change initiatives, one has to hit at least four of these drivers at the same time to make change happen . . . one doesn't have to use all these levers of change, but you can't use just use one and expect to succeed."[81] People need a sense that their work world has changed before they will change their own behavior and adapt.

Shea goes on to say that constant change requires constant choices and the development of new skills—along with constant attention to the environment within which the organizations exists. Shea's advice is as follows:

> I have seen very talented managers and executives, in the classroom and in my consulting, chewed up and spit out by this environment. They thrash about and even drown in change. The environment is relentless. They tried to meet a relentless environment, a permanent white-water environment, with their old skills. They took a scull or crew boat down the Grand Canyon. Not a good idea. The world has changed and we need new ways of meeting it.[82]

Shea on How to Choose *What* to Change

In a world where things change every day, it is necessary to choose both what to focus on and what *not* to focus on. In fact, Gregory Shea says that one of the most important things to do at work today (especially if you are a manager or leader) is to *choose what not to do*. It is impossible to address everything, and if you try to do so, you will likely fail at everything, or at least not meet even your own standards.[83]

You will want to *focus* on things that are important. To determine what's really important, however, you have to know whether the issues you are aware of are real and require immediate attention. For example, when Toyota faced the need to recall thousands of vehicles in 2009 and 2010 because of problems with their accelerator pedals, the company's leaders knew that these very real problems would require employees, managers, and executives at all levels and in many functions to spend lots of time managing the recall process, fixing the problem, and attending to Toyota's image.

According to Shea, there are three other ways to categorize situations to help you decide what to do (or not). Some things don't seem important, but in fact they are. Shea calls these *bombs*. Some things truly are unimportant, and you should ignore them. And some things are a *waste of time* because although unimportant, they capture your attention and tempt you to spend time on them.

So, what happens when something does not capture your attention but is, in fact, really important? The now-defunct financial services firm Lehman Brothers found out the hard way—the company seemed to ignore a bomb that blew up in a big way. Interestingly, there were numerous important clues that Lehman Brothers' banking practices could lead to difficulties. Presumably, no one paid attention or realized how important these clues were. Too many people inside and outside the organization ignored these very important issues, and a century-old company went out of business, taking with it thousands of jobs and many people's life savings.

Or take the example of the financial services firm Merrill Lynch (now part of Bank of America). Late in 2008, in the middle of one of the biggest financial meltdowns in history, a decision was made to remodel the new CEO's office to the tune of $1.2 million.[84] This is a classic example of *wasting time* while a ticking *bomb* (public opinion) was being *ignored*. Surely people had better things to worry about, but somehow, due to a combination of tradition, policy, and possibly the CEO's and other peoples' desires, the remodeling went ahead. Needless to say, the press got hold of this information and the bomb soon exploded. The company's reputation was badly damaged, and the time and effort spent on defending, explaining, and apologizing for these actions most likely took away from dealing with more pressing issues related to the financial crisis.

A less disastrous but more common example of a bomb at work is ignoring people's feelings about factors such as working conditions. For instance, within organizations, it is common to hear about people's pleasure or displeasure with their offices, cubicles, or workspaces. As a manager, you may decide to ignore this (which might be the right decision in some cases). However, when situations affect people's status or physical comfort, emotions can run very high. People care about their spaces, and managers must decide when it is important to pay attention to these types of issues and when not to.

But how do you know when issues are unimportant, rather than bombs waiting to explode? It's not easy deciding what to pay attention to. Far too often, people in organizations spend countless hours on things that simply aren't important. It takes careful consideration, critical thinking, and intuition to determine what to simply ignore. It would seem that something that isn't important will not make anyone's priority list and that people will not waste time on it. That is not always the case, however. For example, many people spend an inordinate amount of time dealing with e-mails that have nothing to do with their work and that truly aren't important. One reason people receive unnecessary (but distracting and time-consuming) e-mails is because others are trying to protect themselves by copying *everyone*. They want to be sure that no one can come back and say "I didn't know" or "Why didn't you ask me?" Your job is to figure out which e-mails to read and which to ignore.

Sometimes, people waste a lot of time on things like complaining about their bosses or colleagues without trying very hard to change anything. This is a tremendous waste of time—but you can't stop it just by telling people it's not acceptable. You can, however, consider this kind of behavior to be a symptom, and you can attempt to discover the source of the real problem. Maybe, for example, the culture encourages this kind of behavior—in such an environment, he or she who complains loudest has the most power. Or maybe there are one or two troublemakers—"bad apples" so to speak. Only by getting to the source of this behavior can you begin to change it.

To understand where to focus your time and attention, especially when it comes to change management, questions such as "Should we consider if this is important *now*?" and "Will it be important later?" should be asked regularly. That's because in today's volatile world, things are changing all the time—and priorities need to change too. Gregory Shea encourages us to think critically and to continue to evaluate our views about how important (or not) an activity is, as well as to review how we spend our time and energy.

In the preceding two sections, you focused on models that help you understand organizational change. Kurt Lewin's change model explains that there are both forces for and forces against change. Peter Vaill and others say that change is constant in society, the economy, and organizations. John Kotter helps you see that there are stages in the organizational change model, and each one is crucial. Finally, Gregory Shea's model helps you understand where you can focus your efforts to change organizations and how to constantly evaluate your choices. All of these models assist you in understanding what change is and how it can be integrated into organizations. Next, we turn our attention to people, looking specifically at what makes people want to change and what keeps them going even when change is difficult.

Most Popular » Discussion Questions

1. Think about a time you have tried to get others to change (in your family, a group, or a team at school or work). What did you do to ensure that they were ready for change? Did it work? Why or why not?

2. Consider Shea's levers of change. In your experience (at work, in teams, and so on), which lever is most important? Which is least important? Use real experiences to support your answer.

3. Review Shea's advice about how to categorize issues and determine how to spend your time. In your life at school or work, is there anything in the "bomb" category that actually needs your attention? Why are you not spending any time on this, and should you reevaluate your behavior?

6. How Do *People* Change?

Organizations change only if people do. That's why we have to understand a bit about how people respond to change psychologically and how to manage our responses to both positive change and changes that are not as welcome. With a deeper understanding about how people deal with change, we can turn our attention to a model that helps us create a change process that actually works for individuals: the intentional change model, developed by noted scholar Richard Boyatzis.

Change: It Is Not Always Easy for People

Learning and change come easy to children. With adults, however, this is often not the case. Scholars have long been interested in how our minds respond to change—basically, how adults learn new behaviors and different ways of dealing with the world.

For most adults, change can be painful. It makes us feel uncomfortable. Part of the reason is that when things remain the same, our minds can function efficiently along well laid out neural pathways—conscious attention is not needed. However, as changes occur, our working memory is limited, and memory overload can lead quickly to fatigue. The act of simply paying attention corresponds to real chemical and physical changes that occur in the brain as we form new neural pathways. This takes effort. As we pay more attention and practice new ways of thinking, these pathways become stronger and more efficient.[85] Psychologist Paul Waring has referred to this process as "coaching the brain."[86]

The process of taking in information from our five senses and processing the information is also complicated. One of the first things we do with information is process it in a part of our brains called the limbic system. This complicated system holds our emotional memories, and these help us determine whether what we see, hear, or experience is a threat or not, or whether what we encounter is a call to nurture others, care for, or even pursue a relationship. Parts of our limbic system (such as the amygdala and the thalamus) process information before messages are sent to our prefrontal lobe—where decisions are made and actions are planned.

Understanding and being able to manage your emotions isn't necessarily easy, nor does it always come naturally. That is because our emotions serve a purpose: They focus our attention on both threats and opportunities. In fact, emotions are a primal driver of attention, focus, and ultimately our behavior. Scholars Daniel Goleman, Richard Boyatzis, and Annie McKee have looked at how to harness emotions related to change.[87]

We need to cultivate and develop emotional intelligence competencies such as self-awareness and self-management to ensure that the emotions *guide* our thoughts and behaviors, rather than *hijacking* our limbic system. When our emotions are hijacked, we often act before we think. We can be hijacked by anxieties or fears that have little to do with survival; in addition, things like attraction to another person can also hijack us.[88] In either case, we often do things that we would not have done if we'd thought about it—even for a moment. Let's take this a bit further and look at exactly how some emotions affect our capacity for learning, change, and resilience.

The Psychology and Neuropsychology of Individual Change

Positive emotions matter when dealing with change because emotions impact our ability to stay focused and succeed at whatever we are doing. Environments that are characterized by positive emotions, challenge, and excitement can be highly motivating and results-oriented. If we look to psychology to explain why, we find that

■Exhibit **7.14**

Positive and Negative Emotional Attractors	
Positive Emotional Attractors	**Negative Emotional Attractors**
Hope	Fear
Joy	Despair
Compassion	Anger
Excitement	Resentment
Challenge	Jealousy
Serenity	Mistrust
Growth and learning	Forced compliance
Love	Hate
Respect	Disdain

Positive emotional attractor
A psychological state of well-being and hope that engages the parasympathetic nervous system and can counter the effects of stress.

Negative emotional attractor
A psychological state characterized by negative emotions that is linked to the sympathetic nervous system and that can cause people to feel defensive, threatened, and stressed.

when people experience what scientists call positive emotional attractors, they are resilient, creative, and open to new ideas and ways of doing things.[89] A **positive emotional attractor** is a psychological state of well-being and hope that engages the parasympathetic nervous system and can counter the effects of stress. The concept of emotional attractors is derived from chaos theory, a recent and popular approach to understanding human systems and human behavior.[90]

Unfortunately, and not surprisingly, a negative emotional attractor has the opposite effect. A **negative emotional attractor** is a psychological state characterized by negative emotions that is linked to the sympathetic nervous system and that can cause people to feel defensive, threatened, and stressed. When such emotions are pervasive in our organizations and teams, a dissonant climate is created, which causes people to shut down, avoid risks, and generally suboptimize their performance. That's not the best state to be in when approaching change. The negative emotional attractors can be activated by factors such as a fear of doing things differently, being forced to change against one's will, or a lack of clarity about what the changes entail or how they affect us personally.

How we deal with and manage emotion has a strong effect on how we approach change—both around us and in ourselves. ■Exhibit 7.14 lists some positive and negative emotional attractors. You can see how these states of mind will affect how you feel and perform. Let's look at how leaders put this into action, paying special attention to a model that can help us *use* emotions proactively to engage in change.

Intentional Change

Some leaders understand how to help people manage their emotions so there is an appropriate mix of positive and challenging responses to change. That is the case with Mark McCord-Amasis, Head of Global Facility Strategy for GlaxoSmithKline (GSK). As mentioned earlier, under the leadership of Andrew Witty, 2009 and 2010 saw GSK take bold and powerful steps to begin to change how the business operates and how the company sees its responsibility to the world's people—especially the poor.[91] These important and impressive actions are rippling through the organization, causing leaders everywhere to engage their people in profound change. Mark McCord-Amasis, an inspiring and insightful leader, shows us how to do this in a manner that engages people's energy and enthusiasm—as well as their talent and commitment.

**Mark McCord-Amasis,
Head of Global Facility Strategy
for GlaxoSmithKline**

Mark McCord-Amasis, Head of Global Facility Strategy for GlaxoSmithKline, is a creative and dedicated leader. He leads a full and exciting life, and he's inspiring.

The essential act of leadership is to envision the preferred future you want to create for your business or organization and put that into words. It is important to involve people in this process, as you are committing them and the organization to that future. Just as you need to feel inspired and optimistic about where you are going, so does every single person who will be involved in the hard work of implementing change. Once that vision is collectively defined, it should be a communication tool to convey your ideas to the rest of the organization and external stakeholders.

The vision is what lays the foundation for all subsequent strategic planning activities for the organization. When you are facing big changes and need to respond with a strategy to address the issues you face, you've got to get key stakeholders in the room, and develop a coherent and collectively aligned strategy. And this starts with the leaders and managers who will have to bring about the changes and make the strategy come alive. They've got to be involved in the dialogue: Where are we now? Where do we want our business to be in 5 or 10 years time? What are the issues important for us? What are the factors critical for success? How do we monitor our progress?

My approach is not to tell them what to think or do, but to facilitate an interactive strategic planning session with key leaders and managers. What I bring to that interactive session is a clear idea of where we need to go. I don't take this process lightly; I prepare. I make sure that I have really thought about where we need to go, what the issues are, what my vision is. Then, together, we can discuss and develop our vision elements and brainstorm the key issues. We then categorize our "vision elements" and the issues we think are important and come to real agreement about what matters most in terms of our goals and objectives. We understand critical success factors and barriers and develop strategies to address them. As people go through this process, there is a sense of engagement and ownership of the whole strategic plan and the issues. Everything is transparent. WE are excited and committed.

We're now ready to go to the next step: planning how to implement our strategy. We're ready to reach out to others—the managers and staff who are closest to the business operations and logistics. We're ready to get them as excited and engaged as we are. This process isn't necessarily easy, and it takes time. But it's worth it. As we move into the hard work of implementation, we have a single, coherent strategy that we have all contributed to, feel good about, and buy into.

Source: Personal interview with Mark McCord-Amasis conducted by Annie McKee, 2009.

Most approaches to individual learning and change focus people's attention first on their deficiencies. But as Mark McCord-Amasis teaches us, that's not where you need to start. You need to start knowing where you want to go and involving people in personally creating this picture. Intentional change theory, developed by Richard Boyatzis, shows exactly how this works.[92] This theory backs McCord-Amasis up: People need a compelling personal vision as a starting point for the change and development processes. People need *hope*.

Hope and its sister optimism allow you to control your emotions and guide where to focus your attention. **Hope** is the emotional experience of looking forward to a future that seems feasible and enticing.[93] **Optimism** is a positive outlook on life, coupled with the belief that good things will come and that bad things are only temporary and can be overcome.[94] Optimists typically perceive bad situations as challenges and opportunities for learning to try harder. Both hope and optimism change the way you perceive the world, which has an effect on health, decision making, and productive change.[95] Encouraging hope, optimism, and other positive emotions helps us deal with the stress inherent in change and cultivate the resiliency needed to focus on attaining our change goals.[96]

The intentional change model was developed by Professor Richard Boyatzis after many years of research into how people actually change behavior and competencies.[97] The model includes several distinct and yet interrelated steps, as you can see in ■Exhibit 7.15. The model is different from other individual change models

Hope
The emotional experience of looking forward to a future that seems feasible and enticing.

Optimism
A positive outlook on life, coupled with the belief that good things will come and that bad things are only temporary and can be overcome.

■Exhibit **7.15**
The intentional change model.

My Ideal Self
1

Experimenting
4

Supporting Relationships

My Real Self
2

My Learning Agenda
3

Source: Goleman, Daniel, Richard Boyatzis, and Annie McKee. 2002. Primal Leadership. Boston: Harvard Business School Press, p. 110. © 2002 Daniel Goleman. For more information on Intentional Change Theory see Boyatzis, Richard E. 2006. Intentional change theory from a complexity perspective. *Journal of Management Development* 25(7): 607–623.

Gestalt cycle of experience
A model that helps us understand how to mobilize and sustain energy, direct our attention, and choose actions that result in change in ourselves and in groups.

in a significant way: It starts with a positive vision of one's future, rather than focusing on personal deficiencies.

Take an example from personal life. Imagine that you believe you have gained too much weight as a result of studying (and partying) too much. You might say, "I look terrible, and I need to lose weight." You plan to eat less and exercise more. However, after a few days, you are back to fast food and sodas. If you follow a process of intentional change, however, you might first identify a future state that is important to you. For example, you might know of a race two months in the future. You know that if you run the race, you can raise money for breast cancer research, which is something that is important to you. You know that at the moment, you cannot run the race, so you plan a training schedule that includes eating well and walking, running and cross training four days a week. You are energized and motivated to continue with the program because you consider the goal to be noble and worthy. In the process, you lose weight![98]

This happens because a vision of one's *ideal self* sparks a psychological state that supports the hard work of learning, whereas focusing on one's shortcomings is actually demotivating.[99] Change processes enable us to identify our *ideal self*, examine our current state (the *real self*) to identify gaps, and then create a personal learning plan that actually works. By following this process and actively seeking and accepting the support of others, we can learn and develop complex competencies, change long-held patterns of behavior, and become better leaders.[100]

Now that you know a bit about how to mobilize your own energy for change, let's look at a model that helps us understand what comes next for us—and how we can help others mobilize their energy. To begin a change process that really works, it is important to understand how to manage awareness, energy, and action.

Leading Change in Groups, Organizations, and Communities

One of the primary tasks of employees, managers, and leaders is to ensure that people join change processes as opposed to resisting them. This is not as easy as saying "You have to" or "Trust me, this is good for you." Oftentimes, these approaches spark more resistance. In this section, we will explore the **Gestalt cycle of experience**, a model that helps us understand how to mobilize and sustain energy, direct our attention, and choose actions that result in change in ourselves and in groups.

Gestalt Cycle of Experience Applied to Change

To engage people in a change process, you have to find ways to engage their hearts and minds, help them get over resistance, and prepare them to share their ideas, energy, and commitment. One of the best ways to ensure that people are ready to support change is to focus on how aware people are of the need to change, then help them manage their energy and enthusiasm throughout the change process. The Gestalt cycle of experience explains this.

The Gestalt cycle of experience cannot be traced to any one particular source, but some scholars give credit to Fritz and Laura Perls in the 1950s as two key drivers of many of the

▪Exhibit 7.16

The Gestalt cycle of experience.

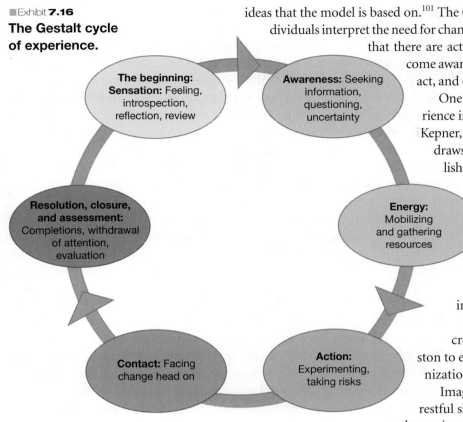

ideas that the model is based on.[101] The Gestalt cycle of experience focuses on how individuals interpret the need for change and how they respond.[102] This model shows that there are actually a number of steps that help people become aware of the need for change, mobilize their energy, act, and evaluate the change process.

One of the first people to describe the cycle of experience in its modern form was Gestalt therapist Elaine Kepner, and the example depicted in ▪Exhibit 7.16 draws from her work in 1980 as well as work published by organizational scholar David Kolb. Kolb's work was presented in 1984 and drew on ideas from a number of other scholars, including education philosopher John Dewey, sociologist Kurt Lewin, and Gestalt practitioners.[103]

This model illustrates that, in fact, what we do and feel before changing actually impacts how ready we are to engage in change and stick with it. Let's use a simple example created by scholar-practitioner Frances Johnston to explain each step and then apply it to an organizational situation.[104]

Imagine a lioness, just waking from a long and restful sleep. It's dusk, and she sniffs the air and scans the environment—she *senses* something. Slowly, she becomes aware that she is uncomfortable. Is there danger? She sniffs again and decides all is well. Is she still tired? Lying down again, she feels restless. It's not sleepiness. Her cubs sense her uneasiness, and they become restless because they too begin to feel anxious and uncomfortable.

The lioness gets up, stretches, and becomes *aware* that she is hungry. Aha! That's it—and if she's hungry, she knows her cubs are too. All of a sudden, she feels more awake and *energized*: She is ready to *move*. The lioness is focused on her hunger, and she *acts* on her desire to get rid of this feeling and to feed her cubs. She gracefully leaves the forest and stealthily walks to a favorite watering hole. The cubs follow, now aware that they are hungry and that they need to *do* something.

Then it happens: The lioness sees her prey, tenses, prepares, and pounces! She's made *contact* with what she desires—a way to alleviate her hunger and a way to feed her cubs. They eat, totally focused, until their hunger is gone. After a while, the lioness and her cubs sense *resolution* and *closure*—there's nothing driving them to search for food anymore. They all become bored with their meal, *withdraw their attention*, and find another good spot for a nap.

The story of the lioness and her cubs shows us that for change to occur, we need to first pay attention to what we are sensing and what we are aware of. This directs our attention—the beginning of mobilizing our energy for action—for making contact with what we need to address or change. Once action is taken, we can then reflect on and evaluate what has occurred—likely sparking a new cycle of experience.

The Gestalt Cycle of Experience and Change in Groups, Organizations, and Communities

Now, let's look at how this works in an organization and what can happen if steps in this change model are skipped, which they often are. Take the example of a company that manufactures food products. During the late 1990s, the growth of this company slowed down—something executives soon *sensed* was a trend. Leaders spent countless hours exploring the trend, finally coming to *awareness* and collective agreement that many of the company's products were outdated—too high in fats, sugars, and preservatives, to which the market was beginning to object. This conclusion *energized* them. They believed they had a line of sight on a solution, and they created and then *acted* on a massive change process that included changing product brand images, ingredients, and formulas.

So far, so good—or so they thought. The top executives had indeed attended carefully to the sensation that something was wrong and worked to come to the point of understanding what was wrong (awareness). They were energized, and they acted. In fact, their actions were reasonable considering the issue. However, as they began to roll out the change plan, they met huge resistance from other senior leaders, managers, and employees. How could this be? From the top leaders' point of view, it was time for change.

What they missed, however, was that outside their small group (of about eight people), no one else truly sensed a need for change, nor was anyone else aware of the real problems. Therefore, most managers and employees were not energized or motivated to act. Instead, they were resistant—they argued and interfered with change activities at every turn.

Luckily, this organization was led by an individual who recognized what was happening. He slowed the process down—stopped it, in fact. Then, he began a process of "cascade" events that enabled ever-larger groups of people from the senior executives down to first-level employees to personally engage in processes that heightened sensation and awareness of the issues. The process also helped people see how the change would benefit them personally and enable them to reach for their dreams.

It worked: People began to be highly energized, and they mobilized for action. When the change process resumed, more people were ready to constructively support the change process and to act, in whatever capacity was needed. During the next two years, people and the company made great strides as they tackled and truly made contact with some of the most difficult (and expensive) problems related to changing products and brand image. They made tremendous headway and success led to a feeling of resolution. The market responded well and growth figures began to improve. Over time, executives and managers evaluated and assessed positively for progress. They were free to withdraw their attention from this change process and focus on other important issues.

As this example shows, conscious and uninterrupted movement throughout the Gestalt cycle produces optimal change. Let's look at how it can work in groups—even when the issues are complicated and controversial.

The Gestalt Cycle of Experience: It Works for Groups Even When Controversial Changes Need to Be Explored

Enabling and managing the cycle of experience and change requires recognition of and attention to each step, the identification of potential blockages, and engaging everyone along the way. The *Business Case* shows that when this process is used in a group or organization, it is important to ensure that everyone involved in the change experiences each step of the cycle of experience personally.

As you have seen, a number of steps in the Gestalt cycle of experience can help ensure that change actually happens. Common mistakes, such as skipping steps, lead to problems. One technology organization we know, for example, has an HR department that has the tendency to jump to solutions long before anyone is really clear on what the problems or opportunities are. Needless to say, this means that lots of people waste lots of time. Employees recognize this pattern of course, and the HR department has become a joke. No one wants to engage in anything the department is involved in (even though some programs are necessary and quite good).

Another type of blockage occurs when an individual or organization becomes stuck in a stage. For example, it's not uncommon for people and organizations to be stuck in

Cambodia

Combatting the Spread of HIV

Leadership scholar-practitioners Frances Johnston and Eddy Mwelwa point out the relevance of involving everyone in change and add that the cycle of experience does not begin and then end. Instead, it is continuous, because change occurs in cycles that overlap. Energy flows from awareness to action in recurring sequences that allow for the possibility for change. This requires leadership.[105] Let's look at how skilled change agents Johnston and Mwelwa used this model to lead a large-scale social change initiative.

Johnston and Mwelwa, along with a talented team of change agents, worked with an organization in Cambodia to support leaders from all walks of life in addressing the growing problem of HIV and AIDS. In 2001, UNAIDS estimated that 170,000 people (about 1.3 percent) were living with HIV/AIDS in Cambodia. The change team's first step was to build their own awareness and understanding of the challenges facing them. This was partially accomplished by obtaining information in the form of statistics about the prevalence and spread of the virus, as well as how it was spread (largely through heterosexual sexual practices, as is true in most of the world).

Scholar-Practitioners Frances Johnston and Eddy Mwelwa

However, such information is insufficient without also having an awareness of the cultural, social, and emotional realities of Cambodian life. Information about Cambodian life was gathered through communication and observation, interviews with dozens of people, and trust building with key stakeholders. Through this information-gathering process, the researchers were able to identify gender inequality as an important contributing factor in the spread of the disease. This, of course, was not an easy topic to bring up or discuss, nor would an intellectual understanding necessarily lead to the kind of change necessary. The team members realized that they needed to ensure that the people they were working with *sensed* the issue and became informed and more *aware* of the issue. They had to create a situation in which individuals and the group would become energized through open dialogue between men and women that empowered everyone to consider the decisions they made about their relationships and sexual practices. Without awareness, understanding, and empowerment, there can be no meaningful action resulting in change.[106]

How did they foster this kind of dialogue? Johnston and Mwelwa explain it like this:

- *We created activities that led to the group being able to talk about the issues openly and to appreciate that the most common spread of infection was through individual sexual behavior, which was under personal control.*
- *We raised awareness and mobilized energy through giving people experiences that caused them to feel deep empathy and compassion. For example, we arranged visits to families living with HIV/AIDS, orphanages, clinics/hospitals, and brothels to experience the realities of what was happening and the very real emotional impact on people. Visiting places like these (which were often in the center of towns and villages but largely ignored), we were able to heighten aware-*ness of the implications of the disease and its impact on organizations and the country.
- *We also supported raising awareness and energy mobilization by including people living with HIV and AIDS in the group. That was particularly powerful in terms of reducing stigma and prejudices. For most of the participants, it was the first time they had actually been in close contact with anyone living with the virus. Having people living with the virus in the group ensured that the issues regarding HIV and AIDS were faced head on rather than avoided.*
- *To really prepare people for change, we started with a powerful vision. We had group members envision a different and desired Cambodia without the stigma associated with the disease. What would it look like if men's and women's relationships supported respect and good health? What would the country look like as it left the brutality of the Pol Pot regime behind?*

The dictator Pol Pot's regime had decimated the country. Under the Khmer Rouge, Cambodian citizens were tortured, murdered and brutalized until Pol Pot and his regime were driven out of power by neighboring Vietnam. It is estimated that between one and two million people were killed—14 to 27% of the population at the time.[107] For five years prior to an intervention, the UN had been assisting in setting up a sustainable democratic government. What would Cambodia look like as the new democratic government took hold and schools, businesses and employment led to a country which could once again be proud of itself and its people? To answer this question, we arranged a visit to Angkor Wat, one of the greatest works of art and architecture on earth.

These experiences were deeply meaningful to people—they were touched and inspired—they wanted the vision they saw. They were ready to act.

The Cambodians took charge of the issues. Teams from the group crafted plans to work in their communities on every issue imaginable: education for children and adults about how HIV and AIDS is spread; work with prostitutes to help them (and their clients) remain virus-free; work with men about their feelings and treatment of their wives and other women; anti-discrimination laws were passed in the Senate; education and support for women as they took on a new, more empowered way of dealing with life.

Six years later, adult HIV prevalence is 0.09%—down more than 50%, 78% of HIV-infected people are receiving antiretroviral therapy, and the Ministry of Education has included HIV/AIDS education in the national curriculum.[108] By taking a pragmatic and multidisciplinary approach to change that included activities at every level of society, and that involved emotional, legal, educational and multi-sectorial interventions, Cambodia has been able to reverse a very dangerous trend. Local leaders have learned how to collaborate, to mobilize energy for change, and to craft change projects that resulted in increased awareness and action in order to achieve the Cambodia they desired.

sensation or awareness. Signs that this is happening include an obsessive focus on analyzing problems (sometimes called *analysis paralysis*) or endless complaining and a general sense of hopelessness about organizational challenges.

Most Popular » Discussion Questions

1. Think about a situation that caused you to feel hopeless about changing something in your life. What was the impact of this emotion on your behavior? Now,
   think about a situation that caused you to feel inspired and hopeful about your
   life. What aspects of the situation caused you to feel this way? How did these
   emotions impact what you actually did in your life?

2. Choose a simple example of a situation in which you need to mobilize energy to
   change something (such as getting up to go to class or work, or starting to
   study). Imagine applying the Gestalt cycle of experience to this situation. What
   would happen at each stage?

3. Give an example of how you might apply the intentional change model to something you need to change in your life.

---

7. What Can HR Do to Foster Effective Change?

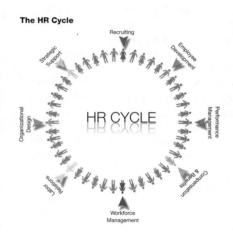

The HR Cycle

HR CYCLE

Change does not occur magically. It requires individual energy, effort, and support. To
start this section, we will review *organization development*, a set of change activities that
HR often leads. Then, because HR departments and professionals need to understand
how to engage the organization's members in research processes that help to identify an
organization's strengths and challenges, we will continue our discussion of *action research*.

Finally, because HR professionals are responsible for teaching others the skills and
competencies needed to manage change, we will conclude with how they can create
leadership development programs that work.

Organization Development Defined

Organization development (OD) refers to a systematic, scientific, and research-based
approach to change in organizations.[109] The goals of OD are often to improve the organization's competitive advantage through changing the organization's culture and leadership practices and to improve problem-solving and change management skills.[110]
According to the *NTL Handbook of Organization Development and Change*, Kurt Lewin
is considered by many to be the father of both action research and organization development because he links two important ideas, which are the study and effective use of
group dynamics and the application of an action research methodology.[111]

There are many different approaches to OD, but all of them essentially focus on *planned*
change at the organizational level—structures, processes, culture, and so forth. Planned
change starts with the view that the organization is a complex system composed of many elements, each influencing and influenced by the other elements of the system.[112] The process
starts with examination of the organization, followed by a "diagnosis" and then strategic
change management, which engages the organization at different levels of the system.[113]

Because so much of an "organization" is people, HR has a huge role to play in collaborating with employees and leaders in OD work. Unfortunately, in too many cases, HR
departments and professionals do not see this as a priority. Douglas McGregor and Joel
Cutcher-Gershenfeld, authors of *The Human Side of Enterprise*, noted that limits to collaborative and OD work in the organization are not *human* limits but rather a failure

of HR creativity and leadership.[114] Another problem is that because HR leaders are not well integrated into organizational strategy, some OD interventions are not linked to strategy and result in "dysfunctional outcomes."[115] To avoid this, and to be able to conceptualize changes and change processes that work, HR professionals can learn new ways to study their own organizations, such as action research. This can help HR leaders rethink issues about where change may need to occur in the organization, what stakeholders need, and how to bring about positive change.

Action Research

Kurt Lewin first coined the term *action research* in 1946 in a paper discussing research to address issues concerning minorities in society.[116] The approach has been used and expanded by a number of scholars and practitioners in fields as varied as organization development, education, race relations, environmental sustainability, and social justice.[117] This was at the heart of powerful research done by the educational scholar Paolo Freire, who was concerned with the issues of social justice and empowerment. Action research has also been used successfully in communities and organizations around the world.[118]

Lewin believed that any intervention into a group, organization, or community (even research about group dynamics or culture) actually affects the driving and restraining forces that either help or hinder change. Depicted in ■Exhibit 7.17, he called interventions that simultaneously investigate and change human systems *action research*.[119] Let's look at how action research differs from more traditional research, and how it can support learning and change.

Action research, like all research, is done to further knowledge and understanding. Traditionally, change tends to be what you do *after* research is concluded. This is not the case for action research. As mentioned, action research assumes that the very act of studying a group, organization, or community results in change—regardless of whether the researchers intend this or not. That means that while we study systems, we need to understand and manage the changes that occur because of our research. Another difference between traditional research and action research is that traditional research separates the researcher from the problem that is being examined. Action research makes no such artificial separation, placing the researcher in a role of both researcher and participant in the situation.

Action research starts with a research plan to explore an issue, a concern, or an opportunity. Many different approaches can be taken in action research, but the important aspect of all of these methods is the focus on understanding interrelationships through hands-on participation in your research. In other words, you are a participant and a researcher at the same time: a participant-researcher.[120] In most cases, HR professionals or external experts join with organization members to conduct this research, which includes conversations, reflection, and activities involving many people beyond the research team.

As research continues, results are continually reevaluated, and new research is conducted, observed, reflected, and acted on. The spiral continues. In other words, action research is an iterative process designed to shift people and perspectives and to affect the problem or opportunity until it is resolved or leveraged.[121] The use of a feedback loop to engage constant improvement has also been called *organizational cybernetics* and can be found, among other places, in the practices of total quality management (an organizational control process that will be covered in Chapter 12).[122]

Leadership Competency Development and Change

The process of developing leadership competencies as an approach to supporting and managing complex organizational change has been greatly expanded in recent years. In fact, the American Society for Training and Development (ASTD) reported an estimated $134.39 billion was spent on developing competencies in the United States during 2007.[123] Such an approach can be supportive of individual and organizational effectiveness in change processes *only* when the competencies that are developed are the *right* competencies.

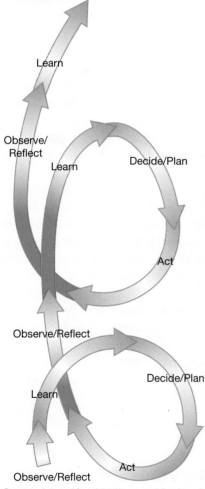

■Exhibit **7.17**

The action research cycle.

Learn

Observe/
Reflect

Learn

Decide/Plan

Act

Observe/Reflect

Learn

Decide/Plan

Act

Observe/Reflect

Source: Adapted from http://www.worldbank.org/afr/ik/commun_toolkit/pictures/Learning-spiral-final.gif

However, in many companies, the popularity of the competency model approach has led HR professionals and others to cobble together models that are ineffective for people and jobs in today's organizations. For example, so-called "competencies" observed in some organizational models often include a mixture of observable behaviors, personal values, vague terms more related to personality, and even allusions to organizational values. Although all of these might be valuable in certain situations, they are not competencies, and it is hard to link these confusing mixtures directly to performance—or to effective change management.

So, if HR professionals take on the responsibilities related to teaching employees, managers, and leaders, the first thing they need to do is to create an architecture for leadership development that enables employees to learn the right competencies at the right time. When it comes to change, many of the right competencies relate to social and emotional intelligence. For example, to understand and manage change, it is essential to develop one's capacity for social awareness: *empathy* and *organizational awareness*. To create and implement change initiatives you need to read people's needs and desires accurately and understand how various factors (such as culture and politics) affect the organization.

In addition to discovering *what* to teach, HR professionals need to reflect on *how* to teach. What kinds of leadership development processes actually work? Many HR professionals and others struggle with this question. In fact, research indicates that far too many leadership development programs and processes are simply a waste of time. Often, the competencies and models that are taught do not lead to more effective leadership, and the learning methods that are employed do not support learning or retention of knowledge.

Researchers are stepping in to help resolve this problem. For example, Richard Boyatzis and colleagues have been engaged for years in what are called *outcome studies*.[124] These studies involve the creation of learning and development programs that focus on competencies, such as those related to social and emotional intelligence, that are shown to improve leadership development.[125] These leadership development programs, particularly those that employ the intentional change model, enhance learning and retention of knowledge.

A final note on leadership development: Although the development of programs focused on leadership development is one of the most common interventions used to improve performance and provide people with the tools to address change, it is certainly not the only approach that is needed. Some scholars believe that training is a much overused approach to fixing organizational problems and that a large portion of the hundreds of billions of dollars spent yearly on these programs is wasted.[126]

HR Leadership Roles

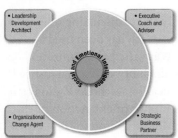

- Leadership Development Architect
- Executive Coach and Adviser
- Organizational Change Agent
- Strategic Business Partner

Social and Emotional Intelligence

Most Popular » Discussion Questions

1. Draft a plan to interview people about a group or organization to which you belong. Now, generate a list of things that might happen to the group or organization as a *result* of your interviews (e.g., people would be curious about what you are doing or they might talk to each other about your questions).
2. Considering the organization from Question 1, how could you design your research activities so people would be more engaged and ready for change?

---

8. What Can We All Do to Support Change?

Today, virtually everyone in most organizations is involved in change. Just like leadership, change is up to all of us, no matter what role we hold. In this section, we explore two very practical approaches to contributing positively to change processes: by becoming a change agent and by learning how to care for others during a change process. Then we look at the last important issue: how to face changes that are truly unwelcome.

Become a Change Agent

Much has been written about the role of individuals in organizations to act as agents of change—people who are able to make an impact on organizational goals, processes, and resources. Clearly, change agents need to have good interpersonal skills related to social and emotional intelligence and the ability to access and control the flow of information—networking skills.[127]

At a more fundamental level, change agents need to have an understanding of and the ability to manage politics and power as influential levers of change within the organization.[128] Scholars have identified three skills related to power that change agents need:[129]

• The power to enlist organizational resources. Of course, this can be difficult, especially if you don't have formal authority. However, it is possible. You just need to learn how to influence those who *do* control resources.
• The power to affect the agenda and participate in decision making. This is easier in organizations that empower people. However, even in those that do not, it is often possible to "get your voice heard" by identifying people who listen, talking to them (this takes courage), and mobilizing other people to use systems (such as employee surveys) to make a point (this takes inspirational leadership).
• The power to use the current culture and "the way we do things around here" to enlist people and to begin to see new ways of being and working. This has been referred to as *management of meaning*.[130]

Effectively accessing and mobilizing different forms of power, managing politics, and utilizing interpersonal communication skills to further a change agenda are all skills related to social and emotional intelligence.[131] This has led some scholars to proclaim that the essential role of a leader is as a change agent, and the ability to be effective in that role is through the development of the skills of emotional intelligence.[132] Emotionally intelligent change agents are able to demonstrate resilience in the face of uncertainty, partly because they see the big picture. A systems perspective helps us to recognize that current problems can be overcome and to understand and address others' reservations regarding new endeavors.[133]

Caring for Others during Change: Empathy, Inspiration, and Managing Resistance

Through any organizational change, people expect and deserve care and attention from leadership. As you can see in ■ Exhibit 7.18, emotional and behavioral responses to change range from acceptance to active resistance. Resistance can be obvious or subtle and can occur immediately or be delayed by days or even months.

Exhibit 7.18 covers a wide range of behaviors. The first tip for managing resistance to change is to stop assuming that resistance will be people's automatic response. This is a common assumption and is in fact not true. If you assume the people will resist, you might actually be the one who adopts an approach that is either forceful, negative, or manipulative.

There are many ways people respond to change, as you can see in ■ Exhibit 7.19. People do not, however, like being forced to change. They want to choose. You need to give people as much freedom of choice as possible (and that's usually more than most managers give). People can handle change, and they often have

■ Exhibit **7.18**
How people may respond to change.

Acceptance
• Cooperation
• Support
• Resignation

Indifference
• Apathetic
• Ambivalent
• Minimally compliant

Passive Resistance
• Strict compliance to unproductive rules or procedures
• Minimizing work output
• Failing to develop new skills or knowledge
• Overlooking or failing to correct errors

Active Resistance
• Overt rudeness
• Disobedience
• Sabotage

Source: Based on A. S. Judson. 1991. *Changing behavior in organizations: Minimizing resistance to change*, p. 48. Cambridge, MA: Basil Blackwell.

■Exhibit **7.19**

The Smart Way to Lead Change

1. Become aware of and manage your own emotional response to change first.
2. Don't assume people will resist change; it's only one of many possible responses.
3. Don't force people to change (unless it's life or death).
4. Don't try to control everything (or everyone).
5. Be empathetic. Change is hard sometimes.
6. Inspire people with a vision that is meaningful to them.
7. Face real resistance with hope, resolve, and courage.
8. Negotiate where and when you must; do it in good faith and respectfully.
9. Tell the truth.
10. Be a role model.

good ideas about the specifics of change and how to implement it. Let people contribute. Don't feel you have to control everything, because that in itself sparks resistance.

You can do a number of things personally to help others respond to change (see Exhibit 7.19). How people respond to change is partly dependent on how *you* respond. Again, start with emotional intelligence: self-awareness and self-management. If you are enthusiastic and committed, people are more likely to "catch" your emotions and contribute positively. Similarly, if you are secretly (much less overtly) resentful or fearful, people know it—no matter how much you try to hide it. People are smart that way. In times of turmoil or when we feel threatened, we take emotional cues from others, especially formal and informal leaders.

As we mentioned, you don't assume people will always resist change, so you don't need to force people. Forcing things on people or over-controlling everything sparks resistance. You can be empathetic with people as they go through change. Change is hard sometimes, even when it is welcomed. Truly seeking to understand people's experiences and being supportive can go a long way toward minimizing potential resistance. In practice, this might mean providing emotional support, giving time off after a demanding period, or providing training in new skills.

You can work on being inspirational: Paint a vision for where the group is going and make sure it links to people's individual dreams. To do this, you have to *know* what people's dreams are. When you face real resistance, don't despair. Face the difficulties with optimism, hope, resolve, and courage. Negotiate where and when you must, and do it in good faith and respectfully. Tell the truth. Be a role model.

Facing Change with Courage

In this chapter, you have learned many ways to deal with change, manage change, and lead change. These skills will serve you well at work and in life. There's one more thing we need to address, however: What do we do when the changes we face are unwelcome? What about when something really bad happens—how do we face this kind of change? What happens when the changes that occur are things that we would never, ever have chosen?

Throughout our lives, we all have to deal with changes that we do not want to face. Natural disasters destroy homes and communities, wars break out, and people engage in crimes that hurt innocent people. Relationships break up, people get sick, and loved ones die. No one welcomes these changes—we don't want things like this to happen, and it's hard to deal with the difficult changes and tragedies. So how can we deal with changes that aren't welcome and that hurt rather than help us?

The answer to this question is complicated—so complicated that most of the world's religions and many of its great philosophers have tried to discover the secret. In the end, there's no easy answer. However, there are some things that you can do to help yourself when change is hard.

First, remember what neuroscience teaches us: When we feel hopeful, we are more open to learning, more able to solve problems creatively, and more resilient.[134] So, in whatever situation you find yourself, try as hard as you can to find something to be hopeful about. It might be small—like knowing you are a strong person and have faced difficult times before. Or, maybe you can find hope in the learning that comes from surviving a difficult experience. Alternatively, if things are really bad, you may just hold on to the belief that at some point, things will work out and get better.

Second, cultivate practices of mindfulness. When we are mindful, we are awake and aware and attuned to ourselves and other people. As tempting as it might be to hide from changes we don't like—to deny what's happened and our feelings about it—doing this just postpones the inevitable. Ultimately, we all have to deal with what life brings us. When we live life mindfully, taking time to reflect and to build our resilience and our capacity for awareness, we are more prepared to stay calm and grounded when things are tough.

Finally, get help. As humans, we're not meant to deal with problems or sadness alone. We need other people, especially when facing difficulties in our lives. What you can do now to help yourself prepare for the inevitable ups and downs of life is to make sure you build strong relationships with people who care for you—people who will do anything for you. Then, you can be there for each other.

In the following *Student's Choice*, we can see how even the worst challenges can be faced with courage and hope when people come together to help each other. And in this case, people go even further—they've looked to the healing power of horses to help wounded veterans find health and confidence once again.

Student's Choice

Horses as Healers

Juliane C. Wigsten

Although the value of the horse-human relationship carries profound historical significance, the organized practice of therapeutic riding is relatively new. Nearly 40 years ago, 23 individuals gathered in Middleburg, Virginia, to create the groundwork for what is now called the North American Riding Association for the Handicapped (NARHA). NARHA's mission statement is to enrich the lives of people by "promoting excellence in equine-assisted activities."[135] Today, NARHA centers exist across the country, offering equine-assisted therapeutic programs to individuals with psychological and physical handicaps. These programs are inspiring for everyone involved. Today, these programs are providing an incredibly important service: Helping veterans wounded in war regain both their health and their confidence.

According to the U.S Department of Veterans Affairs (VA), VA medical centers nationwide nation are networking with NARHA equine professionals to develop therapeutic riding programs and other equine-assisted activities (such as grooming and cleaning stalls) for wounded veterans. Being around horses helps treat veterans who are suffering from psychological issues, including post-traumatic stress disorder (PTSD), social anxiety, and depression. Equine therapy also helps these soldiers recuperate from physical injuries.

At Stable Hands, near Yreka, California, co-founder Marcia Cushman manages a six-week therapeutic riding program called "Horses for Heroes" for wounded Marines who served tours of duty in Iraq. One participant, Craig Coggins, age 39, had sustained moderate brain trauma and a severe back injury in Iraq, and he struggles with PTSD as a result of his experience. Coggins mentions how his physical pain levels always decreased after a 45-minute ride and describes that "the only time I didn't feel pain was in the saddle." Similar to Coggins, Loren Carrell, age 25, has problems with short-term memory due to a mild head injury, and he also has terrible flashbacks as a result of PTSD. After his first riding lesson on a horse named Keeper, Carrell suffered the usual forgetfulness—he couldn't remember how he'd groomed, tacked, and prepared Keeper for the ride. By his fourth session, however, he had gained the confidence to perform the sequence of grooming activities more independently.

Coggins summarizes the program best by saying the following: "While working with Keeper, I began to feel as though I was changing inside. I felt better about myself overall and it gave me a new perspective on my medical issues. . . . I could not have become the person I am today without the help of Stable Hands and the wonderful people who have formed Horses for Heroes to help veterans like myself."[136]

Horses are sensitive and intelligent creatures in that they make humans work to gain their trust through loving care, affection, and dedication. So, in equine therapy, veterans have a profound and meaningful experience because they engage mind, body, heart, and spirit. The time spent in or out of the saddle helps teach wounded veterans how to better combat their personal struggles, reintegrate themselves into society, and live normal, satisfying, and fulfilling lives.

Source: Adapted from a case by Juliane C Wigsten.

Hope, mindfulness, and the help of others are a few of the keys to living through hard times, when changes are not welcome or even tragic. Approaching life's most difficult times in this way will help you be a better person—and be ready to help others when they need it.

Most Popular » Discussion Questions

1. Consider a change that you would like to bring about in a group at work or at school. Look at Exhibit 7.18 to review the various ways people respond to change. Analyze each of the members of the group (including yourself) and determine how you believe they will respond to the change and why.

2. Now, look at Exhibit 7.19. For each of the 10 tips on managing resistance and leading change, note some concrete actions you can take to help bring about change in a group at work or at school.

---

9. A Final Word on Change

Regardless of whether people resist change or thrive on it, change is never easy. Even the word "change" evokes different reactions from people and organizations because each person and every organization defines "change" in a different way. Those who do thrive on change see change as an opportunity to grow and learn. To manage change among others, you must first determine how to get the best response from people to change, and then leverage that response in an organization. Inspiring people with a vision of a better tomorrow, even if it means hard work in the short term, is how the world's best companies continue to be competitive.

Key Terms

1. What Is Change and How Do You React to It? (pp. 212–214)

Key Terms

Change To alter, adjust, modify, or transform someone or something. p. 212

2. Why Do Organizations Change? (pp. 214–219)

Key Terms

Diversity The varied perspectives and approaches to work that members of different groups bring. p. 216

3. What Is the Difference between Incremental and Transformational Change? (pp. 220–224)

Key Terms

Top-down changes Changes that are introduced by leaders and managers, who define the agenda and create the overarching plan for the change effort. p. 220

Bottom-up changes Changes that occur when employees or managers at various levels spark a movement for change, influence one another and leaders, and contribute to the planning and implementation of change. p. 220

Investment banks Institutions that raise capital, trade securities, and assist with mergers and acquisitions. p. 222

Net capital rule Rule that guides how much debt an institution can hold. p. 222

Leveraging money A practice that allows financial institutions to increase the amount of debt they handle in proportion to the amount of money they hold. p. 222

Subprime lending The practice of lending money to people who normally would not qualify for a mortgage because they have maxed-out credit cards, a poor debt-to-income ratio, or bad credit. p. 223

4. Which Models Can Help Us Understand Change? (pp. 224–228)

Key Terms

Permanent white water Metaphor that refers to the fact that organizational systems face unrelenting turbulence and constant change. p. 228

5. What Practical Models Can Help Us Manage Change in Organizations? (pp. 228–234)

Key Terms None

6. How Do *People* Change? (pp. 235–242)

Key Terms

Positive emotional attractor A psychological state of well-being and hope that engages the parasympathetic nervous system and can counter the effects of stress. p. 236

Negative emotional attractor A psychological state characterized by negative emotions that is linked to the sympathetic nervous system and that can cause people to feel defensive, threatened, and stressed. p. 236

Hope The emotional experience of looking forward to a future that seems feasible and enticing. p. 237

Optimism A positive outlook on life coupled with the belief that good things will come, and that bad things are only temporary and can be overcome. p. 237

Gestalt cycle of experience A model that helps us to understand how to mobilize and sustain energy, direct our attention, and choose actions that result in change in ourselves and in groups. p. 238

7. What Can HR Do to Foster Effective Change? (pp. 242–244)

Key Terms None

8. What Can We All Do to Support Change? (pp. 244–248)

Key Terms None

9. A Final Word on Change (p. 248)

Key Terms None

Chapter 7 Visual Summary

8. Workplace Essentials: Creativity, Innovation, and a Spirit of Entrepreneurship

7. Change: A Focus on Adaptability and Resiliency

9. Organizing for a Complex World: Structure and Design

Planning and Change

6. The Human Side of Planning: Decision Making and Critical Thinking

5. Planning and Strategy: Bringing the Vision to Life

1. What Is Change and How Do You React to It? (pp. 212–214)

Summary: Whether you call it an about-face or a modification, whether you say that you're adjusting or tampering with the situation, you're talking about change, which is all around us. Both employees and managers need to be aware of how pervasive change is today and their personal attitudes to it. We need to adapt and change ourselves to meet the different and ever-changing demands of the world around us.

2. Why Do Organizations Change? (pp. 214–219)

Summary: Three words drive a great deal of the change we face today: technology, globalization, and environmentalism. Technology affects how we work and what we can do at work. Globalization has brought diversity of all sorts to work as well as shifted which economies are growing, and which remain at the status quo. Social changes such as a far more diverse workforce, rebalancing of the world's economies, and an increased focus on sustainability require us, and organizations, to embrace change.

3. What Is the Difference between Incremental and Transformational Change? (pp. 220–224)

Summary: Tuning, adaptation, reorientation, and re-creation describe four approaches to change. Tuning and adaptation are incremental approaches to change. Reorientation and re-creation are transformational approaches. Traditionally, incremental change has been seen as easier to manage. However, even slow changes can be difficult to manage and even dangerous if ignored: witness the recent recession and global financial industry meltdown, which was the result of years of incremental changes.

Top Three Blockbuster Drugs in 2005

1. Lipitor
   a. Treats: High blood pressure
   b. Annual Sales: $12.9 billion
   c. Annual Growth: 6.4%
   d. Manufacturer: Pfizer
   e. Approved: December 1996
   f. Patent Expiration: June 2011[70]
2. Plavix
   a. Treats: Heart disease
   b. Annual Sales: $5.9 billion
   c. Annual Growth: 16%
   d. Manufacturer: Bristol-Myers Squibb and Sanofi-Aventis
   e. Approved: November 1997
   f. Patent Expiration: November 2011[71]
3. Nexium
   a. Treats: Heartburn
   b. Annual Sales: $5.7 billion
   c. Annual Growth: 16.7%
   d. Manufacturer: AstraZeneca
   e. Approved: March 2000
   f. Patent Expiration: 2019, but on 27 May 2014, AstraZeneca will license this drug to another manufacturer to settle a lawsuit[71]

4. Which Models Can Help Us Understand Change? (pp. 224–228)

Summary: Kurt Lewin's force field analysis model is useful when considering change in an organization. He postulates three steps: an unfreezing phase; a changing phase; and a freezing phase that sets the new status quo. Peter Vaill suggests that, instead of existing in either frozen or changing phases, organizations instead are in permanent white water—that is, in a constant state of change.

5. What Practical Models Can Help Us Manage Change in Organizations? (pp. 228–234)

Summary: John Kotter created an eight-stage model to approach organizational change, beginning with "Ensure that people feel an urgent need for change" and ending with "Solidify the change in the organizational culture." He argued that each step must be attended to in order to ensure that change does not fail. Gregory Shea created a work systems model identifying organizational levers that can be attended to during change processes. Because change is constant, we have to determine what to pay attention to, what to change, and what to ignore.

9. A Final Word on Change (p. 248)

Summary: Change is a difficult process that elicits a broad range of reactions from people. You must understand how to get the best response from people in order to effectively manage change. This will make the hard work of change less daunting and help your organization stay competitive.

8. What Can We All Do to Support Change? (pp. 244–248)

Summary: There are two useful approaches to becoming a positive contributor to change in your organization: by becoming a change agent and by using empathy to manage resistance during a change process. A change agent needs to be able to access, or know how to access, organizational resources, decision-making opportunities, and the current culture in the organization, and have the emotional intelligence and people skills to move that culture toward the path of change. Being positive and committed to change can help manage the resistance of those around you. Being empathetic and inspirational are helpful too. That said, even those of us who are most adept at managing change will encounter changes that we don't want and would never choose. When this happens, we need courage and the support of others.

7. What Can HR Do to Foster Effective Change? (pp. 242–244)

Summary: HR often leads change through engaging in organizational development—systematic processes to improve organizational systems, culture, and leadership practices. One tool that is very helpful in diagnosing groups and organizations is called action research. Action research furthers knowledge, but sees a researcher as a participant in a situation, not just an observer. This can lead to better and more precise knowledge of what aspects of an organization must be changed and how to do it.

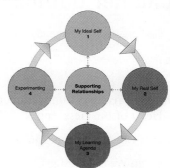

6. How Do *People* Change? (pp. 235–242)

Summary: We know from our own experience that individual change is difficult, and can lead to stress and both physical and emotional resistance. One way to think about change positively is to think about where you want to go, and use hope and optimism to focus your attention and your energy to get there. When leading change in your organization, it helps to think about the Gestalt cycle of experience, which focuses on moving energy in the right direction, toward sustainable change.

Workplace Essentials:

Creativity, Innovation, and a
Spirit of **Entrepreneurship**

Chapter Outline

Find out what you already know about the concepts in
this chapter by going to www.mymanagementlab.com
and taking the **Pre-Test**. Your results will generate a customized
study plan for Chapter 8.

1. Why Are Creativity, Innovation, and Entrepreneurship at
   the Heart of Business? (pp. 254–255)

2. What Is Creativity? (pp. 256–259)

3. How Can We Encourage Creativity at Work? (pp. 259–261)

4. What Is Innovation and Why Is It Important? (pp. 262–267)

5. How Can We Foster Innovation in People and Companies?
   (pp. 267–270)

6. What Is Entrepreneurship? (pp. 270–274)

7. How Does a New Business Get Started? (pp. 274–281)

8. What Is Intrepreneurship? (pp. 282–283)

9. What Is HR's Role in Supporting Creativity, Innovation,
   and Entrepreneurship? (pp. 284–285)

10. What Can We All Do to Be More Creative, Innovative, and
    Entrepreneurial? (pp. 285–287)

11. A Final Word on Creativity, Innovation, and
    Entrepreneurship (p. 287)

Go back to www.mymanagementlab.com and take the **Post-Test**
to verify your understanding of the concepts. **To experience and apply**
the concepts, explore the additional material associated with Chapter 8.

Part 1: Leading and Managing for Today and the Future (Chapters 1, 2, 3, 4)
> **Part 2:** Planning and Change (Chapters 5, 6, 7, **8**, 9)
Part 3: Organizing Human Systems (Chapters 10, 11)
Part 4: Controlling Quality, Culture, and Yourself (Chapters 12, 13)
Part 5: Leading and Managing for the Future (Chapters 14, 15, 16)

8. Workplace Essentials: Creativity, Innovation, and a Spirit of Entrepreneurship

Planning and Change

8. Workplace Essentials: Creativity, Innovation, and a Spirit of Entrepreneurship

7. Change: A Focus on Adaptability and Resiliency

9. Organizing for a Complex World: Structure and Design

6. The Human Side of Planning: Decision Making and Critical Thinking

5. Planning and Strategy: Bringing the Vision to Life

Organizing Human Systems

10. Teams and Teambuilding: How to Work Effectively with Others

11. Working in a Virtual World: Technology as a Way of Life

Leading and Managing for Today and the Future

16. Managing and Leading for Tomorrow: A Focus on Your Future

1. Managing and Leading Today: The New Rules

14. Globalization: Managing Effectively in a Global Economic Environment

2. The Leadership Imperative: It's Up to You

4. Communication: The Key to Resonant Relationships

3. Motivation and Meaning: What Makes People Want to Work?

15. Sustainability and Corporate Social Responsibility: Ensuring the Future

12. Organizational Controls: People, Processes, Quality, and Results

Controlling Quality, Culture, and Yourself

13. Culture: It's Powerful

1. Why Are Creativity, Innovation, and Entrepreneurship at the Heart of Business?

Hypercompetition
A state of constant and escalating competition.

To stay relevant in an ever-changing world, leaders must foster an environment that encourages creativity, innovation, and an organization-wide spirit of entrepreneurship. The new rules for success in business include learning how to excel in an environment of **hypercompetition**—a state of constant and escalating competition. Organizational leaders also need to avoid defensive reactions to change, like overfocusing on short-term results and controlling people. Instead, we all need to be creative, to bring our ideas to life in innovative products and services, and to approach our work with the attitude of an entrepreneur—empowered, energized, and totally committed to our mission.

Hypercompetition

Professor Richard D'Aveni is credited with coining the term *hypercompetition*. In his book of the same name, he argues that hypercompetition is characterized by a rapid escalation of competition in pricing, quality, development of new technologies and processes, and market position, as well as competition to enter new global markets.[1] Companies' increasingly bold and aggressive actions result in constant changes in the market, which can be seen in the shortening of product life cycles (how long a product is viable) and product design cycles (how long it takes to design new products), as well as the rush to develop new technologies. Think about cell phones—new ones come out almost every day. Is this the case because companies think you really need a new phone? Or is it because these companies will be left behind if they don't innovate as fast as their competitors?

Another source of hypercompetition is the frequent entry of new competitors onto the scene, which makes competitive advantages difficult to maintain. This leads companies to compete on price or quality, or to increase efficiencies in the production of goods or delivery of services, and to rely on innovation.[2] For example, Apple's iPhone was unveiled on January 9, 2007.[3] Its original price was $599, according to *Macworld*.[4] By September, to ensure that it kept high market share as competitors' answers to the iPhone came out, Apple decided to decrease the cost of the phone to $399 and give a $100 gift certificate to those who had bought the product earlier at the full price (∎Exhibit 8.1).[5]

Hypercompetition increases uncertainty. Scholars have argued that due to the constant change present in hypercompetitive environments, managers cannot rely on traditional frameworks for making sense of the competitive landscape (such as SWOT analysis and the BCG matrix).[6] Today's competitive environment calls for constant attention to creativity, innovation, and entrepreneurship. Simply put: We need to learn how to do things differently.

Adopt a Long-Term Outlook and Embrace Innovation

Sometimes, the response to change is to react defensively and slip into crisis management. Too often in business, this means focusing on measures of success that can actually harm a company over time, such as focusing on short-term outcomes or overcontrolling people and processes. When a company puts too much emphasis on short-term financial results while cutting corners on investments in new products and services, it can find itself unable to compete, out of date, or even out of business within a few years.

Another common but erroneous assumption is that when in crisis, leaders should become more autocratic. In some situations this may be true, such as when there is a fire in the building and people aren't walking toward the exits. However, in most cases, allowing followers to make decisions will yield better results. When everyone feels that

∎Exhibit **8.1**

The Apple iPhone is popular and has decreased in price over time.

D. Hurst/Alamy Images

they each have a stake in business results and employees are empowered, letting go of control allows for decisions to be made closest to where the opportunities and problems exist. This also supports the generation of new knowledge, creativity, and innovation.[7]

Controlling employees too tightly or overfocusing on short-term financial results rarely supports creativity, innovation, or an entrepreneurial mind-set. Yet, we see short-term and overcontrolling mind-sets in many companies. In this chapter, we look at how employees, managers, and leaders can create environments that support entrepreneurship, creativity, and innovation. We examine how we can all think and behave in ways that help people and companies rise to the top in our exciting—but challenging—turbulent environments. Specifically, we explore the art and science of creativity and innovation, and we look at how to foster a spirit of entrepreneurship at work.

To begin, let's consider what Joe Steier, CEO of Signature HealthCARE and a finalist for a regional 2007 Ernst and Young Entrepreneur of the Year award, has to say about inspiring people to be creative, innovative, and entrepreneurial.[8]

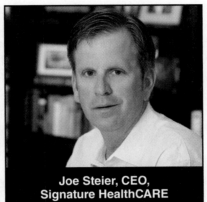

Perspectives

Joe Steier, CEO, Signature HealthCARE, has insight on how to inspire pople to be creative.

I want to keep my top talent challenged. The most creative people want challenge, and I need to keep these people. They are the future. So how do you keep the best and brightest?

First, it's my belief that most people don't want to work "for" someone their whole lives. They want something they can call their own, they want to create, they want to succeed in bringing their ideas to life. And their ideas, innovation, and creativity come from their dreams. They want to realize those dreams! Most of the time, though, they can't realize their dreams at work, so the best people often leave.

Joe Steier, CEO, Signature HealthCARE

I don't want the best and brightest, most creative, most innovative entrepreneurs to leave this company, and I want them to be fulfilled, challenged, and excited about the work they are doing. What we've done at Signature HealthCARE is to create a "Dream Factory." First of all, everyone is encouraged to think about how to do things better, what new businesses we can create inside the company. We encourage them to bring these ideas to us. When the ideas are great, which they often are, we support them in getting the business off the ground in the company. We grow people by opening the creative process.

Source: Personal interview with Joe Steier conducted by Annie McKee, 2009.

Joe Steier is a well-respected entrepreneur and his approach is unique. Later in this chapter, you will see how he brings entrepreneurship to life in his company. In this chapter, you will also explore how creative ideas can be turned into innovations that support businesses, organizations, and communities. You will learn what it takes to be an entrepreneur and what you can do to be successful. Finally, you will consider some of the things you will need to understand about HR in small businesses, as well as what we can all do to develop our own creativity.

Most Popular » Discussion Questions

1. Have you ever been in a situation where a manager, teacher, or another "authority figure" was controlling your actions too much? What did that do to your desire to be creative and to help that person achieve his or her goals?
2. Have you ever dreamed of owning your own business? Which aspects of this idea are attractive to you? Which are daunting or frightening, and which don't you understand very well yet?

2. What Is Creativity?

Why is creativity so important today? There's a simple answer: The way we work, manage, and lead organizations has changed, because the environment has changed. We need to find new ways to build, organize, and position businesses for success, new ways to engage and motivate employees at all levels, and new ways to face even more changes. We need curiosity and courage and we need new ideas. All of these require creativity.

Creativity Defined

Creativity
The process of imagining and developing something new.

Creativity is the process of imagining and developing something new. We often associate creativity with artists and writers, but it is at the heart of all work. Creativity can be the source of an idea that explains something (like gravity or the theory of relativity), or it can manifest as something tangible (such as a work of art, a consumer product, or a new process). For example, the marketing professional who devises a new slogan is using his or her creativity. Likewise, the factory worker who continually encounters a bottleneck (an area where production slows due to limits of equipment, supplies, or other resources) and thinks of ways to relieve it is also being creative.

Are you creative? Do you know friends or family who are? Many people do not see themselves as very creative. They reserve the term for musicians, artists, dancers, and the like, as well as the special few, such as Facebook founder Mark Zuckerberg, Microsoft founder Bill Gates, or Apple's Steve Jobs. In actuality, we can all be creative. As you can see in ■Exhibit 8.2, many factors affect creativity, all of which are available to you and many of which can be developed.

■Exhibit **8.2**

Which Factors Affect Creativity?	
Factors Affecting Creativity	**Explanation**
Knowledge	Creativity does not occur in a vacuum. It always involves a combination of new ideas and existing knowledge.[9]
Age	An important area of the brain for creativity and memory, the prefrontal cortex, does not fully mature until we reach our early 20s. This area may also be one of the first to deteriorate as we get older.[10]
Positive outlook	Research has connected positive emotions to performance on cognitive tests.[11] There is also a connection between positive emotions and the ability to take in new information.[12]
Cognitive flexibility	Cognitive flexibility is a person's ability to break out of traditional or conventional patterns of thought, as well as to identify more abstract concepts and principles.[13] Replacing the language of "certainty" with the language of "possibility" removes mental barriers and allows for more cognitive flexibility.[14] Finally, cognitive flexibility can include the ability to embrace paradoxical ideas.[15]
Working memory and sustained attention	Working memory is critical to the ability to focus attention for a sustained period of time. Sustained attention can be limited by how much information can be held in working memory.[16]
Self-esteem	People who have high self-esteem are able to engage in independent thought and action despite criticism.[17] They also tend to have a more positive outlook, which affects their ability to learn and to stay motivated.[18]
"Rogue" behavior and avoiding conformity	People who defy the status quo are less inclined to slip into traditional mind-sets and more inclined to challenge assumptions that never were or no longer are valid.[19]
Mindfulness	Mindfulness is the act of sustaining attention and awareness while in the act of doing something.[20] This involves an effective working memory, but it also involves the ability to focus attention.[21]

Creativity resides within all of us. Our brains are literally wired for it—we just need to cultivate this complex ability and use it more often. In the following sections, we will look at some common ways of talking about and explaining creativity, and then we will discuss research as to how our brains support creative thinking and actions.

Convergent and Divergent Thinking

It is not easy to describe creativity. Part of the reason for this difficulty is that creativity happens inside an individual or among individuals as they work together. Because creativity is so hard to "see," people often take shortcuts to explain it. In fact, research on how people think has been oversimplified to explain creativity. For example, it is commonly thought that outcome-oriented or "convergent" thinking is not creative, whereas more open thought processes are creative. Similarly, you have probably heard people talking about "left brain" and "right brain" to explain how we approach logic and creativity. This research has also been oversimplified and even inaccurately applied to creativity. Let's look at both of these frameworks and then turn to more recent and more accurate research that links brain function to creativity.

Convergent thinking
An analytical thought process that follows the steps and rules of logic.

Divergent thinking
A thought process that relies on the generation of many ideas, random connections, observations, and interpretations.

Convergent thinking is an analytical thought process that follows the steps and rules of logic.[22] **Divergent thinking** is a thought process that relies on the generation of many ideas, random connections, observations, and interpretations. Divergent thinking is often spontaneous and relies more on deep understanding and pattern recognition than on isolated facts and logic to work out problems.

The confusion about how creativity links to convergent and divergent thinking has existed for years.[23] Specifically, it has been argued that creativity is linked most directly to divergent thinking.[24] This view would mean that logic and creativity are in opposition to each other—that somehow, logic is the absence of creativity, and vice versa. Neuroscience researcher Arne Dietrich wishes to destroy the myth that creativity and divergent thinking are synonymous, and that convergent thinking is not involved in creative thinking.[25] His stance is that creativity can be a process of convergent thinking just as much as it is a process of divergent thinking.[26]

Creativity is a complicated process that involves many parts of the brain, not just those that link to divergent thought. As long as we continue to promote the myth that only divergent thinking involves creativity, we are less likely to recognize creativity in ourselves or to help others develop creativity in themselves. Another common myth that we need to examine (and do away with) is that creativity is linked to one half of the brain and not the other.

The Left vs. Right Brain Myth

Dr. Arne Dietrich also attacks another myth about creativity: the idea that creative thought occurs only in the right brain, and logical thought occurs only in the left brain. There is no evidence that creativity is controlled by the right brain.[27] Many regions, processes, and types of neurological activities are involved in creativity (■Exhibit 8.3). Depending on the type of creative work being done, these activities can be both profoundly different and located in different parts of the brain.[28]

The idea that there are right-brained and left-brained people is a popular myth, and it receives widespread coverage in the popular press despite all scientific evidence to the contrary.[29] Back in 1980, an early pioneer of split brain research, Michael Corballis, warned that thinking of creativity in terms of right versus left brain was not something that could be supported by actual research.[30] So why does this myth continue? Political economist Catherine Weaver calls the left-brain/right-brain hype "dichotomania," and suggests that the myth says more about society's need to classify and categorize than it does about logic or creativity.[31] Let's examine some of the more recent research about the neuroscience of creativity.

■Exhibit **8.3**

Many regions of the brain are active during creative moments.

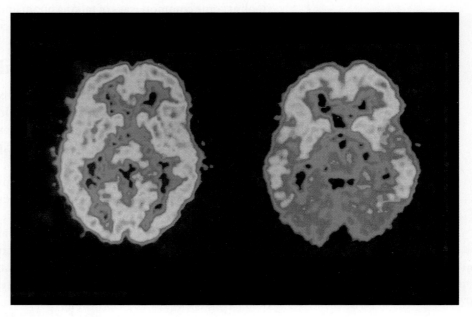

Medical-on-line/Mediscan/Alamy

The Neuroscience of Creativity: Thinking *and* Feeling

Neurological activities related to creativity are difficult to isolate.[32] For one thing, there appear to be many different types of creativity. For another, even as creative activity occurs, other activities are also occurring—for instance, a person may be playing with an idea while taking a walk and enjoying the views of nature. One of these actions is a creative activity, another is a neuromuscular activity, and the third is a visual activity. Still, all three activities draw on the same pool of mental resources, such as long-term memory, working memory, and emotions.

According to scholar Arne Dietrich, two streams of neurological activity seem to be related to creativity. One is the *knowledge domain*, which includes both thoughts and feelings. The other is the *processing mode*, which includes sustained, deliberate effort and spontaneous generation of creative thoughts.[33] Research has also shown that during focused creative activity, the brain actually shuts down certain regions, blocking unnecessary information in order to preserve cognitive resources for the creative effort.[34] In other words, specific parts of the brain slow down their processing some kinds of information so that the conscious mind can focus on the creative task at hand. However, when the task involves certain kinds of manipulation of language, this slowed-down processing state is not activated, suggesting that there is a difference between verbal and nonverbal creativity in how the brain functions.[35]

Based on information learned about the knowledge domains and processing modes of creativity, Dietrich proposes that there are *four different domains of creativity*, depending on whether the brain processes information through its emotional centers or through its cognitive centers, and whether the process is deliberate or spontaneous.[36] These four types of creativity are shown in ■Exhibit 8.4.

Clearly creativity is complicated. Yet, it is a process that is natural for human beings and one that we can all access. Thoughts, feelings, knowledge, experience, age, and several other factors affect our creativity, as do conditions in our workplaces.

■Exhibit **8.4**

Four Types of Creativity

		Knowledge Domain	
		Emotional	**Cognitive**
Processing Mode	*Deliberate*	Insights start in the prefrontal cortex, which recruits attention processes to locate and access emotional memories, which are stored in emotional structures. Example: Insight during therapy or coaching	Insights start in the prefrontal cortex, which recruits attention processes to enhance perception and to direct the search in long-term memory for relevant information. Example: Thomas Edison's inventing style, which was systematic and exhaustive
	Spontaneous	Insights begin in the limbic system, and then higher-level emotional processing is continued in other parts of the brain, such as areas of the prefrontal cortex.[37] Example: Artistic inspirations, epiphanies, revelations	Insights originate in the areas that process perceptions (possibly where unconscious learning and automatic behavior occur and originate). These unconscious thoughts "break into" the working memory of the prefrontal cortex, where they can then be consciously processed. Example: The "Eureka!" moment

Source: Dietrich, Arne. 2004. The cognitive neuroscience of creativity. *Psychonomic Bulletin and Review,* 11(6): 1011–1026.

Most Popular » Discussion Questions

1. Review Exhibit 8.2, the factors that affect creativity. For each of these factors, identify a situation in which the factor helped you be creative.
2. Think about a time when you were very creative at work or in school. What was the situation? What did you think or do? What conditions supported you in being creative? How did people respond?
3. Review the four domains of creativity in Exhibit 8.4. Which is most comfortable and natural for you? Which is uncomfortable and unnatural?

---

3. How Can We Encourage Creativity at Work?

Many people believe that creativity is something people are born with, but creativity *can* be developed. Creativity can be encouraged in the workplace to meet all kinds of challenges, such as unexpected opportunities, falling sales, rising costs, unsafe working conditions, and so on. The ability to approach these challenges in new ways is important to both short- and long-term success. Leaders can develop an organizational culture where creativity is viewed as valuable.[38] Specific steps leaders can take to foster creativity include challenging the status quo, ensuring that the workforce is diverse, supporting people in taking risks, and providing a work environment that supports relaxation and conversation.

Developing a Culture Where Creativity is Valued

Challenge the status quo: Some companies struggle with creativity because they keep employees within a narrow set of parameters, and policies and procedures remain as they have been for decades. Companies where challenging the status quo is encouraged will be competitive because doing things the same way as in the past does not work in the twenty-first century. An example of a company that breaks the status quo barrier is Procter & Gamble. Creative P&G employees are supported in questioning the "unquestionable." One result is that the common household mop was completely redesigned. The new "Swiffer" is P&G's twenty-first-century mop, and it uses electrostatic attraction rather than water to remove dirt.[39]

Build a diverse workforce: Creativity among employees occurs more often when groups and the entire workforce are composed of people with different perspectives. Companies who continually hire the same types of people end up with "cookie-cutter" employees who all think alike. This is not how innovation and creativity happen. Creativity and innovation emerge when varying perspectives are applied to problems. Different perspectives come from people who have different cultures, backgrounds, experience, training, education, and careers. Unilever, the multinational company with brands including Dove, Axe, Vaseline, and Lipton, believes strongly in diversity as a foundation for creativity and innovation. For Unilever, diversity means everything from age and gender to level of expertise and years with the company. For this firm, the broad diversity in its research and development function has resulted in highly creative products and marketing.[40]

Encourage risk-taking: Employees should feel comfortable taking risks and making mistakes. One roadblock to creativity occurs when people feel that offering up a suggestion flies in the face of accepted operating procedures. People will simply not make their ideas known if they believe they won't be heard. They surely won't share creative ideas if they fear being punished for taking risks.

Provide a comfortable, thought-provoking work environment: Managers can foster creativity by providing physical spaces for groups to meet and thoughts to flow. Designating conference spaces for brainstorming and quiet places for reflection and holding off-site meetings are just a few examples of how this can be done. For instance, employees working for the American Industrial Hygiene Association in Virginia decided to create their own space for creative thoughts. They worked together to choose color schemes, furniture, and so on, and for around $2,300 they crafted a creativity room for employee use.[41]

The suggestions in this section are useful guidelines for promoting creativity: They are practical and even somewhat obvious, albeit if harder to do than to talk about. Let's now look at a few more radical suggestions.

"The Weird Rules of Creativity"

Well-known scholar Robert Sutton takes ideas about how to foster creativity much further in his article entitled "The Weird Rules of Creativity." As he puts it, "Managing for creativity, I've discovered, means taking most of what we know about management and standing it on its head."[42] He proposes a set of rules that are not only counterintuitive, but are in some ways heretical in that they suggest radical ways to behave when hiring, rewarding, guiding, and pursuing new ideas. As you can see in ■Exhibit 8.5, Sutton's rules do indeed challenge the status quo.

As you review Exhibit 8.5, you are probably thinking things like "That's funny!" or "I would love to try that at work" or "No way!" Sutton's suggestions do indeed spark strong reactions because the new rules are radical and provocative. Of course, many of these suggestions are not meant to be applied all the time—people and companies could get in big trouble, for example, if employees ignored their bosses when it comes to ethical issues. Sutton is in no way suggesting that the old rules be thrown out entirely, but rather that we must have new rules as well. That is because for the most part, traditional management behavior and belief systems sought to control people and processes to ensure that they remained the same: predictable, efficient, and easily managed. That is just not the way to spark creativity in people.

■Exhibit **8.5**

Robert Sutton's "Weird Rules for Creativity"	
Typical Actions	**Weird Rules for Creativity**
Decide to do something that will probably succeed—_then convince yourself and everyone else that success is certain._	**Decide to do something that will probably fail—**_then convince yourself and everyone else that success is certain._
Reward—_success; punish failure and inaction._	**Reward—**_success and failure; punish inaction._
Seek out—_and be attentive to people who will evaluate and endorse the work._	**Seek out—**_ways to avoid, distract, and bore customers, critics, and anyone who just wants to talk about money._
Take your past successes—_and replicate them._	**Take your past successes—**_and forget them._
Use job interviews—_to screen candidates and, especially, to recruit new employees._	**Use job interviews—**_to get new ideas, not to screen candidates._
Think of some—_sound or practical things to do, and plan to do them._	**Think of some—**_ridiculous or impractical things to do, and plan to do them._
Ignore people—_who have never solved the exact problem you face._	**Ignore people—**_who have solved the exact problem you face._
Find some happy people—_and make sure they don't fight._	**Find some happy people—**_and get them to fight._
Hire—_"fast learners" (of the organizational code)._ **Hire—**_people who make you feel comfortable and whom you like._ **Hire—**_people you (probably) do need._	**Hire—**_"slow" learners (of the organizational code)._ **Hire—**_people who make you uncomfortable, even those you dislike._ **Hire—**_people you (probably) don't need._
Encourage people—_to pay attention to and obey their bosses and peers._	**Encourage people—**_to ignore and defy their bosses and peers._
Summary—_efficiency indicates effectiveness in the implementation and use of proven ideas._	**Summary—**_creative companies and teams are inefficient (and often annoying places to work)._

Source: Sutton, Robert. 2001. The weird rules of creativity, _Harvard Business Review_ (September): 97.

In this section we have looked at creativity—what it really is and how we can nurture it in our organizations and ourselves. Now we turn to what we _do_ with creativity: We innovate.

Most Popular » Discussion Questions

1. When do you feel most creative? Mornings? Nights? What kinds of physical spaces do you find to be the most conducive to creativity?
2. Consultants and HR professionals use a wide variety of role-plays, games, and other experiential exercises to foster creativity in training sessions. One such exercise involves presenting a mundane object to participants, who must generate a list of all possible uses for this object. With two or three of your friends or classmates, see how many uses you can think of for a nail, leaf, penny, and spoon.
3. Think about a group that you participated in that included people with differing backgrounds, experiences, and points of view. When managed effectively, diverse groups like this can be much more creative than homogeneous groups. Was your group creative? Why or why not?

4. What Is Innovation and Why Is It Important?

Innovation
The process of implementing new ideas.

The word *innovation* is everywhere in the business press. Scholars study it, consultants and advisers promise to foster it, and leaders obsess about it. But why? What is it? **Innovation** is the process of implementing new ideas. Businesses, organizations, and communities of all kinds have reasons to focus on innovation, starting with the fact that our social, economic, political, technological, and environmental conditions have changed tremendously in recent years.

Spenser Wigsten is an engineering student at Binghamton University and the local director for the university's branch of Doctors without Borders, an organization that provides medical services in poor, remote, and war-torn parts of the world. When asked to write a case on change and innovation, Spenser pointed out that we all share responsibility for innovation in society, business, and education. You can see what Spenser had to say in the following *Student's Choice* feature.

Student's Choice

Spenser Wigsten

Innovation: It's Everywhere

Inspirational leaders promote innovative ways of looking at society, business, and our responsibility in and to the world. Creativity is essential today. Independent thinkers, inventors, and "renaissance" people are revolutionizing the way society operates to enhance the lives of others. I see three areas where creativity and innovation are really important: our community, business, and supporting people around the world through education.

Our Collective Responsibility for Leadership and Innovation in Our Communities

I recently watched President Barack Obama deliver his 2010 State of the Union address. He evoked a sense that we are all in it together, and that we need to put our differences aside. I was watching with my friends: Everyone in the room was inspired to contribute their opinions to the debate about how we need to go forward. He was talking about all of us in the U.S. We argued our points of view about President Obama's ideas and proposed policies. But one thing we all agreed on was the need to become more innovative. As President Obama put it:

> [W]e need to encourage American innovation. Last year, we made the largest investment in basic research . . . that could lead to the world's cheapest solar cells - or treatment that kills cancer cells but leaves healthy ones untouched. And no area is more ripe for such innovation than energy.

President Obama reminds us that America needs inspirational leadership and innovation to prosper in our communities and in business.

Innovation in Business

Steve Jobs is also an unequivocal inspiration when it comes to innovation. As CEO of Apple, Jobs has transformed the way

the world communicates. The millions of applications, online resources, and venues for social connection started by Apple's product lines have fostered interconnectedness of users around the world and inspired creativity and new ways to learn. That, in itself, is inspiring.

Innovation in Education for Everyone

Education is the key to making our world a better place—and it is very hard to get in some parts of the world. And as technology becomes more and more fundamental to how we communicate and learn, we have to find ways to help people access things like computers.

The One Laptop per Child campaign is an initiative that aims to foster learning and computer literacy by providing strong, simple, and even solar-powered computers to children who otherwise wouldn't have them. Matt Keller is the Director for Global Advocacy for the organization. In an IBM-sponsored forum on smartplanet.com, Mr. Keller recently spoke on the relief efforts in Haiti and future plans for product innovation. In this venue, he is a representative leader of the organization and reflects the desire to expand it worldwide. Keller notes that these computers are:

> [D]esigned with the real world in mind, considering everything from extreme environmental conditions such as high heat and humidity, to technological issues such as local language support. As a result, the XO laptop is extremely durable, brilliantly functional, energy-efficient, responsive, and fun.[43]

The most successful people and organizations in the world, in my opinion, consist of passionate people who truly want to increase the quality of life of humanity as a whole. By recognizing and accepting change and by fostering innovation in our communities, businesses, and the world, we act as leaders. We inspire others to hope, to be creative, and to support change the right way.

Source: Adapted from a case written by Spenser Wigsten.

Spenser's take on innovation is one we should pay attention to: Innovation is happening everywhere, at every level of society and in business. For example, the One Laptop per Child campaign is innovative on all three levels Spenser mentions. Let's look at that effort in a bit more depth.

Nicholas Negroponte is the inspiration behind the One Laptop per Child campaign (OLPC). This not-for-profit's mission is to help eliminate poverty by providing educational opportunities to the impoverished children of the world by giving them access to their own laptop computers, using donated money.[44] The company states that the laptop "is a tool—a gateway—to creativity and experimentation, sharing and discovery for a generation of people who've never used a computer."[45]

There have been controversies surrounding the program. For instance, ideological differences regarding use of proprietary Windows operating system software in addition to free, open-source Linux software led to the resignation of OLPC president Charles Kane.[46] Other issues have been the continued high cost of laptops, as well as issues surrounding privacy and safety. Some fear that the use of these computers may allow governments in developing countries to spy on users through the laptops.[47]

Problems and criticisms notwithstanding, as of early 2010, the OLPC organization had purchased more than a million XO laptops (the so-called $100 laptops, although prices have remained about $200) and shipped them to 24 countries worldwide—including Peru, Uruguay, and Haiti. Volunteers across the globe include a wide range of professionals and students who work in classrooms and orphanages to help children with disabilities learn to use their new computers.[48]

In the next section we will focus on one of the themes highlighted by the OLPC program: innovation in business. Organizations around the world are seeking ways to be competitive on a global scale. They want new ways to reach new customers and clients with new products and services. Organizations also want to find ways to lead and manage diverse employees who have very different expectations of work than people did in the past.

Innovation: What It Looks Like in the World of Business

In 1993, organizational scholar Peter Drucker proclaimed that knowledge was "the only meaningful resource."[49] But knowledge itself does not lead to innovation. Rather, it is knowledge applied in new, meaningful, and creative ways that result in innovation. Take the example of Netflix, an online movie-rental company. Netflix has revolutionized the video rental industry since it was founded in 1997. The company went public in 2002.[50] By 2010, it had 12 million active subscribers.[51] The company literally has no physical stores to contend with, which drives down overhead. Its main competitor, Blockbuster, was built around the traditional bookstore model of people coming into a physical location and browsing for titles, which limited the selection and required customers to come into the store. Although Blockbuster eventually moved toward a Netflix-type model, it was reluctant to let go of its physical presence, and by 2010, it was faced with the forced closure of a thousand stores and filed for bankruptcy.

On the other hand, Netflix had to overcome a different limitation—a time delay of several days between customers' selection of a video and ability to watch it. One way the company overcame this obstacle was by offering its customers amnesty from late fees. In other words, customers could return a title any time they wished. Another way the company overcame this limitation was to reframe customers' perceptions. In a store, customers select titles just before rental. In contrast, with an online service, customers can select multiple titles in which they are interested and place them in a "queue." The company then sends out the next title in the queue whenever it receives a video back from the customer. The perception of time delay diminishes as a result. Of course, as technology improves, so do the services of this innovative company. For instance, when

■Exhibit **8.6**

Netflix has changed the way people rent and watch movies.

NetPics/Alamy Images

streaming video became feasible for movies, Netflix offered instant access to videos through its Web site (■Exhibit 8.6).[52]

Another innovation offered by the company is the Netflix Prize, which is an award of $1 million to anyone who offers ideas "to substantially improve the accuracy of predictions about how much someone is going to enjoy a movie based on their movie preferences."[53] Netflix takes these innovative ideas and runs with them, constantly upgrading the technology of its Web site to help steer customers to videos that they are most likely to enjoy, thus saving them money and improving their experience.

Some companies have gone beyond innovating their products and services to looking at new ways of creating, marketing, pricing, and disposing of product waste when the consumer is done with the product.[54] These companies consider not only what people want and need, but how the product should "fit" into the overall environment (both business and natural). Consider the following *Business Case* on Seventh Generation, a company that produces green cleaning products.

Seventh Generation   **Business** Case

Innovation and a Long-Term View

Many breakthroughs in human history were driven by challenges to long-held assumptions and beliefs. One prominent challenge facing the world today is as follows: Can an organization sell environmentally friendly products and still make a profit? Many people see sustainability and profitability as incompatible. Others, however, have tested the waters and found that there is no contradiction, and that producing and selling sustainable products can actually be highly profitable. Seventh Generation shows us that it is the challengers who teach us new truths, ideas, and ways of doing things.

In 2009, Vermont-based Seventh Generation was the largest American wholesale distributor dedicated to environmentally friendly household products, from diapers to cleaning and laundry products and paper solutions.[55] In 2008, the company recorded sales of more than $150 million.[56] Given Seventh Generation's two decades of success, many say they were the first company to understand the potential value of green products in the U.S. market even before "going green" became a key competitive advantage.[57]

Innovation in Product Lifecycle

Clearly, Seventh Generation's product line is innovative (although more and more companies are getting into the business of green products). What is equally interesting is the innovative business model they have pursued. To start, the name "Seventh Generation" comes from the teachings of the Native American Iroquois Confederacy: "In our every deliberation, we must consider the impact of our decisions on the next seven generations."[58] Seventh Generation takes a strong stand that for a business to succeed, it must take this long-term view in everything it does: from the type of products it manufactures, to relationships it builds with customers and suppliers, to the way employees work.[59] This company's belief is that economic, environmental, and social systems are actually influenced by each individual activity of an organization, so the organization is responsible for attending to its actions at all levels of the value chain, including outside the company itself.[60]

In addition, Seventh Generation has adopted a truly innovative way to think about what products *really* cost. Their approach goes beyond consideration of the costs of raw materials, production, people, and transportation of goods to market. Instead, the company also considers the costs of resource utilization and production in terms of their impact on the environment.[61] Here's what this looks like: At this time, organic and green products tend to cost more than the same products that are produced without consideration of the environment. That is because organic and green products can be more expensive to produce. Seventh Generation's point of view, however, is that if you tally the *real* cost of both sets of products, *nongreen products are more expensive in the long term* because of their negative impact on the environment, so they should cost more than green products.[62] This new approach promotes the understanding of an organization's responsibility to cover not only the cost of producing goods, but also the cost of replacing raw materials, as well as costs for the disposal and potential reuse of goods.[63] This is a truly innovative approach.

Innovators like Seventh Generation discover new ground and make us think differently about what we are doing, buying, and selling. As CEO Jeff Hollender puts it: "Seventh Generation is really in the business of helping people make more thoughtful and conscientious choices about how they lead their lives. Raising consciousness is a large part of why we are in business."[64]

Photo Source: Mopic/Shutterstock

Most Innovative Companies and Products

Innovative companies like Seventh Generation and Netflix are not alone in focusing an incredible amount of energy, time, and money on finding new and better ways to position themselves and their products in the marketplace. In fact, this issue is so important that a number of prominent business magazines track the most innovative companies and the most innovative products. In ■Exhibit 8.7, you can see what *BusinessWeek* had to say about the most innovative companies of 2009. A much more interesting list of innovative companies and products comes from *Fast Company*'s Web site (■Exhibit 8.8).[65] Their list for 2009 gives "Team Obama" the top prize for most innovative company. *Fast Company*'s list is creative, because it looks at many more issues than financial performance or short-term impact on the market (as evidenced by the pick of Team Obama). Both *BusinessWeek* and *Fast Company* try to choose innovative companies and institutions that matter to real people. Let's look in ■Exhibit 8.9 at what some 20-somethings think were the most innovative products of the past decade or so.

When it comes to business, innovation is a key long-term strategy. Many times when we see lists like this, we assume that a few geniuses are coming up with the products and services, but that is not usually the case. Most innovations in products and services take years of effort and tremendous investment. But when it pays off, a product or service can pay off big and take the market by storm—as the Apple iPhone did, for example.

■Exhibit **8.7**

BusinessWeek's Most Innovative Companies of 2009

Each year, *BusinessWeek* publishes an article describing what it believes to be the 50 most innovative companies in the world. The magazine doesn't really specify any criteria for inclusion on the list other than phenomenal success in the market.[66] The magazine's top 10 companies for 2009 are as follows:

1. *Apple:* In choosing Apple, *BusinessWeek* points specifically to the company's growth in the cell phone market, the success of its online iPhone App Store, and the continuing popularity of its Mac and iPod products.
2. *Google:* Although *BusinessWeek* acknowledges that Google did cut back somewhat in light of economic conditions, it also cites the company's incredible array of new services (including Google Voice and targeted advertising) as examples of its continuing commitment to innovation.
3. *Toyota:* Here, *BusinessWeek* was impressed not just by Toyota's long-standing leadership in "green" automaking initiatives, but also by the company's commitment to further improve its Prius product by making it roomier and incorporating solar-powered electrical features.
4. *Microsoft: BusinessWeek* included Microsoft on the list because of the company's many innovations in the field of "cloud computing." At the same time, the magazine also listed Microsoft's failed attempt to buy Yahoo! as a bit of a disappointment.
5. *Nintendo: BusinessWeek* was impressed by Nintendo's regular release of new game titles, as well as by the company's ability to reach customers of all ages through its innovative, family-friendly Wii products.
6. *IBM: BusinessWeek* mentions IBM's "Smart Planet" initiative as a prime example of the company's leadership in incorporating new computing technologies into nearly all aspects of public service planning and provision.
7. *HP:* HP earned a spot on *BusinessWeek*'s list as a result of its ability to cut research and development costs by nearly two-thirds while simultaneously introducing multiple practical advances into the marketplace, such as new uses for touchscreen technology.
8. *Research in Motion:* Here, *BusinessWeek* cites Research in Motion's continued success as Apple's primary competitor in the development and sale of applications for handheld computing devices.
9. *Nokia:* According to *BusinessWeek,* the need to compete with the iPhone led Nokia to introduce a new and innovative line of touchscreen products. These devices have allowed the company to maintain its position as the worldwide leader in cell phone manufacturing and sales.
10. *Walmart: BusinessWeek*'s decision to include Walmart in its top 10 relates to the retailer's use of technology in developing digital health records, "greener" stores, and even a new social networking platform named "Elevenmoms."

■Exhibit **8.8**

Fast Company's Top 10 Most Innovative Companies of 2009

1. *Team Obama:* Although it does not fit the traditional definition of a business enterprise, metaphorically, this group had a "product" (Senator Obama) for which it "created a market" (voters) and "sold it" (financial supporters), generating huge sums of money in the process.
2. *Google:* Although Google has undergone some tough transitions of late and has cut back on some of its famous perks, the Googleplex has been churning out new ideas and products as fast as ever.
3. *Hulu:* Few believed that a fully online database of current and past television programs would change people's attitudes toward the tube, but Fox and NBC Universal showed them all how it's done.
4. *Apple:* Apple is stronger than it has ever been and has more offerings.
5. *Cisco Systems:* Distributed leadership and encouraging the entrepreneurial spirit keeps this company at the top of the list.
6. *Intel:* Intel redefined the rules of competition yet again with the introduction of the Atom microprocessor, smaller and more energy efficient than anything else on the market.
7. *Pure Digital Technologies:* Flip digital video recorders have changed the way people think about recording.
8. *WuXi PharmTech:* This company contracts out its scientists to conduct R&D. They are in high demand, and WuXi gets the benefit of all their experience. This company may overtake Pfizer in the number of chemists it employs.
9. *Amazon:* Amazon started a revolution with its Kindle electronic reader. Small, lightweight, yet easy to read, this product allows you to take your library with you wherever you go. Also, Kindle downloads offer considerable savings over physical books—and they are good for the environment.
10. *IDEO:* Global design consultancy IDEO now designs experiences as well as products, using a human-centered approach to professional and other services. IDEO's programs can now design for creating behavioral change as the company gets into the organizational learning market.

So far in this chapter, we have looked at what innovation looks like in businesses. This can include a wide range of types of innovations, such as offering better services, more advanced products, increased efficiency, more effective marketing, decreased cost, or innovations that support communities and the environment. Today, innovation needs to be central to most business plans or companies risk becoming obsolete quickly.[67] So how do businesses ensure that they are innovative? We will explore that next.

■Exhibit **8.9**

A Group of 20-Somethings Generates a List of Products They Think Are Innovative

According to a diverse group of young people, the most innovative gadgets range from entertainment products to specific technologies, including GPS systems and mobile phones. The following top-innovative product list was created by this group of 20-somethings. As they put it, "it's not scientific but we had a lot of fun putting it together!!"

1. The **Blackberry** revolution is huge! Statistics indicate that since 2005, 13 million people have become Blackberry users.[68] We love it and are addicted to it.
2. Apple has become **I "Everything!" iPhone, iPods, laptops, iTouch, iPad**—we want them all!!!
3. Nintendo **Wii** and Xbox **Guitar Hero** are fun and engage the mind and body.
4. **Wifi** online anywhere, anytime.
5. EVERYONE uses **Facebook**!

6. **Cisco Telepresence:** Takes video conferencing to a "Star Trek" level where people appear so real on the screen—from anywhere on the planet.[69]
7. Commercialized GPS **"TomTom."** ROAD TRIP!!!!!!
8. **CGI Technology:** 3D . . gotta get used to it. Cool. Feels like we're in the movie.
9. **HDTV:** Clear, classy, and a must.
10. **Kindle:** No more heavy backpacks!

Most Popular » Discussion Questions

1. Review the lists of innovative companies. Choose one and research the company and its products and services. What is appealing to you about the company? What concerns you about this company?
2. Do you think innovation in business is done primarily for market competitiveness and profit? Why else might a business engage in innovation?
3. Is innovation always good? Explain your answer.

5. How Can We Foster Innovation in People and Companies?

The lists in the previous section point to several companies that can teach us about innovation. But these lists also spark a question: Are *companies* themselves innovative, or are the *people* in companies innovative? The answer is both. For a company to be innovative, it must have creative people who can take their own ideas and work with others to turn them into innovative products, services, and ways of doing business that can help the company. Innovation may come from a flash of genius, but most comes from a conscious search for opportunity. This can be hard work, take a long time, and require skills that have not necessarily been taught to us in school or in our first jobs.

Many of us have simply not been taught how to transform our creativity and good ideas into something that can be developed for use. There is growing awareness in a variety of sectors that teaching creativity and innovation and linking both to leadership is a first step in ensuring that a company can make it to one of these top 10 lists. Leaders everywhere are beginning to see that we actually need to foster innovation in people so they, in turn, can foster it in their organizations and communities. For example, Dato' Nooraishah Ahmad Tajuddin, deputy director of the Centre for Leadership Training, is the inspiring and innovative leader of an exciting new division of the Ministry of Education in Malaysia called AKEPT. AKEPT's mission is to support the transformation of higher education in Malaysia, focusing especially on developing people's capacity to manage and lead. Dato' Nooraishah is inspiring and also challenging in her vision of what we need to do in our higher educational systems to foster innovation. Let's look at what she has to say in the following *Perspectives* feature.

Perspectives

Dato' Nooraishah Ahmad Tajuddin, Deputy Director of the Centre for Leadership Training, Malaysian Ministry of Education, looks for ways to inspire education.

[Today, people] simply don't stress innovation enough in higher education. We talk about it all the time, but our curriculum does not support it, nor does the way many professors teach or grade students' work. There has always been too much emphasis on academic achievement—but in today's world, getting is not enough, especially when we get them for memorizing facts. Of

Dato' Nooraishah Ahmad Tajuddin, Deputy Director of the Centre for Leadership Training, Malaysian Ministry of Education

course this is an important part of learning, but we need to also focus on curiosity, creativity, and especially innovation.

The fact that we don't stress innovation is not really surprising. Schools have been the place we learn about others' ideas, not necessarily our own. From primary school, we have been taught to listen and remember, rather than listen and challenge, or listen and go beyond what is known. From now on, we need to find ways to help even our primary students learn to be innovative. The challenges our young people face in the workplace and our global environment are very real. This

Continued on next page>>

Dato' Nooraishah is a wise and committed leader. She and her team are actively pro-moting innovation in higher education—one of the sectors most likely to impact Malaysia and the region in powerful and positive ways. The programs she and AKEPT are developing are based in part on an "each one teach one" philosophy, preparing peo-ple to share their knowledge and to support others in leading through innovation, in whatever sector they work. Dato' Nooraishah has supported the development of a cul-ture of innovation and backed it up by creating practical organizational structures (such as employee idea-generating groups) that help people bring their best ideas to the table.

Structures That Promote Innovation

Structures that encourage innovation have been used for decades. From customer fo-cus groups to new venture teams to Skunk Works®, the intent is the same: Get new ideas and then get them up and running. Today, some common structures that promote in-novation include Skunk Works® and idea incubators.

Skunk Works®

Skunk Works®
A term used in business to describe a group within an organization that is given a high degree of autonomy and is unhampered by bureaucracy. The term is trademarked by Lockheed Martin.

Bureaucracy and traditional decision-making processes can be a serious hindrance to the development of new technologies and designs.[70] **Skunk Works®** is a term used in business to describe a group within an organization that is given a high degree of autonomy and is unhampered by bureaucracy. Entrepreneurial research teams and divisions designed in this way focus on breakthrough ideas, providing highly tal-ented individuals the time and freedom to be creative. The work within such teams is often secretive.

The term Skunk Works® is trademarked by Lockheed Martin, where it was first used as the official nickname of an entrepreneurial branch of the company that is actually called Advanced Development Programs. This structure was created in the mid-twentieth century and continues today. Under the leadership of Kelly Johnson, and later Ben Rich, the Skunk Works® team developed such legendary craft as the U2 spy plane, the SR-71, and the stealth bomber. The division was created because Lockheed Martin realized that the creativity and innovation the company needed was hampered tremendously by its bureaucracy: "What allowed Kelly to operate the Skunk Works® so effectively and efficiently was his unconventional organizational approach. He broke the rules, challenging the current bureaucratic system that sti-fled innovation and hindered progress."[71]

Although Skunk Works® is a registered trademark of Lockheed Martin, many peo-ple use it to describe their own companies' entrepreneurial research teams and divi-sions. Many companies, however, honor the trademark and have chosen different names. For example, Boeing has its "Phantom Works," while the U.S. Air Force has Area 51. Similarly, in 2006, Ford Motor Company's chief diesel engineer Adam Gryglak mod-eled his own advanced development project team, called "Project Scorpion," to fast-track innovation and help bring competitive advantage back to Ford.[72]

Idea Incubators

Idea incubator
Part of the research and development (R&D) branch of an organization that focuses on the development of entrepreneurial ideas.

An **idea incubator** is another way to facilitate innovation. An idea incubator is usually part of the research and development (R&D) branch of an organization that focuses on the development of entrepreneurial ideas. The metaphor is not accidental, because the "incubator" protects and nurtures an idea until it is viable and healthy, just as an incubator protects and nurtures premature infants. When business ideas are first generated, they are incapable of surviving without some form of support. New ideas require supportive challenge and examination, and they may need to change their scope to enhance feasibility.[73] A plan for implementation might also be created and the idea might require support from key stakeholders. All of this needs to be done in a safe environment.

For example, the U.S. Army has an idea incubator called the Army Suggestions Program. This program offers cash awards for military personnel or civilians who develop ideas that result in tangible savings for the army. On average, 100 suggestions are submitted per year, and some of these suggestions have saved the army millions of dollars.[74] Universities are developing their own idea incubators as well. The University of Pennsylvania's Graduate School of Education teamed up with the Milken Family Foundation in 2009 to sponsor an educational entrepreneurial program in the form of a competition. People from around the world were encouraged to submit business plans "to tackle the biggest issues at all levels of education" and compete to win the top prize of $25,000 or a second prize of $15,000.[75]

Innovative Divisions Outside an Organization's Bureaucratic Hierarchy

One interesting example of an innovation structure that is technically outside the organization is Disney's Imagineering, a permanent division of the organization whose purpose is to dream up wild ideas about new things a guest at Disneyland might experience.

Walt Disney Imagineering is the branch of Disney that is involved in creative development and planning of major projects, as well as research and development.[76] To support innovation, the group draws on more than 150 different disciplines in the creation of new resorts, theme parks, real estate projects, and media. The name *Imagineering* is a play on *imagination* and *engineering*, as the group blends advanced technology and creativity to develop innovative and distinct storytelling. The company owns more than 100 patents in ride systems, fiber optics, audio, special effects, and interactive technologies.[77]

Imagineering has been an integral part of the Disney franchise since 1952, when it was formed as an independent company to help create Disneyland.[78] Recently completed projects include the *Space Mountain* ride at Disneyland in 2005, the 2008 *Spaceship Earth* attraction at Orlando's Disneyworld (Exhibit 8.10), and the 2009 *Turtle Talk with Crush* in Tokyo DisneySea park.

Another innovation that supports people in sharing new ideas is Disney ImagiNations. Disney ImagiNations is a Walt Disney Imagineering-sponsored design competition that promotes diversity and allows students to develop their talents and knowledge in creative design. Finalists in the competition receive an all-expenses-paid trip to present their work to Imagineering executives, and many are chosen for internships.[79]

To this point in the chapter, you have learned about creativity and innovation. We have examined how creativity and innovation are important for you as an employee, manager, or leader. We

■Exhibit **8.10**

In 2008, Walt Disney Imagineering redesigned the famous Spaceship Earth attraction at Disneyworld in Orlando, Florida, to include an interactive time machine ride.

© Mervyn Rees/Alamy

have also looked at how creativity and innovation support existing organizations in continuing to be successful. Now, we will turn our attention to *new* organizations—entrepreneurial ventures. In new businesses (start-ups), creativity and innovation are essential, as is an understanding of what it takes to be an entrepreneur.

Most Popular » Discussion Questions

1. In this chapter you have learned that innovation is not just about new products or services. Innovation is also about how businesses and organizations are structured and managed. Brainstorm a list of ways a small business such as a coffee shop, local restaurant, or auto repair garage might change the way it does business to more effectively meet the needs of its clientele.
2. Imagine that you have been hired by a large retail clothing chain to consult on innovative marketing and advertising ideas. Brainstorm a list of suggestions you would give the company about attracting the 20- to 25-year-old customer.
3. Brainstorm a list of innovations that would help you be more efficient or have more fun in your daily life.

---

6. What Is Entrepreneurship?

Entrepreneurship
The process of identifying an opportunity, developing resources, and assuming the risks associated with starting a new business.

Entrepreneur
A person who starts a new business.

■Exhibit **8.11**

Tony Blair and Gerhard Schröder argue that all societies need entrepreneurs.

Entrepreneurship is the process of identifying an opportunity, developing resources, and assuming the risks associated with starting a new business. An **entrepreneur**, then, is a person who starts a new business. The word *entrepreneur* is borrowed from French. Although we, as a society, have attached a number of meanings to this term, its original and fundamental meaning is "one who undertakes or manages."[80] Entrepreneurship is about creating and taking ownership of new ideas, plans, business activities, or responsibilities.[81] This view of entrepreneurship includes being creative and innovative—that is, having an "entrepreneurial spirit."[82] Many people argue that the opportunities and challenges we face today require all of us to develop an entrepreneurial approach to work and life, and even politicians are talking about the need for an entrepreneurial spirit.

Former British Prime Minister Tony Blair and former German Chancellor Gerhard Schröder argue that in the twenty-first century, we need to ignite a new entrepreneurial spirit across all levels of society and we need people who are ready and eager to adopt responsibilities (■Exhibit 8.11).[83] More recently, President Barack Obama called on the American people to focus on innovation in areas related to renewable energy for the purposes of long-term sustainability and creation of jobs.[84]

We often think about entrepreneurs as individual people whose creative genius results in a technological breakthrough or an invention that results in hugely profitable or popular businesses. Bill Gates of Microsoft, Steve Jobs of Apple, and Craig Newman of Craigslist are examples of this type of entrepreneur. Most entrepreneurs, however, are everyday people in your neighborhood or city who are providing products and services to their customers and earning a modest living.

Entrepreneurs come from all walks of life. If you walk around your town, you will see different types of businesses and service organizations. Despite the fact that many small entrepreneurial businesses have been swallowed up in recent years by "giants" such as Walmart, most communities have small grocery stores, coffee shops, dry cleaners, and landscape companies. In

Torsten Leukert/vario images/Alamy Images

office parks and office buildings, you will find firms that specialize in fields such as research, technology, fashion design, consulting, and manufacturing. Entrepreneurship is alive and well in almost every single industry and in not-for-profits in all communities.

The Importance of Small Businesses in Our Economies

When you think about it, every single business or organization started as an entrepreneurial venture, and most started *small*. Entrepreneurial ventures are an extremely important part of many economies. Oftentimes in the study of management, we don't pay much attention to small businesses. That's a big mistake. In the United States and many other countries, small businesses are the backbone of the economy. For example, in the U.S. Small Business Administration's "Frequently Asked Questions" publication, one of the questions is "How important are small businesses to the U.S economy?" The question is answered in this way: *"Small businesses:*

- *Represent 99.7 percent of all employer firms.*
- *Employ just over half of all private sector employees.*
- *Pay 44 percent of total U.S private payroll.*
- *Have generated 64 percent of net new jobs over the past 15 years.*
- *Create more than half of the nonfarm private gross domestic product (GDP).*
- *Hire 40 percent of high-tech workers (such as scientists, engineers, and computer programmers).*
- *Are 52 percent home-based and 2 percent franchise.*
- *Made up 97.3 percent of all identified exporters and produced 30.2 percent of the known export value in FY 2007.*
- *Produce 13 times more patents per employee than large patenting firms; these patents are twice as likely as large firm patents to be among the one percent most cited."*[85]

Just think about it: 99.7 percent of companies that employ people are small businesses. More than half of private-sector employees work for small businesses.

Small businesses are also important in other countries, and they do not always look the way we might expect. For example, in some countries, many entrepreneurial ventures are not the typical one-person owner, employing a few people to provide services or sell goods. Instead, they are owned and operated by entire communities. Let's hear what Chikasha Muyembe has to say about "cooperatives" in Zambia in the following *Student's Choice* feature.

Cooperative
An organization made up of a group of people who come together voluntarily to meet common economic, social, and cultural needs through a jointly owned and democratically controlled enterprise.

Student's Choice

Cooperatives in Zambia

Chikasha Muyembe

Population increase is a major problem that affects many developing nations, such as Zambia. Zambia's population grew about 15% between 2003 and 2009, and it now stands at 11,862,740.[86] With the right policies in place, a large population can positively influence economic development and growth through its large labor force and consumer base. However, population increase can make it difficult for an economy to sustain the large number of people, as has been the case in Zambia. In that country, there just aren't enough jobs and the unemployment rate is very, very high—in 2000, it was approximately 50%. In a quest to reduce unemployment levels, the Zambian government has been encouraging skills development and entrepreneurship—both of which come alive through the formation of cooperatives.

A **cooperative** (or co-op for short) is an organization made up of a group of people who come together voluntarily to meet common economic, social, and cultural needs through a jointly owned and democratically controlled enterprise. Chaisa Multipurpose Co-operative is one of the oldest in Zambia, situated about 5 kilometers away from the central business district of Lusaka. Formed in 1982, this co-op has a membership of 150 people and is involved in several different business activities, including selling a variety of consumer goods, carpentry, and metal working.

Continued on next page>>

Mr. Dube, the chairperson of the co-op, has been a member for over 15 years. In 2008, Dube and six other members were elected to the board of directors. This leadership structure helps the cooperative have a path through which it can achieve its goals. It is the duty of the chairperson together with the board of directors to see to it that the cooperative's objectives are carried out.

Benefits of the Cooperative to the Members and the Community

- The joint ownership of the cooperative creates a sense of belonging and brings about unity in the society.
- There are over 400 people who use the facilities of the cooperative. These people get to help each other, especially when one has a bereavement.
- The co-op is a huge source of income for the members and creates employment for the people in the surrounding community. This means that many people are able to earn income through the co-op's activities and through the dividends from the cooperative.

- All economic benefits are kept within the cooperative.
- Because cooperatives are legal entities, it is far easier for them to borrow money than if a single individual was starting a business.
- Cooperatives help create employment and help improve the standard of living of their members and the surrounding communities.

People who decide to form a cooperative are entrepreneurs, because they take risks by investing in a cooperative, developing businesses and taking their products and services to the marketplace. One of the most important aspects of this type of entrepreneurial venture is that it empowers people. As the co-op becomes more successful, both members and employees become better equipped and more empowered to open their own businesses. In other words, co-ops start a cycle of entrepreneurship, which in my country is so necessary and so inspiring.

Source: Adapted from a case by Chikasha Muyembe.

Chikasha's example of the Chaisa Multipurpose Co-operative is inspiring. Just think about what it would take for people to create such a business: Many of them would come to the venture unemployed and with very little income. However, they would also come with passion, commitment, many talents, and a powerful and palpable spirit of entrepreneurship.

Entrepreneurs can also be found in unlikely places, such as the world of music and television. As you can see below, a lot of celebrities you know are entrepreneurs:[87]

1. Actresses Mary-Kate and Ashley Olsen are no strangers to entrepreneurial activity, and they have built a huge business empire. In February 2010, the sisters launched a new line of clothing and accessories called Olsenboye, which is available through JCPenney.
2. Another pair of celebrity sisters, Khloe and Kourtney Kardashian, along with sister Kim, own clothing boutiques in Beverly Hills and Miami.
3. Comedian Will Ferrell has a line of sunscreens portraying him in comedic bare-skin situations. Proceeds from the line fuel scholarships for former and current cancer patients.
4. Actress Melissa Joan Hart and her mother own a confections and frozen yogurt store called "Sweet Harts" in Sherman Oaks, California.
5. Comedian actor Steve Carell bought Marshfield Hills General Store in Marshfield, Massachusetts—his hometown. The store is run by family members.
6. Actor/director Clint Eastwood owns a 22-acre hotel in Carmel, California.
7. Legendary rocker Bono is founder and managing director of a private equity firm, Elevation Partners, that invests in media and entertainment.

Similarly, many celebrities have used their fame and fortune to help spur efforts for social change. Consider the examples listed below:

- *Bono:* The lead singer of U2 co-founded an organization called ONE to find solutions to extreme poverty and disease in the developing world, especially in Africa. This grassroots organization has generated support from more than 2 million people. ONE works in conjunction with African leaders and policy makers to support equitable development policies, aid, and trade reform.[88]

- *Sting:* In 1980, Sting and his wife Trudie Styler formed the Rainforest Foundation to protect the South American rainforest and the cultures of the indigenous people who live there. The organization now operates in dozens of countries through a network of four independent organizations. The Rainforest Foundation lobbies for the rights of indigenous peoples, sustainable development, and policy reform.[89]
- *Oprah Winfrey:* The talk-show host founded the Oprah Winfrey Leadership Academy in 2007, a school for girls in South Africa who could not otherwise obtain an education because of poverty or because they live in remote rural areas. As Oprah puts it, "The school will teach girls to be the best human beings they can ever be; it will train them to become decision-makers and leaders; it will be a model school for the rest of the world."[90]

People start businesses for many reasons. Some see it as an opportunity to make a fortune. Others want the freedom to make their own decisions and not have to seek approval through corporate bureaucracies. Still others just want to know if they can do it. They want and enjoy the challenge. Other people want to contribute to their communities in a different way, and they cannot find a way to do it in more traditional organizations. But who becomes an entrepreneur? Does it take a special kind of person?

Profile of an Entrepreneur

So what does an entrepreneur look like? Are there common traits we can point to and say, "That person would make a good entrepreneur"? Do certain distinguishing characteristics make one person a more successful entrepreneur than his or her competitors? The reality is that too many factors influence the success of any entrepreneurial venture to be able to sum up the profile of an entrepreneur in a simple list. Every demographic characteristic you can imagine—race, gender, age, national origin, education, and so on—is represented among successful entrepreneurs. So what makes entrepreneurs different from their peers in society?

Successful entrepreneurs do seem to share some characteristics. Probably the most important factor is that entrepreneurs *embrace risk*.[91] A leap of faith into the world of owning your own business is not easy and requires courage. It is a difficult step, but one that many entrepreneurs take on simply because they enjoy the challenge. But this idea of risk taking should be understood as *calculated risk*. Perhaps President John F. Kennedy summed it up best when he noted: "There are risks and costs to a program of action. But they are far less than the long-range risks and costs of comfortable inaction."[92] In other words, those with an entrepreneurial spirit do take risks—as does anyone who actually seeks to make a change in the world—but by far, the biggest risk is to watch the world change around you without doing anything to protect your long-term survival.

Entrepreneurs also *take the initiative*.[93] They are *self-starters*. They are not content to develop ideas and idly sit by without putting them into practice. Entrepreneurs have a *strong need for achievement*. When they see something that can be done better, they do it. Along with this achievement drive, entrepreneurs have a high level of *self-esteem*, and they may even be a bit self-centered.[94] Additionally, entrepreneurs *see the "big picture"* while taking care of the details of the business as well. They have to. A new venture rarely has available to it the skills of a large organization, so the entrepreneur must have a hand in a wide variety of tasks, such as communicating a vision, raising capital, coming up with new ideas, and solving a range of problems as they crop up. Their minds and bodies are always engaged in tasks.[95] Finally, many entrepreneurs are *engaged learners*.[96] Whether they spend evening hours on the Internet looking for best practices or attend trade shows to find out the latest in what makes businesses like theirs do well, entrepreneurs passionately pursue learning. Finally, and given all of the other things in this list of characteristics, entrepreneurs tend to be *energetic*. Entrepreneurs can be found throughout society—in business, of course, but also in education, medicine, law, agriculture, psychology, consulting—literally every field lends itself to entrepreneurship. Let's look at how social entrepreneurship is capturing attention today.

Social Entrepreneurship

Social entrepreneurship
The activity of identifying opportunities to help society in some way, with financial gain taking a secondary position if it factors in at all.

Social entrepreneurship is the activity of identifying opportunities to help society in some way, with financial gain taking a secondary position if it factors in at all. Social entrepreneurs see the chance to do public good through promoting social change. The work is neither charity nor business in any strict sense, although it can lead to more effectiveness for both.[97]

For example, Josh Nesbit, a Stanford University student, became a social entrepreneur when he took 100 reconditioned cell phones and a laptop to doctors in Malawi.[98] Using open-source software, health care providers in this African country are able to keep in touch through text messages about patient conditions and emergencies.[99] Also, using this text messaging platform provided by FrontlineSMS, Nesbit and others including Ken Banks, the founder of another social entrepreneurship organization called kiwanja.net, have created organizations that help improve life for people in Malawi and other places in Africa.[100]

Another well-known example of social entrepreneurship is the solar cooker known as the Kyoto Box. In 2009, this solar cooker was developed by Norwegian inventor Jon Bohmer, who is based in Kenya, to meet the needs of the rural poor in an environmentally friendly way.[101] This cooker, which is a modern adaptation of a 1767 invention, was developed for the HP-sponsored *Forum for the Future Climate Change Challenge*, held in 2009.[102] The 15-euro machine won the top prize of U.S. $75,000, which is being used to fund large-scale trials in 10 countries.[103] The cooker, which derives all its energy needs from the sun, produces no smoke and requires no other resources to operate. It can cook, bake, clean water, and dry food while at the same time reducing environmental damage caused by CO_2, deforestation, and electricity production.[104]

Social entrepreneurs have many of the same characteristics as entrepreneurs, but they have a greater desire to pursue opportunities that help others. They are *intrinsically motivated* in their work, which sustains them, encourages them to work hard, and inspires them to think creatively.

Most Popular » Discussion Questions

1. Would you like to own your own business one day? Why? What specifically attracts you to the idea of becoming an entrepreneur?
2. If you were to start your own business, what would it be? Why?
3. Think about a social issue that is important to you. Brainstorm a few ideas for entrepreneurial ventures that could address this issue. Pick one of your ideas and explore in some detail what it would take to launch your social entrepreneurship venture.

---

7. How Does a New Business Get Started?

Suppose you have an idea for a business. It's new. It's unique. You think you can really make it work. Unfortunately, many great ideas end right there. The idea might have come to you or it may have developed over time, slowly gaining momentum until you could actually see how to turn it into a business. Either way, many people cannot seem to take the next step: going from idea to reality. They tell themselves that their idea will never work, or that they don't have enough money or business experience. Sometimes, they simply don't know how to take the idea forward in a concrete manner.

Starting a business, however, is likely to result in success if you understand some basics, such as:

- Knowing the right questions to ask
- Knowing how to write a business plan
- Determining how to secure funding
- Understanding the life cycle of a start-up
- Knowing how to avoid common pitfalls
- Leading and managing for success

In the next few sections, we will explore each of these very important topics so you *can* be a successful entrepreneur if you choose.

Questions to Ask When Starting a Business

Say you have a good idea for a business. Maybe you even think it is a great idea and you can't wait to start. You know, however, that many, many new businesses fail in the first two years.[105] You'd like to be one of the businesses that "makes it" and is around for a long time. So, you do some soul searching, ask yourself some tough questions and do research to find the answers. As you can see in the following list, the questions you might ask yourself are not easy, but you need to be honest with yourself if you want to get off to the right start:

- How much will it really cost me to get this business off the ground? From ordering supplies to paying cell phone costs, and from securing office space to buying insurance, all expenses must be accounted for.
- What taxes will I need to pay? Many entrepreneurs fail to realize that taxes can be substantial. If you plan on hiring employees, you will have payroll taxes. You will also have to pay taxes on your income. You may have property taxes; city, state, and federal taxes on revenue; and the like. Depending on what your business does, you may also need to collect sales tax from customers.

Break-even point
The point at which expenses equal income.

- What is my break-even point? A **break-even point** is the point at which expenses equal income. For example, let's say you add up all of the costs associated with running your new business for a year (payroll, supplies, taxes—everything). Your yearly costs add up to $120,000 (including paying yourself). Let's assume the revenue you bring in each month from the sales of your products or service is about $15,000 per month. Since $15 \times 8 = 120$, it will be eight months into the year before you cover the costs of doing business. Knowing your break-even point is vital because it shows you the importance of budgeting.
- What will be my personal income? What if I need to forego an income for some period of time? Many start-ups require personal financial sacrifices. You must have a candid discussion with your family and be realistic with yourself to determine whether you can afford to live without any personal income for many months or even a year or two. Will your lifestyle be impacted if it takes over a year to finally bring a paycheck home?
- How will you pay for things like health care costs, insurance (home, renter, office, business inventory, car, etc.)? You will want to be especially careful about health care costs, because they can be extremely expensive for small businesses in the United States.
- Are you and your family up for the 24/7 work that most start-ups require? How will you take care of yourself and your relationships?

These are just a few of the questions you will need to explore. Depending on the type of business you are opening and your needs as a person, there may be many more. As tedious as it might seem, it will be more than worth the time and effort to think through these questions so you can understand what you are getting into and what you need to do to prepare yourself and your family. In addition, asking these questions will help you get to the next step: writing a business plan.

Writing a Business Plan

Business plan

A formal document that states the nature of a business and its goals and outlines how the business will succeed.

The formal outline of a business venture is often captured in a business plan. A **business plan** is a formal document that states the nature of a business and its goals and outlines how the business will succeed. Many business plans also include other information, such as the background of the entrepreneur, financial statements, and an analysis of the industry. ▪Exhibit 8.12 illustrates the elements of a business plan to give you a better idea of how to write one.

A business plan is important for several reasons. First, if an entrepreneur is seeking a loan from a third-party source, such as a bank, the financial lender will want to review the business plan to ensure it is realistic. For example, if you went to a bank and asked for half a million dollars but could not adequately explain your great idea, why the business was relevant, how the business would be marketed, and how long it will take to break even, then the bank will probably not lend you any money.

▪Exhibit **8.12**

Elements of a Typical Business Plan[106]

Elements of a Business Plan
1. **Cover sheet**
2. **Statement of purpose**
3. **Table of contents**
   - **I. The business**
      - A. Description of business
      - B. Marketing
      - C. Competition
      - D. Operating procedures
      - E. Personnel
      - F. Business insurance
   - **II. Financial data**
      - A. Loan applications
      - B. Capital equipment and supply list
      - C. Balance sheet
      - D. Break-even analysis
      - E. Pro forma income projections (profit and loss statements)
      - F. Three-year summary
      - G. Detail by month, first year
      - H. Detail by quarters, second and third years
      - I. Assumptions on which projections were based
      - J. Pro forma cash flow
   - **III. Supporting documents**
      - A. Tax returns of principals for last three years
      - B. Personal financial statement (all banks have these forms)
      - C. For franchised businesses, a copy of franchise contract and all supporting documents provided by the franchisor
      - D. Copy of proposed lease or purchase agreement for building space
      - E. Copy of licenses and other legal documents
      - F. Copy of resumes of all principals
      - G. Copies of letters of intent from suppliers, etc.

Second, even if you are not attempting to secure outside funds, having a business plan helps structure the idea behind the business. In other words, outlining how success will be measured will keep you on track. The very characteristics that make entrepreneurs successful—creativity, risk taking, and action orientation—can cause them to fail because they lose sight of where they are going.

Where Does the Money Come From?

As most entrepreneurs quickly discover, starting a new business is expensive. It takes money to get the process rolling. Some people use their personal savings to finance the venture. Others use credit cards to pay for the initiative—obviously, a potentially dangerous solution. As an alternative, many entrepreneurs seek funding from a third party, such as investors, venture capitalists, and financial institutions.

Investor

Someone who provides money as a loan and is, in return, paid back with interest.

Angel investor

A person or a small group of people who offer money to a start-up in exchange for a stake in the business.

Venture capitalist firm

A company that seeks to earn a profit through investments in start-up firms or companies that are undergoing dramatic change.

Before venturing too far from home, an entrepreneur might look to family and friends as investors. An **investor** is someone who provides money as a loan and is, in return, paid back with interest. Investors can also be people you don't know. For instance, a local trade association might have funds available to budding entrepreneurs, or perhaps you know of someone who wants to invest in something other than the stock market. These investors are sometimes referred to as angels. An **angel investor** is a person or a small group of people who offer money to start-ups in exchange for a stake in the business. They will often seek a 30 percent return on their investment over five years.[107]

Similarly, a **venture capitalist firm** is a company that seeks to earn a profit through investments in start-up firms or companies that are undergoing dramatic change.[108] When venture capitalists get involved in an entrepreneurial venture, they often enter into a financial partnership with the entrepreneur. Though the entrepreneur may have operating control of the business, a venture capitalist retains some, most, or in some cases all of the legal ownership of the company. Venture capitalists are very selective, choosing to invest in only about six of every thousand business plans they review.[109] However, because of their ownership stake, when they do invest, the money is often substantial. It is estimated that venture capitalists invest nearly $30 billion each year in the United States alone.[110]

Finally, perhaps the most common source of third-party funds is financial institutions. Financial institutions are organizations such as banks and credit unions that receive, hold, invest, and lend money. With a well-crafted business plan in hand, an entrepreneur may seek a business loan from a financial institution. He or she may have to show proof of collateral or personal investment in the business. In addition, a payment schedule is determined and, in most cases, repayment begins immediately. Some financial institutions have been designated as Small Business Investment Companies (SBICs). An **SBIC** is a financial institution that makes loans to entrepreneurs under the auspices of the Small Business Administration, a U.S. federal government agency.

SBIC

Small Business Investment Company; a financial institution that makes loans to entrepreneurs under the auspices of the Small Business Administration, a U.S. federal government agency.

The Life Cycle of a Start-Up Business

As an entrepreneur starts a business, he or she is setting forth on a journey of exploration and discovery. It is exciting and frightening at the same time because of the "unknowns" that lie ahead. There will be successes and challenges. However, successful entrepreneurs take these all in stride and move the business forward, no matter what. As an entrepreneurial venture matures, it goes through four stages: start-up, growth, maturity, and decline/renewal.[111] Each stage is discussed in the following subsections.

Stage 1: Start-Up

This is the first stage in launching a business. It is here that the first steps are taken to transform a dream into reality. Early on, it is critical for the entrepreneur to have a good grasp of the business's financials. It is easy to become overextended if expenses are not understood. A name must be chosen, physical or virtual locations secured, all legal issues associated with setting up the venture must be completed, and the initial marketing of products or services must be carried out. Organizational scholars have also referred to this stage as "birth" and note that successful leaders in this stage develop their systems of operation and successfully manage the inevitable crises that occur.[112] Scholars also note that what works for a mature organization just doesn't cut it for a start-up.[113] For instance, sales structures have to be tactical and quickly evolving.

Stage 2: Growth

If a venture survives the start-up stage and begins showing a profit, it may then enter the growth stage. Revenue and profits may increase. More employees might need to be hired, and operations and processes become more firmly established. Issues such as marketing, good customer service, strategic human resources, budgeting, purchasing, and upgrading of equipment take precedence.[114] The venture is now viable, as long as it is managed well.

It is also at this point that the vision of the business owner becomes critical to future development. Entrepreneurs often have choices about how much to grow, and these decisions need to be made consciously. A successful business need not be a "growing" business. Many owners are perfectly content to see their businesses remain a small and manageable size rather than pursue continual growth.[115]

Stage 3: Maturity

In the growth stage, an organization may increase in size rapidly. When an organization reaches maturity, that rapid growth slows down. Competition is looked at differently. Rather than "capturing" a market share or a customer base, organizations think more about "protecting" those things and maintaining stability.[116] A great deal of focus, then, goes into cultivating a long-term strategy through effective marketing and good customer service. Another way of protecting long-term viability at the maturity stage is to invest more time and energy in technical efficiency and quality control.[117] Enhancing production methods, improving marketing efforts, exceeding customers' expectations, and training employees are all important at this stage.

Stage 4: Decline or Renewal

At some point, an organization may become entrepreneurial again, seeking renewal and additional growth, or it may enter into a stage of decline. As the environment changes, many factors may be outside the control of the mature organization that has focused on stability and strength. Changes such as a tough economy or societal transformations can threaten a mature organization and cause it to go into decline. In fact, an organization that is over-focused on stability may be more at risk of decline than one that is more adaptable. Scholars have argued that organizational decline is often due to too much bureaucracy that prevents the organization from responding to changing market conditions.[118]

On the other hand, decline may occur because of inability to keep up with threats. For example, Napster, an online music distribution channel, started out as a free site where people could exchange music files. The company was hailed as revolutionary, but it also faced huge threats from the more traditional music industry. After only a few years in business, the company was shut down, because courts found that Napster was violating copyright laws.[119] Let's look at what happened.

Napster was founded in 1999 by Shawn Fanning and Sean Parker, and it became an instant success. By December of that year, the Recording Industry Association of America filed a lawsuit against the company in federal court, followed by another lawsuit brought by music group Metallica. Within a few months, the courts ruled that Napster did not enjoy protection under the Digital Millennium Copyright Act, and two months later, an injunction against the company was granted.

In 2002, another music organization from Germany agreed to buy the struggling company's assets for $8 million, but after Napster filed for bankruptcy, a judge blocked the sale. The bankruptcy court allowed Roxio to buy the bankrupt company for $5.3 million at the end of 2002, and it reopened the next year under Roxio's ownership and with a different model that no longer allowed free file sharing. Napster continued to struggle for many years, but was eventually bought by Best Buy for $121 million. The company is still around, and it is currently still owned by Best Buy.[120]

We can see from the example of Napster that its birth and growth were dynamic and rapid, but the company was challenged early and beset by many obstacles. It never reached the maturity stage before decline set in. But, after coming out of bankruptcy, Napster was rejuvenated, found stability, and went through a five-year process of growth before being bought by Best Buy.

When things go wrong, business owners may turn their business around by dramatically altering business strategy, processes, and operations, as happend at Napster. Sometimes, however, the forces against survival are just too powerful. What can you do if this happens? Again we can look at what happened at Napster. When the controversies and lawsuits hit, the owners were no doubt concerned. Maybe they asked the question, "How do we get out of this without losing too much money?" In this case, the owners filed for bankruptcy and ultimately sold the company.

Decline of a business can be fast or slow. Outcomes are varied: Sometimes owners can sell their business to a competitor or allow employees to buy it. This might mean that the organization continues, although in a different form. And of course, sometimes owners will simply close the business.

How to Avoid Common Pitfalls and Succeed as an Entrepreneur

There are tremendous opportunities for entrepreneurs in terms of financial success or the satisfaction that comes from supporting people through a not-for-profit venture. But there are also risks. Business and social entrepreneurs have the ultimate responsibility for the success or the failure of an enterprise. If employees—whether they are family, friends, or strangers—are hired into the business, their livelihoods depend on the decisions the entrepreneur makes. Unfortunately, many entrepreneurial ventures fail.

In 2005, the U.S. Bureau of Labor Statistics determined that about two-thirds of all new businesses lasted at least two years and that after four years, 44 percent were still in existence.[121] Said another way, one-third fail in the first two years, and 56 percent fail within four years. This failure rate is significant and keeps many people from even attempting to start their own business. We will now explore what you can do to ensure that your business succeeds.

Good Leadership and Management Will Result in Success

As you might suspect, being able to lead and manage effectively is a must for an entrepreneurial venture.[122] Very often, entrepreneurs are highly achievement oriented, under a lot of pressure, and somewhat individualistic. This often results in micromanaging—overcontrolling employees, processes, and everything else related to the business. This usually backfires. Even entrepreneurs who do manage well often skip the leadership part. Don't forget that people will need inspiration. They will need you to create a culture that focuses on effectiveness and innovation, as well as a climate that is ripe with optimism, excitement, and a feeling of "we're all in it together."

Develop Your Employees

Training and development of employees is not only for giant corporations. Even if you have only one other employee besides yourself, that person deserves to be sufficiently trained in what he or she does. Local community colleges and other educational institutions often have low-cost seminars and classes in all aspects of business. Building the skills of your employees not only helps them improve their own abilities, but it will ultimately help your business as well.

Remember Your Business Plan and Understand Your Finances

Drafting a comprehensive business plan is a must.[123] Too many entrepreneurs jump right in with little if any planning, resulting in a blueprint for failure. In fact, many people skip writing a business plan altogether. They believe that their ideas are so good and the business opportunity so compelling that a detailed plan isn't necessary. In addition, writing a plan might just seem too daunting. Whatever the reason, skipping this step is risky. Your business plan provides guidance and keeps you focused on your mission and vision for your company. You simply need to do it.

In addition, many entrepreneurs have the technical expertise and the passion to start a business, but they do not understand finance.[124] Get the advice and help you need regarding financial matters.

Stay Flexible

Change is inevitable. Something unexpected *will* occur in a new venture (that's part of the fun). The advantage of a small business is that you can be nimble and move quickly—more quickly than your larger competitors. You can decide to change and then do it—you'll have less need to secure permissions, approvals, and the like. So, avoid setting up too much bureaucracy, and be ready to adapt. Flexibility means shifting the business model in a way that keeps your company moving forward.

Manage Growth and Measure Success

Controlled growth should be your entrepreneurial mantra. As profits begin to increase and you find yourself with more cash, the temptation is to grow the business as fast as you can—but this is faulty logic. Uncontrolled growth can result in overextension to the point that you and your employees can't keep up and quality slips. A very common response to the possibility of growth is overborrowing and overspending. Growing the business is fine—it's expected—but growing too quickly will hurt the company in the long run.

Also be sure to measure your success. There is an old axiom in business: "What gets measured gets done." This speaks to the notion that those activities that are monitored for progress on a regular basis are the ones that are typically more successful.

Marketing Matters

Effective marketing is a must. Many entrepreneurs fail to realize how important marketing is to their business. You may believe that your products or services are fabulous and assume that others will automatically recognize this. Unfortunately, that is rarely the case. You have to let your potential customers know that you exist. You have to market to your buyers. If customers do not know your company exists, how will they find you?[125] As with financial planning, if you don't know how to market your company, get advice and help. Marketing is a professional field—it is not nearly as easy as it looks.

Focus on Customer Service

One way to ensure repeat business is through outstanding customer service. What is the formula for great customer service? First, you truly need to care about your clients. You need to listen to what customers really want from your business.[126] You also need to let them know you have heard them, that you value their input, and that you will do whatever it takes to make them happy. This will require you, as the owner, to model this kind of behavior. You will also need to provide motivation, inspiration, and training for employees who face your customers.

Be a Good Community Member

Successful entrepreneurs recognize that they are part of larger communities and networks—both physical and online. You should become involved in community events, get to know other business owners, and take pride in the town or county where you work. The following *Business Case* features a pair of entrepreneurs who exemplify excellent leadership and business management, as well as good community relations. Being a good community member also means being socially responsible and exhibiting strong ethical standards in your business practices, as Kathleen and Rhett Reddell of R&R Health and Fitness Center show us.

R&R Health and Fitness Center   **Business** Case

Kathleen and Rhett Reddell

In the tiny town of Hillsboro, Texas, located between Dallas and Austin, Kathleen and Rhett Reddell have started a business that embodies outstanding community relations. This husband and wife team—both competitive bodybuilders—work hard to ensure that their company, R&R Fitness, supports the community in a positive and powerful way. Between the two of them, the Reddells have served on or volunteered for the Rotary Club, the Hillsboro Chamber of Commerce, local ministries, schools, hospitals, community centers, civic organizations, the Boys and Girls Club, various fundraisers—the list goes on. R&R Fitness caters to a town with only 8,000 citizens, but it has more than 1,000 members—that's just over 12 percent of the population who are getting fit in the company's facility. This remarkable number of members is due in part to the Reddells' strong entrepreneurial and management skills, but also to their role in the community.

Good Citizens, Good Business

"We are a part of the community," Kathleen says, "and the community is part of us. The people who come into our business are our neighbors, they are people we attend church with, and we stand in line with them at the grocery store."

"We would like to see every person in this town as a healthy individual," says Rhett. "Our membership fees are very reasonable and our customers get the benefit of our decades of experience." The Reddells provide training programs, dieting advice, and healthy living tips to their customers—and to noncustomers, too. "It doesn't matter if they are a member of our fitness center or not," adds Rhett. "If they ask me for some suggestions on getting rid of belly fat, I'll gladly give them suggestions at no cost. Our job is to promote a healthy lifestyle."

Their focus on community has been a boon to the business. Despite recent downturns in the economy, their sales have steadily increased. The business is doing so well that they will soon be opening a second location.

Most Popular » Discussion Questions

1. Review the questions in this section that you should ask yourself before starting a business. Brainstorm five more questions that relate specifically to your knowledge and expertise, personality, and desired lifestyle.
2. Imagine that you really are starting a business. Given your age, experience, and financial situation, generate a list of possible funding sources. Pick one and make a plan for how to begin securing the money.
3. Of the four stages of a business's life, which stage would be most exciting for you? Why?
4. Do you know someone who has started a business? If it is successful, what factors do you think contributed to its success? If it is failing or has failed, what caused its demise?

8. What Is Intrepreneurship?

Intrepreneur
An employee who behaves like an entrepreneur inside his or her own organization.

Researchers have adopted the term *intrepreneurship* to describe creative and innovative talent and the spirit of entrepreneurship within organizations.[127] The term **intrepreneur** was coined in 1976 to describe an employee who behaves like an entrepreneur inside his or her own organization.[128] Intrepreneurship is a compelling topic today because of the need for creativity and innovation.

In our organizations and businesses it can be very difficult to launch new products or services. Bureaucratic rules, competition for resources, and even organizational culture often inhibit people and companies from starting something new—and yet that is just what most businesses need. Because of this, intrepreneurs need to have some of the same characteristics as entrepreneurs. They especially need to be creative, innovative risk takers.

Intrepreneurship: How It Works in a Health Care Company

As you may remember from the beginning of this chapter, Joe Steier, CEO of Signature HealthCARE, is a passionate entrepreneur, and he runs his company in a manner that allows others to be intrepreneurial. He uses the phrase "Dream Factory" to describe the process he and his team use to spark and support new intrepreneurs and exciting new business inside the boundaries of Signature HealthCARE. This is what Joe has to say about what it takes to support intrepreneurship.

Perspectives

Joe Steier, CEO, Signature HealthCARE, on Risk Taking

It is unfortunate, but many, many people have been taught not to take risks in our companies. Here at Signature HealthCARE, we are doing something very different. We want people to take risks, to be creative and innovative. We want them to succeed—here, in our company. We believe we can outperform the market by encouraging people to dream, and then take the best of those dreams and bring them to life. The first step in the process is to make sure people have a way to talk to us about their ideas. Most good ideas stay in people's minds and are never even shared. Our antidote to that is that we have built a culture where fear of failure does not exist and where people feel safe taking the risk and sharing their ideas.

We also recognize that it is true that many entrepreneurial ventures fail so we do everything we can to ensure people's success. First, of course, we evaluate the idea for a new business against the market needs, our

capacity to grow the new business and the like. Then, to launch the entrepreneur and his or her business, we seek to mitigate the most common risks, such as undercapitalization or too little outside advice, and to build the support that is needed at every step. To mitigate these risks, we:

- Capitalize the start-up appropriately. We believe that if it really is a good idea, we need to invest in it.
- Provide the right kind and amount of advice. Many start-ups have a fundamental flaw at the outset—one that is far easier for an outsider to spot.
- Coach and mentor at every step of the way. Some of us have had a lot of experience with start-ups—our whole careers have been entrepreneurial. We know what the challenges are, and when they are likely to arise. We also know how challenging it is to start a business, with all the concrete and emotional ups and downs. We're there for people when they need us.

Source: Personal interview with Joe Steier conducted by Annie McKee, 2009.

As you can see in the case of Signature HealthCARE, intrepreneurship is the process of identifying an opportunity, developing resources, and assuming some of the risk associated with the idea, all while being employed by an organization.[129] Because less than 10 percent of Americans own their own business, and likely far more would like to, intrepreneurship is one way for everyone to win.[130] What, then, can you do to ensure that your good ideas are used? One of the keys to successful intrepreneurship is making sure ideas surface and are taken up by an organization.

Building Support for Ideas

Creative ideas—ones that truly stand out—can relate to improving products or services, enhancing marketing efforts, making the workplace safer, or cutting costs. All of these are areas where companies like to see their employees and managers taking an interest and offering suggestions. But once you have a great idea, what do you do with it? How do you get others in the company to buy into it?

First, you should constantly be on the lookout for new ideas. Anything that makes the company better, faster, less costly, or safer is fair game. Ideas are everywhere. Do you see cables stretched across common areas that could be dangerous hazards? Have you been thinking about a great new ad campaign for your company's products? Do you see a wasteful practice in the company's warehouse area? Have you identified a way to reduce paper in the office that will also speed up communications? The first step in getting support for good ideas like these is to focus your attention and creativity on problems and opportunities.

You also need to talk about your ideas. Share them with others. You can get others involved by holding regular brainstorming sessions. It's a good way to find innovative ways to build the business, and it also encourages teamwork.[131] Also, be patient, make sure you don't fall into the "I can't do it" trap. If you engage in self-defeating thoughts such as "This will never work" or "We don't have the money to do this," your ideas will lay dormant.

It is one thing to sit around and come up with ideas; it's another entirely to implement those ideas. Thus, another way to build support for your ideas is to clearly articulate how they are to be implemented and demonstrate this to the right people. But who are the right people? That's where the social and emotional intelligence competency of organizational awareness comes in. To build the right kind of support, you must accurately scan your environment. You need to understand who you must bring on board (e.g., your boss), who will be strong supporters, and who will resist. You also need to know who has access to funds to support the implementation of your idea. With this understanding, you will be able to craft an approach for who, where, how, and when to share your ideas. Crafting an action plan that shows in step-by-step fashion how the idea is put into effect will give more credibility to your idea and illustrate its feasibility.

Finally, do not become frustrated. Some ideas simply won't get the support you expected. Due to budget, time, or staffing constraints, suggestions may have to be placed on the back burner until those resources are available. The key is to continue seeking new ideas.

The concept of intrepreneurship is important because it fosters innovation and creative thinking in a safe environment. Today, more and more companies are creating systems that support intrepreneurship tangibly. For example, leaders are more focused on building cultures that tolerate risk. When this works, intrepreneurs have the advantage of a steady, relatively secure income from their employer, and in most cases, they will not lose their jobs if an idea fails or does not live up to expectations.[132] Most organizations truly want employees who have an intrepreneurial spirit.[133] They encourage and reward those employees who think creatively, solve problems, and are innovative.

Most Popular » Discussion Questions

1. Think of yourself as an intrepreneur in your school. What opportunities for innovation can you see? List five areas where you could apply your creativity and innovation to make changes that would support students, faculty, staff, or the community. What support and resources would you need to start this new venture? Who would you need to include in the stakeholder group to take this forward?

2. What obstacles might you run into if you attempted to act as an intrepreneur in your school? How could you overcome them?

3. What are the potential risks and benefits of acting as an intrepreneur in an organization?

9. What Is HR's Role in Supporting Creativity, Innovation, and Entrepreneurship?

As an entrepreneur, you might end up as "chief cook and bottle washer." You will likely be the CEO, CFO, director of marketing, and VP of HR (as well as holding down your day job). For this reason, we will use this section of the chapter to present two very important aspects of the HR-type work that you will likely have to do yourself: knowing and communicating laws regarding your business, and minimizing bureaucracy.

Laws and Regulations That Entrepreneurs Must Understand

Entrepreneurs face certain legal matters before they ever make their first sale. For example, one of the first steps an entrepreneur usually takes is to think of a name for the new business. In the United States, you need to apply for an assumed name. An **assumed name**—sometimes called a "doing business as" (DBA) name—is the name of the business to be started. A local or statewide search is often conducted to determine if a particular name exists, and if no matching name is on record, the entrepreneur now has an official name for the firm.

Other legal issues must be considered as well. For example, the concept of intellectual property is one that can be troublesome. **Intellectual property** refers to the ownership of a creative thought or idea and legal control over the representation of the thought or idea. Ownership is usually established in the form of a patent, copyright, or trademark.

A **patent** is a legal grant given by the U.S. Patent and Trademark Office that prevents anyone other than the grant holder from manufacturing, selling, or utilizing a particular invention. Typically, a patent is applied for when an entrepreneur develops something new and wants to protect it from being copied by someone else. In 2008, nearly half a million patents were applied for in the United States; this is up from only 150,000 in 1988.[134] In the United States, a patent is granted for 20 years. During this time, the patent holder has a virtual monopoly over the use of the product. However, after 20 years and assuming there are no enhancements or design changes to the original patent, the patent protection ends, and others can legally copy the product or process.

A **copyright** is the exclusive rights granted to the creator of an orginal work, which includes the rights to copy, distribute, and adapt. These rights can be licensed or transferred. Copyright is granted for things like books, articles, music, lyrics, and art. A copyright can be secured through the U.S. Copyright Office and is designated by the symbol ©. It lasts the entire lifetime of the creator of the work, plus 70 years.[135]

A **trademark** is any distinctive sign, image, slogan, etc., used to identify a product or service as originating from a particular individual, business, or legal entity. This can include symbols (such as the Nike "swoosh"), names (Starbucks), logos (Intel's name in its distinctive circle), designs (Coca-Cola's bottle), or words, phrases, and slogans (Magic™ tape). In other words, a trademark must be truly distinctive. Unlike patents and copyrights, though, a trademark remains in the originator's possession as long as it is continually used—there is no expiration. It is represented by the symbols ™ and ®. ™ signifies an unregistered trademark, while ® represents a trademark that has been officially registered with the U.S. Patent and Trademark Office. Both types of trademark offer certain legal protections, but officially registering a trademark makes legal action much smoother in the event of a violation of the entrepreneur's intellectual property.

Legal "rules" are an important part of any business. They provide boundaries that a company must honor. This can sometimes feel constraining, but in the long run, these "rules" are very helpful. Other "rules" that are put in place may not be as necessary or as helpful—for example, bureaucratic policies and procedures that interfere with creativity and innovation or that waste time.

Assumed name
Sometimes called a "doing business as" (DBA) name, this is the name of the business to be started.

Intellectual property
The ownership of a creative thought or idea and legal control over the representation of the thought or idea.

Patent
A legal grant given by the U.S. Patent and Trademark Office that prevents anyone other than the grant holder from manufacturing, selling, or utilizing a particular invention.

Copyright
The exclusive rights granted to the creator of an original work, which includes the rights to copy, distribute, and adapt. These rights can be licensed or tranferred.

Trademark
Any distinctive sign, image, slogan, etc., used to identify a product or service as originating from a particular individual, business, or legal entity.

Minimize Bureaucracy to Support Creativity and Innovations

One way HR managers can foster entrepreneurship is to reduce bureaucratic constraints. Policies and procedures that get in the way of creative ideas become major roadblocks for employees and may eventually get in the way of creativity and innovation. Most rules and regulations are put in place to guide behavior, and as you will see in Chapter 12, controlling for effectiveness, quality, and efficiency is important. However, far too many bureaucratic policies and procedures are unnecessary. HR professionals are in a unique position to influence all levels of management in an organization. That influence can be a powerful force to remove bureaucratic obstacles. Note that as many as 42 percent of professionals have considered quitting their job solely because of the bureaucracies that exist in their companies.[136] As an entrepreneur, you simply can't afford this.

Most Popular » Discussion Questions

1. What is your opinion about people who violate copyright laws? Justify your "for," "against," or "situational" opinion.
2. In your opinion, how do layers of bureaucracy emerge in businesses?
3. Imagine that you own a small, high-end landscaping business. The business is three years "old" and growing. You now have five full-time, year-round employees and 25 seasonal employees. Generate a list of rules you believe you need to run the business. Examine each rule for its impact on employees' creativity and innovation.

---

10. What Can We All Do to Be More Creative, Innovative, and Entrepreneurial?

Luckily, we can all learn to be more creative. In this section, we will focus on how you can develop your creativity. Creativity supports both innovation and entrepreneurship. Let's look at some simple rules you can adopt relatively easily. Then, you will learn about a specific technique to support creative thinking called mind mapping.

Becoming More Creative

So how can you support yourself in being more creative in life and at work? Scholar Mihaly Csikszentmihalyi has spent a lifetime exploring how to find fulfillment in creative work. His advice, shown in ■Exhibit 8.13, is useful—and profound.

■Exhibit **8.13**

Mihaly Csikszentmihalyi's Suggestions for Enhancing Creativity

Here are a few suggestions for enhancing your personal creativity and happiness:

- Try to be surprised by something every day.
- Try to surprise at least one person every day.
- Write down each day what surprised you and how you surprised others.
- When something strikes a spark of interest, follow it.
- Recognize that if you do anything well, it becomes enjoyable.
- To keep enjoying something, increase its complexity.
- Make time for reflection and relaxation.
- Find out what you like and what you hate about life.
- Start doing more of what you love and less of what you hate.
- Find a way to express what moves you.
- Look at problems from as many viewpoints as possible.
- Produce as many ideas as possible.
- Have as many different ideas as possible.
- Try to produce unlikely ideas.

Source: Csikszentmihalyi, M. 1997. Happiness and creativity. *The Futurist*: 31(5).

Thinking Outside the Box

Another tip on how to be more creative is to adopt practices and to use tools that cause you to think "outside the box." For example, whether taking down information, strategizing a problem, or developing a concept, you can use a creative tool called *mind mapping*, which is illustrated in ■Exhibit 8.14.[137]

As you can see, mind maps are diagrams with a central idea from which other concepts branch off, with more important concepts nearer the idea and lesser ones further away. These branches show relationships between concepts.[138] Mind mapping allows us to take notes or to capture our ideas as they occur, and to link our thoughts and information in ways that support creative thinking.

The reason this process sparks creativity is that it encourages us to think in a non-linear fashion and allows us to indicate emphases and relationships between ideas. Taking notes is a linear process in which we capture ideas and information as it is presented to us, or as it occurs to us—in a chronological order. Mind mapping, on the other hand, starts with a central image or idea and radiates out, using multiple colors, visual imagery, and key words. Lines connecting concepts are used, and these lines can also represent the level of importance (through thickness, color, solid or dashed, etc.). They can also represent the directionality of influence using such things as loops and arrows.

Images can also be used to represent the emotional content associated with ideas, concepts, problems, and so forth. The important thing is to come up with a code that makes sense—both cognitively and emotionally.[139] You can use mind mapping in the traditional way—pen and paper—or find one of the wonderful computer programs that are available.

■Exhibit **8.14**

This is an example of a mind map.

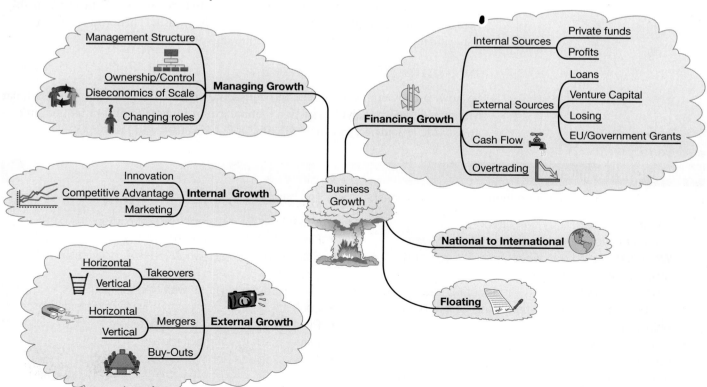

> **Most Popular »** Discussion Questions
>
> 1. Have you worked or been a student in a highly bureaucratic organization? What was the impact on you of the many "rules and regulations"?
> 2. Have you ever met people who "follow the rules" no matter what? How do these people impact your and other people's abilities to be creative?
> 3. Review the suggestions for being creative in Exhibit 8.14. Choose three or four of the suggestions and try them out for a week or so. Take notes during the week on what you did and what outcomes you noticed in yourself and others.
> 4. Try using mind mapping the next time you and a group are brainstorming about a project or an assignment.

11. A Final Word on Creativity, Innovation, and Entrepreneurship

This chapter has touched on a number of topics that are important today as the pace of change continues to drive the need for creativity, innovation, and an entrepreneurial spirit in all of our organizations. So, rather than ending here, let's look at what some prominent entrepreneurs have to say about what might be coming in the future. In 2010, the *Global Human Capital Journal* asked 17 entrepreneurs to make predictions for the future of Web 2.0 (the newest technology supporting interactive information sharing and integrated use of applications in cyberspace). They made 12 observations about trends to be expected in the second decade of the twenty-first century:[140]

- Web 2.0 is bringing with it a "seismic shift" in the way that organizations market their services and products.
- "Gamification" of work means that the boundary between work and play will increasingly become blurred.
- The government will respond to modern technologies by shedding old patterns of business at federal, state, and local levels.
- The green revolution will take off in developing nations, who will look to extreme innovation to leapfrog infrastructure limitations straight into globalism.
- The position of "digital salesperson" will become an exciting new career.
- Print media will increasingly seek creative alliances to keep from becoming obsolete.
- Because of the explosion in ideas and information, organizations will pay more attention to finding ways of nurturing ideas and maximizing individuals' engagement.
- Enterprise 2.0 (social network software used in business contexts) will face many challenges, but it will continue to make headway.
- The commercial real estate and other service industries will continue to move toward going digital.
- There will be a global explosion of mobile social networking.
- Latin American countries that hold state monopolies on telecommunications will founder in developing the next generation of network infrastructure.
- More focus will be given to developing trusted relationships and improving the quality of interpersonal interactions to quantify and add value to social networks.

Our economies, the rapid pace of change, and technological advances require us to think ahead and to think differently. As such, creativity, innovation, and a spirit of entrepreneurship are increasingly prevalent in our organizations. The best part about this is that it is *fun*.

Key Terms

1. Why Are Creativity, Innovation, and Entrepreneurship at the Heart of Business? (pp. 254–255)

Key Terms

Hypercompetition A state of constant and escalating competition. p. 254

2. What Is Creativity? (pp. 256–259)

Key Terms

Creativity The process of imagining and developing something new. p. 256

Convergent thinking An analytical thought process that follows the steps and rules of logic. p. 257

Divergent thinking A thought process that relies on the generation of many ideas, random connections, observations, and interpretations. p. 257

3. How Can We Encourage Creativity at Work? (pp. 259–261)

Key Terms   None

4. What Is Innovation and Why Is It Important? (pp. 262–267)

Key Terms

Innovation The process of implementing new ideas. p. 262

5. How Can We Foster Innovation in People and Companies? (pp. 267–270)

Key Terms

Skunk Works® A term used in business to describe a group within an organization that is given a high degree of autonomy and is unhampered by bureaucracy. The term is trademarked by Lockheed Martin. p. 268

Idea incubator Part of the research and development (R&D) branch of an organization that focuses on the development of entrepreneurial ideas. p. 269

6. What Is Entrepreneurship? (pp. 270–274)

Key Terms

Entrepreneurship The process of identifying an opportunity, developing resources, and assuming the risks associated with starting a new business. p. 270

Entrepreneur A person who starts a new business. p. 270

Cooperative An organization made up of a group of people who come together voluntarily to meet common economic, social, and cultural needs through a jointly owned and democratically controlled enterprise. p. 271

Social entrepreneurship The activity of identifying opportunities to help society in some way, with financial gain taking a secondary position if it factors in at all. p. 274

7. How Does a New Business Get Started? (pp. 274–281)

Key Terms

Break-even point The point at which expenses equal income. p. 275

Business plan A formal document that states the nature of a business and its goals and outlines how the business will succeed. p. 276

Investor Someone who provides money as a loan and is, in return, paid back with interest. p. 277

Angel investor A person or a small group of people who offer money to a start-up in exchange for a stake in the business. p. 277

Venture capitalist firm A company that seeks to earn a profit through investments in start-up firms or companies that are undergoing dramatic change. p. 277

SBIC Small Business Investment Company; a financial institution that makes loans to entrepreneurs under the auspices of the Small Business Administration, a U.S. federal government agency. p. 277

8. What Is Intrepreneurship? (pp. 282–283)

Key Terms

Intrepreneur An employee who behaves like an entrepreneur inside his or her own or organization. p. 282

9.   What Is HR's Role in Supporting Creativity, Innovation, and Entrepreneurship? (pp. 284–285)

Key Terms

Assumed name   Sometimes called a "doing business as" (DBA) name, this is the name of the business to be started. p. 284

Intellectual property   The ownership of a creative thought or idea and legal control over the representation of the thought or idea. p. 284

Patent   A legal grant given by the U.S. Patent and Trademark Office that prevents anyone other than the grant holder from manufacturing, selling, or utilizing a particular invention. p. 284

Copyright   The exclusive rights granted to the creator of an original work, which includes the right to copy, distribute, and adapt. These rights can be licensed or transferred. p. 284

Trademark   Any distinctive sign, image, slogan, etc., used to identify a product or service as originating from a particular individual, business, or legal entity. p. 284

10.   What Can We All Do to Be More Creative, Innovative, and Entrepreneurial? (pp. 285–287)

Key Terms   None

11.   A Final Word on Creativity, Innovation, and Entrepreneurship   (p. 287)

Key Terms   None

Chapter 8 Visual Summary

8. Workplace Essentials:
Creativity, Innovation, and
a Spirit of Entrepreneurship

7. Change: A Focus
on Adaptability
and Resiliency

9. Organizing for
a Complex World:
Structure and Design

Planning
and Change

6. The Human Side of
Planning: Decision Making
and Critical Thinking

5. Planning and
Strategy: Bringing
the Vision to Life

1. Why Are Creativity, Innovation, and Entrepreneurship at the Heart of Business? (pp. 254–255)

Summary: In the constantly changing climate of modern organizations, relevancy is based on the ability of leaders to encourage creativity, innovation, and entrepreneurship. These concepts are important because they shift the focus from short-term outcomes and overcontrolling people to fostering sustainable growth and development. In the long run, this gives rise to innovations that support businesses and communities and enables everyone within an organization to feel successful.

2. What Is Creativity? (pp. 256–259)

Summary: Creativity is the process of thinking about and developing something new. Creativity happens at all levels of organizations—from the factory floor to the board room—and it is not limited to people who are considered artistic. Unfortunately, some of us don't realize our full creative potential because we've been taught that logical thinking and creativity are mutually exclusive activities carried out by different sides of our brains. In truth, we are all creative and can employ both cognition and emotion in our creative efforts.

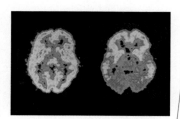

3. How Can We Encourage Creativity at Work? (pp. 259–261)

Summary: Managers need to develop organizational cultures where creativity is viewed as valuable, the status quo is challenged, the workforce is diverse, employee risk taking is supported, and creative spaces are provided. This enables organizations to step beyond the processes and products of the past to embrace new, more competitive ways of doing things and developing goods. Encouraging this kind of creativity requires a rethinking of traditional rules and an incorporation of some rules that scholar Robert Sutton describes as "weird." These weird rules don't take the place of the traditional rules; rather, they represent a supplementary set of rules that can help spark creativity.

4. What Is Innovation and Why Is It Important? (pp. 262–267)

Summary: Innovation is the process of implementing new ideas, and is a central component of modern organizations because it prevents obsolescence. In the business world, innovation does not just apply to the production of technological gadgets (although many of these devices certainly are innovative); it applies to new ways of providing service, employing sustainable practices, and increasing efficiency. Innovation is a long-term strategy for organizations of all types today. Despite the huge investments of time, effort, and money it requires, in the long run, innovation pays off for individuals, organizations, and communities.

5. How Can We Foster Innovation in People and Companies? (pp. 267–270)

Summary: In order for a company to be innovative, it must employ people with the creativity and drive to turn ideas into products and services that will help the company. Innovation is something that is often neglected in formal education and entry-level jobs, and some organizations have combated this by adopting business structures that promote innovation, including "Skunk Works"® teams that fast-track innovation and idea incubators that focus on research and development. Other organizations form partnerships with outside companies for the sole purpose of conceptualizing and building innovative products and processes. Regardless of how it is encouraged, innovation supports organizations in the quest for continued success.

8. What Is Intrepreneurship? (pp. 282–283)

Summary: Intrepreneurship is the process of using creative and innovative talents and an entrepreneurial spirit within an organization. True intrepreneurship can be difficult to find in today's organizations because bureaucracy and organizational cultures inhibit people's desire to speak up and launch a new project. As a result, intrepreneurship tends to thrive only in those organizations that actively support innovative ideas and provide a safe environment for creative thinking. Most organizations, however, are on the lookout for intrepreneurial employees, even if their structure is not entirely conducive to the process, and it is essential that intrepreneurs do not become frustrated with the process.

7. How Does a New Business Get Started? (pp. 274–281)

Summary: Understanding the basics of starting a business—which questions to ask, how to write a business plan, how to secure funding, what the business life cycle is, and how to lead and manage for success—increase the likelihood that a new venture will be successful. Even if you think your idea is great and that other people will feel the same way, there is no substitute for preparing yourself emotionally and financially by doing your homework. It is also important to understand that, no matter how well prepared you are, unexpected things will crop up that will require you to rethink your strategies. You will weather these storms successfully if you train your employees well, stay flexible, focus on customer service, and seek outside help when you need it.

6. What Is Entrepreneurship? (pp. 270–274)

Summary: Entrepreneurship is the process of identifying an opportunity, developing resources, and assuming the risks associated with a new venture. Even though many of us think of entrepreneurs as creative geniuses, most entrepreneurs are average people who own small companies in local communities that all of us do business with on a regular basis. These small businesses are an important component of the national economy, and innovative, energetic risk takers who are active learners are behind them. Not all entrepreneurs are in business for profit; social entrepreneurs devote the same skills and time to endeavors to improve the world around them.

9. What Is HR's Role in Supporting Creativity, Innovation, and Entrepreneurship? (pp. 284–285)

Summary: Many entrepreneurs must assume the HR roles within their own businesses, and two of the most common HR functions these individuals are faced with involve understanding laws and regulations and minimizing bureaucracy. In terms of laws and regulations, it is essential for entrepreneurs to understand how to protect their intellectual property through patents, copyrights, and trademarks. Entrepreneurs should also learn how to structure policies and procedures within their organizations in such a way that they do not hinder employees' creativity.

10. What Can We All Do to Be More Creative, Innovative, and Entrepreneurial? (pp. 285–287)

Summary: Developing your creative skills will help you be more innovative in all aspects of your life and more entrepreneurial in your work. Noted scholar Mihaly Csikszentmihalyi offers many suggestions for enhancing creativity—and happiness—by taking joy in the surprises life offers, recognizing and reflecting on the things you enjoy, and producing diverse ideas. Mind maps can also help you in your efforts by enabling you to create visual representations of your ideas and their conceptual connections. Regardless of the method you use to support your creativity, it is key that you engage your senses whenever you can and that you view things both cognitively and emotionally.

11. A Final Word on Creativity, Innovation, and Entrepreneurship (p. 287)

Summary: Creativity, innovation, and entrepreneurial spirit are driven by the pace of change in organizations today. Each of these concepts is important to organizational survival and will continue to be so well into the future. As we move into the future, innovation in several key sectors will change the way we do business.

Organizing for a Complex World:

Structure and **Design**

Chapter Outline

Find out what you already know about the concepts in this chapter by going to www.mymanagementlab.com and taking the Pre-Test. Your results will generate a customized study plan for Chapter 9.

1. Why Study Organizational Structure? (p. 294)

2. How Do Traditional Concepts Affect Our Views about Organizational Structure Today? (pp. 294–299)

3. What Is an Organizational Chart? (pp. 299–301)

4. How Can We "See" Organizations and Their Structures in Nontraditional Ways? (pp. 301–308)

5. How Are Organizations Classified and Legally Structured? (pp. 308–315)

6. What Are Common Contemporary Organizational Structures? (pp. 315–323)

7. How Is Work Structured? (pp. 323–325)

8. What Factors Affect the Design of Organizational Structures? (pp. 325–328)

9. What Is HR's Role in Organizational Design and Structure? (pp. 329–330)

10. What Can We All Do to Work Effectively within Our Organizations' Structures? (pp. 330–333)

11. A Final Word on Organizational Structure (p. 333)

Go back to www.mymanagementlab.com and take the Post-Test to verify your understanding of the concepts. To experience and apply the concepts, explore the additional material associated with Chapter 9.

Part 1: Leading and Managing for Today and the Future (Chapters 1, 2, 3, 4)
Part 2: Planning and Change (Chapters 5, 6, 7, 8, **9**)
Part 3: Organizing Human Systems (Chapters 10, 11)
Part 4: Controlling Quality, Culture, and Yourself (Chapters 12, 13)
Part 5: Leading and Managing for the Future (Chapters 14, 15, 16)

8. Workplace Essentials: Creativity, Innovation, and a Spirit of Entrepreneurship

7. Change: A Focus on Adaptability and Resiliency

9. Organizing for a Complex World: Structure and Design

Planning and Change

6. The Human Side of Planning: Decision Making and Critical Thinking

5. Planning and Strategy: Bringing the Vision to Life

16. Managing and Leading for Tomorrow: A Focus on Your Future

1. Managing and Leading Today: The New Rules

14. Globalization: Managing Effectively in a Global Economic Environment

Organizing Human Systems

10. Teams and Teambuilding: How to Work Effectively with Others

11. Working in a Virtual World: Technology as a Way of Life

9. Organizing for a Complex World: Structure and Design

Leading and Managing for Today and the Future

2. The Leadership Imperative: It's Up to You

4. Communication: The Key to Resonant Relationships

3. Motivation and Meaning: What Makes People Want to Work?

15. Sustainability and Corporate Social Responsibility: Ensuring the Future

12. Organizational Controls: People, Processes, Quality, and Results

Controlling Quality, Culture, and Yourself

13. Culture: It's Powerful

1. Why Study Organizational Structure?

Most of this book is about how you can be most effective personally while helping your organization succeed. You've learned how to be a good leader (regardless of your role at work), how to motivate, and how effective communication will set you apart. You've also learned that excellent planning, strategizing, decision making, and critical thinking are essential for your success. You now know how to deal with change in life and at work, and how creativity, innovation, and a spirit of entrepreneurship are some of the more exciting and important aspects of work today.

But regardless of how well you lead, motivate, or inspire others, the context in which you work—your organization's structure—will have a tremendous impact on you and your organization. Organizational structure affects your behavior, your accomplishments, and your attitude about work. Organizational structure affects your organization's agility, efficiency, and effectiveness. We study organizational structure because it is so crucial to the overall performance and well-being of organizations and employees.

Think about a few companies you know: a favorite clothing store, restaurant, or mobile phone store, for example. Imagine what it is like to work in these organizations. What do employees do every day? When you are in the store, can you tell who is a manager and who is not? How? How many people seem to report to the manager? How many employees are in the store? How many employees are in the company? Are there senior managers? What do they do? What would the leaders of these organizations be responsible for? What sorts of jobs does the organization have, and what tasks do people do? All of these questions and more are related to how the organization is structured.

Understanding how organizations are structured—who does what; how people, groups, and divisions work together; and how jobs are designed—will help you be a better leader, manager, and employee. As an introduction to this chapter, we will examine several key concepts that are traditionally important in organizational structure and design. Then we will analyze several intriguing and modern concepts that pertain to how we can understand organizations and their structures today. Following this, we will explore how organizations are classified and learn about business ownership models. In the remainder of the chapter, you will learn about some popular contemporary organizational structures and how jobs fit into them. You will study the factors that managers and leaders consider when designing an organizational structure, such as the organization's strategy, the environment in which the organization operates, and its technology, size, and geographic dispersion. Finally, the chapter concludes with a look at what HR and all of us can do to create and sustain a healthy organizational structure.

> **Most Popular »** Discussion Questions
>
> 1. Think about your family as an organization. Who is/are the leader(s)? Who makes major decisions? How does your family organize household work?
> 2. How does the way your family is organized affect you?

2. How Do Traditional Concepts Affect Our Views about Organizational Structure Today?

An **organization** is a group of people assembled to perform activities that will allow the entity to accomplish a set of strategic and tactical goals and to realize its mission. The term **organizational structure** refers to the way in which the division of labor, communication, and movement of resources among the parts of an organization are coordinated to accom-

Organization
A group of people assembled to perform activities that will allow the entity to accomplish a set of strategic and tactical goals and to realize its mission.

Organizational structure
The way in which the division of labor, communication, and movement of resources among the parts of an organization are coordinated to accomplish tasks and goals.

Organization design
The process of creating an organizational structure.

plish tasks and goals. A broader definition of organizational structure includes all of the physical, social, and legal mechanisms that enable an organization to accomplish its goals.

Organizational structure and organization design are two terms that are often used interchangeably, but they really mean two different things. **Organization design** is the process of creating an organizational structure. Said another way, organizational structure is the outcome of organization design.

To illustrate these three concepts, consider your school. Your school is an organization. Within its geographic and virtual structure, groups of people are organized in ways that enable them to advance and share knowledge, among other things. Your school's mission includes educating students, and it has a strategy to fulfill that mission. The strategy likely includes processes for identifying students who fit the mission, enrolling them, and ensuring that they receive a good education. All of these activities require that work, communication, and resources be coordinated.

Over the years, your school's employees have engaged in organization design to create an organizational structure that can support the school in implementing its strategy through finding, enrolling, and educating students. For instance, it is likely that your school has an admissions department. Within this part of the organizational structure, employees select potential students who meet the school's standards for entering the institution. In many schools, selecting students is a process conducted by an admissions committee. This committee is a team structure within a departmental structure. Imagine if the admissions department did not exist: How would the school select students who fit the school's mission? Would the president select students? Would students have to write to an instructor and ask to be admitted?

Your school no doubt also has a registration department and a finance department. Whereas the registrar coordinates enrollment for the entire school and for individual classes, the finance department collects tuition, pays employees, and manages financial aid. Imagine the chaos that would ensue if there were no registrar. How would students enroll in classes? How would class sizes be controlled? What if 500 students wanted to attend a particular course and there was only room for 30? Whose problem would that be? Would each instructor have to collect tuition and fees from every student each semester? How would employees get paid? How would financial aid be dispersed?

Finally, your school has academic departments. Academic departments foster ease of communication among faculty whose jobs and interests are similar. These departments are structured to provide a sense of identity for both students and faculty. They house classes, study groups, and research projects that enable faculty members to advance and share knowledge and support students in furthering their education.

In this example, you can see how your school—an organization—has been designed in ways that allow people to simplify, divide, and coordinate work processes. Many of our organizations (likely including your school) have designed their organizational structures around three traditional concepts: hierarchy, span of control, and centralization of decision making, all of which we consider next.

Hierarchy in Organizational Structures

Hierarchy
A way of organizing people and groups according to formal authority.

In an organization, a **hierarchy** is a way of organizing people and groups according to formal authority. A simple organizational hierarchy looks like a pyramid, with one person on the top (e.g., the president), a few below him or her (vice presidents), several beneath each of them (managers), and on down until you get to first-level employees at the bottom.

Organizational hierarchies can be "tall" or "flat." Tall organizational structures have many layers of management, whereas flat organizations have few. We will discuss the implications of how tall or flat a structure is later in the chapter. For now, you can see an example of a typical organizational hierarchy in ■Exhibit 9.1, which depicts part of the Dallas Independent School District Service Centers.[1]

■Exhibit **9.1**

The Dallas Independent School District Service Centers organizational chart illustrates a hierarchy.

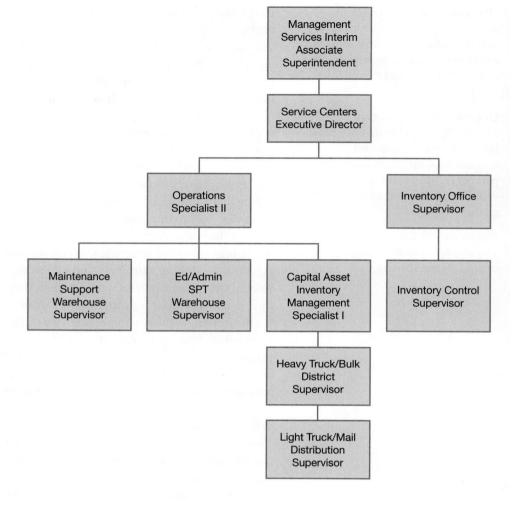

A hierarchy includes reporting relationships—who reports to whom. This is sometimes called the *chain of command.* Three concepts related to hierarchies and reporting relationships are important when it comes to how people behave within a hierarchical structure: authority, responsibility, and accountability.

Authority

Authority
The legitimate right of a person in a particular job to make certain decisions, allocate resources, and direct certain other people's activities.

Authority in an organization is defined as the legitimate right of a person in a particular job to make certain decisions, allocate resources, and direct certain other people's activities. Note that in this definition, we mention a job—that is because in the traditional sense, authority is associated with jobs, not people. If, for example, you were called by the university president today and told you'd been hired to teach this course, you would have the authority to ask students to complete assignments and grade them. This example shows why it is important to understand the person–job fit, which we will discuss later in the chapter.

Within a traditional organizational hierarchy, the job at the top of the structure has the most authority, and the jobs at the bottom have the least. Everyone within the hierarchy accepts his or her level of authority and honors others' levels of authority both above and below their own. For instance, in this management class, your professor is at the top of the hierarchy. Maybe there is a teaching assistant who is one step below the professor in the hierarchy. Then there is you (and the other students), located below the teaching assistant. If this is a "perfect" hierarchy, you will know exactly what level of authority the teaching assistant has compared to your professor. This knowledge allows you to honor the hierarchy by, for example, approaching the teaching assistant with certain questions, rather than your professor.

Responsibility
The obligation to satisfactorily accomplish the tasks associated with a job.

Responsibility

A second important traditional concept related to organizational hierarchy is responsibility. In an organization, **responsibility** is defined as the obligation to satisfactorily accomplish the tasks associated with a job. As a student, you are likely responsible for reading the assignments and preparing for and attending class. Similarly, your professor is responsible for sharing information with you in a manner that will enable you to learn.

Accountability
An individual's willingness to report job success or failure regarding expected job outcomes to his or her manager or other superiors in the chain of command.

Accountability

Along with authority and responsibility comes accountability. **Accountability** is an individual's willingness to report success or failure regarding expected job outcomes to his or her manager or other superiors in the chain of command.[2] For example, say you are a manager in a bookstore. You are responsible for managing the daily finances of the shop, which in turn means overseeing the cashiers and ensuring that they balance their registers correctly every evening. If one of the cashiers is short or over, *you* are accountable for the situation and must report it to your manager.

Accountability has received a great deal of attention recently in terms of one particular aspect of work: ethical conduct on the job. Many senior-level jobs explicitly include ethical guidelines, and many organizations have explicit ethical codes of conduct as well. Partly as a result of gross ethical transgressions in some businesses, employees, managers, and leaders are now being held increasingly accountable for transparent and ethical behavior.

Span of Control in Organizational Structures

Span of control
The number of jobs that report to a position at the next higher level in a hierarchy.

The second key traditional consideration in organizational structure is span of control. The term **span of control** refers to the number of jobs that report to a position at the next higher level in a hierarchy. Let's go back to the college classroom example: In a very large class, a professor might have five teaching assistants (TAs) reporting to him or her. This means that the professor's span of control is five. Similarly, if each teaching assistant is responsible for twenty students, each TA's span of control is twenty.

But does the professor *really* control the teaching assistants? Do the teaching assistants control the students? In both cases, this is unlikely. A more realistic way of describing this concept might be span of management, or even better, span of leadership. **Span of leadership** refers to the number of jobs reporting to a person who is responsible for influencing, inspiring, and developing the people who hold those jobs.

Span of leadership
The number of jobs reporting to a person who is responsible for influencing, inspiring, and developing the people who hold those jobs.

A key question related to span of leadership is how many jobs/people should report to any one job/individual. The practical consideration is clear: How many individuals can one leader actually influence, inspire, and develop? Twenty employees? One hundred? One thousand? Most research indicates that when aspects of the leader's responsibility include direct in-person supervision in a traditional hierarchy, a reasonable expectation for span of leadership is probably around ten jobs/people.

Although this formula might hold true in many cases, today's organizational designers must address at least two serious issues when considering span of leadership. First, in many organizations, maintaining a span of leadership that small is simply too expensive. Second, in recent years, the trend has been to move away from many layers of hierarchy, to fewer levels and more empowered employees. By definition, this means that span of leadership is much larger than in the past.

These changes lead to several conclusions: Organizations will need to provide managers with the skills to lead more people; organizational structures will need to be created that support individuals and groups working autonomously; and/or people at all levels will need to use critical thinking skills to make more and better decisions on their own. Whereas in the past, many of the most important decisions were made at the top of an organization, in many cases, this is no longer true in organizations today. This means we need to understand yet another traditional concept—the degree to which decision making is centralized in an organization.

Centralization of Decision Making in Organizational Structures

Centralized decision making
Structural model in which the vast majority of decision-making power is concentrated, typically among those at the top of the organizational hierarchy.

Centralized decision making refers to a structural model in which the vast majority of decision-making power is concentrated, typically among those at the top of the organizational hierarchy. One advantage of this model is that responsibility and accountability are very clear—everyone knows who can decide what. Another advantage is greater consistency within an organization around key processes. For example, if leadership development is centralized in the senior HR group, it is more likely that the organization will have one leadership model, one set of training programs, and so forth. A downside of centralized decision making is that it can be extremely inefficient, slow, and unresponsive to internal organizational needs or to changes in the external environment. For this reason, many organizations adapt a decentralized decision-making approach when possible.

Decentralized decision making
Structural model in which decision-making power is distributed among the people closest to the relevant information, those who will be affected by the decision, or those who will have to implement the decision.

Decentralized decision making is a structural model in which decision-making power is distributed among the people closest to the relevant information, those who will be affected by the decision, or those who will have to implement the decision. In an organizational structure, then, decentralizing decision making means that people lower in the hierarchy and most directly involved in a given situation are empowered to make decisions. Decentralization is characterized by a more dispersed and shared decision-making process—a "leaderless" or distributed leadership model.

Decentralized decision making offers many advantages. First, most people enjoy having some control over their actions and decisions. Empowered employees are committed employees. Second, employees closest to the problems and opportunities often have the best solutions and ideas. For example, say the chairs in your classroom are extremely uncomfortable. Who would make a better decision about criteria for new chairs—students, or administrators who never sit in these chairs?

A third advantage of decentralized decision making is that things can happen *fast*. This is important in many organizations today because the environment changes rapidly, calling for new and better responses. Related to this, decentralized decision making allows an organization to decipher and respond to customers' actual needs in a timely manner, rather than waiting for far-away research teams to collect data, analyze trends, and begin the process of adjusting products or services.

Decentralized decision making also has disadvantages. First, the quality of such decisions is wholly dependent on the individuals making them. This means that these employees must have excellent critical thinking skills and highly developed competencies such as pattern recognition, systems thinking, and social awareness. They need to be able to see the big picture, and how their decisions fit into the organization. If employees do not have these skills, serious errors will occur.

Second, decentralized decision making can result in the development of practices at the local level that should be—but are not—consistent with organization-wide systems, such as ethics policies, financial management processes, human resource processes, customer service and leadership models, and so forth.

For this reason, and also to ensure that decision-making models fit the organization's strategy, leaders need to pay careful attention to which kinds of decisions are centralized and which are decentralized. Employees, managers, and leaders can be more effective in their jobs if they understand and learn how to navigate an organization's structure. In the next section, we will examine a visual tool that helps us simplify this structure in order to study it.

1. Imagine that you have taken a job for which the typical span of leadership is 30 people. You find yourself reporting to a manager who can't possibly train you directly. Brainstorm some ways to get the training and attention you need.
2. Have you ever worked in an environment that used centralized decision making? If so, what did you like and dislike about it? Similarly, have you ever worked in an environment in which decision making was decentralized? If so, what did you like and dislike about it?

3. What Is an Organizational Chart?

An organizational chart depicts the hierarchy and areas of responsibility within an organization. In other words, an **organizational chart** is a visual representation of how roles, jobs, authority, and responsibility are distributed within an organization. ■Exhibit 9.2 shows a simple organizational chart for a small restaurant.

Organizational chart
A visual representation of how roles, jobs, authority, and responsibility are distributed within an organization.

As you can see, the general manager is at the top of the chart. This person is responsible for the entire organization. The general manager is accountable to the owners for realizing the restaurant's mission (to serve healthy and delicious food), making the business profitable, and leading an organization in which employees can be and do their best while learning and having fun (also part of the restaurant's mission). The general manager has the authority to make, approve, or disapprove all decisions. Two managers report to the general manager, and various other positions report to those managers.

Each of the boxes on this chart represents a job that includes certain responsibilities and is granted a certain level of authority. The people doing these jobs hold roles (e.g., busser, server, head chef, etc.) that are distinct and different. For example, bussers may pour water, clear tables, and support servers in delivering food. They have the authority to determine when a customer needs water and to provide it. Servers are responsible for taking and delivering orders. They are not responsible for cooking the food—the chefs are. Among the chefs, the assistant chefs are responsible for prepping and cooking food. They have the authority to decide if food is spoiled and to replace a certain amount as necessary, but they do not have the authority to change the menu—the head chef has the authority to do this for certain items, and the general manager has authority for significant changes to the menu. A shift manager is responsible for coordinating all activities during his or her shift and preparing the restaurant for the next shift. He or she has the authority to schedule workers but shares this authority with the other shift managers.

■Exhibit **9.2**

An organizational chart for a restaurant depicts the business's reporting structure.

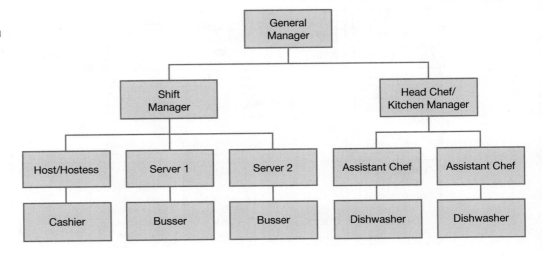

This hierarchy facilitates communication, organization of tasks and resources, and management and leadership of people in different functions (i.e., the restaurant floor and the kitchen). Organizational charts are helpful because they show hierarchy, jobs, and roles. However, the picture an organizational chart portrays doesn't tell even half the story about how an organization is really structured. To illustrate this, look at ■ Exhibit 9.3. This organizational chart includes the U.S. Department of Homeland Security's mission statement at the top.

Considering what the Department of Homeland Security does, do you think this chart represents the way things actually work? What about when the director of the Domestic Nuclear Detection Office needs to put a team together with people in the Coast Guard? Can that director call the commandant? Or does the director ask his or her boss: the secretary or deputy secretary? Who is her boss, anyway? You can see that a line from the secretary goes all the way through each level. In a flat organizational structure like this, all of the positions technically report to the secretary. So how can the secretary manage the 27 people who report to him or her? Or, what if one of the directors is close to the president of the United States? Would that affect this director's power in the organization? Or, say two individuals worked their way "up" in the government and have had interpersonal problems. Would this get in the way of interdivisional coordination?

The questions one could ask about the Department of Homeland Security illustrate that reporting relationships are only one determinant for how people work and coordinate tasks. Formal and informal communication, power relationships, and even phys-

■Exhibit **9.3**

The complete organizational chart for the U.S. Department of Homeland Security is 25 pages long.

"This Department of Homeland Security's overriding and urgent mission is to lead the unified national effort to secure the country and preserve our freedoms. While the Department was created to secure our country against those who seek to disrupt the American way of life, our charter also includes preparation for and response to all hazards and disasters. The citizens of the United States must have the utmost confidence that the Department can execute both of these missions."

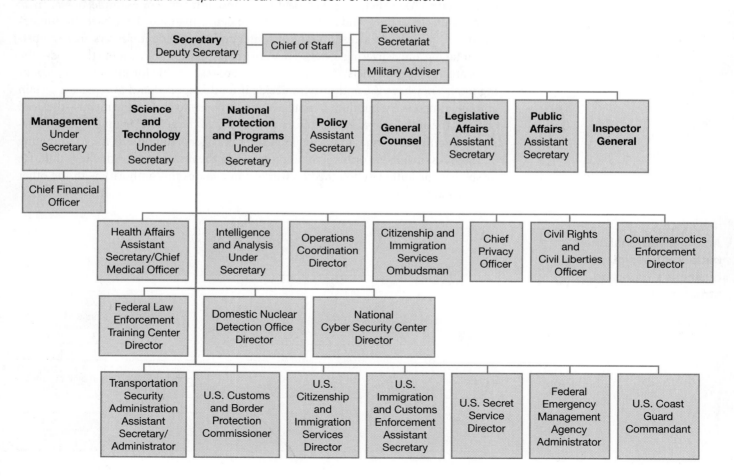

ical proximity are examples of some of the complex factors that also affect how work is coordinated and accomplished. An organizational chart can help us talk about some aspects of structure, but in the end, it is only a two-dimensional picture of jobs, roles, and hierarchical reporting relationships—nothing more, nothing less.

In this section, we have covered important concepts that claim a rightful place in the study of how organizations are designed. As helpful as these ideas are, however, they don't tell the whole story. Organizations are groups of *people*, and people are complicated. Accordingly, in the next section, we will explore several models and metaphors that allow us to consider organizational structure in more sophisticated and creative ways.

Most Popular » Discussion Questions

1. Draw an organizational chart for your family. In what ways does this chart demonstrate "how things really work" in the family? In what ways does it not capture things like communication, power relationships, and coordination of work and chores?
2. Join together with three other people. Without looking at each others' work, draw the organizational chart for your school. Now compare the charts: Are your hierarchies the same or different? If they are different, why might that be?

---

4. How Can We "See" Organizations and Their Structures in Nontraditional Ways?

Although organizational charts and topics such as hierarchy are very important to understanding organizations, we also need to be more creative when we think about organizations and their structures. That's because organizations are full of *people*—and people make choices about what to do based on how they perceive their relationship to others and to the organization, the organizational culture, and internal and external pressures. In addition, organizations and their structures are becoming even more complex as the external environment changes and as technologies become central to the workplace.

In this section, we'll look at four innovative ways of seeing organizations: organizations as open systems, mechanistic versus organic structures, metaphors describing organizations, and organizations as "spiders" and "starfish."[3]

Open Systems Theory: No Organization Is an Island

Open systems theory
A theory stating that any human system, such as an organization, is constantly influenced by and is influencing its environment.

Open systems theory states that any human system, such as an organization, is constantly influenced by and is influencing its environment.[4] As you can see in ■Exhibit 9.4, organizations are not closed, bounded entities. Both an organization and its environment are constantly changing each other.[5]

Organizations Are Naturally Open to Their Environments

Borrowed from the natural sciences, open systems theory is the idea that a system is made up of individual parts that create a whole system, and it is also part of the environment within which it exists. The organizational environment includes factors like economic and social systems (such as capitalism and national cultures), educational systems that prepare employees, raw materials, and customers. Within the boundaries of an organization are elements such as employees, technology, organizational culture, work and communication processes, and leadership practices. All of these serve to link various organizational subsystems, creating a complex whole that has the capacity to manage internal work and processes and also interact with the environment.[6]

■Exhibit **9.4**

Organizations function as open systems and are affected by the environment in which they operate.

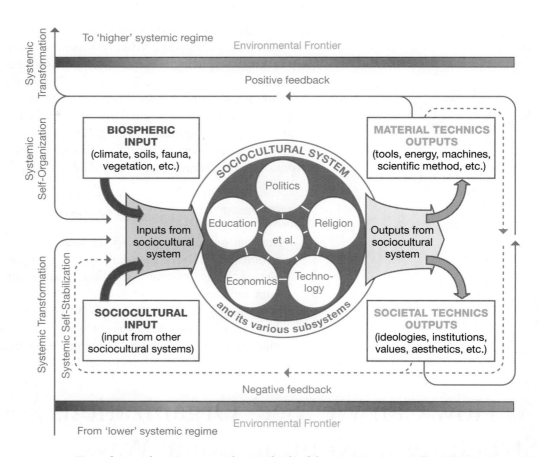

To understand open systems theory, think of the organization as a living being. It receives inputs from the environment, processes those inputs, and shares outputs with the environment. For example, British Petroleum (BP), a huge multinational corporation headquartered in the United Kingdom, has operations in dozens of countries. As one of the largest corporations in the world and extremely important in the United Kingdom, BP can exert a great deal of influence on its environment: the British economy, the economies of the different oil-producing countries in which it operates, and so forth. But BP is still powerfully influenced by its environment in terms of the demand for and price of oil, the stability of governments throughout the world, the local cultures of its employees and customers, international conflicts, piracy, and local, national, and international laws, to name a few factors.

BP affects the physical environment—its geography and atmosphere—through the operations of extracting oil, refining it, and selling it. Companies like BP are well aware of their impact on the natural environment. They are both mandated by law and voluntarily driven to take responsibility for how their operations affect the air, water, land, plants, and animals in areas in which they do business. BP's relationship to the natural environment became painfully clear in 2010, when an explosion destroyed a deep-water oil platform in the Gulf of Mexico owned and operated by a company named Transocean. Yet another company, Halliburton, had been contracted to apply a special cement to cap the bore hole that tapped the sub-sea oil reservoir. The explosion killed 11 workers and injured several others. The next tragedy involved the oil itself, which flowed nearly unrestricted out of the uncapped well 5,000 feet below the surface for months after the explosion, endangering the ocean, all kinds of sea life, and the livelihoods of thousands of people who depend upon the ocean.[7] This example, while tragic and extreme, points out that no organization can ever be separate from the environment within which it operates.

At the same time, the physical environment has an impact on companies such as BP through things like weather patterns and geological formations. To understand BP, then, means also being able to understand something about a great many different things and how they interact—geology, politics, culture, meteorology, economics, and trade, for example. Both the organization and its environment are constantly providing feedback to each other, and the organization adapts to the environment as appropriate. This output-as-feedback indicates the degree to which the environment or the organization is healthy. For example, feedback that can contribute to the general health of the environment depends on the organization's health, and vice versa.

Understanding Open Systems and Complex Issues

Earlier in the chapter, we mentioned how important it is for you to understand organizational structure. Sometimes, students think that this topic is more important for senior managers or perhaps the HR professionals who help design organizations. In reality, though, in any job you have, it helps to understand how your company or institution is structured and how it relates to other organizations. One bright and dedicated student highlighted this idea when she wrote about how her country's government is attempting to control malaria. Mulenga Mwenda has done field work that allowed her to see the incredible level of organization it takes to fight this deadly disease.

Mulenga Mwenda

Student's Choice

Organizing to Fight Malaria

Malaria is an enormous global public health problem that affects some 350 to 500 million people every year. In sub-Saharan Africa, this devastating disease kills somewhere between 1 and 3 million people each year, mostly children under the age of 5 and pregnant women.

Malaria is endemic throughout Zambia, a sub-Saharan African country. How can a disease that is so widespread and that is transmitted by mosquitoes be addressed? Due to the negative impact of malaria on national development, the Zambian government considers controlling the disease a top priority. Accordingly, in 2006 the government set up a program specifically devoted to the control of malaria known as the Zambia National Malaria Control Program, which is run at National Malaria Control Center. These two "umbrella" organizations coordinate activities all over the country. Specifically, they coordinate activities related to the control of mosquitoes, how and where the disease is spread, and how progress in fighting malaria is evaluated and monitored.

Organizing to Control Mosquitoes

Looking at just a portion of Zambia's program allows us to better understand how it works. The country's Entomology Department, for example, helps control mosquitoes, and it also helps people avoid catching malaria. This department is managed by the chief entomologist, who works with various research assistants and staff in the management and control of mosquitoes. These individuals also coordinate departments and people to oversee and disseminate prevention tools, such as insecticide-treated mosquito nets (ITNs) and indoor residual spraying (IRS). To understand the complexity of this work, you have to imagine the countryside: In Zambia, there are only a few large cities; roads make travel difficult and even impossible during the rainy season; and most of the population lives in remote rural areas with no modern infrastructure.

Staff often brave these difficulties to go into the field to collect mosquito species and bring them back to the laboratory, where they are reared under favorable conditions until they are able to reproduce. These newborn mosquitoes are then sub-jected to the chemicals used in IRS to see if the substances are effective in the control of mosquitoes or if the insects have become resistant to them.

Finding Mosquitoes and Preparing for Treatment

Elsewhere in the National Malaria Control Program, the Parasitology Department is run by the chief parasitologist. This person and his or her team identify the mosquito species present in Zambia. Four species of the malaria parasite can cause human malaria: *Plasmodium ovale*, *Plasmodium malariae*, *Plasmodium vivax*, and *Plasmodium falciparum*, which is the most deadly. By determing the location of each species in the countryside, the Parisitology Department can make recommendations to the Ministry of Health to assist them in the distribution of drugs to hospitals, clinics, and rural health centers. It is also the duty of the parasitologists to determine which drugs are still effective in treating malaria and which are not.

Evaluating Strategies to Combat Malaria

In any complex coordinated effort, evaluation of strategies is essential. In the case of fighting malaria in Zambia, this process is organized by the Ministry of Health. Departments within the ministry coordinate many evaluation activities, such as administering a survey every two years to determine whether people are using the ITNs, the effectiveness of IRS, and the mortality rates in children and pregnant women due to malaria. These surveys are known as the National Malaria Indicator surveys.

The fight against malaria is huge and it is important. Success will only come about if each department, each agency, and each person can coordinate activities. As of 2010, the head of the National Malaria Control Center was Dr. Kamuliwo, who was appointed by the Zambian Ministry of Health Permanent. Many people have great faith in Dr. Kamuliwo—in only his first two years at the center, he showed leadership skills and qualities that are admired by many. For one thing, he and his staff realize that the control of malaria cannot be accomplished single-handedly by any one agency. This incredibly complex work requires a great deal of coordinated effort from many different organizations and governmental departments.

Source: Adapted from a case written by Mulenga Mwenda.

As you can see in this example, organizational structure is complicated. That's why it's important for us to look at the topic carefully and not oversimplify it. Let's turn to a few other viewpoints that can help us understand how organizational structure works.

Mechanistic and Organic Organizations

An organization can also be described in terms of how flexible it is. This is a particularly important concept today because of the rapid pace of change—most organizations *need* to be flexible or they will not survive. Let's look at what is meant by the terms *mechanistic* and *organic* when applied to organizations and their level of flexibility.

A **mechanistic organization** is characterized by routine job functions, a high degree of specialization, and division of labor. *Job specialization* is a term that is often linked to division of labor. **Division of labor** is the process of reducing work to the smallest, simplest, and most easily repeated tasks possible. A mechanistic organization may also be hierarchical and bureaucratic, with processes and standard operating procedures that are routine.[8] **Standard operating procedures**, or **SOPs**, are detailed and specific instructions for carrying out routine tasks. A mechanistic organization is inflexible and formal, and it often has centralized decision making.

In comparison, an **organic organization** is characterized by a high degree of flexibility, low levels of specialization, less formality, and decentralized decision-making processes. The greatest strength of an organic organization is its flexibility. It can change and adapt, depending on internal and external conditions and demands.

Organic organizations are adaptable and open to the environment and to change.[9] As organizational scholar Gareth Morgan puts it, there is a constant "exchange with their environment," but different parts have different degrees of "openness" in this exchange so the organization can function well internally while also adapting to the environment.[10] This means that parts of the organization are structured differently depending on the specific functions and purposes of each subsystem, like specialized organs within the human body. For example, we would expect to see manufacturing structured differently than marketing, because manufacturing tends to have more routine functions and marketing requires more creativity. Additionally, processes in manufacturing have to be stable and predictable in order to ensure quality in production. This is not the case in marketing, which adapts to different technologies, venues, and customer populations based on a number of environmental factors, such as what is currently popular, the current state of competition, and what venues are currently available for marketing programs. By enabling different parts of the organization to be more or less open to the environment, the organization can maintain what is called homeostasis—an internal self-regulation that keeps it healthy, in balance, and distinct from its environment.

Because environments change, organizations have to change with them: They need to evolve and adapt to stay competitive and to function properly.[11] Organic organizations are also adaptive organizations. An **adaptive organization** is one that is very flexible and readily responds to feedback—to internal and external changes in conditions and the overall environment.[12] In an adaptive organization, leadership and management practices, organizational culture, and structure are designed to ensure that people can respond to threats and opportunities quickly and effectively.

Scholars have taken a number of approaches when studying adaptive organizations. For instance, researchers Dessein Wouter and Tano Santos argue that adaptive organizations may empower employees to structure their work processes to meet the needs, opportunities, and demands of the local environment.[13] This approach requires a great amount of coordination in a geographically dispersed organization. These researchers also make the case that adaptive organizations need to rely less on specialization because this can lead to ignoring "local knowledge."[14] In other words, when the division of labor becomes too specialized, employees can lose perspective about how their work

Mechanistic organization
An organization characterized by routine job functions, a high degree of specialization, and division of labor.

Division of labor
The process of reducing work to the smallest, simplest, and most easily repeated tasks possible.

Standard operating procedures (SOPs)
Detailed and specific instructions for carrying out routine tasks.

Organic organization
An organization characterized by a high degree of flexibility, low levels of specialization, less formality, and decentralized decision-making processes.

Adaptive organization
An organization that is very flexible and readily responds to feedback—to internal and external changes in conditions and the overall environment.

fits with the local economic, cultural, and political environments. Examples of this are abundant in multinational organizations that apply company-wide standards to regions around the world where the context is quite different.

Consider safety standards, for example. European Union and U.S. requirements are far stricter than the standards in many parts of Asia, so there are likely to be complicated compliance issues. For instance, environmental hazards in the workplace are strictly regulated in the United States by the Occupational Safety and Health Administration (OSHA), but such standards are not internationally adopted, and the processes outlined in the United States may not even be appropriate in another country. The United Kingdom has its own standards as well, which differ from those of the rest of the European Union. So, a compliance measure that was crafted at a company's U.S. headquarters may be difficult to implement in other countries; or worse, it may make no sense because the laws don't match or because the needs of the foreign subsidiary might be completely different.

Organizational scholar Karl Weick describes adaptive organizations as "loosely coupled." A loosely coupled organization is one in which there is less centralized control and greater flexibility within and among parts of the organization.[15] Because of this flexibility, there is a greater ability to adapt to changing environmental conditions.

An example of the importance of loosely coupled but coordinated activity lies in the case of natural and man-made crises. Researchers have studied the global crisis network that was put in place to respond to the threat of a deadly pandemic of severe acute respiratory syndrome (SARS) in 2002 and 2003. SARS had a high mortality rate (9.6 percent) and had spread globally before being identified.[16] Luckily, even though the disease was highly contagious and had spread to dozens of countries, the global crisis network was able to contain it and fewer than a thousand people died.[17] The researchers found that the combination of loosely coupled, "decoupled," and tightly coupled (highly coordinated and centrally controlled) interactions gave the organization the amount of flexibility it needed to respond effectively to the crisis while at the same time averting chaos.[18]

Gareth Morgan's Metaphors for Organizations

Unconsciously, we often adopt ways of seeing our organizations that affect what aspects of structure and human processes we pay attention to. In other words, we "see" organizations differently depending on the lens through which we view people and systems. To bring this cognitive process into our awareness, researchers such as Gareth Morgan use metaphors when describing organizations. Metaphors allow us to describe organizational structures and functioning in familiar and simple ways. A few useful metaphors or images of organizations are listed in ■Exhibit 9.5.[19]

Metaphors help us think creatively. Sharply different images come to mind when we think of organizations as "machines," "organisms," and "brains." These different images help us see the different ways in which organizations function and can be structured. They also show us different ways organizations can interact with the environment. A newer metaphor for organizations as "spiders" or "starfish" shows us yet another way to look at organizations today.

Organizations as Spiders and Starfish

Authors Ori Brafman and Rod Beckstrom believe that given the changing nature of organizations in the twenty-first century, we must look at our organizations in radically different ways. They use the metaphors of "spiders" and "starfish" to describe traditional and adaptive organizations, respectively.[20]

Spider organizations are traditional, hierarchical, and mechanistic. Decisions are made higher up and then pushed down the chain of command. The information required to

■Exhibit **9.5**

Our Metaphors for Organizations Affect What We Pay Attention to and Do		
Metaphor	**How We See the Organization**	**What We Do**
The organization as a machine	How do the "parts" fit together? Are the "gears" well oiled (e.g., effective and efficient supply chain, intake, and output)?	Manage for efficiency; attend to flow of inputs and outputs; reduce jobs to their simplest form.
The organization as an organism	What does the organization need in order to be healthy? How can we ensure that the entity has the "food" it needs (e.g., raw materials, committed people)?	Commit to employee health and welfare; scan the environment for changes; adapt to those changes.
The organization as a brain	How does the "brain" control the organization? Are our leaders smart enough? Are our employees high in IQ and emotional and social intelligence?	Develop excellent knowledge management systems; focus on leadership development.
The organization as a culture	How do our values and beliefs affect our actions inside and outside the organization? Is our sense of identity, commitment, and purpose clear and shared among all of us?	Focus on ethical conduct inside and outside the organization; show customers how we live our values through our business practices.
The organization as an instrument of power and domination	Do we exploit our people and our customers? Are we focused on winning at *any* cost? Or, are we focused on empowerment and activities that support ourselves and others in our external environment?	Consciously manage personalized and socialized power; consider ethical implications of actions.

■Exhibit **9.6**

Traditional organizations can be described as spiders, in which decisions are centralized.

Eureka/Alamy/Bob Elsdale

make these decisions must pass through numerous bureaucratic barriers before it can reach those with the authority to make decisions, so response to change is slow, inefficient, and often ineffective.

Power is centrally organized at the top of spider organizations. The head and brain of the spider represent centralized power and control in the organization, and the legs are the collective actions of divisions, departments, and groups. (See ■Exhibit 9.6.) Literally everything is dependent upon the head and central nervous system of the spider. If the head dies, the whole organism dies with it. The legs do what the head tells them—nothing more and nothing less. They only work together with the support of the head, and if one of the legs dies, the others have to find a way to walk without it—out of balance and overburdened. If two legs die, the problem becomes worse, and if more die, the spider will be unable to function and it will die too.

Starfish are very different from spiders. First, the "legs" of a starfish act independent of one another, smoothly and gracefully moving over and around obstacles. Also, the starfish's brain isn't

Adaptive organizations can be described as starfish, in which decisions are decentralized.

WILDLIFE GmbH/Alamy Images

making all of the decisions or controlling all of the action: All the knowledge for the activities needed to stay healthy, adapt, and change is self-contained in various parts of the starfish. If you cut off one of the creature's legs, a new leg will grow back. In fact, in some species of starfish, each piece will regenerate into a whole new organism. This animal is built to adapt, to survive threats, and to thrive in the face of adversity. (See ■Exhibit 9.7.)

The decentralized "starfish" organization has appeared many times in human history, and each time it has thrived and in some cases brought about significant social change. A twentieth-century example is the Alcoholics Anonymous organization. This organization gets its power from the fact that each group is locally autonomous; members hear about it by word of mouth and stay because it is beneficial rather than because someone tells them to. There is no supreme "owner" of the organization. Rather, there is local, collective ownership. Each meeting and each group is different, yet all of them function with the common goal of sobriety.

In the twenty-first century, many examples of decentralized, networked organizations have appeared. Brafman and Beckstrom cite Al Qaeda as a powerful starfish organizations that is changing how nations defend themselves.[21] They also point out that a number of relatively new organizations and structures including Wikipedia, Craigslist, peer-to-peer (P2P) networks, and open-source software rely on participatory membership, collective ownership, and commitment to a new and different way of interacting.

Taking the metaphor of the starfish a step further, Brafman and Beckstrom describe how the starfish organization is vastly different from the hierarchical spider organizations we are used to. They identify five distinct characteristics of a decentralized starfish organization, which they refer to as the five "legs" of the starfish.[22]

The first leg is that such organizations are organized as "circles" that are essentially social networks. Groups that are organized in this way do not rely on centralized authority or rules because each network is locally autonomous. Rather, in order to function, the social network collectively establishes norms that individuals subscribe to, and such norms develop implicitly through interaction.

Leg two of the starfish organization is what the authors call the catalyst. This is the person or persons who have the "big ideas" and are effective at inspiring others to action. The catalyst sparks activity, but it is not necessarily involved in the activity itself—it continues on its own steam without the catalyst. The main role of the catalyst is to ensure localized empowerment of the different groups that spring forth to take up the call for action.

The third leg of the starfish is a collectively shared ideology, such as sobriety in the case of Alcoholics Anonymous. Leg four involves turning a preexisting network into a decentralized organization. The fifth leg is related to the fact that in such organizations, having a catalyst (an inspirational leader) is not enough. There must also be a champion—an individual who is involved from an early stage in doing a lot of the work—a die-hard activist, if you will, who turns the vision into a reality.

In this section, you have learned how to view organizations in many different ways. This knowledge allows you to consider basic information about organizational structures in a more sophisticated manner. We will now turn our attention to common types of organizations and ownership models. As you read about these, continue to think creatively about how you can seek to understand the ways in which organizational structure affects individual behavior and overall organizational success.

5. How Are Organizations Classified and Legally Structured?

Think about the businesses and organizations in your hometown. You probably have restaurants, retail stores, manufacturers, and banks. You may also have a theater, charitable organizations, churches, local government offices, fraternal organizations, and so forth. To help us study organizational structure, we will start with how various types of organizations are classified. We will then look at common ownership models that all students of management and leadership needs to understand.

Organizations can be classified in many ways, including by how large or small they are or whether they provide goods or services. They can also be categorized by industry: consumer goods, electronics, telecommunications, apparel, luxury goods, and so forth. In addition, organizations may be classified by where they do business: locally, nationally, or globally. ■Exhibit 9.8 presents some common types of organizations that you are likely to encounter.

■Exhibit **9.8**

Common Types of Organizations		
Type of Organization	**Definition**	**Examples**
For-profit organization	Any business whose mission includes making profit for owners	Williams-Sonoma, Inc. (headquarters in San Francisco); Sanrio Co. Ltd (Tokyo)
Not-for-profit organization	An organization that provides goods or services and that invests profits in pursuit of organizational goals as opposed to sharing profit among owners	The Conference Board (New York); National Association for the Advancement of Colored People (NAACP) (Baltimore, Maryland)
Governmental organization	An organization that leads, manages, and controls a nation, state, province, town, or so forth	U.S. Senate (Washington, D.C.); Parliament of the United Kingdom of Great Britain and Northern Ireland (London)
Nongovernmental organization (NGO)	An organization that is not directly or solely linked to one or more governments and that seeks to support human or social issues; NGOs are usually not-for-profit and often voluntary	World Wildlife Fund (U.S. headquarters in Washington, D.C.); Amnesty International (London), Human Rights Watch (U.S. headquarters in New York)

Continued **on next page>>**

■Exhibit **9.8** **Continued**

Common Types of Organizations

Type of Organization	Definition	Examples
Small business	Any organization that is organized for profit, independently owned, and not dominant in its market	WilliamsTown Communications (Indianapolis, Indiana); Rebec Vineyards (Amherst, Virginia)
Local organization	Any organization that operates in a defined geographic area	Hal's Delicatessen and Sandwich (Ithaca, New York); Simi Valley Chamber of Commerce (Simi Valley, California)
International organization	Any organization that has substantial operations in multiple countries	African Development Bank (headquarters in Tunis-Belvédère, Tunisia); Teleos Leadership Institute (headquarters in Elkins Park, Pennsylvania)
Multinational corporation	Any for-profit business that has formalized operations in many countries	Toyota Motor Corp. (headquarters in Toyota, Japan); Nestle S.A. (headquarters in Vevey, Switzerland)
Importer	Any organization that specializes in importing goods or services from another country or countries	Atlas Coffee Importers, LLC (Seattle, Washington); Vanilla, Saffron Imports (San Francisco)
Exporter	Any organization that specializes in exporting goods or services to another country or countries	Future Generation Company Ltd. (Hanoi, Vietnam); DeBeers Diamonds (Jaipur, India)
Public charity	A type of not-for-profit organization that is organized for purposes beneficial to the public	International Federation of Red Cross/Red Crescent Societies (Geneva, Switzerland); Save the Children (Westport, Connecticut); Lance Armstrong Foundation (Austin, Texas)
Private foundation	A type of organization set up by an individual, family, or group of individuals for philanthropic purposes; although not public charities, they are often an important source of funding for charities through grants	Bill and Melinda Gates Foundation (Seattle, Washington); Carnegie Foundation (San Francisco)
Virtual organization	Any organization that provides some or all of its products or services via information and telecommunications technologies, particularly the Internet	Amazon.com (headquarters in Seattle, Washington); eBay Inc.(headquarters in San Jose, California)

Classifications are helpful when talking about organizations. However, they are really just shorthand because many organizations can be described by more than one of these classifications. For example, an international organization can also be a small business and a local organization such as a food bank can also be not-for-profit. Organizations may even be set up and funded by the government but not owned or managed by that government, such as state schools, hospitals, or universities.[23] The case becomes even more complicated in the not-for-profit category. In many instances, there are laws and governmental regulations affecting not-for-profits, even though the government doesn't "run" these entities. For example, in the United States, one type of legal entity is called a "501(c)(3)," which can be a corporation, community chest, fund, or foundation run for educational, scientific, religious, charitable, literary, or other purposes. Let's turn our attention now to forms of business ownership.

Common Forms of Ownership

Business ownership models affect many aspects of organizational life, including leadership models and practices, organizational culture, and structure. To the casual observer, ownership may not be apparent, other than indications on a company's letterhead such as "Inc." or "LLC."

Company ownership can take many forms. Each form of ownership is based on a number of factors and comes with its own set of pros and cons for the owner(s) related to taxes, legal restrictions, and governance models. ■Exhibit 9.9 shows several common forms of business ownership, each of which is discussed in the following sections.

Sole Proprietorship

Sole proprietorship
An ownership model in which a single individual owns a business.

As the name implies, a **sole proprietorship** is an ownership model in which a single individual owns a business. Legal requirements for setting up a sole proprietorship vary from town to town and state to state in the United States. A good source of information on starting and running a sole proprietorship in the United States is the Small

■Exhibit **9.9**

Common Forms of Ownership		
Form of Ownership	Definition	Example
Sole proprietorship	A business that is owned by an individual and has not been registered as a corporation or partnership. A sole proprietorship can be a limited liability company if the owner elects not to treat it as a legal corporation or partnership.[24]	figureplant (San Francisco); Creative English.net (United Kingdom)
Partnership	A legal structure for a business with two or more people is called a general partnership when qualifiers such as "limited" or "limited liability" are not used. Partners share profits and are each personally liable for all business debts, and each partner also claims a portion of the business income (or losses) on his or her individual tax return.	Smock Sterling (Lake Bluff, Illinois); Community Orthopedic Medical Group Partnership (Mission Viejo, California)
Corporation	A corporation is a legal entity and is treated as such by the government. The corporation owns the business, whereas individuals, called shareholders, own a percentage of the corporation. Publicly owned corporations have ownership shares traded on a stock exchange.	DryShips, Inc. (Athens, Greece); First Solar, Inc. (Tempe, Arizona)
Limited liability company (LLC; in some countries, this is referred to as a public limited corporation or PLC)	Relatively new to the United States, this is a hybrid form of ownership that combines elements of a partnership and a corporation. As a partnership, the liability of owners is "limited," and partners may also take ownership of corporate losses to offset taxes. Member-owners can be people, corporations, other LLCs, and/or foreign entities.[25]	3H Technology, LLC (Reston, Virginia); 51 Minds Entertainment, LLC (Los Angeles)

Business Administration, a governmental organization that provides guidance and support to small business owners.[26] The simplicity of this type of ownership (at least in the United States) is a distinct advantage. There are few legal restrictions on how the owner operates his or her business.

One major disadvantage of a sole proprietorship in the United States is the financial liability of this form of ownership: A sole proprietor is personally responsible for all financial assets and debts. All money earned by a sole proprietor (after expenses) is taxed as personal income, all loans are personal loans (which are often difficult to obtain), and all debts incurred by the business are seen as personal debts.

Similarly, a sole proprietor is liable for any and all events that occur on his or her property or as a result of business-related activities. For example, if a customer falls and is hurt on business property, or is harmed by a business product, practice, or service, the business owner is liable for damages. Although a primary home or primary vehicle is exempt from seizure, any other possessions can be seized by the courts to pay for unpaid debts associated with the business.

Partnership

Partnership
An ownership model in which two or more individuals share the ownership of a business.

A **partnership** is an ownership model in which two or more individuals share the ownership of a business. Control of the business is often split 50/50, but it can be split 80/20, 60/40, or in any other combination, as long as all partners are in agreement. Whatever is decided, the partners should have a legally binding partnership agreement. This document outlines principles such as ownership shares, how profits are to be distributed, resolution of disputes, and how a partner can leave the partnership. In the event that the business is sold or goes out of business, the partnership agreement also specifies how the profits or debts are to be divided among the partners.

The advantages to this form of ownership revolve primarily around the saying "two heads are better than one," as well as the fact that there may be more capital for start-up and growth activities than in a sole proprietorship. The drawback is that personal liability is still an issue. Also, if the business depends on one partner more than another, and if that person becomes ill, dies, or simply no longer has an interest in the business, the business will likely suffer.

Corporation

Corporation
An organization that is legally recognized as a unique entity, pays taxes, and can be sued, and that does not have the personal liability issues of sole proprietorships and partnerships.

In 1819, Supreme Court Justice John Marshall famously declared that a corporation is "an artificial being, invisible, intangible, and existing only in contemplation of law . . . and may act as a single individual . . . to manage its own affairs, and to hold property. . . ."[27] We define a **corporation**, then, as an organization that is legally recognized as a unique entity, pays taxes, and can be sued, and that does not have the personal liability issues of sole proprietorships and partnerships. Like other forms of ownership, specific laws governing corporations differ from state to state.[28]

Ownership of a corporation is usually distributed among many people or groups. Individuals or groups such as other businesses buy stock (shares) in the corporation as an investment. In other words, they buy pieces of the corporation in hopes that the value of the corporation will go up, and that their share of the corporation will become more valuable over time. Profits are regularly distributed among shareholders (these are called dividends). The more shares that an owner purchases, the more money that owner stands to gain—or lose. A shareholder's personal liability is limited only to his or her amount of ownership in the business at the time when the shares were purchased. This means that if a company becomes heavily in debt, the shareholder may lose the money he or she invested initially, but no more than that. This is different from a partnership, in which individual owners are personally responsible for the debt of the entire company.

A corporation exists on its own, separate from those who may have ownership of it. In fact, it continues to exist even if the shareholders are no longer around to manage it or are even alive. Shares can be bought and sold. The business can also sell additional shares of stock to generate income.

One disadvantage of the corporation, especially for very small businesses, concerns taxes. The business is taxed as a separate entity, and owners who draw a salary are also taxed on their personal income. Another disadvantage is that setting up a corporation is a more complex and expensive process than setting up other forms of ownership.

How Corporations and Partnerships Can Be Structured Legally: S Corporations and LLCs

Two other forms of ownership are S corporations and limited liability companies (LLCs). These have emerged as relatively easy and less expensive forms of ownership for entrepreneurs.

An **S corporation** is a type of corporation that has 100 or fewer shareholders and does not pay federal income taxes. Instead, income, losses, deductions, and credit are passed on to the shareholders for federal tax purposes.[29] S corporations have only one class of stock.[30] With this type of setup, the owner(s) avoids double taxation because the corporation is *not* taxed on earnings and losses, which pass directly to the shareholders.[31] The S corporation is a very common form of ownership, with well over 3 million S corporations in the United States.[32]

An **LLC** is a hybrid form of ownership that provides limited personal liability to the owners of a business. It combines characteristics of a corporation with characteristics of a sole proprietorship or partnership.[33] The greatest advantage of an LLC in the United States is that it can be taxed according to what the owners or members of the LLC designate as most appropriate—either as a corporation, S corporation, partnership, or sole proprietorship. This is because the U.S. federal government does not recognize an LLC classification for tax purposes.[34] In addition, the owners are protected from many of the debt liabilities associated with the business. In the next section, we will expand our discussion of ownership models to include structures that allow organizations to expand their reach through agreements with individuals or other organizations.

S corporation
A type of corporation that has 100 or fewer shareholders and does not pay federal income taxes.

LLC
A hybrid form of ownership that provides limited personal liability to the owners of a business.

Structural and Legal Relationships with Outside Entities

In addition to the forms of ownership we have discussed so far, additional relationships exist between businesses. These include cooperative contracts, licensing agreements, franchises, strategic alliances, and wholly owned affiliates.

Cooperative Contracts

Cooperative contracts
Friendly business agreements that result from equity joint ventures, which are also known as equity alliances.

Cooperative contracts are friendly business agreements that result from equity joint ventures, which are also known as equity alliances.[35] Equity alliances come in two forms. In the case of partial acquisitions, a company takes a minority stake (less than 50 percent ownership) in the other company. In contrast, cross-equity alliances occur when each company takes a stake in the other, essentially exchanging shares.[36]

Equity alliances carry less risk than either buying or building a company, which makes them attractive. A company can focus on its core business while at the same time exploring other options. This can be especially helpful when expanding into overseas markets, where a company may not have the cultural knowledge, expertise, or manpower to operate or oversee operations.

One highly successful international cross-equity alliance has been Fuji Xerox in Japan, with equal equity ownership by both companies. Although Fuji and Xerox hold equal equity, nearly all members of the executive board are Japanese, and one of the members also sits on the board of Xerox International. When Xerox suffered contraction in the United States, the alliance served as an important source of revenue.[37]

Licensing Agreements

Licensing agreement

A business agreement in which the owner of trademarked material authorizes an individual or company to use that material to sell or market products or services in exchange for a fee.

A **licensing agreement** is a business agreement in which the owner of trademarked material authorizes an individual or company to use that material to sell or market products or services in exchange for a fee. Licensing is an increasingly popular method by which companies can expand their business by granting other entities the right to use trademarked material.[38] This trademarked material is sometimes referred to as intellectual property (IP), and the owner of the IP is the licensor. The licensor, in effect, rents his or her IP to a licensee, who is then allowed to create products based on the IP in exchange for fees or royalties.[39] Some licensing agreements require the licensee to submit products bearing the IP to the licensor for final approval prior to sale and distribution. This helps the licensor ensure that the IP is being used in a suitable fashion and that the quality of the product is acceptable.[40]

One familiar example of this model involves clothing bearing a sports team logo. The logo is the intellectual property of the team's owners, and the owners grant a license for the logo's use to a clothing manufacturer. The manufacturer, in turn, produces sweatshirts and t-shirts bearing the logo and pays an agreed-on percentage of the shirts' sales to the team's owners.[41]

Licensing agreements can be beneficial to both parties involved. In the previous example, for instance, every individual wearing a sweatshirt bearing the licensor's IP is a walking advertisement. Licensees benefit by increasing the desirability of their products via recognizable trademarks. They also enjoy decreased in-house design costs.

Of course, licensing agreements have disadvantages too. For licensors, these are primarily associated with the quality of licensed products and the way in which the trademark is portrayed in those products. For licensees, these are primarily monetary, because some agreements include guaranteed fees that must be paid regardless of how well a licensed product sells.[42]

Franchising

Franchise

An agreement in which the owner of a business grants an individual or group of individuals the right to sell or market products or services under that business name in exchange for a fee.

A **franchise** is an agreement in which the owner of a business grants an individual or group of individuals the right to sell or market products or services under that business name in exchange for a fee. A franchise is a business agreement between two independent parties. The first party, known as the franchisor, owns a particular business and grants the second party, known as the franchisee, the right to market products or services under that business name. In return for this right, the franchisee pays a fee to the franchisor. The two primary types of franchises are business format franchises and product distribution franchises.

Business format franchises are more common, and they dictate the marketing plan and operations procedures the franchisee will use to sell products or services. The majority of fast-food restaurant franchises are business format franchises. Product distribution franchises, on the other hand, do not specify the way in which the franchisee is expected to sell products or services.

When it comes to these types of agreements, one benefit to the franchisor is monetary; franchisees pay a variety of fees and royalties to the franchisor. A second benefit is the wide distribution of products or services and an increase in name recognition. The primary benefit for the franchisee is that they are marketing services or products that customers are already familiar with, so they do not have to spend a great deal of time generating customer awareness.

The disadvantages of franchise agreements are most strongly felt by franchisees who are not given the freedom to establish their own standards for marketing and pricing.[43] For example, Burger King recently ran a $1 double cheeseburger promotion nationwide, forcing franchisees to adopt the pricing despite resultant losses. The franchisees sued Burger King over the promotion; at the time of this writing, the case had not yet been to court.[44]

Wholly Owned Affiliates

Wholly owned affiliate or subsidiary

A company whose stock is completely owned by a second company, referred to as a parent or holding company.

A **wholly owned affiliate or subsidiary** is a company whose stock is completely owned by a second company, referred to as a parent or holding company.[45] The parent company is typically larger than the affiliate and seeks to control, but not dissolve, the internal structure of the affiliate. This arrangement is beneficial from a legal standpoint because it enables the parent and affiliate to remain separate entities, and in most situations, it protects the parent company in the event that the affiliate is sued.[46]

The wholly owned affiliate ownership form is also advantageous because it provides the parent company with the technical expertise of another company without having to share any of its own expertise with a competitor, as sometimes happens with joint ventures.[47] Multinational parent companies may also receive more favorable treatment in terms of taxation via wholly owned affiliates in other countries.[48] Another important benefit to having a wholly owned affiliate is that the parent company may be able to capitalize on name recognition and marketing associated with the affiliate and utilize existing distribution channels already established by the affiliate.[49] Many companies interested in international expansion pursue either outright purchase of an affiliate or purchase of affiliate stock for this very reason.[50]

For instance, cosmetics giant Estée Lauder acquired Aveda, a manufacturer of plant-based and natural beauty products, as a wholly owned affiliate in 1997 for approximately $300 million.[51] This purchase enabled Estée Lauder to enter the hair care market and acquire a private salon distribution channel. At the time of the purchase, Aveda was experiencing pains associated with its rapid growth and welcomed Estée Lauder's centralized purchasing power and policy structure. Aveda has maintained its own manufacturing facility, which uses organic products and sustainable practices, as well as its own executive structure, while Estée Lauder has been reaping the financial benefits of the affiliation.[52]

Of course, wholly owned affiliates do pose several disadvantages to parent companies. Chief among these is that the parent company bears the full cost and risk of business operations should the objective for which it acquired the affiliate fail.[53] Additionally, the parent company must be careful to maintain the affiliate as a separate corporate entity with its own interests and operational procedures.[54] This separation is important when it comes to a range of issues, including taxes and liability. These two issues are chief among the reasons why some companies seeking international expansion opt to pursue joint ventures rather than wholly owned affiliates.[55]

Strategic Alliances

Strategic alliances

Agreements between two or more parties to work together to achieve a common goal.

Strategic alliances are agreements between two or more parties to work together to achieve a common goal. These agreements may or may not be legally binding, but in either case, creating an alliance contract is pivotal to enabling both parties to protect their assets, engage in amiable and beneficial business interactions with one another, and delineate how and under what circumstances the alliance will end.[56] Formation of any alliance, regardless of the strength of the contract, is risky. However, many companies around the world have decided that the benefits in terms of global capabilities, marketplace adaptation, and formation of economies of scale are worth the risk.[57]

Businesses of all sizes and in all sectors are becoming increasingly reliant on strategic alliances as a means of driving growth.[58] Strategic alliances are similar to partnerships or joint ventures in which two companies team up for their mutual benefit in creating or distributing a product. Unlike partnerships and joint ventures, however, strategic alliances typically lack permanence. For instance, strategic alliances may be set up around one or two products or lines, rather than a lifelong agreement.[59]

■Exhibit **9.10**

PepsiCo and Unilever forged a successful strategic alliance.

Vario images GmbH & Co. KG/Alamy/Knut Mueller

For example, two companies may team up temporarily through a strategic alliance because one has the technical expertise to develop a new video gaming system and the other has the resources to build and distribute it.[60] Strategic alliances are especially important in today's economy because they yield greater economic benefits to companies faster than would be possible if companies pursued certain projects on their own. Research and development, licensing, advertising, and distribution costs are shared among the two parties in the alliance, and innovative products and technologies can be made available to the public more quickly across broader market segments.[61]

Strategic alliances are business-to-business collaborations that establish business networks. Sometimes, these networks are vertical and bring together a vendor company and a customer company. Other times, they are horizontal and bring together two vendor companies.[62] In the latter case, the networks created occasionally bring together rival companies. Rival-based alliances are complex because of the vulnerability each company assumes by engaging in information sharing with a competitor, but they can be successful too.

One strategic alliance success story involves a joint venture between PepsiCo and Unilever, the company that produces Lipton tea. The two companies came together to bring bottled teas to stores around the United States in 1991.[63] Lipton, a name long associated with tea, brought brand recognition and manufacturing capabilities to the alliance, whereas PepsiCo brought an established distribution network.[64] By 2003, the bottled beverages produced through this alliance were the leading ready-to-drink teas in the U.S. and Canadian markets, which prompted PepsiCo and Unilever to expand their agreement to include international distribution in 60 additional countries.[65] The alliance continues to be successful and innovative, and it launched its first-ever sparkling tea beverage in 2009 (■Exhibit 9.10).[66]

Now that you know about organizational classification systems and ownership structures, let's turn our attention to how companies organize people and processes to accomplish their goals. The organizational structures discussed in the next section are common in business today, so it is important that you understand the terminology and the differences among them.

Most Popular » Discussion Questions

1. Interview a small business owner to find out what form of ownership model he or she utilizes. Why did the business owner choose that particular form of ownership? What are the pros and cons of the model he or she chose?

2. If you were setting up your own business, which form of ownership would you choose and why?

---

6. What Are Common Contemporary Organizational Structures?

In this section, we will look at several common organizational structures in use today. One reason we focus on specific structures is that at some point in your career, you are likely going to need to weigh in on how to structure your organization, or at least the part of the organization in which you work. In fact, employees at all levels are more and more likely to be asked to weigh in on decisions like these—especially in flatter organizations, which we will explain later in this section.

Another reason why it is important to recognize typical organizational structures is that you will probably feel more or less comfortable working within some organizational structures than others. For example, you may prefer more or less guidance, autonomy, certainty, ambiguity, or change. You might prefer very clear lines of authority, or you might like more networked and informal authority. Recognizing which kinds of organizational structures foster the kind of conditions you enjoy and where you can be at your best will result in making better choices about the organizations you join and the jobs you accept.

We will start this section by looking more deeply at the differences between "tall" and "flat" organizational structures. Then we will discuss departmentalization and how structures differ when jobs are grouped by division, function, product, process, customer, and geography. Finally, we'll conclude by looking at several structures that have emerged in recent years to support organizations in dealing with today's complex environment: matrix, hybrid, and networked structures.

"Tall" and "Flat" Organizational Structures

A vertical organizational structure can be "tall" with several levels of hierarchy, or it can be "flat" with few levels of hierarchy. In theory, tall vertical structures support fluid movement of information and resources up and down the hierarchy, whereas flatter structures facilitate faster and more effective communication horizontally across and among groups in the organization.

Tall vertical structures involve a chain of command that forms a pyramid-type organizational chart, extending from boards of directors and the most senior leaders at or near the top, to managers, supervisors, and then lower-level employees at the bottom. Tall structures can be understood purely in terms of hierarchy, as in the rank system of the U.S. Army. As you can see in ■Exhibit 9.11, enlisted soldiers are classified into 13 hierarchical

■Exhibit **9.11**

The U.S. Army uses 24 rank designations for enlisted soldiers and officers.*

Enlisted Soldiers*			Commissioned Officers		
Insignia	**Rank**	**Designation**	**Insignia**	**Rank**	**Designation**
	Sergeant Major of the Army	E–9		General of the Army (GOA)	0–11
	Command Sgt Major (CSM)	E–9		General (GEN)	0–10
	Sergeant Major (SGM)	E–9		Lieutenant General (LTG)	0–9
	First Sergeant (1SG)	E–8		Major General (MG)	0–8
	Master Sergeant (MSG)	E–8		Brigadier General (BG)	0–7
	Sergeant First Class (SFC)	E–7		Colonel (COL)	0–6
	Staff Sergeant (SSG)	E–6		Lieutenant Colonel (LTC)	0–5
	Sergeant (SGT)	E–5		Major (MAJ)	0–4
	Corporal (CPL)	E–4		Captain (CPT)	0–3
	Specialist (SPC)	E–4		First Lieutenant (1LT)	0–2
	Private-First Class (PFC)	E–3		Second Lieutenant (2LT)	0–1
	Private (PVT2)	E–2			
NO INSIGNIA	Private (PVT)	E–1			

*Among enlisted soldiers, corporal and above are referred to as non-commissioned officers.

ranks, 9 of which represent the category of "non-commissioned officers" (NCOs). The hierarchy of "commissioned officers" (the lowest of which technically outranks the highest ranking enlisted soldier) has 11 different ranks, for a total of 24 hierarchical levels.

A major benefit of clear vertical structures is that the hierarchy tends to work as a cohesive whole, and information sharing up and down the chain of command can be efficient.[67] One drawback is that different vertical structures within an organization (e.g., marketing, finance, manufacturing) can develop a "silo mentality." The term *silos* is often used to describe parts of an organization that are isolated from and interact less with other parts of the organization.[68]

Many organizations will try to minimize the negative impact of silos by creating cross-functional teams for important organization-wide projects. **Cross-functional teams** consist of individuals from many parts of an organization who are brought together to provide different points of view and skills in the service of organization-wide challenges and opportunities, innovations, and special projects.

Another potential problem in a tall vertical structure is that more managers and executives are needed to make decisions, allocate resources, and the like. This is expensive and can be highly inefficient. That is why in recent decades, many organizations have "downsized" by reorganizing their hierarchies so that fewer managers are needed to oversee operations. In other words, organizations are becoming "flatter." An organization is referred to as "flat" when there are few levels of hierarchy in the organizational structure. Think of a pyramid that is very wide at its base and not very high, and you have the basic concept of what a flat organization is like (■Exhibit 9.12).

In flat organizations, communication can be more effective horizontally across teams, work groups, and departments. Theoretically, resources can flow more easily across the organization. To this end, flat organizations often have team-based structures, less specialization, and wider spans of control and leadership.[69] A flat structure can potentially result in decreased costs and increased speed because there are fewer layers of management to involve in the decision-making process.

A truly flat structure is rare and would only be found in very small organizations. Moreover, many people have a hard time imaging what it would be like to work in a flat organization. Members of the Boston Consulting Group published an article pointing out that contemporary thinking about career paths and peer groups tends to be very much the same as in the past—and both of these are linked to hierarchal models of organizational structure. People want to move "up." In addition, metrics, planning, and budgeting all continue to support the vertical, hierarchical organization.[70]

Cross-functional teams
Teams that consist of individuals from many parts of an organization who are brought together to provide different points of view and skills in the service of organization-wide challenges and opportunities, innovations, and special projects.

■ Exhibit **9.12**
Organizations may be tall or flat.

IDEO

Business Case

Empowering Employees

Companies are not limited to traditional organizational structures. Innovative firms often bypass these structures and create new configurations that allow more freedom for creativity, innovation, and teamwork. Consider the example of IDEO, a global design consultancy firm with over 500 employees worldwide. The word "ideo" is Greek for idea, and one of the company's founders, David Kelley, has become well known as an innovator.

His inventive style in designing products can also be seen in IDEO's unique organizational structure. Kelley recalls working for large corporations early in his career and finding them oppressive. In his words, "You could feel the weight of the organizational chart. My boss was a person I didn't know, who was making decisions about my life." Therefore, when he later started his own company, Kelley wanted to do something different—something he refers to as "employee empowerment."[71]

Continued on next page>>

IDEO Continued

The result of Kelley's innovative thinking was IDEO's current structure. Although the firm's employees can be described as a flat team, they also form "studios" and multidisciplinary "hot teams." Studios are departments that vary in size from 15 to 25 people, with each studio head responsible for the profit and loss of his or her particular group. Studio heads are not hired from the outside but are instead groomed from within IDEO. Hot teams are groups of people with multidisciplinary backgrounds who work together for a certain period of time. The leaders of the hot teams come from within the teams and are not hired to be leaders; rather, these individuals have worked at IDEO for some time and have come to be respected by their colleagues.

Clients and thinkers from outside IDEO are also vital participants in the company's hot teams. This cross-disciplinary approach has contributed to IDEO's success in the completion of

Hot teams spark innovation

design projects such as the Palm V, the Apple mouse, and the Crest Neat-Squeeze Tube for toothpaste. In fact, IDEO has won more *Business Week*/IDSA Industrial Design Excellence Awards than any other firm and has been ranked among the 25 most innovative companies by both *Fast Company* and Boston Consulting Group.[72] David Kelley attributes his company's success partly to its use of teams: "We have the advantage of working in multiple industries. Let's say we are working on a chair, but we've learned something in the automobile industry before. Maybe we learned about a certain kind of spring in the automobile industry. We just cross-pollinate that into the chair, and now we have an innovation in the furniture industry."[73]

Source: Case written by Laura Town; **Photo Source:** Shutterstock

---

Departmentalization
The process by which individuals or activities are grouped together into departments according to function, geography, product, process, or customer, as well as how the departments are coordinated and how they fit within the larger organization.

■Exhibit **9.13**

General Electric's organizational chart illustrates its divisional structure.

When a flat structure is implemented, the changes in employee attitudes and organizational culture can be both beneficial and challenging. For instance, researchers have found that when a firm "flattens," employees feel empowered but have less access to feedback. Additionally, involvement increases, but identification with the organization can suffer. Finally, intrinsic motivation tends to rise dramatically, but this can be at the cost of decreased satisfaction in important extrinsic motivators such as pay and job security.[74]

Departmentalization and Organizational Structure

Within an organizational hierarchy, jobs are often grouped in ways that allow people, resources, and processes to be coordinated for efficiency and effectiveness. This is called departmentalization. **Departmentalization** is the process by which individuals or activities are grouped together into departments according to function, geography, product, process, or customer, as well as how the departments are coordinated and how they fit within the larger organization. Departmentalization can also support matrix, hybrid, and network structures. Let's examine each of these departmental groupings in turn.

Divisional Structures

Divisions are structures within a company that include all of the departments necessary to achieve particular organizational goals. For example, a global consumer goods company might have a "Foods Division" that is a self-contained organization including departments such as marketing, sales, human resources, and supply chain—everything that is needed to produce, distribute, market, and sell the company's products. In some cases, each division operates as if it is a separate business with its own hierarchy, top leaders, and even board of directors.[75] As you can see in ■Exhibit 9.13, a large company may also choose a divisional structure to support separate and self-contained structures for the production of a certain product or service line. In

General Electric Company
├─ GE Capital Services
│   ├─ Capital Real Estate
│   └─ Commercial Lending and Leasing
└─ GE Industrial
    ├─ Consumer and Industrial
    │   ├─ Lighting LLC (Kentucky)
    │   └─ Lighting Ltd (UK)
    └─ Sensing and Inspection Technologies

Exhibit 9.13, the top two levels of the company, GE Capital Services and GE Industrial, are divisions. Within each division are departments necessary to manage the entire production-to-market cycle.

"Pure" divisional structures would not need or have any hierarchical or reporting relationships with the parent company, except through the division's leader. In practice, however, it is more common for certain business units and functional groups such as HR and finance to have secondary "dotted line" reporting relationships into the central organization to ensure consistency in vital organizational processes.[76]

Functional Departmentalization

Functional departmentalization
Method of grouping jobs based on the nature of the work being performed.

Functional departmentalization is a method of grouping jobs based on the nature of the work being performed. Most organizations have five functional areas: operations (all the jobs related to what the organization does, produces, or provides), marketing, sales, human resources, and finance. Many organizations also have other functions that support their particular business or institution. ■Exhibit 9.14 illustrates functional departmentalization at the executive level of an organization, showing the president at the top of the organization and five vice presidents (VPs) of each functional area.

■Exhibit **9.14**
Functional departmentalization groups jobs based on the type of work being performed.

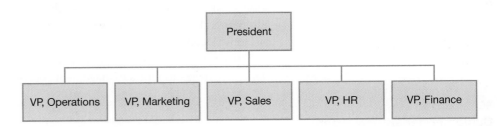

One benefit of functional departmentalization is that each functional area works as a cohesive whole, and information sharing within each function can be efficient.[77] A drawback is that the different functions can develop the "silo mentality" mentioned earlier because they may interact less with other functions of the organization.[78]

Product Departmentalization

Product departmentalization
A method of grouping jobs based on the products made or services offered.

In some larger corporations, departmentalization occurs along product lines. For example, Fortune Brands owns various brands of alcohol including Jim Beam, Canadian Club, and Maker's Mark. The company also manufactures kitchen and bath faucets under the brand name Moen and produces Titleist golf balls.[79] This diversified company uses a product departmentalization structure. **Product departmentalization** is a method of grouping jobs based on the products made or services offered.

In a large diversified organization, having separate departments devoted to particular products or services helps cut costs related to getting goods and services to market.[80] One drawback to this type of departmentalization, however, is that there is redundancy in the jobs being done across the organization. For example, if a company has an entire division devoted to making soap, another to making shampoo, a third to toothpaste, and a fourth to hair gel, each of those divisions will need HR professionals, a finance group, and a marketing group. ■Exhibit 9.15 shows an example of product departmentalization for a frozen food company.

■Exhibit **9.15**
Product departmentalization groups jobs based on the products or services offered.

Division President, Frozen Foods

Director, Desserts   Director, Entrees   Director, Gourmet

Process Departmentalization

Process departmentalization
A method of grouping jobs based on the sequential steps of the work people do to produce products or services or engage in other business activities.

Process departmentalization is a method of grouping jobs based on the sequential steps of the work people do to produce products or services or engage in other business activities. Let's say you work in a manufacturing plant where soda is produced, bottled, and prepared for market. Using process departmentalization, one department would have all the jobs

■Exhibit **9.16**
Process departmentalization groups jobs based on the sequential steps required to create a good or provide a service.

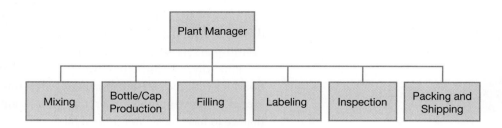

associated with mixing the soda. Another department would be involved in manufacturing the glass bottles and metal caps. A third would involve pouring the soda into individual bottles and capping those bottles. The fourth department would include all jobs related to labeling the bottles, and the fifth department would be responsible for inspection and quality control. Finally, one department would be responsible for packing the bottles into boxes and shipping them out. ■Exhibit 9.16 illustrates this particular process structure.

Customer Departmentalization

Customer departmentalization
A method of grouping jobs based on the needs of customers, consumers, or clients.

Customer departmentalization is a method of grouping jobs based on the needs of customers, consumers, or clients. Focusing attention on the specific customers who purchase products or services can enhance customer satisfaction because it often means a team of individuals—or an entire division—is devoted to the best customers. For example, Newell Rubbermaid has teams of sales representatives dedicated to their largest customers, such as Home Depot and Lowe's. As with some other types of departmentalization, however, this structure suffers from job redundancy. ■Exhibit 9.17 shows an example of customer departmentalization for a management consulting firm.

■Exhibit **9.17**
Customer departmentalization is a structure that groups jobs based on the needs of customers, consumers, or clients.

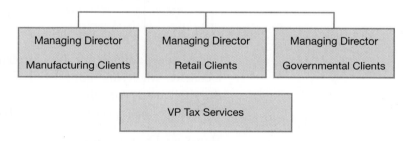

Geographic Departmentalization

Geographic departmentalization
A method of grouping jobs based on their physical location.

Geographic departmentalization is a method of grouping jobs based on their physical location. This is often seen within sales divisions of large organizations (■Exhibit 9.18).

Departmentalization structures are complex, no matter what form they take, because it is always challenging to coordinate complex vertical structures (e.g., the hierarchy) and even more daunting to coordinate among departments, because they have inherent "walls" between them. Nevertheless, several popular new structures have been developed to eliminate some of the problems inherent in structures that hamper communication, creativity, and speed. We look at three of these structures next: matrix, hybrid, and networked structures.

Matrix
A structure in which departments within an organization are linked directly to one unit in the vertical organization and to another unit in the horizontal organization.

■Exhibit **9.18**
Geographic departmentalization groups jobs based on their physical location.

Matrix Structure

A **matrix** is a structure in which departments within an organization are linked directly to one unit in the vertical organization and to another unit in the horizontal organization. The purpose of a matrix structure is to maximize the positive attributes of vertical structures while also supporting effective coordination, communication and agility across the organization. A common type of matrix is organized by function and geography, as shown in ■Exhibit 9.19.

The horizontal and vertical dimensions of a matrix structure can be any of the structures

■Exhibit **9.19**

A basic matrix structure combines vertical and horizontal structures.

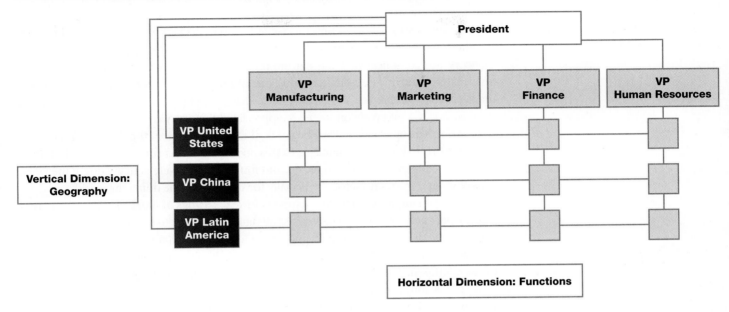

studied so far: divisional, functional, product, process, customer, or geographic. Sometimes, organizations will create a matrix structure for special projects, innovation teams, or any group that needs the support and control inherent in a vertical chain of command as well as the expertise from a department in the horizontal organization.

A matrix structure often helps shift the organizational culture away from a silo mentality in which each department or division is isolated from the rest of the organization. At its best, this type of structure allows for optimal control in the hierarchical organization while also ensuring maximum efficiency and effective coordination of the horizontal organization.

The downside of the matrix structure is that it can be very confusing. Most people are used to working within a single hierarchy. In a basic matrix structure, people often report formally to two bosses. Even if the structure does not have everyone reporting formally to two bosses, the department itself is responsible for the outcomes required by two distinct and different parts of the organization—each of which has its own goals. Sometimes, the required outcomes can be in conflict with one another. This can cause a great deal of tension in the organization and result in overburdening the senior leader or leaders who have to resolve conflicts.

Hybrid structure
A structure that incorporates more than one type of structure in the overall organization.

■Exhibit **9.20**

The hybrid structure in this cancer center incorporates more than one type of structure.

Hybrid Structure

A **hybrid structure** incorporates more than one type of structure in the overall organization. For example, ■Exhibit 9.20 depicts part of the structure of a large cancer center. The structure is divisional, but it also includes flat team structures within the clinical investigations and clinical affairs divisions.

As many variations of hybrid structures exist as there are combinations of organizational structures. One structure that is worth mentioning because it hardly ever shows up on an organizational chart is the vertical structure created within a team. As mentioned earlier in the chapter, many people have been socialized to view hierarchy as the most important aspect of organizational structure. We tend to be most comfortable with the rules of hierarchies (even if we don't like them). For this and other reasons, people often gravitate toward implementing a hierarchy, even when it is not officially called for in the organizational structure.

You may have experienced this on a project team in the past. When you started to work together, members were equal, with the exception that there was a designated leader. Maybe the work was complicated, it was hard to meet the deadlines, or your leader was busy or unavailable. Suddenly (it seemed to you), one of the other members was now the "project manager"—he or she was organizing work, delegating tasks, and reporting back to the team leader. Not everyone on the team appreciated this, so two people designated themselves as "subgroup leaders." They began organizing the work of the remaining members and reporting to the project manager. At this point, you had a team of eight people, four of whom were organizing and delegating, and four of whom were actually doing the work. This obviously makes no sense—especially for the four people doing the work!

It is surprising how often this happens in real settings at work. This dynamic may arise in part because some people resist being led and need to learn the art of followership. It may also arise because of poor team leadership—flat structures such as teams are not easy to lead, as you will see in Chapter 10. It takes special skills and a high level of self-confidence to let people work collaboratively without micromanagement.

As more and more organizations adopt flat and hybrid structures, it will serve you well to learn to recognize the signs that a flat structure is turning into a dysfunctional hierarchy. It will also serve you well to learn how to manage and lead groups without the benefit of a formal hierarchical structure. This is particularly true when it comes to flat, networked structures—in which power dynamics are an important part of the overall structure that must be understood and tracked.

Networked Organizational Structures and Power Dynamics

All of the structures we have looked at so far have been described primarily in terms of formal authority, responsibility, and accountability. In other words, these structures revolve around formal and position power. This is not the only important dimension, however, when it comes to organizational structure. Other increasingly important dimensions of organizational success include access to resources, information, and social networks.

An organization is a social network. People are linked in many ways: by similarity in jobs, similarity in level of authority, personal relationships, the need to work together, or common interests, to name just a few. By virtue of where you "sit" in an organization and how you interact with others, you will have more or less access to information. Typically, we think of people in higher-level jobs as having access to more organizational knowledge and resources. This can be true, but take the example of an executive assistant. This person has little position power but might hold a great deal of social power because she constantly makes decisions about who gets access to what information, who has access to her boss, and so forth. Her boss, who has tremendous position power, may have little power in the sense that his information is filtered through a small group of people in the organization.[81]

Organizations can tailor social networks to improve the flow of information, facilitate the spread of innovation, improve decision making, strengthen organizational culture, and remove information "bottlenecks," which occur when too much information is passing through too few individuals.[82] As shown in ■Exhibit 9.21, the networked structure of an organization can also be mapped out in terms of communication and interaction between departments, boards, teams, functional divisions, and so forth. In this case, the focus is not on which individuals are interacting, but rather on which parts of the organization are interacting and in what way.

In this section, we have described numerous contemporary organizational structures, as well as a few of the pros and cons of these structures. One form of organiza-

■Exhibit **9.21**
The network structure at Indymedia.

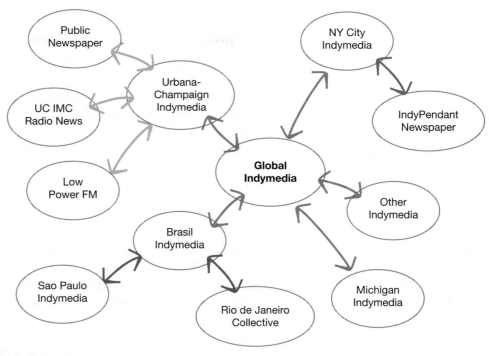

Source: http://www.indymedia.org

tion we have not yet discussed is the virtual organization. Because of advances in information and communication technologies, a vast number of organizations are now at least partially virtual. For this reason, Chapter 11 is entirely dedicated to this topic. Now, let's turn our attention to what happens within all of these structures: work.

Most Popular » Discussion Questions

1. Organizational structure is not always easy to see when we interact with a company, but it is important to understand when taking a job. Brainstorm a list of questions you could ask an interviewer about the company's organizational structure that would help you to determine if it is a place you would like to work. *Note:* "What is this organization's structure?" is a given. See what else you can come up with.
2. How do you think the structure and functions of hot teams contribute to IDEO's success?
3. In a matrix organization, you could have two bosses. What problems might arise in this situation? How could you deal with these problems?
4. In this section, we pointed out that people often feel comfortable with hierarchical structures and will create a mini-hierarchy around themselves, even if the formal structure does not call for it. In addition to our explanations, why do you think people do this?

7. How Is Work Structured?

You can consider overarching organizational structures, such as those described in the previous section, as "templates" within which smaller units and functions operate, jobs get done, and tasks are accomplished. As we have stressed throughout this chapter, organizational structure is an important concept to understand, but as you read on, please remember that numerous other factors, such as leadership, management practices, and organizational culture, are also extremely powerful in determining *how* work gets done, jobs are defined, and organizational goals are accomplished (or not). Let's look briefly at how tasks and jobs fit into the study of organizational structure.

Tasks

Within an organizational structure, *tasks* are the activities that people do regularly as part of their jobs. For example, an administrative assistant answers his boss's phone—this is a task. His job, on the other hand, is to provide support to his boss in a variety of ways, including managing his boss's calendar, editing written materials, arranging travel, and preparing speech and presentations materials. Likewise, a sales representative that completes her monthly expense report is doing a task for which she is responsible. This person's job is to sell products to certain customers within a geographical region.

Jobs

Job
A group of tasks and responsibilities related to accomplishing organizational objectives.

A **job** is defined as a group of tasks and responsibilities related to accomplishing organizational objectives. Like organizations, jobs can be classified in many ways. For example, jobs can be classified by profession or industry, type of workplace, associated tasks, grade or pay level, union or nonunion status, public or private sector status, or paid or unpaid status. As discussed earlier in the chapter, job specialization and division of labor describe how narrowly focused tasks and jobs are. For example, Henry Ford's assembly line in the early twentieth century used division of labor (as do many assembly lines today). Workers were assigned to very few tasks—even just one, which they did over and over—efficient, perhaps, but also mind-numbing.[83]

Job specialization is an old topic. Plato discussed it extensively in his famous work *The Republic*.[84] Centuries later, famed economist Adam Smith explained that specialization increased production output and wealth.[85] In the twentieth century, functional job specialization was explained as a core concept of scientific management by industrial researcher Frederick Taylor.[86] Job specialization, in this sense, has been linked to the movement to subdivide labor into its smallest units, such as what you might see on an assembly line. Organizational design will of course be affected by such processes, but so are people.

Highly specialized work, when taken to the extreme, can result in highly efficient but extremely boring and repetitive tasks and a mechanistic view of the organization.[87] It can lead to feelings of alienation.[88] On the other hand, employee satisfaction can be improved if job enlargement is pursued (i.e., by adding more and more interesting tasks).[89] In advanced industrial societies, scholars have recommended that functional specialization can give way to "flexible specialization," or the ability to quickly and efficiently manufacture customized products at low volume.[90] When this happens, employees are given the opportunity to vary the types of tasks and their order. This flexible specialization has been seen, for instance, in computer assembly based on customer input, which gave Dell Computers a strategic edge at the beginning of the twenty-first century.

When a course of job specialization is pursued, markets for each specialized job tend to emerge. When this occurs, jobs begin to develop outside the firm, and this can lead to outsourcing.[91] Additionally, "integration" of various specialties in organizational design can itself become a specialized function in the firm.[92]

Researchers have suggested that although job specialization is often intended to increase efficiency, it also may create more motivation by requiring deep "expert" knowledge in a specific work area.[93] Other researchers have noted that job specialization is beneficial in high-tech industries. Although in the past, job rotation had been adopted to alleviate the burnout associated with highly specialized work, in high-tech work, deep knowledge of one area of work increases self-efficacy and decreases burnout.[94]

While some jobs are highly specialized, other jobs are broader and include more tasks and activities. For example, the HR director in a manufacturing facility may perform most tasks associated with that position. She may coordinate all of the recruiting, hiring, pay practices, benefits administration, training, employee relations, and safety practices, and she may even craft policies and procedures.

A person who performs a wide variety of tasks is known as a generalist. A specialist, on the other hand, is someone who has a very narrowly focused set of job tasks. Using the HR analogy, in a large corporate center you may have one person responsible for benefits, several people responsible for payroll, a team of corporate trainers, and so forth. These are specialists.

Now that you know quite a lot about jobs, organizations, and how they can be structured, let's look at a few important factors leaders must consider when determining just how to structure—or restructure—an organization.

Most Popular » Discussion Questions

1. Have you ever done a highly specialized job? What was it? What did you like and what did you dislike about it?
2. Would you prefer to be a generalist or a specialist? Why?

---

8. What Factors Affect the Design of Organizational Structures?

We have been discussing structure as if it is something that already exists, something we can see and evaluate—which of course you can. You can step into any one of the types of businesses discussed in the previous section and "see" the structure that exists at that moment in time. But how did it get that way? When the organizational design process is deliberate, leaders and HR professionals consider several important factors: the organization's strategy, the external environment, technology, size, and geography.

The Relationship between Structure and Strategy

Over the years, scholars have debated the relationship between strategy and structure. You will often hear people in organizations say "Structure follows strategy," as if it is a known and unquestionable fact. It's a little more complicated than that, however.

Structure Follows Strategy

Organizational scholar Alfred Chandler was one of the first to propose that structure must follow strategy. The argument is pretty straightforward: An organization exists in a particular environment from which it draws its resources and within which it provides products or services. The decisions about how to position the organization in the environment are part of the organization's strategy. To implement that strategy, the organization makes certain choices about structure. In other words, the organization's structure is part of the outcome of the strategic decision-making process. Hence, structure follows strategy.[95]

Strategy Can Be Determined by Structure

Others have argued just the opposite—that structure *determines* strategy. This argument states that the benefits and limitations of the structure will determine what types of strategies are viable. Because structures can limit the implementation of certain strategies, it is important for organizations to develop a proactive approach to strategy formation. In a proactive organization, strategy and structure are constantly influencing each other. When this is not the case, the strategy is in danger of becoming "the lackey of the structure."[96]

Structure and Strategy: An Iterative Process

Now, let's consider the issue from another perspective. Tactics are actions that are implemented to try to achieve a strategic goal. A particular tactic, however, can only be used if the existing structure allows it (i.e., resources cannot be used by one part of the organization if they are controlled by another in a tall, siloed organization). At the same time, a tactic can be chosen because it is instrumental in changing organizational structure. If this works, different tactical choices become possible down the road. In other words, tactics are the interface between strategy and structure. More scholars are coming to recognize the importance of putting strategy and structure in an iterative relationship—a relationship in which strategy influences structure, structure influences strategy, and both are constantly improving.[97]

The External Environment

The external environment in which an organization operates also plays a key role in the structure of the organization. For example, Nautilus, a Vancouver, Washington–based company that manufactures fitness equipment, recently went through a major restructuring as a result of adverse economic conditions in the business environment. Facing a tough economic environment in 2008, including an $8.9 million loss in just one quarter, the company examined its strategies and structure in an attempt to become more aligned with external conditions.[98]

In an effort to cut costs, Nautilus closed one of its manufacturing facilities and combined two distribution centers. This change in structure meant that other areas of the company would need to handle an increased workload. Additionally, teams were established and given authority and responsibility for specific business units. The company also launched a strategic initiative supporting new product development, to keep the company's products fresh for the market.[99] Thanks to these changes, by the third quarter of 2009, the company was able to reduce its losses, and by the fourth quarter, it began showing profit.[100]

What the company had found was that its business of selling to exercise clubs and hotels was struggling, while consumer sales were doing well. So, in March 2010, Nautilus decided to shed its commercial sales in order to more effectively focus on the portion of the company that was generating profit—direct consumer sales.[101] In response to a changing environment, Nautilus continues to restructure the organization and to refocus its strategy.

How quickly and how well an organization adapts to the environment is also important. The national trucking company Vitran Express immediately took action when fuel prices rose in 2008. They began purchasing biodiesel fuels and ensured that drivers did not exceed 65 miles per hour. This quick adaptation saved the company $375,000 in their Chicago area terminals alone.[102]

In both of these cases, changes in the external environment happened *fast*. This situation is very common today. Positive changes such as advances in technology and the emergence of new markets are the norm, and companies need to be ready to take advantage of these changes. These examples illustrate a fact of organizational life today: The global environment is volatile and uncertain. Major changes can and do happen very quickly.

Environmental uncertainty
A situation in which market conditions are changing rapidly or are unclear.

Environmental uncertainty refers to a situation in which market conditions are changing rapidly or are unclear. Environmental uncertainty can be the result of political instability or changes such as elections or regime changes in influential countries. As another example, when resources are controlled for political reasons (as happens with oil), entire industries can be forced to change what they are doing overnight.

Social changes such as how people are using technology to share information can also cause a good deal of uncertainty. For example, only a few years ago news reporters were usually the ones to find and report stories. Now, anyone with a cell phone camera can do this work. This means that the news industry needs to change dramatically. And because of our increasingly interconnected world, other environmental conditions such as wars, conflicts or potential conflicts, regional environmental regulations, and even local laws can cause environmental uncertainty in places far from an organization's activities.

Competition on a global scale can also create environmental uncertainty. The recession in the late 2000s combined with increased international competition in the auto industry hit U.S. automotive companies especially hard. Since 1990, the 30,000 companies involved in supplying the auto industry have consolidated into 10,000 as a result of failures, mergers, and acquisitions.[103] In the auto industry and many others, environmental uncertainty will continue to affect business profoundly, in turn affecting how businesses and organizations structure people and operations.

Technology

We will discuss the effects of technology on individuals and organizations in depth in Chapter 11. For now, let us simply say that the level of technology in an organization impacts both the structure and strategy. As early as the 1950s, British researcher Joan Woodward found that the structure of an organization is influenced by the technology that it employs. For example, if a manufacturing company uses mass production, the structure might be one in which managers supervise more employees than in a custom manufacturing environment, where there may be fewer employees reporting to each manager.[104] In more modern times, computer technologies have greatly influenced the structure of organizations. Communication within the organizational structure has also adapted to these new technologies.

Company Size and Geography

In addition to strategy, the environment, and technology, numerous other factors can affect how leaders design or redesign an organization. Two that we will mention here are the organization's size and geography.

Company Size

An organization's size affects its structure in obvious ways. If your company has 20 people, you would not have 20 departments—you probably wouldn't even want four departments. If you differentiated that much, you would certainly be wasting resources. Similarly, if your organization has 20,000 people, you wouldn't organize them all in one department. Doing so would be chaotic and unmanageable.

There are no rules that dictate how leaders should design organizations of various sizes. However, in traditional vertical organizations, there seem to be some trends as organizations grow: Power becomes less concentrated; there are increasingly more levels of management, but this levels off as the organization becomes quite large; and more formal policies tend to emerge as a company grows.

Most research on how size affects structure has concentrated on traditional organizations in which the people counted are employees. Considering the fact that there has been a rapid increase in different employment relationships (such as contractors and temporary workers), we now need to look at the relationship of size to structure differently. As social networking continues to affect the "virtual" size of an organization, more research will be conducted as to what actually constitutes a small, medium, or large business, and how the various internal and external groups work together to impact structure—and vice versa.

Geography

How geographically dispersed employees and customers are will have an impact on organizational design. For example, national restaurant chains have hundreds of locations, and thousands of employees are needed to staff the individual restaurant sites. Each restaurant has a manager, but each manager also reports to a district manager. The reason why these district managers are responsible for specific geographical areas is because it would be too difficult to manage thousands of staff from one central corporate office. It would be challenging to maintain consistency, and controls on operations would be very limited.

In addition to the geographical dispersion of employees, geographical distribution of customers is key when it comes to structure. Large consumer products companies such as Procter & Gamble and Black & Decker have sales representatives in territories corresponding to the locations of major customer bases such as Walmart, Home Depot, and Target.

All of the topics presented so far in this section have an effect on organizational design. One would imagine, then, that leaders would always consider such factors before deciding to design, or redesign, an organization. That is not always the case, however, as we will see next.

Organizational Design: It's Not Always Deliberate!

As organizations grow, strategies change, or technology changes, organizational structures often *emerge* without much conscious planning or design. Individual managers and business leaders often make structure decisions for "their" parts of the organization, resulting in something of a hodgepodge over time. This emergent process can support adaptability. On the other hand, it can also result in chaos and redundancy of tasks and functions.

For example, in one very large company we know, the HR function was decentralized in the late 1990s. What this meant was that HR leaders were empowered within each division to make decisions that suited their particular needs with regard to leadership development, hiring practices, and the like. About five years later, the organization bought another large company that had to be integrated into the current organization. Numerous problems were discovered, including the fact that there was no centralized technology system to track "hiring" the employees from the acquired organization—every division used different software. It was impossible to track who went where.

Second, the acquiring organization wisely wanted to ensure that this new, bigger entity's managers and leaders would share a common approach to leadership, values, and culture. As the central HR team began investigating the leadership models that were in use around the business, they found that over the five years of decentralization, no less than 187 new leadership models had been adopted and taught in as many regions and divisions! Imagine trying to coordinate communication about leadership and culture under those circumstances.

As much as empowerment and adaptability are key to success, so is ensuring that the structure used across the organization is coherent. In most organizations, this is accomplished through centralized planning around key issues related to the environment and technology, as well as a host of factors such as the organization's size, geographical dispersion of locations, degree of specialization, and the like.

Most Popular » Discussion Questions

1. In what ways does the external environment influence the structure of your school as an organization?
2. Are there any new technologies that are affecting how work gets done in your school or place of work? If so, what are they, and what impact do they have on work processes?
3. Use the Internet to find the biggest company you can, in terms of number of employees. Now, study the company's structure. How do you think the size of this organization impacted decisions about its structure?

9. What Is HR's Role in Organizational Design and Structure?

HR Leadership Roles

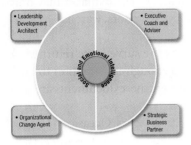

Job analysis
The systematic process of gathering and analyzing information about jobs and the knowledge, skills, and competencies needed to perform these jobs.

Job description
A written document that lists the major tasks and responsibilities of a particular job.

Job specification
A written document that lists all of the necessary knowledge, skills, and abilities that a person must possess in order to perform a particular job.

The HR function is heavily involved in organizational design. Organizational design, however, is not a one-time job—our hypercompetitive, changing environment results in constant pressure on organizations to change quickly and often. In many cases, these changes are structural. HR needs to be ready to sit at the table with leaders to provide advice and counsel, as well as to anticipate, plan for, and implement structural changes that enable the organization to keep up—or stay ahead—of the environment. You can think of this role as relating to the "macro" aspects of organizational design and structure. HR is also responsible for organizational design on the "micro" level—job analysis.

Job Analysis

Job analysis is the systematic process of gathering and analyzing information about jobs and the knowledge, skills, and competencies needed to perform these jobs. Two products emerge from the job analysis process: job descriptions and job specifications. A **job description** is a written document that lists the major tasks and responsibilities of a particular job. A **job specification** is a written document that lists all of the necessary knowledge, skills, and abilities that a person must possess in order to perform a particular job.

Job analysis is important for effective utilization of employees. It becomes the foundation for HR practices such as compensation, labor relations, employee training and development, recruiting, and safety programs. Essentially, every facet of HR is impacted by accurate job analyses, descriptions, and specifications.

The process of job analysis involves seven steps. These are outlined in ■Exhibit 9.22.[105] In the first step, a review of all pertinent and current information about jobs throughout the company is done. HR professionals determine what documentation is already in existence and how relevant and accurate the current job descriptions and job specifications are. Step 2 entails choosing a specific job analysis method. Job analysis methods include surveys, interviews, observations, or any combination of these methods.

In the third step, the data about the jobs is collected. Obviously, this takes a great deal of time and effort. If surveys are used, it takes time out of employees' busy schedules to

■Exhibit **9.22**

Job Analysis Process

Step 1: Review current information about the job or jobs.

Step 2: Choose a job analysis method.

Step 3: Collect data about the job or jobs through surveys, observation, interviews, or focus groups or by studying benchmark jobs.

Step 4: Compile and analyze the data, then create job description and job specification documents.

Step 5: Have employees verify or provide final input to the job description and job specification documents.

Step 6: Seek supervisory approval of the job description and job specification documents.

Step 7: Maintain and update the job descriptions and job specifications as needed.

Source: From Stovall, Steven. *Cases in Human Resource Management,* 1E. © 2005 Custom Solutions, a part of Cengage Learning, Inc. Reproduced by permission www.cengage.com/permissions.

complete these instruments and submit them to the HR department. In large companies, vast amounts of data can be generated that then need to be analyzed—which is also time consuming and complex. To deal with these issues, job analyses may focus on collecting data about benchmark jobs, rather than every job throughout the firm. A **benchmark job** is one that is representative of other similar jobs. For example, rather than surveying every person in the operations department, the HR manager may only send questionnaires to a few randomly selected front-line supervisors, warehouse managers, logistics coordinators, and plant managers.

Step 4 consists of compiling and analyzing the data. As the surveys are returned or observations written up, the HR manager begins to have enough information to craft job descriptions and job specifications. Then, in the fifth step, these documents are sent out to people in those jobs for review and correction.

In the sixth step, input is sought from the job holders' supervisors. Occasionally, people tend to inflate their level of responsibility or the importance of their positions. Having others examine these documents facilitates a more accurate portrayal. The seventh and final step is one of the most critical, but also one that is most often forgotten or ignored. Maintaining these records and updating them as necessary keeps these documents fresh. The use of new technology can render a job description or job specification obsolete very quickly. Additionally, restructuring and process improvements can rapidly cause job descriptions to become outdated.

Benchmark job
A job that is representative of other jobs that are similar in nature.

The HR Cycle

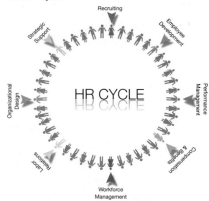

Most Popular » Discussion Questions

1. Conduct a job analysis for a manager you know.
2. Create a job description for a first-year student at your school. Consider all aspects of the job: classes, formal involvement in extracurricular activities, social activities, etc.
3. Find a job search site on the Internet and review job descriptions for several jobs you might like to do at some point in your life. Discuss what is appealing about these jobs, and what you would have to do to qualify for them.

---

10. What Can We All Do to Work Effectively within Our Organizations' Structures?

Given the amount of time you will spend working in your life, you should make the most of it. To do so, you must learn how to function effectively within your organization's structure. You will need to know how to communicate, get and share resources, and learn and innovate within certain constraints—even if you work in a "flat" organization. In this section, we will explore two ways to work effectively within an organizational structure. The first topic we will cover seems contradictory: We will explore how to work effectively *outside* the formal structure. This is an essential skill because no matter how perfect a formal organizational structure is, there is always an informal structure within which people build relationships, manage power dynamics, and get things done.

Next, we will discuss an important skill that you will need to work within a hierarchy: managing "up." Most people think of a hierarchy as a structure in which people above manage people below. But it goes both ways, and it takes special skills to manage your boss.

Managing and Leading the Informal Organization

A formal organization is one in which all departments, jobs, reporting relationships, rules, policies, and procedures are standardized. As an example, consider a company that has many layers of management, each with a clear division of responsibilities and tasks. In this company, people follow rules, policies, and procedures. In fact, the policy manual is a large book, divided into sections, covering everything from how to conduct meetings to what personal items are permitted on your desk. In this company, all employees—no matter what level they are at in the organization—have a set of job duties that are dictated by their manager. Most major decisions require the approval of at least one senior manager, and associates have very little actual authority over how they approach their work. This describes a formal organization.

This imaginary company is not necessarily a "bad" organization. In fact, it is fairly typical of large organizations. However, rules and policies just can't dictate everything, for every situation, every time. It is also not unusual for a formal organization and the structure that goes with it to be somewhat out of synch with how people really communicate and what it takes to make things happen. That is one of the reasons why people find ways around the formal organization, sometimes by creating what is called an "informal organization."

An informal organization includes the organization's social structure, social networks, and culture. You won't find the rules for your informal organization written anywhere, but they exist. For example, in many organizations leaders have an "open door" policy—anyone can contact them at any time (this is an informal structure). In one organization we know where managers and leaders adhere to this informal policy, the CEO abides by different rules. She has a chief of staff who vets all communications, all e-mails, and all meetings. Knowing this, you won't naively send an e-mail to her—you will build a relationship with the chief of staff to the point that he begins to trust you. That's the way to get to your CEO in this particular organization.

Working effectively within an informal organization requires a high degree of social awareness. Understanding how to maneuver within your informal organization is one of the most powerful skill sets you can have at work, so it's worth developing early in your career. Take a look at the *Perspectives* feature to see how one informed and talented leader worked within her informal organization to quickly accomplish a goal that worked out well for everyone at Franklin & Marshall College.

Perspectives

Carol de Wet is the associate dean of the faculty at Franklin & Marshall College, a highly regarded private college in Pennsylvania. Carol is also a professor—she teaches geoscience and is highly regarded by students, faculty, staff, and senior administrators. Carol's track record indicates that she gets things done—things that the university needs and that faculty, students, and staff want. She has led and been involved in several important initiatives, including drawing people's attention to important issues such as the college's benefits package. Through informal organizational structures and social networking, Carol helps people move beyond awareness to actually grappling with issues, finding solutions, and bringing about change. As she put it:

Carol de Wet, Associate Dean, Franklin & Marshall College

Our president needed someone to look at sustainability issues on campus. There are many different viewpoints on the subject, so I knew I needed to make sure everyone had an opportunity to be heard, to be part of the discussion. We began by pulling those people together and creating working groups with faculty, staff, and students—anyone who wanted to participate was welcome. This was a bit unusual—I didn't close the groups, or just invite senior people—anyone could be involved. During these group meetings and in many, many conversations, we began to see pockets of activity—individuals or groups who had some energy for the topic, or who were already doing things themselves. We found that there were actually lots of people on campus—many of whom felt isolated, or not sure what to do to make a contribution to the college around these issues. Together, though, and through open dialogue, we were able to find out what people on our campus really wanted to do around sustainability, and we did it.

Continued on next page>>

We marshaled our energy and wrote a white paper about what Franklin & Marshall students, faculty, and staff could and wanted to do about sustainability on our campus. We created a center to take the initiative into the future more formally, and we even helped one group *of students bring their dream to reality: They created an organic garden on campus.*

Source: Personal interview conducted with Carol de Wet by Annie McKee, 2009.

Carol's work with the informal networks and structures of her college resulted in significant and powerful change to the formal structures of the college. She found people who had something to say, and she motivated people to *act*.

Carol de Wet understands the importance of working with the informal networks of an organization, and she realizes it takes a special kind of leadership behavior to do so. When you are trying to mobilize people, to get them interested and involved, you can't rely on position power or even rewards—the informal network doesn't operate this way. In the informal, networked organization, people get things done by joining rather than forcing, by inspiring rather than telling, and by encouraging rather than criticizing. As Carol put it, leading this way requires "graciousness, honor and humility . . . with a stance that says 'I want to hear from you. I want to know how you understand this issue.' [Then,] we can go farther, faster."

Managing "Up"

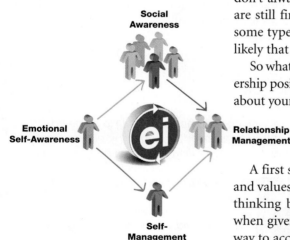

Social
Awareness

Emotional
Self-Awareness

Relationship
Management

Self-
Management

Despite the fact that organizations are becoming flatter, and that traditional hierarchies don't always meet organizations' or their environments' needs, traditional structures are still firmly in place in most organizations. Most organizations in the world have some type of hierarchy, and most people who work in organizations have a boss. It is likely that you will too.

So what can you do to effectively negotiate your relationship with those who are in leadership positions over you? For one, you can remember that your boss probably knows less about your job than you do. He or she has many responsibilities and is not intimate with the day-to-day context of your work. This is why it is important to manage up (or lead up) when and where you can.[106] As career coach Janet Bickel explains, managing up is creating a working partnership with your boss.[107]

A first step is to size up your boss—to understand him or her and to identify needs and values. This takes mindfulness and emotional intelligence as you try to uncover the thinking behind important decisions and read verbal and nonverbal cues.[108] Then, when given requests, if you understand that there is a more efficient or more effective way to accomplish your boss's goals, you can add your idea in a request for directions: "Would you like me to. . . ?"

Another way of managing up is to learn your boss's preferred style of communication and present information in the format he or she is most likely to respond favorably to. These ways of managing up also require you to look at yourself and to understand who you are through the eyes of your boss.[109] Knowing how others see you can become a strong motivation to work on changing those perceptions through modifying your own behaviors in a positive way.

1. Think about a department in your school that you "do business with" or that you belong to (the finance department or the management department, for example). Draw an organizational chart depicting the hierarchy, formal groups, and so forth. Now, draw another chart that reflects the informal organization. The person(s) at the top should be the ones that have the most information about what is really going on in the department—people who "get it" and can get things done. Discuss the implications of this chart, along with the formal chart, for your engagement with this department.

2. Think about a boss you have or have had. Create a plan for "managing up" that would improve your relationship.

11. A Final Word on Organizational Structure

Learning about organizational structure while you are still in school might seem like preparing for a race that you will run in 10 years. Hopefully this chapter has shown you otherwise. First, as we have mentioned many times in this book, our organizations are changing in response to the many economic, social, and technological changes that are occurring. This means that organizational structures will need to change, too. If you can be one of the "thinkers," one of the people who imagine new and better ways to organize ourselves to work in this new age, you will be way ahead of the game. The world's businesses, institutions, and even governments need people like you, who have learned about the many traditional concepts related to organizational design but are creative and can create new and better ways to coordinate people, processes, products, and services.

Key Terms

1.   Why Study Organizational Structure?
(p. 294)

Key Terms None

---

2.   How Do Traditional Concepts Affect Our Views about Organizational Structure Today?
(pp. 294–299)

Key Terms

Organization A group of people assembled to perform activities that will allow the entity to accomplish a set of strategic and tactical goals and to realize its mission. p. 294

Organizational structure The way in which the division of labor, communication, and movement of resources among the parts of an organization are coordinated to accomplish tasks and goals. p. 294

Organization design The process of creating an organizational structure. p. 295

Hierarchy A way of organizing people and groups according to formal authority. p. 295

Authority The legitimate right of a person in a particular job to make certain decisions, allocate resources, and direct certain other people's activities. p. 296

Responsibility The obligation to satisfactorily accomplish the tasks associated with a job. p. 297

Accountability An individual's willingness to report job success or failure regarding expected job outcomes to his or her manager or other superiors in the chain of command. p. 297

Span of control The number of jobs that report to a position at the next higher level in a hierarchy. p. 297

Span of leadership The number of jobs reporting to a person who is responsible for influencing, inspiring, and developing the people who hold those jobs. p. 297

Centralized decision making Structural model in which the vast majority of decision-making power is concentrated, typically among those at the top of the organizational hierarchy. p. 298

Decentralized decision making Structural model in which decision-making power is distributed among the people closest to the relevant information, those who will be affected by the decision, or those who will have to implement the decision. p. 298

3. What Is an Organizational Chart? (pp. 299–301)

Key Terms

Organizational chart A visual representation of how roles, jobs, authority, and responsibility are distributed within an organization. p. 299

4. How Can We "See" Organizations and Their Structures in Nontraditional Ways? (pp. 301–308)

Key Terms

Open systems theory A theory stating that any human system, such as an organization, is constantly influenced by and is influencing its environment. p. 301

Mechanistic organization An organization characterized by routine job functions, a high degree of specialization, and division of labor. p. 304

Division of labor The process of reducing work to the smallest, simplest, and most easily repeated tasks possible. p. 304

Standard operating procedures (SOPs) Detailed and specific instructions for carrying out routine tasks. p. 304

Organic organization An organization characterized by a high degree of flexibility, low levels of specialization, less formality, and decentralized decision-making processes. p. 304

Adaptive organization An organization that is very flexible and readily responds to feedback—to internal and external changes in conditions and the overall environment. p. 304

5. How Are Organizations Classified and Legally Structured? (pp. 308–315)

Key Terms

Sole proprietorship An ownership model in which a single individual owns a business. p. 310

Partnership An ownership model in which two or more individuals share the ownership of a business. p. 311

Corporation An organization that is legally recognized as a unique entity, pays taxes, and can be sued, and that does not have the personal liability issues of sole proprietorships and partnerships. p. 311

S corporation A type of corporation that has 100 or fewer shareholders and does not pay federal income taxes. p. 312

LLC A hybrid form of ownership that provides limited personal liability to the owners of a business. p. 312

Cooperative contracts Friendly business agreements that result from equity joint ventures, which are also known as equity alliances. p. 312

Licensing agreement A business agreement in which the owner of trademarked material authorizes an individual or company to use that material to sell or market products or services in exchange for a fee. p. 313

Franchise An agreement in which the owner of a business grants an individual or group of individuals the right to sell or market products or services under that business name in exchange for a fee. p. 313

Wholly owned affiliate or subsidiary A company whose stock is completely owned by a second company, referred to as a parent or holding company. p. 314

Strategic alliances Agreements between two or more parties to work together to achieve a common goal. p. 314

6. What Are Common Contemporary Organizational Structures? (pp. 315–323)

Key Terms

Cross-functional teams Teams that consist of individuals from many parts of an organization who are brought together to provide different points of view and skills in the service of organization-wide challenges and opportunities, innovations, and special projects. p. 317

Departmentalization The process by which individuals or activities are grouped together into departments according to function, geography, product, process, or customer, as well as how the departments are coordinated and how they fit within the larger organization. p. 318

Functional departmentalization Method of grouping jobs based on the nature of the work being performed. p. 319

Product departmentalization A method of grouping jobs based on the products made or services offered. p. 319

Process departmentalization A method of grouping jobs based on the sequential steps of the work people do to produce products or services or engage in other business activities. p. 319

Customer departmentalization A method of grouping jobs based on the needs of customers, consumers, or clients. p. 320

Geographic departmentalization A method of grouping jobs based on their physical location. p. 320

Matrix A structure in which departments within an organization are linked directly to one unit in the vertical organization and to another unit in the horizontal organization. p. 320

Hybrid structure A structure that incorporates more than one type of structure in the overall organization. p. 321

7. How Is Work Structured?   (pp. 323–325)

Key Terms

Job A group of tasks and responsibilities related to accomplishing organizational objectives. p. 324

8. What Factors Affect the Design of Organizational Structures?   (pp. 325–328)

Key Terms

Environmental uncertainty A situation in which market conditions are changing rapidly or are unclear. p. 326

9. What Is HR's Role in Organizational Design and Structure?   (pp. 329–330)

Key Terms

Job analysis The systematic process of gathering and analyzing information about jobs and the knowledge, skills, and competencies needed to perform these jobs. p. 329

Job description A written document that lists the major tasks and responsibilities of a particular job. p. 329

Job specification A written document that lists all of the necessary knowledge, skills, and abilities that a person must possess in order to perform a particular job. p. 329

Benchmark job A job that is representative of other jobs that are similar in nature. p. 330

10. What Can We All Do to Work Effectively within Our Organizations' Structures? (pp. 330–333)

Key Terms None

11. A Final Word on Organizational Structure (p. 333)

Key Terms None

Chapter 9 Visual Summary

1.   Why Study Organizational Structure?   (p. 294)

Summary: Even if you are a very effective employee and leader, the structure of an organization has a major impact on your success because it affects the way you behave and think about work. It also dictates the efficiency and agility of your organization. Understanding who does what, how people and groups interact, and how jobs are designed in your organization are key to helping you do your best in your role as an employee, a manager, or a leader.

2.   How Do Traditional Concepts Affect Our Views about Organizational Structure Today?   (pp. 294–299)

Summary: Organizational structure is the way in which labor, communication, and resources are coordinated in order to accomplish organizational goals. Structure helps simplify the complexities inherent in most organizations. Traditionally, hierarchy has been an important component of structure because it outlines the relationships among managers and employees and the authority, responsibility, and accountability afforded to each. Span of control is closely related to hierarchy; it refers to the number of jobs that report to a specific job in the next higher level in the hierarchy. Finally, the degree of centralization of decision making impacts the speed with which organizational decisions are made and the quality of those decisions.

3.   What Is an Organizational Chart?   (pp. 299–301)

Summary: An organizational chart is the visual representation of the way in which roles, jobs, authority, and responsibility are distributed within an organization. It helps us to see certain aspects of structure. It is not, however, a complete representation of an organization's structure because roles, reporting relationships, and authority are just a few of many aspects of structure. Formal and informal communication, power relationships, and physical proximity all impact these interactions but are not accounted for in the organizational chart.

8. Workplace Essentials: Creativity, Innovation, and a Spirit of Entrepreneurship

7. Change: A Focus on Adaptability and Resiliency

9. Organizing for a Complex World: Structure and Design

Planning and Change

6. The Human Side of Planning: Decision Making and Critical Thinking

5. Planning and Strategy: Bringing the Vision to Life

4.   How Can We "See" Organizations and Their Structures in Nontraditional Ways?   (pp. 301–308)

Summary: Open systems theory is another way of viewing organizations. This theory states that an organization is constantly influenced by and is influencing its environment. Organizations can also be described as mechanistic or organic. These terms refer to the degree of flexibility, specialization, formality, and centralized/decentralized decision making within an organization. Metaphors allow us to imagine how an organization functions as if it were a machine, an organization, or a brain, for example. The spiders and starfish metaphors present the spider as a hierarchical organization reliant on centralized decision making and the starfish as a flat organization that is decentralized.

5.   How Are Organizations Classified and Legally Structured?   (pp. 308–315)

Summary: Organizations can be classified by size, industry, and location, and most organizations can be classified in multiple ways. From a legal and taxation standpoint, the form of ownership a business has is important because it dictates the restrictions and licensing for the business and its income structure, tax, and reporting procedures. These forms are familiar to most of us and include sole proprietorships, partnerships, corporations, and LLCs. Less familiar and more complex relationships also exist between businesses that coordinate efforts to expand their markets and product lines through cooperative contracts, licensing or franchising agreements, wholly owned affiliates, and strategic alliances.

9. What Is HR's Role in Organizational Design and Structure? (pp. 329–330)

Summary: HR is responsible for many macro and micro aspects of organizational design, including assessing the environment and job analysis. Job analysis is particularly important because it enables the organization to understand job specifications and requirements. A rigorous analysis of jobs can result in a better fit between people and jobs.

8. What Factors Affect the Design of Organizational Structures? (pp. 325–328)

Summary: Although it is commonly held that structure should follow strategy, it is more accurate to say that the two have a symbiotic relationship. The external environment exerts a strong influence over organizational design, often necessitating rapid changes in order for a business to adapt to changing conditions. Technology, company size, and geography also impact the way an organization is designed. Surprisingly, adequate attention is not always given to organizational design, resulting in structures that "emerge" which can be both ineffective and inefficient.

7. How Is Work Structured? (pp. 323–325)

Summary: Work is structured around jobs and tasks. Tasks are the individual activities that, when taken together, form a job. A job, then, is a grouping of tasks that enable an individual to accomplish an objective. Some jobs are specialized, allowing for a high degree of division of labor. These jobs may involve very few tasks, which may be repeated over and over. Other jobs are broader and require people to engage in many and diverse tasks.

6. What Are Common Contemporary Organizational Structures? (pp. 315–323)

Summary: Contemporary organizations are becoming flatter as cost-cutting measures lead companies to turn away from traditional tall hierarchies. A common structure called departmentalization is often used to group jobs by job functions, products, processes, consumers, or geography. Some organizations utilize a matrix structure that links the vertical and horizontal structures in an organization. Other organizations have turned to hybrid structures that combine two or more types of structures. Still others utilize a networked structure, approaching the organization as a social network.

10. What Can We All Do to Work Effectively within Our Organizations' Structures? (pp. 330–333)

Summary: Learning to work effectively within the informal structure of your organization helps you be more effective at work. It is also important that you learn to work effectively with, or "manage," your boss. Being able to identify his or her needs, preferred communication style, and opinions of you will allow you to be more effective and efficient.

11. A Final Word on Organizational Structure (p. 333)

Summary: Organizations change as the world changes economically, socially, and technologically. As a result, organizational structures also need to change. Understanding traditional organizational structures is a first step in developing the skills to creatively improve them.

Teams and Team Building:

How to Work Effectively with **Others**

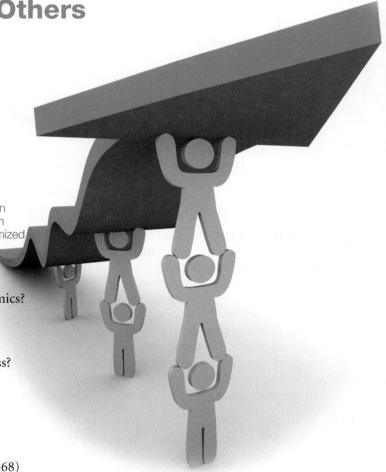

Chapter Outline

Find out what you already know about the concepts in this chapter by going to www.mymanagementlab.com and taking the **Pre-Test.** Your results will generate a customized study plan for Chapter 10.

1. Why Do Leaders Need Teams? (pp. 340–342)

2. How Does Leadership Behavior Affect Group Dynamics? (pp. 342–343)

3. How Do Groups Change over Time? (pp. 344–348)

4. How Do Group Dynamics Impact Team Effectiveness? (pp. 349–359)

5. How Do Teams Function at Work? (pp. 359–362)

6. How Can We Deal with the Challenges of Working in Groups? (pp. 362–366)

7. What Role Does Conflict Play in Groups? (pp. 366–368)

8. How Can HR Support Effective Team Performance? (pp. 369–370)

9. What Can We All Do to Create and Sustain Resonant Teams? (pp. 370–373)

10. A Final Word on Teams and Team Building (pp. 373–374)

Go back to www.mymanagementlab.com and take the **Post-Test** to verify your understanding of the concepts. **To experience and apply** the concepts, explore the additional material associated with Chapter 10.

Part 1: Leading and Managing for Today and the Future (Chapters 1, 2, 3, 4)
Part 2: Planning and Change (Chapters 5, 6, 7, 8, 9)
➤ **Part 3:** Organizing Human Systems (Chapters **10**, 11)
Part 4: Controlling Quality, Culture, and Yourself (Chapters 12, 13)
Part 5: Leading and Managing for the Future (Chapters 14, 15, 16)

8. Workplace Essentials: Creativity, Innovation, and a Spirit of Entrepreneurship

7. Change: A Focus on Adaptability and Resiliency

9. Organizing for a Complex World: Structure and Design

Planning and Change

6. The Human Side of Planning: Decision Making and Critical Thinking

5. Planning and Strategy: Bringing the Vision to Life

16. Managing and Leading for Tomorrow: A Focus on Your Future

Organizing Human Systems

10. Teams and Teambuilding: How to Work Effectively with Others

11. Working in a Virtual World: Technology as a Way of Life

14. Globalization: Managing Effectively in a Global Economic Environment

1. Managing and Leading Today: The New Rules

Leading and Managing for Today and the Future

2. The Leadership Imperative: It's Up to You

4. Communication: The Key to Resonant Relationships

3. Motivation and Meaning: What Makes People Want to Work?

15. Sustainability and Corporate Social Responsibility: Ensuring the Future

12. Organizational Controls: People, Processes, Quality, and Results

Controlling Quality, Culture, and Yourself

13. Culture: It's Powerful

10. Teams and Teambuilding: How to Work Effectively with Others

1. Why Do Leaders Need Teams?

Working in groups comes naturally to us. We are wired to empathize with one another, align around a shared purpose, and collaborate to achieve common goals. Working in groups is natural and it's also necessary. Rarely, if ever, can one individual succeed without others' input, help, and support. Working in groups enables us to have impact beyond our solitary reach. People need other people, and we need effective teams as well.

Good leaders understand that success and effectiveness are linked to creating conditions where individuals *and* teams can be at their very best. Philadelphia's Police Commissioner Charles Ramsey is one such leader. Compelling and inspiring, Chief Ramsey truly understands that great leadership is 100 percent about empowering others.

Charles H. Ramsey   **Business** Case

Philadelphia Police Commissioner Charles H. Ramsey on Leadership

Commissioner Charles H. Ramsey of the Philadelphia Police Department grew up in Chicago at a time when becoming a police officer was hardly the thing to do. As a child, Chuck (as he was called then) never imagined joining the police force, even for a minute. Then, after high school, he started on a pre-med course, working his way through college. Along the way, he got to know a couple of police officers who often came to the store where he worked. These officers were friendly and interesting, and when one of them asked Chuck whether he had ever thought about becoming a cadet, the young man gave the question some serious thought. When Chuck learned that Chicago had a tuition reimbursement program for police cadets, his decision was made.

Ramsey joined the Chicago Police Department in 1968. He loved his job. He was helping people and making a difference in the city he cared so much about. He was working with great people on great teams, and he could see a future that made *sense* for him. This vision crystallized one cold night when Officer Ramsey and a few others were dealing with a homicide. In those days, old-timers were assigned to ambulance detail. While watching the veteran officers, Ramsey had a blinding insight: If his life continued on the path he was on, that would be *him* in thirty years, struggling to carry a body down icy stairs. The very next day, Ramsey signed up for the sergeant exam.

Ramsey passed, of course, and this marked the beginning of a fulfilling journey packed with great experiences, tough situations, and fascinating people. Although Ramsey started out with the right stuff, it was along the way that he *learned* to be a great leader. These leadership abilities didn't go unnoticed, and when the call eventually came for Ramsey to interview for the top police job in Washington, D.C., he was ready for the challenge. And what a challenge! Washington had been suffering for years under poor leadership and a host of social and economic problems, and the city's police force had been beaten down, battered, criticized,

Commissioner Charles H. Ramsey

and disrespected. As the newly appointed chief of police, Ramsey certainly had his work cut out for him.

Person by person and group by group, Chief Ramsey soon learned just what Washington had to offer—and it offered a lot. He found great people, tons of talent, and profound commitment to the city and its police force. Ramsey also learned everything he could about the strengths of the individuals on his team and on the force. Some needed just a bit more attention; some needed guidance; and some needed him to keep distractions at bay. With his team and other groups within the city, Ramsey faced up to Washington's problems. When things didn't work out as planned, he was the first to step up and say that a different direction was needed. Ramsey didn't cast shame or blame anyone; rather, he simply expressed his commitment to making things work.

And make it work they did. For example, when protesters made their way to Washington, D.C., in 2002, many people feared there would be riots, as had occurred the year before in Seattle during the World Trade Organization meetings. Ramsey and the police force had to help the city avoid this fate while maneuvering through complex political dynamics and ensuring that people could gather and speak freely, as is their constitutional right. On the whole, the force acted with restraint and respect. People were able to protest and voice their concerns, but no buildings or property were damaged and no people were harmed.

When planes toppled the World Trade Center and crashed into the Pentagon on September 11, 2001, Ramsey and his strong and renewed force were ready as well. Throughout that dark day and the weeks that followed, the force functioned like a well-oiled machine, protecting not just the citizens of Washington, D.C., but the interests of the country as a whole. In fact, over the eight years that Ramsey served in Washington, D.C., the city's crime rate dropped by 40 percent, and its force earned the reputation of being one of the best urban police forces in the country.[1] Chief Ramsey remembers the moment that he considers his best reward—when an officer walked up to him in a crowd and said, "Chief, you have given us back our pride."

Continued on next page>>

Charles H. Ramsey **Continued**

In 2008, Charles Ramsey was appointed Commissioner of the Philadelphia Police Department, where he immediately began tackling some of the most difficult social and economic issues ever faced in an urban area. The way Ramsey looks at the situation goes something like this: "*I* won't be able to 'fix' these issues in Philadelphia, but *we will.* When the community—all of us—pull together and say, 'No more crime; we want our city to be better than it is now,' that's when change will happen."

Later in the chapter, we'll hear more from Commissioner Ramsey. For now, let's start studying groups by considering some of Ramsey's words of wisdom:

It's great to talk about individual leaders as if they do it all. But that's not what it's all about. Success is about a group of people coming together to do something. If you can be the person to draw people together, that's great. And if you can be part of the group that does something fantastic together, that's great too.[2]

Groups and Teams: Where We Learn, Live, and Work

As Commissioner Ramsey knows, much of what happens at work is done in groups and teams. Generally, a small group is defined as any structure that includes three to approximately 15 people. In comparison, a **team** consists of a small group (ideally 6 to 10 individuals) whose members share a common purpose, hold themselves individually and collectively responsible for goals, and have complementary skills and agreed-on processes for working together.[3] In this chapter, we will use both the word *group* and the word *team*, because the chapter is about *groups at work*, which are usually called teams.

Within organizations, teams can be structured in many different ways. Some teams always meet in person, whereas others interact virtually. Some teams have formal leaders; others do not. Some teams stay together for a very long time, whereas others are formed for specific purposes and then are disbanded when the job is done. Some teams stay in place even when all of their members change. For example, a senior team in an organization will still exist after one CEO resigns and another takes over. The team will also continue to exist even if the new CEO hires new people and lets the "old" members go. In this example, the team members will have changed, and perhaps individual members' roles will be somewhat different, but the governance structure called the senior team still exists.

We need to learn about teams because they are the structures within which most of an organization's work is accomplished. We also study teams because they provide a "home" for us at work: Belonging to a team provides us with a sense of personal identity, and contributing to a team enables us to fulfill our desire to achieve important goals that we could not achieve alone. Groups and teams are the places in which our most important social interactions occur at work. We laugh and learn in our work groups. We build solid collegial relationships and even friendships in our groups at work. We fight and learn how to deal with conflict in groups, and it is in groups and teams that we learn how to respect people who are different from us.

Groups Are Mysterious

Have you ever wondered about the feelings and behaviors that swirled around you as you worked in a group? Have you ever considered why some groups are great at getting things done while others struggle? Have you thought about why you feel motivated to work harder in some groups than in others? Groups are complex and mysterious. That's partly because people are complicated, and it's also partly because you can't always see what is going on between and among people in a group. For instance, you can't really see how people's emotions and moods impact one another, or how people feel when they are included, excluded, looked up to, or ignored in a group. You can't see people's psychological reactions to power—their own or others'—and you can't see the inner satisfaction or struggles people experience when their ideas are accepted or

Team
A small group (ideally 6 to 10 individuals) whose members share a common purpose, hold themselves individually and collectively responsible for goals, and have complementary skills and agreed-on processes for working together.

rejected by a group. You can only see individual behaviors and the collective decisions and actions that are agreed to and implemented.

This chapter is dedicated to helping you demystify what happens in groups and teams and to giving you another lens through which to view leadership and human behavior at work. There are several streams of knowledge and skills that can help you and the groups you belong to become more effective. We will begin by exploring early studies of the impact of leadership behavior on group dynamics, followed by interesting research about how groups develop over time. After that, we will focus on key aspects of group dynamics, including roles, norms, status, power, and diversity. Once you have a solid grounding in how groups develop and function, we will study work teams, paying special attention to various factors that enable high performance. We will discuss the challenges involved in working in groups, as well as the benefits and drawbacks of the conflict that inevitably arises in group settings. Finally, we'll conclude the chapter with a look at how HR can support effective teamwork in organizations and what we can all do to be more effective group members and team leaders.

Most Popular » Discussion Questions

1. Think about the best and worst groups you have ever led or been a part of. For each group, describe the members, the group's purpose, and what the group achieved. In your opinion, why was one group "best" and one "worst"?
2. Success is rarely, if ever, dependent on one person, no matter how good a leader that individual is. Do you agree with this idea? Why or why not? Support your response using examples from your own experience.

---

2. How Does Leadership Behavior Affect Group Dynamics?

■ Exhibit **10.1**

Psychologist Kurt Lewin's experience in Nazi Germany fueled his curiosity about how people behave in groups.

INTERFOTO/Alamy/Personalities

Scholar Kurt Lewin set the stage for a great deal of research about people in work settings, including how people behave in groups. The time Lewin spent in Nazi Germany left him with an enduring interest in the positive and negative influence of groups (■ Exhibit 10.1).

At the time when much of the early research on groups was conducted, most studies of human behavior focused solely on individuals—personality, intelligence, capability, and other personal characteristics. Lewin turned the nature of inquiry into human behavior upside down by moving away from this singular focus on individual characteristics and instead focusing on the group environment as a primary factor in determining what people think, feel, and do. He proposed an intriguing formula that you can see in ■ Exhibit 10.2. In this formula, *behavior* (B) is a *function* (f) of the interaction of the *person* (P) and the *environment* (E).[4]

This formula points out that how a person behaves is linked to both personal characteristics (intelligence, social and emotional intelligence, personality, etc.) and the conditions of the environment. The conditions of a group's environment can include any number of factors, such as a group leader's behavior, the physical conditions in which the group works, the society and organization in which the group operates, pressures on the group from outside, and so on.

Lewin and his colleagues created an experiment to test the effects of different styles of leadership on small groups.[5] Their subjects were young boys working on projects in voluntary teams. Each team was randomly assigned an adult leader who demonstrated one of three styles of leadership: autocratic, democratic, or laissez-

■Exhibit **10.2**

Lewin's Formula

$$B = f(P, E)$$

Autocratic leader

A leader who tends to make decisions without input from others.

Democratic leader

A leader who seeks input and then either makes a decision or engages the group in collective decision making.

Laissez-faire leader

A leader who remains at a distance from the decision-making process, allowing the group to make decisions without leadership intervention.

faire. An **autocratic leader** tends to make decisions without input from others, whereas a **democratic leader** will seek input and then either make a decision or engage the group in collective decision making. A **laissez-faire leader** remains at a distance from the decision-making process, allowing the group to make decisions without leadership intervention.

In this study, the groups were observed as they worked, and their productivity and aggression were analyzed. The researchers found that the autocratic group spent more time "working" than the democratic group, which was, in turn, more productive than the laissez-faire group. Hostility and aggression were highest within the autocratic group. Frequently, the boys in the autocratic group destroyed their work after the work session ended.[6] These findings began a long tradition of research that showed that autocratic leadership has negative consequences over the long term, whereas involving people in a democratic manner increases commitment to both the task and the leader.[7]

For example, one recent study found that group members were less willing to work hard in groups where leaders took an autocratic approach.[8] Another interesting study of people on juries found that jurors' satisfaction with a verdict was in part dependent on how their fellow jurors treated them and listened to them. This supports the idea that a democratic approach to making decisions in groups results in a higher level of satisfaction with the outcomes of a group's work.[9]

In a follow-up to the findings about laissez-faire leadership, research has noted that the style is a "common, but unrealistic and immature" way to manage teams.[10] This is an important point because many people adopt a passive approach to team leadership, thinking they are empowering team members. Unfortunately, delegation of authority to team members is often more about avoiding responsibility than about empowerment. In these cases, productivity, relationships, and innovation tend to suffer.[11]

Good leaders don't take a hands-off approach with their teams, even when team members are empowered to make decisions and do their jobs. It takes effort and action to lead teams and to create an atmosphere where people can give their best.

Over the years, thousands of studies of groups and teams have been conducted in laboratories and in real-world settings (the field), resulting in a wealth of knowledge about what tends to happen in small groups and teams. Many of these studies focused on leadership and leader–member relationships. Other studies focused on how and why groups included or excluded people, how patterns of behavior developed, and how conflict emerged and was dealt with in groups. Some studies also looked at how and why groups changed over time.

The 1980s and 1990s saw an increase in interest and research about group development and group dynamics within many disciplines, including political theory, family systems theory, communication, and organizational development. Today, emerging research on the impact of neuropsychology, emotions, and social networking is adding depth and richness to the research of the previous century. In the next several sections, we will look at how this research can help us understand group development, group dynamics, and how to lead and manage teams today.

Most Popular » Discussion Questions

1. Make a list that includes every group and team you belong to. Choose two of the most important and describe the environmental "conditions" of those groups and teams that affect your behavior and the group's effectiveness.

2. Have you ever been part of a group that was led by an autocratic leader? How did you react to this person? What was the impact on your group's performance?

3. Why do you think people often adopt a laissez-faire approach to leading groups?

3. How Do Groups Change over Time?

Think about a group you have been a member of from the beginning—maybe an athletic team for an entire season or a study group during a whole semester. Did the way in which group members interact change over time? If your group was like most, the way people interacted in the beginning was very different from later on, the way conflict was dealt with changed, and probably the group's effectiveness improved over time.

Beginning with landmark research by scholars Warren Bennis and Herb Shepard about how groups deal with authority, structure, intimacy, and interdependence, a long tradition of research has studied how groups develop over time and how member and leader behavior can be predicted based on a group's stage of development.[12] In this section, we will look at two models of group development devised by researchers Bruce Tuckman and Susan Wheelan.

Bruce Tuckman's model of group development
A model of group development that includes five sequential stages: forming, storming, norming, performing, and adjourning.

Forming
The first stage of group development, during which members start to get to know one another, are polite and friendly, avoid conflict, and seek common ground.

Storming
The second stage of group development, which is characterized by disagreements about how to work together, bids for power, and conflict with leaders.

Norming
The third stage of group development, when the group agrees on common "rules" of behavior for members (group norms), who does what (group roles), and how best to work together.

Group norms
Informal but powerful standards that guide group members' behavior.

Group roles
Shared expectations among members about who does what.

Performing
The fourth stage of group development, during which the group channels energy into tasks rather than into building relationships, resolving conflicts, or deciding how to work together.

Bruce Tuckman's Model of Group Development

In the mid-1960s, researcher Bruce Tuckman synthesized the results of numerous studies and created a model of group development that includes five sequential stages: forming, storming, norming, performing, and adjourning.[13] He and colleague Mary Ann Jensen later added a fifth stage, adjourning.[14] This model suggests that groups mature over time and that during each stage, there are specific ways in which people deal with interpersonal relationships and task behaviors.

Stage 1: Forming

Forming is the first stage of group development, in which members start to get to know one another, are polite and friendly, and avoid conflict. During this stage, people work to *build* a group, and they avoid any topics or interactions that might harm relationships or the development of common ground.

Stage 2: Storming

Storming is the second stage of group development. It is characterized by disagreements about how to work together, bids for power, and conflict with leaders. In this stage, people are more apt to speak up, disagree, and attempt to influence others and the group. It is not uncommon for group members to fight openly with one another and with the leader.

Stage 3: Norming

Norming is the third stage of group development, when the group agrees on common "rules" of behavior for members (**group norms**), who does what (**group roles**), and how best to work together. Group norms are informal but powerful standards that guide group members' behavior. For example, many work groups will establish norms about timeliness, adhering to deadlines, and how people should treat one another.

Group roles are shared expectations among members about who does what. For example, during the norming stage, people might discuss and agree that going forward, a particular member will take on the role of meeting agenda planner, while another will take the role of note taker.

Stage 4: Performing

Performing is the fourth stage of group development, during which the group channels energy into tasks rather than into building relationships, resolving conflicts, or deciding how to work together. Interpersonal relationships now support the group in accomplishing tasks, and roles are more fluid (e.g., anyone can step into the leadership role as the task requires).

Stage 5: Adjourning

Adjourning
The fifth stage of group development during which the group finishes its tasks and decides or is forced to dissolve membership.

Adjourning is the stage during which the group finishes its tasks and decides or is forced to dissolve membership. This stage can cause people to feel sad and to try to hold on to the group even though it no longer serves a purpose. Sometimes at work, groups actually do stay together after their tasks are completed. This can be a source of confusion, contention, and wasted resources. One important group skill, then, is to know when to let go.

Tuckman's model of group development became popular over the years, partly because it is so simple. On the other hand, the model's simplicity has been criticized. In recent years, scholars such as Susan Wheelan have attempted to look at group development in more depth.

Susan Wheelan's Integrated Model of Group Development

Susan Wheelan's integrated model of group development
A model of group development that shows how groups progress through four stages as members gain experience communicating and working together; a fifth stage, termination, can also be included in this model.

By the 1990s, more powerful computers allowed for more sophisticated analyses of people's behavior in groups and how groups develop. Based on such research, Susan Wheelan proposed an integrated model of group development that is similar to other models in that it is linear and outlines the stages through which groups progress.[15] What is different about this model is that Wheelan believes that time is not the only factor that influences group development. She proposes that groups develop and progress through four stages as members gain experience communicating and working together. A fifth stage, termination, can also be included in the model. Like other models of group development, Wheelan's model associates certain kinds of behavior with each stage of group development, as you can see in ■Exhibit 10.3.

Stage 1: Dependency and Inclusion

In the first stage of group development, members are dependent on the leader to tell them what to do.[16] If there is no leader, then a powerful member is needed. Somebody needs to take charge. Members are concerned about emotional safety and issues of inclusion: "How do I fit in?" "Is it safe here?"

In work teams, the dependency and inclusion stage can be awkward because no one knows exactly how to behave or what to do, even if the task is clear. This stage can be frustrating because there is an expectation from team members and managers alike that the team will be productive immediately, which is very hard to do. People usually can't focus their energy on tasks and goals because of the uncertainty surrounding norms and roles. Oftentimes we make the mistake of ignoring the real needs people have during this stage, such as the need to "find their place" on the team, to feel included, and to feel accepted for who they are and the contributions they can bring.

On the other hand, Stage 1 can be exhilarating at first because it seems that everyone gets along, and with direction from a member or leader, things go well for a while. It's fine to enjoy this part of Stage 1, but don't let it fool you. Things almost always change in Stage 2.

Stage 2: Conflict and Counterdependence

Counterdependence
Attitudes and behaviors related to resisting leadership or direction from others.

The group's task during Stage 2 is to develop a unified set of goals, values, and operational procedures. These negotiations inevitably generate conflict. Many times, this conflict is directed at the leader and/or powerful group members, which is a dynamic that is called counterdependence. **Counterdependence** refers to attitudes and behaviors related to resisting leadership or direction from others.[17]

During the conflict and counterdependence stage people argue, form power coalitions with other members to get "their" plan implemented, or even sabotage the leader

■ Exhibit **10.3**

Susan Wheelan's Stages of Group Development

	Stage 1: Dependency and Inclusion	Stage 2: Conflict and Counterdependence	Stage 3: Trust and Structure	Stage 4: Productivity and Work
Role of leader	Allays fears and anxieties. Promotes feelings of safety and competence. Provides direction and confidence. Offers positive feedback. Openly discusses goals, values, and work tasks. Provides supervision and training. Sets work standards and offers guidance. Manages the external environment.	Slowly promotes empowerment to those who seek it. Doesn't respond personally to criticism or challenge. Promotes open discussion to resolve conflicts about values, goals, and leadership.	Supports member involvement in leadership. Encourages the group to review and make changes to group structure if it helps productivity.	Becomes more participatory as an expert team member. Monitors team for signs of loss of cohesion. Conducts regular reviews. Models effective team membership.
Conflict	Members seek security and acceptance from the group and usually do not openly disagree with the leader.	Conflict emerges around group values, goals, and tasks. Dissent is possible because of members' increased feelings of security.	Conflict continues but is managed more effectively. A consensus regarding group goals emerges.	Periods of conflict may be frequent but brief.
Norms	Deviation from emerging norms is rare for members, who seek structure.	Deviation from group norms may begin to occur.	Reorganization of roles and tasks happens in response to evolving team needs. Helpful deviation from group norms is tolerated.	Group norms encourage high performance and quality work. Team members collectively determine participatory decision-making structure.
Communication	Members may be hesitant to speak up. Many important communications come from or are filtered through the leader.	Increased trust and cohesion become possible because communication is less restricted.	Communication becomes more flexible and content becomes more task oriented.	The team spends more time defining, discussing, and planning for the problems it will address.

Source: Adapted from Wheelan, Susan A. 2010. *Creating effective teams: A guide for members and leaders.* Thousand Oaks, CA: Sage.

or other powerful group members. This can be a nasty and unproductive period, especially when conflict becomes personalized or has nothing to do with helping the group learn how to work together or achieve its goals. In these situations, groups often get "stuck" or blow up.

Conflict in groups, however, is a healthy process because it is necessary to establish a climate in which members feel free to disagree. Having individuals who are willing to disagree is great insurance against thoughtless conformity. In order for conflict to be dealt with in a constructive manner, both members and the group leader need to be clear about and committed to the group's purpose.

As the group "survives" conflicts, people begin to feel safer and more willing to share different viewpoints. As members try out their independence and differentiate from one another, they gain confidence and are more willing to take on roles and responsibilities. There is more positive relational and emotional engagement among members and more commitment to the group as a whole. What emerges from this process is a broader range of ways to negotiate differences, make decisions, communicate, and lead.

Stage 3: Trust and Structure

If the group emerges from Stage 2, it is ready to enter Stage 3, the trust and structure stage. In this stage, norms and roles are more clear, and the group is not as dependent on a leader. Members welcome guidance from formal leaders, and they are more open to being led by other members as well. Members understand that structures such as roles and decision processes are helpful, and they use them. They also adjust group norms and roles if needed, rather than hold on rigidly to "the way it is" as sometimes happens in earlier stages. People trust each other more and can more maturely negotiate roles and stay organized, allowing the group to maintain positive working relationships.

In the trust and structure stage, people often feel a sense of relief. They know where they fit and how people relate to one another, and they feel confident that the group can handle conflict without falling apart. People don't take things as personally as they did in the first two stages, because they trust that other members' intentions are good.

Stage 4: Productivity and Work

Having resolved many of the issues of the previous stages, a group in Stage 4 can efficiently and effectively focus most of its energy on goal achievement and task accomplishment. During this productivity and work stage, group members feel clear, committed, and capable of navigating conflicts, and they are able to give and receive both individual and group-level performance feedback.

Stage 5: Termination

Wheelan's model speaks to the termination stage of a group's life as a time when members reflect on task accomplishment and relational memories. Sometimes when a group stays together for a long time, "eras" of the group's life can be tracked by paying attention to what members become nostalgic about.

Group Development: A Useful but Limited Way to Explain What Happens in Groups

Models of group development are useful in that they help members and leaders understand some of what occurs at different times in a group's life. Group development models do not, however, tell the whole story. For one thing, most group development research focused on groups that worked together in person in the laboratory or the field. Today, however, many work groups rarely see one another. They rely on electronic communication and meet more often in subgroups than as a whole. (Virtual teams are discussed in more depth in Chapter 11.) It is not clear whether the same developmental progression occurs in such groups.

Second, developmental models are difficult to apply in a fast-paced organizational environment in which projects and teams change all the time. Third, group development models do not take into account the fact that, in many cases, teams are responsible for significant joint outcomes yet members spend little time working *together*—in such situations, work looks more like a series of hand-offs than a collective effort. Let's look at four possible practical considerations when applying models of group development to teams in organizations today:

- Stages of group development are not as discrete as the models we've studied suggest.[18] Depending on factors such as members' personalities and communication styles, culture, group tasks, and pressure from the outside, groups must deal with issues such as dependency, conflict, and coalitions throughout the life of the group. Sophisticated group members can differentiate stage-related behavior from behavior that is caused by other forces.
- Groups cycle through the developmental processes over and over, engaging with each stage in a different manner depending on why they need to revisit it. For example, at work today, people join and leave groups regularly, and if a new member joins, technically the group is new. When this happens, group members may revert to a stage-one level of dependency, but they can cycle through it very quickly by bringing the new member up to speed on norms, roles, and so forth. Similarly, if a new leader is assigned, a group could easily slip back into stage one or even stage two behavior. These transitions are very important. If you have a really effective team, you are able to flexibly adjust to changes that affect the group's stage of development so that the group does not blindly slip into old or dysfunctional patterns.
- Groups in organizations are often extremely short lived, yet they need to accomplish very sophisticated tasks. Group development models assume that tasks cannot be accomplished well and that either goals will either not be met or results will be compromised if people do not have enough time or enough experience working with each other. Practical experience in organizations today tells us otherwise. For instance, in many groups at work, it can be difficult to tell where one stage ends and another begins.[19] This means that either people are learning to speed through the stages of group development, or they are adapting to new ways of building relationships more quickly and resolving conflicts more effectively even before they really know each other. The need to work this way could be linked to the growing importance of social and emotional skills in the workplace today.

Group development models will continue to be studied, and it is likely that new research will inform how these models can better support groups today. A number of other factors also affect our behavior in groups, such as what roles we play, the expectations we have of one another, and how we manage power and status. In the next section, we will explore these group dynamics more deeply.

Most Popular » Discussion Questions

1. Think about a group that you have belonged to for a long time. What stage of development do you think this group is in? Explain your answer in terms of member–leader relationships, conflict, and communication.
2. Do you think most groups experience conflict in Stage 2? Explain your answer with an experience you have had in a group.
3. Choose a group that you have been part of, or were part of, from the beginning until completion of a project or assignment. Using Wheelan's model and Exhibit 10.3, try to identify events and group member behaviors that support this developmental model. Does this model describe what happened in your group?

4. How Do Group Dynamics Impact Team Effectiveness?

In this section, we will explore four aspects of group dynamics that affect people's behavior and group effectiveness: roles, norms, status and power, and diversity. We will then conclude the section by considering the paradoxes we need to resolve in ourselves and with others in order for our groups to function well.

Group Roles

A role in a group includes expectations about who does what and how they do it, as well as who is responsible for what. Roles can be formal and assigned (e.g., official leader, project manager) or informal (e.g., meeting organizer, snack-bringer) (■Exhibit 10.4). Roles help members because they define responsibilities.

Roles support effectiveness because they help ensure that the group can attend to its tasks and goals; roles also support individual members and the relationships among members. Early group theorists pointed out that, in fact, roles can be associated with *task functions* and *group maintenance functions*.[20] They pointed out that the roles that

■Exhibit **10.4**

Roles can be informal, such as the role of the person who brings donuts to the morning meeting, or they can be formal, such as the role of president of a company.

Top: Daniel Ehrenworth/First Light/Alamy
Bottom: Alex Segre/Alamy Images

accompany these functions are important and deserving of effort and energy on the part of members and leaders.[21]

People who take on task roles engage in behaviors and activities that help the group accomplish tasks and achieve goals. Examples of task roles include:[22]

- Information provider: One who offers facts and research.
- Diagnoser: One who points out the obstacles to successful group work.
- Evaluator: One who measures the accomplishments of the group against set critera.

Group maintenance roles include activities that are important to relationships and to the morale of the group, such as:[23]

- Tension reliever: One who relieves the group's stress.
- Encourager: One who asks for and encourages participation and ideas.
- Trust builder: One who inspires others to take emotional risks.

These roles are people oriented and create an atmosphere that enables each member to contribute maximally.

People often pay more attention to task roles than group maintenance roles. That may be because it is easier to focus on a task than on relationships or because there is often extreme pressure to "perform" at work and in school. Whatever the reason, ignoring roles and activities that support relationships is foolhardy. Groups fail when attention is not given to human beings.

How Roles Develop in Groups

Sometimes people choose a role in a group, such as when someone volunteers to be the person to schedule meetings. Other times, roles are assigned. For example, your instructor might ask you to lead a semester-long study group. In still other instances, a role can emerge over time—no one asks for it and no one assigns it, yet it is real. For example, after a few meetings of a study group, you may realize that you are the one that always asks the group to set deadlines. The group has come to depend on you for this service. They begin to *expect* this from you, and "deadline setter" is now your role. This might be fine if you also see yourself in this role. If, on the other hand, you set deadlines a few times to help the group but believe that others should do so as well, you may find that your group will have to deal with conflict. Conflict about group roles also emerges when members have not fully outlined the tasks associated with each role. This sort of conflict is best addressed by clearly defining the group's expectations regarding who is responsible for completing each critical task.

Roles are a powerful social force: They dictate our behavior, sometimes far more than they should. We've all encountered the person who, when given the role of group leader, becomes a tyrant. We have also all taken on roles and found ourselves acting in ways that didn't really represent who we are. This was made painfully clear in a study done at Stanford University in 1971, famously called the *Stanford prison experiment*.

Stanford Prison Experiment

The Stanford prison experiment was conducted in 1971 at Stanford University in Palo Alto, California (■Exhibit 10.5). In the experiment, volunteers from the university participated in a mock prison, where some volunteers played guards and others played prisoners. The researchers wanted to know things like "What happens when you put good peo-

■Exhibit **10.5**

The Stanford prison experiment demonstrated that roles are a powerful determinant of behavior.

Archives du 7eme Art/Photos 12/Alamy

ple in an evil place? Does humanity win over evil, or does evil triumph?"[24] Only people who were considered highly stable psychologically were chosen to participate in the experiment.

To re-create prison conditions, guards were given uniforms, wooden batons (weapons), and mirrored sunglasses to prevent eye contact with prisoners. The prisoners were given poorly fitting outfits and were called by the numbers assigned to them, which were sewn onto their prison outfits. They also wore chains around their ankles. Guards were explicitly told not to physically harm prisoners, but they were encouraged to find ways to create boredom, fear, and hopelessness.[25]

Over the course of the experiment, the participants adapted to their roles far beyond any of the researchers' expectations. Within a short period of time, guards became cruel and even sadistic. They humiliated and degraded the prisoners. At first, the prisoners revolted, but as their treatment worsened, they began to show signs of extreme emotional disturbance. The situation became so dire that the experiment had to be stopped after six days, more than a week earlier than planned. Interestingly, out of the 50 people who were familiar with the experiment, only one viewed the conditions that had developed as immoral.[26]

The Stanford prison experiment has gained considerable attention in recent years as a result of a scandal involving extreme abuse of prisoners (many of whom had not been convicted of any crime) in Abu Ghraib, a prison run by U.S. military personnel in Iraq.[27] The lesson for us is that roles *do* affect how we see ourselves and others and how we behave. It is very important, then, to be highly self-aware whenever we take on a role, especially a leadership role.

Group Norms

Remember your first day in college or your first day on the job? Chances are you paid careful attention to the behavior of the people around you to get some sense of what was expected of you. What you were searching for, even if you didn't realize it, were "norms." Group norms are informal standards for behavior that guide group members' behavior. Norms are the "way we do things" and how we expect one another to behave. Norms help us predict social interaction—they tell us what we are supposed to do and what we are not allowed to do in certain situations.

For instance, norms guide your behavior in school: You arrive on time, take a seat, and behave as if you are attentive to the lecture. Some instructors set other norms, such as "ask questions" or "participate in class discussions." Societal norms also dictate our behavior. For example, societal norms guide what sort of swimwear we wear and what we wear to bed or to a funeral. If we switched things around and wore pajamas to a funeral or a swimsuit to work, people would be offended. That's a lesson about norms: The surest way to determine whether something is a norm is to violate it—people will let you know.

Norms are a very important aspect of group dynamics. As in society, they become the informal "rule book" that guides individual behavior in groups. Group norms differ depending on things such as the society in which the group is operating, the group's purpose, members' social and cultural backgrounds, and the actual work that the group is expected to perform.

Group Norms Need to Be Explicit

Norms may be clear to all members of a group (explicit), known or sensed by only a few members (implicit), or operating completely below the level of awareness of any group members. Many groups operate primarily around implicit norms: expectations for behavior that members bring to a group based on their backgrounds and prior experiences, but which they do not discuss or agree on. Sometimes implicit norms provide enough guidance, particularly if the group members belong to the same or similar cultures, the same organization, and have worked together in the past.

■Exhibit **10.6**

Our Group Norms

1. Everyone has the responsibility to lead this group when his or her area of expertise is needed.
2. Everyone in this group is responsible for making sure we perform at our very best individually and as a group.
3. We are committed to open dialogue: Everyone *can* speak, and everyone *must.*
4. We respect one another at all times.
5. We put group needs in front of our individual needs.

Most of the time, however, implicit norms are not sufficient to support members in all necessary interactions with each other, nor do unspoken norms necessarily support group effectiveness. For that reason, it is often helpful for work groups to agree on norms when they begin to work together. Common norms that groups might agree to are listed in ■Exhibit 10.6.

Let's now look at norms related to social and emotional competencies that can support group effectiveness.

Emotional Intelligence and Group Norms

Effective groups translate social and emotional intelligence into group norms. At the beginning of the chapter, you read about Commissioner Ramsey of the Philadelphia Police Department, an outstanding leader who knows how to build great teams. Let's see what he has to say about what kind of norms we can adopt to work successfully with others in teams in the following *Perspectives* feature.

Perspectives

Police Commissioner Charles H. Ramsey, Philadelphia

Commissioner Ramsey on leadership: You need to know yourself. And you need to be true to yourself. You're not John Kennedy or General Petraeus or Barack Obama—you are first and foremost yourself. What makes you tick? You've got to do the self assessment, over and over. Take inventory. Until you do this, you're not going to get very far. You've got to know what triggers you, so you can back away or change a situation before you do something you will regret. You can't influence anyone else if you can't control yourself.

And you need to really listen to people—even people you don't like. Their criticism may not be what you want to hear, and most of it might be wrong, but I've found that *when you really listen, even to these people, you're likely to find out that one thing that you really need to know. You can learn so much just by watching others. You'll learn the good and the bad—what you want to do as a leader, and what you'll never do to people.*

And finally, learn to be a good follower. Even the best leaders have to be followers sometimes. When I go to a crime scene, I'm not going to step in and take over. I let the experts do it—the homicide squad or the narcotics officers. My role is to follow them, and to get obstacles out of their way.[28]

Source: Personal interview with Commissioner Charles H. Ramsey conducted by Annie McKee, 2010.

Commissioner Ramsey could write a book on social and emotional competencies and leadership; he truly understands the impact of self-awareness, self-management, and social awareness on a leader's effectiveness and his or her impact on others. As a leader, he sets the stage for those around him to adopt norms that support group and institutional effectiveness.

To help a group be emotionally intelligent, leaders like Commissioner Ramsey create structures such as explicit norms to encourage and guide members to draw on their social and emotional intelligence competencies. The creation of norms that are grounded in social and emotional intelligence supports the development of trust, group identity, and a belief in group efficacy. In fact, scholars Vanessa Druskat and Steven Wolff argue that developing group emotional intelligence is a necessary condition for maximizing effectiveness.[29]

In addition, the group's culture—underlying values, beliefs, and language—should also support emotionally intelligent behavior. If culture and norms support emotional intelligence, members will more naturally adhere to these guidelines. Then, if a member crosses the line and engages in behavior that violates these norms, the group will likely feel more comfortable calling attention to the behavior because it violates the group's identity. You can see an example of an expanded set of group norms that focuses on emotional intelligence in ■Exhibit 10.7.

These norms and others linked to social and emotional intelligence will support group members in trusting one another, working through difficult problems, and enabling members and the group to be most effective. Working in groups that adhere to emotionally intelligent norms can be satisfying and fun. That does not mean, however, that these groups don't experience conflicts. Social and emotional intelligence in groups is not just about group harmony, tight friendships, and the absence of tension. Rather, it is about the ability of members to acknowledge that "when harmony is false, tension is unexpressed."[30]

Group norms and group roles are usually linked to another set of group dynamics related to status and power, which we will now explore.

Status and Power in Groups

Meritocracy

A system in which people are granted power, responsibilities, and roles because of superior intellect, talent, and competencies.

In organizations, team leadership and influence *should* be based on **meritocracy**, in which the person or people with the most expertise in the subject matter or in leading people are granted influential roles. A meritocracy is a system in which people are granted power, responsibilities, and roles because of superior intellect, talent, and competencies. Unfortunately, this does not always happen. In human groups, leadership is

■Exhibit **10.7**

Our Emotionally Intelligent Group Norms

1. Each one of us is to be aware of our impact on others and seek to ensure that our ideas, actions, and emotions support other members and the group as a whole.
2. Each of us is responsible for understanding and managing our own emotions in ways that support the group and its members.
3. Each of us is responsible for being attuned to and empathetic with other members.
4. We will collectively notice and monitor group dynamics for the purpose of managing our team in the most effective way possible.
5. Everyone has the responsibility to lead this group toward achieving our goals and becoming and remaining a healthy and resonant group.
6. Everyone in this group is responsible for making sure we perform at our very best individually and as a group.
7. We put group needs in front of our individual needs.
8. We are committed to open dialogue: Everyone *can* speak, and everyone *must*.
9. We support one another personally even when we are in conflict.
10. We respect one another at all times.

often granted for the wrong reasons, such as social status or a power base that has nothing to do with the group's tasks, goals, or mission.

Social Status

Social status
The relative standing or prestige you have compared with others in groups to which you belong.

The *Merriam-Webster Dictionary* defines status as "a position or rank in relation to others; relative rank in a hierarchy of prestige."[31] **Social status** is the relative standing or prestige you have compared with others in groups to which you belong. Social status can be formal, such as a rank or a position within a hierarchy. It can also be formally recognized through membership in a social class or a caste. Informal social status can be granted through relationships with other high- or low-status individuals and groups. We have all been in situations where status was granted by reputation or association with other powerful people. It happened in school, when the popular students were given leadership roles on sports teams, clubs, or school councils. It happens at work when "friends of the boss" are given special assignments or when we treat them more gingerly or with more respect than others. It happens in life when we meet someone who knows famous people—somehow, the fame rubs off.

How We "Get" Social Status

Different factors affect social status in society. For instance, socioeconomic status—your wealth, education, and occupational history compared to others—is a big determiner of whom you can meet and how you are able to interact with them. Gender, religion, race, and other factors also contribute to social status in different settings.

■Exhibit **10.8**

Social networks can break down the traditional barriers between social groups.

Kevin Britland/Alamy Images

One determiner of social status that has dramatically changed during the past 20 years is the richness of your social network.[32] Richness here refers to the number of people you know and interact with, as well as the variety of their experiences and social positions. This has been changing due to the rise of social networking as an activity available throughout society. Blogs, Twitter, MySpace, and Facebook are just a few tools that allow people to increase the range of social groups to which they belong, which provides opportunities for increasing social status (■Exhibit 10.8).[33]

Social status has a powerful effect on how we see ourselves, who we interact with, and how we are expected to behave. This is why people who join higher status groups often employ coaches to help them learn new ways of behaving, or image consultants to help them learn how to dress and groom themselves to fit in. Every behavior, every mannerism in speech and gesture, our clothing, our jewelry, and many other things communicate something about who we are. All of these things become symbols of our membership in different groups.[34] The more exclusive a group is, the more difficult it is to coordinate all of these different symbols in ways that convince others we truly belong.

Status and Influence in Groups

Status is important because it determines the amount and types of resources you have available to you as a group member. In other words, status and leadership go hand in hand. Research has found that high-status members can more directly influence the outcome of group activities and group processes, such as communication and conflict. Low-status members have less influence on a group, and their attempts to influence the group are weaker, less direct, and often less effective.[35]

A topic that is related yet different from social status is personal power. Personal power in a group can be linked to factors other than social status, providing people with different avenues through which to influence groups.

Personal Power in Groups

Power in a group can be bestowed from outside (designated position power) or earned (such as by being the person who supports the group in achieving goals and helping individuals succeed). Let's look at each in turn. Power is related to the ability to influence others, and there are several sources of personal power. These include:[36]

- The *legitimate* position you hold; for example, you are the official team leader.
- The extent to which people believe you can *reward* them; for example, you manage the project money.
- The extent to which people believe you can *coerce* or *punish* them; for example, you have a special relationship with the boss and have been known to talk badly about other team members.
- Your degree of *expertise;* for example, you are the only one on the team who understands accounting, a skill needed to complete the project.
- Your personal characteristics that people admire (*referent* power); for example, you are inspiring and hopeful, even when the work is difficult.

Each of these sources of power can be useful in group settings, and each is potentially available to you. Let's say you find yourself designated by an authority (an instructor or a manager) as the team's leader. You now have legitimate power, which makes influencing others easier, although you will find you still have to earn people's respect before they will follow you. You can also use reward power. You may not be able to reward people with money, but you can praise them and draw the group's attention to their contributions. You could also punish people in a group through shaming them or pointing out flaws. If you want long-lasting power in a group, however, don't even think about doing this. It will backfire on you.

When it comes to expertise, most groups at work require a wide variety of skills. Surely you have some of them. You just need the confidence to offer your services. Another hallmark of a good leader is that he or she can inspire people. Literally anyone can do this. It takes effort, of course, as well as self-confidence and a commitment to using and developing your social and emotional intelligence.

Power and Influence in a Leaderless Group

It is important to consider the many sources of power in a group because many teams at work and in school do not have formal leaders. "Leaderless" teams can be effective, but usually only when members are skilled at managing group dynamics, equally committed to the team's success, and willing to share leadership as the task requires. These conditions are most often seen in mature teams.

If you find yourself a member of a leaderless team that is not ready for the fluidity of this type of structure, one solution is for the team to designate an individual as the leader for a period of time. This can be difficult if more than one person wants this role, or if no one does. Despite the challenges inherent in choosing a leader, it is often worth doing at the beginning to get things going. Most groups have a difficult time working together in the beginning and, therefore, need a temporary leader. Most managers at work or instructors have little tolerance for delayed projects as a result of dysfunctional team dynamics, so it is important for you to take steps to organize the team for performance when you can.

Even if it is only temporary, taking on leadership of a "leaderless" team requires skill, self-confidence, and humility. Although groups need structure, especially in the beginning, it is also likely that members will resent it (and possibly you). To avoid this or at least minimize it, you should draw on other sources of power, such as your expertise, to gain the team's respect. You will also need to watch team dynamics carefully, using empathy and social awareness competencies to track the team members' response to you and the team's development.

As a designated team leader, you also need to monitor yourself. It is easy to become "drunk on power" because (1) at first the team really needs you; (2) people will praise you a lot—sometimes genuinely, and other times to get your attention; and (3) at some point, people will begin to fight you and it's natural to try to hold on to your position. Self-awareness and self-management are key in these situations. You need to be able to see clearly how power is affecting you, manage your reactions, and always remember that you are there to serve the team as long as it needs you, not vice versa.

We have now discussed several topics that are commonly associated with group dynamics. There are, of course, other topics such as communication and decision making, which you have learned about already in this course. One topic that hasn't always been considered yet but is increasingly critical to understand is the relationship between member diversity and group effectiveness.

Diversity Is a Group Dynamic

If we are to achieve a richer culture, rich in contrasting values, we must recognize the whole gamut of human potentialities, and so weave a less arbitrary social fabric, one in which each diverse human gift will find a fitting place.

—**Margaret Mead**, *Sex and Temperament in Three Primitive Societies* (1935)[37]

Throughout this book we have pointed out that we work in a world of diversity. Everyone knows that working with people who are different from ourselves is a fact of life. Gone are the days when people debated about how to "manage" diversity in the workplace, as if it were something we need to control. We now need to learn how to make the most of the rich and varied perspectives, talents, and social interaction styles of all people in our groups and teams. Elsewhere in this text, we discuss the impact of aspects of human diversity, such as race, gender, age, and culture, on people in the workplace. In this section, we will focus on two other types of diversity that impact group functioning: personality type as measured by the Myers-Briggs® Type Indicator and the Golden™ Personality Type Profiler Test, and learning style, as measured by David Kolb's Learning Style Inventory.

We Differ in How We Take In and Process Information

Psychologist Carl Jung proposed that we all have preferences about how we gather and evaluate information, and we all have rational and nonrational ways of organizing this information (■Exhibit 10.9).

No one way of gathering or processing information is inherently better.[38] In fact, diverse ways of processing information helps groups come to better decisions than individuals would on their own. Over the years, two interesting tests have been developed to help us understand how we process information. These tests are often used in teams at work as ways for members to understand group dynamics.

Personality Tests Can Help Us Understand Diversity

The Myers-Briggs® Type Indicator (MBTI) and the Golden™ Personality Type Profiler tests are useful tools for helping team members understand group dynamics because they identify specific differences in individuals' ways of processing information and their approaches to making decisions. There are three dimensions that are similar in both tests:

Intuiting-sensing: Intuitive-type people tend to like abstract concepts, value insight and hunches, and begin with the big picture and work down from there. These are positive attributes, of course, yet intuitives can run into trouble because turning abstract goals into realizable tasks can be difficult. In comparison, sensing-type people are more pragmatic, rely on facts and examples, and prefer to work with data and details. Their problem might be that they are unable to see the "big picture".[39]

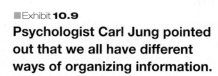

■Exhibit **10.9**
Psychologist Carl Jung pointed out that we all have different ways of organizing information.

Mary Evans Picture Library/Alamy Images

Thinking-feeling: Thinking-type people analyze data dispassionately—what we call being "objective." They are ordered and logical in their interpretation of information. Feeling-type people, on the other hand, don't interpret; they use emotions as an important input to their interpretations.[40] Rather than rely on objective facts, they see all information as subjective. They look at relationships, rely on communication, and follow their heart.[41]

Introversion-extraversion: Introverts are energized more in isolation within their own thoughts and feelings, whereas extraverts are energized by being around people.[42]

The MBTI® also measures *judging-perceiving.* Judging-type people tend to make decisions based on the data at hand and generally prefer closure. They are plan- and process-oriented individuals who like to have a course of action mapped out. Perceiving-type people are comfortable with ambiguity and change. They play things by ear, preferring matters to remain open ended, and they may change a decision several times before making it final.[43]

The Golden™ Personality Type Profiler also measures *organizing-adapting* and *tense-calm.* Organizing is linked with planning and reliability, while adapting is linked to tendencies toward being open ended and spontaneous. Tense-calm is the dimension that measures being uneasy and unsure versus being more confident and optimistic.[44]

The dimensions that the MBTI® and Golden™ tests measure are popular topics of training programs in organizations. Part of the reason for this is that most people can "see" themselves in these dimensions. Another reason is that the tests categorize people in a nonthreatening way, making it easier to talk about differences in approaches and perspectives. And finally, by using tests such as the MBTI® and the Golden™ Personality Type Profiler, an organization can create teams with complementary approaches.

Another way to look at diversity in teams is to consider how people learn and adapt. One tool used widely for this purpose was developed by well-known scholar David Kolb.

David Kolb's Learning Styles

Educational researcher David Kolb is known for his work on learning styles. Kolb's model illustrates four styles of learning: converger, diverger, assimilator, and accommodator. *Convergers* are people who like working with abstract concepts and devising experiments to test these concepts. They are the applied scientists of the world. *Divergers* tend to focus on concrete experiences and to reflect deeply and generate lots of possibilities. They come up with ideas and look at them through different lenses. These are the artists of the world. *Assimilators* live in the world of abstract ideas, which they create through observation and reflection. They are the theoreticians of the world. Finally *accommodators* are "doers." They live in the world of concrete experience and experimentation. They are practitioners.[45] All of these styles are measured by the Learning Style Inventory, a test developed by David Kolb that is widely used around the world.[46]

When people learn differently, they tend to pay more or less attention to certain kinds of information and make decisions differently. Different learning styles can be a barrier to communication in groups, simply because people don't understand one another's approach to discovering new ways of doing things. For example, when faced with a problem to solve, a diverger will want to seek as much information as possible, to brainstorm, and to think out of the box—he will resist coming to a conclusion. This can be frustrating for a converger, who will have identified what she thinks is the most relevant information quickly and is ready to make a decision. People with different learning styles can get very frustrated with one another. On the other hand, the diversity in styles on a team can, when well managed, ensure that the group balances creativity with closure, research with experimentation, and reflection with action.[47]

You now have a solid understanding of several important aspects of group dynamics: roles, norms, status, power, and diversity of perspective. Understanding these dynamics should help you decipher what happens in the groups you work with, as well as social groups. We will conclude this section by looking at one more way to understand what it's like to live and work in groups: as a series of paradoxes that must be resolved in order for individuals and the collective to be most effective.

Paradoxes of Group Life

A paradox is any situation in which two opposing facts are both true at the same time, yet cannot be true at the same time. For example, you can feel hunger yet not want to eat. Or, in physics, quantum mechanics states that light is a particle and is also a wave.[48] By definition, if something is a wave it cannot be a particle, and vice versa. But light is both a particle and a wave. That is a paradox.

According to scholars Kenwyn Smith and David Berg, what happens to us in groups can be paradoxical as well.[49] The paradoxes we experience in groups stem from basic dualities within human beings. For example, we have a deep and abiding desire to be independent, and we have an equally strong, almost primal, drive to be accepted by others and to be part of groups—family, friends, school, workplace, and society. We feel tension when this paradox is activated, such as when our group requires us to give up some independence.

We also want to be unique, to be different, but our personal differences are almost always tied to our membership in certain groups. For example, take a moment to describe yourself as a unique human being. Perhaps you love dogs, or autumn is your favorite season, or the 1965 Mustang is your favorite car. You are male, female, American, Korean, British, athletic, friendly, passionate, quick to anger. You love baseball, hate football, have an IQ of 120. You are gracious, shy, funny, pretty, tall, Asian, Hispanic, Black, White. As you can see, how you describe your very uniqueness also describes what groups you belong to. Even describing yourself as a "non-joiner" puts you in a certain group: People who don't like to join groups.

This exercise illustrates what Smith and Berg call the paradox of identity: How we define ourselves as individuals requires membership in a variety of groups, yet membership in groups means that we are not unique individuals.[50] Smith and Berg point out that another paradox we experience in groups is related to trust. This paradox is very interesting in that it takes a "leap of faith" to resolve. Here's how it works: Group members need to trust one another for people to feel safe sharing themselves, their ideas, and their talents. But where does that trust come from? Simply put, you have to give trust in order to build trust.[51]

Another paradox involves authority. Authority is inherently paradoxical. Those in authority have power over others, yet only if others accept their authority. In other words, your power over others comes from people's willingness to comply—their power over you is their decision to follow. As Smith and Berg put it, "one develops power as one empowers others."[52]

The final paradox we will discuss here is the paradox of courage. Smith and Berg note that to really *belong* to a group demands a great deal of courage.[53] It is courage that allows us to submit to the will of a group, and to give up our individual choice in favor of the needs of the group, while at the same time trusting the group to meet our needs as they arise. This requires engagement, disclosure, and willingness to be empowered and to help empower others. It takes courage to realize that self-preservation requires taking care of the group, while group preservation requires taking care of yourself.[54]

These paradoxes and others that Smith and Berg write about affect us deeply when we work in groups, but we rarely talk about them. As you learn to manage group dynamics, you may want to explore some of these complicated but fascinating paradoxes to see how they affect you, other group members, and the dynamics of the group as a whole.

5. How Do Teams Function at Work?

As long as human beings have been alive, we have organized ourselves to get things done in groups. Flash forward thousands of years, and here we are today, getting things done in teams at work and in school. In fact, teams are one of the most important structures in most modern organizations. Teams are where ideas are generated, decisions get made, and work gets done. As well-known authors Jon Katzenbach and Douglas Smith said in their influential book on teams, "a real team—appropriately focused and rigorously disciplined—is the most versatile unit organizations have for meeting both performance and change challenges in today's complex world."[55]

Describing Work Teams

There are many ways to describe work teams in organizations, as you can see in ■Exhibit 10.10. This exhibit classifies teams by their purpose, structure, type of participant, and assignment. The list is not exhaustive, and teams can actually have more than one designation. For example, a team whose purpose is research may also be self-directed and cross-functional.

You will likely encounter each type of team at some point, even early in your career. One type of team structure that is important to pay attention to is the self-directed work team, because it is increasingly common for teams to be self-directed or self-managed at work.

Self-Directed Work Teams

Self-directed work teams
Teams in which there is no formally designated leader and members organize their own activities.

Self-directed work teams deserve special mention because they are becoming much more common in organizations. In self-directed work teams, there is no formally designated leader and members organize their own activities. Self-directed teams grew in favor and number during the implementation of total quality management (TQM; see Chapter 12). TQM relies on the initiative and insight of employees to solve problems and improve processes in the areas with which they are intimately familiar. The key characteristic is that the teams themselves take responsibility for their work, finding solutions to problems they identify, providing performance feedback, meeting goals, and monitoring performance.

When working in a self-directed work team, it is important to understand group development, group dynamics, and how to build effective working relationships among members. That's also true in teams that do have designated leaders as well. Let's look now at key ideas about what it takes to create and sustain highly effective work teams in organizations today.

■Exhibit **10.10**

Common Ways Teams Are Described in Organizations

Teams Described by Assignment

- Project team (often named for the specific project)
- Research team
- Innovation team
- "Green" team

Teams Described by Purpose

- Motivation or employee morale team
- Quality team
- Safety and environmental team
- Employee wellness team
- Workplace diversity team
- Incident response team
- Action learning team

Teams Described by Structure

- Self-directed/self-managed work team
- Virtual team
- Co-led team
- Ad hoc team

Teams Described by Participant Type

- Leadership team
- Cross-functional team
- Global/international team

High-Performance Teams

Authors Jon Katzenbach and Douglas Smith believe that teams, as opposed to working groups, have shared leadership roles, mutual accountability, and collective work products.[56] The distinction is important, they argue, because teams have a unique culture and discipline structure that sets them apart from the wider organization, which allows them to become high-performing collective units. These scholars encourage the use of teams as a way of increasing performance by circumventing organizational hierarchies and boundaries. Hierarchy and boundaries get in the way of organizational and team performance, which is why Katzenbach and Smith argue that team members, especially those in leadership positions, should be carefully selected for their skills and not because of status or seniority.[57] Katzenbach and Smith's research on teams has uncovered numerous findings, such as the following:[58]

- "Real" teams are more frequently engendered in organizations with high-performance standards.
- High-performance teams are the exception, not the rule.
- Teams are the most efficient method of integrating ideas and performance across hierarchical and structural organization boundaries.
- A real team naturally integrates learning and performance.

It's hard to generalize, of course, but it is safe to say that in many organizations, too little attention is paid to the development, dynamics, or support that teams need in order to be effective. During the past two decades, this has begun to change as researchers have helped us see how effective work teams can be structured and managed for maximum use of individuals' talents and to support the collective energy, knowledge, and wisdom of the team. In this section, we will discuss what it takes to be a highly effective team. To start, let's look at how one such team is led at the University of Colorado at Boulder.

Emily King

Sean Planchard

Student's Choice

Mark Arnoldy—GlobeMed

Many college students talk about making social change, but few have the confidence and drive to take action on the scale that Mark Arnoldy did. At the end of his junior year at the University of Colorado at Boulder, Mark decided to take some time off from school. He chose to delay his senior year, graduation, and medical school ambitions to embark on a unique social venture in Nepal that focused on improving nutritional health for children by providing them with peanut butter, which is packed with energy and high in protein, healthy fats, iron, niacin, and fiber. After seeing first-hand the potential for change in Nepal, Mark brought his ideas back to Boulder and co-founded the university's chapter of Globe-Med, a national, student-run nonprofit organization that partners university students with grassroots non-government organizations (NGOs) in the movement for global health equity. The story of Mark's involvement with GlobeMed and the founding of his chapter is inspiring, but even more impressive was his ability to mobilize and empower 50 students to become involved.

At its core, GlobeMed is about bringing students together to fight health inequality. But there is something that sets GlobeMed apart from the rest of the chapters across the country: the leadership that Mark Arnoldy and three other extraordinary individuals bring to the team. Prior to joining GlobeMed, many staff members probably couldn't have pointed out Nepal on a map; less than a year later, 50 students are sacrificing sleep, school, and free time to do whatever they can to support the goal of providing primary health care in Nepal. How did it happen? First, Mark was able to convey his passion for the work in a way that other students could relate to, and this vision has translated into a team of college kids raising tens of thousands of dollars for nutritional supplements in Nepal in just a few short months.

Mark came up with the idea to begin each staff meeting with one team member taking a few minutes to discuss his or her motivations for joining GlobeMed and passion for global health equity. In any organization, it's easy to get bogged down in the day-to-day, trivial details and lose sight of the bigger picture. At GlobeMed, however, this 'why we're here' activity allows every staff member—from the co-president to the campaign team leader to the staff member that just joined last week—to take on a leadership role and contribute to the shared vision.

At 22, Mark's accomplishments are astounding. He has achieved more in his short adult life than some people do in their entire lives. But the fact of the matter is that Mark is a game-changer, the type of player that simply seems to make magic happen. And this leader's story has just begun!

Source: Adapted from a case by Emily King and Sean Planchard.

High-performance team

A team that performs beyond "all reasonable expectations," as compared with other teams in similar situations.

Mark Arnoldy is leading what authors Jon Katzenbach and Douglas Smith call a high-performance team. A **high-performance team** is a team that performs beyond "all reasonable expectations," as compared with other teams in similar situations.[59] According to Katzenbach and Smith, attributes of high-performance teams include the following:[60]

1. Small size (fewer than 12 members)
2. Members have complementary skills
3. Members are united under a common purpose
4. Members have a mutually agreed-on set of performance goals
5. Members agree on an approach to the work
6. Members share accountability for performance and work products[61]

Other researchers have also focused on what can be done to ensure that teams are effective. Professor Richard Hackman has written extensively about team performance perspectives and concludes that groups, like people, need the support of organizational systems in order to be most effective.[62] For example, he suggests that reward systems, systems of learning how to do the expected task(s), information management systems, resource needs and allocations, and clear project timelines are structures that support group effectiveness.

6. How Can We Deal with the Challenges of Working in Groups?

In this section, we will address a set of common challenges that almost every team deals with: membership, participation, communication, influence, social loafing, and emotions. Then we will look at how dangerous conformity can be in groups.

The Big Six Challenges We Face in Groups

As you have read this chapter, you have probably had some insights about how the teams you have been part of developed, the dynamics that affected you and the team, and how your teams might have been more effective. To take the next step, you can learn more about six challenges that everyone faces when working with groups: membership, participation, communication, influence, social loafing, and emotions. These are issues *you* can do something about right away.

Membership

A major concern for group members is the degree of acceptance or inclusion in the group. Different patterns of interaction may develop in the group that provide clues to the degree and kind of membership each person wants and needs. By tracking these patterns and taking corrective action, you can ensure that group members feel appropriately welcomed and included. For example, you might ask yourself the following questions:

- Do some people seem to be "outside" the group? Do some members seem to be "in"? How are those "outside" treated?
- Are there subgroups? Sometimes two or three members may consistently agree and support each other, or they may consistently disagree and oppose one another. This causes an in-group/out-group dynamic that can be destructive.
- Do some members physically move in and out of the group, for example, leaning forward or backward in their chairs or moving their chairs in and out? Under what conditions do they move in or move out? The physical setup of a group often indicates who feels "in" and who feels "out." Similarly, if people are consistently late for meetings or do not respond to e-mails regularly, these could be signs that these individuals feel as if they are on the outside of the group.

Participation

The most effective groups enable everyone to share their best ideas in a timely manner. If you notice that participation in your group is uneven or that certain members dominate, you have an issue to address. To better diagnose what is going on, you might ask:

- Who are the high and low participators?
- Has there been any shift in participation? For example, have high participators become quiet? Have low participators suddenly become talkative?
- Do you see any possible reason for changes in the group's interaction pattern?
- How are the silent people treated? Is silence interpreted as consent? Disagreement? Lack of interest? Fear?
- Who talks to whom? Why might certain people talk, or not talk, to certain other people?
- Who keeps the ball rolling?

Communication

In any group or team, constructive communication is crucial to effective performance. Communication problems can manifest in many ways. Some typical communication problems to watch out for include:

- *Silence:* Although some silence is good, members may avoid speaking up even when their thoughts can benefit the group. Members can encourage each other to communicate through appropriate verbal and nonverbal signals, as well as through directly soliciting opinions from less talkative members. Making communication more democratic—for instance, by using a round-table technique—can be a useful way to encourage participation.
- *Cynicism:* Anger and resentment are often communicated through cynicism. Rather than shutting down members when they express cynicism, you need to find out the source of these feelings and deal with it. Often, when participants' views are calmly listened to, their anger dissipates and they feel more involved in the group.
- *Interruptions:* In most conversations, speakers tend to overlap one another's comments to some degree. There is a difference, however, between talking at the same time as another person and actively seeking to interrupt him or her. Interruptions that silence the voice of some members should not be tolerated.
- *Rambling:* Some people take longer to get to the point than others, so there should be some tolerance for "rambling." Additionally, cultures have different degrees of directness when attempting to make a point. Talk should be periodically summarized and compared to the group's goals. If talk meanders away from those goals, then effort to bring participation back into focus is needed.
- *Arguing:* Disagreements allow for a close inspection of assumptions and biases that can, if not checked, lead to poor group performance. However, some arguments can become personal and lead to relational conflict. In addition, some arguments result from the illusion of differences of opinion. A good practice is to make sure that people are actually talking about the same thing when they are arguing.

Influence

Influence, participation, and communication are related, but they are not the same. Some people may speak rarely, yet they capture the attention of the whole group. Others may talk a lot but are not listened to by other group members. Effective groups manage influence in ways that allow the person with the most relevant experience and knowledge to influence the group when this experience or knowledge is most needed. To track how well your group is managing influence, ask yourself:

- Which members are high in influence, and which are low in influence? Why do these people have different levels of influence on the group?
- Are there any shifts in influence patterns? What has shifted and why?
- Do you see any rivalry in the group? Is there a struggle for leadership?

Social Loafing

Social loafing is exactly what it sounds like: Someone decides to take a free ride and let the rest of the group do the work. Sometimes it is hard to tell at first that someone is taking advantage of the team. Social loafers are clever. They have a million and one excuses, most of which are plausible. Some indications that you are dealing with social loafing and not legitimate excuses for missing work and deadlines include the following:

- Leaving group meetings before assignments are handed out
- Pairing up with another member because it will be "fun" or "better" even when a task is obviously suited to one person
- Bragging to others outside the group about how little work he or she has to do
- Stepping up and getting involved only when authorities are around

One extensive study found that social loafing is a frequent occurrence, but it does not happen as much when team members feel that the task or the team itself is important.[63] Therefore, one way to minimize social loafing is to organize teams and groups around tasks that are important to members, and to build an identity within the team that reinforces the feeling of commitment to the team. One thing you don't want to do with social loafers is to protect them from being "caught" by managers, instructors, and so forth. You're just hurting yourself and your team if you do that.

Emotions

During any group discussion, interactions will frequently generate emotions among members that are seldom discussed openly. You may have to make guesses about what people are feeling based on tone of voice, facial expressions, gestures, and many other forms of nonverbal cues. If you are aware of people's feelings, you will be better able to deal with them individually or on a group level in a way that is helpful, rather than harmful, to the individuals and the group. To "diagnose" feelings, you might ask questions such as:

- What feelings seem to be "allowed" in the group? What purpose do these feelings serve in the group?
- Who expresses which emotions in the group? Is there a pattern?
- What emotions are not allowed in the group or remain unexpressed?
- What do you commonly notice in people's body language?
- Do you see any attempts by group members to block the expression of feelings, particularly negative feelings? How is this done? Does anyone do this consistently?

In this section, we have provided you with some tips for "diagnosing" what is happening in groups. This skill is tremendously helpful in just about any career: If you can figure out what is happening in groups, you can usually help them be more effective. Let's now turn to yet another problem that you can help groups avoid: too much conformity.

Conformity and Groupthink

Between 1951 and 1956, psychologist Solomon Asch published a series of studies that examined independence and conformity among individuals. The work, collectively known as the *Asch conformity studies*, typically conducted "vision" tests on groups of students, in which only one student was actually the subject. The other group members were secretly working for the experimenter. The question was how the student-subject would respond when all other group members seemed to agree and he or she alone had a different opinion. In these studies, the researchers asked group members to compare the lengths of lines that were written on cards and to choose the ones that were the same.

After making the "real" subject comfortable, the research assistants started giving wrong answers. The research assistants posing as group members gave their answers first, and they always gave the same answer as each other. The majority answer was clearly wrong, but surprisingly, test subjects wound up giving incorrect answers 32 percent of the time, and 74 percent of test participants answered at least one question wrong.[64]

Why did the student-subjects do this? They felt pressure to conform. The experimenters knew that conformity was a factor because in other experimental conditions where there was no pressure to conform, only 3 percent of test participants ever offered an incorrect answer.[65]

However, some recent researchers have been reexamining the Asch studies and suggest the answer may not be as simple as first explained. When faced with a situation such as that in Asch's experiment, participants must make a number of decisions that balance the importance of many different values and relationships, and it is the negotiation of these conflicts that results in conformity. In particular, group decisions are frequently linked to people's beliefs that consensus is the most important group goal.[66] Because there was little opportunity to reach consensus in other ways, the lone participant in Asch's studies was forced to demonstrate consensus by conforming to the majority opinion of the single task of the group within which he found himself a member.

Conformity can lead to groupthink. According to researcher Irving Janis, **groupthink** is "a collective pattern of defensive avoidance that leads people in a group to adopt a singular view even when there is evidence to the contrary."[67] What Janis meant by this is that when there is strong pressure to arrive at a consensus in groups, members may come to hold the same views and then vigorously defend this consensus as consistent with their own opinion. Groupthink has been blamed in a number of incidents including the Bay of Pigs invasion, the Space Shuttle *Challenger* disaster, and even some activities in financial services companies that contributed to the the recession that began in 2007 (■Exhibit 10.11).[68]

Avoiding Dysfunctional Conformity in Groups

Groupthink is a significant problem among business teams. When groupthink occurs, team members may truly "shut down" because they do not want to go against the group. Team leaders can ameliorate this by ensuring that everyone gets a turn to speak, that one individual does not dominate the discussion, and that more dominant members avoid providing their opinions too early in the decision-making process.

Another way of combating groupthink is to bring outsiders into the group to critically evaluate the group's work and offer contrasting opinions and new information. Another tactic is for groups to create a norm in which someone is formally designated the "devil's advocate" to question group opinions and decisions.

One way of avoiding the negative effects of conformity in groups is to implement processes that encourage teams to revisit and reexamine decisions and their effects.[69] Going back to Solomon Asch's studies, this research revealed another interesting pattern. If there was even one other person in the group who gave the same answer as the subject, the subject would not simply go along with the group of participants who knowingly chose the wrong answer. This fact has important implications for understanding how to mitigate group pressure on individuals. For instance, you should ensure that group norms are set up that encourage people to voice their opinions. That way, the best answer is likely to be voiced and supported, and individuals are more likely to "stick by their guns" even when others disagree.[70]

Groupthink
"A collective pattern of defensive avoidance that leads people in a group to adopt a singular view even when there is evidence to the contrary."

■ Exhibit **10.11**
Groupthink was one of the contributing factors to the Space Shuttle *Challenger* disaster.

Horizon International Images Limited/Alamy Images

Perhaps the best way of avoiding conformity is to ensure that group norms *value* differing opinions. Selecting individuals for membership in a group because of their different views—as in international or cross-functional teams—can also help if proper team building is done to build trust among members.[71]

In this section we have discussed what happens when people go along with each other too much. But what if the opposite is true? What if people can't agree on anything? Let's look at both the upsides and the downsides of conflict in groups.

Most Popular » Discussion Questions

1. Consider the "big six" common challenges in groups. Of the six, which are *you* most likely to have problems with? Why do you think you do this? Can you think of some strategies to overcome this problem?
2. What do you do when you have a social loafer in a group? Is your strategy for dealing with this effective? If not, what else could you do?
3. Have you ever been in a group where members conformed too much? If so, what could you have done to help the group be more effective?

---

7. What Role Does Conflict Play in Groups?

Many forms of ritualized group conflict are an important part of our society. For instance, just about every community has some form of team sports, and in most major cities, we have dedicated huge buildings and tracts of land so thousands of fans can watch these teams play games that involve competition and conflict.

Other forms of conflict have more negative consequences—they weaken the effective functioning of groups and teams, cause emotional damage, and may even lead to violence. Researcher Karen Jehn conducted a study in organizations and found that conflict involving relationships had negative consequences for both performance and satisfaction with the organization.[72] In high-performance teams, relationship conflicts were almost nonexistent except when projects neared deadlines, when this type of conflict suddenly rose.[73] So how can we determine when conflict is necessary—and even healthy—and when it is destructive?

Functional and Dysfunctional Conflict

Functional conflict
Involves allowing or encouraging differences of opinions among team members in order to yield better group outcomes.

Conflict can be either functional or dysfunctional. **Functional conflict**, sometimes called constructive conflict, involves allowing or encouraging differences of opinions among team members in order to yield better group outcomes. A moderate amount of conflict has been indicated as good for group creativity and group problem solving.[74] Organizational research has shown that the absence of functional conflict among team members can lead to complacency and the loss of a competitive edge. On the other hand, dysfunctional conflict, sometimes called destructive conflict, is counterproductive and results in poor performance and poor team cohesion. **Dysfunctional conflict** can involve aggression, personal attacks, or ways of expressing differences that undermine group success.

Dysfunctional conflict
Involves aggression, personal attacks, or ways of expressing differences that undermine group success.

Sources of Conflict

Where does conflict come from? At one level, we can say that all conflict arises out of attempts to access or maintain position and/or resources, either personally or for a group.[75] This is certainly true of political conflicts, border disputes between countries, and com-

■Exhibit **10.12**

Sources of Conflict in Groups	
Sources of Conflict	**Explanation**
Resource conflict	Conflicts of interest within a group frequently happen when resources are scarce and each group member desires more rather than less of those resources.[76]
Cognitive conflict	Conflict can occur when group members share the same group goals but disagree on how to best achieve the desired result.[77]
Relationship conflict	Relationship conflict has to do with "personal" conflict among members of the team. This kind of conflict has been seen to negatively impact group performance.[78]
Process conflict	Process conflict refers to conflict within teams about who should be doing what and how the group should operate.[79]
Task interdependency conflict	Task interdependency is another source of conflict, and one to which you can probably relate. As you may have experienced when working on group projects, your entire team depends on each individual member to complete his or her tasks. When one person misses a deadline, everyone is affected. Naturally, conflict results in this situation because the project is not complete until all participants have accomplished their respective tasks.[80]
Overlapping authority conflict	Overlapping authority is also a source of conflict when two or more people claim authority for the same tasks or functions. In many instances, redundant work by two different business units results in an overlap of managerial authority and employee scheduling.
Reward conflict	Finally, different evaluation and reward systems can cause conflict among departments and divisions. If one division is evaluated by how low they keep their overhead while another division in the same organization is evaluated on how much they sell despite overhead costs, conflict can result from opposing systems of evaluation and rewards for work effort.

petition for market share of a product. Conflict in groups within organizations can also be the result of a number of other factors, as shown in ■Exhibit 10.12.

Conflict can be examined at three different levels: intrapersonal, interpersonal, and group. At the intrapersonal level, conflict is experienced inside a person. For example, sometimes we experience clashes between our values and what we are expected to do, or we might be exposed to facts that challenge our way of seeing the world.

Interpersonal conflict occurs between people, often as the result of challenges to identity, bids for power, protecting one's "turf," and other similar situations.

At the group level, there is always a dynamic tension between the identity of the individual and the identity of the group. Conflict can result when individuals challenge group values and processes, or when group norms are inconsistent with individual beliefs and behavior. It can also arise when the group becomes too focused on and involved in one member's life and contributions, or when members get caught up too heavily in group life.[81] Or, when an individual member's needs and interests are served by the group at the expense of other members' needs and interests, conflict may arise. For instance, if a person feels she is not getting enough support or recognition from the group, she may develop anger or resentment toward other members and toward the group in general.

An individual can get too caught up in the needs of the group, as well, and this can lead to conflict. For instance, when the demands of a group at work are high, this may leave little time for fulfillment of family roles, leading to conflict within the individual.[82] These feelings can affect how the person relates to groups at work and at home.[83] Another source of conflict is when power is not equally distributed in groups. When some people accumulate a disproportionate amount of power, the group may serve those people more than other members.

Trust: The Basis for All Conflict Resolution Strategies

A cohesive group requires a great deal of trust among its members. If that trust never fully develops or if it is threatened, individuals may feel that they are not accepted by the group, and people may not be willing to fully contribute.[84] This can result in conflict and the danger of the group falling apart. For these reasons, there are often ritualized processes of induction in groups where trust is a must (such as elite military outfits and secret societies).

Trust is particularly important when a group is experiencing conflict. That's because people need to rely on one another's goodwill and good intentions to resolve conflict. So, trust is at the heart of conflict resolution, no matter what approach is chosen.[85]

Several conflict resolution strategies are typically employed when a team is faced with strife. One of these strategies is compromise. Compromise involves a give-and-take approach that may require concessions by both parties. Collaboration, on the other hand, requires that the parties work together to solve problems or achieve goals.

Other conflict management strategies include accommodation, which occurs when the party with less power defers to the other, more powerful party, and avoidance, which occurs when both parties ignore a problem, hoping the conflict will disappear. This strategy doesn't work, however, because conflicts fester and spread rather than simply disappearing. Finally, competition can often occur when each party tries to best the other by maximizing its own position of power without considering the other party's needs or goals.

One of the best *practical* conflict management strategies is to call a group meeting and get the various perspectives about relationships, processes, and issues out in the open.[86] The team leader, or a strong group member, needs to take responsibility for structuring the conversation and facilitating the group to reevaluate its norms and procedures, or simply support appropriate expressions of "I am sorry."

Conflict Management: Negotiating to Find the Win-Win

Successful conflict management strategies rely on negotiation, a conflict resolution method in which both parties give, take, and make concessions, to achieve an agreeable solution to a conflict. Several different scenarios are possible when negotiation tactics are used. In a lose-lose scenario, neither party gets what it desires or needs from the negotiation. The distributive negotiation approach creates a win-lose scenario (also popularly referred to as a *zero-sum* negotiation), in which one party reaches its desired goal in the negotiation while the other party does not.[87] In another approach, integrative bargaining, a win-win scenario results. In this scenario, both parties maximize their desired goals by finding common ground to integrate their interests, and the conflict is resolved.[88] This approach requires cooperation by both parties and uses a win-win frame of mind to achieve the best possible outcome for all and to preserve relationships.

Most Popular » Discussion Questions

1. Describe a functional conflict in which you were involved. How do you know it was functional? Now, do the same analysis for a dysfunctional conflict in which you were involved.
2. How do you normally approach conflict, and how do you feel about it? Explain your approach and your feelings.
3. Analyze a conflict you have witnessed in school or at work. What were the reasons (or sources) for the conflict?

8. How Can HR Support Effective Team Performance?

HR plays an important role in supporting effective team performance. In this section we will begin with a few ideas about how HR can focus attention on teams. Then, we will share some tips on how to engage a group in a team-building retreat.

Focus on Teams: HR's Contributions

The HR Cycle

The following is a list of helpful things HR can do to support the groups and teams for which they are responsible:

- Provide training and development to team leaders about how to set up and lead teams.
- Pay attention to the personal transitions in and out of teams, especially at the leadership level.
- Provide high-quality professional development and support for teams, especially in the important formation phase.
- Develop processes to evaluate team performance that include level of team effectiveness in addition to goal achievement.
- Recognize outstanding teams—teams that get results and that people are happy to join. Highlight their best practices so other teams can learn from them.
- Develop team-based incentive programs.
- Model all of the above and establish high-performance HR teams.

These are just a few ideas about how HR professionals can design systems and processes to support team effectiveness. In addition, HR professionals can design processes that enable teams to grapple with the inevitable challenges inherent in working in groups.

Resonant Team Building

HR Leadership Roles

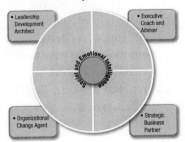

This section is intended to provide a picture of how you can use intentional team retreats and processes to build, sustain, and renew effective teams. Processes like these are often led by HR professionals, but you can do it too.[89]

Resonant Team Building: Getting Started

If you can, plan to take people out the office or classroom. Find a location that is really different and preferably close to nature. Maybe you will find a lodge in the mountains. Maybe you will simply go to someone's backyard. Wherever you go, plan carefully. Make sure you will have privacy, relative comfort, and safety. Make sure the environment doesn't inadvertently single people out—for example, if there are people in your group who are not physically fit, make sure they can participate safely and without shame.

Ahead of time, you should select a few discussion topics and activities that will enable people to get to know each other. Ensure that the flow of conversation moves from light and safe to more intense and just a bit risky. Set ground rules; for example, be respectful, don't violate one another's privacy, and keep people's confidences. Think about how you will move people through actually doing the exercises and how you will talk about what comes up and make conclusions about the team or organization.

Even group members who have worked together for years find the experience of "meeting each other" by sharing more of themselves and their lives to be enlightening. One way to do this is to give people the chance to do, and then talk about, exercises that will help them reflect on and share their personal visions and life stories.

For this to work, you need to create resonance by establishing an environment that is optimistic, energized, and focused on building constructive relationships. People need to be open to possibilities, and your leadership presence in this phase is critical. You need to consciously manage yourself so that you can help people feel comfortable, engaged, and ready to work on becoming a better team.

Resonant Team Building: Visioning

How do you help a group work together to create a collective vision? First, you need to find out what personal visions are shared among the members. It is more than likely that people's personal visions have a few commonalities—hopes for families, lifestyle, professional success, kinds of group they want to be part of, ways of working together, and so forth. Don't let these similarities go unnoticed. When conversations about people's personal hopes are authentic and respectful, openness to a shared vision grows. A parallel and linked process can unfold as people consider their team's vision and connect it to their own dreams.

Once people have shared personal visions, you can go back to your team's mission, purpose, and current challenges. Review together the reason the team exists, the organization's strategy, and how the team's work supports the organization's goals. Consider your team's emotional reality in terms of whether your norms, habits, and culture will support you in attaining your vision: Do your patterns of interaction support you in working effectively? What is your team's explicit charge? Its implicit charge? Are you all on the same page? Will you get in your own way? A clear picture of your team's objective and emotional realities provides you with a platform to build a full picture of what your group can be and do in the future.

Then, for each member, clearly work through accountabilities: What are our expectations of each other? Who will be responsible for leading the different elements of our work together? What is the plan to take the process forward? How will energy be sustained? How will each individual continue to grow and develop along the way?

An occasional team retreat can dramatically renew a tired team. Every so often teams need to be refreshed; they need to revisit their purpose and renew their relationships. When we get into deep, authentic, emotional contact with each other, our mood almost always elevates and we feel renewed hope and connection.

To strengthen this process, you should try to come away with team members' commitments to engage in group processes that support people in working more effectively together. This might be as simple as reserving 15 minutes at the end of each team meeting to ask, "How are we doing?" The process can also be much more complex—maybe you need to change your performance management and incentive systems to encourage people to work toward group goals. However simple or complex your "support systems" need to be, the most important thing is that you *continually* take actions to support your team's effectiveness. The stress and pressure of work are the enemy of effective teams. Make sure you attend to your group's health through occasional team renewal sessions. Regular process "check-ups" can make all the difference in your overall effectiveness.

Most Popular » Discussion Questions

1. Have you ever participated in a retreat, whether with fellow workers, a school group, or another organization? Where did you go? What happened? How did the experience impact the relations of the group?
2. If you can, plan a mini-retreat for a team you are on at work or school. Start by bringing up the idea with other members, and if people are interested, partner with someone to use ideas in this section to help the members of your group talk with one another about their collective effectiveness.

---

9. What Can We All Do to Create and Sustain Resonant Teams?

You now understand what happens as teams develop, how group dynamics affect people and teams, what a high-performance team looks like, and how to help teams to be

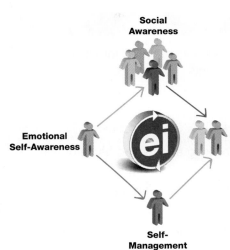

Social Awareness

Emotional Self-Awareness

Relationship Management

Self-Management

more effective. All of these theories and models are useful and have their place. When it comes right down to it, however, *people* make or break teams. What each one of us says, does, and believes affects whether our teams will be great or miserable. In this section, we will share a few practical tips about one skill that is crucial to team leadership: listening. We will home in on skills related to listening because many problems arise in teams because people simply don't listen to one another. Then, we will share tips about how to lead a resonant team.

Listening to What People Actually Say

Listening is a foundational skill on which other communication and team skills are built, including the abilities to ask relevant questions, be attentive, offer appropriate feedback, and negotiate effectively, among other skills.[90] It is important to appreciate that listening and hearing are not the same thing. Hearing is the passive reception of incoming messages, whereas listening requires full engagement with another person. Effective listening requires that you attend to people's words and the feelings—which, by the way, takes more energy than speaking. Some tips for better listening include the following:

- *Concentrate:* Do not be distracted. Focus your attention fully on the person (what is being said, what is *not* being said, body language, *everything*).
- *Listen empathetically:* Empathy is crucial to effective listening. By focusing on the person and the emotions that underlie his or her message, you are more likely to receive the full message, including that which is not said directly. Also, when the other person experiences you as empathetic, he or she is much more likely to trust you and expand and extend the message as necessary.
- *Listen for facts and feelings:* Remember that what someone says contains facts, opinions, beliefs, values, and emotions. You need to be able to tell the difference between the many messages people send when they are expressing themselves.
- *Avoid jumping to conclusions:* Always wait until you have heard everything before jumping to conclusions. This sounds obvious, but poor listeners are often impatient and will interpret a message prematurely. Some people even jump in and interrupt the other person, wasting time and confusing the process as they provide what turns out to be inappropriate interpretations.
- *Judge content, not delivery:* If someone has poor communication skills, this does not excuse you from being a good listener. Your job remains to seek to understand and respond to the other person.
- *Provide feedback:* Remember that feedback is part of what makes communication meaningful. Eye contact, nods, note-taking, and other nonverbal responses let people know that you are paying attention and that you understand what they are saying, as do brief verbal responses. Asking clarifying questions or restating the message can also help ensure that you understand the message completely.

This last point—providing feedback as part of the listening process—is particularly important because it allows you and the person you are communicating with to come to a much deeper understanding. Learning a technique called "active listening" will help you hone this skill.

Active Listening

Active listening is the process of attending and responding to what people say more deeply and consciously in order to really understand what they mean. At the heart of active listening is an interest in both the person and in what is being said, as well as respect and authenticity.[91]

Active listening involves listening fully to what is being expressed. Instead of interpreting, commenting on, or even building on what is said, an active listener will reflect back to the speaker what he or she heard, including both facts and feelings.

■Exhibit **10.13**

Active Listening Skills

- Pay attention to your speaker by directing your attention to the speaker and blocking out other things that compete for your attention, such as other activity in the room or even your thoughts.
- Adopt appropriate body language to communicate respect and attention, such as making eye contact, facing your whole body toward the speaker, and not fidgeting.
- Withhold judgment of the speaker or the content of the message.
- Practice empathy by trying to really understand *what* the person is actually thinking and feeling as he or she communicates, not *why*.
- Reflect on what is actually being communicated—and what is not said. Much of what is communicated is transmitted through avoided topics, choice of words, and body language.
- Use feedback to clarify what you are hearing or to request clarification (e.g., this might simply involve repeating the main points of what someone has just said and waiting for confirmation).
- Summarize what is being said (another level of clarification).
- Share your evaluations of what you have heard.

Source: From Hoppe, Michael H. 2006. *Active listening: improve your ability to listen and lead.* Greensboro, NC: Center for Creative Leadership.

Active listening is a process that involves a number of distinct skills that are used simultaneously, as listed in ■Exhibit 10.13.[92] Active listening involves cultivating a frame of mind that allows you to mindfully focus on the person speaking. Emotional intelligence and empathy are required to withhold judgment until you have heard all of what the person has to say. An active listener should try to understand what is being said from the speaker's own perspective or point of view. This is a process that involves empathy, and it is closely related to social and emotional intelligence.

To understand someone else's perspective, you must listen for total meaning, which includes both the objective and the subjective content of what is being said—in other words, facts and feelings. The objective content involves the meaning of what is actually said, whereas the subjective content includes details about the speaker's feelings or attitudes about the information. Scholars refer to this information as the speaker's stance.[93] An active listener will respond to feelings and pay attention to all communication cues, both verbal and nonverbal.[94]

Active listening helps us avoid common traps such as listening with the goal of influencing the speaker toward your point of view. People also routinely send out signals that request or challenge the listener to agree or to disagree with what they have said. Responding to requests for advice, information, and judgments can result in a conversation that closes prematurely—the speaker hasn't expressed him or herself fully, and the listener hasn't expressed him or herself at all.

As an active listener, of course, you cannot just listen. Eventually, you must share your own thoughts and questions and also give feedback.

Leading a Resonant Team

Have you ever had the experience of being in or leading a truly resonant team—a team in which you and a few other people acted, thought, and felt as one? When a group is at its best, it is able to accomplish amazing feats. Resonant teams create an experience, a condition—together—that transcends the boundaries of individual human beings. This state is elusive, yet if you have had such an experience, it remains a touch point for you about what is possible for teams.

If you follow the tips listed in ■Exhibit 10.14, you can create and sustain a resonant team. Pay attention to the emotional life of the team members, to establishing and re-

■Exhibit **10.14**

Leading a Resonant Team

1. *Start with yourself:* All the rules, roles, and guidelines for creating and sustaining resonance in a team start with you. As Chief Ramsey said earlier in the chapter, it all starts with knowing yourself.

2. *Build resonance with people around you:* Resonance doesn't happen by accident. You need to reach out to people, connect with them, show them a vision of what the team can be, and demonstrate how the team can help them achieve their personal goals and dreams.

3. *Seek to understand the emotional reality of your team:* It's not always easy to see the "emotional reality" of a group—the feelings that swirl around, and the team's stance and attitudes about certain things. But you need to know these things. Watch group dynamics carefully, and take the time to talk with people more deeply about what they are thinking and how they feel about the team.

4. *Engage people's hearts and minds:* It's easy to get caught up in the pressure of deadlines and deliverables. To create resonance on a team, however, you need to slow down enough to engage your own and others' imagination and passion around the work and the team itself.

5. *Capture the dream:* People need a dream to hold on to, especially when work is hard and the team is facing obstacles. Find ways to remind yourself and others about why you're working so hard. Remember the noble purpose of your work.

Source: Adapted from McKee, Annie, Boyatzis, Richard, and Johnston, Frances. 2008. *Becoming a Resonant Leader: Develop your emotional intelligence, renew your relationships, sustain your effectiveness.* Boston, HBP.

inforcing trust in the group, and to making sure you have clarity about team goals. Be sure that the team feels excited by the challenge. Add in the use of humor, loving feedback, and having fun while pursuing your goals, and you've got a resonant team.

Most Popular » Discussion Questions

1. Today you will most likely have dozens of conversations. In at least one of these, consciously monitor your listening habits. Do you concentrate? Jump to conclusions? Judge people? Do you really empathize? Review the sections on listening and active listening, and note one or two areas where you can improve your listening skills.

2. Think about a team in which you are involved. Using the guidelines in Exhibit 10.14 for leading a resonant team, identify at least one action you can take for each of the points listed that will result in improving your team.

10. A Final Word on Teams and Team Building

One foundation of democracy is the idea that concentrating decision-making power in the hands of too few individuals can lead to injustice in society. For this reason, we have instituted collective decision-making bodies throughout society. We have juries to judge guilt or innocence, branches of governments where officials elected by people work in groups to create laws and policies, and boards of directors to guide organizations. As the saying goes, two heads are better than one.

Researchers have compared group performance to individual performance on a number of different tasks and found that groups indeed tend to outperform individuals.[95] Groups can pool resources and have more opportunities to identify and correct errors. Additionally, when a group member works with another member with better skills, the less-skilled individual tends to perform at a higher level. That's why we spend so much time and energy trying to understand groups and how to use them effectively at work: You can get better results when people work together and collaborate on tasks—at least when these large teams are functioning effectively.

When team dynamics are dysfunctional, or even when we underattend to our team's norms, roles, and leadership, it's a very different story. In these groups, decision making and collective work can take an inordinate amount of time, the most competent individuals' contributions can be ignored, the morale of the entire team can suffer, and results can be compromised.[96] In situations like this, it's often impossible for a group to come together around a shared purpose. In fact, just the opposite often happens: People fall prey to groupthink.[97]

What all of this means for us at work is that we must pay attention to how teams function. Great teams don't just happen; they are created and sustained by people who understand group dynamics. In every single team you work with, you have the chance to create an environment where people can share their talents and ideas, have fun, and create outstanding results.

You will probably lead many teams during your career. As you do, it will help to think about some of the guidance shared with us by prominent businessman and well-known leader Niall FitzGerald. FitzGerald, deputy chairman of the board of directors of Thomson Reuters, puts it this way:

> *Leaders are defined by the actions of their followers. The very few really great leaders I have encountered have had:*
>
> *CLARITY (of vision)*
> *COURAGE (to take risks and be unpopular)*
> *EMPATHY (for those they lead)*
> *HUMILITY (which is real)*
> *INSPIRATION (which all followers need)*
> *SIMPLICITY (of expression)*
> *SELF-AWARENESS (of themselves and their impact on others)*
> *TRUST (which they give to others)*
> *WILLPOWER (which drives people and process)*
>
> *The best leaders also understand that they will only sustain success if they gather around them people who are more talented than themselves and give these people the freedom to act and grow. Ultimately leaders will be defined by their willingness to live by the credo that "there are few limits to achievement providing we have no concern for who gets the credit."*

The kind of leaders that Niall FitzGerald is talking about get things done and help each of us grow as citizens and human beings.

Key Terms

1. Why Do Leaders Need Teams? (pp. 340–342)

Key Terms

Team A small group (ideally 6 to 10 individuals) whose members share a common purpose, hold themselves individually and collectively responsible for goals, and have complementary skills and agreed-on processes for working together. p. 341

2. How Does Leadership Behavior Affect Group Dynamics? (pp. 342–343)

Key Terms

Autocratic leader A leader who tends to make decisions without input from others. p. 343

Democratic leader A leader who seeks input and then either makes a decision or engages the group in collective decision making. p. 343

Laissez-faire leader A leader who remains at a distance from the decision-making process, allowing the group to make decisions without leadership intervention. p. 343

3. How Do Groups Change over Time? (pp. 344–348)

Key Terms

Bruce Tuckman's model of group development A model of group development that includes five sequential stages: forming, storming, norming, performing, and adjourning. p. 344

Forming The first stage of group development during which members start to get to know one another, are polite and friendly, avoid conflict, and seek common ground. p. 344

Storming The second stage of group development, which is characterized by disagreements about how to work together, bids for power, and conflict with leaders. p. 344

Norming The third stage of group development, when the group agrees common "rules" of behavior for members (group norms), who does what (group roles), and how best to work together. p. 344

Group norms Informal but powerful standards that guide group members' behavior. p. 344

Group roles Shared expectations among members about who does what. p. 344

Performing The fourth stage of group development, during which the group channels energy into tasks rather than into building relationships, resolving conflicts, or deciding how to work together. p. 344

Adjourning The fifth stage of group development during which the group finishes its tasks and decides or is forced to dissolve membership. p. 345

Susan Wheelan's integrated model of group development A model of group development that shows how groups progress through four stages as members gain experience communicating and working together; a fifth stage, termination, can also be included in this model. p. 345

Counterdependence Attitudes and behaviors related to resisting leadership or direction from others. p. 345

4. How Do Group Dynamics Impact Team Effectiveness? (pp. 349–359)

Key Terms

Meritocracy A system in which people are granted power, responsibilities, and roles because of superior intellect, talent, and competencies. p. 353

Social status The relative standing or prestige you have compared with others in groups to which you belong. p. 354

5. How Do Teams Function at Work? (pp. 359–362)

Key Terms

Self-directed work teams Teams in which there is no formally designated leader and members organize their own activities. p. 359

High-performance team A team that performs beyond "all reasonable expectations," as compared with other teams in similar situations. p. 361

6. How Can We Deal with the Challenges of Working in Groups? (pp. 362–366)

Key Terms

Groupthink "A collective pattern of defensive avoidance that leads people in a group to adopt a singular view even when there is evidence to the contrary." p. 365

7. What Role Does Conflict Play in Groups? (pp. 366–368)

Key Terms

Functional conflict Involves allowing or encouraging differences of opinions among team members in order to yield better group outcomes. p. 366

Dysfunctional conflict Involves aggression, personal attacks, or ways of expressing differences that undermine group success. p. 366

8. How Can HR Support Effective Team Performance? (pp. 369–370)

Key Terms None

9. What Can We All Do to Create and Sustain Resonant Teams? (pp. 370–373)

Key Terms None

10. A Final Word on Teams and Team Building (pp. 373–374)

Key Terms None

Chapter 10 Visual Summary

1. Why Do Leaders Need Teams?
(pp. 340–342)

Summary: Working in groups is natural and necessary for humans. It is difficult for an individual to be successful without the ideas, help, and support of others—and this includes leaders. Understanding team structures is important because most organizational work is completed in teams and teams function as work families that support and uplift us. They motivate us to work and lead in satisfying, powerful ways.

2. How Does Leadership Behavior Affect Group Dynamics? (pp. 342–343)

Summary: The scholar Kurt Lewin and colleagues started a long tradition of research that looked beyond the individual to determine why people behave as they do. In particular, this research focused on how behavior is a function of the person and the environment. Research in this area looked at leadership as one important aspect of the environment. Both early and more recent studies have looked at the effects of autocratic, democratic, and laissez-faire leadership on group members' behavior. Not surprisingly, democratic leadership has proven most successful in field and laboratory studies because it provides sufficient structure and support to individuals without dictating what they should do. Autocratic leadership breeds hostility in group members and laissez-faire leadership is actually not leadership at all—it's an abdication of responsibility.

■Exhibit **10.2**

Lewin's Formula

$$B = f(P, E)$$

3. How Do Groups Change over Time?
(pp. 344–348)

Summary: Researchers Bruce Tuckman and Susan Wheelan developed two widely accepted group development models that describe group formation, learning how to work together, trust building, performance, and dissolution phases. During each stage, some aspects of member and leader behavior are typical, such as politeness in the forming stage and conflict when learning how to work together. Stages are not as discrete as the models suggest and outside forces do influence groups, but understanding these models is key to appreciating the ways groups change over time.

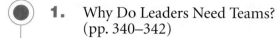

10. Teams and Teambuilding: How to Work Effectively with Others

Organizing Human Systems

11. Working in a Virtual World: Technology as a Way of Life

4. How Do Group Dynamics Impact Team Effectiveness? (pp. 349–359)

Summary: Group roles can be divided into task roles that focus on task performance and maintenance roles that focus on supporting group members emotionally. Norms are another important dynamic for groups because they help group members understand and internalize the way things are done. Status and power represent a third dynamic because they strongly impact group functioning in either positive or negative ways. Diversity is a group dynamic that extends beyond the culture, race, or nationality of group members to their personality types and tendencies. Finally, groups have inherent paradoxes that must be resolved, such as how to place one's trust in a group before the group has had time to prove that trust is deserved.

5. How Do Teams Function at Work?
(pp. 359–362)

Summary: Work teams can be defined in many ways—by function/purpose, structure, participant type, or assignment. No matter what their purpose, many teams are self-directed. Self-directed work teams are becoming increasingly common and they rely on employees to take responsibility for identifying and correcting problems themselves. High-performance teams utilize members' talents and skills in complementary ways that enable the team to function at an optimal level. This, in turn, allows the team to be self-motivated and makes membership its own reward.

8. How Can HR Support Effective Team Performance? (pp. 369–370)

Summary: HR contributes to teams by ensuring that people are trained, supported, and rewarded for group performance. Additionally, HR professionals can facilitate resonant team building that helps individuals learn more about one another and their group as a whole. These opportunities not only help teams focus on a shared vision and establish expectations, they refresh and motivate team members.

■Exhibit **10.14**

Leading a Resonant Team

1. *Start with yourself;*
2. *Build resonance with people around you;*
3. *Seek to understand the emotional reality of your team;*
4. *Engage people's hearts and minds;*
5. *Capture the dream.*

7. What Role Does Conflict Play in Groups? (pp. 366–368)

Summary: Conflict in groups is not inherently bad and, in many situations, promotes creativity, improved processes, and problem solving. Unfortunately, if not handled properly, the advantages of conflict are lost and it becomes dysfunctional. Understanding the various sources of conflict and how to resolve them is a good first step to ensuring positive results. When resolving conflict, trust is the starting point. Allowing group members to explain their positions and utilizing appropriate, win–win negotiation strategies also enables conflict to be constructive.

6. How Can We Deal with the Challenges of Working in Groups? (pp. 362–366)

Summary: Every team is faced with challenges that threaten its ability to perform—membership and inclusion needs, participation, communication, influence, social loafing, and emotions all require thoughtful attention. These issues need to be diagnosed and dealt with by leaders and intuitive group members to ensure a healthy level of discussion and shared responsibility within a group. Conformity and groupthink are two specific group challenges that may also arise. These destructive patterns involve group members going along to get along and defending group actions at all costs, even when it means agreeing to things they would never agree to as individuals.

9. What Can We All Do to Create and Sustain Resonant Teams? (pp. 370–373)

Summary: One of the most important things you can do to improve team dynamics is develop your listening skills, because they form the basis of effective communication. Active listening enables you to accurately interpret what is being said and shows respect for the person speaking by reflecting back to the speaker what you have heard. Listening is a good first step. To go on to build and lead truly resonant teams, you can: start with yourself; build resonance with people; understand your team's emotional reality; engage people's hearts and minds; and capture the dream.

10. A Final Word on Teams and Team Building (pp. 373–374)

Summary: Knowing the basics of team dynamics and understanding the decades of research on the topic will prepare you for your working life. Even as organizations change in our modern world, the basic skills of being a good teammate and leader—clarity, courage, and empathy, to name a few—will help you sustain success no matter the changes you face. Understanding that you can't do everything alone and that you need the support of your team will also enable you to grow as a leader and a person.

Working in a Virtual World:

Technology as a
Way of Life

Chapter Outline 🔍

Find out what you already know about the concepts in this chapter by going to www.mymanagementlab.com and taking the Pre-Test. Your results will generate a customized study plan for Chapter 11.

1. How Do Advances in Information and Communication Technologies Change Life and Work? (pp. 380–382)

2. How Did Technology Affect Life and Work during the Industrial Revolutions? (pp. 382–389)

3. How Have Computing and Telecommunication Technologies Evolved? (pp. 389–392)

4. How Do People Use ICTs at Work? (pp. 392–397)

5. Where and How Is Virtual Work Conducted? (pp. 397–401)

6. What Is a Virtual Organization? (pp. 401–407)

7. What Are the Challenges of Working in a Virtual World? (pp. 408–410)

8. What Can HR Do to Support Virtual Work? (pp. 411–412)

9. What Can We All Do to Work Most Effectively in a Virtual World? (pp. 412–414)

10. A Final Word on Working in a Virtual World (p. 414)

Go back to www.mymanagementlab.com and take the Post-Test to verify your understanding of the concepts. To experience and apply the concepts, explore the additional material associated with Chapter 11.

Part 1: Leading and Managing for Today and the Future (Chapters 1, 2, 3, 4)
Part 2: Planning and Change (Chapters 5, 6, 7, 8, 9)
➤ **Part 3:** Organizing Human Systems (Chapters 10, **11**)
Part 4: Controlling Quality, Culture, and Yourself (Chapters 12, 13)
Part 5: Leading and Managing for the Future (Chapters 14, 15, 16)

8. Workplace Essentials: Creativity, Innovation, and a Spirit of Entrepreneurship

7. Change: A Focus on Adaptability and Resiliency

9. Organizing for a Complex World: Structure and Design

Planning and Change

10. Teams and Teambuilding: How to Work Effectively with Others

Organizing Human Systems

11. Working in a Virtual World: Technology as a Way of Life

6. The Human Side of Planning: Decision Making and Critical Thinking

16. Managing and Leading for Tomorrow: A Focus on Your Future

1. Managing and Leading Today: The New Rules

14. Globalization: Managing Effectively in a Global Economic Environment

5. Planning and Strategy: Bringing the Vision to Life

Leading and Managing for Today and the Future

2. The Leadership Imperative: It's Up to You

4. Communication: The Key to Resonant Relationships

3. Motivation and Meaning: What Makes People Want to Work?

15. Sustainability and Corporate Social Responsibility: Ensuring the Future

12. Organizational Controls: People, Processes, Quality, and Results

Controlling Quality, Culture, and Yourself

13. Culture: It's Powerful

11. Working in a Virtual World: Technology as a Way of Life

1. How Do Advances in Information and Communication Technologies Change Life and Work?

When technologies change, work changes. In the words of the respected scholar Krishnan Kumar, "Work, play, education, family relationships . . . gradually adapt or succumb to the pressures and opportunities of the new technological forces."[1] Technologies of all sorts have dramatically changed every field imaginable, and the convergence of two vital technologies, computers and telecommunications, has had the greatest impact on work life of any innovation in human history. Almost every aspect of our lives is now inexorably linked to **information and communication technologies (ICTs)**—the hardware and software related to electronic communication and information sharing.

Information and communication technologies (ICTs)
All of the hardware and software related to electronic communication and information sharing.

ICTs now help us with most basic human actions such as determining how we meet our partners and mates, where we work and how we do it, how we create and enjoy music and the arts, and how religions are shared and disseminated. In this chapter we will explore the many ways in which ICTs affect our communication at work.

The Winning Formula: ICTs + People = Successful Communication and Information Sharing

One of the challenges in studying ICTs is that it is tempting to focus only on the technology—what it allows us to do, how we can best put it to use, and how it can be improved. However, if we study ICTs this way, we will miss an important point: ICTs are *tools* that *people* use to get things done. ICTs are part of the equation when it comes to working in a virtual world, but people are still the most important factor.

For example, suppose your school introduces a new application that allows you to communicate with your professors and other students more effectively via e-mail, groupware, and videoconferencing (see ■Exhibit 11.1). You and other students like the new program and adapt quickly—but your professor does not. He or she likes the old program, is under pressure to do research, and does not believe taking the time to learn the new one is "worth it." So, your professor refuses to use the new program and forces you to stick with the old one. You think he or she is a dinosaur.

Now, say that this is a widespread problem at your school, and the administration gets involved. They recognize that professors are not using the new system, and they jump to the conclusion that professors don't know how to use the technology. The administration distributes instruction manuals and "tip sheets" and even offers classes. Few professors take advantage of these services.

■Exhibit **11.1**

Technology allows for ease of information sharing and communication.

Next, the administration decides that the new technology must be too complicated, so they eliminate some of what the students consider the best features. Still nothing changes, because the problem is that professors aren't rewarded for learning new technologies—they are rewarded for research and publishing. Taking time to learn and use the new system isn't worth it to them. In addition, now the students don't like the program either. Both professors and students are frustrated and relationships have begun to deteriorate among the three groups—students, professors, and the administration. The school now has an even bigger problem.

This example shows that an improvement in technology does not necessarily result in improvement overall unless the social side of the equation is addressed. In this case, the administration would have

Yuri Arcurs/Shutterstock

needed to recognize and deal with the fact that professors believed that they should not waste time learning new technologies. When it comes to ICTs and innovation at work, we need to pay attention to the *interaction* between technology and people.

Sociotechnical Systems Theory

Sociotechnical systems theory
Theory that examines both social and technical characteristics of tasks and how work is organized, focusing on the interaction between people and technologies.

The dilemma and problems described in the previous example are not new. As various forms of technologies have appeared on the scene, people have had to learn how to change individual behavior, work processes, and organizational cultures. One especially useful theory for understanding how to support people and organizations in linking people and technology is called sociotechnical systems theory, or *sociotech*. As its name implies, **sociotechnical systems theory** examines both social and technical characteristics of tasks and how work is organized, focusing on the interaction between people and technologies. The two primary principles of this theory are:[2]

1. Organizational performance is tied to the interaction of social *and* technical factors. Technological advances alone do not necessarily lead to organizational success. Social factors—what people choose to do, how they feel about it, and the culture of the organization—are equally if not more important.
2. Optimization of either social or technical elements alone increases the unpredictability of relationships and can lead to less effective performance. Therefore, a coordinated optimization of both elements is needed.

Sociotechnical systems theory can be traced back to 1951, when scholars Eric Trist and Ken W. Bamforth presented a case study of an organization that had suffered from decreased productivity although it had improved its technology. Despite human resource interventions such as increased pay and benefits, employee absenteeism rose following the technological changes. Trist and Bamforth found that these changes had the unpredicted effect of increasing the bureaucratic structure of the organization, which in turn had a negative effect on employee productivity.[3]

Sociotechnical systems theory was further developed by scholars Fred Emery and Eric Trist during the 1960s, with many others following through to the present time.[4] In the 1980s, after reviewing more than 130 studies, noted sociotech scholar William Pasmore concluded that the research made a strong and valid point: More attention should be paid to the effects of technological changes on individual behavior.[5] The best technology in the world is worthless if people won't use it, and organizations can actually be harmed, rather than helped, if the people side of the equation is ignored. As you read this chapter keep in mind that people are still at the heart of an organization's success. It's up to managers and leaders to support people in changing behaviors, values, and norms as technologies are introduced. Attention to the people side of the equation is even more important in our world today, because technologies are changing constantly.

ICTs and Working in a Virtual World

Today's business environment is characterized by rapid, discontinuous, often unpredictable change. Also, partly as a result of ICTs and other technologies, the global market has become hypercompetitive. Slow-moving companies are at a major disadvantage, especially if they continue to organize work, ICTs, and people as they did in the past. Again, *people* are the key to successfully maneuvering this new environment.

Technologically savvy communication competencies, delegation skills, and the ability to participate in and manage virtual teams are only a few of the skills people will need to develop in order to be successful at work today. Social and emotional intelligence competencies are also important because the use of ICTs adds a dimension of complexity to building and maintaining effective relationships. To deal with this complexity, we all need to be highly self-aware and self-managing and able to practice empathy, positive influencing skills, and coaching and mentoring skills—even with people we never meet face to face.[6] To this list, former U.S. Secretary of Labor Robert Reich adds four additional capabilities: abstract reasoning, systems thinking, collaboration, and the ability to experiment.[7]

In the remainder of this chapter, we take a close look at the precise ways in which ICTs are changing how people live and work and what you need to learn in order to be successful. We start with a brief review of how technological changes have impacted human societies and how people worked in the past. Then, we explore some of the recent technological innovations that have revolutionized how people communicate and work, including the Internet and Web 2.0. After that, we look at how ICTs are used at work, virtual work structures such as telecommuting and virtual teams, and virtual organizations. Lastly, we examine what HR can do to support effective virtual work (and workers), as well as what we can all do to be as effective as possible in an increasingly virtual world.

Most Popular »   Discussion Questions

1. List the ICTs you use each day beginning with the most important device and ending with the least important. Consider the top three items on the list: Why are they so important to you?

2. Access to ICTs is not equal across the globe. On the Internet, find one country where ICTs are widely used and one that you believe has less access (e.g., in the developing world). What social and economic outcomes could occur if imbalances like this continue?

3. Visit three shops in your community and observe how people work. What conclusions can you make about the extent to which the stores' managers and employees are considering sociotechnical systems to organize the space and the workflow? What could be done to improve the link between people, the physical space, and technology?

---

2. How Did Technology Affect Life and Work during the Industrial Revolutions?

Technology
The use of tools and knowledge to influence the environment.

Broadly defined, **technology** is the use of tools and knowledge to influence the environment. People have been using and improving technology since prehistoric times. For example, our ancient ancestors first used rocks and sticks to forage and kill game. Later, the invention of the wheel enabled the ancients to transport goods more efficiently—making it possible for people to live in one place for longer periods of time. Art, storytelling, and writing are technologies that developed over time too—they allowed people to share history, religion, and culture from one generation to the next.

For more than 90 percent of our history, changes in how our species lived and worked were gradual. People lived in small groups of 30 to 150 people, foraging, gathering, and hunting food in order to survive.[8] Technologies were passed from generation to generation and with a few rare inventions (such as gunpowder and the printing press), most advances caused people to *adjust* their lifestyles rather than fundamentally changing the way they lived or worked. This remained the case until the onset of the Industrial Revolution, which marked the beginning of rapid technological advances.

Technology and the First Industrial Revolution

Industrial Revolution
The period in the eighteenth and nineteenth centuries during which major advances in technology, manufacturing, and transportation changed people's way of life, mainly in England, the United States, and parts of continental Europe.

The **Industrial Revolution** refers to the period in the eighteenth and nineteenth centuries during which major advances in technology, manufacturing, and transportation changed people's way of life, mainly in England, the United States, and parts of continental Europe. This revolution didn't simply "happen"; it occurred over time.[9] Key events that took place during this period included the shift from manual and animal labor to the use of machinery in manufacturing; the harnessing of steam power; and the improvement of older technologies such as water power.[10]

Throughout the Industrial Revolution, changes in technology drove widespread changes in society. For example, as factories were built to produce textiles and other goods, massive numbers of people moved from rural areas into cities. People whose families had farmed or worked as craftsmen for generations, were now living in crowded cities, earning wages, and buying things they had always made themselves. Ways of life that had been in place for hundreds of years disappeared in a short period of time.

During much of this time a philosophical transformation was also sweeping through the Western world. This movement, now known as the **Age of Enlightenment**, fueled radical new ideas about government, science, economic systems, and wealth across Europe and parts of North America.[11] This philosophy inspired Western society to see logic and reason as the greatest of human gifts, and to believe that self-interest is a primary driver of human behavior.

The Scottish philosopher Adam Smith was one of the leading figures of the Enlightenment. His writings addressed the relationship between reason, the production of goods in a free-market economy, self-interest, and wealth (■Exhibit 11.2). One of Smith's transformative ideas was his belief that self-interest is a primary source of both action and innovation. In other words, what we do is linked to our assessment of whether its personally good for us or not. Smith also believed that self-interested behavior ultimately serves the larger society, an idea he elaborated most famously in his book *The Wealth of Nations*:

> It is not from the benevolence of the butcher, the brewer, or the baker that we expect our dinner, but from their regard to their own self-interest. We address ourselves, not to their humanity, but to their self-love, and never talk to them of our own necessities but of their advantages.[12]

Smith's second transformative idea related to how wealth is created.[13] He believed that a free market creates order in an economic environment by guiding the amount of goods produced (what people want) and the price the market will bear for those goods (what people will pay), resulting in the optimum use of society's resources. This stance, coupled with the belief that self-interested behavior is beneficial for individuals and societies, helped to legitimize the power and high social status of the new "owner" class—the individuals who owned and operated the means of production. During this period of time, wealth became more concentrated in the hands of this new class of people and the divide between the owner class and the worker class grew.

Later, influential thinkers such as Karl Marx sought to expose the inherent problems in the world of "haves" (capitalist owners) and "have nots" (workers).[14] For instance, Marx believed that a society in which workers had little or no access to the wealth they produced would ultimately result in an unsustainable social and economic systems.

During the time the philosophies represented by the writings of Adam Smith and Karl Marx were taking hold, a new manufacturing and goods-consuming society and shifts in the concentration of wealth dramatically altered life in England, the United States, and parts of Europe. This was just the beginning: continuing technological advances catapulted even more of the world's people into a new era.

Technology and the Second Industrial Revolution

Sometimes referred to as the **Second Industrial Revolution**, the period from the mid-nineteenth century through approximately 1915 was marked by the development of several life-altering technologies including electricity, motors, synthetics, internal

Age of Enlightenment
Primarily eighteenth-century movement that fueled radical new ideas about government, science, economic systems, and wealth across Europe and parts of North America.

■Exhibit **11.2**
Scottish philosopher Adam Smith championed the free market as a way to help the whole of society in *The Wealth of Nations*.

Classic Image/Alamy Images

Second Industrial Revolution
The period from the mid-nineteenth century through approximately 1915 that was marked by the development of several life-altering technologies, including electricity, motors, synthetics, internal combustion, and mass production techniques.

combustion, and mass production techniques.[15] This period also witnessed Henry Ford's creation of the assembly line, which allowed for scientific precision in the division of labor and created new possibilities for mass production. As a result of assembly lines, traditional forms of labor-intensive work were automated and eliminated, and in many cases, workers began to specialize in only one or two of the thousands of functions involved in complex manufacturing processes.[16]

New means of communication such as the telegraph and the telephone also transformed life during the Second Industrial Revolution. Organizations could now be managed more efficiently, even when work sites and workers were geographically dispersed. At the same time, wealth-sharing structures such as wider access to stock ownership, increases in manufacturing wages, and the slow transition of landowners from lenders to borrowers began emerging. Together, these developments allowed more people to be involved in the growing industrialized economy and helped to spread the wealth that had formerly been concentrated in the hands of the elite owner class.[17]

As you have seen, industrialization brought about fundamental shifts in societies and work in several countries in the Western world. These countries' experiences during the Industrial Revolutions helped to shape societies and businesses. But what was happening elsewhere during this period? To better understand global dynamics today, it's important to take time out to review what was happening in the rest of the world during the 200-plus years that saw England, the United States, and much of Europe become industrialized nations.

Africa, India, South America, and China during the Era of Western Industrialization

Why is it so important to study how other parts of the world were developing during this period? First, many countries and regions that used to be uninvolved in the global economy are not only players today—now they are leaders. With the advancement of ICTs comes globalization and more equal access: People everywhere now have an opportunity to be vitally involved in global economic and social changes that can provide a better quality of life. Finally, because many parts of the world—most of it, in fact— did not industrialize in the same way or at the same time that England, parts of Europe, and the United States did, we face vast differences in the experiences people and entire countries have had with respect to business and work. To get a better picture of these differences, let's consider what was happening in Africa, India, South America, and China during the era of industrialization.

Africa during the Era of Industrialization

Despite its proximity to Europe, much of Africa remained largely closed to the outside world until well after the end of World War II. While Africa's eastern coastline was part of an important trade route between India and Europe as early as the 1500s, most ships did little more than stop to replenish supplies, wait out harsh weather, or purchase slaves and raw materials. Europe's imperialist powers penetrated Africa's interior very little other than along the coastal ports and the few large rivers on the eastern side of the continent.

Throughout this period, Western Africa also remained relatively isolated. As with the eastern coast, there was little to no interest in exploring the interior or setting up ongoing trade, which might have led to the development of larger cities and industrialization. Portuguese and other Western explorers found few centralized tribal governments, the terrain was harsh, and there were tropical diseases to contend with. Also, much of Africa was densely populated with tribes who were well armed and hostile toward outsiders. There was therefore little contact between most of Africa and the West, with one major exception: traders who found easy access to gold, ivory, gum, wax, and especially slaves.[18]

■Exhibit **11.3**

Statue of a slave couple in Dakar, Senegal.

Friedrich Stark/Alamy Images

Since at least the seventh century and continuing through the twentieth century, Arab traders enslaved some 18 million East Africans. The Atlantic slave trade, which began several centuries later and ended a century earlier, enslaved 7 to 12 million Africans, most of whom ended up in the Americas (■Exhibit 11.3).[19] The slave trade was largely one sided, as was the trading of raw materials like gold and diamonds. In other words, traders took out much more than they brought in. There was also little spread of technological innovations that might have fostered industrialization. Even after European colonialism began in earnest in Africa during the nineteenth century, there was little change in Western nations' unbalanced and oppressive relationship with African communities.

Another horrific reason why the continent was not part of the Industrial Revolution was the widespread belief among white Europeans and North Americans that African cultures were "too primitive" to adapt to a more modern way of life. Multicultural consultant Paula Rothenberg notes that racist attitudes led many to perceive the failure of modernization in Africa as evidence of Africans' inferiority, rather than the result of trade practices and colonialist systems. These inequitable and brutal systems kept many Africans in menial and labor intensive jobs, often accompanied by repressive and even brutal treatment (as was the case in the Americas as well).[20]

India during the Era of Industrialization

By the sixteenth century, several European powers had established trading ports in India, which developed into colonies over time. As the British expanded their political power in India, a system emerged that included a class of wealthy landlords who heavily taxed the peasantry.[21] Although Indians attempted to rebel in 1857, the uprising resulted in a harsh crackdown on Indian citizens by the British-run regime.[22]

During the many years of British rule, Indian craftsmanship became virtually worthless, primarily because the country's residents were required to buy products that were imported from England. Indian soldiers and administrators were kept in low-level jobs, while the best jobs were reserved for the British.[23] Meanwhile, the textile industry, which fueled the Industrial Revolution in England and other Western countries, was virtually destroyed in India through high taxes and a British embargo on Indian exports. Subsequently, many industrial towns fell into decline.[24] In short, British colonial rule effectively and systematically compartmentalized labor and destroyed any opportunity for industrialization in India.

South America during the Era of Industrialization

Although South America had been the target of European interest since the days of the conquistadors, it too remained relatively unaffected by industrialization. The continent's "discovery" by European powers during the late 1400s and early 1500s first brought the conquistadors, whose sole purpose was to lay waste to wealthy indigenous civilizations such as the Aztecs and the Incas and bring treasure back to Europe. As a result, highly sophisticated agrarian societies were destroyed.[25] Soon after the early conquistadors, missionaries arrived with the goal of converting local populations to Christianity. This too resulted in fundamental changes to local societies, including replacing local governance structures with church and/or foreign leaders.[26] Over time, several European nations—primarily Spain and Portugal—established colonial governments throughout South America, and they continued to rule until the 1800s when many South American colonies won their independence.[27] Still, despite (or perhaps because of) years of colonization, the continent remained somewhat isolated and underdeveloped, and trade was mainly in the form of raw materials and cash crops produced by cheap labor on large plantations.

From the mid-1800s up through the first few decades of the twentieth century, economic growth remained slow in the region, partially as a result of many South American nations' unwillingness to be dependent upon foreign powers as a more global economy emerged.[28] During this period and continuing through most of the 1980s, many South American countries industrialized to some extent and produced goods locally. Weak ties with industrialized nations for so many years caused problems in some ways, but there was a pronounced upside: Isolation helped much of the continent to escape the worst effects of the Great Depression and World War II.[29] By the late 1980s, however, social unrest, wars, political intervention by world superpowers, collapsing South American economies and widespread debt pushed many countries away from their isolationist policies and toward a more open economic stance.[30]

China during the Era of Industrialization

China was not a major contributor to the Industrial Revolution of the eighteenth and nineteenth centuries. Part of the reason for this relative noninvolvement may have been the nation's severe restriction of information and repression of writers, known as the "literary inquisition," during the eighteenth century.[31] This meant that some of the philosophies and ideas that supported industrialization and subsequent social changes in the West were not widely disseminated in China.

It is still somewhat surprising that China was so late to industrialize; after all, Chinese society had the infrastructure, the technological means, and the labor to do so. So, why didn't industrialization happen earlier? For one thing, despite established relations with the West, the nation's military empire severely restricted trade, accepting only precious metals from the West in exchange for Chinese goods such as silks and ceramics.[32] Another possible answer lies in China's severe restrictions on women working outside the home.[33] Particularly in England and the United States, women were a major part of the labor force in factories. In China women were not only prohibited from working outside the home, but the practice of binding their feet (which continued until the late nineteenth century) ensured that they had limited mobility—and limited capacity to work.[34]

Among the working poor, there were severe restrictions on Chinese men's access to females: Widows were not allowed to remarry, and wealthy households kept several female concubines, so many poor men had no wives. As a result, poor farming families often had few children. This meant that for several generations, offspring would often stay on and work a family's small plot of land.[35] The trend was different in Europe, where high birth rates and the decline of feudal systems caused young people from the lower classes to move to the growing cities to seek work.

A final word on Chinese industrialization: The rise of Communism after World War II resulted in widespread destruction in the countryside, which was already decimated by war. Much of the infrastructure and industrial means of production that had been developed during the early twentieth century was compromised, as was much of the infrastructure in large cities. As Mao Zedong claimed power, private farms were obliterated, to be replaced by collectives. The idea was that the money generated by farm collectives would finance industrialization and the building/rebuilding of the country's economic and industrial infrastructure. During this period, there was widespread famine, violence, and repression, as well as almost complete isolation from Western economies.

The World Economic Stage as Western Industrialization Waned

Africa, India, South America, and China changed a great deal during the two to three centuries of Western industrialization. They did not, however, develop either the technological infrastructure or socioeconomic structures that by the mid-twentieth century governed many Western nations' politics, economies, and cultures. By the time advances in technologies allowed for increasing interdependence among the world's economies, there was a vast difference in how various countries could or would engage.

By the early to mid-twentieth century, technological changes, increased global trade, decline of political structures such as colonialism, and the rise of the working middle class had resulted in vastly different social and economic systems around the world. The stage was set for the next, even more radical (and faster) social and technological revolution. This time, the revolution has the potential to include everyone, even the most remote and isolated countries.

The Post-Industrial Society and the Third Industrial Revolution

By the 1960s, it was becoming clear that another massive change was under way in many parts of the world. The technological innovations that had previously shifted work from farms to factories in industrialized societies were once again poised to shift many people's work from mass production to the generation and dissemination of knowledge and services.[36] In 1973 futurist Daniel Bell described this "post-industrial" society as one in which the manufacturing workforce would be replaced by a workforce of professionals and service providers.[37] Whereas during the First and Second Industrial Revolutions, wealth was linked to the means of production, during the latter half of the twentieth century, wealth became more and more linked to the ability to create, acquire, and share knowledge.

Third Industrial Revolution
The period beginning in the mid- to late-twentieth century through today when economic activities are marked by an increased focus on information and communication technologies, along with greater attention to issues of environmental sustainability and economic competition.

As the twenty-first century neared, the so-called Third Industrial Revolution began to emerge. The **Third Industrial Revolution** describes a period of time beginning in the mid- to late-twentieth century through today when economic activities are marked by an increased focus on ICTs along with greater attention to issues of environmental sustainability and economic competition. According to social thinker Jeremy Rifkin, the convergence of ICTs, the focus on environmental sustainability, and economic competition will, "require a wholesale reconfiguration of the transport, construction and electricity sectors, creating new goods and services, spawning new businesses, and providing millions of new jobs."[38]

This "wholesale reconfiguration," along with the need to move away from reliance on fossil fuels and to respond to climate change, will bring about great transformations in how energy is created and used, as well as in manufacturing processes. In the words of writer Kurt Anderson, this new era can therefore be thought of as the "reset economy"—an opportunity to correct the wrongs of past business practices, promote clean energy, clean up the environment, and invest in social goods and services such as health care and education.[39] The dawn of this social and technological revolution is certain to bring profound changes in political, economic, and social structures all over the world.[40] Let's look at some of the changes we are seeing *now*.

Information + Communications Technology = Profound Social Change

During the past few decades, changes in many of the social structures that developed alongside industrialization have begun to shift, often in unpredictable ways. Let's look at just a few of the social changes related to ICTs that are occurring today, as well as their far-reaching consequences:

- The nation-state is now rivaled by social structures (such as Al Qaeda) that are not located in one geographical area or centered in a single nation, yet wield tremendous power on the international stage. Groups like this can create and support sophisticated governance and communication structures, all as a result of information technology.
- News and information can now be shared around the world in a matter of milliseconds.
- Access to information is currently less dependent on wealth or social class than it was in previous decades, and unprecedented numbers of people have access to communication networks.

- Developing nations are often "leapfrogging" certain aspects of industrialization (e.g., many countries are not making massive investments in land-line telephone technology) because newer, more advanced (and often cheaper) alternatives are already available.[41]

Social Change = Changes at Work

ICTs are increasingly at the center of how people learn and work.[42] The spread of computer networks has made communication across long distances increasingly feasible and affordable, and this has greatly aided organizational communication. As a result, today's workers can collaborate, share, and access information more efficiently and easily than ever before, and managers have a vast array of technological tools for coordinating and monitoring work.

Closely related to these changes has been an inexorable move toward globalization and interconnectedness. For example, transportation technologies have made it possible to move goods (and people) more quickly and easily, allowing for organizational models such as "just-in-time" inventory management to be used more efficiently and effectively. A vast number of products are not produced in one location anymore. Intel, for example, has manufacturing facilities in Argentina, China, Costa Rica, India, Ireland, Israel, Malaysia, Mexico, the Philippines, Poland, Russia, and Vietnam.[43] Similarly, the raw materials required to create a single product often come from numerous parts of the world. For example, the gold used in a computer's circuit board could have come from mines in Africa, the silicon may have been mined in Brazil, and the plastics may have been created from oil that was pumped out of the ground in the Middle East but processed in the United States. To manage the complex supply chains that are necessary for this kind of production process, businesses use highly sophisticated ICTs and workflow management systems.[44]

■ Exhibit **11.4**

Global logistics has changed how ships load and unload cargo.

Phil Degginger/Alamy Images

In today's work environment, even employees who never leave their local sites may find it necessary to interact with people from a range of cultures, nationalities, and ethnicities on a regular basis.[45] To better illustrate the interconnectedness of these sorts of changes in ICTs, society, and work, let's look at two examples of major shifts that are currently under way in the modern workplace: job migration and global logistics.

Job Migration

One defining characteristic of today's information society is the rapid expansion of globalization, which has resulted in an international division of labor that can be used to maximize efficiency and profits. Given the desire to maximize profits—and the abundance of lower priced labor in less-developed countries—many companies have moved some of their operations far from home. This has been especially true in the manufacturing sector. For example, in the United States the number of manufacturing jobs declined by 19 percent between 1998 and 2005.[46] This drop and others like it are due in large part to jobs and operations moving elsewhere. This is far more possible now than in the past because of ICTs.[47]

Global Logistics

Advanced global logistics processes are made possible in part by a satellite tracking technology, an advanced form of ICTs. The term *global logistics* refers to how goods are processed, transported, and stored along a supply chain. Given that so many products are manufactured in one place and sold in another, and/or include parts made in various places around the world, global logistics is an increasingly complicated and important part of how goods are made and sold. Advances in global logistics have allowed for business integration, streamlined operations, and leaner organizations. Companies such as UPS have been able to perfect certain aspects of the process and now sell their services to other organizations.[48]

Consider how technology has changed one aspect of global logistics: the docks where ships load and unload cargo (■Exhibit 11.4). Since 1968, the amount of cargo flowing through U.S. docks has increased by about 500 percent, while the number of employees has decreased by nearly half.[49] In the face of advancing technology, dock workers were understandably worried about the future of their jobs and their industry.

For example, in 2002, after a three-month failure to renegotiate a union contract and an alleged work "slowdown" (a type of strike), the Pacific Maritime Association instituted a 10-day lockout of International Longshore and Warehouse Union (ILWU) employees, costing billions of dollars.[50] The dispute was settled with an agreement between the Pacific Maritime Association and the ILWU regarding the role of technology. Ultimately, the union accepted the use of new technologies and the related loss of 400 jobs, with the guarantee that the 400 employees would be retrained and put to work elsewhere on the docks. In addition, the union negotiated for a large wage and benefits increase.[51]

As you can see, many of the changes under way in the world during the past 200 to 300 years are the result of shifts in technology, especially ICTs. In the next section, we will take a closer look at the development of the World Wide Web and telecommunications technology, as well as how these things support us on a daily basis as we work.

Most Popular » Discussion Questions

1. Search the Internet to find out what parts of the world are currently industrializing. How is this wave of industrialization different than the Industrial Revolution of the eighteenth and nineteenth centuries? How might this new wave of industrialization affect global business? Has it affected you? If so, how?

2. Through social networking, connect with a college student in Africa, India, South America, or China. Discuss how industrialization has affected your respective countries, and how more recent advances in ICTs have affected each of you personally.

3. Explain why recent advances in ICTs are contributing to changes in social structures such as economics and politics. Begin your discussion by focusing on how people's lives and work have changed in your community. Then, consider how ICTs are driving changes in parts of the world far from your home.

---

3. How Have Computing and Telecommunication Technologies Evolved?

ICTs are important drivers of new ways of working. In this section, we will consider how computers and telecommunications are revolutionizing the way work is conducted and organized in modern organizations. We'll also explore how the Internet, intranets, extranets, and the cloud facilitate information sharing and collaboration among and between people at work.

Computing Technology: From a U.S. Defense Strategy to Web 2.0

The birth of the Internet can be traced back to 1962, when MIT computer scientist Joseph Licklider first began working for the Advanced Research Projects Agency (ARPA), a Cold War agency of the U.S. Department of Defense.[52] By 1968, a plan for the creation

The Internet was preceded by ARPANET.

Alex Segre/Alamy Images

Internet
A global system of interlinked, hypertext documents contained within an electronic network that connects computers and computer networks around the world.

Web 2.0
The second generation of Web technology and software development that allows for increased interactivity, user design and control, and collaboration.

Intranet
An internal company network that is usually accessible only to employees.

Extranet
A computer network designed for an organization to communicate in a secure environment with certain external stakeholders, such as customers.

of an information-sharing network called ARPANET was approved. Within months, a permanent ARPANET link was established between two computers at UCLA and Stanford Research Institute. Electronic mail was now possible, and in 1971, the first e-mail message was sent between two ARPANET-linked computers that sat side by side.[53]

Although ARPANET was a success, this technology was used by only a handful of individuals for almost two decades, and most people weren't even aware of its existence.[54] This all began to change in 1989, when researcher Tim Berners-Lee used the idea of interlinked hypertext documents (Web pages) to develop the "WorldWideWeb" (one word).[55] Later, the terms "World Wide Web" (WWW or "the Web") became interchangeable with the term "Internet." The **Internet** is a global system of interlinked, hypertext documents contained within an electronic network that connects computers and computer networks around the world (■Exhibit 11.5).[56] In 1993, the code for developing Web pages was released to the public. At the time, there were only 130 Web pages—but that wouldn't be the case for long. Indeed, by 2004, Google had indexed approximately 8 billion pages, and by 2008, that number had hit the 1 trillion mark.[57]

Today, much of the excitement in the tech- and networking-related sectors is around "Web 2.0." **Web 2.0** is often described as the second generation of Web technology and software development that allows for increased interactivity, user design and control, and collaboration. Web 2.0 applications permit faster sharing of greater quantities of information, greater ease of use, and more opportunities for people to interact with the technology and with one another.

Specific examples of technologies associated with Web 2.0 include social networking sites, virtual worlds in which "real" activities can occur, multiperson gaming, wikis, blogs, peer-to-peer networks, and hosted services. One particular benefit of many of these applications is that they are not dependent on a single brand or manufacturer of hardware (e.g., PC or Mac). This allows organizations and individuals greater control of their own data and has expanded the types of applications available to many people at work.[58]

For businesses that sell products and services, Web 2.0 has facilitated far more communication and interaction with customers and between organizations than ever before. For example, online user reviews of products and services can lead to more informed buying and increased power for the consumer. And, according to author Amy Shuen, the real benefit of bigger, faster, more interactive information-sharing networks is increased traffic—which means that more people can access business, and businesses can market to more people faster.[59] Shuen cites Google, eBay, Skype, and Wikipedia as prime examples of networks benefiting from the positive impact of network traffic.[60]

The Internet, Intranets, Extranets, and the "Cloud"

The Internet, as you know, is a computer network that enables data transmission among computers all over the world. Some of the technology at the heart of the Internet is also used by companies to manage their own internal communication. Frequently, this involves creation of an **intranet**, or an internal company network that is usually accessible only to employees. To keep company information secure, intranets have firewalls and other security features that prevent outsiders from gaining access. An **extranet** is a computer network designed for an organization to communicate in a secure environment with certain external stakeholders, such as customers.

Cloud computing
Hosted services offered via the Internet that are available on demand, are highly flexible in terms of the amount of service users have access to, and are fully managed by the provider.

Many companies in the past two decades have built extensive computer networks to manage information flow and storage. In the past few years, however, processes for working electronically have been increasingly shifting away from company-maintained networks to vast data structures located in third-party run computing centers.[61] This is referred to as **cloud computing**. Cloud services are different from traditional local hosting services in that they are offered on demand, are highly flexible in terms of the amount of service users have access to, and are fully managed by the service provider.[62]

Cloud computing is not a new concept. Early computers operated on a "hub-and-spoke" structure that provided multiple users access to a host of services. Computing, therefore, was a somewhat centralized technology. When personal computers arrived on the scene in the 1980s, people were thrilled that they no longer had to "buy time" on a network but could manage and store documents and applications themselves. We still value this benefit but even the most powerful new personal computers and local networks cannot keep up with people's needs for massive storage capacity and increasingly powerful infrastructures, platforms, and software services. One current example of cloud computing is Google Docs. With this online word-processing and spreadsheet application, documents are stored on a server run by Google, and they are instantly accessible via the Internet to any invited collaborator. Because the document is centrally located, it no longer has to be passed around from person to person by e-mail for multiple rounds of editing.[63] Another example is the Amazon Elastic Compute Cloud (Amazon EC2), which offers virtual IT services.[64] Also, Apple's MobileMe offers applications hosting and data storage, along with applications integration.[65]

Work in many organizations today depends on the ability to communicate effectively and rapidly across distance and time. Computers, networks, and the cloud allow us to transmit a wide variety of information digitally. Of course, this capability is greatly enhanced by advances in telecommunications technology.

The Evolution of Telecommunications

The history of mobile telecommunications is one of industry competing with military institutions during and after the Cold War. During that period, technology did not allow for much "traffic" over the airways. Therefore, business leaders found it difficult to convince governments to allow for the nonmilitary use of mobile telecommunications.[66] As new digital technologies emerged and the Cold War ended, all of this began to change. By all accounts, the digital cell phone revolution began in 1991, when Finland launched the world's first 2G public network using new telecommunications technology. The phrase *2G* refers to the second generation of cellular phone technology, which used digital rather than analog technology (we're now potentially moving beyond even *4G*).

The new cellular technology was a tremendous success, and it soon spread across the planet. The International Telecommunication Union (ITU) reported that by December 2008, the number of mobile phone subscribers worldwide had passed 4 billion, up from 3 billion just 18 months earlier. By mid-2009, there were more than 276 million cell phone subscribers in the United States alone, and the world's two most populous countries, China and India, surpassed 700 million and 500 million subscribers, respectively.[67] In addition to these cell phone figures, there were also a reported 1.27 billion fixed lines, 1.54 billion Internet users, and close to 800 million broadband subscribers, including 430 million mobile broadband users.[68]

What that means is that people can connect in ways unimaginable a few decades ago. This has changed our lives, and it has certainly changed work. The spread of cell phones and other mobile devices has literally put computing in the palms of our hands. Your cell phone or smart phone probably has more and often better computing power than large desktop computers of the past, not to mention cameras, the ability to play music, and keyboards to write e-mail and text messages.

Information and communication technologies have paved the way for entirely new modes of working. In the next section, we will look at the many ways people can work and communicate via electronic technologies.

Most Popular » Discussion Questions

1. Talk to a relative or friend over age 45 about phone and computer technologies when they were young. How does your experience with this technology differ from theirs?
2. Some of the technologies that ultimately supported the development of mobile phones existed early in the last century. Brainstorm a list of reasons why it took so long for cell phones to be commercially developed.

---

4. How Do People Use ICTs at Work?

In many jobs, ICTs are the basis upon which work is planned, conducted, shared, and evaluated. We use computers to capture and share ideas, plan projects, evaluate performance, and calculate costs, expenditures, revenues, profits, and debt. We track inventory, create graphics, market our products and services, conduct research—the list goes on and on. In this section, we will focus on certain types of ICTs that enable communication, learning, and knowledge sharing at work: e-mail, texting, teleconferencing, videoconferencing, Web conferencing, and social networking. The reason we are focusing on these few is that no matter what job you have, what school you attend, or what type of work you do, you will need to use these applications effectively and professionally.

E-Mail

The high speed and low cost of e-mail make it a highly efficient channel for both internal and external communication at work. E-mail has all the value of traditional written communication but with a number of added benefits. For one, e-mail is fast—almost immediate—and it provides for a quick feedback loop if all parties are online and actively reading and responding. E-mail also allows us to communicate with any number of people in any part of the world with one efficient message. In addition, e-mail is essentially democratic, theoretically allowing anyone to communicate with anyone else in an organization, regardless of their positions in the hierarchy.

Of course, despite all of its benefits, e-mail is also a source of numerous communication problems. Consider the following examples:

- E-mail is one of the leading causes of information overload.
- Much of the e-mail sent and received is simply a waste of time.
- E-mail lends itself to lazy communication.
- Unless the users are skilled, e-mail tends to lessen the likelihood that the right amount of information is shared and that the content of the information includes enough context.
- It is difficult to communicate and interpret emotion in e-mail communication.

For a better idea of why it's so important to communicate the right information in *the right way* via e-mail, consider the words of Rachel Kamau, Director of Reimbursements at Signature HealthCARE. Rachel Kamau's advice is helpful when considering how to use e-mail, because we often ignore some of the most important rules she out-

Rachel Kamau, Director of Reimbursements, Signature HealthCARE

Signature HealthCARE is an innovative network of health care centers, and Rachel Kamau is a highly respected leader in her role as Director of Reimbursements. Because of Signature HealthCARE's network structure, it is essential that people within the organization learn how to get and share information effectively. Rachel has mastered the art and science of communicating in a networked organization. As she puts it:

In order to do my job well, I need to be involved and understand globally where we are going and where my department fits in. So, there are a few things I do, that we can all do, to be sure that when we communicate with people, we get the information we need. It's not only about getting the information, sending the e-mails, etc. It's about people.

Respect is the first rule. And probably the most important rule. Second, you need to use common sense and be sure to include enough background information about what you are sharing, or asking, so people can understand what to do and what you need. And third: ask questions. Ask a lot of questions. I approach life and my work with great curiosity. I look at each day as a chance to pursue something, to learn something. No one is born knowing everything—it's curiosity and practice, practice, practice that results in continuous learning.

You have to have the attitude that you can ask any question—that's how you find out what's really going on. You have to ask "Why?" one, two, three, even four times. Remember: It's the fourth question, not the first, that gets you the truth.

I believe we have a lot more control over what we learn and how we learn it. But it takes courage, belief in yourself, and a willingness to take the time you need to get, and share, the right kind of information, while keeping relations positive.

Source: Personal interview with Rachel Kamau conducted by Annie McKee, 2009.

lines: respect, using common sense about what to share, and asking enough questions to get what you need.

Sometimes, though, no matter how skilled the users are, e-mail is simply not the right way to communicate certain messages. E-mail is not the best avenue for sensitive messages or messages that can be easily misunderstood. For example, if someone has made a mistake, it's not a good idea to offer criticism by e-mail; pick up the phone or meet face to face for difficult conversations. And don't forget that e-mail is a permanent and public form of communication: *Nothing is confidential in an e-mail message.* Even when messages are deleted, they exist on record and are retrievable.

Another potential problem is that transmitting emotion via e-mail is a tricky process. The first mistake many people make is to assume that electronic written communication channels are emotionless. Communication *always* includes emotion, so we must seek ways to appropriately express our emotions even when we communicate via technology.[69]

Not understanding how emotion comes across in e-mail affects more than our personal relationships—it can also result in problems at work. Frequent mistakes include the following:

- Assuming that your reader understands your intended emotions
- Overstating emotions in e-mail to make sure receivers get the point
- Assuming that all readers will interpret the emotions expressed in an e-mail in the same way
- Failing to recognize that emotion can be magnified when interpreted and received in e-mail communications—especially negative emotions.

It is critical to remember that in contrast to face-to-face communication, where people can help one another regulate their emotions, people are on their own in managing their emotions when writing or receiving an e-mail. This can result in communication that is confusing or lacking empathy—even when the sender intended otherwise.

Text Messages

A popular alternative to e-mail is text messaging, which can take the form of instant messaging (IM) via the Internet or transmission of text (or SMS) messages via cell phone. Texting involves real-time communication in short bits. Text messaging can speed up the communication process, but it also has drawbacks.

Text messages tend to be very brief. Some forms of texting, like Twitter, allow very few characters—140 in this case. Like e-mail, however, texting isn't without its problems:

- Text messages are short and incomplete.
- They include acronyms and "codes" for certain words that some people do not understand.
- They require that everyone be logged on to a computer or attending to a phone.
- They interrupt work.
- It is difficult to accurately send and interpret emotions in texts.

Constant attention to text messages also hinders—and can harm—communication and relationships. Consider how you would feel if you were interviewing for your dream job and your interviewer, the vice president of the company, was texting during the entire interview! This is exactly what happened to our colleague recently.

Using Emoticons

Emoticons
Letters and symbols combined to represent emotions.

To overcome some of the drawbacks of sending and interpreting emotion in e-mail and text messaging, we sometimes use emoticons. The word *emoticon* is a combination of *emotion* and *icon*. **Emoticons** are letters and symbols combined to represent emotions—a clever way to indicate feelings. There are now hundreds, if not thousands, of well-known emoticons, some of which are illustrated in ■ Exhibit 11.6.

Although the use of emoticons in work-related e-mail is still generally unacceptable, this is rapidly changing, especially in less formal communications, such as among peers. Before using shortcuts like this, however, you should be sure that these methods are "allowed" in any new group or organization with which you need to communicate.

Teleconferences, Videoconferences, and Web Conferencing

Together, teleconferencing, videoconferencing, and Web conferencing have greatly increased our ability to link people who are geographically distant from one another. Teleconferences can include just a few people, or they might involve hundreds. One of the advantages of teleconferencing over e-mail is that it allows for better feedback and potentially more accurate interpretation of messages and emotion. It also permits interaction among participants, which can increase people's sense of belonging and allow for more complete information sharing. Videoconferencing has all of the qualities of teleconferencing, with the added benefit of video images that allow people to convey other communication-enhancing forms of body language, such as gestures and facial expressions.

Web conferencing enables participants to view the same information on their computers at the same time, often while on a tele-or videoconference. This enables workers to complete interdependent tasks that used to require people to be in the same room or same building.

All of these technologies, of course, have limitations. Teleconferences become less interactive as more and more people are involved, as do video and Web conferences. None of these methods allows for full use of nonverbal communication, and it is often difficult for people to join the conversation because normal social cues are not easy to give or interpret. This can mean that certain people may tend to dominate interactions, some people may not get a chance to talk, or participants may find it awkward to interrupt a speaker. Finally, teleconferences, videoconferences, and Web conferences can be tedious if the meetings are long.

■Exhibit **11.6**

Emoticons Communicate Emotions via Written Communications		
Facial Expression	Emoticon Text	Emotion
1.	:-)	Happy
2.	:-(	Sad
3.	>:-<	Angry
4.	:-		Disappointed
5.	:-$	Embarrassed
6.	: P	Joking with tongue sticking out
7.	: - D	Laughing
8.	: ~ /	Mixed up
9.	: ->	Sarcastic
10.	: -O	Surprised

Groupware

Groupware
A wide variety of software and technological applications that enable people to work collaboratively via information and communication technologies.

Groupware is a term that encompasses a wide variety of software and technological applications that enable people to work collaboratively via ICTs. We've already introduced Web conferences as one way for people to work together via electronic communication. Other common groupware includes wikis, blogs, and additional applications that allow users to share documents with ease.

Wikis are inexpensive and effective applications that allow users to create and edit Web documents without passing them back and forth on e-mail. Wikis can be highly efficient—indeed, the name comes from *wikiwiki,* the Hawaiian word for "fast," because they permit real-time collaboration while archiving the history of what the participants create together.

Blogs are another example of groupware. The word *blog* is shorthand for "Web log," or an online site that allows people to share ideas. Blogs originally served as a way to share observations, ideas, and commentary. Today, however, most blogs provide a "comments" section so people can respond. The result is that blogs can contain a public, recorded feedback loop. Blogs have become an especially popular way for companies to share new ideas and policies with employees, to solicit feedback, and to market products (either by setting up their own blogs or by asking popular bloggers to review their products). Leaders of organizations also use blogs to enhance internal communication and reinforce organizational culture. Externally, blogs are the tool of choice to gauge or increase interest, gather consumer information and feedback, and educate the general public.

A more recent innovation is microblogging in which users send short messages instantaneously to subscribers (e.g., Twitter). Because microblogging can be done via cell phones, and messages can reach wide audiences very efficiently, the technology has become exceptionally useful in situations where information is hard to get or changing rapidly, such as during natural disasters.

Social Networks

Social networks such as Facebook, YouTube, Flickr, MySpace, LinkedIn, and Friendster have exploded across the technological landscape, as have "closed" social networks such as Ning. Social networking sites provide an interactive forum in which people can share information and take advantage of professional and personal networks. Within the workplace, social networking sites are often an electronic manifestation of the grapevine, enabling workers to connect with one another even in large or geographically dispersed organizations. Organizations can also communicate with current customers and potential new ones through social networks, and they sometime use these networks to share information with shareholders, financial analysts, and other stakeholders.

As useful as social networks can be, some organizations have banned their use at work fearing that employees will spend too much of their time tending to personal communication instead of working. Also, the public nature of social networks presents a challenge to the security of an organization's proprietary information, and there is the additional danger that employees will communicate sensitive information via these networks. Many organizations have reduced such security risks by using software and Internet applications that are specifically designed for business use. Applications such as Yammer and Socialtext, for example, are well suited to business because they maintain security behind a firewall, are more easily integrated into e-mail systems, and are more amenable to archiving and searching functions.

Putting It All Together: When Business Goes Multimedia

Today's organizations need an integrated approach to business that harnesses as many of the benefits of ICTs as possible. Given the rapid pace of innovation, the most successful organizations will be those that remain flexible in the face of constant change—ones that adapt their business processes as they integrate these evolving ICTs. As an example, let's look at how Shelia Robinson, Founder and Publisher of *Diversity Woman*, has managed to use ICTs to totally transform her business.

Perspectives

The Information Age has brought great changes to the publishing world. Sheila Robinson, Founder and Publisher of *Diversity Woman*, has managed to take challenges and turn them into opportunities by using technology to connect with readers.

My industry is filled with challenges—the Internet, the environment, the economy. It can be very difficult for a magazine, especially for one that is focused on the leadership advancement of women in corporate America and needs of women entrepreneurs. Diversity Woman is an Internet magazine as well as a traditional one. We're also on Twitter, Facebook, LinkedIn, and we have an RSS feed. And this is what we need to do to support leadership and executive development for women—we have to get the information out there to support a more diverse workforce. This is a form of leadership that I hope creates more great leaders. For instance, right now I follow about 3,000 people on Twitter and

Sheila Robinson, Founder and Publisher of *Diversity Woman*

over 5,000 follow us. That number has been growing by 1,000 per month. That's the power of social networking.

The workforce is changing, too. You have three or four different generations all in the workforce at the same time, and each one has its preferred way of getting and delivering information. You need diversity in how you deliver the content, and if we are going to support that, we have to embrace not just traditional conceptions of diversity, but also all these different types of technology available to us. That's why we call ourselves a multimedia company.

The future of communication is always changing. So for us, instead of shutting down, we've been integrating to keep up with these challenges. For instance, we are hosting events and conferences, and the events are advertised in the magazine and online. We can link customers, sponsors,

Continued **on next page**>>

and events because we have a platform for sponsoring the events. Our corporate sponsors have access to all these different channels of communication, rather than just a print ad, and it increases their exposure and value. A lot of our revenue now comes from these sponsorships and partnerships that we build into a multichannel message.

The role of the Internet helps us both inside and outside Diversity Woman. The team that puts together our magazine

is all over the country. We have people in California, New York, and here in Greensboro, North Carolina, that all work together. If everybody were housed inside this one building, we wouldn't be able to tap into all that talent the way we can by having a virtual team. At the same time, though, you cannot discount that face-to-face contact. I physically meet with everybody on our team at least once or twice a year.

Source: Personal interview conducted with Sheila Robinson by Annie McKee, 2010.

Doing business today requires flexibility, adaptability, and openness toward constantly evolving ICTs. Sheila Robinson has taken her magazine company in the direction it needs to go to fulfill its mission. But in the case of many other companies, the task can seem daunting. Further, though ICTs encourage efficient virtual approaches to work, human relations and face-to-face communication are still important and cannot be replaced completely—a topic we will return to throughout later sections.

In this section we have focused on a few ways in which people use ICTs at work and to redefine the work that their organizations do. Next, we will look at a few of the ways that people can work "virtually."

Most Popular » Discussion Questions

1. Imagine that you are managing a team of six people—all of whom live in different countries (e.g., the United States, England, Italy, and South Africa). Taking into consideration time zone differences and the need for effective collaboration, create a three-month communication plan. (Assume the team will have two face-to-face meetings during the three-month project, with other types of telecommunication occurring between meetings.)
2. The next time you need to write an e-mail related to work or school, experiment with communicating your thoughts and emotions as fully as possible while still remaining concise and professional. After sending your e-mail, ask for feedback from the receiver.
3. Try this experiment: For one day (24 long hours), try not to use or be exposed to any ICTs. First, is this possible? Second, to the extent that you were successful, how were you affected? Be sure to take your reflection/discussion beyond the inevitable frustration you will experience.

---

5. Where and How Is Virtual Work Conducted?

Virtual is an adjective that describes something as having the essence of the real thing, even though it is not the same as the real thing. For example, you might say that a snowstorm is "a virtual blizzard" even if it technically lacks the heavy snow and extreme wind associated with an actual blizzard. Similarly, in information technology, *virtual* means that technology is mimicking real life (such as in virtual reality games). Virtual technologies imitate physical reality through the digital creation of images, sights, sounds, and opportunities to do things such as "talk" with people, play, learn, work, write, or buy and sell goods and services. In this section we will discuss virtual work—which, by the way, is *real* work.

Unlike traditional work that is conducted in one physical location among a group of people, virtual work depends on ICTs as the primary vehicles for interaction, creativity, collaboration, and doing business. Of course, even virtual work is done in a physical setting—somewhere, someone is using a computer, on the phone, etc. Virtual work also requires a social setting—a psychological and relational "space" where people connect. Of course, virtual work is also conducted via virtual technologies. Scholar Matti Vartiainen shows us that even the most virtual of all jobs takes place in *physical, mental/social,* and *virtual spaces.*[70]

To bring this framework to life, consider the example of Steven, a telemarketer who has been hired to conduct surveys about consumers' preferences. Steven has been briefed by his manager, along with several other new telemarketers, about the company, its goals for the project, and the manner in which the phone interviews are to be conducted. This particular company places high value on professionalism, friendliness, and respect—all of which are translated into norms of communication, which in turn have been translated into performance measures that Steven and the others must seek to achieve. The company also has specific metrics—for instance, how many calls must be made each day, how long they should last, and what data the telemarketers must collect. This kind of socialization to the company gives Steven a clear picture of what is expected of him. As a result, he feels that he is part of a team whose members all *share the same mental and social space.*

When Steven makes calls, he relies on *virtual spaces* such as the telephone. He is also connected to several networked computer applications that allow him to enter the data he gathers into a shared database. Steven's *physical space* is the dining room of his home, which is off-limits to his two small children so it will be quiet while he is on the phone. All three spaces—shared mental and social space, virtual settings, and physical space— are essential for Steven to do his job well.

Telecommuting

In the previous example, Steven was an example of a telecommuter—someone who works for a company in a different location than the company's offices. The trend toward telecommuting first emerged about 20 years ago, as people began to see the possibilities of using technology to work from home. And as travel became more necessary for global business, more people needed to work from places other than their offices.

Examples of telecommuting abound. For instance, many catalog operations have employees who work from their homes using special phones connected to an 800 number. Cruiser, an experimental system at Bell Communications Research, uses small video cameras, a central computer, and an onscreen "window" to allow users to visit colleagues' offices without ever leaving their desks.[71] People also routinely work in coffee shops, on trains, and on airplanes. Indeed, many jobs today are so knowledge centered that wherever a computer and/or phone can be used, work can be done.

In the United States, the number of people reporting that they telecommute regularly grew steadily from 1996 to 2006, from a total of 9 to 32 percent. However, only 12 percent of those polled in 2006 responded that their employer encouraged more frequent telecommuting, such as one or more days per week.[72]

A 2008 poll by the same organization found that since 2006, the number of Americans who even occasionally telecommute has dropped from 32 to 30 percent.[73] This may be a result of an increase in contracting work with outside individuals or companies— nonemployees who were not included in the poll. Also, telecommuting seems to be a perk that is reserved for the upper middle class, with those people earning more than $75,000 being twice as likely as those earning between $30,000 and $75,000 to have telecommuted. In addition, telecommuting was about 20 percent more likely to occur outside of regular business hours (another indication that the boundary between home and work is becoming more blurred).[74]

Despite all the benefits of telecommuting, many employees simply seem to prefer physically "going" to work. There may be many reasons for this, such as the enjoyment and effectiveness of face-to-face interaction, distractions at home, or even fears about being left out or overlooked by management. For these and many other reasons, new forms of hybrid structures are developing, in which people work some of the time in their company's physical setting and some of the time elsewhere.

The Hybrid Worker

More and more people are engaging in work both at the office and "on the road." In light of this trend, many organizations are creating work spaces specifically designed for temporary use. Instead of having their own offices or cubicles, people reserve or share space that is not designated for any one person. The spaces are mobile ready: electronic connections, wireless networks, Internet cables, conference phones, and video technology all await the user.

This practice, aptly called *hoteling*, allows for itinerant workers to reserve a station to plug into the network and conduct in-office work whenever they are in the facility.[75] For example, PricewaterhouseCoopers (PwC) is a global accounting firm with offices in 166 countries around the world. Currently, the organization serves 16 industries, including governments, educational institutions, financial firms, and nonprofit organizations. PwC is a leading proponent of global workforce mobility. Web conferencing is a standard form of team communication, and PwC has invested in the development of extensive online databases to allow for rapid creation, sharing, and retrieval of information.[76]

Virtual Teams

Virtual team
A group of individuals who collaborate on work projects while operating from different locations and using ICTs to establish shared goals, coordinate work, manage work processes and outcomes, and build effective relationships and team norms.

It is fast becoming the norm for organizations to rely on virtual, cross-functional, and culturally diverse teams to promote stability, increase efficient use of resources, and to keep up with changing markets.[77] A **virtual team** is a group of individuals who collaborate on work projects while operating from different locations and using ICTs to establish shared goals, coordinate work, manage work processes and outcomes, and build effective relationships and team norms.[78] Virtual teams often exist in an extremely dynamic, changing state.[79] Such teams are typically project based or task focused and can be stable in membership or quite fluid. The task itself usually provides the initial motivation to work together across time and space.[80]

Today, many teams within organizations (including schools) combine traditional face-to-face work with virtual work. In other words, many teams combine work done virtually with face-to-face interactions. One approach to describing virtual teams has been to view the "virtualness" of the team as based on the amount of face-to-face contact among members: the lower the time spent in face-to-face interactions, the more virtual the team is.[81]

Making Virtual Teams More Effective

Given how hard it can be for conventional teams to maintain effective working relationships, why would organizations choose to create geographically dispersed teams that may never engage each other face to face? Virtual teams offer several benefits that are not available with conventional teams. These include cost savings, increased ability for employees to accommodate their personal and professional lives, and the possibility of assigning individuals to multiple teams or projects regardless of physical location. Also, virtual teams may lead to higher levels of creativity as a result of their greater openness, flexibility, diversity, and access to information.[82]

Research has identified a number of strategies for maximizing the effectiveness of virtual teams:

1. Explicit and detailed communication about roles and relationships and how to use ICTs
2. Agreement around team norms
3. Agreement on which ICTs to use when
4. Agreement on how to manage knowledge and information sharing and storage
5. Clarity regarding members' responsibilities and contributions to the team
6. Establishment of clear work processes
7. Shared, explicit understanding of problems and challenges[83]

In addition to these tips, members of virtual teams need to find ways to deal with and manage conflict and minimize uncertainty. This means that team norms must in some way deal with how to manage differences of opinion and how to bring conflicts in the open to discuss and resolve them. Virtual teams can also manage conflict by actively engaging in the development of standard practices, which help reduce ambiguity. This includes collectively deciding on the mix of communication technologies and when they will be used; selecting proper documentation processes; defining and clarifying the roles and responsibilities of all team members; coming up with an explicit collective description of problems to be addressed by the team; and keeping a log of past activities and processes to solve problems.[84]

Trust and Accountability in Virtual Teams

Two additional dimensions must be considered when attempting to ensure that virtual teams are truly effective: trust and accountability. Trust in virtual relationships is important for several reasons. First, virtual work has to be based on trust and minimal supervision, because it is very difficult to supervise and control people and activities from a distance.[85] In traditional organizations, managers oversee how employees spend their time and what they do. In a virtual workplace managers must rely heavily on trust and processes that aid in monitoring output. To be most effective with virtual teams, managers need to shift their focus from time to results, and they must develop supervisory skills that include building and managing relationships virtually.

Moving from a "face time" orientation to a results orientation is necessary within virtual teams. People simply have to trust one another to do what is expected and to carry out their tasks. We do not yet know how trust develops in virtual teams, but we do know that the process is not the same as in face-to-face groups. In fact, a team of researchers investigating trust in virtual and face-to-face teams found that virtual team members started out with a lower level of trust but after a few weeks they caught up with their face-to-face counterparts. These researchers also noted that people were more likely to make inflammatory remarks at the outset of virtual team work when members had never met each other, and they attributed the slower development of trust to this.[86] What this means is that virtual teams might have to pay more attention to building trust explicitly in the early stages of team development in order for members to be able to hold one another accountable from the start.

Scholars Gina Hinrichs, Jane Seiling, and Jackie Stavros describe what you can do to create constructive accountability in virtual teams.[87] Behaviors focused on explicit communication and purposeful interaction help virtual teams communicate effectively; therefore, to increase virtual team performance, build a shared understanding of information, tasks, and relationships, and build shared accountability (■Exhibit 11.7).

■Exhibit **11.7**

Scholars Have Offered Many Tips for Building Constructive Accountability and Trust in Virtual Teams
Build meaningful relationships by encouraging full participation and contribution in meetings and conversations, whether conducted face-to-face or in virtual spaces.
Mindfully engage in critical thinking by listening for differences and similarities in the views of others, asking for clarifications, and challenging assumptions—your own, as well as others'.
Openly share information and resources you have available that would support team goals.
Actively engage in collective virtual brainstorming.
Advocate for the team or individual team members.
Make clear and explicit time commitments, and communicate with others immediately when these commitments cannot be met.
Organize extra virtual meetings to get to know each other and discuss new issues.
A virtual relationship is a relationship. Engage in casual communication by swapping stories and sharing some personal information.
Communicate with all key stakeholders, solicit feedback, and make others feel that they are part of a collaborative effort.

Source: Based on Hinrichs, Gina, Jane Seiling, and Jackie Stavros. 2008. Sensemaking to create high-preforming virtual teams, in *Handbook of high-performance virtual teams: A toolkit for collaborating across boundaries,* ed. Jill Nemiro, Michael M. Beyerlein, Lori Bradley, and Susan Beyerlein, 131–52. San Francisco: Jossey-Bass.

Communication, role clarity, effective norms, trust, and accountability are at the heart of a virtual team's success. They are also essential within any virtual work structure. Telecommuting, hybrid work, and hoteling all require people to connect and collaborate with few or no face-to-face meetings and often with limited, indirect, or no formal supervision. In order for people to work effectively under these conditions, we all need to take responsibility for paying attention to our interactions, our roles, and our responsibility for contributing to building healthy virtual work relationships. In the next section we will go beyond looking at what people need to do and be in order to work virtually, and look instead at the virtual workplace itself.

Most Popular » Discussion Questions

1. Consider groupthink, which you studied in Chapter 10. Can groupthink happen in a virtual team? Why or why not? If you believe it can happen, how might you prevent it?
2. How can you avoid social loafing in virtual teams?
3. Consider a virtual work project or school team that you have been part of (even if it was only partially virtual). What did you do to help the team build effective relationships and esprit de corps? What more could you have done?
4. Review the guidelines in Exhibit 11.7. Now, using the guidelines as a checklist, evaluate a virtual or partially virtual team that you have worked in or are currently part of.

---

6. What Is a Virtual Organization?

Organizations have traditionally been structured around hierarchies, or chains of command between levels and people that guide responsibility for work output and accountability for results. This basic design emerged from the Confucian civil service model in ancient China, early models of military organizations, and the Catholic Church, which, for centuries, was the most powerful organization in Europe.[88] When companies that relied on few leaders and many workers began to emerge during the early part of the Industrial Revolution, these companies were typically modeled after those earlier organizations. The hierarchical model continues to shape many businesses today.

However, there has been a shift in organizational design as we adapt to our increasingly virtual world. Companies are moving away from vertical hierarchies to flatter networked structures in order to take advantage of rapidly flowing information and to adapt to a constantly changing global environment. Today, "[t]he network is the paradigm, not the Catholic Church or the military," according to former president of PepsiCo and CEO of Apple Computer, John Scully.[89] In other words, many organizations are becoming more virtual. **Virtual organizations** usually consist of diverse people, groups, and networks that are geographically dispersed and that rely on information and communication technologies for communication and coordination of activities.[90]

Virtual organizations
Organizations that consist of diverse people, groups, and networks that are geographically dispersed and that rely on information and communication technologies for communication and coordination of activities.

Virtual organizations have defined and shared goals, have limited physical presence (e.g., distribution sites rather than office buildings), and rely on ICTs for the coordination of employees, suppliers, and customers as they produce, distribute, or provide goods or services. Although it is true that the trend toward virtual organizations is greatly magnified today, this trend is not entirely new. In fact, one organization, Avon,

Avon

Ahead of Its Time

For more than 100 years, Avon's business model has focused on empowering a network of entrepreneurial women. Avon's story began a century ago, in a bookstore where the owner gave away free perfume along with each book sale. Soon, the owner realized that women were very successful in convincing one another to try this or that perfume. He had a brainstorm: These women were a ready-made sales force for perfumes and maybe other products as well. He soon went from selling books to organizing women to sell perfume, followed shortly by other products. The Avon network was born.[91] Today, this company is a prime example of an organization that adds value throughout the network, uses virtual technology to connect its members, and keeps an entrepreneurial spirit alive despite its size and age.[92]

The company delivers close to 2,000 new products a year in the beauty, fashion, jewelry, and apparel categories in more than 100 countries, earning more than $10 billion per year.[93] These products are marketed and sold by a network of some 5.8 million individual businesses, many of which consist of single representatives selling products to friends, neighbors, and customers on the Internet.[94] In addition to this massive network of owner/sales representatives, Avon also employs 42,000 people to oversee centrally managed functions like brand marketing and logistics.[95]

Many representatives in the Avon network sell products as a hobby, earning only small amounts of money. However, there are notable exceptions to this trend. One example is Lisa Wilber of New Hampshire. Lisa was previously employed as a temp worker, not making enough money and definitely not reaching her potential. Now, Lisa manages huge businesses, overseeing hundreds of Avon representatives.[96] She is a millionaire, and she credits Avon for lifting her out of poverty.

Avon's network model continues to have multiple benefits, chief of which is its owner/operator sales force, which connects with the powerful central organization through ICTs. This sales network may be one of the easiest to manage in the world: Sales representatives are entirely self-driven, paid on commission, and manage their own schedules, budgets, and marketing plans.[97] Also, because Avon's representatives are in direct contact with the market, they can quickly spot trends.

There are inherent challenges, of course, in Avon's network-based business model. In recent years, the biggest of these challenges has been increased competition. Historically, Avon relied on its owner/operators for marketing. However, given the increased accessibility of products via the Internet and the decrease in working women's time for face-to-face interaction, the company's one-to-one sales model must be revisited.[98] To deal with these current and potential challenges, Avon is in the midst of a multiyear restructuring plan that encourages sophisticated use of ICTs to interact with customers—especially the new, younger market the company is planning to attract with an entirely new product line.[99]

Photo Source: iStock

Avon: A network based on trust

---

has been successfully using a hybrid virtual structure for many years. Let's look at what this company does.

Avon can be described as a hybrid organization—part virtual, part more traditional. During the first decade of this century, we have experienced dramatic increases in the number and types of organizations that are adopting networked and virtual structures, or expanding the use of ICTs in existing networks, as Avon has done. Let's take a closer look at some of these characteristics that distinguish virtual organizations from more traditional organizational models.

Components of Virtual Organizations

Virtual organizations differ from traditional models in that employees are often not located in the same place, customers may never visit a physical store, information is shared digitally, and money is transferred electronically. In addition, according to scholars Geraldine DeSanctis and Peter Monge, all virtual organizations are characterized by the four key components listed in ■Exhibit 11.8.

DeSanctis and Monge's early work on virtual organizations is helpful in that it permits us to see general characteristics can be seen in most virtual organizations. In the years since this study, there has been a tremendous amount of additional research conducted on virtual organizations, and scholars are now able to identify several specific models of virtual organizations, as described in the following section.

■Exhibit **11.8**

Four Key Components of Virtual Organizations

1. Dynamic processes, such as rapid, customized, relationship-based communication (e.g., e-mail, Web conferencing), along with a high degree of collaboration using wikis, social network environments, and groupware.
2. Contractual relationships among entities, including temporary or short-term partnerships or collaborations with "experts" for the duration of a project or task. A virtual organization that manufactures a product, for instance, may partner with an outside marketing firm to handle all of its sales instead of hiring its own sales staff.
3. Permeable boundaries, meaning a customer may directly order a product from a company's online catalog, but in reality, five distinct and separate organizations are involved in the process of designing, creating, marketing, managing, and delivering the product.
4. Structures that allow for swift adaptation to meet the needs of the marketplace.

Source: Adapted from DeSanctis, Geraldine, and Peter Monge. 1998. Communication process for virtual organizations. *Journal of Computer-Mediated Communication*, p. 6.

Models of Virtual Organizations

Models of virtual organizations can be understood in a number of ways, depending on whether you focus on an organization's function/purpose or on the structure of its network. For example, researchers Janice Burn, Peter Marshall, and Martin Barnett classify virtual organizations into four functional and seven structural models. From the functional, or purpose-based, standpoint, their four models are as follows:[100]

- *Destination sites:* This category consists of online storefronts, advertising sites, and content sites that offer services such as searchable databases for a fee, either to the user or to sponsors who advertise on the site. Questia is one example of a destination site model.
- *Traffic control sites:* This category consists of virtual malls, "incentive sites" (e.g., free e-mail and free Web page hosting sites), and free Internet service providers. NetZero is an example of a traffic control model.
- *Business portals:* This category consists of sites that are shared by businesses within a particular industry. For example, travel planning sites such as Expedia.com use the business portal model.
- *Auction sites:* These are sites where sellers and customers join together to buy, sell, or trade goods and services. eBay is perhaps the best-known auction site company.

When it comes to virtual organizational structures, Burn, Marshall, and Barnett have identified seven common structural models, which are described in ■Exhibit 11.9.

The seventh structural model (virtual space), if taken literally, does not exist. Somewhere, people are in a physical space creating, maintaining, and managing the services. PayPal, for example, is dependent on virtual interaction, but it also has a very large building in California where employees work together physically.

An eighth structure known as a peer-to-peer network (P2P) can also be added to this list. The P2P networks are common in virtual project work, because they allow all members of a network to be directly linked and to have direct access to one another.[101] This model differs from the star alliance/hub-and-spokes model in that members do not have to rely on the central organization for transfer of information or resources among

■ Exhibit **11.9**

Seven Structural Models of Virtual Organizations		
Model	**Description**	**Examples**
Virtual face model	An online store as an extension of a physical store; a "clicks-and-bricks" model	Target.com
Co-alliance model	A structure linking two organizations that offer complementary services	Netflix and Xbox[102]
Star alliance model	A "hub-and-spokes" model linking several member organizations through a central, core organization[103]	Airline companies united under Star Alliance
Value alliance model	Operates on a supply chain principle to link "a range of products, services, and facilities based on the value or supply chain";[104] has been described elsewhere simply as a supply chain model[105]	Travel booking companies that link transportation plans, rentals, hotels, and tours in a single package
Market alliance model	A highly networked supply chain that offers a range of products and services, although only one core organization might serve as the virtual face for the entire network	Amazon.com
Virtual broker model	Model in which one core organization "provides structure around specific business information services"[106]	eBay
Virtual space	Model that is completely dependent on virtual interaction	Some cloud computing services

Source: Adapted from Burn, Janice, Peter Marshall, and Martin Barnett. 2002. *E-business strategies for virtual organizations*. Woodburn, MA: Butterworth-Heinemann.

themselves. P2Ps flourish on the Internet, where users can access each other through a service and swap information, files, programs, and so on. Napster started out as a P2P network that facilitated free file sharing of music, threatening the music industry.[107]

Today, a wide variety of organizations conduct all or part of their operations virtually—this includes everything from public schools, such as the kindergarten through grade 12 Agora Cyber Charter School in Pennsylvania, to virtual stores such as eBay, to stock trading organizations such as eTrade. Virtual organizations are sometimes called e-businesses. For example, Amazon.com and Craigslist are two examples of real companies that interface with customers and sellers by way of a virtual marketplace. In e-businesses and virtual organizations like these, people can engage in certain activities that would normally—or that used to—occur in a physical location. Let's take a closer look at how several specific industries have evolved thanks to this sort of virtual technology.

Traditional Organizations Are Evolving to Better Use and Offer Virtual Services

The way goods and services are created, marketed, and sold has changed, and so has the way work is organized, conducted, and managed. To illustrate how traditional organizational forms have evolved to include more and more aspects of virtual organizations, consider what has occurred in banking, the consumer goods industry, and education and training.

The Evolution of Virtual Banking

One of the earliest virtual banking services was the credit card, which has been around since the early twentieth century. These cards were originally made of paper and issued by oil companies and department stores.[108] The first nonproprietary credit card not issued by a company was issued in 1966, and by 1970 only 6 percent of households used credit cards. By 1995 it was 65 percent and in 2002 the Gallup organization reported that only one in six Americans did not have access to a credit card, and 81 percent of adults had their own card.[109] This dramatic rise in credit card usage is linked to the increasingly widespread use of computing technologies which allow merchants to plug into the central banking companies that manage credit.[110]

During the second half of the twentieth century, cash also began flowing through electronic funds transfer networks, first through the use of ATMs and debit cards, and later through fully online banking systems that are accessible via the Internet.[111] The first ATM was actually installed at Rockefeller Center in Manhattan in 1969, but it was part of an offline network.[112] This machine read cards with a magnetically encoded strip that contained enough bank account information for limited cash withdrawals, but it could not perform other teller services.[113] It wasn't until the early 1980s that computerization allowed for online banking and widespread distribution of ATMs at grocery and convenience stores, along with point-of-sale use of debit cards.

A 2002 research report found that institutions that offered Internet banking were more profitable than those that did not.[114] Not surprisingly, findings like these encouraged banks to join the virtual revolutions—some even went completely virtual, such as ING Direct (owned by Internationale Nederlanden Groep). ING Direct opened in Canada in 1997, and shortly thereafter began operating in Spain and the United States.[115] Although ING Direct is wholly online, it operates cafes in most major cities providing customers with access to computer terminals and agents for support (■Exhibit 11.10).[116]

More innovations are occuring in the financial services industry as information technology advances. For example, eBay-owned PayPal is an online service that acts as an intermediary between buyers and sellers in Internet purchasing arrangements. The service acts as a buffer that protects individuals from disclosing financial information.[117] Or, consider Kiva, a virtual company that manages small peer-to-peer loans. This microlending Web site specializes in loans as small as a few dollars to people in developing nations, who usually pay back their debt in 6 to 12 months.[118] Let's look at what student Chris Allen Thomas has to say about Kiva.

■Exhibit **11.10**

Internet banking has become popular during the past decade.

Security/Alamy Images

Microfinance
The practice of providing financial services on an extremely small scale.

Chris Allen Thomas

Using the Internet to Change Lives: One Entrepreneur at a Time

Microfinance is the practice of providing financial services on an extremely small scale, including things like loans as small as $25. Microfinancing has been used in various parts of the world to support local entrepreneurs in starting their businesses, especially where small amounts of money can have an impact.

With Kiva.org, microfinancing has gone global in a big way, bringing ordinary people together with entrepreneurs around the world. It all started in 2003 at Stanford, when then-student Jessica Flannery was fortunate enough to listen to a speech by Nobel Laureate Muhammad Yunus about microlending. The talk affected her profoundly and as a result Jessica joined a nonprofit organization called the Village Enterprise Fund and went to Africa to help people start businesses.

When Jessica's soon-to-be husband Matt visited her in Africa, the two started exploring how to use the Internet to help people access microloans. The couple founded Kiva in October 2005 as a nonprofit organization with the mission of fighting global poverty through "enabling people to connect with and make personal loans to low-income entrepreneurs in the developing world."[119] Kiva works by doing two things. This microfinancing organization enlists the support of volunteer

Continued on next page>>

lenders through its Web site, which also showcases entrepreneurs identified by local organizations. Second, Kiva partners with microlending institutions in countries around the world that manage the loans locally. Member microlending institutions post profiles of entrepreneurs on Kiva's website. Lenders can browse these profiles and then make loans through PayPal, which offers the service without charging a fee to the lender or to Kiva. Because Kiva is a not-for-profit organization, lenders do not receive interest on their loans, but it doesn't matter because the experience of doing this service is highly rewarding.

As of March 2010, the total value of loans through Kiva exceeded $127 million, provided by 438,964 lenders to 320,983 entrepreneurs, with a reported repayment rate of 98.47%. More than 82% of Kiva's funded entrepreneurs in the developing world have been women.[120] Kiva operates in 54 countries and partners with 111 regional microfinance institutions, and has made 178,143 loans. The average loan size is just under $400, with many loans at amounts much less than that.[121] To put the power of microlending into perspective, a $400 loan is about 1% of the 2009 per capita Gross Domestic Product (GDP) of the U.S., while it is 31% of Uganda's per capita GDP and 133% of Congo's per capita GDP for the same time period.[122] So, what we consider a very small loan in the United States, can be a lifeline for a business entrepreneur in her home country. Just a little effort on our part can change the lives of hundreds of people and reduce global poverty—through the Internet, one person (and one click) at a time.

Source: Case by Chris Allen Thomas.

The Evolution of Virtual Consumer Sales

As far back as when the Silk Road was filled with traders, people have been placing "orders" for goods from remote and distant places. When we look at the evolution of virtual sales in more modern times, a good starting point is catalog shopping in the United States, which began in the nineteenth century and became especially popular in the early part of the twentieth century. During this period, the Sears and Roebuck catalog sold everything from medicines to dry goods, clothing, tools, and even houses. In some cases, catalogs like this were the only way people could shop for goods, as was the case in many small towns across the United States.

Today, all large department stores and thousands of specialty stores have Web sites to complement their physical businesses and/or catalogs. Some companies have no storefront at all. For example, Amazon.com is heralded as one of the most successful virtual shopping sites. Founded in 1994 and launched the following year, Amazon is a virtual store that began by selling books and later diversified to offer many other products. Amazon has an advantage over many brick-and-mortar stores in that its offerings are not limited by physical space; similarly, unlike mail-order retailers, Amazon is not limited by the size of its catalog.[123] In recent years, Amazon has implemented a model that incorporates third-party sellers into its vast online sales network, effectively linking its Web site to sellers and resellers around the world who hold accounts with Amazon.[124] A similar model of networked third-party sellers is used by eBay. However, eBay acts only as a virtual marketplace and does not sell products at all except through third parties that set up their own auctions and online stores.[125]

The Evolution of Virtual Education and Training

Distance learning has been around for a long time in the form of correspondence courses, in which assignments were completed without supervision and submitted to an instructor via mail. Most courses were quite basic and did not allow for much, if any, teacher–student or student–student interaction. The introduction of the Internet, however, changed this model for delivering and submitting educational content. Computers allowed for much more complexity in the information shared, more engaging instructional materials, and eventually meaningful online interaction between and among teachers and students.

The first e-learning course was introduced in 1995.[126] Since then, Internet-based learning has expanded to include K-12 education, higher education, corporate universities, and various types of training programs. Virtual education and training programs have moved far beyond the traditional classroom model and now include services to

■Exhibit **11.11**

Four Cycles in the Evolution of Virtual Learning Technologies

- *Cycle 1:* The first cycle enhances the existing traditional course structure through the use of online materials, e-mail communication, multimedia materials, and prepackaged software.
- *Cycle 2:* The second cycle involves the use of course management systems such as Blackboard, a virtual platform for both blended and fully online courses.
- *Cycle 3:* The third cycle involves the importation of course objects by instructors and facilitators, such as compressed video and interactive simulations.
- *Cycle 4:* The last cycle involves re-engineering the learning structure, fully integrating learning systems, and developing configurations that blend synchronous, asynchronous, and face-to-face interaction in effective and innovative ways.

Source: Adapted from Zemsky, R., and W. Massey. June 2004. *Thwarted innovation: A Learning Alliance report,* p. 11. West Chester, PA: Learning Alliance.

support faculty in designing and preparing courses, multimedia to support learning and interaction, and a variety of groupware processes that encourage collaboration.

One big advantage of virtual learning is that it has begun to level the playing field in terms of peoples' access to education and training. For companies, training can now be delivered to any employee, wherever they are and whenever they need it. Similarly, when it comes to general education, populations that are far from bricks-and-mortar institutions now have ever-increasing access to learning as more computers find their way to remote corners of the world. In addition, educational institutions can offer a greater variety of niche programs because they can aggregate learners nationally or even globally.[127]

As these examples suggest, virtual learning comes in a variety of forms. Adult learning scholars Bob Zemsky and William Massey have identified four distinct cycles of evolution in virtual learning, as listed in ■Exhibit 11.11.[128]

Clearly, organizations have been and are continuing to change dramatically in the virtual age. This has implications for all of us: employees, managers, and leaders alike. The technological revolution brings tremendous opportunities, yet it also means we must learn new ways of interacting with our work and with peers, managers, and networked colleagues. In the next section of the chapter, we will explore virtual work even further by looking at how people can face challenges associated with virtual work so that they can be most effective.

Most Popular » Discussion Questions

1. Do you know any business that does not have a virtual component? Should it? Why or why not?
2. Consider an organization that you believe has the components listed in Exhibit 11.8 on page 403. What do you believe are the primary management challenges for this organization?
3. Imagine that you own and manage a virtual business (say an auction site). Brainstorm ways to motivate your employees.
4. Online banking and shopping have contributed to a rise in identity theft. Research what you can do to avoid becoming a victim of this crime.
5. What are the advantages and disadvantages of online learning programs? Give some examples from your own experience.

7. What Are the Challenges of Working in a Virtual World?

Technology has improved our lives and made many aspects of work easier, faster, cheaper, and more fun. That said, there are some definite downsides to living and working in a virtual world, which we will now explore. First, we will consider the challenges individuals face in the 24/7 world of virtual work. Then, we will look at the impact of information overload. Finally, we will examine problems related to knowledge management.

The Challenges of the 24/7 Virtual Work World

Working virtually offers several benefits to employees and organizations alike. For one, business continuity can be maintained 24 hours a day if people are working in different time zones around the world, or when a workplace has been lost or temporarily closed due to catastrophe.[129] A company and its employees might also experience cost savings due to a decrease in real estate costs and expenses such as meals and transportation. Working from home can also decrease employees' and organizations' carbon footprints and save utility costs, and virtual workers develop skills that are useful for being part of diverse teams and virtual collaboration.[130]

Still, virtual work has several notable downsides. First, because it breaks up the traditional nine-to-five workday, people can feel like they are on-call all the time. Advances in ICTs have blurred the lines between personal and professional time, making it easier for work to reach us once we have left the office, and making it harder for us to disengage from our work when we should be enjoying free time. We can feel like we are *always* working. On the other hand, many people now find it easier to use organizational time and resources for personal activities. That said, the separation of a person's home and work life can become blurred, and heightened levels of stress can be the result of isolation.[131]

When it comes to virtual relationships, conflict may become more problematic if communication and work norms are not clear and agreed on.[132] Also, because virtual work requires independence and less oversight, problems can arise when role clarity and responsibilities are not firmly established. Additionally, there is the potential for loss of quality and efficiency due to some reduction of direct control and oversight, as well as a decrease in face-to-face communication.[133]

Other challenges relate to the sheer amount of information we receive every day in the form of e-mails, texts, downloads to our computers, and the like—taken together, we can easily find ourselves drowning in information.

Technology and Information Overload

Information overload has become especially problematic in recent years. People have turned to e-mail as a primary communication channel, our cell phones are with us constantly, and any time we log on to a computer, others can find us. These and other technologies have made it easier for us to send and receive information, but in doing so, they have exponentially multiplied the amount of time we spend communicating. You could probably spend most of your time reading and responding to e-mails, texts, and social media messages, but is that the best use of your time?

One study has found that the average worker who sits at a computer all day checks his or her e-mail 50 times, instant messages 77 times, and visits 40 Web sites a day. In addition, in the United States alone, more than $650 billion a year in productivity is lost because of unnecessary interruptions—most of them unimportant.[134] Think about your own experience as you have read this chapter: How many e-mails, text messages, phone calls, or social networking alerts have you received? As welcome as these distractions may have been, they most likely haven't helped you study productively.

Information overload comes with a high price. First, the sheer volume of communication at work can take up a huge amount of time—time needed to *work*. Second, when we are barraged with communication, it becomes difficult to prioritize work tasks—typically, the most immediate bit of information gets our attention while more important tasks are left for later. Third, more communication doesn't necessarily mean better communication—too often, the information shared via e-mail, texts, and social networks is peripheral (at best) to the task at hand.

Microsoft, Google, Intel, and IBM are among the organizations that formed the Information Overload Research Group in 2008 to examine and address the problem of too much information.[135] These companies are also trying to devise remedies for information overload within their own organizations. Intel, for instance, started the Next Generation Solutions program specifically with the purpose of reducing information overload. The company began by encouraging a team of employees to limit both electronic and in-person communication just one morning a week so they could focus on their other work. They also experimented with a program called Zero E-Mail Fridays, in which people were asked to avoid e-mail as much as possible on Fridays. The program met with limited success; most employees continued using e-mail on Fridays because they found it essential. Still, 60 percent of the employees recommended the program for wider use following certain modifications.[136] What this example illustrates is that simply going back to how we worked before e-mail isn't an option—yet we must do something.

In the next section, we will look at some of the challenges managers and employees face in trying to manage the huge volume of information that is generated at work today.

The Challenge of Knowledge Management

Managing the vast amount of constantly changing information that is traveling at light speed into, around, and out of organizations is profoundly challenging for people. Even more challenging is organizing this information so that multiple people can access and use it.

Just leaving this task up to individuals doesn't work. We need systems to capture, store, and disseminate information and knowledge. A deadly example of how difficult this can be is found in the stories of information that was available prior to the Christmas day bombing attempt in the United States in 2009. In this case, different individuals or groups held different pieces of information about the situation, but these pieces were not shared among the parties in ways that allowed the information to be pieced together. For example, the suspect's father had reported concern over his son's "radicalization and associations" to the U.S. Embassy in Nigeria in 2007, and his name was added to a terrorist-related activities database in November 2009.[137] But this and other small pieces of information were not wholly available to certain key authorities such as government security bodies, embassy officials, and airline personnel. In the end, nobody could see the entire picture. As a result, the United States suffered a frightening breach of security.

The consequences of inadequate knowledge management systems at work aren't usually so dire, but they still matter. For example, when a sales employee in Malaysia learns something important about a customer, competitor, or supplier, you need to have a structure in place for getting that information back to the organization, as well as a process for disseminating critical data to the right employees. Or what about the vast amount of time wasted when people "re-create the wheel," designing presentations, proposals, or reports that have been done many times before?

■Exhibit **11.12**

Some Common Myths about Knowledge Management Technology

- **Myth Number 1: Knowledge management technologies can deliver the right information to the right person at the right time.** Businesses can no longer predict what will be needed when, where, or in what form, so automated or static knowledge management systems do not always work. Nor can businesses predict who will need what information at any given time. Knowledge management systems now need to be designed to anticipate change, to include processes for quickly updating information, and to anticipate how to share it across the organization (even with unlikely functions or people).

- **Myth Number 2: Knowledge management technologies can store human intelligence and experience.** Technologies such as databases and groupware applications store bits and pixels of data, but they can't store the rich schemas that people possess for making sense of this data. Information is context sensitive—meaning the same data can evoke different responses from different people. ICTs don't think. People do. Storing a static representation of some aspects of a person's knowledge is not tantamount to storing human intelligence and experience.

- **Myth Number 3: Knowledge management systems should replicate traditional filing systems.** Data archived in computer files is often irrelevant to any situation other than the one for which it was created. Such systems do not account for renewal of existing knowledge and creation of new knowledge. The best knowledge management systems enable people to find what they need quickly—even when information related to a "new" situation is housed in many places and in many ways. Organizations need knowledge management systems that allow people to quickly sort through irrelevant data and to interpret relevant information in order to find gaps in the information, patterns, surprises, and anomalies.

Source: Adapted from Malhotra, Yogesh. 2000. *Knowledge management and new organization forms: A framework for business model innovation*, pp. 7–8. Hershey, PA: Idea Group Publishing.

All of these examples point to the fact that organizations must create systems to capture, organize, and disseminate knowledge so it can be easily accessed by those who need it. This is a huge challenge. One way to address this challenge is to first understand what knowledge management systems *cannot* do. Accordingly, some common myths about knowledge management systems can be debunked (■Exhibit 11.12).

All of these myths add up to one simple fact: Knowledge management technologies do not take the place of human beings. *People* need to ensure that the knowledge generated and stored makes sense. This requires repetitive questioning, critical thinking, and revision of the assumptions underlying information.[138]

Most Popular » Discussion Questions

1. In your life at school or work today, is there ever a time when you "unplug" from ICTs? Why or why not? How connected do you need to be in order to be effective at school and at work? What impact does it have on your quality of life and health?

2. Under what circumstances do you experience information overload? For example, does it result from too much e-mail, text messaging, and social networking? Or does it happen when you are tired or stressed? What can you do to manage this situation?

3. Examine the knowledge management system you have in place for organizing e-mail, texts, schoolwork, work-related projects, and so on. Is your technology up to the task? Are you using it to full advantage? What can you do to improve your system?

8. What Can HR Do to Support Virtual Work?

The HR Cycle

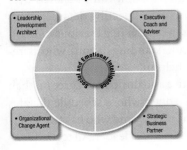

Managing virtual work is everyone's job in organizations today. However, HR professionals contribute to this process in particularly important ways. First, HR is often responsible for understanding and applying emerging laws and regulations that affect virtual work, such as those related to workplace privacy. Second, HR is responsible for creating guidelines that support workers and managers in using technology (such as social networks) in an appropriate manner at work.

The Privacy Question: HR's Role in Monitoring Employee Electronic Communications

In addition to tracking and ensuring compliance with laws involving e-commerce and related topics, HR is at the center of a growing debate about the privacy of communication in the workplace. Today, employers can easily access and monitor employees' e-mails, Internet searches, phone calls, and text messages. The debate over these practices is complex and heated. In many countries, individual privacy is a deeply held cultural value—one that is backed by the power of the law. When an employee is using company property (computers or cell phones) or company time to engage in personal communication, who actually "owns" the information that is communicated? Also, does an employer have the right to ensure that employees are working, as opposed to engaging in personal communication or surfing the Web?

It appears to be only a matter of time before legal precedents will be set to either further protect employee privacy or erode it, at least to some degree. In the meantime, it is often HR's responsibility to create and enforce policies that both protect employees from privacy violations and ensure that communication within the organization serves its stated goals.

Establishing Guidelines for On-the-Job Social Networking

HR is also often responsible for creating and enforcing guidelines and policies related to social networking. Interactive applications such as Facebook and LinkedIn, as well as applications such as Twitter, have given rise to mass networking for both personal and professional purposes. To date, there have been few studies about how much time employees spend on social networking. However, the perception is that as the number of people or groups in an individual's network increases, the more time that individual will spend during the workday reading postings and updates that have nothing to do with work. Some organizations have banned access to these tools at work because of violations of trust in the working relationship (e.g., spending time with friends on the network instead of working).

The vast majority of social networking sites were originally designed with a focus on *personal* (rather than professional) social networks. LinkedIn is slightly different in that it began as a professional tool, but there is no regulation for how individuals use this site. Thus, there are currently as many personal notices posted on LinkedIn as there are professional ones. Given these observations, organizations must carefully weigh the advantages and disadvantages of engaging social media for business use. As with any technology, clear communication about company rules and guidelines and the provision of appropriate training will lend itself to the effective use of social networking applications.

HR Leadership Roles

9. What Can We All Do to Work Most Effectively in a Virtual World?

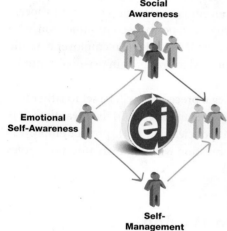

Social Awareness

Emotional Self-Awareness

Relationship Management

Self-Management

Communication and relationships are at the heart of virtual work. Some people even say that effective communication should be the primary focus when it comes to understanding and designing virtual work processes. All relationships require effort to build and maintain, and virtual relationships are no exception. This means you have to consciously attend to how you relate to people and they to you in the virtual work space. In this section we will look at how you can build healthy relationships virtually, how to use e-mail effectively at work, and how to help virtual teams be successful.

Virtual Relationships Are *Real* Relationships

Factors that are critical when working in an office, store, or factory are just as important when working virtually: mutual trust, respect, morale, constructive influencing behaviors, and dealing with conflict effectively. This can be tricky in the virtual world, however, because face-to-face meetings where we have the benefit of nonverbal communication and social cues are often missing. Media that allow for visualization, such as Web conferencing and videoconferencing, address some of these issues, but not completely.

To be most effective when working virtually, you must focus on the development of skills that allow you to build effective working relationships—often with people you rarely see or may not ever meet. It is important to develop communication norms that create a common way of signaling and interpreting relational information, such as emotions.

Humans are emotional beings. Our brains are physically wired to pick up subtle cues that help us interpret others' emotions.[139] Emotions are key to communicating, collaborating, accomplishing goals, and creating an environment in which people can be at their best. In short, emotions are central to building effective relationships at work. It also helps to make communication norms explicit in advance and to establish procedures for reconciling differences in communication practices that emerge as you work across personal, cultural, and professional boundaries. Some of these can be quite simple and straightforward. For example, an agreement about what sort of information can be shared over e-mail (e.g., project planning documents, factual information, meeting details) versus what should be communicated either over the phone or in person (e.g., serious difficulties with the project, interpersonal conflicts, or misunderstandings about who is responsible, accountable, and so forth) can be extremely helpful.

Some norms that need to be discussed are more sensitive and difficult to agree on than others. For example, when people are in different time zones, whose schedule dictates when meetings will be held? Whose schedule is "most important" and who has to accommodate? Also, many virtual teams do not have a designated formal leader. All team members therefore need to understand and agree on who is leading what, when, and how.

Tips for Using E-Mail Effectively at Work

Sending E-Mail

- Use clear, informative subject lines.
- Avoid "mass" e-mails. Be judicious with the "Reply All" button and include only those people who need to see the message.
- Assume that management will read your e-mail.
- Assume that your e-mail will be seen by people outside of your organization.
- Do not send inappropriate or critical messages.

Receiving and Interpreting E-mail

- Look at subject lines to see whether you want to open an e-mail.
- If your organization has not already installed them, use e-mail filters to avoid spending time deleting spam.
- If you receive an e-mail that causes you to have a strong emotional reaction, do not respond immediately. Calm down, reflect on the message, and then respond appropriately—which may or may not be via e-mail.
- Don't let e-mail pile up: Answer it, move it to an appropriate folder, or delete it.
- Purge your inbox folder regularly.

In addition to learning to build and maintain relationships virtually, you need several explicit communication competencies, including how to use e-mail effectively.

Using E-Mail Effectively at Work

Another way to improve your communication effectiveness in the world of virtual work is to master one of its core technologies: e-mail. You have likely used e-mail for years and are quite proficient, as are many (if not most) of the people you interact with. Nonetheless, misuse of e-mail is prevalent in organizations today. From overuse, to sending messages with too little or too much context and information, to including the wrong people in communications for the wrong reasons—problems abound. These problems contribute significantly to information overload, miscommunication, misunderstandings, and even damaged relationships. Given these potentially negative effects, it is critical that you learn to use e-mail responsibly at work. Several methods for using e-mail more effectively are outlined in ■Exhibit 11.13.

Taking Charge of Virtual Teams

The very nature of virtual work and virtual teams means that more of us will have to take on leadership more often, and in many cases without a formal role or designation. You need to be well versed in the variety of communication tools, strategies, and techniques that are needed for virtual collaboration. However, technological mastery is only one factor in providing leadership or even being a member of a virtual team. Other critical factors involve the same kind of leadership competencies that are important in face-to-face interactions.[140]

Virtual teams need good leaders. They need members to be open to feedback, willing to adapt their usual approach to work, and able to manage the stress and frustration that sometimes go along with virtual work. You can lead virtual teams more effectively if you actively create explicit norms for communication, attempt to decrease ambiguity, encourage interaction and help the team collectively develop goals.[141] In fact, some scholars have found a strong relationship between team members' perceptions of the quality of the goal setting process and project managers' perception of team effectiveness.[142]

You can also help a virtual team be more effective by empowering people and delegating management functions.[143] This approach casts the leader more in the role of a facilitator than that of the traditional manager.[144] One study that examined 35 virtual teams found that the less face-to-face contact there was among team members, the more crucial empowerment was to team effectiveness.[145]

Managers of virtual teams will find that self-management, influence, and inspirational leadership are critical competencies for team members. So, what can you do to encourage development of these behaviors? First, you can help team members create a connection both interpersonally and with the task at hand. For example, one study of 29 global virtual teams that communicated strictly by e-mail for six weeks indicated that three factors were central to the teams' success: (1) initial messages that were social and allowed members to get to know one another well, (2) establishment of clear roles for each member, and (3) establishment of the norm that all communications during the project should be positive and action oriented.[146]

Working virtually is fun and exciting. The rewards that come from focusing on one's own skills as a leader while simultaneously empowering others are huge—not just for you, but also for the team members and the organization.

Most Popular » Discussion Questions

1. Think about a relationship at work, in school, or in your social life in which you use e-mail, texting, or social networking a great deal. How do you ensure effective and full communication in that relationship? How do you build trust using these technologies?
2. From your own experiences, create a list of "dos and don'ts" for how to manage relationships virtually.

---

10. A Final Word on Working in a Virtual World

ICTs have changed how we work and live. These technologies are also changing our world's societies. Thomas Friedman's popular book *The World Is Flat* addresses how people across the globe are dramatically more interconnected now than ever before, which has in turn resulted in greater opportunities for intense cooperation and competition.

The metaphor of the "flat world" centers on the idea that computers and telecommunications have vastly increased the competitive advantage for people in developing nations while simultaneously decreasing the competitive advantage for people in developed nations. This "flattening" marks the beginning of a global revolution. Many believe that these changes will occur so quickly and have such far-reaching effects that the world in the twenty-first century will look nothing like the world we knew in the twentieth century.[147]

Digital divide
The lack of access to and lack of skill in using Internet communication technologies among various underprivileged groups and residents of lesser developed countries.

However, while more people around the world have the potential to participate and contribute, we can also see a disturbing sociological trend emerging. The term **digital divide** refers to the lack of access to and lack of skill in using Internet and communication technologies among various underprivileged groups and residents of lesser developed countries. In Cambodia, for instance, there is only one Internet user per 200 people, whereas in Canada, more than 75 out of every 100 people use the Internet, indicating a strong digital divide that leaves Cambodians potentially unprepared for work opportunities that require skill in modern technologies.[148] Even in industrialized countries that are quick to embrace digital technologies, older employees may find it difficult to develop competitive skills in these technologies. Other groups who face socioeconomic and educational challenges may also find it challenging, if not impossible, to develop the critical computer-based skills that are required for many jobs in an information society.[149]

The changes we are seeing in our societies can either support the development of a more just and equitable world—or not. It's up to us. Human beings—and their knowledge, creativity, and passion—are still, and always will be, at the heart of personal, organizational, and societal success.

Key Terms

1. **How Do Advances in Information and Communication Technologies Change Life and Work?** (pp. 380–382)

Key Terms

Information and communication technologies (ICTs) All of the hardware and software related to electronic communication and information sharing. p. 380

Sociotechnical systems theory Theory that examines both social and technical characteristics of tasks and how work is organized, focusing on the interaction between people and technologies. p. 381

2. **How Did Technology Affect Life and Work during the Industrial Revolutions?** (pp. 382–389)

Key Terms

Technology The use of tools and knowledge to influence the environment. p. 382

Industrial Revolution The period in the eighteenth and nineteenth centuries during which major advances in technology, manufacturing, and transportation changed people's way of life, mainly in England, the United States, and parts of continental Europe. p. 382

Age of Enlightenment Primarily eighteenth-century movement that fueled radical new ideas about government, science, economic systems, and wealth across Europe and parts of North America. p. 383

Second Industrial Revolution The period from the mid-nineteenth century through approximately 1915 that was marked by the development of several life-altering technologies, including electricity, motors, synthetics, internal combustion, and mass production techniques. p. 383

Third Industrial Revolution The period beginning in the mid- to late twentieth century through today when economic activities are marked by an increased focus on information and communication technologies, along with greater attention to issues of environmental sustainability and economic competition. p. 387

3. **How Have Computing and Telecommunication Technologies Evolved?** (pp. 389–392)

Key Terms

Internet The global system of interlinked, hypertext documents contained within an electronic network that connects computers and computer networks around the world. p. 390

Web 2.0 The second generation of Web technology and software development that allows for increased interactivity, user design and control, and collaboration. p. 390

Intranet An internal company network that is usually accessible only to employees. p. 390

Extranet A computer network designed for an organization to communicate in a secure environment with certain external stakeholders, such as customers. p. 390

Cloud computing Hosted services offered via the Internet that are available on demand, are highly flexible in terms of the amount of service users have access to, and are fully managed by the provider. p. 391

4. **How Do People Use ICTs at Work?** (pp. 392–397)

Key Terms

Emoticons Letters and symbols combined to represent emotions. p. 394

Groupware A wide variety of software and technological applications that enable people to work collaboratively via information and communication technologies. p. 395

5. **Where and How Is Virtual Work Conducted?** (pp. 397–401)

Key Terms

Virtual team A group of individuals who collaborate on work projects while operating from different locations and using ICTs to establish shared goals, coordinate work, manage work processes and outcomes, and build effective relationships and team norms. p. 399

6. **What Is a Virtual Organization?** (pp. 401–407)

Key Terms

Virtual organizations Organizations that consist of diverse people, groups, and networks that are geographically dispersed and that rely on information and communication technologies for communication and coordination of activities. p. 401

Microfinance The practice of providing financial services on an extremely small scale. p. 405

7. **What Are the Challenges of Working in a Virtual World?** (pp. 408–410)

Key Terms None

8. **What Can HR Do to Support Virtual Work?** (pp. 411–412)

Key Terms None

9. **What Can We All Do to Work Most Effectively in a Virtual World?** (pp. 412–414)

Key Terms None

10. **A Final Word on Working in a Virtual World** (p. 414)

Key Terms

Digital divide The lack of access to and lack of skill in using Internet communication technologies among various underprivileged groups and residents of lesser developed countries. p. 414

Chapter 11 Visual Summary

1. How Do Advances in Information and Communication Technologies Change Life and Work?   (pp. 380–382)

Summary: Information and communication technologies have the power to change the way we communicate in all aspects of our lives. Technology, however, is not the only factor we need to pay attention to. If we neglect the human factors, technology will not necessarily help us to be successful. This is where sociotechnical systems theory comes into play. This theory is based on the idea that organizational performance is tied to the interaction of social and technical factors and that implementation of one without the other may be harmful. The theory calls on you to utilize your creativity, empathy, and emotional intelligence when facing the challenges presented by ICTs.

10. Teams and Teambuilding: How to Work Effectively with Others

Organizing Human Systems

11. Working in a Virtual World: Technology as a Way of Life

2. How Did Technology Affect Life and Work during the Industrial Revolutions?   (pp. 382–389)

Summary: Technological developments have been a key to societal progression since prehistoric times. Major shifts in how we live and work came as a result of the First Industrial Revolution. Advances in technology during this period dramatically changed work and life for people in England, the United States, and portions of continental Europe. The Second Industrial Revolution brought electricity, automobiles, and mass production and further moved some Western societies away from their rural, cottage-industry roots to an urban consumer culture. The current Third Industrial Revolution is gradually replacing manufacturing jobs with professional and service jobs, is generating international business networks, and is creating a kind of alternate route to industrialization for those countries that were not involved in the previous revolutions.

4. How Do People Use ICTs at Work? (pp. 392–397)

Summary: Most people use ICTs in both their personal and work lives. E-mail is perhaps the most commonly used ICT at work due to its low cost and ease of use. Text messaging is another ICT that is gaining popularity. Conferencing hardware and software, groupware, and social networks are additional ICTs that promote collaborative working relationships between individuals and groups in remote locations. It is important to remember, however, that communication via ICTs is more limited than face-to-face communication and can open the door for misinterpretation of emotion and intent.

3. How Have Computing and Telecommunication Technologies Evolved?   (pp. 389–392)

Summary: Computing as we know it today started out small—with just two computers linked to each other via the earliest form of the Internet. The technology has grown by leaps and bounds in a very short time to the point that Web 2.0 and other advances are paving the way for continuous and rapid development and new ways to communicate, live, and work. Modern telecommunications have also seen rapid changes from government-regulated cellular technologies for military use to a vast private network that connects billions of civilians. These advances have led to completely new ways of working.

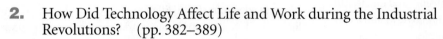

■Exhibit **11.6**

Emoticons Communicate Emotions via Written Communications		
Facial Expression	Emoticon Text	Emotion
1.	:-)	Happy
2.	:-(	Sad
3.	>:-<	Angry
4.	:-|	Disappointed
5.	:-$	Embarrassed

10.   A Final Word on Working in a Virtual World   (p. 414)

Summary: Computers and telecommunications have impacted modern work more than any other innovation, and have led to great competitive and cooperative opportunities. However, you must remember that ICTs are not a substitute for human knowledge, creativity, or passion. Additionally, some nations, socioeconomic groups, and age groups experience a digital divide, or knowledge gap, when it comes to using ICTs. As a society, it is important to be mindful of this divide and strive to overcome socioeconomic, educational, and age-related challenges in the virtual world.

9.   What Can We All Do to Work Most Effectively in a Virtual World?   (pp. 412–414)

Summary: Working in the virtual world requires you to build relationship skills that transcend face-to-face communication and help you forge bonds with people you may never meet. An important first step in this process is appreciating the fact that virtual relationships are real relationships that involve real people with real emotions that must be attended to. You also must establish communication norms in advance that clarify the types of information you will share via particular communication channels, and understand the limitations presented by e-mail. Finally, you must be prepared to lead your virtual team and be mindful of the ways in which virtual communication requires you to alter your approach to leadership and collaboration.

8.   What Can HR Do to Support Virtual Work?   (pp. 411–412)

Summary: HR professionals in many organizations are involved in two key aspects of controlling virtual communication: understanding personal privacy laws and creating guidelines that support organizational members' use of technology. Privacy is often difficult to balance in the workplace as individuals use company property—computers and cell phones specifically—to stay in contact with friends outside of the office and take care of personal needs. A related issue that HR often has to manage is the creation of rules for the use of social networking and other non-business Web sites during work hours. Both of these issues require HR professionals to carefully weigh the importance of such communication to the individuals involved and the organization as a whole.

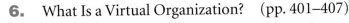

■ Exhibit **11.13**
Tips for Using E-Mail Effectively at Work

Sending E-Mail
- Use clear, informative subject lines.
- Avoid "mass" e-mails. Be judicious with the "Reply All" button and include only those people who need to see the message.
- Assume that management will read your e-mail.
- Assume that your e-mail will be seen by people outside of your organization.
- Do not send inappropriate or critical messages.

Receiving and Interpreting E-mail
- Look at subject lines to see whether you want to open an e-mail.
- If your organization has not already installed them, use e-mail filters to avoid spending time deleting spam.
- If you receive an e-mail that causes you to have a strong emotional reaction, do not respond immediately. Calm down, reflect on the message, and then respond appropriately—which may or may not be via e-mail.
- Don't let e-mail pile up: Answer it, move it to an appropriate folder, or delete it.
- Purge your inbox folder regularly.

7.   What Are the Challenges of Working in a Virtual World?   (pp. 408–410)

Summary: Some aspects of the virtual world make our work faster and simpler; other aspects introduce stress and complications that must be managed. One of these is the constant accessibility of workers and managers through laptops and smart phones at the expense of their personal time. Another challenge is information overload. Finally, we must manage knowledge effectively and appreciate that people generate knowledge and determine the flow of information through ICTs.

6.   What Is a Virtual Organization?   (pp. 401–407)

Summary: Virtual organizations are made up of diverse people and networks that are geographically dispersed and rely on ICTs to share information and coordinate activities. Many virtual organizations tend to be flat, rather than hierarchical, in order to maximize the rapid exchange of information. Some virtual organizations have only a small physical presence and complete a majority of their business transactions online. Online storefronts, auction sites, and business portals are a few common examples of virtual organizations. Many industries are beginning to increase their virtual presence, as can be seen in the banking industry, consumer sales, and education.

5.   Where and How Is Virtual Work Conducted?   (pp. 397–401)

Summary: All virtual work is conducted in three spaces—shared mental and social space, virtual settings, and physical space. Telecommuting is one example of a virtual work structure that involves performance of essential work functions outside of traditional offices via ICTs. Hybrid work is another form of virtual work and involves individuals who travel from company facilities to other locations and rely on their ICTs to link up and work with others. Finally, virtual teams connect individuals in different locations with one another using an agreed-on mix of ICTs to complete project- and task-based work.

Organizational Controls:

People, Processes, Quality,
and Results

People

Processes

Quality

Results

Chapter Outline

Find out what you already know about the concepts in this chapter by going to www.mymanagementlab.com and taking the **Pre-Test.** Your results will generate a customized study plan for Chapter 12.

1. What Is the Organizational Control Process? (p. 420)

2. What Historical Perspectives Help Us Understand Control in Organizations? (pp. 421–425)

3. What Are Common Control Systems? (pp. 425–428)

4. What Conventions and Forces Guide Organizational Control Processes? (pp. 429–433)

5. What Are the Typical Steps in the Control Process? (pp. 433–437)

6. What Should Companies Control? (pp. 437–447)

7. What Can HR Do to Help Control for Effectiveness and Efficiency at Work? (pp. 447–450)

8. What Can We All Do to Enhance Effectiveness and Efficiency at Work? (pp. 450–451)

9. A Final Word on Organizational Control (pp. 451–452)

Go back to www.mymanagementlab.com and take the **Post-Test** to verify your understanding of the concepts. **To experience and apply** the concepts, explore the additional material associated with Chapter 12.

Part 1: Leading and Managing for Today and the Future (Chapters 1, 2, 3, 4)
Part 2: Planning and Change (Chapters 5, 6, 7, 8, 9)
Part 3: Organizing Human Systems (Chapters 10, 11)
➤ **Part 4:** Controlling Quality, Culture, and Yourself (Chapters **12**, 13)
Part 5: Leading and Managing for the Future (Chapters 14, 15, 16)

8. Workplace Essentials: Creativity, Innovation, and a Spirit of Entrepreneurship

7. Change: A Focus on Adaptability and Resiliency

9. Organizing for a Complex World: Structure and Design

10. Teams and Teambuilding: How to Work Effectively with Others

Planning and Change

Organizing Human Systems

6. The Human Side of Planning: Decision Making and Critical Thinking

16. Managing and Leading for Tomorrow: A Focus on Your Future

14. Globalization: Managing Effectively in a Global Economic Environment

11. Working in a Virtual World: Technology as a Way of Life

5. Planning and Strategy: Bringing the Vision to Life

1. Managing and Leading Today: The New Rules

Leading and Managing for Today and the Future

2. The Leadership Imperative: It's Up to You

4. Communication: The Key to Resonant Relationships

3. Motivation and Meaning: What Makes People Want to Work?

15. Sustainability and Corporate Social Responsibility: Ensuring the Future

12. Organizational Controls: People, Processes, Quality, and Results

12. Organizational Controls: People, Processes, Quality, and Results

Controlling Quality, Culture, and Yourself

13. Culture: It's Powerful

1. What Is the Organizational Control Process?

■Exhibit **12.1**

A MINI dealership uses controls for quality service.

BG Motorsports/Alamy Images

Control process
An organization's systems for establishing standards to achieve goals, monitoring and measuring performance, comparing performance to standards, and taking corrective action as necessary.

If you've ever been in a MINI Cooper dealership, you know their image: hip, inviting, and *fast* (■Exhibit 12.1). Spencer Phillips, the sales manager at a dealership in Pennsylvania, talks about how different the car buying process is today: "People come in and they already know so much; you've got to convey informed enthusiasm and impart useful information to them as fast as they can get it on the Internet." Phillips goes on to say, "without customers, the lights don't go on, so we have instituted the 10-foot rule." This rule means that if anyone in the dealership is within 10 feet of a customer, they need to have a friendly, warm interaction by either saying "hello" or asking if there's anything the customer needs. "Some form of interaction should take place, and whatever the interaction is, it should leave the customer more informed and in a better position to make a good decision for themselves about what they want."[1]

The case of the MINI dealership illustrates that managing a business involves controlling multiple aspects of what happens in the organization. This can include anything from establishing and meeting financial goals ("Without customers, the lights don't go on"), to determining and communicating the organization's beliefs and values ("You've got to convey informed enthusiasm . . . through warm, friendly interaction"), to promoting behaviors that support these goals ("We have instituted the 10-foot rule"). These are all organizational control processes. An organization's **control process** includes systems for establishing standards to achieve goals, monitoring and measuring performance, comparing performance to standards, and taking corrective action as necessary.

Controls are created and used to monitor and regulate how an organization performs in relation to its strategic goals and objectives. Controls are typically applied to employee behaviors, financial processes, resource allocation and use, customer experience, and quality. Controls allow organizations to stay on track or change as necessary over time. In this chapter, you will learn about the historical perspectives that influenced the control processes used in organizations today, and you'll explore several common types of control systems, including the familiar bureaucratic system. You'll then examine some of the forces that organizations choose to—or must—consider in their control processes, such as corporate governance and laws. Next, you'll investigate typical steps in the control process, as well as what sorts of things organizations typically need to control. After that, the chapter's focus turns to what companies should be controlling, with special attention given to several popular quality control processes, including business process reengineering, Total Quality Management, Six Sigma, and Lean Management. Finally, the chapter concludes with a discussion of how HR can support control processes in organizations, along with a look at what we all can do to ensure that our performance—and others' contributions—are outstanding.

Most Popular » Discussion Questions

1. Think of an organization you know well. How does this organization control behavior? Resources? Finances?
2. Have you ever been part of a workplace that lacked sufficient controls? How did this impact the organization? How did you and other team members respond?
3. Make a list of five things that you do to control your own performance in school.

2. What Historical Perspectives Help Us Understand Control in Organizations?

Karl Marx argued against management controlling the lives of workers.

North Wind Picture Archives/Alamy Images

Scientific management
An approach that involves organizing work for maximum efficiency.

In his *Economic and Philosophic Manuscripts,* written in 1844, German philosopher Karl Marx first elaborated his theory of alienation, arguing that laborers do not have any control over their work and that they lose control of their lives in a capitalistic system that forces them to produce goods and services for others (■Exhibit 12.2). Marx asserted that in such situations, work is meaningless because the worker has no say in how to accomplish the owner's objectives. Therefore, according to Marx, workers do not gain any personal satisfaction from their accomplishments.[2]

Thinking back to the horrid factory conditions prevalent during the mid-nineteenth century, it's easy to see how Marx came to these conclusions. In Marx's view, management really *did* control workers' lives, and laborers were treated like machines. Little or no attention was paid to workers' physical needs beyond what was minimally necessary for them to get the job done, and virtually no attention was given to their feelings, goals, or aspirations. It is not surprising that concerns about the relationship between workers and factory owners swept across the industrialized world, with the study of management emerging as one of the results. Indeed, during this period, several early management theorists—notably Frederick Taylor, Elton Mayo, and Mary Parker Follett—played particularly prominent roles in setting the stage for how work and workers would be managed in organizations for years to come.

Frederick Taylor and Scientific Management

Frederick W. Taylor (1856–1915) was an engineer who made a case for redesigning work processes for greater efficiency by studying the relationship between people and the tasks they performed. Known as the "Father of Scientific Management," Taylor also promoted the idea that management should be viewed as an academic discipline. **Scientific management** is an approach that involves organizing work for maximum efficiency.

Taylor argued that all aspects of society were riddled with waste and inefficiency, and that organizations could be improved if experts studied and determined the best way to carry out work. Accordingly, he focused on how work could be broken down into manageable tasks, and how these tasks could be broken down into discrete actions, so that both time and motion could be managed more efficiently. Operating from this point of view, Taylor proposed four principles of scientific management:[3]

1. Develop a science for each element of work.
2. Scientifically select and train all workers.
3. Ensure that all of the work is being done in accordance with the scientific method (i.e., that techniques are developed to maximize efficiency based on observation and experimentation).
4. Divide work between managers and workers. Managers must scientifically plan the work, and workers must carry it out.

Stories about how Taylor applied these principles are legendary. For example, when studying how men shoveled coal, Taylor noticed that if the shovel blade was designed to hold what an "average" worker could lift, that worker could be more efficient and move more coal each day (■Exhibit 12.3). Taylor drew many such conclusions as he consulted to many organizations about workplace efficiency. However, because Taylor's clients were company owners and managers, it is not surprising that his findings tended to support management's desires to find ways for people to do more with less.[4]

Despite questionable findings, the efficiency movement caught on and even came to be called "Taylorism." Some say that the efficiency movement went far beyond organizations

■Exhibit **12.3**
Frederick Taylor proposed ways to maximize workers' productivity.

Mike Greenslade/Alamy Images

Human relations movement
A movement that started around the beginning of the twentieth century and emphasized placing people, interpersonal relationships, and group behavior at the center of workplace studies.

Hawthorne Studies
A series of research projects demonstrating that when workers perceived that management cared about them and/or when they felt they were getting special treatment, both morale and productivity improved.

and has affected countless aspects of the way we live. Kitchens, for example, are designed so that minimum steps and effort are required as the cook moves between the stove, sink, and refrigerator. Although it is true that Taylor's work has had a profound impact on how we work and live, it is important to mention that even during his lifetime, Taylor was at the center of a number of controversies. Most of these controversies centered on many people's belief that Taylor's approach to work design focused on efficiency at any cost—even when the cost involved harming workers. With regard to Taylor's coal-shoveling observation, for instance, many people suspected that few human beings could actually lift the amount of weight Taylor recommended for very long.

Although Taylor certainly has an important place in the history of management, his theories aren't necessarily a good fit for the twenty-first-century workplace. Present-day workplaces and employees are profoundly different from the factories and manual laborers of the late 1800s and early 1900s. In today's knowledge economy, efficiency equations rarely involve something as simple as changing the shape of a shovel. Also, in the current service economy, efficiency is only part of the effectiveness equation.

Scientific management is not nearly robust enough a theory for today's organizations. However, it is still the basis for many of the control processes seen in modern organizations. Total Quality Management, Six Sigma, and Lean Management are just a few examples of current methods that incorporate aspects of Taylor's principles. Each of these methods will be discussed in depth later in the chapter. First, however, let's explore two other early approaches to the relationship between management, employees, and work processes: those proposed by Elton Mayo and Mary Parker Follett.

Elton Mayo and the Hawthorne Studies

In comparison to Taylor, Elton Mayo championed a different approach to management that focused less on tasks and work processes and more on the relationship between managers and workers. Mayo is considered to be one of the founders of the **human relations movement**, which started around the beginning of the twentieth century and emphasized placing people, interpersonal relationships, and group behavior at the center of workplace studies.

Mayo is best known for a series of experiments conducted at the Western Electric Company between 1924 and 1932 called the **Hawthorne Studies**. These studies involved a series of research projects demonstrating that when workers perceived that management cared about them and/or when they felt they were getting special treatment, both morale and productivity improved. In the earliest of the Hawthorne studies, certain physical conditions (e.g., lighting) were altered and changes in employee productivity were monitored. The results revealed that lighting itself actually had very little effect on productivity, unless it became too dark for the workers to see at all. What did have an effect on productivity and morale, however, was the workers' belief that management cared about them and their working conditions, and that they were somehow "special." Subsequent studies found that an employee's work group also had an effect on productivity, because social pressure (in the form of group norms) dictated acceptable levels of productivity and even people's attitudes about work and management.[5]

These findings are relevant today and, in fact, the term *Hawthorne effect* is still used to describe the improvement in productivity and morale that occurs when management pays attention to people. These studies put the relationship between employees and managers firmly at the center of the organizational success equation. In the wake of the Hawthorne studies, more and more scholars began to make the case that to increase productivity, managers and leaders must be educated about how to motivate people and create environments that make employees feel special and cared for. Scholars also began to focus on how managers could become more adept at creating work groups with behavioral norms that support productivity and positive attitudes. In short, the Hawthorne Studies legitimized common sense: It makes good business sense to attend to workers' feelings and related factors that affect how they think about their work, and it also makes good sense to support the development of group norms that encourage productivity and high morale.

Mary Parker Follett: Control Is More Than Telling People What to Do

As the Hawthorne Studies suggested, controlling people's behavior involves far more than simply telling people what to do or enhancing physical conditions in the workplace. This perspective is closely linked to the work of yet another highly influential theorist: Mary Parker Follett.

Follett is considered by many management experts to be a visionary in the fields of human relations, democratic organization, and management. Her work regarding the importance of the relationship between leaders and employees, the impact of groups on people's behavior, conflict management, and the role of informal leadership in the workplace led to outstanding contributions in the 1920s that were decades ahead of their time. In recent years, Follett's work has drawn widespread attention and acclaim, to the point that famous management author Peter Drucker has called her his "guru."[6]

Follett's writings focused on exploring the interdependent relationships between employees, leaders, and organizations. She believed that organizational results are an outcome of the interplay between people, systems, processes, and organizational culture. Follett also believed that the best people to solve problems are those closest and most familiar with the issues. In particular, she argued that power (and decision making) should be fluid and should go to the people who have the most knowledge and ability, not necessarily the most senior people in the hierarchy. When it came to control in the workplace, Follett suggested what must have been a revolutionary way of looking at power: Managers should emphasize "power with" as opposed to "power over" people, thus empowering people at all levels of an organization. Further, she believed that such empowerment would both enable and motivate the employees closest to a problem to find the best solution possible.[7]

The Human Touch

Mary Parker Follett set the stage for modern theories of leadership and organizational behavior. Many other theorists followed her lead, and one clear finding from their decades of research is that leaders, managers, and employees have mutually dependent relationships that benefit from certain types of controls. Specifically, the best types of controls are those that focus on people *and* processes *and* results. As you will see in this chapter, these can take the form of rules, guidelines, and measurement systems. Many effective forms of organizational control are linked to the field of psychology as well. For example, the command-and-control approach to managing people has been studied and critiqued as a relatively ineffective way to build organizational climates that foster high performance. The phrase "command and control" is often used to describe an approach to management that relies on powerful managers who dictate what needs to be done and obedient employees who do what they are told. Research has shown that outside of life-threatening situations (e.g., when a fire breaks out), this approach is not useful because it does not result in maximum performance over time. In fact, organizations that employ this approach tend to breed dissonance and dissent. Negativity permeates the walls, and employees feel guarded and even despondent—which means they don't perform at their best.[8]

Organizational culture also has a profound effect on people and organizational results. In particular, resonant cultures that employees and customers experience as positive, inclusive, and focused on excellence have been found to be powerful drivers of people's behavior and effectiveness. These kinds of organizational climates are often empowering, which means that people are vitally involved in how work gets done, as well as in how effectiveness and efficiency are monitored and controlled. These environments tend to be places in which people feel supported, valued, and recognized for their contributions.[9]

Work climates that embody the "spirit" of an organization and support empowerment significantly impact productivity in a positive direction. In cultures that support positive attitudes and productivity, the people who do the actual work are often the ones to create appropriate mechanisms to improve work processes and systems.[10] As illustrated in the following *Student's Choice* feature, leaders have a special role when it comes to creating resonant cultures—especially when times are tough. It isn't as hard as one might think to create an environment in which everyone can be at their best, solve problems together, and jointly control quality.

Student's Choice

Bob Kern

Spartan Surfaces

Kevin Jablon is the founder and owner of Spartan Surfaces, a wholesale business-to-business flooring distributor located in Forest Hill, Maryland. Since opening for business at the beginning of 2007, Spartan Surfaces has become a very successful flooring distributor on the East Coast of the United States.

Through experience, patience, perseverance, and a clear-cut set of values, Jablon has created his own destiny and has become a respected example of a truly great leader. It has not been easy, however. In the first three years of business, Jablon was confronted with many challenges that tested his leadership skills.

Let's look at how this dynamic young person learned to lead. Twenty-three years old and new to the workforce, Jablon recognized that he was not mature enough to embark on building a successful business—so he waited, observed, and listened. He developed an apprentice mentality. He learned from every person he came in contact with, adopting the positive qualities of the leaders he met. He also learned what qualities *not to adopt* from the bad leaders he encountered. Maybe most importantly, he honed the values that would see him through good times and bad. Operating a business with honesty and integrity is vital to success, Jablon says, and trust is crucial to building relationships. Surrounding oneself with talented and trustworthy people helps too.

After 11 years of gaining experience in four different positions in the industry, Jablon decided it was time to make his dream a reality by starting his own business. He drew on his vision, passion, and knowledge about what it takes for people to succeed and hired individuals who were passionate, who loved their work, and who knew how to have fun.

Although Jablon's vision was solid and his people were fantastic, the rapidly changing economic landscape in 2007–2008 caused him to redesign his business model many times. Lack of control over the economic climate was by far the biggest challenge that Jablon and the Spartan team had to overcome. In fact, at the height of the recession in 2008, the company saw a huge decrease in sales. Times were more than tough—they were dire.

Jablon's passion and drive kept the business going, but he recalls being irritable and snapping at his employees. Somehow, he was losing all of the great skills he had developed over the years, and he realized that even his core values weren't enough to keep him on track as a good leader. Luckily, he quickly caught himself: This behavior was killing motivation and morale. He realized that his drive for success could get the best of him and that he needed to be less impulsive. He needed to tap into self-awareness and improve his self-control. To truly be a great leader, he needed to step back and reflect on how his emotional reactions to stress were affecting him and his employees.

Many factors have led to Jablon's success, but some of the most significant were his core values, self-awareness, and self-control during difficult times. With these in place, he could—and did—create the kind of culture in which people were able to do their very best. Together, they made it through the recession. And it wasn't a miracle. It was good leadership, self-control, and creating a culture that supports resonance and results.

Source: Adapted from a case written by Bob Kern.

In this case, Kevin Jablon practiced self-awareness, first by knowing his needs before trying to start his business, and later by reflecting on how his own personality and emotions could create an environment that either discouraged or encouraged people to perform their best. By being self-aware and mindful, Kevin was able to see how his own mental state affected others, and by focusing on self-control and his relationships, he was able to create a resonant environment—one in which people were actively involved, excited, and committed to shared goals.[11] This case demonstrates that when it comes to organizational controls, people matter. In Chapter 13, you will learn more about organizational culture and its role in the control process. For now, as you read about the sometimes complex systems that have been designed to control people and processes in organizations, remember that people are at the center of it all.

Most Popular » Discussion Questions

1. Consider a job you have had (paid or unpaid) in which efficiency was important. Using Frederick Taylor's first principle of scientific management, develop a "science" for one of the tasks you had to do. Break the task into as many components as possible, and describe how the task could be done most efficiently in terms of time and motion.
2. Have you ever experienced the "Hawthorne effect" at work or at school? If so, what happened, and how did your manager's or teacher's attention affect your morale and productivity?
3. According to Mary Parker Follett, what is the difference between using "power over" people and using "power with" people? Describe a situation in which the "power with" strategy would be more effective.

---

3. What Are Common Control Systems?

Now that we've seen how the science of managing others has evolved during the past century, let's examine some of the ways in which present-day companies try to control for efficiency and effectiveness. Among the most common of these methods are bureaucratic control and normative control. In recent years, more and more organizations have also begun to employ a model known as the levers of control system.

Bureaucratic Control Systems

Bureaucratic control systems
Control processes that use specific rules, standards, and hierarchical authority to achieve planned and desired organizational outcomes.

Bureaucratic control systems are control processes that use specific rules, standards, and hierarchical authority to achieve planned and desired organizational outcomes. Sometimes referred to as a "compliance" model, the bureaucratic system mandates that employees abide by established rules, policies, and standards. This type of control system focuses on roles rather than individuals. In other words, responsibilities and duties are linked to jobs and roles, and people who hold certain roles are expected to behave in a prescribed manner.[12]

Managing a bureaucratic control system involves comparison of performance to established standards, operating procedures, and metrics to determine whether people and/or the organization are meeting strategic goals. In this system, if standards are not adhered to or metrics are not met, corrective action is taken. Bureaucratic control systems are designed to ensure that output is predictable, and they are prominent in organizations that are managed in a highly structured fashion and in those that rely heavily on hierarchy and authority to influence behaviors.

You have probably experienced bureaucratic control in schools and organizations. For example, it is likely that you had to fill out a form asking for specific personal information

■Exhibit **12.4**

At work and school, ID cards are often part of bureaucratic control systems.

David Adamson/Alamy Images

before you could receive your student identification card (■Exhibit 12.4). This is part of a bureaucratic control system that ensures only students can obtain such cards. Later on, you likely used your ID in yet another bureaucratic control system when you either showed your card to someone or slid it through an electronic reader. This process enables the school to control who enters which building, as well as to monitor people's comings and goings. Bureaucratic controls are widespread in organizations of all types. They include such things as safety protocols, signing in and out of work, tracking vacation and sick time, the procedures managers must use to request raises for their employees, systems that track and monitor goods when they are shipped—and on and on.

In a bureaucratic control system, policies and rules are valued above using one's own judgment. Let's see what this means by returning to the example of your school ID card. Most likely, you are fully capable of determining which building you should enter for class on your own—you don't *need* a card that provides or limits access. However, at some point, the school's leaders determined that they needed to control student behavior so they could gather information or make sure all students did certain things in the same way. It's the same in many businesses—rather than leaving matters up to the individual, businesses rely on standard processes that ensure that decisions can be monitored at the organizational level and that all employees complete specific tasks in the same manner.

Besides actual rules and policies, bureaucratic control systems also rely on social control mechanisms to create common value systems, understandings, and expectations among employees.[13] In many instances, aspects of the bureaucratic control system become inseparable from an organization's culture. The social rules associated with this informal system may not be written down or even articulated—but they are nevertheless powerful. For example, in the hierarchical system of reporting relationships, employees are often expected to deal directly with their own managers when problems arise. There may be no rule that prohibits going to a manager in another division or to your boss's boss about a problem. Still, the social pressure that prohibits such actions can be extreme, and in some cases, people may even be fired for violating rules in this less formal part of the control system.

Bureaucratic control systems are pervasive and the rules and regulations are often robust and effective. These systems, however, can inhibit innovation and honest communication and breed an environment where good judgment is suspended in favor of following the rules. For many of us, the idea of being discouraged from using our own common sense paints a picture of a repressive work environment. In fact, when taken to the extreme, such formal, rules-bound organizations can become dissonant and even toxic.[14]

Furthermore, too much bureaucracy can introduce layers of administrative activity and radically slow down decision making. The trick to leveraging bureaucratic control systems is to use them in settings where they promote better performance and safety, such as manufacturing facilities. But even in these cases, steps should be taken to limit the detrimental effect that excessive regulation can have on the positive climate needed to bring out the best in an organization's people.[15]

Adhering to Rules versus Objective Assessment of Behavior and Outputs

In traditional bureaucracies, following the rules actually can become more important than the quality of work that gets done. When objectivity is valued, however, behavior and work outputs are considered in addition to whether rules are adhered to. This type of control is "objective" because of its focus on observables—managers observe how employees behave and monitor work outputs to assess performance.

Two important aspects of objective control are output control and behavior control. In **output control**, outcomes are measured against financial performance and other clearly articulated metrics, such as customer retention. With this system, incentives and

Output control
Type of control in which outcomes are measured against financial performance and other clearly articulated metrics, such as customer retention.

rewards are tied to meeting or surpassing a set of predetermined metrics; thus, clarity of expectations, measurable and achievable targets, and transparency around measurement and evaluation of goals are essential. Output control allows managers and employees a relative amount of freedom when determining how to best meet goals, without too much direct supervision.[16]

Behavior control

Type of control in which an organization tries to shape the behaviors of its employees in order to attain the desired outcomes that will lead to organizational success.

Behavior control focuses on what employees actually do in order to attain desired outcomes. Within bureaucratic control systems, managers closely monitor and evaluate employee behavior, addressing any deviations from expectations.[17] The most obvious form of behavior control is seen in the supervisor–employee relationship. Here, supervisors watch over employees, assist them in developing the skills required to perform their duties, and monitor their effectiveness and efficiency to ensure they are acting in accordance with expectations. In this system, incentives are often given to those individuals who exhibit the desired behaviors. In other words, employees are rewarded for behaving in accordance with expectations, and they are also punished for deviations from expectations.

Objective control systems involve the development and implementation of mechanisms such as measurement processes.[18] Behavior and outputs are often controlled and measured through standards and procedures (sometimes called standard operating procedures, or SOPs). Once these standards and procedures are in place, objective control operates through the use of hierarchical controls, chains of command, and communication.[19]

Normative Control

Normative control

A control system that involves sharing and embedding an organization's values and beliefs so they act as a guide for employees' behavior.

Normative control is about sharing and embedding an organization's values and beliefs so they act as a guide for employees' behavior. When normative control is effective, organizations typically have fewer formal rules and standard operating procedures. Rather, employees are encouraged to use their best judgment and the organization's values to guide their behavior. With this type of system, new employees look to more seasoned colleagues (rather than a policy manual) for clues and cues about acceptable behaviors.

Normative control is most often enforced through an organization's culture (discussed in Chapter 13), and it works well when the "fit" between employees and the organization is good—in other words, when individual employees' values, beliefs, and expectations about work behavior are aligned with those of the organization. This means that organizations that rely on normative control need to be very selective in their hiring process, looking for people who have compatible attitudes and values. One scholar who studies control systems notes that the most important (and often underutilized) form of control is retaining the best employees.[20]

In the case of Ticketfly, a social marketing and online ticketing company that serves American music clubs, founder Dan Teree notes that, "Everyone here takes accountability and can point to a variety of accomplishments and say 'I did that!' and feel great about it."[21] This is an example of how values can be at the center of a normative control system that guides people's behavior.

Levers of Control

Levers of control

A control system that relies on various levers such as organizational values, rules, feedback systems, and focused involvement in decision making.

One of the more recent and more innovative control systems in use today is the **levers of control** model proposed by Harvard professor Robert Simons.[22] A lever can be thought of as a simple machine that gives the user a mechanical advantage. Imagine prying a large rock out of the ground with a bar—when you push down on one end, very little effort is needed to lift the heavy weight on the other end. Levers work the same way when it comes to controls in an organization. In the example, only one lever is needed to move the rock, but if the rock were very large or heavy, several levers could be combined to move it. This is also the case in organizations: The more levers you use, the more likely you are to change and control aspects of work and outcomes.

■Exhibit **12.5**

Simons's Levers of Control[23]		
Lever	**How It Works**	**Examples**
Belief Systems	Defines the core values of an organization and its members	Credos, mission statements, and values statements
Boundary Systems	Defines territory or span of control for people within the organization	Rules, proscriptions, and regulations of the organization
Diagnostic Control Systems	Feedback system that allows the organization to monitor standards	Systems to measure output, as well as incentives and goals
Interactive Control Systems	Allows managers to plan how to regularly involve themselves personally in their subordinates' decision-making activities	Project management systems, knowledge management systems, and scheduling systems

This model attempts to integrate some of the best aspects of other models; accordingly, it includes belief systems, boundary systems, diagnostic control systems, and interactive control systems, as illustrated in ■Exhibit 12.5.

The levers of control model expands our understanding of the factors that contribute to organizational performance, allowing us to pay close attention to the people- and process-oriented, relational aspect of getting things done. Levers of control are about creating and maintaining a cultural mindset that contributes to behaviors within an organization in addition to putting systems and processes into place.

Within control systems, employees may have various levels of input and involvement. In some organizations, control systems are a top-down set of rules that cannot be changed and must be obeyed. In other organizations, control systems are more participative, and people have opportunities to be involved in the creation and implementation of the control process. In the latter case, people are seen as an asset whose cooperation and input is essential to full realization of the organization's goals and potential.

When considering control systems in organizations, it is important to consider the various forces that organizations choose to—or must—incorporate in their control processes, including corporate governance, audits, laws, and customers. Each of these forces will be examined in greater detail in the next section of the chapter.

Most Popular » Discussion Questions

1. Brainstorm a list of some of the bureaucratic controls that guide your behavior as a student. Which of these do you believe are necessary or helpful, and which do you believe are unnecessary or harmful? Explain.

2. Have you worked in a job or attended a school that had a highly controlled environment? What were the effects of this environment on your behavior (both positive and negative)?

3. Consider a process that you see implemented at school or at work every day, such as cleaning the classrooms or offices. What controls seem to be in place to ensure effectiveness and efficiency? Are the employees who perform these jobs involved in controlling their work output? If so, how?

4. What Conventions and Forces Guide Organizational Control Processes?

In this section, you'll learn about two conventional structures organizations often use as part of their control processes: corporate governance and audits. You'll also explore how legislation impacts the control process, and how today's most innovative organizations seek to involve customers in their control systems.

Corporate Governance

Corporate governance
The way in which an organization is controlled, administered, or directed as described by laws and the processes, policies, regulations, and customs of that organization.

Corporate charter
An articulation of policies, rules, and procedures that address a variety of governance issues, such as the legal name and location of the business, along with the business's mission, rules relating to its board of directors, and classes of securities (stocks) that are issued.

Corporate governance refers to the way in which an organization is controlled, administered, or directed as described by laws and the processes, policies, regulations, and customs of that organization. With respect to finance, corporate governance is the method by which suppliers of capital ensure returns on their investment in the company.[24] Corporate governance can also be described as the set of rules, policies, and procedures for managing an organization and ensuring that the organization's behavior and practices are aligned with market forces and internal control structures.[25]

Corporate governance is frequently spelled out in a corporate charter. A **corporate charter** is an articulation of policies, rules, and procedures that address a variety of governance issues, such as the legal name and location of the business, along with the business's mission, rules relating to its board of directors, and classes of securities (stocks) that are issued.

Corporate governance involves three primary sets of players: the board of directors, management, and selected stakeholders. Together, these parties are responsible for ensuring that the company's mission, values, and legal obligations are upheld.

The board of directors usually includes individuals who are not employed by the company and who may have expertise that will be helpful to management. These individuals are called "independent directors," and they are often paid a stipend for their service (which can be quite a lot of money in some cases). The board of directors also usually includes representatives from the top of the organization, such as the CEO, CFO, and general counsel. The board helps guide the organization's strategy and ensure that the organization is meeting both its own objectives and the expectations of stakeholders. In many companies, the board of directors has ultimate fiduciary and legal accountability for the organization.

The second major player in the corporate governance equation is management, which, of course, is responsible for ensuring that the organization is governed according to its charter and that it—and all its employees—uphold all applicable laws. Management is charged with making sure that all stakeholders are satisfied.

Privately held company
A company that is wholly owned by an individual or group of individuals and does not sell shares of ownership on the open market.

Publicly traded company
A company that issues shares of ownership, or stocks, that are traded on the open market.

Selected stakeholders are the third major party involved in corporate governance. The selection of which stakeholders to include in corporate governance differs depending on whether a company is privately held or publicly traded. A **privately held company** is a company that is wholly owned by an individual or a group of individuals and does not sell shares of ownership on the open market. In privately held companies, special stakeholders can include advisers, experts in areas such as finance or community relations, and even friends and family. A **publicly traded company** is a company that issues shares of ownership, or stocks, that are traded on the open market. In publicly traded companies, stakeholders usually include experts in various functional areas (finance, accounting, etc.), as well as senior-level advisers such as ex-CEOs or sitting senior members of other companies. They also include a company's shareholders, or the individuals or groups that own shares of the company. These individuals and/or groups have purchased shares either through employee stock options or on the open market. Other stakeholders that may have a say in governing an organization include community representatives, founders, and employees, to name just a few.

A last word on governance: Regardless of how a board is structured, its members need to share an understanding of the company's mission, vision, and goals. Furthermore, members must offer positive and constructive advice to management. As obvious as this seems, the governance process is often complicated and even undermined because not everyone is on the same page. In addition, the relationship between external board members and management is extremely important and must be designed to support open communication, mutual respect, and effective governance.

Audits

Audit

A formal review to make sure that certain processes have been fully and accurately managed and reported.

Corporate governance is the umbrella control mechanism under which an organization functions. Beneath that umbrella, audits are one of several means for ensuring that people and the organization as a whole are doing what they are supposed to be doing. An **audit** is a formal review to make sure that certain processes have been fully and accurately managed and reported. For example, an audit might be conducted to check that a financial statement has been completed accurately. Although audits are usually associated with accounting tasks like this one, they can actually be performed on a wide range of processes. For instance, an audit could be conducted to ensure that environmental protection laws are being followed; human resources might conduct an audit to ensure that the company is complying with federal labor laws; or a company may carry out an audit of its safety practices.

Audits are sometimes internal and conducted by employees such as accountants, environmental specialists, or HR professionals.[26] External audits employ independent professionals or firms. One especially common practice for medium-to-large businesses is to hire outside accountants to audit the finances of the company. These auditors ensure that financial records are accurate, complete, and prepared according to GAAP (generally accepted accounting principles), as well as state and federal regulations.

Legislation and Sarbanes-Oxley

All businesses and industries are controlled to some extent by government regulations. Let's first look at how laws affect businesses in general, then consider a piece of important special legislation (Sarbanes-Oxley) that has been instituted in recent years.

Legislation and Controls

Regulations can be local, such as zoning laws that dictate what kind of business can be conducted where. State or provincial laws also control how business is carried out, how employees are treated, and the like. Businesses must additionally abide by applicable national or federal laws, such as the Civil Rights Act in the United States, which protects the rights of employees in the workplace.[27] In many cases, these laws are supported and upheld by regulatory agencies, such as the U.S. Food and Drug Administration (FDA) and the Environmental Protection Agency (EPA). Through legislation and agencies such as these, the government exerts control over a wide range of business practices. For example, the government regulates how products are labeled and advertised, including whether they can be called "certified organic" or "fair trade."

All countries have these sorts of laws and regulatory bodies, and they greatly impact how, when, and where a company can do business. In addition, international organizations that govern trade and business practices, such as the World Trade Organization (WTO), can have an impact on issues such as pricing, what goods are sold by whom, and where goods are sold.

Many of these laws and regulations have been implemented to ensure that businesses act in a fair and responsible manner with respect to the communities and people they serve. Often, they are intended to provide balance to the profit-seeking imperative of market economies. This could mean looking out for the interests of workers, consumers, or society, and it may involve local, national, or international regulating bodies or agencies.

Sarbanes-Oxley and Controls

Sarbanes-Oxley Act of 2002
Formally known as the Public Company Accounting Reform and Investor Protection Act, this act sets new or enhanced standards for publicly traded companies' boards, managers, and public accounting firms.

In recent years, one set of regulations in particular has been instituted to ensure that businesses operate in a fair and ethical manner. These regulations and standards are the result of the **Sarbanes-Oxley Act of 2002**, commonly abbreviated as SOX and formally known as the Public Company Accounting Reform and Investor Protection Act. SOX is critical to all publicly traded companies in the United States because it sets new or enhanced standards for these companies' boards, managers, and public accounting firms.

SOX was enacted as a result of a number of major corporate and accounting scandals in the early 2000s, including those at Enron, Arthur Andersen, Tyco International, Adelphia, Peregrine Systems, and WorldCom. These scandals caused the companies' financial infrastructures to collapse, which cost employees and investors billions of dollars. The fraud involved in these scandals, and the government's inability to detect and stop the fraud, shook public confidence in the nation's companies and in government regulators.

SOX applies only to public companies, not to privately held companies. The act contains 11 sections that cover topics ranging from additional corporate board responsibilities to criminal penalties for violation of standards, and it requires the Securities and Exchange Commission (SEC) to implement rulings regarding compliance with the new laws. The act created a new agency called the Public Company Accounting Oversight Board, which is charged with overseeing, regulating, inspecting, and disciplining accounting firms (see ■Exhibit 12.6). The act also covers issues such as auditor independence, corporate governance, internal control assessment, and enhanced financial disclosure.

Debate continues about the perceived benefits and costs of SOX. Supporters contend that the act was necessary and that it has restored public confidence in U.S. business and oversight procedures by strengthening corporate accounting controls. Opponents of SOX claim that it has reduced America's international competitive edge by introducing an overly complex regulatory environment.[28]

So far, we have discussed how companies set standards to ensure adherence to both internal governance criteria and laws originating outside the organization. In the next section, we will look at a third, more innovative approach to control—letting customers in on the processes of product design and marketing.

■Exhibit **12.6**

Sarbanes-Oxley Public Company Accounting Oversight Board

The Public Company Accounting Oversight Board shall:[29]

1. Register public accounting firms;
2. Establish or adopt, by rule, auditing, quality control, ethics, independence, and other standards relating to the preparation of audit reports for issuers;
3. Conduct inspections of accounting firms;
4. Conduct investigations and disciplinary proceedings, and impose appropriate sanctions;
5. Perform such other duties or functions as necessary or appropriate;
6. Enforce compliance with the Act, the rules of the Board, professional standards, and the securities laws relating to the preparation and issuance of audit reports and the obligations and liabilities of accountants with respect thereto;
7. Set the budget and manage the operations of the Board and the staff of the Board.

When Customers Control

Often, companies *must* comply with certain controls, such as those created by government legislation. Some companies, however, start at the other end of the spectrum: They *seek* to be controlled. This is the case in the growing number of organizations that strive to involve customers in product design and quality control. Consider the example of Threadless in the following *Business Case* feature.

Threadless

Business Case

Customer Control

Jake Nickell, founder of online T-shirt retailer Threadless, had no intention of creating a revolution in management or rewriting books on organizational design. As a 20-year-old part-time student, he spent much of his time browsing design sites, interacting with members on forums, and designing Web pages.[30] The trigger event that eventually caused him to launch Threadless came when Nickell won a competition at the New Media Underground festival for a T-shirt logo he designed. There was no prize money—not even a copy of the shirt he designed—but it was validation.

Together with his friend Jacob DeHart, Nickell decided to host an online T-shirt design contest. The first contest was held in November 2000, and the response was just under 100 submissions. The prize? Two free shirts and a promise from the company that all proceeds would go to funding the next competition. Two dozen copies of the five most popular designs were printed up as T-shirts and priced at $12 each. They sold out very quickly.

By 2002, with over $100,000 worth of T-shirt stock and over 100,000 site members, Nickell and DeHart realized that they had much more than a hobby on their hands. They formed a company, named it Threadless, and brought more people on board. Just four years later, in 2006, Threadless's sales hit $16 million, with a profit of roughly $6 million, and the company had a member base of around 700,000.[31] By 2009, Threadless was selling 100,000 T-shirts every month and was regularly approached by venture capitalists.[32]

As these figures demonstrate, Threadless is a tremendous success both financially and in terms of customer loyalty. Today, there is even an unofficial Threadless fan blog (www.lovesThreadless.com), a Threadless Facebook site with 89,000 fans, and a Threadless Twitter account with 1,359,851 followers (as of November 2009), along with competitions to spot celebrities wearing Threadless T-shirts.

Part of Threadless's popularity is due to the fact that instead of restricting customers to the role of buyer, the company takes every opportunity to encourage their participation in designing products, voting, or just spreading the word. Nickell and his crew

Threadless Customers: Masters of Design

spend much of their time discussing and participating with members on their forums, and members seem to relish the openness of the company, as shown by the exponential growth in the company's customer base and sales.

When it came to building the Threadless brand, the company didn't spend a cent—not in real money, anyway. What they did spend was *time*. So far, Threadless's primary marketing channel has been straightforward, simple word of mouth. In fact, fans of the company were responsible for setting up the company's Facebook page and other fan sites. Although Nickell and DeHart briefly experimented with advertising, they soon abandoned the idea because it didn't produce the desired effect and elicited a negative reaction from their existing customer base. In Nickell's own words:

> With our company, it's all about trust and honesty and we just don't like the idea of pushing our brand on people who otherwise wouldn't hear about it . . . organically, naturally. It's not that we don't market; we just don't advertise.[33]

When it comes to employee selection at Threadless, the topic of trust plays a major role. "It's pretty much the only thing we talk about when we interview," Nickell says.[34] The idea is to find people who can work on their own, without supervision. Many of the employees are designers themselves or have art degrees. In fact, 75 percent of the company's employees were Threadless Web site members before ever working for the company.[35]

Threadless has big plans. The company has already opened a retail store in Chicago, initially as a flagship marketing channel with only a few products. The majority of the space is dedicated to displaying the work of emerging artists. Although the store was opened with the expectation of losing money, it became profitable within six months, and it currently attracts customers from all over the country. Threadless is also considering expansions and opening regional warehouses, which would enable European customers to get their T-shirts faster.[36] Another idea is to extend the range of community design products to children's apparel, clothing accessories, and even dishware. The opportunities are truly unlimited.

Photo Source: R. Gino Santa Maria/Shutterstock.

As described in the case study, Threadless challenges the traditional approach to controlling business practices and marketing. Although every business is intuitively aware of the importance of consumer loyalty and brand trust, Threadless is proof that consumer-controlled product design and marketing can be a company's core competence and its most important asset. Threadless is clearly employing a very different business model;

though not yet that common, it will doubtless be explored by more organizations as technology and social networking take on ever greater importance in our day-to-day lives.

You have now read about several common control systems, as well as some new and innovative ways of looking at the control process. In the next section, you'll get a better idea of how these systems operate as you learn about the typical steps in control processes.

Most Popular » Discussion Questions

1. Imagine you are hired as a consultant to a boutique clothing store. What control processes would you recommend that the owners create to monitor finances, people, and adherence to laws?
2. Do you believe that laws such as the Sarbanes-Oxley Act were a reasonable or effective response to the corporate accounting scandals of the time? Why or why not?
3. You may be part of a group that has a charter (e.g., a fraternity or sorority). Review this charter or the charter for another group at your college. Do you believe the charter truly guides and controls the group or organization? Explain your answer.
4. Research several companies that involve their customers in product design via the Internet. What is your opinion about involving customers in design and other control processes? What are the benefits? What are the drawbacks?

---

5. What Are the Typical Steps in the Control Process?

■Exhibit **12.7**
The business process model shows the points at which control processes can be applied.

Control systems can be applied at any point in the business process, from input (e.g., monitoring the quality and price of raw materials), to throughput (e.g., measuring the efficiency of manufacturing processes), to output (e.g., applying quality standards to the finished product). (See ■Exhibit 12.7.) At all of these stages, an organization's goals can be transformed into specific quality and efficiency standards and metrics, such as baselines for cost and quality of raw materials, expectations for internal production processes, standards for employee performance, product quality specifications, timelines for getting products to market, and so on. Indeed, almost any aspect of the business process can be measured and monitored as an organization attempts to meet its goals and objectives.

Systems Model

External Environment

People, Materials, Money, Information → Inputs → Throughputs → Outputs → Goods and Services

Feedback

Creating Standards and Metrics

Standards and metrics
Measures established to define quality and efficiency criteria.

Standards and metrics are measures established to define quality and efficiency. Standards and metrics can come from internal analyses of behaviors and systems that lead to desired outcomes. Alternatively, they can be determined by talking to customers about their preferences. In addition, they may be established by benchmarking an organization's results against those of other companies in the same industry.

Standards can be either quantitative (e.g., "A retail clerk is to sell 25 pieces of clothing per shift") or qualitative (e.g., "A retail clerk is to treat customers in a friendly, respectful manner"). The logic behind standards and metrics is as follows: If the right standards and metrics are created, and if all standards and metrics are met or exceeded, then the organization should meet its goals. Standards and metrics also serve as a basis for comparison, giving employees and managers guidelines for performance.

An example of quantitative controls is measuring how many items, such as MP3 players, are manufactured within an hour.

Peter Alvey/Alamy Images

To see how standards affect workers' daily tasks, let's consider two fictitious workers: Will and Tiffany. Will works in a factory. He must ensure that 60 MP3 players are produced per hour (■Exhibit 12.8). In addition, the players must conform to the specific dimensions defined in the product specifications (five inches tall by two inches wide). These controls are quantitative.

In comparison, Tiffany works in a call center, where she must make five outbound calls per hour and answer an additional five inbound calls per hour. She is expected to keep each call to five minutes, and to then document each call in a period of one minute. These are quantitative measures. When on a call, Tiffany is also expected to be helpful and engaging. These are qualitative measures. Thus, the standards that Tiffany must meet are both quantitative and qualitative.

Measuring Performance

After determining standards and metrics, another important step in the control process is measuring the extent to which organizational performance is meeting, falling short of, or exceeding expectations. Answering this question might include looking at levels of production, safety records, customer retention rates, or monthly revenues. Measurements are then recorded for use in the next phase of the control process as a benchmark for determining what, if any, corrective action needs to be taken.

To illustrate how this works, let's look at the differences in how Will's and Tiffany's performances are measured. Will's performance is measured by the quantity of MP3 players produced per hour and by the dimensions of what is produced. Will, therefore, has two quantitative controls that are used to judge his performance. Quantitative controls like this are common in manufacturing environments. Tiffany's managers have a more difficult job because her performance is not only measured quantitatively (by how many calls she makes and receives), but also qualitatively (by the tone of her voice and her friendliness as she talks to customers). This is typical in a customer service or sales environment.

Comparing Performance to Standards

Following performance measurement, the next step in the control process is to compare an organization's actual performance with desired standards. The clearer and more precise these standards are, the easier it is to make this comparison. For instance, emergency rooms often have standards regarding the average amount of time patients must wait before seeing a doctor. According to data from the U.S. Centers for Disease Control and Prevention, in 2004, patients spent an average of about 3.3 hours in the emergency department from arrival to discharge.[37] This is a benchmark that a hospital can use to gauge its own performance. If a hospital's goal is to improve the patient experience or to become the local hospital of choice for emergency treatment, then that hospital might implement a standard that is significantly less than the benchmark, say, two hours or less.

So, how do Tiffany's and Will's performances compare to the standards set by their managers? Will needs to produce 60 MP3 players per hour, and these devices need to meet certain size specifications. Say that from 2:00 P.M. to 3:00 P.M. on October 25, Will produces 51 MP3 players with the correct dimensions. This is nine fewer than the standard calls for, and it represents a downward deviation of 15 percent. This is a control loss: a downward deviation from the benchmark.

Meanwhile, Tiffany made five outbound calls but only answered four inbound calls during the same hour-long period on October 25. This represents a control loss of 20 percent against the standard for incoming calls, and a loss of 10 percent against her overall requirements for calls of all types. On these nine calls, Tiffany's attitude was helpful and engaging in seven of them, but in the remaining two calls, the manager who reviewed Tiffany's audiotapes judged her to be unhelpful and to sound irritated.

Taking Corrective Action

After comparing actual performance to standards, the next phase in the control process involves reconciling the gap. In the event that standards were exceeded, this may mean that performance was stellar or that the standard was set too low. If performance was low and standards were not met, then managers must decide whether and how to address the situation through corrective action.

Before taking action, however, it is important to understand the reasons why standards were not met. In some cases, it's simple to see cause and effect—for instance, employees were late for work; therefore customers could not get into the store until one hour after the scheduled opening time and sales were down. However, many other reasons for failing to meet standards are not as easy to understand.

Let's look at the reasons behind Will's and Tiffany's failures to meet standards. Will's manager interviewed Will and his coworkers to determine why they were all 15 percent below their production targets. Through these interviews, the manager determined that Will's team was engaging in conversation with the other workers and not focusing on the task. Will's production team was issued a verbal warning and informed that they would receive a written warning if this production shortfall occurred again within the next 30 days.

Meanwhile, at the call center, Tiffany's manager reviewed the notes Tiffany made about each call and determined that she was only able to take four inbound calls (instead of the standard five) because two of the other calls were with customers who required extra attention and help. Because these customers had special needs, the manager did not take corrective action. However, the manager issued a warning to Tiffany about her tone of voice and lack of helpfulness with customers. Tiffany did not believe her tone was inappropriate, but she promised to try to improve nonetheless.

This example points to what can be a big problem when managers take action to correct an employee's behavior: They need to have judged that behavior accurately, and they also need to help the employee see the situation the same way. In this case, Tiffany's manager judged her to be unhelpful and irritated. If this manager is highly skilled and emotionally intelligent, he will have "read" Tiffany's behavior accurately, and he will have correctly judged the impact that Tiffany had on customers. But what if this manager isn't skilled in reading human behavior? Or what if he was in a rush, and he didn't take the time to listen to the entire audiotape? These sorts of problems are extremely common when it comes to making judgments about human interaction—yet another reason why employees and managers need to develop skills that will enable them to build strong, positive relationships and accurately assess behavior.

■Exhibit **12.9**

Feedback is an essential part of the control process.

Ron Rovtar/Alamy Images

Feedback Processes

Without feedback, the control process does not work (■Exhibit 12.9). Usually, when people hear the word *feedback*, they automatically think about getting information after the fact—which is often the case in organizations. Feedback of this kind is discussed first. Then, we will review two additional types of information and input that factor into many control systems: feed-forward control and concurrent control.

Feedback Control

Feedback control
Type of control in which information about performance is gathered and shared after the fact.

Feedback control is a type of control in which information about performance is gathered and shared after the fact, which can be costly to an organization. Sometimes feedback is simply too late and the damage can't be undone. For instance, when safety standards in a factory are ignored, feedback in the form of an injured employee is not something that can be rectified for that individual. Or, if ethics standards were breached but not noticed until afterward, the damage will have already been done.

How might feedback control operate in Will's situation? If Will's boss hears from an electronics retailer that red MP3 players are outselling blue MP3 players, then he will want to increase production of red MP3 players. However, it takes time to switch the production process so that more red players can be manufactured. Here, the retailer's feedback may have been communicated too late, resulting in a missed opportunity.

Feed-Forward Control

Feed-forward control
Type of control system that anticipates potential issues or problems before they arise.

In contrast to feedback control, **feed-forward control** is a type of control system that anticipates potential issues or problems before they arise. It is a "best guess" approach that proactively sets a course to control for potential problems and opportunities early on, rather than waiting for the problems or missed opportunities to occur. For example, Will's employer might actually research production machinery and buy the most stable equipment before the factory starts producing the players. This feed-forward control is designed to prevent problems from happening in the first place or at least to reduce the number of equipment repairs required later.

Concurrent Control

Concurrent control
The process of collecting "real-time" information to decrease the lag time between performance deficiencies and corrective action.

Finally, **concurrent control** is the process of collecting "real-time" information to decrease the lag time between performance deficiencies and corrective action. For instance, with the introduction of software that performs real-time tracking, an entertainment venue's managers could see, at any time, how many tickets have sold for an upcoming concert without having to wait for monthly or weekly sales reports. If sales are down, the managers will know immediately, and they can take corrective action such as more advertising. Some airline reservation systems use this type of control to determine cost per seat as the plane fills up. Here, prices can be increased or decreased to maximize revenue and capacity usage.

Let's consider how concurrent control might work at Tiffany's call center. Say the center is constantly monitored by managers through the use of real-time audio monitoring, report generation, and software that tracks numbers of calls and time spent on each call. Tiffany and her manager are provided with this information at frequent intervals, which allows them to immediately take corrective action if standards are not being met.

Integrating Feedback

The control process is one manifestation of an organization's values, and it communicates to employees what the organization's leaders deem most important. Furthermore, the feedback that employees receive can affect them either positively or negatively. If feedback is delivered and perceived in a positive way, then employees are more likely to use this feedback and to integrate it so their performance improves. In contrast, if feedback is seen as unrealistic, or if it is delivered in a caustic or demeaning manner, employees are less likely to improve.

In the cases of Will and Tiffany, Will's manager delivers his feedback in a positive way. He always begins by telling Will what he did right and lets him know how to improve. Tiffany's manager is different. He is capricious—it's hard to know how he will react to things. He tends to be dismissive and disrespectful, and he doesn't always have his facts straight. So, although in this case Tiffany assured her manager that she would try to do better, she was angry and unmotivated.

Of course, employees are ultimately accountable for their own behavior. Still, the responsibility for using the steps in the control process to support and motivate workers falls squarely on the shoulders of managers and leaders—and this is no easy task! The best leaders and managers keep a balanced perspective on how controls affect the quality of products and services and on how those same controls act to motivate and support employees to perform their jobs. When employees feel supported and processes are aligned with values and objectives, organizations perform better over time.

Most Popular » Discussion Questions

1. We've all worked for organizations with bosses who we believed judged our performance unfairly or gave us inaccurate feedback. Think back to one of those times, and consider how it affected your behavior. If you had been your manager back then, what would you have done to make sure this feedback was delivered more effectively?
2. Do you generally feel compelled to "follow the rules" at work? Why or why not?
3. Think about the last time you wrote a paper or report for school. Consider how to create standards, how to measure your performance, how to compare your performance to standards, and how to take corrective action to create a control process that will enable you to get an A on the next paper you write.

---

6. What Should Companies Control?

Now that you understand how organizational controls work, it's time to consider *what* organizations usually need to control. It's obvious that organizations want to control certain things like financial performance and employee productivity. However, it is actually quite difficult to know what to control in many organizations, as well as to determine how much emphasis should be placed on various control processes. For example, most businesses want to produce quality products or deliver excellent service, yet they also need to manage costs to ensure that they are profitable and can stay in business. However, these two areas—quality and cost—are often in conflict with one another: It costs money to provide quality goods and services, and cutting costs can harm quality.

As this typical conflict demonstrates, all areas of a business are interrelated. An improvement in performance in one area can have a detrimental affect in another area. In 2008, for example, Hershey decided to control costs by replacing cocoa butter with vegetable oil in some of its candy bars. Sales of Almond Joy subsequently dropped, and customers complained. So, in trying to control costs, sales and profitability were lost. After months of declining sales and increasing complaints, Hershey went back to its original recipe for the Almond Joy bar.[38]

In this section, we will examine how businesses often control three important areas: finance, customer service, and quality. To illustrate important points in each section, we'll use the fictitious example of small business owner Tameka Jenkins and her company LearnIT, which creates online educational courses for information technology professionals. Let's follow Tameka as she considers how she should control her business and what controls to use (■Exhibit 12.10).

■Exhibit **12.10**

Tameka Jenkins has to determine how to control her business's performance.

Bill Bachmann/Alamy Images

Controlling Financial Performance

Part of what makes a company financially healthy is its managers' and leaders' ability to control expenses and produce profit. To measure how a company is performing financially, there must be financial plans (budgets) and ways of analyzing how money is being earned and spent (profit and loss statements and cash flow analyses). Each of these controls, as well as an interesting and more recent process called *Beyond Budgeting,* is discussed in the following sections.

Financial Controls

Financial controls are used to plan how money is earned and spent, to track financial activities such as costs and revenues, and to provide guidelines to manage expenditures. One of the most common financial controls is a budget. A **budget** is a document that outlines when and how money is spent within a company and who is spending it. In many organizations, budgets are created for the entire company for a specific period of time. Within the company's overall budget, various divisions and departments have their own budgets. For example, a company's HR department will have its own budget that outlines the amount of money it will receive for a given period of time and what it must do with that money. Each departmental budget may be broken down even further to reflect the allocation of funds to specific departmental projects and activities. For example, within the HR department's budget, training and development initiatives may have their own budget, and this will determine how much and what sort of learning activities are provided to employees.

Budgets represent a plan of action outlined in quantitative terms for a specified period of time. Accounting professor David Otley argues that budgets also do the following:[39]

1. Compel strategic planning and a process for implementation
2. Provide a set of expectations from managers
3. Motivate managers and employees
4. Promote communication among people and units

If budgets are well thought out, they can be a powerful financial control mechanism. Of course, managers must sometimes revisit budgets and adapt them in response to unforeseen circumstances, such as changes in the business environment, the emergence of a new competitor, variations in the cost of raw materials, or changes in customer demand.

So, how might Tameka approach the budgeting process? When Tameka started LearnIT, she had to project what her expenses would be, so she created a budget that defined her expectations for research and development, marketing, office space and utilities, taxes and start-up fees, salaries, and benefits. Tameka thought that she would be able to hire the right people for her company at a certain salary level, which was represented in her budget. However, once she began interviewing and offering jobs, she recognized that she would have to pay more than she had anticipated in order to hire the best people. Tameka had to revisit her budget to see whether she could decrease the amount of money allocated to another area in order to increase the amount of money allocated to salaries and benefits. Alternatively, Tameka could have chosen to hire fewer employees than originally planned until she had more revenue coming in.

Accounting Controls

In addition to budgets, there are a number of **accounting controls** that provide documentation of what an organization owes and is owed, as well as its assets and liabilities. Three of the most common accounting controls are the cash flow analysis, the balance sheet, and the profit and loss statement.

A **cash flow analysis** looks at the money coming in and going out of an organization in a given time frame, either current or projected. The cash flow analysis from LearnIT is depicted in ∎Exhibit 12.11. This table shows that the company will have $136,283 in cash on hand at the end of the year. It also shows that LearnIT's largest cash outflow is the money paid to suppliers and employees, although the company has paid out less money than it has taken in from sales.

Financial controls
Controls that are used to plan how money is earned and spent, to track financial activities such as costs and revenues, and to provide guidelines to manage expenditures.

Budget
A document that outlines when and how money is spent within a company and who is spending it.

Accounting controls
Controls that provide documentation of what an organization owes and is owed, as well as its assets and liabilities.

Cash flow analysis
A document that looks at the money coming in and going out of an organization in a given time frame, either current or projected.

■Exhibit **12.11**

Cash Flows for LearnIT

Cash Flows from (Used in) Operating Activities

	Line Item	Totals
Cash receipts from customers	$250,000	
Cash paid to suppliers and employees	($122,217)	
Cash generated from operations (sum)	$50,000	
Interest paid	($2,000)	
Income taxes paid	($60,000)	
Net cash flows from operating activities		$115,783
Cash Flows from (Used in) Investing Activities		
Proceeds from the sale of equipment	$500	
Loans received	$10,000	
Net cash flows from investing activities		$10,500
Cash Flows from (Used in) Financing Activities		
Dividends paid	($10,000)	
Net cash flows used in financing activities		($10,000)
Cash Flow Totals for the Year		
Net increase in cash and cash equivalents		$116,283
Cash and cash equivalents, beginning of the year		$20,000
Cash and cash equivalents, end of the year		$136,283

Balance sheet
A document that provides a snapshot of a company at a particular moment in time, highlighting both its assets and its liabilities.

Profit and loss statement
Also called a P&L or an income statement, this document itemizes revenues and expenses and provides insight into what can be done to improve a company's results.

A **balance sheet** provides a snapshot of a company at a particular moment in time, highlighting both its assets and its liabilities. For instance, LearnIT's balance sheet, as depicted in ■Exhibit 12.12, shows that the company has an equal amount of assets and liabilities.

A **profit and loss statement** (also called a P&L or an income statement) itemizes revenues and expenses and provides insight into what can be done to improve a company's results. P&Ls use the fundamental accounting equation (profit equals revenues minus expenses) to show the profitability of an organization and whether owner/stakeholder equity is going up or down. Together, the cash flow analysis, the balance sheet, and the P&L are often used by senior management and business leaders to assess how well a company's current strategy is working and what, if anything, needs to be adjusted.

■Exhibit **12.12**

Balance Sheet for LearnIT

Assets		Liabilities and Owners' Equity	
Cash	$136,283	**Liabilities**	
Accounts receivable	$6,200	Notes payable	$36,400
Tools and equipment	$5,000	Accounts payable	$3,994
		Owners' Equity	
		Capital stock	$88,289
		Retained earnings	$18,800
Total Assets	$147,483	*Total Liabilities and Equity*	$147,483

■Exhibit **12.13**

Profit and Loss Statement for LearnIT, Year Ending December 31, 2011		
Revenues		
Gross profit		$300,000
Interest*		$2000
Net revenue		$302,000
Expenses		
Advertising	$6,300	
Bank and credit card fees	$ 244	
Bookkeeping	$3,350	
Employees	$90,000	
Entertainment	$3,550	
Insurance	$1,750	
Legal and professional services	$1,575	
Licenses	$632	
Printing, postage, and stationery	$325	
Rent	$13,000	
Utilities	$1,491	
Taxes	$60,000	
Total Expenses		($182,217)
Net Income		$119,783

*Some companies use profit and loss statements that do not capture interest and taxes.

LearnIT's profit and loss statement for 2011 is shown in ■Exhibit 12.13. Looking at this statement, Tameka wonders where she can make adjustments in order to increase her profit. She is considering trying to renegotiate her office rent, because she sees that rent is her highest category of expenses after employee salaries, benefits and taxes.

Like any type of financial reporting, these statements are only indicators, and they do not tell the whole story of an organization. Often, companies take short-term losses in order to make important long-term investments that will improve their market position. So expanding the view beyond monthly and annual financial data to include mission, environmental impact, and other indicators is important.

Beyond Budgeting

Beyond Budgeting
A control model that is intended to support more adaptive, decentralized, responsive, and ethical organizations.

Beyond Budgeting is a control model that is intended to support more adaptive, decentralized, responsive, and ethical organizations. This method has emerged in response to the growing belief that centralized financial management of organizations can be both inefficient and insufficient. Proponents of the Beyond Budgeting model believe that its benefits include faster response to issues, greater innovation, and lower costs through local negotiations with vendors, all of which result in more loyal customers.

Beyond Budgeting is based on 12 major principles.[40] Six are classified as *adaptability* principles:

1. Outperform the competition
2. Reward teams for their successes
3. Continually focus on strategy, making it an inclusive process
4. Use resources as needed
5. Develop highly coordinated "cross-country interactions" that mimic market forces
6. Offer fast and open information built around multi level control

The remaining six principles are classified as *decentralization* or *devolution* principles:

1. Develop a climate of performance that is based on sustained competitive success
2. Build committed teams that are united under a shared purpose, values, and rewards
3. "Devolve strategy" by a process of decentralization that gives teams local decision-making power
4. Be financially conservative, and question the value that all resources are believed to add to the organization
5. Create a dynamic network that allows teams to serve the customer more efficiently
6. Support transparency and open availability of information

Controlling Service: Customer Relationship Management

Every business, including this Moroccan pastry shop, must work to earn its customers' loyalty in order to be successful.

Anne-Marie Palmer/Alamy Images

Customer relationship management (CRM)
A customer-centric approach to business with the aim of implementing a customer intimacy strategy or establishing a customer-friendly brand image—or both.

Although the financial perspective is critical to the success of a business, even the brightest accountants cannot save a company if it does not have enough customers or clients (■Exhibit 12.14). This is obvious, of course, but creating processes to ensure customer satisfaction is not necessarily easy.

Customer relationship management (CRM) is a customer-centric approach to business with the aim of implementing a customer intimacy strategy or establishing a customer-friendly brand image—or both. CRM evolved in the 1990s, as many businesses moved away from transactional customer interactions toward more relational customer interactions.[41] CRM focuses on building and maintaining a loyal customer base over the long term, rather than simply maximizing the number of transactions in the short term.

A CRM focus includes mechanisms to measure customer data, but it goes far beyond the technology of collecting information through surveys and the like. When a real CRM strategy is adopted, the focus is evident in the organization's mission statement and values, as well as in its leadership behaviors and culture. Indeed, attention to the customer is obvious in almost everything anyone in the organization does.

The success of CRM strategies is measured in both financial terms and the degree of customer loyalty and retention. Although technology plays an important supportive role in tracking and managing relationships and things like customer loyalty, if relationships with customers are poor, technology often hurts rather than improves customer relations.[42] That is because communication via technology is often impersonal, and the feedback channel is relatively weak. This can make customers feel even more dissatisfied. For example, they may not be able to communicate directly or they may not feel "heard" if they respond to a survey and never see the results.

Some companies, however, have mastered the art of tracking the customer experience. Constant Contact is an online business-to-business (B2B) service provider used by many small- and medium-sized companies to manage their online marketing efforts, such as e-newsletters. According to Gail Goodman, chairman, president, and CEO of the company, "When we say 'Focus on the Customer,' we back it up with metrics and incentives at every level of the organization." Because most of Constant Contact's growth comes from happy customers referring new customers, the company has instituted what Goodman calls "customer-driven metrics and controls."[43] In Goodman's words, this means that "Everyone at the company who has a customer-facing role gets daily, weekly, and monthly feedback." Moreover, a supervisor randomly listens in on four calls per month with every customer service representative and scores the call using 30 criteria. These criteria cover things like attitude, tone, help with features, and the like.

Then, once per month, the supervisor meets with every customer representative and coaches them on their development and customer relations skills. The representatives' performance is also reinforced through monthly bonuses. According to Goodman:

These results are always shared with the senior managers every month so that everyone in the company is connected to business performance and to customer experience. In fact, customer service metrics are weighed more heavily than financial metrics in our company. We don't focus on quarterly results according to Wall Street. We focus on our own internal capabilities and performance according to the customer. That feels consistent with who we are.[44]

As Gail Goodman knows, it only takes one mistake to lose a customer. That's why Constant Contact dedicates so much time, attention, and money to ensuring that its customers have a great experience. Of course, in order to survive in the long term, companies must balance this focus on quality and the effectiveness of processes with a focus on efficiency and cost containment. Thus, over the past several decades, a number of processes have been developed to help organizations attain quality results while operating efficiently. Let's take a look at some of those methods.

Quality Control

Operations management
The transformation of inputs—materials, labor, and ideas—into outputs, such as products or services.

Operations management is the transformation of inputs—materials, labor, and ideas—into outputs, such as products or services. A number of approaches are used to design and measure operations management processes while controlling for quality. These include quality initiatives such as business process reengineering, Total Quality Management, Six Sigma, and Lean Management. Each of these approaches is described in the following sections, followed by a discussion of ISO 9000 and 14000—well-known management systems for ensuring quality and adhering to environmental standards. The section concludes with a discussion of the Baldrige Award, an honor bestowed on companies in recognition of outstanding quality.

Business Process Reengineering

Business process reengineering (BPR)
A management approach that utilizes available technology and management science to redesign business processes, products, and systems to increase efficiency and focus attention on customer needs.

Business process reengineering (BPR) is a management approach that utilizes available technology and management science to redesign business processes, products, and systems to increase efficiency and focus attention on customer needs. According to Thomas Davenport and James Short, two leaders in the field, reengineering is a process that starts from scratch. Rather than simply modifying the design of existing processes, the goal is to redesign from the ground up, even if the result is a radical reconceptualization of the organization.[45]

Scholars Michael Hammer and James Champy argue that BPR is "the fundamental rethinking and radical redesign of business processes to achieve dramatic improvements in critical, contemporary measures of performance, such as cost, quality, service and speed."[46] Whereas Taylor's scientific management approach sought to divorce decision making from labor by pushing decisions up the organizational hierarchy, Hammer and Champy point out "Workers themselves now do that portion of a job that, formerly, managers produced."[47] BPR includes the customer as well: It is a process that is customer-centric, not technology-centric.[48]

The twentieth century was dominated by the notion of a mass market, and the response was mass production for an abstract mass customer. In contrast, in BPR, the notion of "*the* customer" is replaced by "*this* customer," resulting in a refocus on individual customer needs.[49] Information technology is often at the center of the redesign, with the intended outcome being creation of added value for the customer.

Davenport and Short suggest that BPR be incorporated into an organization by way of a five-step approach.[50] The first step in BPR is to define the business vision and objectives. The second step is to identify which business processes need to be reengineered and which changes will make the biggest impact. The third step is to understand what is and what isn't working. The fourth step is to determine which IT systems and functions should influence the business process reengineering. The last step is to design the new process and build a pilot project or prototype based on the new design.

While other approaches such as Total Quality Management (discussed next) offer incremental improvements, BPR seeks improvements through a fundamental rethinking and redesign of business. Describing the goal of BPR, Thomas Davenport notes, "Today firms must seek not fractional, but multiplicative levels of improvement—10X rather than 10%."[51]

Although critics have pointed out that BPR has ultimately led to downsizing and a more stifling workplace environment, the approach was quickly adopted by many companies in the early 1990s. In fact, it is estimated that by 1993, more than 80% of large companies in North America had adopted BPR.[52] It's important to note that if BPR is not performed rigorously, the results can have a strong negative impact on the business, especially for small- and medium-sized enterprises, which are more fragile than large, stable organizations. Research suggests that for such businesses, owners and managers can facilitate success by demonstrating knowledge of and support for the BPR process.[53]

Total Quality Management

Total Quality Management (TQM)
A quality control philosophy that supports the elimination of deficiencies and removes variation in output quality through employee involvement in decision making, continuous improvement in processes, and a strong focus on the customer.

Kaizen is a Japanese philosophy that underlies the model known as Total Quality Management. **Total Quality Management (TQM)** is a quality control philosophy that supports the elimination of deficiencies and removes variation in output quality through employee involvement in decision making, continuous improvement in processes, and a strong focus on the customer. TQM revolves around the idea that, rather than wiping a slate clean, life and organizations should be incrementally and constantly improved. The central principles of this approach are described in ■Exhibit 12.15.

■Exhibit **12.15**

Fundamental Principles of TQM[54]

1. *Kaizen:* A focus on continuous process improvement, often through incremental changes. Kaizen involves the following five elements that facilitate the elimination of waste:[55]
   - Teamwork
   - Personal discipline
   - Improved morale
   - Quality circles (employee groups that seek solutions for quality problems)
   - Suggestions for improvement.
2. *Atarimae hinshitsu:* The idea that "things" will work according to their function and purpose (e.g., a pen will write).
3. *Kansei:* The idea that understanding the way people use products leads to the improvement of these products.
4. *Miryokuteki hinshitsu:* The idea that manufactured products should have an aesthetic quality.

TQM has been widely used in manufacturing industries, as well as in call centers and technical fields such as aerospace. It is important to note, however, that TQM is not just used in big manufacturing companies. In fact, Rafidah Mohamad Noor, an assistant director of AKEPT, describes in the following *Perspectives* feature the principles of employee participation in problem solving can be used in any organization with great results.

AKEPT is a higher education leadership academy created under the Ministry of Education in Malaysia in 2008. AKEPT's mission is to revitalize and improve higher education in Malaysia. The agency's goal is inspiring: It wants to prepare the country's higher education system to better serve the needs of students and faculty from all over Asia. As Rafidah Mohamad Noor put it:

Rafidah Mohamad Noor, Assistant Director, AKEPT

We want AKEPT to be truly successful, so we are always looking for ways to move us forward. We have an important mission at AKEPT, and we have big challenges. When you think about the kinds of changes that will be needed to reach our goal, and what we need to do in a very short time, it is clear that we will have to focus on innovation and enhancing the quality of our work.

We are faced with new challenges and new activities every day, and we are constantly reminded that things will be different, and we need to be able to adapt and change to improve how we work. We are always focusing on how we can improve ourselves and AKEPT. One of the ways we want to do this is to be sure everyone's opinion can be heard, no matter what role they have in our institution. When everyone's voice is heard, they can have discussions, spot problems, capture ideas, and find solutions.

Source: Personal interview conducted with Rafidah Mohamad Noor by Annie McKee, 2009.

Six Sigma

Six Sigma

A management strategy that employs quality management methods in a specific sequence to either reduce costs or increase profits.

Originally developed by Motorola in an effort to eliminate defects in their manufacturing processes, **Six Sigma** is a management strategy that employs quality management methods in a specific sequence to either reduce costs or increase profits. It has evolved into a business management strategy that is used to improve a wide array of manufacturing and business processes.[56] People trained in Six Sigma are placed into a hierarchical infrastructure with "Champions" at the top. After "Champions," the descending levels of expertise are termed as follows: Master Black Belts, Black Belts, Green Belts, and Yellow Belts.[57]

Companies such as GE, Boeing, Caterpillar, and Raytheon have implemented Six Sigma. It is worth noting that these companies are among the largest in the world. Large companies have the expansive financial resources required for implementation of Six Sigma, whereas smaller companies may not. Training one person to attain Yellow Belt status, for example, can cost more than $1,000.[58] In larger organizations, hundreds if not thousands of employees receive Six Sigma training, making it a significant investment of time and money.

The goal of Six Sigma is to limit defects through a process of incremental adjustments and attention to even the smallest details of the manufacturing process. Two common uses of the Six Sigma method are for process improvement and for new product or service development. These two situations require different approaches, as seen in ■Exhibits 12.16 and ■12.17.

The results of Six Sigma implementation have been mixed. GE, for example, boasts of a $10 billion gain through cost reduction and/or increased profits over the initial five-year period following implementation.[59] 3M, however, found that the implementation of Six Sigma

■Exhibit **12.16**

Six Sigma for Process Improvement: Define, Measure, Analyze, Improve, and Control

- *Define* high-level project goals and the current process.
- *Measure* key aspects of the current process and collect relevant data.
- *Analyze* the data to verify cause-and-effect relationships.
- *Improve* or optimize the process based on data analysis.
- *Control* to ensure that any deviations from the target are corrected before they result in defects.

■Exhibit **12.17**

Six Sigma for New Product and Service Development: Define, Measure, Analyze, Design, and Verify

- *Define* design goals that are consistent with customer demands and the enterprise strategy.
- *Measure* and identify *CTQs* (characteristics that are *Critical To Quality*), product capabilities, production process capability, and risks.
- *Analyze* to develop and design alternatives, create a high-level design, and evaluate design capability to select the best design.
- *Design* details, optimize the design, and plan for design verification.
- *Verify* the design, set up pilot runs, implement the production process, and hand it over to the process owners.[60]

dampened creativity and innovation.[61] This conflict between innovation and the efficiency improvements from Six Sigma has been explored by author Stephen Ruffa, who points to data that show the Six Sigma program did little to help Ford Motor Company.[62] Despite widespread critiques, Six Sigma initiatives are still widely pursued by companies today.

Lean Management

Lean Management
A management approach that organizes manufacturing and logistics to maximize efficiency and eliminate waste by reducing variation in every process.

Lean Management is a management approach that organizes manufacturing and logistics to maximize efficiency and eliminate waste by reducing variation in every process. Although the term "Lean Management" has appeared sporadically in various contexts in Europe since the 1980s, it was popularized in a 1990 book on Japanese lean production systems.[63] Currently, one of the best-known lean production methodologies is the Toyota Production System, which relies on the following Lean Management goals to eliminate waste and maximize efficiency:[64]

1. *Improve quality:* To be competitive, a company must have a quality product that exceeds customers' expectations.
2. *Eliminate waste:* There are several different types of waste, including overproduction, downtime, defects, and rework. All such waste must be eliminated to stay "lean" and profitable.
3. *Reduce time:* Time from the beginning of the manufacturing process to the end must be reduced in order to stay competitive.
4. *Reduce total costs:* Any extra costs, such as those that come from keeping an unnecessary inventory of parts or finished projects, hinder a company's profitability and should be reduced.

Lean management, and indeed all lean systems, improves efficiency primarily by reducing wasted time, space, effort, materials, and so forth. This can be done, for instance, by identifying and removing redundancies.[65] Although many Lean Management principles are common sense and can result in greater efficiency, when taken to the extreme and/or when efficiency trumps effectiveness and quality, results can be catastrophic. There have been occasions in companies such as Toyota, where despite control processes like Lean Management, product quality has been compromised significantly. Therefore, when processes like Lean Management are employed, it is important to ensure that processes are not so "lean" that they can't adapt or that human errors become more likely.[66]

ISO 9000 and 14000

The ISO 9000 and 14000 families of management system standards are some of the best known in the world, and they have been implemented by more than 1 million organizations in approximately 175 countries.[67] The ISO (International Organization for Standardization) is an international standards-setting body composed of national-level representatives. ISO 9000 and 14000 address quality management and environmental management, respectively. While widely used in the automotive and industrial sectors, the standards are not specific to any one industry.[68] In fact, the ISO strongly encourages small- and medium-sized enterprises across all industries to consider adoption of these standards, particularly ISO 14000, so that they can reap the economic benefits they offer.[69]

The ISO 9000 standards are auditable international standards that have guided quality control since 1987, when they were first published.[70] Revised repeatedly since then, the standards are rooted in eight quality management principles that are designed to enable companies to exceed the quality requirements of their customers and enhance customer satisfaction while at the same time meeting regulatory requirements.[71] These principles include focusing on the customer, providing leadership, involving people, utilizing a process approach, employing a systems approach to management, striving for continual improvement, implementing a factual approach to decision making, and developing mutually beneficial supplier relationships.[72]

In support of these eight principles, ISO 9000 requires that any company using the system produce documentation in support of quality management, such as a quality manuals and procedural instructions.[73] Companies can also seek independent certification, or registration, of their quality management system that recognizes successful maintenance of standard requirements. This certification is not required of companies that implement ISO 9000, but it is often beneficial in terms of marketing and securing customers that require certification.[74]

ISO 14000 was developed in 1992.[75] The goal of this set of standards is to encourage environmental responsibility within the business community by helping companies reduce their environmental impact and increase their long-term sustainability.[76] The key points of ISO 14000 are identifying the ways in which companies impact the environment, improving environmental product labeling, promoting company life cycle analyses, and evaluating environmental performance on an ongoing basis.[77] Ultimately, this will lead companies to get more out of their inputs and develop positive relationships with their stakeholders.[78] Companies may pursue ISO 14000 certification via an independent audit in much the same manner that they seek ISO 9000 certification. This certification signals that the company is going above and beyond minimum government regulations regarding waste disposal and pollution control.[79]

ISO 9000 and ISO 14000 standards are not intended to dictate specific quality or environmental practices. Rather, they are designed to provide a framework and a systematic approach to evaluating processes.[80] Both systems take time and money to implement, but both lead to improved profits by way of more effective management; moreover, they also enable companies to be more ethically responsible to their customers and the environment.[81] Perhaps that is why so many companies worldwide have adopted these standards as part of their day-to-day operations.

Baldrige Award

The need for quality assurance and improvement in industry is not solely a concern of the private sector; it is a governmental concern as well, as evidenced by the Malcolm Baldrige National Quality Award. This award was established by U.S. Public Law 100-107 in 1987, and it was first awarded in 1988. It is named for Malcolm Baldrige, U.S. Secretary of Commerce from 1981 through 1987.[82] During his tenure as secretary, Baldrige espoused the idea that long-term economic improvement in the United States was closely tied to quality management, and he put these concepts into practice within the Commerce Department. Under his leadership, the department's budget and administrative overhead were drastically reduced, and its effectiveness and efficiency greatly improved.[83]

The Baldrige award is presented each year by the president of the United States to manufacturing and service businesses, educational institutions, health care enterprises, and nonprofit organizations of all sizes. Companies apply for the award themselves and are judged on their performance in seven specific areas: leadership; strategic planning; customer and market focus; measurement, analysis, and knowledge management; workforce focus; process management; and results. Award winners typically exercise good citizenship and public responsibility as well as superior relationships with customers and employees. In addition, they exhibit outstanding production and delivery processes that are aligned with organizational objectives.[84] Far from simply recognizing exceptional companies, however, the Baldrige criteria have become a "way of organizational life" for many businesses that have introduced them into their daily operating standards.

When applied to business operations as a whole, the Baldrige principles assist organizations in focusing on strategy-driven performance, and they promote organizational sustainability.[85] To that end, Baldrige Award winners are asked to share their performance strategies with others in order to perpetuate a culture of excellence in industry.[86] It is this culture of excellence that helps keep U.S. companies vital to the world economy and keeps the Malcolm Baldrige National Quality Award relevant in our ever-changing business climate.

Most Popular » Discussion Questions

1. Have you ever worked for—or been served by—an organization in which the customer really was the center of all decisions? How was this organization different from others you have experienced?
2. Imagine that your school or workplace plans to implement TQM, Six Sigma, or Lean Management. What changes might you see in how resources are used? In how people are managed?

---

7. What Can HR Do to Help Control for Effectiveness and Efficiency at Work?

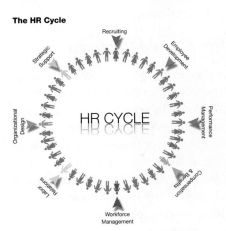

The HR Cycle

Human resources management has a central role in developing and enforcing controls within an organization. Sometimes it's a highly enviable job: developing top performers and preparing them for increasing opportunity and responsibility. Other times, it is the toughest job in the organization and requires a tremendous amount of emotional sensitivity and compassion. In this section, we will focus on performance management—a powerful control mechanism in the workplace.

The Performance Management Process

Performance management is a tremendous responsibility that is entrusted to managers and HR professionals within organizations. By directly working with employees or supporting managers who are tracking the performance of the people in their groups, HR has a significant role in creating processes that enable people to improve their performance and that help the organization track employee strengths and developmental needs.

Performance management processes set standards, monitor performance, and help people leverage strengths and overcome deficiencies. When performance management systems work well, they focus less on simple monitoring of behavior and more on measuring contributions and accomplishments that lead to organizational success, as shown in ■Exhibit 12.18.[87]

■Exhibit **12.18**

Five Steps in the Performance Management Process
1. Planning work and setting expectations
2. Continually monitoring performance
3. Developing people's capacity to perform
4. Completing periodic performance reviews
5. Rewarding good performance and correcting underperformance

HR professionals can be instrumental in the development of robust performance management systems that follow all of the steps in Exhibit 12.18, and they can go beyond this to engage leaders, managers, and employees in linking performance management to virtually everything they do. One very common—but possibly not optimal—performance management approach is called management by objectives. Let's begin by looking at some pros and cons of this method.

Management by Objectives: Use with Caution

Management by objectives (MBO) is a performance tool used to help people set goals for themselves in the context of an organization's goals. MBO is often thought to be passé, but it is still widely used or adapted for use in organizations today.[88] The method is based on the notion that employees can participate in setting meaningful goals for themselves to help accomplish the organization's goals. The process is based on the idea that if employees receive regular feedback, and are then properly rewarded, they will be motivated, satisfied, and successful. The idea behind this philosophy is to focus employees'—and the manager's—attention on outcomes rather than just activities.[89]

Some companies do it right, but more often than not, the MBO process withers on the vine. That's because without open communication, trust, and excellent facilitation of an MBO program, employees can be very reluctant to be involved in the planning and goal-setting processes.[90] Numerous problems can get in the way, such as lack of training for managers or a hostile culture that makes it unsafe for employees to be open about shortcomings. Or, the process becomes just that: a process. Everyone fills in the blanks on the form once a year, but the form is never looked at again. These problems point out how important it is that a performance review process includes robust ways to gather and share information about employee performance.

Gathering Information about Employee Performance

To evaluate performance and help employees develop, managers need to collect accurate information about employees' behavior on the job. Performance data can consist of the manager's observations, data collected and measured through metrics (e.g., how much revenue a sales representative generated), self-appraisal (in which the employee reflects on his or her own performance), feedback gathered from people who work with the employee, customer feedback, or a combination of all or some of these things.

There are many ways to gather information about employees' performance. Some methods are straightforward, such as those used for performance that can be easily quantified (e.g., did the employee meet targets for revenue generation through sales, meet the agreed-upon number of customers, or hit production targets?). Other aspects of performance are harder to quantify but are nevertheless essential. These can include demonstration of job-specific and social and emotional intelligence competencies, both of which are key to individual and group success. HR is often responsible for crafting the process by which robust data about employees' performance is gathered and for teaching managers how to use and share this information.

One form of data collection that has become very popular in recent years is called a 360-degree review. A **360-degree review** is a process in which a picture of an employee or man-

360-degree review
A review process in which a picture of an employee or manager is created through self-assessment along with feedback from peers, managers, customers, and other relevant stakeholders.

HR Leadership Roles

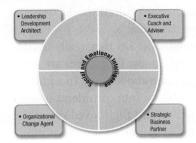

ager is created through self-assessment along with feedback from peers, managers, customers, and other relevant stakeholders. This information can be gathered via an anonymous questionnaire about competencies. The data can then be tabulated to provide the employee with a report that shows how the various groups view him or her. The second way 360-degree data can be gathered is for a manager, HR professional, or outside consultant to conduct structured, confidential conversations about the employee with relevant individuals. This data is then analyzed to discover themes, which are subsequently presented to the employee (without divulging who said what, of course). This offers the employee a more well-rounded perspective with a wider range of information about how others perceive him or her.

A 360-degree review is a powerful tool because it offers a robust perspective of an employee's effectiveness. However, like any process that involves people's opinions of others, it must be used carefully. First of all, a 360-degree review is far more effective when used for development as opposed to identifying weaknesses. Second, how the feedback is shared is almost as important as what the data says.

Performance Review

Once performance data has been collected, managers and HR professionals often share it with employees in what is called a performance appraisal. A **performance appraisal** is the process of sharing an evaluation of an employee's performance in (ideally) a face-to-face meeting that usually takes place between an employee and his or her manager, although in some organizations, this appraisal is delivered by a human resources manager. Of course, even pristine performance data is useless unless it is shared with employees in a positive way.

Unfortunately performance appraisal processes are often highly ineffective. Rather than engaging employees in healthy conversations, managers or HR professionals often share feedback in ways that spark resistance, defensiveness, anger, and hurt feelings. It's HR's job to ensure that performance appraisals are positive and helpful, as opposed to negative and destructive.

To do this, HR professionals can develop a performance appraisal process that supports managers and employees during these conversations. This process can include creating a timeline for such conversations: Do they happen once a year or more often? How long should each conversation last? Simple guidelines like these can make a big difference because both managers and employees know what to expect.

HR professionals can also craft a process to follow before, during, and after the performance appraisal conversation. Robust processes include preparation for both the manager and the employee (e.g., structured data collection that includes self-reflection and self-appraisal). Such processes also include a structured way to have the conversation, often using a written document created by the manager that includes relevant data about performance as well as how it was measured. This document provides the guideline for the conversation. One example of such a process is the Balanced Scorecard.

The **Balanced Scorecard** was developed by scholars at Harvard Business School in the 1990s, and it is considered a significant move beyond the traditional concept of performance measurement, which often focuses a tremendous amount of attention on financial measures of success. The Balanced Scorecard takes a more holistic view of success and measures several factors related to performance.[91] With the Balanced Scorecard, four areas are usually measured: financial performance, customers, business processes, and learning and growth. Each of these may be further broken down into subcategories of measurement. When used in performance management, a scorecard can be developed in different ways for different levels and functions within the organization. The scorecard, then, can link employees' performance with the organization's goals and priorities.

The third way in which HR professionals can support effective performance appraisal processes is by training managers to engage in conversations that are meaningful, non-threatening, and honest. This is harder than it sounds. Having direct, supportive,

Performance appraisal

Process of sharing an evaluation of an employee's performance in (ideally) a face-to-face meeting that usually takes place between an employee and his or her manager, although in some organizations this appraisal is delivered by a human resources manager.

Balanced Scorecard

A review process that takes a holistic view of success and measures several factors related to performance.

honest, and caring conversations with employees requires a high degree of emotional intelligence. In order for these conversations to be perceived as helpful, employees need to believe that managers' assessments are accurate, unbiased, and fair.

Employees also need to experience managers as empathetic: Do they really understand the employees' jobs, working conditions, goals, and hopes? Employees are most likely to respond well to feedback if they believe managers care about them. In addition, research strongly suggests that the most effective appraisals take into consideration employees' lives and personal goals and dreams for themselves and their loved ones. The art and science of establishing developmental goals during appraisals involves finding meaningful intersections between the employee's life and his or her professional aspirations and the needs of the organization.[92]

Most Popular » Discussion Questions

1. Have you ever had a performance conversation with a supervisor? Describe the interaction, and consider how it made you feel before, during, and after.
2. Make a list of your life goals. Next to that, make a list of the goals of an organization to which you belong. Are there areas of overlap? How can your goals support those of the organization and vice versa?

---

8. What Can We All Do to Enhance Effectiveness and Efficiency at Work?

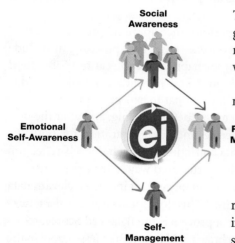

There are many ways in which you can contribute to an effective control system in your organization. From involvement in the creation of processes, to constant attention to improvements, to being personally committed—all of these matter tremendously. In this section, we will look at two things that only you can do: self-management and emotional self-control.

Self-management and emotional self-control are probably the most important control mechanisms we have at work. Ultimately, we all choose what to do and what not to do. External control measures such as rules, regulations, and even culture have a powerful effect on our attitudes, values, and behavior—but when it comes right down to it, we make choices about how we work, which rules we obey, and how we impact others.

No matter what the organization dictates, we have choices about setting goals for ourselves related to personal or professional development, such as learning a second language, completing our assigned tasks, or supporting the development of new members of our teams. This is self-management—and only you can do it. Interestingly, effective self-management is often seen in organizations that set a tone of positivity, trust, and high expectations for their people.[93] This may be because empowering organizations actually create a positive loop: Trust engenders self-management and effectiveness, which, in turn, engenders more trust, and so on.

In addition to managing our behavior at work, we have choices about how to manage our emotions when we are under pressure, when we are challenged by having to learn new ways of doing things, or when we have the chance to share optimism and excitement about our work. This is called emotional self-control—a fundamental emotional intelligence competency that is at the core of good leadership.[94] This is because when others look to us for guidance—whether as a formal leader, a mentor, or someone they look up to—they pay a lot of attention to our emotions. In fact, a leader's emotions are part of what people factor into the equation when determining how effective that leader is—and whether to follow him or her.

As we have stressed throughout this book, everyone is a leader in one way or another in today's organizations. As a result, it is important for you to understand how your emotions can affect others. In one study, researchers investigated the effect of the emotional displays of leaders on the emotional states of observers. This study found that the display of negative emotions had a significant, detrimental effect on others' assessments of the leader's effectiveness.[95]

Emotions are also contagious.[96] This means that if you are angry, upset, or stressed, chances are that others around you will feel this way as well—or at the very least be anxious about your state of mind. We know from research in cognitive psychology that when people experience extreme or chronic negative emotions, they are not as effective, do not make the best decisions, and are less creative.[97] On the other hand, when people are appropriately challenged, excited, and optimistic, their performance can soar.

This means that you, as a leader, can have an impact on others' performance simply as a result of managing your emotions. This starts, of course, with recognizing your emotions (that is, with emotional self-awareness). You can improve your ability to recognize and interpret your own emotions by more consciously monitoring your feelings during everyday activities. Then, as you notice how you feel, you can extend your awareness to track how others are responding to you. This simple—but profound—practice can dramatically improve your capacity for self-awareness and self-management.

Most Popular » Discussion Questions

1. Considering a group, team, or organization you belong to, reflect on the ways in which you take personal responsibility for controlling your own—and others'—effectiveness and efficiency. What do you do? What could you do more or less of to improve your contribution to the control process?

2. Think about a group situation in which you are a leader (formal or informal). Now, think about a challenge this group has faced and your emotional response to this challenge. How do you think your emotions impacted other people, the situation, and the outcomes?

3. Consider a challenging situation you face with a team and reflect on how you can harness positive emotions to help the group overcome this challenge. What can you do, exactly?

---

9. A Final Word on Organizational Control

Frederick Taylor and other early scholars set the stage for now nearly 100 years of research on how to increase efficiency in organizations. This focus continues today, and with the advent of technologies, we have a number of complex and powerful tools we can use to help us be more efficient and improve the quality of our products and services. Still, as positive as these tools and the efficiency/quality movement have been and despite our fascination with this stream of research, these practices have led to some problems.

First, in some organizations, efficiency and cost savings have become primary goals. When this happens, the mission of an organization can become obliterated—noble goals such as providing safe vehicles, safe workplaces, and contributing to society take a backseat to maximizing human and organizational output and financial results. Second, when controls become the goal rather than an enabler of organizational success, organizational cultures can become toxic. In companies where people are constantly under pressure and stressed, it is difficult to sustain creativity and innovation, and people are often not able to do and be their best.

Having said all this, we *need* controls in our organization. We welcome ways to work more efficiently, and all leaders want to produce quality products and services. So the question isn't whether we need controls at work; it is "How can we use control processes to help us realize all aspects of our organization's mission and also create a workplace that is inspired and inspiring?" Luckily, researchers have been pursuing this stream of thought.

Throughout this book, you have been reading about scholars, managers, and leaders who seek to understand how to empower people at work and how to create an environment that supports people in making good decisions about how they work and solve problems. Empowerment is at the heart of positive and powerful organizational controls systems. You've also read about leaders who put ethics first rather than cutting corners, which can foster even more success in the long term. Ethical behavior and cultures that support all of us in making the right choices are key to healthy organizational controls. Finally, you've also learned that when we develop social and emotional intelligence competencies, we can all be great leaders. When we see ourselves as leaders, we take responsibility for guiding people to work in the most effective ways. This, too, is at the heart of the best organizational control systems.

Key Terms

1. What Is the Organizational Control Process? (p. 420)

Key Terms

Control process An organization's systems for establishing standards to achieve goals, monitoring and measuring performance, comparing performance to standards, and taking corrective action as necessary. p. 420

2. What Historical Perspectives Help Us Understand Control in Organizations? (pp. 421–425)

Key Terms

Scientific management An approach that involves organizing work for maximum efficiency. p. 421

Human relations movement A movement that started around the beginning of the twentieth century and emphasized placing people, interpersonal relationships, and group behavior at the center of workplace studies. p. 422

Hawthorne Studies A series of research projects demonstrating that when workers perceived that management cared about them and/or when they felt they were getting special treatment, both morale and productivity improved. p. 422

3. What Are Common Control Systems? (pp. 425–428)

Key Terms

Bureaucratic control systems Control processes that use specific rules, standards, and hierarchical authority to achieve planned and desired organizational outcomes. p. 425

Output control Type of control in which outcomes are measured against financial performance and other clearly articulated metrics, such as customer retention. p. 426

Behavior control Type of control in which an organization tries to shape the behaviors of its employees in order to attain the desired outcomes that will lead to organizational success. p. 427

Normative control A control system that involves sharing and embedding an organization's values and beliefs so they act as a guide for employees' behavior. p. 427

Levers of control A control system that relies on various levers such as organizational values, rules, feedback systems, and focused involvement in decision making. p. 427

4. What Conventions and Forces Guide Organizational Control Processes? (pp. 429–433)

Key Terms

Corporate governance The way in which an organization is controlled, administered, or directed as described by laws and the processes, policies, regulations, and customs of that organization. p. 429

Corporate charter An articulation of policies, rules, and procedures that address a variety of governance issues, such as the legal name and location of the business, along with the business's mission, rules relating to its board of directors, and classes of securities (stocks) that are issued. p. 429

Privately held company A company that is wholly owned by an individual or group of individuals and does not sell shares of ownership on the open market. p. 429

Publicly traded company A company that issues shares of ownership, or stocks, that are traded on the open market. p. 429

Audit A formal review to make sure that certain processes have been fully and accurately managed and reported. p. 430

Sarbanes-Oxley Act of 2002 Formally known as the Public Company Accounting Reform and Investor Protection Act, this act sets new or enhanced standards for publicly traded companies' boards, managers, and public accounting firms. p. 431

5. What Are the Typical Steps in the Control Process? (pp. 433–437)

Key Terms

Standards and metrics Measures established to define quality and efficiency criteria. p. 433

Feedback control Type of control in which information about performance is gathered and shared after the fact. p. 436

Feed-forward control Type of control system that anticipates potential issues or problems before they arise. p. 436

Concurrent control The process of collecting "real-time" information to decrease the lag time between performance deficiencies and corrective action. p. 436

6. What Should Companies Control? (pp. 437–447)

Key Terms

Financial controls Controls that are used to plan how money is earned and spent, to track financial activities such as costs and revenues, and to provide guidelines to manage expenditures. p. 438

Budget A document that outlines when and how money is spent within a company and who is spending it. p. 438

Accounting controls Controls that provide documentation of what an organization owes and is owed, as well as its assets and liabilities. p. 438

Cash flow analysis A document that looks at the money coming in and going out of an organization in a given time frame, either current or projected. p. 438

Balance sheet A document that provides a snapshot of a company at a particular moment in time, highlighting both its assets and its liabilities. p. 439

Profit and loss statement Also called a P&L or an income statement, this document itemizes revenues and expenses and provides insight into what can be done to improve a company's results. p. 439

Beyond Budgeting A control model that is intended to support more adaptive, decentralized, responsive, and ethical organizations. p. 440

Customer relationship management (CRM) A customer-centric approach to business with the aim of implementing a customer intimacy strategy or establishing a customer-friendly brand image—or both. p. 441

Operations management The transformation of inputs—materials, labor, and ideas—into outputs, such as products or services. p. 442

Business process reengineering (BPR) A management approach that utilizes available technology and management science to redesign business processes, products, and systems to increase efficiency and focus attention on customer needs. p. 442

Total Quality Management (TQM) A quality control philosophy that supports the elimination of deficiencies and removes variation in output quality through employee involvement in decision making, continuous improvement in processes, and a strong focus on the customer. p. 443

Six Sigma A management strategy that employs quality management methods in a specific sequence to either reduce costs or increase profits. p. 444

Lean Management A management approach that organizes manufacturing and logistics to maximize efficiency and eliminate waste by reducing variation in every process. p. 445

7. What Can HR Do to Help Control for Effectiveness and Efficiency at Work? (pp. 447–450)

Key Terms

360-degree review A review process in which a picture of an employee or manager is created through self-assessment along with feedback from peers, managers, customers, and other relevant stakeholders. p. 448

Performance appraisal Process of sharing an evaluation of an employee's performance in (ideally) a face-to-face meeting that usually takes place between an employee and his or her manager, although in some organizations this appraisal is delivered by a human resources manager. p. 449

Balanced Scorecard A review process that takes a holistic view of success and measures several factors related to performance. p. 449

8. What Can We All Do to Enhance Effectiveness and Efficiency at Work? (pp. 450–451)

Key Terms None

9. A Final Word on Organizational Control (pp. 451–452)

Key Terms None

Chapter 12 Visual Summary

12. Organizational Controls: People, Processes, Quality, and Results

Controlling Quality, Culture, and Yourself

13. Culture: It's Powerful

1. What Is the Organizational Control Process? (p. 420)

Summary: The control process includes systems for establishing standards, monitoring and measuring performance, comparing performance to standards, and taking corrective action when needed. These systems apply to a variety of areas—from employee behavior to product quality—and help organizations become more flexible and responsive when change is necessary. Many control processes are used today, some of which are rooted in historical perspectives on business performance.

2. What Historical Perspectives Help Us Understand Control in Organizations? (pp. 421–425)

Summary: Three theorists figured prominently in the early study of management and organizational control: Frederick Taylor, Elton Mayo, and Mary Parker Follett. Taylor, with his concept of scientific management, was primarily concerned with reducing waste and inefficiency in production processes, often with little regard for the individuals performing work tasks. Mayo and Follett, on the other hand, were particularly interested in the people aspects of management, including how employees and managers interacted, how power was used, and how the personal and production aspects of work interact. These people-centric theories, particularly those developed by Follett, are largely responsible for the modern movement toward empowerment and resonant leadership.

3. What Are Common Control Systems? (pp. 425–428)

Summary: Bureaucratic control systems use rules, standards, and hierarchical authority to achieve desired outcomes in a ways that involves little individual judgment. Objective controls focus on measurable behaviors and outputs, and normative control focuses on using organizational values to guide people's behavior. Finally, the levers of control model combines the best aspects of several control systems to ensure a people- and process-oriented control system.

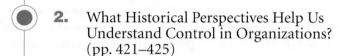

Simons's Levers of Control[23]		
Lever	How It Works	Examples
Belief Systems	Defines the core values of an organization and its members	Credos, mission statements, and values statements
Boundary Systems	Defines territory or span of control for people within the organization	Rules, proscriptions, and regulations of the organization
Diagnostic Control Systems	Feedback system that allows the organization to monitor standards	Systems to measure output, as well as incentives and goals
Interactive Control Systems	Allows managers to plan how to regularly involve themselves personally in their subordinates' decision-making activities	Project management systems, knowledge management systems, and scheduling systems

4. What Conventions and Forces Guide Organizational Control Processes? (pp. 429–433)

Summary: Corporate governance is often part of the control process, and it dictates the ways in which the company is administered based on internal policies and external laws. To ensure that people and the organization as a whole are doing what they should, a formal review or audit may be used as an evaluation tool. Both of these structures are increasingly important for ensuring that a company's legal obligations are met, particularly since the passage of the Sarbanes-Oxley Act and increased oversight of publicly held companies. Recently, some companies are shifting from a compliance mentality to inviting guidance from key stakeholders, such as customers. This concept is likely to gain popularity in the future thanks to social networking and the desire of consumers to have a hand in making decisions about the things they purchase.

9. A Final Word on Organizational Control (pp. 451–452)

Summary: Organizational control processes need to strike a balance between financial goals, customer goals, and the overall mission of the organization. We need to be careful not to rely too much on tools and processes that foster efficiency, and to balance this with empowerment, ethics, and resonant leadership—three keys to truly effective control systems in organizations.

8. What Can We All Do to Enhance Effectiveness and Efficiency at Work? (pp. 450–451)

Summary: Self-management and emotional self-control are two things that all of us can develop to improve the effectiveness and efficiency of our organizations. Emotional self-control is important because negative emotions can interfere with one's effectiveness. Emotions are also contagious, so a leader's emotions, both positive and negative, can impact others' performance.

7. What Can HR Do to Help Control for Effectiveness and Efficiency at Work? (pp. 447–450)

Summary: Performance management as a control mechanism is often the responsibility of the HR professionals within an organization. In order for performance management systems to be effective, we need adequate structures and processes for gathering data about people's performance and sharing it with them. It is essential for feedback to be delivered in a constructive, compassionate way to ensure positive employee response. Appraisals should also help employees set goals for their careers that strike a meaningful balance between their professional and personal aspirations and the goals of the organization.

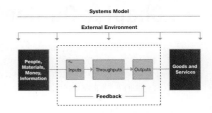

6. What Should Companies Control? (pp. 437–447)

Summary: Companies typically seek to control finances, customer service, and quality; these three areas are tied together such that adjustments in one area impact the other two. A budget is one of the most basic financial controls used by a company, as are accounting controls that include cash flow analyses, balance sheets, and P&L statements. Customer service controls are directed toward monitoring and improving customer service, with the goal of building and maintaining a loyal customer base. Finally, quality controls strive to ensure that inputs are being transformed into ideal outputs through systems like TQM, Six Sigma, Lean Management, and the ISO family of standards.

5. What Are the Typical Steps in the Control Process? (pp. 433–437)

Summary: Control systems can be engaged during any stage in the business process and are typically used to determine the efficiency and quality of business processes and/or the goods or services produced or provided. Both quantitative and qualitative measurements can be used measure performance against goals and corrective actions must be taken when specifications aren't met or opportunities are being missed.

Culture:

It's **Powerful**

Chapter Outline

Find out what you already know about the concepts in
this chapter by going to www.mymanagementlab.com
and taking the Pre-Test. Your results will generate a customized
study plan for Chapter 13.

1. What Is Culture? (pp. 458–460)

2. Why Is Culture Important at Work? (pp. 461–462)

3. What Are the Dimensions of National and Organizational
   Culture? (pp. 462–468)

4. How Can We Describe Organizational Cultures? (pp. 468–471)

5. How Can We Study Organizational Culture? (pp. 472–478)

6. Organizational Culture: What's Important Today? (pp. 479–484)

7. How Can HR Support the Development of Positive
   Organizational Cultures? (pp. 484–489)

8. What Can We All Do to Create Positive and Powerful
   Organizational Cultures? (pp. 489–491)

9. A Final Note on the Power of Culture (p. 491)

Go back to www.mymanagementlab.com and take the Post-Test
to verify your understanding of the concepts. To experience and apply
the concepts, explore the additional material associated with Chapter 13.

Part 1: Leading and Managing for Today and the Future (Chapters 1, 2, 3, 4)
Part 2: Planning and Change (Chapters 5, 6, 7, 8, 9)
Part 3: Organizing Human Systems (Chapters 10, 11)
> **Part 4:** Controlling Quality, Culture, and Yourself (Chapters 12, **13**)
Part 5: Leading and Managing for the Future (Chapters 14, 15, 16)

8. Workplace Essentials: Creativity, Innovation, and a Spirit of Entrepreneurship

7. Change: A Focus on Adaptability and Resiliency

9. Organizing for a Complex World: Structure and Design

Planning and Change

6. The Human Side of Planning: Decision Making and Critical Thinking

5. Planning and Strategy: Bringing the Vision to Life

16. Managing and Leading for Tomorrow: A Focus on Your Future

1. Managing and Leading Today: The New Rules

14. Globalization: Managing Effectively in a Global Economic Environment

10. Teams and Teambuilding: How to Work Effectively with Others

Organizing Human Systems

11. Working in a Virtual World: Technology as a Way of Life

Leading and Managing for Today and the Future

2. The Leadership Imperative: It's Up to You

4. Communication: The Key to Resonant Relationships

3. Motivation and Meaning: What Makes People Want to Work?

15. Sustainability and Corporate Social Responsibility: Ensuring the Future

12. Organizational Controls: People, Processes, Quality, and Results

Controlling Quality, Culture, and Yourself

13. Culture: It's Powerful

13. Culture: It's Powerful

1. What Is Culture?

Culture
Everything that the people in a society have learned and share through traditions, pass on to children, and teach new members; this includes religion, beliefs, political ideologies, values, customs, foods, language, gender roles, sexuality, and many other aspects of everyday life.

■Exhibit **13.1**

Anthropologist Margaret Mead was best known for her study of Samoan culture.

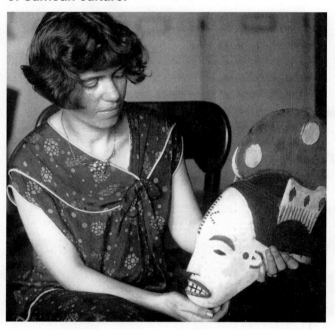

Pictorial Press/Alamy Images

The famous anthropologist Margaret Mead defined **culture** as everything that people in a society have learned and share through traditions, pass on to children, and teach new members (■Exhibit 13.1). According to this view, culture includes religion, beliefs, political ideologies, values, customs, foods, language, gender roles, sexuality, and many other aspects of everyday life.[1]

Culture is a powerful force in our lives because it guides our beliefs, our values, and almost everything we do at home, in our communities, and at work. We learn about culture from the moment we are born. The language we learn is part of our culture. The food we eat is part of our culture. Our manners and how we behave are part of our culture. Culture and cultural expectations affect how we think, feel, and act. Often invisible, culture is so much a part of us that we may not realize we are following its "rules." Rather, these "rules" are simply the way things are supposed to be. As organizational scholar Geert Hofstede puts it, culture is the "collective programming of the mind."[2]

To be an effective leader, manager, or employee, you must appreciate how culture affects people, influences relationships, and impacts organizations. In this chapter, you will study aspects of culture that affect people at work and in other relationships. You will also learn about models of culture in organizations. In addition, you'll evaluate the types of organizational cultures that are important today, HR's role in creating and maintaining healthy cultures, and what we can all do to create powerful organizational cultures. Let's start by developing a deeper understanding of the ways in which values, attitudes, and commonly held expectations of behavior relate to culture.

Values

Values are ideas that a person or a group believes to be right or wrong, good or bad, attractive or undesirable.[3] Values related to a society's culture often include ideas about principles like freedom, democracy, truth, and justice. Values also include ideas about things such as sex, marriage, and raising children. For example, you might have certain values associated with family life: Should you be married before having children? Should adult children care for elderly parents at home, rather than moving them to a nursing facility? Should family members be loyal no matter what someone does? You may have strong opinions about these questions and feel less intensely about others. That's because values aren't just abstract ideas—they often help to define who we are and can therefore produce very strong emotions.

Deeply held values are profound drivers of our behavior at work and in life. People will fight and even die for values that are important to them, such as justice, freedom, or those linked with religious beliefs. Do you know which values are most important to you and why? Do you know how your values affect you at work? Understanding your values will help you in life and at work.

One example of a personal value that can impact how people feel and behave in the workplace is "fairness." People who place a high value on fairness will often act in ways that enhance justice and equality. Individuals who hold this value typically favor use of the merit system, and they believe that employees should be rewarded for their performance. In addition, these people are generally on the alert for any signs of injustice. If such signs are detected, people who value fairness may become angry, frustrated, and demoralized at work.

Organizations often promote specific values that guide behavior among employees, customers, stakeholders, and behavior related to property and the natural environment. One example of an organizational value that is commonly espoused in companies goes something like this: "People are our greatest asset." Companies that hold this value tend to place special emphasis on supporting people's learning, development, health, and well-being.

In companies that put a high value on people, you might expect that managers who mistreat employees would be chastised and maybe even let go. Indeed, this was recently the case in one U.S. law firm. This firm was a partnership—meaning that the senior lawyers owned the business together. In this sort of business structure, it is very difficult to fire people. Nevertheless, this particular company decided that some of its partners were not living up to the firm's values when it came to how to treat people. These partners were not supporting the young attorneys' development, they often communicated in harsh and unprofessional ways, and they were causing employees to burn out. The firm's leadership felt that this violation of values was serious—and they fired several senior partners as a result.

Attitudes

Sometimes we hear people say things like "He has a bad attitude" or "Her attitude is so positive!" These types of statements are often shorthand for any number of beliefs, values, and behaviors that affect a person, how he or she relates to others, and how he or she is seen at work. When we hear statements like these, it is important for us to go beyond the shorthand and find out exactly what the speaker means.

Attitudes are a group of ideas, values, beliefs, and feelings that predispose a person to react to a thing, a situation, another person, or a group in a certain way.[4] What is your attitude toward school? Do you value learning and feel generally positive about your classes, and do you usually see the benefits of attending school? Or do you resent having to go to school? How does your attitude about school affect your study habits?

Attitudes matter when it comes to how we perceive situations and judge people, and, in turn, how those people see and judge us. Strongly held attitudes evoke strong emotions in people in much the same way that values do. Many people don't spend much time thinking about their values or attitudes, or about which of these are most important and which are less so. That's because values and attitudes are so much a part of "who we are" that they often go unexamined.

Good leaders, however, do not leave values or attitudes unexamined. They constantly push themselves to understand what is driving them, which values are sacrosanct, and which attitudes may need to change. Understanding our own values and attitudes—and the emotions we attach to them—is critical because it helps us understand our behavior and develop a personal code of ethics. Knowing our values also helps us better understand other peoples' values, and it permits us to examine the values that our organizations ask us to uphold. Values and attitudes are also important because they affect behaviors and norms.

Norms

Norms are internalized standards for behavior that support agreed-upon ways of doing things and what people expect of one another within a cultural group. For example, norms guide how we dress and behave at a formal dinner, how we greet one another, and how we behave with friends versus family versus coworkers.

Norms are often unspoken, and in some cases, people may not even recognize them until they are violated. For instance, in the United States, people go to the end of the line at a counter in a store and wait until it is their turn to pay for their merchandise. No one has to tell us to do that—it's just what happens. Now, imagine what you would think and feel if someone walked to the front of the line and pulled out his wallet. You'd probably be irritated, because the person was violating a norm. Or, imagine how you would feel if someone joined you on an elevator and stood several inches closer than normal. What

Attitudes
A group of ideas, values, beliefs, and feelings that predispose a person to react to a thing, a situation, another person, or a group in a certain way.

Norms
Internalized standards for behavior that support agreed-upon ways of doing things and what people expect of one another within a cultural group.

Folkways
The routine conventions of everyday life.

Mores
Norms that are central to the functioning of society.

■Exhibit **13.2**
Unusual haircuts are often seen as a violation of folkways.

blickwinkel/Teister/Alamy

would you do? What would you think of the person? Your thoughts and feelings would be in part related to the fact that the person was violating norms about personal space.

Some norms function like guidelines, whereas others are more like social rules. Accordingly, scholars have identified two distinct categories of norms: folkways, which are like guidelines, and mores, which are stricter social rules. **Folkways** are the routine conventions of everyday life. They include aspects of culture such as appropriate dress and good social manners. People who violate folkways may be perceived as odd or weird, but not necessarily as evil or bad (■Exhibit 13.2). For example, if you jumped fully dressed into a crowded pool, others would view you as an oddball. Folkways also exist at work, and they might include such things as how you greet senior managers, how you are expected to behave at an office party (e.g., don't drink too much), or how carefully you attend to the start and end times of meetings.

As opposed to folkways, **mores** (pronounced "morays") are norms that are central to the functioning of society or a group. More like rules than guidelines, mores might include a society's stance on murder, rape, sexuality, or childrearing practices. When people violate mores, they can face serious reprisals, often because many of our mores are codified into laws. For example, in many societies, people face trial and possible jail time for theft, murder, or incest.

Societies differ, of course, and mores are not universal from one culture to the next. For instance, several countries, including the United States, have laws that prohibit polygamy. The nation of Senegal, however, does not have mores prohibiting polygamy. In Senegal, polygamy is allowed and practiced alongside marriages between one man and one woman. Indeed, one researcher found that 15 percent of Christian men and 28 percent of Muslim men in Senegal reported having polygamous marriages in the year 2000. This equaled about 29 percent of the country's population at the time.[5]

Within the work environment, mores often revolve around core business practices and ethics. For example, many businesses expect their employees to refuse to take or offer bribes for any reason or in any situation. Another example of a more might relate to the protection of corporate secrets, such as the formulas involved in preparing products like Kentucky Fried Chicken or Coca-Cola.

Understanding how values and norms differ in cultures is critical in business today. That's because so many businesses—both domestic and international—conduct operations outside their home country and/or employ people whose cultures differ.

To work effectively together, people need to understand and respect one another's norms and values. For example, it is often said that the failure of the auto industry merger between Daimler-Benz (maker of Mercedes-Benz) and Chrysler was linked to irreconcilable differences in culture and the inability of the company's leaders to bridge these gaps.[6] In the next section, we will look at other aspects of culture and how they affect us at work.

Most Popular » Discussion Questions

1. Brainstorm a list of things that you believe define your national culture, such as beliefs, values, traditions, foods, and religion. Share with others from your own culture and from another. How are your lists the same? How are they different?
2. Give two examples of folkways at your school.
3. Have you ever experienced a new and different culture? If so, how did you learn about the norms of that culture?
4. What are your core values—those values that define who you are as a person and guide you in some of the most important arenas of your life, including family, relationships, and work?

2. Why Is Culture Important at Work?

Most of us take culture for granted. Why, then, do we need to study culture in a course on management? There are several answers to this question. First, today's organizations often consist of individuals from multiple countries, and peoples' national cultures guide what they do, feel, think, and believe. This impacts how they work and relate to others. In addition, within many countries (including the United States), numerous cultures exist—and need to coexist—in organizations. Diversity is therefore a fact of life in modern organizations.

People from different cultures often have different ways of expressing their values, different ways of building and maintaining relationships, and diverse needs and habits. In fact, in today's organizations, we can't even assume that people will speak the same native language. These differences can be tricky to navigate in a corporate setting, so we need to find a way to build bridges across our differences. People must understand their own and others' cultures in order to work together effectively.

Many leaders and companies today take culture and diversity seriously. They focus time and attention on helping leaders build the skills necessary to navigate the differences inherent in working globally. Take, for example, CSL Behring, a global plasma-based pharmaceutical company that specializes in protein biotherapeutics—making life-saving drugs from the proteins found in human plasma.[7] Let's look at how one great leader talks about working in a multicultural organization.

Perspectives

Michael Gaines, director of Global Commercial Development at CSL Behring, is a dynamic and powerful leader. Michael's team is colocated in the United States and in Switzerland, and his company does business all over the world. Michael's keen intelligence and, in particular, his emotional intelligence are evident in the way he builds great relationships and gets immense results when working in a multicultural environment:

First, you need to have patience. It takes a while for people to trust each other across cultures. It helps to ask a lot of questions that will ultimately leverage and also validate colleagues' knowledge and experience. You need to spend time on projects, at dinner, over lunch. You need to really listen, and you need to build relationships that are effective. It takes a lot of time, and it takes a lot of air miles to build these kinds of relationships!

You also need to pay attention to your language. Precision is important—you have to be constantly aware of the gaps in communication that will occur.

And this next one is hard—you have to understand that cultural perceptions exist about your own culture, as well as others. We don't like admitting that such perceptions exist, but they are present. If you know them, you can either leverage them or break them down.

Michael Gaines, Director of Global Commercial Development at CSL Behring

In a word, you need to be open. You need to immerse yourself in the culture, and immerse yourself in how business is conducted in that culture. You need to show respect for other countries and other cultures.

Michael goes on to describe how learning to work successfully in a multicultural environment can help people become great leaders:

Working in a multicultural environment teaches us something about great leadership. If you approach this situation openly with intense focus on maintaining your self-awareness, you will have the ability to connect with people even if their point of view is in opposition to your perspective on a project. Even if they're diametrically opposed to your point of view, you will be able to respectfully discuss and "reach them" regarding your point of view on the issues. If you take this approach, people will sense that you are seeking, "What can I learn from you?" They will feel more inclined to learn from you as well. You will be seen as approachable—someone who looks at things from different points of view. You will be seen as a person with a high level of integrity—one who treats people fairly and someone people can trust.

Source: Personal interview with Michael Gaines conducted by Annie McKee, 2009.

Like CSL Behring, many organizations employ a multicultural workforce and also do business outside their home countries. For example, Unilever, a large consumer goods company based in London, has operations in more than 100 countries; Exxon-Mobil lists 40 countries in which it does business; and Nike is based in Beaverton,

Oregon, but employs people in Europe, the Middle East, Africa, Asia, and the Americas.[8] Global business isn't just for large companies, either. Consider the case of a small consulting firm called the Teleos Leadership Institute. Teleos is based in Philadelphia and has less than 20 full-time employees, but the company provides services in over a dozen countries. It also employs full-time and associate staff from several nations.[9]

Yet another reason why it is important to study culture is that culture is an incredibly powerful force in organizations. Each and every organization develops its own specific culture that is related to—but distinct from—the national and regional cultures from which it emerged. Therefore, each organization has its own unique blend of values, customs, habits, traditions, and beliefs. Moreover, culture is a form of control in organizations, and it can have a tremendous impact on individual behavior and, ultimately, on an organization's success or failure. Organizational culture regulates behavior both implicitly and explicitly, and it can direct people's actions more effectively than standard control systems.[10] This is the case because, unlike rules and directives that come from outside an individual, culture tends to be internalized—it is part of who we are.

Most Popular » Discussion Questions

1. How would you describe the culture of your school? How does your school's culture guide your behavior?
2. How do cultural differences affect people's relationships in your school? Give an example from your own experience.
3. Have you ever experienced a misunderstanding as the result of a cultural difference between two groups? If so, describe that experience.

---

3. What Are the Dimensions of National and Organizational Culture?

Organizational culture
A set of shared values, norms, and assumptions that guide peoples' behavior within a group, business, or institution.

Building on the concepts of culture in the previous sections, **organizational culture** is a set of shared values, norms, and assumptions that guide peoples' behavior within a group, business, or institution.[11] Organizational culture contributes significantly to the effectiveness of an organization.[12]

In this portion of the chapter, you'll learn about various dimensions of culture that are found in national groups and also in organizations. Much of this information can be traced to the groundbreaking research conducted by psychologist Geert Hofstede in the 1960s and 1970s.[13] More recently, research by the Global Leadership and Organizational Behavior Effectiveness (GLOBE) project has extended Hofstede's work by identifying nine dimensions in which cultures differ. Dimensions of culture are important to understand, in part because they give us simple ways to describe how cultures and subcultures affect us at work.

Hofstede's Dimensions of Culture

During the late 1960s and early 1970s, Geert Hofstede studied the attitudes and values of over 70,000 IBM employees working in 40 countries. This was the beginning of decades of studies involving many more people and countries. In his research, he identified four di-

■Exhibit **13.3**
Hofstede's five dimensions of culture.[14]

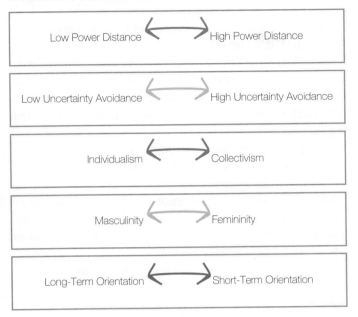

Low Power Distance	⟷	High Power Distance
Low Uncertainty Avoidance	⟷	High Uncertainty Avoidance
Individualism	⟷	Collectivism
Masculinity	⟷	Femininity
Long-Term Orientation	⟷	Short-Term Orientation

Power distance
The extent to which people in societies accept the idea that power is distributed unequally.

Uncertainty avoidance
The degree to which people can tolerate unpredictable, ambiguous, or uncertain situations.

Individualism
The degree to which people prefer to act in their own self-interest instead of acting on what is best for the group as a whole.

Collectivism
The degree to which people prefer to act as members of a group (rather than as individuals) in exchange for loyalty and the benefits of membership.

Masculinity/femininity
The extent to which society values achieving (masculine) versus nurturing (feminine).

mensions that he proposed represent differences across cultures: power distance, uncertainty avoidance, individualism/collectivism, and masculinity/ femininity. Several years later, Hofstede added a fifth dimension, long- versus short-term orientation.[15] Each of these dimensions is described in ■Exhibit 13.3.

Hofstede's first dimension is power distance. **Power distance** is the extent to which people in societies accept the idea that power is distributed unequally. In high power distance cultures, people accept wide variance in the amount of power possessed by different individuals and groups. Titles, rank, and status are important in these societies. Within organizations in these societies employees show great respect for individuals in positions of authority. In low power distance cultures, people downplay power and authority and do not see these characteristics as legitimate ways to differentiate people. In a low power distance society, people might be focused on minimizing the difference between the rich and poor. In organizations with low power distance, employees might feel they have the right to disagree with their managers, and managers might be more inclined to involve employees in making decisions. Moreover, managers may be empowered to make decisions and take risks even when they are farther down in the leadership hierarchy.

The second dimension in Hofstede's model is uncertainty avoidance. **Uncertainty avoidance** reflects the degree to which people can tolerate unpredictable, ambiguous, or uncertain situations. In high uncertainty avoidance cultures, people feel threatened by ambiguity and change, and they may be less tolerant of new ideas. In such cultures, we often see a need for written rules and regulations. In organizations characterized by the tendency to avoid uncertainty, managers are often closely involved with details and activities tend to be highly structured. In comparison, managers in cultures that accept uncertainty are more comfortable with taking risks: uncertainty and change are a way of life and are easily accepted.

Individualism/collectivism is the third dimension in Hofstede's model. **Individualism** refers to the degree to which people prefer to act in their own self-interest instead of acting on what is best for the group as a whole. High individualism cultures tend to place importance on personal time, freedom, autonomy, and challenge. People from individualist cultures are expected to look after their own interests and those of their immediate families and individual decisions are frequently considered better than group decisions. **Collectivism** is the degree to which people prefer to act as members of a group (rather than as individuals) in exchange for loyalty and the benefits of membership. Collectivists expect people in the group to look after and protect them, just as they look after and protect others. In cultures high in collectivism, group decisions are viewed as better than individual decisions, and employees are often very loyal to their companies.

The fourth component in Hofstede's model is **masculinity/femininity**. This dimension focuses on the extent to which a society values achieving (masculine) versus nurturing (feminine). It is important to note that this does *not* necessarily mean that certain traditional roles, behaviors, or emotions are the sole responsibility of one gender or the other.

Masculinity refers to the preference for achievement, assertiveness, and/or the acquisition of money and material goods. In masculine cultures, the dominant approach can be summarized as "live to work" and emphasis is placed on independence and decisiveness. In cultures that are high in masculinity, women must adopt certain behaviors associated with masculinity in order to succeed. The same would be true for men who don't naturally tend toward the cultural traits that Hofstede termed "masculine."

Within Hofstede's model femininity refers to a preference for relationships, cooperation, and quality of life. Accordingly, in cultures that are high in femininity, the dominant approach can be described as "work to live," and there is an emphasis on interdependence. In organizations that embody this trait, women and men high on the feminine side of the equation would not have to adopt more masculine behaviors in order to be successful. Rather, everyone would be required to exhibit behaviors that strengthen relationships or place quality over quantity.

Long-term orientation
Refers to a greater concern for the future and for values such as thrift, perserverance, and avoidance of shame.

Short-term orientation
Refers to a desire for gratification of personal needs, as well as a focus on tradition and meeting social obligations.

The fifth and final dimension in Hofstede's model is long- versus short-term orientation. **Long-term orientation** refers to a greater concern for the future and for values such as thrift, perseverance, and avoidance of shame. In cultures with a long-term orientation, people focus on the future and on value persistence. On the other hand, **short-term orientation** refers to a desire for gratification of personal needs, as well as a focus on tradition and meeting social obligations.[16] The long- versus short-term orientation dimension was added as a result of additional studies conducted both at IBM and in China. Interestingly, this dimension was first called Confucian dynamism, because it called attention to traditional Confucian values.[17]

In the years since initial publication in 1980, Hofstede's work has formed the basis for a vast number of studies about organizational culture. One of these efforts has gained traction with both researchers and practitioners because it both supports and extends Hofstede's work. This study is known as the GLOBE project.

The GLOBE Project Value Dimensions

Using data from 18,000 managers in 62 countries, the research team behind the GLOBE project proposed nine dimensions of culture in 2004 (■Exhibit 13.4).[18] Two of the GLOBE value dimensions are similar to Hofstede's dimensions: power distance and uncertainty avoidance. Also, GLOBE's future orientation is much like Hofstede's long- versus short-term orientation, and its institutional collectivism is akin to Hofstede's individualism/collectivism dimension. The remaining five dimensions offer additional insights into culture. These five dimensions are assertiveness, gender differentiation, in-group collectivism, performance orientation, and humane orientation.

As a leader, it's important for you to understand how cultures differ. In seeking to bridge gaps related to cultural differences, you can begin by studying the dimensions presented in both the Hofstede and the GLOBE models. For example, say that you are an American manager who has been asked to manage a subsidiary in Sweden. Based on your knowledge of the GLOBE model, you might be prepared for differences in how you and the people in the subsidiary approach assertiveness. Partly because of the influence of American culture and partly because of your own personal style of interaction, you tend to be highly assertive at work. You are often the first to propose or push an idea at a meeting, for instance, and when you notice that people are not participating in a discussion, you tend to publicly draw them out. However, because you are aware that people in Sweden generally score low on assertiveness, you decide that it would be wise to adjust your usual approach. Otherwise, you are likely to offend people, or at the very least confuse them. In this situation, you must also work to understand what your Swedish employees value and how this affects their behavior.

■Exhibit **13.4**

GLOBE Project Value Dimensions[19]		
GLOBE Project Dimension	Description	**Country Examples**
Power Distance The degree to which members of a society expect an unequal distribution of power.	Societies high on power distance focus on status and power, and leaders expect deference from their subordinates. Societies low on power distance favor participative decision making and egalitarian relationships.	**HIGH:** Russia 　　　Spain 　　　Thailand **MED:** England 　　　France 　　　Brazil **LOW:** Denmark 　　　Netherlands 　　　South Africa
Uncertainty Avoidance The extent to which members of a society rely on social norms and procedures to diminish unpredictability.	Societies high on this dimension value structure and clear expectations. Societies low on this dimension do not value rules and procedures and accept ambiguity.	**HIGH:** Austria 　　　Denmark 　　　Sweden **MED:** Israel 　　　United States 　　　Mexico **LOW:** Russia 　　　Greece 　　　Venezuela
Future Orientation The extent to which a society encourages and rewards future-oriented behaviors.	Societies high on future orientation plan for the future and delay gratification. Societies low on this dimension focus on short-term results and seek instant gratification.	**HIGH:** Denmark 　　　Canada 　　　　(English speaking) 　　　Singapore **MED:** Slovenia 　　　Ireland 　　　India **LOW:** Russia 　　　Argentina 　　　Italy
Institutional Collectivism The extent to which the members of a society are encouraged and take pride in being part of collective actions.	An institutional emphasis on collectivism allocates resources so that all members can participate in economic, social, and political processes. A greater emphasis is placed on group goals than individual goals. Low emphasis on collectivism encourages self-interest. Here, rewards are based on individual performance.	**HIGH:** Denmark 　　　Japan 　　　Sweden **MED:** United States 　　　Poland 　　　Egypt **LOW:** Argentina 　　　Greece 　　　Italy
Assertiveness The extent to which a society encourages people to be tough, assertive, and confrontational.	A high value for assertiveness represents a society that encourages and rewards toughness, a certain degree of forcefulness, and competitiveness. A low value for assertiveness refers to a society that values gentleness and modesty.	**HIGH:** Spain 　　　United States 　　　Austria **MED:** Egypt 　　　France 　　　Ireland **LOW:** Sweden 　　　Switzerland 　　　Japan

Continued **on next page>>**

■Exhibit **13.4**   **Continued**

GLOBE Project Value Dimensions[19]

GLOBE Project Dimension	Description	Country Examples
Gender Differentiation The extent to which a society maximizes gender role differentiation and how much status and decision-making responsibility is given to women.	Societies high on this dimension grant one gender higher status. Societies that score low on gender differentiation grant more equal status to men and women.	**HIGH:** South Korea Egypt China **MED:** Italy Brazil Venezuela **LOW:** Sweden Denmark Poland
In-Group Collectivism The extent to which members of a society take pride in being members of *small groups* within the society, such as families, close circles of friends, teams, and the organizations in which they work.	Societies high on this dimension will likely provide benefits for families or have structures encouraging groups to get together to socialize. Societies low on this dimension might place less emphasis on the importance of the nuclear family and more on allegiance to country.	**HIGH*:** China India Egypt **MED:** Japan Italy Israel **LOW:** Denmark Sweden Finland
Performance Orientation The degree to which a society rewards group members for performance improvements and excellence.	Societies high on this dimension value training and development and believe in taking initiative. People who live in societies that are low on this dimension may feel uncomfortable with feedback.	**HIGH:** United States Taiwan Singapore **MED:** Sweden Japan England **LOW:** Russia Greece Italy
Humane Orientation The degree to which a society encourages and rewards people for being fair, altruistic, generous, and kind to others.	Societies high on this dimension focus on human relations and sympathy. Societies low on this dimension are motivated by material possessions.	**HIGH:** Indonesia Egypt Ireland **MED:** Sweden United States Hong Kong **LOW:** Germany (Former West) France Spain

*A high score corresponds to collectivism and a low score corresponds to individualism.[20]

Source: Robert House, Paul J. Hanges, Mansour Javidan, and Peter W. Dorfman (eds.), *Culture, Leadership, and Organizations: The GLOBE Study of 62 societies* (Thousand Oaks, CA: Sage Publications, 2004).

Culture: It's Complicated!

As you can see, considering the most effective ways to bridge cultural differences can be complicated. After all, it's extremely difficult to account for all of the many values, norms, and other dimensions of a culture. That is partly because dimensions and values are by no means "pure" or truly shared by every member of a society. Why is this? First, multiple strong subcultures always exist within a society's dominant culture and second, culture is always changing.

Subcultures

Rarely (if ever) do all members of a broader culture share the same values, attitudes, beliefs, and norms. This is the case because every culture functions much like an umbrella under which many smaller subcultures exist. Examples of subcultures abound. Consider, for instance, some of the regional subcultures found in the United States, including those associated with the South, the Northeast, the Midwest, New York City, and California. Different values, attitudes, and norms exist in each of these different subcultures, although all of these subcultures still reflect elements of the broader national culture. Consider religious groups—these too are subcultures.

Have you ever had roommates? Chances are you and they came from different subcultures. What differences in culture were most obvious to you? How did these similarities and differences affect your relationships? Which were easiest to get used to? Which were the most difficult to accept?

Subcultures are important to understand for the same reasons culture is: The values and norms of subcultures affect our behavior in life and work. Another reason subcultures are important is that they are often where changes that affect the larger culture begin.

Culture Change

Every culture is dynamic and constantly changing, if only in small and almost invisible ways. Consider the current controversy in the United States regarding who can and cannot be married. Values have influenced laws, and until recently, only heterosexual couples could legally marry. Today, however, many people believe that same-sex couples should have the legal right to marry. This is a sign that American subcultures and the overarching culture are changing. These changing values and the resulting attempts to change the law didn't arise overnight, they've actually been brewing for roughly four decades.

The battle over same-sex marriage dates back to at least 1970, when Jack Baker and James Michael McConnell requested a marriage license in Minnesota and were refused. (Keep in mind that for Baker and McConnell to even reach the point where they could make this request, values and culture must have already been changing.) The couple subsequently sued, and the resulting case (*Baker v. Nelson*) was won by the State of Minnesota.[21] A later appeal to the U.S. Supreme Court was dismissed without being heard. Fifteen years later, two California cities (Berkeley and West Hollywood) granted benefits for and recognition of same-sex domestic partnerships, but this fell short of an official recognition of marriage. Currently, same-sex marriages are performed in a handful of states and a few other states will recognize such marriages granted by other countries or states.[22] The situation is in constant flux. For example, California briefly allowed same-sex marriages to be performed (June 16 to November 4, 2008). Although the law permitting such marriages was rescinded by popular vote, all marriages performed during that time are still recognized (■Exhibit 13.5).

Debates about same-sex marriage continue to rage across the United States and other countries around the world. Views about this culture change

■Exhibit **13.5**

Gay rights supporters demonstrate on the day California upheld Proposition 8, which legalized same-sex marriage. It was later overturned.

Peter Bennett/Ambient Images Inc./Alamy

seem to split along traditional conservative/liberal lines (these too are subcultures). Indeed, this clash of values erupted into a bitter and public debate in the United States during the 2004 presidential race between George W. Bush and John Kerry—with Bush becoming associated with the "no-never" side of the argument, and Kerry suggesting same-sex unions as a compromise that would address the call for change (while not going so far as changing what "marriage" means in American culture). In the midst of extremely important issues such as war, the fight against terrorism, serious problems with health care, and looming economic problems, the issue of gay marriage often took center stage.[23]

As this heated debate illustrates, cultural changes often cause a great deal of internal conflict for people as they begin to question the values they have learned and adopted, or as their values are threatened. This happens in organizations as well. For example, in the early 1990s, Powell Flute Company of New England was known for making the best handcrafted flutes in the world. So, when the company's leaders learned of a new technology related to the placement of holes on the flute body, there was a great deal of debate as to whether Powell could adopt the so-called "Cooper scale" and still retain its identity. After all, making this change meant more than just adopting a new methodology—for the craftsmen, it meant taking in and accommodating something new and very different, something foreign to their practice that challenged their identity, their ideas about how flutes should be made, and the company's organizational culture.[24]

Research has helped us to understand dimensions of culture that impact organizations. In the next section, we will look at how scholars and practitioners classify organizational cultures.

Most Popular » Discussion Questions

1. Use the Hofstede and GLOBE models to describe your national culture and one other culture you know well. How do the two cultures compare? What implications do the similarities and differences between these cultures have for work relationships?
2. Consider your school or place of work. Choose two of Hofstede's dimensions or two of the GLOBE dimensions and describe how they apply to this organization's culture.
3. Generate a list of values and norms in your primary culture that have changed or are in the process of changing. Why do you think they are changing?
4. What are some of the subcultures in your organization and/or school? What is the impact of these subcultures on people?

---

4. How Can We Describe Organizational Cultures?

In this section, we turn our attention to how scholars have classified organizational cultures. First, we will explore one popular categorization scheme called the competing values model. Then, we will look at cultures in another way—by considering the degree to which they are strong or weak and examining how this difference in intensity affects people's behavior.

Competing values framework
A model that shows how cultures can be measured along two axes: structure (stability versus flexibility) and focus (internal versus external).

The Competing Values Model of Organizational Culture

One popular model that helps explain the relationship between organizational culture and organizational performance is the **competing values framework**. This model

■Exhibit **13.6**

The competing values framework.[25]

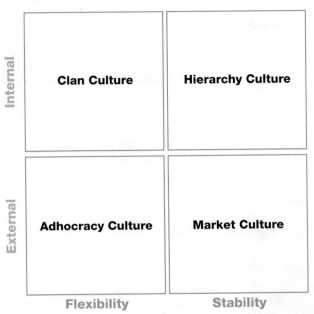

Clan culture
A culture that has an internal focus and encourages flexibility.

Hierarchy culture
A culture that has an internal focus and encourages stability and control.

Adhocracy culture
A culture that has an external focus and encourages flexibility.

Market culture
A culture that has an external focus and encourages stability and control.

Balanced culture
A culture that has values linked to each of the culture domains of the competing values framework, and all of these values are perceived to be important and are held by organization members quite strongly.

Strong culture
A culture in which central values and norms are shared and strongly upheld by most members of the organization.

shows how cultures can be measured along two axes—structure (stability versus flexibility) and focus (internal versus external)—as depicted in ■Exhibit 13.6.[26]

The focus dimension of the competing values framework includes internal focus and external focus. An organization with a high internal focus dedicates most of its attention to factors inside the organization, such as employee satisfaction. An organization with a high external focus directs attention to factors outside the organization, such as how the organization fits into and/or affects its environment. The structure dimension of the framework measures the degree of flexibility an organization has versus its need for stability. Thus, an organization with high flexibility has a tolerance for self-directed behavior, whereas an organization with high stability has more systems to regulate employees' behavior. Using this framework as a starting point, researchers have identified four distinct types of organizational cultures: clan culture, hierarchy culture, adhocracy culture, and market culture.[27]

A **clan culture** has an internal focus and encourages flexibility instead of stability and control. This culture values collaboration among organizational members and promotes cohesion by focusing on things such as agreement and job satisfaction. Clan cultures often devote significant resources to recruitment, selection, and employee development.

A **hierarchy culture** has an internal focus and encourages stability and control. In general, organizations with this type of culture have structured work environments and numerous control mechanisms to ensure reliability and efficiency.

An **adhocracy culture** has an external focus and encourages flexibility. In adhocracy cultures, organizations concentrate on innovation and creativity, and they are adaptable and respond well to changes in the environment. This type of culture supports members who seek new ways to do things.

A **market culture** has an external focus and encourages stability and control. Organizations with market cultures emphasize competition and are driven by results and profitability. Members of such organizations are therefore expected to deliver timely, quality products.

In other research, a fifth type of culture is added: the balanced culture.[28] A **balanced culture** has values linked to each of the culture domains of the competing values framework, and all of these values are perceived to be important and are held by organization members quite strongly. In such cultures, organization members are supported in adapting their behavior to specific situations.

Although all types of cultures can support organizational effectiveness in certain circumstances, the clan and balanced cultures seem to have the most positive effects on effectiveness and outcomes.[29] This is because these two cultures provide the most support for their members and are most adaptable to environmental changes.

"Strong" and "Weak" Cultures

Organizational cultures also differ in the degree to which they impact people's values, attitudes, and behavior. For instance, in a **strong culture**, central values and norms are shared and strongly upheld by most members of the organization. In addition, most managers also share a set of business practices.[30] Strong cultures empower employees to perform at a higher level because they are committed and self-confident.[31] Companies with strong cultures are also more likely to be successful in the short term and to produce a return on investment for investors.[32] Many researchers support the idea that strong cultures lead to enhanced commitment and increased productivity and performance.[33]

Sometimes, cultures may be so strong that they continue to affect people even after they have left the group. As illustrated in the *Business Case*, McKinsey and Company (a global business consulting firm) is one company for which this holds true.

McKinsey

They Get You for Life

The desire to belong to a group is a basic human need. When asked to talk about ourselves, most people start with talking about the groups they belong to, such as our professions, organizations, and schools. The Japanese language includes important words defining "in-groups" (*uchi*) and "out-groups" (*soto*).[34] The groups that we belong to determine who we are. They also define who we are *not*.

You would think, then, that once you leave a group you are no longer "in." That's not true of former McKinsey employees. They belong to a very strong in-group, and the personal network connecting them is one of the most admired in the business world.

McKinsey is an "up or out" company.[35] This means that employees must climb the company's career ladder toward partnership and if they cannot meet the standards, they must leave. Not everyone makes it. And in addition to those who *have* to leave, a good number of McKinsey employees *choose* to leave—often to join one of McKinsey's client organizations at very senior positions. To some, this seems like a brutal system that would result in resentment among employees who are pushed out and disappointment among teammates when a "star" employee

Some companies value and instill long-term loyalty

departs. McKinsey, however, has learned how to capitalize on this process.

When people leave—or have to leave—the company supports them in finding good jobs, very often with clients.[36] In the long run this is advantageous for both the employees and the firm. Consider the example of Westinghouse Electric Corporation's Michael H. Jordan, who gained his experience with McKinsey during the late 1960s and 1970s, left the firm to work for one of its clients, and now regularly hires McKinsey for consulting work. "It's still a bit of a fraternity," says Jordan, "A lot of my close friends are people I worked with at McKinsey."[37]

Although some people don't like the exclusive nature of the club (they call it the "McKinsey mob") the fact is that this network is powerful.[38] The company's culture places great value on loyalty to the company and there is a lasting feeling that they are part of an in-group that shares values about work standards, loyalty, and business practices.[39] These beliefs and behaviors are part of McKinsey's culture—a culture that is strong enough to guide people even when they no longer work for the company.

Photo Source: Zsolt Nyulaszi/Shutterstock

Strong cultures are often found in partnership organizations like McKinsey. Entrepreneurial start-ups and family-owned firms also tend to have strong cultures. One of the benefits of a strong culture, especially in the start-up phase, is that shared values and commitment to a common vision can hold people together during the challenging early days. Let's look at how this played out in a start-up called Vineyard Vines.

Leah Despain

Tying One On at Vineyard Vines: Poised for Progress, Maintaining Family Culture

In 1997, brothers Shep and Ian Murray realized that their Wall Street jobs left them feeling less than satisfied.[40] They wanted out, and they wanted to bring more of the family spirit they remembered from their childhood summers on Martha's Vineyard to their work lives. Then, during Christmas dinner with

their parents, the two young men came up with an idea: Create high-end, printed silk neckties with patterns that reminded them of Martha's Vineyard and the summers they longed for. Their idea represented a simple dream to turn their passion for the "good life" into apparel.

Shortly after devising their plan, the Murrays ripped the "Clothing Manufacturers" page out of the Manhattan Yellow Pages and started making calls. With $8,000 in credit card debt, the brothers quit their day jobs in advertising and public relations, took their prototype ties to clothing boutiques in Martha's Vineyard, and convinced the shop owners to sell their

Continued on next page>>

Student's Choice   Continued

products on consignment. The Murrays also made similar arrangements with several high-end Boston menswear retailers. They even sold ties out of their backpacks at bars and on beaches across New England. Gradually, business began to take off, and Vineyard Vines was born.[41]

During the next few years, the Murrays continued to explore novel ways to publicize their products. For instance, they sent Vineyard Vines ties to media personnel and network anchors until the ties eventually made their national television debut on a news program. This appearance marked the beginning of a media blitz as Shep and Ian took the brand national. By 2004, the Murray's bright, whimsical ties were a hit on Wall Street and Main Street. In fact, both George W. Bush and John Kerry donned the ties while on the campaign trail.[42]

The Murray brothers seized upon the growing demand for their preppy duds by expanding their line to include men's and women's apparel, shoes, and accessories. As the product line grew, the presence of Vineyard Vines apparel swelled. Today, the Murrays' products are available from more than 600 retailers, as well as eight company-owned stores with a total of 120 employees. In 2006 alone, Vineyard Vines posted sales of over $37 million, according to *Entrepreneur Magazine*.[43]

The culture of the "good life" is felt the moment you walk into any Vineyard Vines store. There's a family feel to the place—energetic, fun, and committed. The salespeople make it a point to learn their customers' names and occupations, and there's always lively conversation. Just like the Vineyard Vines clothes, the mood in the store is bright and upbeat, yet casual and comfortable.[44] With the opening of each new store, however, the Murrays take great pains to preserve the strong culture of the company.

Source: Adapted from a case written by Leah Despain.

Weak culture
A culture in which the values and norms are shared by a limited group of people and employees' goals may not be in line with management's goals.

In contrast to strong cultures like Vineyard Vines and McKinsey, a **weak culture** is one in which the values and norms are shared by a limited group of people. In an organization, this can mean that employees' goals may not be in line with management's goals. It would seem natural to conclude that strong cultures are better than weak cultures, because they control people more effectively. But strong cultures are not necessarily always best. As it turns out, strong cultures can inhibit an organization's ability to adapt to environmental changes because they control people's beliefs and behavior so tightly. Scholars refer to this phenomenon as "value engineering."[45] A strong culture may regulate and control behavior so strictly that it limits the possibility of innovation, and this in turn can decrease organizational effectiveness.[46] Thus, in stable environments, strong cultures enhance performance, but when the environment changes, the benefits of this type of culture decrease dramatically.[47]

Some scholars have concluded that diverse and/or international companies might be able to perform better when they do not have strong overarching organizational cultures, but rather have distinct, strong subcultures within each of their business units.[48] In these companies, employees must embrace uncertainty and rely on the combined expertise of the diverse components of the overall organization.[49] The central underlying value that organizes the firm, then, is a strong orientation to learning and adaptation.

You have probably had experiences with both strong and weak organizational cultures, and you can probably describe various types of organizational cultures in simple language based on your observations of people's values and how they behave. In the next section, we will explore how you can get better at "diagnosing" organizational cultures. Knowing how to study cultures will help you to choose the right organization when accepting a job. It will also help you to support the development of healthy cultures wherever you work.

Most Popular » Discussion Questions

1. Using the competing values framework, discuss Vineyard Vines. Is its culture likely to be more flexible or more stable? Is it more internally or more externally focused? Of the four types of culture, which do you think Vineyard Vines practices, and why?

2. Is the culture of your school or workplace strong, or weak? What evidence do you have to support your opinion? How does the strength of the culture impact students? Faculty? Staff?

5. How Can We Study Organizational Culture?

Culture is often difficult to understand. However, it's critical to learn how to study organizational culture because it has such a powerful effect on people's values, attitudes, and behaviors. Culture also affects organizational results. In this section, you'll begin by considering two ways to "look" at culture. The first method enables you to see three levels of culture—from more obvious to less. The second method draws your attention to stories, traditions, taboos, and the way in which language is used in organizations—all of which are powerful indicators of culture. After that, we discuss practical methods for studying culture—methods that managers can actually use.

■Exhibit **13.7**

We can observe some parts of culture, but other parts are less obvious.

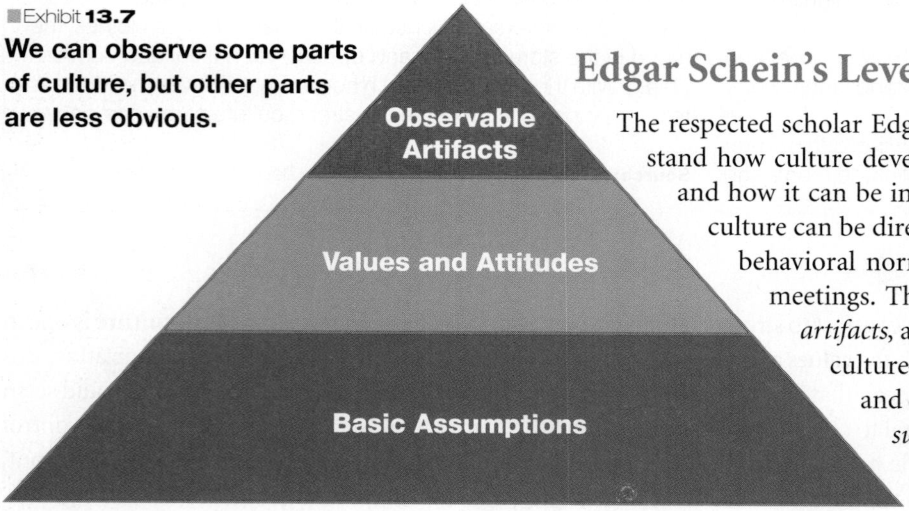

Observable Artifacts

Values and Attitudes

Basic Assumptions

Edgar Schein's Levels of Culture

The respected scholar Edgar Schein has done much to help us understand how culture develops in organizations, how it is maintained, and how it can be improved.[50] Schein notes that some aspects of culture can be directly observed, including language, dress, and behavioral norms such as how late or early people are for meetings. These aspects are what Schein calls *observable artifacts*, as depicted in ■Exhibit 13.7. Other aspects of culture—values, for example—are not as easy to see, and even less visible are what Schein calls *basic assumptions*.[51] Let's look at each of these levels of culture and how they might play out in an organization.

Observable Artifacts: The Top Level of Schein's Organizational Culture Model

Observable artifacts are those aspects of a culture that can be seen, heard, or experienced by an organization's members. Observable artifacts can often be easily determined just by asking questions. Some common examples of observable artifacts:

- *Dress code:* An organization's dress code may be written or unwritten, but in either case the organization has a clear expectation of how employees should dress for work. To determine a company's dress code, try asking the following types of questions: Can you wear jeans to work, or would that be cause for dismissal? Do men wear ties? Do people pay a lot of attention to things like polished shoes? Do some people wear uniforms but other people wear their own clothes?
- *Language and jargon:* Language and jargon are clues to what people value and pay attention to in a culture. When studying language and jargon, ask yourself the following questions: Do people use words that have meaning only to organization members? Are acronyms frequently used? Is slang used? By whom and how? In a multicultural organization, is one language the norm for senior leaders?
- *Interpersonal relationships:* Organizations have cultural "rules" about how people relate to one another. When determining the relational norms, you can start by asking: Do people know much about one another's personal lives? Do people do things together outside of work? Do people treat each other with respect and consideration, or do they relate more instrumentally around tasks?
- *Technology:* How people use technology is linked to beliefs and norms around work. To explore how technology relates to people's beliefs, ask the following sorts of questions: Are Macs or PCs used? Do employees communicate mainly through e-mail, or do they talk to each other directly?

- *Workspace:* Where people do their work is an indication of communication norms, power dynamics, and the like. You can study this by asking: Do the big bosses have special offices? Is management close to staff or far away? Does everyone have a desk in an open space? If it's a virtual organization, does technology support group work?
- *Ceremonies, rituals, and awards:* Ceremonies, rituals, and awards indicate what is valued in a culture. To explore this, you can ask: Are there events that can't be missed and that people will cancel vacations to attend? Do managers always bring food to early morning meetings? Are there "prizes" for certain outcomes, such as hitting sales targets?

There are many observable indicators of culture. Learning how to question what you see will enable you to draw conclusions about some of the less visible and yet very powerful aspects of organizational culture, such as values.

Values: The Middle Level of Schein's Organizational Culture Model

Espoused values
Explicit values that are preferred by an organization and communicated deliberately to the organization's members.

The **espoused values** of an organization are explicit values that are preferred by the organization and communicated deliberately to the organization's members. Founders and leaders have an important role in shaping these values, which are often listed in the company's marketing materials, mission statement, and employee training materials. Note, however, that the term *espoused values* refers only to what is said, and not necessarily to what is actually done. For example, a company can communicate to its employees and customers that one of its core values is quality, but if the organization does not have a quality control department and does not measure defects, then these values are merely espoused (rather than enacted).

Enacted values
The values that are actually exhibited in an organization.

Enacted values are the values that are actually exhibited in an organization. These values can be seen, for example, in how people treat customers or how people treat each other at work. Enacted values are also often evident in people's ethics, in policies regarding sustainability, and in the behaviors for which employees are rewarded.

Basic Assumptions: The Deepest Level of Schein's Organizational Culture Model

In Schein's system the deepest level of organizational culture consists of basic assumptions, or the *core* beliefs that are deeply embedded in the organization and that are largely invisible. Organization members are usually unaware of these assumptions or how they guide behavior, and they are often taken for granted. For example, a basic assumption may be that people are opportunists and will steal when given the opportunity. In this situation, you may never hear anyone say that people are untrustworthy, and if asked, people might not admit to this basic assumption. You would see, however, that managers are highly vigilant, inventory is checked regularly, security is tight, and monitoring cameras are used throughout the organization's facilities. Another example of a common basic assumption is that only leaders can fix organizational problems. Again, people would not say this directly and if asked would not necessarily agree. But the basic assumption would be evident in things like the number of small decisions made at senior meetings.

This brings us back to the importance of carefully observing and interpreting observable artifacts. These, and both espoused and enacted values, are the clues to "what's really going on around here." To deepen your understanding, you can also look at other indicators of culture: organizational myths and heroes, taboos, sacred symbols, and language.

Myths and Heroes, Taboos, Sacred Symbols, and Language

Culture is rarely communicated directly. More often, it is conveyed through the stories people tell about themselves, through what is considered good or evil, and through the ways in which language is used. When seeking to learn about an organization's culture, therefore, it is especially helpful to consider the organization's myths, heroes, taboos, sacred symbols, and language. These types of cultural expression are linked to values and basic assumptions, and they drive members' behavior because they are part of what people look to when they make decisions about what to think, believe, and do.[52]

Myths and Heroes

Myths

Exaggerated stories that are told and retold to communicate values and to emphasize norms.

In anthropology, myths are stories that describe ideologies.[53] An organization's **myths** are exaggerated stories that are told and retold to communicate values and to emphasize norms. These stories usually involve important events or people, such as the founder of the organization, setbacks that occurred long ago, heroes who overcame problems, or even examples of "perfect" or "evil" behavior.[54] Myths point to what an organization values, and they also communicate which behaviors are desirable and which are considered taboo. Because they bind people together around a common vision of good and bad behavior, myths demonstrate what it takes to succeed in a company.

Hero

A legendary person who embodies the highest values of a culture.

Myths often center on the actions of a hero. Here, a **hero** is defined as a legendary person who embodies the highest values of a culture. He or she defends the organization against external or internal forces that threaten values, beliefs, or the best way to do things. Schein notes that in the mythologies of many organizations, stories are told of managers and engineers who have fallen into disfavor for bucking an organizational norm only to later become heroes in some other context.[55]

For example, author William Rogers relates a story about a low-level IBM employee who refused to admit the chairman of the board to a secure area without proper identification. When others in the group verbally assaulted the employee, the chairman rewarded his behavior by silencing the critics and obtaining the requested identification.[56] This particular story communicates the idea that rule breaking is unacceptable, even for the highest status members of IBM.[57] The employee who challenged the chairman became elevated to the status of folk hero through the telling and retelling of the story. Stories like this show how heroes uphold organizational values even when facing danger. Heroes are courageous and bigger than life.

How do you know a hero story when you hear one? Chances are, the person at the center of the story will be talked about a lot in the organization. In addition, people tend to employ strong language when talking about heroes, using words like *amazing*, *incredible*, *brilliant*, *unbelievably creative*, and *charismatic*. He or she will be referred to with respect and perhaps even reverence.

Socialization

The process of teaching new members about a culture.

Myths and hero stories are important because they support **socialization**, or the process of teaching new members about a culture. They also provide a way to explain current practices and shape the future.[58]

Taboos

Taboos

Strong prohibitions against certain activities.

Hero stories frequently describe what people should do in organizations. In contrast, taboos tell people what *not* to do. **Taboos** are strong prohibitions against certain activities, and they are often associated with what a group considers sacred or profane.[59] In many societies' cultures, they involve such things as food, sexuality, religious practice, and death. Taboos essentially act as unwritten laws that forbid various activities, thoughts, and even feelings. Violations can lead to severe sanctions, such as shaming, ostracism, or, in some societies, losing one's life.

Every culture has taboos, and this includes organizational cultures. For instance, some organizational cultures include an unspoken rule that you should never get mad at your boss. Other common examples include taboos around whom employees can date—sometimes, other employees are off limits, and oftentimes, clients are as well. In addition, some scholars who study conflict between men and women believe that many cultures have strong taboos against men and women arguing or disagreeing with one another.[60] You can see how this would not be helpful in organizations, because disagreement often leads to better solutions.

Other researchers have focused specifically on taboos related to an organization's willingness to engage in socially responsible behavior. One scholar has identified three taboos that inhibit corporate social responsibility: the taboo against seeing business as having moral responsibility; the taboo against questioning the goal of continuous economic growth; and the taboo against becoming involved in the "politics" around social responsibility.[61] Of the three, the taboo against interfering with continuous economic growth is perhaps strongest. For most of the twentieth century, growth was the "Holy Grail" and anything that interfered with it seemed to be taboo.[62]

Sacred Symbols

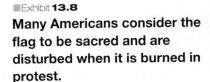

Sacred symbols
Things, people, and events that are untouchable and unquestionable within a culture.

A culture's **sacred symbols** are the things, people, and events that are untouchable and unquestionable. Consider how people sometimes feel about their nation's flag: It's just a piece of cloth, really, but it holds such special meaning that it is often protected from harm by laws and taboos (■Exhibit 13.8). Thus, to some people in some cultures, the flag is sacred.

The same sort of thing happens in organizations. Certain objects, people, or events take on such special meaning that they cannot be harmed, removed, or changed. Consider the proverbial "corner office." In some organizations, status and power come with sacred trappings like the corner office, or perhaps a private washroom or a special cafeteria. These privileges are viewed as sacred symbols of having "made it" in the organization.

When something becomes sacred, it is extremely difficult to change. This can even apply to products, such as Coca-Cola. Coca-Cola company's management found out the hard way that consumers weren't going to tolerate any changes to their beloved drink. When "New Coke" was introduced in the mid-1980s consumers rebelled. In fact, some people actually stockpiled "real" Coke before the change, and many people felt betrayed by the company.

What's especially interesting about the "New Coke" example is that the Coca-Cola Company had changed Coke's recipe numerous times since the product was first introduced in the mid-1880s. Back then, the drink was known as "Cocawine," and its recipe included both alcohol and derivatives of coca leaves, which are used in the production of cocaine. By the 1930s, however, the company had phased out these ingredients, eventually arriving at the formula we know today.

Few people complained when the company adjusted its recipe between 1880 and 1930, yet when Coke's formula was changed in the mid-1980s, people rebelled. Maybe

■Exhibit **13.8**

Many Americans consider the flag to be sacred and are disturbed when it is burned in protest.

Sergey Kamshylin/Shutterstock

it was because the recipe had been the same for more than 50 years, and two or three generations had grown up with the "old" taste, logo, bottles, and packaging. Or maybe it was because Coke had become a symbol of something much more profound than a sweetened drink—it had become an American icon, and for some a symbol of freedom. Indeed, before the end of the Cold War in the late 1980s, whenever Coke's advertising appeared on the streets of a Communist country, some people believed that progress was being made toward establishment of a less restrictive society.[63]

Whatever the reason, one thing remained certain: New Coke wasn't Coke, and it really didn't matter if the updated version was "better" or not. Ultimately, this public outcry convinced the Coca-Cola Company to switch back to the previous formula.[64] In doing so, the company had to take on the cost and time burdens associated with two major changes in production and marketing within a short time frame.

Sometimes events unfold in the opposite direction of the "New Coke" debacle. In such cases, companies refuse to change their products or services or wait too long to do so because their products or services have historically been part of the company's image. These products and services are therefore viewed by the company as sacred and untouchable, even when the market no longer wants or needs them. For example, for some years now there has been more awareness that fast-food restaurants often serve foods that are high in fats, sugar, and the like, and that these are not good for you. One would think that these restaurants would have paid attention to the trend. In fact, they appeared to do so when, in the late 1990s, we started seeing things like "chicken Caesar salads" appear on menus. Customers soon discovered, however, that these salads often had more fat and more calories than burgers! It is only recently that truly healthy foods have begun to show up on fast-food menus.

Language

How people use words, which native language is paramount in multicultural organizations, and even body language are powerful indicators of culture. An organization's culture can therefore be studied by looking at how language and symbols relate to ideologies and practices that unify an organization.[65]

Because spoken language is a key form of communication, familiarity with the sayings, slang, jargon, and/or acronyms specific to an organization is useful when seeking to understand that organization's culture. Consider the following expression: *"I can't believe the butterbar went VFR direct to the Old Man!"*[66]

Can you translate this? Unless you belong or have belonged to a military subculture that uses this language, you probably won't have a clue what is meant. In this case, a butterbar is a second lieutenant, the lowest officer rank in the army. The derogatory term refers to the yellow color of the single bar insignia. VFR is an acronym for "visual flight rules" and means to take the most visually direct path. Here, VFR becomes a metaphor for circumventing the chain of command to reach the top (the "Old Man") officer, a taboo in the military and many other cultures. This illustrates problems related to the use of slang, jargon, and the like: Although this language tends to unify members inside an organization, it also serves to keep other people out. In addition, unique language can establish a barrier between an organization and its customers, consumers, and vendors. In today's flat, complex, international organizations, this can be destructive.

Many companies today have a much bigger problem than simply controlling the use of jargon and acronyms: today, members of many organizations speak different native languages. Consider the example of a large European financial services company with senior managers whose native languages are Italian, German, and English. Several managers prefer using their native Italian, several others prefer doing business in German, and one or two prefer English. In most subsidiaries, employees speak only the local language. How does a company like this manage language—and how can language be effective in supporting culture if people can't speak to one another? Situations like this are common today. Thus, in recent years, many organizations have had to develop "language policies" to guide which language(s) are used on the job and what language(s) employees must learn in order to be promoted.[67]

The intricate and inseparable relationship between language and culture means that a choice of one language over others has an organization-wide impact on how power is perceived and who has access to it. To return to the previous example, the company's leaders eventually decided that English was the preferred language for business. This decision caused a great deal of conflict and disagreement, because it was seen as a sign that the company was going to adopt more British and/or American ways of doing business. Many of the Italian and German managers were highly displeased with the decision and the implications for the organization's culture.

Nonverbal communication provides us with another means for understanding a culture. By examining people's facial expressions, body language, posture, tone of voice, and so forth, you can gain a significant amount of information. For example, if you notice that people tend to lower their eyes and speak softly when talking with senior managers, this might indicate high power distance—or a large status differentiation between lower level employees and upper management.

Language, nonverbal communication, and the stories people tell about their cultures are powerful in that they can help maintain and strengthen that culture. This is fine when the culture supports the goals of the organization—but that isn't always the case, especially in today's rapidly changing world. For instance, when myths are really just questionable beliefs that are protected by taboos, or when heroes' behavior is actually harmful, myths and hero stories can be destructive.[68] Similarly, when things that are sacred really need to be changed, or when taboos prevent people from doing the right things, culture becomes a barrier to success. Accordingly, one powerful way to begin to change a culture is to examine the various aspects of that culture, then consciously use those aspects that support positive outcomes and change those that don't. In the next section of the chapter, you'll learn how to study culture to better understand which aspects of culture help an organization and which get in the way.

Leaders and Managers as Ethnographers

Observing, myths, heroes, taboos, sacred symbols, and language can help tremendously in understanding a culture. Sometimes, however, you need to go beyond simple observation and interpretation. You need to also find out from people themselves about their culture. Most of the time you can't simply ask questions because peoples' culture is so deeply buried that they don't consciously recognize it. For that reason, students of organizational culture—and good managers and leaders—must become ethnographers.

Ethnography is the systematic study of human cultures. An ethnographic approach includes observation and co-inquiry. In a co-inquiry process, people observe and collaborate with one another to truly understand what is happening within their group or organization. This is sometimes called *participant observation*, and it isn't necessarily comfortable.[69] It's hard to really look at your culture. That's because when we co-inquire into an organization's culture, we attempt to explore the unspoken aspects of the culture—things that are a part of "who we are" but that might need to change. When faced with this challenge, good leaders can remember a quote widely attributed to Plato: "We can easily forgive a child who is afraid of the dark. The real tragedy of life is when men are afraid of the light."[70]

Through observation and inquiry, we can literally shine a light on an organization's culture. Dynamic inquiry is a co-inquiry approach developed by scholars Annie McKee and Cecilia McMillen. This process enables organization members to uncover cultural values and the basic assumptions that drive people's behavior as well as how leadership practices affect people and the organization.[71] Authors Daniel Goleman, Richard Boyatzis, and Annie McKee describe the process this way:

> Many large companies have processes in place for systematically evaluating employee attitudes, values, and beliefs—a kind of proxy for the emotional reality. These processes can be very helpful, but the problem is that surveys measure only what they set out to measure—and they rarely tap the more subtle layer of . . . complex norms

Ethnography
The systematic study of human cultures.

that flow through an organization. This blind spot can result in simply measuring what people want to know, but not what they don't want known. . . .

Dynamic inquiry offset[s] the "find what you look for" effect of most surveys and enable[s] leaders to begin to address the underlying cultural issues that are getting in their way. . . . Through the process of discovering the truth about their organization, people begin to create a shared language about what's really going on as well as what they'd like to see—their ideal vision of the company.

Dynamic inquiry involves focused conversations and open-ended questions intended to get at people's feelings. . . . It is only when people talk about their feelings that they begin to uncover root causes of problems in the culture and the true sources of inspiration around them. . . . They create a language that captures the real truth about the forces that affect people's day-to-day lives in the organization as well as their hopes for the future. . . . Once people are engaged in this kind of open dialogue about their culture and their dreams, it is very difficult to put the lid back on the box. . . . The creation of a shared language that is based on feelings as well as facts is a powerful driver of change. This shared language provides a sense of unity and resonance, and the resulting momentum helps people to move from talk to action. They feel inspired and empowered, willing to work together to address their collective concerns.[72]

Another ethnographic method often used to discover the underlying attributes of culture focuses exclusively on what's working in a group or organization. Developed by David Cooperrider, *appreciative inquiry* is a process that explores people's and the organization's strengths—in other words, everything that stimulates both people and the organization to become healthy and productive.[73] Appreciative inquiry is a form of ethnographic research that often includes interviews and large-group meetings where people can identify cultural and organizational strengths and opportunities and explore these together. This method can be particularly powerful when a company's employees have lost sight of what their unique contributions are, or when morale is so low that people need to build psychological strength to face challenges.

Methods such as dynamic inquiry and appreciative inquiry are built on the assumption that as a *study* of an organization is conducted, *change will begin to occur.* In other words, these methods are forms of action research, or research that seeks to effect organizational change as part of the study process.[74] With this type of research, all people who are involved in the interview process are also viewed as active participants in change management.[75]

Studying culture isn't reserved for experts or consultants—we all need to learn how to do it—employees, managers, and leaders alike. Understanding an organization's culture can help us to make the right choice about joining a company. Equally important is the fact that understanding culture can help us to be effective in a company. In the next section, we will look at what kinds of cultures leaders are attempting to create and foster in order to help their companies to be successful in today's complex environment.

Most Popular » Discussion Questions

1. How do things like dress, language, spatial arrangement, technology, relationships, and rituals reflect the cultural values of your school or place of work?
2. Articulate several core values for a group to which you belong. Now, try to determine the underlying basic assumptions that drive these values.
3. Think about some taboos in your family, workplace, or at school. How do these taboos affect how people interact and/or how effective the group is?
4. Using a co-inquiry approach, interview a classmate about the culture of your school, then have him or her interview you. Together, identify themes that relate to the culture of your school.

6. Organizational Culture: What's Important Today?

Today's managers and leaders are increasingly struggling with issues related to organizational culture. One reason for this is that many organizational cultures have developed with very little guidance. Indeed, for much of the last century, managers and leaders paid little attention to the "people issues" in their organizations, including culture. Many organizational cultures, therefore, have been developed in haphazard ways. Many current cultures are also problematic in that they feature norms, values, and attitudes that supported simpler ways of doing business that worked a few decades ago but do not adequately support the complexity of today's business environment.

For these and other reasons many leaders are struggling to change their organizational cultures to better support long-term organizational sustainability, excellence, and success in today's environment. The next few sections explore organizational cultures that focus in turn on innovation, customer service, diversity, ethics, sustainability, and supporting employees in becoming the best they can be.

Innovative Cultures

Organizations must be innovative to remain competitive in today's global marketplace. An innovative culture can support employees in creative problem solving, formulating breakthrough ideas, developing new products and services, and finding more effective and efficient ways to work. Research demonstrates that when a culture has little bureaucracy, gives people autonomy, and allows them to take risks, then innovation flourishes.[76] Furthermore, when employees perceive their work environments to be original and imaginative, there is an increased level of creativity in their own work.[77] Of course, an innovative culture must be supported by management and organizational reward systems, and employees must not be burdened by excessive workloads and pressures, because these can inhibit development of this type of culture.[78]

■Exhibit **13.9**
The Ritz-Carlton employees follow a credo.

Elan Fleisher/LOOK Die Bildagentur,der Fotografen GmbH/Alamy

Customer Service Cultures

Another way companies can distinguish themselves from their competitors is by providing superior service to their customers. For example, the Ritz-Carlton Hotel Company's credo includes the following statement: "We are ladies and gentlemen serving ladies and gentlemen"[79] (■Exhibit 13.9). This philosophy highlights that Ritz-Carlton's goal is to excel at providing service with a high degree of professionalism.

In a study of best practices in the U.S. lodging industry, one common characteristic shared by all of the leading companies was that their hotels created a service culture. Consider the Four Seasons & Regent Hotel and Resorts, for instance.[80] This company has a comprehensive orientation and training program designed to teach its employees the value of personal service. Then, to support employees in delivering such service, the company keeps a higher than normal ratio of employees to guests. Finally, senior management collects data from focus groups, guests, and managers to ensure that a service culture is not just created, but successfully maintained.

Many organizations far removed from the lodging industry also focus on creating cultures that support excellent customer service. In businesses ranging from banks to clothing stores to software companies, service has become a priority. Interestingly, researchers note that successful customer and market orientation—and the cultures that support these characteristics—are highly dependent on good leadership.[81]

Diversity Cultures

Innovation and customer service can capture customers' attention—as well as their business. Even innovation and great customer service, however, aren't enough to make a business successful over the long term. To achieve lasting success, people must be able to effectively work together inside the organization—and one potential challenge to this ability lies in the area of demographics.

The demographics in many business organizations have changed rapidly in recent years, and they continue to change today. For example, according to the research organization Catalyst, in 2008 more than half of management and professional occupations were held by women.[82] However, only 6.2 percent of top earners at Fortune 500 companies were women, and only 3 percent of Fortune 500 CEO positions were held by females. Still, in 2008, women held 15.2 percent of Fortune 500 board seats, compared to only 11.7 percent in 2000.[83]

Companies are also becoming increasingly diverse in terms of ethnicity and race. According to U.S. Bureau of Labor Statistics (BLS) projections, 68.3 percent of entrants into the labor force from 2006 to 2016 will be people of color or women, and 22.3 percent of this total will be Hispanic.[84] It is expected that the fastest rate of growth will be among Asian and Hispanic employees.[85] Also, many modern organizations—even small- and medium-sized companies—are international and have employees, suppliers, and vendors from more than one country, as well as customers and consumers all over the world. Finally, diversity in the workplace also includes differences in sexual orientation, religion, and physical abilities.[86]

Given the realities of the current business environment, it is essential that leaders and managers take steps to create more inclusive and diverse workplaces. Research indicates that diverse perspectives lead to better decisions, and they also help companies attract the best employees. Nonetheless, diversity can also be a source of conflict—when people have different ways of engaging with each other, different ways of working, or different cultures, clashes sometimes ensue. Thus, diversity is more likely to produce benefits if an organization focuses on integration and learning, which can help people better understand these sorts of differences.[87]

Some companies already know how to leverage diversity in the workforce to ensure that both employees and the company thrive. For one example of a culture that promotes diversity, consider the efforts of Johnson & Johnson, a global pharmaceutical company based in the United States. Chairman and CEO William C. Weldon and his management team believe that diversity increases competitive advantage, and their efforts have propelled Johnson & Johnson to the number-one spot on Diversity Inc.'s list of the Top 50 Most Diverse Companies of 2009.[88]

Weldon and his team are vitally involved in the company's many concrete efforts to build a culture that supports diversity, as depicted in ■Exhibit 13.10. For example, Weldon meets regularly with employees to discuss diversity initiatives. These types of meetings between the CEO and rank-and-file employees are rare in most companies. Another notable example of the company's diversity efforts is that Johnson & Johnson offers benefits to employees' same-sex partners.

Companies like Johnson & Johnson aren't leaving the development of a diverse workforce up to chance. Rather, they are actively engaged in building cultures that support everyone in contributing their best, and they also help employees develop the skills necessary to work effectively across cultural boundaries. In today's global business environment, this isn't just a "nice-to-have" characteristic—it's a must.

Ethical Cultures

Yet another attribute that distinguishes companies from one another is their commitment to ethics. Social pressure for people and companies to act in an ethical manner has

■Exhibit **13.10**

Johnson & Johnson's Diversity Efforts[89]	
Diversity Area	**Johnson & Johnson's Efforts**
CEO commitment	Chairman and CEO William Weldon regularly meets with employee-resource groups. Weldon has the company's chief diversity officer as a direct report. More than 6 percent of the bonuses for Weldon's direct reports are tied to meeting the diversity targets set forth in their goals and strategies. Johnson & Johnson has a diverse board of directors: among the 11 directors, African Americans, Asians, Latinos, and women are represented.
Company-wide commitment	Johnson & Johnson gets a perfect score on work/life benefits and on the benefits it offers to employees' same-sex domestic partners. Both the company's overall workforce and its management populations reflect the demographics of the communities Johnson & Johnson serves in the United States. Thirty-one percent of the most senior-level executives (CEO and direct reports) and nearly half of the company's top 10 percent, highest paid employees were women. Johnson & Johnson has excellent employee resource groups, including a group for employees of Middle Eastern and North African heritage.
Supplier diversity	Johnson & Johnson sponsors business-school programs for key diverse suppliers. The company also sponsors memberships and other professional development for diverse suppliers, such as participation in the National Minority Manufacturing Institute.

been increasing steadily for years, and recent high-profile cases of business leaders acting unethically have caused this movement to gain momentum.

Employees today are faced with numerous dilemmas, and for many of them, working in an organization that rewards ethical decisions is important. That's one reason why having an ethical culture is critical: When values and norms support ethical behavior, there is pressure for employees throughout a company to behave ethically in all circumstances.[90]

Research suggests that it is important for ethics to be institutionalized—but what does this mean? For some organizations, the process of institutionalizing ethics means explicitly encoding ethics in rules and guidelines. For example, companies may prohibit bribery, have rules about how to dispose of toxic waste, or set policies for investing employees' retirement funds. These rules protect the companies' ethical stance on a variety of social issues. However, explicit institutionalization of ethics is not enough. If an organization adopts guidelines that support ethical decision making but its managers don't follow these guidelines or not everyone has to observe them, then the organization's employees are bound to receive mixed signals.

This is why implicit institutionalization of ethics is important. Implicit institutionalization is the integration of ethics into the organizational culture. This process must include having management make a commitment to ethical leadership, as well as promoting a culture of personal responsibility when making ethical choices. To give an example, consider the previous example where the IBM employee refused to admit the chairman because he lacked the required credentials. He was following the rules, but in doing so potentially violating a company norm (deference to leaders). Facing an ethical dilemma, he chose to do the "right thing," in part because he had internalized the company's stance on security.

Scholars have found that when ethics are not mandated but are instead internalized, they have a much more powerful effect on employees' belief that the workplace is ethical.[91] This is linked to another reason to focus on implicit institutionalization of an ethical culture: Research suggests that implicit institutionalization leads to job satisfaction and high morale, whereas explicit institutionalization alone does not.[92]

How, then, can companies build an ethical culture? Luis Ramos, CEO of The Network, a company that provides ethics and compliance services, suggests the following:[93]

- A company's ethical code should be thought of as a living document—historical, yet modern. The code of ethics should therefore be an accessible resource which can easily be read by others.
- Ethics is a way of doing business; it is not a "program," which means it is a dynamic and continuous process.
- Ethics training is always relevant and, with the right attitude, it can be fun. If a company's ethics training is relevant, employees will more likely be interested in participating.
- Make sure that employees are actively engaged members of the organization and are aligned with the company's culture.

These actions support both ethical values and ethical behavior, two key aspects of an ethical culture.[94]

So, what types of companies carry out these activities successfully? One example is Cisco Systems, a firm that creates and supplies network management products for the Internet. Cisco wants its more than 65,000 employees to know that ethics are at the core of its business practices. In support of this goal Cisco rewrote its code of ethics to make it more user-friendly, and the company helps promote ethics and two-way communication by having monthly meetings for employees.

When a culture does not support ethical behavior people can get away with bad behavior. Consider Bernie Madoff, former non-executive chairman of the NASDAQ stock exchange, who was recently exposed for defrauding thousands of investors out of more than $60 billion. Although Madoff claimed that he was solely responsible for this scheme, authorities questioned whether he could have conducted such a vast fraud on his own. On August 11, 2009, Frank DiPascali, Jr., a former Madoff deputy, was taken into custody after admitting guilt to 10 felony counts of fraud. DiPascali was a cooperating witness in the Madoff trial, and he was the second insider to admit criminal responsibility in Madoff's scheme. Although Madoff insisted that he acted by himself, DiPascali implicated others in the criminal enterprise.[95]

Managing the details of a fraud of this magnitude would have been a monumental job, and it is not likely that one person, or even two or three, could have done it alone. So, although we can only speculate, it is certainly possible that Madoff's company had developed a culture that supported actions that ultimately resulted in fraud. One can easily imagine some of the unspoken norms and beliefs in such a culture—perhaps "Don't ask questions," "Do as you are told," or "The founder can do no wrong."

Cultures That Support Sustainability and Service

Today, companies of all types are choosing—or being forced—to reduce their impact on the environment and to do business in a socially responsible manner. Many companies are finding that to become responsible stewards of the environment and to be socially responsible they need to change their cultures. What might such a culture look like? Unilever, the Dutch/British manufacturer of consumer goods including Lipton tea and Dove soap, is an example of a company that infuses its business projects with a focus on sustainability. One Unilever project that reflects this commitment is the company's Cleaner Planet Plan. As a result of this plan, since 1995, Unilever claims to have reduced energy-related greenhouse gas emissions from its laundry product factories by 44 percent, disposal waste by 70 percent, and water consumption by 76 percent per metric ton of production.[96] Indeed, Unilever is currently ranked by an organization called "Global 100" as one of the top 100 global companies with regard to sustainability."[97]

Yet another Unilever project highlights the corporation's focus on a socially responsible approach to marketing. Specifically, in its "Campaign for Real Beauty," Unilever has deliberately moved away from traditional stereotypes of women and attractiveness. One element in this campaign is the now-famous "Dove Evolution," a short documentary film produced by the Dove Self-Esteem Fund.[98] This short film and the marketing campaign for Dove soaps and beauty products depict women of all ages, races, and sizes as beautiful and strong—which is markedly different from some of the more typical marketing images that limit beauty to the young and slender.

The movement toward sustainable business practices and social responsibility requires significant cultural changes. Instead of viewing the world as "us and them," people must come to visualize the entire planet as "us." Also, the practice of seeking individual success at any cost must end. To thrive, an organization's culture will have to support both success *and* acceptable practices, especially with respect to the natural environment and the wider communities within which an organization exists.

Cultures That Support the Whole Person: Mind, Body, Heart, and Spirit

In recent years, the amount of attention paid to employees' health, psychological well-being, work/life balance, and even spirituality has increased dramatically. The idea that companies should support employees in reaching their full potential as both workers and unique individuals has embraced by a wide variety of organizations. One primary reason behind this focus on the "whole person" is that our society is changing, and people now have different expectations about what work—and the culture of the workplace—can and should provide. Also, during the past 50 years, women have entered the workforce in unprecedented numbers. This means that work is now a family affair. In addition, people are living longer than ever before in many parts in the world. Today, individuals frequently work well into their seventies, so being employed is no longer something to do while you wait to retire.

Moreover, technology has made it possible to work around the clock from almost anywhere. This is both good and bad—theoretically more can be done, but people can easily burn out, too. Finally, the global workforce is far more mobile now than in the past. People move more often, change jobs more often, and even change careers more often than in the past. One of the outcomes of these changes is that people don't have to stay in organizations that treat them poorly.

When employees feel satisfied, fulfilled, physically resilient, and committed to their work and the organization, results can soar. It makes good business sense for leaders to create cultures that focus on the mind, the body, the heart, and the spirit. In practical terms, focusing on "the mind" might mean creating a culture that enables people to learn and grow and to develop their intellect and their talents. Similarly, focusing on "the body" might mean ensuring that the culture supports physical health.

But what about focusing on "the heart" and "the spirit"? A culture that supports people's "hearts" is one that values productive relationships, positive and effective communication, respect, and compassion. Recent research in psychology and neuroscience indicates that when people are excited, appropriately challenged, and experiencing positive emotions, they are more creative, flexible, and resilient.[99] In comparison, a culture that supports spirituality is one that focuses on ensuring that work is meaningful and that people feel connected in working together toward an important mission.[100] People naturally seek meaning in life, so a sense of meaningfulness in the workplace can be highly motivating. As more and more businesses have recognized this fact, the term *workforce spirituality* has become increasingly popular in recent years. An important note—the term workforce spirituality refers to meaningfulness in work and the organization's goals, not religion. At the time of this writing, searching Google for "workforce spirituality" resulted in more than 222,000 links.[101] But why is workplace spirituality important? Scholars highlight the following points:[102]

1. Workplace spirituality can facilitate organizational effectiveness and productivity. For instance, one study revealed that employees who experienced workplace spirituality were more likely to increase their work unit performance.[103]
2. Workplace spirituality may facilitate ethical behavior. When employees are focused on connectedness as opposed to individual self-interest, they may be more likely to think about how their decisions influence others and whether they are ethical.[104]
3. The incorporation of spirituality in the workplace can be increasingly important in providing employees with feelings of connectedness, empowerment, and work/family balance. These conditions are becoming increasingly important to people today.[105]

Research therefore proves that people seek meaning in their work, and leadership that seeks to integrate ways for people to feel deeply fulfilled in the workplace can have a significant impact on employee motivation.[106] Creating a culture that supports people in finding meaning in their work will support positive organizational performance.

Most Popular » Discussion Questions

1. Of the types of cultures discussed in this section (innovation, customer service, diversity, ethics, sustainability, and cultures that support the whole person) which is the most appealing to you? Why?
2. Discuss the role of ethics and spirituality in your life at school or at work.
3. Consider a team with which you have worked in recent months. Examine the cultures and backgrounds of each team member. What was the nature of the diversity on this team? How did the team deal with diversity?

---

7. How Can HR Support the Development of Positive Organizational Cultures?

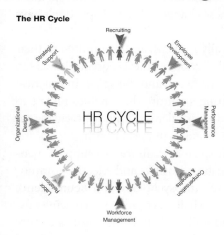

The HR Cycle

HR CYCLE

The human resource function—and human resource professionals themselves—can have a profound effect on an organization's culture. One way that HR can support the development and maintenance of a healthy organizational culture is through a "push strategy"—compelling people to comply with rules and regulations that support the kind of culture the organization's leaders want and need. Conversely, HR can also use a "pull strategy"—guiding people in positive ways to adopt cultural values and engage in behaviors that support organizational effectiveness.

HR's Role in Creating an Inclusive Culture: A "Push" Strategy

HR engages in push strategies to control employee behavior when it codifies and enforces culture via organizational policies and rules. Policies, rules, and laws all reinforce "how we do things around here." These things may be based on the values and basic assumptions that form the culture, or they may reinforce an ideal culture that the organization's leaders are striving to create.

Promoting Diversity and Inclusion in the Workplace and the EEOC

To illustrate how HR pushes culture in the right direction, consider the issue of diversity in the workplace. For example, many companies are striving to hire and promote talented individuals without consideration of gender, race, national origin, religion, sexual orientation, age, or disability status. That's because these companies and their leaders understand that they are doing business in an environment where talent is essential, and that the characteristics listed above have nothing to do with talent.

Unfortunately, not all individuals or all companies are this smart. Discrimination still occurs in the United States and elsewhere, and people are still denied access to jobs, training, and equal pay because of gender, race, national origin, religion, or age. Similarly, people are still victims of sexual harassment, and people continue to be discriminated against because of their sexual orientation or disabilities. Because discriminatory practices like these have been and continue to be problematic, updates in the law have been necessary to support cultural change in the United States. In 1965 the **Equal Employment Opportunity Commission (EEOC)** was created as part of the Civil Rights Act of 1964. The EEOC is a division of the U.S. Department of Justice. It deals with complaints about discrimination and can punish organizations for engaging in discriminatory practices. An organization's leaders, managers, and employees must take steps to comply with all federal anti-discrimination laws. If they don't, serious consequences can and do occur.

■Exhibit 13.11 shows a number of the **equal opportunity (EEO) laws** that have been passed by the U.S. government during the past 45 years to ensure that organizations provide equal opportunities for all people. These laws "push" organizations to change their cultures and practices.

HR is responsible for ensuring that all of the laws listed in Exhibit 13.11 are known to employees—and enforced. Although all of these laws are extremely important, we would like to discuss more fully the prohibitions against sexual harassment.

Equal Employment Opportunity Commission (EEOC)

A federal commission created as part of the Civil Rights Act of 1964 that handles complaints of discrimination against organizations.

Equal opportunity (EEO) laws

Federal regulations that ensure that organizations provide equal opportunities for all people.

■Exhibit **13.11**

Equal Opportunity Laws		
Law	Year Passed	Coverage
Executive Order 11246	1965	Prohibits covered federal contractors and subcontractors from discriminating on the basis of race, color, religion, sex, or national origin, and requires affirmative action to ensure equal employment opportunity without regard to those factors.
Age Discrimination in Employment Act	1967	Protects the rights of employees 40 years of age or older from discrimination on the basis of age in hiring, promotion, discharge, compensation, or terms, conditions, and privileges of employment.
Title IX Sex Discrimination in Educational Programs and Federally Funded Activities	1972	Prohibits discrimination on the basis of sex in educational programs and activities that receive federal financial assistance.
Rehabilitation Act	1973	Protects qualified individuals with disabilities in federally funded activities and contracts.
Vietnam Era Veterans' Readjustment Assistance Act, amended (Disabled Veterans Act)	1974	Protects qualified veterans with disabilities in federally funded activities and contracts. Requires affirmative action in projects that cost more than $25,000.
Employee Retirement Income Security Act (ERISA)	1974	Sets minimum standards for most voluntary pension and health plans in private industry to protect individuals in these plans.
Age Discrimination Act	1975	Prohibits discrimination on the basis of age in federally assisted programs.
The Migrant and Seasonal Agricultural Worker Protection Act (MSPA)	1983	Protects migrant laborers in their dealings with contractors, agricultural employers, and migrant housing providers.

Continued on next page>>

■Exhibit **13.11**   Continued

Equal Opportunity Laws

Law	Year Passed	Coverage
The Consolidated Omnibus Budget Reconciliation Act (COBRA)	1985	Protects workers and their families who lose health benefits due to job loss or reduction in hours by giving them the right to choose to continue group health insurance for a limited time.
The Americans with Disabilities Act (ADA)	1990	Title I prohibits employers of 15 or more workers, employment agencies, and labor organizations of 15 or more workers from discriminating against qualified individuals with disabilities. Title II prohibits state and local governments from discriminating against qualified individuals with disabilities in programs, activities, and services.
Family and Medical Leave Act (FMLA)	1993	Protects workers' rights to family and medical leave under certain circumstances. A new final rule (as of January 2009) grants eligible workers the right to take up to 12 or 26 weeks of unpaid military family leave.
Uniformed Services Employment and Reemployment Rights Act (USERRA)	1994	Protects the jobs of employees who have been called to active duty.
Health Insurance Portability and Accountability Act (HIPAA)	1996	Provides rights and protections for participants and beneficiaries in group health plans; protects against exclusions for preexisting conditions; prohibits discrimination against employees and dependents based on health status; and allows a right to purchase individual coverage for those who have no group health plan coverage available and have exhausted COBRA or other continuation coverage.
Workforce Investment Act	1998	Section 188 protects qualified individuals with disabilities in all WIA Title I financially assisted programs or activities.
Veterans Employment Opportunities Act	1998	Requires an agency to allow eligible veterans to apply for government jobs when the agency will accept applications from individuals outside its own workforce; allows preference in certain circumstances.
Veterans Benefits and Health Care Improvement Act (VBHCIA)	2000	Protects veterans with regard to health care and educational benefits. Title III protects jobs during redeployment and provides protections for veterans with disabilities.
Executive Order 13166	2000	Protects limited-English speakers' rights to access federally conducted or federally assisted services.
Jobs for Veterans Act	2002	The final rule expands the coverage of veterans with disabilities; expands Disabled Veterans Act to cover veterans of wars other than the Vietnam Conflict.
Fair Minimum Wage Act	2007	Increases federal minimum wage standards in increments.
Lilly Ledbetter Fair Pay Act	2007	Eases statute of limitations restrictions to make it easier for employees who have been discriminated against to file lawsuits (signed into law in January 2009).
Americans with Disabilities Act Amendments Act (ADAAA)	2008	Increases protections under the ADA (became effective January 1, 2009).

Preventing Sexual Harassment in the Workplace

In the United States and many other countries, it is illegal to discriminate against people in the workplace based on their race, gender, religion, sexual orientation, ethnicity, or physical abilities. One form of discrimination that is covered in these laws is sexual harassment, and HR is often responsible for preventing this from happening at work.

According to the EEOC, **sexual harassment** is defined as "unwelcome sexual advances, requests for sexual favors, and other verbal or physical conduct of a sexual nature such that submission to or rejection of this conduct explicitly or implicitly affects an individual's employment, unreasonably interferes with an individual's work performance, or creates an intimidating, hostile, or offensive work environment."[107]

Sexual harassment does not necessarily have to cause economic suffering or include threats. The behavior of the harasser must only be unwelcome. Although most sexual harassment cases consist of a man harassing a woman, sexual harassment can come from men or women and can be directed toward members of the same sex or the opposite sex. In fact, in recent years, the percentage of sexual harassment charges filed by men has risen.[108] The harasser can be the victim's supervisor, a subordinate, a coworker, a client, a supervisor in another area, or a nonemployee. The victim does not need to be the person to whom offensive behavior was directed; anyone affected by the offensive behavior has the right to report it.[109] By 1998, 95 percent of large employers in the United States had harassment grievance policies, and 70 percent of U.S. companies provided training related to sexual harassment.[110] Unfortunately, however, most people who experience sexual harassment do not report it, so the behavior may continue and create ongoing high costs to the employee and employer.[111]

It can be difficult to measure the cost of sexual harassment. There are litigation costs, settlement costs, and productivity costs. The EEOC keeps track of the monetary settlements paid out for sexual harassment charges. Between 1997 and 2009, the total average yearly monetary cost was $48 million in non-litigation settlements alone.[112] However, the highest costs may come from loss of productivity. A survey of U.S. federal government employees estimated that sexual harassment cost the U.S. government $327 million between 1992 and 1994 alone due to issues such as those listed in ∎Exhibit 13.12.[113] A study of organizational productivity costs for same-sex harassment in the U.S. Army in 1999 found these costs to exceed $95 million.[114]

Sexual harassment

"Unwelcome sexual advances, requests for sexual favors, and other verbal or physical conduct of a sexual nature such that submission to or rejection of this conduct explicitly or implicitly affects an individual's employment, unreasonably interferes with an individual's work performance, or creates an intimidating, hostile, or offensive work environment."

∎Exhibit **13.12**

Sexual Harassment Is Costly to Employees and Employers

To the Employee

Increase in sick leave and time away from work
Decrease in individual productivity of individual victims of sexual harassment
Lost productivity of work groups in which harassment occurs
Job turnover, including job transfers, firings, and resignations
Stress, depression, and other emotional and physical consequences, including alcohol-, sleep-, and weight-related problems.

To the Employer

Decrease in employee productivity
Higher staff turnover
Increase in sick leave and other types of leave, as well as higher medical payouts
Damaged company reputation (leading to difficulties associated with retention and attraction of employees)
Decrease in teamwork
Poor staff morale
Possible legal and consultant costs.

So, what can HR do about sexual harassment? Basically, there are two streams of activities that HR professionals can direct when it comes to preventing sexual harassment in the workplace. The first stream of activity is related to education and awareness. HR is often responsible for ensuring that employees understand what sexual harassment is, what the law says about it, and what the company's policies are. Education and awareness activities include (but are not limited to) training programs, company-wide communication via the Web, brochures, statements by company leaders, one-on-one coaching sessions with managers, and small group discussions with employees.

A second area of activity that HR must support with respect to sexual harassment relates to compliance and consequences. This set of activities often includes creating processes for reporting sexual harassment and investigating the reported incidents. This is obviously a complex and sensitive process. Oftentimes, employees are hesitant to report sexual harassment for fear of reprisal. This means that HR and other managers must provide safe and confidential processes that encourage employees to come forward. On the other hand, claims must be investigated and proven true or false—false claims are extremely damaging as well.

One would hope that at some point, laws won't be required to ensure a fair and equitable workplace. For now, however, they are necessary—and HR is responsible for ensuring that these laws are enforced. Meanwhile, HR professionals are also responsible for exploring and developing an organization's culture via "pull" strategies.

How HR Can Help Diagnose and Develop Culture: A "Pull" Strategy

In addition to pushing employees, leaders, and managers to create and maintain a healthy organizational culture, HR professionals can lead people, or pull them, in the right direction. First of all, HR can be strategic business partners with the organization's leaders and managers, helping them determine what kind of culture would best fit the mission, vision, and goals of the organization.

Then, HR leaders can develop skills and competencies that enable them to diagnose culture and help change it. Skills that support such a diagnosis include selecting appropriate measurement tools (such as surveys) and correctly interpreting the collected information in order to identify key cultural issues. As mentioned earlier in this chapter, however, surveys tend to result in finding little other than what you were expecting to find in the first place.[115] Thus, HR professionals must also hone the skills and competencies that enable them to conduct dynamic inquiry and other ethnographic research techniques. These methods will help uncover an organization's deeper norms, values, and basic assumptions.

For example, HR professionals can be trained to conduct interviews and to analyze the information obtained in these interviews for themes related to culture. This is a process called *thematic analysis* and it results in identifying patterns in the values, norms, and assumptions that drive employee behavior.[116] By dealing with patterns as opposed to isolated situations, feelings, or behavior, HR professionals and organization management can more effectively deal with both the culture's strengths and its problems.

Recently, this process was effective with employees inside a large financial services company. In this situation, certain HR professionals were selected to participate in a program aimed at enhancing their abilities to be executive coaches and advisers, leadership development and facilitation experts, strategic business partners, and change agents—four key roles for HR today. As part of this program, the HR team was trained in dynamic inquiry and thematic analysis. Then, team members interviewed approximately 75 HR professionals and 75 business professionals throughout the company. The

HR Leadership Roles

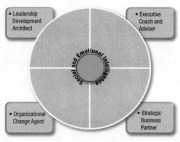

interviews were analyzed, and the themes were presented to management. Key cultural drivers of effectiveness were identified, as were aspects of the culture that were hindering the organization.

Armed with this information, leaders, managers, and their HR business partners were much more prepared to create plans designed to change those aspects of the culture that were harmful and to support those aspects that were helpful. These are just a few examples of how HR can help develop, maintain, and enhance a powerful and positive organizational culture. Businesses today recognize how important HR's role is in these critical "pull" activities, and many forward-thinking organizations are investing in the skills and competencies of their HR professionals.

Most Popular » Discussion Questions

1. Have you ever completed diversity or antidiscrimination training or sexual harassment awareness and education? What was the impact of the training on you? What do you think the impact of such training was on the culture of the organization to which you belonged during the training?
2. How does your university or workplace create and promote an inclusive culture? Try to come up with five examples.

---

8. What Can We All Do to Create Positive and Powerful Organizational Cultures?

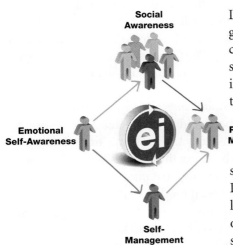

Leaders and managers have a powerful effect on culture, and you, as a member of an organization, can have impact, too. Powerful, positive cultures foster resonance. In such cultures, emotional and social intelligence enable people to create and sustain relationships and an environment where positive values drive behaviors. Social and emotional intelligence competencies support what's called cultural intelligence, and these competencies also enable us to lead cultural change.

People who use the social and emotional competency empathy to understand an organization's culture can be leaders within the organization.[117] That's because people who can manage culture well are able to use self-awareness, self-management, and empathy to bridge differences. Researcher Daniel Goleman emphasizes the importance of empathy in social interactions. "Fast, low-road empathy" involves complex connections in our brains, allowing us to read others' emotions and even catch their moods very quickly. He also emphasizes that a slower form of empathy involves our thinking brain to a greater degree. When we use this form of empathy we imagine ourselves in the situation of the other person and think about how it would feel to be in that position. This allows us to truly examine and understand another individual, or a group, along with the accompanying cultural values and norms.[118]

Develop Your Cultural Intelligence

Employees and managers who are most successful in managing and leading across cultures are adaptable, patient, and flexible—in other words, they exhibit the behaviors associated with cultural intelligence. *Cultural intelligence* is a term that some scholars use to describe a set of behaviors that are related to social and emotional intelligence that focus specifically on a person's ability to interpret values and behavior.[119] Important aspects of cultural intelligence include the use of reasoning and observational skills to interpret unfamiliar behavior and situations (cognitive abilities), willingness to "stick with it" when encountering a new culture (emotional/motivational abilities), and a willingness to adopt body languages and gestures (physical abilities). These three sources of cultural intelligence can be described this way:[120]

- *Cognitive cultural intelligence* encompasses a person's observational and learning skills. It's the ability to pick up factual information about important values and norms of behavior.
- *Emotional cultural intelligence* deals with a person's self-confidence and motivation. Adapting to a new culture is not always easy, and it may involve setbacks and obstacles. Thus, it's important that people have self-efficacy—they need to believe in themselves, avoid becoming discouraged, and not give up.
- *Physical cultural intelligence* is a person's ability to adapt his or her speech patterns, expressions, and body language to those of another culture. By adopting these patterns and mannerisms, a person can better understand what it's like to be part of that culture.

Note that there are two complementary types of cultural intelligence.[121] The first involves to the ability to understand values, norms, and the like within one's own culture. The other, often called cross-cultural intelligence, involves the ability to adjust quickly and with little stress to the mores of cultures other than one's own when and where needed.

Leading Culture Change

What we hear most often about culture from leaders today is: "Our culture needs to change. We need to change the mind-set of our people. We need to preserve our most precious values, and change—or get rid of—some of the beliefs that just don't serve us anymore."

But how can leaders and managers address this challenge? Scholars Daniel Goleman, Richard Boyatzis and Annie McKee have compiled guidelines for leading cultural change based on their research and work in organizations. The following guidelines can support examination and the subsequent transformation of an organization's culture:[122]

- *"Respect the group's values and the organization's integrity.* Visions change, but as the vision evolves, the leader needs to be sure that the 'sacred center'—what everyone holds as paramount—remains intact. That's the first challenge: Knowing what the sacred center actually is—from the perspective of others, not just oneself. The second challenge is seeing clearly what *must* change, even when it is held dear, and getting other people to see it too."[123]
- *"Slow down in order to speed up.* A target-shooting coach we know tells his students, 'If you're in a combat situation, you can't miss fast enough to save your life.' So too with building resonance and an emotionally intelligent organization—the shotgun approach to change doesn't work. The process of slowing down and bringing people into the conversation about their systems and their culture is one we don't see enough in organizations but that nevertheless is critical. Processes such as dynamic inquiry require a supportive, coaching approach and democratic style: The leader must really listen to what people have to say"—and this takes time.[124]
- *"Start at the top with a bottom-up strategy.* Top leadership *must* be committed to facing the truth about the emotional reality of the organization, and they must be committed to creating resonance around a vision of the ideal. But that's not enough: A bottom-up strategy is needed as well, because powerful resonance only develops when everyone is attuned to the change. This means engaging formal and informal leaders from all over the organization in con-

versations about what is working, what is not, and how exciting it would be if the organization could move more in the direction of what *is* working. Taking time out to discuss these kinds of issues is a powerful intervention. It gets people thinking and talking, and it shows them the way. Once the excitement and buy-in builds, it's more possible to move from talk to action. The enthusiasm provides momentum. But the movement needs to be directed: toward the dream, toward collective values, and toward new ways of working together. Transparent goals, an open change process, involvement of as many people as possible, and modeling new behaviors provide a top-down, bottom-up jump-start for resonance."[125]

Leadership today means embracing all members within the larger culture of an organization, taking the time to engage all stakeholders in the process of culture change, and carefully negotiating the right balance between core values and new demands. Creating and maintaining a positive organizational culture takes work. Cultural intelligence, and the ability to lead change effectively and empathically, are critical skills that can facilitate that work.

Most Popular » Discussion Questions

1. When you are in a situation with people from another culture, how do you employ empathy? How could you do this better?
2. Do you think you use cultural intelligence in your interactions with people at school or at work? If so, how and where.
3. Consider a group or an organization you belong to that would benefit from examining its culture. Choose one of the guidelines from the "Leading Culture Change" sections and describe how you would use this advice to help the group or organization.

---

9. A Final Note on the Power of Culture

In this chapter you have explored culture at several levels—what it means for you, how it affects nations and communities, and how it impacts organizations. You've learned how to study culture, and how we can shift organizational culture to make our groups and organizations more effective.

Maybe the most important lesson to take from this chapter is that when it comes to personal, group, or organizational culture and effectiveness, *it's not all about individual behavior.* Culture is a powerful force in our lives, and it affects virtually everything we do. If we want to be successful personally, or in our organizations or even our nations and communities, we must focus on ensuring that our cultural "rules" are in synch with our visions and goals.

Key Terms

1.   What Is Culture? (pp. 458–460)

Key Terms

Culture Everything that the people in a society have learned and share through traditions, pass on to children, and teach new members; this includes religion, beliefs, political ideologies, values, customs, foods, language, gender roles, sexuality, and many other aspects of everyday life. p. 458

Attitudes A group of ideas, values, beliefs, and feelings that predispose a person to react to a thing, a situation, another person, or a group in a certain way. p. 459

Norms Internalized standards for behavior that support agreed-upon ways of doing things and what people expect of one another within a cultural group. p. 459

Folkways The routine conventions of everyday life. p. 460

Mores Norms that are central to the functioning of society. p. 460

2.   Why Is Culture Important at Work? (pp. 461–462)

Key Terms None

3.   What Are the Dimensions of National and Organizational Culture? (pp. 462–468)

Key Terms

Organizational culture A set of shared values, norms, and assumptions that guide peoples' behavior within a group, business, or institution. p. 462

Power distance The extent to which people in societies accept the idea that power is distributed unequally. p. 463

Uncertainty avoidance The degree to which people can tolerate unpredictable, ambiguous, or uncertain situations. p. 463

Individualism The degree to which people prefer to act in their own self-interest instead of acting on what is best for the group as a whole. p. 463

Collectivism The degree to which people prefer to act as members of a group (rather than as individuals) in exchange for loyalty and the benefits of membership. p. 463

Masculinity/femininity The extent to which society values achieving (masculine) versus nurturing (feminine). p. 463

Long-term orientation Refers to a greater concern for the future and for values such as thrift, perseverance, and avoidance of shame. p. 464

Short-term orientation Refers to a desire for gratification of personal needs, as well as a focus on tradition and meeting social obligations. p. 464

4.   How Can We Describe Organizational Cultures? (pp. 468–471)

Key Terms

Competing values framework A model that shows how cultures can be measured along two axes: structure (stability versus flexibility) and focus (internal versus external). p. 468

Clan culture A culture that has an internal focus and encourages flexibility. p. 469

Hierarchy culture A culture that has an internal focus and encourages stability and control. p. 469

Adhocracy culture A culture that has an external focus and encourages flexibility. p. 469

Market culture A culture that has an external focus and encourages stability and control. p. 469

Balanced culture A culture that has values linked to each of the culture domains of the competing values framework, and all of these values are perceived to be important and are held by organization members quite strongly. p. 469

Strong culture A culture in which central values and norms are shared and strongly upheld by most members of the organization. p. 469

Weak culture A culture in which the values and norms are shared by a limited group of people and employees' goals may not be in line with management's goals. p. 471

5.   How Can We Study Organizational Culture? (pp. 472–478)

Key Terms

Espoused values Explicit values that are preferred by an organization and communicated deliberately to the organization's members. p. 473

Enacted values The values that are actually exhibited in an organization. p. 473

Myths Exaggerated stories that are told and retold to communicate values and to emphasize norms. p. 474

Hero A legendary person who embodies the highest values of a culture. p. 474

Socialization The process of teaching new members about a culture. p. 474

Taboos Strong prohibitions against certain activities. p. 474

Sacred symbols Things, people, and events that are untouchable and unquestionable within a culture. p. 475

Ethnography The systematic study of human cultures. p. 477

6. Organizational Culture: What's Important Today? (pp. 479–484)

Key Terms None

7. How Can HR Support the Development of Positive Organizational Cultures? (pp. 484–489)

Key Terms

Equal Employment Opportunity Commission (EEOC) A federal commission created as part of the Civil Rights Act of 1964 that handles complaints of discrimination against organizations. p. 485

Equal opportunity (EEO) laws Federal regulations that ensure that organizations provide equal opportunities for all people. p. 485

Sexual harassment "Unwelcome sexual advances, requests for sexual favors, and other verbal or physical conduct of a sexual nature such that submission to or rejection of this conduct explicitly or implicitly affects an individual's employment, unreasonably interferes with an individual's work performance, or creates an intimidating, hostile, or offensive work environment." p. 487

8. What Can We All Do to Create Positive and Powerful Organizational Cultures? (pp. 489–491)

Key Terms None

9. A Final Note on the Power of Culture (p. 491)

Key Terms None

Chapter 13 Visual Summary

1. What Is Culture? (pp. 458–460)

Summary: Culture is an important force that affects much of what we do at home, at work, and in life. Culture includes values, traditions, language and all that a group or society shares. Values and attitudes refer specifically to the ideas or groups of ideas that people hold dear and that predispose them to react to certain things in certain ways. Norms are standards of behavior held by a culture that are, to some extent, based on the values and attitudes of its people.

2. Why Is Culture Important at Work? (pp. 461–462)

Summary: Understanding culture is important because culture is a powerful driver of people's behavior and organizational results. In addition, many organizations do business in multiple countries and employ a workforce with diverse cultural backgrounds. In order for these cultures to peacefully coexist, respect for and understanding of differences must be developed.

12. Organizational Controls: People, Processes, Quality, and Results

Controlling Quality, Culture, and Yourself

13. Culture: It's Powerful

3. What Are the Dimensions of National and Organizational Culture? (pp. 462–468)

Summary: Organizational culture is commonly studied using two models: the Hofstede model and the GLOBE model. Each of these models rates cultures as either high or low on a number of dimensions. In general, these models seek to describe the way some cultures view the importance of power, how they handle unpredictability, whether they favor assertiveness (masculine) or relational (feminine) behaviors, whether or not they engage in forward-looking activities, and whether they value individual or group achievement as being most important. The study of culture is complex because of the many factors to consider, including the subcultures that exist within larger cultures and the constantly changing nature of culture.

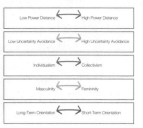

Low Power Distance	⟷	High Power Distance
Low Uncertainty Avoidance	⟷	High Uncertainty Avoidance
Individualism	⟷	Collectivism
Masculinity	⟷	Femininity
Long-Term Orientation	⟷	Short-Term Orientation

4. How Can We Describe Organizational Cultures? (pp. 468–471)

Summary: Categorization of organizational culture is often done according to the competing values framework, which examines whether cultures tend to be focused internally or externally and whether they are flexible or more stable. Following the line of thinking in this framework, scholars have classified cultures as clan cultures, hierarchy cultures, adhocracy cultures, market cultures, and balanced cultures. Cultures can also be described as strong or weak, depending on the degree to which culture impacts members' values, attitudes, and behaviors.

5. How Can We Study Organizational Culture? (pp. 472–478)

Summary: Understanding culture in organizations is key to knowing how to maintain and improve it. Edgar Schein proposes that we can study culture by looking at observable artifacts, values, and basic assumptions. These reveal both the obvious and the deeply embedded elements of an organization's culture. We can deepen our study of culture by looking at myths, heroes, taboos, sacred symbols, and language. To study culture more formally, managers can take an ethnographic approach, combining observation with co-inquiry and analysis of people's own sense of their culture's attributes. This approach allows employees and leaders to create a collective, dynamic picture of an organization's culture.

9. A Final Note on the Power of Culture (p. 491)

Summary: The study of organizational culture is important because it points out that the forces affecting our behavior and our success at work are not linked to just individual talents or even leadership. Instead, culture is a collective phenomenon that affects people profoundly.

8. What Can We All Do to Create Positive and Powerful Organizational Cultures? (pp. 489–491)

Summary: Powerful, positive cultures are the responsibility of everyone in an organization, and the keys to accomplishing this are social, emotional, and cultural intelligence skills . These skills enable you to understand your own culture and to adapt quickly and easily to other cultures and to changes within your own culture. Cultural change is sometimes necessary and can be difficult to achieve, but you can support change by respecting the values and integrity of the organization as it changes, and learning how to slow down, study your culture carefully, and choose shifts in values and behavior that will help the organization and its people.

7. How Can HR Support the Development of Positive Organizational Cultures? (pp. 484–489)

Summary: HR professionals in many organizations are responsible for and have a profound effect on culture. HR uses "push" strategies to ensure that an organization's culture and employee behavior are in line with important societal rules and laws (such as those related to EEOC and sexual harassment). HR can also use "pull" strategies to help leaders and employees study, evaluate, and change their organization's culture when necessary. Together these strategies create a more positive and productive work environment for employees.

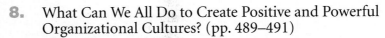

6. Organizational Culture: What's Important Today? (pp. 479–484)

Summary: Some organizations struggle with issues related to their culture because, for many years, the "people issues" at the heart of culture have been ignored and cultures have developed organically in ways that do not support the well-being of employees. In recent years, some business leaders have made a point of supporting innovative, customer service-oriented, diversity, and ethical cultures with great success. Leaders are also focusing more deliberately on developing cultures that support sustainability, social responsibility, and whole-person well-being at work.

Globalization:

Managing Effectively in a
Global Economic Environment

Chapter Outline

Find out what you already know about the concepts in this chapter by going to www.mymanagementlab.com and taking the **Pre-Test**. Your results will generate a customized study plan for Chapter 14.

1. What Is Globalization and Why Does It Matter? (pp. 498–500)

2. How Have International Political and Economic Changes Fostered Globalization? (pp. 500–503)

3. What Key Economic Factors Are Affecting Global Business? (pp. 504–505)

4. What Must Be Considered When Developing a Global Strategy? (pp. 505–508)

5. What Are the Opportunities and Risks in a Global Business Environment? (pp. 508–511)

6. What Opportunities Exist in Emerging Markets? (pp. 511–529)

7. How Has the Growth of Worldwide Trade Alliances Affected Globalization? (pp. 529–532)

8. How Do Global Regulators Affect Economies and Social Issues? (pp. 533–535)

9. What Is HR's Role in Supporting Global Business? (pp. 535–537)

10. What Can We All Do to Succeed in a Global Environment? (pp. 537–539)

11. A Final Word on Globalization (p. 539)

Go back to www.mymanagementlab.com and take the **Post-Test** to verify your understanding of the concepts. **To experience and apply** the concepts, explore the additional material associated with Chapter 14.

Part 1: Leading and Managing for Today and the Future (Chapters 1, 2, 3, 4)
Part 2: Planning and Change (Chapters 5, 6, 7, 8, 9)
Part 3: Organizing Human Systems (Chapters 10, 11)
Part 4: Controlling Quality, Culture, and Yourself (Chapters 12, 13)
> **Part 5:** Leading and Managing for the Future (Chapters **14**, 15, 16)

8. Workplace Essentials: Creativity, Innovation, and a Spirit of Entrepreneurship

7. Change: A Focus on Adaptability and Resiliency

9. Organizing for a Complex World: Structure and Design

10. Teams and Teambuilding: How to Work Effectively with Others

Planning and Change

Organizing Human Systems

6. The Human Side of Planning: Decision Making and Critical Thinking

11. Working in a Virtual World: Technology as a Way of Life

5. Planning and Strategy: Bringing the Vision to Life

16. Managing and Leading for Tomorrow: A Focus on Your Future

14. Globalization: Managing Effectively in a Global Economic Environment

1. Managing and Leading Today: The New Rules

Leading and Managing for Today and the Future

2. The Leadership Imperative: It's Up to You

4. Communication: The Key to Resonant Relationships

3. Motivation and Meaning: What Makes People Want to Work?

14. Globalization: Managing Effectively in a Global Economic Environment

15. Sustainability and Corporate Social Responsibility: Ensuring the Future

12. Organizational Controls: People, Processes, Quality, and Results

Controlling Quality, Culture, and Yourself

13. Culture: It's Powerful

1. What Is Globalization and Why Does It Matter?

Imagine you own an interior design company, and operate it out of your home. You need new accounting software, so you decide to visit a small computer store located down the street. When you arrive, the store's employees ask about the specifics of your business, and they recommend a software package. You purchase the software, confident that you've made the right choice and feeling good that you have supported a local business.

A few hours later you begin the software installation process, and you notice the disc was made in China. You insert the CD into your computer and follow the instructions that appear on screen. Soon, a problem arises—you cannot install the new software because it conflicts with another program on your computer. You call the computer store for help, and the manager says she is not familiar with the problem you're experiencing. On her advice, you dial the software manufacturer's toll-free customer assistance hotline. Your call is answered almost immediately by a staffer in Mumbai, India. After listening to your description of the problem, the staffer says that he will need to consult with the company's programmers to determine what's going wrong. Unfortunately, it will take him several hours to get an answer, because the programming office isn't located in Mumbai, but in Moscow.

This scenario is one example of just how dramatically **globalization**—the global flow of money, products, information, services, and expertise—has transformed both the business environment and society in recent years. Of course, nations have traded with one another for centuries, and ideas have been passed among different groups of people forever. Within the past few decades, however, globalization has come to permeate every aspect of our daily lives. Whether we're eating, sleeping, working, playing sports, or just relaxing, chances are we're using a product that was to some extent designed or manufactured somewhere outside our national borders.

Globalization means that businesses and people from all corners of the globe are now more closely connected—and more reliant on one another—than ever before. This is in part because of advances in technology, especially information and communication technologies (ICTs). Let's look at how technology fosters globalization and how this combination is changing our cultures and our lives.

Globalization
The global flow of money, products, information, services, and expertise.

McDonald's has 32,000 restaurants around the world, including this one in Beijing.

Dennis Cox/Alamy Images

Technology's Role in Fostering Rapid Globalization

It is impossible to conceive an interconnected global economy without technology. Former U.S. Secretary of Labor Robert Reich points out that the shift toward globalization began several decades ago:

> [Starting in] *the 1970s . . . large firms became far more competitive, global, and innovative. . . . The shift began when technologies developed by government to fight the Cold War were incorporated into new products and services. This created possibilities for new competitors, beginning in transportation, communications, manufacturing, and finance. This . . . forced all companies to compete more intensively for customers and investors.*[1]

Since the period described by Reich, there have been rapid advances in ICTs. People now know more about what is going on outside of their communities, which has resulted in global demand for access to products and services as varied as automobiles, food, music, and movies. For example, moviegoers from all areas of the world want to see the latest films from Hollywood. This worldwide demand has created a system in Hollywood (and now in India's Bollywood) in which some movies are made with the international audience in mind rather than just American or Indian audiences. Similarly, global demand for Big Macs and fries has resulted in 32,000 McDonald's restaurants in 120 countries worldwide (■Exhibit 14.1).[2]

As information about other people and places becomes more accessible, cultures begin to change. The result? Businesses change and respond as well. Changes in technologies related to transportation and manufacturing, for example, have enabled goods to be distributed in new and cheaper ways, leading to revolutionary changes in the way business is conducted in many industries. These and other changes allow companies to arrange for the production, marketing, distribution, and sale of goods and services far from home more cheaply and more efficiently than ever before.

Globalization Matters Because It Is Changing Our Lives

Globalization is changing all of our lives. It changes how we think about college, how we choose a career, and how we move up the career ladder. For example, 30 years ago, if you wanted a career in aerospace engineering with Boeing, you might be competing with 100 aerospace engineers who wanted to work in Seattle, Washington. Now, thanks to globalization, you are competing with people from all over the world for positions in offices all over the globe. The most successful professionals today are people who are willing to learn new skills, work in diverse organizations, and even move their homes and families.

Globalization has done a tremendous amount of good around the world. As individuals, we now have more choices in terms of purchasing goods, where we work, and what types of jobs we have. Globalization has helped entire groups of people across societies, such as the worldwide middle class, which continues to expand.[3] Supporters of globalization argue that the end result will be increased prosperity for many of the world's poor, as corporations and governments invest in undeveloped regions.[4] It has also been argued that increased integration of economies and technologies will make war less likely—or at least more costly.[5] This perspective is based on the idea that when all of the world's countries are potential markets, and when people are more interconnected, going to war anywhere affects individuals everywhere.

Still, some people do oppose globalization. Anti-globalization advocates have been vocal and occasionally violent in their protests (■Exhibit 14.2). They see progress toward globalism as a capitalist movement with built-in inequities that are designed to hurt the average citizen and destroy the autonomy of the developing world and indigenous cultures.[6] Unfortunately, these people have good reason to be concerned. For example, a report prepared for the United Nations (UN) found that millions of farmers in both developing and developed countries were losing their farms and their livelihoods in the name of progress and globalization.[7] Water rights are also a concern, as rivers are dammed or diverted, underwater aquifers disappear, and weather patterns change as a result of global warming.

These issues are contentious. In a global economic environment, whose needs are more important? Farmers? Developers? Businesses? What about when jobs migrate en masse away from certain countries (such as the United States) to other countries (like China and India)? Whose well-being should be considered? In light of these issues, many people now advocate a form of responsible globalization that incorporates democratic freedoms and representation, as well as protection of the environment and human rights through fair trade and development.[8]

Regardless of whether we like the results, changes in the way we think, do business, and interact culturally and interpersonally are here to stay. Countries that will be successful in the era of globalization are those that are open to change. Consider the following words of advice from Jerry Rao, CEO of IT firm MphasiS and head of the Indian high-tech trade association:

■Exhibit **14.2**

An anti-globalization protestor.

Islemount Images/Alamy

Cultures that are open and willing to change have a huge advantage in this world. My great-grandmother was illiterate. My grandmother went to grade two. My mother did not go to college. My sister has a master's degree in economics, and my daughter is at the University of Chicago. We have done all this in living memory, but we have been willing to change. . . . You have to have a strong culture, but also the openness to adapt and adopt from others. The cultural exclusivists have a real disadvantage.[9]

Globalization has huge implications for companies, institutions, and people. In this chapter, we will examine some critical political and economic events that have helped foster globalization. We will also explore key aspects of global business and how organizations develop and implement a global strategy. After that, we'll look at some of the major opportunities and risks associated with global business, paying special attention to four key emerging markets: Brazil, Russia, India, and China. We will also consider how trade agreements and international regulatory bodies affect worldwide business relationships. Finally, to conclude the chapter, we'll explore HR's role in supporting an organization's global strategy, as well as what we can all do to be successful in an increasingly interconnected world.

Most Popular » Discussion Questions

1. How has globalization affected the community in which you grew up?
2. Do you have a passport? If so, and if you're American, you are in a minority in the United States. If you do have a passport, why did you get it? If you do not have one, how might this affect you as the globalization of business continues?

---

2. How Have International Political and Economic Changes Fostered Globalization?

Globalization didn't just happen: It is the result of a number of factors that came together during the past few decades. Chief among these are the end of the Cold War, shifts in the nature and balance of power among nation-states, and changes in economies around the world. The following sections look at each of these factors in greater depth.

The End of the Cold War

Beginning in the 1980s, a number of political events helped transform the global landscape from one of clear national boundaries and spheres of influence to one of increasing transparency, cooperation, and interconnectedness. Perhaps the most dramatic of these events was the end of the **Cold War.** This "war" was a political and ideological conflict between the Soviet Union and the United States that lasted from the end of World War II until the early 1990s. It was characterized by military antagonism and economic competition between the two nations.

During this period, the United States and the former Soviet Union (USSR) were locked in intense competition for world power, with the United States seeking to spread democracy and the USSR supporting new and existing Communist regimes. This was most obvious in Germany: The country was divided into West Germany and East Germany after World War II with control given to the United States and the USSR, respectively. The city of Berlin was physically split by the Berlin Wall, which soon became symbolic of the **Iron Curtain**, or the seemingly impenetrable physical and political boundary that separated democracy-favoring Western Europe from Communism-favoring Eastern Europe and the Soviet Union (■Exhibit 14.3).

Over time, most major countries around the world chose sides—or were forced to. The Soviet Union widened its sphere of political and economic influence through mili-

Cold War
A political and ideological conflict between the Soviet Union and the United States that lasted from the end of World War II until the early 1990s. It was characterized by military antagonism and economic competition between the two nations.

Iron Curtain
The seemingly impenetrable physical and political boundary that existed during the Cold War and separated democracy-favoring Western Europe from Communism-favoring Eastern Europe and the Soviet Union.

■Exhibit **14.3**

The Berlin Wall became a symbol of the divide between democracy and Communism during the Cold War.

Norbert Michalke/Alamy Images

tary occupation of areas such as Hungary, the Baltic States, Czechoslovakia, Romania, and Afghanistan. Meanwhile, the United States sought to protect democracy and the world-wide balance of power by providing military and economic aid and by sponsoring various dissidents and regimes that tried to drive the Soviets out of their homelands.

China was also involved in the Cold War, although not controlled by either power. As political scientists Andrew Nathan and Robert Ross put it, "During the Cold War, China was the only major country that stood at the intersection of the two superpower camps, a target of influence and enmity for both."[10] During this time, China played a central role in two wars that presented major difficulties for the United States: the Korean War and the Vietnam War. The primary reason the United States became involved in both of these wars was to prevent the spread of Communism.

Events That Shook the World during the Cold War

Even though the United States and the Soviet Union never met directly in combat during the Cold War, this period was anything but peaceful because the two superpowers were constantly fighting each other by way of proxy wars. **Proxy wars** are wars that are encouraged or triggered by powerful nations but in which those nations don't necessarily participate in combat against each other. Instead, the nations use less-powerful third parties to represent their competing interests. Several prominent proxy wars of the Cold War era include the Korean War, the Vietnam War, and conflicts in Afghanistan, Israel, and various Arab states, each of which involved groups that either the United States or the USSR supported for political or economic reasons.

Another common Cold War tactic was widespread use of **propaganda**, or various forms of communication that are meant to further a specific agenda and/or weaken the position of a competing party. During the Cold War, American and Soviet propaganda took many forms, with the two countries frequently demonizing each other, incorporating inaccurate (and frightening) information in school curricula, and convincing their citizens that what they read about the other country was the absolute truth and what the other country said about them was pure lies. Some of this propaganda was based in real fears, such as the ongoing threat of nuclear war. In fact, from the late 1940s through the early 1960s, U.S. schoolchildren regularly practiced nuclear fallout drills, learning to "duck and cover" by hiding under their desks.[11]

U.S.–Soviet competitions such as the development of weapons systems and the "race to the moon" were regularly played out in the press and on television in the United States, and this contributed to the dedication of massive resources to these efforts. For example, when

Proxy wars
Wars that are encouraged or triggered by powerful nations but in which those nations don't necessarily participate in combat against each other. Instead, the nations use less-powerful third parties to represent their competing interests.

Propaganda
Various forms of communication that are meant to further a specific agenda and/or weaken the position of a competing party.

the Soviets clearly took the lead in creating and launching spacecraft in the late 1950s, NASA was born.

The Lasting Impact of the Cold War

Sadly, the events of the Cold War brought great harm to all parties involved. For example, during the Vietnam War alone, hundreds of thousands of American soldiers were killed or injured, as were far more North and South Vietnamese soldiers and civilians.[12] At the time, television was making its way into more and more homes, so for the first time in history, American citizens watched death, destruction, and defeat on the evening news. The debate over what was happening in Vietnam divided Americans, and bitter fights ensued.

Later, in Afghanistan, the United States provided arms and money to local guerillas in an attempt to assist them in driving out the Soviets. Helping the guerillas seemed a reasonable way to support the Afghan dissidents in promoting democracy. Unfortunately, many of the people who received this top-notch American weaponry and training would later become terrorists.

Finally, the economies of the USSR and most of Eastern Europe suffered profound negative effects as a result of the Cold War. Poverty; inability to access information, goods, and services; and a system that stifled innovation left many countries in shambles.

After many years of diplomacy and weakening economies in Eastern Europe, the Berlin Wall came down in November 1989 and East and West Germany were reunified. Soon other Communist governments behind the Iron Curtain fell—including those in Poland, Hungary, Czechoslovakia, and Romania—and were replaced with more democratic or socialist regimes. By 1991, the Soviet Union itself was no longer a Communist nation. As the Cold War concluded, the tenuous balance of power that had existed since the end of World War II shifted dramatically.

Fluid Boundaries and the Softening of the Nation-State

Scholar Francis Fukuyama described the end of the Cold War as the "end of history" and wrote the following in his influential essay of the same name:

> What we may be witnessing is not just the end of the Cold War, or the passing of a particular period of postwar history, but the end of history as such: that is, the end point of mankind's ideological evolution and the universalization of Western liberal democracy as the final form of human government.[13]

What Fukuyama meant was that democracy would ultimately prevail globally with the fall of Communism. In fact, as the Cold War ended, the rigid and ideological debates of previous years—those of capitalism versus communism and democracy versus socialism—began to change. The demise of the Soviet empire discredited top-down totalitarian Communism as a legitimate form of government in almost every corner of the globe. Countries including Brazil, India, and even China—all of which had been influenced by Communism—began to open their economies to outsiders. With this openness came a greater level of interaction among people, businesses, and governments. As Nobel Prize–winning economist Amartya Sen once said,

> The Berlin Wall was not only a symbol of keeping people inside East Germany—it was a way of preventing a kind of global view of our future. We could not think globally about the world when the Berlin Wall was there. We could not think about the world as a whole.[14]

With the end of the Cold War, both U.S. President George H. W. Bush and Soviet Premier Mikhail Gorbachev used the phrase "new world order" to describe a new era of cooperation between the two powers and between nations on either side of the ideological divide.[15] Emerging cooperation among nations was not the only change on the horizon. Several countries in the Middle East had been growing wealthier as oil reserves were discovered and exploited. By the 1970s, it was clear that some regimes in the region could, if they

■Exhibit **14.4**

Former Russian leader Boris Yeltsin marshals support from the people during the demise of the Soviet Union.

Nikolai Ignatiev/Alamy Images

Exporting
The transportation and sale of domestic goods to foreign markets.

Importing
The transportation and sale of foreign goods to a domestic market.

chose, strangle the global economy by controlling the amount of oil on the market. Against a backdrop of ongoing tensions between Israel and several Arab states, this change in the balance of world power was cause for deep concern across the globe.[16]

During this time there was also a rise in religious fundamentalism, which affected internal politics and international relations in countries including the United States and many Middle Eastern nations. Partly as a result of this movement, citizens of countries such as Saudi Arabia, Iran, Iraq, and Afghanistan were at times recipients of violent repression from forces within their own governments.

Alongside the rise of religious fundamentalism, transnational extremist groups like Al Qaeda began to exert more power, often through terrorist activities such as the first bombing of the World Trade Center in 1993 and the infamous September 11, 2001, terrorist attacks on the United States. New transnational powers like Al Qaeda were often tied to specific philosophical orientations and fundamentalist perspectives, rather than to any particular nation.

Social and Economic Changes Sweep across the World

Political events alone weren't responsible for the rise of globalization in the late twentieth and early twenty-first centuries. As the Iron Curtain fell and technology advanced, people everywhere had more access to information about other cultures and lifestyles, as well as products and services that were available in other parts of the world. For instance, people in some countries had been convinced that living conditions were even worse in the United States than in their homelands. Even Boris Yeltsin, the Russian leader who succeeded Mikhail Gorbachev, believed this propaganda despite having a good education and a privileged place in Soviet society (■Exhibit 14.4). Writing about a 1989 visit to a U.S. grocery store, Yeltsin said, "When I saw those shelves crammed with hundreds, thousands of cans, cartons, and goods of every possible sort, for the first time I felt quite frankly sick with despair for the Soviet people. That such a potentially super-rich country as ours has been brought to a state of such poverty! It is terrible to think of it."[17]

As people on the other side of the Iron Curtain learned more and more about the democratic West, they called for change. Countries that were just beginning to industrialize—China, South Africa, and Brazil, to name just a few—similarly desired better lifestyles and stronger economies. The end result was a rapid increase in global business in terms of **exporting** (the transportation and sale of domestic goods to foreign markets) and **importing** (the transportation and sale of foreign goods to a domestic market), as well as a rise in the production of goods far from a company's home base.

> **Most Popular »** Discussion Questions
>
> 1. Ask several Americans who were born in the 1940s or 1950s how the Cold War affected their lives, what they remember being taught about the USSR and China, and what they recall learning about the threat of nuclear attack. Then, if you can, ask several people from China and/or the former Soviet Union what they were taught about America.
> 2. Research how spies and counterspies operated during the Cold War. How do you think demand for goods that supported spying affected the development of technologies and cultures in both the United States and the USSR?
> 3. How might economic factors have contributed to the rise of transnational fundamentalist organizations such as Al Qaeda?
> 4. What shifts have you seen in the U.S. economy that can be linked to the end of the Cold War?

3. What Key Economic Factors Are Affecting Global Business?

The list is endless when it comes to economic and social factors that affect globalization. In this section, we will focus on several key economic factors: global trade, investment, and finance and debt.

Global Trade

For many years in the last century, North America, Western Europe, and Japan were responsible for more than 70 percent of the world's manufactured exports. As the Cold War ended, however, technology advanced rapidly and governments began deregulating international trade.[18] Deregulation was particularly beneficial to developing countries and newly industrialized economies because it simplified the process of exporting goods, thereby enabling them to better compete with larger, well-established nations.[19] As a result, the end of the twentieth century marked the beginning of a dramatic shift in the balance of international trade. For example, as the U.S. and other industrialized nations became heavily involved in the technology and service sectors, newly industrialized economies entered and eventually dominated the textiles and manufacturing export markets.[20]

The economic benefits realized by countries involved in the export process are numerous. For one, the development of stable foreign markets insulates the economies of individual nations from internal booms and busts. Free trade also stabilizes world markets.[21] In fact, because private sector exports have such an important effect on national economies, many governments help companies get started in foreign markets, and nations the world over have formed free-trade agreements designed to eliminate trade barriers.[22] These agreements are examined in depth later in this chapter.

Of course, there is another side to this situation: Shifts in the balance of trade also mean that some countries and companies lose market share, which translates to lost jobs at home. This has been the case for many U.S.-based manufacturing companies during the past several decades. The result is a growing trade imbalance.[23]

Global Investment

Global investment is generally a positive force because it helps countries finance their infrastructure. It can, however, also have negative effects. For example, global investors own trillions of dollars' worth of U.S. stocks, bonds, and other securities. Some economists have suggested that the vast amount of money funneled into the U.S. market by foreign investors allowed American financiers to engage in sloppy credit practices in the first decade of the twenty-first century simply because there was so much money that the risks seemed smaller than they actually were. As economist Robert Samuelson put it, "Too much money chased too few good investment opportunities."[24]

Global Finance and Debt

Global finance is the supply and demand of money on a worldwide stage. Today our businesses are so interconnected that changes in some economies have the potential for global impact. For example, during the recession that began in 2007, banks in the United States retracted the supply of money, made fewer loans, and charged higher interest rates. For businesses that rely on lines of credit or need money to hire workers or invest in equipment, lack of access to money means slow or no growth or even bankruptcy. Because the world of business is so interconnected, the ripple effect from situations like this in a few countries has been felt far away.

Another reason why U.S. banks needed to slow the flow of money during this period had to do with national debt. By 2008, China had financed the public and private debt of the United States to the tune of $2 trillion, leaving the United States economically exposed and facing political dilemmas as well.[25] For instance, because of this financing, U.S. leaders could be hamstrung as to what demands they can make of the Chinese on topics such as the environment, human rights, or intellectual piracy, fearing that the Chinese might demand immediate repayment of loans. This would cause the dollar to plummet, adversely affecting the lives of all Americans and harming economies around the world.

In late 2008, James Fallows, a writer for *The Atlantic Monthly*, interviewed Gao Xiqing, one of the overseers of China's holdings in the United States. In the interview, Xiqing stated the following about America's dependence on foreign loans:

> *The simple truth today is that your economy is built on the global economy. And it's built on the support, the gratuitous support, of a lot of countries. So why don't you come over and . . . I won't say kowtow, but at least be nice to the countries that lend you money.*[26]

You now understand some of the key factors that affect global business—but what does this mean for individual organizations? In the next section, we will attempt to answer this question by looking at globalization from a practical standpoint, focusing on those things companies must consider when planning and implementing a global strategy.

Most Popular » Discussion Questions

1. Check the label on your clothes, phone, television, computer, or bedding. Where were these items made?
2. Listen to a few of your favorite songs. What indications of globalization can you hear in the words and music?
3. Watch your favorite TV show or music video channel. List as many indicators of globalization as you can.

---

4. What Must Be Considered When Developing a Global Strategy?

Numerous factors need to be explored and understood when developing and implementing a global business strategy, starting with market needs and maintaining the quality of goods and services. Other issues are also important, such as trade regulations, laws, organizational design, and cultural considerations—not to mention myriad technical issues around such things as availability of raw materials, environmental impact, transportation, and the like. In this section, we'll take a closer look at legal and organizational design issues and also explore the interaction of global business and international differences, such as those related to culture.

Reviewing Legal and Organizational Design Issues

A company that wants to "go global" has a wide array of options for structuring both its legal agreements and its organizational design, including the following:

- **Cooperative contracts:** These are agreements in which two or more organizations pool their needs and place a single order with a vendor for the purchase of goods or services. They are "cooperative" or friendly business agreements that result from equity joint ventures, which are also known as equity alliances.[27]
- **Licensing:** Licensing refers to a business agreement in which the owner of trademarked or otherwise branded material authorizes an individual or company to use that material to sell or market products or services in exchange for a fee. Licensing is an increasingly popular method by which companies can expand their business by granting other entities the right to use trademarked material.[28]

Cooperative contracts
Agreements in which two or more organizations pool their needs and place a single order with a vendor for the purchase of goods or services.

Licensing
A business agreement in which the owner of trademarked or otherwise branded material authorizes an individual or company to use that material to sell or market products or services in exchange for a fee.

Franchising
A business agreement in which the owner of a business grants an individual or group of individuals the right to sell or market products or services under that business name in exchange for a fee.

Strategic alliances
Business agreements in which two companies temporarily team up for their mutual benefit in creating or distributing products or services.

Wholly owned affiliates
Companies that are controlled by another company, most commonly through ownership of all common stock.

Global new ventures
Start-up companies that open globally before firmly establishing a domestic presence.

Outsourcing
The process by which companies subcontract specific jobs or work functions to non-employees or other companies.

- **Franchising:** Franchising is a business agreement in which the owner of a business grants an individual or group of individuals the right to sell or market products or services under that business name in exchange for a fee.
- **Strategic alliances:** These are business agreements in which two companies temporarily team up for their mutual benefit in creating or distributing products or services.[29]
- **Wholly owned affiliates:** This term refers to companies that are controlled by another company, most commonly by ownership of all common stock. The owner company is often referred to as a parent or holding company.[30]
- **Global new ventures:** These are start-up companies that open globally before firmly establishing a domestic presence. The global new venture start-up model calls for infant companies to go global before securing significant domestic market shares, thereby securing resources and marketing channels in multiple countries simultaneously.[31]
- **Outsourcing:** Outsourcing is the process by which companies subcontract specific jobs or work functions to non-employees or other companies.[32]

Although the choice of how to structure a business is critical, it is equally important to create and implement a global strategy thoughtfully, carefully, and attentively. Let's look at some of the major issues that should be considered with respect to culture and how to position an organization on the global stage.

Global Strategy and Culture

In a 1993 article in *Foreign Affairs*, Samuel Huntington argued that world politics was entering a phase in which the predominant source of conflict would not be ideological or economic, but cultural.[33] This scenario might play out through so-called "McDonaldization" or, alternatively, through hybridization.[34]

"McDonaldization" refers to a form of global scientific management that leads to the creation of a single world culture based on efficiency and standardization.[35] What this means in practice is that things like products, services, music, art, and so on are transferred around the globe without adaptation. These become part of local cultures, and ultimately, cultures look very much the same from one place to the next. This is disturbing to many people.

Hybridization represents a more positive outlook, because it suggests that interconnectedness will not destroy individual cultures. This viewpoint holds that as globalization continues, we will see the development of a superimposed "hybrid" culture that gathers together the best of many cultures without losing distinctiveness.[36] Let's look at two examples that illustrate the importance of thoughtfully considering cultures when developing and implementing a global strategy.

Exporting Disney

Exporting can be an important part of a global growth strategy. To be successful, companies need to evaluate the potential of particular products to make money within foreign markets, shipping methods, documentation, and government regulations both at home and abroad.[37] Companies also need to understand the cultures of the foreign markets they hope to serve. Let's look at what happened to one company when culture was not adequately addressed at first.

EuroDisney theme park opened in Paris in 1992 and lost approximately $1 billion during its first 18 months (■Exhibit 14.5).[38] A recession in Europe was partially responsible for these losses, but Disney's failure to understand the differences between European and American culture was a major reason why the park faced so many problems.[39]

■Exhibit **14.5**

EuroDisney's introduction to France was difficult.

Lourens Smak/Alamy Images

Some of these cultural differences led to problems in the park's operations, such as the fact that designers failed to account for the European tradition of dining after 8 P.M. As a result, dinner time at EuroDisney involved long lines and overcrowded dining facilities not seen at the American parks, where the dinner hour is more fluid.[40] Cultural differences also contributed to difficulties with staffing and labor relations because workers were unaccustomed to company-dictated dress codes and the American management style.[41] Other Disney policies struck at long-held traditions of the French people—especially a ban on alcohol at a theme park located in the heart of Europe's wine-making region.[42]

As the park's debt mounted, executives had to learn how to make EuroDisney succeed in a decidedly non-American environment. Sweeping changes were enacted to help the park fit into the local and regional culture. In addition, a massive marketing campaign was launched that included renaming the park Disneyland Paris, lowering ticket prices, adding new attractions, and carefully targeting marketing efforts to individual countries within Europe. These changes proved successful and, as of 2008, the park was making a profit.[43]

Crafting an *International* Strategy

Disney started its venture in Europe by trying to share its distinctive culture—along with American culture. Like many companies that do business outside their home country, this is a legitimate strategy: Build organizational cohesiveness by building a common culture everywhere—regardless of differences in local cultures. Other companies, however, have found that in order to focus on local customer needs, it is important to have both foundational business practices and an understanding of local culture. That is precisely the policy of global telecommunications company Vodafone, as discussed in the following *Perspectives* feature.

Perspectives

Vittorio Colao, CEO of Vodafone, is one of the world's best leaders when it comes to crafting a global strategy that enables a company to succeed—*no matter where it is operating.* Currently, Vodafone is the largest mobile telecommunications company in the world. The company does business in more than 40 countries, using a variety of legal structures.

One structure in particular, called Partner Market Agreements, is interesting in that it enables this global business to operate in a truly international fashion, honoring the local culture while allowing everyone in the company to share the same basic set of values. According to Vodafone's Web site, Partner Market Agreements "[enable] Vodafone and its partner operators [to] co-operate in the marketing of global products and services with varying levels of brand association. This strategy enables Vodafone to implement services in new territories and to create additional value to their partners' customers and to Vodafone's travelling customers."[44]

But, as Colao and Vodafone's other leaders understand very well, it isn't just the company's structure that makes it work—rather, it's how the business is led and managed, and how its leaders and managers create an environment based on the foundational values of speed, simplicity, and trust; focus on customers; and servant leadership.

Vittorio Colao, CEO of Vodafone

Colao is a brilliant and dynamic leader—a powerful man who sees himself serving his customers and his company above all. As he puts it:

You serve as a leader. For a period of time, you are empowered to bring about changes and to build the company. People trust you to see that your employees are part of changes and that they feel as if they are doing something meaningful. And you are trusted to understand your customers. For me, that means being totally in tune with who our customers are, wherever they are in the world.

There is no such thing as a "global culture." People in each country, each region of the world are proud of their own distinctiveness. Today of course, many people do the same things: They use mobile phones, text, and Facebook. They listen to the same music and even share some values. But the way people do things and the way they express their values is different from one part of the world to another.

A simple example: I recently visited some of our companies and stores. In every single one, people were proud of our company values, but they expressed them in different ways. In Ghana, they created a song about who and what we are; in Portugal, they created a painting. Somewhere else, it might be a formal plaque

Continued on next page>>

on the wall: "Speed, Simplicity, Trust." At Vodafone, we encourage this kind of difference. The expression of our values is different, but we all share core values and agree on core business practices.

We are committed to being close to our customers. And we do something about it. We have begun to dedicate one day a month solely to our customers. We sim-

ply call it "Customer Day." On this day, there are no internal meetings. Everyone focuses directly on customers. Everyone. Even me and my executive team. This symbolic and very real commitment to staying close to our customers is reshaping the way we do business.

Source: Personal interview with Vittorio Colao conducted by Annie McKee, 2009.

As you can see, a company's formal business model is important, but it takes more than a good structure, good lawyers, and good accountants to succeed in a business that serves customers around the world. It takes a philosophy. For Vittorio Colao and all of Vodafone's leaders, managers, and employees, this philosophy involves respect and the celebration of distinctive cultures around the world.

Most Popular » Discussion Questions

1. Do a quick Internet search to study some major aspects of U.S. and French culture related to food and entertainment. Based on your findings, why do you think Disney had such trouble when it first opened its theme park in France?
2. On the Internet, find two or three stores that you patronize regularly that have international operations. Based on what you read on the Web, discuss aspects of the companies' values, ethics, and culture that you believe the companies want visible in their stores everywhere. Can you see any indication that the Web sites you reviewed are also tailored specifically to U.S. culture? If so, please discuss.

5. What Are the Opportunities and Risks in a Global Business Environment?

Globalization offers opportunities and risks for societies and also for businesses that wish to compete internationally. Businesses that want to "go global" are usually enticed by the potential of improved sales, improved quality, improved costs, and improved lead time. When expanding internationally, however, many companies run up against the dangers of uncertainty, growing too fast, engaging in poor partnerships, and encountering political and popular resistance. Each of these opportunities and risks is explored in the following sections.

Opportunity: Expand Markets and Sales

Selling products in new markets opens up new revenue streams. Considering just the populations of India and China (each has more than 1 billion people), it's staggering to think of how much buying power these countries alone will possess as their middle classes grow. It isn't unreasonable to think that in the next 50 years, Indian and Chinese consumers could be driving the world economy. Beyond these two huge countries, the world's population is increasing, as are the number of people with income to spend on products and services. Much of this growth in markets will be seen in what is now the developing world. Companies that reach these markets with the right products and services will prosper.

Opportunity: Access to Expertise While Saving Money

In some cases, a business may want to outsource or offshore work to other countries to take advantage of expertise and less costly labor. Recall that outsourcing is the process by which companies subcontract specific jobs or work functions to non-employees or other companies. **Offshoring** is a form of outsourcing in which companies transfer jobs to countries other than their own to reduce labor and other expenses.

Offshoring
A form of outsourcing in which companies transfer jobs to countries other than their own to reduce labor and other expenses.

A qualification to the opportunities inherent in outsourcing and offshoring is that with these practices, someone usually loses. For example, many workers, such as autoworkers in the United States, are concerned that their skilled jobs may disappear altogether so that companies can increase their profits. Another controversial example of taking advantage of expertise and low wages overseas can be found in the tuna industry. Samoa Packing Company (makers of Chicken of the Sea) and StarKist have used workers in American Samoa to clean and prepare tuna since the first Samoan cannery opened in 1954.[45] Until recently, these companies have been exempted from U.S. minimum wage standards. As a result, it was common for cannery workers to receive as little as $3.60 an hour. In light of this situation, Congress passed the Fair Minimum Wage Act of 2007, which stated that the canneries have to raise their wages by $0.50 per year until the minimum wage in the Samoa equals that in the 50 states. In response to this act, Samoa Packing left the island altogether to seek cheaper labor, and 2,041 employees were laid off, accounting for almost half of all Samoan cannery workers.[46]

Opportunity: Improve Operations

Increasing openness to the globalization of business means that it is becoming easier for companies to set up operations in foreign countries. For instance, a U.S.-based business that wants to sell apparel in China may find that the cumbersome process of shipping is costly, takes a great deal of time, and is unpredictable. In recognition of the fact that "time is money," the company's leadership may decide to build factories in China.

Similarly, a company that has a huge project to complete may find that it does not have enough local talent to complete the task. A new software release, for example, may require engineers, developers, and testers from around the world in order to make the deadline. A company might also be able to take advantage of unpaid help. Microsoft, for example, allows amateur software junkies to be beta testers for their new products. These individuals test the products and then communicate with others in chat rooms, Microsoft portals, and other venues regarding problems with the software, what features they like, what features they don't like, and what they feel is missing. Microsoft takes advantage of this global community of users to improve its products before their release to the public.

Risk: Uncertainty Due to Government Involvement and Political Instability

Despite the recession that began in 2007, the American economy remains one of the most stable economies in the world. The reason for this is that the U.S. has a predictable political system in which elections are held on a routine basis. Also, the separation of powers makes it impossible for sweeping changes to occur quickly. In addition, America's government does not interfere in businesses to the degree that some other governments do.

Depending on a country's political climate, your business situation could change quickly. For example, according to the *CIA World Factbook*, Nigeria is the tenth richest country in terms of proven oil reserves, making it an attractive place to do business.[47] However, political instability erodes many of these advantages, as Royal Dutch Shell (Shell) has discovered. In particular, attacks on facilities or pipelines can cost lives, dramatically reduce production, and cost a company vast amounts of money. For instance, repeated attacks on Shell's oil facilities by militant groups beginning in 2006 led to the company's decision to sell three of its Nigerian oil leases to a multinational concern after production dropped by 150,000 barrels of oil per day.[48]

Risk: Growing Too Fast and False Economies of Scale

During periods of global expansion, companies are frequently tempted to grow too fast. When this sort of growth occurs, leaders often take shortcuts and compromise on quality, which can lead to a business's downfall. In addition, a rapid increase in the number of employees is extremely difficult to manage. Just the technical aspects of recruiting and hiring at a rapid pace can be extremely time consuming. Similarly, in times of rapid growth, it can be difficult to ensure that the organization's culture develops as leaders want it to.

Economy of scale
The process of taking advantage of the power that comes with large operations to reduce costs and redundancy of efforts.

One issue that is both a positive and negative factor in business expansion is called **economy of scale**. Economy of scale is the process of taking advantage of the power that comes with large operations to reduce costs and/or redundancy of efforts. For example, in searching for ways to save money, Toyota used the same auto parts on many of its models. By buying in bulk this way, Toyota was able to significantly cut expenses. However, this practice also exposed Toyota to the risk that if one of its widely used parts was faulty, then the fallout could cause global quality problems.

Unfortunately, this is exactly what happened in 2009 and 2010, when Toyota was forced to recall 5.3 million vehicles around the world and nearly 3 million more in the United States due to "sticky" gas pedals. A total of 8.1 million vehicles were ultimately affected by early 2010. In light of this recall, Toyota even halted production and sales on many of its models, including the popular Camry and Avalon. The number of vehicles involved made this recall effort unprecedented in terms of both scope and expense.[49] Maybe more importantly, Toyota's reputation as the standard bearer of quality in the auto industry was badly damaged.

Risk: Partnerships Can Increase Exposure

Because of increased global interconnectedness, when one partner in a business deal has a problem, others may as well. For example, Toyota was not the only company affected by the vehicle recall of 2009 and 2010. French automaker Peugeot had to join the recall as well, because its Peugeot 107 and Citroen C1 cars were made in a Czech plant that operated as part of a joint venture with Toyota.[50] Pontiac also had to recall its Vibe cars because they were built with parts similar to those used in Toyota vehicles.[51]

These relationships between Toyota and the other car manufacturers highlight the fact that partnerships can be tricky. Partners must be chosen carefully, and mutually agreed-upon standards must be met in order for a partnership to be successful. Otherwise, the fortunes or misfortunes of one company can affect not only that company's consumers, but the partner business and its consumers as well.

Risk: Political and Popular Disapproval

In the United States and many other nations, the migration of jobs overseas has been going on for quite some time. This has been and continues to be a subject of massive controversy. According to some estimates, more than 5 million manufacturing jobs were lost in the United States during the 25-year period from 1979 to 2004, with more than half of these losses occurring since 2000.[52] Indeed, in 1950, about 30 percent of all

American jobs were in the area of manufacturing; but by 2004, that figure had dropped to just 11 percent.[53]

More recently in the United States, computer science, software engineering, and information technology jobs are also migrating elsewhere. The reason behind this trend is the same as that behind the migration of manufacturing jobs: access to cheaper and in some cases more-skilled labor.[54] Ironically, one of the United States' and other developed countries' most prominent exports is higher education, which actually helps support migration of jobs. Scholar Doug Lynch notes that in 2005, higher education (both traditional and distance postsecondary learning) was America's fifth-largest export, and as developing countries increase their wealth, the demand only becomes greater.[55]

As you can see, the opportunities and risks inherent in global business are complicated. In many cases, what is considered a risk in one context is actually an opportunity in another context. This complexity is magnified exponentially when doing business in developing nations. Therefore, in the next section, we'll consider some special opportunities and risks associated with doing business in emerging markets, including those in Brazil, Russia, India, and China.

Most Popular » | Discussion Questions

1. Imagine you have been asked to transfer abroad to work for an indefinite period of time. What opportunities might this provide for you as a person and a professional? What concerns would you have, and how might you address them?
2. Research job loss in the United States due to outsourcing and/or offshoring. Now, research job creation that has occurred when industries and companies have moved to the United States to do business, or when U.S. companies have begun providing services to other nations. How might these trends affect your career?
3. Research a company that has run into trouble due to the sale of foreign-made products or ingredients (e.g., pet food companies, toy manufacturers). What could this company have done to avoid these problems?

---

6. What Opportunities Exist in Emerging Markets?

In 2001, a Goldman Sachs team led by Jim O'Neill coined the acronym *BRIC*, which stands for Brazil, Russia, India, and China—the world's four largest emerging markets. This team made the prediction that these countries' collective GDP would constitute more than 10 percent of global output by 2009. The BRIC economies actually surpassed this prediction, reaching 15 percent of global output by the end of 2008.[56] Stock indexes in the BRIC countries also outperformed U.S. stock indexes in 2009.

To better understand why the BRIC nations have had so much success in recent years, take a look at the data in ▪Exhibit 14.6. As you can see, India and China dwarf the other countries in the table (and indeed, all other countries in the world) in terms of population, which gives them an advantage in terms of number of available workers and consumer potential. Also, note that U.S. government spending has far outpaced spending in other countries, as evidenced by America's immense national debt. Finally, notice that all of the countries in the table import and export billions (if not trillions) of dollars' worth of goods, which creates opportunities for the global economy—especially in countries with growing middle classes, including all four BRIC nations. For a more thorough understanding of these emerging BRIC markets, along with their benefits and risks, let's look at each country individually, beginning with Brazil (▪Exhibit 14.7).

■ Exhibit **14.6**

Economic and Demographic Comparison of the United States and the Four BRIC Nations, 2008–2009[57]					
	United States	**Brazil**	**Russia**	**India**	**China**
Population	307.2 million	198.7 million	140.0 million	1.166 billion	1.339 billion
*Total GDP (official exchange rate)**	$14.44 trillion	$1.573 trillion	$1.677 trillion	$1.207 trillion	$4.758 trillion
*Total GDP (PPP)***	$14.44 trillion	$1.998 trillion	$2.271 trillion	$3.304 trillion	$8.767 trillion
GDP per Capita (PPP)	$47,500	$10,200	$16,100	$2,900	$6,500
Birth Rate (per 1,000 people)	13.83	18.43	11.1	21.76	14.0
Death Rate (per 1,000 people)	8.38	6.35	16.06	6.23	7.06
Life Expectancy at Birth	78.11 years	71.99 years	66.03 years	69.89 years	73.47 years
Number of Internet Users	231 million	64.948 million	45.25 million	81 million	298 million
Literacy Rate	99%	88.6%	99.4%	61%	90.9%
Value of Imports	$2.117 trillion	$173.1 billion	$291.9 billion	$315.1 billion	$921.5 billion
Value of Exports	$1.277 trillion	$197.9 billion	$471.6 billion	$187.9 billion	$1.194 trillion
Public Debt (amount owed by national government, expressed in % of GDP)	37.5%	38.8%	6.5%	56.4%	18.2%
External Debt (total amount owed to creditors outside the country)	$13.75 trillion	$262.9 billion	$483.5 billion	$229.3 billion	$347.1 billion
Media Ownership	Private	Both private and state owned	Both private and state owned, although private media companies have close links to the national government	Both private and state owned	Exclusively state run

*"Official exchange rate" refers to values calculated using global currency exchange rates. Therefore, these values reflect the weakness of various nations' currencies on the international market.
***"PPP" or "purchasing power parity" amounts are calculated using rates that equate the price of a set amount of goods in a particular country to the price of the same set of goods in the United States. This method attempts to compensate for the weakness of various national currencies.

Brazil

Although it has enjoyed positive growth for most of the past decade, Brazil has not experienced long-term economic stability or widespread prosperity. This lack of economic strength is primarily the result of a past marked by drastic shifts in political ideology and ineffective economic policy.

Brazil: The Past (1889–1985)

Brazil was established as a Portuguese colony in 1534. From then until the end of the eighteenth century, slave-supported sugar plantations brought prosperity to some regions. This wealth, however, was controlled by plantation owners, who spent much of it on imported goods rather than local products. Similarly, the discovery of gold and di-

■Exhibit **14.7**
Brazil, Russia, India, and China are the world's four largest emerging markets.

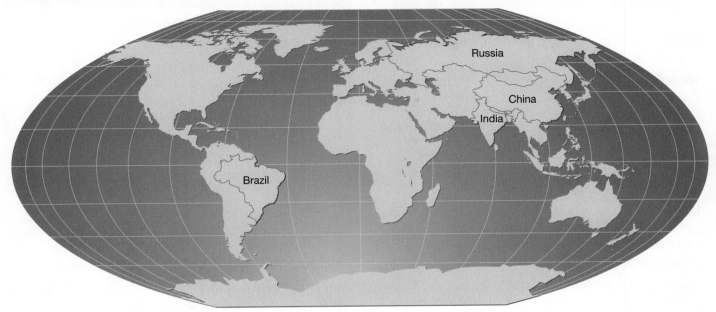

amonds during the 1700s profited individual prospectors but contributed little to the overall domestic economy.[58]

Brazil's fortunes began to improve when the Portuguese royal family fled to Rio de Janeiro in 1808 to escape the Napoleonic Wars in Europe. As you can see in ■Exhibit 14.8, this resulted in some progress as well as a great deal of economic, political, and social uncertainty during the next 170 years or so.

From the mid-1970s until 1985, Brazil remained under military rule, although the government was gradually becoming more open, with the goal of full democratization by 1985. Still, throughout this period, the country's protectionist stance allowed little importation of goods and kept Brazil largely removed from the world economy.

Brazil: The Present (1985–2009)

In 1985, military rule came to an end when Brazil's parliament elected Tancredo Neves president. Neves died several weeks later, and Vice President José Sarney assumed the presidency, which he retained until 1989.[59] Under Sarney, Brazil approved a new constitution that extended civil rights to all citizens and gave state and local governments greater authority. However, Sarney's time in office was plagued by inflation and little economic development.[60]

Sarney was replaced by Fernando Collor de Mello in 1989. He was the first president chosen via direct election in 29 years. Collor was unsuccessful at curbing Brazil's rapidly rising inflation, and corruption and political scandal forced him to resign in 1992.[61] Vice President Itamar Franco then stepped into the presidency and employed a new approach for addressing the nation's crippling hyperinflation.[62] Among many other reforms, Franco appointed a new minister of the treasury, Fernando Cardoso, who launched a reform effort called the Plano Real.[63] Under this plan, the government issued a new currency called the *real* and linked its value to the U.S. dollar (at least initially). This helped Brazil's inflation rate drop into the single digits within just one year.[64]

Cardoso's economic "miracle" made him popular, and he was elected president in 1994. As president, he continued to push financial reforms, including privatization of government-owned telecommunications, mining, and energy enterprises. In 1998, Cardoso led Brazil out of another financial crisis, this one related to a burgeoning deficit, climbing interest rates, and devaluation of the real.[65]

■Exhibit **14.8**

Key Events in Brazil's History, 1808–1975	
Year and Event	**Effects on Brazil's People and Economy**
1808: The Portuguese royal family arrives in Rio de Janeiro.	Colonial shipping restrictions are relaxed.
1822: Brazil gains independence from Portugal and establishes a constitutional monarchy under Dom Pedro I.	The country enters a period of relative peace and prosperity, and the size of its middle class increases.
1889: Dom Pedro II is overthrown. Brazil becomes a constitutional democracy, although the government remains under the control of wealthy planters and the military.[66]	Ordinary citizens lose many of their freedoms and coffee becomes Brazil's primary cash crop.[67] European immigration increases and is followed by industrialization.
1930: A military coup results in suspension of Brazil's national legislature and constitution. Meanwhile, demand for coffee decreases due to the Great Depression.	The drop in coffee demand weakens the economy, and the government establishes social security benefits and wage regulations.[68] These efforts improve the status of the lower classes and overall national prosperity.[69]
1935: After an attempted Communist coup, the president seizes dictatorial power. Society and the economy are subsequently organized into "corporations," each of which represents a major interest group.[70]	Many industries are nationalized, and state-owned iron and steel production facilities are developed using foreign funding.[71] Labor organizations are formed to oversee these enterprises, although they are largely ineffective.[72]
Post–World War II: The government continues to develop state-owned monopolies and expand protectionist trade policies.	Inflation skyrockets and the working-class standard of living declines. As the deficit increases, the government simply prints more money.
1954–1964: A new military regime arises that attempts to promote economic growth and borrows heavily from foreign governments. This regime evolves into a repressive dictatorship.[73]	Although oppressive, the new government ushers in an era of political stability and economic growth.
Mid-1970s: The existing regime moves toward democratization of Brazil's political system and eases its repressive policies. At the same time, the world economy begins to slow down.[74]	Hyperinflation sets in, and the national deficit grows significantly while financial markets and exchange rates collapse. Brazil finds itself unable to repay its large foreign debt.[75]

When Luiz Inacio Lula da Silva became president in 2002, Brazil was in a period of relative stability (■Exhibit 14.9). For the first six years of Lula's administration, the country's economy grew rapidly, with its gross domestic product (GDP) increasing 5.7 percent in 2007 and 5.1 percent in 2008.[76] Still, when worldwide recession hit in 2007, Brazil was not immune. However, the country's GDP decreased by only 0.8 percent in the first quarter of 2009.

Even with this downturn, Brazil weathered the storm better than many emerging economies, largely as a result of proactive government efforts. For instance, when global markets began to show signs of distress, the Lula administration cut interest rates, offered tax cuts to businesses, and introduced more than U.S. $100 billion in cash into the country's economy. Since these actions were taken, Brazil's economy has shown multiple indicators of growth, including decreasing unemployment, only moderate inflation, increasing export levels, and increased inflow of cash from foreign investors.[77]

Brazil: The Future (2010 and Beyond)

In the years to come, Brazil is likely to experience continued economic growth and greater recognition on the world stage. The national government is dedicated to strengthening the country's economy and combating poverty.[78] If these efforts are successful, Brazil's middle class will continue to expand, and the demand for consumer products will rise.

■ Exhibit **14.9**

Luiz Inacio Lula da Silva became president of Brazil in 2002.

But where will the money for growth come from? Most likely, much of it will involve agricultural exports. Brazil is already the world's largest grower of coffee and oranges and a leading exporter of soybeans, corn, livestock (especially beef cattle), rice, and forest products.[79] Brazil is also expected to profit from global interest in plant-based biofuels. As of 2008, Brazil was already the world's largest producer of biofuels—much of it in the form of sugarcane-derived ethanol.[80] Demand for plant-based fuels will likely grow as concern about the use of fossil fuels and global warming intensifies.[81]

Brazil can also benefit from its natural resources, including large reserves of potassium, tin, copper, uranium, phosphate, tungsten, lead, graphite, chrome, and iron ore.[82] In addition, the nation is already one of the world's top 20 oil producers, and the recent discovery of vast offshore reserves means that it could become a top 10 producer within the next two decades.[83] These valuable mineral and oil deposits have led to the development of extensive mining and refining operations, as well as the growth of manufacturing industries that rely on these substances. For instance, Brazil is a global leader in steel production, which contributes to its thriving aircraft, machinery, motor, and auto parts industries.[84] Brazil also houses large reserves of niobium and tantalite, both of which are used in superconductors and electronic components.[85] As worldwide demand for electronics grows, Brazil stands to profit, and its emerging tech industry will no doubt grow as well.

Finally, after years of being referred to as a "sleeping giant" or "the country of the future," it appears that Brazil is ready to assume a greater leadership role on the world stage.[86] The nation has spearheaded diplomatic and trade efforts within the Western Hemisphere, and it is a founding member of the Union of South American Nations (UNASUR), Mercosur, and the Latin American Integration Association (ALADI).

Globally, Brazil has played a leading role in World Trade Organization negotiations, sent troops to United Nations peacekeeping efforts, and signed several prominent nuclear nonproliferation treaties. In addition, Brazil is a member of the G-20 group of nations, and in 2009, it became one of several countries that contribute to the International Monetary Fund in order to help poorer nations bolster their economies.[87]

Advantages and Disadvantages of Doing Business with Brazil

Brazil is becoming increasingly attractive to international firms. As shown in ■ Exhibit 14.10, Brazil offers many advantages beyond the factors mentioned earlier, including economic

■ Exhibit **14.10**

Advantages and Disadvantages of Doing Business with Brazil

Advantages	Disadvantages
Economic Stability: Brazil's economy has grown at an average annual rate of 3 percent since 1993.[88] Recently, the government has enacted policies to increase the liquidity of the economy, reduce interest rates, and cut taxes in the manufacturing sector.[89]	**Aversion to Imports:** In its trade negotiations, Brazil pushes an agenda of liberalization for its exports and protectionism from foreign imports. As a result, its tariffs tend to be high. Brazil has better import relationships with other South American countries than with the United States.[90]
Openness to Foreign Investment: Brazil's government welcomes foreign investment, particularly by U.S. companies. Public–private partnerships are strongly encouraged, especially in the area of infrastructure improvements.[91]	**Potential for Political Upheaval:** Radical changes aren't expected as a result of Brazil's 2010 presidential election, but the contest brings some uncertainty.[92] Changes in governments can be more disruptive in developing countries than in developed countries.
Engagement in Global Exports: Brazil is heavily engaged in the export market, with its products being sent to the United States, the European Union, Asia, and Latin America. The country's exports reflect a wide mix of raw, semi-manufactured, and manufactured goods.	**Differing Standards for Meat:** Brazil is the global leader in meat exports, but the prevalence of foot-and-mouth disease prevents the sale of fresh or frozen beef and chicken in the United States.[93] These factors also limit access to meat markets worldwide and contribute to lowered export values of Brazilian meat.[94]

stability, openness to foreign investment, and engagement in the global export market. Of course, there are also several potential disadvantages to conducting business in Brazil, including continued aversion to imports, the potential for political instability, and health concerns related to meat exports.

Russia

Although a fast-growing economy, Russia faces significant obstacles to becoming a true economic powerhouse. Most of these obstacles can be traced to Russia's authoritarian roots and its lack of economic sophistication due to years of participating in a **centrally planned socialist economy**. Centrally planned socialist economies have a variety of characteristics that make them different than **capitalist economies**. The most important difference is that in centrally planned economies, the government dictates every aspect of the economic system, including what goods are produced by whom, how much these goods cost, how much people are paid for their work, and the like. In contrast, in a capitalist economy, what is produced and sold, as well as how much goods and services cost, is determined by the market. This means that the supply of and demand for goods and services determines prices, wages, and so forth.

Russia: The Past (1917–1989)

Russia's history reflects a combination of outward aggression and inward oppression. Through conquest, annexation of other lands, and exploration, a series of tsars built the Russian Empire of the eighteenth century into the second-largest contiguous empire in the history of the world. This empire existed from 1721 until the Bolshevik Revolution of 1917. During the reign of the tsars and of the Bolsheviks who took their place, citizens enjoyed few rights and civil liberties. Freedom of speech, freedom of religion, freedom of press, and even the freedom to earn a living in the manner one desired were often denied. This repressive internal environment, combined with the country's desire to promote the spread of Communism after the Bolshevik revolution, triggered the series of events that shaped the nation and its economy during the next seventy years, as outlined in ■Exhibit 14.11.

Russia: The Present (1989–2009)

Although the USSR had begun to institute reforms as early as 1985, the fall of the Berlin Wall in 1989 was the most dramatic indicator that the Cold War era was finally drawing to a close. By this time, many satellite countries and republics that had once been part of the USSR were breaking away and forming their own governments, thereby leaving Russia less powerful.

Throughout this period, great changes were happening inside Russia as well. Most notably, the Russian people held a democratic election for the first time in their history, and Boris Yeltsin was installed as president. Winning 57 percent of the vote, Yeltsin was popular both domestically and internationally for casting himself as a democrat and embracing a free-market economy.

Upon taking office, Yeltsin immediately set about transitioning Russia's economy from one of command and control to one that embraced free trade. Unfortunately, this was no simple task, and numerous "growing pains" soon became evident in the form of a severe downturn in the Russian economy. During the 1990s, Russia's GDP fell by 50 percent, and the country sank into a serious economic depression. Yeltsin, in a surprising move, resigned at the end of 1999, stating, "I want to beg forgiveness for your dreams that never came true. And I would also like to beg forgiveness not to have justified your hopes."[95]

Following Yeltsin's resignation, Prime Minister Vladimir Putin served as acting president until the 2000 presidential election, which he won. In his role as president, Putin governed Russia in a more authoritarian manner than Yeltsin. He also oversaw a period of economic recovery in which the country's GDP increased by 72 percent and the number of Russians who lived in poverty was cut in half.[96] Thanks in part to these statistics, Putin was reelected in 2004.

Centrally planned socialist economy
An economy in which the government dictates every aspect of the economic system, including what goods are produced by whom, how much these goods cost, how much people are paid for their work, and the like.

Capitalist economy
An economy in which what is produced and sold, as well as how much goods and services cost, is determined by the market. This means that the supply of and demand for goods and services determines prices, wages, and so forth.

■Exhibit **14.11**

Key Events in Russia's History, 1917–1989[97]

Year and Event	Impact on Russia's People and Economy
1917: The Bolsheviks, a group of Marxist revolutionaries led by Vladimir Lenin, overthrow the tsarist autocracy and establish a centralized government that tightly controls all aspects of Russia's economy, politics, and culture.	Ordinary citizens are subject to widespread repression, including potential imprisonment or death for anti-Bolshevik activities. Private property is confiscated and the central government takes control of industries, professions, and businesses. Incomes are redistributed and the state assumes responsibility for all social services. These events mark the rise of Communism.
1922–1927: Communist Russia merges with several surrounding states to form the Union of Soviet Socialist Republics (USSR). Lenin's death results in a power struggle, with Josef Stalin eventually emerging as supreme leader.	Existing restrictions on political, economic, and religious freedoms are tightened as Stalin consolidates his power. During the next 10 years, Soviet intelligence agencies are granted increased authority; political dissidents are purged; millions of citizens (especially certain ethnic groups) are deported or relocated; farms are collectivized; and government policies contribute to widespread famine.
1939–1945: The USSR joins with the United States and the United Kingdom to help defeat Germany in World War II.	Following Nazi surrender, the Cold War begins as the USSR and the United States attempt to gain influence over lands previously held by Germany. Stalin's government takes over numerous Eastern European countries. People within the Soviet sphere of influence are subject to continued political and cultural oppression, as well as increasing economic distress as a result of government policy, trade embargoes, and geographic isolation.
1953–1985: After Stalin's death in 1953, the USSR is controlled by a series of Communist leaders (Nikita Khrushchev, Leonid Brezhnev, Yuri Andropov, and Konstantin Chernenko), each of whom differs in his approach to domestic policies and relations with the West.	Under Stalin's successors, residents of the USSR and its satellite countries are subject to alternately relaxed and tightened restrictions on basic civil liberties. The nation devotes massive sums to aeronautics, the military, the sciences, and creation of an educational system that identifies "future stars" deemed worthy of development (including Olympic athletes). The vast majority of citizens suffer under increasing poverty and heavily rationed goods and services (including food). The country engages in a series of wars and skirmishes with satellite countries and other nations (e.g., Afghanistan).
1985–1989: Mikhail Gorbachev is elected premier in 1985. Soon thereafter, he spearheads a series of landmark reforms, including *glasnost* (openness), *perestroika* (restructuring), *demokratizatsiya* (democratization), and *uskoreniye* (acceleration of economic development).	Gradually, the economies of the USSR and its satellite nations begin to open. The movement in support of democracy and capitalism gains ground as more and more citizens demand greater freedoms and access to international products. The United States and other Western nations increase the amount and visibility of the pressure they place on the Soviet government.

Throughout his time as president, Putin approached the West with an attitude of antagonism. Rarely supporting the United States or Western Europe in international endeavors, he also blamed the West for many of Russia's ills while promoting an attitude of Russian nationalism and anti-Americanism.[98] Due in part to propaganda on behalf of the Putin administration, almost half of Russians polled in 2008 said they believed that America actively sought the complete destruction of Russia.[99]

By law, Putin could not run for a third term as president in 2008. Instead, he became premier of Russia (a title that was created for him). President Dmitry Medvedev was elected in March 2008 and inaugurated two months later. Although Medvedev had never before held elected office, his ascension was not surprising. For one, Medvedev faced no serious competition at the polls. More importantly, he was Vladimir Putin's hand-picked successor, and before the election even took place, he declared his intention to appoint Putin prime minister. Analysts believe that this combination of factors accounts for the fact that Medvedev scored a whopping 70 percent of all votes cast.[100]

Given Putin's current visibility and power as prime minister, along with his role in Medvedev's election, many critics—especially those in the West—predicted that the Medvedev administration would amount to little more than a continuation of the Putin administration. Medvedev was himself aware of such predictions, and he has repeatedly declared his intentions to employ a "softer style" than his predecessor while simultaneously pushing for needed economic, political, and judicial reforms.[101] Still, as of 2010, few reforms had materialized, the national government remained filled with Putin appointees, and, in the words of one commentator, "Medvedev [gave] no serious public display of independence from Putin when it [came] to policy."[102] In fact, according to a May 2009 poll, most Russians viewed Putin as the most powerful man in their country.[103]

Russia: The Future (2010 and Beyond)

In 2010, Russia is at a political and economic crossroads. Although Medvedev portrayed himself as a liberalizer, there has been little evidence of radically breaking with Putin's record of authoritarian tactics and antagonism with the West. Financially, Russia's continued heavy dependence on oil and gas exports does not bode well because the country lacks economic diversification. In the words of U.S. ambassador to Russia John Beyrle:

> *Russia's goals, to become the fifth-largest economy in the world by 2020 and to raise living standards to the current level in Europe, are achievable. But they will not be built on the basis of commodity exports and cheap foreign capital. It will require a different set of policies.*[104]

On the positive side, Beyrle also notes that Russia has a GDP in excess of $1 trillion, and as of 2009, its economy was the ninth largest in the world. In fact, until the economic crisis that began in 2007, the Russian economy had been growing at a rate of roughly 7 percent per year. Moreover, Russia's middle class—nonexistent before the 1990s—made up 25 percent of the population in 2010.[105] Russia therefore has an economy that is poised for growth, as well as a population that can support it.

Advantages and Disadvantages of Doing Business with Russia

While it simply wasn't possible to do business in Russia during much of the twentieth century, more and more international companies are now looking to Russia as a place to outsource work. Among the advantages of outsourcing are Russians' high level of education and expertise, their strong work ethic and geographic proximity to the West, and their low wages in comparison to workers in most Western countries.

Still, even after record growth in the nation's economy between 2000 and 2008, Russia's financial sector remains weak. As Vice President Joseph Biden stated in an interview with the *Wall Street Journal*, Russians "have a shrinking population base, have a withering economy, [and] have a banking sector and structure that is not likely to withstand the next 15 years."[106] Although this remark angered Moscow and may have hindered the U.S. State Department's attempts to improve relations with Russia, what Biden said is true. These and other areas of weakness, along with several advantages of doing business in Russia, are summarized in ■ Exhibit 14.12.

■ Exhibit **14.12**

Advantages and Disadvantages of Doing Business with Russia	
Advantages	**Disadvantages**
Education and Expertise: Russia has a highly educated and technologically savvy population. The nation's literacy rate is 99.4 percent, and more than half of the adult population has a university-level education.[107]	**Population Decline:** In recent years, Russia's population has declined at an annual rate of 0.5 percent, due to a combination of poverty, poor health, and a death rate that significantly exceeds the nation's birth rate.[108] Currently, the country has more yearly abortions than live births, as well as one of the world's highest suicide rates.[109] Moreover, an estimated 10 million Russian women are sterile because of poor health and botched abortions.[110]
Cultural Proximity to the West: Cultural conventions in Russia are similar to those in Europe and North America, which makes Russia attractive to Western companies that worry about the cultural difficulties that often arise in Asian operations. Also, a strong work ethic is an important part of the Russian identity, and after years of oppression, many Russians have a pent-up desire for more variety in their career choices.[111]	**Weak Economy:** Russia's per capita GDP is lower than the GDPs of most of its former satellites.[112] Output and employment are on the decline, and the ruble lost a third of its value during the recession that began in 2007. In addition, a large portion of Russian business and industry remains under the control of the inefficient central government, less-than-scrupulous politicians, or their affluent businessman friends.[113]
Geographic Proximity to the West: Russia's relative proximity to most European countries means that time differences and travel concerns are negligible. Also, the latter part of the Russian business day coincides with the beginning of the business day in most American offices,[114] and it has become increasingly easy to get a direct flight to Moscow from many major U.S. cities.	**Weak Banking Sector:** Russia's financial sector is plagued by a shortage of banks. As more and more money flowed into the country's economy during the past 15 years, many financial institutions simply couldn't keep up with the increase in demand, which meant that a handful of large, powerful banks were able to consolidate their control of the market. In fact, of the 1,178 banks operating in Russia in March 2007, only 30 controlled roughly 70 percent of all assets. Moreover, of the remaining banks, 60 percent operated with an incredibly low capital base of less than €5 million (about U.S. $7 million).[115]
Low Wages: In 2009, the averge Russian wage earner brought in approximatley $600 per month.[116] Accordingly, many Russian professionals (including engineers and IT staffers) receive approximately one-fourth the wages of their American counterparts.[117]	**Weak Rule of Law:** Within Russia, there is no firm guarantee that citizens' rights will be upheld or that legal matters will be decided fairly and uniformly. This is the result of multiple factors, including a poorly paid, poorly trained judiciary; a legal system that does not operate on the principle of precedent; and widespread corruption and strong-arm tactics undertaken by various criminal factions.[118] These conditions make Russia unattractive and sometimes even physically dangerous for foreign investors.

India

Since 1991, India has been in the midst of a financial boom fueled by liberalization of its economic policies and improved political relations with the West. According to many current scholars, India's unique approach to management and leadership is a distinct and powerful advantage on the global scene.[119] Today, India offers opportunities to foreign investors and business interests, but it must overcome significant hurdles before it can regain the economic prestige it enjoyed in centuries past (see ■Exhibit 14.13).

■Exhibit **14.13**

Key Events in India's History, 1757–1990	
Year and Event	**Impact on India's People and Economy**
1757–1857: The British East India Company assumes control of a large portion of India in 1757, ousting both the French and the Mughals.[120] The company gradually takes over the areas that make up present-day Pakistan, Bangladesh, and Sri Lanka.	The Indian people lose control of their government, their economy, and to some extent, their way of life. India remains one of the largest economies in the world, although an increasing percentage of its products are sent directly to Britain.
1857: Control of India is transferred from the East India Company to the British crown. The British government assumes direct authority over the region and grants some measure of self-government to its Indian subjects.	The British government establishes provincial councils composed of Indian members and appoints Indian advisers to the British viceroys governing the country.[121] These moves are meant to appease India's middle class but do not quell the call for an end to British rule.
1858–1919: India's self-rule movement intensifies, reaching a fever pitch by the end of World War I. Although India's economy still remains among the world's largest, the country loses ground to other nations, including the United States and Germany.	After sacrificing on behalf of the British war effort, many Indian citizens feel it is time to demand independence.[122] The spread of industrialization means that India's handicraft-based economy disappears in favor of an economy based on mass-produced goods.
1920: Mohandas K. Gandhi rallies people against British rule. His message of nonviolent resistance and noncooperation with the colonial government garners millions of followers and makes it difficult for Britain to fight the movement (■Exhibit 14.14).	More and more Indians refuse to cooperate with the British government. Meanwhile, industrialization continues to spread across India. Rapid population growth means that India must begin widespread importation of food products for the first time.
1947: Britain decides to abandon its control of India. Independence is finally realized on August 15, 1947, when India becomes a dominion within the British Commonwealth and Jawaharlal Nehru is named the country's first prime minister (Exhibit 14.14).	India faces a devastating array of problems. The country's population has swelled to nearly 360 million, and its infrastructure and social services cannot support so many people.[123] Hostilities with Pakistan result in ongoing tensions and full-scale war.[124] Without Britain as a primary trade partner, India has no market for its products; also British exploitation has left the country without the internal industry necessary for self-sufficiency. As a result, India's share of the overall world income drops.[125] Crippling poverty grips most of the country.
1950s to early 1980s: India's leaders feel that industrialization will cure the country's financial woes, specifically championing a form of this process inspired by the USSR. Consequently, they launch a centralized planning program in which nearly every aspect of the country's industrial sector is either owned or heavily regulated by the national government.	India's GDP grows at an average rate of just below 4 percent, which is significantly less than that of surrounding nations. The country's inefficient bureaucracy and business licensing processes consume a large portion of the national budget, make it extremely difficult for people to start or run businesses, and make foreign investment in India almost impossible. Between 40 and 50 percent of the population suffers from extreme poverty and high unemployment, especially in rural areas.[126]
Mid- to Late 1980s: India's leaders acknowledge that the socialist system of the previous 40 years has failed to build the economy or improve the plight of the population. The fall of the Soviet Union, the phenomenal growth of other Asian economies, and India's near financial collapse due to an inability to pay for imports illustrate that a new approach is needed.[127]	The stage is set for widespread economic reform.

India: The Past (2500 B.C.E. to 1990)

India is home to one of the oldest continuous civilizations on Earth, and for much of its history, the country was a center for global trade. For instance, the Indo-Aryan culture of the Indus River valley developed heavily traveled trade routes that unified the Indian subcontinent.[128] This extensive trade system fostered the development of handicraft-based industries such as textile weaving and metal smithing, as well as a flourishing market for Indian-grown teas and spices.

Not surprisingly, India's commercial wealth and vast supply of spices attracted the attention of many foreigners over the years. Among the first was Alexander the Great, who took control of much of the subcontinent during the fourth century B.C.E. Alexander was followed by Roman traders, Turkish and Afghan invaders, and Mongol conquerors over several centuries.[129] By the time Portuguese explorers landed in 1498, the Indian population had already been exposed to a wide range of foreign influences.[130]

During the 1500s and 1600s, the Portuguese, French, Dutch, and British all sought a foothold in India in order to obtain spices, tea, silk, and other goods. The British East India Company soon became the dominant Western presence in the country, and for over a century, a peaceful relationship with India's ruling Mughal Empire was maintained. When regional clashes and wars erupted in the country in the mid-1700s, however, Great Britain and France began to battle each other for a greater share of control in India. This marked the beginning of a nearly 250-year-long series of events that dramatically altered India's politics and social structures.

India: The Present (1991–2009)

India began to take major steps toward liberalization of its economic policies in 1991, thanks to the leadership of Finance Minister Manmohan Singh. Under Singh, the business licensing process was dramatically simplified—entrepreneurs now required only four or five licenses to start a new business, as opposed to the 80 they needed in previous years.[131] The Indian government also reduced tax rates, opened the economy to more foreign and large-business investment, decreased tariffs on incoming goods, and overhauled the nation's banking system.[132]

■Exhibit **14.14**

Jawaharlal Nehru and Mohandas Gandhi were the most influential figures in modern India.

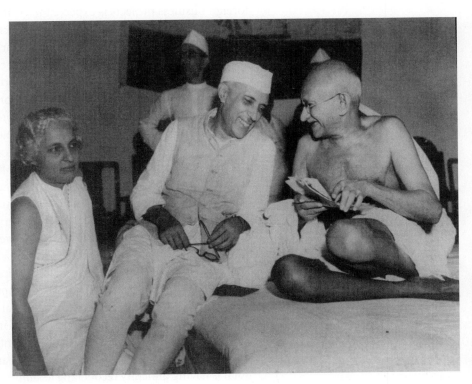

The results of this market liberalization were rapid and astounding. By 1993, India's GDP was increasing at a rate of 5.1 percent per year, and since 1997, that rate has risen to an annual average of over 7 percent, topping out at 9 percent in 2007.[133] Moreover, the proportion of the nation's GDP linked to imports and exports has quadrupled since 1985, and foreign direct investment jumped from $165 million in 1991 to over $2.54 billion in 2005.[134] India is now the world's third-largest economy, and it accounts for nearly 7 percent of the overall world GDP.[135]

Even with this phenomenal growth, India's economy is not problem free. For one, as much as 62.6 percent of the nation's GDP is based on the provision of services, and a full 34 percent of the country's laborers are employed in service-related occupations. This is no surprise to most observers, as India is widely recognized as a world leader in technical support and computer services. This sector has promoted an economic boom and contributed to the emergence of the middle class. The dominance of this sector, however, means that the country has a feeble industrial sector, with only 14 percent of Indians employed in industry.[136] Another problem is that the majority of the wealth obtained through the provision of services remains in the hands of the middle class, most of whom reside in urban or suburban areas. This concentration of wealth is the result of vast inequities in the Indian educational system and lingering class divisions linked to the traditional Hindu caste system. The net result is that millions of Indians, especially those in rural areas, continue to live in abject poverty.

Finally, lingering political conflicts with neighboring countries, especially Pakistan and China, continue to make some foreigners hesitant to invest in India. In fact, as the country began to acquire and test nuclear weapons as part of escalating tensions with Pakistan in the 1980s and 1990s, the United States and other Western countries enacted various sanctions against India. By the early 2000s, the U.S. government recognized India as a valuable strategic and financial partner and lifted many of these restrictions, thereby permitting vast amounts of American capital to flow into the now-flourishing Indian economy.[137]

India: The Future (2010 and Beyond)

The Indian government is dedicated to continued economic growth and has set a GDP growth rate target of 10 percent by 2011.[138] To achieve this target, liberal approval of foreign business projects is expected to continue, with emphasis on the telecommunications and services sectors and infrastructure development.[139] In addition, India's biotechnology sector has become particularly attractive to investors due to the large domestic talent pool, and it was poised to become a $5 billion industry in 2010.[140]

These foreign investments are a primary driver of India's growing middle class. In turn, this expansion has increased disposable income and created shifts in spending that are leading to even more industrial growth. The processed food, paper, and mobile broadband industries in particular are experiencing rapid expansion and are expected to continue growing through 2015.[141] Industrial growth is also expected to come from privatization of government-owned industries as a means of offsetting the national deficit.[142] These efforts, coupled with vast reserves of coal, iron ore, and bauxite, could lead India to become one of the top five suppliers of steel in the world during the next decade.[143] Privatization efforts are also likely to benefit the electricity industry, partially through increased access to coal reserves and partially through improved delivery systems.[144]

Current industrial growth has led to a steady decline in the share of GDP held by India's agricultural sector, and this decline is likely to continue. This is a positive signal for India's economy because it will reduce the impact of agrarian crises on the national economy.[145] Still, during the past few years, natural disasters and poorly managed food distribution chains have led to rapid increases in inflation.[146] The target inflation rate set by Indian authorities is between 5 and 5.5 percent; during the first quarter of 2010, however, this rate reached 8.5 percent.[147] The Reserve Bank of India is taking steps to fight inflation, but it is having difficulty reconciling its aims with those of the Indian government.[148] The effects of inflation on the Indian economy, therefore, are difficult to predict.

Next—and importantly—the current population of India has a dedication to economic progress. This is due in large part to the relative youth of the Indian population, with more than 54 percent of citizens under age 25. These individuals were raised in a globally driven economy rather than a socialist economy and are interested in using their talents and education for the betterment of their lives, their families, and their communities.[149]

Finally, scholars believe that India's management and leadership practices, which are quite different from American or other Western approaches, are at the heart of the country's current and future growth and economic development. Wharton professors Peter Cappelli, Harbir Singh, Jitendra Singh, and Michael Useem point out that greater attention paid to people and culture, more adaptability and creativity, a long-term focus, and a commitment to values, mission, purpose, and community set India's businesses apart.[150] Many of these attributes are in stark contrast to the short-term profit orientation of Western businesses.

Advantages and Disadvantages of Doing Business with India

India offers a number of advantages to international companies. These include a large pool of educated workers, a growing middle class, and widespread fluency in English. As with many emerging nations, however, there are certain disadvantages to working with India. The most prominent of these are the extreme poverty of certain portions of the population, insufficient infrastructure, and social prejudices held over from the days of the caste system. These advantages and disadvantages are summarized in ■Exhibit 14.15.

■Exhibit **14.15**

Advantages and Disadvantages of Doing Business with India

Advantages	Disadvantages
Large Pool of Educated Workers: In India, strong emphasis is placed on education—but only for those who can afford it. The public education system is in need of reform, but the private system provides a very good education to millions of students.[151] Many Indians receive higher education; in fact, India sends more college-aged students to the United States than any other country in the world.	**Poverty:** As much as 25 percent of India's population (nearly 300 million people) lives in poverty.[152] Just a decade ago, as many as 130 million people lacked even basic health care, and up to 226 million had no access to safe drinking water.[153] This far-reaching poverty is reflected in the nation's average per capita GDP, which, at about $2,900 in 2009, gives India the rank of 165th in the world.[154]
Growing Middle Class: India already has a large middle class, estimated at roughly 50 million people. This population is growing rapidly and is expected to reach 583 million by 2025, accounting for more than 40 percent of the country's residents.[155] By that same year, India's discretionary income will rise to 70 percent of all spending from its 2009 level of 39 percent.[156]	**Poor Infrastructure:** India's infrastructure is inadequate to support the nation's population—let alone business expansion. Roads are too small to accommodate high volumes of traffic in urban areas, and in rural areas, many roadways have deteriorated.[157] Other infrastructure problems include inadequate airports and bridges, too little clean water, and unreliable electricity.
Fluency in English: India has the second-largest English-speaking population in the world after the United States. With 21.09 percent of the country's population conversant in English, 226,449 people in India speak English as a first language, 132 million speak it as a second language, and 100 million speak it as a third language.[158]	**Social Prejudices:** Caste-based discrimination is illegal in India, and in many urban areas, members of different castes mingle freely. In rural communities, however, caste discrimination is a problem.[159] Economic development may improve conditions for the lower castes, but the social divisions are unlikely to disappear and may negatively impact India's future growth.[160]

China

Breaking free from the shackles of a centrally planned economy in the 1990s, China quickly became an economic powerhouse thanks to the sheer size of its population and its commitment of tremendous resources to modernization and economic growth. Today, an unusual mix of authoritarian controls and free-market practices creates both opportunities and obstacles for companies that want to do business in China.

China: The Past (1912–1989)

China is one of the world's oldest civilizations, and it was ruled by a series of powerful dynasties from 2100 B.C.E. until 1912, when Sun Yat-sen of the Nationalist Party was proclaimed president of the new Chinese republic. However, power struggles ensued, and it wasn't until the late 1920s that both the party and the country as a whole were unified under the leadership of Nationalist Chiang Kai-shek. Although the Nationalist Party was initially unchallenged, this would not be the case for long. Beginning in 1927, the Western-supported Nationalists went to war with the Soviet-supported Communists for control of China. The war was fought intermittently and continued to occur in parallel with China's second modern war with Japan.[161] These and other important events between 1925 and 1989 dramatically transformed many aspects of China's economy, government, and culture, as depicted in ■Exhibit 14.16.

■Exhibit **14.16**

Key Events in China's History, 1925–1989	
Year and Event	**Impact on China's People and Economy**
1925: Following the death of Sun Yat-sen, the Nationalist party is united under Chiang Kai-shek, beginning a period of one-party rule.	Despite political instability, China dramatically increases its trade with the Soviet Union (■Exhibit 14.17). Still, high unemployment affects nearly 128 million Chinese citizens, many of whom are farmers.[162]
1927: The Western-supported Nationalist Party and the Soviet-supported Communist Party engage in intermittent warfare for control of China; meanwhile, the country battles Japan in the Second Sino-Japanese War.	The ruling Nationalist Party launches a forced purge of Communists and other dissidents, resulting in the death of nearly 12,000 people in Shanghai alone. Many Communists flee into rural areas, where they work to consolidate their power. The country begins to see significant modernization, especially in military-related industries.[163]
1935: Chiang Kai-shek's attempted final purge of the Chinese Communist movement chases Mao Zedong and 200,000 of his followers across China in what becomes known as the Long March.[164]	Only a handful of Communists survive the Long March, but they form the core of a successful Communist Party. Ongoing warfare and efforts to defeat the Communists drain Chiang Kai-shek's resources, leaving him vulnerable to both Japanese and Russian influence.[165]
1937: The Second Sino-Japanese War continues, leading to an uneasy alliance between China's Nationalist and Communist parties.	The Nationalists are forced to accept Mao Zedong's assistance in fighting the Japanese, their common enemy. Meanwhile, Japan enters an alliance with Germany's Adolf Hitler and Italy's Benito Mussolini, forming what would become the Axis powers of World War II. The Second Sino-Japanese War begins to wind down, but only after nearly 20 million Chinese have died and the country's industries have been crushed. Following Japan's surrender, China's civil war resumes.[166]

Continued on next page>>

■Exhibit **14.16** **Continued**

Key Events in China's History, 1925–1989	
Year and Event	**Impact on China's People and Economy**
1949: China's civil war ends. Mao Zedong takes control of mainland China (now known as the People's Republic of China). Chiang Kai-shek and his Nationalist followers retreat to Taiwan. Both call themselves the "true China."[167]	Mainland China undergoes a period of economic restoration from 1949 to 1952. The banking system is nationalized, and the monetary system is unified with the government's guarantee to back all currency. By the end of 1952, nearly all of China's industries have been similarly nationalized.
1958: The Great Leap Forward, an ambitious economic and social restructuring plan, is implemented.	The Chinese government rejects the Soviet model of industrialization, instead placing emphasis on agricultural reform and rural industrialization, as well as establishment of farm collectives. Economic disaster and famine result, leading to 30 million deaths.[168]
1966: Mao Zedong launches the Cultural Revolution in response to the disaster of the Great Leap Forward. In doing so, he seeks to purge all Western and "old" Chinese influence. Red Guards (a cadre of 11 million youths) terrorize the country. Red Guards nearly undermine the Chinese Communist Party and are subsequently dismantled. Many members of the group are sent to the countryside.[169]	Temples and churches are destroyed throughout China. In Shanghai, municipal power is undermined, and with it, links to the West are severed. Chinese "intellectuals" (defined as anyone with a middle-school education or higher) are sent to the countryside. Red Guard activity leads to production decreases throughout the country. Later (between 1970 and 1974), the country's universities reopen and Chinese isolationism ends. As a result, foreign investment resumes, and China's industrial output grows by 8 percent per year.[170]
1978: Deng Xiaoping becomes leader, ushering in an era of post-Maoist economic reforms.[171]	The introduction of market mechanisms leads to increased efficiency. Centralized control of China's economy is scaled back, and the country begins to experiment with merit pay and free enterprise. Most communes are dissolved, and the Chinese standard of living rises. Special economic trade zones are established.[172]

China: The Present (1989–2009)

While the West was preparing to tear down the Berlin Wall, Chinese dissidents staged a protest of their own, centered directly in the heart of China: Beijing's Tiananmen Square. Led primarily by students and intellectuals, the protestors lacked a unified cause, but all were disillusioned by China's Communist Party and its continuing authoritarian rule. The protests, some of which involved as many as 100,000 people at a time, lasted seven weeks before the government took action. At that point, tanks were dispatched to Tiananmen Square, and the military chased away, imprisoned, and killed untold numbers of protestors. It is not known exactly how many people died, although the Chinese Red Cross initially estimated 2,600 before retracting the statement.[173]

Known in many parts of the world as the Tiananmen Square massacre, this event unfolded on television news, and it greatly affected how people across the globe viewed (and continue to view) China. After the debacle was over, the Chinese government arrested protestors and their supporters and banned foreign press from the country. Even high-ranking members of the Communist Party who voiced support for the protesters were put under house arrest. Widespread international condemnation of the Chinese government ensued.

China experienced significant economic losses as a result of the incident. For example, the World Bank and governments around the world suspended loans to China. Tourism revenue from the United States decreased to half its previous level, and the European Union and the United States enacted an embargo on weapons sales that remains in place today. As late as 2008, the United Nations Committee Against Torture urged China to apologize for the massacre, conduct an investigation of what happened, and

A propaganda poster of Josef Stalin and Mao Zedong reads "Long live indestructible friendship and cooperation."

Photos 12/Oasis/Alamy

release any protesters still held in prison. Discussion of the event is now taboo in China, and any press mention of it is censored inside the country (■Exhibit 14.18). Still, the protesters were not entirely defeated, and many continue to speak out to this day, although they risk their lives in doing so.

Despite ongoing and nearly universal condemnation of the Tiananmen Square incident, China was successful in joining the World Trade Organization (WTO) in 2001. Many critics felt that China should be kept out of the organization due to the government's repression of free speech. Others, however, argued that making China a global partner would help promote increased freedom. By becoming part of the WTO, the international business community began to believe that China was not going to return to a centrally planned economy.[174] This inspired confidence and by November 2001, 400 of the companies in the Fortune 500 had invested in more than 2,000 projects in mainland China.[175] Similarly, a 2006 report by the Organization for Economic Cooperation and Development states that China has become a leading destination for foreign direct investment.[176]

China: The Future (2010 and Beyond)

On the global stage, China remains powerful, both in terms of its economy and its military. China is currently the world's largest producer of coal, steel, and cement, as well as the third-largest importer of oil.[177] In addition, it owns trillions of dollars in U.S. treasury securities, which puts the United States at a disadvantage in negotiations. China will likely continue to be a powerful economic force.

Still, China faces several major obstacles as it continues to improve its economy. For one, as the country's standard of living continues to rise, its laborers will likely demand higher salaries. In light of these demands, many companies may choose to leave China in search of cheaper labor, as is happening even now. Another prominent obstacle relates to China's educational system, which does not yet fully compete with those of the United States, India, or Russia. Of course, the issue of human rights also looms: Businesses and governments routinely need to address issues such as unfair labor practices and censorship.

Advantages and Disadvantages of Doing Business with China

Many businesses already have operations in China, and still others are poised to enter the country in the near future. From a purely financial perspective, it makes sense to do business in China because of such factors as the size of the population, the rapid growth of the middle class, and the relatively low wages and benefits paid to the average worker.

Although the advantages of doing business with China may seem straightforward, some of the disadvantages in working with China are extremely complicated. Many of these drawbacks stem from the country's authoritarian government and its lack of

Soldiers at Tiananmen Square.

The Photolibrary Wales/Alamy Images

regard for human rights. In China, the state is viewed as an ultimate power that needs protection and service from the people, and individuals are not regarded as highly as in many other countries. As a result, Chinese citizens are told what they can and cannot say and do, and their safety and health are often compromised by government actions. These and other prominent advantages and disadvantages of working with China are explored in greater depth in ■Exhibit 14.19.

■Exhibit **14.19**

Advantages and Disadvantages of Doing Business with China

Advantages	Disadvantages
Population: With roughly 1.339 billion people, China has the largest population in the world.[178] More than 160 Chinese cities have populations of 1 million or greater.[179]	**Human Rights Violations:** Widespread reports of child laborers in Chinese factories have drawn worldwide condemnation. In addition, freedom of speech is greatly curtailed in China. Citizens are prohibited from studying subjects like Tibet, the Dali Lama, and Tiananmen Square, and access to print- and Web-based information is strictly limited.[180]
Growing Middle Class: China's middle class is growing, and the members of this group have more discretionary income and buy more goods and services than ever before. This growth is the result of globalization and an influx of jobs into the cities. Currently, more than 80 million people are part of China's middle class, and this number is expected to reach 700 million by 2020.[181]	**One-Child Policy:** Since the late 1970s, the Chinese government has allowed most couples to have only one child. This has led to higher adoption and abortion rates and even the murder of babies after birth. Many parents prefer sons, which means that the proportion of females in the population is shrinking. Some estimates predict that by 2020, nearly 30 million Chinese men will be unable to find a wife.[182]
Wages and Benefits: Wages are projected to rise in China, but they will continue to be low by American standards. The average wage for a factory worker is $150 per month, or less than one-tenth of what an American factory worker earns over the same period.[183]	**Environmental Sustainability:** China's rapid industrialization has led to high levels of pollution, smog, and degradation of natural resources. The world's 10 most polluted cities are in China.[184] The country is also the world's largest emitter of carbon dioxide.
Low Health Care Costs: Health care costs remain low in China for several reasons, including the absence of a legal system that tolerates medical malpractice lawsuits, as well as a lack of expensive equipment and facilities that need to be maintained. Also, China's low wages mean that health care providers must keep their prices down if they wish to stay in business.[185]	**Software Piracy and Counterfeiting:** The software piracy rate in China is one of the highest in the world (more than 20 percent of consumer products in Chinese markets are counterfeit).[186] Every year, U.S. companies lose over $1 billion as a result of this piracy. When China joined the WTO in 2001, one of its provisions for acceptance was strengthening of the country's intellectual property laws. However, enforcement of these measures has been inadequate because of corruption and a lack of training among officials, dedication of only limited resources to the problem, and a complicated system for handling complaints.[187]
	Lax Safety Standards: Chinese manufacturers do not always adhere to the same safety standards that American and European Union companies do. In recent years, this has been evidenced by massive recalls in pet food products and children's toys that contained Chinese components.[188] In addition, many pharmaceutical products that are manufactured in China contain unregulated and impure chemical ingredients.[189]

A Final Word on Emerging Markets

In this section, we've focused on the BRIC countries because of the allure they hold for countless organizations in the United States and elsewhere. As described, all of these countries are significantly industrialized and are already global players. Of course, numerous other countries are not as far along the path to industrialization and modernization, yet they too are globalizing—often as a result of tourism. Such is the case for Zambia, a landlocked but resource-rich country in southern Africa. For a brief look at some of the challenges and opportunities this country faces, consider the following *Student's Choice* case study.

Student's Choice

Mwitwa Muyembe

Zambia: On the Threshold of Globalism

Zambia is a country endowed with abundant natural resources, many of which are tourist attractions that earn the country income and attention from the rest of the world. Perhaps its most famous attraction is Victoria Falls, which has been called one of the seven natural wonders of the world.[190] The country also boasts several national parks and game reserves, the largest of which is South Luangwa National Park, which is packed with elephants, lions, zebras, giraffes, and other amazing wildlife.[191]

Zambia is much more connected to the world than it was only a few years ago. Today, people from all corners of the globe flock to Zambia to view its wildlife and other natural attractions. In fact, in 2007 (the most recent year for which tourism statistics are available), 805,059 tourists visited Zambia; this represents a 6.5 percent increase over the previous year and a 77 percent increase over the average number of visitors from 1998 to 2002.[192] Tourism is undeniably a critical source of income for a country in which the per capita GDP is only U.S. $1,500.[193]

As a developing nation, Zambia faces many challenges. As of 2010, 65 percent of Zambia's population lives in rural areas and depends primarily on natural resources for their livelihood.[194] Because these resources are also central to the nation's tourism industry, it is critical that Zambia properly manage and care for them, which can be difficult for a developing country. To further its efforts in this area, the Zambian government has created the Ministry of Tourism, Environment, and Natural Resources, through which it hopes to promote the concept of environmental and economic sustainability.

Of course, in a country where widespread poverty forces many people to rely on whatever resources are available, it is a challenge to get locals to see the value of environmental conservation. This challenge is intensified by Zambia's high illiter-

acy and mortality rates (the latter of which is the third highest in the world), as well as its low median age of just 17 years, which is less than half of that in many developed countries.[195] These factors not only hamper conservation and education efforts, but they also mean that many Zambians are becoming increasingly disconnected from their traditions and cultural heritage.

There are external threats to Zambia's economy and environment as well, such as climate change and barriers to engaging in international trade. Zambia has taken a strong stand on climate change, and it is making its position known on the world stage. For example, after the disappointments of the Copenhagen summit on climate change in 2009, Zambia's government registered a complaint with the United Nations Framework Convention on Climate Change, noting the following:

> *Zambia is one of the most vulnerable countries to the adverse effects of climate change and adaptation remains Zambia's top priority. For the country to implement its adaptation programmes . . . and to ensure that national sustainable development goals are met, adequate support from the international community is required.*[196]

When it comes to trade, a recent study conducted by the World Bank concluded that both globalization and domestic reforms are needed to improve life in Zambia. For instance, if the country had the necessary information and physical infrastructure, it could have greater access to world agricultural markets, which could increase the quality of life for all Zambians.[197] This would require a shift from focusing on tourism to focusing on self-development, and for this the nation would need global support of "liberalization of world agricultural markets."[198] Therefore, Zambia's environmental and economic sustainability aren't just subjects for its citizens to deal with—they require the participation of people from far beyond the country's borders, and gathering this level of support is sure to be a tremendously difficult task.

Source: Adapted from a case by Mwitwa Muyembe.

Most Popular » Discussion Questions

1. How would you need to prepare yourself to live and work in Brazil, Russia, India, or China? Consider all aspects of life, not just work.
2. Review the advantages and disadvantages of working and doing business in Brazil, Russia, India, and China. Which advantages are most appealing to you and why? Which disadvantages concern you the most and why?
4. Research Zambia on the Internet, including its history, current economic and political state, and natural resources and game parks. What will help Zambia more fully enter the market as a global tourist destination?

7. How Has the Growth of Worldwide Trade Alliances Affected Globalization?

The concept of globalization is fairly new, but trade between peoples and countries has existed since the Stone Age, when obsidian was first exchanged for flint. If we fast-forward to the twentieth century, we see that international trade has become complicated by countries' competing desires to attain goods and to protect homegrown industries. This tension has led to various forms of protectionism and agreements between nations to attempt to create a fair and equitable system.

In this section, we will look first at several powerful trade alliances, and then turn our attention to global regulatory groups.

World Trade Organization

The World Trade Organization (WTO) began in 1995 to help regulate and encourage international trade of capital goods between its 153 member nations, including the United States.[199] Based in Geneva, Switzerland, the WTO has two main functions: to oversee international trade and to provide an objective forum to settle trade disputes. Today, more than 95 percent of the world's trade is conducted among WTO nations. The five basic tenets of the WTO are as follows:

1. Nondiscrimination, meaning that all member nations must receive equal treatment from other member nations
2. Exclusion of reciprocity, meaning deals cannot be struck in one contract to gain favor in another
3. Legally binding contracts
4. Transparency, meaning members must make trade policies public
5. The ability to restrict trade when necessary

The WTO is the largest trade organization in the world in terms of numbers of members, so it wields enormous influence.

The European Union

It's easy to see why the United States and Russia were superpowers in the twentieth century. For one, these countries' sizes gave them great advantages in terms of natural resources. In addition, the size and education of their populations gave the two nations considerable intellectual capital. Many European countries, in contrast, have individually struggled to compete. Part of the reason is that during World War II, many European countries' infrastructures were damaged or destroyed. Cities were laid to waste, and roads, bridges, and factories were decimated. It took years to rebuild.

European Union (EU)
An economic and political union of 27 European nations (as of 2010).

Supranationalism
A type of structure in which members transfer a portion of their power to the union in exchange for certain benefits.

In an effort to compete economically, European nations began experimenting with powerful trade alliances in the 1950s, first with the Treaty of Paris, which eventually became the **European Union (EU)**. Founded in 1993, the EU is an economic and political union of 27 nations (as of 2010). The EU is an example of **supranationalism**, a type of structure in which members transfer a portion of their power to the union in exchange for certain benefits. With a structure like supranationalism, nations lose part of their individual identities and perhaps even their unique currency, but they gain the power and protection of a large economic bloc. Today, the EU also deals with treaty negotiation, foreign relations, legal matters, energy programs, coordination of development, and several other arenas.

The formation of the EU has impacted trade on many levels. One basic change was the adoption of a standardized currency called the *euro*. (Some EU members, such as the United Kingdom, still use their own currency, which continues to be a point of contention.) A more far-reaching change has been the creation of a single-market system, which has eliminated trade and immigration barriers among member countries, resulting in a powerful joint economy. For example, the gross domestic product of the EU surpassed that of the United States in 2004.[200] In addition, the EU is the world's largest exporter of goods, and the United States is the EU's largest trading partner, followed by China and Japan.[201] Although the population of the EU makes up only about 7 percent of the global population, it accounts for nearly 20 percent of total world trade.[202] As these statistics demonstrate, the creation of the EU has made this group of relatively small nations a powerful force in the global economy.

For all the strengths of such a union, there are definitely drawbacks as well. This was brought into stark relief in 2010 when one member nation—Greece—faced economic disaster partly as a result of poorly structured debt. The EU had to step in, costing member nations a great deal of money and further destabilizing economies still reeling from recession.

The North American Free Trade Agreement

North American Free Trade Agreement (NAFTA)
An accord between the United States, Canada, and Mexico that lifts tariffs and other trade barriers among the three nations.

The **North American Free Trade Agreement (NAFTA)** is an accord between the United States, Canada, and Mexico that lifts tariffs and other trade barriers among the three nations.[203] A similar agreement has existed between Canada and the United States since 1988. NAFTA also includes two additional agreements that address collaboration to improve environmental and labor practices across North America.

Although the United States has a long history of trade with Canada, it does not have the same formal history with Mexico. Remaining cool to the idea of trade, the United States' agreements with Mexico were limited to those that were ratified in the context of the WTO in the 1980s. However, this anti-trade attitude changed in the 1990s when the United States began searching for ways to form a trade bloc that would counterbalance those forming in Europe and Asia. After much debate, NAFTA was signed by the leaders of the three countries. In 1993, the agreement passed through the U.S. Congress under President Bill Clinton.

NAFTA is controversial. To start, it is not technically a treaty, although many people refer to it as such. To pass, treaties require a two-thirds majority—67 votes—in the U.S. Senate, but NAFTA passed as an "agreement" with only 61.[204] The debate over NAFTA has been so bitter that it even spawned a movement that led Ross Perot, a successful businessman, to form a third party and run for president largely on the basis of his protectionist stance against NAFTA. Perot spent millions of his own dollars on infomercials in which he talked about how NAFTA would be bad for the United States. In these ads, he urged Americans to listen for the "giant sucking sound" of American jobs heading to Mexico after NAFTA's ratification.[205]

Although it is difficult to fully assess NAFTA's impact on the American economy, trade among the three countries has definitely increased, which has led to greater integration of the three economies.[206] Some experts say this was the original intent of the agreement's architects. In general, however, the United States' trade deficit has worsened under NAFTA: Exports to Canada and Mexico have increased, but imports have increased even more.[207] In addition, although NAFTA may have benefited American corporations, the Economic Policy Institute, a liberal think tank, estimated that by 2006, more than 1 million American workers had been displaced into lower paying jobs as a result of the agreement.[208]

Central America Free Trade Agreement

United States–Dominican Republic–Central America Free Trade Agreement (CAFTA)
A trade agreement among seven nations: the United States, the Dominican Republic, Costa Rica, El Salvador, Guatemala, Honduras, and Nicaragua.

The United States has several other free-trade agreements with countries in the Western Hemisphere, such as the **United States–Dominican Republic–Central America Free Trade Agreement (CAFTA)**. The agreement applies to trade among seven nations: the United States, the Dominican Republic, Costa Rica, El Salvador, Guatemala, Honduras, and Nicaragua. These countries' relationship with the United States is a close one because of the Floridian gateway. More specifically, Florida serves as the main gateway to many countries in South and Central America, and approximately 300 multinational firms from these countries have their regional headquarters in Florida.

CAFTA is not recognized as an official treaty in the United States because it did not receive a two-thirds majority vote in the Senate. However, both U.S. houses narrowly passed the CAFTA bill in 2005.[209] This agreement removes tariffs and other trade barriers among the signatory nations. Tariffs on 80 percent of exports from the United States were eliminated immediately, with the rest following during the next several years.[210] The goals of CAFTA are to increase competitiveness, promote agricultural and rural development, improve environmental management, and ensure civil rights and fair labor practices.[211]

Supporters of CAFTA hope that it will accomplish all of these goals and, in addition, promote democracy in member countries. In contrast, CAFTA's detractors say that this agreement leaves member nations vulnerable to larger powers such as the United States. In fact, several participants have seen their debt to the United States increase and their internal foreign investment decrease under CAFTA.[212] Despite pluses and minuses of agreements like these, the United States has negotiated or is currently negotiating additional free-trade agreements with several other Latin American nations, including Chile, Panama, Peru, Columbia, Ecuador, and Bolivia.[213]

South American Trade Alliances

Union of South American Nations (UNASUR)
A political alliance that moves South America closer to its overall goal of forming an EU-like bloc with a common currency, parliament, and passport.

The **Union of South American Nations (UNASUR)** is a political alliance that moves South America closer to its overall goal of forming an EU-like bloc with a common currency, parliament, and passport.[214] All independent South American countries have signed the agreement; however, only two UNASUR countries—Bolivia and Venezuela—have actually ratified it.

Like the EU, UNASUR strives to create a single market system, phasing out tariffs over a five-year period from 2014 to 2019. A major step toward the ultimate goal of a single currency was achieved with the launch of a central bank in 2007. Another EU-style objective is to have a single passport, allowing free movement among citizens of all member nations. Visa requirements were lifted from several countries in 2006. Cooperation on infrastructure construction and environmental initiatives are also UNASUR goals.

Progress on ratifying the trade bloc has been slow, mainly because of disputes between countries. For example, when Colombia raided a guerilla camp in neighboring Ecuador, the incursion brought protests from Venezuela and Ecuador. Likewise, Venezuelan President Hugo Chavez has taken several actions, such as supporting groups classified as terrorists by the United States and Europe, which have deepened rifts between his country and other member nations.[215]

As of early 2010, the future of UNASUR was unclear because a 2009 deadline passed without full ratification by all member states. When and if UNASUR receives full support, its member nations will collectively form the fourth-largest population base and the fifth-largest economy in the world.[216] In addition, UNASUR will be culturally united in that the vast majority of its population shares a common history, religion, and language.

Asian Trade Alliances

Asian nations have also formed alliances to accelerate their own economic growth while promoting stability in their regions.[217] In particular, ASEAN and APEC have both seen success within their respective trading blocs.

Association of Southeast Asian Nations

The Association of Southeast Asian Nations (ASEAN) dates back to 1967 and was created during the Vietnam War. It began as a five-member organization and has grown to 10 member states: Indonesia, Malaysia, the Philippines, Singapore, Thailand, Brunei, Myanmar, Cambodia, Laos, and Vietnam. ASEAN is a political union with three ambitious goals: political security, economic growth, and cultural development.[218] Like other alliances, ASEAN also provides a central forum for settling disputes among the nations. To achieve the goal of economic prosperity, ASEAN is working toward establishment of a unified ASEAN Economic Community (AEC) by 2015.[219] The free-trade component of the future AEC already exists and is known as the ASEAN Free Trade Area, or AFTA.

ASEAN has also negotiated free-trade agreements with non-ASEAN Asian countries such as China and Japan. Other ASEAN goals are a single aviation market, unified cultural activities, and a network of universities. According to Fidel Ramos, one-time president of the Philippines, "ASEAN could marshal the still untapped potentials of this rich region through more substantial united action."[220]

Asia-Pacific Economic Cooperation

Unlike the EU or ASEAN, the Asia-Pacific Economic Cooperation (APEC) is not a political or cultural union, but one based strictly on economic growth for the Asia-Pacific region (some members also belong to ASEAN). Its three goals are freeing up trade and investments, making it easier for member nations to do business with one another, and increasing cooperation in economic and technical ventures. Like ASEAN, APEC has a consortium of study centers at large universities.

APEC seeks to achieve a free-market trade area by lifting tariffs to industrialized countries by 2010 and to developing countries by 2020. Since its inception, trade involving APEC nations has grown nearly 400 percent.[221]

Beyond trade blocs, countries often come together to discuss economic issues that affect the entire world. Leaders have several different forums for conducting these discussions, and we will explore a few of them in the next section of the chapter.

Most Popular » Discussion Questions

1. Within the EU, people can move freely between countries and can work in any member country without a visa. This is not true under NAFTA provisions. What are the pros and cons of each approach?
2. In the United States, there is bitter debate about the topic of immigration, and this debate often focuses on Mexico. What is your opinion on this issue? Be sure to support your argument with research from both sides of the debate.
3. Using the Internet, find several reliable sources that describe how one American company has been hurt by NAFTA and another has been helped.

8. How Do Global Regulators Affect Economies and Social Issues?

Another way in which global economic matters are regulated is through global monetary policies that are developed by international bodies such as the Group of Twenty, the World Economic Forum, and the United Nations Economic and Social Council. Each of these bodies is discussed in turn in the next three sections.

Group of Twenty

Group of Twenty (G-20)
Representatives of 20 major economies who meet at least once a year to help secure global economic cooperation.

The **Group of Twenty (G-20)** includes representatives of 20 major economies who meet at least once a year to help secure global economic cooperation. The goal of the G-20 is to encourage economic cooperation for the collective good rather than support individual countries' interests.[222] Combined, the group members' economies add up to 90 percent of the world's GDP, 80 percent of global trade, and 67 percent of the world's population.[223] All three North American countries—the U.S., Canada, and Mexico—are represented. Argentina and Brazil are the sole South American participants, and the European Union as a single entity is a member, along with France, Germany, Italy, and the United Kingdom, which have distinct representation as well. The two Eurasian member economies are Russia and Turkey, and the Asian and Middle Eastern countries in the G-20 are China, India, Indonesia, Japan, Saudi Arabia, and South Korea. Australia and South Africa are also members.

International Monetary Fund (IMF)
A United Nations agency that promotes currency stability and lends reserve currencies to nations with trade deficits.

World Bank
An international banking organization that provides capital supplied by member governments to underdeveloped nations.

The G-20 also includes the managing director of the IMF and the president of the World Bank, two financial bodies that support global finance.[224] The **International Monetary Fund (IMF)** is a United Nations agency that promotes currency stability and lends reserve currencies to nations with trade deficits. The **World Bank** is an international banking organization that provides capital supplied by member governments to underdeveloped nations.

Each year, the financial minister of one G-20 nation acts as chairperson for the group. The chair is one-third of a revolving management team, known as the Troika, along with the previous year's chair and the chair for the following year.[225] The chair's country hosts the annual summit of the G-20 leaders. In 2008 and 2009, two summits were held each year due to the global economic crisis, and two meetings were planned for 2010.

Each summit results in an action plan, which is implemented by various G-20 working groups. Working groups are co-chaired by representatives from one established economy and one emerging economy. As of 2009–2010, working groups are focusing on the following areas: regulation and transparency, cooperation and integrity, International Monetary Fund reform, and policy examination of the World Bank and other multilateral development banks.

To achieve its goal of global economic cooperation, the G-20 promotes five major points: global trade and investment; financial supervision and regulation; international financial institution funding and reform; inclusive, sustainable market building; and confidence, growth, and job building.[226] These points support efforts to build a strong global economy by encouraging members to reject protectionist tariffs and increase regulation of their own financial systems. Member countries also promise to support emerging and troubled nations. Finally, the G-20 stresses the importance of protecting and providing for world citizens through economic activities and interventions.[227] By creating a forum for leaders to understand global interconnectedness, the G-20 represents a powerful supporting force to the world's overall financial health.

The World Economic Forum

World Economic Forum
A not-for-profit organization that claims no ties to political, partisan, or national agendas and brings together business, political, social, and intellectual leaders from around the world.

The World Economic Forum is also called the Davos Economic Forum after the Swiss village in which the annual meeting is held. The **World Economic Forum** is a not-for-profit organization that claims no ties to political, partisan, or national agendas and brings together business, political, social, and intellectual leaders from around the world.[228]

The mission of the World Economic Forum is to improve the overall state of the world. Unlike the IMF or the World Bank, the World Economic Forum does not accomplish this by providing funding to nations in need. Rather, it engages its members in ongoing projects to address what it identifies as the major challenges facing today's world.[229] For example, in 2002, members of the forum contributed funds for research trials of a microbicide designed to protect women in Africa from HIV/AIDS.[230] Today, the World Economic Forum focuses on diverse projects such as sustainable food production, disaster recovery, global education, and humanitarian relief, as well as business, management, and economic issues.[231]

In addition to these projects, the group promotes the idea of responsible governance among its 1,200 corporate members as a means of generating stability within the global economy.[232] The World Economic Forum bases all of these efforts on the idea that no single sector—governmental, business, or social—can meet today's challenges alone, and only through continuous collaboration can these three sectors successfully improve the world.[233]

Although the ideals of the World Economic Forum are admirable, critics object to what they view as the World Economic Forum's acceptance of free trade, market capitalism, and deregulation of business.[234] Some even suggest that the economic downturn of the late 2000s was the result of policies embraced by the forum and its members within the business community.[235] Still, the World Economic Forum remains an important force for shaping social initiatives and corporate practices around the world.

United Nations Economic and Social Council

The United Nations (UN) influences the world's economy primarily through the development of loan and aid programs designed to promote higher standards of living within UN member states. Up to 70 percent of these loans and aid are overseen by the Economic and Social Council (ECOSOC).[236]

In addition to the ECOSOC, UN bodies act to support people and nations through programs tied to international relations. These programs provide much needed help, but can be difficult to manage. Such was the case with the Oil-for-Food program developed by the UN Security Council in 1995. Designed to ensure that average Iraqi citizens were able to obtain clean water, sufficient food, and basic supplies despite UN sanctions against the nation, the program provided the Iraqi government with the opportunity to export oil to member states with the understanding that the profits from these sales would finance humanitarian efforts.[237] The program was successful in lessening the impact of economic sanctions on Iraqi citizens by increasing their nutrition levels.[238] Unfortunately, the program also suffered from mismanagement and allegations of wrongdoing. It is estimated that through the program, Saddam Hussein's government made several billion dollars of profit by embezzling funds and smuggling oil out of the country illegally.[239]

These problems arose primarily because the office established to oversee the program lacked the authority and the resources necessary to prevent them.[240] Enforcement of the agreement was ultimately the responsibility of individual UN member states, some of which were allegedly engaged in illegal trade with the Iraqi government.[241] Situations such as these give additional credence to experts' calls for UN reforms.

Trade agreements and regulatory bodies have an important role in globalization. Still, when it comes down to what happens within a company and between the company and its host countries, individual people make decisions about what to do and how to do it. Accordingly, many companies do their utmost to prepare people to live and work abroad, as described in the next section.

Most Popular » Discussion Questions

1. A number of powerful associations and regulatory bodies have been established to impact global business. What is your opinion about outside entities controlling aspects of international business? Back up your opinion with research on both sides of the issue.
2. Why do you think people care enough about what the G-20 does to protest the organization and risk getting hurt or arrested?
3. In your opinion, why is the G-20 the subject of far more protests than the World Economic Forum or the United Nations?

---

9. What Is HR's Role in Supporting Global Business?

If a global business is to be successful, every part of the business must be aligned and able to "do its part"—often far from home and in difficult situations. Things like company rules, guidelines, ethical codes, pay structures, and travel policies all contribute to individual employees' understandings about how to behave, make decisions, and thrive personally in a global business environment. This is especially true when people move house, home, and family to another country to work. To prepare people for this exciting and challenging experience, HR is often charged with creating and supporting workforce development programs to help people succeed in countries other than their own. In this section, we will first look at a case study to see how teams can be used to help a company understand its global market, then at competencies that can help employees succeed globally.

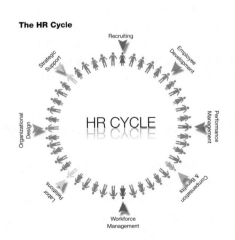

The HR Cycle

The Expat Experience: Team-Based Learning

Expatriate or "expat" employees are those who work outside their home country, sometimes for extended periods of time. Multinational organizations and governments rely on expatriates to act as knowledge transfer agents and representatives.[242] These jobs are important and also challenging. First, conducting business in a foreign country, even one where people speak the same language, requires a deep understanding of the local cultural, business, and legal environment, as well as the culture of the organization in that country.[243] When it comes to finding the best way to develop talented employees and prepare them for an international assignment, we can learn some lessons from IBM, as discussed in the *Business Case*.

What IBM did with these programs is an excellent example of effective workforce development. The company clearly identified the need to prepare people and give them the experience of working internationally. Then, HR and others fostered a very

IBM

Building a Culture of Collaboration

In the early 1990s, IBM wasn't what most people would describe as a highly effective, high-performing, and collaborative working environment.[244] To deal with this, leaders made a considerable investment in stimulating a new culture, tightening up HR, and developing programs that fostered new and more effective ways for employees to work together.[245] Among the many initiatives IBM undertook, three in particular stand out in terms of their impact: the Extreme Blue internship program, the IBM Speed Teams Initiative, and the Corporate Services Corps.

The Extreme Blue™ internship program puts together teams from across IBM to stimulate creativity in key projects. The four-person teams, each covering a mix of technical and business knowledge, are deployed every summer to support more than 50 projects across the United States, Europe, China, India, Brazil, and Canada.[246] An extension of this program, called the IBM Speed Teams initiative, is used to induct and engage new talent by setting up teams around real IBM business needs.[247] Both programs also benefit from the practice of mentoring and shadowing that allows team members access to top experts in fields related to their projects.

Innovative programs at IBM foster collaboration

All of these projects help employees work with people far from their home offices—learning from one another about cultures, business in certain regions, and local practices.

Building on these two successful examples, IBM next decided to foster collaboration in its emerging markets through its Corporate Service Corps. In this program, IBM creates teams of high-performing, experienced employees and sends them into month-long interventions in markets such as Romania, Turkey, Ghana, Vietnam, the Philippines, and Tanzania.[248] Over the course of the month, each member of the team works with local organizations to contribute their expertise while learning about the local culture, specific business needs, and creative ways IBM can be involved.[249] These efforts have yielded results far beyond the specific projects on which the teams worked. As IBM's vice president of corporate citizenship Stanley Litow notes, "The premier new emerging markets are in places where most big companies don't yet do a lot of business—and we want to build a leadership cadre that learns about these places and also learns to exchange their diverse backgrounds and skills."[250]

Photo Source: Kuzma/Shutterstock

visible and important company-wide initiative to promote individual employees' knowledge and understanding about other countries and cultures.

Coaching for Success: Helping Employees and Managers Adjust to Globalization

HR Leadership Roles

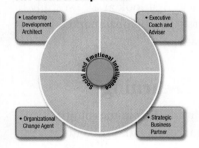

Managing an international or global organization is challenging for many reasons, not the least of which relates to helping employees interact with one another when their cultures are very different. Preparation for even a brief period of working abroad is important. But what about when people are sent to another country for an extended period of time? How can HR support employees in dealing with the many personal and professional challenges that come with long-term living and working abroad?

One important way that HR can help in this situation is to provide expat employees with coaches. Trained coaches can provide much-needed guidance on the complex issues related to working outside of one's home country.

Executive coaching has become very popular in recent years. In the early days of the profession, many coaches were retired employees coming back to give advice, and others were psychologists. As the field of coaching began to mature, many more people entered the field: therapists, consultants, even people with little or no training in organizational behavior, leadership, or management. This resulted in many problems: Untrained coaches can do a great deal of harm to individuals and even companies. In addition, the popularity of coaching resulted in some organizations hiring dozens, even hundreds, of coaches, none of whom coordinated with one another and none of whom were managed by the organization. Because of these problems, more and more organizations are formally training HR professionals to be coaches. The best training programs, such as those certified by the International Coach Federation, include training in coaching ethics and coaching competencies (e.g., active listening, establishing trust, and self-awareness).[251]

Coach training is important in any setting, and it is absolutely essential in a cross-cultural environment because of the added complexity. Tips for coaching success in such an environment include the following:

- Understand your client's culture and the host country culture.
- Deliberately build a strong, trusting, and confidential relationship.
- Have a plan for the overall coaching engagement (e.g., what will be worked on for the first third of the time period, the second third, and so on).
- Ensure that you help your client focus on the future and his or her dreams, not just the problems he or she faces at the present time.
- Do not prolong the coaching relationship beyond the time you are needed.

We are fortunate to have the opportunity to live and work abroad or to work with people who come from places far from our homes. We have many choices about how to make these interactions and our cross-cultural workplaces most effective. Our HR departments can help tremendously. And we can also help a great deal ourselves, as we will see in the next section.

Most Popular » Discussion Questions

1. Think about an experience you have had working or living in a community and culture not your own. If you haven't had an international experience, consider a time when you joined a new organization at your school or when you took a new job. How did you learn about the business practices and culture in the new setting?
2. When you visit a country or a region that has a different culture than your own, what do you do to try to "fit in"?

---

10. What Can We All Do to Succeed in a Global Environment?

Globalization requires us to learn and change. Often, our attitudes, values, and even ethics will be challenged when working abroad or working with people from other cultures. In this section, we'll look at two key areas that you will need to attend to in order to be successful in our global work environment: values and ethics, and your emotional and social competencies.

The Intersection between Personal Ethics, Societal Ethics, and Company Ethics

Professor Ronald Sims argues that ethical failures at the organizational level are failures of leadership to integrate the values and ethics of key stakeholders.[252] What that means for you is that you need to be clear about your own values and ethics, as well as those of

■Exhibit **14.20**

Knowing where the intersection between personal ethics, societal ethics, and company ethics lies is key to operating successfully in a country other than your own.

your society and your organization. You need to be able to see where differences lie and seek to resolve them, as shown in ■Exhibit 14.20.

Understanding values and ethics this way requires thoughtfulness, openness, and critical thinking. That is partly because it is easy to underestimate or ignore differences between cultures when it comes to ethics and values. If you can't see differences, you are unlikely to resolve them. In addition, it's easy to assume that people will always follow an organization's code of ethics. However, this simply doesn't happen all the time. People don't always defer to an organization's code of ethics, in part because personal values may be a more powerful driver of behavior.

Another potential problem is that external codes of ethics (like an organization's ethical code) can be seen to constrain behavior, which many people resist. Values, on the other hand, are motivating because they are deeply held beliefs about right and wrong, good and bad. In other words, ethics act as a kind of legal code that tells us what not to do and reminds us of the consequences, whereas values propel us toward what we want to obtain or achieve.[253]

So, whose values and ethics win? That is one of today's biggest leadership challenges. The resolution starts with each of us examining what we believe and finding ways to craft codes of ethics that work for us, our societies, and our companies—even when it means changing some of our values and ethics in support of healthy businesses and healthy societies.

Competencies That Support Working Abroad

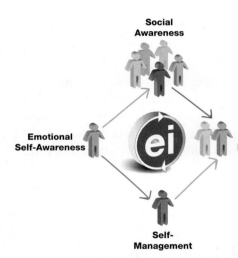

International managers report that communication is a very important skill to consider when choosing employees for expatriate assignments.[254] For example, international business communication researcher Lena Zander conducted a study of leadership preferences in 16 countries and among 15,000 employees. She found that even when the languages were similar, leaders differed in their communication preferences in important areas, such as general and personal communication, achievement reviews, and feedback.[255]

In addition to communication, other competencies are central to success when you work abroad, such as many of the emotional and social competencies you have learned about in this book.

For example, exploring your emotions is important because working in a culture other than your own tends to provoke strong emotions such as excitement, confusion, and anxiety. If you know what you are feeling, you are much more likely to engage in self-management and not say or do things that are inappropriate. Organizational awareness will support you in assessing both the organizational environment and the culture within which your organization operates—again, helping you behave in an appropriate and even inspiring manner. Of course, adaptability is essential. You simply can't do or say many things the way you do at home. You need to be willing to adjust your approach to teamwork, management, and social relationships.

To develop your competencies, you'll want to start with a vision of why this learning is important to you. Maybe you envision yourself working abroad, or you want to be considered a global citizen. Or, maybe you want a life that includes travel. Whatever your dream, being clear about it will give you energy for the learning process as you develop your social and emotional competencies.

> **Most Popular »** Discussion Questions
>
> 1. Choose a company that does business in the United States and in several countries that have different values and ethics when it comes to things like nepotism, bribery, and negotiating the price of goods. What dilemmas might employees face? How would you deal with these ethical dilemmas?
> 2. Which competencies and personal strengths do you have that would help you work in a country other than your own? Consider social and emotional intelligence competencies, personal resiliency, and your experience with other cultures.
> 3. What personal challenges do you believe would interfere with your effectiveness working in a country other than your own? What can you do to minimize the impact of these problems?

11. A Final Word on Globalization

Globalization is touching virtually every aspect of our lives, from what we can and want to buy, to music, to culture, to work. Although this trend has emerged over several centuries of social, political, and economic change, it is now moving fast, and the effects are rippling across the planet.

Looking back 50 years from now, people may say that the technological, environmental, and social changes we are currently experiencing were the beginning of a "new world order." As you engage in this exciting and challenging time of globalization, you have a chance to impact the world in ways unimaginable to your grandparents. What will you do to help your friends, family, community, nation, and world adopt practices that will enable us all to connect positively and effectively across the globe? What will you do at work to ensure that your company benefits from globalization while also supporting places and people far from home?

Today's global environment offers tremendous opportunity. Take advantage of it!

Key Terms

1. **What Is Globalization and Why Does It Matter?**   (pp. 498–500)

Key Terms

Globalization The global flow of money, products, information, services, and expertise. p. 498

2. **How Have International Political and Economic Changes Fostered Globalization?** (pp. 500–503)

Key Terms

Cold War A political and ideological conflict between the Soviet Union and the United States that lasted from the end of World War II until the early 1990s. It was characterized by military antagonism and economic competition between the two nations. p. 500

Iron Curtain The seemingly impenetrable physical and political boundary that existed during the Cold War and separated democracy-favoring Western Europe from Communism-favoring Eastern Europe and the Soviet Union. p. 500

Proxy wars Wars that are encouraged or triggered by powerful nations but in which those nations don't necessarily participate in combat against each other. Instead, the nations use less-powerful third parties to represent their competing interests. p. 501

Propaganda Various forms of communication that are meant to further a specific agenda and/or weaken the position of a competing party. p. 501

Exporting The transportation and sale of domestic goods to foreign markets. p. 503

Importing The transportation and sale of foreign goods to a domestic market. p. 503

3. What Key Economic Factors Are Affecting Global Business? (pp. 504–505)

Key Terms None

4. What Must Be Considered When Developing a Global Strategy? (pp. 505–508)

Key Terms

Cooperative contracts Agreements in which two or more organizations pool their needs and place a single order with a vendor for the purchase of goods or services. p. 505

Licensing A business agreement in which the owner of trademarked or otherwise branded material authorizes an individual or company to use that material to sell or market products or services in exchange for a fee. p. 505

Franchising A business agreement in which the owner of a business grants an individual or group of individuals the right to sell or market products or services under that business name in exchange for a fee. p. 506

Strategic alliances Business agreements in which two companies temporarily team up for their mutual benefit in creating or distributing products or services. p. 506

Wholly owned affiliates Companies that are controlled by another company, most commonly through ownership of all common stock. p. 506

Global new ventures Start-up companies that open globally before firmly establishing a domestic presence. p. 506

Outsourcing The process by which companies subcontract specific jobs or work functions to non-employees or other companies. p. 506

5. What Are the Opportunities and Risks in a Global Business Environment? (pp. 508–511)

Key Terms

Offshoring A form of outsourcing in which companies transfer jobs to countries other than their own to reduce labor and other expenses. p. 509

Economy of scale The process of taking advantage of the power that comes with large operations to reduce costs and redundancy of efforts. p. 510

6. What Opportunities Exist in Emerging Markets? (pp. 511–529)

Key Terms

Centrally planned socialist economy An economy in which the government dictates every aspect of the economic system, including what goods are produced by whom, how much these goods cost, how much people are paid for their work, and the like. p. 516

Capitalist economy An economy in which what is produced and sold, as well as how much goods and services cost, is determined by the market. This means that the supply of and demand for goods and services determines prices, wages, and so forth. p. 516

7. How Has the Growth of Worldwide Trade Alliances Affected Globalization? (pp. 529–532)

Key Terms

European Union (EU) An economic and political union of 27 European nations (as of 2010). p. 530

Supranationalism A type of structure in which members transfer a portion of their power to the union in exchange for certain benefits. p. 530

North American Free Trade Agreement (NAFTA) An accord between the United States, Canada, and Mexico that lifts tariffs and other trade barriers among the three nations. p. 530

United States–Dominican Republic–Central America Free Trade Agreement (CAFTA) A trade agreement among seven nations: the United States, the Dominican Republic, Costa Rica, El Salvador, Guatemala, Honduras, and Nicaragua. p. 531

Union of South American Nations (UNASUR) A political alliance that moves South America closer to its overall goal of forming an EU-like bloc with a common currency, parliament, and passport. p. 531

8. How Do Global Regulators Affect Economies and Social Issues?   (pp. 533–535)

Key Terms

Group of Twenty (G-20) Representatives of 20 major economies who meet at least once a year to help secure global economic cooperation. p. 533

International Monetary Fund (IMF) A United Nations agency that promotes currency stability and lends reserve currencies to nations with trade deficits. p. 533

World Bank An international banking organization that provides capital supplied by member governments to underdeveloped nations. p. 533

World Economic Forum A not-for-profit organization that claims no ties to political, partisan, or national agendas and brings together business, political, social, and intellectual leaders from around the world. p. 533

9. What Is HR's Role in Supporting Global Business?   (pp. 535–537)

Key Terms None

10. What Can We All Do to Succeed in a Global Environment?   (pp. 537–539)

Key Terms None

11. A Final Word on Globalization   (p. 539)

Key Terms None

Chapter 14 Visual Summary

1. What Is Globalization and Why Does It Matter? (pp. 498–500)

Summary: Globalization is the flow of money, products, information, services, and expertise around the world, and it has drastically changed the business environment during the past few decades. This is due in large part to technologies that enable us to connect with other nations and people. Globalization is a transformational force that is changing the way we think about school, work, and life. It is a process that requires organizations to be open to and responsible about change in order to be successful.

2. How Have International Political and Economic Changes Fostered Globalization? (pp. 500–503)

Summary: The conclusion of the Cold War ended decades of conflict between Communist and capitalist nations, bringing about new opportunities for growth and understanding in both. Ultimately, these opportunities led citizens around the world to demand better products and an improved quality of life that can only come about through cooperation among the nations of the world. At the same time, concerns over oil reserves and the growing strength of terrorist groups have also affected and changed economies and political balances around the world. These changes suggest that globalization is more than just a business phenomenon; it is a social and economic phenomenon.

16. Managing and Leading for Tomorrow: A Focus on Your Future

14. Globalization: Managing Effectively In a Global Economic Environment

1. Managing and Leading Today: The New Rules

Leading and Managing for Today and the Future

2. The Leadership Imperative: It's Up to You

4. Communication: The Key to Resonant Relationships

3. Motivation and Meaning: What Makes People Want to Work?

15. Sustainability and Corporate Social Responsibility: Ensuring the Future

3. What Key Economic Factors Are Affecting Global Business? (pp. 504–505)

Summary: Global trade is one of the predominant factors affecting global business, due in large part to deregulation and relaxation of trade restrictions after the Cold War. Increased international trade has led to an interconnectedness of world economies that has given rise to investment and financial opportunities on a global scale. Culture is yet another important aspect of global business and a potential casualty of globalization if leaders do not take care to hybridize, rather than standardize, characteristics of groups and nations.

Exhibit 14.9

Key Events in Brazil's History, 1808–1975

Year and Event	Effects on Brazil's People and Economy
1808: The Portuguese royal family arrives in Rio de Janeiro.	Colonial shipping restrictions are relaxed.
1822: Brazil gains independence from Portugal and establishes a constitutional monarchy under Dom Pedro I.	The country enters a period of relative peace and prosperity, and the size of its middle class increases.
1889: Dom Pedro II is overthrown. Brazil becomes a constitutional democracy, although the government remains under the control of wealthy planters and the military.[66]	Ordinary citizens lose many of their freedoms and coffee becomes Brazil's primary cash crop.[67] European immigration increases and is followed by industrialization.
1930: A military coup results in suspension of Brazil's national legislature and constitution. Meanwhile, demand for coffee decreases due to the Great Depression.	The drop in coffee demand weakens the economy, and the government establishes social security benefits and wage regulations.[68] These efforts improve the status of the lower classes and overall national prosperity.[69]
1935: After an attempted Communist coup, the president seizes dictatorial power. Society and the economy are subsequently organized into "corporations," each of which represents a major interest group.[70]	Many industries are nationalized, and state-owned iron and steel production facilities are developed using foreign funding.[71] Labor organizations are formed to oversee these enterprises, although they are largely ineffective.[72]
Post–World War II: The government continues to develop state-owned monopolies and expand protectionist trade policies.	Inflation skyrockets and the working-class standard of living declines. As the deficit increases, the government simply prints more money.
1964–1984: A new military regime arises that attempts to promote economic growth and borrows heavily from foreign governments. This regime evolves into a repressive dictatorship.[73]	Although oppressive, the new government ushers in an era of political stability and economic growth.
Mid-1970s: The existing regime moves toward democratization of Brazil's political system and eases its repressive policies. At the same time, the world economy begins to slow down.[74]	Hyperinflation sets in, and the national deficit grows significantly while financial markets and exchange rates collapse. Brazil finds itself unable to repay its large foreign debt.[75]

4. What Must Be Considered When Developing a Global Strategy? (pp. 505–508)

Summary: A variety of structures can be used for organizing global business—cooperative contracts, licensing, franchising, strategic alliances, and others—but each one requires research into the environmental and cultural differences among countries. It is important for anyone engaging in global business to understand that there is no single global culture; even where cultural values are the same, the way these values are expressed may differ from place to place. Taking care to appreciate this will make it easier to focus on international customers and employees as individuals and will lead to a successful global strategy.

5. What Are the Opportunities and Risks in a Global Business Environment? (pp. 508–511)

Summary: As with any business venture, globalization presents both opportunities and risks that must be carefully weighed by organizations interested in multinational growth. Expanding markets and improving sales by reaching untapped markets, improving quality by incorporating new knowledge, and lowering costs by accessing cheaper labor are some of the opportunities presented by globalization. On the other hand, economic uncertainty in some countries, growth that outpaces the ability to expand, and popular disapproval of certain globalization policies all represent risks. Opportunities and risks will differ by company and environment and, in some cases, a risk for one company will represent an opportunity for another.

8.   How Do Global Regulators Affect Economies and Social Issues?   (pp. 533–535)

Summary: Several regulatory organizations comprised of representatives from around the world currently exist to promote ethical trade policies and social improvements. The G-20 provides an open forum to discuss global trade and investment, sustainable market building, and financial system regulations. The World Economic Forum is a not-for-profit organization that seeks to bring governmental, business, and social leaders together to complete projects that address economic and societal challenges. Finally, the United Nations develops loan and aid programs designed to promote higher standards of living within its member states.

7.   How Has the Growth of Worldwide Trade Alliances Affected Globalization? (pp. 529–532)

Summary: The World Trade Organization is an alliance that strives to oversee trade and settle disputes on a global level. Regional trade alliances exist as well. The European Union, the NAFTA and CAFTA alliances, the Union of South American Nations, and the Association of Southeast Asian Nations are just a few of the current trade alliances that affect global business today. Each of these has a general goal of improving trade for the benefit of the member nations, and each has achieved varying levels of success and public support.

6.   What Opportunities Exist in Emerging Markets? (pp. 511–529)

Summary: Four emerging markets—Brazil, Russia, India, and China—are collectively known as the BRIC countries. They have been identified as extremely important to the world economy. The first of these markets, Brazil, is enjoying its newfound prosperity as a result of increased political and economic stability, a growing alternative-fuel industry, and its wealth of mineral reserves. Russia's well-educated populace, low wages, and cultural and geographic proximity to Western Europe and the United States have contributed to its growth. Like Russia, India's educated masses have proved advantageous to the economy, as has the overall English proficiency of its people and its increasing middle class. Finally, China's low wages and benefit structure, low health care costs, and sheer population size have contributed to its success. Along with the positive changes these countries will bring to global business, they also bring a number of potential and very real challenges such as poverty, corruption, and problems with human rights.

9.   What Is HR's Role in Supporting Global Business?   (pp. 535–537)

Summary: As more and more businesses become involved in globalization, HR is increasingly asked to prepare employees for working abroad through workforce development initiatives. Additionally, work on global and cross-cultural teams is becoming more important and more common. HR professionals can help by providing one-on-one support for expat executives in the form of executive coaching.

10.   What Can We All Do to Succeed in a Global Environment? (pp. 537–539)

Summary: Knowing where personal, societal, and company ethics intersect with one another is one key to success in a global business environment. This knowledge makes it possible for you to perform your job in a way that does not compromise you or your company and does not clash with the culture in which you find yourself. It also provides you with a way to identify what might need to change—even with respect to your own values and ethics. It is also important to have strong emotional and social competencies—self-management, organizational awareness, and adaptability—when working as an expatriate.

11.   A Final Word on Globalization   (p. 539)

Summary: Globalization impacts both the personal and professional aspects of our lives, and is changing our needs, wants, and culture. The skills you learn today will help you lead in the global environment now and in the future.

Sustainability and Corporate Social Responsibility:

Ensuring the **Future**

Chapter Outline

Find out what you already know about the concepts in
this chapter by going to www.mymanagementlab.com
and taking the Pre-Test. Your results will generate a customized
study plan for Chapter 15.

1. Why Are Sustainability and Corporate Social Responsibility
   Important in Today's World? (p. 546)

2. What Is Sustainability? (pp. 546–553)

3. What Are the Three Pillars of Sustainability? (pp. 553–556)

4. What Is Environmental Sustainability? (pp. 556–566)

5. What Is Social Sustainability? (pp. 566–572)

6. What Is Economic Sustainability? (pp. 572–575)

7. What Is Corporate Social Responsibility? (pp. 575–578)

8. How Can Companies Approach Corporate Social
   Responsibility? (pp. 578–581)

9. What Is HR's Role in Sustainability and Corporate Social
   Responsibility? (pp. 581–583)

10. What Can We All Do to Support Sustainability and
    Corporate Social Responsibility? (pp. 584–585)

11. A Final Word on Sustainability and Corporate Social
    Responsibility (p. 585)

Go back to www.mymanagementlab.com and take the Post-Test
to verify your understanding of the concepts. To experience and apply
the concepts, explore the additional material associated with Chapter 15.

Part 1: Leading and Managing for Today and the Future (Chapters 1, 2, 3, 4)

Part 2: Planning and Change (Chapters 5, 6, 7, 8, 9)

Part 3: Organizing Human Systems (Chapters 10, 11)

Part 4: Controlling Quality, Culture, and Yourself (Chapters 12, 13)

> **Part 5:** Leading and Managing for the Future (Chapters 14, **15**, 16)

8. Workplace Essentials: Creativity, Innovation, and a Spirit of Entrepreneurship

7. Change: A Focus on Adaptability and Resiliency

9. Organizing for a Complex World: Structure and Design

Planning and Change

6. The Human Side of Planning: Decision Making and Critical Thinking

5. Planning and Strategy: Bringing the Vision to Life

16. Managing and Leading for Tomorrow: A Focus on Your Future

1. Managing and Leading Today: The New Rules

14. Globalization: Managing Effectively in a Global Economic Environment

10. Teams and Teambuilding: How to Work Effectively with Others

Organizing Human Systems

11. Working in a Virtual World: Technology as a Way of Life

Leading and Managing for Today and the Future

2. The Leadership Imperative: It's Up to You

4. Communication: The Key to Resonant Relationships

3. Motivation and Meaning: What Makes People Want to Work?

15. Sustainability and Corporate Social Responsibility: Ensuring the Future

15. Sustainability and Corporate Social Responsibility: Ensuring the Future

12. Organizational Controls: People, Processes, Quality, and Results

Controlling Quality, Culture, and Yourself

13. Culture: It's Powerful

1. Why Are Sustainability and Corporate Social Responsibility Important in Today's World?

In recent decades, the world has witnessed environmental, technological, and social changes that have had profound effects on individuals, families, communities, and governments. These changes have affected the ways in which businesses and organizations are designed, organized, managed, and led—as well as the ways in which people do their jobs and relate to one another at work. Technology has sparked a communication revolution, economies have become truly global, and previously underdeveloped countries have begun to industrialize at an incredible pace.

When we consider the massive changes that have occurred, along with those that are currently under way, one thing becomes crystal clear: All people are fundamentally interconnected, and a primary consequence of this interconnectedness is that the actions of individuals, institutions, and businesses in any one part of the world have the potential to affect us all. Indeed, in recent years, a seemingly endless list of highly publicized environmental accidents and ethical violations have illustrated that people everywhere can be negatively affected by the activity of even a single business. So, although we often derive great benefit from the products and services businesses provide, we must also figure out how to avoid and address any long-term negative consequences from business activities.

Many people believe that we are at a turning point and must face the major challenges of our day head-on—especially the threats of climate change and global warming. Also, in light of serious industrial accidents, lapses in business ethics, and the worldwide recession that began in 2007, it has become clear that people everywhere must reach an agreement about precisely what business is responsible for when it comes to the health of our environment, society, and global economy. The call for increased social responsibility among businesses is greater now than ever before.

In this chapter, we explore how organizations and individuals are approaching the closely related topics of sustainability and social responsibility. The chapter begins with a definition of sustainability, followed by a brief look at the history of this practice and the primary reasons why sustainability is critical in today's world. Next, we introduce the three "pillars of sustainability"—environmental sustainability, social sustainability, and economic sustainability—and examine what each of them entails. After that, our focus turns to corporate social responsibility, including ways that organizations have integrated this idea into their daily operations. Finally, the chapter concludes with a look at what HR can do to support sustainability and social responsibility at work, as well as what we all can do to ensure that our organizations and communities are positioned for success both today *and* tomorrow.

Most Popular » Discussion Questions

1. List some of the major environmental, technological, and social changes that have occurred in the past five years. Which of these changes are most likely to affect you at work?
2. What are some possible environmental implications of the rapid industrialization currently under way in large, powerful countries like China and India?

---

2. What Is Sustainability?

Sustainability means different things to different people. In fact, there are more than 350 documented definitions of *sustainability* and *sustainable development*.[1] One of the most popular definitions comes from the United Nations (UN), which describes

Sustainability
The process of meeting present needs without compromising the ability of future generations to meet their needs.

sustainability as "the process of meeting present needs without compromising the ability of future generations to meet their needs."[2] Notice that this definition includes time as a dimension. Looking at sustainability in this way allows us to consider how our current activities impact the health of our social and ecological systems in the short term and in the more distant future.

Sustainability: People Have Been Practicing It for Generations

Although it's become a hot topic in recent years, sustainability is hardly a new idea. This concept can be traced back to prehistoric times, when our ancient ancestors recognized that biodiversity had to be maintained and the consumption and replenishment of resources had to be balanced if humans were to survive. About 10,000 years ago, the development of agriculture allowed our prehistoric ancestors to "create" some of the resources they needed, and this led to the gradual development of population-dense cities, as well as increases in the overall population.[3]

Before the rise of agriculture, our ancestors were hunters and gatherers. Whenever resources became scarce, perhaps because of overforaging or overhunting, tribes were forced to migrate to prevent starvation and possible extinction. Some early groups of people were perpetually nomadic, following the migratory routes of their animal prey or forever traveling in search of better weather, water supplies, and grazing lands. When these nomadic bands became too large for the available resources, members often splintered off to form new groups. Alternatively, competing tribes sometimes fought wars so they could lay claim to particularly desirable pieces of land. In other cases, multiple tribes formed loose confederations in an attempt to work out territorial rights and join together to fight off outside invaders.[4]

We know these things not only because of artifacts from that time that have been discovered, but also because in some areas of the globe, some tribes and nomadic bands continue to exist using technologies that have remained relatively unchanged for hundreds or even thousands of years.[5] For instance, not many years ago the Dani tribes of New Guinea engaged in warfare practices that helped the tribe to maintain balance with available resources. Today, aspects of these practices still exist, although they are now ritualistic. Similarly, the semi-nomadic Maasai people, who inhabit regions of the Rift Valley in present-day Kenya and Tanzania, were historically known as fierce warriors. Partly to maintain balance with natural resources, they often displaced other groups through warfare.[6] Today, however, the Maasai are pastoral and live off the products of their cattle, while also maintaining ceremonies and traditions that support values related to balancing their human needs with the needs of their environment.[7]

The Maasai have developed an incredibly finely tuned, symbiotic relationship with their animals, although in times of drought or disease, they have had to turn to hunting or agriculture to survive.[8] In part because of their ability to manage themselves and their environment, the Maasai have been able to maintain their sustainable way of life, despite two centuries of some of the most intense imperialist pressures of any region in the world.[9] Still, even this healthy balance is threatened today. Increasing reliance on trade with the outside world has made the future of the Maasai culture uncertain, largely because this reliance threatens the precarious balance between people, neighboring tribes, and the environment.[10]

Why Sustainability Is Important Today: The "Big Three" Reasons

Today, of course, sustainability means more than simply ensuring that we have adequate food and water supplies or that our populations can be supported by the immediate environment. In the twenty-first century, sustainability also involves responding to widespread global changes in how we interact with each other and with our planet. As you have seen throughout this text (and as you know from experience), technology is a primary driver of change in the modern world—but it's not the only force at work. The question of sustainability has also been brought into stark relief by at least three major issues that have captured our attention in recent years:

1. Climate change and the potential effects of such change on people, businesses, communities, and countries
2. Massive lapses of judgment and unethical business practices that have ruined many people's lives and brought formerly great companies to their knees
3. A global economic crisis that happened, in part, because changes in key financial policies in certain parts of the world had grave effects on people, businesses, and communities far removed from the world's stock markets and financiers

The following sections examine each of these factors in greater detail.

1. Climate Change and Global Warming

Changes in Earth's climate profoundly affect the planet's entire ecosystem. As past events have shown, when temperatures rise or fall by even a degree or two over a prolonged period of time, water levels change and weather patterns are altered, resulting in stress on the ecosystem. Thousands of species struggle, while only a handful tend to thrive during such times. Therefore, the threat of climate change—and global warming in particular—represents a potential challenge to humankind's ability to live and thrive on planet Earth.

But what is global warming, and how might it affect us and our planet's ecosystem? The term **global warming** is used to describe a fairly recent increase in the temperature of Earth's lower atmosphere (the air we breathe) and the land and water that make up Earth's surface. The causes and effects of global warming are matters of heated international debate. To better understand this debate, let's first consider several elements of the controversy.

Global warming is normally a natural phenomenon. In fact, scientists know that gradual warming and cooling of the global climate is a regular occurrence, and they point out that throughout human history, there have been many significant changes in global climate, such as the Ice Age and the "thaw" that followed it. Notable changes also happened during the "little ice age," which began around 1300 and lasted into the nineteenth century, ending around the same time that the Industrial Revolution went into high gear.[11]

Another widely held position is that changes in the planet's temperature are due in part to a phenomenon called the *greenhouse effect*. The **greenhouse effect** is a phrase that describes how air, water, and land temperatures are affected by certain gases in Earth's atmosphere. These gases trap infrared energy, which leads to an increase in the planet's atmospheric and surface temperatures. Greenhouse gases include water vapor (the most prevalent), carbon dioxide, ozone, nitrous oxide, and methane, all of which to a certain extent occur naturally. In fact, the greenhouse effect has occurred for eons, and we should all be grateful for it. Scientists estimate that without the greenhouse effect, vastly lower temperatures would render much of our planet uninhabitable.[12] Although it appears likely that the greenhouse effect contributes to global warming, just how much these trapped gases are affecting our climate is a point of debate.

Today, few people dispute that average temperatures are rising all across the planet. In fact, several agencies keep track of global temperatures, including NASA, whose data show that the five-year mean global temperature has risen about 0.65°C since 1970. This increase is more than triple the temperature rise that occurred between 1900 and 1970.[13] Therefore, it's not the increase in temperatures but rather the *reasons* for and the *relative speed* of this increase that are a source of controversy.

One side of this debate is represented by individuals who cite solar changes and other natural, cyclical climate cycles as the primary reasons behind the rise in temperatures.[14]

Global warming
Term used to describe a fairly recent increase in the temperature of Earth's lower atmosphere (the air we breathe) and the land and water that make up Earth's surface.

Greenhouse effect
Term used to describe how air, water, and land temperatures are affected by certain gases in Earth's atmosphere. These gases trap infrared energy, which leads to an increase in the planet's atmospheric and surface temperatures.

Environmentalists argue that global warming is causing the polar ice caps to melt.

blickwinkel/Rose/Alamy Images

These people argue that humans have little or no impact on Earth's temperatures—and accordingly, they believe that government measures aimed at imposing stricter requirements on emissions, manufacturing practices, and waste control are unnecessary and perhaps even unfair to businesses. In addition, some proponents of this position point out that the results of global warming may not be as adverse as claimed by many media reports.

On the other side of the global warming debate are those who argue that humans have indeed been responsible for much of the increase in Earth's temperatures (■ Exhibit 15.1). For example, the United Nations Intergovernmental Panel on Climate Change (IPCC) has published reports stating that current levels of global warming are the direct result of human activity.[15] Similarly, many scientists support the finding that human activity is contributing to an "enhanced" greenhouse effect.[16] In fact, the IPCC concluded that most of the temperature increases observed during the past century were caused by human-initiated deforestation and combustion of fossil fuels. Both of these activities increase the amount of greenhouse gases in the atmosphere, which in turn has the potential to raise temperatures.

The question of how much global warming is caused by human activity and how much is the result of natural processes is hotly debated among scientists, business leaders, and governments. Whatever the cause of this rise in temperature, however, one fact remains: Our climate is getting warmer, and this will likely affect people's lives in numerous ways.

Potential Effects of Climate Change and Global Warming

How, exactly, might climate change and global warming affect life in the years to come? In 2007, the IPCC identified a variety of current and potential impacts of global warming, as outlined in ■ Exhibit 15.2.[17]

Clearly, we have much to consider when it comes to global warming and climate change. Changes like the ones listed in Exhibit 15.2 may have already begun, and if so, they will have a profound effect on individuals, communities, and nations, not to mention businesses and other organizations. In addition, even if these sorts of changes don't happen in the near future, widespread public concern about their eventual possibility means that companies and government officials are wise to consider climate issues when making long-term decisions. But thinking about these topics is not the responsibility of business and political leaders alone.

■Exhibit **15.2**

Current and Potential Effects of Global Warming

Effects on the Ecosystem

- Climate change could potentially alter many ecosystems, and some researchers predict that it will bring disturbances such as floods, droughts, fires, insect overpopulation, and acidic oceans.
- An estimated 20 to 30 percent of plant and animal species may be more threatened by extinction if global average temperature increases exceed 1.5° to 2.5°C.
- Global warming may trigger changes in water quality that will likely have an adverse effect on many freshwater species and their ecosystems.

Effects on Food Supplies

- In mid- and higher-latitude regions, crop yields will likely increase with a rise in average temperature. However, in lower-latitude regions, this yield will likely decrease, especially in drier and more tropical climates. In turn, decreased crop outputs in these areas may increase the risk of famine.
- Overall food production is predicted to rise with an increase in temperature of 1° to 3°C but decrease at temperatures in excess of this amount.

Effects on Coastlines

- Many researchers estimate that global warming will increase rates of coastal erosion due to rising sea levels. Human land use may exacerbate this phenomenon.
- By the late twenty-first century, yearly floods are predicted to affect millions more people, particularly in densely populated river deltas and on small islands.

Effects on Industry and Associated Populations

- According to many researchers, coastal industries and populations, as well as areas of rapid urban development, will likely be most vulnerable to the negative effects of climate change. This seems particularly true for industries and societies that are economically dependent on resources that are sensitive to disruptions caused by global warming.
- Impoverished communities in high-risk areas are predicted to be most vulnerable overall.

Effects on Health

- Increased malnutrition, diseases, injuries, and deaths may occur as a result of extreme weather events. Higher concentrations of ground-level ozone might increase the prevalence of cardiorespiratory diseases. Diarrheal diseases may also become more common.
- Should Earth's climate become warmer, the range and infectiousness of some diseases (e.g., malaria) are expected to increase, in part because warmer temperatures provide a more hospitable environment for many pathogens.
- Fewer deaths and injuries due to exposure to extreme cold are expected.
- Many experts predict that inadequate education, health care, public health programs, and economic development may lead to health crises.

Effects on Water Supplies

- Should climate change, population growth, and urbanization continue, water resources will likely be increasingly stressed.
- Water resources in the form of mountain snowpacks and glaciers have already been reduced, and this reduction is predicted to accelerate, which could lead to a drop in freshwater availability.
- Changes in rainfall and temperature patterns could result in a 10 to 40 percent increase in runoff in high latitudes and wet tropical regions, whereas a 10 to 30 percent decrease is expected in dry, mid-latitude regions and the dry tropics. Semi-arid regions will likely lose water resources, which could adversely affect farming, energy, and health.
- Up to 20 percent of Earth's population could live in areas with high flood potential by the end of the century.
- Water quality and drinkability are predicted to decrease. Groundwater is predicted to rise in salinity.

Source: Adapted from IPCC's *Climate Change 2007*.

Facing the Threat of Climate Change: It's Up to All of Us

The potential effects of global warming could be far reaching and devastating. But who is responsible for dealing with the threat of climate change? Scientists? The United Nations? Government leaders? Businesses and organizations? Most likely, the answer is "all of the above"—plus each one of us. That's because our planet is facing more challenges than climate change alone, as serious as that threat might be.

For one, the human population is increasing rapidly, which means there are more people cutting down trees for farmland and burning fuel to cook and heat their homes. A growing population means there is increased demand for energy—more electricity for homes and businesses, more oil and gas for cars and machines, and so on. In turn, as energy consumption rises and developing nations industrialize, greenhouse gases will likely be produced at an alarming rate.

Beyond climate change and an increasing demand for energy and goods, we are facing another change that relates directly to how companies operate. Today, business practices that would have previously remained hidden are now instantaneously available to millions of people—each of whom has an opinion. That's why, in addition to the challenge of environmental sustainability, there is growing demand for businesses everywhere to operate in a more socially responsible manner.

2. The Call for Business Ethics and Social Responsibility

In recent years, the public has learned of countless scandals in companies that once seemed to be positive contributors to the economy and to society in general. The list of such companies and the people who led them astray is lengthy: Enron, Tyco, Arthur Andersen, Parmalat, WorldCom, Adelphia, Royal Ahold, and Bernie Madoff are just a few examples. The list goes on and on—as does the list of companies whose practices have been questioned in recent years, even when no criminal activities took place. For instance, in the 1990s, the public questioned Nike as to whether children were working in its factories in China. Unfortunately, the answer to this question was yes.[18]

More recently, Walmart's labor practices and compensation scheme fell under public scrutiny. Was the company forcing workers to skip meal breaks? Was it underpaying them? In 2004, a report outlining several unethical and illegal labor practices in Walmart's stores in California was published by the United States House of Representatives Committee on Education and the Workforce. The report included assertions that employees were forced to skip breaks, paid wages that kept them below the poverty level, encouraged to seek welfare, and denied health insurance. In addition, there was strong evidence that Walmart's unfair labor practices targeted women, who were paid significantly less than men and underrepresented in management positions. The report concluded that a 200-employee Walmart store actually cost the government more than $420,000 a year in subsidized housing, health care, utilities, low-income tax credits, and meals.[19]

Yet another recent controversy involved the question of whether Yahoo! revealed to the Chinese government the identity of its Chinese users, including dissidents, while they were residing outside mainland China. Again, this really did happen, which caused human rights groups to question the company's role in government censorship.[20]

Questionable practices and scandals like these have soured many individuals on the idea of "big business." As a result, people—consumers of businesses goods and services, potential and actual employees, investors, community groups, and even governments—are fighting back. More and more often, stakeholders do not want to support companies that pollute rivers, steal from investors, or fail to give back to the community in meaningful ways. Likewise, employees do not want to work for companies that are engaged in unethical or unsustainable business practices. Most of us would cringe if we found out, for example, that our company is actively destroying the Brazilian rain forest, dumping waste, or hiring children to work in its factories.

Some debate surrounds the topic of whether companies and their leaders are engaging in a greater number of unethical or questionable practices now than in the past. The answer to this question is unclear. What is clear is that almost everything a company does can be discovered and shared around the world within a matter of seconds. In the past, workers (and perhaps their unions) were often the only groups directly challenging businesses' practices. Today, however, millions of people are involved in discussions about companies' labor policies, working conditions, environmental impact, and executive compensation.

People care what companies do, and they care a lot. Individuals far removed from businesses can and do weigh in with opinions and demands. This has become increasingly apparent in recent years, as business leaders have been called on to take responsibility for the conditions that resulted in the recession that began in 2007—a global economic crisis of a magnitude not seen since the Great Depression. Let's take a closer look at what happened.

3. An Economic Crisis That Swept the World

The global economic crisis that began in 2007 exploded in 2008, causing an untold amount of damage to individuals, families, businesses, not-for-profit organizations, governments, communities, and countries. This crisis was caused by many factors, including the widespread financial industry practice of approving "subprime" mortgages—loans to people who would have difficulty repaying them. There is no doubt that the economic crisis was and continues to be harmful—devastating, in fact, for the many people who lost their jobs, homes, and life savings. However, there might be a silver lining of sorts. In particular, the crisis was so bad, and business's role in it was so clear, that it is now apparent that companies must adopt a different outlook on their role in society.

Niall FitzGerald is a world-renowned leader who understands how important it is for individuals—and for businesses—to recognize how interconnected we all are, and what this means in terms of leadership and responsibility. Among his many accomplishments, FitzGerald was chairman of Unilever, a global consumer goods company, from 1996 through 2004. During this period, the company fundamentally remade itself—reducing its number of brands, changing its marketing strategy, and focusing explicitly on environmental sustainability and corporate social responsibility.

In 2006, FitzGerald spearheaded the Investment Climate Facility for Africa, a not-for-profit organization that supports economic development in that continent.[21] Today, FitzGerald serves as chairman of the board of the British Museum and as deputy chairman of Thomson Reuters. As you might imagine, FitzGerald understands business and finance, and he also knows what it means to work in today's interconnected world. This is just a small part of what he had to say at the 2009 Tyburne Lecture in England:

> I believe the economic events [related to the recession that began in 2007] have brought the business world to a crossroads. If business is to recover, it is vital that we choose the right turn. . . . [This crisis] invites us to create a business world in which the world can have future trust and confidence, to rebuild our business institutions on stronger and sustainable foundations. . . . I believe that social responsibility has to become a core value of the business, a central tenet that affects the way it works. . . . Businesses should be explicit about these values and ensure that all employees understand that they will be judged on their contribution to this core value of social responsibility as much as they are judged on such things as production and sales.[22]

As FitzGerald points out, companies can no longer justify their performance based solely on financial figures. Today's best leaders know that the decisions they make can have far-reaching effects—and that their actions impact people, communities, and ecosystems far beyond the walls of their corporate offices. Sustainability and corporate social responsibility are therefore much more than faddish buzzwords: They are philosophies that are here to stay, and they will increasingly impact how we conduct business. In the following sections, we will discuss sustainability in greater depth, focusing on the "three pillars" of this practice: environmental sustainability, social sustainability, and economic sustainability.

Most Popular » Discussion Questions

1. Make a list of businesses, organizations, or industries that have been affected by either global warming or climate change. Choose one business from your list and analyze global warming's effects on it to date, considering social, political, and financial factors. Next, consider how climate change may affect this company or industry during the next five years.
2. Have you been affected by climate change? If so, how?
3. Conduct a five-minute search on the Internet of business ethics issues in the news recently. How many can you find? Are there any similarities shared across the group? For example, are concerns focused largely on one industry? Are the complaints similar in any way?
4. How have you, or people you know, been affected by the economic crisis that began in 2007?

---

3. What Are the Three Pillars of Sustainability?

Environmental sustainability
Term that refers to the preservation of environmental resources and biodiversity, creation of sustainable access to safe drinking water, and enhancement of quality of life among the most impoverished.

Social sustainability
Term that refers to the improvement of daily life for the greatest number of people through improving fair income distribution; promoting gender equality; ensuring equal access to land ownership, employment, and education; investing in basic health and education; and enlisting the participation of beneficiaries.

Economic sustainability
Term that refers to an economy's capacity to regularly produce outcomes consistent with long-term economic development.

The United Nations describes "three pillars of sustainability": environmental sustainability, social sustainability, and economic sustainability.[23] In this model, **environmental sustainability** means preservation of environmental resources and biodiversity, creation of sustainable access to safe drinking water, and enhancement of quality of life among the most impoverished.[24] **Social sustainability** refers to the improvement of daily life for the greatest number of people through improving fair income distribution; promoting gender equality; ensuring equal access to land ownership, employment, and education; investing in basic health and education; and enlisting the participation of beneficiaries.[25] Finally, **economic sustainability** is "an economy's capacity to regularly produce outcomes consistent with long-term [economic development]."[26] The UN model, illustrated in ▪ Exhibit 15.3, is extremely valuable when considering how businesses and organizations must think about sustainability.[27]

At no time in history has the topic of sustainability been taken up as globally and as powerfully as today, and business is a leader in this conversation. That's because there is growing recognition that no company is an island and that the social, economic, and environmental spheres are indelibly linked. Negative effects to the environment can adversely affect economic stability, and these events might even cause social upheaval if they are harmful enough. For example, imagine what would happen if a natural disaster destroyed many oil production facilities. Certainly, gas prices would be sky-high, people would suffer economically, and this could cause social unrest. Or, consider the short- and long-term effects of the oil well disaster in the Gulf of Mexico in 2010. This situation has and will continue to affect water, sea life, coastal biodiversity, and people's livelihoods. The disaster also sparked heated social debate about oil companies' responsibility for preventing such catastrophes. Let's look in some detail at another far-reaching disaster: what happened in Bhopal, India, where an accident and lax standards resulted in devastation for the natural environment and for thousands of people.

The Bhopal Disaster

On the night of December 3, 1984, near Bhopal, India more than 40 tons of deadly toxins were accidentally released into the atmosphere. These chemicals were released from

■Exhibit **15.3**

Sustainability is important in three spheres: environmental, social, and economic.[28]

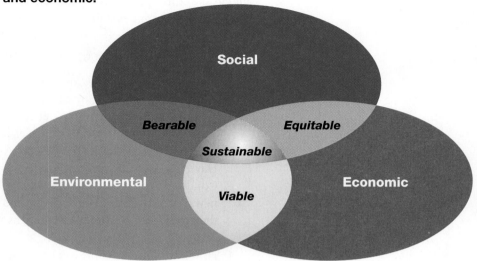

Source: Based on a report from the United Nations World Summit on Sustainable Development, August 26–September 4, 2002. Retrieved May 27, 2010, from http://www.un.org/events/wssdsummaries/envdevj8.htm.

a pesticide plant owned by the American company Union Carbide Corporation and operated by Union Carbide India Limited, its Indian subsidiary.[29] The nearly half-million people who lived in Bhopal at the time were immediately exposed to a variety of harmful chemicals, including methyl isocyanate gas, which degrades into an even more deadly gas when exposed to high temperatures like those present in the plant.

In the aftermath of the disaster, many Bhopal residents suffered from cyanide poisoning.[30] The official death toll was 2,259 people, although the local government later confirmed about 1,500 additional deaths. Still other estimates put the toll at 8,000 to 10,000 lives within the first 72 hours, with the ultimate cost in human lives at roughly 20,000.[31] Those victims who died first were the poor who lived in the slums adjacent to

■Exhibit **15.4**

Bhopal disaster victims are examined by their doctor.

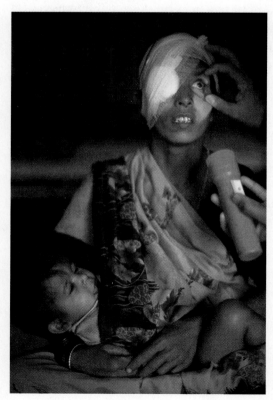

the plant. Of course, the cyanide gas that was released from the factory didn't just kill humans; pets, wildlife, and livestock, including cattle—which are sacred to Hindu people—also died.[32]

The Bhopal disaster precipitated a number of long-term actions. In the spring of 1985, India passed the Bhopal Gas Leak Disaster Act, making the government the "sole representative of the victims in legal proceedings both within and outside India," and it eventually had all claims filed in the United States transferred to India.[33] The court-recognized official death toll was only around 3,000, so the settlement of $470 million did not include many of the people who died later, and it recognized only 102,000 victims who had permanent disabilities. Even today, the long-term effects of the disaster result in an estimated 4,000 daily visits to health clinics in the Bhopal region (■Exhibit 15.4). In June 2010, more than 25 years after the Bhopal disaster, former officials were convicted of criminal negligence, leading the Prime Minister of India to set up a new Bhopal panel to example the fairness of the settlement.[34]

Union Carbide's Bhopal factory was closed in 1985 and 1986, and some of the facility's equipment was subsequently cleaned and sold. However, many toxic materials were left on site, where they continue to infiltrate the soil and water. Because the area around the plant was used as a toxic dumping ground, the water there is toxic to fish, and there is evidence that the groundwater supply has been contaminated by a long list of chemicals. Lead, mercury, and organochlorines have been detected in the breast milk of nursing mothers.[35]

In addition, some of the many poisons found in and around the former factory cause mutations, which means they have affected subsequent genera-

Mark Downey/Alamy Images

tions of humans and animals with various diseases and deformities.[36] More than 25 years after the incident, the region's high court finally ruled to have the more than 350 metric tons of toxic waste removed through incineration.[37] This is a promising development, but it comes far too late for the thousands of people and animals who suffered, as well as the land, water, and vegetation that won't recover for many years.

Obviously, sustainability is not just about avoiding disasters. It is also about daily business practices that enable people to attend to environmental, social, and economic concerns while simultaneously maintaining the profitability and viability of the organizations to which they belong.

Tracking Companies That Focus on Sustainability

The Global 100 Most Sustainable Corporations in the World is a project that attempts to track and measure business activities and identify those companies whose approach to sustainability is outstanding. The Global 100's position is as follows:

> [S]ocial, environmental, and governance factors are increasingly relevant to financial performance, and the companies which show superior management of these issues are fast gaining an edge over their competitors—an edge which we believe will translate into outperformance in the long haul. The Global 100 companies are, therefore, sustainable in the sense that they have displayed a better ability than most of their industry peers to identify and effectively manage material environmental, social, and governance factors impacting the opportunity and risk sides of their business.[38]

In 2009, the Global 100 list included companies such as Adidas, Dell, GlaxoSmithKline, Intel, L'Oreal, and Unilever. Twenty companies based in the United States made the list, followed by nineteen companies from the United Kingdom and fifteen Japanese companies. The Global 100 is not the only group that tracks companies' sustainability records, however. The Dow Jones also has an index, and *Newsweek* tracks companies headquartered in the United States. *Newsweek*'s top-five companies for 2009 are listed in ■Exhibit 15.5.

In the following sections, we will explore the three pillars of sustainability in some depth to see how people, communities, and companies alike can join the movement to promote environmental, social, and economic sustainability.

■ Exhibit **15.5**

Newsweek's 2009 Top-Five Green U.S. Companies

1. *Hewlett-Packard* has created programs to help reduce greenhouse gas emissions throughout its entire supply chain. The company has also worked to decrease the number of harmful toxins in its products.
2. *Dell* company headquarters is fueled using 100% renewable sources of energy. In 2008, Dell achieved carbon neutrality. By 2010, the company planned for all Dell desktop and laptop computers to consume as much as 25% less energy. Also, its product return and recycling programs continue to be among the best in the computer industry.
3. *Johnson & Johnson* holds the distinction of having the largest fleet of hybrid vehicles worldwide.
4. *Intel* is the largest corporate purchaser of renewable energy in the United States, using about 46% green energy for its company operations. Energy efficiency is also key to the company's product development, where the focus is on reducing the energy consumption of its chips while increasing speed. Intel exemplifies strong leadership through its environmental management, including lowering its production of toxic materials and waste.
5. *IBM* began supporting environmental policies in the early 1970s. With a strong focus on reducing carbon waste, the company has been rewarded with the EPA's Climate Protection Award twice. An IBM pilot program that focused on reducing traffic in Stockholm helped lower inner-city greenhouse gases by 40%. IBM plans to work with London next. The company also spends nearly $1 billion per year to expand its data centers without increasing energy consumption. In addition, IBM has instituted environmental awareness training for new employees.

Source: Newsweek. September 21, 2009. Green rankings: The 2009 list. Retrieved June 2, 2010, from http://greenrankings.newsweek.com/.

1. How does your school approach the three pillars of sustainability? Research and compile relevant data, such as information about mission statements, programs, and community activities.
2. Do you think your school is doing enough in the area of social sustainability? Why or why not?
3. Research several industrial accidents that have occurred in the United States. What short- and long-term effects did these accidents have on the environment, people, and the local economy?
4. Research one of the companies on *Newsweek*'s 2009 green companies list. What is this company actually doing to support environmental, social, and economic sustainability? (Be specific.) How do you think these activities support or detract from the company's business goals?

4. What Is Environmental Sustainability?

Many people believe that unless we find a way to ensure environmental sustainability, both social and economic sustainability are impossible. For that reason, we will explore the environmental aspect of sustainability in some depth. First, we will look at the history of the conservation and ecology movements in the United States—precursors to today's environmental movement—and we'll consider some of the methods nations are currently considering to curb greenhouse gas emissions. Then, we'll look at an *unsustainable* source of energy: fossil fuels. Finally, we'll conclude the section with an exploration of some of the ways that U.S. businesses and government are working to promote greater environmental sustainability.

The History of the Conservation and Ecology Movements in the United States

For well over a century, America's leaders and philanthropists have recognized that land, water, and clean air are precious and need to be protected. From the 1800s through the present, numerous acts of Congress, as well as state and local ordinances, have been passed with the goal of protecting the country's land, timber, plants, animals, and waterways.

Land conservation in particular has a robust history in the United States. Yellowstone became the first protected national park in 1872.[39] Later, in 1897, the federal government set aside many areas as national forests, and in 1903, President Theodore Roosevelt created the United States' first wildlife refuge. Just over a decade later, the National Park Service was formed on August 25, 1916. Today, with a budget of just under $3 billion, the agency manages 84.4 million acres, including nearly 400 units of nationally protected land, 59 of which are national parks.[40]

U.S. citizens and governmental agencies did not stop their conservation efforts with the creation of parklands, however. By the middle of the twentieth century, it became clear that industrial pollution was seriously harming land, water, air, and people. Attention to pollution issues grew, partly because the growing number of televisions in American homes allowed people to see what was happening to natural resources all over the country. Thus, in 1970, the U.S. Environmental Protection Agency (EPA) was established in response to enormous public sentiment in favor of a cleaner environment.

Since its creation, the EPA has been charged with defining and enforcing specific controls and standards for industries and individual polluters. These controls are loosely based on "the best available and best achievable technology for each source of pollution in each industry."[41]

As you can see in ■Exhibit 15.6, tremendous progress has been made in the years since 1970, with Americans currently focusing more attention and resources on protecting the environment than ever before.[42]

Among the EPA's efforts, one especially notable success has been the reduction of sulfur dioxide emissions from electric utility plants. This reduction was spurred in large part by the Clean Air Act Amendments of 1990, which set a cap on total sulfur dioxide emissions. Under the amendments, instead of requiring all power plants to meet a technology-based standard, the EPA allocated electric utilities a share of the maximum allowable national emissions amount. The utilities could then buy or sell emission allowances among themselves, depending on their individual needs. This program has worked well, reducing total control costs by an estimated $750 million to $1.5 billion per year (relative to the cost of the former technology-based standards), while simultaneously meeting or exceeding goals for sulfur dioxide reduction. In recent years, similar programs have also been put in place for CFC (chlorofluorocarbon), particulate, and carbon emissions.

■Exhibit **15.6**

Timeline of the Environmental Movement in the United States Since 1970[43]

1970s

1970: Following celebration of the first Earth Day, the EPA is created. Congress amends the Clean Air Act so that air quality, automobile emission, and antipollution standards can be set and enforced.

1972: The EPA bans use of DDT, a dangerous pesticide that was implicated in the near extinction of the American bald eagle. The United States and Canada agree to improve water quality in the Great Lakes. The Clean Water Act is passed, thereby limiting the release of pollutants into U.S. waterways.

1973: Lead begins to be phased out of gasoline.

1974: The Safe Drinking Water Act is passed, and the EPA is charged with its regulation.

1975: Congress sets fuel economy and emissions standards for automobiles.

1976: Congress passes the Resource Conservation and Recovery Act, which regulates hazardous waste production and disposal. President Ford signs the Toxic Substances Control Act. The EPA begins to phase out production of PCB (a cancer-causing liquid used in numerous applications).

1977: President Carter signs an amendment strengthening the Clean Air Act.

1978: The federal government bans use of chlorofluorocarbons as propellants in aerosol sprays.

1979: The EPA bans PCB manufacture and begins to phase out use of these substances.

1980s

1980: Congress establishes Superfund, a federal program to clean up toxic sites. The program is operated by the EPA.

1982: Congress passes laws to clean asbestos from schools.

1983: Cleanup of the Chesapeake Bay gets under way. The EPA publicizes the dangers of radioactive radon gas and encourages testing.

1985: The EPA sets new limits on the use of lead in gasoline.

1986: Congress passes amendments to the Safe Drinking Water Act.

1987: The EPA mandates sanctions against individual states that fail to meet air quality standards.

1988: After medical and other waste begins washing up on shore in New York and New Jersey, Congress bans the ocean dumping of industrial waste.

1989: The accidental spill of 11 million gallons of oil in Alaskan waters leads to a public outcry.

Continued on next page>>

■Exhibit **15.6** **Continued**

Timeline of the Environmental Movement in the United States Since 1970

1990s

1990: Congress passes more Clean Air Act amendments that require states to demonstrate progress in improving air quality. The EPA creates a Toxic Release Inventory that makes public which pollutants are being released into which communities. President Bush signs the Pollution Prevention Act.

1991: Federal agencies begin to use products that contain recycled components. The EPA launches a voluntary industry partnership to promote energy efficiency.

1993: The EPA begins a campaign against secondhand smoke. President Clinton orders the federal government to buy more recycled and environmentally friendly products.

1994: The EPA issues new emissions standards to reduce air pollution by over 500,000 tons per year.

1995: The EPA offers incentives to reduce sulfur dioxide emissions, which are a primary cause of acid rain.

1996: Suppliers of public drinking water are required to provide information about chemicals and microbes in the water they supply. President Clinton signs the Food Quality Protection Act, which tightens standards for pesticide content on food that is brought to market.

1997: The EPA implements the Food Quality Protection Act.

1998: President Clinton signs the Clean Water Action Plan to protect American waterways.

1999: New standards require auto emissions to be at least 77 percent cleaner. The EPA increases air quality standards for national parks and wilderness areas.

2000s

2000: The EPA establishes new regulations that require 90 percent cleaner diesel fuel engines.

2003: The EPA proposes mercury emissions regulations for power plants.

2004: New ozone and fine particulate standards become effective across the country. Construction and farm engines are required to use cleaner fuels.

2005: The EPA establishes the Clean Air Interstate Rule.

2006: The EPA is the first federal agency to buy 100 percent of its energy from green power sources.

2008: The EPA drastically cuts locomotive and marine diesel pollution.

2009: The EPA officially finds that greenhouse gases endanger public health, which gives it authority to regulate emissions of these gases.

The EPA is responsible for administering numerous laws, a few of which are described in ■Exhibit 15.7. As the laws illustrate, adopting practices that support environmental sustainability means everything from addressing global warming to preventing accidents that harm the ecosystem—and innumerable other things that touch every aspect of business and people's daily lives. Of particular interest to global leaders, businesses, and organizations are activities related to the reduction of greenhouse gas emissions.

Reducing Greenhouse Gas Emissions: World Leaders Try to Agree on a Course of Action

Although there is general consensus that regulating air, water, and ground pollution is in the best interests of people across the globe, precisely what to regulate and how to regulate it has long been an area of controversy. This controversy has played out very publicly in meetings organized by the United Nations and other international bodies in an attempt to get world leaders to agree on a course of action for curbing the effects of greenhouse gases. Perhaps the most famous of these meetings was held in Kyoto, Japan,

■Exhibit **15.7**

Laws Administered Either Wholly or in Part by the EPA[44]	
Law	**EPA's Role in Administration**
Atomic Energy Act (1946)	The EPA offers guidance for federal and state agencies that set radiation protection requirements. It also works with states to establish and administer radiation protection programs.
Clean Air Act (1970)	The EPA establishes and reviews emission standards for hazardous air pollutants.
Occupational Safety and Health Act (1970)	The EPA establishes standards for workplace health and safety and enforces compliance in all 50 states.
Clean Water Act (1972)	The EPA implements programs to control water pollution, including industry wastewater standards.
Superfund (1980)	The EPA cleans up toxic waste sites in all states and territories when the culprit cannot be identified or compelled to act.
Emergency Planning and Community Right-to-Know Act (1986)	The EPA oversees the emergency planning and notification activities of local governments and facilities. It also enforces community right-to-know rules regarding hazardous chemicals through the use of publicly available Material Safety Data Sheets (MSDS).
Executive Order 13045: Protection of Children from Environmental Health Risks and Safety Risks (1997)	The EPA evaluates the effectiveness of planned regulations related to environmental health or safety risks to children and recommends alternative approaches when necessary.
Executive Order 13211: Actions Concerning Regulations That Significantly Affect Energy Supply, Distribution, or Use (2001)	The EPA determines whether a regulatory action or activity is likely to significantly and adversely impact the supply, distribution, or use of energy.
Federal Food, Drug, and Cosmetic Act (2002)	The EPA is authorized to set maximum limits for the presence of pesticide residues on foods. Foods that exceed these limits are subject to seizure.

in 1997. Another more recent meeting of great importance to the greenhouse gas debate occurred in Copenhagen, Denmark, in December 2009.

The Kyoto Protocol

Kyoto Protocol
An international agreement drafted during the 1997 United Nations Framework Convention on Climate Change for the purpose of supporting and enforcing the reduction of greenhouse gas emissions.

The **Kyoto Protocol** is an international agreement drafted during the aforementioned 1997 meeting in Kyoto, formally known as the United Nations Framework Convention on Climate Change. The purpose of this agreement is to support and enforce the reduction of greenhouse gas emissions worldwide. Although the Kyoto Protocol recognizes that all nations must engage in activities to support this initiative, it places a heavier burden on developed nations. The rationale behind this decision is that developed nations are largely the cause of the current situation, and developing nations should not be prevented from advancing because of the financial burdens associated with greenhouse gas reduction.

Under the Kyoto Protocol, a three-pronged approach to averting climate change has been developed:[45]

- The first prong, emissions trading (often called the carbon market), is the best known among Americans. Carbon trading is based on agreed-to limits for member countries on the amount of greenhouse gases (most notably, carbon) they can release into the atmosphere in a given period. The basic principle is that if a country is producing more airborne carbon than it is allotted, it can buy emission allowances from other countries that are producing less than their allotment. Within countries, businesses and industries can also participate in buying, selling, and trading emissions credits.

During the past several years, the carbon trading mechanism has been expanded to include what is commonly called "cap and trade." Under the cap-and-trade plan, companies purchase annual emissions credits, and fewer credits are available each year per a federal "cap" on emissions.[46] The reduced supply drives up the cost of the credits, which encourages companies to create new business methods that do not result in the release of as many greenhouse gases. Cap-and-trade legislation is one component of a comprehensive bill passed by the U.S. House of Representatives in June 2009, and it is part of President Obama's commitment to "closing the carbon loophole and cracking down on polluters."[47]

- The second prong created under the Kyoto Protocol is the clean development mechanism (CDM). Under the CDM, countries that are actively involved in an emission reduction or limitation commitment may start projects in developing countries to help those countries reduce emissions while also developing their industries and economies. The goal is to encourage sustainable development yet permit industrialized countries flexibility in how they meet their emission targets.[48]
- The third prong consists of joint implementation (JI) projects. These projects were designed to allow Kyoto Protocol member countries to earn credits for helping reduce or remove emissions in another member nation—even a developed one.[49]

According to the Kyoto Protocol, developed nations must monitor, report, and reduce their greenhouse gas emissions by 2012 relative to a 1990 baseline, or else they will face significant financial penalties. Reduction amounts vary by country, but the overall goal is a reduction of 5.2 percent. The total target reduction for the European Union (EU), for example, is 8 percent; Japan's target is 6 percent; and the United States' is 7 percent.[50]

As of the end of 2009, 187 governing entities have signed and ratified the Kyoto Protocol, including 36 developed nations. Several countries have not signed the agreement, while others have signed but not ratified it. The United States is the only developed nation to fall into the latter category—in fact, Congress has never even been asked to ratify the Kyoto Protocol. Why? The principal argument is that complying with the Kyoto Protocol would cripple the American economy, which many other nations depend on for their financial survival. Also, there is tremendous debate about the heavier burden of responsibility placed on developed nations. For instance, 4 of the top 10 emitters—Brazil, Russia, India, and China (the BRIC nations) are exempt from any emissions reductions under the protocol.[51] Many people consider this a significant problem, especially because China and India have the world's fastest rates of emissions growth.[52]

Another problem, some say, is that the protocol delays the impact of global warming by only four years, yet it costs trillions to implement.[53] For these and other reasons, the Senate unanimously passed a resolution in 1997 stating that the United States should not sign a binding agreement that did not address emissions by developing nations.[54] Also, it's important to note that even though the United States has not ratified the Kyoto Protocol and Congress has not passed legislation on emissions reduction, many U.S. states have stringent guidelines and effective enforcement policies and practices. In fact, more than half the states have existing climate legislation, and California, the world's eighth-largest economy since 2008, has some of the most stringent legislation in the world.[55]

Although debate continues as to what each country, state, and business must do to curb global warming, the problem of climate change is becoming more pronounced. Thus, in 2009, the world's leaders and scientists met in Copenhagen to try to iron out a new agreement and further the cause of reducing greenhouse gas emissions.

The United Nations Climate Change Conference of 2009

In December 2009, the United Nations Climate Change Conference was held in Copenhagen, Denmark, and attended by 192 countries. The goal of the Copenhagen summit was to produce a framework for mitigating the effects of climate change beyond the year 2012.[56]

The fact that the United States federal government had not passed legislation on emissions reduction or ratified the Kyoto Protocol weighed against the United States as discussions began. In fact, China and other developing countries started the summit by strongly criticizing wealthy developed countries, including the United States, the EU, and Japan, for setting themselves low targets for emissions reduction. In response, the EU proposed a 20 percent cut, and Japan proposed a 25 percent cut but made it contingent on legally binding cuts from developing nations.[57]

Meanwhile, President Obama expressed U.S. commitment to reduce emissions 17 percent from 2005 levels by 2020, although the American proposal was not met with enthusiasm, especially from developing countries.[58] Other news was seen as extremely promising. In particular, the Obama administration announced that the U.S. EPA now officially recognizes six greenhouse gases, including carbon dioxide, as dangerous pollutants and hazardous to human health. The official identification of these gases as dangerous to health allows the EPA to develop emissions standards for industry and automobiles, bypassing Congress in the process.[59]

Despite some progress, by the end of the conference, international media had concluded that the summit faced significant problems.[60] Much of the trouble resulted from strenuous opposition from developing countries to the efforts and promises of developed nations, as well as their fear that the Kyoto Protocol would be abandoned in favor of more stringent demands on countries that were exempt from its requirements.[61]

When talks broke down, the United States, China, India, South Africa, and Brazil met privately and developed an agreement known as the Copenhagen Accord, which recognizes the importance of keeping temperature increases below 2°C without outlining what commitments are required to meet that goal. This agreement also contains a pledge of U.S. $30 billion to developing nations over three years.[62] The accord has been widely criticized, including by some of the countries that signed it. Critics say one major flaw is the nonbinding nature of the agreement.[63] In other words, it is not enforceable.

As you can see, reducing greenhouse gases is difficult, complicated, and controversial. Ultimately, regulations can only do so much. For that reason, we must also look at a major source of greenhouse gas emissions that "regular" people use all the time—fossil fuels. Since the onset of the Industrial Revolution, people have relied heavily on these fuels. However, not only do fossil fuels help create greenhouse gases, but their supply will eventually be depleted.

Reliance on Fossil Fuels: It Can't Last Forever

Underneath many of the environmental issues linked to global warming is the use of fossil fuels for energy. According to the *CIA World Factbook*, the United States is the world's largest consumer of oil at close to 20 million barrels per day, which is about 25 percent more than the entire European Union, even though it has 200 million more people than the United States. In comparison, China, the world's most populous country, uses about 40 percent of what the United States consumes in oil each day, and India, which has four times as many people as the United States, uses only 15 percent.[64] The United States produces less than half of the oil it consumes, which means that it is dependent on other countries for a great deal of its energy.

In part because of this imbalance in production and use, and in part because of the political agendas of some countries that produce much of the oil used in the United States, American dependence on fossil fuels is considered not just an environmental issue, but also a security issue. Of course, oil use and production represent an important economic issue as well. For example, when a consortium of oil producing and exporting countries (OPEC) enacted an embargo against the United States in 1973 in response to American policies in the Middle East, oil prices quadrupled in less than a year.[65] In this situation, control of oil output was effectively used as an economic weapon. Similarly, after the Iranian Revolution of 1979, loss of that country's oil on the world market caused widespread panic and economic devastation, and the price of oil reached its highest ever price (adjusted for inflation) until March 2008.[66]

As more countries industrialize, demand for oil is rising, and with this jump in demand come higher prices and increased competition. The situation is only going to get worse if warnings that the world has already passed its peak oil-production capabilities are true.[67] This doesn't mean, of course, that it is possible to simply stop using fossil fuels. In fact, virtually every source of energy used today is somehow linked to fossil fuels. As U.S. Secretary of the Interior Ken Salazar put it in 2009, "We must recognize that we will likely be dependent on conventional sources—oil, gas, and coal—for a significant portion of our energy for many years to come."[68] To this end, the U.S. government has sold leases for lands for offshore drilling, and it has also proposed some new ideas about how to reduce the country's dependence on foreign oil.

Through an array of initiatives to promote and fund increases in solar energy, wind energy, hydropower, and hybrid and electric vehicles, the Obama administration is aggressively pursuing policies to help the United States become less dependent on fossil fuels. In fact, in 2009, President Obama pledged $150 billion over the next 10 years in the areas of clean energy research and development. Ideally, these activities will help move the nation toward a so-called "green economy."

The Green Economy and Green Jobs

As previously discussed, overdependence on fossil fuels is both risky and ultimately unsustainable. A new way of considering our economy is based on the idea of human interdependence with the natural world, with a focus on renewable energy sources such as wind energy, biofuels, and so on (■Exhibit 15.8). This new perspective is often called the **green economy**—an economic model that focuses on development and use

Green economy
An economic model that focuses on development and use of renewable energies such as wind, biofuels, and so on to displace traditional fossil fuels and move businesses and communities toward environmental sustainability.

■Exhibit **15.8**

Green workers install solar panels.

Alamy/Ambient Images Inc/Peter Bennett

Green-collar jobs
Jobs related to providing
environmentally friendly products
or services.

of renewable energies such as wind, biofuels, and so on to displace traditional fossil fuels and move businesses and communities toward environmental sustainability.

With the emergence of the green economy, several other new terms have entered the business vocabulary as well. For example, **green-collar jobs** are jobs related to providing environmentally friendly products or services.[69] Green-collar jobs pay more than blue-collar jobs and have been promoted as a way to help the lower and middle classes while simultaneously helping the economy.[70] The list of green-collar jobs includes positions such as organic farmers, environmental consultants and trainers, solar-power engineers, architects, recycling experts, and compliance officers. In 2008, there were approximately 8.5 million green-collar jobs in the United States, with the expectation that there will be as many as 40 million such positions by 2030.[71] In fact, President Obama has pledged to create an additional 5 million green jobs by 2018.[72]

Another aspect of the green economy is the growth of construction practices that have fewer negative effects on the environment. Today, as companies build new manufacturing, warehousing, and corporate offices, greater attention is being paid to addressing environmental concerns. For example, Discovery Communications, parent company of media entities including the Discovery Channel, TLC, Animal Planet, and FitTV, recently built a new corporate headquarters outside Washington, D.C. The building itself is so environmentally friendly that in 2007, it was only one of nine U.S. structures certified by the U.S. Green Building Council with a Platinum-Level Leadership in Energy and Environmental Design designation.[73] This designation considers everything from the materials used in construction to how the building is heated and cooled.

In addition to climate change and fossil fuels, businesses and organizations also need to attend to other issues related to environmental sustainability, such as pollution, waste, and biodiversity. Let's look at these topics next.

Pollution, Waste, and Environmental Sustainability

The United States has been regulating pollution for decades. The nation's current set of pollution control laws regulates the use of numerous materials that are potentially harmful to both human health and the environment. There is a great deal of variation in terms of expectations and penalties for violators, and these often depend on the risks associated with the materials involved.

One of these statutes—the Comprehensive Environmental Response, Compensation, and Liability Act, commonly called "Superfund"—is of particular note. According to the EPA Web site, "Superfund is the federal government's program to clean up the nation's uncontrolled hazardous waste sites."[74] Superfund is operated by the EPA, which is authorized to identify those parties responsible for toxic pollution and compel them to clean up hazardous sites. As of November 2009, approximately 600 Superfund sites were operating in the mid-Atlantic region alone.[75]

Issues about how to deal with waste have been hotly debated for decades. Although problems remain, the United States and other countries have made great headway in developing and promoting technologies and human habits related to recycling. Currently, most communities in the United States provide the services necessary for recycling aluminum, plastic, and paper. In fact, in today's world, just about anything can be recycled—not only paper, metal, and plastic, but also oil, batteries, and even nuclear waste.

France is currently the world leader in the recycling of nuclear waste, in part because the French (unlike many Americans) embrace nuclear energy.[76] In fact, more than 75 percent of France's electricity came from nuclear sources in 2010.[77] France first became heavily involved in nuclear recycling in the 1970s, when it modernized its recycling plant in La Hague.[78] Since then, the plant has never had a serious accident, although it does release tiny amounts (below legal limits) of radioactive substances into the atmosphere and into the water of the English Channel.[79] The facility is able to recycle 96 percent of nuclear waste, resulting in uranium that is stockpiled so that it can be reused at a later date, as well as plutonium that can be blended with fresh uranium for fresh fuel. Ultimately, the process reduces 528 spent fuel rods into two canisters' worth of material, each a little over one meter tall.[80]

Compare this situation with that at Yucca Mountain, a facility located in the middle of the Mojave Desert about 100 miles northwest of Las Vegas. In 1987, with stockpiles of nuclear waste accumulating across the country, the U.S. government decided to convert the mountain into a dump where this waste would be buried deep underground.[81] This plan has generated a great deal of controversy, because no one wants a nuclear waste facility in their backyard—not even 100 miles away. To the relief of many Nevadans, one of the first things President Obama did after taking office was to effectively kill the Yucca Mountain plan. However, this leaves the U.S. government with no other plan for disposing of deadly radioactive materials.[82]

In the years to come, we are likely to see more efforts aimed at managing waste products in a manner that supports environmental sustainability. This will include complex and controversial disposal plans for dangerous materials such as nuclear waste. It will also include how to deal with more mundane things like household trash. Indeed, one of the most promising streams of technology emerging in today's green economy is the push to find ways to turn trash into energy—a movement that will result in new technologies, new jobs, and a cleaner environment.

Plants, Animals, and Environmental Sustainability

Within the United States, endangered species are protected by the U.S. Fish and Wildlife Service per the terms of the Endangered Species Act of 1973.[83] As of April 2010, this agency classifies 2,018 species as endangered, and 594 of these species have important habitats in the United States.[84] The Fish and Wildlife Service also acts as consultant on a wide range of environmental safety and sustainability issues, and it actively works to plan habitat conservation and recover damaged habitats. In addition, the agency operates fisheries to replenish threatened fish populations, as well as "conservation banks"—parcels of land that are set aside for the conservation of various species.[85]

All over the world, the leading cause of species loss is destruction of natural habitats.[86] The most species-rich habitats such as rain forests are often the most threatened.[87] According to some scholars' estimates, rain-forest loss and other habitat destruction could result in the extinction of as many as 12 percent of plants and 11 percent of birds in the medium-range future.[88]

Another prominent threat to biodiversity is species invasion. This refers to the transplantation of species to new habitats, which frequently occurs as a result of global trade. In a new environment, a new species may have no natural predators, which means it can easily overpopulate. Also, the introduction of non-native species may threaten native plants and animals to the point that they become endangered or are driven to extinction.[89]

The introduction of non-native species to islands is especially harmful because of the delicate balance that must be maintained in a limited space.[90] A particularly salient example took place on the big island of Hawai'i. Early shipping introduced rats to the island, and these rats subsequently threatened the large bird populations by eating their eggs. To get rid of the rats, the mongoose was introduced to the island, but no one accounted for the fact that rats are nocturnal and mongooses hunt by day. The two species rarely meet, so of course, the mongooses have not eliminated the rats. Worse yet, mongooses also eat bird's eggs, so the island's native bird species were even more threatened.[91] Since its introduction to the big island, the mongoose has spread to all but two of the major islands of Hawai'i.

Although protection of native species is clearly required to protect biodiversity, problems arise when efforts to prevent habitat loss come into conflict with business interests and the need for jobs. Another example, also in Hawai'i, involves the billion-dollar 30-meter telescope (which will be the largest telescope on Earth) to be constructed at an observatory atop Mauna Kea. Of all the arguments community members and groups like the Sierra Club put forth, the one that almost won the day was that a small insect lives among the cinder cones where the telescope is to be built. Because the mountaintop is this insect's sole habitat, the land is protected.[92] This points out the very difficult choices that must be made as we try to balance environmental sustainability with social and economic sustainability.

What Else Are We Doing to Foster Environmental Sustainability?

Everyone who is involved in producing and consuming goods and services has a role in environmental sustainability. This includes customers, suppliers, manufacturers, and service providers. Manufacturers are sometimes among the most visible proponents of adopting sustainable practices and marketing the resulting products to consumers. Ford Motor Company, for example, has developed a "blueprint for sustainability" that outlines ways to more power out of more efficient engines, such as by building cars that perform like they have an eight-cylinder engine when they have only six cylinders.[93]

Many firms incorporate this sort of strong environmental commitment into their marketing efforts. In 2009, for instance, Toyota ran a series of commercials for its hybrid automobile, Prius, which featured the tag line "Where man's wants and nature's needs agree" (■Exhibit 15.9).[94]

Despite some progress, laws and policies that do not promote environmental sustainability continue to exist. For example, even though businesses have received tax credits for purchasing hybrid vehicles, up until recently, they also received tax credits for buying gas-guzzling Hummers. This was the result of a law passed in the 1970s with the original intent of allowing small farmers and self-employed workers to buy trucks without being subject to the luxury car tax that was in place at the time. Laws or loopholes such as these do not automatically change with the times, so Congress must intervene when necessary. Until Congress takes action, outdated laws can and often do reward behavior that does not promote sustainability.[95]

Of course, even new laws and programs crafted by proponents of environmental sustainability are not without controversy. For instance, in response to the economic recession

■Exhibit **15.9**

The Toyota Prius is advertised as being a "green" car because of its relatively high gas mileage.

David Hancock/Alamy Images

that began in 2007, Congress passed a "Cash for Clunkers" program that gave Americans a tax credit of $3,500 to $4,500 for each old, inefficient car they got rid of. The Cash for Clunkers program was intended to get inefficient cars off the road and replace them with cars with better gas mileage, while also supporting the auto industry. The program was deemed a success, because approximately 700,000 cars were traded in over the span of a few weeks.[96] But did the program really reflect sound principles of sustainability? To answer this question, let's consider some of the arguments against the program:

- Those consumers who received a $3,500 rebate had to improve their mileage by only four miles per gallon. This is not much of an improvement, and it makes little difference in the long run.[97]
- Consumers could use their rebates toward new cars only; used cars weren't eligible, even if they had better gas mileage than new cars. This triggered a demand for certain models (e.g., hybrids) that could not be met. As a result, auto companies resumed production of several high-demand models. However, by producing more new cars, these companies also used more resources and fossil fuels and thereby contributed to existing environmental problems.
- All of the "clunkers" turned in through the program were destroyed, save for a few exotic cars with historical or financial value. The destruction of these assets left fewer cars to be donated to charities that rely on such donations to fund their operations.

Still, once the Cash for Clunkers program ended, the federal government reported that the cars purchased under the program averaged a 58 percent improvement in miles per gallon (from 15.8 to 24.9 miles per gallon).[98] This means that buyers went far beyond the mandated 4 miles per gallon improvement. In light of this and the arguments above, would you say that the program promoted environmental sustainability? What about economic sustainability?

As technologies advance and research continues, your role as a manager and leader will become increasingly focused on supporting your company in providing goods and services while respecting environmental sustainability. That's not the whole story, however. Partly because of our increasingly interconnected world, there is also a growing awareness of the importance of fostering social sustainability—which, of course, is linked to environmental sustainability. In the next section, we will explore a few aspects of social sustainability that are particularly critical to organizations, businesses, and responsible leaders.

Most Popular » Discussion Questions

1. What is your opinion about the Kyoto Protocol's requirement that developed nations take on a heavier burden than developing countries in reducing greenhouse gas emissions?
2. Using the Internet, research a company that supports environmental sustainability. Would you want to work for this company? Why or why not?
3. What can you do in your life today to help reduce greenhouse gas emissions? What effect would this action have on your life?

---

5. What Is Social Sustainability?

As you saw earlier in the chapter, social sustainability focuses on improving people's lives through equity, equality, and access to health care and education. Social sustainability examines the ways in which natural resources, education, skills, and social institutions build human quality of life. Similar to other sustainability concepts, social sustainability is concerned with meeting the social needs of the present population while ensuring a healthy social climate for future generations. Although closely related to both environmental and economic sustainability, social sustainability steps beyond its sister concepts in its recognition that the conditions of equality, equity, education, opportunity, and protection of all basic human rights are pivotal to the creation of a truly sustainable global society.[99]

There are numerous ways to look at social sustainability with respect to people around the world. Three particularly important issues are poverty, access to education, and global health. Many organizations are attempting to address these issues, including Ashoka, as described in the following *Business Case.*

Ashoka

A Proactive Approach to Social Sustainability

Ashoka is an organization that's clearly focused on social sustainability. Founded in Washington, D.C., in 1980 by Bill Drayton, Ashoka began with the premise that "the most effective way to promote positive social change is to invest in social entrepreneurs who have innovative solutions to society's problems that are sustainable and replicable, both nationally and globally."[100] A social entrepreneur is a person who identifies social issues and organizes people, resources, and networks to address these problems. Once Ashoka locates such individu-

als, it chooses some of them to be "fellows." The company then supports each fellow with guidance, expertise, and funding as he or she launches and grows a business.

One Ashoka fellow, chosen in 2008, is Molly Barker. With Ashoka's help, Barker founded Girls on the Run, an organization that helps girls and women eliminate the social barriers they face and helps them make positive choices while reducing risky behavior. Today, the venture has many sponsors, including Kellogg, New Balance, Goody, and Horizon Fitness, which together fund Girls on the Run's $1.5 million annual budget.

Ashoka promotes positive social change

Photo Source: pidjoe/iStock

Ashoka is a bit unusual among companies in that its mission is to directly support social sustainability. Although most companies don't have this as their primary focus, they too can support social sustainability through their business practices. Several key issues are currently of particular importance in the world and to business today: child labor, slavery, and workplace safety.

Child Labor

There is little doubt that most companies today would object to the use of child labor—so why does this practice continue to exist? To answer this question, let's consider a bit of history. First, in our species' past, children have always worked alongside family members on farms and in small businesses. How children were treated varied widely. While in many cases these situations were likely quite brutal, many others were likely fair, just, and even loving ways for families to live and get by. Therefore, children doing tasks is itself not necessarily the problem. What *is* a problem, however, is when children are subject to brutality, denied education, and forced into poor working conditions without legal protections. This sort of exploitation of child workers first came to public attention in the United States during the Industrial Revolution. What followed was a movement in which American society recognized the evils of forcing children to work in dangerous factories and sweatshops, and this movement eventually resulted in the eradication of child labor from most American industries.[101] Today, many other countries also have laws against exploitation of children in the workplace.

But global statistics paint a very different picture. A 2009 report by the U.S. Department of Labor cited statistics estimating 200 million children were working in hazardous conditions worldwide.[102]

The problem of child labor can be tricky for companies, especially when cultural differences collide on a global scale. For example, in 2006, after it was revealed that Nike products were made with child labor, the company severed its ties with Pakistani supplier Saga in order to repair its public image in the United States and other countries. Saga was severely affected by this loss, and it estimated that as many as 20,000 Pakistani families may have been impacted as well.[103] Nasir Dogar, chief executive of the Independent Monitoring Association for Child Labor, notes that although Saga was in the wrong, Nike may have intensified the damage by relying on child labor and then suddenly cutting ties as soon as public pressure mounted.[104]

Most companies intend to act in a responsible manner, especially when it comes to issues such as child labor. But then there's the issue of global competition. When countries allow child labor or companies find ways to exploit children illegally, costs of doing business are lower. Indeed, if companies in some parts of the world can hire child workers and pay them very little to work in a dangerous environment, then these companies can make a cheaper product that other nations will likely buy. What that means for responsible businesses and consumers is that we need to be informed, and we need to learn to make choices based on values and ethics—not just cost of doing business or price of goods.

Today, ever more people and organizations are getting the message that globalization does not simply mean exploitation for the sake of profit. For instance, the Fair Trade Federation, whose stamp of approval began appearing on coffee years ago, is one of several watchdog organizations that ensure the products they endorse create opportunities for economically disadvantaged regions. Products that bear the Fair Trade seal are produced by businesses that participate in transparent trade, offer reasonable pay for labor and materials in developing countries, and protect children and other workers from exploitation.[105]

Today, the Fair Trade label can be found on clothing, chocolate, and a wide variety of other products whose manufacture has traditionally involved labor exploitation. Equal Exchange is another organization similar to the Fair Trade Federation, and it too issues a stamp of approval for certain products. Lots of consumers now look for things like the Equal Exchange and the Fair Trade stamps of approval to help them make informed choices about what they buy. Both of these labels are growing quickly in popularity, and they are a symbol for how people are changing the way they think about corporate social responsibility.[106]

Slavery in the World Today

When we think about slavery, we often focus only on that shameful period of history when millions of Africans were taken from their homes and sold as slaves in places like the Caribbean, South America, and the United States. The practice of enslaving people and forcing them to work in plantations, ships, homes, and other businesses during the sixteenth through nineteenth centuries left a lasting and terrible mark on many communities around the world. However, that period was not the only time in which people enslaved others, robbing them of freedom and dignity in order to foster their own (usually economic) interests. As shown in ■Exhibit 15.10, slavery has existed for an incredibly long time.

Let's look more closely at what slavery is and how it is still present today. The term *slavery* refers to a type of forced labor in which people are essentially the property of others. According to the United Nations Educational, Scientific, and Cultural Organization (UNESCO), most definitions of slavery focus on the practice as a legal institution, which is rare, so these definitions are not very useful for understanding modern slavery.[107] In today's world, slavery is rampant but largely illegal. Women and children tend to be the victims—as sex slaves, child soldiers, and sweatshop workers (■Exhibit 15.11).

■Exhibit **15.10**

A Few Examples of Slavery throughout History			
Masters	**Time Frame**	**Sources of Slaves**	**Types of Work**
Ancient Greeks[108]	Roughly 6th to 3rd century B.C.E.	Primarily war, but also piracy and trade	Agricultural laborers; domestic servants; tradesmen; mine workers
Han Dynasty of China[109]	206 B.C.E to 220 C.E.	Penal enslavement; children born of illegal unions; children of slave parents; darker-skinned border people	Laborers; servants; concubines
Aztecs[110]	Roughly 14th to 16th century C.E.	War prisoners from neighboring peoples	Human sacrifices for religious ceremonies, among other things
Buganda[111] (present-day Uganda)	Probably before 19th century B.C.E. until well into the 20th century	Captives of war, primarily women and children	Domestic servants; laborers; concubines

Not everyone agrees how many people are enslaved today. According to a United Nations estimate, in 2005 there were 27 million slaves in the world. This is more than double the number of Africans who were sent to the Americas during the 400 years of the African slave trade.[112] According to the International Labour Office (ILO), at the turn of the twenty-first century, 8.4 million children between the ages of 5 and 17 were victims of human trafficking, forced/bonded labor, armed conflict, prostitution, pornography, and other illegal activities.[113] A later report by the ILO calculates that, at minimum, 12.3 million people worldwide are victims of forced labor, with 2.4 million of these cases involving human trafficking.[114] Although these estimates differ, they have one thing in common: The number of people who are likely enslaved today is huge.

■Exhibit **15.11**

These two West African children work as slaves.

Alamy/Trinity Mirror/Mirrorpix

Sex trafficking is one of the most pervasive and hardest to eliminate forms of modern slavery. In January 2010, the Indian Supreme Court issued a demand that the country's government do more to stop sex tourism in the country, which has been a source of international embarrassment. Some experts estimate that more than 70 percent of Indian sex workers are children under the age of 18.[115] Sex slavery exists in all corners of the world, even in the United States. For instance, in 2007, both MSNBC and the *Today* show featured the story of Ukrainian women who had been forced to work in a Detroit strip club after coming to the United States to study English. These women were kidnapped at an American airport by Russian human traffickers and were imprisoned with 15 other slaves.[116] A lot of women have been tricked into slavery in Eastern Europe as well, often with enticements of legitimate work offers.[117]

The stories and statistics are nothing less than shocking—and it's even more shocking to imagine what these statistics actually *mean*. The concept of social sustainability is meaningless if we allow practices like this to continue.

So why does this practice exist? Obviously there are many reasons, but when it comes to business, globalization and increasing consumer demand for cheap products have led to the perpetuation of practices that decrease costs, such as exploitation of children and slave labor. In 2009, the U.S. Department of Labor released a list of countries that engage in slave and child labor along with the following statement:

> As a nation and as members of the global community, we reject the proposition that it is acceptable to pursue economic gain through the forced labor of other human beings or the exploitation of children in the workplace. However, we are aware that these problems remain widespread in today's global economy. Indeed, we face these problems in our own country.[118]

Excepting pornography, the industries identified by the Department of Labor are all in the agricultural, mining, and manufacturing sectors. Particular instances of slave labor cited in the report include the following:[119]

- Garment manufacturers in Argentina
- Cotton farmers in Benin
- Agricultural workers in Bolivia and Brazil
- Cotton farmers and gold miners in Burkina Faso
- Mining, brick making, and agricultural workers in Myanmar
- Workers in a host of industries in China
- Toy and drug manufacturers in Colombia
- Cocoa and coffee growers in the Ivory Coast
- Sugarcane farmers in the Dominican Republic
- Fishery workers in Ghana
- Garment, textile, quarry, and agricultural laborers in India
- Garments workers in Jordan
- Cotton and tobacco farmers in Kazakhstan
- Tobacco workers in Malawi
- Garment manufacturers in Malaysia
- Agricultural laborers in Mali
- Textile and quarry workers in Nepal
- Cocoa growers and quarry workers in Nigeria
- Mine laborers in North Korea
- Agricultural workers in Pakistan
- Cattle workers in Paraguay
- Mining and agricultural laborers in Peru
- Pornography workers in Russia
- Diamond miners in Sierra Leone
- Cotton growers in Tajikistan

- Garment and fishery workers in Thailand
- Cotton growers in Turkmenistan and Uzbekistan

One reason why this report was released was to help American companies and consumers make informed buying decisions based on information about how and under what conditions goods are produced. The Department of Labor's Bureau of International Labor Affairs has published over 20 such reports since 1993, and it has provided a total of $720 million to more than 80 countries as part of its efforts to combat child and slave labor.[120]

But what can you do to help? First, you need to become informed by reading reports such as the one released by the Department of Labor. Then, you need to investigate. Are any of the organizations, businesses, or groups that you typically engage with involved in such practices? It may seem unlikely, but during the past 10 years or so, a number of well-respected manufacturers, hotels, farms, and other businesses have been revealed to use people in a way that is essentially slavery. If we are to claim that we support social sustainability, then we each have a responsibility to find out where our money is going and to refuse to do business with companies that use these horrific practices.

Safety and Risk at Work

In some cases, work can be dangerous or even deadly. For example, one of the worst workplace accidents in U.S. history occurred in 1947, when a harbor explosion in Texas City, Texas, claimed the lives of 576 people both on land and at sea.[121] In China, there are reports of lead poisoning from industrial facilities affecting hundreds of factory workers and thousands of children, and many families have been forced to relocate because of pollution.[122] In Thailand, a 1993 fire in a toy factory claimed the lives of 188 workers, mostly young females, and seriously injured 500 more.[123]

While these dramatic incidents capture our attention, employees and companies everywhere struggle to create and maintain safe work environments. Sales organizations face car accidents; manufacturing plants deal with machine accidents; chemicals spill or are used inappropriately. The list goes on and on. And it's not just company conditions or policies that are problematic—employees often make very bad decisions: Sales people don't use seat belts and die in crashes; machine operators try to fix equipment while it's running and lose hands; employees walk through hazardous chemical spills. These things happen. But why would people do such stupid things? There are many reasons, including inadequate safety standards and/or compliance processes, habit, organizational cultures that encourage speed or results even when safety is compromised, over-tiredness, and stress. Whatever the reasons, organizations that want to support social sustainability within their boundaries need to attend to creating conditions where people can be, and choose to be, safe.

And in an age of globalization, workplace safety is no longer just a concern for individual employees, their companies, or their immediate communities. Global trade means that dangerous materials used in a factory in one country can poison and even kill humans and animals in other countries worldwide. Pollution does not respect national boundaries—for instance, nuclear waste from the Chernobyl nuclear reactor disaster in the former Soviet Union (now Ukraine) traveled halfway across the globe.[124] Also, companies and countries are no longer protected from repercussions related to risky decisions. International lawsuits are on the rise, and assets can be seized in other countries.[125]

Most of the world's governments have some sort of system in place to regulate workplace safety. In the United States, that system is the Occupational Safety and Health Administration (OSHA), which is run by the U.S. Department of Labor. OSHA was created by President Nixon in 1970, following the signing of the Occupational Safety and Health Act.[126] Beyond keeping track of occupational accidents, OSHA is responsible for regulating the safety of American workplaces through an array of policies and

■Exhibit **15.12**

Example OSHA Regulations and Guidelines

- Use of guards on all moving parts of industrial machines[127]
- Permissible exposure limits for approximately 600 chemicals[128]
- Requirements regarding the use of personal protective equipment (e.g., gloves, clothing, earplugs, face shields, respirators) when handling chemicals and operating in industrial environments[129]
- Turning off energy sources when conducting repairs[130]
- Use of two-person crews and air sampling when working in confined spaces[131]
- Hazard communication policies that require developing and communicating information about dangerous workplace chemical products[132]
- Regulations to protect health care workers against bloodborne pathogens such as HIV and hepatitis B[133]
- Safeguards for workers in excavations or deep trenches to prevent collapses or cave-ins[134]
- Asbestos exposure safety regulations[135]

requirements, some of which are outlined in ■Exhibit 15.12.[136] Since its formation, OSHA has had a significant impact on many businesses and industries.

Some companies are especially vigilant when it comes to protecting their workers. For example, "America's Safest Companies" is an annual award presented by watchdog organization EHS to companies that take extra steps to ensure safety. Organizations that receive this award excel at matters such as innovative solutions to workplace safety challenges, injury and illness rates below national averages, and strong safety training programs, among other criteria.[137]

Most Popular » Discussion Questions

1. Do you think it's a company's responsibility to "police" its suppliers to make sure they are complying with laws and the company's ethical code when it comes to issues such as child labor? Why or why not?
2. Research child labor on the Internet. Which countries seem to engage in this practice the most? What do you think should be done about this situation?
3. Research slavery in the world today. Who tends to be enslaved? Why do you think this is the case? How do you feel about this issue, and what can you and others do to combat it?
4. Take two hours and walk around your school's campus. What evidence do you see that suggests the school is proactive about employee and student safety?

---

6. What Is Economic Sustainability?

Economic sustainability refers to an economy's ability to create and maintain economic conditions that foster current economic health and long-term economic development. Also referred to as sustainable development, this activity is recognized by the United Nations as a shared responsibility of both world governments and private institutions, such as businesses. Contained within the UN definition of economic sustainability are two key concepts: a focus on the needs of the world's poor, "to which overriding priority should be given"; and responsible use of natural resources in a manner that benefits present and future generations and has a positive impact on worldwide economic health and growth.[138]

The concept of sustainable development has drawn criticism from environmentalists, who dislike the way it assigns value to resources based on their usefulness to mankind, as well as from more traditional economists, who dislike the emphasis it places on efficacy and equity in the long term rather than profit now.[139] Nevertheless, economic sustainability and the notion of sustainable development are gaining popularity as concerns related to the environment, the exploitation of resources in underdeveloped nations, and the ability of future generations to continue enjoying a high standard of living create uncertainty and apprehension about the future.

How does a focus on sustainability impact our capitalist economic system? Are the two at odds? Not according to Al Gore and David Blood of Generation Investment Management, who are the subject of the following *Business Case* feature.

Generation Investment Management   **Business** Case

Al Gore and David Blood

Few people would argue against environmental or social sustainability from an ethical point of view. But can sustainability be the right ethical choice *and* the right way for firms to invest and manage their money? Al Gore and David Blood think so. Together, they run Generation Investment Management, an asset management firm that promotes sustainable capitalism.

Gore and Blood believe that the only way human civilization can continue is by taking a long-term view of how businesses impact both people and the environment. They see a combination of sustainability and commercial acumen as the key to long-term value and business success.[140] The philosophy behind Generation Investment Management's simple but transformational solution is that rather than looking at a long checklist of sustainability criteria, a business should develop a strategy that incorporates both a focus on business initiatives that meet market needs and a focus on sustainability—thereby positively impacting profitability in the long term as well as the short term.[141] When asked for examples of successful companies that have implemented this approach, Blood states the following:

Al Gore

A company like Johnson Controls, for example . . . [has] a focus on the demand side [of] energy efficiency. About 50% of its business is batteries for hybrid cars and products to run buildings efficiently; the other 50% is automotive interiors and controls. We think it's the former that's going to be growing and driving that company. They understand that their products will help reduce their clients' environmental footprint. This strategy is completely revenue driven.[142]

Another example of a project that reflects Gore and Blood's philosophy is in Mexico, where homebuilders are linking demographic trends, environmentally sustainable construction practices, and the demand for affordable housing.[143] Yet another example is Unilever's Project Shakti, a rural entrepreneurship pro-

gram.[144] This program involves the creation of self-help groups in Indian villages, where Unilever recruits people to become salespersons called *shakti amma*. These individuals go to surrounding villages to sell products and distribute health information. This is helpful because it provides the people (largely women) with an income, and it also gives Unilever access to rural areas—markets that are traditionally very difficult for outsiders to reach.[145]

Despite these good examples, investing in long-term sustainability is still far from mainstream.[146] This is partly because it requires a mindset change from corporations as vehicles for short-term profit gain to corporations as important drivers of long-term sustainability within and beyond their boundaries. Another mindset change is to shift from a focus on *stockholders* to a focus on *stakeholders*.[147] In addition, Gore and Blood believe that we need to shift our collective mindset toward acknowledging that every organization's successes and challenges have numerous immediate and long-term effects on world economic, social, and political systems.[148]

Gore and Blood also state that we need to bridge the disconnect between sustainability indicators and financial indicators. Actions and investments that support long-term sustainability cost money, and they can negatively impact profitability in the short term—something many companies avoid at all costs. However, Gore and Blood's position is that unless companies take these actions, the long-term sustainability of not only the business but also the environment and the communities it serves is at risk.[149]

Gore and Blood see a powerful link between focusing on sustainability, long-term financial success, and a company's reputation and attractiveness to customers and employees.[150] Their question is not whether businesses can learn to successfully put sustainability at the forefront of their strategy, but rather how fast and how effectively they can do it.

Photo Source: Stocklight/Shutterstock

Al Gore and David Blood manage Generation Investment Management in ways that allow them to support businesses in making decisions with the long term in mind while simultaneously maintaining short-term viability. This is not easy, because for many years, short-term profitability (especially in publicly traded companies) has been the sole measure of business success. The move from a short-term orientation to a long-term orientation takes time and collaboration from virtually all stakeholders—and some companies are making this commitment.

For example, Sonoco, a South Carolina–based supplier of industrial and consumer packaging, states that "we believe that sustainability and business success are not only compatible but are inextricably linked and that by embracing both, we will benefit our shareholders for the long term."[151] Similarly, WholeSoy, a California-based maker of soybean-based products, incorporates sustainability into many of its processes and practices. For example, the company pays a living wage to all of its employees, offers company-funded health benefits, and has located its facilities near public transportation. In fact, the company proudly notes that only one employee actually drives to work![152]

Economic sustainability can take many forms, and it doesn't always involve big business. To illustrate this, let's look at a partnership between college students and a small town in Ecuador in the following *Student's Choice* feature.

Student's Choice

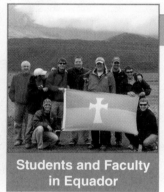

Students and Faculty in Equador

Passion and Partnership: One Road to Economic Sustainability

The Salinas Foundation is a cooperative organization in Quito, Ecuador, that consists of several microindustries that produce and sell products made from Salinas's natural resources. When the organization began some decades ago, only a handful of companies were involved, but today, there are a variety of vibrant small businesses that have helped Salinas immensely.[153]

In 2009, a group of students from Arkansas State University (ASU) traveled to Salinas to get a firsthand idea of the local environment and consult with the businesses located there. After a week in Salinas, the students generated ideas and advice as to how the companies could increase their production, run more efficiently, and lower their costs. One issue of particular in-

terest to the students was how to expand the businesses' markets. As of 2009, the town's enterprises sold products in only two countries outside of South America—Japan and Italy.[154] The students came upon one solution: open a store back in the United States to sell the foundation's products. When the students returned from Ecuador, they began working to fulfill this dream, taking steps to open a store in their hometown that would sell some of the products made in Salinas.

The ASU–Salinas partnership has the potential to dramatically affect many lives. The students hope that their store will bring joy and prosperity to the people of Salinas. As demand for the products of Salinas grows, so will the industries and the town itself. This venture will also have long-lasting effects on the students, providing them with knowledge that will not only help them in business, but will have a deep impact on their personal lives.

Photo: Front left to right of photo (kneeling) Jonathan McCoy and Joshua Adkerson; Back left to right (standing) Dr. Clint Relyea, Jared Jacks, Reid Robertson, Seth Holifield, Brian McFarlane, John Mooney, Austin Allen. Special Thanks: Reid Robertson.

This case shows that more and more sectors of society are becoming engaged in the move toward an increased focus on the environment, the health and well being of people everywhere, and the long-term economic viability of communities, organizations, and industries. As we become more interconnected globally in our businesses and organizations, governments will play a significant role in encouraging sustainability at every level. Meanwhile, the scientific and not-for-profit communities provide research, innovation, and watchdog functions, and many businesses and organizations are increasingly facing the issues proactively rather than simply complying with rules and regulations. Perhaps most importantly, individuals—such as you, your friends, and your colleagues—are working to ensure that environmental, social, and economic sustainability become a lasting way of life.

Most Popular » Discussion Questions

1. Search the Internet for information about businesses that foster or support economic sustainability. Is there a common thread with respect to these organizations' philosophies or work? If so, what is it? If not, why do you think differences exist?
2. What is your definition of a successful organization? When formulating your answer, consider economic sustainability and the organization's impact on all of its stakeholders.
3. Research the largest city near your home. What programs exist in the city to support economic development? How effective are these programs, in your opinion?

7. What Is Corporate Social Responsibility?

Corporate social responsibility (CSR)
A form of corporate self-regulation that builds sustainability and public interest into business decision making and activities.

Philanthropy
Giving money, time, services, or products in the service of supporting people's well-being.

Corporate social responsibility (CSR) is a form of corporate self-regulation that builds sustainability and public interest into business decision making and activities. Broadly defined, CSR is the term used to describe how businesses and institutions address environmental, social, and economic sustainability.

Corporate social responsibility has its roots in corporate philanthropy. The word *philanthropy* is derived from the Greek words *phil*, which means "love," and *anthropos*, which means "mankind." So, philanthropy is a word that means to love mankind.[155] In a practical sense, **philanthropy** means giving money, time, services, or products in the service of supporting people's well-being. Philanthropy is not a new idea and it continues today, as you can see in ■Exhibit 15.13.

■Exhibit **15.13**

Famous Philanthropists Past and Present	
Name	**Philanthropic Efforts**
Benjamin Franklin	Franklin is credited with being the father of American philanthropy. In 1727, he founded a 12-person club called Junto, which evolved into a think tank for philanthropic ideas. His newspaper, the *Philadelphia Gazette*, was routinely used for mobilization of the public, recruitment of volunteers, and fund-raising. Among his many public service works, Franklin founded the University of Pennsylvania, the country's first public library, the country's first volunteer fire department, and a hospital.[156]
Andrew Carnegie	The Scottish-American magnate was known as a ruthless baron of the steel industry and a devout Christian. After selling out his share of U.S. Steel in 1901, he became heavily involved in activism for world peace, giving away most of his vast fortune. He created the Carnegie Endowment for International Peace in 1910 with a gift of $10 million. The following year, he created the Carnegie Corporation of New York "to promote the advancement and diffusion of knowledge and understanding." Another foundation, the Carnegie Institute, operates four museums in Pittsburgh, including the Andy Warhol Museum. He also founded what is now known as Carnegie Mellon University.[157]
Bill and Melinda Gates	The cofounder of Microsoft has given more money to charity than anyone in history. Bill Gates set up the Bill and Melinda Gates Foundation in 2000, and in 2008, it had a $34 billion endowment to improve global health and learning. Warren Buffet donated an additional $31 billion to the foundation in 2008—at the time, half of his fortune. The foundation has paid out more than $20 billion since its inception.[158]

Continued on next page>>

■ Exhibit **15.13**   **Continued**

Famous Philanthropists Past and Present	
Name	**Philanthropic Efforts**
Bono	The lead singer of immensely popular rock band U2 has been internationally recognized for his ongoing philanthropic efforts. He was involved in Band Aid and Live Aid in 1984 and 1985 to raise money for famine relief in Ethiopia. In 2002, he cofounded DATA (Debt, AIDS, Trade in Africa) to work for equality and justice in Africa through debt relief, improving trade, and fighting the AIDS epidemic.[159]
Jet Li	Li Lianjie is better known as Jet Li, the famous Chinese director and actor of martial arts films. Li founded the Jet Li One Foundation shortly after he became ambassador for the Red Cross Society of China. His interest in philanthropy was greatly influenced by a near-death experience when he and his 4-year-old daughter were caught in a tsunami in 2004. The foundation's four principles are education, health, care for the environment, and relief of poverty. It works closely with the Red Cross to meet these goals.[160]
Marcos de Moraes	De Moraes, a dynamic Brazilian businessman, has focused on education with his foundations Zip Educação and Instituto Rukha. Through his institutions, he has worked to take children off the streets and enroll them in school. He has also provided free Web services to 6 million students. De Moraes works with a global circle of philanthropists called the Synergos organization.[161]
Rohini Nilekani	Nilekani, social activist and journalist wife of Infosys CEO Nandan Nilekani, began to look for ways of productively giving away money as soon as it started rolling in. She built two foundations: the Akshara Foundation, which is dedicated to education, and the Arghyam Trust, which focuses on clean water.[162]

■ Exhibit **15.14**

Dimensions of Corporate Social Responsibility		
Dimension	**Context**	**How Companies Talk about the Dimension**
Environmental	The natural environment	"A cleaner environment" "Environmental stewardship"
Social	The relationship between corporations and society	"Contribute to a better society" "Consider the full scope of impact on communities" "Integrate social concerns in business operations"
Economic	Socioeconomic or financial elements of operation	"Contribute to economic development" "Preserving profitability while also thinking about the future"
Stakeholder	All stakeholders or stakeholder groups	"There are many stakeholders we need to consider" "How we interact with our employees, suppliers, customers, and communities matters a lot"
Voluntariness (willingness)	Whether or not actions are prescribed by law	"We engage in CSR because it's the right thing to do" "We are acting on our values and ethics, beyond legal obligations"

Source: Adapted from Dahlsrud, Alexander. 2008. How corporate social responsibility is defined: An analysis of 37 definitions. *Corporate Social Responsibility and Environmental Management* 15(1): 4.

It has become common practice for owners of companies and other wealthy individuals to donate money to philanthropic organizations, partly out of a sense of duty (or commitment to sustainability) and partly to create goodwill throughout the community. Is philanthropy, however, the only measure of corporate responsibility? Consider Kenneth Lay, former (and now deceased) CEO of Enron. As CEO of Enron, Lay donated millions to philanthropies throughout Texas and the United States, in part to generate goodwill for his company—and it worked. Enron and Lay were thought of highly in both social and political spheres. In terms of corporate social responsibility, however, we could never hold up Enron as a paragon. As a result of the company's illegal business practices, thousands of people lost their jobs at Enron and other companies affected by the fallout, and many also lost their life savings that had been invested in Enron stock.[163] Giving money isn't enough to brand an organization as socially responsible, and in fact there are other important ways companies engage in CSR. For example, in one notable study, five common dimensions emerged: environmental, social, economic, stakeholder, and voluntariness (willingness). As you can see in ■Exhibit 15.14, these dimensions cover a broad set of definitions and ways of expressing commitment to CSR.

One outstanding example of a company that is building CSR into everything it does is McCain Foods Limited, a Canadian-based company that manufactures and distributes frozen foods around the world.

Perspectives

CSR is a pillar within McCain Food's strategic business model, guiding business decisions and how the company relates to its employees, customers, consumers, suppliers, and communities in which it operates. Mary McNevin, President of McCain Learning Centre, the organization accountable for developing McCain's people, has a keen sense of what it means to incorporate social responsibility into everything everyone does at the company. She describes the company's approach this way:

Mary McNevin, President, McCain Learning Centre

We build our pillars of Corporate Social Responsibility—Respecting the Environment, Inspiring Wellness, and Positively Impacting Our People—into everything we do. It's all about caring for our key stakeholders and focusing our efforts on ensuring that we do the right things in the right way to benefit both these stakeholders and our shareholders. For example, we have a global energy reduction program—the Search for Joules—which reduced our energy consumption by 5 percent between 2005 and 2009, as well as a similar water reduction program called the Search for Pools.

We also focus on the communities where we work and do business. For example, vegetable agronomy and the transfer of knowledge to contract growers have played key roles in McCain Foods' worldwide success. Our role is to share our research, knowledge, and expertise with our grower partners to ensure their operations have the least impact on the environment and deliver quality product and a profitable return. In India, for example, farming is traditionally done manually, but after McCain's arrival just 10 years ago, partner growers have learned the technology of sowing and reaping with machines and the value of applying fertilizers. The result has been record breaking, with yields from one acre of land once averaging 1 to 10 tons of potatoes increasing to 15 tons today. Further, McCain has helped reduce farmers' expenditures by 35 percent and increase income by 104 percent. In China, where similar initiatives were implemented when we entered this market in 1998, our supply of raw product, which was 100 percent grown by McCain corporate farms just three years ago, is 95 percent supplied by the local growing community today.

We also focus on developing our people into leaders at all levels of the organization. After all, if we have better leaders, it's so much more fun to come into work every day, and our company and our people thrive.

Source: Personal interview with Mary McNevin conducted by Annie McKee, 2009.

Mary McNevin explains what corporate social responsibility really means. She shows us that, in fact, this approach is not an add-on, or a nice-to-have, or something to do so you look good. It's essential to good business.

Most Popular » Discussion Questions

1. In your opinion, do you have to be wealthy in order to be a philanthropist? Why or why not?
2. Consider this quote: "If you think you are too small to make an impact, try going to bed with a mosquito in the room" (attributed to various authors). In light of the quote, do you think all companies should be involved in CSR, regardless of their size? Why or why not?
3. Do you donate time or money to causes in which you believe?

---

8. How Can Companies Approach Corporate Social Responsibility?

People today are demanding to do business with companies that make social responsibility part of their core values—and with today's communication technologies, they can readily find out if a company acts in a socially responsible way or not.[164] By the same token, investors and employees also prefer to interact with a company that has a firm foothold in socially responsible approaches, at least for innovative firms.[165] After all, would you want to work for a firm that you knew was not socially responsible? How would you feel if your employer was constantly in the news for ethical violations, unfair labor practices, or environmental contamination? Of course, leaders do not want to be in the headlines for engaging in socially irresponsible practices. The high costs of bad publicity are immeasurable for individuals and companies alike.

It would seem that CSR makes sense, but there are many competing priorities in organizations, and CSR can easily slip to last place. This is especially true when a company is experiencing financial strain due to economic conditions, competition, or the need to invest in innovations or new technology.

When it comes down to it, CSR is a choice—a choice all stakeholders have a say in. Scholars note that the justification for CSR should not lie in its relation to the bottom line but rather to principles of social justice.[166] And many companies have discovered that engaging in CSR is most powerful when it is at the heart of strategy.[167] Take global pharmaceutical company Johnson & Johnson (J&J), for example. J&J focused on corporate social responsibility long before it was popular. Known simply as "the Credo," J&J's mission statement was created by Robert Wood Johnson in 1943. As you can see in ■Exhibit 15.15, the Credo spells out how the company should operate in light of its obligations to individuals who use or administer its products, its stakeholders, and society. The Credo begins with a focus on doctors, nurses, patients, mothers and fathers, and anyone who uses the company's products, then moves to employees, communities, and the environment. It *ends* with stockholders and business management—where many companies both start and end.[168]

As the J&J Web site states, "Our Credo is more than just a moral compass. We believe it's a recipe for business success. The fact that Johnson & Johnson is one of only a handful of companies that have flourished through more than a century of change is proof of that."[169]

Like J&J, many companies have discovered that it actually makes economic sense to engage in socially responsible activities. Many people, managers, and leaders look at CSR from the perspective that it is indeed the right thing to do—and also the smart

■Exhibit **15.15**

The Johnson & Johnson Credo

We believe our first responsibility is to the doctors, nurses and patients,
to mothers and fathers and all others who use our products and services.
In meeting their needs everything we do must be of high quality.
We must constantly strive to reduce our costs
in order to maintain reasonable prices.
Customers' orders must be serviced promptly and accurately.
Our suppliers and distributors must have an opportunity
to make a fair profit.

We are responsible to our employees,
the men and women who work with us throughout the world.
Everyone must be considered as an individual.
We must respect their dignity and recognize their merit.
They must have a sense of security in their jobs.
Compensation must be fair and adequate,
and working conditions clean, orderly and safe.
We must be mindful of ways to help our employees fulfill
their family responsibilities.
Employees must feel free to make suggestions and complaints.
There must be equal opportunity for employment, development
and advancement for those qualified.
We must provide competent management,
and their actions must be just and ethical.

We are responsible to the communities in which we live and work
and to the world community as well.
We must be good citizens — support good works and charities
and bear our fair share of taxes.
We must encourage civic improvements and better health and education.
We must maintain in good order
the property we are privileged to use,
protecting the environment and natural resources.

Our final responsibility is to our stockholders.
Business must make a sound profit.
We must experiment with new ideas.
Research must be carried on, innovative programs developed
and mistakes paid for.
New equipment must be purchased, new facilities provided
and new products launched.
Reserves must be created to provide for adverse times.
When we operate according to these principles,
the stockholders should realize a fair return.

Source: Johnson & Johnson. Our Credo. Retrieved April 10, 2010, from http://www.jnj.com/wps/wcm/connect/
c7933f004f5563df9e22be1bb31559c7/our-credo.pdf?MOD=AJPERES.

thing to do. But how does a firm determine if it is successful in its CSR efforts? This is
not an easy question to address, because CSR is both a stance and the sum of all actions
every manager, employee, and leader takes on a day-to-day basis. Let's look at how approaches to CSR can be evaluated.

■ Exhibit **15.16**

Organizations can approach corporate social responsibility in at least four different ways.

Obstructionist	Defensive	Accommodative	Proactive

From the board of directors to the senior executive team, from managers to each and every employee, CSR is enacted—or not—every day. Many companies take CSR very seriously. In fact, one recent study showed that about half of the people holding jobs that ensure that a company is socially responsible reported directly to the CEO or to a board member.[170] To an outside observer, this could be an indication that a company takes CSR seriously.

But how can we really know whether a company is engaged in CSR in a meaningful way? Let's look at how scholars have categorized various approaches to CSR. The visible behaviors associated with these approaches enable us to evaluate how a company is dealing with CSR. ■Exhibit 15.16 illustrates a continuum of these four approaches.

The Obstructionist Approach

With the obstructionist approach, a firm gives little or no attention to social responsibility. For managers in these companies, social responsibility takes a distant backseat to profits and operations. Obstructionists engage in unethical and sometimes illegal actions in order to hide their socially irresponsible behavior.

One early example of the obstructionist approach occurred in 1892 at Andrew Carnegie's Homestead Steel Mill, when 3,000 workers went on strike in pursuit of higher wages and safer working conditions. Instead of talking to the workers and trying to come to an agreement, the company hired a private army to stop the strikers. The confrontation between the workers and the strikers led to the death of 12 people. Even in the late 1800s, such an extreme approach was uncommon.[171] It is interesting to note that later in life, Carnegie was a champion of some aspects of social responsibility.

The Defensive Approach

If a company takes a defensive approach to CSR, then it is only engaging in those activities that it is legally required to do. It won't necessarily try to hide anything or go to extremes, but it will comply only with the minimum legal requirements. Food companies and restaurants that failed to provide caloric content, ingredients, or percent daily values until legal requirements dictated their compliance are examples of firms that used the defensive approach.

The Accommodative Approach

In an accommodative approach, the organization is more positive in its view of social responsibility. In this case, it does everything that it is legally required to do, but it also goes beyond this by addressing those areas that managers feel are important from an ethical standpoint. For example, the standard for a particular industry may be that only 1 out of 20 executive positions are held by women. But, using an accommodative approach, a firm may make an effort to have 25 percent of its executive positions filled by women.

The Proactive Approach

As the name suggests, a proactive approach means that a company is actively engaging in socially responsible activities and attempting to set the highest industry standard possible. The goal is for the company to be the leader in the industry and the epitome of social responsibility.

Interface Global, a manufacturer of carpet and floor tiles, uses a proactive approach to CSR. In 1994, Interface CEO Ray Anderson read Paul Hawken's book *The Ecology of Commerce* and had an epiphany about how he could, and must, make his company sustainable. He immediately set out to achieve "Mission Zero." Mission Zero is Interface's promise to "eliminate any impact Interface has on the environment by 2020." Of his efforts, Anderson says:

> Costs are down, not up, dispelling a myth and exposing the false choice between the economy and the environment, products are the best they have ever been, because sustainable design has provided an unexpected wellspring of innovation, people are galvanized around a shared higher purpose, better people are applying, the best people are staying and working with a purpose, the goodwill in the marketplace generated by our focus on sustainability far exceeds that which any amount of advertising or marketing expenditure could have generated.[172]

The debate about CSR and its relationship to business strategy has been going on for decades. Some people believe business is for business and that any focus on environmental, social, or economic sustainability actually *harms* a company's ability to provide goods and services—thereby harming people. However, given the "big three" you learned about at the beginning of this chapter—climate change, growing intolerance for compromised business ethics, and the meltdown of the economy that began in 2007—people are far less tolerant of businesses that are simply out for themselves. Taking a more positive viewpoint, there is increasing evidence that far from being bad for business, CSR is good for business. It's a double win: good for business *and* the right thing to do.

Most Popular » Discussion Questions

1. Does your university have an articulated stance on its approach to CSR? What is it? Do you believe that it is an appropriate stance? Why or why not?
2. Consider Johnson & Johnson's Credo: Stockholders and business practices are listed last, after individuals who use the product, employees, communities, and the environment. Argue for and against this order of priorities (e.g., Why might this be good for business? How might it inhibit business?).
3. On the Internet, find companies that seem to use an obstructionist, defensive, accommodative, or proactive approach to CSR. Give evidence to support your choices.
4. In this chapter, Andrew Carnegie is mentioned as a famous philanthropist and as someone who was involved with a company that violently obstructed CSR efforts. How can these two images of Carnegie be reconciled? What other examples can you find? Explain your reasoning.

---

9. What Is HR's Role in Sustainability and Corporate Social Responsibility?

Because HR is central to designing work, HR professionals hold an important role in moving a company toward sustainable business practices. One way in which they can do this is to be aware of, and willing to use, technology in ways that minimize travel and commuting. HR can also help organize programs that foster a culture that supports social sustainability by supporting employees in providing service to their local communities or through activities that support global citizenship.

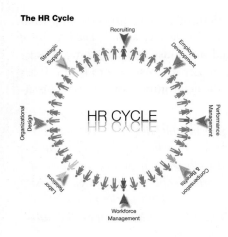

The HR Cycle

Telecommuting

One way to reduce our dependency on oil and decrease emissions is to provide employees with the opportunity and freedom to telecommute. As a candidate and as president, Barack Obama pushed for the expansion of telecommuting.[173] A report published in 2008 estimated that 45 million Americans telecommuted to work at least once per week.[174] Considering the monetary advantages telecommuting offers employers and the personal advantages it offers employees, it is easy to understand why this practice has become so popular.[175] Telecommuting also offers environmental advantages. In fact, some states offer incentives to companies that allow employees to telecommute as a way of making this environmentally friendly work phenomenon more attractive to employers.[176]

The most obvious environmental benefit of telecommuting is the fact that it decreases the number of cars on the road, thus decreasing fuel consumption and automobile emissions. Some estimates even suggest that as many as 1.35 billion gallons of gas and 26 billion pounds of carbon dioxide emissions could be saved if every employee who was able to telecommuted approximately two days per week.[177]

The energy savings, however, are not strictly limited to automotive gas consumption. Fewer cars, trains, and buses need to be produced when more people telecommute, meaning less energy is expended in their production, and fewer office buildings require heat, air conditioning, and light. Beyond energy consumption, telecommuting also means less consumption of land surface area for buildings, parking lots, and roadways, which could equate to more green space and parks in communities nationwide.[178]

One might argue, of course, that construction of fewer cars, buildings, and offices will negatively impact the economy, because it means fewer jobs. This is probably true. However, as manufacturing jobs decline, we will concurrently see a rise in jobs related to technology and the green economy. Think about it: People who are working from home will require better information and telecommunications technology, as well as other products and services that allow them to work effectively far from the organization.

One potential downside to the increase in telecommuting is that it opens the door to more outsourcing. The "permanent temporary workforce" is becoming a reality, and increasing numbers of people are now working as individual contractors instead of as long-term employees.[179] In fact, approximately 26 percent of the U.S. workforce fit this category as of 2010.[180]

What's the problem with this? Contract workers often do not have typical employee benefits, such as sick days, paid vacation, or employer-supported health insurance. They don't get severance when they are laid off, and they are easier to lay off because neither the company nor the employee has built the kind of bond that is typical in an employee–employer relationship. In essence, economic sustainability (in the short term, at least) wins out in this model. The employees—and ultimately, social sustainability—may be the big losers.

HR has a tremendous challenge as this and similar trends emerge. The challenge is to find new and innovative ways to support all three pillars of sustainability—to foster economic viability for the organization, while also attending to the environment and treating employees in ways that are fair, just, and equitable.

Supporting CSR through Employee Service Programs

HR can also look for ways in which the company can support the larger community by providing needed services. In its broadest sense, **service** is giving of oneself without any expectation of a return. Many companies sponsor programs that allow employees to serve their local communities, stakeholders, or even the global community. For example, companies may organize to serve their local communities by sponsoring service

Service
Giving of oneself without any expectation of a return.

HR Leadership Roles

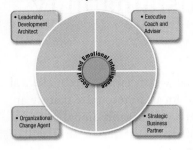

Global citizenship
Involves understanding one's place in and one's impact on the world community and engaging in activities that support global environmental, social, and economic sustainability.

days where employees can volunteer at an event that helps the community instead of going to work. Some firms provide the expertise of their employees to community groups. For instance, a corporate accountant may assist a community theater with its financial records, a human resources manager may help recruit volunteers at a thrift shop, or employees might use their business expertise to help local not-for-profit boards of directors.

Service can be organized to support people and groups far from home as well, enabling employees to act as global citizens. **Global citizenship** involves understanding one's place in and one's impact on the world community and engaging in activities that support global environmental, social, and economic sustainability. One company that is making strides in global citizenship is eBay, the online auction firm. eBay has launched three different programs that help people around the world. First, MicroPlace is a service that connects the working poor with investors through micro-loans. Investors need only put up a minimum of $20 to invest in a start-up small business. Second, WorldofGood.com is a Web site where customers can purchase from fair trade manufacturers and other socially responsible organizations. Buyers know that purchases made through this site support fair labor practices. Third, eBay allows sellers to donate part or all of the proceeds from sales to any of 18,000 certified nonprofit organizations around the world.[181]

To see some different ways in which companies can give back to the community and the world, let's look at pharmaceutical company Eli Lilly. Eli Lilly, headquartered in Indianapolis, won the U.S. Spirit Award from the United Way in 2009. Lilly's contributions included the following:

- Lilly employees volunteered more than 160,000 hours in 2008 during their Global Day of Service. Volunteers in more than 55 countries made it one of the largest single-day initiatives undertaken by any U.S.-based company.
- More than 600 Lilly employees were recruited as tutors to fourth- and fifth-grade students.
- Lilly donated approximately 5,000 volunteer hours of skills-based Six Sigma training to nonprofits.[182]

Some companies make it easy for employees to serve. A small business and accounting consulting firm in the Cleveland area, Skoda Minotti, even pays employees for the time they spend volunteering with local organizations. In one recent year, employees of the company logged more than 1,700 hours volunteering.[183] Or another example: Employees of Allied Bank, a financial institution located in Pakistan, contributed portions of their salaries and provided food, clothing, and medicine to victims of the earthquake that struck the region in October 2005.[184]

The benefits to communities that receive such services are clear. What's less obvious, but also very important, is that people who engage in service activities reap tremendous benefits as well. From learning new skills, to learning how to work cross culturally with people whose backgrounds are very different from your own, to the sheer satisfaction you can derive from giving of yourself—service is worth it.

Most Popular » Discussion Questions

1. Would you enjoy telecommuting? Why or why not?
2. Have you ever provided service to your community through volunteer work sponsored by your school or workplace? What did you do? What did your community get from this experience? What did *you* get?

10. What Can We All Do to Support Sustainability and Corporate Social Responsibility?

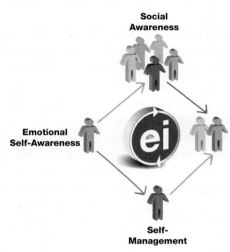

Social Awareness

Emotional Self-Awareness

Relationship Management

Self-Management

Servant leadership
A leadership style in which the leader seeks to serve followers and stakeholders, as opposed to dominating them.

We started this chapter by pointing out that the massive social and technological changes currently under way have resulted in the need for us to recognize that we are fundamentally interconnected, and that our individual and organizational activities have impact far beyond ourselves or the walls of our offices. What that means for all of us is that we have to become conscious of how important sustainability and social responsibility really are. From global warming to business ethics to economic woes around the world, we are facing serious problems that will take all of our efforts to address. We all need to understand how our organizations affect our communities and the world, and we must be ready to do something if, in fact, we—or our organizations—are causing damage to the environment, society, or the long-term economic viability of our communities.

We can all be part of the solution to the challenges we face in our world today. One thing you can do right now is to begin to see yourself as a steward of the environment, a servant to the people you lead, and a member of the communities you touch. In other words, you can begin to see yourself as a servant leader.

First coined by Robert Greenleaf in 1970, the term **servant leadership** describes a leadership style in which the leader seeks to serve followers and stakeholders, as opposed to dominating them.[185] Greenleaf's concept of servant leadership grew out of a Herman Hesse novel *(Siddhartha)* that inspired him to consider servitude and leadership not as opposites but as two roles that operate dynamically.[186] According to Greenleaf, a servant leader is a servant first—a person who has the desire to serve as his or her first priority. A servant leader makes sure that the most pressing needs of others are taken care of. Servant leadership is an approach that starts with concern for the welfare of others and sincere and selfless motivation behind our actions—which almost always brings tremendous loyalty, commitment, and outstanding contributions from the people we serve.[187]

Many times, we think of leaders who get other people to do things for them. In this model, however, doing for others comes first. This is empowering for followers: As their needs are addressed, people begin to grow and become more mature and self-reliant.

The Greenleaf Center has identified 10 ways in which you can enact servant leadership:[188]

- Listening
- Empathy
- Healing
- Awareness
- Persuasion
- Conceptualization
- Foresight
- Stewardship
- Commitment to the growth of people
- Building community

Are you a servant leader? How do you demonstrate your servant leadership? How do you find out what others on the team need, and what do you do about this? Why do you think people follow you? These questions are important for every leader, no matter what position you hold. Learning to lead means learning to serve—at home, in our communities, and in our businesses.

1. Think about an opportunity you have to lead (formally or informally) at work or in school. If you decided to truly enact servant leadership, what three things might you do differently in this situation?
2. Consider a few leaders whom you admire. Do they serve others? If so, how?

11. A Final Word on Sustainability and Corporate Social Responsibility

Environmental, social, and economic sustainability are very complex topics that generate passion and commitment all over the world in families, communities, nations, and businesses. These topics generate controversy as well. In this chapter, you have learned how our world is coming together in dialogue and debates about how we can cooperate to ensure that our actions support healthy communities and businesses. This dialogue will no doubt continue throughout your lifetime. This means that you have a wonderful opportunity to shape how today's businesses and organizations will contribute to future generations.

Key Terms

1. Why Are Sustainability and Corporate Social Responsibility Important in Today's World? (p. 546)

Key Terms None

2. What Is Sustainability? (pp. 546–553)

Key Terms

Sustainability The process of meeting present needs without compromising the ability of future generations to meet their needs. p. 547

Global warming Term used to describe a fairly recent increase in the temperature of Earth's lower atmosphere (the air we breathe) and the land and water that make up Earth's surface. p. 548

Greenhouse effect Term used to describe how air, water, and land temperatures are affected by certain gases in Earth's atmosphere. These gases trap infrared energy, which leads to an increase in the planet's atmospheric and surface temperatures. p. 548

3. What Are the Three Pillars of Sustainability? (pp. 553–556)

Key Terms

Environmental sustainability Term that refers to the preservation of environmental resources and biodiversity, creation of sustainable access to safe drinking water, and enhancement of quality of life among the most impoverished. p. 553

Social sustainability Term that refers to the improvement of daily life for the greatest number of people through improving fair income distribution; promoting gender equality; ensuring equal access to land ownership, employment, and education; investing in basic health and education; and enlisting the participation of beneficiaries. p. 553

Economic sustainability Term that refers to an economy's capacity to regularly produce outcomes consistent with long-term economic development. p. 553

4. What Is Environmental Sustainability?
(pp. 556–566)

Key Terms

Kyoto Protocol An international agreement drafted during the 1997 United Nations Framework Convention on Climate Change for the purpose of supporting and enforcing the reduction of greenhouse gas emissions. p. 559

Green economy An economic model that focuses on development and use of renewable energies such as wind, biofuels, and so on to displace traditional fossil fuels and move businesses and communities toward environmental sustainability. p. 562

Green-collar jobs Jobs related to providing environmentally friendly products or services. p. 563

5. What Is Social Sustainability?
(pp. 566–572)

Key Terms None

6. What Is Economic Sustainability?
(pp. 572–575)

Key Terms None

7. What Is Corporate Social Responsibility?
(pp. 575–578)

Key Terms

Corporate social responsibility (CSR) A form of corporate self-regulation that builds sustainability and public interest into business decision making and activities. p. 575

Philanthropy Giving money, time, services, or products in the service of supporting people's well-being. p. 575

8. How Can Companies Approach Corporate Social Responsibility?   (pp. 578–581)

Key Terms None

9. What Is HR's Role in Sustainability and Corporate Social Responsibility?
(pp. 581–583)

Key Terms

Service Giving of oneself without any expectation of a return. p. 582

Global citizenship Involves understanding one's place in and one's impact on the world community and engaging in activities that support global environmental, social, and economic sustainability. p. 583

10. What Can We All Do to Support Sustainability and Corporate Social Responsibility?   (pp. 584–585)

Key Terms

Servant leadership A leadership style in which the leader seeks to serve followers and stakeholders, as opposed to dominating them. p. 584

11. A Final Word on Sustainability and Corporate Social Responsibility   (p. 585)

Key Terms None

Chapter 15 Visual Summary

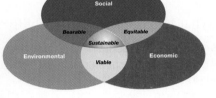

16. Managing and Leading for Tomorrow: A Focus on Your Future

14. Globalization: Managing Effectively in a Global Economic Environment

1. Managing and Leading Today: The New Rules

Leading and Managing for Today and the Future

2. The Leadership Imperative: It's Up to You

4. Communication: The Key to Resonant Relationships

3. Motivation and Meaning: What Makes People Want to Work?

15. Sustainability and Corporate Social Responsibility: Ensuring the Future

1. Why Are Sustainability and Corporate Social Responsibility Important in Today's World?   (p. 546)

Summary: The increasing interconnectedness of the world has brought sustainability and corporate social responsibility to the forefront of the business agenda. This interconnectedness is the result of advances in technology, economic interdependence, and continued industrialization. The changes we are experiencing in much of the world are positive; unfortunately, they can also have negative consequences for the environment, our society, and the economy. As a result, it is crucial that leaders understand the ways in which their organizations impact the planet and its people.

2. What Is Sustainability? (pp. 546–553)

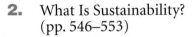

Summary: Sustainability is the ability of current generations to meet their needs without compromising the ability of future generations to do the same. This is not a new concept; in fact, many tribal peoples practiced sustainability for thousands of years, and some of these tribes continue to exist today. However, in today's world, climate change, lapses in business ethics, and global economic crises put people all over the planet at risk. Therefore, curbing trends related to things like global warming and questionable business practices is no longer just the responsibility of corporations and governments, but of each and every responsible citizen.

3. What Are the Three Pillars of Sustainability?   (pp. 553–556)

Summary: According to the United Nations, the three pillars of sustainability are environmental sustainability, social sustainability, and economic sustainability. Each of these pillars has a major impact on organizations, communities, and the people of the world. The Bhopal disaster of 1984 is one devastating example of business practices that did not support sustainability, and the aftermath of that event continues to affect many people. More and more companies are attending to issues of sustainability to avoid such disasters, and some companies are even being recognized through tracking projects like the Global 100 Most Sustainable Corporations.

4. What Is Environmental Sustainability? (pp. 556–566)

Summary: Environmental sustainability is the preservation of environmental resources and biodiversity, creation of sustainable access to safe drinking water, and enhancement of quality of life among the most impoverished. The conservation and ecology movements in the United States were early attempts at environmental sustainability, and they resulted in the creation of government agencies like the National Park Service and the Environmental Protection Agency. More recently, international alliances have attempted to impact energy use in the United States, but these efforts have met resistance. As nations seek to find ways to collaborate around environmental issues, other problems, such as dwindling fossil fuels, add even more complexity. There are many positive outcomes of the world's leaders attending to environmental sustainability, such as the promotion of green energy technologies that will support new jobs and new answers to environmental problems.

5.　What Is Social Sustainability?　(pp. 566–572)

Summary: Social sustainability is the improvement of daily life for the greatest number of people through improving fair income distribution; promoting gender equality; ensuring equal access to land ownership, employment, and education; investing in basic health care and education; and enlisting the participation of beneficiaries.

　　Child labor and slavery gravely impair social sustainability, and they are important considerations even in countries that closely regulate these practices within their own borders. Due to the global nature of our economy, many consumers unknowingly purchase products produced in nations where child labor and slavery are commonplace; sustainability labeling is gaining popularity as a method to combat this lack of knowledge. Workplace safety is also an important aspect of social sustainability today, and it is at the forefront of many business agendas.

6.　What Is Economic Sustainability?　(pp. 572–575)

Summary: Economic sustainability is an economy's capacity to regularly produce outcomes consistent with long-term economic development.

　　Such long-term development can be difficult to achieve in the modern business world, where short-term profit has traditionally been the measure of success. However, more and more large and small companies recognize that profitability and sustainability are inextricably linked, and they have started focusing on all of their stakeholders as a result. These companies, in turn, are positively impacting the environment, health, and well-being of both local and global communities.

7.　What Is Corporate Social Responsibility?　(pp. 575–578)

Summary: Corporate social responsibility (CSR) is a form of corporate self-regulation that builds sustainability and public interest into business decision-making activities. Corporate social responsibility has a long history, with its roots in philanthropy. At its best, CSR is the smart thing to do in terms of the bottom line and the right thing to do in terms of serving stakeholders. This is why corporations such as Johnson & Johnson have found that it makes financial sense to embrace CSR.

11. A Final Word on Sustainability and Corporate Social Responsibility (p. 585)

Summary: We are in the midst of a massive global transformation that is improving on a daily basis our ability to communicate, live, and work. Our global population is also expanding, and it is important that we use our knowledge and skills to support ourselves and our planet in the midst of this boom. Many old ways of doing things have become inadequate, wasteful, and even harmful, and we must challenge ourselves to change. By working together as a single global community and utilizing our collective knowledge, resources, and abilities in responsible ways, we can learn how to manage these challenges.

Obstructionist   Defensive   Accommodative   Proactive

10. What Can We All Do to Support Sustainability and Corporate Social Responsibility? (pp. 584–585)

Summary: The first step in supporting sustainability, corporate social responsibility, and service is understanding how your company's actions affect current and future generations. What you can do now to be part of the solution is to begin to see yourself as a servant leader. This approach to leadership requires you to serve followers and stakeholders and be sincerely concerned about their welfare. Servant leadership revolves around selfless motivation, generates loyalty among followers, and can be incredibly fulfilling.

9. What Is HR's Role in Sustainability and Corporate Social Responsibility? (pp. 581–583)

Summary: HR can have a powerful effect on an organization's CSR efforts. For example, work design can include telecommuting, which provides clear environmental and economic benefits but potential social downfalls as more and more people work as contractors without traditional employee benefits. In addition, HR professionals can look for ways to incorporate service into organizational CSR activities. Creating programs that allow employees to serve local and global communities is beneficial for everyone involved.

8. How Can Companies Approach Corporate Social Responsibility? (pp. 578–581)

Summary: In today's world where there is ready public access to information, companies have a strong motive for acting in socially responsible ways. CSR builds goodwill with customers, employees, governments, and communities. Four approaches to CSR have been identified: the obstructionist approach, which ignores CSR; the defensive approach, which does the bare minimum in terms of CSR; the accommodative approach, in which CSR acitivites are above average; and the proactive approach, which attempts to set the industry standard for CSR.

Managing and Leading for Tomorrow:

A Focus on Your **Future**

Chapter Outline

Find out what you already know about the concepts in this chapter by going to www.mymanagementlab.com and taking the **Pre-Test.** Your results will generate a customized study plan for Chapter 16.

1. Why Do "Great Leaders Move Us"? (pp. 592–593)

2. What Are "Moon Shots for Management"? (pp. 593–595)

3. How Can You Continue Your Journey to Becoming a Resonant Leader? (pp. 595–596)

4. What Can You Do to Develop Your Leadership? (pp. 596–606)

5. A Final Word on Managing Yourself (p. 606)

Go back to www.mymanagementlab.com and take the **Post-Test** to verify your understanding of the concepts. To experience and apply the concepts, explore the additional material associated with Chapter 16.

Part 1: Leading and Managing for Today and the Future (Chapters 1, 2, 3, 4)
Part 2: Planning and Change (Chapters 5, 6, 7, 8, 9)
Part 3: Organizing Human Systems (Chapters 10, 11)
Part 4: Controlling Quality, Culture, and Yourself (Chapters 12, 13)
Part 5: Leading and Managing for the Future (Chapters 14, 15, **16**)

8. Workplace Essentials: Creativity, Innovation, and a Spirit of Entrepreneurship

7. Change: A Focus on Adaptability and Resiliency

9. Organizing for a Complex World: Structure and Design

Planning and Change

6. The Human Side of Planning: Decision Making and Critical Thinking

5. Planning and Strategy: Bringing the Vision to Life

16. Managing and Leading for Tomorrow: A Focus on Your Future

10. Teams and Teambuilding: How to Work Effectively with Others

Organizing Human Systems

11. Working in a Virtual World: Technology as a Way of Life

14. Globalization: Managing Effectively in a Global Economic Environment

1. Managing and Leading Today: The New Rules

Leading and Managing for Today and the Future

2. The Leadership Imperative: It's Up to You

4. Communication: The Key to Resonant Relationships

3. Motivation and Meaning: What Makes People Want to Work?

16. Managing and Leading for Tomorrow: A Focus on Your Future

15. Sustainability and Corporate Social Responsibility: Ensuring the Future

12. Organizational Controls: People, Processes, Quality, and Results

Controlling Quality, Culture, and Yourself

13. Culture: It's Powerful

1. Why Do "Great Leaders Move Us"[1]?

In this book, you have learned what it means to work in today's organizations—how to be a great employee and team member, an effective manager, and an outstanding leader. You have explored many of the theories and models that have guided us for decades as well as new ideas and new research that will help you be successful in our changing world. In this chapter, you will have a chance to explore a little bit more about yourself: your leadership strengths, some things you would like to develop, and contributions you can make at school, in your community, at work, and ultimately in the world. Before we turn to a model and some exercises that will help you do this, let's hear from one of the most brilliant, insightful and funny leaders we have ever met: Chade-Meng Tan—better known as "Meng"—of Google.

Perspectives

Meng was a very successful engineer in Singapore ("he knew it was successful because no one offered to fire him").[2] Then, after attending graduate school at University of California at Santa Barbara ("mainly for the beach, but I didn't mind the graduate degree either"[3]), Meng became one of the pioneer engineers at Google.[4] He focused great effort on ensuring quality in the new system and after several years he moved to Google University (later renamed "GoogleEDU"),

Chade-Meng Tan, Google

where he is the Head of Personal Growth. One of his favorite programs is called Search Inside Yourself—"a mindfulness-based emotional intelligence program which he hopes will contribute to world peace in a meaningful way."[5] He's known to everyone at Google, and to many of the world's celebrities and dignitaries as he is the official "greeter" at Google.[6]

Meng is a genius, there's no doubt about that. And what he had to say to us about leadership is not only smart and funny, it's wise:

Being a leader humbles you, in a way that motivates you to help people. Leadership is essentially about character *and* compassion.

It's hard to measure character. What would you say— "In order to be a good leader you need 10% more character?" It's not that easy to quantify. You have to do the right thing. That's character. You have to realize that you can't do anything alone. *You have to be big enough and have a strong enough ego to know you can do something, and that you are small enough—egoless enough—to know you need other people. You need to let go of total control, while*

still making things happen, and let go of your ego while still holding onto your belief in yourself.

There are a lot of leaders who are just good enough to get things done. But they can't create breakthroughs. To create breakthroughs you need to be able to create a sense of exhilarating discomfort, and to operate with egoless-ego and selfless glory. This is the exact opposite of becoming obsessed with yourself (what those just-get-things-done leaders often do).

And compassion is the antidote to excessive self obsession. Compassion has three parts:

- *Cognitive: "I understand you,"*
- *Emotion: "I feel for you," and*
- *Motivation: "I want to help you."*

When you are engaged in compassionate endeavors, people are inspired by you. They want to be near you, and they want to help you. If you are a leader who people like and respect, and your "heart is in the right place," you can do a lot.

Meng's final words were perhaps the most inspiring—he talked about fun and happiness, and how all of us should be able to experience fun and happiness at work.

Happiness is a state of mind that frees you to do a lot. Good leaders need to be happy. Good leaders need to be fun. I want to see every workplace in the world to be a fountain of happiness and enlightenment.

Source: Personal interview with Chade-Meng Tan conducted by Annie McKee, 2009.

Meng is a leader, and he has powerful advice for the rest of us. Part of the reason his advice is so good is that he points us to very new ways to think about work, management, and leadership. Like Meng, it's about time for all of us to start thinking differently about what it means to be successful at work. We live in a world that is very different from that in which many management theories and practices were developed. Today, the opportunities and challenges presented by changes in information and telecommunications technology, global warming, and the call for ethical and responsible business require us to find new ways of working, managing, and leading. Let's take one last look at what leading scholars are calling for when it comes to management in the twenty-first century.

Most Popular » Discussion Questions

1. Chade-Meng Tan says that leadership takes character. How do you describe character?
2. Do you think it is important for leaders to be happy? To be "fun"? To inspire others to laugh? Why or why not?
3. What do you think Meng means by "egoless-ego"?

---

2. What Are "Moon Shots for Management"[7]?

In 2008, the *Harvard Business Review* published a report of an ambitious project undertaken by scholars, business leaders, and consultants to compile a list of the top priority challenges for twenty-first century management research and practice. The report, called "Moon Shots for Management," identified 25 changes and challenges we need to address if we are to learn how to manage and lead our organizations more responsibly.[8]

As you can see in ■Exhibit 16.1, the report calls for some very bold changes in how we understand management. Several of the "moon shots" are related to overcoming the

■Exhibit **16.1**

Moon Shots for Management: Important Challenges for Twenty-First Century Management, as Identified by Top Scholars, Business Leaders, and Consultants

1. *Ensure that the work of management serves a higher purpose.* Management, both in theory and practice, must orient itself to the achievement of noble, socially significant goals.
2. *Fully embed the ideas of community and citizenship in management.* There is a need for processes and practices that reflect the interdependence of all stakeholder groups.
3. *Reconstruct management's philosophical foundations.* To build organizations that are more than merely efficient, we will need to draw lessons from such fields as biology, political science, and theology.
4. *Eliminate the pathologies of formal hierarchy.* There are advantages to natural hierarchies, where power flows up from the bottom and leaders emerge instead of being appointed.
5. *Reduce fear and increase trust.* Mistrust and fear are toxic to innovation and engagement and must be wrung out of tomorrow's management systems.
6. *Reinvent the means of control.* To transcend the discipline-versus-freedom trade-off, control systems will have to encourage control from within rather than constraints from without.
7. *Redefine the work of leadership.* The notion of the leader as a heroic decision maker is untenable. Leaders must be recast as social-systems architects who enable innovation and collaboration.
8. *Expand and exploit diversity.* We must create a management system that values diversity, disagreement, and divergences as much as conformance, consensus, and cohesion.
9. *Reinvent strategy making as an emergent process.* In a turbulent world, strategy making must reflect the biological principles of variety, selection, and retention.
10. *De-structure and disaggregate the organization.* To become more adaptable and innovative, large entities must be disaggregated into smaller, more malleable units.
11. *Dramatically reduce the pull of the past.* Existing management systems often mindlessly reinforce the status quo. In the future, they must facilitate innovation and change.
12. *Share the work of setting direction.* To engender commitment, the responsibility for setting goals must be distributed through a process in which share of voice is a function of insight, not power.

Continued on next page>>

■Exhibit **16.1**   **Continued**

Moon Shots for Management: Important Challenges for Twenty-First Century Management, as Identified by Top Scholars, Business Leaders, and Consultants

13. *Develop holistic performance measures.* Existing performance metrics must be recast, since they give inadequate attention to the capabilities that drive success in the creative economy.

14. *Stretch executive time frames and perspectives.* We need to discover alternatives to compensation and reward systems that encourage managers to sacrifice long-term goals for short-term gains.

15. *Create a democracy of information.* Companies need information systems that equip every employee to act in the interests of the entire enterprise.

16. *Empower the renegades and disarm the reactionaries.* Management systems must give more power to employees whose emotional equity is invested in the future rather than the past.

17. *Expand the scope of employee autonomy.* Management systems must be redesigned to facilitate grassroots initiatives and local experimentation.

18. *Create internal markets for ideas, talent, and resources.* Markets are better than hierarchies at allocating resources, and companies' resource allocation processes need to reflect this fact.

19. *Depoliticize decision making.* Decision processes must be free of positional biases and should exploit the collective wisdom of the entire organization and beyond.

20. *Better optimize trade-offs.* Management systems tend to force either-or choices. What's needed are hybrid systems that subtly optimize key trade-offs.

21. *Further unleash human imagination.* Much is known about what engenders human creativity. This knowledge must be better applied in the design of management systems.

22. *Enable communities of passion.* To maximize employee engagement, management systems must facilitate the formation of self-defining communities of passion.

23. *Retool management for an open world.* Value-creating networks often transcend the firm's boundaries and can render traditional power-based management tools ineffective. New management tools are needed for building and shaping complex ecosystems.

24. *Humanize the language and practice of business.* Tomorrow's management systems must give as much credence to such timeless human ideals as beauty, justice, and community as they do to the traditional goals of efficiency, advantage, and profit.

25. *Retrain managerial minds.* Managers' deductive and analytical skills must be complemented by conceptual and systems-thinking skills.

Source: Hamel, Gary. 2009. Moon shots for management. *Harvard Business Review* 87(2): 91–98.

limitations of the twentieth-century focus on scientific management, while others are directed toward furthering the agenda of business ethics, organizational culture, organizational learning, and strategy. Let's consider some of the main points of this report.

Perhaps because the brainstorming session that spawned this report came on the heels of the worst global economic disaster since the Great Depression of the 1930s, the number one challenge in the report is to ensure that management's activities serve a purpose higher than mere accumulation of wealth. The group of top scholars and practitioners stated that business goals *must* be socially significant. In fact, the top three moon shots are focused on management ethics, such as finding ways of embedding the ideas of community and citizenship into management processes and reconstructing the philosophical foundations of management to take greater advantage of knowledge from other disciplines, including biology, theology, and political science.

Two other moon shots are interesting in that they challenge some of the more dysfunctional behaviors that have been rampant in our organizations for decades. These moon shots call for eliminating the pathologies of hierarchical power so that leaders and leadership practices can emerge in a more organic manner. They also call for the elimination of fear and mistrust, which are toxic to innovation.

Some of the moon shots for management listed in Exhibit 16.1 are familiar, and the best leaders and organizations have been seeking to implement them for some time now. Others are new, and it's up to all of us to define exactly what they mean in practice.

1. Do you find any of the moon shots reported here particularly important? Why?
2. Given all that you have learned in this course about changes in societies, technologies, and the world's economies, what other "moon shots for managers" do we need to focus on in the next 10 years?
3. Choose one of the moon shots, or one that you believe should be added to the list, and identify five actions *you* can take now to address the issue/challenge/change.

3. How Can You Continue Your Journey to Becoming a Resonant Leader?

Our vision for this book is that it will truly help you to be a powerful and positive leader. But we don't imagine this as something that will happen in the future. It is our profound hope that you will see yourself as a leader *now*, rather than thinking you have to wait until later in your career. To conclude, we'd like to share a few final ideas, and then suggest some ways to continue your journey to becoming a resonant leader.

First, as we have emphasized throughout this book, ***everyone needs to be a leader today.*** As our organizations and management systems foster greater autonomy, empowerment, and input into decision-making processes at all levels, you will need to be a leader each and every day—often without the benefit of a formal title. This means you need to explore the secrets of great leadership: social and emotional intelligence, ethics, and responsible use of power. You need to make these your very own.

Second, ***you can embrace change and be part of the solution***, as opposed to being part of the problems we face in our organizations and in the world today. Change is constant in life and work—fighting it does no good and is, in fact, destructive. You have the opportunity to develop your capacity for adaptability, flexibility, and optimism; these qualities will help your organization and your local and global communities face today's challenges with courage, as well as maximize the opportunities available to all of us.

Third, ***you must learn how to use your power for the good of the groups, organizations, and communities to which you belong.*** For too long, too many people have used their power and influence to further their own agendas or to benefit *their* group, *their* organization, *their* community or nation. Internal competition, self-serving agendas, fear, and mistrust have been prevalent for too long. It takes courage to refuse to play the game this way—you'll have to stand up for what's right, even when it's inconvenient or risky. Each of us has the responsibility to use our power for good and for others.

Fourth, ***you can and you must demand that the organizations with which you do business and where you work support your values and ethics.*** In this day and age, employees and consumers can easily find out what companies are doing vis-à-vis the environment, society, and the broader economy. Learning to do the right thing with the right people in the right way takes initiative, self-management, and the ability to inspire others to join you. You can and must make your voice heard.

Fifth, ***you need to become a lifelong learner.*** Social, economic, political, and technological changes will not slow down, nor will globalization. You have the opportunity to learn every single day from people who are very different from yourself. Don't miss the opportunity. It is up to you, and you alone, to tap into your natural curiosity, imagination, and passion, and to make learning a part of life and work every day.

You can prepare yourself for these challenges in a number of ways. In the next section we share how you can tap into your dreams and your passion, learn a bit more about your leadership strengths and challenges, and chart a course for the future.

1. Where in your life can you take up leadership? How will you demonstrate leadership and how will this behavior help others?
2. What aspects of your life or work are currently changing? What might you do to embrace these changes positively—to become part of the solution?
3. Consider the organizations where you go to school, do business, or work. Do they support your values and ethics? How so? If they do not, what can or should you do about it? Will you do these things? Why or why not?

4. What Can You Do to Develop Your Leadership?

By taking this course and reading this textbook, you have taken a huge step toward becoming a more effective leader. You are now equipped with the knowledge of what makes a great leader as well as the challenges we face in our world today. You have the information you need to be successful at work and as a global citizen.

If you are like most people, however, it is sometimes hard to translate knowledge into actions. Just reading about emotional intelligence, for example, or ethics, or how to use power, doesn't mean that you will simply turn around and improve overnight. The same thing is true for skills related to communication, planning, decision making, organizing, controlling resources, and working in a virtual world or a diverse, global organization. Learning the skills that go along with this knowledge takes deliberate and focused action.

Most of the time when people attempt to learn something new (especially something related to work, like leadership skills), they start with a focus on what's not working: "I'm not a good team leader." "My communication skills are terrible." "I lose my temper all the time and get in trouble at work." We all have these kinds of thoughts sometimes, and often we try to act on them to improve. But have you ever noticed how hard it is to stay focused on a goal when we are trying to overcome a deficiency? Let's use examples from life to illustrate this point. Pick one of the following—something you have faced:

- "I need to lose weight."
- "I need to quit smoking."
- "I need to study more and party less."

If you are like most people, some of the feelings that go along with goals like this are "I'm too fat," "I'll die if I don't quit smoking," or "I'm going to fail this semester unless I stop going out with my friends so much." However compelling these feelings might be, new research tells us that thoughts and feelings like this make it very hard to stay focused on a goal.[9] This is because of the emotions that accompany these thoughts: they tend to be negative, self-critical, and pessimistic. These kinds of feelings cause us to want to get away from whatever is making us feel that way. It's the fight-or-flight response—in the face of a threat, even a psychological one, most people shut down and focus only on what will allow them to escape the threat or the source of pain. This means that when it comes to goals, negative thoughts and feelings are usually not helpful and, in fact, can interfere with achieving our goals, especially if the goals are challenging.

Making Leadership Development Fun—and Effective

So what can you do? Our research indicates that if you want to make meaningful and lasting changes in the skills and competencies related to leadership, you need to first focus on why these changes are important to you. You need to develop a powerful and positive view of the future—one where the changes you envision will help you live the

■ Exhibit **16.2**
The intentional change model charts a path to your future.

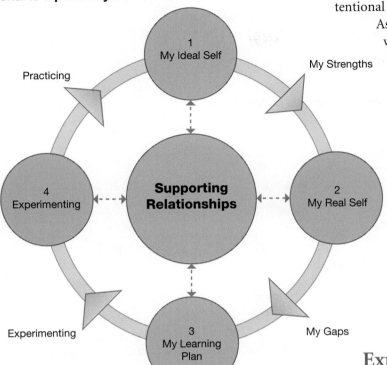

Source: Goleman, Daniel, Richard Boyatzis, and Annie McKee. 2002. *Primal Leadership*. Boston: Harvard Business School Press, p. 110. © 2002 Daniel Goleman. For more information on Intentional Change Theory see Boyatzis, Richard E. 2006. *Intentional change theory from a complexity perspective*. Journal of Management Development 25(7): 607–623.

life you want and become your "ideal self." This is the beginning of a process that noted scholar Richard Boyatzis has been studying for several decades, called "intentional change."

As you can see in ■Exhibit 16.2, intentional change begins with identifying your life vision and your ideal self. The hope, excitement, and other positive emotions this vision sparks actually provide you with energy and resilience—enough so that you can do the hard (and sometimes emotional) work of looking at both your strengths and your weaknesses. Looking at your real self—where you are today in your life, what's working and what's not—takes resilience and courage. Once you have a balanced and clear view of your real self, it is easy to see where some of the gaps are, and you can create a learning plan that is truly meaningful to you.

To give you a head start on this process, the next section includes several exercises that will help you explore your ideal self and where you are now. They'll also help you practice writing a learning goal.

Exploring Your Vision and What You Want to Change

Here we provide seven exercises that will help you begin the process of intentional change (see ■Exhibits 16.3 through 16.9). The first few exercises will help you identify what is most important to you—your values and beliefs. Next, you will explore who you

■ Exhibit **16.3**
The lottery: If I could, I would . . .

The Lottery: If I Could, I Would . . .

You just won the super lottery and received 50 million dollars or the equivalent in your currency after tax. How would your life and work change?

....
....
....
....
....
....
....
....
....
....

Source: Adapted from McKee, Annie, Richard Boyatzis, and Frances Johnston. 2008. *Becoming a resonant leader: Develop your emotional intelligence, renew your relationships, and sustain your effectiveness* (p. 79). Boston: Harvard Business School Press.

■Exhibit **16.4**

My life in the year 20_____.

My Life in the Year 20___

Project yourself into the future. It is 10 years from today. Picture what you most hope your life and work will be on that day.

In 20___, I am ___ years old.

If I am working, my work is best described as ....

....

....

My major work responsibilities are ....

....

....

The people I will see or talk to today include ....

....

....

The people with whom I live and socialize are ....

....

....

My most important possessions are ....

....

....

If someone were describing me to a friend today, they would say that I am .....

....

....

When I have some free time, I spend it ....

....

....

My leisure or fun activities in a typical week include ....

....

....

At least once a year, I try to ....

....

....

Source: Adapted from McKee, Annie, Richard Boyatzis, and Frances Johnston. 2008. *Becoming a resonant leader: Develop your emotional intelligence, renew your relationships, and sustain your effectiveness* (p. 81). Boston: Harvard Business School Press.

are now. Finally, you will "take stock." You will probably see a pattern in what you have written. You'll see some themes in what you say you want to be and do in life and how your strengths can help you get there. Maybe you will even see some gaps that you would like to close or some things you would like to learn.

As a result of these exercises (and this course!) you probably have a lot of ideas about how you can be effective in the many roles you will play at work. As you think about this, it helps to remember *why* you want to be effective: your purpose in life, the special talents and gifts that you bring, and the contributions you can make.

■Exhibit **16.5**
My fantasy job.

My Fantasy Job

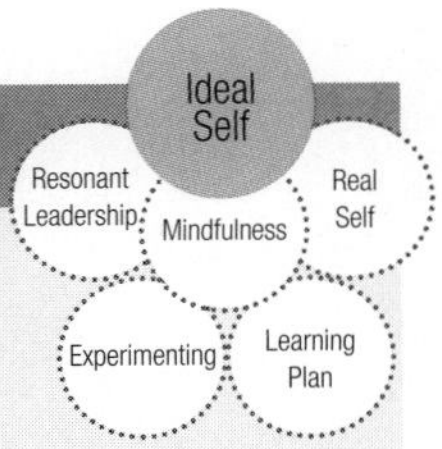

This is an opportunity to imagine yourself doing the kind of work that you sometimes wonder about: "What would it be like if I were doing X?"

Make believe that:

1. You enter a new machine called a Neurophysiological Remaker. Using genetic reengineering and non-invasive neural implants, a few minutes inside the machine gives you the body, knowledge, and capability to do any job—and do it well.

2. You have been given the financial resources to do any job you want, and you are free of all personal, social, and financial responsibilities.

List several jobs that you would love to do or try. Consider a wide variety of jobs like those in other countries and jobs in sports, music, medicine, politics, agriculture, and religion. Consider jobs you have heard about or seen in the movies or on television.

....
....
....
....
....
....

Choose the three jobs in your list that most interest you or seem the most exciting or rewarding. Describe each of them below, including what you would enjoy or look forward to the most about each job.

1. _____

   _____

2. _____

   _____

3. _____

   _____

Continued on next page>>

My Fantasy Job

Sometimes a person describes a fantasy job as one he or she really wants to do. Other times, the job represents some interesting or exciting activities or conditions. In other words, sometimes it is not the job that is the fantasy, but some aspect of it or conditions under which the job is done.

As you read your descriptions of the jobs you would most like to do or try, do you notice themes or patterns? How are these different jobs similar? Are there activities (such as being outdoors) that are part of each? Are there conditions of the work (such as working with a team) that are part of each? Are there outcomes (such as being famous) that are a part of each? List those themes or patterns below.

....

....

....

....

....

....

....

....

....

....

....

....

....

....

....

....

Source: Adapted from McKee, Annie, Richard Boyatzis, and Frances Johnston. 2008. *Becoming a resonant leader: Develop your emotional intelligence, renew your relationships, and sustain your effectiveness* (pp. 82–83). Boston: Harvard Business School Press.

■ Exhibit **16.6**
My values.

My Values

Beliefs, Principles, and Personal Characteristics That Guide My Life

Below is a list of values, beliefs, or personal characteristics for your consideration. Each of the steps in this process will help you identify which are most important to you and which are guiding principles in your life. It is difficult to choose, of course, because many of these values and characteristics will be at least somewhat important to you. It is also hard to choose because you might find yourself thinking, "I should value X and put it first on my list," even though it really isn't. So, force yourself to choose, and choose based on your true feelings, not the "shoulds" in life.

You might find it useful to determine degrees of importance by imagining how you would feel if you were forced to give up believing in or acting on a particular value, belief, or personal characteristic. Or, think about how you would feel if your life really revolved around certain values, beliefs, or characteristics. How would this make you feel? Sometimes, you might find it helpful to consider two values at a time, asking yourself about the relative importance of one over the other.

1. Start by circling the fifteen or so values that are most important to you.
2. Then, from this list of fifteen or so, identify the ten that are the most important to you and write them in a list.
3. From this list of ten, circle the five that are the most important to you.

List of Values, Beliefs, or Desirable Personal Characteristics

Accomplishment	Control	Independence	Reliable
Achievement	Cooperation	Improving society	Religion
Adventure	Courageous	Innovative	Respectful
Affection	Courteous	Integrity	Responsible
Affectionate	Creativity	Intellectual	Restrained
Affiliation	Dependable	Involvement	Salvation
Ambitious	Disciplined	Imagination	Self-controlled
Assisting others	Economic security	Joy	Self-reliance
Authority	Effective	Leisurely	Self-respect
Autonomy	Equality	Logical	Sincerity
Beauty	Excitement	Love	Spirituality
Belonging	Fame	Loving	Stability
Broad minded	Family Happiness	Mature Love	Status
Caring	Family Security	National Security	Success
Challenge	Forgiving	Nature	Symbolic
Cheerful	Free choice	Obedient	Taking risks
Clean	Freedom	Order	Teamwork
Comfortable life	Friendship	Peace	Tidy
Companionship	Fun	Personal Development	Tender
Compassion	Genuineness	Pleasure	Tranquility
Competent	Happiness	Polite	Wealth
Competitiveness	Health	Power	Winning
Contribution to others	Helpfulness	Pride	Wisdom
Conformity	Honesty	Rational	Other:
Contentedness	Hope	Recognition	
			_____

Continued on next page>>

■ Exhibit **16.6**
Continued

My Values

My Ten Most Important Values

1. _____   6. _____
2. _____   7. _____
3. _____   8. _____
4. _____   9. _____
5. _____   10. _____

Finally, rank each of your five most important values, beliefs, or characteristics with "1" being the most important value to you and "5" being the least important of these five important values.

1. _____   4. _____
2. _____   5. _____
3. _____

Source: Adapted from McKee, Annie, Richard Boyatzis, and Frances Johnston. 2008. *Becoming a resonant leader: Develop your emotional intelligence, renew your relationships, and sustain your effectiveness* (pp. 90–91). Boston: Harvard Business School Press.

■ Exhibit **16.7**
Strengths I see in myself.

Strengths I See in Myself

Strengths can be elements that you were born with or things you have learned. They are extremely valuable or useful abilities, assets, or qualities. What are your strengths? What do you consider your character assets?

Complete this sentence: I am a person who...

....

....

List ten things that have served you well and of which you are most proud. For each strength, notice the sensations or feelings that come up for you as you write it down and reflect on your successes.

My Strengths	Sensations/Feelings
1. _____	_____
2. _____	_____
3. _____	_____
4. _____	_____
5. _____	_____

Continued on next page>>

■Exhibit **16.7**
Continued

Strengths I See in Myself

My Strengths	Sensations/Feelings
6. _____	_____
7. _____	_____
8. _____	_____
9. _____	_____
10. _____	_____

Do any of these sensations or feelings surprise you? Why do these things stand out to you? How do these strengths relate to the core values you explored in Chapter 4?

....

....

....

....

....

Summarize what you consider to be personal and leadership strengths. These elements are likely to be things you enjoy about yourself, and which others like about you. They are energizers for you.

....

....

....

....

....

....

....

....

Source: Adapted from McKee, Annie, Richard Boyatzis, and Frances Johnston. 2008. *Becoming a resonant leader: Develop your emotional intelligence, renew your relationships, and sustain your effectiveness* (pp. 132–134). Boston: Harvard Business School Press.

■Exhibit **16.8**
Personal balance sheet.

Personal Balance Sheet

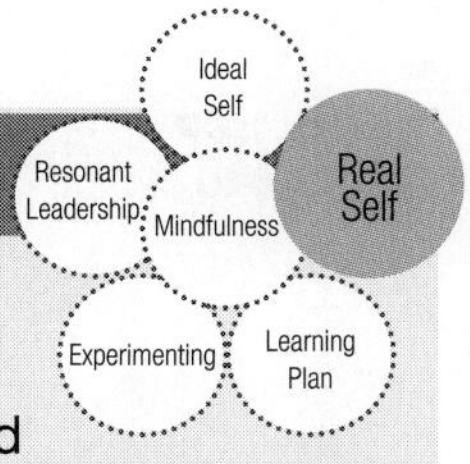

Like assessing the value of a business, a balance sheet is a way to summarize our personal assets and liabilities. Using all of the assessments and reflection you have done so far and the form that follows, we invite you to create your Personal Balance Sheet.

My Assets	My Liabilities
My Distinctive Strengths—things I know I do well and strengths that others see in me	**My Weaknesses**—things I know that I don't do well and I want to do better
My Potential Strengths—things I could do better or more often if I focused, or things I do well in some situations and could begin to apply more broadly	**Weaknesses I Want to Change**—things that I know I don't do well and want to change
My Enduring Dispositions that support me—this includes traits, habits, behaviors that I do not want to change and that help me to be successful	**My Enduring Dispositions that sometimes get in my way**—this includes traits, habits, behaviors that I do not want to change and that sometimes cause me to be less effective

Source: Adapted from McKee, Annie, Richard Boyatzis, and Frances Johnston. 2008. *Becoming a resonant leader: Develop your emotional intelligence, renew your relationships, and sustain your effectiveness* (p. 150). Boston: Harvard Business School Press.

■ Exhibit **16.9**

My learning edge.

My Learning Edge

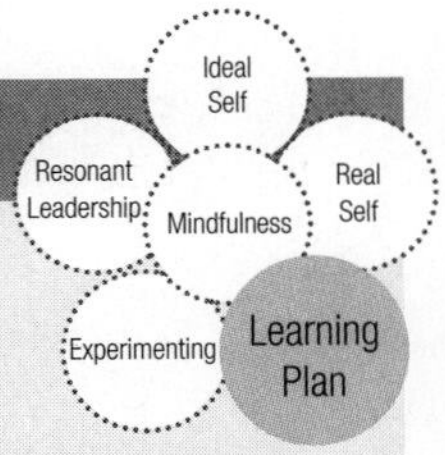

To begin the process of articulating learning goals, it helps to review all that you have learned and done so far in this book. Find a quiet place to sit, and go back through the exercises. Think about your Personal Vision and then look at your Personal Balance Sheet. Read some of your notes about your past, your present, and your future.

What stands out to you about how your current strengths will help you move toward your Personal Vision for life and work?

....
....
....
....

Are there gaps between who you are now and who you want to be in the future or how you want to live your life?

....
....
....
....

What major changes might you need to make if you are to achieve your vision?

....
....
....
....

Identify two to five themes of what you would like to do, be, or achieve.

....
....
....
....
....
....
....
....

Source: Adapted from McKee, Annie, Richard Boyatzis, and Frances Johnston. 2008. *Becoming a resonant leader: Develop your emotional intelligence, renew your relationships, and sustain your effectiveness* (pp. 163–164). Boston: Harvard Business School Press.

> **Most Popular »** Discussion Questions
>
> 1. Which exercises did you find the most revealing?
> 2. In working through the exercises, what were you surprised to learn about yourself?
> 3. Ask yourself one last question: What can I do today to help achieve my dreams?

5. A Final Word on Managing Yourself

Our world needs all that you can give: your brilliance and creativity, values and ethics, enthusiasm, hope, and inspiration. We are facing some very big challenges today—as a leader, you can help your organization and your community to rectify the mistakes of the past and step into a new and exciting era.

Chapter 16 Visual Summary

1. Why Do "Great Leaders Move Us"? (pp. 592–593)

Summary: Being a great leader is about more than knowing leadership theories; it is about knowing yourself and acknowledging both your strengths and your weaknesses. Chade-Meng Tan of Google exemplifies this and points out that egoless-ego, compassion, and fun are essential for truly inspiring followers. This type of inspiration is especially important in light of the challenges facing the world today.

2. What Are "Moon Shots for Management"? (pp. 593–595)

Summary: Moon shots for management are 25 changes and challenges essential for leading organizations today. These guidelines encourage us to lead responsibly and shift away from antiquated forms of management toward ethical and community-oriented behavior. The moon shots focus on socially significant business practices to eliminate many of the dysfunctions seen in today's organizations, such as stifling hierarchies. Moon shots are not designed to be a specific set of instructions; rather, they are guiding principles that must be interpreted meaningfully by individual organizations and their leaders.

3. How Can You Continue Your Journey to Becoming a Resonant Leader? (pp. 595–596)

Summary: Leadership is not a distant career goal; it is a journey that you can begin now. As autonomy and empowerment become the norm in business, you need to lead, embrace change, and become a lifelong learner in order to solve organizational and community problems. It is also essential that you use your power as a leader to benefit those around you and ensure that your organization lives up to your personal values and ethics.

Leading and Managing for Today and the Future

16. Managing and Leading for Tomorrow: A Focus on Your Future

14. Globalization: Managing Effectively in a Global Economic Environment

1. Managing and Leading Today: The New Rules

2. The Leadership Imperative: It's Up to You

4. Communication: The Key to Resonant Relationships

3. Motivation and Meaning: What Makes People Want to Work?

15. Sustainability and Corporate Social Responsibility: Ensuring the Future

4. What Can You Do to Develop Your Leadership? (pp. 596–606)

Summary: Translating leadership theory into action can be tough, particularly if you set goals that focus solely on personal deficiencies. In order for you to achieve meaningful change, you need to think positively about your ideal self and engage in the process of intentional change. This process involves identifying your personal vision, exploring who you are, and planning to develop strengths that are meaningful to you.

5. A Final Word on Managing Yourself (p. 606)

Summary: You are in a position to help your organizations and community today. The world needs all your talents, competencies, and creativity as we face tremendous challenges and opportunities.

Endnotes

Chapter 1

1. Goleman, Daniel, Richard Boyatzis, and Annie McKee. 2002. *Primal leadership.* Boston: Harvard Business School Press; McKee, Annie, and Richard Boyatzis. 2005. *Resonant leadership.* Boston: Harvard Business School Press.
2. McKee, Annie, Richard Boyatzis, and Frances Johnston. 2008. *Becoming a resonant leader.* Boston: Harvard Business School Press.
3. *Oxford English Dictionary.* Retrieved August 20, 2009, from http://dictionary.oed.com.
4. Mintzberg, Henry. 1975. *The nature of managerial work.* New York: Harper and Row.
5. Ibid.
6. Hollander, Edwin P. 1992. Leadership, followership, self, and others. *Leadership Quarterly* 3(1): 43–54.
7. Kellerman, Barbara. 2008. *Followership: How followers are creating change and changing leaders.* Boston: Harvard Business School Press.
8. Kellerman, Barbara. 2007. What every leader needs to know about followers. *Harvard Business Review* 85(12): 84–91.
9. Kellerman, Barbara. 2007. What every leader needs to know about followers. *Harvard Business Review* 85(12): 84–91; Hollander, Leadership, followership, self, and others.
10. Kellerman. What every leader needs to know about followers.
11. Bennis, Warren. 2007. The challenges of leadership in the modern world: Introduction to the special issue. *American Psychologist* 62(1): 2–5.
12. Pina e Cunha, Miguel, and Arménio Rego. 2010. Complexity, simplicity, simplexity. *European Management Journal* 28(2): 85–94.
13. Useem, Michael. 2003. *Leading up: How to lead your boss so you both win.* New York: Three Rivers Press.
14. Hooley, Tristram. 2009. *Followership.* Adventures in Career Development (July 19). Retrieved March 10, 2010, from http://adventuresincareerdevelopment.posterous.com/followership.
15. FitzGerald, Niall. 2009, May 20. Corporate responsibility in the 21st century. Tyburn Lecture, Tyburn Convent, London, England.

Chapter 2

1. Boyatzis, Richard E. 2008. Competencies in the 21st century (Guest Editorial). *Journal of Management Development* 27(1): 5–12; Spencer, Lyle M., and Signe M. Spencer. 1993. *Competence at work: Models for superior performance.* New York: John Wiley and Sons; Boyatzis, Richard E. 1982. *The competent manager: A model for effective performance.* Hoboken, NJ: Wiley-Interscience.
2. McClelland, David C. 1973. Testing for competence rather than for "intelligence." *American Psychologist* 28: 1–14.
3. Thorndike, R. L., and E. Hagen. 1959. *10,000 careers.* New York: Wiley.
4. Boyatzis, Competencies in the 21st century.
5. Ibid.
6. Ibid.
7. Boyatzis, *The competent manager.*
8. Ibid.
9. Ibid.
10. Goleman, D. 1995. *Emotional intelligence.* New York: Bantam Books; Goleman, D. 2006. *Social intelligence.* New York: Bantam Books.
11. Boyatzis, R., and A. McKee. 2005. *Resonant leadership: Sustaining yourself and connecting with others through mindfulness, hope, and compassion.* Boston: Harvard Business School Press.
12. Gardner, H. 1983. *Frames of mind: The theory of multiple intelligences.* New York: Basic Books; Bar-On, R. 1997. *Bar-On Emotional Quotient Inventory: Technical manual.* Toronto: Multi-Health Systems; Goleman, *Emotional intelligence*; Bar-On, R. 1992. *The development of a concept and test of psychological well-being.* Unpublished manuscript. Tel Aviv: Reuven Bar-On.
13. Goleman et al., *Primal leadership*; McKee, A., R. E. Boyatzis, and F. Johnston. 2008. *Becoming a resonant leader: Develop your emotional intelligence, renew your relationships, sustain your effectiveness.* Boston: Harvard Business School Press; Goleman, D. 1998. *Working with emotional intelligence.* New York: Bantam Books.
14. Goleman et al., *Primal leadership;* Boyatzis and McKee, *Resonant leadership.*
15. Goleman, *Social intelligence.*
16. Goleman et al., *Primal leadership*; Boyatzis and McKee, *Resonant leadership*; McKee et al., *Becoming a resonant leader*; Lewis, Thomas, Fari Amini, and Richard Lannon. 2000. *A general theory of love.* New York: Random House.
17. McKee et al., *Becoming a resonant leader* p. 31.
18. Butcher, David, and Martin Clarke. 2008. *Smart management: Using politics in organisations.* Basingstoke, UK: Palgrave.
19. Runde, Craig E., and Tim A. Flanagan. 2007. *Becoming a competent leader: How you and your organization can manage conflict effectively.* San Francisco, CA: John Wiley & Sons.
20. Goleman et al., *Primal leadership.*
21. The Beyster Institute. 2009. Southwest Airlines President Emeritus Colleen Barrett on the power of an ownership culture. *The Beyster Institute Newsletter* (May). Accessed November 18, 2009, from http://rady.ucsd.edu/beyster/newsletter/Southwest.html; Boyatzis and McKee, *Resonant leadership.*
22. Bowne, D. E., and E. E. Lawler. 1992. Empowerment of service workers: What, why, how and when. *Sloan Management Review* 33(3): 31–39; Pastor, J. 1996. Empowerment: What it is and what it is not. *Empowerment in Organizations* 4(2): 5–7.
23. Spreitzer, G. M. 2007. Giving peace a chance: Organizational leadership, empowerment, and peace. *Journal of Organizational Behavior* 28: 1077–95.
24. Bakker, A. B. 2005. Flow among music teachers and their students: The crossover of peak experiences. *Journal of Vocational Behavior* 66: 26–44; Reeve, J., H. Jang, D. Carrell, S. Jeon, and J. Barch. 2004. Enhancing students' engagement by increasing teachers' autonomy support. *Motivation and Emotion* 28: 147–69; Ouchi, W. G. 1981. *Theory Z: How American business can meet the Japanese challenge.* Reading, MA: Addison-Wesley.
25. Spreitzer, G. M. 1995. Psychological empowerment in the workplace: dimensions, measurement, and validation. *Academy of Management Journal* 38: 1442–65.
26. Lucas, Victoria, Heather K. Spence Laschinger, and Carol Wong. 2008. The impact of emotional intelligent leadership on staff nurse empowerment: The moderating effect of span of control. *Journal of Nursing Management* 16: 964–73; Erstad, M. 1997. Empowerment and organizational change. *International Journal of Contemporary Hospitality* 9(7): 325–33.
27. Ouchi, William. G. 1981. *Theory Z: How American business can meet the Japanese challenge.* Reading, MA: Addison-Wesley.
28. Ibid.
29. Pellegrini, E. K., and T. A. Scandura. 2008. Paternalistic leadership: A review and agenda for future research. *Journal of Management* 34(3) 566–93.
30. Forrester, R. 1993. Empowerment, *Academy of Management Executive* 14: 67–90.
31. Levine, David I. and Laura D'Andrea Tyson, "Participation, Productivity, and the Firm's Environment," in Alan Blinder, ed. *Paying for Productivity* (Brookings Institution, 1990) pp. 203–204.
32. Beck, Sanderson. 2004. Greece & Rome to 30 BC. Retrieved August 7, 2009, from http://www.san.beck.org/EC22-Aristotle.html.
33. Wills, Garry. 2001. *Saint Augustine's childhood.* New York: Penguin Putnam.
34. Princeton Wordnet. Ethical Code. Retrieved August 29, 2010, from http://wordnetweb.princeton.edu/perl/webwn?s=ethical+code&o2=&o0=1&o7=&o5=&o1=1&o6=&o4=&o3=&h=.
35. Ferguson, W. C. 1997. Ethical foundations. *Executive Excellence* 14(6): 15–16(p. 16).

36. Rokeach, Milton. 1973. *The nature of human values.* New York: Free Press. http://faculty.weber.edu/molpin/healthclasses/1110/bookchapters/valueschapter.htm.

37. Epstein, Edwin M. 1989. Business ethics, corporate good citizenship and the corporate social policy process: A view from the United States. *Journal of Business Ethics* 8(8): 583–95.

38. AICPA code of professional conduct: Preamble. Retrieved February 26, 2010, from http://www.aicpa.org/About/code/et_50.html.

39. Bauman, Zygmunt. 1998. *Globalization: The human consequences.* New York: Columbia University Press.

40. Ess, Charles. 2006. Ethical pluralism and global information ethics. *Ethics and Information Technology* 8(4): 215–26.

41. Bauman, Zygmunt. 1993. *Postmodern ethics.* Blackwell, Oxford.

42. Sarbanes-Oxley Act. Retrieved July 9, 2009, from http://en.wikipedia.org/wiki/Sarbanes-Oxley_Act.

43. U.S. Department of State. International Anticorruption and Good Governance Act. Retrieved February 26, 2010, from http://www.state.gov/p/inl/rls/rpt/c6696.htm.

44. Clegg, Stewart, Martin Kornberger, and Carl Rhodes. 2007. Business ethics as practice. *British Journal of Management* 18(2): 107–22.

45. President and Fellows of the Harvard College. 2009. Great American business leaders of the twentieth century. Retrieved September 12, 2009, from http://www.hbs.edu/leadership/database/leaders/katharine_m_graham.html.

46. The Pulitzer Prizes. 1998. Katharine Graham—biography. Retrieved September 13, 2009, from http://www.pulitzer.org/biography/1998-Biography-or-Autobiography.

47. NPR News. 2001, July 17. Katharine Graham: A life remembered. Retrieved September 12, 2009, from http://www.npr.org.

48. Dweck, Carol. 2006. *Mindset: The new psychology of success.* New York: Random House.

49. The Washington Post Company. 2001, July 18. Katharine Graham: 1917–2001. Retrieved September 12, 2009, from http://www.washingtonpost.com/wp-dyn/content/article/2006/03/20/AR2006032000789.html.

50. Barsh, Joanna, Susie Cranston, and Rebecca A. Craske. 2008 (September). Centered leadership: How talented women thrive. Retrieved September 12, 2009, from http://www.mckinseyquarterly.com/Centered_leadership_How_talented_women_thrive_2193.

51. Ibid.

52. Fisher, Marc. 2001, July 28. Katharine Graham never lost sight of her city. Retrieved September 12, 2009, from http://www.washingtonpost.com/wp-dyn/content/article/2006/03/16/AR2006031601396.html.

53. Ibid.

54. Brin, S., and L. Page. Google code of conduct. Retrieved July 5, 2009, from http://investor.google.com/conduct.html.

55. Madoff investment scandal. Retrieved August 13, 2009, from http://www.wikipedia.com; Appelbaum, Binyamin, David S. Hilzenrath, and Amit R. Paley. 2008, December 13. All just one big lie. *Washington Post.* Retrieved September 10, 2009, from http://www.washingtonpost.com/wp-dyn/content/article/2008/12/12/AR2008121203970.html?hpid=topnews.

56. Biggs, Barton. 2009, January 13. The Affinity Ponzi scheme. *Newsweek.* Retrieved August 13, 2009, from http://www.newsweek.com/id/177679.

57. Madoff trading statement, November 2008. Retrieved February 26, 2010, from http://www.scribd.com/doc/8976754/Madoff-Trading-Statement-November-2008.

58. Arvedlund, Erin E. 2001, May 7. Don't ask, don't tell. *Barron's.* Retrieved February 26, 2010, from http://online.barrons.com/article/SB989019667829349012.html.

59. Appelbaum et al. All just one big lie.

60. McClean, Elkind, and Alex Gibney. 2005. *Enron: The smartest guys in the room.* Directed by Alex Gibney. Distributed by Columbia Pictures.

61. Halbesleben, Jonathon R. B., Anthony R. Wheeler, and M. Ronald Buckley. 2005. Everybody else is doing it, so why can't we? Pluralistic ignorance and business ethics education. *Journal of Business Ethics* 56(4): 385–98.

62. Hardin, Garrett. 1968. The tragedy of the commons. *Science* 162(3859): 1243–48.

63. Kohs, S. C., and K. W. Irle. 1920. Prophesying army promotion. *Journal of Applied Psychology* 4(1): 73–87: Tead, Ordway. 1929. *Human nature and management.* New York: McGraw-Hill; Page, David P. 1935. Measurement and prediction of leadership. *American Journal of Sociology* 41(1): 31–43; Bellingrath, George C. 1930. *Qualities associated with leadership in the extra-curricular activities of the high school.* New York: Teacher's College Contributions to Education; Gowin, E. B. 1927. *The executive and his control of men.* New York: Macmillan Company.

64. Jenkins, W. O. 1947. A review of leadership studies with particular reference to military problems. *Psychological Bulletin* 44: 54–79.

65. Bass, Bernard M. 1990. *Bass & Stogdill's handbook of leadership: Theory, research and managerial applications.* New York: The Free Press.

66. Contributors to Exhibit 2.10, (individual contributions undifferentiated): Bass, Bernard M. 1990. *Bass & Stogdill's handbook of leadership: Theory, research and managerial applications.* New York: The Free Press; Kirkpatrick, Shelley A., and Edwin A. Locke. 1991. Leadership: Do traits matter? *Academy of Management Executive* 5(2): 48–60; Mishra, Aneil K. 1996. Organizational responses to crises: The centrality of trust. In *Trust in organizations,* ed. Roderick M. Kramer and Thomas Tyler, 261–87. Newbury Park, CA: Sage; Bryman, A. 1993. *Charisma and leadership in organizations.* London: Sage; George, Jennifer M. 2000. Emotions and leadership: The role of emotional intelligence. *Human Relations* 53(8): 1027–55; Judge, Timothy A., and Joyce E. Bono. 2000. Five-factor model of personality and transformational leadership. *Journal of Applied Psychology* 85(5): 751–65; Mumford, Michael D., Stephen J. Zaccaro, Francis D. Harding, T. Owen Jacobs, and Edwin A. Fleishman. 2000. Leadership skills for a changing world: Solving complex social problems. *Leadership Quarterly* 11(1): 11–35; Conger, Jay A., and Rabindra N. Kanungo. 1987. Towards a behavioral theory of charismatic leadership in an organizational setting. *Academy of Management Review* 12: 637–47; Conger, Jay A., and Rabindra N. Kanungo. 1994. Charismatic leadership in organizations: Perceived behavioral attributes and their measurement. *Journal of Organizational Behavior* 15(5): 439–52; Hartog, Deanne N., Robert J. House, Paul J. Hanges, and S. Antonio Ruiz-Quintanilla. 1999. Culture specific and cross-culturally generalizable implicit leadership theories: Are attributes of charismatic/transformational leadership universally endorsed? *Leadership Quarterly* 10(2): 219–56; Covey, S. R. 1996. Three roles of the leader in the new paradigm, in *The leader of the future: New visions, strategies, and practices for the next era,* ed. F. Hesselbein, M. Goldsmith, and R. Beckhard, 149–59. New York: Jossey Bass; Covey, S. R. 1990. *Principle-centered leadership.* New York: Simon and Schuster; Russell, Robert F., and A. Gregory Stone. 2002. A review of servant leadership attributes: Developing a practical model. *Leadership & Organization Development Journal* 23(3/4): 145–57; Zaccaro, S. J., C. Kemp, and P. Bader. 2004. Leader traits and attributes. In *The nature of leadership,* ed. J. Antonakis, A. T. Cianciolo, and R. J. Sternberg, 101–24. Thousand Oaks, CA: Sage; Zaleznik, Abraham. 1992. Managers and leaders: Are they different? *Harvard Business Review* (March–April): 126–35; Goleman et al. *Primal leadership.*

67. Fleishman, E. A. 1957. A leader behavior description for industry, in *Leader behavior: Its description and measurement,* ed. R. M. Stogdill and A. E. Coons. Columbus, OH: Bureau of Business Research; Fleishman, E. A., E. F. Harris, and H. E. Burtt. 1955. *Leadership and supervision in industry.* Columbus, OH: Bureau of Educational Research, Ohio State University; Fleishman, E. A., and D. A. Peters. 1962. Interpersonal values, leadership attitudes, and managerial success. *Personnel Psychology* 15: 127–43. See also Fiedler, F. E. 1958. *Leader attitudes and group effectiveness.* Urbana, IL: University of Illinois Press.

68. Fleishman, E. 1973. Twenty years of consideration and structure, in *Current developments in the study of leadership: A centennial event,* ed. E. A. Fleishman and J. Hunt, 1–40. Carbondale, IL: Southern Illinois University Press.

69. Likert, R. 1979. From production- and employee-centeredness to systems 1–4. *Journal of Management* 5: 628–41.

70. Blake, R., and J. Mouton. 1964. *The managerial grid: The key to leadership excellence.* Houston: Gulf Publishing Co; Blake, R., J. Mouton, L. Barnes, and L. Greiner. 1964. Breakthroughs in organization development. *Harvard Business Review* 42(6): 133–55; Blake, R., and J. Mouton. 1981. Management by grid® principles or situationalism: Which? *Group and Organization Studies* 6(4): 439–55; Blake, R., and J. Mouten. 1985. *The managerial grid III.* Houston: Gulf Publishing Co.

71. Blake, R., and J. Mouton. 1978. *The new managerial grid.* Houston, TX: Gulf Publishing Co; Blake, R. R., and J. S. McCanse. 1991. *The managerial grid illuminated: Leadership dilemmas grid solutions.* Houston, TX: Gulf Publishing Co; Blake, R., and J. Mouton. 1994. *The managerial grid.* Houston, TX: Gulf Publishing Co; McKee, R. K., and B. Carlson. 1999. *The power to change.* Austin, TX: Grid International, Inc.

72. Blake and Mouton, *The managerial grid*.

73. Fiedler, F. E. 1967. *A theory of leadership effectiveness*. New York: McGraw-Hill.

74. Fiedler, F. 1965. Engineer the job to fit the manager. *Harvard Business Review* 43(5): 115–22; Fiedler, F., and M. M. Chemers. 1984. *Improving leadership effectiveness: The leader match concept* (rev. ed.). New York: Wiley.

75. Hersey, P., and K. Blanchard. 1982. *Management of organizational behavior*. Englewood Cliffs, NJ: Prentice Hall.

76. House, R. J. 1971. A path-goal theory of leader effectiveness. *Administrative Science Quarterly* 16: 321–38; Wofford, J. C., and L. Z. Liska. 1993. Path-goal theories of leadership: A meta-analysis. *Journal of Management* 19: 857–76.

77. Keller, R. 1989. Test of path-goal theory of leadership with need for clarity as moderator in research and development organizations. *Journal of Applied Psychology* 74: 208–12.

78. Kerr, S., and J. M. Jermier. 1978. Substitutes for leadership: Their meaning and measurement. *Organizational Behavior and Human Performance* 22: 375–403.

79. Burns, James M. 1978. *Leadership*. New York: HarperCollins.

80. Knowledge@Wharton. 2005. Tyco's Edward Breen: When leadership means firing top management and the entire board. Retrieved October 15, 2009, from http://www.wharton.universia.net/index .cfm?fa= viewArticle&id=1094&language=english.

81. Ibid.

82. Bloomgarden, Kathy. 2007. *Trust: The secret weapon of effective business leaders*. New York: St. Martin's Press; Useem, Michael. 2006. How well-run boards make decisions. *Harvard Business Review* 84(6): 130–38.

83. Knowledge@Wharton. Tyco's Edward Breen.

84. Conger, J. A., and R. N. Kanungo, eds. 2008. *Charismatic leadership in organizations*. Thousand Oaks, CA: Sage Publications.

85. McKee, Annie, and Frances Johnston. *The four HR leadership roles* (Elkins Park, PA: Teleos Leadership Institute, 2010) slides.

86. Ibid.

87. Laycayo, Ricardo and Ripley, Amanda. 2002. Persons of the year 2002: Cynthia Cooper, Colleen Rowley and Sherron Watkins. *Time* (December 22, 2002). Accessed September 8, 2009, from http://www .time.com/time/subscriber/personoftheyear/2002/poyintro.html.

88. Lloyd-LaFollette Act. Retrieved September 8, 2009, from http://en .wikipedia.org/wiki/Lloyd-La_Follette_Act.

89. U.S. Securities and Exchange Commission. Whistleblower Protection Act information. Retrieved September 8, 2009, from http://www.sec .gov/eeoinfo/whistleblowers.htm.

90. *Garcetti v. Ceballos*. Retrieved September 8, 2009, from http://en .wikipedia.org/wiki/Garcetti_v._Ceballos.

91. OpenCongress. H.R. 985—Whistleblower Protection Enhancement Act of 2007. Retrieved September 8, 2009, from http://www.opencongress .org/bill/110-h985/show.

92. George, B., P. Sims, A. N. McLean, and D. Mayer. 2007. Discovering your authentic leadership. *Harvard Business Review* 85(2): 129–38.

93. Avolio, Bruce J., and William L. Gardner. 2005. Authentic leadership development: Getting to the root of positive forms of leadership. *Leadership Quarterly* 16(3): 315–38.

94. Kernis, Michael H. 2003. Toward a conceptualization of optimal self-esteem. *Psychological Inquiry* 14(1): 1–26.

95. Gillespie, Nicole A., and Leon Mann. 2004. Transformational leadership and shared values: The building blocks of trust. *Journal of Managerial Psychology* 19(6): 588–607; Hosmer, Larue Tone. 1995. The connecting link between organizational theory and philosophical ethics. *Academy of Management Review* 20(2): 379–403.

96. Gillespie and Mann, Transformational leadership and shared values.

97. Molière, J. B. 1664. *Tartuffe*, Act 5, scene 1.

98. Brown, Michael E., and Linda K. Treviño. 2005. Ethical leadership: A social learning perspective for construct development and testing. *Organizational Behavior and Human Decision Processes* 97: 117–34.

99. Den Hartog, D. N., R. J. House, P. J. Hanges, S. A. Ruiz-Quintanilla, P. W. Dorfman, et al. 1999. Culturally specific and cross-culturally generalizable implicit leadership theories: Are attributes of charismatic/transformational leadership universally endorsed? *Leadership Quarterly* 10: 219–56.

100. Waddock, Sandra. 2007. Leadership integrity in a fractured knowledge world. *Academy of Management Learning & Education* 6(4): 543–57.

101. Palanski, Michael E., and Francis J. Yammarino. 2009. Integrity and leadership: A multi-level conceptual framework. *Leadership Quarterly* 20(3): 405–20.

102. Redmoon, Ambrose H. 1991. No peaceful warriors! *Gnosis: A Journal of the Western Inner Traditions* 21(Fall): 40–45.

103. Hightower, Jim, and Susan DeMarco. 2008. *Swim against the current: Even a dead fish can go with the flow*. Hoboken, NJ: John Wiley & Sons.

104. Kouzes, J., and B. Posner. 2003. *The leadership challenge*. New York: Jossey-Bass.

105. Ibid.

Chapter 3

1. Latham, Gary P., and Craig C. Pinder. 2005. Work motivation theory and research at the dawn of the twenty-first century. *Annual Review of Psychology* 56: 485–516.

2. Frankl, Victor. 1963. *Man's search for meaning*. New York: Pocket Books.

3. Ryan, J. J. 1977. Humanistic work: Its philosophical and cultural implications. In *A matter of dignity: Inquiries into the humanization of work*, ed. W. J. Heisler and J. W. Houck, 11–22. Notre Dame, IN: University of Notre Dame Press.

4. Csikszentmihalyi, Mihaly. 1975. *Beyond boredom and anxiety: Experiencing flow in work and play*. San Francisco: Jossey-Bass; Csikszentmihalyi, Mihaly. 1990. *Flow: The psychology of optimal experience*. New York: HarperCollins; Keller, J., and H. Bless. 2008. Flow and regulatory compatibility: An experimental approach to the flow model of intrinsic motivation. *Personality and Social Psychology Bulletin* 34: 196–209.

5. Adapted from Nakamura, Jeanne, and Mihaly Csikszentmihalyi. 2002. The concept of flow. In *Handbook of positive psychology*, ed. R. Snyder and Shane Lopez. Oxford: Oxford University Press.

6. Boyatzis, Richard, and Annie McKee. 2005. *Resonant leadership: Renewing yourself and connecting with others through mindfulness, hope and compassion*. Boston: Harvard Business School Press; Snyder, C. R., K. L. Rand, and D. R. Signon. 2002. Hope theory: A member of the positive psychology family. In *Handbook of positive psychology*, ed. C. R. Snyder and S. J. Lopez, 257–76. New York: Oxford University Press.

7. Boyatzis and McKee, *Resonant leadership*; Snyder, C. R., C. Harris, J. R. Anderson, S. A. Holleran, L. M. Irving, S. T. Sigmon, L. Yoshinobu, J. Gibb, C. Langelle, and P. Harney. 1991. The will and the ways. *Journal of Personality and Social Psychology* 60: 570–85.

8. Boyatzis and McKee, *Resonant leadership*.

9. Goleman, Daniel, Richard Boyatzis, and Annie McKee. 2002. *Primal leadership: Realizing the power of emotional intelligence*. Boston: Harvard Business School Press.

10. Csikszentmihalyi. *Beyond boredom and anxiety*.

11. Ryan, Richard M., and Edward L. Deci. 2000. Self-determination theory and the facilitation of intrinsic motivation, social development, and well-being. *American Psychologist* (January): 68–78; Deci, E., and R. Ryan. 2008. Facilitating optimal motivation and psychological well-being across life's domains. *Canadian Psychology* 49: 14–23; Deci, Edward L., and Richard M. Ryan, eds. 2002. *Handbook of self-determination research*. Rochester, NY: University of Rochester Press; Deci, Edward L., and Richard M. Ryan. 1985. *Intrinsic motivation and self-determination in human behavior*. New York: Plenum Press; Mruk, Christopher J. 2006. *Self-esteem research, theory, and practice*. New York: Springer Publishing Company.

12. Deci, Edward L., and Richard M. Ryan. 2008. Self-determination theory: A macrotheory of human motivation, development, and health. *Canadian Psychology* 49(3): 183; Guay, Frédéric, Catherine F. Ratelle, and Julien Chanal. 2008. Optimal learning in optimal contexts: The role of self-determination in education. *Canadian Psychology* 49(3): 233–40; Joussemet, Mireille, Renée Landry, and Richad Koestner. 2008. A self-determination theory perspective on parenting. *Canadian Psychology* 49(3): 194–200; Baard, Paul P., Edward L. Deci, and Richard M. Ryan. 2004. Intrinsic need satisfaction: A motivational basis of performance and well-being in two work settings. *Journal of Applied Social Psychology* 34(10): 2045–68.

13. Deci and Ryan, *Intrinsic motivation*.

14. Gagné, Marylène, and Edward L. Deci. 2005. Self-determination theory and work motivation. *Journal of Organizational Behavior* 26: 331–62.

15. Deci, Edward L. 1972. Intrinsic motivation, extrinsic reinforcement, and inequity. *Journal of Personality and Social Psychology* 22(1): 113–20.

16. Google Inc. 2009. The Google culture. Retrieved September 12, 2009, from http://www.google.com/corporate/culture.html.

17. Ibid; Kumar, Reshma. August 24, 2008. Google's free food being cut. *Silicon Valley WebGuild.* Retrieved September 23, 2009, from http://www.webguild.org/2008/08/googles-free-food-being-cut.php.

18. The most desirable employers. 2009. *BusinessWeek.* Retrieved September 12, 2009, from http://bwnt.businessweek.com/interactive_reports/most_desirable_employers/index.asp.

19. Battelle, John. December 1 2005. The 70 percent solution. CNNMoney.com. Retrieved September 12, 2009, from http://money.cnn.com/magazines/business2/business2_archive/2005/12/01/8364616/index.htm; Princeton University. December 22, 2008. Princeton University learning process. *Learning & Development.* Retrieved September 12, 2009, from http://www.princeton.edu/hr/l&d/l&d_learning_process.htm; Casnocha, B. April 24, 2009. Success on the side. Retrieved September 12, 2009, from http://www.american.com/archive/2009/april-2009/Success-on-the-Side.

20. Help wanted: Google. January 22, 2008. CNNMoney.com. Retrieved March 16, 2010, from http://money.cnn.com/galleries/2008/fortune/0801/gallery.BestCo_Google_help.fortune/7.html.

21. Battelle, John. The 70 percent solution.

22. Ibid.

23. Rotter, J. B. 1954. *Social learning and clinical psychology.* New York: Prentice Hall; Rotter, Julian B. 1966. Generalized expectancies for internal versus external control reinforcement. *Psychological Monographs:* General and Applied. Vol 80(1): 1–28.

24. Thurstone, L. L. 1934. The vectors of the mind. *Psychological Review* 41: 1–32; Goldberg, L. R. 1981. Language and individual differences: The search for universals in personality lexicons, *Review of personality and social psychology, Vol. 2,* ed. L. Wheeler, 141–165. Beverly Hills, CA: Sage.

25. Allport, G. W., and H. S. Odbert. 1936. Trait names: A psycholexical study. *Psychological Monographs* 47: 211.

26. Goulden, R., P. Nation, and J. Read. 1990. How large can a receptive vocabulary be? *Applied Linguistics* 11(4): 341–63.

27. Cattell, R. B. 1946. *The description and measurement of personality.* New York: World Book.

28. Thurstone, The vectors of the mind; Cattell, *The description and measurement of personality;* Norman, W. T. 1963. Toward an adequate taxonomy of personality attributes: Replicated factor structure in peer nomination personality ratings. *Journal of Abnormal and Social Psychology* 66: 574–83; Goldberg, Language and individual differences; McCrae, R. R., and P. T. Costa. 1987. Validation of the five-factor model of personality across instruments and observers. *Journal of Personality and Social Psychology* 52(1): 81–90.

29. Bono, J. E., and T. A. Judge. 2004. Personality and transformational and transactional leadership: A meta-analysis. *Journal of Applied Psychology* 89(5): 901–10.

30. Barrick, M. R., G. L. Stewart, and M. Piotrowski. 2002. Personality and job performance: Test of the mediating effects of motivation among sales representatives. *Journal of Applied Psychology* 87(1): 43–51.

31. Maslow, Abraham. 1968. *Toward a psychology of being.* New York: D. Van Nostrand Co.

32. Alderfer, Clayton P. 1972. *Existence, relatedness, and growth: Human needs in organizational settings.* New York: Free Press.

33. Herzberg, Frederick. 1959. *The motivation to work.* New York: Wiley.

34. Wall, Toby D., and Geoffrey M. Stephenson. 1970. Herzberg's two-factor theory of job attitudes: A critical evaluation and some fresh evidence. *Industrial Relations Journal* 1(3): 41–65.

35. Herzberg, F., B. Mausner, and B. B. Snyderman. 1959. *The motivation to work.* New York: Wiley; Parker, Sharon K., and Toby D. Wall. 1998. Work design: Learning from the past and mapping a new terrain. In *Handbook of industrial, work, and organizational psychology,* Vol. 1, ed. Neil Anderson, Deniz S. Ones, Handan K. Sinangil, and Chockalingam Viswesvaran, 90–109. Thousand Oaks, CA: Sage Publications.

36. McClelland, David C. 1985. *Human motivation.* Glenview, IL: Scott Foresman and Company; Wheatley, Margaret. 1999. *Leadership and the new science: Discovering order in a chaotic world.* San Francisco: Berrett-Koehler; Wheatley, Margaret. 2005. *Finding our way: Leadership for uncertain times.* San Francisco: Berrett-Koehler; Boyatzis, Richard. 2006. An overview of intentional change theory from a complexity perspective. *Journal of Management Development,* 25(7): 607-623; Goleman, Daniel, ed. 2003. *Destructive emotions: How can we overcome them? A scientific dialogue with the Dalai Lama.* New York: Bantam Books.

37. Hofer, Jan, Athanasios Chasiotis, Wolfgang Friedlmeier, Holger Busch, and Domingo Campos. 2005. The measurement of implicit motives in three cultures: Power and affiliation in Cameroon, Costa Rica, and Germany. *Journal of Cross-Cultural Psychology* 36: 689–716; Sokolowski, Kurt, Heinz-Dieter Schmalt, Thomas A. Langens, and Rosa M. Puca. 2000. Assessing achievement, affiliation, and power motives all at once: The multi-motive grid (MMG). *Journal of Personality Assessment* 74(1): 126–45; Yamaguchi, Ikushi. 2003. The relationships among individual differences, needs and equity sensitivity. *Journal of Managerial Psychology* 18(4): 324–44.

38. McClelland, David C. 1982. The need for power, sympathetic activation, and illness. *Motivation and Emotion,* 6(1): 31–41; McKee, Annie, Richard Boyatzis, and Frances Johnston. *Becoming a Resonant Leader: Develop your emotional intelligence, renew your relationships and sustain your effetiveness.* Boston: Harvard Business Press. 2008.

39. McClelland, D. C. 1961. *The achieving society.* New York: Van Nostrand-Rheinhold.

40. Boyatzis and McKee, *Resonant leadership;* McClelland, *Human motivation,* 1982, p. 71.

41. McClelland, D. C., W. N. Davis, R. Kalin, and H. E. Wanner. 1972. *The drinking man.* New York: Free Press; Schultheiss, O. C., K. L. Campbell, and D. C. McClelland. 1999. Implicit power motivation moderates men's testosterone response to imagined and real dominance success. *Hormones and Behavior* 36: 234–41.

42. Ibid.

43. Schultheiss, Campbell, and McClelland. Implicit poor motivation moderates men's testosterone reponse to imagined and real dominance success.

44. Brown, Michael E., and Linda K. Treviño. 2006. Socialized charismatic leadership, values congruence, and deviance in work groups. *Journal of Applied Psychology* 91(4): 954–62; Kanungo, Rabindra N., and Manuel Mendonca. 1996. *Ethical dimensions in leadership.* Beverly Hills, CA: Sage Publications.

45. Mandela, Nelson, interviewed and presented on video http://www.youtube.com/watch?v=ODQ4WiDsEBQ.

46. Nussbaum, Barbara. 2003. African culture and Ubuntu: Reflections of a South African in America. *World Business Academy* 17: 1; Nussbaum, Barbara. 2003. Ubuntu: Reflections of a South African in our common humanity. *Reflections* 4: 4; Nussbaum, Barbara. 2003. Ubuntu and business . . . reflections and questions. *World Business Academy* 17: 3.

47. McKee, Annie, Frances Johnston, Eddy Mwelwa, and Suzanne Rotondo. 2009. Resonant leadership for results: An emotional and social intelligence program for change in South Africa and Cambodia. In *Handbook for developing emotional and social intelligence,* ed. Marcia Hughes, Henry L. Thompson, and James Bradford Terrel, 49–71. San Francisco: Pfeiffer.

48. McClelland, *The achieving society;* McClelland, D. C. 1975. *Power: The inner experience.* New York: Irvington; Murray, Henry A. 1938. *Explorations in personality.* New York: Oxford University Press.

49. Aronow, Edward, Kim Weiss, and Marvin Reznikoss. 2001. *A practical guide to the Thematic Apperception Test: The TAT in clinical practice.* Philadelphia: Taylor and Francis.

50. McClelland, David C. 1958. Methods of measuring human motivation. In *Motives in fantasy, action and society,* ed. John W. Akinson, 12–13. Princeton, NJ: D. Van Nostrand Co..

51. Adams, J. Stacey. 1965. Inequity in social exchange. In *Advances in experimental social psychology,* Vol. 2, ed. Leonard Berkowitz, 267–99. New York: Academic Press.

52. Festinger, Leon. 1957. *A theory of cognitive dissonance.* Stanford, CA: Stanford University Press; Brehm, Jack, and Arthur Cohen. 1962. *Explorations in cognitive dissonance.* New York: Wiley.

53. Brown, Michael E., and Linda K. Treviño. Ethical leadership: A review and future directions. *Leadership Quarterly* 17: 595–616.

54. Schor, Juliet. 1991. *The overworked American.* New York: Basic Books.

55. Schoen, John W. August 11, 2009. Americans working much harder—for less pay. *MSNBC.* Retrieved December 11, 2009, from http://www.msnbc.msn.com/id/32374533/ns/business-eye_on_the_economy.

56. Goleman et al., *Primal leadership;* Lewis, Thomas, Fari Amini, and Richard Lannon. 2000. *A general theory of love.* New York: Random House.

57. Vroom, Victor H. 1964. *Work and motivation.* New York: Wiley; Atkinson, J. W. 1958. Towards experimental analysis of human motivation in terms of motives, expectancies, and incentives. In *Motives in fantasy, action and society,* ed. J. W. Atkinson, 288–305. New York: D. Van Nostrand Co.

58. Galbraith, Jay, and Larry L. Cummings. 1967. An empirical investigation of the motivational determinants of past performance: Interactive

effects between instrumentality, valence, motivation and ability. *Organizational Behavior and Human Performance* 2: 237–57.

59. Vroom, *Work and motivation.*

60. Altvater, Elmar. 2003. The growth obsession. In *2002: A world of contradiction, socialist register 2002*, ed. Leo Panitch and Colin Leys, 73–92. London: Merlin Press.

61. Latham, Gary, and Edwin Locke. 1990. *A theory of goal setting and task performance.* Englewood Cliffs, NJ: Prentice Hall; Latham, G., and Edwin Locke. 2002. Building a practically useful theory of goal setting and task motivation. *American Psychologist* 57(9): 705–17.

62. Locke, Edwin. 1968. Toward a theory of task motivation and incentives. *Organizational Behavior and Human Performance* 3(2): 157–89.

63. Doran, George T. 1981. There's a S.M.A.R.T. way to write management's goals and objectives. *Management Review* 70(11): 35–36.

64. Vermeeren, Douglas. July 3, 2005. Want to be a top achiever? Stop setting goals! Retrieved July 9, 2009, from http://www.myarticlearchive .com/articles/7/305.htm.

65. Siegert, Richard J., and William J. Taylor. 2004. Theoretical aspects of goal-setting and motivation in rehabilitation. *Disability and Rehabilitation* 26(1): 1–8.

66. Skinner, B. F. 1971. *Beyond freedom and dignity.* New York: Alfred A. Knopf; Thorndike, E. L. 1911. *Animal intelligence: Experimental studies.* New York: Macmillan.

67. Braithwaite, John. 2000. Shame and criminal justice. *Canadian Journal of Criminology* 42(3): 281–98; Tangney, June P. 1990. Assessing individual differences in proneness to shame and guilt: Development of the self-conscious affect and attribution inventory. *Journal of Personality and Social Psychology* 59(1): 102–11.

68. Kohn, Alfie. 1994. The risks of rewards. *ERIC Digests*, ED376990, 1–6.

69. Bandura, Albert. 1969. Social-learning theory of identificatory processes. In *Handbook of socialization theory and research*, ed. David A. Goslin, 213–62. Chicago: Rand McNally & Co.; Bandura, Albert. 1977. *Social learning theory.* Englewood Cliffs, NJ: Prentice Hall; Bandura, Albert. 977b. Self-efficacy: Toward a universal theory of behavioral change. *Psychological Review* 84(2): 191–215.

70. Tarde, G. 1903. *The laws of imitation.* New York: Henry Holt and Co.; Vygotsky, Lev S. 1962. *Thought and language.* Cambridge, MA: MIT Press; Vygotsky, L. S. 1978. *Mind in society.* Cambridge, MA: Harvard University Press; Bandura, A. 1965. Vicarious processes: A case of no-trial learning. In *Advances in experimental social psychology, Vol. 2* (1–57), ed. L. Berkowitz, New York: Academic Press.

71. Rotter, J. B. 1954. *Social learning and clinical psychology.* Englewood Cliffs, NJ: Prentice Hall.

72. Bandura, Albert, Dorothea Ross, and Sheila A. Ross. 1961. Transmission of aggression through imitation of aggressive models. *Journal of Abnormal and Social Psychology* 63: 575–82.

73. Bandura, Albert. 1986. *Social foundations of thought and action: A social cognitive theory.* Englewood Cliffs, NJ: Prentice Hall.

74. Bandura Albert. 1997. *Self-efficacy: The exercise of control.* New York: H. Freeman.

75. Bandura, Albert. 1997. Self-efficacy: Toward a unifying theory of behavioral change. *Psychological Review* 84(2): 191–215.

76. Pajares, Frank. 2004. Albert Bandura: Biographical sketch. Retrieved August 5, 2009, from http://www.emory.edu/EDUCATION/mfp/bandurabio.html.

77. Bandura, Albert. 1994. Self-efficacy. In V. S. Ramachaudran (ed.) *Encyclopedia of human behavior.*, Vol. 4. (71–81). New York: Academic Press.

78. Bandura, Albert. 1973. Social learning theory of aggression. In *The control of aggression*, ed. John F. Knutson, 201–52. Piscataway, NJ: Transaction Publishers.

79. LIVESTRONG: Lance Armstrong Foundation. 2009. Retrieved from http://www.livestrong.org/site/c.khLXK1PxHmF/b.2660611/k.BCED/Home.htm.

80. Yenkins, Sally. 2001. *It's not about the bike: My journey back to life.* New York: Berkley Publishing Group. http://www.livestrong.org/site/c.khLXK1PxHmF/b.2660611/k.BCED/Home.htm.

81. Kirkman, Bradley L., and Debra L. Shapiro. 1997. The impact of cultural values on employee resistance to teams: Toward a model of globalized self-managing work team effectiveness. *Academy of Management Review* 22(3): 730–57.

82. Hackman, J. R., and G. R. Oldham. 1976. Motivation through the design of work: Test of a theory. *Organizational Behavior and Human Performance* 16: 250–79.

83. Heathfield, Susan M. 2008. Five factors every employee wants from work. Human_Resources_About.com. Retrieved July 16, 2009, from http://humanresources.about.com/od/managementtips.

84. Goleman et al. *Primal leadership*; Boyatzis and McKee, *Resonant leadership.*

85. Preston, Stephanie D., and Frans B. M. de Waal. 2002. Empathy: Its ultimate and proximate bases. *Behavioral Brain Science* 25: 1–72; de Vignemont, Frederique, and Tania Singer. 2006. The empathic brain: How, when and why? *Trends in Cognitive Sciences* 10(10): 435–41; Hoffman, M. L. 2000. *Empathy and moral development: Implications for caring and justice.* New York: Cambridge University Press.

86. Goleman, Daniel. 2006. *Social intelligence: The new science of human intelligence.* New York: Bantam Dell; Boyatzis and McKee, *Resonant leadership*; Goleman et al., *Primal leadership.*

87. Kao, H. S. R., and N. Sek-Hong. 1997. Work motivation and culture. In *Motivation and culture*, ed. D. Munro, J. F. Schumaker, and S. C. Carr, 119–32. New York: Routledge.

88. Thinkexist.com Sigmund Freud Quotes. http://thinkexist.com/quotation/love_and_work_are_the_cornerstones_of_our/166402.html. Accessed November 14, 2009.

Chapter 4

1. Pearce, Terry. 2003. *Leading out loud: Inspiring change through authentic communication.* San Francisco, CA: Jossey-Bass; Boyatzis, Richard, and Annie McKee. 2005. Primal and *Resonant leadership: Renewing yourself and connecting with others through mindfulness, hope and compassion.* Boston: Harvard Business School Press.

2. Gorman, Carol K. 2004. *"This isn't the company I joined": How to lead in a business turned upside down.* National City, CA: KCS Publishers.

3. Klein, E. 1969. *Klein's comprehensive etymological dictionary of the English language.* Stockholm: Elsevier.

4. Chomsky, Noam. 1988. *Language and problems of knowledge: The Managua lectures,* p. 183. Cambridge, MA: MIT Press; Chomsky, Noam. 2005. Three factors in language design. *Linguistic Inquiry* 36(1): 1–22; Chomsky, Noam. 2006. *Language and mind.* Cambridge: Cambridge University Press.

5. Corballis, Michael C. 2002. *From hand to mouth: The origins of language,* p. 3. Princeton, NJ: Princeton University Press.

6. Deacon, Terrence W. 1997. *The symbolic species: The co-evolution of language and the brain.* New York: W. W. Norton & Company; Merlin, Donald. 1991. *Origins of the modern mind: Three stages in the evolution of culture and cognition.* Boston: Harvard University Press; Lieberman, Paul. 1991. *Uniquely human: Speech, thought, and selfless behavior.* Boston: Harvard University Press.

7. World Federation of the Deaf Homepage. Retrieved April 2, 2010, from http://www.wfdeaf.org.

8. Gallaudet University FAQ Page. Retrieved April 2, 2010, from http://library.gallaudet.edu/Library/Deaf_Research_Help/Frequently_Asked_Questions_(FAQs)/Sign_Language/ASL_Ranking_and_Number_of_Speakers.html.

9. Gallaudet University FAQ Page. Retrieved April 2, 2010, from http://library.gallaudet.edu/Library/Deaf_Research_Help/Frequently_Asked_Questions_(FAQs)/Sign_Language/ASL_Ranking_and_Number_of_Speakers.html.

10. Ibid.

11. Sutton-Spence, Rachel, and Bencie Woll. 1999. *The linguistics of British Sign Language: An introduction.* Cambridge: Cambridge University Press.

12. British Deaf Association. 1975. *Gestuno: International sign language of the deaf.* Carlisle, England: BDA.

13. Birdwhistell, Ray L. 1970. *Kinesics and context: Essays on body motion communication.* Philadelphia, PA: University of Pennsylvania Press.

14. Mehrabian, Albert, and Susan R. Ferris. 1967. Inference of attitudes from nonverbal communication in two channels. *Journal of Consulting Psychology* 3(3): 248–52.

15. McKee, Annie, Richard Boyatzis, and Frances Johnston. 2008. *Becoming a resonant leader: Develop your emotional intelligence, renew your relationships, and sustain your effectiveness.* Boston: Harvard Business School Press; Boyatzis, Richard, and Annie McKee. 2005. *Resonant leadership: Renewing yourself and connecting with others through mindfulness, hope and compassion.* Boston: Harvard Business School Press; Goleman, Daniel, Richard Boyatzis, and Annie McKee. 2002. *Primal leadership: Realizing the power of emotional intelligence.* Boston: Harvard Business School Press; Pearce, *Leading out loud*; Lewis, Thomas,

Fari Amini, and Richard Lannon. 2000. *A general theory of love*. New York: Random House

16. Ekman, Paul. 1975. *Unmasking the face: A guide to recognizing emotions from facial clues*. Upper Saddle River, NJ: Prentice Hall; Ekman, Paul. 2005. *Emotions in the human face*. Oxford: Oxford University Press.

17. Ibid.

18. King, L. A., and R. A. Emmons. 1990. Conflict over emotional expression: Psychological and physical correlates. *Journal of Personality and Social Psychology* 58: 864–77.

19. Emmons, R. A., and P. M. Colby. 1995. Emotional conflict and well-being: Relation to perceived availability, daily utilization, and observer reports of social support. *Journal of Personality and Social Psychology* 68: 947–59.

20. Ekman, Paul. 1985. *Telling lies: Clues to deceit in the marketplace, politics, and marriage*. London: W. W. Norton & Company.

21. Katz, I. M., and J. D. Campbell. 1994. Ambivalence over emotional expression and well-being: Nomothetic and idiographic tests of the stress-buffering hypothesis. *Journal of Personality and Social Psychology* 67: 513–24; King, L. A., and R. A. Emmons. 1990. Conflict over emotional expression: Psychological and physical correlates. *Journal of Personality and Social Psychology* 58: 864–77; Emmons and Colby, Emotional conflict and well-being.

22. George, Jennifer. 2000. Emotions and leadership: The role of emotional intelligence. *Human Relations* 53(8): 1027–55.

23. Goffman, Erving. 1959. *The presentation of self in everyday life*. New York: Doubleday.

24. Goffman, Erving. 1955. On face-work: An analysis of ritual elements in social interaction. *Journal for the Study of Interpersonal Processes* 18: 213–31.

25. Brown, Penelope, and Stephen C. Levinson. 1987. *Politeness: Some universals in language usage*. New York: Cambridge University Press.

26. Ibid.

27. Ibid.

28. Wilbur, Ken. 1996. *A brief history of everything*. Boston: Shambhala Publications, Inc.

29. Ibid.

30. Shannon, Claude, and Weaver, Warren. 1949. *The mathematical theory of communication*. Urbana, IL: University of Illinois Press.

31. Schramm, Wilbur. 1954. How communication works. In *The process and effects of communication*, ed. Wilbur Schramm, 3–26. Urbana, IL: University of Illinois Press.

32. Shannon and Weaver, *The mathematical theory of communication*.

33. Mortensen, C. David. 1972. *Communication: The study of human communication*. New York: McGraw-Hill.

34. Roszak, Theodore. 1986. *The cult of information*. Berkeley, CA: University of California Press.

35. Schramm, How communication works.

36. Berlo, David K. 1960. *Process of communication: An introduction to theory and practice*. New York: Holt, Rinehart and Winston.

37. Daft, R., R. Lengel, and L. Trevino. 1987. Message equivocality, media selection, and manager performance: Implications for information systems. *MIS Quarterly* 17: 355–66; Rice, R. 1992. Task analyzability, use of new media, and effectiveness: A multi-site exploration of media richness. *Organization Science* 3: 475–500.

38. Carlson, John R., and Robert W. Zmud. 1999. Channel expansion theory and the experiential nature of media richness perceptions. *Academy of Management Review* 42(2): 153–70.

39. Reinfeld, Fred. 1966. *Pony express*. New York: Macmillan.

40. Carter, Kimberly A. 2003. Type me how you feel: Quasi-nonverbal cues in computer-mediated communication. *ETC: A Review of General Semantics* 60(1): 29–40.

41. Richards, Howard, and Harris Makatsoris. 2002. The metamorphosis to dynamic trading networks and virtual corporations. In *Managing virtual web organizations in the 21st century: Issues and challenges*, ed. Ulrich Franke, 65. Hershey, PA: Idea Publishing Group.

42. Gibson, Cristina B., and Susan G. Cohen. 2003. *Virtual teams that work*, p. 220. San Francisco, CA: John Wiley and Sons.

43. Friedman, Barry A., and Lisa J. Reed. 2007. Workplace privacy: Employee relations and legal implications of monitoring employee e-mail use. *Employee Responsibilities and Rights Journal* 19(2): 75–83; Allen, Myria W., Stephanie J. Coopman, Joy L. Hart, and Kasey L. Walker. 2007. Workplace surveillance and managing privacy boundaries. *Management Communication Quarterly* 21(2): 172–200; Halpern, David,

Patrick J. Reveille, and Donald Grunewald. 2008. Management and legal issues regarding electronic surveillance of employees in the workplace. *Journal of Business Ethics*, 80(2): 175–80.

44. Linden Research, Inc. 2009. How meeting in Second Life transformed IBM's technology elite into virtual world believers. Retrieved September 12, 2009, from http://secondlifegrid.net/casestudies/IBM.

45. IT News Online. 2008. IBM opens IBM virtual healthcare island on Second Life. *IT News Online* (February 25).

46. Linden Research, How meeting in Second Life transformed IBM's technology elite.

47. Ibid.

48. Beechler, Schon L., and Allan Bird. 1998. *Japanese multinationals abroad: Individual and organizational learning*, p. 118. New York: Oxford University Press.

49. Adler, Carlye. 2003. Colonel Sanders' march on China. *Time Magazine*. Retrieved March 31, 2010, from http://www.time.com/time/magazine/article/0,9171,543845,00.html.

50. Agha, Asif. 2007. *Language and social relations*. Cambridge: Cambridge University Press.

51. Labov, William. 1966. *The social stratification of English in New York City*. Washington, DC: Center for Applied Linguistics.

52. Agha, *Language and social relations*.

53. Trompenaars, Fons, and Charles Hampden-Turner. 1998. *Riding the waves of culture: Understanding diversity in global business*. New York: McGraw-Hill.

54. Hymes, Dell. 2001. On communicative competence. In *Linguistic anthropology: A reader*, ed. Allesandro Duranti. Malden, MA: Blackwell Publishers.

55. Hargie, Owen, and David Dickson. 2004. *Skilled interpersonal communication: Research, theory and practice*. New York: Routledge.

56. Ting-Toomey, Stella, and Atsuko Kurogi. 1998. Facework competence in intercultural conflict: An updated face-negotiation theory. *International Journal of Intercultural Relations* 22(2): 187–225.

57. Ibid.

58. Kouzmin, Alexander, and Nada Korac-Kakabadse. 1997. From phobias and ideological prescription: Towards multiple models in transformation management for socialist economies in transition. *Administration and Society* 29(2): 139–88.

59. Ibid.

60. Kouzmin, Alexander, R. Leivesley, and A. Carr. 1996. From managerial dysfunction, towards communicative competence: Re-discovering dramaturgy and voice in communicating risk. In *Handbook of administrative communication*, ed. J. L. Garnett and A. Kouzmin, 661–79. New York: Marcel Dekker; Kouzmin, Alexander, and Nada Korac-Kakabadse. 2000. Mapping institutional impacts of lean communication in lean agencies: Information technology, illiteracy, and leadership failure. *Administration and Society* 32(1): 29–69.

61. Catalyst. 2003. *Women in U.S. corporate leadership: 2003*. New York.

62. Ibid.

63. Trompenaars and Hampden-Turner, *Riding the waves of culture*.

64. Hall, Edward T. 1976. *Beyond culture*. Oxford: Anchor Books.

65. Thomas, David A. 2004. Diversity as strategy. *Harvard Business Review* 82(9): 98–108.

66. Gray, John. 1999. *Men are from Mars, women are from Venus*. New York: HarperCollins; Tannen, Deborah. 1990. *You just don't understand: Women and men in conversation*. New York: William Morrow.

67. Gilligan, Carol. 1984. New maps of development: New visions of maturity. In *Annual progress in child psychiatry and child development, 1983*, ed. Stella Chess and Alexander Thomas, 98–116. New York: Brunner/Mazel.

68. Tannen, Deborah. 1986. *That's not what I meant: How conversational style makes or breaks relationships*. New York: Random House.

69. Brody, Leslie R. 2000. The socialization of gender differences in emotional expression: Display rules, infant temperament, and differentiation. In *Gender and emotion: Social psychological perspectives*, ed. Agneta H. Fischer, 24–47. New York: Cambridge University Press; Hall, Judith A., Jason D. Carter, and Terrence G. Horgan. 2000. Gender differences in nonverbal communication of emotion. In *Gender and emotion: Social psychological perspectives*, ed. Agneta H. Fischer, 97–117. New York: Cambridge University Press.

70. Lakoff, Robin. 1973. Language and woman's place. *Language in Society* 2(1): 45–80.

71. Ibid.

72. Tannen, D. 1994. *Talking from 9 to 5: How women's and men's conversational styles affect who gets heard, who gets credit, and what gets done.* New York: William Morrow & Co.

73. Oakley, Judith G. 2000. Gender-based barriers to senior management positions: Understanding the scarcity of female CEOs. *Journal of Business Ethics* 27: 321–34.

74. Claes, Marie-Thérèse. 1999. Women, men, and management styles. *International Labour Review* 138(4): 431–46; Boyatzis and McKee, *Resonant leadership.*

75. Ridgeway, Cecelia L., and Lynn Smith-Lovin. 1999. The gender system and interaction. *Annual Review of Sociology* 25: 191–216.

76. Randstad USA. 2008. *Limited interaction among generations in the workplace identified as key indicator of coming skilled worker crisis.* Atlanta, GA: Randstad, U.S.A.

77. Liberty Building Systems Webpage. Retrieved April 2, 2010, from http://www.libertybuildings.com/content/article_182.shtml.

78. Idle, Anthony. 2009. A message from the general manager: Internal changes benefit Liberty's customers. *The Liberty Letter* 4(2): 8 pp.

79. Ibid.

80. Ibid. Idle, Anthony. 2009. A message from the general manager. *The Liberty Letter* 4(3): 4 pp.

81. De Mare, G. 1989. Communicating: The key to establishing good working relationships. *Waterhouse Review* 33: 30–37.

82. Crampton, Suzanne M., John W. Hodge, and Jitendra M. Mishra. 1998. The informal communication network: Factors influencing grapevine activity. *Public Personnel Management* 27(4): 569–83.

83. Keyes, Ralph. 2006. *The quote verifier: Who said what, where, and when.* New York: St. Martin's Press.

84. Byrne, Dennis. 2010. When all else fails, blame the system. *Chicago Tribune* (January 4). Retrieved January 11, 2010, from http://www.chicagotribune.com/news/opinion/chi-oped0105byrnejan05,0,6556064.column.

85. Milbank, Dana. 2010. Obama administration says there was no smoking gun before attempted airline bombing. *Washington Post* (January 8). Retrieved January 11, 2010, from http://www.washingtonpost.com/wp-dyn/content/article/2010/01/07/AR2010010704069.html?hpid=topnews.

86. Coombs, W. Timothy. 2007. *Ongoing crisis communication: Planning, managing, and responding.* Thousand Oaks, CA: Sage Publications.

87. Weick, Karl E. 2004. A bias for conversation: Acting discursively in organizations, in *The Sage handbook of organizational discourse,* ed. David Grant, Cynthia Hardy, Cliff Oswick, and Linda Putnam, 405. Thousand Oaks, CA: Sage Publications.

88. Davenport, Thomas H., and Laurence Prusak. 1998. *Working knowledge: How organizations manage what they know.* Boston: Harvard Business School Press (p. 5).

89. Gabriel, Yiannis. 2000. *Storytelling in organizations: Facts, fictions, and fantasies.* New York: Oxford University Press.

90. Forster, Nick, Martin Cebis, Sol Majteles, Anurag Mathur, Roy Morgan, Janet Preuss, Vinod Tiwari, and Des Wilkinson. 1999. The role of storytelling in organizational leadership. *Leadership and Organizational Development Journal* 20(1): 11–17.

91. Kouzes, J., and B. Posner. 2005. *The leadership challenge.* New York: Jossey-Bass.

92. Grice, H. P. 1975. Logic and conversation. In *Syntax and semantics. Vol. 1: Speech acts,* ed. P. Cole and J. L. Morgan, 41–58. New York: Academic Press.

93. Brown and Levinson, Politeness: Some universals in language usage; Grice, Logic and conversation.

94. Weick, A bias for conversation.

95. Cross, Rob, Andrew Parker, and Stephen P. Borgatti. 2002. *A bird's-eye view: Using social network analysis to improve knowledge creation and sharing.* Somers, NY: IBM Institute for Business Value.

Chapter 5

1. McCaskey, Michael B. 1974. A contingency approach to planning: Planning with goals and planning without goals. *Academy of Management Journal* 17(2): 281–91; McCaskey, Michael B. 1977. Goals and direction in personal planning. *Academy of Management Review* 2(3): 454–62; McKee, Annie. 1991. *Individual differences in planning for the future.* Dissertation. Cleveland, OH: Case Western Reserve University.

2. Csikszentmihalyi, Mihaly. 1975. *Beyond boredom and anxiety: Experiencing flow in work and play.* San Francisco: Jossey-Bass; Csikszentmihalyi, Mihaly. 1990. *Flow: The psychology of optimal experience.* New York: HarperCollins; Keller, J., and H. Bless. 2008. Flow and regulatory compatibility: An experimental approach to the flow model of intrinsic motivation. *Personality and Social Psychology Bulletin* 34: 196–209.

3. Online Etymology Dictionary. "Teleos." Retrieved April 2, 2010, from http://www.etymonline.com/index.php?search=teleos&searchmode=none.

4. Mintzberg, Henry. 1994. *The rise and fall of strategic planning: Reconceiving roles for planning, plans, planners,* p. 12. New York: The Free Press.

5. Ibid.

6. Wang, Xuemei. 1994. Learning planning operators by observation and practice. In *Proceedings of the Second International Conference on AI Planning Systems, AIPS-94,* pp. 335–340, Chicago, IL.

7. McCaskey, A contingency approach to planning; McCaskey, Goals and direction in personal planning.

8. Online Etymology Dictionary. "Plan." Retrieved October 2, 2009, from http://www.etymonline.com/index.php?term=plan.

9. Lane, Terry, and Leslie P. Kaelbling. 2001. Toward hierarchical decomposition for planning in uncertain environments. Workshop on planning under uncertainty and incomplete information. Paper presented at International Joint Conferences on Artificial Intelligence (Seattle, WA: August 4–10).

10. *The American Heritage Dictionary of the English Language,* 4th ed. 2006. Boston: Houghton Mifflin Company.

11. Online Etymology Dictionary. "Goal." Retrieved December 1, 2009, from http://www.etymonline.com/index.php?search=goal&searchmode=none.

12. Doran, George T. 1981. There's a S.M.A.R.T. way to write management's goals and objectives. *Management Review* 70(11): 35–36.

13. Sarasvathy, S. D., and S. Kotha. 2001. Effectuation in the management of Knightian uncertainty: Evidence from the Realnetworks case. In *Research on Management and Entrepreneurship, Vol. 1,* ed. J. Butler, 31–62. Greenwich, CT: IAP Inc.

14. Lakoff, George, and Mark Johnson. 1980. *Metaphors we live by.* Chicago: University of Chicago Press.

15. Helmert, M., P. Haslum, and J. Hoffmann. 2007. Flexible abstraction heuristics for optimal sequential planning. In *Proceedings of ICAPS 2007,* pp. 176–183. Menlo Park, CA: AAAI Press.

16. Markov, A. A. 1913/2006. Classical text in translation: An example of statistical investigation of the text "Eugene Onegin" concerning the connection of samples in chains. *Science in Context* 19(4): 591–600; Markov, A. A. 1971. Extension of the limit theorems of probability theory to a sum of variables connected in a chain. Reprinted in Appendix B of *Dynamic probabilistic systems, Vol. 1: Markov chains,* ed. R. Howard. New York: John Wiley and Sons.

17. Watkin, Michael, and Christopher Rozell. 2004. *A Markov chain analysis of black jack.* Course material for Math 502 at Rice University (26 pp.). Retrieved September 29, 2009, from http://www-ece.rice.edu/~crozell/courseproj/MCBJ.pdf.

18. Wack, Pierre. 1985. Scenarios: Uncharted waters ahead. *Harvard Business Review* 63(5): 74.

19. Kourdi, Jeremy. 2008. "Business ideas: I am the greatest." *Accountancy Age* (May): 19. Retrieved March 30, 2010, from http://www.pcmag.co.uk/accountancyage/features/2215594/business-ideas-greatest.

20. Abrahams, Jeffrey. 1999. *The mission statement book: 301 corporate mission statements from America's top companies,* 2d ed., p. 14. Berkeley, CA: Ten Speed Press.

21. Big Brothers Big Sisters. "About us." Retrieved October 21, 2009, from http://www.bbbs.org/site/c.diJKKYPLJvH/b.1539781/k.4319/Mentors__The_Largest_Youth_Mentoring_Programs_from_Big_Brothers_Big_Sisters.htm.

22. Toyota Website FAQ. Retrieved October 21, 2009, from http://www.toyota.com/help/faqs/company-what_are_toyotas_mission_and_vision_statements.html.

23. Stovall, Steven Austin. 2009. Is your vision a hallucination? *Podiatry Management* 28(1): 142.

24. Manasse, A. Lorri. 1985. Vision and leadership: Paying attention to intention. *Peabody Journal of Education* 63(1): 150–73.

25. Stovall, Steven Austin. 2009. Change your culture, change YOUR future. *Bed Times* 134 (12): 10.

26. Malnight, Tom. 2008. *Strategically engaging your organization: Assessing your current reality.* Lausanne, Switzerland: IMD International, 5 pp.

27. Ibid.

28. Carey, Denis, Michael Patsalos-Fox, and Michael Useem. 2009. Leadership lessons for hard times. *McKinsey Quarterly Review* (July). Retrieved September 12, 2009, from http://www.mckinseyquarterly .com/Leadership_lessons_for_hard_times_2413.

29. Ibid.

30. Ibid.

31. Von Hippel, Eric, Stefan Thomke, and Mary Sonnack. 1999. Creating breakthroughs at 3M. *Harvard Business Review* (September). Retrieved September 12, 2009, from http://hbr.harvardbusiness.org/1999/09/creating-breakthroughs-at-3m/ar/1.

32. Ibid.

33. Beinhocker, Eric D. 2006. The adaptable corporation. *McKinsey Quarterly Review* (May). Retrieved September 12, 2009, from http://www.mckinseyquarterly.com/The_adaptable_corporation_1757.

34. Expert Choice Inc. 2009. 3M case study. Retrieved September 12, 2009, from http://www.expertchoice.com/xres/uploads/resource-center -documents/3M_casestudy.pdf.

35. Donlon, J. 2009. Best companies for leaders: What makes a company attractive for talent, and what kind of company develops the best leaders? (January 31) Retrieved September 12, 2009, from http://www.chiefexecutive.net/ME2/Audiences/dirmod.asp?sid=&nm= &type=Publishing&mod=Publications%3A%3AArticle&mid=8F3A70 27421841978F18BE895F87F791&tier=4&id=BF3221D721F74109BD2 FA95B404E4AC6&AudID=AFC68D68FF0A49299D8688CFDAD5F871.

36. Ibid.

37. Von Hippel et al., Creating breakthroughs at 3M.

38. Shor, Rita. 2009. Managed innovation: 3M's latest model for new products—Guest editorials. *Manufacturing and Technology News*. Retrieved March 20, 2010, from http://www.manufacturingnews.com/news/editorials/shor.html.

39. Von Hippel et al., Creating breakthroughs at 3M.

40. Ibid.

41. Shor, Managed innovation.

42. Courtney, Hugh, John T. Horn, and Jayarta Kar. 2009. Getting into your competitor's head. *McKinsey Quarterly Review* (February). Retrieved September 12, 2009, from http://www.mckinseyquarterly.com/Getting_into_your_competitors_head_2281.

43. Aufreiter, Nora A., Teri L. Lawver, and Candace D. Lun. 2000. A new way to market. *McKinsey Quarterly Review* (May). Retrieved September 12, 2009, from http://www.mckinseyquarterly.com/A_new_way_to _market_801.

44. Casnocha, Ben. 2009. Success on the side. (April 24, Retrieved September 12, 2009, from http://www.american.com/archive/2009/april-2009/Success-on-the-Side.

45. Costello, Brid, and Jennifer Weil. 2008. Annick Goutal outlines global growth strategy. *Women's Wear Daily* 196(128): 21.

46. Laube, James, and Daniel Sogg. 2004. Wine giant to acquire Mondavi for $1 billion. *Wine Spectator* 29(15): 14.

47. Landi, Heather. 2007. 'Tis the season . . . for mergers and acquisitions. *Beverage World* 126(12): 10.

48. Yanow, Dvora. 2000. Seeing organizational learning: A cultural view. *Organization Articles* 7(2): 24–268.

49. Tierney, Jim. 2009. Lore of Frederick's brings back the sexy sell. *Multichannel Merchant* 5(6): 9.

50. Daimler. Cerberus Takes Over Majority Interest in Chrysler Group and Related Financial Services Business for EUR 5.5 Billion (7.4 billion) from DaimlerChrysler. Retrieved May 22, 2010, from http://www .daimler.com/dccom/0-5-7145-1-858191-1-0-0-0-0-0-11979-0-0-0-0-0 -0-0-0.html.

51. Puranam, Phanish, Harbir Singh, and Maurizio Zollo. 2006. Organizing for innovation: Managing the coordination-autonomy dilemma in technology acquisitions. *Academy of Management Journal* 49(2): 263–80.

52. Piekkari, R., E. Vaara, J. Tienari, and R. Santti. 2005. Integration or disintegration? Human resource implications of the common corporate language decision in a crossborder merger. *International Journal of Human Resource Management* 16(3): 333–47; Vaara, E., J. Tienari, R. Piekkari, and R. Santti. 2005. Language and the circuits of power in a merging multinational corporation. *Journal of Management Studies* 42(3): 595–623.

53. Thomas, Chris A. 2008. Bridging the gap between theory and practice: Language policy in multilingual organizations. *Language Awareness* 17(4): 307–25.

54. San Francisco Bay Joint Venture. Retrieved October 19, 2009, from http://www.sfbayjv.org.

55. Walmart Stores.com: India. Retrieved March 30, 2010, from http://walmartstores.com/aboutus/276.aspx?p=251.

56. Gulati, Ranjay, and Harbir Singh. 1998. The architecture of cooperation: Managing coordination costs and appropriation concerns in strategic alliances. *Administrative Science Quarterly* 43(4): 781–814.

57. Grossman, Lev. 2007. Invention of the year: The iPhone. *Time South Pacific (Australia/New Zealand edition)*: 44.

58. Boguslauskas, Vytautas, and Goda Kvedaraviciene. 2009. Difficulties in identifying company's core competencies and core processes. *Inzinerine Ekonomika-Engineering Economics* 62(2): 75–81.

59. Porter, Michael E. 1979. How competitive forces shape strategy. *Harvard Business Review* 57(2): 137–45; Porter, Michael E. 2008. The five competitive forces that shape strategy. *Harvard Business Review* 86(1): 79–93.

60. Mariani, John. 2006. Lessons of the low-carb diets. *Restaurant Hospitality* 90(1): 18.

61. Gillin, Paul. 2007. Twitter strikes community chord. *B to B* 92(15): 11.

62. Franco, Joanna. 2009. Shell to pay $5.8 million in Clean Air Act penalties. *World Refining and Fuels Today* 4(79): 8.

63. OSHA fines Imperial Sugar $8.77 million. *Occupational Hazards* 70(9): 12.

64. Luce, Thomas F., and Anita A. Summers. 1987. *Local fiscal issues in the Philadelphia metropolitan area.* Philadelphia: University of Pennsylvania Press.

65. Philadelphia Forward. *How business taxes compare.* Retrieved October 19, 2009, from http://www.philadelphiaforward.org/node/45.

66. Ruilson, Larry. 2003. City tops in business tax burden. (October 10) *Philadelphia Business Journal.* Retrieved October 19, 2009, from http://philadelphia.bizjournals.com/philadelphia/stories/2003/10/13/story1 .html; *Philadelphia Forward.* Eliminate the BPT. Retrieved October 19, 2009, from http://www.philadelphiaforward.org/eliminate_the_bpt.

67. *Philadelphia Forward.* The status of tax reform. Retrieved October 19, 2009, from http://www.philadelphiaforward.org/node/41.

68. Jamison, Nancy. 2007. Datria fast forwards warehouse speech opportunities. *Speech Technology Magazine* 12: 9. Retrieved December 1, 2009, from http://www.speechtechmag.com/Articles/Column/Voice-Value/Datria-Fast-Forwards-Warehouse-Speech-Opportunities-40051.aspx.

69. Green, Heather. 2008. The greening of the corporation. *Business Week Online* 10. Retrieved December 1, 2009, from http://www.businessweek .com/technology/content/dec2008/tc20081211_004876.htm.

70. Porter, How competitive forces shape strategy.

71. Ibid.

72. Nalebuff, B. J., and A. M. Brandenburger. 1996. *Co-opetition.* London: HarperCollins.

73. Van der Laan, Joost W. 2000. Online food retailing. *RetailEconomics.* Retrieved March 4, 2010, from http://www.retaileconomics.com/online-food-retailing.html.

74. McConnon, Aili. July 1, 2009. The issue: FreshDirect focuses on customer service. *BusinessWeek.* Retrieved March 4, 2010, from http://www.businessweek.com/managing/content/jun2009/ca20090630 _154481.htm.

75. ALC. 2009. A website's work is *never* done. *The Rest of the Story* 4(1): 6–7. Retrieved March 4, 2010, from http://www.alc.com/newsletters/ALC_Spring09.pdf.

76. Braddock, Rick. 2009. Lessons of Internet marketing from FreshDirect. *Wall Street Journal* (May 11, 2009). Retrieved March 4, 2010, from http://online.wsj.com/article/SB124205175154206817.html.

77. Ibid.

78. Mitchell, Ronald K., Bradley R. Agle, and Donna J. Wood. 1997. Toward a theory of stakeholder identification and salience: Defining the principle of who and what really counts. *Academy of Management Review* 22(4): 853–86.

79. Freeman, R. E. 1984. *Strategic management: A stakeholder approach.* Boston: Pitman.

80. UNESCO-IHE–UNEP/GPA. 1970. Stakeholder analysis I. Retrieved October 5, 2009, from http://www.training.gpa.unep.org/ content .html?id=109.

81. *The ripple effect: Why failure of the Big 3 is not an option.* 2008. Report published by the Office of the House Majority Leader, compiled by House Representative Carolyn B. Maloney. Retrieved October 19, 2009, from http://majorityleader.house.gov/docUploads/TheRippleEffect121008.pdf.

82. Einstein, Paul. 2009. Toyota's reputation takes a pounding. *MSNBC*. Retrieved October 12, 2009, from http://www.msnbc.msn.com/id/33192916/ns/business-the_drivers_seat.

83. How a new strategic plan saved a century-old nonprofit. 2005. *Nonprofit World* 23(4): 1.

84. Ginter, Peter M., Andrew C. Ruck, and W. Jack Duncan. 1985. Planners' perceptions of the strategic management process. *Journal of Management Studies* 22(6): 582.

85. Ireland, Duane R., Michael A. Hitt, Richard A. Bettis, and Deborah A. De Porras. 1987. Strategy formulation processes: Differences in perceptions of strength and weaknesses indicators and environmental uncertainty by managerial level. *Strategic Management Journal* 8: 469–85.

86. Barney, Jay B. 1995. Looking inside for competitive advantage. *Academy of Management Executives* 9(4): 49–61.

87. Earls, Alan. 2009. BASF procurement gets deep into R&D. *Purchasing* 138(6): 31–33.

88. Roberto, Michael A., Richard M. J. Bohmer, and Amy C. Edmondson. 2006. Facing ambiguous threats. *Harvard Business Review* 84(11): 106–13.

89. Hill, Terry, and Roy Westbrook. 1997. SWOT analysis: It's time for a product recall. *Long Range Planning* 30(1): 46–52.

90. Houben, G., K. Lenie, and K. Vanhoof. 1999. A knowledge-based SWOT-analysis system as an instrument for strategic planning in small and medium sized enterprises. *Decision Support Systems* 26: 125–35.

91. Hill and Westbrook, SWOT analysis.

92. Hambrick, Donald C., Ian C. MacMillan, and Diana L. Day. 1982. Strategic attributes and performance in the BCG matrix—A PIMS-based analysis of industrial product businesses. *Academy of Management Journal* 25(3): 511.

93. Sacco, Al. 2007. In-stat: Worldwide smartphone market to grow more than 30 percent each year through 2012. *CIO.com*. Retrieved October 23, 2009, from http://www.cio.com/article/155001/In_Stat_Worldwide_Smartphone_Market_to_Grow_More_Than_30_Percent_Each_Year_Through_2012.

94. Davidsson, P., F. Delmar, and J. Wiklund. 2006. *Entrepreneurship and the growth of firms*. Northampton, MA: Edward Elgar Publishing.

95. Calandro, Joseph, and Scott Lane. A new competitive analysis tool: The relative profitability and growth matrix. *Strategy and Leadership* 35(2): 30–38.

96. Bruner, Jerome S. 1956/2005. On perceptual readiness. In *Social cognition: Key readings*, ed. D. L. Hamilton, 108–14. New York: Psychology Press.

97. Bossidy, Larry, and Ram Charan. 2002. *Execution: The discipline of getting things done*. New York: Crown Publishing Group.

98. Ibid.

99. Charan, Ram, and Geoffrey Colvin. June 21, 1999. Why CEOs fail. *Fortune*, pp. 68–80.

100. Mankins, Michael C., and Richard Steele. 2005. Turning great strategy into great performance. *Harvard Business Review* (July–August): 1–11.

101. Killing, Peter, Tom Malnight, and Tracy Keys. 2005. *Must-win battles: Creating the focus you need to achieve your key business goals*. Upper Saddle River, NJ: Wharton School Publishing.

102. Stovall, Steven Austin. 2006. *Cases in human resources management*. Cincinnati, OH: Atomic Dog Publishing.

103. Stovall, Steven Austin. 2006.

104. Needleman, Sarah. 2009. A new job just a tweet away. *Wall Street Journal Online*. Retrieved March 30, 2010, from http://tweetmyjobs.com/docs/wsj.pdf.

105. Dwyer, Jim, and Kevin Flynn. 2005. *102 minutes: The untold story of the fight to survive inside the twin towers*. New York: Times Books.

106. Marquez, Jessica. 2006. Learning from 9/11 recovery. *Workforce Management* 85(17): 1–36.

107. Boyatzis, Richard E., Elizabeth C. Stubbs, and Scott N. Taylor. 2002. Learning cognitive and emotional intelligence competencies through graduate management education. *Academy of Management Learning and Education* 1(2): 150–62.

108. Margolis, Howard. 1987. *Patterns, thinking and cognition: A theory of judgment*. London: University of Chicago Press.

109. Kass, Steven J., Daniel A. Herschler, and Michael A. Companion. 1991. Training situational awareness through pattern recognition in a battlefield environment. *Military Psychology* 3(2): 105–12.

110. Wiig, Karl M. 2003. *A knowledge model for situation-handling*. Arlington, TX: Knowledge Research Institute.

111. Langer, Ellen J. 1989. *Mindfulness*, p. xiv. Reading, MA: Addison-Wesley/Addison Wesley Longman. Quote from abstract retrieved October 9, 2009, from http://psycnet.apa.org/psycinfo/1989-97542-000.

112. Boyatzis, Richard E. 2008. Leadership development from a complexity perspective. *Consulting Psychology Journal: Practice and Research* 60(4): 298–313.

113. McKee, Annie, Richard Boyatzis, and Frances Johnston. 2008. *Becoming a resonant leader: Develop your emotional intelligence, renew your relationships, sustain your effectiveness*. Boston: Harvard Business School Press.

Chapter 6

1. Drake, R. A. 1987. Effects of gaze manipulation on aesthetic judgments: Hemisphere priming of affect. *Acta Psychologica* 65: 91–99; Merckelbach, Harald, and Patricia Van Oppen. 1989. Effects of gaze manipulation on subjective evaluation of neutral and phobia-relevant stimuli. *Acta Psychologica* 70: 147–51; Schiff, Bernard B., and Sandra A. Rump 1995. Asymmetrical hemispheric activation and emotion: The effects of unilateral forced nostril breathing. *Brain and Cognition* 29: 217–31.

2. Boyatzis, Richard, and Annie McKee. 2005 *Resonant leadership: Renewing yourself and connecting with others through mindfulness, hope and compassion*. Boston: Harvard Business School Press; Goleman, Daniel, Richard Boyatzis, and Annie McKee. 2002. *Primal leadership*. Boston: Harvard Business School Press.

3. Soelberg, Peer. 1966. Unprogrammed decision making. *Academy of Management Proceedings* 3.

4. March, James G., and Chip Heath. 1994. *A primer on decision making: How decisions happen*. New York: The Free Press.

5. Bornat, Richard. 2005. *Proof and disproof in formal logic: An introduction for programmers*. New York: Oxford University Press.

6. Ibid.

7. Abelson, Robert P., Roger C. Schank, and Ellen J. Langer, eds. 1994. *Beliefs, reasoning, and decision making: Psycho-logic in honor of Bob Abelson*. Hillsdale, NJ: Lawrence Erlbaum Associates.

8. Fiske, S. T., and P. W. Linville. 1980. What does the schema concept buy us? *Personality and Social Psychology Bulletin* 6: 543–57.

9. Piaget, Jean. 1970. Piaget's theory. In *Carmichael's manual of child psychology, Vol. 1*, 3d ed., ed. P. H. Mussen. New York: Wiley.

10. Ibid.

11. Greenwald, Anthony G., and Mahzarin R. Banaji. 1995. Implicit social cognition: Attitudes, self-esteem, and stereotypes. *Psychological Review* 102(1): 4–27.

12. Thorndike, Edward L. 1920. A constant error on psychological rating. *Journal of Applied Psychology* 4: 25–29; Rozenweig, Phil. 2007. *The halo effect ... and the eight other business delusions that deceive managers*. New York: The Free Press.

13. Asch, Solomon. 1946/2005. Forming impressions of personality. In *Social cognition: Key readings in social psychology*, ed. David L. Hamilton, 362–71. New York: Psychology Press.

14. Nisbett, R. E., and T. D. Wilson. 1977. Telling more than we can know: Verbal reports on mental processes. *Psychological Review* 84(3): 231–59.

15. Bechara, Antoine. 2004. The role of emotion in decision making: Evidence from neurological patients with orbitofrontal damage. *Brain and Cognition* 55(1): 30–40.

16. Porges, Stephen W. 1998. Love: An emergent property of the mammalian autonomic nervous system. *Psychoneuroendocrinology* 23(8): 837–61.

17. Critchley, Hugo D., Rebecca Elliott, Christopher J. Mathias, and Raymond J. Dolan. 2000. Neural activity relating to generation and representation of galvanic skin conductance responses: A functional magnetic resonance imaging study. *Journal of Neuroscience* 20(8): 3033–40.

18. Tversky, Amos, and Daniel Kahneman. 1981. The framing of decisions and the psychology of choice. *Science* 211(4481): 453–58.

19. Read, Stephen J., and Carol L. Miller. 1994. Dissonance and balance in belief systems: The promise of parallel constraint satisfaction processes and connectionist modeling approaches. In *Beliefs, reasoning, and decision making: Psycho-logic in honor of Bob Abelson*, ed. Robert P. Abelson, Roger C. Schank, and Ellen J. Langer. New York: Lawrence Erlbaum Associates.

20. Definition of intuition—What is intuitive decision making? 2010. Time for Change. Retrieved March 23, 2010, from http://timeforchange.org/definition-of-intuition-intuitive.

21. Ibid.

22. Burke, L. A., and M. K. Miller. 1999. Taking the mystery out of intuitive decision making. *Academy of Management Executive* 13(4): 91–99; Dane, Erik, and Michael G. Pratt. Exploring intuition and its role in managerial decision making. *Academy of Management Review* 32(1): 33–54.

23. Dane and Pratt, Exploring intuition.

24. Simon, Herbert A. 1987. Making management decisions: The role of intuition and emotion. *Academy of Management Executive* 1(1): 57–64.

25. Epstein, Seymour. 1994. Integration of the cognitive and the psychodynamic unconscious. *American Psychologist* 49: 709–24. Hogarth, Robin M. 2005. Deciding analytically or trusting your intuition? The advantages and disadvantages of analytic and intuitive thought. In *The routines of decision-making*, ed. T. Betsch and S. Haberstroh, 67–82. Mahwah, NJ: Lawrence Erlbaum Associates.

26. Hammond, Kenneth R., Robert M. Hamm, Janet Grassia, and Tamra Pearson. 1987. Direct comparison of the efficacy of intuitive and analytical cognition in expert judgment. *IEEE Transactions on Systems, Man, and Cybernetics* 17: 753–70.

27. Goleman, Daniel, and Boyatzis, Richard. 2008. Social intelligence and the biology of leadership. *Harvard Business Review* 86(9): 74–81.

28. Nicosia, F. 1966. *Consumer decision processes.* Englewood Cliffs, NJ: Prentice Hall.

29. Lacey, Hoda. 2006. Don't let your bosses make wrong decisions. *Travel Trade Gazette UK and Ireland* (No. 2701): 45–45.

30. Simon, Herbert. 1957. *Models of man: Social and rational—Mathematical essays on rational human behavior in a social setting.* New York: Wiley; Roach, John M. 1979. Decision making is a "satisficing" experience. *Management Review* 68(1): 8.

31. Retrieved April 4, 2010, from http://www.google.com/search?q =decision+making&rls=com.microsoft:en-us:IE-SearchBox&ie =UTF-8&oe=UTF-8&sourceid=ie7&rlz=1I7GGLL_en.

32. Kant, Immanuel. 1785/1993. *Grounding for the metaphysics of morals*, 3d ed. Trans. James W. Ellington. Indianapolis, IN: Hackett.

33. Simon, *Models of man.*

34. Ibid.; March, James G. 1978. Bounded rationality, ambiguity, and the engineering of choice. *Bell Journal of Economics* 9(2): 587–608.

35. Simon, *Models of man*; March, Bounded rationality, ambiguity, and the engineering of choice; Kahneman, Daniel, and Amos Tversky. 2004. Prospect theory: An analysis of decision under risk. In *Preference, belief, and similarity*, ed. Amos Tversky, 549–82. Cambridge: Massachusetts Institute of Technology.

36. Kahneman, Daniel and Amos Tyersky. 2004. Prospect theory: an analysis of decision under risk. In A. Tversky (ed.), *Preface, belief, and similarity* (549–582). Cambridge, MA. MIT Press.

37. Kahneman, Daniel. 2003. Maps of bounded rationality: Psychology for behavioral economics. *American Economic Review* 93(5): 1449–75.

38. Tversky, Amos, and Daniel Kahneman. 2004. Judgment under uncertainty: Heuristics and biases. In *Preference, belief, and similarity*, ed. Amos Tversky, 203–20. Cambridge, MA: MIT Press.

39. Kahneman, Maps of bounded rationality.

40. Simon, *Models of man*; Roach, Decision making is a "satisficing" experience.

41. Juran, Joseph M. 1975. The non-Pareto principle—Mea culpa. *Quality Progress* 8: 8–9; Bunkley, Nick. 2008. Joseph Juran, 103, pioneer in quality control, dies. *New York Times* (March 3): 23.

42. Emiliani, M. L. 2000. Cracking the code of business. *Management Decision* 38(2): 60–79.

43. Watson, G. B., and E. M. Glaser. 1994. *Watson-Glaser Critical Thinking Appraisal Form S manual.* San Antonio, TX: Harcourt Brace.

44. Taylor, Chris. 2005. It's a wiki, wiki world. *Time Magazine* (May 29). Retrieved September 12, 2009, from http://www.time.com/time/ magazine/article/0,9171,1066904-1,00.html.

45. Miller, Robin ("Roblimo"). July 28, 2004. Wikipedia founder Jimmy Wales responds. *Slashdot.org.* Retrieved September 12, 2009, from http://interviews.slashdot.org/article.pl?sid=04/07/28/1351230.

46. Cunningham, Ward. 2003. Correspondence on the etymology of Wiki (November). Retrieved September 12, 2009, from http://c2.com/doc/ etymology.html.

47. Taylor, It's a wiki, wiki world.

48. Wikipedias or wiki world. 2006. *Solar Navigator.* Retrieved September 12, 2009, from http://www.solarnavigator.net/wikipedias.htm.

49. Taylor, It's a wiki, wiki world.

50. Tapscott, D., and A. D. Williams. 2006. *Wikonomics: How mass collaboration changes everything.* New York: Portfolio.

51. Hammond, John S., Ralph L. Keeney, and Howard Raiffa. 1998. The hidden traps in decision making. *Harvard Business Review* 76(5): 47–58.

52. Edwards, M. O. 1966. Tips on solving problems creatively. *Management Review* 55(3): 28.

53. Rowe, Gene, and George Wright. 1999. The Delphi technique as a forecasting tool: Issues and analysis. *International Journal of Forecasting* 15(4): 353–75.

54. Mehr, Robert I., and Seev Neumann. 1970. Delphi forecasting project. *Journal of Risk and Insurance* 37(2): 243.

55. Langer, Ellen J. 1997. *The power of mindful learning.* Reading, MA: Perseus Books; Kabat-Zinn, Jon. 1990. *Full catastrophe living: Using the wisdom of your body and mind to face stress, pain and illness.* Cambridge, MA: Perseus Publishing.

56. Boyatzis, Richard, and Annie McKee. 2005. *Resonant leadership: Renewing yourself and connecting with others through mindfulness, hope and compassion.* Boston: Harvard Business School Press.

57. McKee, Annie, Richard, Boyatzis, and Frances Johnston. 2008. *Becoming a resonant leader: Develop your emotional intelligence, renew your relationships and sustain your effectiveness.* Boston: Harvard Business School Press; Goleman, Daniel, Richard Boyatzis, and Annie McKee. 2002. *Primal leadership.* Boston: Harvard Business School Press.

58. Ruggiero, V. R. 1996. *Becoming a critical thinker.* Boston, MA: Houghton Mifflin.

59. Argyris, C., and D. Schön. 1978. *Organizational learning: A theory of action perspective*, Reading, MA: Addison Wesley; Argyris, C., and D. Schön. 1974. *Theory in practice: Increasing professional effectiveness*, San Francisco, CA: Jossey-Bass; Forrester, J. W. 1971. *World dynamics.* Cambridge, MA: MIT Press.

60. Argyris, Chris. 1976. *Increasing leadership effectiveness.* New York: Wiley.

Chapter 7

1. Wallechinsky, David, and Irving Wallace. 1978. *The people's almanac #2, issue 2.* New York: William Morrow and Company.

2. Whorf, Benjamin. 1940. Science and linguistics. *Technology Review (MIT)* 42(6): 229–31, 247–48.

3. Goodwin, Charles. 1996. Practices of color classification. *Ninchi Kagaku* (Cognitive Studies: Bulletin of the Japanese Cognitive Science Society) 3(2): 62–82.

4. Thesaurus.com. Change. Retrieved March 29, 2010, from http:// thesaurus.reference.com/browse/change.

5. Ibid.

6. Ibid.

7. James, Jesse. 2009. Career transitioning not just a symptom of the economy (November 1). AC Associated Content. Retrieved January 31, 2010, from http://www.associatedcontent.com/article/2346770/ career_transitioning_not_just_a_symptom.html?cat=3.

8. Bureau of Labor Statistics. 2008. Employee Tenure Summary (September 26). Retrieved May 10, 2010, from http://www.bls.gov/news .release/tenure.nr0.htm.

9. Ibid.

10. Bell, D. 1973. *The coming of post-industrial society.* New York: Basic Books.

11. Friedman, Thomas L. 2008. *Hot, flat and crowded: Why we need a green revolution and how it can renew America.* New York: Farrar, Straus and Giroux.

12. Rifkin, Jeremy. 2010. *The empathic civilization: The race to global consciousness in a world in crisis.* New York: Tarcher-Penguin.

13. Patagonia. Patagonia's history. Retrieved from http://www .patagonia.com/web/us/patagonia.go?slc=en_US&sct=US&assetid=33 51. Retrieved May 10, 2010.

14. Ibid.

15. Chouinard, Yvon. 1993. Patagonia: The next hundred years. In M. Katakis (ed.), *Sacred trusts: Essays on stewardship and responsibility* (pp. 112–121). San Francisco: Mercury House.

16. Patagonia. Footprint chronicles: Green business practices. Retrieved from http://www.patagonia.com/pdf/en_US/green_and_business.pdf. Retrieved May 10, 2010.

17. Chouinard, Patagonia.

18. Chouinard, Yvon. 2005. *Let my people go surfing: The education of a reluctant businessman*, p. 1. New York: Penguin Group.

19. Friedman, Thomas. 2005. *The world is flat.* New York: Farrar, Straus and Giroux.

20. Anderson, Chris. 2008. *The long tail: Why the future of business is selling less of more.* New York: Hyperion Books; Bauman, Zygmunt. 2007. *Consuming life.* Cambridge: Polity Press; Watson, Joe. 2006. *Without excuses: Unleash the power of diversity to build your business.* New York: St. Martin's Press.

21. Norton, Seth W. 2004. Towards a more general theory of franchise governance. In J. Windsperger and G. Hendrikse (eds.), *Economics and management of franchising networks* (pp. 17–37). New York: Physica-Verlag Heidelberg.

22. Disney. Walt Disney Imagineering. Retrieved May 10, 2010, from http://corporate.disney.go.com/careers/who_imagineering.html.

23. Avery, Derek R., Patrick F. McKay, David C. Wilson, and Scott Tonidandel. 2007. Unequal attendance: The relationships between race, organizational diversity cues, and absenteeism. *Personnel Psychology* 60(4): 875–902.

24. Anderson, *The long tail.*

25. Thomas, Chris Allen, Wendy Green, and Doug Lynch. 2010. Online learning: An examination of contexts in corporate, higher education, and K–12 environments. In *Encyclopedia of information communication technologies and adult education integration*, ed. Victor Wang. Hershey, PA: IGI Global.

26. Thomas, David A., and Robin J. Ely. 2007. Making differences matter. In *The Jossey-Bass reader on educational leadership*, ed. Michael Fullan, p. 270. San Francisco: Jossey-Bass.

27. Bureau of Labor Statistics. Retrieved February 1, 2010, from http://www.bls.gov/cps/cpsaat39.pdf.

28. Women CEOs. 2009. *Fortune* (May 4). Retrieved February 11, 2010, from http://money.cnn.com/magazines/fortune/fortune500/2009/womenceos.

29. Ibid.

30. Bureau of Labor Statistics.

31. Catalyst. 2010. Women in U.S. information. Retrieved February 1, 2010, from http://www.catalyst.org/publication/157/women-in-us-information.

32. U.S. Census Bureau. International data base. Retrieved February 1, 2010, from http://www.census.gov/ipc/www/idb/region.php.

33. Ibid.

34. Ibid.

35. Ibid.

36. Ibid.

37. Jagota, Mukesh. 2010. India expects strong economic growth this fiscal year. *Wall Street Journal* (January 11). Retrieved April 4, 2010, from http://online.wsj.com/article/SB126292793623121229.html.

38. Trading Economics. United States. GDP. Retrieved May 10, 2010, from http://www.tradingeconomics.com/Economics/GDP-Growth.aspx?symbol=USD.

39. Chakravarthy, B., and P. Lorange. 2008. Driving renewal: The entrepreneur manager. *Journal of Business Strategy* 29: 14–21.

40. Nadler, David A., and Michael L. Tushman. 1989. Organizational frame bending: Principles for managing reorientation. *The Academy of Management Executive* 3(3): 194–204.

41. General Electric. Our history. Retrieved January 26, 2010, from http://www.ge.com/company/history/index.html; General Electric Company. Retrieved January 26, 2010, from http://www.fundinguniverse.com/company-histories/General-Electric-Company-Company-History.html.

42. General Electric. Ecomagination. Retrieved May 10, 2010, from http://ge.ecomagination.com/index.html.

43. Frogland-The boiled frog. Retrieved May 10, 2010, from http://allaboutfrogs.org/stories/boiled.html.

44. Krugman, Paul. 2009. Reagan did it. *New York Times* (May 31). Retrieved January 28, 2010, from http://www.nytimes.com/2009/06/01/opinion/01krugman.html?_r=1.

45. Stiglitz, Joseph E. 2009. Capitalist fools. *Vanity Fair* (January). Retrieved January 28, 2010, from http://www.vanityfair.com/magazine/2009/01/stiglitz200901.

46. Labaton, Stephen. 2008. Agency's '04 rule let banks pile up new debt. *New York Times* (October 2). Retrieved January 28, 2010, from http://www.nytimes.com/2008/10/03/business/03sec.html?em.

47. Holmes, Steven A. 1999. Fannie Mae eases credit to aid mortgage lending. *New York Times* (September 30). Retrieved January 28, 2010, from http://www.nytimes.com/1999/09/30/business/fannie-mae-eases-credit-to-aid-mortgage-lending.html; Board of Governors of the Federal Reserve System. Open Market Operations. Retrieved May 10, 2010, from http://www.federalreserve.gov/fomc/fundsrate.htm. Federal

Deposit Insurance Corporation. 2006. Challenges and FDIC efforts related to predatory lending. Report No. 06-011. Arlington, VA: FDIC. Retrieved January 28, 2010, from http://www.fdicoig.gov/reports06/06-011.pdf.

48. Andrews, Edmund L. 2008. Greenspan concedes error on regulation. *New York Times* (October 23). Retrieved February 1, 2010, from http://www.nytimes.com/2008/10/24/business/economy/24panel.html.

49. Ip, Greg. 2008. His legacy tarnished, Greenspan goes on defensive. *Wall Street Journal* (April 8). Retrieved March 11, 2010, from http://online.wsj.com/article/SB120760341392296107.html.

50. Bartlett, Bruce. 2009. Who saw the housing bubble coming? *Forbes.com* (January 2). Retrieved February 1, 2010, from http://www.anderson.ucla.edu/faculty/edward.leamer/documents/01-02-2009%20Forbes%20-%20Who%20saw%20bubble%20coming.pdf.

51. CSI: Credit crunch. 2007. *The Economist* 385 (October 20): 4–8.

52. Joint Center for Housing Studies of Harvard University. 2008. The state of the nation's housing 2008. President and fellows of Harvard College. Retrieved January 28, 2010, from http://www.jchs.harvard.edu/publications/markets/son2008/son2008.pdf; Labaton, Agency's '04 rule let banks pile up new debt.

53. Engdahl, F. William. 2004. Is a USA economic collapse due in 2005? Centre for Research on Globalisation. Retrieved February 1, 2010, from http://www.globalresearch.ca/articles/ENG407A.html.

54. Glass, Ira. 2009. This American life: Giant pool of money wins Peabody. (April 5). Public Radio International. Retrieved February 1, 2010, from http://www.pri.org/business/giant-pool-of-money.html.

55. Volcker, Paul A. 2005. An economy on thin ice. *Washington Post* (April 10). Accessed March 11, 2010, from http://www.washingtonpost.com/wp-dyn/articles/A38725-2005Apr8.html.

56. BBC News. 2003. Buffett warns of investment "time bomb." Retrieved January 28, 2010, from http://news.bbc.co.uk/2/hi/business/2817995.stm.

57. Salmon, Felix. 2009. Recipe for disaster: The formula that killed Wall Street. *Wired Magazine* 17 (February 23). Retrieved January 28, 2010, from http://www.wired.com/techbiz/it/magazine/17-03/wp_quant.

58. Lewin, Kurt. 1951/1964. *Field theory in social science: Selected theoretical papers.* New York: Harper Torchbooks.

59. Ibid., 229.

60. Burnes, Bernard. 2004. Kurt Lewin and complexity theories: Back to the future? *Journal of Change Management* 4(4): 309–25.

61. Lewin, Kurt. 1943. Psychological ecology. In *Field theory in social science,* 1952, ed. D. Cartwright. London: Social Science Paperbacks; Lewin, Kurt. 1947. Frontiers in group dynamics. In *Field theory in social science,* 1952, ed. D. Cartwright. London: Social Science Paperbacks; Burnes, Kurt Lewin and complexity theories.

62. Levy, Steven. 2005. Honey, I shrunk the iPod. A lot. *Newsweek* 146(12): 58.

63. Ibid; Sutton, R. L. 2001. The weird rules of creativity. *Harvard Business Review* 79(8): 94–103.

64. Lewin, Kurt. 1952. Group decision and social change. In *Readings in social psychology,* ed. G. E. Swanson, T. N. Newcomb, and E. L. Hartley. New York: Holt; Schein, E. H. 1987. *Organizational culture and leadership.* San Francisco: Jossey-Bass.

65. Ibid. Schein, Edgar H. 2002. Models and tools for stability and change in human systems. *Reflections* 4(2): 13.

66. Vaill, Peter. 1989. *Managing as a performing art: New ideas for a world of chaotic change.* San Francisco: Jossey-Bass.

67. Shea, Gregory, and Robert Gunther. 2009. *Your job survival guide: A manual for thriving in change.* Upper Saddle River, NJ: Pearson Education.

68. Vaill, Peter. 1996. *Learning as a way of being: Strategies for survival in a world of permanent white water.* San Francisco: Jossey-Bass.

69. Herper, Matthew, and Peter Kang. 2006. The world's ten best-selling drugs. *Forbes* (March 22). Retrieved January 29, 2010, from http://www.forbes.com/2006/03/21/pfizer-merck-amgen-cx_mh_pk_0321topdrugs.html.

70. Crabill, Steven C. 2009. Pfizer wins patent extension on cholesterol drug (January 29). Nj.com. Retrieved January 29, 2010, from http://www.nj.com/business/index.ssf/2009/01/pfizer_wins_patent_extension_o.html.

71. U.S. judge upholds Bristol, Sanofi patent on Plavix. 2007 (June 19). Reuters. Retrieved January 29, 2010, from http://www.reuters.com/article/idUSN1931607820070619?pageNumber=1.

72. AstraZeneca. 2008. AstraZenica settles US Nexium patent litigation with Ranbaxy (April 15). Retrieved January 29, 2010, from http://www.astrazeneca.com/media/latest-press-releases/2008/5387?itemId=3892250.

73. Piribo. 2008. Pharmaceutical market trends, 2008–2012 (140 pp.). Retrieved January 29, 2010, from http://www.piribo.com/publications/general_industry/pharmaceutical_market_trends_2008_2012.html.

74. GlaxoSmithKline. 2009. Creating a pool of intellectual property to fight neglected tropical diseases. Retrieved February 14, 2010, from http://www.gsk.com/collaborations/patentpool.htm.

75. Delfanti, Alessandro. 2010. Open lab tackles neglected diseases. P2P Foundation Blog. Retrieved February 14, 2010, from http://blog.p2pfoundation.net/category/p2p-healthcare.

76. Nature Editorial. 2010. Learning to share. *Nature* 463: 401; Butler, Declan. 2009. Drug patent plan gets mixed reviews. *Nature* 457: 1064–65.

77. Witty, Andrew. 2010. GSK investor presentation at JP Morgan 28th Annual Healthcare Conference, San Francisco (January 12). Retrieved February 11, 2010, from http://www.gsk.com/investors/presentations/2010/JP-Morgan-12January2010.pdf.

78. Shea, Gregory P. 2001. Leading change. In *Medicine and business: Bridging the gap*, ed. S. Rovin, p. 47. Gaithersburg, MD: Aspen Publishers.

79. Personal correspondence with Gregory Shea, January 30, 2010.

80. Thomas, Chris A., and Brett Lee. 2010. Language liaisons: Language planning leadership in health care. *Language Problems and Language Planning*, 34. In press.

81. Wharton ebuzz. Innovation requires change. Retrieved January 28, 2010, from http://executiveeducation.wharton.upenn.edu/ebuzz/0611/classroom.html.

82. Shea, G. 2008. Riding the waves during the recession: An interview with authors Gregory Shea and Robert Gunther, e-BIM. Retrieved July 9, 2009, from http://www.humanresourcesig.com.

83. Shea, Gregory P. 2001. Leading change. In*Medicine and business: Bridging the gap.* ed. S. Rovin, Gaithersburg, MD: Aspen Publishers. Block, Peter. 2002. *The answer to how is yes: acting on what matters.* San Francisco: Berrett-Koehler Publishers, Inc.

84. Green, Peter S. 2009. Merrill's Thain said to pay $1.2 million to decorator. (January 23). Bloomberg.com. Retrieved March 11, 2010, from http://www.bloomberg.com/apps/news?pid=20601087&sid=aFcrG8er4FRw&refer=home.

85. Waring, Paul. 2008. Coaching the brain. *The Coaching Psychologist* 4(2): 10–16.

86. Ibid.

87. Goleman, Daniel, Richard E. Boyatzis, and Annie McKee. 2002. *Primal leadership: Learning to lead with emotional intelligence.* Boston: Harvard Business School Press.

88. Ibid.

89. Boyatzis, Richard E. 2006. An overview of intentional change from a complexity perspective. *Journal of Management Development* 25(7): 607–23; Howard, Anita. 2006. Positive and negative emotional attractors and intentional change. *Journal of Management Development* 25(7): 657–70; Boyatzis, Richard, and Annie McKee. *Resonant leadership: Renewing yourself and connecting with others through mindfulness, hope and compassion.* Boston: Harvard Business School Press.

90. Dolan, S. L., S. Garcia, and A. Auerbach. 2003. Understanding and managing chaos in organizations. *International Journal of Management* 20(1): 23–35; Van der Ven, Andrew H., and Marshall S. Poole. 1995. Explaining development and change in organizations. *Academy of Management Review* 20(3): 510–40.

91. Richwine, Lisa. 2009. Update 1—Glaxo proposes patent pool for neglected diseases (February 13). Forbes.com. Retrieved March 11, 2010, from http://www.forbes.com/feeds/afx/2009/02/13/afx6052325.html.

92. Snyder, C. R. *The psychology of hope: You can get there from here.* New York: Simon & Schuster; Boyatzis, Richard, and Annie McKee. 2005. *Resonant leadership.* Boston, MA: Harvard Business School Press. Boyatzis, An overview of intentional change theory from a complexity perspective; Boyatzis, Richard E. 2001.

93. McKee, Annie, Richard Boyatzis, and Frances Johnston. 2008. *Becoming a resonant leader.* Cambridge: Harvard University Press.

94. Seligman, Martin. 1998. *Learned optimism: How to change your mind and your life.* New York: Pocket Books.

95. Ibid.

96. Boyatzis and McKee. 2005. *Resonant leadership;* Seligman, Martin. *Learned optimism.*

97. Boyatzis, An overview of intentional change theory from a complexity perspective; Boyatzis, Richard E. 2001. Developing emotional intelligence. In *The emotionally intelligent workplace*, ed. C. Cherniss, R. E. Boyatzis and D. Goleman, 234–53. San Francisco: Jossey-Bass; Kolb, David A., and Richard E. Boyatzis. 1970. Goal setting and self-directed behavior change. *Human Relations* 23(5): 439–57; Boyatzis, Richard E. 2008. Leadership development from a complexity perspective. *Consulting Psychology Journal* 60(4): 298–313.

98. Goleman et al., *Primal leadership*; Boyatzis, Richard E., and Kleio Akrivou. 2006. The ideal self as the driver of intentional change. *Journal of Management Development* 25(7): 139.

99. Goleman et al., *Primal leadership*; Boyatzis and Akrivou, The ideal self as the driver of intentional change.

100. Goleman, Daniel, Richard Boyatzis, and Annie McKee. 2002. *Reawakening your passion for work.* Boston: Harvard Business School Press.

101. New York Institute for Gestalt Therapy. Home page. Accessed May 10, 2010, from http://www.newyorkgestalt.org/index/html.

102. Critchley, B., and D. Casey. 1989. Organizations get stuck too. *Leadership and Organization Development Journal* 10(4): 3–12.

103. Kepner, Elaine. 1980. Gestalt group process. In *Beyond the hot seat: Gestalt approaches to group*, ed. Bud Feder and Ruth Ronall, 5–25. Highland, NY: Gestalt Journal Press; Kolb, David. 1984. *Experiential learning: Experience as the source of learning and development.* Upper Saddle River, NJ: Prentice Hall.

104. Interview with Frances Johnston, January 2010.

105. Johnston, Frances, and Eddy Mwelwa. 2009. Making the HIV/AIDS problem visible in Cambodia. In *Mending the world*, ed. Joseph Melnick and Edwin C. Nevis, 287–309. Bloomington, IN: Xlibris Publishing.

106. Ibid.

107. *CIA World Factbook*, Cambodia. Retrieved May 10, 2010, from https://www.cia.gov/library/publications/the-world-factbook/geos/countrytemplate_cb.html.

108. United States Agency Internal Development. USAID/Cambodia. Retrieved May 10, 2010, from http://www.usaid.gov/our_work/global_health/aids/Countries/asia/cambodia_profile.pdf.

109. Burke, W. Warner. 1987. *Organization development: A normative view.* Reading, MA: Addison-Wesley.

110. French, Wendell. 1969. Organization development: Objectives, assumptions, and strategies. *California Management Review* 12: 23–34.

111. Hinkley, Stanley R. 2006. A history of organization development. In *NTL handbook of organization development and change: Principles, practices, and perspectives*, ed. Brenda B. Jones and Michael Brazzel, 28–45. San Francisco: Pfeiffer; Weisbord, M. R. 2004.*Productive workplaces revisited: Dignity, meaning and community in the 21st century.* San Francisco: Pfeiffer.

112. Cummings, T. G., and C. G. Worley. 2009. *Organization development and change.* Mason, OH: South-Western Cengage Learning.

113. Ibid.

114. McGregor, Douglas, and Joel Cutcher-Gershenfeld. 2006. *The human side of enterprise.* New York: McGraw-Hill.

115. Leskiw, Sheri-Lynne, and Parbudyal Singh. 2007. Leadership development: Learning from best practices. *Leadership and Organization Development Journal* 28(5): 444–64.

116. Lewin, Kurt. 1946. Action research and minority problems. *Journal of Social Issues* 2(4): 34–46.

117. Reason, P., and H. Bradbury, eds. 2008. *Sage handbook of action research: Participative inquiry and practice*, 2d ed. London: Sage Publications; http://www.bath.ac.uk/management/news_events/pdf/lowcarbon_insider_voices.pdf.

118. Freire, P. 1970. *Pedagogy of the oppressed.* New York: Herder & Herder.

119. Lewin, Action research and minority problems; Burnes, Kurt Lewin and complexity theories.

120. Reason, Peter and Hilary Bradbury. 2001. Inquiry and participation in search of a world worth of human aspiration. In P. Reason and H. Bradbury (eds.), *Handbook of action research: participative inquiry and practice* (1–14). Thousand Oaks, CA: Sage Publications; McKee, Annie, and Frances Johnston. 2006. The impact and opportunity of emotion in organizations. In B. B. Jones and M. Brazzel (eds.), *The NTL Handbook of Organizational Development and Change* (407–423). San Francisco: Pffeifer; London, Anne (Annie McKee), and McMillan, Cecilia. 1992. Discovering social issues: Organizational development in a multicultural community. *Journal of Applied Behavioral Sciences* 28: 445–460.

121. Kemmis, Stephen, and Robin McTaggart. 2005. Participatory action research: Communicative action and the public sphere. In *SAGE*

handbook of qualitative research, ed. Norman K. Denzin and Yvonna S. Lincoln, 559–604. Thousand Oaks, CA: Sage Publications.

122. Schwaninger M. 2000. Managing complexity: The path toward intelligent organizations. *Systemic Practice and Action Research* 13(2): 207–41; Schwaninger, Markus. 2004. Methodologies in conflict: Achieving synergies between system dynamics and organizational cybernetics. A cyberkinetic model to enhance organizational intelligence. *Systems Research and Behavioral Science* 21: 411; Schwaninger, Markus. 2003. A cyberkinetic model to enhance organizational intelligence. *Systems Analysis Modelling Simulations* 43(1): 53–65.

123. American Society of Training and Development. 2008. *State of the industry report: ASTD's annual review of trends in workplace learning and performance.* Alexandria, VA: A. Paradise.

124. Boyatzis and McKee. Resonant leadership; Boyatzis, Richard E., A. Baker, D. Leonard, K. Rhee, and L. Thompson. 1995. Will it make a difference? Assessing a value-based, outcome oriented, competency-based professional program. In *Innovation in professional education: Steps on a journey from teaching to learning*, ed. Richard E. Boyatzis, S. S. Cowen, and D. A. Kolb, 167–202. San Francisco: Jossey-Bass; Boyatzis, Richard E., and Argun Saatcioglu. 2008. A 20-year view of trying to develop emotional, social and cognitive intelligence competencies in graduate management education. *Journal of Management Development* 27(1): 92–108.

125. McKee, Annie, Richard Boyatzis, and Frances Johnston. 2008. *Becoming a resonant leader: Develop your emotional intelligence, renew your relationships, and sustain your effectiveness.* Boston: Harvard Business School Press.

126. Bunch, Kay J. 2007. Training failure as a consequence of organizational culture. *Human Resource Development Review* 6(1): 142–63.

127. Buchanan, D., and D. Boddy. 1992. *The expertise of the change agent.* New York: Prentice Hall.

128. Dawson, P. 1994. *Organizational change: A processual approach.* London: Paul Chapman; Hardy, C. 1994. *Managing strategic action: Mobilizing change—Concepts, readings and cases.* London: Sage; Hardy, S. 1996. Understanding power: Bringing about strategic change. *British Journal of Management* 7 (Special Issue): S3–S16; Kanter, R. M. 1983. *The change masters: Corporate entrepreneurs at work.* London: Allen & Unwin; Pettigrew, A. M. 1985. *The awakening giant: Continuity and change in Imperial Chemical Industries.* Oxford: Blackwell.

129. Balogun, Julia, Pauline Gleadle, Veronica H. Hailey, and Hugh Willmott. 2005. Managing change across boundaries: Boundary-shaking practices. *British Journal of Management* 16(4): 261–78.

130. Ibid., 263.

131. Goleman, Daniel. 1995. *Emotional intelligence.* New York: Bantam Books; Goleman, Daniel. 1998. *Working with emotional intelligence.* New York: Bantam Books.

132. Cangemi, Joseph P., Bill Burga, Harold Lazarus, Richard L. Miller, and Jaime Fitzgerald. The real work of the leader: A focus on the human side of the equation. *Journal of Management Development* 27(10): 1026–36; Vakola, M., I. Tsaousis, and I. Nikolaou. 2004. The role of emotional intelligence and personality variables on attitudes toward organizational change. *Journal of Managerial Psychology* 19(2): 88–110.

133. Boyatzis and McKee, *Resonant leadership.*

134. Boyatzis and McKee, *Resonant leadership.*

135. NARHA.org. Retrieved on April 23, 2010.

136. Hester, Amanda. Vanguard. "High In The Saddle." VA's Employee Magazine. March/April 2010. Vol. LV1 NO. 1 Published online by the Office of Public Affairs. Retrieved on April 23, 2010 from http://www.va.gov/opa/publications/vanguard_10_marchapril.pdf.

Chapter 8

1. D'Aveni, Richard A. 1994. *Hypercompetition: Managing the dynamics of strategic maneuvering.* New York: The Free Press.

2. Ibid.

3. Honan, Matthew. 2007. Apple unveils iPhone. *MacWorld* (January 9). Accessed March 9, 2010, from http://www.macworld.com/article/54769/2007/01/iphone.html; Huffman, Mark. 2007. Apple cuts price of most expensive iPhone. Consumeraffairs.com (September 6). Accessed March 9, 2010, from http://www.consumeraffairs.com/news04/2007/09/iphone_price.html.

4. Snell, Jason. 2007. The iPhone: Complete review. *Macworld* (July 3). Accessed March 9, 2010, from http://www.macworld.com/article/58733/iphone_rev.html?loomau_ow=t0:s0:a38:g26:r12:c0.000890:b21003931:z0.

5. Huffman, Apple cuts price of most expensive iPhone.

6. Bogner, William C., and Pamela S. Barr. 2000. Making sense in hypercompetitive environments: A cognitive explanation for persistence of high velocity competition. *Organization Science* 11(2): 212–26.

7. Amar, A. D., Carsten Hentrich, and Vlatka Hlupic. 2009. To be a better leader, give up authority. *Harvard Business Review* 87(12): 22–24, 126.

8. Ernst and Young. "The Ernst and Young Entrepreneur of the Year awards program—Southeast area Florida 2007 awards recipients." Accessed March 14, 2010, from http://www.ey.com/US/en/About-us/Entrepreneur-Of-The-Year/SEA_FL_Article_2007_Award_Recipients."

9. Dietrich, Arne. 2004. The cognitive neuroscience of creativity. *Psychonomic Bulletin and Review* 11(6): 1011–26.

10. Ibid.

11. Ibid.

12. Krashen, Stephen. 1985. *The input hypothesis: Issues and implications.* White Plains, NY: Longman; Carson, Shelley H., and Ellen J. Langer. 2006. Mindfulness and self-acceptance. *Journal of Rational-Emotive and Cognitive Behavior Therapy* 24(1): 29–43.

13. Dietrich, The cognitive neuroscience of creativity.

14. Langer, E. J., and M. Moldoveanu. 2000. The construct of mindfulness. *Journal of Social Issues* 56(1): 1–9.

15. Carson and Langer, Mindfulness and self-acceptance; Csikszentmihalyi, Mihaly. *Finding flow: The psychology of engagement with everyday life.* New York: Basic Books. 1997.

16. Dietrich, The cognitive neuroscience of creativity.

17. Sutton, Robert I. 2001. The weird rules of creativity. *Harvard Business Review* 79(8): 94–103.

18. Deci, E. L., and R. M. Ryan. 1995. Human autonomy: The basis for true self-esteem. In *Efficacy, agency, and self-esteem*, ed. M. Kemis, 31–49. New York: Plenum; Carson and Langer, Mindfulness and self-acceptance.

19. Sutton, The weird rules of creativity.

20. Carson and Langer, Mindfulness and self-acceptance.

21. Dietrich, The cognitive neuroscience of creativity.

22. Mölle, Mattias, Lisa Marshall, Werner Lutzenberger, Reinhard Pietrowsky, Horst L. Fehm, and Jan Born. 1996. Enhanced dynamic complexity in the human EEG during creative thinking. *Neuroscience Letters* 208: 61–64.

23. Indefrey, P., and W. J. Levelt. 2004. The spatial and temporal signatures of word production components. *Cognition* 92(1–2): 101–44.

24. Cattell, R. 1971. *Abilities: Their structure, growth, and action.* New York: Houghton-Mifflin; Guilford, J. P. 1975. Creativity: A quarter century of progress. In *Perspectives in creativity*, ed. I. A. Taylor and J. W. Getzels, 37–59. Chicago: Aldine.

25. Dietrich, Arne. 2007. Who's afraid of a neuroscience of creativity? *Methods* 42(1): 22–27.

26. Ibid.

27. Ibid.

28. Dietrich, The cognitive neuroscience of creativity.

29. Victoria, *Herald Sun.* 2007. Right brain v. left brain (October 9). Retrieved May 11, 2010, from http://www.heraldsun.com.au/news/right-brain-v-left-brain/story-e6frf7jo-1111114603615.

30. Corballis, Michael C. 1980. Laterality and myth. *American Psychologist* 35(3): 288.

31. Weaver, Catherine. 2009. IPE's split brain. *New Political Economy* 14(3): 337–46.

32. Fink, Andreas, Mathias Benedek, Roland H. Grabner, Beate Staudt, and Aljoscha C. Neubauer. 2007. Creativity meets neuroscience: Experimental tasks for the neuroscientific study of creative thinking. *Methods* 42(1): 68–76.

33. Dietrich, The cognitive neuroscience of creativity.

34. Fink et al., Creativity meets neuroscience.

35. Ibid.

36. Dietrich, The cognitive neuroscience of creativity.

37. Damasio, A. R. 1994. *Descartes' error: Emotion, reason, and the human brain.* New York: Putnam.

38. Scase, Richard. 2009. "Herding cats": Managing creativity. *Market Leader* 44: 58–61.

39. Nussbaum, Bruce, Robert Berner, and Diane Brady. 2005. Get creative! *BusinessWeek* 3945: 60–68.

40. Mostert, Nel M. 2007. Diversity of the mind as the key to successful creativity at Unilever. *Creativity and Innovation Management* 16(1): 93–100.

41. ASAE & the center for association leadership. Idea bank: A room of their own. 2006. *Associations Now* 2(2): 13.

42. Sutton, Robert. 2001. The weird rules of creativity. *Harvard Business Review.* 79(8): 94–103.

43. One laptop per child. Home page. Retrieved April 1, 2010, from http://laptop.org/en.

44. Ibid.

45. Lawton, Chuck. 2009. The XO laptop two years later: Part I: The vision (June). Retrieved February 24, 2010, from http://www.wired.com/geekdad/2009/06/the-xo-laptop-two-years-later-part-1-the-vision.

46. Talbot, David. 2008. $100 laptop program's new president. *Technology Review* (May 2). Accessed March 14, 2010, from http://www.technologyreview.com/Biztech/20711/page1.

47. Barras, Colin. 2008. Laptops could betray users in the developing world. *New Scientist* (June 5). Accessed March 14, 2010, from http://www.newscientist.com/article/mg19826596.100-laptops-could-betray-users-in-the-developing-world.html?feedId=electronic-threats_rss20.

48. Global Case Challenge. Home page. Retrieved May 11, 2010, from http:// www.globalcasechallenge.com/about.html.

49. Drucker, Peter. 1993. *Post-capitalist society.* New York: HarperCollins, 38.

50. Yahoo! Finance. Netflix, Inc. (NFLX). Retrieved May 11, 2010, from http://finance.yahoo.com/q?s=NFLX.

51. Netflix. About Netflix. Retrieved May 11, 2010, from http://cdn-0.nflximg.com/us/pdf/Consumer_Press_Kit.pdf.

52. Ibid.

53. Netflix, Netflix Prize. Retrieved May 11, 2010, from http://www.netflixprize.com.

54. Salzman, Alex. 2008. *What gets Seventh Generation's "director of corporate consciousness" out of bed in the morning?* (May 19). Retrieved September 12, 2009, from http://www.alternativechannel.tv/blog/en/comments/what_gets_seventh_generations_director_of_corporate_consciousness_out_of_bed.

55. Heimert, Chrystie. 2009. Seventh Generation names PepsiCo/Quaker Oats veteran as CEO (June 1). Retrieved September 12, 2009, from http://www.csrwire.com/press/press_release/27044-Seventh-Generation-Names-PepsiCo-Quaker-Oats-Veteran-as-CEO.

56. Seventh Generation, Inc. Company profile. Retrieved March 14, 2010, from LexisNexis Corporate Affiliations Database.

57. Heimert, Seventh Generation Names PepsiCo/Quaker Oats Veteran as CEO.

58. Seventh Generation, Inc. About Seventh Generation. Retrieved September 12, 2009, from http://www.seventhgeneration.com/about.

59. Ibid.

60. Werbach, Adam. 2009. When sustainability means more than "green." *McKinsey Quarterly* (July). Retrieved September 12, 2009, from http://www.mckinseyquarterly.com/When_sustainabillity_means_more_than_green_2404.

61. Rushe, Dominic. 2009. Eco firm Seventh Generation is riding high in Obama revolution. *Sunday Times* (February 15). http://business.timesonline.co.uk/tol/business/entrepreneur/article5733543.ece.

62. Ibid.

63. Werbach, When sustainability means more than "green."

64. Hollender, Jeffrey. 2008. Corporate consciousness report 2008. Retrieved September 7, 2009, from http://www.seventhgeneration.com.

65. Fast Company. 2009. The world's most innovative companies. Retrieved May 11, 2010, from http://www.fastcompany.com/fast50_09.

66. *Bloomberg BusinessWeek.* The most innovative companies 2009. Retrieved May 11, 2010, from http://images.businessweek.com/ss/09/04/0409_most_innovative_cos/42.htm.

67. Volberda, Henk W. 1996. Toward the flexible form: How to remain vital in hypercompetitive environments. *Organization Science* 7(4): 359–74.

68. BBGEEKS. Blackberry news, reviews, and information. Retrieved May 11, 2010, from http://www.bbgeeks.com/blackberry-guides/the-history-of-the-blackberry_88296.

69. Davis, David. 2009. What is Cisco Telepresence and what does it take? Petri IT Knowledgebase (January 7). Retrieved May 11, 2010, from http://www.petri.co.il/cisco-telepresence-what-is-it-what-does-it-take-video-conferencing-hdtv.htm.

70. Rich, Ben, and Leo Janos. 1996. *Skunk Works: A personal memoir of my years at Lockheed.* Boston: Little, Brown and Company.

71. Lockheed Martin. Skunk Works. Retrieved May 11, 2010, from http://www.lockheedmartin.com/aeronautics/skunkworks.

72. Kiley, David. 2009. Putting Ford on fast-forward. *BusinessWeek* (October 26). Retrieved February 24, 2010, from http://www.thefreelibrary.com/PUTTING+FORD+ON+FAST+FORWARD-a01612033904.

73. Davidsson, Per, Erik Hunter, and Magnus Klofsten. 2006. Institutional forces: The invisible hand that shapes venture ideas? *International Small Business Journal* 24(2): 115–31.

74. Kowal, Eric. 2008. Army suggestion program can thicken your wallet. *U.S. Army Military News* (November 21). Retrieved February 28, 2010, from http://www.army.mil/-news/2008/11/21/14451-army-suggestion-program-can-thicken-your-wallet.

75. PennGSE. PENN and Milken Family Foundation launch business plan competition to improve education. Retrieved May 11, 2010, from http://www.gse.upenn.edu/node/1176.

76. Disney. Walt Disney Imagineering. Retrieved May 11, 2010, from http://corporate.disney.go.com/careers/who_imagineering.html.

77. Ibid.

78. Marling, Karal. 1997. *Designing Disney's theme parks.* New York: Flammarion.

79. Disney. ImagiNations. Retrieved May 11, 2010, from http://disney.go.com/disneycareers/imaginations.

80. Online Etymology Dictionary. Entrepreneur. Retrieved May 11, 2010, from http://www.etymonline.com/index.php?search=entrepreneur&searchmode=none.

81. McClelland, D. C. 1961. *The achieving society.* Princeton, NJ: D. Van Nostrand Company.

82. Lemke, C., and B. Lesley. 2009. *Advance 21st century innovation in schools through smart, informed state policy.* Los Angeles: The Metiri Group; Soriano, D. R., and J. M. C. Martínez. 2007. Transmitting the entrepreneurial spirit to the work team in SMEs: The importance of leadership. *Management Decision* 45(7): 1102–22; Blair, Tony, and Gerhard Schröder. 2003. Europe: The third way/Die neue mitte. In *The new Labour reader*, ed. A. Chadwick and R. Heffernan. Malden, MA: Blackwell Publishing.

83. Blair and Schröder, Europe: The third way.

84. Lytle, Tamara. 2010. Obama vows to increase jobs, cut debt and stay course for health care reform. AARPBulletintoday (January 28). Retrieved May 11, 2010, from http://bulletin.aarp.org/yourworld/politics/articles/state_of_the_union.html?CMP=KNC-360I-GOOGLE-BULL&HBX_OU=50&HBX_PK=jobs_state_of_the_union&utm_source=Google&utm_medium=cpc&utm_term=jobs%2Bstate%2Bof%2Bthe%2Bunion&utm_campaign=G-Your%2BWorld%2B-%2BArticles.

85. Kobe, Kathryn. April 2007. The small business share of GDP, 1998–2004, p. 1. Retrieved March 28, 2010, from http://www.sba.gov/advo/research/rs299tot.pdf; CHI Research, February 27, 2003. Small serial innovators: The small firm contribution to technical change. Retrieved March 28, 2010, from http://www.sba.gov/advo/research/rs225tot.pdf; Small Business Administration Office of Advocacy. September 2009. Frequently asked questions: Advocacy: The voice of small business in government. Retrieved May 19, 2010, from www.sba.gov/advo/stats/sbfaq.pdf.

86. *CIA World Factbook.* Zambia. Retrieved April 11, 2010, from https://www.cia.gov/library/publications/the-world-factbook/geos/za.html.

87. ABC News/Money. Photos: Celebrity entrepreneurs. Retrieved May 11, 2010, from http://abcnews.go.com/Business/popup?id=4941699.

88. ONE International. About. Retrieved May 11, 2010, from http://www.one.org/international/about.

89. Rainforest Foundation. About us. Retrieved May 11, 2010, from http://www.rainforestfoundation.org/about-us.

90. The Oprah Winfrey Leadership Academy Foundation. Building a dream. Retrieved May 11, 2010, from http://oprahwinfreyleadershipacademy.o-philanthropy.org/site/PageServer?pagename=owla_about.

91. Resnick, Rosalind. 2009. Can you handle the risk? Make sure your risk tolerance and investment strategy align. *Entrepreneur Magazine* (January). Retrieved February 28, 2010, from http://www.entrepreneur.com/magazine/entrepreneur/2009/january/199022.html.

92. John F. Kennedy University. About us. Retrieved May 11, 2010, from http://www.jfku.edu/about/story.

93. Hornaday, John A., and John Aboud. 1971. Characteristics of successful entrepreneurs. *Personnel Psychology* 24(2): 141–53.

94. Hines, John L. 2004. Characteristics of an entrepreneur. *Surgical Neurology* 61(4): 407–08.

95. Ibid.

96. Lans, Thomas, Harm Biemans, Jos Verstegen, and Martin Mulder. 2008. The influence of the work environment on entrepreneurial learning of small-business owners. *Management Learning* 39(5): 597–613.

97. Robison, Jennifer. 2008. Will social entrepreneurship save the world? *Gallup Management Journal Online.* Retrieved February 24, 2010, from

http://gmj.gallup.com/content/112915/will-social-entrepreneurship-save-world.aspx#1.

98. Mobiles in Malawi. "Going global" and www.jobsa.org. Retrieved May 11, 2010, from http://mobilesinmalawi.blogspot.com.

99. Ibid.

100. Banks, Ken, and Josh Nesbit. 2008. Witnessing the human face of mobile in Malawi. PC World Business Center (June 27). Retrieved February 28, 2010, from http://www.pcworld.com/businesscenter/article/147679/witnessing_the_human_face_of_mobile_in_malawi.html; http://www.frontlinesms.com/what; http://www.kiwanja.net.

101. Forum for the Future. FT Climate Change Challenge. Retrieved May 11, 2010, from http://www.forumforthefuture.org/FT-climate-challenge.

102. KYOTO: Free is the sun. KYOTO Retrospective. Retrieved May 11, 2010, http://www.kyoto-energy.org/history.html.

103. Ibid.; Forum for the Future. FT Climate Change Challenge. Retrieved May 11, 2010, from http://www.forumforthefuture.org/FT-climate-challenge.

104. Ibid.

105. SBA Office of Advocacy. Frequently asked questions.

106. Small Business Administration. How to write a business plan. Retrieved February 24, 2010, from http://www.sba.gov/smallbusinessplanner/plan/writeabusinessplan/SERV_WRRITINGBUSPLAN.html.

107. Woo, Kevin. 2009. Don't let angel investors bedevil you. Forbes.com. Retrieved August 2, 2009, from http://www.forbes.com/2009/07/28/investor-backer-business-leadership-angel_print.html.

108. Kahn, Sharon. 2009. The venture game. *Fortune Small Business* 19(4): 60.

109. National Venture Capital Association. 2009. Frequently asked questions about venture capital. Retrieved February 24, 2010, from http://www.nvca.org/index.php?option=com_content&view=article&id=119&Itemid=147.

110. Ibid.

111. Zoltners, Andris A., Prabhakant Sinha, and Sally E. Lorimer. 2006. Match your sales force structure to your business life cycle. *Harvard Business Review* 84(7/8): 83.

112. Lippitt, Gordon L., and Warren H. Schmidt. 1967. Crises in a developing organization. *Harvard Business Review* 45: 102–12.

113. Zoltners et al., Match your sales force structure to your business life cycle.

114. Quinn, Robert E., and Kim Cameron. 1983. Organization life cycles and shifting criteria of effectiveness: Some preliminary evidence. *Management Science* 29(1): 33–51; Teeter, Ryan A., and Karen S. Whelan-Berry. 2008. My firm versus our firm: The challenge of change in growing the small professional service firm. *Journal of Business Inquiry* 7(1): 43–52.

115. Teeter and Whelan-Berry. My firm versus our firm; Churchill, N. C., and V. L. Lewis. 1983. The five stages of business growth. *Harvard Business Review* 61(3): 30–50.

116. Dodge, H. Robert, Sam Fullerton, and John E. Robbins. 1994. Stage of the organizational life cycle and competition as mediators of problem perception for small businesses. *Strategic Management Journal* 15(2): 121–34.

117. Azides, I. 1979. Organizational passages: Diagnosing and treating life cycle problems in organizations. *Organizational Dynamics* 9: 3–24.

118. Quinn and Cameron, Organization life cycles and shifting criteria of effectiveness.

119. How to pay the piper. 2003. *Economist* 367(8322): 62.

120. Ambrosek, Renee. 2007. *Shawn Fanning: The founder of Napster.* New York: Rosen Publishing Group; Weiss, Joseph W. 2009. *Business ethics: A stakeholder and issues management approach.* Mason, OH: South-Western Cengage Learning; Napster profile. Retrieved March 14, 2009, from Lexis-Nexis Corporate Affiliations Database.

121. Knaup, Amy E. 2005. Survival and longevity in the business employment dynamics data. *Monthly Labor Review* 128(5): 51.

122. Williams, Geoff. 2007. Dead zone. *Entrepreneur* 35(3): 76.

123. Henricks, Mark. 2008. Do you really need a business plan? *Entrepreneur* 36(12): 92.

124. Diamond, Mike. 2006. Why companies fail. *Reeves Journal: Plumbing, Heating, Cooling* 86 (10): 103.

125. Levinson, Jay Conrad, and Al Lautenslager. 2005. Mind over market. *Entrepreneur* 33(3): 66.

126. Colombo, George. 2004. Are you really listening to your customers? *Business Credit* 106(6): 66.

127. Parker, S. C. 2009. Intrepreneurship or entrepreneurship? *Journal of Business Venturing* 24(5): 519–32.

128. McCrae, N. 1982. Intrapreneurial now. *The Economist* (April 17): 67–72.

129. Pinchot, Gifford. 1999. *Intrapraneuring in action*, p. 1. San Francisco: Berrett-Koehler Publishers.

130. Entrepreneurs in the U.S. economy. 2007. *Monthly Labor Review* 130, (12): 38.

131. Stovall, Steven Austin. 2005. Entrepreneurial spirit isn't just for startups. *Bed Times* (October): 38.

132. Help wanted: A mix of skills. 2006. *eWeek* 23(28): 46.

133. Nelson, S. J., Birchard, B. Raffone, I., and Schrange, M. Starting new businesses–Inside the organization. 1999. *Harvard Management Update* 4(12): 1.

134. U.S. Patent and Trademark Office. Patent applications filed. Retrieved August 2, 2009, from http://www.uspto.gov/web/offices/com/annual/2008/oai_05_wlt_02.html.

135. U.S. Copyright Office. Frequently asked questions. Accessed April 7, 2010, from http://www.copyright.gov/help/faq/faq-duration.html#duration.

136. Charan, Ram. 2008. Stop whining, start thinking. *BusinessWeek*, No. 4097: 58.

137. Buzan, Tony, and Berry Buzan. 1996. *The mind map book.* New York: Penguin.

138. Cross, Jay. 2005. Useful things. *Chief Learning Officer* 4(6): 14.

139. Ibid.; Buzan, Tony, and Raymond Keene. 1994. *Buzan's book of genius: And how to unleash your own.* London: Random House.

140. Global Human Capital Journal. 17 enterprise visionaries release 2010 predictions for social networks, web 2.0. Retrieved May 11, 2010, from http://globalhumancapital.org/?p=1103.

Chapter 9

1. Window on State Government. 2001. Purchasing and contract management. Retrieved April 27, 2010, from http://www.window.state.tx.us/tspr/dallas/chapt8b.htm.

2. Siegel-Jacobs, Karen, and J. Frank Yates. 1996. Effects of procedural and outcome accountability on judgment quality. *Organizational Behavior and Human Decision Making* 65(1): 1–17.

3. Brafman, Ori, and Rod A. Beckstrom. 2006. *The starfish and the spider: The unstoppable power of leaderless organizations.* New York: The Penguin Group.

4. Emery, Merrelyn. 2000. The current version of Emery's open systems theory. *Systemic Practice and Action Research* 13(5): 623–43.

5. Starnes, Becky J. 2000. Achieving competitive advantage through the application of open systems theory and the development of strategic alliances: A guide for managers of not-for-profit organizations. *Journal of Not-for-Profit and Public Sector Marketing* 8(2): 15.

6. Katz, D., and R. L. Kahn. 1978. *The social psychology of organizations.* New York: John Wiley & Sons.

7. Long, Mark, and Angel Gonzalez. 2010. Transocean seeks limit on liability (May 13). *Wall Street Journal.* Retrieved May 17, 2010, from http://online.wsj.com/article/SB10001424052748704635204575241852606380696.html; Efstathiou, Jim, 2010. BP, Halliburton, Transocean blame each other in Gulf oil spill (May 10). *Bloomberg Businessweek.* Retrieved May 17, 2010, from http://www.businessweek.com/news/2010-05-10/bp-halliburton-transocean-blame-each-other-in-gulf-oil-spill.html.

8. Morand, David A. 1995. The role of behavioral formality and informality in the enactment of bureaucratic versus organic organizations. *Academy of Management Review* 20(4): 831–72; Harvey, Edward. 1968. Technology and the structure of organization. *American Sociological Review* 33(2): 247–59; McCaskey, Michael B. 1974. A contingency approach to planning: Planning with goals and planning without goals. *Academy of Management Journal* 17(2): 281–91; Burns, T., and G. M. Stalker. 1961. *The management of innovation.* Tavistock: London.

9. Covin, Jeffrey G., Dennis P. Slevin, and Randall L. Schultz. 1994. Implementing strategic missions: Effective strategic, structural and tactical choices. *Journal of Management Studies* 31(4): 481–505; Morand, The role of behavioral formality and informality; McCaskey, A contingency approach to planning; Burns and Stalker, *The management of innovation.*

10. Morgan, Gareth. 1998. *Images of organization*, p. 40. Thousand Oaks, CA: Sage.

11. Ibid.

12. Dooley, Kevin J. 1997. A complex adaptive systems model of organization change. *Nonlinear Dynamics, Psychology, and Life Sciences* 1(1): 69–97.

13. Wouter, Dessein, and Tano Santos. 2006. Adaptive organizations. *Journal of Political Economy* 114(5): 956–95.

14. Ibid., 956.

15. Weick, Karl E. 2002. The aesthetic of imperfection in orchestras and organizations. In Ken N. Kamoche, Miguel Pina e Cunha, and Joao Vieira da Cunha (eds.), *Organizational improvisation* (pp. 163–180). London: Routledge.

16. Van Baalen, Peter J., and Paul C. van Fenema. 2009. Instantiating global crisis networks: The case of SARS. *Decision Support Systems* 47: 277–86.

17. World Health Organization. Summary of probable SARS cases with onset of illness from 1 November 2002 to 31 July 2003. Retrieved April 27, 2010, from http://www.who.int/csr/sars/country/table2004_04_21/en/index.html.

18. Van Baalen and van Fenema. 2009. Instantiating global crisis networks.

19. Morgan Earth. 1998. *Images of organization,* Thousand Oaks, CA: Sage Publications.

20. Brafman and Beckstrom, *The starfish and the spider.*

21. Ibid.

22. Ibid.

23. Department of Treasury. Publication 557: Tax exempt status for your organization. Retrieved May 14, 2010, from http://www.irs.gov/pub/irs-pdf/p557.pdf.

24. Internal Revenue Service. Limited liability company (LLC). Retrieved April 27, 2010, from http://www.irs.gov/businesses/small/article/0,,id=98277,00.html.

25. Ibid.

26. FindLaw. Local start-up requirements for small businesses. Retrieved May 14, 2010, from http://smallbusiness.findlaw.com/starting-business/starting-business-licenses-permits/starting-business-licenses-permits-local.html.

27. *Trustees of Dartmouth College v. Woodward,* 17 U.S. (4 Wheaton) 518 (1819); Menez, Joseph Francis, John R. Vile, and Paul Charles Bartholemew. 2004. *Summaries of leading cases on the Constitution.* Lanham, ME: Rowman & Littlefield.

28. Internal Revenue Service. Definition of corporation—Section 527 political organizations. Retrieved April 27, 2010, from http://www.irs.gov/charities/political/article/0,,id=204994,00.html.

29. Internal Revenue Service. S corporations. Retrieved April 27, 2010, from http://www.irs.gov/businesses/small/article/0,,id=98263,00.html.

30. Ibid.

31. Standard Legal Law Library. S-corporations: Eliminating "double taxation." Retrieved May 17, 2010, from http://www.standardlegal.com/law-library/S-Corporation.html.

32. Internal Revenue Service. 2005. IRS launches study of S-corporation reporting compliance (July 25). Retrieved August 2, 2009, from http://www.irs.gov/newsroom/article/0,,id=141441,00.html.

33. Internal Revenue Service. Limited liability company (LLC).

34. Ibid.

35. Folta, Paul H. 2005. Cooperative joint ventures: Savvy foreign investors may wish to consider the benefits of this flexible investment structure. *China Business Review* (January–February): 18–23.

36. Pekar, Peter, and Marc S. Margulis. 2003. Equity alliances take center stage: The emergence of a new corporate growth model. *Ivey Business Journal Online* (May/June).

37. Ibid.

38. Beshel, Barbara. An introduction to franchising. International Franchise Association Educational Foundation. Retrieved December 15, 2009, from http://franchise.org/uploadedFiles/Franchise_Industry/Resources/Education_Foundation/Intro%20to%20Franchising%20Student%20Guide.pdf.

39. International Licensing Industry Merchandisers' Association. Introduction to licensing. Retrieved December 15, 2009, from http://www.licensing.org/education/licensing-introduction.php.

40. International Licensing Industry Merchandisers' Association. Why license? Retrieved December 15, 2009, from http://www.licensing.org/education/why-license.php.

41. International Licensing Industry Merchandisers' Association. Types of licensing. Retrieved December 15, 2009, from http://www.licensing.org/education/licensing-types.php.

42. Ibid.

43. Beshel, An introduction to franchising.

44. CBSNews.com. 2009. Food fight: Burger King franchisees sue (November 12). Retrieved December 15, 2009, from http://www.cbsnews.com/stories/2009/11/12/business/main5631870.shtml.

45. *Investor Glossary.* Wholly owned subsidiary. Retrieved December 16, 2009, from http://www.investorglossary.com/wholly-owned-subsidiary.htm.

46. The Free Dictionary. Subsidiary, in *Legal dictionary.* Retrieved December 16, 2009, from http://legal-dictionary.thefreedictionary.com/Wholly+owned+subsidiary.

47. West Virginia University College of Business and Economics. International strategy: Entry modes. Retrieved December 16, 2009, from http://www.be.wvu.edu/divmim/mgmt/insch/International%20Strategy-1.ppt.

48. The Free Dictionary, Subsidiary.

49. Ibid.

50. Chang, Peng S. 1995. International joint ventures vs. wholly owned subsidiaries. *Multinational Business Review* (Spring). Retrieved December 16, 2009, from http://findarticles.com/p/articles/mi_qa3674/is_199504/ai_n8729617/.

51. Aveda Customer Service. Frequently asked questions. Retrieved January 6, 2010, from http://www.aveda.com/customerservice/faq.tmpl; Canedy, Dana. 1997. Estée Lauder is acquiring maker of natural cosmetics. *New York Times* (November 20). Retrieved January 6, 2010, from http://www.nytimes.com/1997/11/20/business/Estée-lauder-is-acquiring-maker-of-natural-cosmetics.html?pagewanted=1.

52. Company profile: Aveda. 2009/2010. *GreenMoney Journal* 18:2. Retrieved January 6, 2010, from http://www.greenmoneyjournal.com/article.mpl?newsletterid=11&articleid=86; Sacks, Danielle. 2007. It's easy being green. *Fast Company* (December 19). Retrieved January 6, 2010, from http://www.fastcompany.com/magazine/85/aveda.html.

53. West Virginia University College of Business and Economics, International strategy: Entry modes.

54. The Free Dictionary, Subsidiary.

55. Chang, International joint ventures vs. wholly owned subsidiaries.

56. Reuer, Jeffrey J., Africa Ariño, and Antoni Valverde. The perfect "pre-nup" to strategic alliances: A guide to contracts. Association of Strategic Alliance Professionals Best Practice Bulletins. Retrieved December 16, 2009, from http://www.strategic-alliances.org/membership/memberresources/bestpracticebulletin.

57. Small Business Notes. Strategic alliances. Retrieved December 16, 2009, from http://www.smallbusinessnotes.com/operating/leadership/strategicalliances.html.

58. Small Business Notes, Strategic alliances.

59. Reuer et al., The perfect "pre-nup" to strategic alliances.

60. Wharton Executive Education. Strategic alliances: Creating growth opportunities. Wharton School at the University of Pennsylvania. Retrieved December 16, 2009, from http://executiveeducation.wharton.upenn.edu/open-enrollment/strategy-management-programs/strategic-alliances-growth-opportuities.cfm.

61. Caltech Industrial Relations Center. Strategic alliances. California Institute of Technology. Retrieved December 16, 2009, from http://www.irc.caltech.edu/p-105-strategic-alliances.aspx.

62. Small Business Notes, Strategic alliances.

63. PepsiCo. Our history: 1991 milestones. Retrieved January 6, 2010, from http://www.pepsico.com/Company/Our-History.html#block_1991.

64. Reference for Business. Strategic alliances. In *Encyclopedia of business* (2d ed.). Retrieved January 6, 2010, from http://www.referenceforbusiness.com/encyclopedia/Sel-Str/Strategic-Alliances.html.

65. Food and Drink Europe. 2003. Unilever, PepsiCo join forces to meet ice tea challenge (October 15). Retrieved January 6, 2010, from http://www.foodanddrinkeurope.com/Products-Marketing/Unilever-PepsiCo-join-forces-to-meet-ice-tea-challenge.

66. PepsiCo, Our history: 2009 milestones. Retrieved May 20, 2010, from http://www.pepsico.com/Company/Our-History.html#block_2009.

67. Hitt, Michael A., R. Duane Ireland, and Robert E. Hoskisson. 2009. *Strategic management: Competitiveness and globalization: Concepts and cases.* St. Paul, MN: South-Western Cengage Learning; Stalk, George, and Jill E. Black. 1994. The myth of the horizontal organization. *Canadian Business Review* 21(4): 26–29.

68. Tiernan, Siobhan D., Patrick C. Flood, Eamonn P. Murphy, and Stephen J. Carroll. 2002. Employee reactions to flattening organizational structures. *European Journal of Work and Organizational Psychology* 11(1): 47–67.

69. Ibid.

70. Stalk and Black, The myth of the horizontal organization; Cornelissen, Joep, Tibor van Bekkum, and Betteke van Ruler. 2006. Corporate communications: A practice-based theoretical conceptualization. *Corporate Reputation Review* 9(2): 114–33.

71. Designed chaos: An interview with David Kelley, founder and CEO of IDEO. Retrieved May 20, 2010, from http://www.va-interactive.com/inbusiness/editorial/bizdev/articles/ideo.html.

72. IDEO fact sheet. Retrieved May 20, 2010, from http://www.ideo.com/to-go/fact-sheet/.

73. Designed chaos: An interview with David Kelley, found and CEO of IDEO.

74. Tiernan et al., Employee reactions to flattening organizational structures.

75. Hitt et al., *Strategic management*.

76. Cornelissen et al., Corporate communications.

77. Hitt et al., *Strategic management*; Stalk and Black, The myth of the horizontal organization.

78. Tiernan et al., Employee reactions to flattening organizational structures.

79. Fortune Brands. Homepage. Retrieved May 20, 2010, from http://www.fortunebrands.com/.

80. Malone, Thomas W. 1987. Modeling coordination in organizations and markets. *Management Science* 33(10): 1317–32.

81. Cross, R., A. Parker, S. P. Borgatti. 2002. A bird's-eye view—Using social network analysis to improve knowledge creation and sharing. IBM Institute for Knowledge-Based Organizations. Retrieved from http://www-304.ibm.com/jct03001c/services/learning/solutions/pdfs/.

82. Carpenter, Mason. 2009. *An executive's primer on the strategy of social networks*. New York: Business Expert Press; Cross et al., A bird's-eye view.

83. Useem, Jerry. 2005. 1914: Ford offers $5 a day. *Fortune* 151(13): 65.

84. Plato. 1946. *The republic* (Benjamin Jowett, trans.). Cleveland: World Publishing Company.

85. Smith, Adam. 1776. *The wealth of nations*. Lawrence, KS: Digireads.

86. Taylor, Frederick W. 1911. *The principles of scientific management*. Ithaca: Cornell University Library.

87. Lindbeck and Snower, Multitask learning and the reorganization of work: from Tayloristic to holistic organization. *Journal of Labor Economics,* 18(3): 353–376.

88. Shepard, Jon M. 1969/1970. Functional specialization, alienation, and job satisfaction. *Industrial and Labor Relations Review* 23: 207–219.

89. Ibid.

90. Burgess, Thomas F. 1994. Making the leap to agility. *International Journal of Operations and Production Management* 14(11): 23–34.

91. Aoki, Masahiko. 1986. Horizontal vs. vertical information structure of the firm. *American Economic Review* 76(5): 971–983.

92. Ibid.

93. Morgeson, F. P., and M. A. Campion. 2002. Avoiding tradeoffs when redesigning work: Evidence from a longitudinal quasi-experiment. *Personnel Psychology* 55: 589–612.

94. Hsieh, An-Tien, and Hui-Yu Chao. 2004. A reassessment of the relationship between job specialization, job rotation, and job burnout: Example of Taiwan's high-technology industry. *International Journal of Human Resource Management* 15(6): 1108–23.

95. Chandler, Alfred D. 1990. *Strategy and structure: Chapters in the history of the industrial enterprise*. Cambridge, MA: MIT Press; Hall, David J., and Maurice A. Saias. 1980. Strategy follows structure! *Strategic Management Journal* 1(2): 149–63.

96. Hall and Saias. Strategy follows structure!, 155.

97. Hall and Saias, Strategy follows structure!; Miller, Danny. 1986. Configurations of strategy and structure: Towards a synthesis. *Strategic Management Journal* 7(3): 233–49; Pacheco, Jorge M., Arne Traulsen, and Martin A. Nowak. 2006. Coevolution of strategy and structure in complex networks with dynamical linking. *Physical Review Letters* 97: 25.

98. Shaver, Jennipher. 2008. Nautilus down $8.9M in second quarter 2008, focusing on retail. *Fitness Business Pro* 24(9): 28–30.

99. Ibid.

100. Nautilus Q4 sales fall. 2010. *Puget Sound Business Journal* (March 1). Retrieved March 28, 2010, from http://seattle.bizjournals.com/seattle/stories/2010/03/01/daily7.html?ana=yfcpc.

101. Nautilus to incur $13M charge to shed commercial business. 2010. *Puget Sound Business Journal* (March 8). Retrieved March 28, 2010, from http://seattle.bizjournals.com/seattle/stories/2010/03/08/daily5.html?ana=yfcpc.

102. Fuel economy is more than MPG. 2009. *Fleet Equipment* 35(8): 46–47.

103. Sherefkin, Robert. 2007. Dauch to U.S. industry: Don't fear trouble. *Automotive News* 81(6239): 30.

104. Woodward, Joan. 1966. *Management and technology*. London: HM Stationary Office.

105. Stovall, Steven Austin. 2006. *Cases in human resources management*. Cincinnati, OH: Atomic Dog.

106. Gabarro, John J., and John P. Kotter. 1993. Managing your boss. *Harvard Business Review* 71(3): 150–7; Useem, Michael. 2001. *Leading up: How to lead your boss so you both win*. New York: Crown.

107. Bickel, Janet. 2007. Managing "up": Achieving an effective partnership with your boss. *Academic Physician and Scientist* (February): 4–5.

108. Ibid.

109. Ibid.

Chapter 10

1. Philadelphia Police Department. Charles H. Ramsey. Retrieved May 15, 2010, from http://www.phillypolice.com/about/leadership/charles-h-ramsey/.

2. Information in this case derived from a personal interview with Annie McKee, 2010.

3. Katzenbach, Jon R., and Douglas K. Smith. 1993. The discipline of teams. *Harvard Business Review* 71(2): 111–20; Katzenbach, J. R., and D. K. Smith. 2003. *The wisdom of teams: Creating the high-performance organization*. New York: HarperCollins Publishers; Wheelan, Susan A. 2010. *Creating effective teams: A guide for members and leaders*. Thousand Oaks, CA: Sage.

4. Lewin, Kurt. 1951. *Field theory in social science*. New York: Harper.

5. Lewin, Kurt, Ronald Lippitt, and Ralph White. 1939. Patterns of aggressive behavior in experimentally created "social climates." *Journal of Social Psychology* 10: 271–99; White, Ronald K., and Ralph Lippitt. 1968. Leader behavior and member reaction in three "social climates." In *Group dynamics: Research and theory*, 3d ed., ed. D. Cartwright and A. Zander, 318–35. New York: Harper & Row.

6. Ibid.

7. Van Vugt, Mark, Sarah F. Jepson, Claire M. Hart, and David De Cremer. 2004. Autocratic leadership in social dilemmas: A threat to group stability. *Journal of Experimental Social Psychology* 40(1): 1–13.

8. De Cremer, David. 2006. Affective and motivational consequences of leader self-sacrifice: The moderating effect of autocratic leadership. *Leadership Quarterly* 17(1): 79–93.

9. Gastil, John, Stephanie Burkhalter, and Laura W. Black. 2007. Do juries deliberate? A study of deliberation, individual difference, and group member satisfaction at a municipal courthouse. *Small Group Research* 38(3): 337–59.

10. Fricher, Josef. 2006. *Laissez-faire leadership versus empowering leadership in new product development*, 1. Aalborg, Denmark: Danish Centre for Philosophy and Science Studies.

11. Ibid.

12. Bennis, W., and H. Shepard, 1956. A theory of group development. *Human Relations* 9: 415–37; Tuckman, B. W., 1965. Developmental sequence in small groups. *Psychological Bulletin* 63: 384–99.

13. Tuckman, Developmental sequence in small groups.

14. Tuckman, Bruce W., and Mary Ann C. Jensen. 1977. Stages of small group development revisited. *Group and Organizational Studies* 2: 419–27.

15. Wheelan, Susan A. 1994. *Group processes: A developmental perspective*. Boston: Allyn and Bacon; Wheelan, Susan A., Barbara Davidson, and Felice Tilin. 2003. Group development across time: Reality or illusion? *Small Group Research* 34: 223–45.

16. Wheelan, Susan A. 2010. *Creating effective teams: A guide for members and leaders*. Thousand Oaks, CA: Sage; Bion, W. R. 1952. Group dynamics: A review. *International Journal of Psychoanalysis* 33(2): 235–47; Bion, W. R. 1961. *Experience in groups*. New York: Basic Books; Cholden, L. 1953. Group therapy with the blind. *Group Psychotherapy* 6: 21–29.

17. Bennis and Shepard, A theory of group development.

18. Forsyth, Donelson R. 2009. *Group dynamics*. Belmont, CA: Wadsworth Cengage Learning.

19. Dias de Figueiredo, António, and Afonso Ana Paula. 2006. Context and learning: A philosophical framework. In *Managing learning in virtual settings: The role of context*, ed. António Dias de Figueiredo and Afonso Ana Paula. Hershey, PA: IGI Global.

20. Benne, Kenneth D., and Paul Sheats. 1948. Functional roles of group members. *Journal of Social Issues* 4(2): 41–49.

21. Johnson, D. W., and F. P. Johnson. 1975. *Joining together: Group theory and group skills.* Upper Saddle River, NJ: Prentice-Hall.

22. Adapted from Johnson, D. W., and F. P. Johnson, 1975. *Joining together: Group theory and Group skills.* Upper Saddle River, NJ: Prentice-Hall.

23. Ibid.

24. Zimbardo, Philip G. 2009. Stanford prison experiment: A simulation study of the psychology of imprisonment conducted at Stanford University. Retrieved April 30, 2010, from http://www.prisonexp.org/.

25. Zimbardo, Stanford prison experiment; Haney, Craig, Curtis Banks, and Philip Zimbardo. 1973; Interpersonal dynamics in a simulated prison. *International Journal of Criminology and Penology* 1: 69–97.

26. Zimbardo, Philip. 2007. *The Lucifer effect: Understanding how good people turn evil.* New York: Random House; Zimbardo, Stanford prison experiment; Haney et al., Interpersonal dynamics in a simulated prison.

27. Zimbardo, *The Lucifer effect.*

28. Personal interview with Annie McKee, 2010.

29. Druskat, Vanessa U., and Steven B. Wolff. 2001. Building the emotional intelligence of groups. *Harvard Business Review* 79(3): 80–91

30. Ibid., 86.

31. Merriam-Webster Dictionary Online. Status. Retrieved April 2, 2010, from http://www.merriam-webster.com/dictionary/status.

32. Lin, Nan. 2001. *Social capital: A theory of social structure and action.* New York: Cambridge University Press.

33. Boyd, Danah. 2008. Why youth ♥ social network sites: The role of networked publics in teenage social life. In *Youth, identity, and digital media,* ed. David Buckingham, 119–42. Cambridge, MA: The MIT Press.

34. Agha, Asif. 2007. *Language and social relations.* Cambridge: Cambridge University Press.

35. Bourdieu, Pierre. 1983. The forms of capital. In *Handbook of theory and research for the sociology of education,* ed. John G. Richardson, 241–58. New York: Greenwood Press; Asante, Molefi, and Alice Davis. 1985. Black and white communication: Analyzing work place encounters. *Journal of Black Studies* 16: 77–93; Kirchmeyer, Catherine, and Aaron Cohen. 1992. *Group and Organization Management* 17(2): 153–170.

36. French, John R. P., and Bertram Raven. The bases of social power. In J. Thomas Wren, Douglas A Hicks, and Terry L Price (eds.), *The international library of leadership,* vol. 2, 150–67. Northampton, MA: Edward Elgar Publishing, Inc.

37. Mead, Margaret. 1977. *Sex and temperament in three primitive societies.* London: Routledge (p. 322).

38. Progoff, Ira. 1999. *Jung's psychology and its social meaning.* London: Routledge.

39. Myers-Briggs Foundation. Sensing or intuition. Retrieved April 5, 2010, from http://www.myersbriggs.org/my-mbti-personality-type/mbti-basics/sensing-or-intuition.asp; Golden LLC, Golden Personality Type Profiler frequently asked questions. Retrieved April 5, 2010, from http://www.goldenllc.com/about_GPTP_FAQ.htm.

40. Progoff, *Jung's psychology and its social meaning.*

41. Myers-Briggs Foundation. Thinking or feeling. Retrieved April 5, 2010, from http://www.myersbriggs.org/my-mbti-personality-type/mbti-basics/thinking-or-feeling.asp; Golden LLC, Golden Personality Type Profiler frequently asked questions.

42. Myers-Briggs Foundation. Extraversion or introversion. Retrieved April 5, 2010, from http://www.myersbriggs.org/my-mbti-personality-type/mbti-basics/extraversion-or-introversion.asp; Golden LLC, Golden Personality Type Profiler frequently asked questions.

43. Myers-Briggs Foundation. Judging or perceiving. Retrieved April 5, 2010, from http://www.myersbriggs.org/my-mbti-personality-type/mbti-basics/judging-or-perceiving.asp; Golden LLC, Golden Personality Type Profiler frequently asked questions.

44. Golden LLC. About Golden LLC Products. Retrieved April 29, 2010, from http://www.goldenllc.com/About_GPTP.htm; Golden Personality Type Profiler frequently asked questions.

45. Kolb, David. 1984. *Experiential learning: Experience as the source of learning and development.* Englewood Cliffs, NJ: Prentice-Hall.

46. Kolb, David A. 1999. *Learning style inventory: Technical manual.* Boston: Hay/McBer.

47. Kolb, *Experiential learning.*

48. Greiner, Walter. 2001. *Quantum mechanics: An introduction.* New York: Springer.

49. Smith, Kenwyn K., and David N. Berg. 1987. *Paradoxes of group life: Understanding conflict, paralysis, and movement in group dynamics.* San Francisco: Jossey-Bass.

50. Ibid.

51. Ibid.

52. Ibid., 135.

53. Ibid.

54. Ibid.

55. Katzenbach, Jon R., and Douglas K. Smith. 1993. *The wisdom of teams: Creating the high-performance organization.* New York: HarperCollins, xiii.

56. Katzenbach, Jon R., and Douglas K. Smith. 1993. The discipline of teams. *Harvard Business Review* 71: 111–20.

57. Ibid; Katzenbach, Jon R., and Douglas K., Smith. 1994. Teams at the top. *McKinsey Quarterly* 1: 71–79.

58. Katzenbach and Smith. *The wisdom of teams.*

59. Katzenbach, Jon R., and Douglas K. Smith. 1993. *The wisdom of teams: Creating the high-performance organization.* Boston: Harvard Business School Press, 65.

60. Katzenbach and Smith. *The wisdom of teams.*

61. Ibid.

62. Hackman, Richard. 1987. The design of work teams. In *Handbook of organizational behavior,* ed. J. Lorsch. Englewood Cliffs, NJ: Prentice Hall; Hackman, J. R., & Morris, C. G., 1975. Group tasks, group interaction process, and group performance effectiveness: A review and proposed integration. In *Advances in experimental social psychology,* vol. 8, ed. L. Berkowitz, 45099. New York: Academic Press.

63. Karau, S. J., and K. D. Williams. 1993. Social loafing: A meta-analytic review and theoretical integration. *Journal of Personality and Social Psychology* 65: 681–706.

64. Asch, Solomon E. 1951. Effects of group pressure upon the modification and distortion of judgments. In *Groups, leadership and men,* ed. H. Guetzkow, 177–90. Pittsburgh, PA: Carnegie Press; Asch, Solomon E. 1955. Opinions and social pressure. *Scientific American* 193(5): 31–35; Asch, S. E. 1956. Studies of independence and conformity: A minority of one against a unanimous majority. *Psychological Monographs* 70(9): (Whole No. 416).

65. Ibid.

66. Hodges, Bert H., and Anne L. Geyer 2006. A nonconformist account of the Asch experiments: Values, pragmatics, and moral dilemmas. *Personality and Social Psychology Review* 10(1): 2–19.

67. Janis, I. L., and L. Mann. 1977. *Decision making: A psychological analysis of conflict, choice, and commitment,* 129. New York: The Free Press.

68. Sims, Ronald R. 1992. Linking groupthink to unethical behavior in organizations. *Journal of Business Ethics* 11: 651–62; Adler, Stephen J. 2009. Beware groupthink on the economy. *Business Week* (February 16), 00077135, Issue 4119.

69. Argyris, Chris. 1977. Double-loop learning in organizations. *Harvard Business Review* 55(5): 115–25.

70. Napier, Matti K. and Gershenfield, Rodney W. 2007. Groups: theory and experience (edition 7). Hillside, NJ: Lawrence Erlbaum Associates, 133.

71. Jassawalla, Avan R., and Hemant C. Sashittal. 1993. Building collaborative cross-functional new product teams. *Academy of Management Executive* 13(3): 50–63.

72. Jehn, Karen A. 1997. A qualitative analysis of conflict types and dimensions in organizational groups. *Administrative Science Quarterly* 42(3): 530–57.

73. Jehn, Karen A., and Elizabeth A. Mannix. 2001. The dynamic nature of conflict: A longitudinal study of intergroup conflict and group performance. *Academy of Management* 44(2): 238–51.

74. Paulas, P. B., and B. A. Nijistad. 2003. *Group creativity: Innovation thought collaboration.* Oxford, UK: Oxford University Press; Laughlin, P. R., M. L. Zanderr, E. M. Knievel, and T. K. Tan. 2003. Groups perform better than the best individuals on letter-to-numbers problems: Informative equations and effective strategies. *Journal of Personality and Social Psychology* 85: 684–94.

75. Hardin, Russell. 1995. *One for all: The logic of group conflict.* Princeton, NJ: Princeton University Press.

76. Ansari, Shahzad, Frank Wijen, and Barbara Gray. 2009. Averting the 'tragedy of the commons': An institutional perspective on the construction and governance of transnational commons. *Academy of Management Proceedings* 2009: 1–6; Hardin, Garrett. 1968. The tragedy of the commons. *Science* 162(3859): 1243–1248.

77. Brehmer, B. 1976. Social judgment theory and the analysis of interpersonal conflict. *Psychological Bulletin* 83: 985–1003.

78. De Drue, C. K. W., and L. R. Weingart. 2003. Task versus relationship conflict, team performance, and team member satisfaction: A meta-analysis. *Journal of Applied Psychology* 86: 1191–201.

79. Jehn, Karen A., and Elizabeth A. Mannix. 2001. The dynamic nature of conflict: A longitudinal study of intragroup conflict and group performance. *Academy of Management*, 44(2): 238–251.

80. Ibid.

81. Smith and Berg, *Paradoxes of group life*.

82. Greenhaus, Jeffrey H., and Nicholas J. Beutell. 1985. Sources of conflict between work and family roles. *Academy of Management Review* 10(1): 76–88.

83. Smith and Berg, *Paradoxes of group life*.

84. Ibid.

85. Tindale, R. S., A. Dykema-Engblade, and E. Wittkowski. 2005. Conflict within and between groups. In *Handbook of group research and practice*, ed. S. Wheelan. Thousand Oaks, CA: Sage.

86. Deutsch, M. 1973. *The resolution of conflict*. New Haven, CT: Yale University Press.

87. Harvard Business Essentials. 2003. *Negotiation*. Boston: Harvard Business School Publishing.

88. Ibid.

89. McKee, Annie, Richard Boyatzis, and Frances Johnston. 2008. *Becoming a resonant leader: Develop your emotional intelligence, renew your relationships and sustain your effectiveness*. Boston: Harvard Business School Press.

90. Hargie, Owen, and David Dickson. 2004. *Skilled interpersonal communication: Research, theory and practice*. New York: Routledge; Barbara, Dominick A. 1959. The art of listening. *Communication Quarterly* 7(1): 5–7; West, Richard, and Lynn H. Turner. 2006. *Understanding interpersonal communication: Making choices in changing times*. Boston: Wadsworth Cengage Learning.

91. Rogers, Carl R., and Richard E. Farson. 1987. Active listening. In *Communication in business today*, ed. R. G. Newman, M. A. Danziger, and M. Cohen. Washington, DC: Heath and Company.

92. Hoppe, Michael H. 2006. *Active listening: Improve your ability to listen and lead*. Greensboro, NC: Center for Creative Leadership.

93. Goodwin, Charles. 2007. Participation, stance and affect in the organization of activities. *Discourse & Society* 18(1): 53–73.

94. Rogers and Farson, Active listening.

95. Hill, Gayle W. 1982. Group versus individual performance: Are *N* + 1 heads better than one? *Psychological Bulletin* 91(3): 517–39.

96. Ibid.

97. Janus, Irving L. 1982. *Groupthink: Psychological studies of policy decisions and fiascoes*. Boston: Houghton Mifflin. Cox, Taylor H., and Stacey Blake. 1991. Managing cultural diversity: Implications for organizational competitiveness. *Academy of Management Executive* 5(3): 45–56.

Chapter 11

1. Kumar, Krishnan. 1995. *From post-industrial to post-modern society*, 62. Malden, MA: Blackwell Publishing.

2. Emery, F. 1959. *Characteristics of sociotechnical systems*. London: Tavistock Institute for Human Relations; Herbst, P. G. 1974. *Socio-technical design*. London: Tavistock Institute for Human Relations.

3. Trist, Eric L., and K. W. Bamforth. 1951. Some social and psychological consequences of the long wall method of coal-getting. *Human Relations* 4(1): 3–38.

4. Emery, F. L., and E. L. Trist. 1969. Socio-technical systems. In *Systems thinking*, ed. F. E. Emery, 281–96. London: Penguin; Pasmore, William, Carole Francis, Jeffrey Haldeman, and Abraham Shani. 1982. Sociotechnical systems: A North American reflection on empirical studies of the seventies. *Human Relations* 35(12): 1179–1204; Damanpour, Fairborz, and William M. Evan. 1984. Organizational innovation and performance: The problem of "organizational lag." *Administrative Science Quarterly* 29(3): 392–409.

5. Pasmore et al., Organizational innovation and performance; R. W. Woodman and W. A. Pasmore, 235–313. Greenwich, CT: JAI Press.

6. McKee, Annie, Richard Boyatzis, and Frances Johnston. 2008. *Becoming a resonant leader: Develop your emotional intelligence, renew your relationships and sustain your effectiveness*. Boston: Harvard Business School Press.

7. Reich, Robert. 2008. *The work of nations: Preparing ourselves for 21st century capitalism*. New York: Simon and Schuster.

8. Rifkin, Jeremy. 2010. *The empathic civilization: The race to global consciousness in a world in crisis*. New York: Jeremy P. Tarcher/Penguin.

9. Mokyr, Joel. 1999. Editor's introduction: The new economic history and the Industrial Revolution. In *The British Industrial Revolution: An economic perspective*, ed. Joel Mokyr, 1–31. Boulder, CO: Westview Press.

10. Landes, David. 1999. The fable of the dead horse; or, the Industrial Revolution revisited. In *The British Industrial Revolution: An economic perspective*, ed. Joel Mokyr, 128–59. Boulder, CO: Westview Press.

11. Gay, Peter. 1977. *The Enlightenment: An interpretation*, Vol. 2. New York: Norton.

12. Smith, Adam. 2000. *The wealth of nations*, 15. New York: Modern Library.

13. Smith, *The wealth of nations*.

14. Marx, Karl. 1988. *The Communist manifesto*, ed. Frederic L. Bender. New York: W. W. Norton.

15. Landes, David. 1969. *The unbound Prometheus: Technological change and industrial development in Western Europe from 1750 to the present*. New York: Cambridge University Press.

16. Drucker, Peter F. 1942. *The future of industrial man*. Omaha, NE: John Day Company.

17. Adams, Brooks. 1901. The new Industrial Revolution. *Atlantic Monthly* (February): 165; Lauck, W. Jett. 1929. *The new Industrial Revolution and wages*. New York: Funk and Wagnalls.

18. Braudel, Fernand. 1979. *Civilization and capitalism: 15th–18th century*. Berkeley: University of California Press.

19. Lovejoy, Paul E. 1983. *Transformations in slavery: A history of slavery in Africa*. New York: Cambridge University Press; Encyclopædia Britannica Guide to Black History. 2009. Slavery. Retrieved December 30, 2009, from http://www.britannica.com/blackhistory/article-24156.

20. Rothenberg, Paula S. 2006. *Beyond borders: Thinking critically about global issues*. New York: Worth Publishers.

21. Know India. 2008. Indian freedom struggle (1857–1947). Retrieved December 31, 2009, from http://india.gov.in/knowindia/history_freedom_struggle.php; Rothenberg, *Beyond borders*.

22. Amin, Samir. 1976. *Unequal development*. New York: Monthly Review Press.

23. Know India, Indian freedom struggle.

24. Amin, *Unequal development*.

25. Wood, Michael. 2000. *Conquistadors*. Los Angeles: University of California Press.

26. Rieger, Joerg. 2007. *Christ and empire: From Paul to post-colonial times*. Minneapolis, MN: Fortress Press.

27. O'Brien, Patrick Karl. 1997. Intercontinental trade and the development of the Third World since the Industrial Revolution. *Journal of World History* 8(1): 75–133.

28. Ibid.

29. Maddison, Angus. Explaining the economic performance of nations, 1820–1989. In *Convergence of productivity: Cross-national studies and historical evidence*, ed. William J. Baumol, Richard R. Nelson, and Edward N. Wolff, 20–61. New York: Oxford University Press.

30. Hirschman, Albert O. 1968. The political economy of import-substituting industrialization in Latin America. *Quarterly Journal of Economics* 82(1): 1–32; Naim, Moises. 1993. Latin America: Post-adjustment blues. *Foreign Policy* 92: 133–150.

31. Wong, Kam C. 2000. Black's theory on the behavior of law revisited IV: The behavior of Qing law. *International Journal of the Sociology of Law* 28: 327–374.

32. Teng, Ssu-yü, and John King Fairbank. 1954. *China's response to the West: A documentary survey, 1839–1923*. Boston: President and Fellows of Harvard College.

33. Goldstone, Jack A. 1996. Gender, work, and culture: Why the Industrial Revolution came early to England but late to China. *Sociological Perspectives* 39(1): 1–21.

34. Ibid.

35. Lavely, W., and R. Bin Wong. 1990. *Population and resources in modern China: Institutions in the balance*. Unpublished manuscript; Lavely, W., and R. Bin Wong. 1992. Family division and mobility in North China. *Comparative Studies in Society and History* 3(4): 439–463.

36. Machlup, Fritz. 1962. *The production and distribution of knowledge in the United States*. Princeton, NJ: Princeton University Press.

37. Bell, D. 1973. *The coming of post-industrial society*, 127. New York: Basic Books.

38. Foundation on Economic Trends. The hydrogen economy. Retrieved January 19, 2010, from http://www.foet.org/lectures/lecture-hydrogen-economy.html.

39. Anderson, Kurt. 2009. *Reset: How this crisis can restore our values and renew America*. New York: Random House.

40. Rifkin, *The empathic civilization*.

41. Thomas, Chris Allen. 2009. Using technology to reintegrate learning and doing: IBM's approach and its implications for education. In *Handbook*

of research on e-learning applications for career and technical education: Technologies for vocational training, 2009, ed. Victor Wang, 59–70. Hershey, PA: IGI Global; Liu, Jianxun, Shensheng Zhang, and Jinming Hu. 2005. A case study of an inter-enterprise workflow-supported supply chain management system. *Information and Management* 42(3): 441–54.

42. Thomas, Using technology to reintegrate learning and doing.

43. Corporate Affiliations. Intel hierarchy. Retrieved May 11, 2010, from http://corporateaffiliations.ecnext.com.

44. Liu et al., A case study of an inter-enterprise workflow-supported supply chain management system.

45. Lustig, Myron W., and Jolene Koestner. 1996. *Intercultural competence: Interpersonal communication across cultures*. New York: HarperCollins College Publishers.

46. Bureau of Labor Statistics. 2006. *International comparisons of manufacturing productivity and unit labor cost trends, 2005*. Washington, D.C.: United States Department of Labor.

47. Bell, *The coming of post-industrial society*; Friedman, Thomas. 2006. *The world is flat*. New York: Farrar, Straus, and Giroux.

48. Quinn, James B. 1999. Strategic outsourcing: Leveraging knowledge capabilities. *Sloan Management Review* 40(4): 9–21.

49. Ackman, Dan. 2002. Dock deal historic in more ways than one. *Forbes* (November 25). Retrieved January 4, 2010, from http://www.forbes.com/2002/11/25/cx_da_1125topnews.html.

50. Sridhar, V. 2002. Locked out of the docks. *Frontline* 19:23. Retrieved January 4, 2010, from http://www.thehindu.com/fline/fl1923/stories/20021122001408800.htm.

51. Arabe, Katrina C. 2002. The aftermath of the West Coast port shutdown. *Industry Market Trends* (December 12). Retrieved January 4, 2010, from http://news.thomasnet.com/IMT/archives/2002/12/the_aftermath_o.html.

52. Hafner, Katie, and Matthew Lyon. 1996. *Where wizards stay up late: The origins of the Internet*. New York: Touchstone.

53. Tomlinson, Ray. The first network e-mail. Retrieved January 5, 2010, from http://openmap.bbn.com/~tomlinso/ray/firste-mailframe.html.

54. Leiner, Barry M., et al. 2009. A brief history of the Internet. *ACM SIGCOMM Computer Communication Review* 39(5): 22–31.

55. Berners-Lee, Tim, Robert Cailliau, A. Lontonen, H. F. Nielsen, and A. Secret. 1994. The world-wide web. *Communications of the ACM* 37: 76–82.

56. Ibid.

57. Google. Corporate history. Retrieved December 22, 2009, from http://www.google.com/corporate/history.html; Google. The official Google blog. Retrieved April 10, 2010, from http://googleblog.blogspot.com/2008/07/we-knew-web-was-big.html.

58. O'Reilly, Tim. 2005. *What is Web 2.0: Design patterns and business models for the next generation of software*. Sebastopol, CA: O'Reilly Media. Retrieved April 10, 2010, from http://www.oreillynet.com/pub/a/oreilly/tim/news/2005/09/30/what-is-web-20.html?page=1.

59. Shuen, Amy. 2008. *Web 2.0: A strategy guide*. Sebastopol, CA: O'Reilly Media.

60. Ibid.

61. Hayes, Brian. 2009. Cloud computing: As software migrates from local PCs to distant Internet servers, users and developers alike go along for the ride. *Communications of the ACM* 51(7): 9–11.

62. TechTarget.com. Cloud computing. Retrieved December 31, 2009, from http://searchcloudcomputing.techtarget.com/sDefinition/0,,sid201_gci1287881,00.html.

63. Google. GoogleApps. Retrieved April 10, 2010, from http://www.google.com/apps/intl/en/business/index.html#utm_campaign=en&utm_source=en-ha-na-us-bk&utm_medium=ha&utm_term=google%20apps.

64. Amazon Web Services. Amazon Elastic Compute Cloud. Retrieved April 10, 2010, from http://aws.amazon.com/ec2.

65. Apple. Mobileme. Retrieved April 10, 2010, from http://www.apple.com/mobileme.

66. Gruber, Harold. 2005. *The economics of mobile telecommunications*. New York: Cambridge University Press.

67. CTIA. 2009. Background on CTIA's semi-annual wireless industry survey. Retrieved January 19, 2009, from http://files.ctia.org/pdf/CTIA_Survey_Midyear_2009_Graphics.pdf; People's Daily Online. 2009. *Over 700 million mobile phone users in China* (September 3). Retrieved January 19, 2009, from http://english.people.com.cn/90001/90778/90857/90860/6747627.html; Telecom Regulatory Authority of India. 2009. Telecom subscription data as on 30th November 2009. Retrieved January 19, 2009, from http://www.trai.gov.in/WriteReadData/trai/upload/PressReleases/712/pr23dec09no79.pdf.

68. International Telecommunication Union. 2009. *ITU corporate annual report 2008*. Retrieved January 18, 2009, from http://www.itu.int/dms_pub/itu-s/opb/conf/S-CONF-AREP-2008-E06-PDF-E.pdf.

69. McKee, Annie, and Richard Boyatzis. 2005. *Resonant leadership: Renewing yourself and connecting with others through mindfulness, hope and compassion*, 24. Boston: Harvard Business School Press.

70. Vartiainen, Matti. 2006. Mobile virtual work—Concepts, outcomes, and challenges. In *Mobile virtual work: A new paradigm?*, ed. J. H. Erik Andriessen and Matti Vartiainen. New York: Springer.

71. Lucas, Henry C. 1994. The role of information technology in organization design. *Journal of Management Information Systems*, v10 (4): p. 7.

72. Jones, Jeffrey M. 2006. One in three U.S. workers have "telecommuted" to work. *Gallup* (August 16). Retrieved December 28, 2009, from http://www.gallup.com/poll/24181/One-Three-US-Workers-Telecommuted-Work.aspx.

73. Saad, Lydia. 2008. Telecommuting still a rare perk. *Gallup* (August 15). Retrieved December 28, 2009, from http://www.gallup.com/poll/109546/Telecommuting-Still-Rare-Perk.aspx.

74. Ibid.

75. BusinessDictionary.com. Hoteling. Retrieved April 10, 2010, from http://www.businessdictionary.com/definition/hoteling.html.

76. Rees, Paul. 2008. Shifting sands. *Communications Review* (PricewaterhouseCooper publication) 13: 2.

77. Richards, Howard, and Harris Makatsoris. 2002. The metamorphosis to dynamic trading networks and virtual corporations. In *Managing virtual web organizations in the 21st century: Issues and challenges*, ed. Ulrich Franke, 75. Hershey, PA: Idea Publishing Group.

78. McDaniel, Christie L. 2008. Removing space and time: Tips for managing the virtual workplace. In *Handbook of research on virtual workplaces and the new nature of business practices*, ed. Pavel Zemliansky. Hershey, PA: IGI Global.

79. Nemiro, Jill, Lori Bradley, Michael M. Beyerlein, and Susan Beyerlein, eds. 2008. *The handbook of high-performance virtual teams*. San Francisco: Jossey-Bass.

80. Burn, Janice, Peter Marshall, and Martin Barnett. 2002. *E-business strategies for virtual organizations*. Woodburn, MA: Butterworth-Heinemann.

81. Fiol, C. Marlene, and Edward J. O'Conner 2005. Identification in face-to-face, hybrid, and pure virtual teams: Untangling the contradictions. *Organization Science* 16(1): 19–32.

82. Nemiro, Jill. 2000. The glue that binds creative virtual teams. In *Knowledge management and new organization forms: A framework for business model innovation*, 102. Hershey, PA: Idea Group Publishing.

83. Malhotra, Arvind, Ann Majchrzak, Robert Carman, and Vern Lott. 2001. Radical innovation without collocation: A case study at Boeing-Rocketdyne. *MIS Quarterly* 25(2): 229–49.

84. Braga, David, Steve Jones, and Dennis Bowyer. 2008. Problem solving in virtual teams. In *The handbook of high-performance virtual teams: A toolkit for collaborating across boundaries*, ed. Jill Nemiro, Michael M. Beyerlein, Lori Bradley, and Susan Beyerlein, 391–404. San Francisco: Jossey-Bass.

85. Lucas, The role of information technology in organization design.

86. Wilson, Jeanne M., Susan G. Straus, and Bill McEvily. 2005. All in due time: The development of trust in computer-mediated and face-to-face teams. *Organizational Behavior and Human Decision Processes* 99(1): 16–33.

87. Hinrichs, Gina, Jane Seiling, and Jackie Stavros. 2008. Sensemaking to create high-performing virtual teams. In *The handbook of high-performance virtual teams: A toolkit for collaborating across boundaries*, ed. Jill Nemiro, Michael M. Beyerlein, Lori Bradley, and Susan Beyerlein, 131–52. San Francisco: Jossey-Bass.

88. Ronfeldt, David. 1996. *Tribes, institutions, markets, networks: A framework about societal evolution*. Santa Monica, CA: RAND; Arquilla, John, and David Ronfeldt. 1996. *The advent of netwar*, 30. Santa Monica, CA: RAND National Defense Research Institute.

89. Sculley, John. 1992. Quoted in Forbes ASAP. *Forbes* 150(13): 26.

90. DeSanctis, Geraldine, and Peter Monge. 1998. Communication process for virtual organizations. *Journal of Computer-Mediated Communication*: 3(4): 2.

91. Mortimer, Ruth. Avon calling for a new generation. Retrieved September 12, 2009, from http://www.marketingweek.co.uk/trends/avon-calling-for-a-new-generation/2065550.article.

92. Ibid.

93. Alliston, Ackerman. 2008. Avon connects worldwide innovation efforts. *Consumer Goods Technology Online* (September 18). Retrieved April 10, 2010, from http://www.consumergoods.com/ME2/dirmod.asp?sid=234FFCB1E8DF4FACBAFF60DFFD8AD37C&nm=Sample+Navigation&type=MultiPublishing&mod=PublishingTitles&mid=A533BDC658 2947448BBFA37BFF6394FF&tier=4&id=96BD83235435486798B178D A3537D300.

94. Ibid.

95. Avon Products. 2009. Avon annual report 2008 (March 26). Retrieved September 12, 2009, from http://www.avoncompany.com/investor/annualreport/pdf/annualreport2008.pdf.

96. Rodewald, Wendy. 2007. Avon calling: How three 40+ women found their dream jobs. *MORE Magazine* (January 17). Retrieved September 12, 2009, from http://www.more.com/2009/3184-avon-calling—how-three-40-.

97. Bosman, Julie. 2006. For the Avon lady, a world beyond ringing doorbells. *New York Times* (May 1). Retrieved April 10, 2010, from http://query.nytimes.com/gst/fullpage.html?res=9E04EFDF113FF932A 35756C0A9609C8B63.

98. Mortimer, Avon calling for a new generation.

99. Bosman, For the Avon lady.

100. Burn et al., *E-business strategies for virtual organizations*.

101. Katzy, Bernhard, Chungyan Zhang, and Hermann Löh. 2005. Reference models for virtual organizations. In *Virtual organizations: Systems and practices*, ed. Luis M. Camarinha-Matos, Hamideh Afsarmanesh, and Martin Ollus, 45–58. New York: Springer Science+Business Media.

102. Netflix. Finish Netflix free trial sign up. Retrieved April 10, 2010, from http://www.netflix.com/NRD/Xbox?mqso=80025846.

103. Burn et al., *E-business strategies for virtual organizations*, 46.

104. Katzy et al., Reference models for virtual organizations.

105. Burn et al., *E-business strategies for virtual organizations*, 46.

106. Katzy et al., Reference models for virtual organizations.

107. Ambrosek, Renee. 2007. *Shawn Fanning: The founder of Napster*. New York: Rosen Publishing Group.

108. Sienkiewicz, Stan. 2001. *Credit cards and payment efficiency*. Philadelphia: Federal Reserve Bank of Philadelphia.

109. Moore, David W. 2002. Only one in six Americans is without a credit card. *Gallup* (May 22). Retrieved January 20, 2010, from http://www.gallup.com/poll/6067/Only-One-Six-Americans-Without-Credit-Card.aspx.

110. Ibid.

111. Hayashi, Fumiko, Richard Sullivan, and Stuart E. Weiner. 2003. *A guide to the ATM and debit card industry*. Kansas City, MO: Federal Reserve Bank of Kansas City.

112. Ibid.

113. Robat, Cornelis, ed. 2006. ATM automatic teller machines. The history of computing project. Retrieved January 20, 2010, from http://www.thocp.net/hardware/atm.htm.

114. Furst, Karen, William W. Lang, and Daniel E. Nolle. 2002. Internet banking. *Journal of Financial Services Research* 22(1): 95–117.

115. ING Bank of Canada. ING Direct. Retrieved April 10, 2010, from http://www.ingdirect.ca/en/; Wikipedia. ING Group. Retrieved April 10, 2010, from http://en.wikipedia.org/wiki/ING_Direct.

116. ING Direct. About us. Retrieved April 10, 2010, from http://home.ingdirect.com/about/about.asp.

117. PayPal. About us. Retrieved April 10, 2010, from https://www.paypal-media.com/aboutus.cfm.

118. Kiva.org. About us. Retrieved April 10, 2010, from http://www.kiva.org/about.

119. Kiva.org. Loans that change lives. Retrieved April 10, 2010, from http://media.kiva.org/KIVA_brochure_6.1.07.pdf.

120. Kiva.org. About us.

121. Ibid.

122. Central Intelligence Agency. World Factbook: United States. Retrieved April 10, 2010, from https://www.cia.gov/library/publications/the-world-factbook/geos/us.html; Central Intelligence Agency. World Factbook: Uganda. Retrieved April 10, 2010, from https://www.cia.gov/library/publications/the-world-factbook/geos/ug.html; Central Intelligence Agency. World Factbook: Democratic Republic of the Congo. Retrieved April 10, 2010, from https://www.cia.gov/library/publications/the-world-factbook/geos/cg.html.

123. Spector, Robert. *Amazon.com: Get big fast: Inside the revolutionary business model that changed the world*. New York: Random House.

124. Amazon.com. Sell on Amazon. Retrieved April 10, 2010, from http://www.amazonservices.com/content/sell-on-amazon.htm?ld=AZFSSOA.

125. Collier, Marsha. 2009. *eBay for dummies*. Indianapolis, IN: Wiley Publishing.

126. Bates, T. 2001. National strategies for e-learning in post-secondary education and training. In *Fundamentals for educational planning*, no. 70, 1–135. Paris: United Nations Educational, Scientific and Cultural Organization (UNESCO).

127. Thomas, Chris Allen, Wendy Green, and Doug Lyncy. 2010. Online learning: An examination of contexts in corporate, higher education, and K-12 environments. In *Encyclopedia of information communication technologies and adult education integration*, ed. C. X. Victor. Hershey, PA: IGI Global.

128. Zemsky, R., and W. Massey. 2004. *Thwarted innovation: A Learning Alliance report*, 11. West Chester, PA: Learning Alliance. Retrieved January 6, 2010, from http://www.immagic.com/eLibrary/ARCHIVES/GENERAL/UPENN_US/P040600Z.pdf.

129. Riswadkar, Amit, and A. V. Riswadkar. 2009. Balancing the risks of remote working: Walking the telecommuting line. *John Liner Review* 23(2): 89–94.

130. Ibid.

131. Bernthal, Paul R., Karen Colteryahn, Patty Davis, Jennifer Naughton, William J. Rothwell, and Rich Wellins. 2004. *Mapping the future: New workplace learning and performance competencies*. Alexandria, VA: ASTD Press.

132. Offstein, Evan H., and Jason M. Morwick. 2009. *Making telework work: Leading people and leveraging technology for high-impact results*. Boston, MA: Nicholas Breatley Publishing.

133. Ibid.

134. Richtel, Matt. 2008. Lost in e-mail, tech firms face self-made beast. *New York Times* (June 14). Retrieved April 10, 2010, from http://www.nytimes.com/2008/06/14/technology/14email.html.

135. Information Overload Research Group. Homepage. Retrieved May 12, 2010, from http://iorgforum.org.

136. Richtel, Lost in e-mail, tech firms face self-made beast.

137. Eggen, Dan, Karen DeYoung, and Spencer S. Hsu. 2009. Plane suspect was listed in terror database after father alerted U.S. officials. *Washington Post* (December 27). Accessed April 10, 2010, from http://www.washingtonpost.com/wp-dyn/content/article/2009/12/25/AR2009122501355_2.html?sid=ST2009122601151.

138. Malhotra, Yogesh. 2000. *Knowledge management and new organization forms: A framework for business model innovation*, 11. Hershey, PA: Idea Group Publishing.

139. Boyatzis et al., *Resonant leadership*, 29.

140. Duarte, Deborah L., and Nancy Tennant Snyder. 2006. *Mastering virtual teams: Strategies, tools, and techniques that succeed*. San Francisco: Jossey-Bass.

141. Hinrichs et al., Sensemaking to create high-performing virtual teams.

142. Hertel, G., U. Konradt, and B. Orlikowski. 2004. Managing distance by interdependence: Goal setting, task interdependence and team-based rewards in virtual teams. *European Journal of Work and Organizational Psychology* 13: 1–28.

143. Duarte and Snyder, *Mastering virtual teams*.

144. Kayworth, T. R., and D. E. Leidner. 2001. Leadership effectiveness in global virtual teams. *Journal of Management Information Systems* 18: 7–40.

145. Kirkman, B. L., B. Rosen, P. E. Tesluk, and C. B. Gibson. 2004. The impact of team empowerment on virtual team performance: The moderating role of face-to-face interaction. *Academy of Management Journal* 47: 175–92.

146. Cascio, Wayne. 2000. Managing a virtual workplace. *Academy of Management Executive*; Vol. 14 (3) 84.

147. Friedman, *The world is flat*.

148. International Telecommunication Union. Cambodia. Retrieved April 10, 2010, from http://www.itu.int/ITU-D/icteye/Reporting/ShowReportFrame.aspx?ReportName=/WTI/InformationTechnologyPublic&RP_intYear=2008&RP_intLanguageID=1.

149. World Summit on the Information Society. 2006. *Report of the Tunis phase of the World Summit on the Information Society: Tunis, Kram Palexpo, November 16–18, 2005*. Retrieved December 22, 2009, from http://www.itu.int/wsis/index-p2.html.

Chapter 12

1. Interview with Spencer Phillips, conducted by Suzanne Rotondo on September 29, 2009.
2. Marx, Karl. 1959. *The economic and philosophic manuscripts of 1844.* Trans. Martin Milligan. Moscow: Progress Publishers.
3. Taylor, Frederick Winslow. 1911. *Principles of scientific management.* New York: Harper and Brothers.
4. Stewart, Matthew. 2009. *The management myth: Why the experts keep getting it wrong.* New York: Norton.
5. Ibid.
6. Follett Foundation. 2010. Mary Parker Follett. Retrieved April 5, 2010, from http://www.follettfoundation.org/mpf.htm.
7. Mockler, Robert J. 1970. *Readings in management control.* New York: Appleton-Century-Crofts; Graham, Pauline, ed. 2003. *Mary Parker Follet: Prophet of management.* Frederick, MD: Beard Books.
8. Goleman, Daniel, Richard E. Boyatzis, and Annie McKee. 2002. *Primal leadership: Learning to lead with emotional intelligence.* Boston: Harvard Business School Press; Boyatzis, Richard, and Annie McKee. 2005. *Resonant leadership; Renewing yourself and connecting with others through mindfulness, hope and compassion.* Boston: Harvard Business School Press; Bowen, Benjamin, and David Bowen. 1995. *Winning the service game.* Boston: Harvard Business School Press.
9. Boyatzis and McKee, *Resonant leadership.*
10. Smith, Vernon. 2003. Constructivist and ecological rationality. *American Economic Review* 93(111): 485–508.
11. Boyatzis and McKee, *Resonant leadership.*
12. Nguyen, Vu, Ronald Lee, and Kaushik Dutta. 2006. An aspect architecture for modeling organizational controls in workflow systems. Paper presented at DESRIST conference, February 24–25 (Claremont, CA): 172–191.
13. Ferner, Anthony. 2007. The underpinnings of "bureaucratic" control systems: HRM in European multinationals. *Journal of Management Studies* 37(4): 521–40.
14. Frost, Peter. 2003. *Toxic emotions at work.* Boston: Harvard Business School Press.
15. Ouchi, William G. 1979. A conceptual framework for the design of organizational control mechanisms. *Management Science* 25(9): 833–48.
16. Eisenhardt, Kathleen M. 1985. Control: Organizational and economic approaches. *Management Science* 31(2): 134–49.
17. Leifer, Richard, and Peter K. Mills. 1996. An information processing approach for deciding upon control strategies and reducing control loss in emerging organizations. *Journal of Management* 22(1): 113–37.
18. Snell, Scott A. 1992. Control theory in strategic human resource management: The mediating effect of administrative information. *Academy of Management Journal* 35(2): 292–327.
19. Ouchi, William G. 1977. The relationship between organizational structure and organizational control. *Administrative Science Quarterly* 20: 95–113.
20. Horngren, Charles T. 2006. *Cost accounting: A managerial emphasis,* 12th ed. Upper Saddle River, NJ: Prentice-Hall.
21. Interview with Dan Teree, conducted by Suzanne Rotondo on October 1, 2009.
22. Simons, Robert. 1994. *Levers of control: How managers use innovative control systems to drive strategic renewal.* Boston: Harvard Business School Press.
23. Ibid.
24. Schleifer, Andrei, and Robert W. Vishny. 1997. A survey of corporate governance. *Journal of Finance* 52(2): 737–83.
25. Berglöf, Erik, and Ernst-Ludwig von Thadden. 1999. The changing corporate governance paradigm: Implications for transition and developing countries. In *Corporate governance and globalization: Long range planning issues,* ed. Stephen S. Cohen and Gavin Boyd, 275–306. Northampton, MA: Edward Elgar Publishing.
26. Jensen, Michael. 1998. *Foundations of organisational strategy.* Boston: Harvard Business School Press.
27. Civil Rights Act of 1964. Title VII: Equal employment opportunities. 42 USC Chapter 21.
28. A study commissioned by New York City Mayor Michael Bloomberg and U.S. Sen. Charles Schumer cites this as one reason why America's financial sector is losing market share to other financial centers worldwide. See http://schumer.senate.gov/new_website/record.cfm?id=267787&.
29. U.S. House of Representatives. USC Chapter 98. Retrieved May 12, 2010, from http://uscode.house.gov/download/pls/15C98.txt.
30. Taylor, William C. 2006. To charge up customers, put customers in charge. *New York Times* (June 18). Retrieved November 11, 2009, from http://www.nytimes.com/2006/06/18/business/yourmoney/18mgmt.html.
31. Ibid.
32. Lindberg, Oliver. 2009. The secrets behind Threadless "success." techradar.com (May 28). Retrieved September 12, 2009, from http://www.techradar.com/news/internet/the-secrets-behind-Threadless-success-602617.
33. Ibid.
34. Chafkin, Max. 2008. The customer is the company. *Inc.* (July 1). Retrieved September 12, 2009, from http://www.inc.com/magazine/20080601/the-customer-is-the-company.html.
35. Ibid.
36. Ibid.
37. Centers for Disease Control and Prevention. 2006. Advance Data No. 372 (June 23).
38. Coffey, Laura T. 2008. Chocoholics sour on new Hershey's formula. MSNBC (September 19). Retrieved April 16, 2010, from http://www.msnbc.msn.com/id/26788143.
39. Otley, David. 1999. Performance management: A framework for management control systems research. *Management Accounting Research* 10: 363–82.
40. Hope, Jeremy, and Robin Fraser. 2003. *Beyond Budgeting: How managers can break free from the annual performance trap.* Boston: Harvard Business School Press.
41. Peelen, Ed. 2005. *Customer relationship management.* Upper Saddle River, NJ: Financial Times/Prentice Hall; Heskett, James, W. Earl Sasser, and Leonard Schlesinger. 1997. *The service profit chain.* New York: Free Press.
42. Jayachandran, Satish, Subhash Sharma, Peter Kaufman, and Pushkala Raman. 2005. The role of relational information processes and technology use in customer relationship management. *Journal of Marketing* 69 (October): 177–92.
43. Interview with Gail Goodman, conducted by Suzanne Rotondo on September 11, 2009.
44. Ibid.
45. Davenport, Thomas H., and James E. Short. 1990. The new industrial engineering: Information technology and business process redesign. *Sloan Management Review* (Summer): 11–26.
46. Hammer, Michael, and James Champy. 2001. *Reengineering the corporation: A manifesto for business revolution,* 35. New York: HarperCollins.
47. Ibid. 56.
48. Hammer, Michael. 1990. Reengineering work: Don't automate, obliterate. *Harvard Business Review* 68(4): 104–12.
49. Hammer and Champy, *Reengineering the corporation,* 21.
50. Davenport and Short, The new industrial engineering; Davenport, Thomas. 1993. *Process innovation: Reengineering work through information technology.* Boston: Harvard Business School Press.
51. Davenport, *Process innovation,* 1.
52. Raymond, Louis, Francios Bergeron, and Suzanne Rivard. 1998. Determinants of business process reengineering success in small and large enterprises. *Journal of Small Business Management* 36(1): 72–85.
53. Goel, Sanjay, and Chen, Vicki. 2008. Integrating the global enterprise using Six Sigma: Business process reengineering at General Electric Wind Energy. *International Journal of Production Economics* 113: 914–27.
54. Wikipedia. Total quality management. Retrieved August 14, 2009, from http://en.wikipedia.org/wiki/TQM.
55. Imai, Masaaki. 1986. *Kaizen: The key to Japan's competitive success.* New York: McGraw Hill.
56. Antony, Jiju. Pros and cons of Six Sigma: An academic perspective. Retrieved October 28, 2009, from http://www.onesixsigma.com/node/7630.
57. Ibid.
58. Acuity Institute. Lean Six Sigma Black Belt certification. Retrieved April 16, 2010, from http://www.acuityinstitute.com/six-sigma-black-belt.html.
59. Six Sigma. New to lean Six Sigma. Retrieved April 16, 2010, from http://www.isixsigma.com/sixsigma/six_sigma.asp.
60. Brady, J. E., and T. T. Allen. 2006. Six Sigma literature: A review and agenda for future research. *Quality and Reliability Engineering International* 22: 335–67.

61. Hindo, Brian. 2007. At 3M, a struggle between efficiency and creativity. *Business Week* (June 6). Retrieved October 28, 2009, from http://www.businessweek.com/magazine/content/07_24/b4038406.htm?chan=top+news_top+news+index_best+of+bw.

62. Ruffa, Stephen A. 2008. *Going lean: How the best companies apply lean manufacturing principles to shatter uncertainty, drive innovation, and maximize profits*. New York: AMACOM.

63. Womac, James P., Daniel T. Jones, and Daniel Roos. 1990. *The machine that changed the world: The story of lean production*. New York: Rawson Associates.

64. Ohno, Taiichi. 1995. *Toyota Production System: Beyond large-scale production*. New York: Productivity Press.

65. Trent, Robert J. 2008. *End-to-end lean management: A guide to complete supply chain improvement*. Fort Lauderdale, FL: J. Ross Publishing.

66. Ibid.; Brun, Yuriy, and Nenad Medvidovic. 2007. Fault and adversary tolerance as an emergent property of distributed systems' software architectures. Paper presented at 2007 Workshop on Engineering Fault Tolerant Systems, Dubrovnik, Croatia, September 4. Retrieved March 20, 2010, from http://portal.acm.org/citation.cfm?id=1316550.1316557.

67. International Organization for Standardization. ISO 9000 and ISO 14000. Retrieved December 2, 2009, from http://www.iso.org/iso/iso_catalogue/management_standards/iso_9000_iso_14000.htm.

68. American Society for Quality. Organization-wide approaches: ISO 9000 and other standards. Retrieved December 2, 2009, from http://www.asq.org/learn-about-quality/iso-9000/overview/overview.html.

69. International Organization for Standardization. ISO 14000:2004 and SMEs. Retrieved December 2, 2009, from http://www.iso.org/iso_catalogue/management_standards/iso_9000_iso_14000/iso_14001_2000_and_smes.htm.

70. American Society for Quality, Organization-wide approaches: ISO 9000 and other standards.

71. ISO9000Council.org. Welcome to ISO9000Council.org. Retrieved April 5, 2010, from http://www.iso9000council.org.

72. International Organization for Standardization. Quality management principles. Retrieved December 2, 2009, from http://www.iso.org/iso/iso_catalogue/management_standards/iso_9000_iso_14000/qmp.htm.

73. ISO9000Council.org, Welcome to ISO9000Council.org.

74. Ibid.

75. Minority Business Development Agency. ISO 14000 Standards. U.S. Department of Commerce. Retrieved December 2, 2009, from http://www.mbda.gov/?id=5&bucket_id=163&content_id=2478&well=entire_page.

76. Hanson, Arthur J. Global green standards. International Institute for Sustainable Development. Retrieved December 2, 2009, from http://www.iisd.org/greenstand/default.htm.

77. International Organization for Standardization. ISO 14000 essentials. Retrieved December 2, 2009, from http://www.iso.org/iso/iso_catalogue/management_standards/iso_9000_iso_14000/iso_14000_essentials.htm.

78. Hanson, Global green standards.

79. International Organization for Standardization. Certification. Retrieved December 2, 2009, from http://www.iso.org/iso/iso_catalogue/management_standards/certification.htm; Minority Business Development Agency, ISO 14000 Standards.

80. International Organization for Standardization. ISO 9000 essentials. Retrieved December 2, 2009, from http://www.iso.org/iso/iso_catalogue/management_standards/iso_9000_iso_14000/iso_9000_essentials.htm.

81. ISO9000Council.org, Welcome to ISO9000Council.org.

82. Baldrige National Quality Program. The Malcolm Baldrige National Quality Improvement Act of 1987—Public Law 100-107. National Institute of Standards and Technology. Retrieved December 2, 2009, from http://www.baldrige.nist.gov/Improvement_Act.htm.

83. Baldrige National Quality Program. Biography of Malcolm Baldrige. National Institute of Standards and Technology. Retrieved December 2, 2009, from http://www.baldrige.nist.gov/Biography.htm.

84. National Institute of Standards and Technology. Frequently asked questions about the Malcolm Baldrige National Quality Award. Retrieved December 2, 2009, from http://www.nist.gov/public_affairs/factsheet/baldfaqs.htm.

85. Turner, Sam. 2009. Baldrige criteria can help utility industry: How the Baldrige Criteria for Performance Excellence can help today's utility industry meet tomorrow's challenges. *Quality Digest* (November 12). Retrieved December 2, 2009, from http://www.qualitydigest.com/inside/quality-insider-article/baldrige-criteria-can-help-utility-industry.html.

86. National Institute of Standards and Technology, Frequently asked questions.

87. U.S. Government Office of Personnel Management. 2001. *Workforce compensation and performance service publication*, PMD-013 (September). Retrieved from http://miha.ef.uni-lj.si/_dokumenti3plus2/196128/Otley-1999-PM-aframeworkforMCSresearch.pdf.

88. Drucker, Peter F. 1954. *The practice of management*. New York: Harper & Brothers.

89. Romani, Paul N. 1997. MBO by any other name is still MBO. *Supervision* 58(12): 6–8.

90. Thomas, Gail Fann, Roxanne Zolin, and Jackie L. Hartman. 2009. The central role of communication in developing trust and its effect on employee involvement. *Journal of Business Communication* 46(3): 291.

91. Kaplan, Robert S., and David P. Norton. 1996. *The Balanced Scorecard: Translating strategy into action*. Boston: Harvard Business School Press.

92. Goleman et al.*Primal leadership*; Frost, P., J. Dutton, M. Worline, and A. Wilson. 2000. Narratives of compassion in organizations. In *Emotion in organizations*, ed. S. Fineman. Thousand Oaks, CA: Sage Publications; Graen, G., and M. Uhl-Bien. 1995. Relationship-based approach to leadership development of leader-member exchange (LMX) theory of leadership over 25 years: Applying a multi-level, multi-domain perspective. *Leadership Quarterly* 6: 219–47; Higgins, M. C., and K. E. Kram. 2001. Reconceptualizing mentoring at work: A developmental network perspective. *Academy of Management Review* 26(2): 264–88; Kanov, J. M., S. Maitlis, M. C. Worline, J. E. Dutton, P. J. Frost, and J. M. Lilius. 2004. Compassion in organizational life. *American Behavioral Scientist* 47(6): 808–27.

93. Kram, Kathy E. 1996. A relationship approach to career development. In *The career is dead—Long live the career*. San Francisco: Jossey-Bass.

94. McKee, A., and R. E. Boyatzis. 2008. *Becoming a resonant leader: Develop your emotional intelligence, renew your relationships, and sustain your effectiveness*. Boston: Harvard Business School Press.

95. Lewis, Kristi M. 2000. When leaders display emotion: How followers respond to negative emotional expression of male and female leaders. *Journal of Organizational Behavior* 21(special issue): 221–34.

96. Ibid.

97. Langer, Ellen. 1989. *Mindfulness*. Reading, MA: Addison-Wesley.

Chapter 13

1. Mead, Margaret. 1953. *Cultural patterns and technical change*, 9–10. Deventer, Holland: UNESCO.

2. Hofstede, Geert. 1980/1984. *Culture's consequences: International differences in work-related values*, 14. Newbury Park, CA: Sage Publications.

3. Mead, R. 1994. *International management: Cross-cultural dimensions*. Oxford: Blackwell Business.

4. Hofstede, Geert. 1998. Attitudes, values, and organizational culture: Disentangling the concepts. *Organization Studies* 19(3): 477–92; Rokeach, Milton. 1972. *Beliefs, attitudes, and values*. San Francisco: Jossey-Bass.

5. Lagarde, Emmanuel, Catherine Enel, Karim Seck, Aïssatou, Gueye-Ndiaye, Jean-Pierre Piau, Gilles Pison, Valerie Delaunay, Ibrahima Ndoye, and Souleymane Mboup. 2000. Religion and protective behaviors towards AIDS in rural Senegal. *AIDS* 14: 2027–33.

6. Finkelstein, S. 2002. The DaimlerChrysler merger. Business case no. 1-0071. Retrieved April 17, 2010, from http://mba.tuck.dartmouth.edu/pdf/2002-1-0071.pdf.

7. CSL Behring. About CSL Behring. Retrieved April 17, 2010, from http://www.cslbehring.com/about.

8. Unilever. Powered by people. Retrieved April 17, 2010, from http://www.unilever.com/careers; ExxonMobil. Country, regional business and brand sites. Retrieved April 17, 2010, from http://www.exxonmobil.com/corporate/about_where_countries.aspx; Nike. Careers. Retrieved November 18, 2009, from http://www.nikebiz.com/careers.

9. Teleos Leadership Institute. Who we are. Retrieved November 18, 2009, from http://www.teleosleaders.com/teleos_who_we_are.html.

10. Pfeffer, J. 1981. Management as symbolic action: The creation and maintenance of organizational paradigms. In *Research in organizational behavior*, vol. 3, ed. L. L. Cummings and B. M. Staw, 1–52. Greenwich, CT: JAI Press.

11. Schein, E. H. 1985. *Organizational culture and leadership*. San Francisco: Jossey-Bass.

12. Schein, *Organizational culture and leadership*; Likert, R. 1961. *New patterns of management*. New York: McGraw-Hill; Gregory, B. T., S. G. Stanley, A. A. Armenakis, and C. L. Shook. 2009. Organizational culture and effectiveness: A study of values, attitudes, and organizational outcomes. *Journal of Business Research* 62: 673–79.

13. Hofstede, *Culture's consequences*; Hofstede, Geert. 1994. The business of international business is culture. *International Business Review* 3(1): 1–14.

14. Hofstede, *Culture's consequences*.

15. Hofstede, Geert, and Michael H. Bond. 1988. The Confucius connection: From cultural roots to economic growth. *Organizational Dynamics* 16: 5–21; Franke, Richard H., Geert Hofstede, and Michael H. Bond. 2002. National culture and economic growth. In *Handbook of cross-cultural management*, ed. Martin J. Gannon and Karen L. Newman, 5–15. Malden, MA: Blackwell Publishers.

16. Hofstede, Geert, Bram Neuijen, Denise D. Ohayv, and Saunders Geert. 1990. Measuring organizational cultures: A qualitative and quantitative study across twenty cases. *Administrative Science Quarterly* 35(2): 286–317; Chinese Culture Connection. 1987.

17. Ibid; Yeh, Ryh-Song, and John J. Lawrence. 1995. Individualism and Confucian dynamism: A note on Hofstede's cultural root to economic growth. *Journal of International Business Studies* 26(3): 655–69; Hofstede and Bond, The Confucius connection; Chinese values and the search for culture-free dimensions of culture. *Journal of Cross-Cultural Psychology* 18: 143–64.

18. House, Robert, Paul J. Hanges, Mansour Javidan, and Peter W. Dorfman, eds. 2004. *Culture, leadership, and organizations: The GLOBE study of 62 societies*. Thousand Oaks, CA: Sage Publications.

19. Ibid.

20. Javidan, M., and R. J. House. 2001. Cultural acumen for the global manager: Lessons from Project GLOBE. *Organizational Dynamics* (Spring): 289–305.

21. *Baker v. Nelson*, 291 Minn. 310 (1971).

22. Freedom to Marry.org. States. Retrieved August 11, 2009, from http://www.freedomtomarry.org/states.php.

23. Lewis, Gregory B. 2005. Same-sex marriage and the 2004 presidential election. *PS: Political Science and Politics* 38: 195–99.

24. Yanow, Dvora. 2000. Seeing organizational learning: A cultural view. *Organization Articles* 7(2): 247–68.

25. Cameron, Kim S., and Robert E. Quinn. 2006. *Diagnosing and changing organizational culture: Based on the competing values framework*. San Francisco: Jossey-Bass.

26. Quinn, R. E., and J. A. Rohrbaugh. 1983. A spatial model of effectiveness criteria: Towards a competing values approach to organizational analysis. *Management Science* 29: 363–77; Quinn, R. E., and G. M. Spreitzer. 1991. The psychometrics of the competing values culture instrument and an analysis of the impact of organizational culture on quality of life. In *Research in organizational change and development*, vol. 5, ed. R. W. Woodman and W. A. Pasmore, 115–42. Greenwich, CT: JAI Press; Cameron, K. S., and S. J. Freeman. 1991. Cultural congruence, strength, and type: Relationships to effectiveness. In *Research in organizational change and development*, vol. 5, ed. R. W. Woodman and W. A. Pasmore, 23-58. Greenwich, CT: JAI Press.

27. Gregory et al., Organizational culture and effectiveness; Quinn, R. E. 1988. *Beyond rational management*. San Francisco: Jossey-Bass; Cameron, Kim S. 1984. Cultural congruence, strength, and type: Relationships to effectiveness. Working Paper No. 401b, Graduate School of Business Administration, University of Michigan; Denison, D. R., and G. M. Spreitzer. Organizational culture and organizational development: A competing values approach. In *Research in organizational change and development*, vol. 5, ed. R. W. Woodman and W. A. Pasmore, 1–21. Greenwich, CT: JAI Press; Cameron, K. S., R. E. Quinn, J. Degraff, and A. V. Thakor. 2006. *Creating values in leadership*. Northampton, MA: Edward Elgar; Cameron, K. S., and R. E. Quinn. 1999. *Diagnosing and changing organizational cultures*. New York: Addison-Wesley.

28. Gregory et al., Organizational culture and effectiveness.

29. Ibid.; Quinn, R. E., *Beyond rational management*.

30. Kotter, J., and J. Heskett. 1992. *Corporate culture and performance*. New York: Free Press; O'Reilly, C. A., and J. A. Chatman. 1996. Culture as social control: Corporations, culture and commitment. In *Research in organizational behavior*, vol. 18, ed. B. M. Staw and L. L. Cummings, 157–200. Greenwich, CT: JAI Press.

31. Pascale, R. 1985. The paradox of "corporate culture": Reconciling ourselves to socialization. *California Management Review* 27: 26–41; Posner, B., J. Kouzes, and W. Schmidt. 1985. Shared values make a difference: An empirical test of corporate culture. *Human Resource Management* 24: 293–309.

32. Sorenson, J. B. 2002. The strength of corporate culture and the reliability of firm performance. *Administrative Science Quarterly* 47: 70–91. Denison, Daniel R. 1984. Bringing corporate culture to the bottom line. *Organizational Dynamics* 13(2): 4-22; Denison, Daniel R. 1990. *Corporate culture and organizational effectiveness*. New York: Wiley; Gordon, G., and N. DiTomaso. 1992. Predicting corporate performance from organizational culture. *Journal of Management Studies* 29: 783–98.

33. Collins, C., and J. Porras. 2002. *Built to last: Successful habits of visionary companies*. New York: HarperCollins; Schrodt, Paul. 2002. The relationship between organizational identification and organizational culture: Employee perceptions of culture and identification in a retail sales organization. *Communication Studies* 53: 189–202.

34. Dakan, Myles. 2007. What is uchi, what is soto: The cultural implications of Japanese grammar. *Daily Gazette* (February 12). Retrieved September 12, 2009, from http://daily.swarthmore.edu/2007/2/12/what-is-uchi-what-is-soto-the-cultural-implications-of-japanese-grammar.

35. Byrne, John A., and Gary McWilliams. 1993. The alumni club to end all alumni clubs. *Businessweek* (September 20). Retrieved September 12, 2009, from http://www.businessweek.com/archives/1993/b333748.arc.htm.

36. Ibid.

37. Ibid.

38. Hirst, Clayton. 2002. The might of the McKinsey mob. *The Independent* (January 20). Retrieved April 23, 2010, from http://www.independent.co.uk/news/business/analysis-and-features/the-might-of-the-mckinsey-mob-664081.html.

39. Byrne, John A. 2002. Inside McKinsey. *BusinessWeek* (July 8). Retrieved September 12, 2009, from http://www.businessweek.com/magazine/content/02_27/b3790001.htm.

40. Vineyard Vines. Our story. Retrieved April 17, 2010, from http://www.vineyardvines.com/content_ourstory.

41. Murray, Shep, and Ian Murray. 2005. For the love of it. In *Chicken soup for the entrepreneur's soul: Advice and inspiration for fulfilling dreams*, ed. Jack Canfield, Mark V. Hansen, and Dahlynn McKowen, 162–66. Deerfield Beach, FL: Health Communications.

42. Manlow, Veronica. 2007. *Designer clothes: Culture and organization of the fashion industry*. New Brunswick, NJ: Transaction Publishers.

43. *Entrepreneur*'s hot 500. 2007. *Entrepreneur Magazine* (August). Retrieved March 6, 2010, from http://www.entrepreneur.com/hot500/industry/APPAREL.html.

44. Off the Cuff. 2009. Vineyard Vines: An American original (March 26). Retrieved March 6, 2010, from http://offthecuffdc.blogspot.com/2009/03/vineyard-vines-american-original-part-i.html.

45. Martin, Joanne, Peter J. Frost, and Olivia A. O'Neill. 2006. Organizational culture: Beyond struggles for intellectual dominance. In *The handbook of organisation studies*, 2d ed., ed. S. R. Clegg, C. Hardy, T. B. Lawrence, and W. R. Nord, 725–53. Newbury Park, CA: Sage Publications.

46. Shrivastava, P. 1985. Integrating strategy formulation with organizational culture. *Journal of Business Strategy* 5: 103–11.

47. Sørensen, Jesper B. 2002. The strength of corporate culture and the reliability of firm performance. *Administrative Science Quarterly* 47(1): 70–91.

48. Gordon, George G. 1991. Industry determinants of organizational culture. *Academy of Management Review* 16(2): 396–415.

49. Michel, Alexandra, and Stanton Wortham. 2008. *Bullish on uncertainty: How organizational cultures transform participants*. New York: Cambridge University Press.

50. Schein, *Organizational culture and leadership*.

51. Ibid., 3–27.

52. Yanow, Dvora. 2000. Seeing organizational learning: A cultural view. *Organization Science* 7(2): 247–68; Lytle, James H. 1996. The inquiring manager. *Phi Delta Kappan* 77(10): 664–66.

53. Bowles, M. L. 1989. Myth, meaning, and work organization, *Organization Studies*, Vol. 10 No. 3, pp. 405–21.

54. Schein, E. H. 1983. The role of the founder in creating organizational culture. *Organization Dynamics* (Summer): 13–28.

55. Schein, *Organizational culture and leadership.*

56. Rogers, William. 1969. *Think: A biography of the Watsons and IBM.* New York: Stein & Day.

57. Martin, Joanne, Martha S. Feldman, and Mary Jo Hatch. 1983. The uniqueness paradox in organizational stories. *Administrative Science Quarterly* 28(3): 438–53.

58. Pettigrew, A. M. 1979. On studying organizational cultures. *Administrative Science Quarterly* 24: 570–81.

59. Durkheim, E. 1965. *The elementary forms of religious life.* New York: Free Press.

60. Martin, Joanne. 1990. Deconstructing organizational taboos: The suppression of gender conflict in organizations. *Organization Science* 1(4): 339–59.

61. Kallio, Tomy J. 2007. Taboos in corporate social responsibility discourse. *Journal of Business Ethics* 74: 165–75.

62. Ibid.

63. Kontakt: The Arts and Civil Society Program of Erste Group. Cold War and Coca-Cola. Retrieved April 23, 2010, from http://www.kontakt.erstegroup.net/report/stories/Issue20_07_Kalter+Krieg+und+Coca+Cola/en.

64. LaTour, Kathryn, Michael S. LaTour, and George M. Zinkhand. 2009. Coke is it: How stories in childhood memories illuminate an icon. *Journal of Business Research* 63(3): 328–36.

65. Barley, Stephen R. 1983. Semiotics and the study of occupational and organizational cultures. *Organizational Culture* 28(3): 393–413; Eco, Umberto. 1986. *Semiotics and the philosophy of language.* Bloomington, IN: Indiana University Press.

66. Military slang. Retrieved July 30, 2009, from http://www.spiritus-temporis.com/military-slang/v.html.

67. Thomas, Chris Allen. 2008. Bridging the gap between theory and practice: Language policy in multilingual organizations. *Language Awareness* 17(4): 307–25.

68. Kallio, Taboos in corporate social responsibility discourse.

69. Yanow, Seeing organizational learning; Reason, Peter. *Human inquiry in action: Developments in new paradigm research.* Thousand Oaks, CA: Sage; Schein, Edgar H. 2001. Clinical inquiry/research. In *Handbook of action research,* ed. Peter Reason and Hilary Bradbury, 228–237. Thousand Oaks, CA: Sage; Lytle, The inquiring manager.

70. Plato. 1908. *The republic of Plato,* ed. Benjamin Jowett, 517D. Oxford: Clarendon Press.

71. London, Anne (Annie McKee) and M. C. McMillen. 1993. Discovering social issues: Organization development in a multicultural community. *Journal of Applied Behavioral Sciences* 28(3): 445–60.

72. Goleman, Daniel, Richard E. Boyatzis, and Annie McKee. 2002. *Primal leadership: Realizing the power of emotional intelligence,* 198–200. Boston: Harvard Business School Press.

73. Cooperrider, David L. 2004. Appreciative inquiry: New horizons in strength-based organization development. In *Sixth annual best of organizational development summit,* 79–107. Burlington, MA: Linkage Inc.; Cooperrider, D. L., and S. Srivasta. 1987. Appreciative inquiry in organizational life. In *Research in organizational change and development,* Vol. 1, ed. R. W. Woodman and W. A. Pasmore, 129–69. Greenwich, CT: JAI Press.

74. Gustavson, Bjørn. 2001. Theory and practice: The mediating discourse. In *Handbook of action research,* ed. Peter Reason and Hilary Bradbury, 17–26. Thousand Oaks, CA: Sage Publications; Hult, M., and S. Lennung. 1980. Towards a definition of action research: A note and bibliography. *Journal of Management Studies* 17(2): 242–50.

75. Weick, Karl E., and Robert E. Quinn. 1999. Organizational change and development. *Annual Review of Psychology* 50: 361–86.

76. Brown, S. L., and K. M. Eisenhardt. 1998. *Competing on the edge: Strategy as structured chaos.* Boston: Harvard Business School Press; O'Reilly, C. A., J. Chatman, and D. F. Caldwell. 1991. People and organizational culture: A profile comparison approach to assessing person-organization fit. *Academy of Management Journal* 14: 487–516; Scott, S. G., and R. A. Bruce. 1994. Determinants of innovative behavior: A path model of individual innovation in the workplace. *Academy of Management Journal* 37: 580–607; Van de Ven, A., E. D. Polley, R. Garud, and S. Venkataraman. 1999. *The innovation journey.* New York: Oxford University Press.

77. Woodman, R. W., J. E. Sawyer, and R. W. Griffin. 1993. Toward a theory of organizational creativity. *Academy of Management Review* 18: 293–321.

78. Chandler, G. N., C. Keller, and D. W. Lyon. 2000. Unraveling the determinants and consequences of an innovative-supportive organizational culture. *Entrepreneurship Theory and Practice* (Fall): 59–76.

79. Kent, William E. 1990. Putting up the Ritz: Using culture to open a hotel. *Cornell Hotel and Restaurant Administration Quarterly* 31(3): 16–24.

80. Enz, C. A., and J. A. Signaw. 2000. Best practices in service quality. *Cornell Hotel and Restaurant Administration Quarterly* 41: 20–29.

81. Locander, W. B., F. Hamilton, D. Ladik, and J. Stewart. 2002. Developing a leadership-rich culture: The missing link to creating a market-focused organization. *Journal of Market-Focused Management* 5: 149–63.

82. Catalyst. 2008. 2008 census of women corporate officers and top earners of the Fortune 500. *Catalyst Research Report.* Retrieved August 20, 2009, from http://www.catalyst.org/file/266/cote_ca_09.pdf.

83. Catalyst. 2001. *2001 Catalyst census of women board directors.* Retrieved August 20, 2009, from http://www.catalyst.org/file/77/2001%20catalyst%20wbd.pdf.

84. Toossi, Mitra. 2007. Employment outlook: 2006–2016. Labor force projections to 2016: More workers in their golden years. *Monthly Labor Review* (November). Washington, DC: Bureau of Labor Statistics. Retrieved August 20, 2009, from http://www.bls.gov/opub/mlr/2007/11/art3full.pdf.

85. Judy, Richard W., and Carol D'Amico. 1997. *Workforce 2020: Work and workers in the twenty-first century.* Indianapolis, IN: Hudson Institute.

86. Ibid.

87. Ely, R. J., and D. A. Thomas. 2001. Cultural diversity at work: The effects of diversity perspectives on work group processes and outcomes. *Administrative Science Quarterly* 46: 229–73.

88. Diversity Inc. Why is Johnson & Johnson number one? Retrieved July 29, 2009, from http://www.diversityinc.com/public/5449.cfm; Diversity Inc. Announcing the ninth annual Diversity Inc. Top 50 companies for diversity. Retrieved July 29, 2009, from http://www.diversityinc.com/public/5530.cfm.

89. Diversity Inc., Announcing the ninth annual Diversity Inc. Top 50 companies for diversity.

90. Posner, B., J. Kouzes, and W. Schmidt. 1985. Shared values make a difference: An empirical test of corporate culture. *Human Resource Management* 24: 527–38.

91. Singhapakdi, Anusorn, and Scott J. Vitell. 2007. Institutionalization of ethics and its consequences: A survey of marketing professionals. *Journal of the Academy of Marketing Science* 35(2): 284–94.

92. Vitell, S. J., and A. Singhapakdi. 2008. The role of ethics institutionalization in influencing organizational commitment, job satisfaction, and esprit de corps. *Journal of Business Ethics* 81: 343–53.

93. Ramos, Luis. 2009. Outside-the-box ethics. *Leadership Excellence* 26: 19.

94. Ibid.

95. Tse, Tomoeh M. 2009. Judge surprises Madoff deputy by denying bail. *Washington Post* (August 13). Retrieved August 13, 2009, from http://www.washingtonpost.com/wp-dyn/content/article/2009/08/12/AR2009081202970.html?hpid=sec-business.

96. Sevier, Laura. 2009. Cleaner Planet Plan: A green wash or greenwash? *The Ecologist* (August 18): Retrieved August 20, 2009, from http://www.theecologist.org/blogs_and_comments/commentators/other_comments/305015/cleaner_planet_plan_a_green_wash_or_greenwash.html.

97. Global 100. 2009. The Global 100 most sustainable corporations in the world. Retrieved August 20, 2009, from http://www.global100.org.

98. Campaign for Real Beauty. 2006. *Evolution: A Dove film.* Retrieved August 20, 2009, from http://www.dove.us/#/features/videos/default.aspx[cp-documentid=7049579].

99. Boyatzis, Richard, and Annie McKee. 2005 *Resonant leadership: Sustaining yourself and connecting with others through mindfulness, hope, and compassion.* Boston: Harvard Business School Press.

100. Pawar, B. S. 2008. Two approaches to workplace spirituality facilitation: A comparison and implications. *Leadership and Organization Development Journal* 29: 544–67; Giacalone, R. A., and C. L. Jurkiewicz, eds. 2003. *Handbook of workplace spirituality and organizational performance.* New York: M. E. Sharpe.

101. Google search results for "workplace spirituality," August 13, 2009.

102. Pawar, Two approaches to workplace spirituality facilitation; Corner, P. D. 2009. Workplace spirituality and business ethics. *Journal of Business Ethics* 85: 377–89.

103. Duchon, Dennis, and Donde A. Plowman. 2005. Nurturing spirit at work: Impact on work unit performance. *Leadership Quarterly* 16: 807–33.

104. Driscoll, Cathy, and Margaret McKee. 2007. Restorying a culture of ethical and spiritual values: A role for leader storytelling. *Journal of Business Ethics* 73: 205–17; Corner, Workplace spirituality and business ethics.

105. Konz, Gregory N. P., and Francis X. Ryan. 1999. Maintaining an organizational spirituality: No easy task. *Journal of Organizational Change Management* 12(3): 200–10.

106. Fry, Louis W. 2003. Toward a theory of spiritual leadership. *Leadership Quarterly* 14: 693–727.

107. U.S. Equal Employment Opportunity Commission. 2002. Facts about sexual harassment (June 27). Retrieved April 6, 2010, from http://www.eeoc.gov/facts/fs-sex.html.

108. Ibid.

109. Ibid.

110. Dobbin, Frank, and Erin L. Kelly. 2007. How to stop harassment: Professional construction of legal compliance in organizations. *American Journal of Sociology* 112(4): 1203–1243.

111. National Women's Law Center. Sexual harassment in the workplace. Retrieved April 17, 2010, from http://www.nwlc.org/details.cfm?id= 459&section=employment; U.S. Equal Employment Opportunity Commission. 2009. Sexual harassment charges: EEOC and FEPAs combined: FY 1997–FY 2008. Retrieved April 17, 2010, from http://www.eeoc.gov/eeoc/statistics/enforcement/sexual_harassment.cfm; Texas Association Against Sexual Assault. 2008. Confronting sexual harassment brochure (October 1). Retrieved April 6, 2010, from http://www.taasa.org/member/pdfs/csh-eng.pdf.

112. U.S. Equal Employment Opportunity Commission. Sexual Harassment Charges.

113. U.S. Metric Systems Correction Board. 1994. Sexual harassment in the federal workplace: Trends, progress, continuing challenges. Retrieved April 6, 2010, from http://www.mspb.gov/netsearch/viewdocs .aspx?docnumber=253661&version=253948&application=ACROBAT.

114. Faley, Robert H., Deborah E. Knapp, Gary A. Kustis, Cathy L. Z. Dubois, Jill Young, and Brian Polin. 2006. Estimating the organizational costs of same-sex sexual harassment: The case of the U.S. Army. *International Journal of Intercultural Relations* 30(5): 557–77.

115. Goleman et al., *Primal leadership*.

116. Boyatzis, Richard E. 1998. *Thematic analysis: Transforming qualitative information.* Thousand Oaks, CA: Sage.

117. Keyton, Joann. 2005. *Communication and organizational culture.* Thousand Oaks, CA: Sage.

118. Goleman, Daniel. 2006. *Social intelligence: The new science of human relationships.* New York: Bantam Books.

119. Earley, P. Christopher, and Elaine Masakowski. 2004. Cultural intelligence. *Harvard Business Review* (October): 139.

120. Earley, P. Christopher, and Ang Soon. 2003. *Cultural intelligence: Individual interactions across cultures.* Palo Alto, CA: Stanford University Press.

121. Brislin, Richard, Reginald Worthley, and Brent Macnab. 2006. Cultural intelligence: Understanding behaviors that serve people's goals. *Group and Organization Management* 31(1): 40–55.

122. Goleman et al., *Primal leadership*.

123. Ibid., 218–19.

124. Ibid., 219.

125. Ibid., 219–20.

Chapter 14

1. Reich, Robert. 2007. *Supercapitalism*, 7. Knopf: New York.

2. Hoovers. McDonald's Corporation. Retrieved April 13, 2010, from http://www.hoovers.com/company/McDonalds_Corporation/rfskci-1.html.

3. Samuelson, Robert. 2008. A baffling global economy. *Washington Post* (July 16). Retrieved April 13, 2010, from http://www.washingtonpost .com/wp-dyn/content/article/2008/07/15/AR2008071502428.html.

4. BBC News. 2001. Globalisation: Good or bad? *Talking Point* (July 25). Retrieved February 8, 2010, from http://news.bbc.co.uk/2/hi/ talking_point/1444930.stm.

5. Friedman, Thomas L. 2000. *The Lexus and the olive tree.* New York: Farrar, Straus and Giroux.

6. Della Porta, Donatella. 2006. *The global justice movement: Cross-national and transnational perspectives.* New York: Paradigm; Juris, Jeffrey S. 2008. *Networking futures: The movements against corporate globalization.* Durham, NC: Duke University Press.

7. Stiglitz, J. 2004. Economic, social, and cultural rights: The right to food. Report prepared for the United Nations Commission on Human Rights. Retrieved February 8, 2010, from http://www.unhchr.ch/Huridocda/ Huridoca.nsf/0/34441bf9efe3a9e3c1256e6300510e24/$FILE/G0410777 .pdf.

8. Stiglitz, J., and A. Charlton. 2005. *Fair trade for all: How trade can promote development.* New York: Oxford University Press.

9. Friedman, Thomas L. 2006. *The world is flat*, 422. New York: Farrar, Straus, and Giroux.

10. Nathan, Andrew J., and Robert S. Ross. 1997. *The Great Wall and the empty fortress: China's search for security*, 13. New York: W. W. Norton.

11. Zacharias, Pat. 1999. When bomb shelters were all the rage. *Detroit News* (April 1). Retrieved April 13, 2010, from http://apps.detnews.com/ apps/history/index.php?id=48.

12. U.S. Department of Defense. Military casualty information. Retrieved April 27, 2010, from http://siadapp.dmdc.osd.mil/personnel/ CASUALTY/vietnam.pdf.

13. Fukuyama, Francis. 1989. *Have we reached the end of history?* 23. Santa Monica, CA: Rand Corporation.

14. Friedman, *The world is flat*, 53.

15. Russett, Bruce, and James S. Sutterlin. 1991. The U.N. in a new world order. *Foreign Affairs* 70(2): 69–83.

16. U.S. Department of Energy. 1999. Petroleum: An energy profile 1999. Washington, DC: Energy Information Administration.

17. Yeltsin, Boris. 1990. *Against the grain*, 255. New York: Summit Books.

18. World Trade Organization. World trade report 2008. Retrieved December 29, 2009, from http://www.wto.org/english/res_e/booksp_e/ anpre_e/wtr08-2b_e.pdr.

19. Ruggerio, Renato. 1995. Growing complexity in international economic relations demands broadening and deepening of multilateral trading system. Paul-Henri Spaack Lecture at Harvard University (October 16). Retrieved December 29, 2009, from http://www.wto.org/english/ news_e/pres95_e/pr025_e.htm.

20. Gale, Colin, and Jasbir Kaur. 2002. *The textile book.* New York: Berg.

21. Business.gov. Trade agreements. Retrieved December 10, 2009, from http://www.business.gov/expand/import-export/trade-agreements.

22. Business.gov. Import/export. Retrieved December 10, 2009, from http:// www.business.gov/expand/import-export; Business.gov, Trade agreements.

23. Buffett, Warren E., and Carol J. Loomis. 2003. America's growing trade deficit is selling the nation out from under us. *Fortune* (November 10). Retrieved April 27, 2010, from http://money.cnn.com/magazines/ fortune/fortune_archive/2003/11/10/352872/index.htm.

24. Samuelson, A baffling global economy.

25. Fallows, James. 2008. Be nice to the countries that lend you money. *Atlantic Monthly* (December): 62–63.

26. Ibid., 63.

27. Folta, Paul H. 2005. Cooperative joint ventures: Savvy foreign investors may wish to consider the benefits of this flexible investment structure. *China Business Review* (January–February): 18–23.

28. Beshel, Barbara. An introduction to franchising. International Franchise Association Educational Foundation. Retrieved December 15, 2009, from http://franchise.org/uploadedFiles/Franchise_Industry/Resources/ Education_Foundation/Intro%20to%20Franchising%20Student %20Guide.pdf.

29. Reuer, Jeffrey J., Africa Ariño, and Antoni Valverde. The perfect "pre-nup" to strategic alliances: A guide to contracts. Association of Strategic Alliance Professionals best practice bulletins. Retrieved December 16, 2009, from http://www.strategic-alliances.org/membership/ memberresources/bestpracticebulletin.

30. Investor Glossary. Wholly-owned subsidiary. Retrieved December 16, 2009, from http://www.investorglossary.com/wholly-owned-subsidiary.htm.

31. Brown, Erika. 2004. The global startup. *Forbes.com* (November). Retrieved December 16, 2009, from http://www.forbes.com/forbes/ 2004/1129/150.html. Presutti, Manuela, Alberto Onetti, and Vincenza Odorici. Serial entrepreneurship and born-global new ventures: A case study. *Biblioteca.net.* Retrieved December 16, 2009, from http://amsacta .cib.unibo.it/2477/1/Serialentrepreneurshipbornglobal.pdf.

32. Sourcingmag.com. Outsourcing—What is outsourcing? Retrieved December 17, 2009, from http://www.sourcingmag.com/content/ what_is_outsourcing.asp.

33. Huntington, S. P. 1993. The clash of civilizations? *Foreign Affairs* 72(3): 22–49.

34. Pieterse, J. N. 2009. *Globalization and culture: Global mélange.* Lanham, MD: Rowman and Littlefield Publishers.

35. Ritzer, G. 1993. *The McDonaldization of society: An investigation into the changing character of contemporary social life.* Thousand Oaks, CA: Pine Forest Press.

36. Pieterse, *Globalization and culture*.

37. Export.gov. FAQ: Export basics. Retrieved December 10, 2009, from http://www.export.gov/faq/eg_main_017487.asp.

38. Spencer, Earl P. 1995. EuroDisney: What happened? What's next? *Journal of International Marketing* 3(3). Retrieved January 7, 2010, from http://www.jstor.org/pss/25048611.

39. Blalock, Marty. 2005. Listen up: Why good communication is good business. *Wisconsin Business Alumni Update* (December). Retrieved January 7, 2010, from http://www.bus.wisc.edu/update/winter05/business_communication.asp; Recklies, Dagmar. EuroDisney—Case study I. *Themanager.org*. Retrieved January 7, 2010, from http://themanager.org/ME/Disney_1.htm.

40. Liddle, Alan. 1992. Guests walk a not-so-fine line at EuroDisney's attractions. *Nation's Restaurant News* (November 23). Retrieved January 7, 2010, from http://findarticles.com/p/articles/mi_m3190/is_n47_v26/ai_12941855/?tag=content;col1.

41. *The Independent*. 2004. Less a Sleeping Beauty, more a rude awakening at EuroDisney. *The Independent* (August 8). Retrieved January 7, 2010, from http://www.independent.co.uk/news/business/analysis-and-feature/less-a-sleeping-beauty-more-a-rude-awakening-at-euro-disney-555756.html; Blalock, Listen up.

42. *The Independent*, Less a Sleeping Beauty, more a rude awakening at EuroDisney.

43. Sylt, Christian, and Caroline Reid. 2009. The end of EuroDisney's white-knuckle ride? *Spectator* (August 9). Retrieved January 8, 2010, from http://www.spectator.co.uk/business/880491/part_2/the-end-of-euro-disneys-whiteknuckle-ride.thtml.

44. Vodafone. About Vodafone. Retrieved April 13, 2010, from http://www.vodafone.com/start/about_vodafone.html.

45. Stanley, David. Tuna Canneries. Retrieved January 31, 2010, from http://www.americansamoa.southpacific.org/americansamoa/canneries.html.

46. Furchtgott-Roth, Diana. 2009. Thousands lost jobs due to higher federal minimum wage. Reuters (May 14). Retrieved January 31, 2010, from http://blogs.reuters.com/great-debate/2009/05/14/thousands-lose-jobs-due-to-higher-federal-minimum-wage/.

47. *CIA world factbook 2009*. Retrieved February 10, 2010, from https://www.cia.gov/library/publications/the-world-factbook/rankorder/2178rank.html.

48. Bala-Gbogbo, Elisha. 2010. Shell to sell oil leases in Nigeria. *234Next .com* (February 5). Retrieved February 10, 2010, from http://234next.com/csp/cms/sites/Next/Money/Business/5522471-147/story.csp.

49. Woodyard, Chris. 2010. Toyota announces massive repair campaign to end sticky-pedal recall. *USA Today*. (February 1). Retrieved February 1, 2010, from http://content.usatoday.com/communities/driveon/post/2010/02/toyota-announces-massive-repair-campaign-to-end-sticky-pedal-recall/1; Valdes-Dapena, Peter. 2010. Toyota recalls top 5.3 million vehicles. CNNMoney.com (January 28). Retrieved April 27, 2010, from http://money.cnn.com/2010/01/27/autos/toyota_recall_expanded/index.htm; Valdes-Dapena, Peter. 2010. Toyota recalls total 8.1 million vehicles. CNNMoney.com (February 4). Retrieved May 19, 2010, from http://money.cnn.com/2010/02/04/autos/toyota_recall_total/index.htm.

50. Chubb, Daniel. 2010. Honda recall joined by Peugeot: Cars made with Toyota. Product Reviews News (January 10). Retrieved February 1, 2010, from http://www.product-reviews.net/2010/01/31/honda-recall-joined-by-peugeot-cars-made-with-toyota/.

51. Woodyard, C. 2010. Pontiac Vibe: Overlooked step-sister in Toyota recall? *USA Today* (February 1). Retrieved February 1, 2010, from http://content.usatoday.com/communities/driveon/post/2010/02/pontiac-vibe-overlooked-step-sister-intoyota-recall/1?loc=interstitialskip.

52. U.S. Congressional Budget Office. 2004. What accounts for the decline in manufacturing employment? Retrieved February 7, 2010, from http://www.cbo.gov/ftpdocs/50xx/doc5078/02-18-ManufacturingEmployment.pdf.

53. Ibid.

54. Aspray, W., F. Mayadas, and M. Y. Vardi. 2006. *Globalization and offshoring of software: A report of the ACM Job Migration Task Force*. New York: Association for Computing Machinery.

55. Lynch, Doug E. 2005. Success versus value: What do we mean by the business of online education? GSE Publications. Retrieved February 7, 2010, from http://repository.upenn.edu/cgi/viewcontent.cgi?article=1035&context=gse_pubs.

56. Elliott, Dominic. 2009. Fundamentals drive the "BRIC" rebound. *Wall Street Journal* (July 27). Retrieved April 13, 2010, from http://online.wsj.com/article/SB124864236547882043.html.

57. All data taken from *CIA World Factbook* online edition, except for details regarding media ownership. CIA values are based on 2008–2009 estimates and were obtained on January 26, 2010, via the following addresses:
    - United States: https://www.cia.gov/library/publications/the-world-factbook/geos/us.html.
    - Brazil: https://www.cia.gov/library/publications/the-world-factbook/geos/br.html.
    - Russia: https://www.cia.gov/library/publications/the-world-factbook/geos/rs.html.
    - India: https://www.cia.gov/library/publications/the-world-factbook/geos/in.html.
    - China: https://www.cia.gov/library/publications/the-world-factbook/geos/ch.html.

    Media ownership data taken from the BBC News' online country profiles. This information was obtained on January 26, 2010, via the following addresses:
    - United States: http://news.bbc.co.uk/2/hi/americas/country_profiles/1217752.stm#media.
    - Brazil: http://news.bbc.co.uk/2/hi/americas/country_profiles/1227110.stm#media.
    - Russia: http://news.bbc.co.uk/2/hi/europe/country_profiles/1102275.stm#media.
    - India: http://news.bbc.co.uk/2/hi/south_asia/country_profiles/1154019.stm.
    - China: http://news.bbc.co.uk/2/hi/asia-pacific/country_profiles/1287798.stm#media.

58. Watkins, Thayer. The economic history of Brazil: Booms and busts of Brazilian history. San Jose State University Department of Economics. Retrieved January 27, 2010, from http://www.sjsu.edu/faculty/watkins/brazil1.htm.

59. U.S. Department of State. 2009. Background note: Brazil. Retrieved January 29, 2010, from http://www.state.gov/r/pa/ei/bgn/35640.htm.

60. Federal Research Division, U.S. Library of Congress. 1997. *A country study: Brazil*. Retrieved January 29, 2010, from http://lcweb2.loc.gov/frd/cs/brtoc.html.

61. U.S. Department of State, Background note: Brazil.

62. Schemo, Diana Jean. 1999. Tense times on front line of Brazil's battle on hyperinflation. *New York Times* (January 20). Retrieved January 29, 2010, from http://www.nytimes.com/1999/01/20/world/tense-times-on-front-line-of-brazil-s-battle-on-hyperinflation-empty-shops.html?pagewanted=1.

63. Hornbeck, J. F., 2006. *Brazilian trade policy and the United States*. CRS report for Congress (February 3). Retrieved January 29, 2010, from http://www.nationalaglawcenter.org/assets/crs/RL33258.pdf.

64. Schemo, Tense times on front line.

65. *Columbia Electronic Encyclopedia*. 2007. Brazil: History. Retrieved January 29, 2010, from http://www.infoplease.com/ce6/world/A0857011.html.

66. Embassy of Brazil—Ottawa. Economy. Retrieved January 27, 2010, from http://www.brasembottawa.org/en/brazil_in_brief/economy.html.

67. History World. The history of Brazil. Retrieved January 27, 2010, from http://www.historyworld.net/wrldhis/PlainTextHistories.asp?groupid=891&HistoryID=aa88.

68. Brazilian economic performance since 1500: A comparative view. April 4, 2000. Paper presented at XIII Forum de Liberdade. Retrieved January 27, 2010, from http://www.ggdc.net/maddison/ARTICLES/Brazil_500.pdf.

69. History World, The history of Brazil.

70. Watkins, Thayer. The economic system of corporatism. San Jose State University Department of Economics. Retrieved January 28, 2010, from http://www.sjsu.edu/faculty/watkins/corporatism.htm.

71. Embassy of Brazil—Ottawa, Economy.

72. Watkins, The economic system of corporatism.

73. Vignogna, Mary E. 2000. The Brazilian economic crisis. Augusta State University. Retrieved January 27, 2010, from http://www.aug.edu/pkp/2000/conf-2000-vignogna.PDF; History World, The history of Brazil.

74. Brazilian economic performance since 1500.

75. Ibid.

76. U.S. Department of State, Background note: Brazil.

77. Ibid.

78. Ibid.

79. Embassy of Brazil—Ottawa, Economy.

80. Downie, Andrew. 2008. Brazil's counterattack on biofuels. *Time* (April 28). Retrieved February 1, 2010, from http://www.time.com/time/world/article/0,8599,1735644,00.html.

81. Clendenning, Alan. 2008. Brazil's biofuel industry dries up. *Boston Globe* via Associated Press (November 23). Retrieved February 1, 2010, from http://www.boston.com/news/world/latinamerica/articles/2008/11/23/brazils_biofuel_industry_dries_up/.

82. Embassy of Brazil—Ottawa. Natural resources. Retrieved February 1, 2010, from http://www.brasembottawa.org/en/brazil_in_brief/natural_resources.html.

83. Clendenning, Alan. 2007. Offshore discovery could make Brazil major oil exporter. *USA Today* via Associated Press (November 9). Retrieved February 1, 2010, from http://www.usatoday.com/money/industries/energy/2007-11-09-brazil-oil_N.htm.

84. U.S. Department of State, Background note: Brazil.

85. Embassy of Brazil—Ottawa, Natural resources.

86. Phillips, Tom. 2008. The country of the future finally arrives. *The Guardian* (May 10). Retrieved February 1, 2010, from http://www.guardian.co.uk/world/2008/may/10/brazil.oil.

87. U.S. Department of State, Background note: Brazil.

88. Brookings Institution. 2009. Brazil in the global crisis: Still a rising economic superpower? (July 13). Washington, D.C. Retrieved April 13, 2010, from http://www.brookings.edu/~/media/Files/events/2009/0713_brazil/20090713_brazil.pdf.

89. Ibid.; U.S. Department of State, Background note: Brazil.

90. Hornbeck, *Brazilian trade policy and the United States.*

91. U.S. Department of State, Background note: Brazil.

92. Brazil Institute. 2009. The evolving configuration of the October 2010 elections. Woodrow Wilson International Center for Scholars. (September 11). Retrieved February 1, 2010, from http:///brazilportal.wordpress.com/2009/09/11/paulo-sotero-on-election-possibilities-in-brazil/.

93. Ibid.; Valdes, Constanza. 2006. Brazil emerges as major force in global meat markets. *U.S. Department of Agriculture Amber Waves Magazine* (April). Retrieved February 1, 2010, from http://www.ers.usda.gov/AmberWaves/April06/Findings/Brazil.htm; U.S. Department of Agriculture. 2009. Countries/products eligible for export to the United States (December 11). Retrieved February 1, 2010, from http://www.fsis.usda.gov/pdf/Countries_Products_Eligible_for_Export.pdf.

94. Valdes, Brazil emerges as major force in global meat markets.

95. BBC News. 1999. Yeltsin's resignation speech. (December 31). Retrieved April 13, 2010, from http://news.bbc.co.uk/2/hi/world/monitoring/584845.stm.

96. Rutland, Peter. 2005. Putin's economic record. In *Developments in Russian politics*, vol. 6, ed. S. White, Z. Y. Gitelman, and R. Sakwa. Durham, NC: Duke University Press.

97. Federal Research Division, U.S. Library of Congress. 1996. *A country study: Russia.* Retrieved May 28, 2010, from http://memory.loc.gov/frd/cs/rutoc.html.

98. Gee, Alastair. 2008. Rising anti-Americanism in Russia. *U.S. News and World Report* (January 18). Retrieved January 30, 2010, from http://www.usnews.com/articles/news/world/2008/01/18/rising-anti-americanism-in-russia.html.

99. Ibid.

100. Knight, Amy. 2008. The truth about Putin and Medvedev. *New York Review of Books* (May 15). Retrieved January 26, 2010, from http://www.nybooks.com/articles/21353.

101. Fishman, Mikhail. 2009. Who's the boss now? *Newsweek* (May 15). Retrieved January 26, 2010, from http://www.newsweek.com/id/197789.

102. Stack, Megan K. 2009. Medvedev talks like the anti-Putin. *Los Angeles Times* (November 13). Retrieved January 26, 2010, from http://articles.latimes.com/2009/nov/13/world/fg-russia-medvedev13.

103. Fishman, Who's the boss now?

104. Beyrle, John. 2009. Russia and America's shared economic future. Address delivered April 29 at Higher School of Economics in Moscow, Russia. Retrieved January 30, 2010, from http://moscow.usembassy.gov/beyrlerem042909.html.

105. Ibid.

106. Brown, Peter. 2009. Do the math: Why Russia won't be a superpower anytime soon. *Wall Street Journal* (August 26). Retrieved May 27, 2010, from http://blogs.wsj.com/capitaljournal/2009/08/26/do-the-math-why-russia-won%E2%80%99t-be-a-superpower-anytime-soon/.

107. *CIA World Factbook.* Russia. Retrieved January 28, 2010, from https://www.cia.gov/library/publications/the-world-factbook/geos/rs.html.

108. Ibid.

109. Brown, Do the math.

110. Ibid.

111. Friedman, *The world is flat.*

112. Stelzer, Irwin. 2010. Investments will remain a gamble until rule of law comes to Russia. *Wall Street Journal* (January 4). Retrieved April 13, 2010, from http://online.wsj.com/article/SB10001424052748704152804574627841894245048.html.

113. Pan, Philip. 2008. Financial crisis in Russia raises stakes for Putin. *Washington Post* (September 21). Retrieved January 27, 2010, from http://www.washingtonpost.com/wp-dyn/content/article/2008/09/20/AR2008092001858.html.

114. SandHill.com. 2006. Best practices: Offshoring and outsourcing. (February 20). Retrieved April 13, 2010, from http://www.sandhill.com/opinion/daily_blog.php?id=27&post=125.

115. Moser, Evelyn, and Nestmann, Thorsten. August 20, 2007. "Russia's Financial Sector: Financial Deepening Will Support Long-Term Growth," Deutsche Banks Research Report. Retrieved January 27, 2010, from "http://www.dbresearch.com/ PROD/DBR_INTERNET_EN-PROD/PROD0000000000214153.pdf" http://www.dbreasearch.com/PROD/DBR_INTERNET)EN-PROD/PROD0000000000214153.pdf.

116. BOFIT Weekly. 2010. Russia (January 8). Retrieved April 13, 2010, from http://www.bof.fi/NR/rdonlyres/4F59BA5D-D0E0-44E5-BD9F-F7B054E4E423/0/w201001.pdf.

117. Friedman, *The world is flat.*

118. Aron, Leon. 2002. Russia reinvents the rule of law. *AEI Russian Outlook* (Spring). Retrieved January 27, 2010, from http://siteresources.worldbank.org/INTLAWJUSTINST/Resources/aronRussiaJudicialReform.pdf. Collins, James, and Anton Ivanov. 2009. Rule of law in Russia. Public dialogue sponsored by the Carnegie Endowment for International Peace (April 3). Retrieved January 27, 2010, from http://www.carnegieendowment.org/events/?fa=eventDetail&id=1314. Edwards, Lynda. 2009. Russia claws at the rule of law. *ABA Journal* (July 1). Retrieved January 27, 2010, from http://www.abajournal.com/magazine/article/russia_claws_at_the_rule_of_law/.

119. Cappelli, Peter, Harbir Singh, Jitendra Singh, and Michael Useem. 2010. *The India way: How India's top business leaders are revolutionizing management.* Boston: HBP; Spencer, Signe M., Tharuma Rajah, S.A. Naryayan, Seetharaman Lmohan, and Gaurav Lahiri, 2010. *The Indian CEO: A portrait of excellence.* Los Angeles: Response Business Books from Sage.

120. Columbia Electronic Encyclopedia, India: History.

121. U.S. Department of State, Background note: India.

122. *Columbia Electronic Encyclopedia,* India: History.

123. United Nations Population Division. 1999. The twenty most populous countries in 1950, 1999, and 2050. Retrieved February 2, 2010, from http://www.un.org/esa/population/pubsarchive/india/20most.htm.

124. *Columbia Electronic Encyclopedia,* India: History.

125. Singh, Manmohan. 2005. Of Oxford, economics, empire, and freedom. *The Hindu* (July 10). Retrieved February 2, 2010, from http://www.hindu.com/2005/07/10/stories/2005071002301000.htm.

126. British Broadcasting Corporation. 1998. India: The economy (December 3). Retrieved. February 3, 2010, from http://news.bbc.co.uk/2/hi/south_asia/55427.stm.

127. Ibid.

128. *Columbia Electronic Encyclopedia.* 2007. India: History. Retrieved February 2, 2010, from http://www.infoplease.com/ce6/world/A0858782.html.

129. U.S. Department of State, Background note: India.

130. *Columbia Electronic Encyclopedia,* India: History.

131. British Broadcasting Corporation, India: The economy.

132. Organization for Economic Cooperation and Development (OECD). 2007. *Policy brief: Economic survey of India* (October). Retrieved February 3, 2010, from http://www.oecd.org/dataoecd/17/52/39452196.pdf.

133. British Broadcasting Corporation, India: The economy; *CIA world factbook.* 2009. India. Retrieved February 3, 2010, from https://www.cia.gov/library/publications/the-world-factbook/geos/in.html.

134. OECD, *Policy brief*; Singh, Kulwindar. 2005. Foreign direct investment in India: A critical analysis of FDI from 1991–2005. Center for Civil Society, New Delhi. Retrieved February 3, 2010, from http://unpan1.un.org/intradoc/groups/public/documents/APCITY/UNPAN024036.pdf.

135. OECD, *Policy brief.*

136. *CIA world factbook*, India.

137. U.S. Department of State, Background note: India.

138. OECD, *Policy brief.*

139. Ministry of External Affairs. Why India? Government of India. Retrieved February 2, 2010, from http://www.indiainbusiness.nic.in/whyindia.thm.

140. Ministry of External Affairs. Economy: Potential for investment in India. Retrieved February 2, 2010, from http://www.indiainbusiness.nic.in/investment/potential_investment.htm.

141. Ibid.

142. *CIA world factbook*, India.

143. Bhargava, Rajat, Rajat Gupta, and Babar Khan. 2005. Unearthing India's mineral wealth. *McKinsey Quarterly* (September). Retrieved February 3, 2010, from http://www.mckinseyquarterly.com/Energy_Resources_Materials/Strategy_Analysis/Unearthing_Indias_mineral_wealth_1657?gp=1.

144. OECD, *Policy brief.*

145. Ministry of External Affairs, Why India?

146. Joshi, Harsh. 2010. India's taste for inflation fight. *Wall Street Journal* (January 30). Retrieved February 2, 2010, from http://online.wsj.com/article/SB100014240527487033890004575032663512689570.html.

147. OECD, *Policy brief.*; Sircar, Subhadip. 2010. RBI: No early rate hikes if inflation within estimate. *Wall Street Journal* (February 1). Retrieved February 3, 2010, from http://online.wsj.com/article/SB10001424052748704107204575038893625795962.html?mod=WSJ_latestheadlines.

148. Joshi, India's taste for inflation fight.

149. Friedman, *The world is flat.*

150. Cappelli, Singh, Singh, and Useem. The India way: How India's top business leaders are revolutionizing management.

151. OECD, *Policy brief.*

152. *CIA world factbook*, India.

153. British Broadcasting Corporation, India: The economy.

154. *CIA world factbook*, India.

155. Singh, Avantika. 2009. Growth of the middle class in India: Implications for domestic tourism (January 13). Retrieved February 3, 2010, from http://www.4hoteliers.com/4hots_fshw.php?mwi=3690.

156. Ibid.

157. Nath, Kamal. 2010. India's road to progress. *Wall Street Journal* (January 26). Retrieved February 2, 2010, from http://online.wsj.com/article/SB10001424052748703808904575026043518922322.html.

158. Wikipedia.org. List of countries by English-speaking population. Retrieved February 3, 2010, from http://en.wikipedia.org/wiki/List_of_countries_by_English-speaking_population.

159. U.S. Department of State, Background note: India.

160. Majumder, Sanjoy. 2006. Furor reflects India's caste complexities. *BBC News* (May 20). Retrieved February 3, 2010, from http://news.bbc.co.uk/2/hi/south_asia/4998274.stm.

161. Republican China. Retrieved February 1, 2010, from http://www-chaos.umd.edu/history/republican.html#nationalism.

162. Fairbank, J. K., and D. C. Twitchett. 1986. *The Cambridge history of China: Republican China 1912–1949, part 2.* Cambridge: Cambridge University Press.

163. Mayhew, B. 2004. *Shanghai.* United Kingdom: Lonely Planet.

164. Fairbank and Twitchett, *The Cambridge history of China.*

165. Ibid.

166. Ibid.

167. Ibid.

168. MacFarquhar, R., J. K. Fairbank, and D. Twitchett. 1991. *Cambridge history of China: The People's Republic, part 2: Revolutions within the Chinese Revolution, 1966–1982.* Cambridge: Cambridge University Press.

169. Ibid.

170. Ibid.

171. Ibid.

172. Ibid.

173. Beam, Christopher. 2009. Tussle in Tiananmen Square. *Slate.* (June 3). Retrieved February 1, 2010, from http://www.slate.com/id/2219697/.

174. Friedman, *The world is flat.*

175. Friedman, *The world is flat.*

176. Organization for Economic Cooperation and Development (OECD). 2006. *OECD investment policy reviews China: Open policies towards mergers and acquisitions.* Paris: OECD Publications.

177. Zakaria, Fareed. 2005. Does the future belong to China? *Newsweek* (May 9). Retrieved February 3, 2010, from http://www.newsweek.com/id/51964.

178. *CIA world factbook.* 2009. China. Retrieved April 13, 2010, from https://www.cia.gov/library/publications/the-world-factbook/geos/ch.html.

179. Friedman, *The world is flat.*

180. Human Rights Watch. 2009. *World report.* New York: Seven Stories Press.

181. Hodgson, Ann. 2007. China's middle class reaches 80 million. Euromonitor International (July 25). Retrieved February 3, 2010, from http://www.euromonitor.com/Chinas_middle_class_reaches_80_million.

182. Reynolds, James. 2007. Wifeless future for China's men. BBC News. (February 12). Retrieved February 3, 2010, from http://news.bbc.co.uk/2/hi/6346931.stm.

183. Friedman, *The world is flat.*

184. Malone, Robert. 2006. America's most polluted cities. *Forbes.com* (March 22). Retrieved February 3, 2010, from http://www.forbes.com/2006/03/21/americas-most-polluted-cities-cx_rm_0321pollute.html.

185. Friedman, *The world is flat.*

186. China Gateway. Protecting your intellectual property rights (IPR) in China. Retrieved February 3, 2010, from http://www.mac.doc.gov/China/Docs/businessguides/IntellectualPropertyRights.htm.

187. Ibid.

188. Wikipedia.org. Pet food recalls. Retrieved February 3, 2010, from http://en.wikipedia.org/wiki/2007_pet_food_recalls#Affected_brands; Wikipedia.org. Chinese export recalls. Retrieved February 3, 2010, from http://en.wikipedia.org/wiki/2007_Chinese_export_recalls#Mattel.

189. Bogdanich, Walt. 2007. Chinese chemicals flow unchecked onto world drug market. *New York Times* (October 31). Retrieved January 11, 2010, from http://www.nytimes.com/2007/10/31/world/asia/31chemical.html.

190. Seven Natural Wonders. Victoria Falls. Retrieved April 13, 2010, from http://sevennaturalwonders.org/the-original/victoria-falls.

191. ZambiaTourism.com. South Luangwa National Park. Retrieved April 13, 2010, from http://www.zambiatourism.com/travel/nationalparks/sluangwa.htm.

192. Kabalata, Mercy. Developing tourism through smart partnership. Retrieved March 18, 2010, from http://www.times.co.zm/news/viewnews.cgi?category=8&id=1219492976.

193. *CIA world factbook.* 2009. Zambia. Retrieved April 13, 2010, from https://www.cia.gov/library/publications/the-world-factbook/geos/za.html.

194. Ibid.

195. Ibid.

196. Permanent Mission of the Republic of Zambia to the United Nations. 2010. Note no. 56b/2010 (March 9). Retrieved April 13, 2010, from http://unfccc.int/files/meetings/application/pdf/zambiacphaccord.pdf.

197. Balat, Jorge F., and Guido G. Porto. 2005. Globalization and complementary policies: Poverty impacts in rural Zambia. In *Globalization and poverty*, ed. Ann E. Harrison, 373–416. London: University of Chicago Press.

198. Ibid., 411.

199. World Trade Organization. Home page. Retrieved October 20, 2009, from http://www.wto.org/.

200. Europa. Economic activity and trade. Retrieved April 13, 2010, from http://europa.eu/abc/keyfigures/tradeandeconomy/index_en.htm.

201. Ibid.

202. Ibid.

203. Clark, Cynthia, and Elaine Turney. 2003. *Encyclopedia of tariffs and trade in U.S. history*, 280. Westport, CT: Greenwood Press.

204. United States Senate. U.S. Senate roll call votes 103rd Congress, 1st Session. Retrieved April 13, 2010, from http://www.senate.gov/legislative/LIS/roll_call_lists/roll_call_vote_cfm.cfm?congress=103&session=1&vote=00395.

205. Posner, Gerald L. 1996. *Citizen Perot: His life and times.* New York: Random House.

206. Teslick, Lee Hudson. 2009. NAFTA's economic impact. Council on Foreign Relations (July 7). Retrieved April 13, 2010, from http://www.cfr.org/publication/15790/#p4.

207. Faux, Jeff, Carlos Salas, and Robert E. Scott. 2006. Revisiting NAFTA: Still not working for North American workers. Economic Policy Institute (September 28). Retrieved April 13, 2010, from http://www.epi.org/publications/entry/bp173/.

208. Ibid.

209. U.S. House of Representatives Resolution 3045. 2005. Retrieved April 13, 2010, from http://thomas.loc.gov/cgi-bin/bdquery/z?d109:HR03045:@@@R.

210. CAFTA Intelligence Center. Home page. Retrieved May 27, 2010, from http://www.caftaintelligencecenter.com/.

211. World Trade Organization. DOHA development agenda. Retrieved April 13, 2010, from http://tcbdb.wto.org/trta_project.aspx?prjCode=113-0439-03-B&benHostId=116.

212. Bilaterals.org 2007. Two years of CAFTA: Deep impacts in Central America and the Dominican Republic (November). Retrieved April 13, 2010, from http://www.bilaterals.org/article.php3?id_article=15272.

213. CAFTA Intelligence Center. What is CAFTA? Retrieved April 13, 2010, from http://www.caftaintelligencecenter.com/subpages/What_is_CAFTA.asp.

214. Goodman, Joshua. 2007. South American presidents agree to form Unasur bloc. *Bloomberg.com* (May 23). Retrieved April 13, 2010, from http://www.bloomberg.com/apps/news?pid=20601087&sid=abWOMOeJUK7Y&refer=home.

215. Ibid.

216. UNASUR. Retrieved April 13, 2010, from http://www.comunidadandina.org/ingles/sudamerican.htm.

217. Association of Southeast Asian Nations. Overview. Retrieved April 13, 2010, from http://www.aseansec.org/about_ASEAN.html.

218. Ibid.

219. Association of Southeast Asian Nations. 2007. 13th ASEAN summit press statement (November 20). Retrieved April 13, 2010, from http://app.mti.gov.sg/data/article/11702/doc/AEC%20BLUEPRINT PressRelease%28final%29%28formatted%29.pdf.

220. Association of Southeast Asian Nations. The founding of ASEAN. Retrieved April 13, 2010, from http://www.aseansec.org/20024.htm.

221. Asia-Pacific Economic Cooperation. Achievements and benefits. Retrieved April 13, 2010, from http://www.apec.org/apec/about_apec/achievements_and_benefits.html.

222. Giles, Chris. 2009. G20 yet to deliver on early promise. *Financial Times* (November 8). Retrieved April 13, 2010, from http://www.ft.com/cms/s/8e834f02-cc63-11de-8e30-00144feabdc0,Authorised=false.html?_i_location=http%3A%2F%2Fwww.ft.com%2Fcms%2Fs%2F0%2F8e834f02-cc63-11de-8e30-00144feabdc0.html&_i_referer=http%3A%2F%2Fsearch.ft.com%2Fsearch%3FqueryText%3DG20%2BYet%2Bto%2BDeliver%2Bon%2BEarly%2BPromise%26aje%3Dtrue%26dse%3D%26dsz%3D%26x%3D9%26y%3D7.

223. G-20. About G-20. Retrieved April 7, 2010, from http://www.g20.org/about_what_is_g20.aspx.

224. Ibid.

225. Ibid.

226. London Summit 2009. Explanatory guide to the communiqué. Retrieved April 7, 2010, from http://www.londonsummit.gov.uk/en/summit-aims/communique-explanation/.

227. Ibid.

228. World Economic Forum. About the World Economic Forum: Entrepreneurship in the global public interest. Retrieved December 18, 2009, from http://www.weforum.org/en/about/index.htm. World Economic Forum. Frequently asked questions. Retrieved December 18, 2009, from http://www.weforum.org/en/about/FAQs/index.htm.

229. World Economic Forum, Frequently asked questions.

230. World Economic Forum. History and achievements. Retrieved December 18, 2009, from http://www.weforum.org/en/about/History%20and%20Achievements/index.htm.

231. World Economic Forum. What is the role of business in advancing economic development and social progress? Retrieved December 18, 2009, from weforum.org/en/initiatives/index.htm.

232. World Economic Forum, Frequently asked questions.

233. World Economic Forum. Our organization. Retrieved December 18, 2009, from http://www.weforum.org/en/about/Our%20Organization/index.htm.

234. New York Times. 2009. World Economic Forum (Davos). *New York Times* (January 26). Retrieved December 18, 2009, from http://topics.nytimes.com/topics/reference/timestopics/organizations/w/world_economic_forum/index.html.

235. Lendman, Stephen. 2009. Competing ideologies: Davos v. Belem. *Global Research.ca.* (February 3). Retrieved December 18, 2009, from http://www.globalresearch.ca/index.php?context=va&aid=12144.

236. United Nations Economic and Social Council. ECOSOC background information. Retrieved January 11, 2010, from http://www.un.org/ecosoc/about/.

237. Office of the Iraq Programme of the United Nations. About the programme. Retrieved January 11, 2010, from http://www.un.org/Depts/oip/background/index.html.

238. United Nations Foundation. Frequently asked questions about the Oil-for-Food Program. Retrieved January 11, 2010, from http://www.oilforfoodfacts.org/faq.aspx.

239. Otterman, Sharon. 2005. Iraq: Oil for food scandal. Council on Foreign Relations (October 28). Retrieved January 11, 2010, from http://www.cfr.org/publication/7631/iraq.html.

240. United Nations Foundation, Frequently asked questions about the Oil-for-Food Program.

241. Gordon, Joy. 2004. UN Oil for Food "scandal." *The Nation* (November 18). Retrieved January 11, 2010, from http://www.thenation.com/doc/20041206/gordon.

242. Zander, L. 2005. Communication and country clusters: A study of language and leadership preferences. *International Studies of Management and Organization* 35(1): 83–103; Kogut, B., and U. Zander. 1992. Knowledge of the firm, combinative capabilities, and the replication of technology. *Organization Science* 3(3): 383–97.

243. Harzing, A.-W., and A. J. Feely. 2008. The language barrier and its implications for HQ-subsidiary relationships. *Cross-Cultural Management* 15(1): 49–61; Zander, Communication and country clusters.

244. Van Alstyne, Marshall W. 2005. Create colleagues, not competitors. *Harvard Business Review* 83(9): 24–28.

245. Ibid.

246. IBM. 2009. Extreme blue. Retrieved September 12, 2009, from http://www-01.ibm.com/employment/us/extremeblue/index.html; IBM. Extreme blue frequently asked questions. Retrieved April 26, 2010, from http://www-01.ibm.com/employment/us/extremeblue/faq2.html.

247. IBM. 2003. Speed teams (June 23). Retrieved September 12, 2009, from http://www-01.ibm.com/employment/us/extremeblue/article/speed_teams.html.

248. Hymowitz, Carol. 2008. IBM creates volunteer teams to cultivate emerging markets. *Wall Street Journal* (August 4). Retrieved September 12, 2009, from http://online.wsj.com/article/SB121779236200008095.html.

249. Ibid.

250. Ibid.

251. Teleos Leadership Institute. Executive coach development program: Core competencies. Retrieved April 7, 2010, from http://www.coachfederation.org/research-education/icf-credentials/core-competencies.

252. Sims, Ronald R. 2003. *Ethics and corporate social responsibility: Why giants fall.* Westport, CT: Greenwood Publishing.

253. Chippendale, Paul. 2001. *On values, ethics, morals, and principles.* Retrieved February 8, 2010, from http://www.minessence.net/AVI_Accred/pdfs/ValuesEthicsPrinciples.PDF.

254. Franke, J., and N. Nicholson. 2002. Who shall we send? Cultural and other influences on the rating of selection criteria for expatriate assignments. *International Journal of Cross Cultural Management* 2(1): 21–36.

255. Zander, Communication and country clusters.

Chapter 15

1. Interface. What is sustainability? Retrieved April 26, 2010, from http://www.interfaceglobal.com/Sustainability/What-is-Sustainability-.aspx.

2. United Nations. *Our common future, chapter 2: Towards sustainable development.* Retrieved April 26, 2010, from http://www.un-documents.net/ocf-02.htm.

3. Vasey, Daniel E. 1992. *An ecological history of agriculture, 10,000 B.C.–A.D. 10,000.* Ames: Iowa State University Press.

4. Kradin, Nikolay N. 2002. Nomadism, evolution, and world-systems: Pastoral societies in theories of historical development. *Journal of World-Systems Research* 8(3): 368–88.

5. Dawkins, Richard. 2004. *The ancestor's tale: A pilgrimage to the dawn of evolution.* New York: Houghton-Mifflin Company.

6. Saitoti, Tepilit Ole, and Carol Beckwith. 1949. *Maasai.* New York: Abradale Press.

7. Maasai Association. Maasai ceremonies and rituals. Retrieved November 3, 2009, from http://www.maasai-association.org/ceremonies.html.

8. Berntsen, John L. 1976. The Maasai and their neighbors: Variables of interaction. *African Economic History* 2: 1–11.

9. Anderson, David M. 1993. Cow power: Livestock and the pastoralist in Africa. *African Affairs* 92(366): 121–33.

10. Maasai Association, Maasai ceremonies and rituals.

11. Fagan, Brian. 2000. *The little ice age: How climate made history, 1300–1850.* New York: Basic Books.

12. Twicken, Joe. 1999. Greenhouse effect. Retrieved April 29, 2010, from http://nova.stanford.edu/projects/mod-x/id-green.html.

13. National Aeronautics and Space Administration. 2010. GISS surface temperature analysis. Retrieved January 22, 2010, from http://data.giss.nasa.gov/gistemp/graphs.

14. Revkin, Andrew. 2009. Skeptics dispute climate worries and each other. *New York Times* (March 8). Retrieved April 26, 2010, from http://www.nytimes.com/2009/03/09/science/earth/09climate.html.

15. United Nations Intergovernmental Panel on Climate Change (IPCC). 2007. Summary for policymakers. In *Climate change 2007: The physical science basis. Contribution of Working Group I to the Fourth Assessment Report of the Intergovernmental Panel on Climate Change,* ed. S. Solomon, D. Qin, M. Manning, Z. Chen, M. Marquis, K. B. Averyt, M. Tignor, and H. L. Miller. Cambridge, UK: Cambridge University Press.

16. Pittock, I. B. 2007. The enhanced greenhouse effect: Threats to Australia's water resources. *Journal of the Australian Water Association* (August): 36–38; Morales, Pablo, Thomas Hickler, David P. Rowell, Benjamin Smith, and Martin T. Sykes. 2007. Changes in European ecosystem productivity and carbon balance driven by regional climate model output. *Global Change Biology* 13: 108–22; Seidel, Dian J., Qiang Fu, William J. Randel, and Thomas J. Reichler. 2008. Widening of the tropical belt in a changing climate. *Nature Geoscience* 1: 21–24. Retrieved January 23, 2010, from http://www.arl.noaa.gov/documents/JournalPDFs/SeidelEtAl.ngeo.2007.38.pdf.

17. Table adapted from United Nations Intergovernmental Panel on Climate Change (IPCC). 2007. Synthesis report. In *Climate change 2007: Contribution of Working Groups I, II, and III to the Fourth Assessment Report of the Intergovernmental Panel on Climate Change,* ed. R. K. Pachauri and A. Reisinger. Geneva: IPCC.

18. Shaw, Randy. 1999. *Reclaiming America: Nike, clean air, and the new national activism.* Berkeley: University of California Press.

19. Miller, George. 2004. Everyday low wages: The hidden price we all pay for Wal-mart. A report by the Democratic staff of the Committee on Education and the Workforce (February 16). Retrieved January 23, 2010, from http://www.wakeupwalmart.com/facts/miller-report.pdf.

20. Mills, Elinor. 2008. Jerry Yang lobbies for release of Chinese dissidents. *BusinessWeek* (February 25). Retrieved January 23, 2010, from http://www.businessweek.com/globalbiz/content/feb2008/gb20080225_248127.htm?campaign_id=rss_daily.

21. FitzGerald, Niall. 2006. Why the investment climate for Africa deserves U.S. support: A response to the "CGD Note: The Investment Climate Facility for Africa: Does it deserve U.S. support?" Retrieved January 23, 2010, from http://www.cgdev.org/doc/commentary/ICFResponseCGDNote.pdf.

22. FitzGerald, Niall. 2009. Corporate responsibility in the twenty-first century. Tyburn Lecture, May 20, Tyburn Convent, London.

23. United Nations General Assembly. 2005. 2005 world summit outcome (Resolution A/60/1) (September 15). Retrieved November 2, 2009, from http://daccess-dds-ny.un.org/doc/UNDOC/GEN/N05/487/60/PDF/N0548760.pdf?OpenElement.

24. United Nations Millennium Development Goals. Goal 7: Ensure environmental sustainability. Retrieved April 26, 2010, from http://www.un.org/millenniumgoals/environ.shtml.

25. United Nations. Information management for social aspects of sustainable development training module. Retrieved April 26, 2010, from www.un.org/esa/sustdev/natlinfo/indicators/idsd/workshops/workshop10-27-31/02_TRAINING%20MODULE.doc.

26. United Nations Economic Commission for Africa. Transforming Africa's economies, 18. Retrieved April 26, 2010, from www.uneca.org/eca_resources/Publications/books/transforming_africas_economies/ECA_Overview_03.pdf.

27. United Nations Educational, Scientific, and Cultural Organization. 2007. The UN decade of education for sustainable development (DESD 2005–2014): The first two years. Paris: UNESCO. Retrieved April 26, 2010, from http://unesdoc.unesco.org/images/0015/001540/154093e.pdf.

28. United Nations. 2002. World Summit on Sustainable Development (August 26–September 4). Retrieved May 22, 2010, from http://www.un.org/events/wssd/summaries/envdevj8.htm.

29. Broughton, Edward. 2005. The Bhopal disaster and its aftermath. *Environmental Health* 4(6).

30. Ibid.

31. Ibid.; *Encyclopædia Britannica.* 2010. Bhopal disaster. Retrieved January 19, 2010, from http://www.britannica.com/EBchecked/topic/1257131/Bhopal-disaster.

32. Broughton, The Bhopal disaster and its aftermath.

33. Ibid., 3.

34. Kumar, S. 2004. Victims of gas leak in Bhopal seek redress on compensation. *British Medical Journal* 329(7462): 366; Lahri, Tripti. "Three things for the Bhopal Panel to consider." *The Wall Street Journal* (June 16, 2010). Retrieved June 16, 2010, from http://blogs.wsj.com/indiarealtime/2010/06/16/three-things-for-the-bhopal-panel-to-consider/.

35. Bhopal Medical Appeal. Poisoned water: Corporate, municipal, and medical neglect condemn many to death. Retrieved January 19, 2010, from http://www.bhopal.org/index.php?id=111.

36. Power, M. 2004. The poison stream: Letter from Kerala. *Harper's* (August): 51–61.

37. Carbide waste to go: HC. 2008. *Times of India* (December 16). Retrieved January 19, 2010, from http://timesofindia.indiatimes.com/India/Carbide_waste_to_go_HC/articleshow/3847412.cms.

38. Global 100. 2010 Global 100: The definitive corporate sustainability benchmark. Retrieved April 26, 2010, from http://www.global100.org.

39. Mills, Enos A. 1917. Your national parks. Cambridge, MA: Houghton-Mifflin Company.

40. National Park Service. Frequently asked questions. Retrieved November 5, 2009, from http://www.nps.gov/faqs.htm.

41. Crandall, Robert W. 2008. Pollution controls. In *Concise encyclopedia of economics.* Library of Economics and Liberty. Retrieved August 31, 2009, from http://www.econlib.org/library/Enc/PollutionControls.html.

42. United States Environmental Protection Agency. 2009. Environmental progress. Retrieved January 24, 2010, from http://www.epa.gov/earthday/history.htm#1.

43. United States Environmental Protection Agency. Timeline. Retrieved April 26, 2010, from http://www.epa.gov/history/timeline/index.htm.

44. United States Environmental Protection Agency. Laws that we administer. Retrieved May 22, 2010, from http://www.epa.gov/lawsregs/laws/index.html.

45. United Nations Framework Convention on Climate Change. Kyoto Protocol. Retrieved November 7, 2009, from http://unfccc.int/kyoto_protocol/items/2830.php.

46. Carey, John. 2009. Obama's cap and trade plan. *Bloomberg Businessweek* (March 5). Retrieved April 26, 2010, from http://www.businessweek.com/magazine/content/09_11/b4123022554346.htm.

47. The White House. Energy and environment. Retrieved April 29, 2010, from http://www.whitehouse.gov/issues/energy-and-environment.

48. United Nations Framework Convention on Climate Change. Clean development mechanism. Retrieved November 7, 2009, http://unfccc.int/kyoto_protocol/mechanisms/clean_development_mechanism/items/2718.php.

49. United Nations Framework Convention on Climate Change, Joint implementation. Retrieved November 7, 2009, from http://unfccc.int/kyoto_protocol/mechanisms/joint_implementation/items/1674.php.

50. United Nations Framework Convention on Climate Change, Kyoto Protocol.

51. The world's top 25 greenhouse gas emitters. 2008. *Reuters* (November 25). Retrieved April 11, 2010, from http://www.alertnet.org/thenews/newsdesk/LP343601.htm.

52. Global Carbon Project. 2008. Carbon budget and trends 2007. Retrieved September 26, 2008, from http://www.globalcarbonproject.org.

53. Lomborg, Bjørn. 2007. *Cool it: The skeptical environmentalist's guide to global warming.* New York: Alfred A. Knopf.

54. 105th Congress 1st Session. S. Res. 98. Retrieved April 26, 2010, from http://frwebgate.access.gpo.gov/cgi-bin/getdoc.cgi?dbname=105_cong_bills&docid=f:sr98ats.txt.pdf.

55. Northrop, Michael, and David Sassoon. 2009. Ambitious actions by the states push U.S. toward climate goals. *Environment 360* (December 8). Retrieved December 8, 2009, from http://www.e360.yale.edu/content/feature.msp?id=2219.

56. Xinhua News. 2009. Global efforts to fight climate change—from Rio de Janeiro to Copenhagen. *China.org.cn* (December 7). Retrieved January 19, 2010, from http://www.china.org.cn/environment/Copenhagen/2009-12/07/content_19019633.htm.

57. Friedman, Lisa. 2009. The major players in the Copenhagen talks and their positions. *New York Times* (December 8). Retrieved December 8, 2009, from http://www.nytimes.com/cwire/2009/12/08/08climatewire-the-major-players-in-the-copenhagen-talks-an-45792.html.

58. Aljazeera. China attacks rich states at summit. 2009. *Aljazeera.net* (December 9). Retrieved December 9, 2009, from http://english.aljazeera.net/news/europe/2009/12/2009128234918828775.html.

59. Talley, Ian. 2009. EPA declares greenhouse gases a danger. *Wall Street Journal* (December 8). Retrieved December 8, 2009, from http://online.wsj.com/article/SB20001424052748703558004574582190625776518.html; Dlouhy, Jennifer A., and Matthew Tresaugue. 2009. EPA declares greenhouse gases pose health risk. *San Francisco Chronicle* (December 8). Retrieved December 8, 2009, from http://www.sfgate.com/cgi-bin/article.cgi?f=/c/a/2009/12/08/MNDA1B0I89.DTL&type=health.

60. National Public Radio. 2009. UN climate chief urges avoiding blame over summit. (December 23). Retrieved January 19, 2010, from http://www.npr.org/templates/story/story.php?storyId=120160589; Memmott, Mark. 2009. Obama in Copenhagen; climate talks in disarray; urges "action over inaction. "National Public Radio (December 18). Retrieved January 19, 2010, from http://www.npr.org/blogs/thetwo-way/2009/12/obama_in_copenhagen_climate_ch.html; Indo-Asian News Service. 2009. Last day of Copenhagen summit, hope fizzling out. *IBN Live* (December 18). Retrieved January 19, 2010, from http://ibnlive.in.com/news/last-day-of-copenhagen-summit-hope-fizzling-out/107355-11.html.

61. Aljazeera. China attacks rich states at summit; Vidal, John. 2009. Copenhagen: Leaked draft deal widens rift between rich and poor nations. *Guardian* (December 9). Retrieved December 9, 2009, from http://www.guardian.co.uk/environment/2009/dec/09/copenhagen-summit-danish-text-leak.

62. United Nations Framework Convention on Climate Change. 2009. Draft decision -/CP.15: Copenhagen Accord (December 18). Retrieved January 19, 2010, from http://unfccc.int/resource/docs/2009/cop15/eng/l07.pdf.

63. Schneider, Keith. 2009. Climate agreement not accepted, but Copenhagen conference makes it "operational." *Copenhagen Insider* (December 19). Retrieved January 19, 2010, from http://copenhagen.nationaljournal.com/2009/12/climate-agreement-not-accepted.php; Taylor, Paul. 2010. E.U. seeks to regain influence on response to climate change. *New York Times* (January 15). Retrieved January 19, 2009, from http://www.nytimes.com/2010/01/16/business/global/16iht-inside16.html.

64. *CIA world factbook 2009.* Country comparison: Oil consumption. Retrieved January 22, 2010, from https://www.cia.gov/library/publications/the-world-factbook/rankorder/2174rank.html.

65. Mouawad, Jad. 2008. Oil prices pass record set in '80s, but then recede. *New York Times* (March 3). Retrieved January 22, 2010, from http://www.nytimes.com/2008/03/03/business/worldbusiness/03cnd-oil.html?_r=1&hp.

66. Ibid.

67. Hubbert, M. K. 1956. *Nuclear energy and the fossil fuels.* Presented at the Spring Meeting of the Southern District, American Petroleum Institute, Plaza Hotel, San Antonio, Texas, March 7–9. Retrieved January 22, 2010, from http://www.hubbertpeak.com/hubbert/1956/1956.pdf; Brandt, Adam R. 2007. Testing Hubbert. *Energy Policy* 35: 3074–88.

68. Salazar, Ken. 2009. Statement before the U.S. Senate Energy and Natural Resources Committee regarding energy development on the public lands and outer continental shelf (March 17). Retrieved October 15, 2009, from http://www.doi.gov/news/speeches/2009_03_17_speech.cfm.

69. McLean-Conner, Penni. 2009. Green-collar jobs. *Electric Light and Power* 87(3): 10.

70. Giller, Chip. 2008. The future of green jobs. *NOW on PBS* (November 14). Retrieved April 26, 2010, from http://www.pbs.org/now/shows/445/green-jobs.html.

71. MacMillan, Douglas. 2008. Switching to green-collar jobs. *Bloomberg Businessweek* (January 10). Retrieved June 1, 2010, from http://www.businessweek.com/managing/content/jan2008/ca2008018_005632.htm.

72. Organizing for America. New energy for America. Retrieved April 25, 2010, from http://my.barackobama.com/page/content/newenergy_more.

73. Discovery Impact. Our planet. Retrieved April 25, 2010, from http://impact.discovery.com/our-planet.

74. United States Environmental Protection Agency. Cleaning up the nation's hazardous waste sites. Retrieved April 11, 2010, from http://www.epa.gov/superfund/.

75. United States Environmental Protection Agency. Mid-Atlantic Superfund: Alphabetical list of Superfund sites. Retrieved April 11, 2010, from http://www.epa.gov/reg3hwmd/super/allnpl.htm.

76. Fairley, Peter. 2007. Nuclear wasteland. *IEEE Spectrum* (February). Retrieved January 24, 2010, from http://spectrum.ieee.org/energy/nuclear/nuclear-wasteland.

77. World Nuclear Association. Nuclear power in France. Retrieved April 25, 2010, from http://www.world-nuclear.org/info/inf40.html.

78. Ibid.

79. Ibid.

80. Ibid.

81. United States Senate Committee on Energy and Natural Resources. 1988. *Nuclear Waste Policy Amendments of 1987.* Washington, DC.

82. *Washington Post.* 2009. Editorial: Mountain of trouble: Mr. Obama defunds the nuclear repository at Yucca Mountain. Now what? (March 8). Retrieved January 24, 2010, from http://www.washingtonpost.com/wp-dyn/content/article/2009/03/07/AR2009030701666.html.

83. United States Fish and Wildlife Service. 2008. A history of the Endangered Species Act of 1973. Retrieved April 11, 2010, from http://www.fws.gov/Endangered/factsheets/history_ESA.pdf.

84. United States Fish and Wildlife Service. Species reports. Retrieved April 25, 2010, from http://www.fws.gov/ecos/ajax/tess_public/.

85. United States Fish and Wildlife Service. 2009. ESA basics. Retrieved November 9, 2009, from http://www.fws.gov/Endangered/factsheets/ESA_basics.pdf.

86. Pimm, Stuart L., and Peter Raven. 2000. Biodiversity: Extinction by numbers. *Nature* 403 (February 24): 843–45.

87. Ibid.

88. Ibid.; Walter, K. S., and H. J. Gillett. 1998. IUCN red list of threatened plants. Gland, Switzerland: International Union for Conservation of Nature; Collar, N. J., M. J. Crosby, and A. J. Stattersfield. 1994. *Birds to watch 2.* Washington, DC: Smithsonian Institution Press.

89. Sax, Dov F., and Steven D. Gaines. 2008. Species invasions and extinction: The future of native biodiversity on islands. *Proceedings of the National Academy of Sciences* 105(1): 11490–97.

90. Ibid.

91. Baldwin, Paul H., Charles W. Schwartz, and Elizabeth R. Schwartz. 1952. Life history and economic status of the mongoose in Hawai'i. *Journal of Mammalogy* 33(3): 335–56.

92. Englund, R. A., D. J. Preston, A. E. Vorsino, S. Myers, and L. L. Englund. 2009. Results of the 2007–2008 alien species and wekiu bug (*Nysius wekiuicola*) surveys on the summit of Mauna Kea, Hawai'i Island. Final report prepared for Office of Mauna Kea Management, University of Hawaii at Hilo.

93. Johnson, Jim. 2009. Ford holds the line on enviro initiatives. *Waste and Recycling News* 15(8): 15.

94. Toyota. Prius 10. Retrieved April 26, 2010, from http://www.toyota.com/prius-hybrid/.

95. MacDonald, Jay. 2005. Hummer tax break gets hammered. Bankrate.com (January 20). Retrieved April 26, 2010, from http://www.bankrate.com/brm/itax/biz_tips/20030403a1.asp.

96. United States Department of Transportation. 2009. DOT 133-09: Cash for Clunkers wraps up with nearly 700,000 car sales and increased fuel efficiency (August 26). Retrieved April 26, 2010, from http://www.cars.gov/files/official-information/August26PR.pdf.

97. Healey, James R. 2009. Q&A: How the "cash-for-clunker" plan would work." *USA Today* (June 10). Retrieved April 26, 2010, from http://www.usatoday.com/money/autos/2009-05-11-chrysler-gm-cash-clunkers_N.htm.

98. United States Department of Transportation, DOT 133-09.

99. McKenzie, Stephen. 2004. Social sustainability: Towards some definitions. *Hawke Research Institute Working Paper Series* 27: 1–25. Retrieved September 11, 2009, from http://www.unisa.edu.au/hawkeinstitute/publications/downloads/wp27.pdf.

100. Ashoka.org. Ashoka facts. Retrieved April 26, 2010, from http://www.ashoka.org/facts.

101. Hindman, Hugh D. 2002. *Child labor: An American history.* New York: M. E. Sharpe.

102. Bureau of International Labor Affairs. 2009. *The Department of Labor's list of goods produced by child labor or forced labor.* Washington, DC: The United States Department of Labor.

103. Montero, David. 2006. Nike's dilemma: Is doing the right thing wrong?: A child labor dispute could eliminate 4,000 Pakistani jobs. *Christian Science Monitor* (December 22). Retrieved January 22, 2010, from http://www.csmonitor.com/2006/1222/p01s03-wosc.html?s=u.

104. Ibid.

105. Fair Trade Organization. 2009. Principles of the fair trade federation members. Retrieved January 22, 2010, from http://www.fairtradefederation.org/ht/d/sp/i/8447/pid/8447.

106. Knox, Robert. 2010. Fair trade importer says it's ripe for success. *Boston Globe* (January 4). Retrieved January 22, 2010, from http://www.boston.com/business/articles/2010/01/04/fair_trade_importer_says_its_ripe_for_success/.

107. Quirk, Joel. 2008. *Unfinished business: A comparative survey of historical and contemporary slavery.* Paris: UNESCO. Retrieved January 18, 2009, from http://www.unesco.org/culture/pdf/UnfinishedBusinessReport2008.pdf.

108. Garlan, Yvon. 1988. *Slavery in ancient Greece.* Ithaca, NY: Cornell University Press.

109. Patterson, Orlando. 1982. *Slavery and social death: A comparative study.* Boston: Harvard University Press.

110. Ibid.

111. Archer, Leonie. 1988. *Slavery and other forms of unfree labor.* London: Routledge.

112. Dodson, Howard. 2005. Slavery in the 21st century. *UN Chronicles* 42(3). Retrieved January 18, 2009, from http://www.un.org/Pubs/chronicle/2005/issue3/0305p28.html; Klein, Herbert S. 2010. *The Atlantic slave trade.* New York: Cambridge University Press.

113. *Every child counts: New global estimates on child labour.* 2002. Geneva: International Labour Office.

114. Belser, P. 2005. *Forced labour and human trafficking: Estimating the profits.* Geneva: International Labour Office.

115. Bhatnagar, Rakesh. 2010. Stop sex tourism, Supreme Court tells govt. *DNA* (January 15). Retrieved January 22, 2010, from http://www.dnaindia.com/india/report_stop-sex-tourism-supreme-court-tells-govt_1335320.

116. Vieira, Meredith. 2007. MSNBC undercover: Sex slaves in America. *MSNBC* (December 3). Retrieved January 22, 2010, from http://www.msnbc.msn.com/id/22056066.

117. European Commission. 2001. Research based on case studies of victims of trafficking in human beings in three EU member states, i.e., Belgium, Italy, and the Netherlands. Commission on the European Communities, DG Justice and Home Affairs, Hippocrates JA/2001/HIP/023.

118. United States Department of Labor. 2009. The Department of Labor's list of goods produced by child labor or forced labor. Washington, DC. Retrieved January 22, 2010, from http://www.dol.gov/ilab/programs/ocft/pdf/2009TVPRA.pdf.

119. Ibid.

120. Ibid.

121. Stephens, Hugh W. 1997. *The Texas City disaster, 1947.* Austin: University of Texas Press.

122. Plant shut amid lead poisoning fear. 2009. *Press Association* (December 29). Retrieved January 22, 2010, from http://www.google.com/hostednews/ukpress/article/ALeqM5jNHD__CRpbPhlUdAP6KKN6VYywLww.

123. Symonds, Peter. 1997. *Industrial inferno: The story of the Thai toy factory fire.* Sydney: Labour Press Books.

124. Medvedev, Zhores. 1990. *The legacy of Chernobyl.* New York: W. W. Norton & Company.

125. Thousands protest reopening of Indorayon pulp plant. 2003. *Down to Earth* 56 (February). Retrieved January 22, 2010, from http://dte.gn.apc.org/56tpl.htm.

126. Occupational Safety and Health Administration. OSHA mission. Retrieved January 22, 2010, from http://www.osha.gov/oshinfo/mission.html.

127. Occupational Safety and Health Administration. Machine guarding. Retrieved April 26, 2010, from http://www.osha.gov/SLTC/machineguarding/index.html.

128. Occupational Safety and Health Administration. Permissible exposure limits. Retrieved April 26, 2010, from http://www.osha.gov/SLTC/pel/index.html.

129. Occupational Safety and Health Administration. Brownfields safety standards. Retrieved April 26, 2010, from http://www.osha.gov/SLTC/brownfields/standards.html.

130. Occupational Safety and Health Administration. Control of hazardous energy. Retrieved April 26, 2010, from http://www.osha.gov/SLTC/controlhazardousenergy/index.html.

131. Occupational Safety and Health Administration. Confined spaces. Retrieved April 26, 2010, from http://www.osha.gov/SLTC/confinedspaces/.

132. Occupational Safety and Health Administration. 1910.1200(a). Retrieved April 26, 2010, from http://www.osha.gov/pls/oshaweb/owadisp.show_document?p_table=STANDARDS&p_id=10099.

133. Occupational Safety and Health Administration. Blood borne pathogens. Retrieved April 26, 2010, from http://www.osha.gov/SLTC/bloodbornepathogens/index.html.

134. Occupational Safety and Health Administration. Confined spaces. Retrieved April 26, 2010, from http://www.osha.gov/pls/oshaweb/owadisp.show_document?p_table=DIRECTIVES&p_id=1659.

135. Occupational Safety and Health Administration. OSHA Instruction CPL 2.87. Retrieved April 26, 2010, from http://www.osha.gov/pls/oshaweb/owadisp.show_document?p_table=STANDARDS&p_id=9995.

136. Occupational Safety and Health Administration. OSHA regulations. Retrieved November 7, 2009, from http://www.osha.gov/pls/oshaweb/owasrch.search_form?p_doc_type=STANDARDS&p_toc_level=0&p_keyvalue=.

137. America's safest companies. 2009. *EHS Today.* Retrieved January 22, 2010, from http://ehstoday.com/safety/asc/.

138. United Nations General Assembly. 1987. Report of the World Commission on Environment and Development. Annex to document A/42/427—Development and International Co-operation: Environment (December 11). Geneva: United Nations Department of Economic and Social Affairs. Retrieved September 10, 2009, from http://www.un-documents.net/wced-ocf.htm.

139. Foy, George. 1990. Economic sustainability and the preservation of environmental assets. *Environmental Management* 12(6): 771–78.

140. Does it add value? 2004. *The Economist* (November 13). Retrieved September 13, 2009, from http://www.highbeam.com/doc/1G1-124864188.html.

141. Oppenheim, Jeremy, and Lenny T. Mendoca. 2007. Investing in sustainability: An interview with Al Gore and David Blood. *McKinsey Quarterly* (May). Retrieved September 13, 2009, from http://www.mckinseyquarterly.com/Investing_in_sustainability_An_interview_with_Al_Gore_and_David_Blood_2005.

142. Ibid.

143. Ibid.

144. Unilever. 2009. India: Creating rural entrepreneurs. Retrieved September 12, 2009, from http://www.unilever.com/sustainability/casestudies/economic—development/creating-rural-entrepreneurs.aspx.

145. Aithal, Rajesh. 2009. Project Shakti going global. Marketing in India Blog (January 9). Retrieved January 24, 2010, from http://rajeshaithal.blogspot.com/2009/01/project-shakti-going-global.html.

146. Lydenberg, Steve, and Graham Sinclair. 2009. Mainstream or daydream? The future for responsible investing. *Journal of Corporate Citizenship* 33: 47–67.

147. Ibid.

148. Oppenheim and Mendoca, Investing in sustainability.

149. Ibid.

150. Ibid.

151. Sonoco. Sustainability statement. Retrieved April 26, 2010, from http://www.sonoco.com/sonoco/Home/Sustainability/sus_sustainability_statement.htm.

152. Whole Soy Company. Sustainability statement. Retrieved April 26, 2010, from http://www.wholesoyco.com/sustainability_statement.html.

153. Gruppo Salinas. Salinas de Bolívar. Retrieved March 30, 2010, from http://www.salinerito.com/.

154. Told to Clint Releya in an interview with the City Council in Salinas and the Salernito Foundation. March and November, 2009.

155. Etymology Online. Philanthropy. Retrieved June 1, 2010, from http://www.etymonline.com/index.php?search=philanthropy&searchmode=none. March 2009/November 2009

156. Grimm, Robert T. 2002. *Notable American philanthropists: Biographies of giving and volunteering.* Westport, CT: Greenwood Publishing Group.

157. Ibid.
158. Bill and Melinda Gates Foundation. 2009. Foundation fact sheet. Retrieved January 22, 2010, from http://www.gatesfoundation.org/about/Pages/foundation-fact-sheet.aspx.
159. National Constitution Center. 2007. 2007 Liberty Medal recipients. Retrieved January 24, 2010, from http://constitutioncenter.org/libertymedal/recipient_2007.html; Tyrangiel, Josh. 2002. Can Bono save the world? *Time*. Retrieved January 24, 2010, from http://www.time.com/time/covers/1101020304/story.html.
160. One Foundation. Retrieved January 24, 2010, from http://www.onefoundation.cn/html/en/beneficence_01.htm; Interview: Jet Li. 2009. *Alliance Magazine* (December 1). Retrieved January 24, 2010, from http://www.alliancemagazine.org/en/content/interview-jet-li.
161. McGee, Suzanne. 2009. The 25 best givers. *Barron's* (November 30). Retrieved January 24, 2010, from http://online.barrons.com/article/SB125935466529866955.html#articleTabs_panel_article%3D1.
162. Nilekani, Nandan. 2009. *Imagining India: The idea of a renewed nation.* London: Penguin.
163. McLean, Bethany, and Peter Elkind. 2003. *The smartest guys in the room: The amazing rise and scandalous fall of Enron.* London: Penguin.
164. Weeks, Edward. 2006. Why firms should embrace CSR. *Lawyer* (December 4): 33.
165. Luo, Xueming, and C. B. Bhattacharya. 2006. Corporate social responsibility, customer satisfaction, and market value. *Journal of Marketing* 70(1): 1–18.
166. Margolis, Joshua D., Hillary A. Elfenbein, and James P. Walsh. 2007. Does it pay to be good? A meta-analysis and redirection of research on the relationship between corporate social and financial performance. Working paper. Boston: Harvard Business School.
167. Garrett, Paul. 2003. Why it pays to be good. *Utility Week* 19(17): 16.
168. McClenahen, John S. 2005. Defining social responsibility. *Industry Week* 254(3): 64–65.
169. Johnson & Johnson. Our Credo. Retrieved April 11, 2010, from http://www.jnj.com/connect/about-jnj/jnj-credo/.
170. Williams, Nadia. 2008. CSR profession no longer the poor relation. *Personnel Today*, 47.
171. Barney, William L. 2006. A companion to 19th century America. Malden, MA: Blackwell Publishing, Ltd.
172. Interface. Toward a more sustainable way of business. Retrieved October 15, 2009, from http://www.interfaceglobal.com/Sustainability.aspx.
173. BarackObama.com. Investing in America's future: Barack Obama and Joe Biden's plan for science and innovation. Retrieved October 15, 2009, from http://www.barackobama.com/pdf/issues/FactSheetScience.pdf.
174. American Electronics Association. 2008. Telework in the information age: Building a more flexible workforce and a cleaner environment. AeA Competitiveness Series, vol. 21 (April). Retrieved April 29, 2010, from http://www.aeanet.org/publications/AeA_CS_Telework.asp.
175. Abate, Tom. 2008. Group touts telecommuting's green benefits. *San Francisco Chronicle* (April 22). Retrieved September 24, 2009, from http://www.sfgate.com/cgi-bin/article.cgi?f/c/a/2008/04/22/BUEC1087U5.DTL.
176. Telework. 2000. Telework (telecommuting): The benefits—and some issues! *European Telework Online* (January 25). Retrieved September 14, 2009. http://www.eto.org.uk/faq/faq03.htm.
177. Abate, Group touts telecommuting's green benefits.
178. Telecommuting Safety and Health Benefits Institute. 1994. Ten advantages to telecommuting: In the areas of conserving energy, protecting the environment, promoting family values, and enhancing worker safety. Retrieved September 14, 2009, from http://www.gilgordon.com/telecommutesafe/telebenefits.html.
179. Coy, Peter, Michele Conlin, and Moira Herbst. 2010. The permanent temporary workforce. *Business Week* (January 18). Retrieved April 26, 2010, from http://www.businessweek.com/magazine/content/10_03/b4163032935448_page_4.htm.
180. Ibid.
181. eBay. Sustainability. Retrieved April 26, 2010, from http://pages.ebay.com/aboutebay/socialventures.html.
182. United Way of America. Eli Lilly and Company responds to U.S. economic challenges, donating millions of dollars, volunteer hours, and life-saving medicines. Retrieved October 15, 2009, from http://www.liveunited.org/NCL/upload/Master_Release_FINAL.PDF.
183. Delivering on the promise. 2008. *Smart Business Cleveland* 20(5):48.
184. Allied Bank. Corporate and social responsibility statement. Retrieved June 1, 2010, from http://www.abl.com/thebank/pdf/annual_report2005/corporate_social_responsibity_statement.pdf.
185. Greenleaf, Robert. 2002. *Servant leadership.* New York: Paulist Press.
186. Greenleaf, Robert K. 1977. *Servant leadership: A journey into the nature of legitimate power and greatness.* Mahwah, NJ: Paulist Press; Hesse, Herman. 1922/2002. *Siddhartha*, trans. Joachim Neugroschel and Ralph Freedman. New York: Penguin.
187. Jaramillo, Fernando, Douglas B. Grisaffe, Lawrence B. Chonko, and James A. Roberts. 2009. Examining the impact of servant leadership on sales force performance. *Journal of Personal Selling and Sales Management* 29(3): 257–75.
188. Greenleaf Center. 1999. *Servant-leadership.* Advanced American Communications, Inc. Retrieved August 21, 2009, from http://www.trainingabc.com/xcart/product_files/P/ServantLeadershipLG.pdf.

Chapter 16

1. Goleman, Daniel, Richard E. Boyatzis, and Annie McKee. 2002. *Primal leadership: Learning to lead with emotional intelligence.* Boston: Harvard Business School Press.
2. Meng's Little Space. Meng's Bio. Retrieved May 27, 2010 from http://www.chademeng.com/meng_bio.html.
3. Ibid.
4. Ibid.
5. Ibid.
6. Lohr, Steve. 2007. Hey, who's he? With Gwyneth? The Google guy. *New York Times* (September 1). Retrieved May 27, 2010 from http://www.nytimes.com/2007/09/01/technology/01google.html.
7. Hamel, Gary. 2009. Moon shots for management. *Harvard Business Review* 87(2): 91–98.
8. Ibid.
9. McKee, Annie, Richard Boyatzis, and Frances Johnston. 2008. *Becoming a resonant leader: Develop your emotional intelligence, renew your relationships, and sustain your effectiveness.* Boston: Harvard Business School Press.

Name Index

Page numbers in *italic* indicate exhibits or special features (Business Cases, Perspectives, or Students' Choices).

A

Abate, Tom, E–34*nn*175, 177
Abelson, Robert P., E–9*n*7
Aboud, John, E–14*n*93
Abrahams, Jeffrey, E–7*n*20
Ackman, Dan, E–20*n*49
Adams, Brooks, E–19*n*17
Adams, John Stacey, *65*, 72, E–4*n*51
Adkerson, Joshua, *574*
Adler, Carlye, E–6*n*49
Adler, Stephen J., E–18*n*68
Aeschylus, 124
Agata, Bonaventure, *60*
Agha, Asif, E–6*nn*50, 52, E–18*n*34
Agle, Bradley R., E–8*n*78
Ahmad Tajuddin, Nooraishah Dato', 267–268, *267–268*
Aithal, Rajesh, E–32*n*145
Alderfer, Clayton P., *65*, 67, E–4*n*31
Alexander the Great, 521
Allen, Austin, *574*
Allen, Myria W., E–6*n*43
Allen, T.T., E–22*n*60
Alliston, Ackerman, E–21*nn*93, 94
Allport, G.W., E–4*n*25
Altvater, Elmar, E–5*n*60
Amar, A.D., E–13*n*7
Ambrose, Renee, E–15*n*120
Ambrosek, Renee, E–21*n*107
Amin, Samir, E–19*nn*22, 24
Amini, Fari, E–5*n*15
Anderson, Chris, E–11*nn*20, 24
Anderson, David M., E–30*n*9
Anderson, Kurt, 387, E–19*n*39
Anderson, Ray, 581
Andrews, Edmund L., E–11*n*48
Andropov, Yuri, *517*
Ansari, Shahzad, E–18*n*76
Antony, Jiju, E–22*nn*56, 57
Aoki, Masahiko, E–17*nn*91, 92
Arabe, Katrina C., E–20*nn*50, 51
Archer, Leonie, E–32*n*111
Argyris, Chris, E–10*nn*59, 60, E–18*n*69
Arino, Africa, E–26*n*29
Aristotle, 30
Armenakis, A.A., E–24*n*12
Armsrong, Lance, *83*
Arnoldy, Mark, *361*
Aron, Leon, E–28*n*118
Aronow, Edward, E–4*n*49
Arvedlund, Erin E., E–2*n*58
Asante, Molefi, E–18*n*35
Asch, Solomon, 264, E–9*n*13, E–18*nn*64, 65
Aspray, W., E–27*n*54
Atkinson, J.W., E–4*n*57
Auerbach, A., E–12*n*90
Aufreiter, Nora A., E–8*n*43
Augustine, Saint, 30
Avery, Derek R., E–11*n*23
Avolio, Bruce J., E–3*n*93
Azides, I., E–15*n*117

B

Baker, A., E–13*n*124
Baker, James, 467
Bakker, A.B., E–1*n*24
Bala-Gbogbo, Elisha, E–27*n*48
Balat, Jorge F., E–29*nn*197, 198
Baldridge, Malcolm, 446
Baldwin, Paul H., E–32*n*91
Balogun, Julia, E–13*nn*129, 130
Bamforth, Ken W., 381, E–19*n*3
Banaji, Mahzarin R., E–9*n*11
Bandura, Albert, 65, 81, E–5*nn*69, 72, 73, 74, 75, 77
Banks, Ken, 274, E–15*n*100
Barch, J., E–1*n*24
Barker, Molly, *567*
Barley, Stephen R., E–25*n*65
Barnett, Martin, 403, E–21*nn*103, 105
Barney, Jay B., E–9*n*86
Barney, William L., E–34*n*171
Barr, Pamela S., E–13*n*6
Barras, Colin, E–14*n*47
Barrett, Colleen, 27, *27*
Barrick, M.R., E–4*n*30
Barsh, Joanna, E–2*nn*50, 51
Bartlett, Bruce, E–11*n*50
Bass, Bernard M., E–2*n*65
Bates, T., E–21*n*126
Battelle, John, E–4*n*19, 21
Bauman, Zygmunt, E–2*nn*39, 40, E–11*n*20
Beam, Christopher, E–29*n*173
Bechara, Antoine, E–9*n*15
Beck, Sanderson, E–1*n*32
Beckstrom, Rod A., E–15*n*3, E–16*nn*20, 21, 22
Beechler, Schon L., E–6*n*48
Beinhocker, Eric D., E–8*n*33
Bell, D., E–10*n*10, E–19*n*37, E–20*n*47
Belser, P., E–32*n*114
Benedek, Mathias, E–13*n*32, 34, 35
Benne, Kenneth D., E–17*n*20
Bennis, Warren, 12, 344, E–17*nn*12, 17
Berg, David N., E–18*n*49, 50, 51, 52, 53, 54, 358, E–19*n*81
Bergeron, Francios, E–22*n*52
Berglof, Eric, E–22*n*25
Berlo, David, 107, E–6*n*36
Bernardo, Dolores, 5
Berner, Robert, E–13*n*39
Berners-Lee, Tim, 390, E–20*nn*55, 56
Bernstein, Carl, 35
Bernthal, Paul R., E–21*n*131
Berntsen, John L., E–30*n*8
Beshel, Barbara, E–16*nn*38, 43, E–26*n*28
Bettis, Richard A., E–9*n*85
Beutell, Nicholas J., E–19*n*82
Beyerlein, Michael M., E–20*n*79
Beyerlein, Susan, E–20*n*79
Beyrle, John, 518, E–28*nn*104, 105
Bhargava, Rajat, E–29*n*143
Bhatnager, Rakesha, E–32*n*115
Bhattaharya, C.B., E–34*n*165
Bickel, Janet, E–17*nn*107, 108, 109
Biden, Joseph, 518
Biemans, Harm, E–14*n*96
Biggs, Barton, E–2*n*56
Bion, W.R., E–17*n*16

Birchard, B., E–15*n*133
Bird, Allan, E–6*n*48
Birdwhistell, Ray, 100, E–5*n*13
Black, Laura W., E–17*n*9
Blair, Tony, 270
Blake, R., E–1*n*70, 71 E–2*n*72
Blake, Robert, 41
Blalock, Marty, E–27*n*39
Blanchard, Ken, 42, E–3*n*75
Bless, H., E–3*n*4, E–7*n*2
Block, Peter, E–12*n*83
Blood, David, *573*, 574
Bloomgarden, Kathy, E–3*n*82
Boddy, D., E–13*n*127
Bogdanich, Walt, E–29*n*189
Bogner, William C., E–13*n*6
Boguslauskas, Vytautas, E–8*n*58
Bohmer, Jon, 274
Bohmer, Richard M.J., E–9*n*88
Bond, Michael H., E–24*n*15
Bono, 272, *576*
Bono, J.E., E–4*n*29
Borgatti, Stephen P., E–7*n*95, E–17*n*81
Born, Jan, E–13*n*22
Bornat, Richard, E–9*nn*5, 6
Bosman, Julie, E–21*nn*97, 99
Bossidy, Larry, E–9*n*97
Bourdieu, Pierre, E–18*n*35
Bowen, Benjamin, E–22*n*8
Bowen, David, E–22*n*8
Bowles, M.L., E–24*n*53
Bowne, D.E., E–1*n*22
Bowyer, Dennis, E–20*n*84
Boyatzis, Richard, 20, 22, 24, 170, 187, 235, 237, 477–478, 490–491, 597, *597, 600, 602, 603, 604, 605*, E–1*nn*1, 2 (ch1), E–1*nn*1, 4, 5, 6, 7, 8, 9, 11, 13 (ch2), E–3*nn*6, 7, 8, 9, E–4*n*36, E–9*nn*2, 107, 112, 113, E–10*nn*27, 56, 57, E–12*nn*87, 88, 89, 92, 93, 96, 97, E–13*nn*124, 125, 133, 134, E–19*nn*89, 6, E–20*n*69, E–21*n*139, E–22*nn*8, 9, 11, E–23*n*94, E–25*nn*72, 99, E–26*n*116, E–34*nn*1, 9
Boyd, Danah, E–18*n*33
Bradbury, Hilary, E–12*n*117, 120, E–25*n*74
Braddock, Rick, *160*, E–8*n*76, *n*77
Bradley, Lori, E–20*n*79
Brady, Diane, E–13*n*39
Brady, J.E., E–22*n*60
Brafman, Ori, 305–307, E–15*n*3, E–16*nn*20, 21, 22
Braga, David, E–20*n*84
Braithwaite, John, E–5*n*67
Brandenburger, A.M., E–8*n*72
Braudel, Fernand, E–19*n*18
Breen, Ed, 44
Brehmer, B., E–18*n*77
Brezhnev, Leonid, *517*
Brin, Sergey, 35–36, E–2*n*54
Brislin, Richard, E–26*n*121
Brody, Leslie R., E–6*n*69
Broughton, Edward, E–31*nn*29, 30, 31, 32, 33
Brown, Erika, E–26*n*31
Brown, Michael, 124
Brown, Michael E., E–3*n*98, E–4*nn*44, 53
Brown, Penelope, 104, E–6*nn*25, 26, 27, E–7*n*93
Brown, Peter, E–28*nn*106, 109, 110

Brown, S.L., E–25n76
Browne, Colin, 26–27
Bruce, R.A., E–25n76
Brun, Yuriy, E–23n66
Bruner, Jerome S., E–9n96
Buchanan, D., E–13n127
Buckley, George, 150
Buckley, M. Ronald, E–2n61
Buffett, Warren E., 223, 575, E–26n23
Bunch, Kay, E–13n126
Burga, Bill, E–13n132
Burgess, Thomas F., E–17n90
Burke, L.A., E–10n22
Burke, W. Warner, E–12n109
Burkhalter, Stephanie, E–17n9
Burn, Janice, 403, E–20n80, E–21n103, 105
Burnes, Bernard, E–11n60
Burns, James M., E–3n79
Burns, T., E–15n8
Busch, Holger, E–4n37
Bush, George W., 124, 198, 222, 468, 471
Butcher, David, E–1n18
Buzan, Berry, E–15n137
Buzan, Tony, E–15nn137, 139
Byrne, Dennis, E–7n84
Byrne, John A., E–24nn35, 36, 37

C
Cailliau, Robert, E–20nn55, 56
Calandro, Joseph, E–9n95
Caldwell, D.F., E–25n76
Cameron, Kim, 118, E–15n114, E–24nn25, 26
Campbell, J.D., E–6n21
Campbell, K.L., 42, 43, E–4n41
Campion, M.A., E–17n93
Campos, Domingo, E–4n37
Cangemi, Joseph P., E–13n132
Cappelli, Peter, 523, E–28n119, E–29n150
Cardoso, Fernando, 513
Carey, Denis, E–8nn28, 29, 30
Carey, John, E–31n46
Carlson, John R., E–6n38
Carman, Robert, E–20n83
Carnegie, Andrew, 575, 580
Carpenter, Mason, E–17n82
Carr, A., E–6n60
Carrell, D., E–1n24
Carrell, Loren, 247
Carrell, Steve, 272
Carroll, Stephen J., E–16nn68, 69, E–17nn74, 78
Carter, Jason D., E–6n69
Carter, Jimmy, 557
Carter, Kimberly, E–6n40
Cascio, Wayne, E–21n146
Casey, D., E–12n102
Casnocha, Ben, E–8n44
Cattell, R.B., E–4n27, E–13nn24, 28
Cebis, Martin, E–7n90
Chafkin, Max, E–22nn34, 35, 36
Chakravarthy, B., E–11n39
Champy, James, 442, E–22nn46, 47, 48, 49
Chandler, Alfred D., 325, E–17n95
Chandler, G.N., E–25n78
Chang, Peng S., E–16nn50, 55
Chao, Hui-Yu, E–17n94
Charan, Ram, 165, E–9n97, E–15n136
Charlton, A., E–26n8
Chasiotis, Athanasios, E–4n37
Chatman, A.J., E–25n76
Chavez, Hugo, 531
Chen, Vicki, E–22n53
Chernenko, Konstantin, 517
Chiang Kai-shek, 524, 524, 525

Chile, 531
Chippendale, Paul, E–30n253
Cholden, L., E–17n16
Chomsky, Noam, 97–98, E–5n4
Chonko, Lawrence B., E–34n187
Chouinard, Yvon, 215, E–10nn15, 17, 18
Chubb, Daniel, E–27n50
Claes, Marie-Therese, E–7n74
Clark, Cynthia, E–29n203
Clarke, Martin, E–1n18
Clegg, Stewart, E–2n44
Clendenning, Alan, E–28nn81, 83
Clinton, Bill, 222, 530, 558
Coffey, Laura T., E–22n38
Coggins, Craig, 247
Cohen, Susan G., E–6n42
Colao, Vittorio, 507–508
Colby, P.M., E–6n19
Collar, N.J., E–32n88
Collier, Marsha, E–21n125
Collins, C., E–24n33
Collor de Mello, Fernando, 513
Colombo, George, E–15n126
Colteryahn, Karen, E–21n131
Companion, Michael A., E–9n109
Confucius, 144–145
Conger, J.A., E–3n84
Conlin, Michele, E–34nn179, 180
Coombs, W. Timothy, 124–125, E–7n86
Cooper, Cynthia, 48
Cooperrider, David L., 478, E–25n73
Coopman, Stephanie J., E–6n43
Corballis, Michael C., E–5n5, E–13n30
Costa, P.T., E–4n28
Costello, Brid, E–8n45
Courtney, Hugh, E–8n42
Covin, Jeffrey G., E–15n9
Coy, Peter, E–34nn179, 180
Coyne, Bill, 151
Crabill, Steven, E–11n70
Crampton, Suzanne, M., E–7n82
Crandall, Robert W., E–31n41
Cranston, Susie, E–2nn50, 51
Craske, Rebecca A., E–2nn50, 51
Critchley, Hugo D., E–9n17, E–12n102
Crosby, M.J., E–32n88
Cross, Jay, E–15nn138, 139
Cross, Rob, E–7n95, E–17n81
Csikszentmihalyi, Mihaly, 59, 62, 285, E–3n4, E–7n2, E–13n14
Cummings, Larry L., E–4n58, E–24n30
Cummings, T.G., E–12n112
Cunningham, Ward, 198, E–10n46
Cushman, Marcia, 247
Cutcher-Gershenfeld, Joel, 242

D
D'Amico, Carol, E–25nn85, 86
D'Aveni, Richard, 254, E–13nn1, 2
Daft, R., E–6n37
Dakan, Myles, E–24n34
Dali Lama, 8
Davenport, Thomas, 442, E–7n88, E–22nn45, 50, 51
Davidson, Barbara, E–17n15
Davidsson, Per, E–9n94, E–14n73
Davis, Alice, E–18n35
Davis, David, E–14n69
Davis, Patty, E–21n131
Davis, R., E–4n41
Dawkins, Richard, E–30n5
Dawson, P., E–13n128
Day, Diana L., E–9n92
Dayton, Bill, 567

De Cremer, David, E–17nn7, 8
De Drue, C.K.W., E–18n78
De Moraes, Marcos, 576
De Porras, Deborah A., E–9n85
de Vignemont, Frederique, E–5n85
de Waal, Frans B.M., E–5n85
de Wet, Carol, 331, 332, 332
Deacon, Terrence W., E–5n6
Deci, E.L., E–13n18
Deci, Edward, 62, 65, E–3nn11, 12, 13, 14, 15
DeHart, Jacob, 432
Delaunay, Valerie, E–23n5
Delfanti, Alessandro, E–12n75
Della Porta, Donatella, E–26n6
Delmar, F., E–9n94
DeMarco, Susan, E–3n103
DeMare, G., E–7n81
Den Hartog, D.N.R., E–3n99
Denison, Daniel R., E–24n32
DeSanctis, Geraldine, 402, 403, E–20n90
Despain, Leah, 470–471
Deutsch, M., E–19n86
Dewey, John, 239
DeYoung, Karen, E–21n137
Diamond, Mike, E–15n124
Dias de Figueiredo, Antonio, E–17n19
Dickson, David, E–6n55, E–19n90
Dietrich, Arne, 257, E–13nn9, 13, 16, 25, 26, 27, 28, 33, 36,
DiPascali, Frank, Jr., 482
DiTomaso, N., E–24n32
Dobbin, Frank, E–26n110
Dodge, H. Robert, E–15n116
Dodson, Howard, E–32n112
Dogar, Nasir, 568
Dolan, Raymond J., E–9n17
Dolan, S.L., E–12n90
Dom Pedro I, 514
Dom Pedro II, 514
Donlon, J., E–8n35, n36
Dooley, Kevin, E–16n12
Doran, George T., E–5n63, E–7n12
Dorfman, Peter W., 466, E–3n99, E–24nn18, 19
Downie, Andrew, E–28n80
Drake, R.A., E–9n1
Drayton, Bill, 567
Driscoll, Cathy, E–26n104
Drucker, Peter, 263, E–19n16, E–23n88
Druskat, Vanessa U., 353, E–18nn29, 30
Duarte, Deborah L., E–21nn140, 143
Dubois, Cathy L.Z., E–26n114
Duchon, Dennis, E–25n103
Duncan, W. Jack, E–9n84
Durkheim, E., E–25n59
Dutton, J.E., E–23n92
Dweck, Carol, E–2n48
Dwyer, Jim, E–9n105
Dykema-Engblade, A., E–19n85

E
Earls, Alan, E–9n87
Early, P. Christopher, E–26nn119, 120
Eastwood, Clint, 272
Edison, Thomas, 259
Edmondson, Amy C., E–9n88
Edwards, M.O., E–10n52
Eggen, Dan, E–21n137
Einstein, Albert, 186
Einstein, Paul, E–9n82
Eisenhardt, Kathleen M., E–22nn13, 16, E–25n76
Ekman, Paul, 102, E–6nn16, 17, 20
Elfenbein, Hillary A., E–34n166
Elis, Richard, 35

Elkind, Peter, E–34n163
Elliott, Dominic, E–27n56
Elliott, Rebecca, E–9n17
Ely, R.J., E–25n87
Emergy, F.L., E–19nn2, 4
Emery, Fred, 381
Emery, Merrelyn, E–15n4
Emiliani, M.L., E–10n42
Emmons, R.A., E–6n18, n19, n21
Enel, Catherine, E–23n5
Engdahl, F. William, E–11n53
Englund, L.L., E–32n92
Englund, R.A., E–32n92
Enz, C.A., E–25n80
Epstein, Edwin, 31, E–2n37
Epstein, Seymour, E–10n25
Ess, Charles, E–2n40

F

Fagan, Brian, E–31n11
Fairbank, John K., E–19n32, E–29nn162, 164, 165,
    166, 167, 168, 169, 170, 171, 172
Fairley, Peter, E–32n76
Faley, Robert H., E–26n114
Fallows, James, 505, E–26nn25, 26
Fanning, Shawn, 278
Farson, Richard E., E–19nn91, 94
Fastow, Andrew, 37
Faux, Jeff, E–29nn207, 208
Feely, A.J., E–30n243
Fehm, Horst L., E–13n22
Feldman, Martha S., E–25n57
Ferguson, W.C., E–1n35
Ferner, Anthony, E–22n13
Ferrell, Will, 272
Ferris, Susan R., 100, E–5n14
Festinger, Leon, E–4n52
Fiedler, Fred, 42, E–3nn73, 74
Fink, Andreas, E–13nn32, 34, 35
Finkelstein, S., E–23n6
Fiol, C. Marlene, E–20n80
Fischer, Agneta H., E–6n69
Fisher, Marc, E–2n52
Fishman, Mikhail, E–28nn101, 103
Fiske, S.T., E–9n8
Fitt, Lawton, 18, 19
Fitzgerald, Jaime, E–13n132
Fitzgerald, Niall, 13, 13–14, 374, 552, E–31n21,
    E–1n15, E–31nn21, 22
Flanagan, Tim A., E–1n19
Flannery, Jessica, 405
Fleishman, E.A., 68, E–2n67
Flood, Patrick C., E–16nn68, 69, E–17nn74, 78
Flynn, Kevin, E–9n105
Follett, Mary Parker, 423
Folta, Paul H., E–16n35, E–26n27
Ford, Gerald, 557
Ford, Henry, 324, 384
Forrester, R., E–1n30
Forster, Nick, E–7n90
Forsyth, Donelson R., E–17n18
Foy, George, E–32n139
Franco, Itamar, 513
Franco, Joanna, E–8n62
Franke, J., E–30n254
Franke, Richard H., E–24n15
Frankl, Victor, 58, 59, 87, E–3n2
Franklin, Benjamin, 212, 212, 575
Fraser, Robin, E–22n40
Freeman, R.E., E–8n79
Freeman, S.J., E–24n26
Freire, Paolo, 243, E–12n118
French, John R.P., E–18n36

French, Wendell, E–12n110
Fricher, Josef, E–17nn10, 11
Friedlmeier, Wolfgang, E–4n37
Friedman, Barry A., E–6n43
Friedman, Lisa, E–32n57
Friedman, Thomas L., 414, E–10nn11, 19, E–21n147,
    E–26nn5, 9, 14, E–28nn111, 117, E–29nn174,
    175, 179, 185
Frost, Peter J., E–22nn13, 14, E–23n92, E–24n45
Fry, Arthur, 150
Fry, John, 7–8
Fry, Louis W., E–26n106
Fu, Qiang, E–31n16
Fukuyama, Francis, 502, E–26n13
Fullerton, Sam, E–15n116
Furchtgott-Roth, Diana, E–27n46
Furst, Karen, E–21n114

G

Gabarro, John J., E–17n106
Gagné, Marylene, E–3n14
Gaines, Michael, 461
Gaines, Steven D., E–32nn89, 90
Galbraith, Jay, E–4n58
Gale, Colin, E–26n20
Gandhi, Mohandas K., 520, 521
Gao Xiqing, 505
Garcia, S., E–12n90
Gardner, H., E–1n12
Gardner, William L., E–3n93
Garett, Paul, E–34n167
Garlan, Yvon, E–32n108
Garud, R., E–25n76
Gastil, John, E–17n9
Gates, Bill, 256, 270, 575
Gates, Melinda, 575
Gay, Peter, E–19n11
Gee, Alastair, E–28nn98, 99
Geert, Saunders, E–24n15
George, B., E–3n92
George, Jennifer, E–6n22
Gershenfield, Rodney, E–18n70
Geyer, Anne L., E–18n66
Gibney, Alex, E–2n60
Gibson, Cristina B., E–6n42, E–21n145
Giles, Chris, E–30n222
Giller, Chip, E–32n70
Gillespie, Nicole A., E–3nn95, 96
Gillett, H.J., E–32n88
Gilligan, Carol, E–6n67
Gillin, Paul, E–8n60
Ginter, Peter M., E–9n84
Glaser, Edwin, 197, E–10n43
Glass, Ira, E–11n54
Gleadle, Pauline, E–13nn129, 130
Goel, Sanjay, E–22n53
Goffman, Erving, E–6nn23, 24
Goldberg, L.R., E–4n24
Goldstone, Jack A., E–19n33
Goleman, Daniel, 16, 22, 90, 187, 235, 477–478, 489,
    490–491, 597, E–1n1,(ch1), E–1nn1, 10, 13, 14,
    16, 20 (ch2) E–3n9, E–4nn36, 56, E–4n56,
    E–9n2, E–10nn27, 57, E–12n98, E–13n131,
    E–22n8, E–23n92, E–25n72, E–26nn115, 118,
    122,123, 124, 125, E–34n1
Gonzalez, Angel, E–15n7
Goodman, Gail, 441, 442, E–22nn43, 44
Goodman, Josh, E–30n214
Goodwin, Charles, E–10n3, E–19n93
Gorbachev, Mikhail, 503, 517
Gordon, George G., E–24n48
Gordon, Joy, E–30n241
Gore, Al, 573, 574

Gorman, Carol K., E–5n2
Goulden, R.P., E–4n26
Grabner, Roland H., E–13nn32, 34, 35
Graen, G., E–23n92
Graham, Katharine, 35
Grassia, Janet, E–10n26
Gray, Barbara, E–18n74
Gray, John, E–6n66
Green, Heather, E–8n69
Green, Peter, E–12n84
Green, Wendy, E–11n25, E–21n127
Greenhaus, Jeffrey H., E–19n82
Greenleaf, Robert, 584
Greenspan, Alan, 222, 223
Greenwald, Anthony G., E–9n11
Gregory, B.T., E–24nn12, 27, 28, 29
Greiner, Walter, E–18n48
Grenleaf, Robert, E–34nn185, 186
Grice, H. Paul, 129, 130, E–7n92
Griffin, R.W., E–25n77
Grimm, Robert T., E–32nn156, 157
Grisaffe, Douglas B, E–34n187
Grodon, G., E–24n32
Grossman, Lev, E–8n57
Gruber, Harold, E–20n66
Grunewald, Donald, E–6n43
Gryglak, Adam, 268
Guay, Frédéric, E–3n12
Guindon-Nasir, Jill, 11
Gulati, Ranjay, E–8n56
Gunther, Robert, 228, E–12n82
Gupta, Rajat, E–29n143
Gustavson, Bjorn, E–25n74

H

Haas, Robert, 97
Hackman, J.R., 85, 361, E–5n82
Hackman, Richard, E–18n62
Hafner, Katie, E–20n52
Hagen, E., E–1n3
Hailey, Veronica H., E–13nn129, 130
Halbesleben, Jonathon R.B., E–2n61
Hall, Edward, 117, E–6n64
Hall, Judith A., E–6n69
Halpern, David, E–6n43
Hambrick, Donald C., E–9n92
Hamel, Gary, 594, E–34nn7, 8
Hamilton, D., E–25n81
Hamm, Robert M., E–10n26
Hammer, Michael, 442, E–22nn46, 47, 48, 49
Hammond, John, 199, E–10n51
Hammond, Kenneth R., E–10n26
Hampden-Turner, Charles, E–6nn53, 63
Hanges, Paul J., 466, E–3n99, E–24nn18, 19
Hanson, Arthur J., E–23nn76, 78
Hardin, Garrett, 38, E–2n62
Hardin, Russell, E–18n75
Hargie, Owen, E–6n55, E–19n90
Hart, Claire M., E–17n7
Hart, Joy L., E–6n43
Hart, Melissa Joan, 272
Hartman, Jackie L., E–23n90
Harzing, A.-W., E–30n243
Haslum, P., E–7n15
Hatch, Mary Jo, E–25n57
Hatch, Shaun, 160
Hawken, Paul, 581
Hayashi, Fumiko, E–21nn111, 112
Hayes, Brian, E–20n61
Healey, James R., E–32n97
Heath, Chip, 182, E–9n4
Heathfield, Susan M., E–5n83
Heimert, Chrystie, E–14n55

Helmert, M., E–7n15
Henderson, Fritz, 155
Henricks, Mark, E–15n123
Hentrich, Carsten, E–13n7
Herbst, Moira, E–34nn179, 180
Herper, Matthew, E–11n69
Herschler, Daniel A., E–9n109
Hersey, Paul, 42, E–3n75
Hertel, G., E–21n142
Herzberg, Frederick, 65, 68, 68, E–4nn33, 35
Heskett, J., E–24n30
Hesse, Herman, 584
Hickler, Thomas, E–31n16
Higgins, M.C., E–23n92
Hightower, Jim, E–3n103
Hill, Gayle W., E–19nn95, 96
Hill, Terry, E–9nn89, 91
Hindman, Hugh D., E–32n101
Hindo, Brian, E–23n61
Hines, John L., E–14nn94, 95
Hinkley, Stanley R., E–12n111
Hinrichs, Gina, 400, E–20n87, E–21n141
Hirschman, Albert O., E–19n30
Hirst, Clayton, E–24n38
Hitler, Adolf, 524
Hitt, Michael A., E–9n85, E–16n67, E–17n77
Hlupic, Vlatka, E–13n7
Hodge, John W., E–7n82
Hodges, Bert H., E–18n66
Hodgson, Ann, E–29n181
Hofer, Jan, E–4n37
Hoffman, M.L., E–5n85
Hoffmann, J., E–7n15
Hofstede, Geert, 458, 462–464, 463, E–23n2, E–24n13, 14, 15, 16, 17
Holifield, Seth, 574
Hollander, Edwin P., E–1n6
Hollender, Jeffrey, 264, E–14n64
Holmes, Steven A., E–11n47
Honan, Matthew, E–13n3
Hooley, Tristram, E–1n14
Hope, Jeremy, E–22n40
Hoppe, Michael H., E–19n92
Horgan, Terrence G., E–6n69
Horn, John T., E–8n42
Hornaday, John A., E–14n93
Hornbeck, J.F., E–27n63, E–28n90
Horngren, Charles T., E–22n20
Hoskisson, Robert E., E–16n67, E–17n77
Houben, G., E–9n90
House, Robert, 466, E–3nn76, 99, E–24nn18, 19, 20
Hsieh, An-Tien, E–17n94
Hsu, Spencer S., E–21n137
Hubbert, M.K., E–32n67
Hult, M., E–25n74
Hunter, Erik, E–14n73
Huntington, Samuel P., 506, E–26n33
Hussein, Saddam, 534
Hymes, Dell, E–6n54
Hymowitz, Carol, E–30nn248, 249, 250

I

Idle, Anthony, 80, 120–121, 121, E–7nn78, 79
Imai, Masaaki, E–22n55
Indefrey, P., E–13n23
Ip, Greg, E–11n49
Ireland, Duane R., E–9n85, E–16n67, E–17n77
Irle, D.W., E–2n63

J

Jablon, Kevin, 424, 425
Jacks, Jared, 574
Jagota, Mukesh, E–11n37
James, Jesse, E–10n7

Jamison, Nancy, E–8n68
Jang, D., E–1n24
Janis, Irving, 365, E–18n67
Janos, Leo, E–14n70
Janus, Irving L., E–19n97
Jaramillo, Fernando, E–34n187
Jassawalla, Avan R., E–18n71
Javidan, Mansour, 466, E–24nn18, 19, E–24n20
Jayachandran, Satish, E–22n42
Jehn, Karen A., 366, E–18nn72, 73, E–19nn79, 80
Jenkins, W.O., E–2n64
Jensen, Mary Ann, 344, E–17n14
Jensen, Michael, E–22n26
Jeon, S., E–1n24
Jepson, Sarah F., E–17n7
Jermier, J.M., E–3n78
Jet Li, 576
Jobs, Steve, 225, 256, 262, 270
Johnson, D.W., E–18nn21, 22, 23
Johnson, F.P., E–18nn21, 22, 23
Johnson, Jim, E–32n93
Johnson, Kelly, 268
Johnson, Mark, E–7n14
Johnson, Robert Wood, 578
Johnston, Frances, 24, 170, 239, 241, 597, 600, 602, 603, 604, 605, E–1n2, 13 (ch2), E–3nn85, 86, E–4nn38, 47, E–5n15, E–9n113, E–10n57, E–12nn93, 104, 105, E–13n125, E–19nn6, 89, E–34n9
Johnston-Peck, Lucas, 182–183
Jones, Daniel T., E–23n53
Jones, Jeffrey M., E–20n72
Jones, Steve, E–20n84
Jordan, Michael, 470
Joshi, Harsh, E–29nn146, 148
Judge, T.A., E–4n29
Judy, Richard W., E–25nn85, 86000
Jung, Carl, 356, 356
Juran, Joseph, 196, E–10n41

K

Kabalata, Mercy, E–29n192
Kabat-Zinn, Jon, 203, E–10n55
Kaelbling, Leslie P, E–7n9
Kahn, R.L., E–15n6
Kahn, Sharon, E–15n108
Kahneman, Daniel, 194–195, E–9n18, E–10nn36, 38, 39
Kalin, R., E–4n41
Kallio, Tomy J., E–25nn61, 62, 68
Kamau, Rachel, 392–393, 393
Kamuliwo (Dr.), 303
Kane, Charles, 263
Kang, Peter, E–11n69
Kanov, J.M., E–23n92
Kant, Immanuel, E–10n32
Kanter, R.M., E–13n128
Kanungo, Rabindra N., E–3n84, E–4n44
Kao, H.S.R., E–5n87
Kaplan, Robert S., E–23n91
Kar, Jayarta, E–8n42
Karau, S.J., E–18n63
Kardashian, Khloe, 272
Kardashian, Kourtney, 272
Kass, Steven J., E–9n109
Katz, D., E–15n6
Katz, I.M., E–6n21
Katzenbach, Jon, 359, 360, E–17n3, E–18nn55, 56, 57, 58, 59, 60
Katzy, Bernhard, E–21nn101, 104, 106
Kaufman, Peter, E–22n42
Kaur, Jasbir, E–26n20
Kayworth, T.R., E–21n144
Keene, Raymond, E–15n139

Keeney, Ralph, 199, E–10n51
Keller, C., E–25n78
Keller, J., E–3n4, E–7n2
Keller, Matt, 262
Keller, R., E–3n77
Kellerman, Barbara, 12, 12, E–1nn7, 8, 9, 10
Kelley, David, 317, 318, E–16n73
Kelly, Erin L., E–26n110
Kemmis, Stephen, E–12n121
Kennedy, Edward (Ted), 33
Kennedy, John, 124, 273
Kent, William E., E–25n79
Kepner, Elaine, 239, E–12n103
Kern, Bob, 424
Kernis, Michael H., E–3n94
Kerr, S., E–3n78
Kerry, John, 198, 468, 471
Keyes, Ralph, E–7n83
Keys, Tracy, E–9n101
Keyton, Joann, E–26n117
Khan, Babar, E–29n143
Khurshchev, Nikita, 517
Kiley, David, E–14n72
Kilgore, Ryan, 121
Killing, Peter, E–9n101
King, Emily, 361
King, L.A., E–6nn18, 21
Kirkman, Bradley L., E–5n81, E–21n145
Klein, E., E–5n3
Klein, Herbert S., E–32n112
Klofsten, Magnus, E–14n73
Knapp, Deborah E., E–26n114
Knaup, Amy E., E–15n121
Knievel, E.M., E–18n74
Knight, Amy, E–28n100
Knox, Robert, E–32n106
Kobe, Kathryn, E–14n85
Koestner, Jolene, E–20n45
Kohn, Alfie, E–5n68
Kohs, S.C., E–2n63
Kolb, David, 239, 357, E–12n97, E–18nn45, 46, 47
Konradt, U., E–21n142
Konz, George, E–26n105
Korac-Kakabadse, Nada, E–6nn58, 59
Korzybski, Alfred, 204
Kotha, S., E–7n13
Kotter, J., Kotter, John P., 228–231, 234, E–17n106, E–24n30
Kourdi, Jeremy, E–7n19
Kouzes, J., E–7n91
Kouzmin, Alexander, E–6nn58, 59, 60
Kowal, Eric, E–14n74
Kozlowski, Dennis, 44
Kradin, Nikolay N., E–30n4
Kram, Kathy E., E–23nn92, 93
Krashen, Stephen, E–13n12
Krugman, Paul, E–11n44
Kumar, Krishnan, 380, E–19n1
Kumar, S., E–31n34
Kurogi, Atsuko, E–6n56
Kustis, Gary A., E–26n114
Kutta, Kaushik, E–22n12
Kvedaraviciene, Goda, E–8n58

L

Labaton, Steven A., E–11n46
Labov, William, E–6nn50, 51
Lacey, Hoda, E–10n29
Ladik, D., E–25n81
Lagarde, Emmanuel, E–23n5
Lahiri, Gaurav, E–28n119
Lakoff, George, E–7n14
Lakoff, Robin, 118, E–6nn70, 71
Landes, David, E–19nn10, 15

Landi, Heather, E–8*n*47
Lane, Scott, E–9*n*95
Lane, Terry, E–7*n*9
Lang, William W., E–21*n*114
Langens, Thomas A., E–4*n*37
Langer, Ellen J., 169, 203, E–9*nn*7, 111
Lannon, Richard, E–5*n*15
Lans, Thomas, E–14*n*96
Lao Tzu, 186
Laschinger, Heather K. Spence, E–1*n*26
Latham, Gary P., 76, E–3*n*1, E–5*n*61
LaTour, Kathryn, E–25*n*64
LaTour, Michael S., E–25*n*64
Laube, James, E–8*n*46
Laughlin, P.R., E–18*n*74
Lautenslager, Al, E–15*n*125
Lavely, W., E–19*n*35
Lawler, E.E., E–1*n*22
Lawrence, John J., E–24*n*17
Lawton, Chuck, E–14*n*45
Lawyer, Teri L., E–8*n*43
Lay, Kenneth, 577
Laycayo, Ricardo, E–3*n*87
Lazarus, Harold, E–13*n*132
Lee, Brett, E–12*n*80
Lee, Ronald, E–22*n*12
Leidner, D.E., E–21*n*144
Leifer, Richard, E–22*n*17
Leiner, Barry M., E–20*n*54
Leivesley, R., E–6*n*60
Lemke, C., E–14*n*82
Lendman, Stephen, E–30*n*235
Lengel, R., E–6*n*37
Lenie, K., E–9*n*90
Lenin, Vladimir, *517*
Lennung, S., E–25*n*74
Leonard, D., E–13*n*124
Leskiw, Sheri-Lynne, E–12*n*115
Lesley, B., E–14*n*82
Lessiter, Julie, *180–181*
Levelt, W.J., E–13*n*23
Levine, David I., E–1*n*30
Levinson, Jay Conrad, E–15*n*125
Levinson, Stephen C., E–6*n*25, E–7*n*93, *n*26, *n*27
Lewin, Kurt, 224–225, *225*, 227, 234, 239, 242, 243, 342, *342*, E–11*nn*58, 59, 61, E–12*n*116, E–17*nn*4, 5
Lewis, Gregory B., E–24*n*23
Lewis, Kristi M., E–23*nn*95, 96
Lewis, Thomas, E–5*n*15
Licklider, Joseph, 389
Liddle, Alan, E–27*n*40
Likert, R., E–2*n*69
Lilius, J.M., E–23*n*92
Lin, Nan, E–18*n*32
Lindberg, Oliver, E–22*nn*32, 33
Linville, P.W., E–9*n*8
Lippitt, Gordon L., E–15*n*112
Lippitt, Ronald, E–17*n*5
Lit, Jet, *576*
Litow, Stanley, *536*
Lmohan, Seetharaman, E–28*n*119
Locander, W.B., E–25*n*81
Locke, Edwin, 65, E–5*nn*61, 62
Lockheed, Martin, E–14*n*71
Loh, Hermann, E–21*nn*101, 104, 106
Lohr, Steve, E–34*n*6
Lombardo, Karen, *96*, 97
Lomborg, Bjorn, E–31*n*53
London, Anne (Annie McKee), E–25*n*71
Long, Mark, E–15*n*7
Lontonen, A., E–20*nn*55, 56
Loomis, Carol J., E–26*n*23
Lorange, P., E–11*n*39

Lore, Linda, *153*
Lorimer, Sally E., E–15*nn*111, 113
Lott, Vern, E–20*n*83
Lovejoy, Paul E., E–19*n*19
Lucas, Henry C., E–20*n*71
Lucas, Victoria, E1*n*26
Luce, Thomas F., E–8*n*64
Lula da Silva, Luiz Inacio, 514, *515*
Lun, Candace D., E–8*n*43
Luo, Xueming, E–34*n*165
Lustig, Myron W., E–20*n*45
Lutzenberger, Werner, E–13*n*22
Lydenberg, Steve, E–32*nn*146, 147
Lynch, Doug E., 511, E–11*n*25, E–21*n*127, E–27*n*55
Lyon, D.W., E–25*n*78
Lyon, Matthew, E–20*n*52
Lytle, Tamara, E–14*n*84

M

MacDonald, Jay, E–32*n*95
MacFarquhar, R., E–29*nn*168, 169, 170, 171, 172
Machlup, Fritz, E–19*n*36
MacMillan, Douglas, E–32*n*71
MacMillan, Ian C., E–9*n*92
Macnab, Brent, E–26*n*121
Maddison, Angus, E–19*n*29
Madoff, Bernie, 18, 36, 482, 551
Magolis, Howard, E–9*n*108
Maitlis, S., E–23*n*92
Majchrzak, Ann, E–20*n*83
Majteles, Sol, E–7*n*90
Majumder, Sanjoy, E–29*n*160
Makatsoris, Harris, E–6*n*41, E–20*n*77
Malhotra, Arvind, E–20*n*83
Malhotra, Yogesh, E–21*n*138
Malnight, Tom, 165, E–7*n*26, E–8*n*27, E–9*n*101
Malone, Robert, E–29*n*184
Malone, Thomas W., E–17*n*80
Manasse, A. Lorri, E–7*n*24
Mandela, Nelson, 71, E–4*n*45
Mankins, Michael C., E–9*n*100
Manlow, Veronica, E–24*n*42
Mann, Leon, E–3*n*95, E–18*n*67
Mannix, Elizabeth A., E–18*n*73, E–19*nn*79, 80
Mao Zedong, 386, *524*, *525*
March, James G., E–9*n*4
Margolis, Joshua D., E–34*n*166
Margulis, Marc S., E–16*nn*36, 37
Mariani, John, E–8*n*60
Markov, Andrey A., 145, E–7*n*16
Marling, Karal, E–14*n*78
Marquez, Jessica, E–9*n*106
Marshall, John, 311
Marshall, Lisa, E–13*n*22
Marshall, Peter, E–20*n*80, E–21*nn*103, 105
Martin, Joanne, E–24*n*45, E–25*nn*57, 60
Marx, Karl, 383, 421, *421*, E–19*n*14, E–22*n*2
Masakowski, Elaine, E–26*n*119
Maslow, Abraham, 65, 67, E–4*n*31
Massey, W., E–21*n*128
Mathias, Christopher J., E–9*n*17
Mathur, Anurag, E–7*n*90
Mausner, B., E–4*n*35
Mayadas, F., E–27*n*54
Mayer, D., E–3*n*92
Mayhew, B., E–29*n*163
Mayo, Elton, 422–423
Mboup, Souleymane, E–23*n*5
McCaskey, Michael, E–7*n*1, *n*7
McClelland, David C., 20, 65, 68, E–1*n*2, E–4*nn*36, 38, 39, 41, 42, 43, 48, 50, E–14*n*81
McClenahen, Johns S., E–34*n*168
McConnell, James Michael, 467
McConnon, Aili, E–8*n*74

McCord-Amasis, Mark, 236, 237, *237*
McCoy, Jonathan, *574*
McCrae, N., E–15*n*128
McCrae, R.R., E–4*n*28
McDaniel, Christie L., E–20*n*78
McElviy, Bill, E–20*n*86
McFarlane, Brian, *574*
McGee, Suzanne, E–34*n*161
McGregor, Douglas, 29, E–12*n*114
McKay, Patrick F., E–11*n*23
McKee, Annie, *5, 8, 11, 19, 147, 237, 352, 397, 444, 461, 477–478, 577, 592, 597, 600, 602, 603, 604, 605,* E–1*nn*1, 2 (ch1), E–1*nn*11, 13, 14, 16, 17, 21 (ch2), E–3*nn*85 (ch2), 6, 7, 8, 9 (ch3), E–4*nn*38, 40, 47, E–5*nn*84, 86 (ch3), E–5*nn*1, 15 (ch4), E–7*n*74 (ch4), E–7*n*1(ch5), E–9*n*113 (ch5), E–9*n*2 (ch6), E–10*nn*56, 57, E–12*nn*87, 89, 92, 93, 96, 100, 120, E–13*nn*124, 125, 133, 134, E–17*n*2, E–18*n*28, E–19, 89 (ch10), E–19*n*6 (ch11), E–20*n*69, E–22*nn*8, 9, 11, E–23*n*94, E–25*nn*71, 72, 99, E–26*n*104, E–34*n*1, 9
McKee, Margaret, E–26*n*104
McLean, A.N., E–3*n*92
McLean, Bethany, E–34*n*163
McClean, Elkind, E–2*n*60
McLean-Conner, Penni, E–32*n*69
McMillen, Cecilia, 477
McMillen, M.C., E–25*n*71
McNevin, Mary, *577*
McTaggart, Robin, E–12*n*121
McWilliams, Gary, E–24*nn*35, 36, 37
Mead, Margaret, E–18*n*37, E–23*n*1
Mead, R., E–23*n*3
Medvedev, Dmitry, 518
Medvedev, Zhores, E–32*n*124
Medvidovic, Nenad, E–23*n*66
Mehr, Robert I., E–10*n*54
Mehrabian, Albert, E–5*n*14
Mendoca, Lenny T., E–32*nn*141, 142, 143, 148, 149, 150
Mendonca, Manuel, E–4*n*44
Merckelbach, Harald, E–9*n*1
Mesa, Leonard, *28*
Michel, Alexandra, E–24*n*49
Milbank, Dana, E–7*n*85
Miller, Carol L., E–9*n*19
Miller, Danny, E–17*n*97
Miller, George, E–31*n*19
Miller, M.K., E–10*n*22
Miller, Richard L., E–13*n*132
Miller, Robin, E–10*n*45
Mills, Elinor, E–31*n*20
Mills, Enos, E–31*n*39
Milne, A.A., 169
Mintzberg, Henry, 9, 10, *10*, E–1*n*4, E–7*n*4
Mishra, Jitendra M., E–7*n*82
Mitchell, Ronald K., E–8*n*78
Mockler, Robert J., E–22*n*7
Mokyr, Joel, E–19*n*9
Moldoveanu, M., E–13*n*14
Molière, J.B., E–3*n*97
Mölle, Mattias, E–13*n*22
Monge, Peter, 402, *403*, E–20*n*90
Montero, David, E–32*nn*103, 104
Mooney, John, *574*
Moore, David W., E–21*nn*109, 110
Morales, Pablo, E–31*n*16
Morand, David A., E–15*n*8
Morgan, Gareth, E–15*nn*10, 11
Morgan, Roy, E–7*n*90
Morgeson, F.P., E–17*n*93
Morris, C.G., E–18*n*62
Mortensen, C. David, E–6*n*33
Mortimer, Ruth, E–21*nn*91, 92, 98

Morwick, Jason M., E–21*nn*132, 133
Moser, Evelyn, E–28*n*115
Mostert, Nel M., E–13*n*40
Mouawad, Jad, E–32*nn*65, 66
Mouton, J., E–2*nn*70, 71, E–3*n*72
Mulder, Martin, E–14*n*96
Murphy, Eamonn P., E–16*nn*68, 69, 78, E–17*n*74
Murray, Ian, 470–471, E–24*n*41
Murray, Shep, 470–471, E–24*n*41
Mussolini, Benito, *524*
Muyembe, Chikasha, 271–272
Muyembe, Mwitwa, *528*
Mwelwa, Eddy, *241*, E–4*n*47, E–12*n*105
Mwenda, Mulenga, 303, *303*
Myers, S., E–32*n*92

N

Nadler, David, 220, 221, E–11*n*40
Nakamura, Jeanne, E–3*n*5
Nalebuff, B.J., E–8*n*72
Napier, Matti K., E–18*n*70
Napolitano, Janet, 124
Naryayan, S.A., E–28*n*119
Nath, Kamal, E–29*n*157
Nathan, Andrew, 501, E–26*n*10
Naughton, Jennifer, E–21*n*131
Ndoye, Ibrahima, E–23*n*5
Needleman, Sarah, E–9*n*104
Negroponte, Nicholas, 263
Nehru, Jawaharlal, *520, 521*
Nelson, S.J., E–15*n*133
Nemiro, Jill, E–20*nn*79, 82
Nesbit, Josh, 274, E–15*n*100
Nestle, S.A., *309*
Nestmann, Thorsten, E–28*n*115
Neubauer, Aljoscha C., E–13*nn*32, 34, 35
Neuijen, Bram, E–24*n*16
Neumann, Seev, E–10*n*54
Neves, Tancredo, 513
Newman, Craig, 270
Newman, Karen L., E–24*n*15
Nguyen, Vu, E–22*n*12
Nicholson, N., E–30*n*254
Nickell, Jake, *432*
Nicosia, F., E–10*n*28
Nielsen, H.F., E–20*nn*55, 56
Nijistad, B.A., E–18*n*74
Nikolauou, I., E–13*n*132
Nilekani, Nandan, *576*, E–34*n*164
Nilekani, Rohini, *576*
Nisbett, R.E., E–9*n*14
Nixon, Richard, 571
Nolle, Daniel E., E–21*n*114
Noor, Rafidah Mohamad, *444*
Norman, W.t., E–4*n*28
Northrop, Michael, E–31*n*55
Norton, David P., E–23*n*91
Norton, Seth W., E–11*n*21
Nowak, Martin A., E–17*n*97
Nussbaum, Barbara, 71, E–4*n*46
Nussbaum, Bruce, E–13*n*39

O

O'Brien, Patrick Karl, E–19*n*27, *n*28
O'Connor, Edward J., E–20*n*81
O'Neill, Jim, 511
O'Neill, Olivia A., E–24*n*45
O'Reilly, C.A., E–25*n*76
O'Reilly, Tim, E–20*n*58
Oakley, Judith, 118, E–7*n*73
Obama, Barack, *262*, 270, 560, 561, 562, 563, 564, 582
Odbert, H.S., E–4*n*25
Offstein, Evan H., E–21*nn*132, 133
Ohayv, Denis D., E–24*nn*15, 16

Ohno, Taiichi, E–23*n*64
Oldham, G.R., 85, E–5*n*82
Oliver, Peter, 122, 123, *123*
Olsen, Ashley, 272
Olsen, Mary-Kate, 272
Oppenheim, Jeremy, E–32*nn*141, 142, 143, 148, 149, 150
Orlikowski, B., E–21*n*142
Otley, David, 438, E–22*n*39
Otterman, Sharon, E–30*n*239
Ottley, Luis, 147, *147*
Ouchi, William, 29, E–1*nn*24, 27, E–22*nn*15, 19

P

Pacheco, Jorge M., E–17*n*97
Page, Larry, 35–36, E–2*n*54
Palanski, Michael E., E–3*n*101
Pan, Philip, E–28*n*113
Pareto, Vilfredo, 196
Parker, Andrew, E–7*n*95, E–17*n*81
Parker, Ben, *215*
Parker, S.C., E–15*n*127
Parker, Sean, 278
Parker, Sharon K., E–4*n*35
Pascale, R., E–24*n*31
Pasmore, William, 381
Pastor, J., E–1*n*22
Patsalos-Fox, Michael, E–8*nn*28, 29, 30
Patterson, Gavin, 195, *195*
Patterson, Orlando, E–32*nn*109, 110
Paula, Afonso Ana, E–17*n*19
Paulas, P.B., E–18*n*74
Pawar, B.S., E–25*nn*100, 102
Pearce, Terry, E–5*n*1
Pearson, Tamra, E–10*n*26
Pedro, Dom II, *514*
Peelen, Ed, E–22*n*41
Pekar, Peter, E–16*nn*36, 37
Pellegrini, E.K., E–1*n*29
Pelosi, Nancy, *8*
Pennoyer, Malinda, *215*
Perls, Fritz, 238–239
Perls, Laura, 238–239
Perot, Ross, 530
Pettigrew, A.M., E–25*n*58
Pfeffer, J., E–23*n*10
Phillips, Spencer, 420, E–22*n*1
Phillips, Tom, E–28*n*86
Piaget, Jean, 183, E–9*nn*9, 10
Piau, Jean-Pierre, E–23*n*5
Piekkari, R., E–8*n*52
Pieterse, J.N., E–26*n*34, E–27*n*36
Pietrowsky, Reinhard, E–13*n*22
Pimm, Stuart L., E–32*nn*86, 87, 88
Pina e Cunha, Miguel, E–1*n*12
Pinchot, Gifford, E–15*n*129
Pinder, Craig C., E–3*n*1
Piotrowski, M., E–4*n*30
Pison, Gilles, E–23*n*5
Pittock, I.B., E–31*n*16
Planchard, Sean, *361*
Plato, 324, 477, E–17*n*84, E–25*n*70
Plowman, Donde A., E–25*n*103
Pol Pot, *241*
Polin, Brian, E–26*n*114
Polley, E.D., E–25*n*76
Poole, Marshall S., E–12*n*90
Porges, Stephen W., E–9*n*16
Porras, J., E–24*n*33
Port, Guido G., E–29*nn*197, 198
Porter, Michael, 159, E–8*nn*59, 70, 71
Posner, B.J., E–3*nn*104, 105, E–7*n*91, E–25*n*90
Posner, Gerald L., E–29*n*205
Power, M., E–31*n*36

Preston, D.J., E–32*n*92
Preston, Stephanie D., E–5*n*85
Preuss, Janet, E–7*n*90
Progoff, Ira, E–18*nn*38, 40
Prusak, Laurence, E–7*n*88
Puca, Rosa M., E–4*n*37
Puranam, Phanish, E–8*n*51
Putin, Vladimir, 515, 517–518

Q

Quinn, James B., E–24*nn*25, 48
Quinn, Robert E., E–15*nn*114, 118, E–24*nn*26, 27, E–25*n*75
Quirk, Joel, E–32*n*107

R

Raffone, B., E–15*n*133
Raiffa, Howard, 199, E–10*n*51
Rajah, Tharamua, E–28*n*119
Raman, Pushkala, E–22*n*42
Ramos, Luis, 482, E–25*nn*93, 94
Ramsey, Charles H., *340, 341, 352*
Randel, William J., E–31*n*16
Rao, Jerry, 499–500
Ratelle, Catherine F., E–3*n*12
Raven, Bertram, E–18*n*36
Raven, Peter, E–32*nn*86, 87, 88
Raymond, Louis, E–22*n*52
Read, Stephen J., E–9*n*19
Reagan, Ronald, 222, *222*, 223
Reason, Peter, E–12*nn*117, 120, E–25*nn*69, 74
Reddell, Kathleen, 281, *281*
Reddell, Rhett, 281, *281*
Redmoon, Ambrose H., E–3*n*102
Reed, Lisa J., E–6*n*43
Reeve, J.H., E–1*n*24
Rego, Arménio, E–1*n*12
Reich, Robert, 382, 498, E–19*n*7, E–26*n*1
Reichler, Thomas J., E–31*n*16
Reid, Caroline, E–27*n*43
Reinfeld, Fred, E–6*n*39
Relyea, Clint, *574*
Resnick, Rosalind, E–14*n*91
Reuer, Jeffrey J., E–26*n*29
Reveille, Patrick J., E–6*n*43
Revkin, Andrew, E–31*n*14
Reynolds, James, E–29*n*182
Reznikoss, Marvin, E–4*n*49
Rhee, K., E–13*n*124
Rich, Ben, 268, E–14*n*70
Richards, Howard, E–6*n*41, E–20*n*77
Richtel, Matt, E–21*nn*134, 136
Richwine, Lisa, E–12*n*91
Ridgeway, Cecelia L., E–7*n*75
Rieger, Joerg, E–19*n*26
Rifkin, Jeremy, 387, E–10*n*12, E–19*nn*7, 40
Ripley, Amanda, E–3*n*87
Riswadkar, Amit, E–21*nn*129, 130
Ritzer, G., E–26*n*35
Rivard, Suzanne, E–22*n*52
Roach, John M., E–10*n*30
Robat, Cornelis, E–21*n*113
Robbins, John E., E–15*n*116
Roberto, Michael A., E–9*n*88
Roberts, James A., E–34*n*187
Robertson, Reid, *574*
Robinson, Sheila, *396–397*
Robison, Jennifer, E–14*n*97
Rodewald, Wendy, E–21*n*96
Rogers, Carl R., E–19*nn*91, 94
Rogers, William, 474, E–25*n*56
Rohrbaugh, J.A., E–24*n*26
Rokeach, Milton, E–2*n*36
Romani, Paul N., E–23*n*89

Ronfeldt, David, E–20*n*88
Roos, Daniel, E–23*n*53
Roosevelt, Theodore, 556
Rosen, B., E–21*n*145
Ross, Dorothea, E–5*n*72
Ross, Robert S., 501, E–26*n*10
Ross, Sheila A., E–5*n*72
Roszak, Theodore, E–6*n*34
Rothenberg, Paula S., 385, E–19*n*20
Rothwell, William J., E–21*n*131
Rotondo, Suzanne, E–4*n*47, E–22*nn*1, 21, 43, 44
Rotter, Julian, 63, 81, E–4*n*23, E–5*n*71
Rowe, Gene, E–10*n*53
Rowell, David P., E–31*n*16
Rozell, Christopher, E–7*n*17
Ruck, Andrew C., E–9*n*84
Ruffa, Stephen A., 445, E–23*n*62
Ruggerio, Renato, E–26*n*19
Ruggiero, V.R., E–10*n*58
Ruilson, Larry, E–8*n*66
Ruiz-Quintanilla, S.A., E–3*n*99
Rump, Sandra A., E–9*n*1
Runde, Craig E., E–1*n*19
Rushe, Dominic, E–14*nn*61, 62
Russett, Bruce, E–26*n*15
Rutland, Peter, E–28*n*96
Ryan, Francis X., E–26*n*105
Ryan, J.J., E–3*n*3
Ryan, Richard M., 62, 65, E–3*nn*11, 12, 13, E–13*n*18

S

Saad, Lydia, E–20*nn*73, 74
Sacco, Al, E–9*n*93
Saint Augustine, 30
Saitoti, Tepilit, E–30*n*6
Salas, Carlos, E–29*nn*207, 208
Salazar, Ken, 562, E–32*n*68
Salmon, Felix, E–11*n*57
Salzman, Alex, E–14*n*54
Samuelson, Robert, 504, E–26*nn*2, 24
Sanger, Larry, *198*
Santos, Tano, 304, *432,* E–16*nn*13, 14
Santti, R., E–8*n*52
Sarasvathy, S.D., E–7*n*13
Sarney, José, 513
Sashittal, Hemant C., E–18*n*71
Sassoon, David, E–31*n*55
Sawyer, J.E., E–25*n*77
Sax, Dov F., E–32*nn*89, 90
Scandura, T.A., E–1*n*29
Scase, Richard, E–13*n*38
Schank, Roger C., E–9*n*7
Schein, Edgar H., 227, 472–473, E–11*n*65, E–23*n*11, E–24*nn*12, 50, 54, 55, 51, E–25*n*69
Schemo, Diana Jean, E–27*nn*62, 64
Schiff, Bernard B., E–9*n*1
Schleifer, Andrei, E–22*n*24
Schmalt, Heinz-Dieter, E–4*n*37
Schmidt, Eric, 63
Schmidt, W., E–25*n*90
Schmidt, Warren H., E–15*n*112
Schneider, Keith, E–32*n*63
Schoen, John W., E–4*n*55
Schor, Juliet, E–4*n*54
Schramm, Wilbur, 107, E–6*nn*31, 35
Schrange, M., E–15*n*133
Schröder, Gerhard, 270, *270*
Schultheiss, O.C., E–4*nn*41, 42, 43
Schultz, Randall L., E–15*n*9
Schwaninger, M., E–13*n*122
Schwartz, Charles W., E–32*n*91
Schwartz, Elizabeth R., E–32*n*91
Scott, Robert E., E–29*n*207, 208
Scott, S.G., E–25*n*76

Sculley, John, E–20*n*89
Scully, John, 301
Seck, Karim, E–23*n*5
Secret, A., E–20*nn*55, 56
Seidel, Dian J., E–31*n*16
Seiling, Jane, 400, E–20*n*87, E–21*n*141
Sek-Hong, N., E–5*n*87
Seligman, Martin, E–12*nn*94, 95
Sen, Amartya, 502
Sevier, Laura, E–25*n*96
Shannon, Claude, E–6*nn*30, 32
Shapiro, Debra L., E–5*n*81
Sharma, Subhash, E–22*n*42
Shaver, Jennipher, E–17*nn*98, 99
Shaw, Randy, E–31*n*18
Shea, Gregory, 228, 231–234, E–12*nn*78, 79, 82, 83
Sheats, Paul, E–17*n*20
Shepard, H., E–17*nn*12, 17
Shepard, Jon M., E–17*nn*88, 89
Sherefkin, Robert, E–17*n*103
Shook, C.L., E–24*n*12
Shor, Rita, E–8*nn*38, 41
Short, James E., E–22*nn*45, 50
Shrivastava, P., E–24*n*46
Shuen, Amy, 390, E–20*nn*59, 60
Shutterstock, Maria, *432*
Siegel-Jacobs, Karen, E–15*n*2
Siegert, Richard J., E–5*n*65
Sienkiewicz, Stan, E–21*n*108
Signaw, J.A., E–25*n*80
Simon, Herbert, 186, 194, E–10*nn*24, 30, 33, 34, 35, 40
Simons, Robert, 427, *428,* E–22*nn*22, 23
Sims, A.N., E–3*n*92
Sims, Ronald R., 537, E–18*n*68, E–30*n*252
Sinclair, Graham, E–32*nn*146, 147
Singer, Tania, E–5*n*85
Singh, Avantika, E–29*n*155
Singh, Harbir, 153, 154, 523, E–8*nn*51, 56, E–28*n*119, E–29*n*150
Singh, Jitendra, 523, E–28*n*119, E–29*n*150
Singh, Manmohan, 218, 521, E–28*n*125
Singh, Parbudyal, E–12*n*115
Singhapakdi, Anusorn, E–25*n*91
Sinha, Prabhakant, E–15*nn*111, 113
Skinner, B.F., 65, 78, E–5*n*66
Slevin, Dennis P., E–15*n*9
Smith, Adam, 324, 383, *383,* E–17*n*85, E–19*nn*12, 13
Smith, Benjamin, E–31*n*16
Smith, Douglas K., 359, 360, E–17*n*3, E–18*nn*55, 56, 57, 58, 59, 60, 61
Smith, Kenwyn K., 358, E–18*nn*49, 50, 51, 52, 53, E–19*nn*81, 83, 84
Smith, Vernon, E–22*n*10
Smith-Lovin, Lynn, E–7*n*75
Snell, Jason, E–13*n*4
Snell, Scott A., E–22*n*18
Snyder, C.R., E–12*n*92
Snyder, Nancy Tennant, E–21*nn*140, 143
Snyderman, B.B., E–4*n*35
Soelberg, Peer, E–9*n*3
Sogg, Daniel, E–8*n*46
Sokolowski, Kurt, E–4*n*37
Sonnack, Mary, E–8*nn*31, 32. 37, 39, 40
Soon, Ang, E–26*n*120
Sørensen, Jesper B., E–24*nn*32, 47
Spector, Robert, E–21*n*123
Spencer, Earl P., E–27*n*38
Spencer, Lyle M., E–1*n*1 (ch2)
Spencer, Signe M., E–1*n*1 (ch2), E–28*n*119
Spreitzer, G.M., E–1*nn*23, 25, E–24*n*26
Sridhar, V., E–20*n*50
Stack, Megan K., E–28*n*102
Stalin, Josef, *517, 526*
Stalker, G.M., E–15*n*8

Stanley, David, E–27*n*45
Stanley, S.G., E–24*nn*12, 24, 27, 28, 29
Starnes, Becky, E–15*n*5
Stattersfield, A.J., E–32*n*88
Staudt, Beate, E–13*nn*32, 34, 35
Stavros, Jackie, 400, E–20*n*87, E–21*n*141
Staw, B.M., E–24*n*30
Steele, Richard, E–9*n*100
Steier, Joe, 255, *255,* 282, *282*
Stelzer, Irwin, E–28*n*112
Stephens, Hugh W., E–32*n*121
Stephenson, Geoffrey M., E–4*n*34
Stewart, G.L., E–4*n*30
Stewart, J., E–25*n*81
Stewart, Matthew, E–22*n*4, *n*5
Stiglitz, Joseph, E–11*n*45, E–26*nn*7, 8
Sting, 273
Stovall, Steven Austin, E–7*nn*23, 25, E–9*n*103, E–15*n*131, E–17*n*105
Straus, Susan G., E–20*n*86
Stubbs, Elizabeth C., E–9*n*107
Styler, Trudie, 273
Sullivan, Richard, E–21*n*111, *n*112
Summers, Anita A., E–8*n*64
Sun Yat-sen, 524
Sutterlin, James S., E–26*n*15
Sutton, Robert, 260, *261,* E–13*nn*17, 19, E–14*n*42
Sutton-Spence, Rachel, E–5*n*11
Sykes, Martin T., E–31*n*16
Sylt, Christian, E–27*n*43
Symonds, Peter, E–32*n*123

T

Talbot, David, E–14*n*46
Talley, Ian, E–32*n*59
Tan, Chad-Meng, 592, *592*
Tan, T.K., E–18*n*74
Tannen, Deborah, 118, E–6*n*68, E–7*n*72
Tapscott, D., E–10*n*50
Tarde, G., E–5*n*70
Taylor, Chris, E–10*nn*44, 47, 49
Taylor, Frederick Winslow, 324, 421–422, 451, E–17*n*86, E–22*n*3
Taylor, Scott N., E–9*n*107
Taylor, William C., E–22*nn*30, 31
Taylor, William J., E–5*n*65
Tayngney, June P., E–5*n*67
Teng, Ssu-yu, E–19*n*32
Teree, Dan, 427, E–22*n*21
Teslick, Lee Hudson, E–29*n*206
Tesluk, P.E., E–21*n*145
Thomas, Chris Allen, 405, *405–406,* E–8*n*53, E–11*n*25, E–12*n*80, E–19*n*41, E–20*n*42, E–21*n*127, E–25*n*67
Thomas, David A., E–6*n*65, E–25*n*87
Thomas, Gail Fann, E–23*n*90
Thomke, Stefan, E–8*nn*31, 32, 37, 39, 40
Thompson, L., E–13*n*124
Thorndike, Edward L., E–9*n*12
Thorndike, R.L., E–1*n*3
Thurstone, L.L., E–4*nn*24, 28
Tienari, J., E–8*n*52
Tiernan, Siobhan, E–16*nn*68, 69, E–17*nn*74, 78
Tierney, Jim, E–8*n*49
Tilin, Felice, E–17*n*15
Tindale, R.S., E–19*n*85
Ting-Toomey, Stella, E–6*n*56
Tiwari, Vinod, E–7*n*90
Tomlinson, Ray, E–20*n*53
Tonidandel, Scott, E–11*n*23
Toossi, Mitra, E–25*n*84
Town, Laura, *317, 318*
Toyoda, Akio, 161
Traulsen, Arne, E–17*n*97

Trent, Robert J., E–23*nn*65, 66
Trevino, Linda K., E–3*n*98, E–4*nn*44, 53, E–6*n*37
Trist, Eric L., 381, E–19*nn*3, 4
Trompenaars, Fons, E–6*nn*53, 63
Tsaousis, I., E–13*n*132
Tse, Tomoeh M., E–25*n*95
Tuckman, Bruce, 344–345, E–17*nn*13, 14
Turner, Sam, E–23*n*85
Turney, Elaine, E–29*n*203
Tushman, Michael, 220, 221, E–11*n*40
Tversky, Amos, E–9*n*18, E–10*n*38
Twicken, Joe, E–31*n*12
Twitchett, D.C., E–29*nn*162, 164, 165, 166, 167, 168,
    169, 170, 171
Tyersky, Amos, E–10*n*36
Tyson, Laura D'Andrea, E–1*n*31

U

Uhl-Bien, M., E–23*n*92
Useem, Jerry, E–17*n*83
Useem, Michael, 12, 523, E–1*n*13, E–8*nn*28, 29, 30,
    E–28*n*119, E–29*n*150

V

Vaara, J., E–8*n*52
Vaill, Peter, 234, E–11*n*66
Vakola, M.I., E–13*n*132
Valverde, Antoni, E–26*n*29
Van Alstyne, Marshall, E–30*nn*244, 245
Van Baalen, Peter J., E–16*nn*16, 18
Van der Laan, Joost W., E–8*n*73
Van der Ven, Andrew H., E–12*n*90, E–25*n*76
van Fenema, Paul C., E–16*nn*16, 18
Van Oppen, Patricia, E–9*n*1
Van Vugt, Mark, E–17*n*7
Vanhoof, K., E–9*n*90
Vardi, M.Y., E–27*n*54
Vartiainen, Matti, 398, E–20*n*70
Vasey, Daniel E., E–30*n*3
Venkataraman, S., E–25*n*76
Vermeeren, Douglas, E–5*n*64
Verstegen, Jos, E–14*n*96
Vieira, Meredith, E–32*n*116
Vignogna, Mary E., E–27*n*73
Vishny, Robert W., E–22*n*24
Vitell, Scott J., E–25*n*91
Volberda, Henk W., E–14*n*67
Volcker, Paul, 223, E–11*n*55
Von Hippel, Eric, E–8*nn*31, 32, 37, 39, 40
von Thadden, Ernst-Ludwig, E–22*n*25
Vorsinos, A.E., E–32*n*92
Vroom, Victor, 65, 75, E–4*n*57, E–5*n*59

W

Wack, Pierre, E–7*n*18
Waddock, Sandra, E–3*n*100
Wagoner, Rick, 155
Wales, Jimmy, *198*
Walker, Kasey L., E–6*n*43
Walker, Mindy, *83*
Wall, Toby D., E–4*nn*34, 35
Wallace, Irving, E–10*n*1
Wallachinsky, David, E–10*n*1
Walsh, James P., E–34*n*166
Walter, K.S., E–32*n*88
Wang, Xuemei, E–7*n*6
Wanner, H.E., E–4*n*41
Waring, Paul, 235, E–12*nn*85, 86
Warren, Weaver, E–6*nn*30, 32
Watkin, Michael, E–7*n*17
Watkins, Thayer, E–27*nn*58, 70
Watson, Goodwin B., 197, E–10*n*43
Watson, Joe, E–11*n*20
Weaver, Catherine, 257, E–13*n*31
Weeks, Edward, E–34*n*164
Weick, Karl E., 125, 305, E–7*nn*87, 94 E–16*n*15,
    E–25*n*75
Weil, Jennifer, E–8*n*45
Weiner, Stuart E., E–21*nn*111, 112
Weingart, L.R., E–18*n*78
Weiss, Kim, E–4*n*49
Weldon, William C., 480, *481*
Wellins, Rich, E–21*n*131
Werbach, Adam, E–14*nn*60, 63
Westbrook, Roy, E–9*nn*89, 91
Wheatley, Margaret, E–4*n*36
Wheelan, Susan A., E–17*nn*3, 15, 16
Wheeler, Anthony R., E–2*n*61
White, Ralph, E–17*n*5
Whorf, Benjamin, E–10*n*2
Wigsten, Juliane C., *247*
Wigsten, Spenser, 262, *262*
Wiig, Karl M., E–9*n*110
Wijen, Frank, E–18*n*76
Wiklund, J., E–9*n*94
Wilber, Lisa, *402*
Wilbur, Ken, 104, E–6*nn*28, 29
Wilkinson, Des, E–7*n*90
Williams, D., E–10*n*50
Williams, Geoff, E–15*n*122
Williams, K.D., E–18*n*63
Williams, Nadia, E–34*n*170
Willmott, Hugh, E–13*nn*129, 130
Wills, Garry, E–1*n*33
Wilson, A., E–23*n*92

Wilson, David C., E–11*n*23
Wilson, Jeanne M., E–20*n*86
Wilson, T.D.W., E–9*n*14
Winfrey, Oprah, 273
Wittkowski, E., E–19*n*85
Witty, Andrew, 230, 236, E–12*n*77
Wolff, Steven, 353, E–18*nn*29, 30
Woll, Bencie, E–5*n*11
Womac, James P., E–23*n*63
Wong, Carol, E–1*n*26
Wong, Kam C., E–19*n*31
Wong, R. Bin, E–19*n*35
Woo, Kevin, E–15*n*107
Wood, Donna J., E–8*n*78
Wood, Michael, E–19*n*25
Woodman, R.W., E–25*n*77
Woods, Tiger, *185*
Woodward, Bob, 35
Woodward, Joan, E–17*n*104
Woodyard, Chris, E–27*nn*49, 51
Worley, C.G., E–12*n*112
Worline, M., E–23*n*92
Wortham, Stanton, E–24*n*49
Worthley, Reginald, E–26*n*121
Wouter, Dessein, 304, E–16*nn*13, 14
Wright, George, E–10*n*53

Y

Yamaguchi, Ikushi, E–4*n*37
Yammarino, Francis J., E–3*n*101
Yanow, Dvora, E–8*n*48, E–24*nn*23, 52, E–25*n*69
Yates, J. Frank, E–15*n*2
Yeh, Ryh-Song, E–24*n*17
Yeltsin, Boris, 503, *503*, 515, E–26*n*17
Yenkin, Sally, E–5*n*80
Yiannis, Gabriel, E–7*n*89
Young, Jill, E–26*n*114
Yunus, Muhammad, *405*

Z

Zacharias, Pat, E–26*n*11
Zakaria, Fareed, E–29*n*177
Zander, Lena, 538, E–30*nn*242, 255
Zanderr, M.L., E–18*n*74
Zemsky, Bob, 407, E–21*n*128
Zhang, Chungyan, E–21*n*101, E–21*n*104, E–21*n*106
Zimbardo, Philip G., E–18*nn*24, 25, 26, 27
Zinkhand, George M., E–25*n*64
Zmud, Robert W., E–6*n*38
Zolin, Roxanne, E–23*n*90
Zollo, Maurizio, E–8*n*51
Zoltners, Andris A., E–15*nn*111, 113
Zuckerberg, Mark, 256

Company/Organization

Page numbers in *italic* indicate exhibits or special features (Business Cases, Perspectives, or Students' Choices).

A

Abu Ghraib, 351
Adelphia, 33, 431, 551
Adidas, 555
Advanced Research Projects Agency (ARPA), 389–390
African Development Bank, *309*
Agora Cyber Charter School, 404
AIG, 223
Air Force, U.S., 268
AKEPT, 267, *267–268*, 443, *444*
Akshara Foundation, *576*
Alcoholics Anonymous, 307
Allied Bank, 583
Al Qaeda, 307, 387, 503
Almond Joy bar, 437
Amazon.com, 216, *216*, 266, *309*, 404, *404*, 406
Amazon Elastic Compute Cloud (Amazon EC2), 391
American Industrial Hygiene Association, 260
American Institute of Certified Public Accountants (AICPA), 32
American Medical Association, 32
American Society for Training and Development (ASTD), 32, 243
Amnesty International, *308*
Annick Goutal, *153*
Antares, *180–181*
Apple, 155, *155*, 164, 225, 254, 256, 262, 265, *265*, *266*, 270, 301
ARAPNET, 390
Area 51, 268
Arghyam Trust, *576*
Arkansas State University, *574*
Army Suggestions Program, 269
Army, U.S., 269, *316*, 316–317, 487
Arthur Andersen, 33, 37, 551
Ashoka, *567*
Asia-Pacific Economic Cooperation (APEC), 532
Association of Southeast Asian Nations (ASEAN), 532
Atlas Coffee Importers, *309*
Aveda, 314
Avon, 401–402, *402*

B

Bank of America, 233
Barron's, 36
BASF, 162–163
BCG (Boston Consulting Group), 164, 317, *318*
Bear Stearns, 223
Bell Communications Research, 398
Best Buy, 279
BestPrice Modern Wholesale, 154, *154*
Bharti Enterprises, 154
Big Brothers and Big Sisters, 148
Bill and Melinda Gates Foundation, *309*, 575
Blackberry, 266, *266*
Blackboard, *407*
Black & Decker, 328
Black Diamond Equipment, *215*
Blockbuster, 263

BlueScope Steel, *120*
Boeing, 268, 444, 499
Boston Consulting Group (BCG), 164, 317, *318*
BP (British Petroleum), *155*, 302
British Deaf Association, 98
British East India Company, 520, *520*
British Museum, 552
British Petroleum (BP), *155*, 302
British Telecom Group, 122, *123*, 195, *195*
Bulgari, 155
Bureau of Labor Statistics, 213, 217, 279, 480
Burger King, 313–314
Business Week, 265, *265*, 318

C

Canadian Club, 319
Cantor Fitzgerald, 167
Carnegie Corporation of New York, *575*
Carnegie Endowment for International Peace, *575*
Carnegie Foundation, *309*
Carnegie Institute, *575*
Carnegie Mellon University, *575*
Catalyst, 116, 480
Caterpillar, 444
Centers for Disease Control and Prevention, 434
Centre for Leadership Training, *267–268*
Cerberus Capital Management, *153*
Chaisa Multipurpose Co-operative, *271–272*, 272
Chicago Police Department, *340*
Chicken of the Sea, 509
Children's Medical Center of Dallas, 232
Chouinard Equipment Company, *215*
Chrysler, *153*, 155, 161, 221, 460
CIA World Factbook, 510, 561
Cisco Systems, 482
Cisco Telepresence, *266*
Clos du Bois, *153*
Coca-Cola Company, 158, 284, 460, 475–476
Committee on Education and the Workforce, U.S. House of Representatives, 551
Community Orthopedic Medical Group Partnership, *310*
Conference Board, the, 32, *308*
Constant Contact, 441–442
Constellation Brands, *153*
Craigslist, 270, 307, 404
Creative English.net, *310*
Cruiser, 398
CSL Behring, 461, *461*

D

Daimler, *153*, 155, 460
Dallas Independent School District Centers, 295, *296*
DATA (Debt, AIDS, Trade in Africa), *576*
Davos Economic Forum, 533–534
DeBeers Diamonds, *309*
Dell, 158, 324, 555, *555*
Department of Homeland Security, U.S., 124, 300, *300*
Department of Justice, U.S., 485
Department of Labor Bureau of International Labor Affairs, 571
Department of Labor, U.S., 567, 570, 571
Digital Millennium Copyright Act, 278
Discovery Communications, 563

Disney, 506–507
Disney ImagiNations, 269
Disneyland, 269
Disneyland Paris, 507
Diversity Inc., 480
Diversity Woman, *396–397*
Doctors Without Borders, 262
Domestic Nuclear Detection Office, 300
Domino's, 159
Donato's, 159
Dove soap, 482, 483
Dow Jones, 555
Drexel University, 7, 8
DryShips, Inc., *310*
Dunkin' Donuts, 163

E

eBay, 216, *309*, 405, 406
The Ecology of Commerce, 581
Economic and Philosophic Manuscripts, 421
Economic and Social Council, United Nations (ECOSOC), 534
Economic Policy Institute, 531
Elevation Partners, 272
Eli Lilly, 583
Encyclopaedia Britannica, 198
Enron, 18, 33, 37, 431, 551, 577
Environmental Protection Agency (EPA), 430, 556, 557, *557*, *559*, 561
Equal Exchange, 568
Estée Lauder, 159, 314
eTrade, 404
EuroDisney, 506–507
expedia.com, 403
Exxon-Mobil, 461

F

Facebook, 158, 256, 266, 354, 396, 411
Fair Trade Federation, 568
Fast Company, 265, 266
Federal Emergency Management Agency (FEMA), 124
Fieldstone Middle School, *147*
51 Minds Entertainment, *310*
Financial Accounting Standards Board, 32
First Solar, Inc., *310*
Fish and Wildlife Service, U.S., 564
Flickr, 396
Food and Drug Administration (FDA), U.S., 430
Ford Motor Company, 161, 221, 268, 445, 565
Fortune Brands, *153*, 319
Forum for the Future Climate Change Challenge, 274
Four Seasons & Regent Hotel and Resorts, 479
Fox, *266*
Franklin & Marshall College, *331*, *332*
Frederick's of Hollywood, *153*
FreshDirect, 159, 160, *160*
Friendster, 396
FrontlineSMS, 274
Fuji, 312–313
Future Generation Company Ltd., *309*

G

Gallup organization, 405
General Electric (GE), 164, 220–221, *318*, 318–319, 444

General Motors, 155, 161, 221
Generation Investment Management, *573*, 574
Geyser Peak, *153*
Girls on the Run, *567*
GlaxoSmithKline, 230, 236, *237*, 555
Global Facility Strategy, GlaxoSmithKline, 236, *237*
Global Human Capital Journal, 287
Global Leadership and Organizational Behavior Effectiveness (GLOBE) project, 50, 462, 464, *465–466*
GlobeMed, *361*
Goldman Sachs, 19, 511
Goodman, Gail, 441–442
Goody, *567*
Google, 5, 35–36, *63*, 164, *265*, 390, 409, *592*
Google Docs, 391
Green Building Council, U.S., 563
Greenleaf Center, 584
Gucci, *155*
Gucci Group, 96

H

Halliburton, 303
Hal's Delicatessen and Sandwich, *309*
Harvard Business Review, 9
Harvard Business School, 12, 449
Hershey, 437
Hewlett-Packard, *265*, 274, 555
Home Depot, 320, 328
Homestead Steel Mill, 580
Horizon Fitness, *567*
HP (Hewlett-Packard), *265*, 274, *555*
Hulu, *266*
Human Rights Watch, *308*
The Human Side of Enterprise, 242

I

IBM, *111*, 158, *262*, *265*, 409, 474, 481, *536*, *555*
IDEO, 266, *317*, *318*
IKEA, 155, *155*
ImagiNations (Disney), 269
Imagineering (Disney), 216, 269, *269*
IMD, 150
Imperial Sugar, 157
Independent Monitoring Association for Child Labor, 568
Indian Supreme Court, 570
Indian Walmart, 154
Indymedia, *323*
Information Overload Research Group, 409
ING Direct, 405
Instituto Rukha, *576*
Intel, 158, *266*, 284, 409, 555
Interface Global, 581
International Coach Federation, 537
International Federation of Red Cross/Red Crescent Societies, *309*
International Labour Office (ILO), 569
International Longshore and Warehouse Union (ILWU), 389
International Telecommunication Union (ITU), 391
Investment Climate Facility, 552
iPad, *266*
iPhone, 155, *155*, 164, 254, *265*, *266*
iPod Nano, 226
ISO (International Organization for Standardization), 445–446
iTouch, *266*

J

JCPenney, 272
Jenkins, Tameka, 437, *437*
Jet Li One Foundation, *576*

Jim Beam, 319
Johnson Controls, *573*
Johnson & Johnson, 149, 480, *481*, *555*, 578–579, *579*
JP Morgan, 230
Junto (club), *575*

K

Kellogg, *567*
Kentucky Fried Chicken (KFC), 112, 216, 460
Kindle, *266*
Kiva, 405, *405–406*
Kyoto Box, 274

L

Lamborghini Gallardo, 155–156
Lance Armstrong Foundation, *83*, *309*
Lao Tzu, 186
Leadership Center, Ritz-Carlton, 11
LearnIt, 437, 438, *439*
Lehman Brothers, 223, 233
Levi Strauss, 97
Liberty Building Systems, *120–121*, 121
Linden Lab, 111
LinkedIn, 396, 411
Lipitor, 229
Lipton, 315
Lipton tea, 482
LIVESTRONG, *83*
Lockheed Martin, 268
L'Oreal, 555
Lowe's, 162, 320

M

Macworld, 254
Magic tape, 284
Maker's Mark, 319
Marshfield Hills General Store, 272
McCain Food, *577*
McDonald's, 498, *498*
McKinsey, *470*
Mercosur, 515
Merriam-Webster Dictionary, 354
Merrill Lynch, 233
Metallica, 278
MicroPlace, 583
Microsoft, 164, 256, *265*, 270, 409, 509, *575*
Milken Family Foundation, 269
MINI, 420, *420*
Mission Zero, 581
MobileMe (Apple), 391
Moen, 319
Molière, 50
Monster.com, 167
Morgan Stanley, 163
Motorola, 444
MphasiS, 499
MySpace, 354, 396

N

Napster, 278–279, 404
NASA, 548
National Association for the Advancement of Colored People (NAACP), *308*
National Malaria Control Center, *303*
National Park Service, 556
Nautilus, 326
Nestle S.A., *309*
Netflix, 263–264, *264*, *404*
The Network, 482
NetZero, 403
New Balance, *567*
Newell Rubbermaid, 164, 320
Newsweek, 555, *555*

New York City Fire Department, 167
New York Times, 35
Nexium, 229
Next Generation Solutions, 409
Nike, *83*, 284, 461–462, 551, 568
Ning, 396
Nintendo, *265*, 266
Nokia, 265
North American Riding Association for the Handicapped (NARHA), *247*

O

Occupational Safety and Health Administration (OSHA), 157, 305, 571–572, *572*
Ohio State University, 40
Olsenboye, 272
ONE, 272
Oprah Winfrey Leadership Academy, 273

P

Pacific Maritime Association, 389
Papa John's, 159
Parliament of the United Kingdom of Great Britain and Northern Ireland, *308*
Parmalat, 551
Patagonia, Inc., *215*
Patent and Trademark Office, U.S., 284
PayPal, 103, 405, *406*
PepsiCo, 301, 315, 401
Peregrine Systems, 431
Peugeot, 510
Pfizer, 229, *266*
PhantomWorks, 268
Philadelphia Business Journal, 158
Philadelphia Gazette, 575
Philadelphia Police Department, *340*
Pontiac, 510
Port Authority of New York and New Jersey, 167
Post-it Notes, *150*
Powell Flute Company of New England, *153*, 468
PricewaterhouseCoopers (PwC), 399
Princeton, 63
Procter & Gamble, 164, 260, 328
Project GLOBE (Global Leadership and Organizational Effectiveness), 50, 462, 464, *465–466*
Project Scorpion, 268
Public Company Accounting Oversight Board, 431, *431*
Pure Digital Technologies, *266*

Q

Questia, 403

R

Rainforest Foundation, 273
RAND Corporation, 202
Randstad USA, 119
Raytheon, 444
Rebec Vineyards, *309*
Recording Industry Association of America, 278
Red Cross Society of China, *576*
Republic, 324
Research in Motion, 265
Reserve Bank of India, 522
Richforth Limited, *155*
Ritz-Carlton, *11*, 479, *479*
Riviana, *28*
Robert Mondavi, *153*
Rolex, 155, *155*
Roxio, 279
Royal Ahold, 551
Royal Dutch Shell, 510

R&R Fitness, *281*
Rubbermaid, 320

S

Saga, 568
Salinas Foundation, *574*
Samoa Packing Company, 509
San Francisco Bay Joint Venture, 154
Sanofi-Aventis, *229*
Sanrio Co. Ltd., *308*
Save the Children, *309*
Sears and Roebuck, 406
Second Life, 111
Securities and Exchange Commission (SEC), 36, 222, 431
Senate, U.S., *308*
Seventh Generation, 264, *264*
Sex and Temperament in Three Primitive Societies, 356
Shell Oil Company, 146, *146,* 157, 510
Siddhartha, 584
Sierra Club, 564
Signature HealthCARE, 255, *255,* 282, *282,* 392–393, *393*
Skoda Minotti, 583
Skype, 390
Small Business Administration, 277, 310–311
smartplanet.com, *262*
Smock Sterling, *310*
Sonoco, *574*
Southwest Airlines, 27
Spartan Surfaces, *424*
Stable Hands, *247*
Stanford Graduate School of Business, Advisory Council, 48–49
Star Alliance, *404*
Starbucks, 163, 284
StarKist, 509
Sting, 273
"Sweet Harts," 272
Synergos organization, *576*

T

Target, 328
Target.com, *404*
Team Obama, 265, *266*
Teleos Leadership Institute, *309,* 462
Thomson Reuters, 13, 18, *19,* 374, 552

Threadless, *432*
3H Technology, *310*
3M, 63, *150–151*
Ticketfly, 427
Time, 155
Titleist golf balls, 319
TomTom, *266*
Toyota, 148, 157, 161, *265, 309,* 510, 565, *565*
Toyota Prius, 157, 565, *565*
Transocean, 302
Twitter, 157, 354, 394, 395, 411
Tyco International, 33, 44, 431, 551

U

U2, *576*
UNAIDS, *241*
UNESCO (United Nations Educational, Scientific, and Cultural Organization), 568
Unilever, 260, 315. *315,* 461, 482–483, 552, 555, *573*
Union Carbide Corporation, 554
Union Carbide India Limited, 554
United Nations (UN), 499, 534, 546–547
United Nations Committee Against Torture, 525–526
United Nations Educational, Scientific, and Cultural Organization (UNESCO), 568
United Nations Framework Convention on Climate Change, *528*
United Nations Intergovernmental Panel on Climate Change (IPCC), 549
University of California at Santa Barbara, *592*
University of Colorado at Boulder, *361*
University of Michigan, 40–41
University of Pennsylvania, *575*
University of Pennsylvania, Graduate School of Education, 269
University of Texas, 41
UN Security Council, 534
UPS, 389
U.S. Air Force, 268
U.S. Army, 269, *316,* 316–317, 487
U.S. Bureau of Labor Statistics, 213, 217, 279, 480
U.S. Copyright Office, 284
U.S. Department of Homeland Security, 124, 300, *300*
U.S. Department of Justice, 485
U.S. Department of Labor, 567, 570, 571
U.S. Department of Veteran Affairs (VA), *247*

U.S. Federal Reserve, 222
U.S. Fish and Wildlife Service, 564
U.S. Food and Drug Administration, 430
U.S. Green Building Council, 563
U.S. Patent and Trademark Office, 284
U.S. Senate, *308*
U.S. Small Business Administration, 271

V

Vanilla, Saffron Imports, *309*
Varco Pruden Buildings, *120*
Veteran Affairs, U.S., *247*
Village Enterprise Fund, 405
Vineyards Vines, *470–471*
Vitran Express, 326
Vodafone, 507, *507–508,* 508

W

Wall Sreet Journal, 218, 518
Walmart, 154, *265,* 551
Walt Disney Imagineering, 216, 269, *269*
Washington Post, 35
The Wealth of Nations, 383
Western Electric Company, 422
Westinghouse Electric Corporation, *470*
Wharton School, 12, 231
WholeSoy, *574*
Wikipedia, 198, *198,* 307, 390
Wild Horse wines, *153*
Williams-Sonoma, *308*
WilliamsTown Communications, *309*
WorldCom, 18, 33, 48, 431, 551
World Trade Organization (WTO), 430, 526, 529
World Wildlife Fund, *308*
WuXi Pharm Tech, 266

X

Xbox, 266, *404*
Xerox, 312–313

Y

Yahoo!, 158, 164, 551
YouTube, 396

Z

Zambia National Malaria Control Program, *303*
Zip Educaçao, *576*

Glossary/Index

Page numbers in *italic* indicate exhibits or special features (Business Cases, Perspectives, or Students' Choices).

A

Absenteeism, *85*, 127, 189
Abu Ghraib prison, 351
Acceptance, of change, *245*
Accommodation The process of adapting one's cognitive categorization system to allow for new information, new schemas, and new ways of understanding information, 183, 206, 368
Accommodative approach to corporate social responsibility, 580
Accommodators, 357
Accountability An individual's willingness to report job success or failure regarding expected job outcomes to his or her manager or other superiors in the chain of command, 297, 334, 400, *400*
Accounting controls Controls that provide documentation of what an organization owes and is owed, as well as its assets and liabilities, 438–439, 453
Achievement-oriented, in path-goal theory, 43
Acquisition strategy A corporate strategy that involves joining with other businesses by buying, merging with, or taking over other companies, 153, *153*, 172
Acronyms, 113–114
Action research, 243, *243*
Action steps, 144
Action-orientation Directing one's full attention to the task at hand, 140, 172
Active listening, 371–372, *372*
Active resistance, to change, *245*
Activists Followers who feel strongly about their organization and leaders and act accordingly, 12, *12*, 14
Adaptability principles, 440
Adaptation, as response to change, 220, *220*
Adaptive organization An organization that is very flexible and readily responds to feedback—to internal and external changes in conditions and the overall environment., 304–305, 334
Adhocracy culture A culture that has an external focus and encourages flexibility, 469, *469*, 492
Adjourning The fifth stage of group development during which the group finishes its tasks and decides or is forced to dissolve membership, 344, 345, 375
Afghanistan, 158, 502, 503
Africa
    age demographics in, *218*
    during era of industrialization, 384–385
African Americans, wage inequities and, 217
Age
    communication and, 118–119
    creativity and, *256*
Age demographics, organizational change and, 217–218, *218*
Age Discrimination Act (1975), *485*
Age Discrimination in Employment Act (1967), *485*
Age of Enlightenment Primarily eighteenth-century movement that fueled radical new ideas about government, science, economic systems, and wealth across Europe and parts of North America, 383, *383*, 415
Agreeableness (personality dimension), 64
AIDS/HIV, *241*
All-channel network A communication network in which all members of a group communicate with everyone else as needed for maximum flow of information, 122, *122*, 133
American Sign Language, 98, 99
Americans with Disabilities Act Amendments Act (ADAAA) (2008), *486*
Americans with Disabilities Act (ADA) (1990), *486*
"America's Safest Companies," 572
Analysis paralysis, 242
Anchoring, as trap in decision making, *200*
Angel investor A person or a small group of people who offer money to a start-up in exchange for a stake in the business, 277, 288
Anti-globalization sentiment, 499, *499*
Appreciative inquiry, 478
Argentina, 388
    GLOBE project dimensions in, *465*
    in Group of 20, 533
    slave labor in, 570
Arguing, in group communication, 363
Arguments, evaluation of, *197*
Army Suggestion Program, 269
ASAP (as soon as possible), 113
Asch conformity studies, 364–365
Asian employees, 480
Asian women, pay gap and, 217
Assembly line, the, 384
Assertiveness, 464, *465*
Assimilation The process of integrating or forcing new information to fit existing cognitive categorization systems, 182, 183, 206
Assimilators, 357
Assumed name Sometimes called a "doing business as" (DBA) name, this is the name of the business to be started, 284, 288, 289
Atlantic slave trade, 385, *385*
ATMs, 405
Atomic Energy Act (1946), *559*
Attitudes A group of ideas, values, beliefs, and feelings that predispose a person to react to a thing, a situation, another person, or a group in a certain way, 459, 492
Auction sites, 403
Audit A formal review to make sure that certain processes have been fully and accurately managed and reported, 430, 453
Australia, 533
Austria, *465*
Authenticity Genuine presentation of one's thoughts, feeling, and beliefs, 49–50, 53
Authority The legitimate right of a person in a particular job to make certain decisions, allocate resources, and direct certain other people's activities, 296, 333
Autocratic leader A leader who tends to make decisions without input from others, 343, 374
Automobile industry, 157, 161
    anticipation of change and, 221
    assembly line, invention of, 384
    "Cash for Clunkers" program, 565–566

control process in, 420
    environmental sustainability and, 565
    offshoring and, 509
    Toyota's vehicle recall, 510
Avatars, 111
Awards, in Schein's organizational culture model, 473
Aztecs, the, *569*

B

Baby Boomers, 118–119
Backward planning, 139
Baker v. Nelson, 467
Balance sheet A document that provides a snapshot of a company at a particular moment in time, highlighting both its assets and its liabilities, 439, *439*, 453
Balanced culture A culture that has values linked to each of the culture domains of the competing values framework, and all of these values are perceived to be important and are held by organization members quite strongly, 469, 492
Balanced Scorecard A review process that takes a holistic view of success and measures several factors related to performance, 449, 453
Baldrige Award, 446–447
Baltic States, 501
Band Aid, *576*
Banking, virtual, 404–405
Banks, federal deregulation of, 222
Basic assumptions, in Schein's organizational cultural model, 472, *472*, 473, *473*
Bay of Pigs invasion, 365
BCG Matrix An analysis tool used to illustrate how a business unit, product, service, brand, or product portfolio is performing in terms of market share and market growth, 164, 164–165, 173
Behavior control Type of control in which an organization tries to shape the behaviors of its employees in order to attain the desired outcomes that will lead to organizational success, 427, 452
Behavioral approaches to leadership, 40–42
    leadership grid, 41–42, *42*
    Ohio State studies, 40
    University of Michigan studies, 40–41
"Behavioral double binds," 118
"Being" goals, 77
Belief systems, *428*
Benchmark information Information that allows HR professionals and managers to compare their scores with the average, high, and low scores of similar organizations, 128, 133
Benchmark job Job that is representative of other jobs that are similar in nature, 330, *330*, 335
Benin, 570
Berlin Wall, 500, *501*, 502, 515
Berlo Model of Communication, 107
Beyond Budgeting A control model that is intended to support more adaptive, decentralized, responsive, and ethical organizations, 438, 440–441
Bhopal disaster (1984), 553–554
Bhopal Gas Leak Disaster Act (1985), 554
Big five theories of personality, motivation and, 64–65

Biodiversity, threats to, 564–565

Blackjack, planning in, 145, *145*

Blockbuster drugs, *229,* 229–230

Blogs, 395

Board of directors, corporate governance and, 429

Body language Hand gestures, facial expressions, eye contact, physical touch, proximity to others, or any other physical gesture that has the capacity to convey meaning, 101, 132
  cross-cultural communication and, 117

Boiling frog, metaphor of, 221

Bolivia, 531, 570

Bolshevik Revolution of 1917, 516

Bombs, in work systems model of change, 233–234

Bottom-up changes Changes that occur when employees or managers at various levels spark a movement for change, influence one another and leaders, and contribute to the planning and implementation of change, 220, 249

Boundary systems, *428*

Bounded rationality An approach to decision making that accepts that all decisions are made under conditions or constraints that limit rationality, 194–195, *195,* 206

Brain, the
  creativity and, 259
  myth of left *vs.* right, 257

Brainstorming The process of generating a list of ideas within a group, 202, 207

Brazil, *465, 466*
  advantages and disadvantages of doing business with, *515,* 515–516
  after the Cold War, 502
  age demographics in, *218*
  Copenhagen Accord and, 561
  economic growth in, 218
  future of (2010 and beyond), 514–515
  in Group of 20, 533
  key events in history of, *514*
  Kyoto Protocol and, 560
  past (1889-1985), 512–513
  present (1985-2009), 513–514
  slave labor in, 570

Break-even point The point at which expenses equal income, 275, 277, 288

BRIC countries, 511, *513,* 528
  Brazil, 512–516, *514, 515*
  China, *524,* 524–527, *525, 526, 527*
  economic and demographic comparisons with U.S., *512*
  India, 519, *520,* 521–523, *523*
  Kyoto Protocol and, 560
  Russia, 516–518, *517, 519*

British Sign Language, 98, 99

Bruce Tuckman's model of group development A model of group development that includes five sequential stages: forming, storming, norming, performing, and adjourning, 344–345, 375

Budget A document that outlines when and how money is spent within a company and who is spending it, 438, 453

Buganda, *569*

Bureaucracy, minimizing, 285

Bureaucratic control systems Control processes that use specific rules, standards, and hierarchical authority to achieve planned and desired organizational outcomes, 425–426, 452

Burkina Faso, 570

Business ethics, 33–36, 551–552
  complexities involved in, 33
  defined through leadership, 35–36
  ethical dilemmas at work, 34–35

role of law and, 33–34

Business plan A formal document that states the nature of a business and its goals and outlines how the business will succeed, *276,* 276–277, 280, 288

Business portals, 403

Business process model, 433, *433*
  See also **Control process**

Business process reengineering (BPR) A management approach that utilizes available technology and management science to redesign business processes, products, and systems to increase efficiency and focus attention on customer needs, 442–443, 453

Business strategies, 155–156, 581

Bystanders Followers who are not engaged, 12, *12,* 14

C

CAFTA (United States-Dominican Republic-Central America Free Trade Agreement), 531

Calculated risk, 273

Cambodia
  combatting spread of HIV in, *241*
  digital divide in, 414

Canada
  digital divide and, 414
  GLOBE project dimensions in, *465*
  in Group of 20, 533
  NAFTA and, 530–531

Cap-and-trade plan, 560

Capitalist, 421, 561

Capitalist economy An economy in which what is produced and sold, as well as how much goods and services cost, is determined by the market. This means that the supply of and demand for goods and services determines prices, wages, and so forth, 421, 516, 540

Carbon trading, 559–560

Caribbean, age demographics in the, 217, *218*

Cash flow analysis A document that looks at the money coming in and going out of an organization in a given time frame, either current or projected, 438, *439,* 453

"Cash for Clunkers" program, 565–566

Caste system, in India, 522, *523*

Celebrities, as entrepreneurs, 272–273

Cell phones, 391

Centralized decision making Structural model in which the vast majority of decision-making power is concentrated, typically among those at the top of the organizational hierarchy, 298, 334

Centrally planned socialist economy An economy in which the government dictates every aspect of the economic system, including what goods are produced by whom, how much these goods cost, how much people are paid for their work, and the like, 516, 524, 526, 540

Ceremonies, in Schein's organizational culture model, 473

CGI Technology, *266*

Chain network A communication network in which information passes in an organized sequence from one person to the next, 122, 133

Challenger disaster, 365, *365*

Change agent, 241

Change To alter, adjust, modify, or transform someone or something, 212, 249
  as constant, 213–214
  cultural, 467–468
  describing, 212, *213*
  diversity and, 216–218
  force field analysis model of, 224–225, *225, 226,* 227

in groups, 344–348
  incremental, *220,* 220–223
  job, 213
  leading to worldwide financial crisis, 221–223
  personal reaction to, 212–213
  reasons for, in organizations, 214–219
  resonant leadership and, 595
  shifts in global economies, 218–219
  transformational, 221
  See also **Organizational change;** Social change; Individual change, 132

Channel The medium through which a message is transmitted from a sender to a receiver, 106, 132
  grapevine, 123–124
  lean, 109
  rich, 108–109

Chaos theory, 236

Character, *592*

Charisma, 45

Chernobyl nuclear reactor disaster, 571

Chess, making decisions in, 186, *187*

Chief executive officers (CEOs)
  gender gap in, 217
  women as, 480

Child labor, 32, 567–568

Chile, 531

China
  advantages and disadvantages of doing business with, 526–527, *527*
  after the Cold War, 502
  age demographics in, *218*
  buying power in, 508
  cell phones in, 391
  Cold War and, 501
  Copenhagen Accord and, 561
  economic growth in, 218, 219
  during era of industrialization, 386
  exports to U.S., 222
  future (2010 and beyond), 526
  GLOBE project dimensions in, *466*
  in Group of 20, 533
  Intel in, 388
  key events in history of, *524–525*
  Kyoto Protocol and, 560
  long-*versus* short-term orientation in, 464
  oil consumption in, 561
  past (1912-1989), 524
  present (1989-2009), 525–526
  slave labor in, 570
  United Nations Climate Change Conference (2009), 561
  U.S. national debt and, 504–505
  Yahoo! controversy and, 551

Chinese Sign Language, 98

Civil Rights Act (1964), 430, 485

Clan culture A culture that has an internal focus and encourages flexibility, 469, *469,* 492

Clean Air Act (1970), 157, *557, 558, 559*

Clean development mechanism (CDM), 560

Clean Water Act (1972), *557, 559*

Clean Water Action Act Plan (1998), *558*

Clean Air Interstate Rule, *558*

Climate change. *See* **Global warming**

Cloud computing Hosted services offered via the Internet that are available on demand, are highly flexible in terms of the amount of service users have access to, and are fully managed by the provider, 391, 415

Coaching and executive coaching, 536–537

"Coaching the brain," 235

Co-alliance model, of virtual organizations, *404*

COBRA (Consolidated Omnibus Budget Reconciliation Act), 486

Coercive power The attempt to influence others through punishment, 26, 52, 355

Cognitive competencies, 2, 22

Cognitive conflict, *367*

Cognitive cultural intelligence, 490

Cognitive dissonance A state of psychological stress arising from the attempt to process conflicting ideas, attitudes, or beliefs, 73, 89, 102

Cognitive flexibility, *256*

Cognitive processing, 182–185
  cognitive costs and, 194–195
  decision making and, 178
  emotions and, 185
  halo effect, 184–185
  schemas, 182–183
  stereotypes and, 183–184

Cold War A political and ideological conflict between the Soviet Union and the United States that lasted from the end of World War II until the early 1990s. It was characterized by military antagonism and economic competition between the two nations, 500, 515, 539

Collectivism The degree to which people prefer to act as members of a group (rather than as individuals) in exchange for loyalty and the benefits of membership, 463, *463,* 464, 492

Colombia, 531, 570

Colonialism, 385–387

Command and control type of management, 423–424

Commercial banks, 222

Communication models, 106–109

Communication networks The pattern of communication among a group of people, 115–116, 121, 133
  organizational, 121–122

Communication The act of conveying a message from one person or group to another person or group, 97, 132
  age and, 118–119
  barriers to effective, 112–116
  channel in, 106
  competence in, 114
  cross-cultural, 116–117
  decoding process, 106
  dialects and, 112–113
  downward, 119
  effective, 108
  efficient, 108
  electronic, 392–396, 411
  e-mail. *See* E-mail
  encoding process, 106
  as essential to work relationships, 96–97
  external, 121
  feedback in, 106–107
  gender differences in, 117–118
  Grice's maxims for, 129–130
  in groups, 363
  in high-context cultures, 117
  horizontal, 120
  human resources and, 126–128
  importance of, at work, *96,* 96–97
  improving, for work relationships, 128–131
  indirect, 104
  information technology used for, 110–111, *111*
  internal, 121
  interpersonal process, 106–109
  jargon and, 113–114
  language, 97–100
  listening and, 114
  in low-context cultures, 117
  managing our image through, 103–104
  message in, 106

noise, 107, 108

nonverbal, 100–101

organizational. *See* Organizational communication

power and, 115–116

receiver in, 106

relationships and, 96–97

"rich" or "lean" channels, 108–109

selective perception and, 114–115

sender in, 106

in a socially diverse world, 116–119

stereotyping and, 115

text messaging, 110, 394

upward, 119

videoconferencing, 110–111

ways of improving our, 128–131

web conferencing, 110–111, 394, 412

Wilbur's model on categorization of information, 104–106

word origin, 97

working abroad and, 538

See also Organizational communication

Communism, 500, 502

Community membership, 281, *281*

Company size, organizational structure and, 327

Compassion, *592*

Compensation package A plan in which wages, bonuses, and "fringe" benefits (such as health insurance, retirement plans, vacation, tuition reimbursement, and stock options) are dispersed to employees, 46, 84–85, 90

Compensation schedule A plan defining how payment structures and terms of payment (including regular pay, commissions, and bonuses) are dispersed to employees, 85, 90

Competencies Capabilities or abilities that include both intent and action and that can be directly linked to how well a person performs on a task or in a job, 20, 52
  cognitive, 2, 22
  deeper aspects of, 20–21
  differentiating, 21
  emotional intelligence, 5, 22, 235
  explained, 20–21
  five components of, 21
  globalization and, 538
  iceberg as metaphor for, *20,* 20–21
  leadership development, 243–244
  relationship with neurophysiology, personality, motives, traits, and values, *24*
  relational, 22
  social and emotional. *See* **Social and emotional intelligence**
  technical, 22
  threshold, 21
  for working abroad, 538

Competency model A set of competencies that are directly related to success in a job and are grouped into job-relevant categories, 22, *22,* 52

Competing values framework A model that shows how cultures can be measured along two axes: structure (stability *versus* flexibility) and focus (internal *versus* external), 468–469, *469,* 492

Competitive advantage Anything that positively distinguishes one organization from others, 147, 172

Complementors, 159

Comprehensive Environmental Response, Compensation, and Liability Act (Superfund), 563

Compromise, 368

Concurrent control The process of collecting "real-time" information to decrease the lag

time between performance deficiencies and corrective action, 436, 453

Conflict
  dysfunctional, 366
  functional, 366
  in groups, *346,* 347
  sources of, 366–367, *367*
  trust and, 368

Conflict management, 368

Conformity, in groups, 364–366

Confucian dynamism, 464

Connotation The associations, feelings, and judgments that accompany a word, 100, 132

Conscientiousness (personality dimension), 64

Conservation, 556–557

Consideration People-oriented behaviors such as respect, openness to employees' ideas and concern for employees' well-being, 40, 53

Consolidated Omnibus Budget Reconciliation Act (COBRA), *486*

Contingency approaches to leadership Models and theories of leadership that take into account leader behavior and various aspects of the organizational situation and/or characteristics of followers, 42–43, 53

Contingency plan, 143

Control mechanisms
  audits, 430
  bureaucratic, 425–426
  performance management, 447–448
  self-management and emotional self-control, 450–451
  See also Organizational control(s)

Control process An organization's systems for establishing standards to achieve goals, monitoring and measuring performance, comparing performance to standards, and taking corrective action as necessary, 420, 452
  See also Organizational control(s); Organizational control systems

Convergent thinking An analytical thought process that follows the steps and rules of logic, 257, 288

Convergers, 357

Cooperative An organization made up of a group of people who come together voluntarily to meet common economic, social, and cultural needs through a jointly owned and democratically controlled enterprise, 271, *271–272,* 288

Cooperative contracts Friendly business agreements that result from equity joint ventures, which are also known as equity alliances, 312–313; Agreements in which two or more organizations pool their needs and place a single order with a vendor for the purchase of goods or services, 505, 540

Copenhagen Accord, 561

Copyright The exclusive rights granted to the creator of an original work, which includes the right to copy, distribute, and adapt. These rights can be licensed or transferred, 284, 289

Core competency An activity that an organization does very well, that is readily identified by customers, and that sets the company apart from its competitors, 155, 172

Corporate charter An articulation of policies, rules, and procedures that address a variety of governance issues, such as the legal name and location of the business, along with the business's mission, rules relating to its board of directors, and classes of securities (stocks) that are issued, 429, 452

Corporate governance The way in which an organization is controlled, administered, or directed as described by laws and the processes, policies, regulations, and customs of that organization, 429–430, 452

Corporate social responsibility (CSR) A form of corporate self-regulation that builds sustainability and public interest into business decision making and activities, 575, 586
accommodative approach, 580
approaches to, 578–581, *580*
company example, *577*, 577–578, *579*
defensive approach, 580
dimensions of, *576*, 577
economic crisis and, 552–553
human resource's role in, 581–583
importance of, 546
Johnson & Johnson Credo, 578, *579*
leadership supporting, 584
obstructionist approach, 580
organizational cultures supporting, 482–483
philanthropy, 575, *575–576*, 577
proactive approach, 580–581
taboos inhibiting, 475

Corporation An organization that is legally recognized as a unique entity, pays taxes, and can be sued, and that does not have the personal liability issues of sole proprietorships and partnerships, 311, *334*
legal structure of, 312
ownership of, 311–312
S, 312

Corrosive power, 26

Cost leadership A business strategy of providing the lowest prices in the industry for a particular product, product line, or service, 155, *155*, 172

Costa Rica, 388, 531

Counterdependence Attitudes and behaviors related to resisting leadership or direction from others, 345, *346*, 347, 375

Country Club Management leadership style, 41

Courage The willingness and ability to face fear, danger, uncertainty, or pain without giving up whatever course of action one believes is necessary and right, 51, 53
facing change with, 246–247

Creativity The process of imagining and developing something new, 256, 288
defined, 256, 257
developing your, 285–286
divergent/convergent thinking and, 257
encouraging, at work, 259–261
factors affecting, *256*
four types of, 258, *259*
human resource's role in supporting, 284–285
innovation and, 262–266
inspiring others toward, *255*
left *vs.* right brain myth and, 257
neuroscience of, 258
suggestions for enhancing, *285*
"weird rules of," 260, *261*

Credit cards, 404–405
Crisis communication, 124–125

Critical thinking The disciplined intellectual process of evaluating situations or ideas and making appropriate judgments or taking certain actions, 197, 206
defined, 197
errors in, 199
importance of, 197–198
thinking skills, *197*
thinking traps, 199–201, *200*
Wikipedia and, *198*

Cross-cultural communication, 116–117

Cross-functional teams Teams that consist of individuals from many parts of an organization who are brought together to provide different points of view and skills in the service of organization-wide challenges and opportunities, innovations, and special projects, 317, 334

C-suite, 113
Cultural diversity, 216
Cultural intelligence, 489–490
Cultural Revolution, *525*

Culture Everything that the people in a society have learned and share through traditions, pass on to children, and teach new members; this includes religion, beliefs, political ideologies, values, customs, foods, language, gender roles, sexuality, and many other aspects of everyday life, 458, 492
adhocracy, 469, *469*
attitudes and, 459
balanced, 469
changes in, 467–468
clan, 469, *469*
communication and, 116–117
for creativity, 259–260
differences in managing our self-image, 104
global business strategy and, 506–508
GLOBE project value dimensions, 464, *465–466*
hierarchy, 469, *469*
Hofstede's dimensions of, 462–464, *463*
importance at work, 461–462
language barriers and, 112
market, 469, *469*
organizational. *See* **Organizational culture**
organizational change and, 227
power and, 25
societal ethics and, 32
strong, 469–470, *470–471*
subcultures, 467
values and, 458–459
weak, 471
working in a multicultural environment, *461*

Customer control, *432*, 432–433

Customer departmentalization A method of grouping jobs based on the needs of customers, consumers, or clients, 320, *320*, 335

Customer relationship management (CRM) A customer-centric approach to business with the aim of implementing a customer intimacy strategy or establishing a customer-friendly brand image—or both, *441*, 441–442, 453

Customer service, 280
Customer service organizational cultures, 479–480
Cynicism, in teams, 363
Czechoslovakia, 501

D

Dani tribes, New Guinea, 547
David Kolb's learning styles, 357–358
Davos Economic Forum (World Economic Forum), 533–534
Debit cards, 405
Decentralization principles, 441

Decentralized decision making Structural model in which decision-making power is distributed among the people closest to the relevant information, those who will be affected by the decision, or those who will have to implement the decision, 298, 334

Decision making A cognitive, emotional, and neuropsychological process involving thoughts, feelings, and neurological functioning that results in making a judgment or choosing from alternatives, 178, 206
at Antares, *180–181*

centralized, 298
cognitive and emotional processes involved in, 181–187
cognitive processing and, 182–185
critical thinking and, 197–201
decentralized, 298
defined, 178
double-loop learning and, 204–205
80/20 rule in, 195
emotions and, 185
halo effect in, 184–185
human resources support for, 201–202
improving our, 203–205
with incomplete information, 194–196
intuition and, 186–187
mindfulness and, 203–204
reason and logic in, 182
schemas in, 182–183
stereotypes in, 183–184
tasks in, 178
in teams, 373–374
thinking traps in, 199–201, *200*

Decisional roles, of managers, *10*

Decision-making process The steps taken when choosing a course of action, 187, 206
allocate weights to decision criteria, 190
analyze alternatives, 191–192
choose alternatives, 192
for complex decisions, 188
eight-stem model, 188, *188*
establish decision criteria, 189–190
evaluate decision, 193
implement decision, 192
list alternatives, 190–191
problem identification, 188–189
systematic approach to, 187–193

Decisions
nonprogrammed, 180
programmed, 179
types of, 178–181

Decoding The process of converting information from one format into another in order to understand it, 106, 132

Deduction, *197*
Defensive approach to corporate social responsibility, 580
Delegating style, in situational leadership theory, 42

Delphi technique A technique in which a panel of experts is asked to reach agreement after responding to a series of questions, 202, 207

Democratic leader A leader who seeks input and then either makes a decision or engages the group in collective decision making, 343, 375

Demographics, 217–218, *218*
Demokratizatsiya, *517*
Denmark, *465, 466*

Denotation The literal or dictionary meaning of a word, 100, 132

Departmentalization The process by which individuals or activities are grouped together into departments according to function, geography, product, process, or customer, as well as how the departments are coordinated and how they fit within the larger organization, 318–320, 334
customer, 320, *320*
functional, 319, *319*
geographic, 320, *320*
process, 319–320, *320*
product, 319

Dependency, in group development, 345, *346*
Deregulation, banking industry, 222
Derivatives, 223

Destination goal, 140

Destination sites, 302

"Developing others" competency, 20

"Devil effect," 184–185

Devolution principles, 441

Diagnostic control systems, *428*

Dialects, 112–113

"Dichotomania," 257

Diehards Followers who are passionate about an idea, a person, or both and will give all for them, 12, *12, 14*

Differentiating competency, 21

Differentiation A business strategy of providing a product or service that is perceived as unique by customers, 155, *155, 172*

Digital cell phone, 391

Digital divide The lack of access to and lack of skill in using Internet communication technologies among various underprivileged groups and residents of lesser-developed countries, 414, *415*

Directional planning The process of identifying a domain (general area of activity) and direction (preferred values and activities) rather than specific goals, 139–140, *172*

Directive, in path-goal theory, 43

Disabled Veteran's Act, *485*

Discrimination
  caste system, in India, *523*
  job, 485
  sexual harassment, 487

Divergent thinking A thought process that relies on the generation of many ideas, random connections, observations, and interpretations, 257, 288

Divergers, 357

Diversified company A company that has two or more distinct divisions that produce different products or services, 164, *173*

Diversity cultures, 480, *481*

Diversity The varied perspectives and approaches to work that members of different groups bring, 216, 249
  communication and, 116–119
  equal opportunity (EEO) laws, 485, *485–486*
  as a group dynamic, 356–358
  learning styles, 357–358
  organizational change and, 216–218
  pay rate and, 217
  personality types, 356–357
  in the workforce, 480
  in the workforce, promoting, 484–485, *485, 486*

Divestiture strategy A corporate strategy in which a company sells off or folds a particular division, business, brand, product, or service line, *153*, 155, *172*

Division of labor The process of reducing work to the smallest, simplest, and most easily repeated tasks possible, 304, *334*

Divisional structures (departmentalization), 318–319

"Doing business as" (DBA) name, 284

"Doing" goals, 77

Dominican Republic, 531, 570

Double binds, 118

Double-loop learning A process that focuses on changing underlying beliefs as well as behavior, 204–205, *207*

Downward communication The flow of information from higher in an organizational hierarchy to lower, 119, *120, 133*

Dress code, in Schein's organizational culture model, *472*

Dynamic inquiry, 477–478

Dysfunctional conflict Involves aggression, personal attacks, or ways of expressing differences that undermine group success, 366, 375

E

East Germany, 500, 502

Eastern Europe, 501, 502, *517*

E-business, 404
  See also **Virtual organizations**

Economic environment, 157

Economic recession
  expectancy theory and, 76
  groupthink and, 365
  See also Global economic recession

Economic regulation. *See* Global economic regulatory agencies

Economic sustainability Term that refers to an economy's capacity to regularly produce outcomes consistent with long-term economic development, 553, 572–574, *573, 585*

Economy
  centrally planned, 516, 524, 526
  free market, 383
  green, 562–563
  shift in balance of power, 218–219

Economy of scale The process of taking advantage of the power that comes with large operations to reduce costs and redundancy of efforts, 510, 540

Ecuador, 531, *574*

Edgar Schein's organizational culture model, *472*, 472–473

Education
  diversity and, 216
  in India, *523*
  in Russia, *519*
  on sexual harassment, 488

Effective communication The result of information conveyed accurately from sender to receiver, 108, *132*

Efficiency, workforce, 421–422

Efficient communication Sharing information using the fewest possible resources (time, money, and effort), 108, *132*

Effort A person's input, which will be affected by the person's perception about whether the effort will lead to an acceptable level of performance, 75, *89*

Egypt, *465, 466*

Eight-stage change model, 228–231, *229*

Eight-step decision making model, 188–193

80/20 Rule, 195, *196*

El Salvador, 531

E-learning, 406–407

Electronic communication, 411
  See also E-mail

E-mail
  advice on using, 392–393, *393*
  benefits of, 392
  communication, 110
  effective use of, 413, *413*
  emotions communicated in, 393, 394, *395*, 415
  human resources monitoring, 411
  problems with, 392
  tips for effective use at work, *413*

Emergency Planning and Community Right-to-Know Act (1986), *559*

Emerging markets. *See* BRIC countries

Emoticons Letters and symbols combined to represent emotions, 394, *395*, 415

Emotion(s)

communicated through e-mail, 393, 394, *395*
  as contagious, 24
  creativity and positive, *256*
  decision making and, 185
  in group interactions, 364
  interpreting, 103
  managing, 450–451
  related to change, 235–236, *236*
  in virtual relationships, 413

Emotional attractors, 236, *236*

Emotional creativity, 258, *259*

Emotional cultural intelligence, 490

Emotional expression(s)
  nonverbal behavior and, 102
  six basic, 102

Emotional intelligence, 5, *11*, 22, 235
  See also **Social and emotional intelligence**

Emotional self-control, control systems and, 450

Emotional stability (personality dimension), 64

Empathy Accurately interpreting the emotions, needs, and desires of others, 24, *49*, 87, 90
  active listening and, 372
  cognitive dissonance and, 73
  communication and, 114, 128
  as a competency, 22, *23*
  effective listening with, 371
  motivation and, 87
  organizational change and, 244, 245–246
  in organizational culture, 489
  performance appraisal and, 450
  reading nonverbal signals and, 101
  as skills for leadership, 4, 5
  virtual work world and, 382, 393

Employee development, 46

Employee engagement surveys, 128

Employee morale The collective mood or spirit in an organization, 127–128, 133

Employee opinion surveys, 128

Employee Retirement Income Security Act (ERISA) (1974), *485*

Employee service programs, 582–583

Employee-oriented behavior, 41

Employees
  adjusting to globalization, 536–537
  Asian, 480
  controlling, 254–255
  diverse, 216
  empowered, 27–28, *317, 318*
  expatriate, 535–537, *536*
  recruiting, 166–167
  selecting the "right," 167
  sexual harassment of, *487*, 487–488
  telecommuting, 582
  training and development of, 279–280
  See also Organizational control(s); Workforce

Empowerment Trusting employees to make decisions and to take responsibility for their decisions and actions, 27–30, 52
  current movement, 29–30
  employee, *317, 318*
  in employees, 27–28, *28*
  in organizations, 28
  Theories X, Y, and Z, 29

Enacted values The values that are actually exhibited in an organization, 473, 492

Encoding The process of converting information from one format into another before sending it, 106, *132*

Endangered species, 564

Endangered Species Act of 1973, 564

Energy efficiency, 158–159

England, *465, 466*

English language, in India, *523*

Entrepreneur A person who starts a new business, 270, 288
  avoiding common pitfalls and succeeding as an, 279–281
  celebrities as, 272–273
  community involvement by, 281, *281*
  different types of, 270–271
  laws and regulations important to, 284
  as managerial role, *10*
  profile of an, 273–274
Entrepreneurship The process of identifying an opportunity, developing resources, and assuming the risks associated with starting a new business, 270, 288
  business plans, *276,* 276–277
  human resource's role in supporting, 284–285
  inspiring others toward, *255*
  investors for, 277
  life cycle of a start-up business, 277–279
  social, 274
  starting a new business, 274–281
Environmental scanning The process of assessing social and natural conditions that have the potential to affect an organization, 157–159, 173
Environmental sustainability Term that refers to the preservation of environmental resources and biodiversity, creation of sustainable access to safe drinking water, and enhancement of quality of life among the most impoverished, 553, 585
  Bhopal disaster (1984) and, 553–555
  in China, *527*
  conservation/ecology movement in U.S., 556–557, *557*
  fossil fuel reliance and, 561–562
  green economy, 562–563
  green-collar jobs, 563
  greenhouse gas emission reduction and, 558–560
  Kyoto Protocol, 559–560
  legislation on, *559*
  nuclear waste and, 563–564
  organizational change and, 215, 220–221
  overdependence on fossil fuels, 561–562
  plants, animals, and, 564–565
  pollution and, 563
  telecommuting and, 582
  Third Industrial Revolution and, 387
  United Nations Climate Change Conference (2009), 561
  waste and, 563
Environmental uncertainty A situation in which market conditions are changing rapidly or are unclear, 326–327, 335
Environmentalism
  as driver of change, 215, *215*
  history of, in U.S., 556–557, *557*–558, 558
Equal Employment Opportunity Commission (EEOC) A federal commission created as part of the Civil Rights Act of 1964 that handles complaints of discrimination against organizations, 485, 487, 493
Equal opportunity (EEO) laws Federal regulations that ensure that organizations provide equal opportunities for all people, 485, *485*–486, 493
Equine therapy, *247*
Equity theory Theory stating that an individual's level of motivation is a result of comparing personal inputs and outcomes, and also of comparing one's efforts and rewards with others' efforts and rewards, 65, *66,* 72–75, 89
  cognitive dissonance, 73

  explained, 72–73
  relevance of, 73–74
  restoring equity and, 74–75
ERG theory Theory that people are motivated to satisfy needs related to existence, relatedness, and growth, and these needs can all be activated at the same time, 65, 66, 67, 89
Espoused values Explicit values that are preferred by an organization and communicated deliberately to the organization's members, 473, 492
Ethical code A system of principles governing morality and acceptable conduct, 30, 52
Ethical cultures, 480–482
Ethical dilemma Situations in which it appears that acting ethically would prevent the achievement of an objective, 34–35, 53
Ethical leadership
  human resources role in supporting, 45–48, *47*
  integrity, courage and, 50–51
Ethics A set of values and principles that guide the behavior of an individual or group, 30–38, 52
  business, 33–36
  developing, 30–31
  in everyday decisions, 36–38
  globalization and, 537–538
  individual, *31,* 31–32
  institutionalization of, 481–482
  levels of, *31,* 31–33
  organizational, *31,* 32, 480–482
  personal responsibility for, 38
  professional, 32
  societal, 32–33
  sustainability and, 551–552
Ethiopia, *576*
Ethnicity, wage gap and, 217
Ethnography The systematic study of human cultures, 477–478, 493
Euro, the, 530
Europe, age demographics in, *218*
European Union (EU) An economic and political union of 27 European nations (as of 2010), 305, 529–530, 540
  United Nations Climate Change Conference (2009), 561
Evaluation of arguments, *197*
Execution of plan, 165
Executive coach and adviser, 47
Executive Order 11246 (1965), *485*
Executive Order 13045: Protection of Children from Environmental Health Risks and Safety Risks (1997), *559*
Executive Order 13166 (2000), *486*
Executive Order 13211: Actions Concerning Regulations That Significantly Affect Energy Supply, Distribution, or Use (2001), *559*
Expatriate employees, 535–536, *536*
Expectancy theory Theory stating that motivation is affected by the relationships among effort and performance, performance and outcomes, and the perceived value of outcomes, 65, 66, 75–76, 89
Expert power The ability to influence others through a combination of special knowledge and/or skills, 26–27, 52, 355
Exporters, *309*
Exporting The transportation and sale of domestic goods to foreign markets, 503, 540
External communication Communication that occurs when members of an organization communicate with people on the outside, 121, 133
External environment, 326–327

External locus of control, 64
Extinction, 79
Extranet A computer network designed for an organization to communicate in a secure environment with certain external stakeholders, such as customers, 390, 415
Extraversion (personality dimension), 64
Extreme Blue internship program, *536*
Extrinsic motivation Motivation that is the result of forces or attractions outside of the self, such as material rewards, social status, or avoidance of unpleasant consequences, 62–63, 88
Eye contact, 101
Eyjafjallojokull volcano, Iceland, 159

F

Face The public representation of an aspect of our identity that we want others to accept, 103, 132
  politeness and, 104
  saving face, 103–104
Face-to-face communication, 109
Facial expressions, 100, 101
Fair Minimum Wage Act (2007), *486,* 509
Fair trade, 499
Fair Trade seal, 568
Family and Medical Leave Act (FMLA) (1993), *486*
Family systems theory, 343
Fantasy job exercise, 599–600
"Fast, low-road empathy," 489
Federal Food, Drug, and Cosmetic Act (2002), *559*
Feedback control Type of control in which information about performance is gathered and shared after the fact, 436, 453
Feedback loop The process of sharing information back and forth between sender and receiver, 106–107, 132
Feedback The process by which a receiver indicates to a sender through words or nonverbal signals that a message has been received or that more communication is desired, 106, 132
  listening and, 371
  organizational control and, 435–437
Feed-forward control Type of control system that anticipates potential issues or problems before they arise, 436, 453
Femininity/masculinity. *See* **Masculinity/femininity**
Fiedler's contingency theory Theory stating that leadership effectiveness is dependent on the characteristics of the leader and the characteristics of the situation, 42, 53
Field theory, 224
Figurehead, as managerial role, *10*
Figureplant, *310*
Filtering The deliberate miscommunication of information, including changing the information or modifying, eliminating, or enhancing particular parts of a message, 120, 133
Finance, global, 504
Financial controls Controls that are used to plan how money is earned and spent, to track financial activities such as costs and revenues, and to provide guidelines to manage expenditures, 438, 453
Financial crisis, 2007, *221,* 221–223
Financial performance, controlling, 437–441
Financial plans, 143
Finland, 391, *466*
First Industrial Revolution, 382–383
Five forces model, 159
Flat organizations Organizations that have few levels of hierarchy, which drives a need for

more people to make decisions, 29, 52, *317*, 317–318, 322, 414
Flexibility, for starting up a business, 280
Flow A state of intense concentration and complete engagement in a task, along with full use of one's talents to accomplish the task, 59, 62, 88
FMLA (Family and Medical Leave Act) (1993), *486*
Folkways The routine conventions of everyday life, 460, *460*, 492
Followers
  innovation and, 254–255
  leaders learning how to be, *352*
  situational leadership theory and, 42
  types of, 11–13
Followership, 11, 12, 322
Food Quality Protection Act (1996), *558*
For-cause termination The dismissal of an employee for breaking a company policy, failing to perform, or failing to adjust to company values, norms, or culture, 168, 173
Force field analysis model of change, 224–225, *225*, *226*, 227
Formal communication Communication governed by distinct and known rules about who can communicate with whom and how they should do it, 122, 133
Forming The first stage of group development during which members start to get to know one another, are polite and friendly, avoid conflict, and seek common ground, 344, 375
For-profit organization, *308*
Fortune 500 companies, 480
Forum for the Future Climate Change Challenge (2009), 274
Forward planning, 139
Fossil fuels, reliance on, 561–562
Framing, as trap in decision making, *200*
France, *465*
  India and, 521
  recycling of nuclear waste in, 563–564
Franchise An agreement in which the owner of a business grants an individual or group of individuals the right to sell or market products or services under that business name in exchange for a fee, 313–314, 334
Franchising A business agreement in which the owner of a business grants an individual or group of individuals the right to sell or market products or services under that business name in exchange for a fee, 506, 540
Fraud, 33–34, 37, 44, 48
  Bernie Madoff and, 482
  Sarbanes-Oxley Act and, 431
  whistle-blowing and, 48
  See also Ponzi scheme
Free market economy, 383
Free trade, 504, 516, 531, 532, 534
French Sign Language, 98
Friendly business agreements, 312–313
Frog and scorpion parable, *226*
Frog fable, 221
Frog parable, 225, *226*
Functional conflict Involves allowing or encouraging differences of opinions among team members in order to yield better group outcomes, 366, 375
Functional departmentalization Method of grouping jobs based on the nature of the work being performed, 319, *319*, 335
Functional strategies Departmental strategies that are developed to help an organization achieve its goals, 156, 172

Future orientation, 464, *465*
Fuzzy logic, 169

G

G-20. *See* **Group of Twenty (G-20)**
Gareth Morgan's metaphors, for organizations, 305, *306*
GDP (gross domestic product)
  of Brazil, 514
  of BRIC countries, 511, *512*
  economic shifts and, 218–219, *219*
  of the European Union (EU), 530
  of India, *520*, 522, *523*
  of Russia, 516, 518, *519*
Gender
  communication and, 117–118
  stereotypes, 183–184
  wage gap and, 217
  See also Women
Gender differentiation, 464, *466*
Generation Y, 118
Geographic departmentalization, 320, *320*
Geographic departmentalization A method of grouping jobs based on their physical location, 320, *320*, 335
Geography, organizational design and, 327–328
Germany
  age demographics in, *218*
  Cold War and, 500
  ethics of child labor in, 32
  GLOBE project dimensions in, *466*
Gestalt cycle of experience A model that helps us to understand how to mobilize and sustain energy, direct our attention, and choose actions that result in change in ourselves and in groups, 238–240, *239*, 242, 249
Ghana, *536*, 570
Glasnost, 517
Global 100 Most Sustainable Corporations in the World, 555
Global business
  culture and, 506–508
  developing a global strategy for, 505–508
  economic factors affecting, 504–505
  human resource's role in supporting, 535–537
  legal and organizational design issues for, 505–506
  opportunities in, 508–509
  risks in, 509–511
Global citizenship Involves understanding one's place in and one's impact on the world community and engaging in activities that support global environmental, social, and economic sustainability, 583, *583*, 586
Global economic recession, *221*, 221–223
  Brazil and, 514
  corporate social responsibility and, 546, 552
  environmental scanning and, 157
  environmental sustainability and, 565–566
  GDP growth rate, 2006-2009, *219*
  global finance/debt and, 504–505
  groupthink and, 365
  organizational change and, 218–219
  Russian and, *519*
  U.S. economy and, 504–505, 509
  workforce reduction and, 168
Global economic regulatory agencies
  Group of Twenty, 5337
  International Monetary Fund (IMF), 533
  United Nations Economic and Social Council (ECOSOC), 534–535
  World Bank, 533
  World Economic Forum, 533–534

Global investment, 504
Global Leadership and Organizational Behavior Effectiveness (GLOBE) project, 50, 462, 464, *465–466*
Global logistics, 388–389
Global new ventures Start-up companies that open globally before firmly establishing a domestic presence, 506, 540
Global trade, 504
Global warming Term used to describe a fairly recent increase in the temperature of Earth's lower atmosphere (the air we breathe) and the land and water that make up Earth's surface, 548–549, *549*, 551, 585
  current and potential effects of, *550*
  debate over, 548–549
  Kyoto Protocol and, 559–560
  personal responsibility for, 551
  potential effects of, 549
  reliance on fossil fuels and, 561–562
  Zambia and, *528*
Globalization The global flow of money, products, information, services, and expertise, 498, 539
  Cold War and, 500–502
  competencies for, 538
  deregulation of trade, 504
  developing a global business strategy, 505–508
  emerging markets. *See* BRIC countries
  ethics of, 33, 537–538
  example of, 498
  global finance and debt, 504–505
  global investment and, 504
  global regulators and, 533–535
  impact of, 499–500
  informational and communications technologies related to, 388
  international trade deregulation and, 504
  job migration and, 388
  language barriers and, 112
  opposition to, 499
  organizational change and, 214
  political changes and, 502–503
  protests against, 499, *499*
  social/economic changes and, 503
  technology's role in, 498–499
  worldwide trade alliances and, 529–532
  See also Global business
GLOBE project, 464, *465–466*
Goal-oriented planning The process of determining the activities and steps from an existing state to a clearly defined end state, 139, *139*, 141, 172
Goals
  defined, 144
  review of, 162
  SMART, 77, 144
Goal-setting
  in organizational planning, 139, 141
  terminology, 144–145
Goal-setting theory Theory which states that people are motivated by the process of identifying and achieving goals, and that the characteristics of these goals will have an impact on motivation, performance, and results, 65, 66, 76–78, 89
Golden Personality Type Profiler, 356, 357
"Golden rule," 38
Golf course, 116
"Good Samaritan" laws, 34
Google Code of Conduct, 35–36
Governmental organizations, *308*
Grammar, 114

Grapevine An informal process of sharing information among and between coworkers about what is happening in an organization, 123–124, 133

Great Britain
  ethics of child labor in, 32
  India and, 521
Great Leap Forward, *525*
"Great Man Approach," 39
Greece, *465, 466,* 530
Green economy An economic model that focuses on development and use of renewable energies such as wind, biofuels, and so on to displace traditional fossil fuels and move businesses and communities toward environmental sustainability, 562–563, 586
Green Revolution, 215
Green-collar jobs Jobs related to providing environmentally friendly products or services, 563, 586
Greenhouse effect Term used to describe how air, water, and land temperatures are affected by certain gases in Earth's atmosphere. These gases trap infrared energy, which leads to an increase in the planet's atmospheric and surface temperatures, 548, 549, 585
  See also **Global warming**
Greenhouse gas emissions, 558–560, 561
Gregory Shea's work systems model of organizational change, 231–232, *232*
  levers of change, 232–233
  selection of what to change, 233–235
Gross domestic product (GDP). *See* GDP (gross domestic product)
Group compensation A plan that bases an individual's compensation on the performance of a group or groups and/or the organization as a whole, 84, 90
Group development models
  limitations of, 347–348
  Tuckman's, 344–345
  a whole, 84, 90
Group dynamics
  changing over time, 344–348
  diversity and, 356–358
  impacting team effectiveness, 349–358
  leadership behavior affecting, 342–343
  norms in, 351–353, *352, 353*
  personal power and, 355–356
  roles in, 349–351
  social status and, 354
Group norms Informal but powerful standards that guide group members' behavior, 344, 351–353, 375
Group of Twenty (G-20) Representatives of 20 major economies who meet at least once a year to help secure global economic cooperation, 533, 541
Group roles Shared expectations among members about who does what, 344, 349–351, 375
  development of, 350
  Stanford prison experiment on, 350–351
  types of, 349–350
Groups
  big six challenges faced in, 362–364
  challenges of working in, 362–366
  as complex and mysterious, 341–342
  conformity in, 364–365, 364–366
  groupthink in, 365
  individual performance *vs.* performance in, 373–374
  norms in, 351–353
  paradoxes experienced in, 358

role of conflict in, 366–368
  See also **Team**
Groupthink "A collective pattern of defensive avoidance that leads people in a group to adopt a singular view even when there is evidence to the contrary," 365, 375
Groupware A wide variety of software and technological applications that enable people to work collaboratively via information and communication technologies, 395, 415
Growth strategy A corporate strategy that involves expansion of operations and/or an increase in market share, 152–153, *153,* 172
Guatemala, 531
Guitar Hero, *266*

H

Haiti earthquake (2010), 221
Halo effect The phenomenon in which we judge something or someone positively based on a previous positive experience or association with someone or something we admire, 184–185, 206
Han Dynasty (China), *569*
Hand gestures, 101, 117
Hawai'i, 564–565
Hawthorne effect, 423
Hawthorne Studies A series of research projects demonstrating that when workers perceived that management cared about them and/or when they felt they were getting special treatment, both morale and productivity improved, 422–423, 452
HDTV, *266*
Health care, ethics over access to, 33
Health Insurance Portability and Accountability Act (HIPAA) (1996), *486*
Hearing, listening *vs.,* 371
Hero A legendary person who embodies the highest values of a culture, 474, 492
Hierarchy A way of organizing people and groups according to formal authority, 295, 333
  in organizational structures, 295–297, *296,* 317, 321–322
  virtual organizations and, 401
Hierarchy culture A culture that has an internal focus and encourages stability and control, 469, *469,* 492
Hierarchy of needs theory A model stating that people are motivated to satisfy physiological, then safety and security, then love and belonging, then self-esteem, and finally self-actualization needs in that order, 65, 66, 67, 89
High-context cultures, 117
High-performance team A team that performs beyond "all reasonable expectations," as compared with other teams in similar situations, 361, 375
HIPAA (Health Insurance Portability and Accountability Act), *486*
Hispanic/Latino employees, 480
HIV/AIDS, *241*
Hofstede's dimensions of culture, 462–464, *463*
Honduras, 531
Hong Kong, *466*
Hope A state of mind that includes optimism, an image of a future that is challenging but realistic, and a belief that we can do something to move toward this vision, 61, 88; The emotional experience of looking forward to a future that seems feasible and enticing, 237, *247, 247,* 249

Horizontal communication The flow of information between individuals at the same or similar levels of an organizational hierarchy, 4, 120, 133
Horses, as healers, 247, *247*
Hoteling, 399
Housing boom, 223
HR (human resources). *See* Human resources (HR) (roles of)
HR cycle, 45–46, *46*
HR inventory An internal system that maintains information about people within an organization, including skills, training needs, career plans, and other information about employees, 166, 173
Hub-and-spoke network, 121–122, 403–404
Human population
  demographics, 217–218, *218*
  growth of, 4, *4,* 551
Human relations movement A movement that started around the beginning of the twentieth century and emphasized placing people, interpersonal relationships, and group behavior at the center of workplace studies, 422, 452
Human resources (HR) (roles of)
  in change, 242–244
  in corporate social responsibility and sustainability, 581–583
  in decision-making, 201–202
  in development of positive organizational cultures, 484–489, *485, 486*
  in ethical leadership development, 47
  in gathering and communicating employee engagement information, 127–128
  labor laws and, 127
  in leadership competency development, 243–244
  leadership roles, 47–48
  organization development interventions by, 242–243
  organizational communication and, 127–128
  in organizational design and structure, 329–330
  in performance management, 447–450, *448, 449*
  in planning and strategy, 166–168
  responsibilities of, 45–46
  role in motivation, 84–86
  in supporting creativity, innovation and entrepreneurship, 284–285
  in supporting ethical and excellent leadership, 45–48
  in supporting global business, 535–537
  in team performance, 369–370
  virtual work and, 411
  whistle-blower protection by, 48
Human rights, in China, *527*
Human trafficking, 569–570
Humane orientation, 464, *466*
Hungary, 501
Hurricane Katrina, 124
Hybrid automobiles, 157, 565
Hybrid organizations, 402
Hybrid structure, 321–322, *322,* 335
Hybrid structure A structure that incorporates more than one type of structure in the overall organization, 321–322, *322,* 355
Hybrid worker, 399
Hybridization, 506
Hygiene factors Both physical and psychological aspects of a job that can lead to dissatisfaction, including salary, working conditions, supervision, relationships with coworkers, and level of job security, 68, 89

Hypercompetition A state of constant and escalating competition, 254, 288

Hyperinflation, 513, *514*

I

Iceberg metaphor, *20*, 20–21

Iceland, 159

Idea incubator Part of the research and development (R&D) branch of an organization that focuses on the development of entrepreneurial ideas, 269, 288

Ideal self, 238

Ideas, building support for, 283

Importers, *309*

Importing The transportation and sale of foreign goods to a domestic market, 503, 540

Impoverished Management leadership style, 41

Inclusion, in group development, 345, *346*

Income statement. *See* **Profit and loss statement**

Incremental change, 220–223

India, 154, 519

  advantages and disadvantages of doing business with, 523, *523*

  age demographics in, 217, *218*

  Bhopal disaster (1984) in, 553–554

  buying power in, 508

  cell phones in, 391

  Copenhagen Accord and, 561

  economic growth in, 218–219

  during era of industrialization, 385

  GLOBE project dimensions in, *465, 466*

  in Group of 20, 533

  Intel in, 388

  key events in history of, *520*

  Kyoto Protocol and, 5607

  past (2500 B.C.E. to 1900), 521

  post-Cold War, 502

  present (1991-2009), 521–522

  sex tourism in, 570

  slave labor in, 570

Indifference, to change, *245*

Indirect communication, 104

Indirect requests, 130–131

Individual change, 235–242

  culture and, 227

  difficulties with, 235

  emotions related to, 235, *236*

  gestalt cycle of experience model, 238–240

  intentional, 236–238, *238*

  intentional change model, 236–238, *238*

  psychology and neuropsychology of, 235–236

Individual compensation A plan in which compensation is determined by considering an individual's performance, 84, 90

Individual ethics A personal code of conduct when dealing with others, *31*, 31–32, 53

Individualism The degree to which people prefer to act in their own self-interest instead of acting on what is best for the group as a whole, 463, *463*, 492

Indonesia, *466*, 533

Industrial Revolution The period in the eighteenth and nineteenth centuries during which major advances in technology, manufacturing, and transportation changed people's way of life, mainly in England, the United States, and parts of continental Europe, 382, 415

  Africa during era of, 384–385

  China during era of, 386

  First Industrial Revolution, 382–383

  India during era of, 385

  Second Industrial Revolution, 383–384

  South America during, 385–386

  Third Industrial Revolution, 387–389

  world economic stage during waning of western, 386–387

Industry A collective group of companies that provide the same or similar products and services, 159, 173

Industry environment, 159

Inference, *197*

Inflation

  in Brazil, 513, *514*

  in India, 522

Influence, in groups, 363

Informal communication Communication that moves through channels other than those that have been explicitly defined within an organization, 122–124, *123*, 133

Informal organizations, 330–332, *331–332*

Information

  differences in processing, 356

  making good decisions with incomplete, 194–196

  Wilbur's model for categorizing, 104–106

Information overload, 408–409

Information and communication technologies (ICTs) All of the hardware and software related to electronic communication and information sharing, 380, 415

  in banking, 404–405

  in consumer sales, 406

  in education and training, 406–407

  e-mail. *See* E-mail

  evolution of, 389–392

  global logistics and, 388–389

  groupware, 395

  interaction between people and, 380–381

  multimedia, 396–397

  social change and, 387–388

  social networks, 396

  sociotechnical systems theory on, 381

  teleconferences, 394

  text messaging, 110, 394

  Third Industrial Revolution and, 387

  used for communicating, 110–111, *111*

  videoconferences, 394

  virtual teams and, 399

  virtual work and, 397

  web conferencing, 394

  working in a virtual world and, 381–382

Informational roles, of manager, *10*

In-group collectivism, 464, *466, 470*

In-groups, *470*

Initiating structure Behaviors related to task and goal orientation, such as giving clear directions, monitoring employees' performance, and planning and setting work schedules and deadlines, 40, 53

Innovation The process of implementing new ideas, 262, 288

  as company strategy, *150–151*

  examples of, 263–264, *264*

  human resource's role in supporting, 284–285

  importance of, 262–263

  inspiring others toward, *255*

  list of innovative products, 266

  long-term outlook for, 254–255

  most innovative companies/products, 265, *265, 266*

  One Laptop per Child Campaign (OLPC), *262, 263*

  outside of bureaucratic hierarchy of organization, 269–270

  personal perspectives on, *267–268*

  structures promoting, 268–269

  student perspective on, *262, 263*

Innovative organizational cultures, 479

Inspirational leaders, 50–51

Inspirational leadership, 22

Institutional collectivism, 464, *465*

Institutionalization of ethics, 481

Instrumental values Preferred behaviors or ways of achieving our terminal values, 31, 52

Instrumentality A person's belief about the degree to which performance will result in realizing certain outcomes, 75, 89

Integrity The quality of steadfastly holding to high moral principles and professional standards, 50–51, 53

Intellectual property The ownership of a creative thought or idea and legal control over the representation of the thought or idea, 284, 289, 313

Intelligence, competence and, 20

Intentional change model, 236–238, *238*, 596–597, *597, 599*

  lottery exercise, 597

  my fantasy job exercise, 599–600

  my learning edge exercise, 605

  my life in the year 20__ exercise, 598

  my values exercise, 601–602

  personal balance sheet exercise, 604

  strengths I see in myself exercise, 602–603

Internal analysis, 162–163

Internal communication Communication that moves through channels other than those that have been explicitly defined within an organization, 121, 133

Internal locus of control, 64

International Anticorruption and Good Governance Act (2000), 34

International Monetary Fund (IMF) A United Nations agency that promotes currency stability and lends reserve currencies to nations with trade deficits, 533, 541

International organization, *309*

International Organization for Standardization (ISO)

  9000, 445–446

  14000, 445–446

International Sign Language, 99

International trade, deregulation of, 504

Internet banking, 405

Internet The global system of interlinked, hypertext documents contained within an electronic network that connects computers and computer networks around the world, 389–391, 415

  human resources monitoring searches on, 411

  technological environment and, 158

Interpersonal relationships, in Schein's organizational culture model, 472

Interpersonal roles, of manager, 10

Interpretation, *197*

Interruptions, in group communication, 363

Intranet An internal company network that is usually accessible only to employees, 390, 415

Intrepreneur An employee who behaves like an entrepreneur inside his or her own organization, 282, 288

Intrepreneurship, 282–283

Intrinsic motivation An internal sense of satisfaction derived from the work itself and/or the desire to engage in activities even in the absence of external rewards in order to feel a sense of satisfaction, to use or improve one's abilities, or to learn, 61, 62, 88

  in flat organizations, 318

  job characteristics model, 85–86, *85*

Introversion-extraversion personality dimension, 357

Intuiting-sensing personality dimension, 356

Intuition Tacit knowledge, or knowledge that we have access to at an unconscious level, 182, 186–187, 206

Investment, global, 504

Investment banks Institutions that raise capital, trade securities, and assist with mergers and acquisitions, 222, 249

Investor Someone who provides money as a loan and is, in return, paid back with interest, 277, 288

Iran, religious fundamentalism and, 503

Iraq, religious fundamentalism and, 503

Ireland, 388, *465*

Iron Curtain The seemingly impenetrable physical and political boundary that existed during the Cold War and separated democracy-favoring Western Europe from Communism-favoring Eastern Europe and the Soviet Union, 500, 502, 539

ISO 9000, 445–446

ISO 14000, 445–446

Isolates Followers who are nonresponsive or indifferent to leaders, 12, 14

Israel, 388, *465, 466*

Italy, *465, 466*

Ivory Coast, 570

J

Japan, 312–313
  China and, 524, *524*
  "face" in, 103
  GLOBE project dimensions in, *465*
  in Group of 20, 533
  United Nations Climate Change Conference (2009), 561

Jargon Terminology that has been specifically defined in relation to certain activities, professions, or groups, 113, 132, 472

Job A group of tasks and responsibilities related to accomplishing organizational objectives, 324–325, 335

Job analysis The systematic process of gathering and analyzing information about jobs and the acknowledge, skills, and competencies needed to perform these jobs, 329–330, *330*, 335

Job changes, frequency of, 213

Job characteristic model Framework that states that people need certain qualities in their job to be intrinsically motivated and satisfied with their work, 85–86, 90

Job description A written document that lists the major tasks and responsibilities of a particular job, 330, 335

Job discrimination, 485

Job enlargement Combining several simple jobs into one larger job, 85, 90

Job enrichment Building intrinsic motivators, such as opportunities for learning, more control over how tasks are accomplished, and leadership opportunities, into the structure of a job, 85, 90

Job loss, globalization and, 511

Job migration, 388

Job rotation Moving employees from one job to one job site to another to increase satisfaction and productivity, 85, 90

Job satisfaction surveys, 128

Job satisfaction/dissatisfaction, 68

Job specification A written document that lists all of the necessary knowledge, skills, and abilities that a person must possess in order to perform a particular job, 330, 335

Jobs for Veterans Act (2002), *486*

Joint implementation (JI) projects, 560

Joint venture A formal arrangement between two or more entities to engage in activities together and to share risk, 154, *154*, 172

Jordan, 570

Judging-perceiving personality dimension, 357

K

Kaizen, 443, *443*

Kansei, 443

Kazakhstan, 570

Kenya, 274, 547

Key stakeholders, 160

Kindle, 266

Knowledge
  competency and, 21
  creativity and, *256*

Knowledge domain, 258, *259*

Knowledge management, 409–410, *410*

Korean War, 501

Kotter's eight-stage change model, 228–231, *229*

Kyoto Box, 274

Kyoto Protocol An international agreement drafted during the 1997 United Nations Framework Convention on Climate Change for the purpose of supporting and enforcing the reduction of greenhouse gas emissions, 559, 561, 586

L

Labor laws, 126, 127

Labor relations, by human resources, 46

Laissez-faire leader A leader who remains at a distance from the decision-making process, allowing the group to make decisions without leadership intervention, 343, 375

Land conservation, 556

Language A systematic form of communication that is composed of a set of sounds and symbols shared by people, 98, 132
  body, 101
  connotative meaning, 100
  defined, 98
  denotative meaning, 100
  dialects, 112–113
  evolution of, 97–98
  getting in the way of communication, 112–114
  jargon, 113–114
  in a multicultural environment, *461*
  in organizational culture, 476–477
  pitch, 101
  rate of speech, 101
  in Schein's organizational culture model, 472
  sign, 98–99
  verbal, 98
  vocal intonation, 101
  voice volume, 101
  written, 99–100

Language barriers, 112

Language variation, 112–114

Latin America
  age demographics in, 217, *218*
  during era of industrialization, 385–386
  in Group of 20, 533
  industrialization and, 385–386
  trade alliances and, 530–532
  See also individual Latin Amercian countries

Latin American Integration Association (ALADI), *515*

Latinos/Hispanic employees, 480

Law(s)
  business ethics and role of, 33–34
  cap and trade, 560
  for entrepreneurs, 284
  equal opportunity, 485, *485–486*
  for not-for-profits, 309
  organizational control and, 430–431

Layoff A termination with the possibility of rehire once conditions improve, 168, 173

Lead customers methodology, 151

Leader(s) A person who is out in front, influencing and inspiring people to follow, 7, 14
  autocratic, 343
  characteristics of great, 374
  democratic, 343
  as ethnographers, 477–478
  expectations of, 4–5, 13–14
  global strategy and, *507–508*
  inspirational, 50–51, 61
  management of emotions by, 450–451
  manager *vs.*, 7–8
  meaning for you, in the workplace, 4–5
  motivating others, 60–61
  in a multicultural environment, *461*
  need for, 4, 18–19
  need for teams, 340–342
  personal perspectives on, *5, 7–8, 237*
  profile of, *592*
  reaction to change, 220–221
  resonant, *11*
  roles of, *6*
  seeing yourself as a, 5–7
  traditional views of, 8–9
  transformational, 44–45
  trust in, 50
  word origin, 7

Leader substitutes model A contingency model of leadership that states that certain characteristics of people or of the situation can make direct leadership unnecessary, 43, 53

Leaderless group, power and influence in, 355–356

Leadership
  behavior models and approaches to, 40–42
  contingency approaches to, 42–43
  for corporate social responsibility and sustainability, 584
  defining ethics through, 35–36
  description of great, *19*
  effective, 20–22
  entrepreneurship and, 279
  ethics and, 30–38
  five styles of, 41–42
  focusing on goal of developing, 596
  human resource's role in supporting ethical and excellent, 45–48
  impact on group dynamics, 342–343
  in informal organizations, 331–332
  intentional change model for developing, 596–605
  as learned, 19
  "Moon Shots for Management," *593*, 593–594, *594*
  motivation and, 60
  power and, 25–30
  of resonant teams, 372–373, *373*
  responsibility for, 18–19
  self-awareness and, 48–50. *See also* **Self-awareness**
  three styles of, 342–343
  trait theories of, 39–40
  for virtual teams, 413–414

Leadership development architect, 47

Leadership grid, *41*, 41–42

Lean communication channel, 109

Lean Management A management approach that organizes manufacturing and logistics to maximize efficiency and eliminate waste by reducing variation in every process, 141, 422, 445, 453

Learning, lifelong, 595

Learning edge exercise, *605*

Learning styles, 357–358

Learning theories, 78–83

operant conditioning theory, 78–81, *79*

social learning theory, *81*, 81–82

Left *vs.* right brain, 257

Legal and tax environment, 157–158

Legal issues

for entrepreneurs, 284

global business and, 505–506

in relationships with outside entities, 312–315

See also Law(s)

Legal structures

of corporations, 312

of organizations, 309

Legitimate power The ability to influence others by right of one's position in an organization, the office held, or formal authority, 26, *26*, 52, 355

Leveraging money A practice that allows financial institutions to increase the amount of debt they handle in proportion to the amount of money they hold, 222, 249

Levers of change (work system model), 232–233

Levers of control A control system that relies on various levers such as organizational values, rules, feedback systems, and focused involvement in decision making, 427–428, *428*, *452*

Lewin's formula, 342, *343*

Liaison, as managerial role, *10*

Licensing A business agreement in which the owner of trademarked or otherwise branded material authorizes an individual or company to use that material to sell or market products or services in exchange for a fee, 505, 540

Licensing agreement A business agreement in which the owner of trademarked material authorizes an individual or company to use that material to sell or market products or services in exchange for a fee, 313, 334

Life in the Year 20__ exercise, 598

Lilly Ledbetter Fair Pay Act (2007), *486*

Limbic resonance Refers to the fact that emotions are contagious and a powerful driver of our feelings, thoughts, and behaviors, 24, 52, 100

Limbic system, 235

Listening, 114, 371–372, *372*

Live Aid, *576*

LIVESTRONG campaign, 83

LLC (limited liability company) A hybrid form of ownership that provides limited personal liability to the owners of a business, *310*, 312, 334

Local organizations, *309*

Locus of control Our perception of the degree to which we have control over what happens in our lives, 63–64, 88

Logic, in decision making, 181–182

Long tail, concept of, 216

Long-term orientation Refers to a greater concern for the future and for values such as thrift, perseverance, and avoidance of shame, *463*, 464, 492

Long-term plans, *143*

Lottery exercise, 597

Low-context cultures, 117

Lying, cognitive behavior conveying, 102

M

Maasai people (Kenya and Tanzania), 547

Maintenance roles, in groups, 350

Malaria, *303*

Malawi, 274, 570

Malaysia, 388, 409, 570

Malcolm Baldridge National Quality Award, 446–447

Mali, 570

Management

corporate governance and, 429

"Moon Shots for Management," *593*, 593–594, *594*

scientific, 421–422

Management by objectives (MBO), 448

Management by walking around, 124

Management competency model, 22, *22*

Management of meaning, 245

Manager(s) An individual who makes plans, organizes and controls people, production and services, and who regulates or deploys resources, 7, 14

adjusting to globalization, 536–537

changing expectations of, 13–14

as ethnographers, 477–478

leader *vs.*, 7–8

performance appraisal by, 449–450

punishment used by, 79–80

reaction to change, 220

restoring equity, 74–75

roles and activities of, 9–11

traditional views of, 8–9

of virtual teams, 414

word origin, 7

Managing up A followership tool that enables followers to influence leaders, 12, 14, 332

Market alliance model, of virtual organizations, *404*

Market culture A culture that has an external focus and encourages stability and control, 469, *469*, 492

Market growth rate A measure of growth in the market for given products or services, 164, 173

Market share The percentage of the market that a product, service, or business unit has captured, *164*, 164–165, 173

Marketing, for start-up businesses, 280

Markov process, 145, *145*

Mars Climate Orbiter, 108

Masculinity/femininity The extent to which society values achieving (masculine) *versus* nurturing (feminine), *463*, 463–464, 492

Matrix A structure in which departments within an organization are linked directly to one unit in the vertical organization and to another unit in the horizontal organization, 320–321, *321*, 335

"McDonaldization," 506

Meaningful work, 58–59

Mechanistic organization An organization characterized by routine job functions, a high degree of specialization, and division of labor, 304, 334

Membership, group, 362

Merit-based compensation A plan in which compensation is determined by the level of performance of an individual or group, 84, 90

Meritocracy A system in which people are granted power, responsibilities, and roles because of superior intellect, talent, and competencies, 353, 375

Message Information, 106

Metaphors, for organizations, 305, *306*

Metrics, planning focusing on, 141

Mexico, 388

economic sustainability and, *573*

GLOBE project dimensions in, *465*

in Group of 20, 533

NAFTA and, 530–531

Microblogging, 395

Microfinance The practice of providing financial services on an extremely small scale, 405–406, 415

Micromanagement The practice of overcontrolling others and their work, as well as paying far too much attention to details and how employees do their work, 28, 52

Micromanagers People who try to do everything themselves and criticize everyone else's efforts, 70, 89

Middle of the Road Management leadership style, 41

Migrant and Seasonal Agricultural Worker Protection Act (MSPA) (1983), *485*

Migratory Bird Treaty Act, 154

Milestones, 144

Millennials (Generation Y), 118–119

Mind mapping, 286, *286*

Mindfulness A state in which we are awake, aware, and attuned to ourselves, others, and our environment, 203, 207

creativity and, *256*

decision making and, 203–204

facing change with, 247

pattern recognition and, 169–170

Miryokuteki hinshitsu, 443

Mission, 141, 142, 147–149, *152*, 162, 174

Mission statement A statement that describes what an organization is, what it does, and what it stands for, 138, 147, 148, *148*, 172

Mobile telecommunications, 391–392

Models of communication, 107

Modular approach to planning, 144–145

"Moon Shots for Management," *593*, 593–594, *594*

Mores Norms that are central to the functioning of society, 460, 492

Motivation, theories of, 65–78

equity theory, 72–75

ERG theory, 67

expectancy theory, 75–76

goal-setting theory, 76–78

hierarchy of needs, 67

integration of, 83

three-needs theory, 69–72

time line of, 65

two-factor theory, 68

visual summary of, 66

Motivation The result of a complex set of psychological influences and external forces or conditions that cause a person to behave in a certain way while maintaining a certain level of effort and degree of persistence, 58, 88

Big Five dimensions of personality and, 64–65

empathy and, 87

explained, 58

extrinsic, 62–63

at Google, 63

hope and, 61

human resource's role in, 84–86

intrinsic, 61, 62

leadership and, 60

learning theories and, 78–83

locus of control and, 63–64

operant conditioning and, 78–81

psychology and, 61–65

self-awareness and, 86–87
self-efficacy and, 82
self-reinforcement and, 81
as up to each individual, 60
Motivator-hygiene theory (Two-factor theory), 65, 66, 68
Motivators Factors that positively impact motivation, such as the needs for recognition, responsibility, achievement, and opportunities for growth and development, 68, 89
Motives, competency and, 21
MSPA (Migrant and Seasonal Agricultural Worker Protection Act) (1983), *485*
Multicultural work environment, *461*
Multimedia, 396–397
Multinational corporation, *309*
Multinational parent companies, 314
Must-win battles, 165
My Fantasy Job exercise, 599–600
My Learning Edge exercise, 605
My Life in the Year 20__ exercise, 598
My Values exercise, 601–602
Myanmar, 570
Myers-Brigg Type Indicator (MBTI), 356–357
Myths Exaggerated stories that are told and retold to communicate values and to emphasize norms, 474, 492

N

NAFTA (North America Free Trade Agreement), 530–531
National debt, U.S., 504–505
Nationalist Party (China), 524, *524*
Natural environment, 158–159
Nazi Germany, 37
Need for achievement (nAch) The desire to engage in challenging and complex activities, meet and exceed personal goals, and to seek excellence, 69, 71, 89
Need for affiliation (nAff) The desire for warm, fulfilling, and close personal relationships, 69, 70, 71, 89
Need for power (nPow) The desire to have influence, control, and responsibility, either directly or through social status, 69, 70–71, 89
Needs theories, 66–68
ERG theory, 67
hierarchy of needs theory, 67
two-factor theory, 68
Negative emotional attractor A psychological state characterized by negative emotions that is linked to the sympathetic nervous system and that can cause people to feel defensive, threatened, and stressed, 236, *236*, 249
Negative politeness, 104
Negative reinforcement, 79
Negotiator, as managerial role, *10*
Nepal, *361*, 570
Nepotism, 34
Net capital rule Rule that guides how much debt an institution can hold, 222, 249
Netflix Prize, 264
Netherlands, *465*
Network structure, 322, *323*
Networks
communication, 115–116
organizational, 121–122
Neurophysiology, competencies and, 24
New business. *See* Small businesses
New Guinea, 547
"New world order," 502
Nicaragua, 531

Niche strategy A business strategy that caters to a narrow segment of the market, *155,* 155–156, 172
Nigeria, 409, 510, 570
Noise Anything that interferes with the transmission or receipt of a message, 107, 108, 132
Nongovernmental organizations (NGOs), *308, 361*
Nonprogrammed decisions Decisions that are not routine and/or involve unique information or circumstances, *179,* 180, 206
Nonverbal communication Any gesture, expression, physical action, or vocal intonation, pitch, or volume that communicates a message either intentionally or unintentionally, 100, 132
body language, 101
cross-cultural communication and, 117
emotional expression with, 102
interpreting emotions, 103
in organizational culture, 477
reading nonverbal signals, 100–101
Normative control A control system that involves sharing and embedding an organization's values and beliefs so they act as a guide for employees' behavior, 427, 452
Norming The third stage of group development, when the group agrees common "rules" of behavior for members (group norms), who does what (group roles), and how best to work together, 344, 375
Norms Internalized standards for behavior that support agreed-upon ways of doing things and what people expect of one another within a cultural group, 459, 492
culture and, 459–460
folkways, 460
group, 351–353, *352*
mores, 460
North American Free Trade Agreement (NAFTA) An accord between the United States, Canada, and Mexico that lifts tariffs and other trade barriers among the three nations, 530–531, 540
North Korea, 570
Not-for-profit organization, *308,* 309
Nuclear waste management, 563–564

O

Observable artifacts, in Schein's organizational culture model, 472, *472*
Obstructionist approach to corporate social responsibility, 580
Occupational Safety and Health Act (1970), *559*
Offshoring A form of outsourcing in which companies transfer jobs to countries other than their own to reduce labor and other expenses, 509, 540
Ohio State Studies, 40
Oil, globalization and, 502–503
Oil producing and exporting countries (OPEC), 562
Oil reserves, in Nigeria, 510
Oil spill, Gulf of Mexico (2010), 302, 553
Oil use and production, 561–562
One Laptop per Child campaign (OLPC), *262,* 263
One-child policy, in China, *527*
One-on-one conversation, 109
Online banking system, 405
Online grocers, 160
Open systems theory A theory stating that any human system, such as an organization, is constantly influenced by and is influencing its environment, 301–304, *302, 303,* 334
Openness to experience (personality dimension), 64

Open-source software, 307
Operant conditioning theory Theory that learning and behavior changes occur when behavior is reinforced, and when behavior is not reinforced or is punished, it will eventually cease, 65, 66, 78, 80–81, 89
Operational plans, 143
Operations management The transformation of inputs—materials, labor, and ideas—into outputs, such as products or services, 442, 453
See also Quality control
Opportunity Any situation, condition, or event that is favorable to an organization, 163, 173
Optimism A positive outlook on life coupled with the belief that good things will come, and that bad things are only temporary and can be overcome, 45, 61, 237, 249
organizational change and, 237
planning and, 139
self-efficacy and, 82
Oral language, 98, *98*
Organic organization An organization characterized by a high degree of flexibility, low levels of specialization, less formality, and decentralized decision-making processes, 304, 334
Organization(s) A group of people assembled to perform activities that will allow the entity to accomplish a set of strategic and tactical goals and to realize its mission, 294, 333
adaptive, 304–305
classification, 308–309
common types of, *308, 309*
defined, 294
empowered, 28
formal, 330–331
forms of ownership, *310,* 310–312
informal, 330–332, *331–332*
mechanistic, 304
metaphors for, 305, *306*
as open systems, 301–304, *302, 303*
organic, 304
relationships with outside entities, 312–315
resonant, 23, 52, 232
spider, 305–306
as spiders and starfish, 305–307
starfish, 306–307
values of, 458–459
virtual services offered by, 404–407
Organization design The process of creating an organizational structure, 295, 333
emergent, 328
geography and, 327–328
human resource's role in, 46, *329,* 329–330, 337
in virtual organizations, 401
without planning, 328
Organization development (OD), 242–243
Organizational awareness
building support for new ideas and, 283
cognitive dissonance and, 73
organizational change and, 244
Organizational change agent, 47
Organizational change
anticipating, 220–221
becoming an agent of, 245
bottom-up, 220
caring for others during, 245–246
competing values model of, 468–469, *469*
eight-stage change model of, 228–231, *229*
gestalt cycle of experience, *239,* 239–240, *241,* 242
human resource's role in fostering effective, 242–244
incremental *vs.* transformational, 220–223

permanent white-water metaphor of, 227–228
personal contribution to, 244–248
reasons for, 214–219
responses to, *245*, 245–246
smart way to lead, *246*
top-down, 220
work systems model of, 231–234, *232*
Organizational chart A visual representation of how roles, jobs, authority, and responsibility are distributed within an organization, *299*, 299–301, *300*, 334
Organizational communication, 119–128
communication flow in, 119–121, *120–121*
crisis, 124–125
formal, 122
grapevine, 123–124
human resources and, 127–128
informal, 122–124, *123*
of labor laws, 127
networks, *121*, 121–122, *122*
storytelling, 125–126
Organizational control(s)
audits and, 430
company example of, *424*, 425
comparing performance to standards, 434
control process, 420
conventions and forces guiding, 429–433
corporate governance and, 429–430
corrective actions, 435
customer control, *432*, 432–433
customer relationship and, *441*, 441–442
emotional self-control/self-management and, 450–451
feedback processes, *435*, 435–437
financial and accounting, 437–441, *439*, *440*
historical perspective on, 421–424
human resource's role in, 447–450
laws/regulations and, 430–431
performance measurement, 434
problems with, 451
quality control and, 442–447
Sarbanes-Oxley Act (2002) and, 431, *431*
steps in process of, 433–437
systems for. *See* Organizational control systems
Organizational control systems
behavior control, 427
bureaucratic, 425–426
levers of control, 427–428, *428*
normative control, 427
output control, 426–427
Organizational culture A set of shared values, norms, and assumptions that guide peoples' behavior within a group, business, or institution, 462, 492
change in, 467
cultural intelligence and, 489–490
customer service, 479–480
diversity, 480, *481*
ethical, 480–481
ethnographic approach to, 477–478
heroes in, 474
human resource's role in creating an inclusive, 484–489, *485*, *486*
innovative, 479
language in, 476–477
leading change in, 490–491
learning to study, 472–478
long-term loyalty, *470*
myths in, 474
normative control and, 427
sacred symbols in, *475*, 475–476
Schein's levels of, *472*, 472–473
supporting sustainability and service, 482–483

supporting the whole person, 483–484
taboos in, 474–475
Organizational cybernetics, 243
Organizational development, 343
Organizational ethics The values and principles that an organization has chosen that guide the behavior of people within the organization and/or what stakeholders expect of the organization, *31*, 32, 53, 480–482
Organizational learning, 125, 266, 594
Organizational planning
complexity of, 142
focusing on goals and metrics, 141
goal-setting and, 139, 141
mission and vision statements, 147, 148
mission clarity for, 147–148
modular approach, 144–145
scenario, 146
terminology, 144–145
thinking about the future and, 138
types of plans, 142–143
in uncertain times, 143–146
vision for, 147, 149
See also **Planning; Strategic planning**
Organizational politics Involve many things, including internal competition and the pursuit of personal goals at the expense of others or the organization, 25, 52
Organizational structure The way in which the division of labor, communication, and movement of resources among the parts of an organization are coordinated to accomplish tasks and goals, 295, 333
centralized decision making in, 298
common contemporary, 315–323
company size and, 327
concepts related to, 294–295
departmentalization and, 318–320
external environment and, 326–327
factors affecting design of, 325–328
hierarchy in, 295–297, *296*
human resource's role in, 329–330
hybrid structure, 321–322, *322*
jobs in, 324–325
matrix structure, 320–321, *321*
networked, 322, *323*
organizational chart showing, *299*, 299–301, *300*
reasons for studying, 294
span of control in, 297–298
strategy and, 325–326
tall vertical, *316*, 316–317
tasks in, 324
technology and, 327
virtual, 403–404, *404*
work in, 323–325
working effectively within, 330–333
OSHA regulations and guidelines, 571, *572*
Out-groups, *470*
Output control Type of control in which outcomes are measured against financial performance and other clearly articulated metrics, such as customer retention, 426–427, 452
Outsourcing The process by which companies subcontract specific jobs or work functions to non-employees or other companies, 506, 509, 540, 582
Overlapping authority conflict, *367*

P

Pacing, in speech, 101
Pakistan, 522, 570, 583
Panama, 531

Paradoxes, of group life, 358
Paraguay, 570
Parent company, 314
Pareto principle, 196
Participants Followers who are actively engaged and make an effort to be supportive and have impact, 12, *12*, 14
Participation, group, 362–363
Participative, in path-goal theory, 43
Participatory style of leadership, 42
Partner Market Agreements, *507*
Partnership An ownership model in which two or more individuals share the ownership of a business, *310*, 311, 334
Passive resistance, to change, *245*
Patent A legal grant given by the U.S. Patent and Trademark Office that prevents anyone other than the grant holder from manufacturing, selling, or utilizing a particular invention, 284, 289
Path goal, 140
Path-goal theory A contingency approach to leadership stating that the leader is responsible for motivating employees to attain goals, 43, 53
Pattern recognition, 21, 22, 169, 257, 298
Peer-to-peer network (P2P), 230, 307, 403–404
People surveys, 128
Perestroika, *517*
Performance appraisal Process of sharing an evaluation of an employee's performance in (ideally) a face-to-face meeting that usually takes place between an employee and his or her manager, although in some organizations this appraisal is delivered by a human resources manager, 449, 453
Performance management process, 46
function of, 447
gathering performance data, 448–449
management by objectives (MBO), 448
performance appraisal, 449–450
steps in, 447, *448*
Performance measurement, 434
Performance orientation, *40*, 464, *466*
Performance The extent to which a task or work is completed successfully, 75, 89
Performing The fourth stage of group development, during which the group channels energy into tasks rather than into building relationships, resolving conflicts, or deciding how to work together, 344–345, 375
Permanent white marker Metaphor that refers to the fact that organizational systems face unrelenting turbulence and constant change, 227–228, 249
Personal Balance Sheet exercise, 604
Personality, motivation and, 64–65
Personality tests, 356–357
Personalized power A need for power that drives people to seek control through assertive or aggressive behavior, often for personal gain, 71, 89
Peru, 531, 570
Pessimism, planning and, 139
Pharmaceutical industry, 229–230
Philanthropy Giving money, time, services, or products in the service of supporting people's well-being, 575, *575–576*, 577, 586
Philippines, the, 388, *536*
Physical cultural intelligence, 490
Physical space, virtual work and, 398
Physical touch, 101
Pidgin A language that uses signs, words, or phrases from more than one language, allowing

people to communicate without learning one another's language, 99, 132

Planning The cognitive, creative, and behavioral process of developing a sequence of activities intended to achieve a goal or move toward an imagined future state, 138, 172
  action-oriented, 140
  defined, 138–139
  directional, 139–140
  goal-oriented, 139
  human resource's role in, 166–168
  probability and, 145
  thinking about the future and, 138, 139
  See also Organizational planning; **Strategic planning**

Plano Real, in Brazil, 513
Platinum-Level Leadership in Energy and Environmental Design, 563
Pluralistic evidence, 37–38
Poland, 388, *465*, *466*
Political environment, 158, 509–510
Politeness, 104
Political theory, 343
Pollution, 556, 563
Pollution Prevention Act (1990), *558*
Polygamy, 460
Pony express, 110
Ponzi scheme, 18, 36
Population demographics, 217–218, *218*, *527*
Portugal, 385

Positive emotional attractor A psychological state of well-being and hope that engages the parasympathetic nervous system and can counter the effects of stress, 236, *236*, 249

Positive politeness, 104
Positive reinforcement, 78–79
Post-industrial society, 387
Poverty
  economic sustainability and, 573
  in India, *523*

Power distance The extent to which people in societies accept the idea that power is distributed unequally, 463, *463*, *465*, 492

Power Influence over or through others, 25, 52
  coercive, 26
  communication and, 115–116
  expert, 26–27
  in groups, 355–356
  influential leadership and, 25–30
  in a leaderless group, 355–356
  legitimate, 26
  need for, 70–71
  need to understand, 25
  personalized, 71
  referent, 27
  resonant leadership and, 595
  reward, 26
  socialized, 71
  sources of, *26*, 26–27
  in spider organizations, 306
  "with" *vs.* "over" people, 423

Power stress, 69–70
Predatory lending, 223
Presence, 45
Primary stakeholders, 160
Prius automobile, 157
Privacy, electronic communication, 411
Private foundations, *309*

Privately held company A company that is wholly owned by an individual or group of individuals and does not sell shares of ownership on the open market, 429, 452

Proactive approach to corporate social responsibility, 580
Probability, planning and, 145
Process conflict, *367*

Process departmentalization A method of grouping jobs based on the sequential steps of the work people do to produce products or services or engage in other business activities, 319–320, *320*, 335

Processing mode, 258, *259*
Product departmentalization, 319, *319*

Product departmentalization A method of grouping jobs based on the products made or services offered, 319, *319*, 335

Production-oriented behavior, 40–41
Productivity and work stage (Susan Wheelan's stages of group development), *346*, 347

Professional ethics Standards that outline appropriate conduct in a given profession, 32, 53

Profit and loss statement Also called a P&L or an income statement, this document itemizes revenues and expenses and provides insight into what can be done to improve a company's results, 439, *440*, 453

Programmed decisions Decisions that are routine in nature and occur with some frequency, 179, 206

Project plan, 143
Project Scorpion, 268

Propaganda Various forms of communication that are meant to further a specific agenda and/or weaken the position of a competing party, 501, 540

Prosocial behavior Any behavior that seeks to protect the welfare of society or the common good, 71, 89

Protests, anti-globalization, 499, *499*
Proximity to others, 101

Proxy wars Wars that are encouraged or triggered by powerful nations but in which those nations don't necessarily participate in combat. Instead, the nations use less-powerful third parties to represent their competing interests, 501, 540

Psychology
  of individual change, 235–236
  motivation and, 61–65

Public charity, *309*
Public Company Accounting Reform and Investor Protection Act (2002), 34, 431
Public limited corporation, *310*

Publicly traded company A company that issues shares of ownership, or stocks, that are traded on the open market, 429, 453

"Pull" strategy, in developing organizational culture, 488–489
Punishment, in operant conditioning, 79–80
Punting, *113*
"Push" strategies, in creating an inclusive organizational culture, 484–488, *485*, *486*

Q

Qualitative controls, 433, 434

Qualitative research A process of gathering and analyzing subjective data, such as information from conversations, interviews, or answers to open-ended questions on a survey, 127, 133

Quality control
  Baldridge Award, 446–447
  business process reengineering, 442–443
  ISO 9000, 445–446
  ISO 14000, 445–446
  Lean Management, 445

  Six Sigma, *444*, 444–445, *445*
  Total Quality Management, 443, *443*
Quantitative controls, 433, 434, *434*

Quantitative research A process of gathering information that can be converted to numbers, then analyzed using statistics and other mathematical tools, 127–128, 133

R

Rainforests, 159
Rambling, 363
Readiness, in situational leadership theory, 42
Real self, 238
Reason, in decision making, 181–182

Receiver A person who receives and decodes a message, 106, 132

Recession. *See* Economic recession; Global economic recession
Recognition of assumptions, *197*
Re-creation, as response to change, 220, *220*

Recruiting The process of attracting qualified candidates for jobs, 46, 166–167, 173

Recycling, 563
Referent, in equity theory, 72–73

Referent power Power that comes from personal characteristics that people value and want to emulate and that cause people to feel respect or admiration, 26, 27, 52, 355

Regulatory agencies. *See* Global economic regulatory agencies
Rehabilitation Act (1973), *485*

Reinforcement Consequences associated with behavior, 78–79, 89

Relational competencies, 22
  See also **Empathy; Self-awareness;** Self-management

Relationship conflict, *367*
Relationship management, *23*, 49

Relationship-oriented leaders Leaders who emphasize good relationships and being liked by employees, 42, 53

Relationships
  communication as essential to work, 96–97
  improving communication, 128–131
  resonant, 97
  saving face in, 103–104
  virtual, 400, 408, 412–413

Relativism, in business ethics, 33
Religious fundamentalism, 503
Reorientation, 220, *220*
Research
  action, 243, *243*
  Asch conformity studies, 364–365
  behavioral approaches to leadership, 40–41
  Hawthorne Studies, 422–423
  qualitative, 127
  quantitative, 127–128
  on traits, 39–40

Resonant environment A work environment characterized by excitement, energy, optimism, efficacy, and hope, 23, 29, 61, *61*, 63, 88
  characteristics of, 61
  organizational control and, 424, *424*, 425
  organizational culture and, 490
  positive reinforcement and, 78–79

Resonant leaders Socially and emotionally intelligent, visionary people who lead and manage in ways that enable everyone to contribute their very best, 23, 52
  continuing your journey for becoming, 595
  social and emotional intelligence of, 22–25, *23*

Resonant leadership, *6*, *11*

Resonant organization Organizations characterized by a powerful and positive culture in which people have a shared sense of excitement and commitment to mutual goals, 23, 52

Resonant relationships Vibrant and supportive relationships that foster respect, inclusion, and open and honest dialogue, 97, 132
communication and, 96, 97, 128–131. *See also* **Communication**
human resources ensuring effective, 126–128

Resonant teams
building, 369–370
creating and sustaining, 370–373
leading, 372–373, *373*

Resource allocator, as managerial role, *10*

Resource conflict, *367*

Resource Conservation and Recovery Act (1976), *557*

Responsibility The obligation to satisfactorily accomplish the tasks associated with a job, 297, 333

Retrenchment strategy A corporate strategy that is adopted when a company needs to regroup and defend itself while turning the business around, 153, 155, 172

Reward conflict, *367*

Reward power The ability to influence others by giving or withholding rewards such as pay, promotions, time off, attractive projects, learning experience, and the like, 26, *26*, 52, 355

Rich communication channel, 108–109

Risk, entrepreneurs embracing, 273

Rituals, in Schein's organizational culture model, 473

Rockefeller Center, Manhattan, 405

Roles
group, 349–351
managerial, 9–11

Romania, 502, *536*

Russia, 388
advantages and disadvantages of doing business with, 518, *519*
age demographics in, 218
centrally planned socialist economy of, 516
future (2010 and beyond), 518
GLOBE Project dimension in, 465, *466*
in Group of 20, 533
key events in history of, *517*
Kyoto Protocol and, 560
past (1917-1989), 515
present (1989-2009), 515–518
slave labor in, 570
as a superpower, 529–530
See also Union of Soviet Socialist Republics (USSR)

Rwanda, 37

S

S corporation A type of corporation that has 100 or fewer shareholders and does not pay federal income taxes, 312, 334

Sacred symbols Things, people, and events that are untouchable and unquestionable within a culture, *475*, 475–476, 493

Safe Drinking Water Act (1974), *557*

Safety standards, 305

Same-sex marriage, *467*, 467–468

Samoa, 509

Sarbanes-Oxley Act of 2002 Formally known as the Public Company Accounting Reform and Investor Protection Act, this act sets new or enhanced standards for publicly traded companies' boards, managers, and public accounting firms, 33–34, 431, *431*, 453

SARS (severe acute respiratory syndrome), 305

Satellite tracking technology, 388

Satisficing Choosing an alternative that is adequate but not perfect, 192, 206

Saudi Arabia, 503, 533

Saving face, 103–104

SBIC (Small Business Investment Company) A financial institution that makes loans to entrepreneurs under the auspices of the Small Business Administration, a U.S. federal government agency, 277, 288

Scenario planning A dynamic, systematic process in which people envision all of the "what if" scenarios for given situations and plan for several likely possibilities, 146, 172

Schein's organizational culture model, *472*, 472–473

Schemas, 46, 73, 182–183, 410

Schramm Model of Communication, 107

Scientific management An approach that involves organizing work for maximum efficiency, 324, 421–422, 442, 452

Scorpion and frog parable, *226*

Search for Yourself program, *592*

Second Industrial Revolution The period from the mid-nineteenth century through approximately 1915 that was marked by the development of several life-altering technologies, including electricity, motors, synthetics, internal combustion, and mass production techniques, 383–384, 415

Second Life environment, 111

Secondary stakeholders, 160

Selection The act of choosing whom to hire from among a group of qualified applicants, 167, 173
of employees, 167

Selective perception Consciously or unconsciously focusing on certain parts of a message and ignoring others, 114–115, 132

Self-actualization, 67

Self-awareness The ability to notice and understand one's emotions and their effects, 23, 52
authenticity and, 49–50
cognitive dissonance and, 73
as a competency, 23
equity theory and, 73
in leaderless groups, 356
motivation and, 60, 86–87
nonverbal signals and, 101
organizational controls and, 425
performance management and, 451
power in communication and, 115
response to change and, 246
as skill for leadership, 4–5, 48–49
social and emotional intelligence and, 24–25
trust and, 50

Self-concept, 21

Self-determination theory (SDT) Theory of motivation that is concerned with people's need for empowerment (to feel competent and have a reasonable degree of autonomy) and their need for relatedness (to care for and be related to others), 6, 62, 66, 88

Self-directed work teams Teams in which there is no formally designated leader and members organize their own activities, 359, 375

Self-efficacy The degree to which a person believes that he or she is capable of successfully performing a behavior, accomplishing a task, or achieving a goal, 82, 89, 90, 89, 490

Self-esteem
authenticity and, 50
creativity and, *256*
in entrepreneurs, 273

Self-management, 20, 21, *23*, 49
control systems and, 450
in leaderless groups, 356
non-verbal signals and, 101
organizational controls and, 450
power in communication and, 115
response to change and, 246
social and emotional intelligence and, 22, 24

Self-reinforcement, 81

Self-starters, 273

Selling style of leadership, 42

Sender A person who encodes and sends a message through a communication channel, 106, 132

Senegal, 460

September 11th terrorist attacks, 167, *340, 503

Servant leadership A leadership style in which the leader seeks to serve followers and stakeholders, as opposed to dominating them, 584, 586

Service Giving of oneself without any expectation of a return, 482–483, 582, 586

Service industries, in India, 522

Severe acute respiratory syndrome (SARS), 305

Sex trafficking, 570

Sexual harassment "Unwelcome sexual advances, requests for sexual favors, and other verbal or physical conduct of a sexual nature such that submission to or rejection of this conduct explicitly or implicitly affects an individual's employment, unreasonably interferes with an individual's work performance, or creates an intimidating, hostile, or offensive work environment," 485, *487*, 487–488, 493

Shakti amma, 573

Shannon-Weaver Model of Communication, 107

Shea's work systems model. *See* Gregory Shea's work systems model of organizational change

Short-term orientation Refers to a desire for gratification of personal needs, as well as a focus on tradition and meeting social obligations, *463, 464*, 492

Short-term plans, 143

Sierra Leone, 570

Sign language, *98*, 98–99, *99*

Silence, in teams, 363

Silo mentality, 317, 321

Singapore, 465, *466*, 592

Single-loop learning A process that results in taking in feedback and changing behavior, but not changing underlying beliefs about one's self, others, or the environment, 204, 207

Single-use plans, 143

Situational leadership theory Contingency model that links leader style with followers' readiness for tasks, 42–43, 53

Six Sigma A management strategy that employs quality management methods in a specific sequence to either reduce costs or increase profits, 422, *444*, 444–445, *445*, 453

Skills, competency and, 21

Skunk Works® A term used in business to describe a group within an organization that is given a high degree of autonomy and is unhampered by bureaucracy. The term is trademarked by Lockheed Martin, 268, 288

Slave trade, 385, *385*, 569

Slavery, 568–571, *569*

Slippery slope argument, 36–37

Slovenia, *465*

Small Business Investment Companies (SBICs), 277

Small businesses, *309*
characteristics of a successful, 279–281
funding sources for, 277

importance of, to economies, 271–272
See also **Entrepreneur; Entrepreneurship**
SMART goals Term describing goals that are specific, measurable, achievable, results-based, and time-specific, 77, *77*, 89, 144
Social and emotional intelligence Competencies linked to self-awareness, self-management, social awareness, and relationship management that enable people to understand and manage emotions in social interactions, 22, *23*, 52
  active listening and, 372
  change and, 235, 244, 245, 246
  cognitive dissonance and, 73
  communication and, 101, 128, 129
  competencies and, 20, 21, 22–25, *23*, 49
  cultural intelligence, 489–490
  as essential to good leadership, 49
  group norms related to, 352–353, *353*
  human resources leadership roles and, 47
  informational and communicational technologies and, 381–382
  in organizational culture, 489
  performance reviews and, 450–451
  resonant leadership and, 22–25
  self-awareness and, 24–25, 49–50
  working abroad and, 538
  See also **Self-awareness;** Self-management
Social awareness, 20, *23*, 49, 244
  See also **Empathy**
Social change
  celebrities working for, 272–273
  changes at work from, 388–389
  combatting spread of HIV, 241
  diversity and, 216–218
  informational and communications technologies related to, 387–388
  sustainability and, 215. *See also* **Sustainability**
Social entrepreneurs, *567*
Social entrepreneurship The activity of identifying opportunities to help society in some way, with financial gain taking a secondary position if it factors in at all, 274, 288
Social learning theory Theory stating that people learn new behaviors by observing others and that self-reinforcement and self-efficacy support learning and behavior change, 65, 66, 81–82, 89, 90
Social loafing, 364
Social networks, 396, *396–397*, 411
Social responsibility, organizational cultures supporting, 482–483
Social status The relative standing or prestige you have compared with others in groups to which you belong, 354, 375
Social sustainability Term that refers to the improvement of daily life for the greatest number of people through improving fair income distribution; promoting gender equality; ensuring equal access to land ownership, employment, and education; investing in basic health and education; and enlisting the participation of beneficiaries, 553, *554*, 585
  child labor and, 567–568
  example of organization's approach to, 567, *567*
  explained, 566–567
  OSHA regulations and guidelines, 571–572, *572*
  slavery, 568–571, *569*
  workplace safety, 571–572, *572*
Socialization The process of teaching new members about a culture, 474, 493
Socialized power An expressed need for power that is based on a desire to support the welfare

of others, a group, society, or the common good, 71, 89
Societal ethics Principles and standards that guide members of society in day-to-day behavior with one another, *31*, 32–33, 53
Sociocultural environment, 157
Sociocultural systems theory, 381
Socioeconomic status, 354
Sociotech, 381
Sociotechnical systems theory Theory that examines both social and technical characteristics of tasks and how work is organized, focusing on the interaction between people and technologies, 381, 415
Software piracy, in China, *527*
Sole proprietorship An ownership model in which a single individual owns a business, *310*, 310–311, 334
Somalia, 158
SOPs (standard operating procedures), 113, 304, 427
Soto, 470
South Africa, *465*
  Copenhagen Accord and, 561
  in Group of 20, 533
South America. *See* Latin America
South Korea, *466*, 533
Soviet Union. *See* Union of Soviet Socialist Republics (USSR)
SOX (Sarbanes-Oxley Act) (2002), 431
Space race (Cold War), 501–502
Space Shuttle *Challenger* disaster, 365, *365*
Spain, 385, *465*
Span of control The number of jobs that report to a position at the next higher level in a hierarchy, 297–298, 334
Span of leadership The number of jobs reporting to a person who is responsible for influencing, inspiring, and developing the people who hold those jobs, 297, 334
Spanish Sign Language, 98
Species invasion, 564
Spider organizations, 305–306
Spirituality, workforce, 483–484
Spokesperson, as managerial role, *10*
Stability strategy A corporate strategy that is intended to maintain a company's current position, *153*, 154–155, 172
Stakeholder analysis An audit of all stakeholders and an analysis of how each stakeholder will be affected by an organization's decisions, and/or how the stakeholder can affect the organization, 159–161, 173
Stakeholders Any constituent potentially impacted by an organization's actions, either inside or outside the organization, 160, 173, *573*
  in business ethics, 33
  corporate governance and, 429
Standard operating procedures (SOPs) Detailed and specific instructions for carrying out routine tasks, 113, 304, 334, 427
Standards and metrics Measures established to define quality and efficiency criteria, *433*, 433–434, 453
Standing plans, 143
Stanford prison experiment, 350–351
Star alliance model, of virtual organizations, *404*
Starfish organizations, 306–307
Status quo
  challenging, creativity and, 259–260
  decision making and, 199–200, *200*
Stereotypes Rigid and often negative biases used to describe or judge individuals based on their membership in a social group, 115, 132

cognitive processing and, 183–184
communication and, 115
Stock indexes, of BRIC countries, 511
Storming The second stage of group development, which is characterized by disagreements about how to work together, bids for power, and conflict with leaders, 344, 375
Storytelling, *125*, 125–126, *126*
Strategic alliances Agreements between two or more parties to work together to achieve a common goal, 314–315; Business agreements in which two companies temporarily team up for their mutual benefit in creating or distributing products or services, 506, 540
Strategic approaches to change, 220–221
Strategic business partner, 47
Strategic planning The process of examining an organization's internal and external environments and determining major goals that will help the company realize its mission and move toward its vision, 143, 156, 172
  environmental scanning process, 157–159
  improving your skills in, 169–170
  pattern recognition skills and, 169
  personal vision and, 170
  process of, 156–161
  stakeholder analysis, 159–161, *161*
  steps in, *161*, 161–165
Strategic support, by human resources, 46
Strategy(ies)
  of 3M, *150–151*
  acquisition, 153–154
  business, 155–156
  components of, *152*
  corporate, 152–155, *153*
  crafting, 163–164
  defined, 150
  evaluation of, 165
  functional, 156
  human resource's role in, 166–168
  implementation of, 165
  organizational structure and, 325–326
  stability, 154–155
  types of, 151–156
Strengths Any positive characteristic or activity that an organization possesses that can have a positive impact on the organization, 162–163, 173
Strengths I See in Myself exercise, 602–603
Stress
  cognitive dissonance and, 73
  need for power and, 70
  negative/positive emotional attractors and, 236
Strong culture A culture in which central values and norms are shared and strongly upheld by most members of the organization, 469–470, *470*, 492
Structure, organizational structure and, 325–326
Subcultures, 467
Subgoals, 144, 145
Subprime lending The practice of lending money to people who normally would not qualify for a mortgage because they have maxed-out credit cards, a poor debt-to-income ratio, or bad credit, 223, 249
Sub-Saharan Africa, age demographics in, 218
Succession plan A plan for filling management positions in the event those positions are vacated, 167, 173
Sudan, 158
Sunk costs, *200*, 200–201
Superfund (Comprehensive Environmental Response, Compensation, and Liability Act), *557, 559,* 563

Supervisors, 40–41

Supply chain All of the resources, products, services, and operations that contribute to producing and selling goods or services, 156, 172

Supranationalism A type of structure in which members transfer a portion of their power to the union in exchange for certain benefits, 530, 540

Susan Wheelan's integrated model of group development A model of group development that shows how groups progress through four stages as members gain experience communicating and working together; a fifth stage, termination, can also be included in this model, 345, *346, 347*, 375

Sustainability The process of meeting present needs without compromising the ability of future generations to meet their needs, 547, 585
  climate change/global warming and, 548–549, *550*, 551
  defined, 546–547
  economic, 553, 572–574, *573*
  ethics and, 551–552
  global economic crisis and, 552–553
  history of, 547
  importance of, 546
  leadership for, 584
  leadership supporting, 584
  organizational cultures supporting, 482–483
  three major issues related to, 547–548
  three pillars of, 553, *554*
  top five green U.S. companies for, *555*
  tracking companies focusing on, 555
  Zambia and, *528*
  See also **Environmental sustainability; Social sustainability**

Sustainable development, 546

Sweden, 464, *465, 466*

Switzerland, 529

SWOT analysis A technique that examines strengths, weaknesses, opportunities, and threats that may affect achievement of strategic mission and vision, 162–163, 173

Sympathetic nervous system, 185

Systems theory. *See* **Open systems theory; Sociotechnical systems theory**

Systems thinking, 21, 22, 149, 169, 298, 382, 594

T

Taboos Strong prohibitions against certain activities, 474–475, 493

Taiwan, *466*

Tajikistan, 570

Tall organizational structures, *316*, 316–317, *317*

Tanzania, *536*, 547

Task interdependency conflict, *367*

Task Management leadership style, 41

Task-oriented leaders Leaders who focus on accomplishments and seek to ensure that employees perform well on the job, 42, 53

Tasks, 324

TAT (Thematic Apperception Test), 71–72

Tax environment, 157–158

"Taylorism," 324, 421–422, 442

Team A small group (ideally 6 to 10 individuals) whose members share a common purpose, hold themselves individually and collectively responsible for goals, and have complementary skills and agreed-on processes for working together, 341, 374
  common descriptions for, 359, *360*
  creating and sustaining resonant, 370–373
  groups and, 341
  high-performance, 360–361

human resource's support for, 369–370
  impact of group dynamics on, 349–358
  leaders of, 374
  need for, 340–342
  self-directed work, 359
  structure of, 341
  virtual, 399–401, 413–414
  See also Groups

Team Management leadership style, 41

Technical competencies, 22

Technological environment, 158

Technology The use of tools and knowledge to influence the environment, 382, 415
  First Industrial Revolution and, 382–383
  impacting organizational structure, 327
  as reason for organizational change, 214
  role in fostering globalization, 498–499
  in Schein's organizational culture model, 472
  Second Industrial Revolution and, 383–384

Telecommunications, 391–392

Telecommuting, 398, 582

Teleconferences, 394

Telling style of leadership, 42

Tense-calm, 357

Terminal value Personal commitments we make to ourselves in relation to our life's goals, 30–31, 52

Termination stage (Susan Wheelan's stages of group development), *346, 347*

Terminations, 168

Terrorism, 503

Text messaging, 110, 394, 411

Thailand, 571

Thematic analysis, 488–489

Thematic Apperception Test (TAT), 71–72

Theories
  learning. *See* Learning theories
  of motivation. *See also* Motivation, theories of

Theory X A belief system that holds that the average employee is inclined to be lazy, without ambition, and irresponsible, 29, 52

Theory Y A belief system that holds that workers are inherently ambitious, responsible, and industrious, and that they will work hard to help an organization reach its goals, 29, 52

Theory Z A belief system that holds that in organization with strong, relational cultures, employees have discretionary freedom in local decision-making and are trusted to work autonomously, 29, 52

Thinking outside the box, 286

Thinking-feeling personality dimension, 357

Third Industrial Revolution The period beginning in the mid- to late twentieth century through today when economic activities are marked by an increased focus on information and communication technologies, along with greater attention to issues of environmental sustainability and economic competition, 387–389, 415

Thought processes, 182–185

Threats Any situation, condition, or event that can negatively impact an organization, 163, 173

360-degree review A review process in which a picture of an employee or manager is created through self-assessment along with feedback from peers, managers, customers, and other relevant stakeholders, 448–449, *449*, 453

Three-needs theory Theory stating that people are motivated by needs for achievement, affiliation, and power, 65, 66, 69–72, 89
  measuring needs, 71–72
  need for achievement, 69–70
  need for affiliation, 70
  need for power, 70–71

Threshold competency, 21

Tiananmen Square massacre, 525–526

Time wasters, in work system model of change, 233–234

Title IX Sex Discrimination in Educational Programs and Federally Funded Activities (1972), *485*

Top 50 Most Diverse Companies of 2009, 480

Top-down changes Changes that are introduced by leaders and managers, who define the agenda and create the overarching plan for the change effort, 220, 249

Total Quality Management (TQM) A quality control philosophy that supports the elimination of deficiencies and removes variation in output quality through employee involvement in decision making, continuous improvement in processes, and a strong focus on the customer, 359, 422, 443, *443*, 453

Tourism, in Zambia, *528*

Toxic Substances Control Act (1976), *557*

Trade
  in Africa, 384
  by Brazil, 515, *515*
  by China, 386, *525*
  deregulation of international, 504
  environmental sustainability and, 564
  globalization and, 498, 503, 504, 529
  by India, 521
  labor exploitation and, 568
  slave, 385, 569
  See also Trade alliances

Trade alliances
  Asia Pacific Economic Cooperation (APEC), 532
  Association of Southeast Asian Nations (ASEAN), 532
  Central American Free Trade Agreement, 531
  European Union (EU), 529–530
  North American Free Trade Alliance (NAFTA), 530–531
  Union of South American Nations (UNASUR), 531–532
  United States-Dominican Republic-Central America Free Trade Agreement (CAFTA), 531
  World Trade Organization (WTO), 529

Trademark Any distinctive sign, image, slogan, etc., used to identify a product or service as originating from a particular individual, business, or legal entity, 284, 289, 505

Traffic control sites, 403

Trait theories Models that attempt to explain leadership effectiveness by articulation of physical, psychological, and social characteristics, as well as abilities, knowledge, and expertise, 39–40, 53

Traits Enduring and distinguishing personal characteristics that may be inherited, learned, or developed, 39, 53
  competency and, 21

Transactional leaders People who follow a traditional approach to management in which leader and follower behavior is an instrumental exchange, 44, 53

Transformational leaders People who have social and emotional intelligence and who can inspire others to seek an extraordinary vision, 44–45, 53

Treaty of Paris, 530

Trust
  as conflict resolution strategy, 368
  in groups, *346, 347*
  self-aware leaders and, 50
  in virtual teams, 400, *400*

Trust and structure stage (Susan Wheelan's stages of group development), 346, 347
Tuckman's model of group development. *See* **Bruce Tuckman's model of group development**
Tuna industry, 509
Tuning, as response to change, 220, *220*
Turkey, 533, *536*
2G public network, 391
Two-factor theory (motivator-hygiene theory) Theory that two distinct sets of factors, called motivators and hygiene-factors, affect job satisfaction, motivation, or job dissatisfaction, 65, 66, 68, 89

U

Ubuntu, 71
Uchi, 470
UNASUR (Union of South American Nations), 531–532
Uncertainty avoidance The degree to which people can tolerate unpredictable, ambiguous, or uncertain situations, 463, *463, 465,* 492
Unethical behavior
    Ponzi scheme, 36
    rationalizing, 37–38
    See also **Ethics**
Uniformed Services Employment and Reemployment Rights Act (USERRA) (1994), *486*
Union of South American Nations (UNASUR) A political alliance that moves South America closer to its overall goal of forming an EU-like bloc with a common currency, parliament, and passport, 515, 531–532, 541
Union of Soviet Socialist Republics (USSR), 500–502, 516, 517, *517,* 571
United Kingdom, 217, *218,* 305
United Nations Climate Change Conference (2009), 561
United Nations Framework Convention on Climate Change, 559
United States
    age demographics in, 217, *218*
    Central America Free Trade Agreement and, 531
    Cold War and, 500
    compared with four BRIC nations, *512*
    Copenhagen Accord and, 561
    economic growth in, 218
    ethics of child labor in, 32
    gender and wage gap in, 217
    global finance and, 504
    GLOBE project dimensions in, *465, 466*
    in Group of 20, 533
    history of conservation and ecology movements in, 556–557, *557–558,* 558
    Kyoto Protocol and, 560
    NAFTA and, 530–531
    national debt of, 504–505
    oil consumption in, 561
    recycling in, 563
    sex trafficking in, 570
    shift in economic growth of, 218, *219*
    slavery in, 569
    as a superpower, 529–530
    United Nations Climate Change Conference (2009) and, 561
United States–Dominican Republic–Central America Free Trade Agreement (CAFTA) A trade agreement among seven nations: the United States, the Dominican Republic, Costa Rica, El Salvador, Guatemala, Honduras, and Nicaragua, 531, 540

University of Michigan Studies, 40–41
Upward communication The flow of information from lower in an organizational hierarchy to higher, 119, *120,* 133
U.S. Spirit Award, 583
USERRA (Uniformed Services Employment and Reemployment Rights Act) (1994), *486*
Uskoreniye, 517
USSR. *See* Union of Soviet Socialist Republics (USSR)
Uzbekistan, 571

V

Valence The value placed on outcomes, 75
Value alliance model, of virtual organizations, *404*
Value engineering, 471
Values Ideas and person or a group believes to be right or wrong, good or bad, attractive or undesirable, 30, 52, 458–459
    competencies and, 24
    culture and, 458–459
    developing, 30–31
    enacted, 473
    espoused, 473
    globalization and, 537–538
    instrumental, 31
    resonant leadership and, 595
    in Schein's organizational culture model, 473, *473*
    terminal, 30–31
Venezuela, *465, 466,* 531
Venture capitalist firm A company that seeks to earn a profit through investments in start-up firms or companies that are undergoing dramatic change, 277, 288
Verbal language, 98
Vertical integration A business strategy of acquiring or developing businesses along the supply chain, *155,* 156, 172
Vertical organizational structures, 316–317
Veterans Benefits and Health Care Improvement Act (VBHCIA), *486*
Veterans Employment Opportunities Act (1998), *486*
Vicarious learning, 81
Videoconferencing, 110–111, 412
Video rental business, 263–264
Videoconferences, 394
Vietnam, 388, *536*
Vietnam Era Veteran's Readjustment Assistance Act (1974), *485*
Vietnam War, 501, 502
Virtual, 397
Virtual banking, 404–405
Virtual broker model, of virtual organizations, *404*
Virtual consumer sales, 406
Virtual education and training, 406–407, *407*
Virtual face model, of virtual organizations, *404*
Virtual organizations Organizations that consist of diverse people, groups, and networks that are geographically dispersed and that rely on information and communication technologies for communication and coordination of activities, 401, 415
    Avon, 401–402, *402*
    components of, 402, *403*
    models of, 403–404, *404*
    organizational design of, 401
Virtual space(s), 398, *404*
Virtual team A group of individuals who collaborate on work projects while operating from different locations and using ICTs to establish shared goals, coordinate work, manage work processes and outcomes, and build effective relationships and team norms, 399–401, 415
    effectiveness of, 399–400

leading, 413–414
    trust and accountability in, *400,* 400–401
Virtual work world
    challenges of, 408–410
    communication in, 111
    downsides of, 408
    global implications of, 414
    human resources's role in, 411, 417
    hybrid workers, 399
    knowledge management in, 409–410, *410*
    relationships in, 308, 412–413
    setting for, 397–398
    technology and information overload in, 408–409
    telecommuting, 398
Vision A description of what an organization wants to become—its future identity—which can be realized through the successful accomplishment of its mission, 147, 149, 172
    getting groups to creative a collective, 370
    personal, 170
    review of, 162
Vision statement An articulation of a company's vision, 147, 148, 172
Vocal intonation, 101
Voice volume, 101

W

Waste management, 563
Waste of time (work systems model of change), 233–234
Watson-Glaser Critical Thinking Appraisal, 197
Weak culture A culture in which the values and norms are shared by a limited group of people and employees' goals may not be in line with management's goals, 471
Weaknesses Any negative characteristic or activity that an organization possesses that can have a negative impact on the organization, 163, 173
Weather patterns, strategic planning and, 159
Web 2.0 The second generation of Web technology and software development that allows for increased interactivity, user design and control, and collaboration, 390
Web conferencing, 110–111, 394, 412
"Weird rules of creativity," 260, *261*
West Germany, 500, 502
Western Europe, age demographics in, 217, *218*
Wheel network (hub-and-spoke network) A communication network in which one person acts as a central conduit for all information, 121, 133
Wheelan's integrated model of group development. *See* **Susan Wheelan's integrated model of group development**
Whistle-blower protection, 48
Whistleblower Protection Act (2007), 48
Whole person, organizational cultures supporting, 483–484
Wholly owned affiliate or subsidiary A company whose stock is completely owned by a second company, referred to as a parent or holding company, 314, 334
Wholly owned affiliates Companies that are controlled by another company, most commonly through ownership of all common stock, 506, 540
Wikipedia, *198–199*
Wikis, 395
Women
    communication of, 118
    in Fortune 500 positions, 480
    marketing images of, 483
    pay equity gap for, 217
    in the workforce, statistics, 217

Work
"flow" experiences in, 59
meaningful, 58–59
structure of, 323–325
Work systems model of change, 231–234, *232*
Workforce
diversity in, 480
growth and reductions in, 166–167
multicultural, 461–462
Workforce data, 127
Workforce Investment Act (1998), *486*
Workforce spirituality, 483–484
Working memory, creativity and, *256*
Workplace safety, 571–572, *572*
Workspace, in Schein's organizational culture
model, 473

World Bank An international banking
organization that provides capital supplied by
member governments to underdeveloped
nations, 525, 533, 541
World Economic Forum A not-for-profit
organization that claims no ties to political,
partisan, or national agendas and brings
together business, political, social, and
intellectual leaders from around the world, 533,
541
World Trade Center bombing (1993), 503
World Wide Web (WWW), 390
Worldwide recession. *See* Global economic recession
Written language, 99–100

X
Xhosa culture, 71

Y
Yellowstone, 556
Yucca Mountains, 564

Z
Z organizations, 29
Zambia, 272, *272–273, 528*
cooperatives in, *271–272*
malaria in, *303*
Zero E-Mail Fridays, 409
Zero-sum negotiation, 368